Introduction to Comparative Politics

CONTRIBUTORS

Ervand Abrahamian
BARUCH COLLEGE

Merilee S. Grindle
JOHN F. KENNEDY SCHOOL OF GOVERNMENT,
HARVARD UNIVERSITY

Richard A. Joseph
EMORY UNIVERSITY

William A. Joseph
WELLESLEY COLLEGE

Mark Kesselman
COLUMBIA UNIVERSITY

Darren Kew
TUFTS UNIVERSITY

Atul Kohli
PRINCETON UNIVERSITY

Joel Krieger
WELLESLEY COLLEGE

Peter Lewis
AMERICAN UNIVERSITY

Al Montero
CARLETON COLLEGE

Scott D. Taylor
SMITH COLLEGE

Introduction to Comparative Politics: Political Challenges and Changing Agendas

SECOND EDITION

GENERAL EDITORS

Mark Kesselman
COLUMBIA UNIVERSITY

Joel Krieger
WELLESLEY COLLEGE

William A. Joseph
WELLESLEY COLLEGE

Houghton Mifflin Company
Boston   New York

To our children, who are growing up in a complex and exhilarating world:
MK—for Ishan and Javed
JK—for Nathan
WAJ—for Abigail, Hannah, and Rebecca

Sponsoring Editor: Melissa Mashburn
Basic Book Editor: Jennifer Sutherland
Editorial Associate: Vikram Mukhija
Project Editor: Gabrielle Stone
Assistant Manufacturing Coordinator: Andrea Wagner
Senior Marketing Manager: Sandra McGuire

Printed in the U.S.A.

Library of Congress Catalog Card Number: 99-71974

ISBN: 0-395-93704-3

3456789-DC-03   02   01   00

BRIEF CONTENTS

CONTENTS

3 France   79

Mark Kesselman

4 Germany   135 — 50 pgs

Christopher S. Allen

5 Japan   187 — 54 pgs

Haruhiro Fukui and Shigeko N. Fukai

7 United States   287 ⌐3z pgs

Louis DeSipio

9 Mexico   377 - 48 pgs

Merilee S. Grindle

10 Russia   425

Joan DeBardeleben

Part ❹ Non-Democracies   484

11 China   485 —60 pgs

William A. Joseph

12 Nigeria   545 ⌐ 60 pgs

Richard A. Joseph, Peter Lewis, Darren Kew, and Scott D. Taylor

13 Iran   607

Ervand Abrahamian

These are exciting yet daunting times to teach comparative politics. After years in which the contours of the subject matter were quite familiar, the democratic revolutions of recent years have challenged scholars and teachers to think anew about the field's geographical, national, and intellectual boundaries. Even as countries ruled for decades by communist and authoritarian regimes adopted democratic institutions, other countries that held out against the democratic tide found themselves on the defensive internationally and at home, while long-established democracies have been buffeted by new economic, cultural, and political challenges. For the countries included in *Introduction to Comparative Politics,* there seems to be no end to history.

Introduction to Comparative Politics: Political Challenges and Changing Agendas is an extensively revamped version of *Comparative Politics at the Crossroads* (1996). We were very gratified by the enthusiastic response to the high level of scholarship, the wealth of information, and the innovative themes in the first edition. We were also pleased to receive many excellent suggestions for changes from reviewers and instructors who assigned the book. In response to many of these suggestions—and to the dramatic changes in the field of comparative politics—we decided that an uncommonly thorough revision was needed.

The book's new title signifies the sweeping nature of the revision. Although we have retained the theoretical framework of *Comparative Politics at the Crossroads,* we have also made some very important changes. First, every chapter has been carefully rewritten to make the book accessible to students with little or no background in political science. We have used simple, sprightly prose and have maximized symmetry among the chapters in order to facilitate comparison. Second, we have updated the material on each of the countries to take account of major events and regime changes that have occurred since 1996.

Third, we have added a new chapter on the United States. We strongly believe that the study of comparative politics is skewed if it does not include close attention to the United States. However, given the fact that most U. S. colleges and universities have a separate introductory course on politics in the United States, the chapter is about half the length of the other country chapters.

Fourth, we have developed a new typology of political systems to replace the former First-Second-Third World classification. The largest group of countries covered in this book are the *long-established democracies:* Britain, France, and the United States, which rank among the most durable democracies; Germany and Japan, industrialized countries whose postwar democratic experience provides lessons in how formerly authoritarian regimes can consolidate democracy; and India, one of the world's most populous and poorest nations, whose democratic institutions have endured for half a century despite severe strains. Next, we discuss a group of *transitional democracies:* Brazil, Mexico, and Russia. Each of these countries has experienced very significant democratization in recent years, but all are still hampered by the persistence of extensive undemocratic elements that make the future of democracy far from certain. For our final three countries—China, Iran, and Nigeria—undemocratic elements are sufficiently powerful as to suggest the need for a third category, *non-democracies,* in *Introduction to Comparative Politics.* (Even as we write, Nigeria has held competitive presidential elections and may be moving toward the category of transitional democracy: a moving target for authors and editors, but that's just what makes the study of comparative politics so exciting!)

We have written this book to help students analyze the problems confronting twelve important countries throughout the world and to equip them with an understanding of where these countries may be headed politically. We have kept in mind the needs of instructors for clear and readable prose, for comparative analysis focused on countries and political systems, and for comprehensive treatment of institutions, political behavior, political economy, and the policy-making process.

A chapter is devoted to each country, and each country chapter consists of five sections. Section 1 treats the historic formation of the modern state and includes a new discussion of the geographic setting. Section 2 describes the political economy of past and current national development. Section 3 outlines the major institutions of governance and policy-making. Section 4 explains the widely varying processes of representation, participation, and contestation. Finally, Section 5 reflects on the major issues that confront the country and are likely to shape its future.

Introduction to Comparative Politics emphasizes patterns of state formation, political economy, domestic politics, and the politics of collective identities within the context of the international political and economic systems. A distinctive feature of the book is the use of four comparative themes to frame the presentation of each country's politics. We explain the themes in Chapter 1 and present an intriguing "puzzle" for each to stimulate student thinking. These themes—treated in each country study—focus attention on the continuities and contrasts among the twelve countries:

- **A World of States** highlights the importance of state formation and the interstate system for political development.

- **Governing the Economy** analyzes state strategies for promoting economic development and stresses the effects of economic globalization on domestic politics.

- **The Democratic Idea** explores the challenges posed by citizens' demands for greater control and participation in both democracies and non-democracies.

- **The Politics of Collective Identities** considers the political consequences of race, ethnicity, gender, religion, and nationality and their complex interplay with class-based politics.

Through our four themes, the methods of comparative analysis come alive as students examine similarities and differences among countries and within and between political systems. This thematic approach facilitates timely and comprehensive analysis of political challenges and changing agendas within countries.

Introduction to Comparative Politics strikes a balance between the richness of national political development and a more general comparative analysis. Chapter 1 explains the comparative method, analyzes the four key themes of the book, and describes core features of political institutions and processes. Each country study presents a clear and thorough treatment of political institutions and their relation to socioeconomic, cultural, and transnational influences.

Several special features assist in the teaching and learning process. At the beginning of each chapter, students will find a page of basic demographic, social, economic, and political information to aid in comparing countries. Throughout the chapters a wide array of maps, tables, charts, photographs, and political cartoons enliven the text

and present key information in clear and graphic ways. Each country study includes four to six boxes that highlight interesting and provocative aspects of politics—for example, the biography of an important political leader, institutional intricacies, or unconventional forms of participation. Key terms are set in boldface when first introduced and are defined in the Glossary at the end of the book. Students will find that the Glossary defines many key concepts that are used broadly in comparative politics.

In *Introduction to Comparative Politics,* we combine an innovative thematic approach and comprehensive coverage of political institutions and processes. We hope that it serves as a stimulating and accessible introduction to the study of comparative politics for your students.

We are grateful for the advice and critical comments of many colleagues, including Amrita Basu, and Graeme Robertson. We also want to thank Shylashri Shankar, Elora Shehabuddin, and Rani Tudor for their assistance in preparing the chapter on India, Andre Leroux for his help with Mexico, and to Maria do Carmo Campello de Souza for her contribution to her first edition. We are especially indebted to those who critiqued the first edition or reviewed portions of the second edition manuscript:

Steve D. Boilard, Western Kentucky University; **George P. Brown,** Boston College; **Daniel P. Franklin,** Georgia State University; **Chris Howell,** Oberlin College; **Peggy Kahn,** University of Michigan, Flint; **Margaret Keck,** Johns Hopkins University; **Nikki Keddie,** University of California, Los Angeles; **Peter R. Kingstone,** University of Vermont; **Stephen Manning,** University of Detroit, Mercy; **Jennie Purnell,** Boston College.

Finally, our thanks to the talented and professional staff at Houghton Mifflin, especially Melissa Mashburn, sponsoring editor; Jennifer Sutherland, basic book editor; Gabrielle Stone, project editor; Vikram Mukhija, editorial associate; and Sandra McGuire, senior marketing manager.

M. K.
J. K.
W. A. J.

Introduction to Comparative Politics

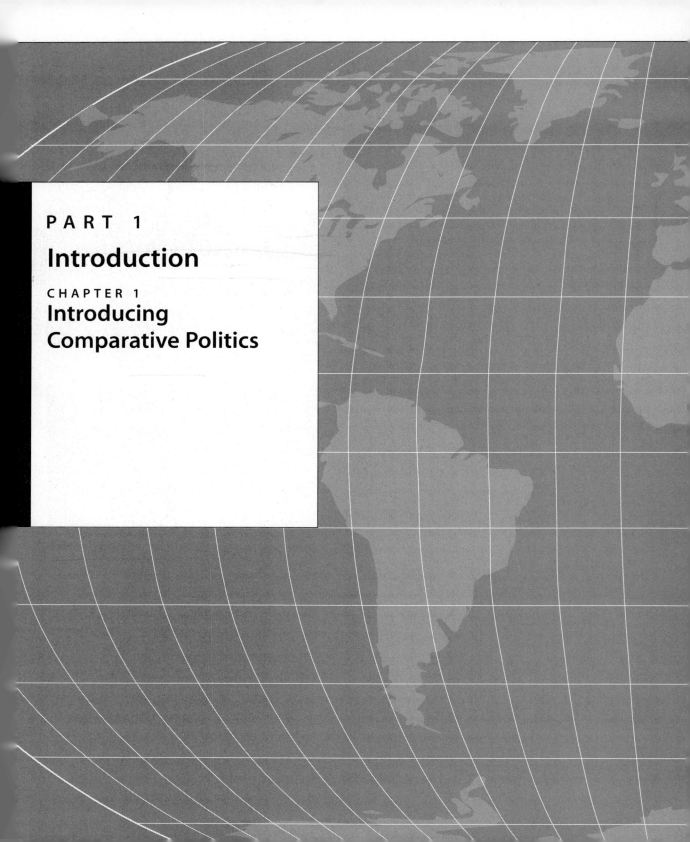

PART 1
Introduction

CHAPTER 1
Introducing Comparative Politics

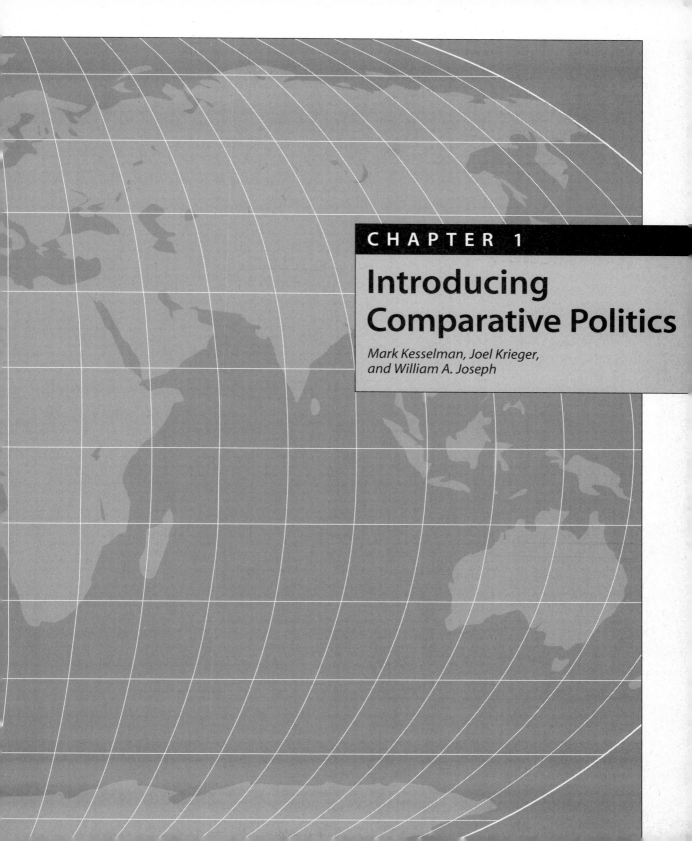

CHAPTER 1

Introducing Comparative Politics

Mark Kesselman, Joel Krieger,
and William A. Joseph

At the start of a new millennium, politics throughout the world is more unsettled than many would have predicted a decade ago. Then, a host of developments heralded a dramatic shift in historic epochs and created the sense that a more harmonious, democratic, and prosperous order might be dawning. The revolutions of 1989 in Eastern and Central Europe marked the disintegration of much of the communist world. When the Berlin Wall—which divided East and West in both physical and symbolic terms—was dismantled brick by brick beginning in November 1989, the architecture of Europe was forever altered. Within a year, Germany was unified after nearly a half-century of **Cold War** division, and by the end of 1991, the Soviet Union, once a formidable superpower, had collapsed into fifteen troubled republics, including a much humbled Russia. Within a few years, Nelson Mandela was transformed from prisoner to president of a newly democratic South Africa and an awkward handshake between Yasir Arafat and Yitzhak Rabin inspired hope for a new era in the Middle East. On July 1, 1997, one hundred and fifty years of British colonial rule in Hong Kong ended when the territory became part of the People's Republic of China.

Today we know that this shift in historical epochs not only created exciting opportunities for human progress but also increased the risks of instability and conflict. As the world has painfully learned in recent years, freedom, peace, and a reasonable standard of living cannot be built on hopes alone. It is desperately hard to make such dreams a reality. Removing dictatorial regimes often proves less difficult than building new democracies, and sustained progress toward peace requires far more than "photo-ops" and paper agreements. In many countries, the rush to democracy awakens new and restless constituencies with demands that neither the government nor the economy can easily meet.

An Uncertain World Order

Post–Cold War political changes and the transformation of the global balance of power have produced new forms of international cooperation and competition—as well as new sources of international tension and violence. The grim but predictable bipolar world of superpower rivalry between the United States and the Soviet Union, reinforced by the North Atlantic Treaty Organization (NATO) and Warsaw Treaty Organization (Warsaw Pact) alliances, has been replaced by the uncertainties of a more fragmented map of global power. During the Cold War, the rivalry between the Soviet Union and the United States was often fought out and contained at a safe distance from the superpowers, as in the Vietnam War or the Middle East conflicts. But now with no superpower standoff to channel and contain conflicts, increasing economic, religious, and ethnic divisions spark tension and crises in every corner of the world.

We have witnessed a surge of brutal clashes between and within countries, along with a quieter dynamic of fierce competition and a rash of trade wars—and perpetual diplomatic combat—among professed allies. The harsh developments are evident in screaming newspaper headlines and heartrending stories on television news. Consider one of the major sources of conflict in the post-cold war world—a wave of violent religious and ethnic conflict. No region of the world is a sanctuary. In Africa, members of the Hutu majority in Rwanda slaughtered hundreds of thousands of the Tutsi minority. In Asia, religious and ethnic minorities in India and Indonesia were savagely attacked and massacred. Europe was also the setting for an onslaught on religious and ethnic groups. In the Balkans, leaders of the Serb majority in Yugoslavia forcibly expelled from their homes and butchered hundreds of thousands of Muslims and ethnic Albanians. The 1990s saw the creation of a new term, "ethnic cleansing," to describe the elimination of minorities within a territory. But the phrase does not convey the inhumanity of the process. Thus, what may have been the most violent century in world history ended as destructively as it began.

The end of the Cold War also failed to resolve other massive problems. Although a major cause of the collapse of communism in the Soviet Union and its allies in

new sources of conflict [handwritten margin note]

3

In a take-off on *The Wizard of Oz,* this cartoon shows that many people who celebrated the collapse of communism in East-Central Europe and elsewhere were not aware of or prepared for the many difficulties involved in making the transition to a capitalist economy. *Source:* © Kevin Kallaugher, Cartoonists & Writers Syndicate.

East Central Europe was that capitalist countries vastly outperformed the communist bloc, the triumph of capitalism has not eliminated poverty for millions of people throughout the world. Quite the contrary. The globalization of trade, investment, and communications has destroyed many traditional communities and the natural environment in many regions of the world. During the 1970s and 1980s, countries in East and Southeast Asia were held up as an economic miracle because of their rapidly growing economies. However, these same countries became an economic nightmare in the late 1990s, as financial crises produced economic recession and sharply reduced living standards for their citizens.

Making Sense of Turbulent Times

It is not surprising that in the flash of newspaper headlines and television sound bites, these upheavals and changes tend to make politics look chaotic beyond comprehension. Although the study of comparative politics can help us understand current events in a rapidly changing world, it involves much more than snapshot analysis or Monday-morning quarterbacking. *Introduction to Comparative Politics* describes and analyzes in detail the government and politics of twelve countries and identifies common themes in their development that explain longer-term causes of both changes and continuities. The book provides cross-national comparisons and explanations based on four themes that we believe are central for understanding politics in today's world. The four key themes are these:

- The interaction of states within the international order.
- The role of the state in economic management.
- The pressures for more democracy and the challenges of democratization.

- The political impact of diverse attachments and sources of group identity, including class, gender, ethnicity, and religion.

We also expect that these four themes will be useful for analyzing where these twelve countries may be heading politically in the opening years of the twenty-first century. Moreover, the themes illustrate how comparative politics can serve as a valuable tool for making political sense of even the most tumultuous times. The contemporary period presents an extraordinary challenge to those who study comparative politics, but the study of comparative politics also provides a unique opportunity for understanding this uncertain era.

In order to appreciate the complexity of politics and political transitions in countries around the world, we must look beyond our own national perspectives. Today, business and trade, information technology, mass communications and culture, immigration and travel—as well as politics—forge deep connections among people worldwide. It is particularly urgent that we adopt a truly global perspective as we explore both the politics of different countries and their growing interdependence.

There is an added benefit: by comparing political institutions, values, and processes in countries around the world, the student of comparative politics acquires analytical skills that can be used at home. After you study comparative politics, you begin to think like a comparativist. As comparison becomes almost automatic, you look at the politics of your own country differently, with a wider focus and new insights.

The contemporary world provides a fascinating laboratory for the study of comparative politics and gives unusual significance to the subject. We hope that you share our sense of excitement and join us in the challenging effort to understand the complex and ever-shifting terrain of contemporary politics throughout the world. We begin by first exploring what comparative politics actually compares and how comparative study enhances our understanding of politics generally.

Section ❷   What—And How—Comparative Politics Compares

To "compare and contrast" is one of the most common human exercises, whether in the classroom study of literature or politics or animal behavior—or in selecting dorm rooms or listing your favorite movies. In the observation of politics, the use of comparisons is very old, dating at least from Aristotle, the ancient Greek philosopher. Aristotle categorized Athenian city-states in the fifth century B.C. according to their form of political rule: rule by a single individual, rule by a few, or rule by all citizens. He added a normative dimension (a claim about how societies should be ruled), by distinguishing ("contrasting") good and corrupt versions of each type. The modern study of comparative politics refines and systematizes the age-old practice of evaluating some feature of X by comparing it to the same feature of Y in order to learn more about it than isolated study would permit.

The term **comparative politics** refers to a field within the academic study of politics (that is, political science), as well as to a method or approach to the study of politics.[1] The subject matter of comparative politics is the domestic politics of countries or peoples.

Within the discipline of political science, comparative politics is one of four areas of specialization. In addition to comparative politics, most political science (or government) departments in U.S. colleges and universities include courses and academic specialists in three other fields: political theory, international relations, and American politics.

Because it is widely believed that students living in the United States should study American politics intensively and with special focus, the two fields remain separate. The pattern of distinguishing the study of politics at home from politics abroad is also common elsewhere, so students in Canada may be expected to study Canadian politics as a distinctive specialty, and Japanese students would likewise be expected to master Japanese politics.

However, because there is no logical reason why study of the United States should not be included within the field of comparative politics—and good reason to do so—we include a chapter on American politics in *Introduction to Comparative Politics*. In fact, many important studies in comparative politics (and an increasing number of courses) have integrated the study of American politics with the study of politics in other countries. Comparative study can place U.S. politics into a much richer perspective and, at the same time, make it easier to recognize what is distinctive and most interesting about other countries.

The comparative approach relies principally on analysis designed to identify the similarities and differences between countries by focusing on selected institutions and processes. As students of comparative politics (we call ourselves **comparativists**) we believe that we cannot make reliable statements about most political observations by looking at only one case. We often hear statements such as: "The United States has the best health care system in the world." Comparativists immediately wonder what kinds of health care systems exist in other countries, what they cost and how they are financed, who is covered by health insurance, and so on. Besides, what does "best" mean when it comes to health care systems? Is it the one that provides the widest access? the one that is the most technologically advanced? the one that is the most cost-effective? the one that produces the healthiest population? We would not announce the "best movie" or the "best car" without considering other alternatives or deciding what specific factors enter into our judgment.

Comparativists often analyze political institutions or processes by looking at two or more cases deliberately selected for their mix of common and contrasting features. The analysis involves actually comparing similar aspects of politics in more than one country—for example, the executive branches of government in the United States, Britain, and Canada.[2] Some comparative political studies take a thematic approach and draw on many different countries to analyze broad issues, such as what causes revolutions.[3]

Levels of Analysis

Comparisons can be very useful for political analysis at several different levels. Political scientists often compare developments in different cities, regions, provinces, or states. Comparative analysis can also focus on specific institutions and processes in different countries, such as the legislature, executive, political parties, social movements, or court systems. The organization of *Introduction to Comparative Politics* reflects our belief that the best way to begin the study of comparative politics is with **countries**. Countries, which are also sometimes referred to as **nation-states**, comprise distinct, politically defined territories that encompass political institutions, cultures, economies, and ethnic and other social identities.

Although often highly divided internally, countries have historically been the most important source of a people's collective political identity and they are the major arena for organized political action in the modern world. Therefore, countries are the natural unit of analysis for most domestic political variables and processes. These include:

- **political institutions**: the formal and informal rules and structured relationships that organize power and resources in society
- **political culture**: attitudes, beliefs, and symbols that influence political behavior
- **political development**: the stages of change in the structures of government.

Within a given country, the state is almost always the most powerful cluster of institutions. But just what is the state? The way the term is used in comparative politics is probably unfamiliar to many students. In the United States, it usually refers to the states in the federal system—Texas, California, and so on. But in comparative politics, the **state** refers to a country's key political institutions that are responsible for making, implementing, enforcing, and adjudicating important policies in that country. The most important state institutions are the national **executive**, notably, the president and/or prime minister and **cabinet**, along with the army, police, and administrative **bureaucracy**, the legislature, and courts. In casual usage, the terms *state* and *government* are sometimes used interchangeably. However, in comparative politics, government often does not refer to the permanent administrative or bureaucratic agencies but to the key officials and offices whose fates are linked by election or appointment to the president or prime minister and who direct major administrative agencies. The use of the term *government* in comparative politics—as in the phrase, "the government of Prime Minister Tony Blair in Britain"—is very similar to the term *administration* in American politics.

States claim, usually with considerable success, the right to issue rules—notably, laws, administrative regulations, and court decisions—that are binding for people within the country. Even democratic states, in which top officials are chosen by procedures that permit all citizens to participate, can survive only if they can preserve enforcement (or coercive) powers both internally and with regard to other states that may pose challenges. A number of countries have highly repressive states whose political survival depends largely on military and police powers. But even in such states, long-term stability requires that the ruling regime have some measure of political **legitimacy**; that is, a significant segment of the citizenry must believe that the state acts with some moral authority. Political legitimacy is greatly affected by the state's ability to "deliver the goods" through satisfactory economic performance and an acceptable distribution of economic resources. Moreover, in the contemporary period legitimacy seems to require that states represent themselves as democratic in some fashion, whether or not they are in fact. Thus, *Introduction to Comparative Politics* looks closely at, first, the state's role in governing the economy and, second, the pressures exerted on states to develop and extend democratic participation.

The fact that states are the fundamental objects of analysis in comparative politics does not mean that all states are the same. Indeed, the organization of state institutions varies widely, and these differences have a powerful impact on political and social life. Hence, each country study in this book devotes considerable attention to variations in institutions of governance, participation, and representation and their political implications. Each country study begins with an analysis of how the institutional organization and political procedures of the state have evolved historically. This process of **state formation** fundamentally influences how and why states differ politically.

Causal Theories

Because countries are the basic building blocks in politics and because states are the most significant political organizations and actors, these two are the critical units for comparative analysis. The comparativist looks at similarities and differences among countries or states and tries to develop causal theories—hypotheses that can be expressed formally in a causal mode: "If X happens, then Y will be the result." Such theories include factors (the independent variables, symbolized by X) that are believed to influence some outcome, and the outcome (the dependent variable, symbolized by Y) to be explained. For example, it is commonly argued that if a country's economic pie shrinks, conflict among groups for resources will intensify. This hypothesis suggests what is called an inverse correlation between variables: as X varies in one direction, Y varies in the opposite direction. As the total national economic product (X) decreases, then political and social conflict over economic shares (Y) increases. Even when the explanation does not involve the explicit testing of hypotheses (and often it does not), comparativists try to identify similarities and differences among countries and to identify significant patterns.

It is important to recognize the limits on just how "scientific" political science—and thus comparative politics—can be. Two important differences exist between the "hard" (or natural) sciences like physics and chemistry and the social sciences. First, social scientists study people who exercise free will. Because people have a margin for free choice, their choices, attitudes, and behavior cannot be fully explained by causal analysis. This does not mean that people choose in an arbitrary fashion. We choose within the context of material constraint, institutional dictates, and cultural prescriptions. Indeed, comparative politics analyzes how these and other factors orient political choices in systematic ways. But there will probably always be a wide gulf between the natural and social sciences because of their different objects of study.

A second difference between the natural and social sciences is that, in the natural sciences, experimental techniques can be applied to isolate the contribution of distinct factors to a particular outcome. It is possible to change the value or magnitude of a factor—for example, the force applied to an object—and measure how the outcome has consequently changed. However, like other social scientists, political scientists and comparativists rarely have the opportunity to apply such experimental techniques.

In the real world of politics, unlike in a laboratory, variables cannot easily be isolated or manipulated. Some political scientists employ techniques that attempt to identify the specific causal weight of a variable in explaining a political outcome. But it is very difficult to measure precisely how, for example, a person's ethnicity, gender, or income influences her or his choice when casting a ballot. Nor can we ever know for sure what exact mix of factors—conflicts among elites, popular ideological appeals, the weakness of the state, the organizational capacity of rebel leaders, or the discontent of the masses—precipitates a successful revolution.

Despite these difficulties and limitations, the study of comparative politics involves the search for just the right balance in an explanation between the specifics of individual cases and universal patterns. One common goal of comparativists is to develop what is called **middle-level theory**. Such a theory explains phenomena found in a limited range of cases, which in comparative politics means a specific set of countries with the same or similar characteristics, political institutions, or processes. If we study only individual countries without any comparative framework, then comparative politics would become merely the study of a series of isolated cases. It would be impossible to recognize what is most significant in the collage of political characteristics that we find in the world's many countries. As a result, the understanding of patterns of similarity and difference among countries would be lost, along with an important tool for evaluating what is and what is not unique about a country's political life.

If we go to the other extreme and try to make universal claims that something is always true in all countries, we would either have to stretch the truth or ignore the interesting differences and patterns of variation. For the political world is incredibly complex, shaped by an extraordinary array of factors and an almost endless interplay of variables. Indeed, after a brief period in the 1950s and 1960s when many comparativists tried—and failed—to develop a "grand theory" that would apply to all countries, most comparativists see the attempt to develop middle-level theory as the most promising.

For example, comparativists have worked hard to analyze the efforts in many countries to replace (or attempt to replace) authoritarian forms of government, such as military **dictatorships** and one-party states, with more participatory and democratic regimes. In studying democratic transitions, comparativists do not treat each national case as unique or try to construct a universal pattern that ignores all differences. Applying middle-level theory, we identify the influence on the new regime's political stability of specific variables such as institutional legacies, political culture, levels of economic development, the nature of the regime before the transition, and the degree of ethnic conflict or homogeneity. Comparativists have been able to identify patterns in the emergence and consolidation of democratic regimes in southern Europe in the 1970s (Greece, Portugal, and Spain) and have compared them to developments in Latin America, Asia, and Africa since the 1980s, and in Eastern and Central Europe since the revolutions of 1989.

The study of comparative politics has many challenges, including the complexity of the subject matter, the fast pace of change in the contemporary world, and the impossibility of manipulating variables or replicating conditions. What can we expect when the whole political world is our laboratory? When we put the method of comparative politics to the test and develop a set of themes derived from middle-level theory, we discover that it is possible to find explanations and discern patterns that make sense of a vast range of political developments and link the experiences of states and citizens throughout the world.

Section ❸ Themes for Comparative Analysis

We began this introduction by emphasizing the extraordinary importance and fluid pace of the global changes currently taking place. Next, we explained the subject matter of comparative politics and described some of the tools of comparative analysis. This section describes the four themes we use to organize the information on institutions and processes in the twelve country chapters in *Introduction to*

Comparative Politics. These themes help explain continuities and contrasts among countries and demonstrate what patterns apply to a group of countries—and why—and what patterns are specific to a particular country. We also suggest a way that each theme highlights some puzzle in comparative politics.

Before we introduce the themes, a couple of warnings are necessary. First, our four themes cannot possibly capture the infinitely varied experience of politics throughout the world. Our framework in *Introduction to Comparative Politics*, built on four core themes, provides a guide to understanding many features of contemporary comparative politics. But we urge students (and rely on instructors!) to challenge and expand on our interpretations. Second, we want to note that a textbook builds from existing theory but does not construct or test new hypotheses. That task is the goal of original scholarly studies. The themes are intended to distill some of the most significant findings in the field of contemporary comparative politics.

Theme 1: A World of States

The theme that we call a world of states reflects the fact that, since the beginning of the modern era about 500 years ago, states have been the primary actors on the world stage. Although international organizations play a crucial role, for the most part it is the rulers of states who send armies to conquer other states and territories. It is the legal codes of states that make it possible for businesses to operate within their borders and beyond. And it is states that regulate the movement of people across borders through immigration law. While courses in international relations focus primarily on interaction among states, courses in comparative politics stress what goes on within a country's borders. In *Introduction to Comparative Politics* we emphasize one key feature of the international arena: the impact on a state's domestic political institutions and processes of its relative success or failure in competing economically and politically with other states.

No state, even the most powerful such as the United States, is unaffected by influences originating outside its borders. Today, a host of processes associated with **globalization** underscore the heightened importance of various cross-national influences. A wide array of international organizations and treaties, including the United Nations, the European Union, the World Trade Organization, the North American Free Trade Agreement, and countless others, challenge the sovereign control of national governments. Transnational corporations, international banks, and currency traders in New York, London, Frankfurt, and Tokyo affect countries and people throughout the world. A country's political borders do not protect its citizens from environmental pollution or infectious diseases that come from abroad. More broadly, developments linked to technology transfer, the growth of an international information society, immigration, and cultural diffusion have a varying but undeniable impact on the domestic politics of all countries. For example, thanks to the global diffusion of radio, television, and the Internet, people everywhere are remarkably informed about international developments. This knowledge may fuel popular local demands that governments intervene in faraway Kosovo, Rwanda, or elsewhere. And this global awareness may make citizens more ready to hold their own government to internationally recognized standards of human rights.

As we cross into the new millennium, nation-states are experiencing intense pressures from an expanding and increasingly complex mix of external influences. In all countries, politics and policy-making are being shaped by influences from beyond their borders. But international political and economic influences do not have the *same* impact in all countries, nor do all states equally shape the institutional form and policy of international organizations in which they participate. It is likely that the more advantaged a state is, as measured by its level of economic development, military power, and resource base, the more it will shape global influences. Conversely, the policies of less advantaged countries are more extensively molded by other states, by international organizations, and by broader international constraints.

The theme we identify as a world of states includes a second important focus: similarities and contrasts among countries in state formation. We study the ways that states have developed historically, diverse patterns in the organization of political institutions, the processes—and limits—of democratization, the ability of the state to control social groups in society and sustain power, and the state's economic management strategies and capacities. We observe the linkage between state formation and the position of states in the international order. Certain countries, such as Britain and India, are connected by colonial histories; others, like China and Russia, share developmental patterns that for decades were shaped by communist ideologies, political structures, and approaches to economic organization.

A puzzle: To what extent do states still remain the basic building blocks of political life? Increasingly the politics and policies of states are shaped by external factors as well as by the more impersonal forces of globalization. At the same time, many states face increasingly restive constituencies who challenge the power and legitimacy of central states. In reading our twelve country case studies, try to assess what impact pressures from both above and below—outside and inside—have had on the role of the state in carrying out its basic functions and in sustaining the political attachment of its citizens. Are states losing their ability to control policy and secure political outcomes?

Theme 2: Governing the Economy

The success of states in maintaining their authority and sovereign control is greatly affected by their ability to assure that an adequate volume of goods and services is produced to satisfy the needs of their populations. Certainly, the inadequate performance of the Soviet economic system was an important reason for the rejection of communism and the disintegration of the Soviet Union. It is very important to analyze, for example, how countries differ in the balance between agricultural and industrial production in their economies, how successful they are in competing with other countries that offer similar products in international markets, and the relative importance of market forces versus government control of the economy. How a country "governs the economy"[4]—how it organizes production and intervenes to manage the economy—is one of the key elements in its overall pattern of political as well as economic development.

An important goal of all countries in the contemporary world is to achieve durable economic development. In fact, effective economic performance is near the top of every state's political agenda. The term **political economy** refers to how governments affect economic performance—and how economic performance in turn affects a country's political processes. We accord great importance to political economy in *Introduction to Comparative Politics* because we believe that politics in all countries is deeply influenced by the relationship between government and the economy, in both domestic and international dimensions.

A puzzle: What political factors promote successful national economic performance? This is a question that students of political economy have long pondered—and to which there are no easy answers. Take, for example, this apparently straightforward question: Are democratic states more or less able to pursue effective developmental strategies? Although all economies, even the most powerful, experience ups and downs, the United States, Canada, and the countries of the European Union—all democracies—have been notable economic success stories (see Figure 1). However, until the Asian economic crisis that began in 1997, several countries with authoritarian regimes achieved remarkable records of development despite having authoritarian governments. The Republic of Korea (South Korea), Taiwan, and Singapore surged economically in the 1960s and 1970s, and Malaysia and Thailand followed suit in the 1980s and 1990s. China has enjoyed the highest growth rate in the world since the early 1990s. Nowadays both democratic and authoritarian governments are facing tremendous challenges to economic governance, although in different ways and to different degrees. Europe faces high unemployment and worries about a loss of competitiveness due to the high costs of wages and social welfare protections that are the result of decades of democratic pressures from center-left parties and working-class interests. Asia is in the throes of an economic crisis and loss of international confidence by investors and international financial organizations such as the IMF who doubt whether authoritarian regimes can effectively reform institutions and stabilize their economies. At another level, all countries are facing trade-offs between more market-driven and more state-regulated economic strategies. As you read the country studies, try to reach your own conclusions about what factors—such as level of democracy and approaches to economic management—lead to economic success and whether any consistent patterns apply across countries.

Figure 1

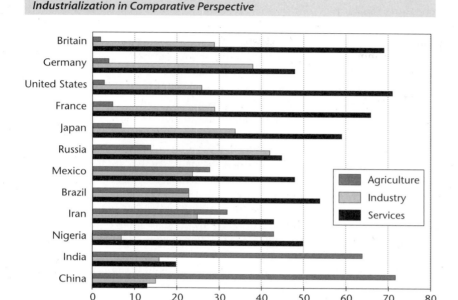

Industrialization in Comparative Perspective

One way to measure the level of industrialization in a country is to look at where people work in the major sectors of the economy. This chart shows the percentage of the labor force in services, industry, and argiculture for all the countries in this textbook. *Source:* United Nations Human Development Report, 1998. Reprinted by permission of the United Nations Development Programme and Oxford University Press.

Theme 3: The Democratic Idea

Our comparative case studies reveal a surprising level of complexity in the seemingly simple fact of the rapid spread of democracy throughout much of the world in recent years. First of all, they show the strong appeal of the democratic idea, by which we mean the claim by citizens that they should, in some way, exercise substantial control over the decisions made by their states and governments. Nevertheless, the cases also show that there is still a lot of **authoritarianism** in the world; that is, there remain many states based on arbitrary and unchecked political power in which citizens cannot freely choose their leaders, openly oppose the government, or question the rulers' decisions.

As authoritarian rulers have recently learned in the former Soviet Union, Brazil, Nigeria, and China, once persistent and widespread pressures for democratic

participation develop, they are hard (although not impossible) to resist. A good indication of the near universal appeal of the democratic idea is that even authoritarian regimes proclaim their attachment to democracy—usually asserting that they embody a superior form to that prevailing elsewhere. For example, leaders of the People's Republic of China claim that their brand of "socialist democracy" represents the interests of the vast majority of citizens more effectively than do the "bourgeois democracies" of capitalist societies.

Second, the case studies draw attention to diverse sources of support for democracy. Democracy has proved appealing for many reasons. In some historical settings, it may represent a standoff or equilibrium among political contenders for power, in which no one group can gain sufficient strength to control outcomes alone.[5] Democracy may appeal to citizens in authoritarian settings because democratic regimes often rank among the world's most stable, affluent, and cohesive countries. Another important pressure for democracy is born of the human desire for dignity and equality. Even when dictatorial regimes appear to benefit their countries—for example, by promoting economic development or nationalist goals—citizens are still likely to demand democracy. Although authoritarian governments can suppress demands for democratic participation, the domestic and (in recent years) international costs of doing so are high.

Third, the country studies show that democracies vary widely in concrete historical, institutional, and cultural dimensions. We pay close attention to different electoral and party systems, to the distinction between parliamentary and presidential systems, and to differences in the values and expectations that shape citizens' demands in different countries.

Fourth, many of the country studies illustrate the potential fragility of democratic transitions. The fact that popular movements or leaders of moderate factions often displace authoritarian regimes and then hold elections does not mean that democratic institutions will prevail or endure: a wide gulf exists between a transition to democracy and the consolidation of democracy. Historically, powerful groups have often opposed democratic institutions because they fear that democracy will threaten their privilege. On the other hand, disadvantaged groups may oppose the democratic process because they see it as unresponsive to their deeply felt grievances. As a result, reversals of democratic regimes have occurred in the past and will doubtless occur in the future. The country studies do not support a philosophy of history or theory of political development that identifies a single (democratic) end point toward which all countries will eventually converge. One important work, published in the early phase of the most recent democratic wave, captured the tenuous process of democratization in its title: *Transitions from Authoritarian Rule: Tentative Conclusions about Uncertain Democracies.*[6] Some suggest that it is far easier for a country to hold its first democratic election than its second. Hence, the fact that the democratic idea is so powerful does not mean that all countries will adopt or preserve democratic institutions.

Finally, our democratic idea theme requires us to examine the incompleteness of democratic agendas in countries with the longest and most developed experiences of representative democracy. In recent years, many citizens in virtually every democracy have turned against the state when their living standards were threatened by high unemployment and economic stagnation. At the same time, antagonistic social movements have targeted the state because of its actions or inactions in such varied spheres as environmental regulation, reproductive rights, and race or ethnic relations. Comparative studies confirm that the democratic idea fuels political conflicts no matter how long-established the democracies because, usually, a large gap separates democratic ideals and the actual functioning of democratic political institutions. Thus, even in countries with impressive histories of democratic institutions, citizens may invoke the democratic idea to demand that their government be more responsive and accountable.

A puzzle: Democracy and stability. Comparativists have intensely debated whether democratic institutions contribute to political stability or, on the contrary, to political disorder. On the one hand, democracy by its very nature permits political opposition: one of its defining characteristics is competition among those who aspire to gain high political office. Political life in democracies is turbulent and unpredictable. On the other hand, the fact that political opposition and competition are legitimate in democracies appears to deepen support for the state even among opponents of a particular government. History reveals far more cases of durable democratic regimes than durable authoritarian regimes in the modern world. In your country-by-country studies, look for the stabilizing and destabilizing consequences of democratic transitions as well as the challenges faced by long-standing democracies.

Theme 4: The Politics of Collective Identity

How do individuals understand who they are in political terms, and on what basis do groups of people come together to advance common political aims? In other words, what are the sources of collective political identity? At one point, social scientists thought they knew the answer. Observers argued that the age-old loyalties of ethnicity, religious affiliation, race, gender, and locality were being dissolved and displaced by economic, political, and cultural modernization. Comparativists thought that **social class**—solidarities based on the shared experience of work or, more broadly, economic position—had become the most important source of collective identity. They believed that most of the time groups would pragmatically pursue their interests in ways that were not politically destabilizing.[7] We now know that the formation of group attachments and the interplay of politically relevant collective identities are far more complex and uncertain.

In the long-established democracies, the importance of identities based on class membership has declined, although class and material sources of collective political identity remain significant in political competition and economic organization. By contrast, contrary to earlier predictions, in many countries non-class identities have assumed growing, not diminishing, significance. These affiliations develop from a sense of belonging to particular groups based on language, religion, ethnicity, race, nationality, or gender.

The politics of collective political identity involves struggles to define which groups are full participants in the political community and which are marginalized or even ostracized. It also involves a constant tug-of-war over relative power and influence—both symbolic and substantive—among groups. Issues of inclusion and priority remain pivotal in many countries, and they may never be resolved.

In addition, questions of representation are very hard to resolve—who is included in an ethnic minority community, for example, or who speaks for the community or negotiates with a governmental authority on its behalf? One reason why conflict around these questions can be so intense is that political leaders in the state and in opposition movements often seek to mobilize support by exploiting ethnic, religious, racial, or regional rivalries and manipulating the issue of representation.

Identity-based conflicts can be found even in long-established countries. In Britain, France, and Germany issues of nationality, citizenship, and immigration—often with ethnic or racial overtones—have been hot-button issues and have often spilled over into electoral politics. These conflicts are often particularly intense in postcolonial countries, such as Nigeria, where colonial powers forced ethnic groups together in order to carve out a country and borders were drawn with little regard to preexisting collective identities. This process of state formation by the imposition of external will sowed seeds for future conflict in Nigeria and elsewhere and threatens the continued survival of many postcolonial countries.

A puzzle: Collective identity and distributional politics. Once identity demands are placed on the political agenda, can governments resolve them by distributing resources in ways that redress the grievances of the minority or politically weaker identity groups? Collective identities operate both at the level of symbols, attitudes, values, and beliefs and at the level of material resources. However, the contrast between material versus nonmaterial-based identities and demands should not be exaggerated. In practice, most groups are animated both by feelings of attachment and solidarity and by the desire to obtain material benefits and political influence for their members. But the analytical distinction between material and nonmaterial demands remains useful, and it is worth considering whether the nonmaterial aspects of the politics of collective identities make political disputes over ethnicity or religion or language or nationality especially divisive and difficult to resolve.

In a situation of extreme scarcity, it may prove nearly impossible to reach any compromise among groups with conflicting material demands. But if an adequate level of resources is available, such conflicts may be easier to resolve because groups can negotiate at least a minimally satisfying share of resources. This process of determining who gets what or how resources are distributed is called **distributional politics**. However, the demands of ethnic, religious, and nationalist movements may be difficult to satisfy by a distributional style of politics. The distributional style may be quite ineffective when, for example, a religious group demands that the government require all citizens to conform to its social practices, or a dominant linguistic group insists that a single language be used in education and government throughout the country. In such cases, political conflict tends to move from the distributive realm to a cultural realm, where compromises cannot be achieved by simply "dividing the pie" of material resources. The country studies will examine a wide range of conflicts involving collective identities. It will be interesting (and possibly troubling) to ponder whether and under what conditions they are subject to the normal give-and-take of political bargaining.

These four themes provide our analytic scaffold.

With an understanding of the method of comparative politics and the four themes in mind, we can now discuss how we have grouped the country studies that comprise *Introduction to Comparative Politics* and how the text is organized for comparative analysis.

Section ❹ Classifying Political Systems

There are nearly 200 states in the world in the present day. How can we classify these nearly 200 regimes in a manageable way? One possibility would be not to classify them at all, but simply to treat each state as different and unique. However, comparativists are rarely content with this solution—or non-solution. It makes sense to highlight clusters of states that share important similarities—just as it is useful to identify what distinguishes one cluster of relatively similar states from other clusters. When comparativists classify a large number of cases into a smaller number of types or clusters, they call the result a **typology**. Typologies facilitate comparison both within the same type as well as between types of states. For example, what difference does it make that Britain has a parliamentary form of government and France has a semi-presidential one? Both are long-established democracies, but their different mix of institutions provides an interesting laboratory case to study the impact of institutional variation.

We can also compare *across* clusters or types. In this type of comparison—comparativists call this **most different case analysis**—we analyze what produces the substantial differences we observe. What difference does it make that the world's two most populous countries—China and India—have two such different political systems? How do their different political regimes affect such important issues as economic development, human rights, and the role of women?

How do we go about constructing typologies of states? Typologies exist as much in the eye of their beholder as in the nature of the beast! Typologies are artificial constructs—they are made rather than born. What counts in evaluating a typology is not whether it is "true" or "false," but whether it is *useful*, and for what purpose. Typologies are helpful to the extent that they permit us to engage in useful comparisons.

What is the most useful typology for classifying states in the present era? In the recent past, political scientists have engaged in a lively debate over the best typology of contemporary states. For more than half a century—from the end of World War II until the 1980s—there was a general consensus on the utility of one typology. Political scientists classified states as industrial (and primarily Western) democracies, the "first world"; communist states as the "second world"; and poor countries in Asia, Africa, and Latin America that had recently gained independence as the "third world." It was imperfect. For example, how should one classify Japan, a country not in the West that rapidly developed in the 1960s and 1970s and became the world's second leading economic power? Nevertheless, the typology was a generally adequate if imperfect way to distinguish broad groups of countries.

Today the first-, second-, and third-world typology is less common because of the large number of countries that no longer fit comfortably within it. For one thing, scores of countries have become democratic in the past two decades that are not highly industrialized nor located in the North Atlantic region, the geographic base of the "first world." From Argentina to Zimbabwe, countries that were formerly colonies or undemocratic states adopted democratic institutions in the last several decades, one of the most important and promising changes in the modern world.

Linked to the swelling of the ranks of democratic countries has been the near-disappearance of countries in the "second world." Beginning in 1989, the implosion of communism in the former Soviet Union and Eastern and Central Europe set off a revolutionary change in world politics. Only a handful of countries in the world—China, Cuba, Vietnam, Laos, and the Democratic People's Republic of (North) Korea—are now ruled by communist parties and declare an allegiance to

Global Connection: *How Is Development Measured?*

One frequently used measure of a country's level of economic development is its gross national product (GNP) per capita. This figure is an estimate of a country's total economic output (including income earned from abroad) divided by its total population. Such estimates are made in a country's own currency, such as pesos in Mexico or rubles in Russia.

In order to make comparisons of GNP per capita across countries, it is necessary to convert the estimates to a common currency, usually the U.S. dollar. This is done using official international currency exchange rates, which, for example, would tell you how many pesos or rubles it takes to buy $1 U.S. But many economists believe that an estimate of GNP per capita in dollars based on official exchange rates does not give a very accurate sense of the real standards of living in different countries because it does not tell what goods and services (such as housing, food, and transportation) people can actually buy with their local currencies.

An alternative and increasingly popular means of comparing levels of economic development across countries is to use exchange rates based on purchasing power parity (PPP). PPP-based exchange rates take into account the actual cost of living in a particular country by figuring what it costs to buy the same bundle of goods in different countries. For example, how many pesos does it take to buy a certain amount of food in Mexico or rubles to pay for housing in Russia? Many analysts think that PPP provides a more reliable (and revealing) tool for comparing standards of living among countries.

The data boxes that are part of each country unit in this text give both GNP per capita at official exchange rates and using purchasing power parity. As you will see, the differences between the two calculations can be quite dramatic, especially for developing countries. For example, China's 1997 GNP per capita according to conventional methods was calculated to be only $860, whereas its PPP-based GNP per capita in the same year was estimated at $3,570!

Because income comparisons based on either GNP per capita or purchasing power parity do not provide a complete picture of a country's level of development, the United Nations has introduced another concept that is useful in making socioeconomic comparisons among nations: the Human Development Index (HDI). Based on a formula that takes into account the three factors of *longevity* (life expectancy at birth), *knowledge* (literacy and average years of schooling), and *income* (according to PPP), the UN assigns each country of the world, for which there is enough data, a Human Development Index decimal number between 0 and 1; the closer a country is to 1, the better its level of human development.

Out of 174 countries ranked according to HDI by the United Nations in 1998, Canada (.960) was at the top and Sierra Leone (.185) was ranked last. Among the countries included in this book, France (2), the United States (4), Japan (8), Britain (14), Germany (19), Mexico (49), and Brazil (62) scored as having "high human development"; Russia (72), Iran (78), and China (106) had "medium human development"; and India (139) and Nigeria (142) were ranked as having "low human development."

communist ideology. It follows that the "second world" is no longer a useful category to classify countries.

Finally, the "third world" has also become less useful as a way to understand the many countries formerly classified in this cluster. Countries that are often called "third world" share few features, other than being less economically developed than industrialized nations (see Global Connection box above). Their colonial legacies have receded further and further into the past. Furthermore, some of them have become more industrialized and economically powerful, including Brazil and Mexico. Nevertheless, even in

the post–Cold War era, the term "third world" retains some significance as a shorthand way to refer to the nearly 130 countries that the United Nations classifies as "developing" and which are still separated from the 50 or so industrialized nations by a vast economic gulf. Within the "third world" there are about four dozen countries—for example, Afghanistan, Ethiopia, and Haiti—that are classified by the UN as "least developed" and are so poor that the term "fourth world" is sometimes used to describe them.

If the "three worlds" method of classification is no longer as useful as it once was, what is a preferred alternative? At present, there is no agreement among comparativists on this question. We provide here a typology that we believe captures some major features that distinguish countries in the contemporary world. We distinguish among *long-established* or *durable democracies*, *newly established* or *transitional democracies*, and *nondemocratic regimes*. We explain why we believe this to be the most useful typology at the present time. But we invite students to evaluate our proposal as they read this book—and to consider constructing a preferable substitute.

What Democracy Is ... and Is Not

Our typology reflects the bedrock distinction between democratic and nondemocratic regimes. Therefore, the first step is to establish what democracy is . . . and is not. We then suggest why the distinction between long-established or durable democracies versus newly established democracies is central to our typology. We conclude this discussion with a description of those features that are shared by countries in the category of nondemocratic regimes.[8]

What is the meaning—or, rather—meanings of the term *democracy*? The wide popularity of the term conceals some important ambiguities. Should democracy be defined solely on the basis of the procedures used to select top governmental officeholders—that is, the requirement that occupants of the highest office(s) of the state be selected on the basis of free and fair elections in which multiple parties are allowed to organize to present candidates and all citizens are entitled to cast a vote? Or, for a state to qualify as democratic, must it respect citizens' civil liberties (including rights of free expression, dissent, and privacy), regardless of whether a particular government departs from these standards? What is the relation between religious practice and the exercise of political power? Some regimes (for example, the Islamic government in Iran) claim to be democratic yet interpret the term to mean that the government must implement a particular religious teaching (in this case, the Qu'ran). What is the relationship between democracy defined in procedural terms, as we do, and

substantive equalities? Must a democratic regime guarantee all citizens certain minimum economic and social rights (such as the right to adequate food, shelter, and medical care) or merely political and civil rights (such as the right to vote and to criticize the government)?

Despite the many debates about the meaning(s) of democracy, a rough consensus has emerged among comparativists. It is generally agreed that, for a political system to qualify as democratic, a country must have the following political characteristics:

- **Political accountability.** There must be formal procedures by which those who hold political power are chosen and held accountable to the people of the country. The key mechanism for such accountability is regular, free, and fair elections in which the voters elect candidates for office.
- **Political competition.** Political parties must be free to organize, present candidates for office, express their ideas, and compete in fair elections. The winning party must be allowed to take office, and the losing party must relinquish power through legal and peaceful means.
- **Political freedom.** All citizens must possess political rights and civil liberties. These include the right to participate in the political process; freedom of assembly, organization, and political expression (including the right to criticize the government); and protection against arbitrary state intrusion into citizens' private lives. A judiciary not subject to direct political control is a common institutional means for safeguarding these freedoms.
- **Political equality.** All citizens must be legally entitled to participate in politics (by voting, running for office, or joining an interest group), and their votes must have equal weight in the political process. Members of political, ethnic, or other minority groups must have equal rights as citizens.

While this is a useful checklist of the political prerequisites of democracy, several qualifications need to be added. First, no government has ever fully lived up to these standards, and all democratic governments have, at various points in their histories, violated them to a greater or lesser extent. For example, the United States did not extend voting rights to women until

1920 and did not effectively protect the rights of racial minorities until the 1960s (and, by some important measures, still has not fully done so).

Second, these ideals are limited, not absolute, in practice. All democracies have laws restricting views, actions, and organizations that are judged to threaten national security or public safety. Such laws place limits on political freedom and sometimes on political competition (as when a "subversive" political party is banned).

Third, the interpretation and implementation of these ideals are often debatable and sometimes become very contentious political issues. For example, the debate over gun control in the United States involves sharply differing perspectives on the meaning of freedom: Some Americans see any ban on weapons or a registration requirement as an infringement of their constitutional right to bear arms, whereas others believe that the government must restrict gun ownership in the name of public safety. In most every other industrial democracy, gun control is not even an issue: Few citizens question the state's authority to limit the possession of weapons.

Fourth, even in democracies, economic inequalities load the political deck. Wealthier citizens, interest groups, and parties can use their more substantial resources to increase their chances of winning an election or influencing public policy. This power creates a tension, to a greater or lesser degree, in all industrial democracies between the formal political procedures (such as voting) in which all are equal, and the actual situation in which the affluent are "more equal than others" because of their greater ability to influence political outcomes and public policy.

The tension between citizens' economic inequalities and their equal right to participate in elections and to try to affect policies is manifest in all industrial democracies. Indeed, it is a perpetual source of political division as governments try to shape distributional politics in a manner that best suits the material interests of social groups who support them. Three key areas of policy difference involve

- **The distribution of taxes.** Although all governments levy taxes on citizens and businesses to support their activities, who pays how much is often a source of intense political debate.
- **Governmental economic priorities.** Should eco-

nomic policy be directed above all toward restraining inflation (a particular concern for the affluent or elderly because inflation reduces the value of their assets and savings) or toward reducing unemployment (which traditionally has harmed working people most)?

- **The extent of governmental spending for social programs.** Typical benefits include the public provision of health care, unemployment compensation, old-age pensions, and assistance to the needy.

There are dramatic variations among industrial democracies in these policy areas. Consider social expenditures, which include programs for the elderly, disabled, and unemployed, often grouped under the term **welfare state**. In some countries where moderate or conservative parties have ruled for long periods, including Japan and the United States, welfare state expenditures constitute around 10 percent of the gross national product (GNP). In many Western European countries, on the other hand, where labor movements have been politically influential within ruling coalitions, the share of social spending may be three times as high. These differences obviously have an important impact on what it means to live in these societies.

Despite these qualifications about the nature of democracy, the prerequisites of democracy—accountability, competition, freedom, and equality—are still useful tools in the study of comparative politics. Not only do they provide a demarcation between democratic and dictatorial political systems, but they also serve as standards against which democracies can be measured and compared. It may be impossible for comparativists to decide whether, for example, France is more or less democratic than Germany. But it is possible (and we hope interesting!) to compare how presidential and parliamentary democracies differ in keeping executives and legislators accountable to the electorate. Such standards can also help us measure (though not precisely) the successes and shortcomings of established democracies in living up to democratic ideals as well as the process of democratization in transitional democracies.

The typology we use in *Introduction to Comparative Politics* makes a fundamental distinction between durable and transitional. Why? At one time, it was thought that once a democratic regime was established, it would remain democratic forever. However, the many examples of democratic reversals taught the sad lesson that establishing a democratic regime is only the beginning of the process of creating a durable democratic system. We first explain why this is the case and then analyze our two categories of democracies.

Democratic Transition and Democratic Consolidation

As noted above, achieving a *transition* to democracy is only the first step toward *consolidating* democracy. In order to achieve a transition to democracy, a non-democratic regime must resign or be toppled and the four prerequisites of democracy we enumerated above—political accountability, political competition, political freedom, and political equality—must be achieved. It is no easy matter to launch a democratic transition. Undemocratic regimes fiercely—usually violently—resist being shunted aside. And yet, however difficult as it may be to take the first steps toward democracy, it is even harder to achieve a durable, stable democracy. In particular, doing so requires achieving much that is not present initially in transitional democracies.

In order to understand the process of consolidating democracy, we draw on a fine account of the *Problems of Democratic Transition and Consolidation*, by two distinguished political scientists, Juan Linz and Alfred Stepan.[9] Linz and Stepan emphasize that, in order to have a democratic regime, there must first be a viable state—which may be no easy matter (recall state disintegration and civil war in the former Yugoslavia in the late 1990s). Once this hurdle has been surmounted, they assert, five conditions are necessary to consolidate a democratic state or regime:

1. "[C]onditions must exist for the development of a free and lively civil society."[10] Civil society consists of self-organized groups, organizations, associations, and relatively independent citizens. A thick network of autonomous organizations constitutes a "school for democracy," in which individuals gain experience in running their own affairs. A vibrant civil society also constitutes a source of independent power that can check arbitrary state action. Unlike the act of toppling a repressive regime, creating a "free and lively civil society" cannot happen at one stroke. This highlights the wide chasm that may separate a democratic transition from democratic consolidation.

2. "[T]here must be a relatively autonomous and valued political society." By political society, Linz and Stepan mean those political institutions and processes—including political parties, electoral rules, and informal arrangements for forming governing alliances—that enable the formal rules of the democratic political game to function. It is not sufficient to hold elections in order to ensure a democratic outcome, for example, if there are twenty or more candidates for a given position. Or if the political parties that gain representation in the legislature cannot form a coalition that allows a stable government to emerge. Or if rules prohibiting political corruption, e.g., bribing candidates, are either nonexistent or not enforced.

3. "[T]here must be a rule of law to ensure legal guarantees for citizens' freedoms and independent associational life." By rule of law, Linz and Stepan mean the need for clear, predictable, fair, and stable laws, if possible enforced by an impartial and powerful judiciary. They also describe this situation as **constitutionalism**. This situation minimizes the chances of naked competition for power or outright chaos.

4. "[T]here must be a state bureaucracy that is usable by the new democratic government." Without a capable and loyal bureaucracy, the democratic state cannot carry out the core functions needed to function: collecting taxes, enforcing the law, and developing and implementing policies that are responsive to electoral majorities.

5. "[T]here must be an institutionalized economic society." By "economic society," Linz and Stepan mean an economy that combines elements of market competition and political direction. If all economic life were controlled by the state (the "command economies" of communist regimes for example, as will be described in the chapter on the People's Republic of China), democracy would probably be impossible, since the state would be all-powerful in this decisive sphere. On the other hand, democracy would not be possible either,

claim Linz and Stepan (and we agree), if there was no possibility of citizens electing a government which would, to apply the terminology of Theme 2 (above), govern the economy in particular ways (for example, by requiring firms to pay minimum wages or observe environmental standards).

Some might disagree with particular elements of Linz and Stepan's argument. But the particular features of the conditions that Linz and Stepan specify are less important than their basic argument: for democracy to endure (and not simply to exist for a brief time), democratic institutions and processes must be *embedded* in a wider set of social, economic, and cultural arrangements.

Durable Versus Transitional Democracies

The discussion of democratic transition and consolidation suggests why there is such an important difference between durable and transitional democracies. The five underlying conditions described above are far more fully developed in long-established democracies. Although there are plenty of conflicts and challenges in these countries, by and large, conflicts are played out within democratic institutions and the rules of the game. By contrast, democratic institutions in the transitional democracies are fragile and vulnerable: conflicts are likely to involve disputes not only *within* existing democratic institutions but *about* the desirability of these institutions. There is less certainty that groups will play by the democratic rules or accept decisions arrived at under these rules. There is less full development of relatively self-organized and autonomous civil society, less effective political society and state bureaucracy, and so on.

Take an important example: elections. In durable democracies, the rules regulating elections are far more fully worked out, stable, and enforced. There are elaborate and reasonable laws concerning campaign finance, such as ceilings on how much private citizens and groups can contribute to political parties and candidates. Most likely, these laws will be obeyed. Again, one must beware of idealizing durable democracies. Note how frequently evidence comes to light of political corruption. But also note that somewhat independent media exist which may expose corruption—

evidence of a well-functioning civil society. By contrast, the violations of democratic procedures in the transitional democracies are more frequent and more flagrant, on the whole. And, most important, they tend to imperil the survival of democratic institutions and processes.

In brief, while all countries fall short on both the four key features of democracy and the five prerequisites for durable democracy, the difference in the *degree* to which these arrangements exist in long-established versus transitional democracies adds up to a difference in *kind*. It is for this reason that our typology divides democracies into the two categories. The broad differences between the two groups are both evident at a given time and affect the probability that a particular country will remain democratic in the future. Not only do durable democracies have a longer *past* history of democracy, the chances are far greater that they will remain democratic in the *future*.

While there is no hard-and-fast division between the two groups, we define durable democracies as those with a record of virtually uninterrupted democratic practice for at least forty years. The countries in *Introduction to Comparative Politics* that we classify as durable democracies are Britain, France, Germany, India, Japan, and the United States. The transitional democracies are Brazil, Mexico, and Russia.

What divides durable democracies from transitional ones? What was the process by which they became consolidated or more durable democracies? Were not the durable democracies newly established at some earlier point in their development? Why use forty years as the basis to divide the two groups?

Although these are important questions, there is insufficient space to consider them here in the Introduction, with the care they deserve. Many country chapters will address these questions. We offer two preliminary observations. First, there is nothing magical about the figure of forty years. However, if a country remains democratic for two or more generations, the chances are good that Linz and Stepan's five conditions will have taken root. Hence, the chances are vastly greater that the country will remain democratic in the future.

A second point concerns the process by which transitional democracies became consolidated: these countries' histories suggest that there is no single path to democratic consolidation. Consider the six durable democracies included in *Introduction to Comparative Politics*. Democracy in the United States emerged from a revolutionary anticolonial struggle, in which perhaps only one-third of the residents of the American colonies actively supported independence. Britain developed democratic institutions through a slow process that took centuries. Democracy developed in France in a quite zigzag fashion. Democracy developed early (following the French Revolution of 1789) but was not consolidated at that time. Instead, there were a succession of regimes in France, some democratic, others undemocratic, until the creation of the quite democratic and durable Fifth Republic in 1958. Germany and Japan became enduring democracies only as a result of defeat in war and military occupation by democratic countries. Although this does not seem a promising recipe for democratic consolidation, both countries have proved quite successful in achieving the five conditions for democratic consolidation described by Linz and Stepan. India was ruled by the British in highly undemocratic fashion for centuries. Nonetheless, in contrast to many colonies that gained their independence in the postwar period, India proved able to create and preserve democratic institutions after it achieved independence in 1947. This was the result of both a long tradition of village-level autonomy in India and the remarkable success of British-style parliamentary institutions.

As varied as the political characteristics of democratic countries may be, their historic—and contemporary—paths to democratic transition and consolidation may show even greater variety. There is not a country in our list of durable democracies whose democratic consolidation always looked like a sure bet. Which of the contemporary transitional cases will achieve a comparable democratic stability in the years ahead, and which will fall back into authoritarianism or greater chaos? We may not know the answer to this critical question for many years.

We return to the questions posed earlier of why and how to distinguish between durable and transitional democracies. We divide democracies into two clusters because there are significant differences between the two groups.

The four key features of democracy and the five prerequisites of durable democracy described earlier provide the tools to understand how durable and transitional democracies differ. As a general matter, durable democracies rank higher on these measures than transitional democracies. This is a broad generalization and many of the country chapters in this book explore the specific characteristics which will enable you to think more fully about this question. Be forewarned that real history is usually messier (and more interesting!) than abstract models.

In durable democracies, the rules of the democratic political game have been achieved, refined, tested, and strengthened through years of practice. While all countries face new challenges, durable democracies have a longer and deeper period of democratic apprenticeship and, hence, are better equipped to face new challenges. In transitional democracies, democratic rules may look wonderful on paper (that is, in the Constitution). But, like new clothes, they may not fit or wear very well.

If space permitted, we might discuss differences between the two groups of democracies with respect to all four core features of democracy and five prerequisites for consolidated democracy. Consider, however, as an illustration of how to explore the question, political accountability. In durable democracies, there is virtually no uncertainty about the fact that periodic elections will be held at times specified by the constitution. It is invariably the case that voters can choose among competing parties presenting alternative programs, that votes will be counted honestly, and that the winning party or parties will be entitled to take control of government. Finally, if the newly elected government is not responsive to citizens' demands, voters can be confident that in the not-too-distant future a new election will be held—at which point they can hold the government accountable and, if a majority so chooses, "throw the rascals out."

Durable democracies vary widely in the particulars of when elections will be held, the procedures used to elect representatives, the way the government is formed, and so on. But the most important point is that, in fact, there are well-established and well-respected procedures for keeping governments accountable.

In transitional democracies, there is far greater uncertainty on all these points, which means that governments in these countries are far less accountable to their citizens. It is clear that Russia and Brazil are transitional democracies. Within recent years, both had authoritarian governments chosen by undemocratic methods. In Brazil, a military junta directed the government; in Russia, a single party, the Communist Party, ruled and elections were a sham. The Mexican case is more complicated. For generations the Mexican Constitution of 1917 stated that political parties were free to compete in elections. However, only in the 1990s did genuine political competition develop. Until then, one party, the Institutional Revolutionary Party (or PRI), had governed Mexico with a heavy hand. The formal promise of democracy in this important sphere (and many others) was simply an illusion.

Chapter 9 will describe how Mexico has taken significant strides toward fulfilling the promise of democracy. Elections now provide citizens with a greater range of alternatives and there is more chance that parties other than the PRI will gain election. Given Mexico's steady progress toward achieving authentic democratic practice, we classify the country as a democracy. But our uncertainty about how deeply rooted its democratic institutions are, and the continued evidence of undemocratic practices, explains why we include it in the category of recently established democracies.

To repeat what we have emphasized, the distinction between transitional and durable democracies is not airtight. Democracy may become more firmly entrenched in Mexico, as measured by our four core features of democracy and five requisites of consolidated democracy, and Mexico may eventually become a durable democracy. Similarly, there is no guarantee that durable democracies will not falter. Although many countries have joined the ranks of democracies in the recent period, some democratic regimes will doubtless abandon democracy in the future. The large number of countries in today's world that are not democratic form the third category of countries in *Introduction to Comparative Politics.*

Non-Democracies

The three countries covered in Part 4 of this book— China, Iran, and Nigeria—have little in common other than that they are not democracies. They are located in three geographically and culturally distinct parts of the world, East Asia, the Middle East, and West Africa. Also, although none of these countries is industrialized, their economies are very different and at varied levels of economic development: China is still a relatively poor country, but with one of the world's fastest growing economies; Iran, because of its oil wealth, is considerably more prosperous, but has been experiencing little economic growth; while Nigeria, also a major oil exporter, remains one of the world's poorest countries.

Most importantly in terms of this book, their political systems represent very different types of nondemocracies. China is a **communist party-state**, a system of government in which a political party that claims allegiance to Marxist-Leninist ideology holds a monopoly on power. Iran is a **theocracy** in which Islamic religious leaders, values, and laws dominate political life. For most of the period since 1966, Nigeria was a **military dictatorship** in which unelected army officers ran the government. Although competitive presidential elections in 1999 held out the possibility that Nigeria might have moved into the camp of transitional democracies, it is too soon to say whether Nigeria has achieved a transition to democracy.

The chapters on these countries discuss the specific political features of these various types of nondemocracies. For now the important point is to clarify why, despite their many differences, they can be classified together in a single category. One way to do so is to refer to four political characteristics of democracy: political accountability, competition, freedom, and equality. Although no country fully lives up to these ideals, the governments of China, Iran, and Nigeria fall far short of meeting even the minimal standards of what constitutes a democracy. As you read the chapters on these countries, take special note of what it is about the structure and distribution of power that limits the accountability of political leaders to the people they govern, prevents competition among political parties, constrains the rights and liberties of citizens, and denies the political equality of all members of society.

You should also watch (both in this text and the real world!) for signs of democratization in China, Iran, and Nigeria. There are elements of democracy in all three. In China, rural villages—home to a majority of the Chinese people—have, in recent years, been conducting competitive local elections, albeit under the watchful eye of the Chinese Communist Party. In Iran, there is fierce electoral competition among political parties espousing very different positions on important policy matters (including relations with the United States), although all parties must operate within the framework of Islamic law. In Nigeria, military leaders who came to power in 1998 promised to hold elections in 1999 and return the country to civilian rule.

What would it take for the seeds of democracy to take root and allow democratic rule to become firmly established in these countries? Remember: elections alone do not a democracy make. Think back to the range of conditions discussed above that are necessary for the consolidation of democracy. Are the governments of China, Iran, and Nigeria easing restrictions on the establishment and functioning of the autonomous citizen organizations that are necessary for a "free and lively civil society"? Is there a democratic "political society"—including truly free competition among political parties and checks on official corruption? Does the rule of law prevail over the dictates of individual leaders, the power of a particular

political party, or the values espoused by a single ideology or religion? Is there a state bureaucracy that effectively and impartially carries out the laws and implements the policies of the government? Does the economy combine elements of market forces and state direction that provide for a democratic balance between private gain and public good?

The spread of democracy to so many countries around the world was one of the most amazing and important political stories of the late twentieth century. And questions about the future of democracy are at the forefront of the political challenges and changing agendas of the new century: Will the trend toward democracy continue and will it bring fundamental political change to non-democratic countries such as China, Iran, and Nigeria? Will the world's many new and transitional democracies—including Russia, Brazil, and Mexico—be able to move to the next step and consolidate democratic rule? How will the United States, Britain, France, Germany, India, and the world's other well-established democracies deal with both long-persisting and newly emerging challenges to their democratic institutions and ideals?

Section ❺ Organization of the Text

The core of this book consists of case studies of twelve countries selected for their significance in terms of our comparative themes and ability to provide a reasonable cross-section of types of political systems and geographic regions. Although each of the country studies makes some important comparative references, the studies are primarily intended to provide detailed descriptions and analyses of the politics of individual countries. At the same time, the country studies have common section and subsection headings to help you make comparisons and explore similar themes across the various cases. The following are brief summaries of the main issues and questions covered in the country studies.

Section 1: The Making of the Modern State

This section provides an overview of the forces that have shaped the particular character of the state. We believe that an understanding of the contemporary

politics of any country requires some familiarity with the historical process by which its current political system was formed. "Politics in Action" uses a specific event to illustrate an important political moment in the country's recent history and to highlight some of the critical political issues it faces. "Geographic Setting" locates the country in its regional context and discusses the political implications of its geographic setting. "Critical Junctures" looks at some of the major stages and decisive turning points in state development. This discussion should give you an idea of how the country assumed its present political order and a sense of how relations between state and society have developed over time. "Themes and Implications" shows how the past pattern of state development continues to shape the country's current political agenda. "Historical Junctures and Political Themes" applies the text's core themes to the making of the modern state: How was the country's political development affected by its place in the world of states? What are the political implications of the state's approach to economic management? What has been the country's experience with the democratic idea? What are the important bases of collective identity in the country, and how do these relate to the people's image of themselves as citizens of the state? "Implications for Comparative Politics" discusses the broader significance of the country for the study of comparative politics.

Section 2: Political Economy and Development

This section traces the country's recent and contemporary economic development. It explores the issues raised by the core theme of "governing the economy" and analyzes how economic development has affected political change. The placement of this section near the beginning of the country study reflects our belief that an understanding of an economic situation is essential for analyzing its politics. "State and Economy" discusses the basic organization of the country's economy, with an emphasis on the role of the state in managing economic life and on the relationship between the government and other economic actors. This section also analyzes the state's social welfare policies, such as health care, housing, and pension programs. "Society and Economy" examines the social and political implications of the country's economic situation. It asks who benefits from economic change and looks at how economic development creates or reinforces class, ethnic, gender, regional, or ideological cleavages in society. "The International Political Economy" considers the country's global role: How have patterns of trade and foreign investment changed over time? What is the country's relationship to regional and international organizations? To what degree has the country been able to influence multilateral policies? How have international economic issues affected the domestic political agenda?

Section 3: Governance and Policy-Making

Here we describe the state's major policy-making institutions and procedures. The section on the "Organization of the State" lays out the fundamental principles—as reflected in the country's constitution,

its official ideology, and its historical experience—on which the political system and the distribution of political power are based. It also sketches the basic structure of the state, including the relationship among different levels and branches of government. "The Executive" encompasses whatever key offices (for example, presidents, prime ministers, communist party leaders) are at the top of the political system, focusing on those who have the most power, how they are selected, and how they use their power to make policy. It looks at the national bureaucracy and its relationship to the chief executive(s) and the governing party and its role in the policy-making. "Other State Institutions" generally include the military, the judiciary and the legal system, state-run corporations, and subnational government. "The Policy-Making Process" summarizes how state policy gets made and implemented. It describes the roles of formal institutions and procedures as well as nonformal aspects of policy-making, such as patron-client relations and interest-group activity.

Section 4: Representation and Participation

The relationship between the state and the society it governs is the topic of Section 4. How do different groups in society organize to further their political interests, how do they participate and get represented in the political system, and how do they influence policy-making? Given the importance of the U.S. Congress in policy-making, American readers might expect to find the principal discussion of "The Legislature" in the Section 3 discussion, "Governance and Policy-Making," rather than in Section 4. But the United States is rather exceptional in having a legislature that is very nearly a coequal branch of government with the executive in the policy process. In most political systems, the executive dominates the policy process—even when it is ultimately responsible to the legislature, as in a parliamentary system. In most countries other than the United States, the legislature functions primarily to represent and provide a forum for the political expression of various interests in government; it is only secondarily (and in some cases, such as China, only marginally) a policy-making body. Therefore, although this section does describe and assess the legislature's role in policy-making, its primary focus is on how the legislature represents or fails to represent different interests in society. "Political Parties and the Party System" describes the overall organization of the party system and reviews the major parties. "Elections" discusses the election process and recent trends in electoral behavior. It also considers the significance of elections (or lack thereof) as a vehicle for citizen participation in politics and in bringing about changes in the government. "Political Culture, Citizenship, and Identity" examines how people perceive themselves as members of the political community: the nature and source of political values and attitudes, who is considered a citizen of the state, and how different groups in society understand their relationship to the state. The topics covered may include political aspects of the educational system, the media, religion, and ethnicity. "Interests, Social Movements, and Protest" discusses how various groups pursue their political interests outside the party system. When do they use formal organizations (such as unions) or launch movements (such as "Green" environmental movements)? What is the relationship between the state and such organizations and movements? When and how do citizens engage in acts of protest that may take them beyond the boundaries of the law? And how does the state respond to such protests?

Section 5: Politics in Transition

In Section 5, each country study returns to the book's focus on the major challenges that are reshaping our world and the study of comparative politics. "Political Challenges and Changing Agendas" lays out the major unresolved issues facing the country and assesses which are most likely to dominate in the near future. "Politics in Comparative Perspective" returns to the four themes and highlights what this case study tells us about politics in other countries that have similar political systems or that face similar kinds of political challenges.

It is quite a challenge to understand the contemporary world of politics. We hope that the timely information and thematic focus of *Introduction to Comparative Politics* will both prepare and inspire you to explore further the endlessly fascinating terrain of comparative politics.

Key Terms

Cold War	dictatorship
comparative politics	globalization
comparativists	political economy
country	authoritarianism
nation-state	social class
political institutions	distributional politics
political culture	typology
political development	most different case
state	analysis
executive	welfare state
cabinet	constitutionalism
bureaucracy	communist party-state
legitimacy	theocracy
state formation	military dictatorship
middle-level theory	

Suggested Readings

Anderson, Benedict. *Imagined Communities: Reflections on the Origins and Spread of Nationalism,* rev. ed. London: Verso, 1991.

Bates, Robert H. *Markets and States in Tropical Africa: The Political Basis of Agricultural Policies.* Berkeley: University of California Press, 1981.

Berger, Suzanne, and Ronald Dore, eds. *National Diversity and Global Capitalism.* Ithaca, NY: Cornell University Press, 1996.

Connor, Walker. *Ethnonationalism: The Quest for Understanding.* Princeton, NJ: Princeton University Press, 1994.

Diamond, Larry, and Marc F. Plattner, eds. *The Global Resurgence of Democracy,* 2d ed. Baltimore: Johns Hopkins University Press, 1996.

Diamond, Larry, Marc F. Plattner, Yun-han Chu, and Hung-mao Tien, eds. *Consolidating the Third Wave of Democracy,* 2 vols. Baltimore: Johns Hopkins University Press, 1997.

Downing, Brian M. *The Military Revolution and Political Change: Origins of Democracy and Autocracy in Early Modern Europe.* Princeton, NJ: Princeton University Press, 1992.

Evans, Peter. *Embedded Autonomy: States and Industrial Transformation.* Princeton, NJ: Princeton University Press, 1995.

Evans, Peter B., Dietrich Rueschemeyer, and Theda Skocpol, eds. *Bringing the State Back In.* New York: Cambridge University Press, 1985.

Greenfield, Liah. *Nationalism: Five Roads to Modernity.* Cambridge, MA: Harvard University Press, 1992.

Hall, Peter A. *Governing the Economy: The Politics of State Intervention in Britain and France.* New York: Oxford University Press, 1986.

Huntington, Samuel P. *The Third Wave: Democratization in the Late Twentieth Century.* Norman: University of Oklahoma Press, 1991.

Inglehart, Ronald. *Modernization and Postmodernization: Cultural, Economic, and Political Change in 43 Societies.* Princeton, NJ: Princeton University Press, 1997.

King, Gary, Robert O. Keohane and Sidney Verba. *Designing Social Inquiry: Scientific Inference in Qualitative Research.* Princeton, NJ: Princeton University Press, 1994.

Lichbach, Mark Irving, and Alan S. Zuckerman, eds. *Comparative Politics: Rationality, Culture, and Structure.* New York: Cambridge University Press, 1997.

Linz, Juan J., and Alfred Stepan. *Problems of Democratic Transition and Consolidation: Southern Europe, South America, and Post-Communist Europe.* Baltimore: Johns Hopkins University Press, 1996.

Marx, Anthony. *Making Race and Nation: A Comparison of the United States, South Africa, and Brazil.* New York: Cambridge University Press, 1998.

O'Donnell, Guillermo A., Philippe C. Schmitter, and Laurence Whitehead, eds. *Transitions from Authoritarian Rule,* 4 vols. Baltimore: Johns Hopkins University Press, 1986.

Przeworski, Adam. *Democracy and the Market: Political and Economic Reforms in Eastern Europe and Latin America.* New York: Cambridge University Press, 1991.

Przeworski, Adam, et al., eds. *Sustainable Democracy.* New York: Cambridge University Press, 1995.

Putnam, Robert, with Robert Leonardi and Raffaella Y. Nanetti. *Making Democracy Work: Civic Traditions in Modern Italy.* Princeton, NJ: Princeton University Press, 1992.

Rueschemeyer, Dietrich, Evelyne Huber Stephens, and John D. Stephens. *Capitalist Development and Democracy.* Chicago: University of Chicago Press, 1992.

Scott, James C. *Seeing Like a State: How Certain Schemes to Improve the Human Condition Have Failed.* New Haven, CT: Yale University Press, 1998.

Skocpol, Theda. *States and Social Revolutions.* New York: Cambridge University Press, 1979.

Stark, David, and Laszlo Bruszt. *Postsocialist Pathways: Transforming Politics and Property in East Central Europe.* New York: Cambridge University Press, 1998.

Tarrow, Sidney. *Power in Movement: Social Movements and Contentious Politics,* 2d ed. New York: Cambridge University Press, 1998.

Tilly, Charles. *Coercion, Capital and European States, AD 990–1992.* Cambridge: Blackwell, 1990.

Endnotes

[1] See Philippe Schmitter, "Comparative Politics," in *The Oxford Companion to Politics of the World,* ed. Joel Krieger (New York: Oxford University Press, 1993), 171–177. This essay provides a comprehensive and insightful discussion of the methods of comparative politics and its evolution, and several elements of the discussion here are drawn from it.

[2] See, for example, Colin Campbell, *Governments Under Stress: Political Executives and Key Bureaucrats in Washington, London, and Ottawa* (Toronto: University of Toronto Press, 1983).

[3] See, for example, Theda Skocpol, *Social Revolutions in the Modern World* (New York: Cambridge University Press, 1994).

[4] This term is borrowed from Peter A. Hall, *Governing the Economy: The Politics of State Intervention in Britain and France* (New York: Oxford University Press, 1986).

[5] This view has been developed well by Adam Przeworski, *Democracy and the Market: Political and Economic Reforms in Eastern Europe and Latin America* (New York: Cambridge University Press, 1991).

[6] Guillermo O'Donnell, Philippe Schmitter, and Laurence Whitehead, eds., *Transitions from Authoritarian Rule: Tentative Conclusions about Uncertain Democracies* (Baltimore: Johns Hopkins University Press, 1986).

[7] For a survey of political science literature on this question, see Mark Kesselman, "The Conflictual Evolution of American Political Science: From Apologetic Pluralism to Trilateralism and Marxism," in *Public Values and Private Power in American Democracy,* ed. J. David Greenstone (Chicago: University of Chicago Press, 1982), 34–67.

[8] Phillipe C. Schmitter and Terry Lynn Karl, "What Democracy Is . . . and Is Not," in Larry Diamond and Marc F. Plattner, eds., *The Global Resurgence of Democracy,* 2d ed. (Baltimore: Johns Hopkins University Press, 1996), ch. 4.

[9] Juan J. Linz and Alfred Stepan, *Problems of Democratic Transition and Consolidation: Southern Europe, South America, and Post-Communist Europe* (Baltimore: Johns Hopkins University Press, 1996).

[10] Ibid., p. 7. All quotes from Linz and Stepan that follow are from p. 7. For a somewhat similar analysis of how the formal trappings of democracy can exist without much of the substance of participation and representation, see Guillermo O'Donnell, "Delegative Democracy," in Larry Diamond and Marc F. Plattner, eds., *The Global Resurgence of Democracy* (Baltimore: Johns Hopkins University Press, 1996), ch. 7.

PART 2

Established Democracies

CHAPTER 2

Britain

Joel Krieger

United Kingdom of Great Britain and Northern Ireland

Land and Population

Capital	London	
Total Area (square miles)	94,251 (Slightly smaller than Oregon)	
Population	59 million	
Annual Average Population Growth Rate (1990–1997)	0.3%	
Urban Population (as % of total)	89%	
Ethnic Composition	English	81.5%
National Identity	Scottish	9.6%
Ethnic Majority	Irish	2.4%
5.5%	Welsh	1.9%
	Ulster	1.8%
	Other (including West Indian, Indian, and Pakistani)	2.8%
Major Language	English	
Religious Affiliation	Anglican	43.5%
	Presbyterian	4.5%
	Methodist	2.2%
	Roman Catholic	9.8%
	Muslim	2.6%
	Other / nonreligious	37.4%

Economy

Domestic Currency	Pound Sterling	
Total GNP (US$)	$1.22 trillion	
GNP per capita (US$)	$20,710	
GNP per capita at purchasing power parity (US$)	$20,520	
GNP average annual growth rate (1996–1997)	3.4%	
GNP per capita average annual growth rate	1996–1997	3.2%
	1980–1995	1.9%
	1965–1980	2.0%
Income Gap: GDP per capita of (US$)	Richest 20% of population $38,164	
	Poorest 20% of population $3963	
Structure of Production (% of GDP)	Agriculture	2%
	Industry	32%
	Services	66%
Labor Force Distribution (% of total)	Agriculture	2%
	Industry	29%
	Services	69%
Exports as % of GDP		28%
Imports as % of GDP		29%
Electricity Consumption per capita (kwh)	6016	
CO$_2$ Emissions per capita (metric tons)	9300	

Society

Life Expectancy	Female	79.4
	Male	74.2
Doctors per 100,000 population		327
Infant Mortality per 1000 live births		6
Adult Literacy		99%

(although the UN estimates that 21.8% of people age 16–65 are functionally illiterate)

Access to Information and Communications (per 1000 people)	Radios	1433
	Television	612
	Telephone Lines	503
	Personal Computers	186

Women in Government and Economy

Women in National Legislature	18.1% (lower house); 8.8% (upper house)
Women at Ministerial Level	9%
Women as % of Total Labor Force	44%
Female Business Administrators and Managers	33%
Female Professional and Technical Workers	44%
1998 Human Development Index ranking (out of 174 countries, 1 = highest)	14

Political Organization

Political System   Parliamentary Democracy/Constitutional Monarchy

Regime History   Long constitutional history, origins subject to interpretation, usually dated from the seventeenth century or earlier.

Administrative Structure   Unitary state with fusion of powers. UK parliament has supreme legislative, executive and judicial authority. Reform in process to transfer limited powers to representative bodies for Scotland, Wales, and Northern Ireland.

Executive   Prime Minister, answerable to House of Commons, subject to collective responsibility of the cabinet; member of Parliament who is leader of party that can control a majority in Commons.

Legislature   Bicameral. House of Commons elected by single-member plurality system with no fixed term but a five-year limit. Main legislative powers: to pass laws, provide for finance, scrutinize public administration and government policy. House of Lords, unelected upper house: limited powers to delay enactment of legislation and to recommend revisions; specified appeals court functions. Reform introduced to eliminate voting rights of hereditary peers and create new second chamber.

Judiciary   Independent but with no power to judge the constitutionality of legislation or governmental conduct. Judges appointed by Crown on recommendation of PM or lord chancellor.

Party System   Two-party dominant, with regional variation. Principal parties: Labour and Conservative; a center party (Liberal Democrats); and national parties in Scotland, Wales, and Northern Ireland.

Politics in Action

The first day of May has long been a day for festivities, as some winter-weary Britons danced around the Maypole to welcome spring and others took to the streets to celebrate labor movements on May Day. In 1997, May Day acquired new significance. The Labour Party, which had been in opposition for eighteen years, was swept into office with a tidal wave of support from every segment of the population and region of the country.

Some twenty electoral records were toppled, as the Labour Party—dubbed "New Labour" by Tony Blair, who had taken over as leader in 1994—won 419 of the 659 seats in Parliament, the largest majority it has ever held. Tony Blair was propelled into office as prime minister with a 10 percent swing from Conservative to Labour, a postwar record. More women (119) and members of ethnic minorities (9) were elected than ever before. In addition, the political undertow of this electoral tsunami was fierce. The Conservative Party, which had been in power since Margaret Thatcher's 1979 victory, and was one of Europe's most successful parties in the twentieth century, was decimated. More cabinet ministers lost their seats than ever before. The Conservatives were nearly wiped off the map in London and other major cities and were shut out altogether in Scotland and Wales.

Pre-election polls had predicted a strong Labour victory, but the extent of the debacle kept millions of Britons glued to their television sets throughout the night and sent television pundits and headline writers into overdrive. Was it merely a "triumph" or was it a "landslide" or a "massacre"? Or as one television analyst put it, was the election "like an asteroid hitting the planet and destroying practically all life on earth"[1]?

Although the last characterization is surely an overstatement, the significance of the election can scarcely be exaggerated. Tony Blair raised expectations throughout the country and excited a new generation of activists by asserting a new brand of politics beyond left and right. Blair committed government to an ambitious program of modernization defined by a set of challenges—to develop top-quality public services especially in education and health, to take tough action on crime, to forge a new partnership with business, to introduce radical constitutional reforms, and to reconfigure Britain's relationship with Europe. In addition, Tony Blair's bold leadership and enormous popularity, backed by a long streak of economic prosperity, have helped make Britain "hot." French entrepreneurs and job seekers are looking for opportunities at the end of the Channel Tunnel and German Chancellor, Gerhard Schröder, is being hailed as "the German Blair."

Tony Blair, with wife Cherie Booth, waving to well-wishers outside 10 Downing Street (5/2/97) before entering for the first time as prime minister. *Source:* Corbis/Bettman.

"Blairism" was widely discussed as a potential "third way" model of government that would meld concerns for social justice with a commitment to market-based economies. As a result, the victory of Blair's New Labour created a rare opportunity for a government to look beyond opinion polls and electoral competition to attempt lasting political change. The ultimate balance sheet on New Labour will offer some important lessons about prospects for political innovation within established democracies.

Geographic Setting

Britain is the largest of the British Isles, a group of islands off the northwest coast of Europe, and encom-

passes England, Scotland, and Wales. The second largest island comprises Northern Ireland and the independent Republic of Ireland. The term *Great Britain* includes England, Wales, and Scotland, but not Northern Ireland. We use the term *Britain* as shorthand for the United Kingdom (U.K.) of Great Britain and Northern Ireland.

Covering an area of approximately 94,000 square miles, Britain is roughly two-thirds the size of Japan or approximately half the size of France. In 1995, the population of the United Kingdom was 58.6 million people; the population is projected to peak at 61.2 million people in 2023.[2] To put this once immensely powerful country in perspective, it is slightly smaller than Oregon.

Although forever altered by the Channel tunnel, Britain's location as an off-shore island adjacent to Europe is significant. Historically, Britain's island destiny made it less subject to invasion and conquest than its continental counterparts, affording the country a sense of security. The geographic separation from mainland Europe has also created for many Britons a feeling that they are both apart from and a part of Europe, a factor that has complicated relations with Britain's European Union partners to this day.

Critical Junctures

Our study begins with a look at the historic development of the modern British state. History shapes contemporary politics in very important ways. Once in place, institutions leave powerful legacies and issues placed on the agenda in one period, but left unresolved, may present challenges for the future.

The Formation of the United Kingdom

In many ways Britain is the model of a unified and stable country with an enviable record of continuity and resiliency. Nevertheless, the history of state formation reveals how complex and open-ended the process can be. Some issues that plague other countries, such as religious divisions, were settled long ago in Britain proper (although not in Northern Ireland). Yet others, such as multiple national identities, remain on the agenda.

British state formation involved the unification of kingdoms or crowns (hence the term United *Kingdom*). After Duke William of Normandy defeated the English in the Battle of Hastings in 1066, the Norman monarchy extended its authority throughout the British Isles. Although Welsh national sentiments remained strong, the prospects for unity with England were improved in 1485 by the accession to the English throne of Henry VII of the Welsh house of Tudor. With the Acts of Union of 1536 and 1542, England and Wales were legally, politically, and administratively united. The unification of the Scottish and English crowns occurred when James VI of Scotland ascended to the English throne as James I. Thereafter, England, Scotland, and Wales were known as Great Britain. Scotland and England remained divided politically, however, until the Act of Union of 1707. Henceforth, a common Parliament of Great Britain replaced the two separate parliaments of Scotland and of England and Wales.

At the same time, the making of the British state included a historic expression of constraints on monarchical rule. At first, the period of Norman rule after 1066 strengthened royal control, but the conduct of King John (1199–1216) fueled opposition from feudal barons. In 1215, they forced the king to consent to a series of concessions that protected feudal landowners from abuses of royal power. These restrictions on royal prerogatives were embodied in the Magna Carta, a historic statement of the rights of a political community against the monarchical state. Soon thereafter, in 1236, the term *Parliament* was first used officially to refer to the gathering of feudal barons which was summoned by the king whenever he required their consent to special taxes. By the fifteenth century Parliament gained the right to make laws.

The Seventeenth-Century Settlement

The making of the British state in the sixteenth and seventeenth centuries involved a complex interplay of religious conflicts, national rivalries, and struggles between rulers and the fledgling Parliament (see Critical Junctures in Britain's Political Development). These conflicts erupted in the Civil War of the 1640s, and the forced abdication of James II in 1688. The bloodless political revolution of 1688, subsequently known as the *Glorious Revolution*, marked the "last successful political coup d'état or revolution in British history."[3] It also confirmed the power of Parliament over the monarchy. Parliament required the new monarchs, William and Mary, to meet with it annually and to agree to regular parliamentary elections. This contrasted dramatically with the arrangement enjoyed in France by Louis XIV (1643–1715), who gained power at the expense of the French nobility and operated without any constraint from commoners.

By the end of the seventeenth century, the framework of a constitutional (or limited) monarchy—which would still exercise flashes of power into the nineteenth century—was established in Britain. For more than 300 years, Britain's monarchs have been answerable to Parliament, which has held the sole authority for taxation and the maintenance of a standing army.

The Glorious Revolution also resolved long-standing religious conflict. The replacement of the Roman Catholic James II by the Protestant William and Mary ensured the dominance of the Church of England (or Anglican church). To this day, the Church of England remains the established (official) religion and approximately two dozen of its bishops and archbishops sit as members of the House of Lords, the upper house of Parliament.

Thus, by the end of the seventeenth century, a basic form of parliamentary democracy had emerged and the problem of religious divisions, which continue to plague countries throughout the world, was settled. Equally important, these seventeenth-century developments became a defining moment for how the British perceive their history to this day. However divisive and disruptive the process of state-building may have been originally, its telling and retelling have contributed significantly to a British political culture that celebrates democracy's continuity, gradualism, and tolerance.

As a result of settling its religious differences early, Britain has taken a more secular turn than most countries in Western Europe. The majority of Britons do not consider religion a significant source of identity, and active church membership in Britain, at 15 percent, is very low in comparison with other Western European countries. In Britain, religious identification has less political significance—in voting behavior or party loyalty—than in many countries. By contrast to France, where devout Catholics tend to vote right of center, there is relatively little association between religion and voting behavior in Britain (although Anglicans are a little more likely to vote Conservative). Unlike Germany or Italy, for example, politics in Britain is secular. No parties have religious affiliation, a factor that contributed to the success of the Conservative Party, one of the most successful right-of-center parties in Europe in the twentieth century.

As a consequence, except in Northern Ireland where religious divisions continue, the party system in the United Kingdom has traditionally reflected class distinctions and remains free of the pattern of multiple parties (particularly right-of-center parties) that occur in countries where party loyalties are divided by both class and religion.

The Industrial Revolution and the British Empire

Although the British state was consolidated by the seventeenth century, its form was radically shaped by the timing of its industrial development and the way that process transformed Britain's role in the world. The Industrial Revolution in the mid-eighteenth century involved rapid expansion of manufacturing production and technological innovation. It also involved monumental social and economic transformations and resulted in pressures for democratization. Externally, Britain used its competitive edge to transform and dominate the international order. Internally, the Industrial Revolution helped shape the development of the British state, and change forever the British people's way of life.

The Industrial Revolution.   The consequences of the Industrial Revolution for the generations of people who experienced its upheavals can scarcely be exaggerated. The typical worker was turned "by degrees . . . from small peasant or craftsman into wage-labourer," as historian Eric Hobsbawm observes. Cash and market-based transactions replaced older traditions of barter and production for local need.[4]

Despite a gradual improvement in the standard of living in the English population at large, the effects of industrialization were often profound for agricultural laborers and particular types of artisans. With the commercialization of agriculture, many field laborers lost their security of employment and cottagers (small landholders) were squeezed off the land in large numbers. The mechanization of manufacturing, which spread furthest in the cotton industry, upset the traditional status of the preindustrial skilled craft workers and permanently marginalized them.

The British Empire.   Britain had assumed a significant role as a world power during the seventeenth century, building an overseas Empire and engaging actively in international commerce. But it was the Industrial Revolution of the eighteenth century that established global production and exchange on a new and expanded scale, with particular consequences for the making of the British state. Cotton manufacture, the driving force behind Britain's growing industrial dominance, not only pioneered the new techniques and changed labor organization of the Industrial Revolution but also represented the perfect imperial industry. It relied on imported raw materials and, by the turn of the nineteenth century, already depended on overseas markets for the vast majority of its sales of finished goods. Growth depended on foreign markets rather than on domestic consumption. This export orientation fueled an expansion far more rapid than an exclusively domestic orientation would have allowed.

With its leading industrial sector dependent on overseas trade, Britain's leaders worked aggressively to secure markets and expand the empire. Toward these ends, Britain defeated European rivals in a series of military engagements, culminating in the Napoleonic Wars (1803–1815), which confirmed Britain's commercial, military, and geopolitical pre-eminence. The Napoleonic Wars also secured a balance of power on the European continent favorable for largely unrestricted international commerce (**free trade**). Propelled by the formidable and active presence of the British navy, international trade helped England take full advantage of its position as the first industrial power. Many scholars suggest that in the middle of the nineteenth century Britain had the highest per capita income in the world (it was certainly among the two or three highest), and in 1870 at the height of its glory, its trade represented nearly one-quarter of the world total and its industrial mastery ensured highly competitive productivity in comparison to trading partners (see Table 1 below).

During the reign of Queen Victoria (1837–1901), the British Empire was immensely powerful and encompassed fully 25 percent of the world's population. Britain presided over a vast formal and informal empire, with extensive direct colonial rule over some four dozen countries, including India and Nigeria. At the same time Britain enjoyed the advantages of an extensive informal empire—a worldwide network of independent states including China, Iran, and Brazil—whose economic fates were linked to England. Britain ruled as the **hegemonic power**, the state that could

---

Table 1

World Trade and Relative Labor Productivity

	Proportion of World Trade (%)	Relative Labor Productivity[a] (%)
1870	24.0	1.63
1890	18.5	1.45
1913	14.1	1.15
1938	14.0	0.92

[a]As compared with the average rate of productivity in other members of the world economy.

Source: Copyright 1984 by Princeton University Press. Reprinted by permission of Princeton University Press.

control the pattern of alliances and terms of the international economic order, and often could shape domestic political developments in countries throughout the world. Overall, the making of the British state observed a neat symmetry. Its global power helped underwrite industrial growth at home. At the same time, the reliance of domestic industry on world markets, beginning with cotton manufacture in the eighteenth century, prompted the government to project British interests overseas as forcefully as possible.

Industrial Change and the Struggle for Voting Rights.   The Industrial Revolution shifted economic power from landowners to men of commerce and industry. As a result, the first critical juncture in the long process of democratization began in the late 1820s, when the "respectable opinion" of the propertied classes and increasing popular agitation pressed Parliament to expand the right to vote (**franchise**) beyond a thin band of men with substantial property, mainly landowners. With Parliament under considerable pressure, the Reform Act of 1832 extended the franchise to a section of the (male) middle class.

In a very limited way, the Reform Act confirmed the social and political transformations of the Industrial Revolution by granting new urban manufacturing centers, such as Manchester and Birmingham, more substantial representation. However, the massive urban working class created by the Industrial Revolution and populating the cities of Charles Dickens's England remained on the outside looking in. In fact, the reform was very narrow and defensive. Before 1832 less than 5 percent of the adult population was entitled to vote—and afterward, only about 7 percent!

In extending the franchise so narrowly, the reform underscored the strict property basis for political participation and inflamed class-based tensions in Britain. Following the Reform Act, a massive popular movement erupted in the late 1830s to secure the program of the People's Charter, which included demands for universal male suffrage and other radical reforms intended to make Britain a much more participatory democracy. The *Chartist movement*, as it was called, held huge and often tumultuous rallies, and organized a vast campaign to petition Parliament, but failed to achieve any of its aims.

Expansion of the franchise proceeded very slowly. The Representation of the People Act of 1867 increased the electorate to just over 16 percent but left cities significantly underrepresented. The Franchise Act of 1884 nearly doubled the size of the electorate, but it was not until the Representation of the People Act of 1918 that suffrage included nearly all adult men and women over thirty. How slow a process was it? The franchise for men with substantial incomes dated from the fifteenth century, but women between the ages of twenty-one and thirty were not enfranchised until 1928! The voting age for both women and men was lowered to eighteen in 1969. Except for some episodes during the days of the Chartist movement, the struggle for extension of the franchise took place without violence, but its time horizon must be measured in centuries. This is British gradualism—at its best and worst (see Figure 1).

World Wars, Industrial Strife, and the Depression (1914–1945)

With the matter of the franchise finally settled, in one sense the making of the British state as a democracy was settled. In another important sense, however, the development of the state was just beginning in the twentieth century with the expansion of the state's direct responsibility for management of the economy and the provision of social welfare for citizens. The making of what is sometimes called the *interventionist state* was spurred by the experiences of two world wars.

The state's involvement in the economy increased significantly during World War I. The state took control of a number of industries, including railways, mining, and shipping. It also set prices and restricted the flow of capital abroad, and channeled the country's resources into production geared to the war effort. After World War I, the state remained active in the management of industry in a rather different way. Amid a set of tremendous industrial disputes, the state wielded its power to fragment the trade union movement and resist demands for workers' control over production and to promote more extensive state ownership of industries. This considerable government manipulation of the economy openly contradicted the policy of laissez-faire (minimal government interference in the operation of economic markets). The tensions between

Figure 1

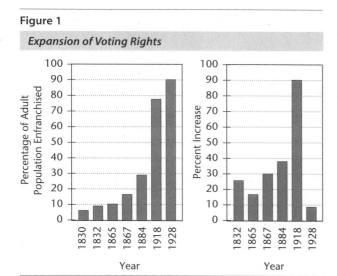

Expansion of Voting Rights

Year

Year

Expansion of the franchise in Britain was a gradual process. Despite reforms dating from the early nineteenth century, nearly universal adult suffrage was not achieved until 1928. *Source:* Jorgen S. Rasmussen. *The British Political Process*, p. 151. Copyright © 1993 Wadsworth Publishing Company. Reprinted with permission of the publisher.

free market principles and interventionist practices deepened with the Great Depression beginning in 1929 and the experiences of World War II. The fear of depression and the burst of pent-up yearnings for a better life after the war helped transform the role of the state and ushered in a period of unusual political harmony.

The Collectivist Consensus (1945–1979)

In the postwar context of shared victory and common misery (almost everyone suffered terrible hardships immediately after the war), reconstruction and dreams of new prosperity and security took priority over ideological conflict. This broad culture of reconciliation and a determination to rebuild and improve the conditions of life for all Britons helped forge a collectivist consensus that endured until the mid-1970s.

Collectivism is the term coined to describe the consensus that drove politics in the harmonious postwar period when a significant majority of Britons and all major political parties agreed that the state should take expanded responsibility for economic governance and provide for the social welfare in the broadest terms. They accepted as a matter of faith that governments should work to narrow the gap between rich and poor through public education, national health care, and other policies of the **welfare state**, and

accepted state responsibility for economic growth and full employment. Collectivism brought class-based actors (representatives of labor and management) inside politics, and forged a very broad consensus about the expanded role of government.

Throughout this period there was a remarkable unity among electoral combatants, as the Labour and Conservative mainstream endorsed the principle of state responsibility for the collective good in both economic and social terms. Although modest in comparative European terms, the commitment to state management of the economy and provision of social services marked a new era in British politics. In time, however, economic downturn and political stagnation caused the consensus to unravel.

Margaret Thatcher and the Enterprise Culture (1979–1990)

In the 1970s, economic stagnation and the declining competitiveness of key British industries in international markets fueled industrial strife and kept class-based tensions near the surface of politics. No government appeared equal to the tasks of economic management. Each party failed in turn. The Conservative government of Edward Heath (1970–1974) could not resolve the economic problems or the political tensions that resulted from the previously unheard-of combination of increased inflation and reduced growth (*stagflation*). The Labour government of Harold Wilson and James Callaghan (1974–1979) fared no better. As unions became increasingly disgruntled, the country was beset by a rash of strikes throughout the winter of 1978–1979, the "winter of discontent." Labour's inability to discipline its trade union allies hurt the party in the election just a few months later in May 1979. The traditional centrist Conservative and Labour alternatives within the collectivist mold seemed exhausted, and many Britons were ready for a new policy agenda.

Margaret Thatcher more than met the challenge. Winning the leadership of the Conservative Party in 1975, she wasted little time in launching a set of bold policy initiatives which, with characteristic forthrightness, she began to implement after the Conservatives were returned to power in 1979. Reelected in 1983 and 1987, Thatcher served longer without interruption than any other British prime minister in the twentieth century and never lost a general election.

Thatcher transformed British political life by advancing an alternative vision of politics. She was convinced that collectivism had contributed to Britain's decline by sapping British industry and permitting powerful and self-serving unions to hold the country for ransom. To reverse Britain's relative economic slide, Thatcher sought to jump-start the economy by cutting taxes, reducing social services where possible, and using government policy to stimulate competitiveness and efficiency in the private sector.

The term *Thatcherism* embraces her distinctive leadership style, her economic and political strategies, as well as her traditional cultural values—prized individual responsibility, commitment to family, frugality, and an affirmation of the entrepreneurial spirit. These values combined nostalgia for the past and a rejection of permissiveness and disorder. Taken together and referred to as the *enterprise culture*, they stood as a reproach and an alternative to collectivism.

In many ways, the period of Margaret Thatcher's leadership as prime minister (1979–1990) marks a critical dividing line in postwar British politics. She set the tone and redefined the goals of British politics like few before her. In November 1990, a leadership challenge within Thatcher's own Conservative

Party—largely over her anti-EC stance and high-handed leadership style—caused her sudden resignation and replacement by John Major. Major served as prime minister from 1990 to 1997, leading the Conservative Party to a victory in the 1992 general election before succumbing to Tony Blair's New Labour in 1997.

New Labour's "Third Way"

After Tony Blair's election in 1997 there was an unmistakable sense in Britain that something extremely interesting and potentially significant was happening. Blair's willingness to experiment with ideas and policy and his call to modernize almost anything in

With characteristic aplomb, Prime Minister Margaret Thatcher greeted the annual Conservative Party Conference at the seaside resort Bournemouth in October 1986.
Source: Stuart Franklin/Magnum Photos, Inc.

Leaders: *Tony Blair*

Born in 1953 to a mother from Donegal, Ireland (who moved to Glasgow after her father's death), and a father from the Clydeside shipyards, Tony Blair lacks the typical pedigree of Labour Party leaders. It is very common in the highest ranks of the Labour Party to find someone whose father or grandfather was a union official or a Labour MP. The politics in the Blair family, by contrast, were most closely linked to Conservatism (as chairman of his local Conservative party club, his father Leo had a good chance to become a Conservative MP). Often, like Tony Blair's two predecessors—Neil Kinnock from Wales and John Smith from the West of Scotland—leaders of the Labour Party also have distinctive regional ties. In contrast, Blair moved to Durham in the north of England when he was five, but spent much of his youth in boarding schools, moved south when he was old enough to set out on his own, studied law at Oxford, and specialized in employment and industrial law in London—and returned to the north only to enter

the House of Commons from Sedgefield in 1983. Thus, Blair has neither the traditional political or regional ties of a Labour Party leader.*

Coming of political age in opposition, Blair joined the Shadow Cabinet in 1988, serving in turn as shadow minister of energy, then employment, and finally as Shadow Home Secretary. An MP with no government experience, he easily won the contest for party leadership after his close friend and fellow modernizer, John Smith, died of a sudden heart attack in the summer of 1994. From the start, he boosted Labour Party morale and raised expectations that the party would soon regain power. As one observer put it, "The new Leader rapidly made a favourable impression upon the electorate: his looks and affability of manner appealed to voters whilst his self-confidence, lucidity and clarity of mind rendered him a highly effective communicator and lent him an air of authority."† Blair has gone from strength to strength, combining winning style with firm leadership, eclectic beliefs, and bold political initiatives. A figure to reckon with—some have predicted he will become the dominant figure in British politics for the next quarter-century—his lack of familiar roots and ideological convictions make Blair, for many, an enigmatic figure.

*See Andy McSmith, *Faces of Labour: The Inside Story* (London: Verso, 1997), 7-96.

†Eric Shaw, *The Labour Party since 1945* (Oxford: Blackwell, 1996), 195.

---

the grasp of government contributed to a sense of political renewal and intellectual ferment in Britain.

New Labour aspired to recast British politics, offering a "third way" alternative to collectivism and Thatcherism. Everything was at issue, from the way politics is organized to the country's underlying values, institutions, and policies. In electoral terms, New Labour rejected the notion of interest-based politics, in which unions and working people naturally look to Labour and business people and the more prosperous look to the Conservatives. Labour won in 1997 by drawing support from across the socioeconomic spectrum. It rejected the historic ties between Labour governments and the trade union movement, choosing instead to emphasize the virtues of a partnership with business.

In institutional and policy terms, New Labour's innovations were intended to reverse the tendency of

previous Labour governments in Britain to provide centralized "statist" solutions to all economic and social problems. Blair promised new approaches to economic, welfare, and social policy, British leadership in Europe, and far-reaching constitutional changes to revitalize democratic participation and devolve (transfer) powers from the central government to component nations (England, Scotland, Wales, and Northern Ireland).

A week is a long time in politics, so Tony Blair (see Leaders: Tony Blair above) will have ample opportunity to disappoint his supporters—or confound his critics. There can be little doubt, however, that Blair displayed effective leadership in his stewardship of the nation during the period after Princess Diana's death and his aggressive efforts to achieve a potentially historic peace agreement for Northern Ireland, with far-reaching constitutional implications.

Not for nothing did Blair's government register higher popularity at the end of its first year than any government at a comparable stage since opinion polling was introduced. Moreover, despite a round of scandals, resignations, and quarrels between ministers in the winter 1998–1999, new Labour was riding high in the polls as it approached the half-way point of its first term in office.

Themes and Implications

Historical Junctures and Political Themes

The processes that came together in these historical junctures continue to influence present developments in powerful and complex ways. Our four core themes, introduced in Part 1, highlight some of the most important features of British politics.

Our first theme suggests that a country's relative position in the world of states influences its ability to manage domestic and international challenges. A weaker international standing makes it difficult for a country to control international events, shape the policy of powerful international organizations, or insulate itself from external pressures. Britain's ability to control the terms of trade and master political alliances during the height of its imperial power in the nineteenth century confirms this maxim. In a quite different way, the world of states theme is also confirmed by Britain's reduced standing and influence today.

As the gradual process of decolonization defined Britain's changing relationship to the world of states, Britain fell to a second-tier status during the twentieth century. Britain's formal empire began to shrink in the interwar period (1919–1939) with the independence of the "white Dominions" of Canada, Australia, and New Zealand. In Britain's Asian, Middle Eastern, and African colonies, the pressure for political reforms leading to independence deepened during World War II and in the immediate postwar period. Beginning with the formal independence of India and Pakistan in 1947, an enormous empire of dependent colonies more or less dissolved in less than twenty years (although the problem of white-dominated Rhodesia lingered until it achieved independence as Zimbabwe in 1980). Finally, in 1997, Britain returned the commercially vibrant crown colony of Hong Kong to China. The process of decolonization ended any realistic claim Britain could make to be a dominant player in world politics.

Is Britain a world power or just a middle-of-the-pack country in Western Europe? It appears to be both. On the one hand, as a legacy of its role in World War II, Britain sits as a permanent member in the United Nations Security Council, a position denied more powerful and populous countries such as Germany and Japan. On the other hand, Britain has remained an outsider in the European Union, more often than not playing second fiddle in its "special relationship" to the United States, and declining in influence in the **Commonwealth** (an association of some fifty states which were once part of the British empire). In particular, British governments face persistent challenges in their dealings with the European Union (EU). As Margaret Thatcher learned too late to save her premiership, Europe is a very divisive issue. Can Britain afford to remain aloof from the fast-paced changes of economic integration symbolized by the headlong rush toward a common currency (the **euro**), thus far endorsed by every leading member state except the United Kingdom? It is clear that Britain does not have the power to control EU policy outcomes. Will British governments, beginning with Tony Blair's, find the right formula for limiting the political fallout of EU politics and, at the same time, find the best approach to economic competitiveness?

A second theme examines the strategies employed in governing the economy and the political implications of economic performance and the choices made by government in the distribution of economic goods and public services. Since the dawn of Britain's Industrial Revolution, prosperity at home relied on superior competitiveness abroad, and this is even more true in today's environment of intensified international competition and global production.

Although forecasters began to observe signs of a potential downturn in 1998, Britain enjoyed a streak of prosperity dating from 1992. Thus, the Blair government came to office in enviable circumstances. It could work to modernize the economy and determine its budgetary priorities from economic strength. Will Britain's "less-is-more" laissez-faire approach to economic governance, invigorated by New Labour's business partnership, continue to compete effectively against the more directive state-centered models of France, Germany, and Japan (which faces its own, far more intense, pressures for modernization)? Can Britain achieve a durable economic model with—or without—fuller integration into Europe? What will be the spending priorities and distributive implications of the "third way" politics of the Blair government? Britain will never again assume the privileged position of hegemonic power. It is positioned well to make the most of its role as competitive middle-of-the-pack European power, but in these perilous times of intense global competition, success is not a given and Britain faces a host of challenges.

A third theme is the potent political influence of the democratic idea, the universal appeal of core values associated with parliamentary democracy as practiced first in the United Kingdom. Even in Britain, issues about democratic governance, citizen participation, and constitutional reform have been renewed with considerable force.

As the traditionally sacrosanct royal family has been rocked by scandal and improprieties, questions about the undemocratic underpinning of the British state are asked with greater urgency. Few reject the monarchy outright but, especially after the perceived insensitivity of the royal family in the aftermath of Diana's death, the pressure to modernize the monarchy, scale it down, and reduce its drain on the budget gained new intensity. Perhaps most significantly, questions about the role of the monarchy helped place on the agenda broader issues about citizen control over government and constitutional reform. As a result, in 1999 the government introduced legislation to eliminate the voting rights of hereditary peers in Britain's upper unelected chamber of Parliament, the House of Lords, and create a new second chamber.

Long-settled issues about the constitutional form and unity of the state have also reemerged with unexpected force in recent years. How can the interests of England, Wales, Scotland, and Northern Ireland be balanced within a single nation-state? Can the perpetual crisis in Northern Ireland be finally resolved? Tony Blair has placed squarely on the agenda a set of policies designed to reshape the institutions of government and reconfigure fundamental constitutional principles to address the "troubles" in Northern Ireland, and to modernize the architecture of the U.K. to recognize the realities of a multi-nation-state. Key policies include the formation of a Scottish Parliament and a Welsh Senedd (or Assembly), and the implementation of a peace agreement for Northern Ireland that would involve a comprehensive set of new political institutions and power-sharing arrangements—some involving the Republic of Ireland—with far-reaching constitutional ramifications. Clearly, democracy is not a fixed result even in the U.K., but a highly politicized and potentially disruptive process, as constitutional reform has taken a place front and center in Tony Blair's bold agenda.

Finally, we come to the fourth theme, collective identities, which considers how individuals define who they are politically in terms of group attachments, come together to pursue political goals, and face their status as political insiders or outsiders by virtue of these group attachments. In Britain, an important aspect of the politics of collective identities is connected to Britain's legacy of empire and its aftermath. Through the immigration of its former colonial subjects to the U.K., decolonization helped create a multiracial society, to which Britain has adjusted poorly. As we shall see, issues of race, ethnicity, and cultural identity have challenged the long-standing British values of tolerance and consensus and now present important challenges for policy and the prospects of cohesion in Britain today. At the same time, gender politics remains a very significant issue, from voting results that show clear differences in the party preferences of men and women (a **gender gap**) to questions of equality in the workplace and in positions of political leadership. Moreover, the specific needs of women for equal employment opportunities and to balance the demands of work and family have assumed an important place in debates about social and employment policies.

Implications for Comparative Politics

Britain's privileged position in comparative politics textbooks—it almost always comes first—seems to follow naturally from the important historical "firsts" it has enjoyed. Britain was the first nation to industrialize and, for much of the nineteenth century, the British Empire was the world's dominant economic, political, and military power, with a vast network of colonies throughout the world. Britain was also the first nation to develop an effective parliamentary democracy (a form of representative government in which the executive is drawn from and answerable to an elected national legislature). As a result of its vast empire, Britain had tremendous influence on the form of government introduced in countries around the globe. For these reasons, British politics is often studied as a model of representative government. Named after the building that houses the British legislature in London, the **Westminster model** of government emphasizes that democracy rests on the supreme authority of a legislature—in Britain's case, the Parliament—and the accountability of its elected representatives. Traditionally, the Westminster model and the values of consensus-building and stability on which it rests have served as one standard (the American political system has been another) for countries struggling to construct democratic political systems. Finally, Britain has served as a model of gradual and peaceful evolution of democratic government in a world where transitions to democracy are often turbulent, interrupted, and uncertain.

Today, more than a century after the height of its international power, Britain's significance in comparative terms must be measured in somewhat different ways. Modernization is the watchword of the Blair government, and Blair's level of public support, the degree of unity within his party, and the strength of the British economy provide a platform for success. Therefore, Blair's ability to succeed—or his failure—in forging a left-of-center business partnership, in constitutional reforms (including Northern Ireland), and in balancing national interest with supranational pressures for European integration will send important signals to governments throughout the world. Is innovation possible in established democracies with powerful institutional and cultural legacies that tend to set limits on radical change? Can a politics beyond left and right develop coherent policies and maintain enduring support? Can constitutional reforms help bind together a multiethnic, multinational state? In fact, contemporary Britain may help define an innovative new model for middle-rank established democracies in a global age.

Section ❷ Political Economy and Development

In addition to its claim as the first industrial nation, Britain is also the country with the longest experience of economic decline. In a way, the country was a victim of its own success and approach to economic development. From the eighteenth century onward, Britain combined its naval mastery and the dominant position created by the Industrial Revolution to fuel expansion based on the foreign supply of raw materials and foreign markets. With plenty of profits available from this traditional overseas orientation, British entrepreneurs became complacent about keeping up with the newest industrial techniques and investing in machinery at home. Secure in the advantages of empire and the priority of international trade over domestic demand, the government stuck to its belief in free trade (low tariffs and removal of other barriers to open markets) in the international realm and a hands-off approach at home. With low investment in the modernization of industrial plants and little effort

to enhance efficiency by grouping small-scale firms into cartels and trusts as the Americans and Germans were doing, Britain slipped behind its competitors in crucial areas: technological innovation, investment in domestic manufacturing, and scale of production facilities.

By the 1890s, Britain's key export—textiles—was slipping, and the international position of the machine-tool industry, which Britain also had dominated, was collapsing even more rapidly. Both Germany and the United States had overtaken Britain in steel production, the key indicator of competitiveness at the time, and the gap was widening. In 1901, the largest U.S. steel company alone was producing more steel than all of England![5] Thus, for more than a century, Britain has been concerned about relative economic decline.

However, by the mid-1990s, the British economy was performing better than most of its major competitors, including its European neighbors who were mired in recession. Among major developed economies, only the United States enjoyed a greater decline in unemployment and stronger growth. At present it appears that the trend has reversed, breathing new life into the old economic doctrine of laissez-faire. How "new" is New Labour's approach to economic management? Are Britons across the spectrum enjoying the fruits of relative prosperity? How has the growing importance of the European Union and the economic processes of globalization changed the political equation? In this section, we analyze the politics of economic management, beginning with a historical overview of Britain's economic development. Then we consider in turn the principles of British economic management, the social consequences of economic developments, and political repercussions of Britain's position in the international economic order.

State and Economy

Whereas late industrializers, like Germany and Japan, relied on powerful government support during their industrial take-off period, England's Industrial Revolution was based more on laissez-faire, or free-market, principles. When the state intervened in powerful ways, it did so primarily to secure free markets at home and open markets for British goods (free trade) in the international sphere.

With control of crucial industries during World War I, and the active management of industry by the state in the interwar years, the British state assumed a more interventionist role. After World War II, the sense of unity inspired by the shared suffering of war and the need to rebuild a war-ravaged country helped crystallize the collectivist consensus. In common with other Western European states, the British state both broadened and deepened its responsibilities for the overall performance of the economy and the well-being of its citizens. The leading political parties and policy-making elites agreed that the state should take an active role in governing the economy.

The state assumed direct ownership of some key industries (nationalization). The state also accepted the responsibility to secure low levels of unemployment (referred to as a policy of "full employment"), expand social services, maintain a steady rate of

growth (increase the output or gross domestic product), keep prices stable, and achieve desirable balance of payments and exchange rates. The approach was characterized by what has come to be called **Keynesian demand management, or Keynesianism** (after the British economist John Maynard Keynes). State budget deficits were used to expand demand in an effort to boost both consumption and investment when the economy was slowing. Cuts in government spending and a tightening of credit and finance were used to cool demand when high rates of growth brought fears of inflation or a deficit in balance of payments. Taken together, this new agenda of expanded economic management and welfare provision, sometimes referred to as the Keynesian Welfare State (KWS), directed government policy throughout the era of the collectivist consensus.

Two central dimensions—economic management and welfare policy—capture the new role of the state. Analysis of these policy areas also reveals how limited this new state role was in comparative terms.

(1) Economic Management

Like all states, whatever their commitment to free markets, the British state intervenes in economic life, sometimes with considerable force. Some states, such as France, Germany, and Japan, exercise strategic control over the economy to guide it and enhance competitiveness. These countries coordinate **macroeconomic policy** (intended to shape the overall economic system at the national level by concentrating on policy targets such as unemployment, inflation, or growth) with **industrial policy** (aimed at enhancing competitiveness by promoting particular industrial sectors).

To this day the British have not developed the institutions for state-sponsored economic planning or industrial policy created by some of their competitors. Instead, apart from its management of nationalized industries, the British state has limited its role mainly to broad policy instruments designed to influence the economy generally (macroeconomic policy) by adjusting state revenues and expenditures. The Treasury and the Bank of England dominate economic policy, which has often seemed reactive and sometimes skittish. As senior officials in these financial institutions respond to fluctuations in the business cycle, the government reacts with short-term political calculations that abruptly shift policy agendas. As a result, state involvement in economic management has been relatively ineffectual. An ongoing stop-go cycle of reversals has plagued policy, which has had relatively little effect on natural business cycles and was unable to prevent recessions during 1979–1981 and 1990–1992.

Despite other differences, this generally reactive and minimalist orientation of economic management strategies in Britain bridges the first two eras of postwar politics in Britain—the consensus era (1945–1979) and the period of Thatcherite policy orientation (1979–1997). How has the orientation of economic policy developed and changed during the postwar period? How new is New Labour when it comes to economic policy?

The Consensus Era.　Before Thatcher became leader of the Conservative party in 1975, Conservative leaders in Britain generally accepted the terms of the collectivist consensus. These Conservatives were also modernizers, prepared to manage the economy in a way consistent with the Keynesian approach and to maintain the welfare state and guarantee full employment.

Declining economic competitiveness made the situation for mainstream Conservatives and, indeed, for any government, more complex and difficult. By the 1970s public officials no longer saw the world as one they understood and could master: it had become a world without economic growth and with growing political discontent. Edward Heath, the Conservative centrist who governed from 1970 to 1974, was the first prime minister to suffer the full burden of recession and the force of political opposition from both traditional business allies and resurgent trade union adversaries. Operating in an era marked by increased inflation and reduced growth (stagflation), Heath could never break out of the political constraints imposed on him by economic decline.

From 1974 to 1979, the Labour government of Harold Wilson and James Callaghan reenforced the impression that governments could no longer control the swirl of events. The beginning of the end came when trade unions became increasingly restive under the pinch of voluntary wage restraints pressed on them by the Labour government. Frustrated by wage increases well below inflation rates, the unions broke with the government in 1978. The number of unofficial work stoppages increased, and official strikes followed, all fueled by a seemingly endless series of leapfrogging pay demands which erupted throughout the winter of 1978–1979 (the "winter of discontent"). There is little doubt that the industrial unrest that dramatized Labour's inability to manage its own allies— the trade unions—contributed mightily to Thatcher's election just a few months later in May 1979. If a Labour government couldn't manage its trade union allies, whom could it govern? More significantly, the winter of discontent helped write the conclusion to Britain's collectivist consensus, and discredit the Keynesian Welfare State.

Thatcherite Policy Orientation.　In policy terms, the economic strategies pioneered by Thatcher and maintained by Major reflected a growing disillusionment with Keynesianism. In its place, **monetarism** emerged as the new economic doctrine. Keynesian demand management assumed that the level of unemployment could be set and the economy stabilized through decisions of government (monetary and fiscal or budgetary policy). By contrast, monetarism assumed that there is a "natural rate of unemployment" determined by the labor market itself. Monetary and fiscal policy should be passive, and intervention limited (so far as this was possible) to a few steps that would help foster appropriate rates of growth in the money supply and keep inflation low.

By implication, the government ruled out spending to run up budgetary deficits as a useful instrument for stimulating the economy. On the contrary, governments could contribute to overall economic efficiency and growth by reducing social expenditure and downsizing the public sector, by reducing its workforce or privatizing nationalized industries. Monetarism reflected a radical change from the postwar consensus regarding economic management. Not only was active government intervention considered unnecessary, it was seen as undesirable and destabilizing.

New Labour's Economic Policy Approach.　Time will tell whether New Labour thinking on macroeconomic policy, backed by new political will, can end the "short-termism" of economic policy and provide the cohesion previously lacking. In British commentaries on New Labour, much has been made of the influence of revitalized Keynesian ideas and reform proposals.[6] In some ways, government policy seems to pursue conventional market reinforcing and pro-business policies (this approach is often referred to as **neoliberalism**). In other ways, the New Labour program stands as an alternative to Thatcherite monetarism and traditional Keynesianism. Whether New Labour's approach to economic management constitutes a distinctive "third way" or a less coherent blend of disparate elements is a matter of political debate.

The first shot fired in the Blair revolution was the announcement within a week of the 1997 election by chancellor of the exchequer (finance minister) Gordon Brown that the Bank of England would be given "operational independence" in the setting of monetary policy. The decision transferred from the cabinet a critical, and highly political, prerogative of government. With Brown attuned to the pressures of international financial markets, and the control of inflation and stability the key goals of macroeconomic policy, the transfer of authority over monetary policy confirmed the neo-liberal market orientation of economic policy.

In other ways, New Labour's approach is refreshingly contemporary in analysis and may signal a "third way." Above all, it emphasizes pragmatism in the face of global economic competition. Since capital is international, mobile, and not subject to control, industrial policy and planning that focus on the domestic economy alone are futile. Rather, government can enhance the quality of labor through education and training, maintain the labor market flexibility inherited from the Thatcher regime, and help attract investment to Britain. Strict control of inflation, low taxes, and tough limits on public expenditure help promote both employment and investment opportunities. At the same time, economic policy is directed at enhancing the competitive strength of key sectors and developing a "partnership" with business through R & D, training, technology, and modernization policies. Blair, his economic policy team, and his supporters hope that this approach will help build a stable and competitive economy, one in which all Britons have a "stake" (New Labour refers to its vision as "the stakeholder economy").[7]

Political Implications of Economic Policy.   Differences in economic doctrine are not what matter most in policy terms. In fact, British governments in the past have never followed any economic theory consistently in the making of economic policy, whether Keynesianism or monetarism. Today, the economic policy of New Labour is, by its very nature, pragmatic and eclectic. The political consequences of economic orientations are more significant: each economic doctrine helps to justify a broad *moral and cultural vision* of society, provide motives for state policy, and advance alternative sets of values. Should the government intervene, work to reduce inequalities through the mildly redistributive provisions of the welfare state, and sustain the ethos of a caring society (collectivism)? Should the government back off and allow the market to function competitively and thereby promote entrepreneurship, competitiveness, and individual autonomy (Thatcherism)? Or should government help secure an inclusive stakeholder economy in which business has the flexibility, security, and mobility to compete, and workers have the skills and training to participate effectively in the global labor market (New Labour)? As these questions make clear, economic management strategies are closely linked to social or welfare policy.

Social Policy

Observers have noted that the social and political role of the welfare state depends as much on policy goals and instruments as on spending levels. Does the state provide services itself or offer cash benefits that can be used to purchase services from private providers? Are benefits limited to those who fall below an income threshold (means-tested) or universal? Are they designed to meet the temporary needs of individuals or to help reduce the gap between rich and poor?

The expanded role of government during World War II and the increased role of the Labour Party during the wartime coalition government led by Winston Churchill prepared the way for the development of the welfare state in Britain. The 1943 Beveridge Report provided a blueprint for an extensive but, in comparative European terms, fairly shallow set of provisions. The principal means-tested program is **social security**, a system of contributory and noncontributory benefits to provide financial assistance (not services directly) for the elderly, sick, disabled, unemployed, and others similarly in need of assistance.

In general, welfare state provisions interfere relatively little in the workings of the market, and policymakers do not see the reduction of group inequalities as the proper goal of the welfare state. The National Health Service (NHS) provides comprehensive and universal medical care and has long been championed as the "jewel in the crown of the welfare state in Britain," but it remains an exception to the rule. Compared to other Western European countries, the welfare state in Britain offers relatively few comprehensive services and the policies are not very generous. For the most part, Britons must rely on means-tested "safety-net" programs that leave few of the recipients satisfied.

The Welfare State under Thatcher and Major. The record on social expenditure by Conservative governments from 1979 to 1997 was mixed. Given Britons' strong support for public education, pensions, and health care, Conservative governments attempted

more limited reform than many at first anticipated. The Thatcher and Major governments encouraged private alongside public provision in education, health care (insurance), and pensions. They worked to increase efficiency in social services, reduced the value of some benefits by changing the formulas or reducing cost-of-living adjustments, and "contracted out" some services (purchased them from private contractors rather than providing them directly). In addition, in policy reforms reminiscent of American "workfare" requirements, they tried to reduce dependency by denying benefits to youths who refuse to participate in training programs.

Despite these efforts, the commitment to reduced spending could not be sustained, partly because a recession triggered rises in income support and unemployment benefits (included under the "Social Security" heading, Figure 2). In addition, the cost of health care rose dramatically in Britain, as in all industrial democracies, because costs were linked to such nonpolicy factors as the increasing age of the population. Looked at in comparative perspective, benefits

Despite efforts to reduce the cost of the welfare state, especially during the period of Conservative governments from 1979 to 1997, Britain experienced real growth in both social services and health care provisions.

Figure 2

Real Growth in Social Security Benefits and National Health Service Expenditure in Britain, 1976–1996

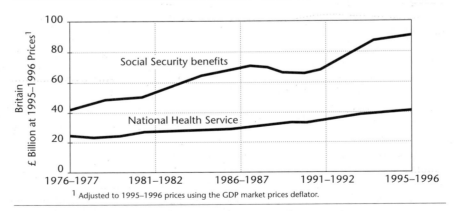

[1] Adjusted to 1995–1996 prices using the GDP market prices deflator.

Source: From *Social Trends* 27, 1997 Edition, ed. Jenny Church p. 137. "Social Trends" Office for National Statistics © Crown, copyright 1997.

Note: In Britain "social security" refers to a variety of social benefits, including pensions, unemployment benefits, sickness benefits, child benefits and one-parent benefits.

per head are below the European Union average, and considerably below those in Germany or the Scandinavian member states (they are higher, however, than in the United States or Japan).

To a degree, however, this general pattern masks specific and, in some cases, highly charged policy changes both in expenditure and in the institutionalized pattern of provision. In housing, the changes in state policy and provision were the most extensive, with repercussions both in electoral terms and in changing the way Britons think about the welfare state. Early on, Thatcher's housing policy became a major test case of her vision of society, as she emphasized private ownership and responsibility. Even before she was prime minister, Thatcher made housing a high-profile issue. During the 1979 campaign, she promised to give all tenants in council (public) housing the opportunity to buy their homes at up to 50 percent below market value.

She kept her promise. By 1990 more than 1.25 million council houses were sold—particularly the attractive single-family homes with gardens (quite unlike American public housing). Two-thirds of the sales were to rental tenants. Thatcher's housing policy was extremely popular. As one observer noted, housing "was electorally crucial in dividing a working-class movement, deeply disillusioned by the apparent inadequacies of the Welfare State and politically embittered by the economic policies pursued by the Labour government after 1976, by its populist appeal to the anti-bureaucratic, individualist and self-sufficient ideology of home ownership."[8] By one calculation, between 1979 and 1983 there was a swing (change in the percentage of vote received by the two major parties) to the Conservative Party of 17 percent among those who bought their council houses.[9] By 1987, the swing by new buyers from Labour to Conservative was down to just 2 percent over the national trend, however. As the rise in adjustable mortgage rates (some 6 percent in 1988–1989 alone!) fueled a steep increase in monthly mortgage payments, the housing issue no longer worked to the advantage of the Conservative Party; it may have started cutting the other way.

Attitudes about the Welfare State: Political Implications.   Despite great Conservative success in the campaign to privatize housing, a strong majority of Britons remain stalwart supporters of the principle of collective provision for their basic needs. Thus, there were limits on the government's ability to reduce social spending or change institutional behavior. For example, in 1989 the Conservative government tried to introduce market practices into the National Health Service (NHS), with general practitioners managing funds and purchasing hospital care for their patients. The British Medical Association (BMA) strongly objected, while many Britons were worried that the creation of an "internal market" would create incentives for doctors or hospitals to cut corners and reduce services to those with the fewest options. Many voiced fears that the reforms would create a two-tier system of medical care for rich and poor.

Major worked to distance himself from Thatcher's perceived disregard for the plight of the less fortunate. In fact, his government increased welfare spending, in part to persuade the electorate that the Conservatives could be trusted on the "caring" issues. Characteristically, and with some quiet success, Major took a pragmatic nonideological turn in welfare policy, looking for cuts and improvements at the same time, within a general framework that preferred means-tested to universal benefits. Nevertheless, the political damage was done. Before the 1992 election, Labour gained a commanding lead over the Conservatives on the health issue: a majority of two-to-one judged it the best party to run the NHS.[10] Clearly, a lack of confidence in the Conservatives on the "caring" issues hurt Major substantially in 1992.

An overwhelming majority of Britons—87 percent—rely exclusively on the NHS for their health care, and nearly all receive most of their critical care in NHS hospitals. As the 1997 election approached, polls made clear that the health service had knocked unemployment out of first place as the most urgent issue on people's minds. Opinion surveys also confirmed that voters usually blamed the Conservatives for problems in these areas, and even blamed Tory social policies for increases in crime. Indeed, a majority of the Conservatives' own supporters worried about what might happen to health and other social services with another Tory government. Nothing propelled the Labour landslide more than the concern for the caring issues.

New Labour Social Policy.   As with economic policy, social policy for New Labour presents an opportunity for government to balance pragmatism and innovation, while borrowing from traditional Labour as well as from Thatcherite options. For example, following his New Democratic counterpart in the United States, the prime minister promises to create a modernized, leaner welfare state, in which people are actively encouraged to seek work. The promised reform of the welfare state emphasizes efficiencies and attempts to break welfare dependency. Efforts to spur entry into the labor market combine carrots and sticks. Positive inducements include extensive training programs, especially targeted at youth, combined with incentives to private industry to hire new entrants to the labor market. The threats include eligibility restrictions and reductions in coverage.

Thus, the Blair government rejects both the attempted retrenchment of Conservative governments that seemed mean-spirited and the egalitarian traditions of Britain's collectivist era that emphasized entitlements. Instead, New Labour focuses its policy on training and broader social investment as a more positive "third way" alternative. At the same time, New Labour draws political strength from the "old Labour" legacy of commitment on the "caring" social policy issues. In this vein, in July 1998, British finance minister Gordon Brown announced new spending plans for social services. The plans call for a three-year increase in public expenditure of more than 10 percent, with dramatic increases in spending on education and health care. The announcement generated quite a furor, with observers sharply divided on the merits of the plan and its implications. Does it represent a return to big government and a retreat from the fiscal conservatism Blair and Brown had promised? Or is it great political theater with relatively modest budgetary or policy implications? After all, as we have seen, social expenditures, and especially health care costs, increased under the Conservatives, and the strong economy should be able to float the increases without undue difficulties. Or does the spending review illustrate a "third way," increasing health care out of necessity and expanding education to achieve the critical goal of a high-skilled competitive workforce for a global age?

Society and Economy

What were the *distributional effects*—the consequences for group patterns of wealth and poverty—of the economic and social policies of Thatcher and Major? To what extent are the policies of Tony Blair's Labour government designed to continue—or to reverse—these trends? How has government policy influenced the condition of minorities and women? It is impossible to ascertain when government policy creates a given distribution of resources and when poverty increases or decreases because of a general downturn or upswing in the economy. The evidence is clear, however, that economic inequality grew in Britain during the 1980s before it stabilized or narrowed slightly in the mid-1990s, and that ethnic minorities and women continue to experience significant disadvantages.

As British journalist Peter Jenkins observed, a host of Thatcher-era policy outcomes—high unemployment, changes in tax policy that increased the tax burdens of the poor relative to the rich, the reduction in the real value of welfare benefits—led to increased inequality. In the 1980s there was much talk in Britain of "two nations" (rich and poor) and a frequent (usually critical) characterization of Thatcher, accordingly, as a "two-nation Tory." Jenkins took the analysis a step further, suggesting that the upward pressure on the top end of the economic scale and the downward pressure on the bottom end had created a three-tiered society of "the haves, the have-nots, and the have-lots."[11]

Data confirm this pattern. Between 1980 and 1990, for those at the ninetieth percentile, incomes grew by 47 percent compared with only 6 percent at the tenth percentile. In the early 1990s the gap stabilized and by 1994 real incomes were growing at both ends of the spectrum and the gap between incomes for the top and bottom 10 percent narrowed. Similarly, the proportion of people whose incomes fell below 40, 50, or 60 percent of the national average grew rapidly throughout the 1980s, but had declined by 1994.[12]

Policy initiated by the Conservative Party particularly during the Thatcher years tended to deepen inequalities. The economic upturn that began in 1992 combined with Major's moderating effects on the Thatcherite social policy agenda served to narrow inequality by the mid-1990s. Labour's commitment on the caring issues, the strong economy inherited by the Blair government, and its promotion of the stakeholding economy augur well for a further modest narrowing of the gap between rich and poor in Britain.

Inequality and Ethnic Minorities

Poverty and diminished opportunity disproportionately characterize the situation of ethnic minorities (a term applied to peoples of non-European origin from the former British colonies in the Indian subcontinent, the Caribbean, and Africa). Official estimates place the ethnic minority population in Britain at around 3.3 million, or just under 6 percent. Indians comprise the largest ethnic minority at 27 percent; Pakistanis and Bangladeshis represent about 23 percent; and Afro-Caribbeans, 23 percent. Due to past immigration and fertility patterns, the ethnic minority population in the U.K. is considerably younger than the white population: more than one-third of the ethnic minority population is younger than 16, nearly half is under 25, and more than four-fifths is under 45. (By contrast, only about one-fifth of whites are under 16, fewer than one-third under 25, and three-fifths under 45.) Thus, despite the often disparaging reference to ethnic minority individuals as "immigrants," the experience of members of ethnic minority groups is increasingly that of a native-born population. Among those under 25, 92 percent of people of Indian descent, 76 percent of Pakistani/Bangladeshi descent, and 80 percent of black people were born in the U.K.[13]

Britain has adjusted slowly and, by most accounts, poorly to the realities of a multicultural society. The postwar period has witnessed the gradual erosion of racial and religious-ethnic tolerance in Britain, and a chipping away at the right of settlement in the U.K. of postcolonial subjects. During the Thatcher era, discussion of immigration and citizenship rights was used for partisan political purposes, and assumed a distinctly racial tone. Ethnic minority individuals, particularly young men, are subject to unequal treatment by the police and considerable physical harassment by citizens. They have experienced cultural isolation as well as marginalization in the educational system, job training, housing, and labor markets.

The sense of cultural isolation within the ethnic minority communities seems strong and these perceptions have deepened ethnic identities or identities based on countries of origin or descent, as distinct from British identities. "In defining ourselves we sometimes say we are English or Welsh or Indian or Jamaican," observed the Afro-Caribbean social theorist and cultural critic Stuart Hall. "Of course this is to speak metaphorically. These identities are not imprinted in our genes. However, we do think of them as if they are part of our essential natures."[14] Few in the minority communities are apt to identify themselves simply as part of a national culture—as English—without reference to their subnational minority identity.

In general, poor rates of economic success reinforce the sense of isolation and distinct collective identities. Variations among ethnic minority communities are quite considerable, however, and there are some noteworthy success stories. For example, among men of African-Asian, Chinese, and Indian descent, the proportional representation in the managerial and professional ranks is actually higher than that for white men (although they are much less likely to be senior managers in large firms). Also, Britons of South Asian—and especially, Indian—descent enjoy a high rate of entrepreneurship. While Britons of Indian descent have enjoyed the greatest mobility into business and professional careers, those of Bangladeshi descent are at the other end of the spectrum. As the latest arrivals and migrants from a predominantly peasant economy, they have faced a set of acute problems: they enter the industrial urban economy of the U.K. with few marketable skills; their proficiency in English is low; and, they are the object of outright discrimination. Despite some variations, employment opportunities for women from all minority ethnic groups are limited. The largest employment concentrations are in the "other non-manual" category (42 percent of Pakistani, 47 percent of Indian, and 54 percent of Afro-Caribbean women), followed by "semi-skilled manual" (45 percent of Pakistani, 34 percent of Indian, and 25 percent of Afro-Caribbean women). There is only limited representation across all other job levels.[15]

A distinct gap remains between the job opportunities available to whites and those open to ethnic minorities in Britain (see Table 2 on p. 48). It is clear that ethnic minority groups are over-represented among low-income households in the U.K. Nearly two-thirds of Pakistani or Bangldeshi households are located within the bottom fifth, while fewer than one-fifth of whites may be found there. Blacks (persons of African or Caribbean descent) are also over-represented in the bottom one-fifth, although not to the same degree.

Inequality and Women

Women's participation in the labor market when compared to that of men also indicates marked patterns of inequality. The Thatcher and Major governments made it clear that management flexibility in hiring part-time workers to lower labor costs would take priority over efforts to reduce gender inequality in the workforce. As a result, the proportion of working women in part-time employment increased. Not only are part-time jobs less secure and lower paid, they also provide fewer pension rights, opportunities for advancement, and employment protections than full-time work. Thus, in the context of cutbacks in provision for home care, employment policy tended to "confirm the old ideas that women worked only for pin money (money to spend for nonessentials) or should stay at home and care for their husbands, children and sick or elderly relatives."[16] In addition, government policy tended to

worsen the often precarious situation of female heads of household when the eligibility for income maintenance was tightened and the value of benefits was reduced.

In fact, most women in Britain work part-time, often in jobs with fewer than sixteen hours of work per week and often with fewer than eight hours (while fewer than one in every fifteen men is employed part-time). More than three-quarters of women working part-time report that they did not want a full-time job, yet more women than men (in raw numbers, not simply as a percentage) take on second jobs. In addition, women are far less likely to be self-employed than men: in 1996, there were roughly three self-employed men for every woman.

A 1997 survey from Eurostat, the statistical arm of the European Union, confirms that employment conditions for women in Britain trail those of their European counterparts. The survey reports that in several EU countries women still get paid substantially less than men, measured in hourly earnings, even when they have comparable education and work in the same industry and occupation. However, the differential is greatest in Britain, where it is just below 25 percent. Moreover, when the overall mix of jobs and the effects of sex segregation in the labor market are taken into account, including both full- and part-time workers, the gap increases to 36 percent—and the gender pay inequality in the U.K. remains the worst in the European Union. To complete the picture, when women move up the job ladder, patterns of inequality actually deepen. Woman in management positions in the U.K. receive only two-thirds the pay of their male counterparts.[17]

The Blair government said that it is committed to gender equality in the workplace and affirmed its resolve to address women's concerns to balance work and family responsibilities. However, the government has continued the Conservative policy of promoting management flexibility, so it seems likely that the general pattern of female labor market participation will change relatively little in the years ahead.

Britain and the International Political Economy

Since the beginning of the Industrial Revolution in the eighteenth century, Britain has been more dependent

---

Table 2

Distribution of Disposable Income in Great Britain by Ethnic Group, 1994–1995		
Ethnic Group	*Percentages*	
	Quintile group of individuals	
	Bottom fifth	Top four-fifths
White	19	81
Black	27	73
Indian	27	73
Pakistani/Bangladeshi	64	36
Other ethnic minorities	36	64
All ethnic groups	20	80

Source: *Social Trends* 27, 1997 Ed., ed. Jenny Church. "Social Trends" Office for National Statistics. © Crown, copyright 1997.

than most countries on international commerce for the creation of wealth. Because Britain's economy is more interdependent with the global economy than most leading industrial powers, it faces considerable external pressures on its economic policy. The dilemmas of European integration most vividly illustrate the interplay between economics and politics in an era of global interdependence.

Britain was humbled when its applications for membership in the European Community (EC) were rejected in 1963 and again in 1967 by France. Worse, since its admission in 1973, Britain's participation in the European Community (in November 1993, it became the *European Union* or EU) has tended to underscore its reduced international power and ability to control regional and global developments. Many Britons remain skeptical about the advantages of Britain's political and economic integration with Europe and are uneasy about the loss of sovereignty that resulted from EU membership.

Economic Integration and Political Disintegration

During the Thatcher and Major years, the issue of economic integration bedeviled the prime minister's office and divided the Conservative Party. The introduction of the European Monetary System (EMS) in 1979 set the stage for the political dramas that followed. The EMS fixed the exchange rates among member currencies (referred to as the Exchange Rate Mechanism or ERM), and permitted only limited fluctuation above or below. Intended to stabilize European economies and promote trade among members, its success depended on the willingness of member states to pursue compatible economic strategies—and on their ability to maintain similar growth rates and levels of inflation. In retrospect, this plan seems highly unrealistic. How likely were Spain, Portugal, Greece—or even Britain—to keep pace with Germany in the period of heady economic competitiveness before unification? But there was tremendous pressure to set up the ERM before political disagreements or recession could close the window of opportunity.

Thatcher opposed British participation in the ERM throughout the 1980s, insisting on British control of its economic policy. However, when her domestic economic policy failed to stem Britain's rampant inflation, Thatcher's anti-EC stance pitted her against senior ministers and leaders of Britain's EC partners as well as against the bulk of the British business community. It seemed that everyone but Thatcher thought participation in European integration would ease inflation in Britain and enhance its competitiveness. In the end, Thatcher succumbed to the pressure to give up a measure of economic sovereignty, in effect, to Germany and its central bank (the *Bundesbank*), whose decisions would force Britain to follow in lock-step. She permitted Britain to join the ERM in October 1990. Ironically, just one month later she was toppled from office by a coup led by those in her own party who most deeply resented her grudging attitude toward integration.

For the new government of Prime Minister Major, participation in the ERM held enormous symbolic and political significance. As chancellor of the exchequer he had quietly pressed Thatcher to join, and as prime minister, he staked his reputation on its success. He hoped that participation would stabilize European trade, reduce inflation, and pull Britain out of a stubborn recession.

The Implications of Maastricht and the Common Currency

The Treaty on European Union (usually called the Maastricht Treaty for the small Dutch town where it was negotiated in 1991) represented a bold agenda for economic and monetary union, and for deeper cooperation on foreign policy and security matters. Maastricht also established a plan to phase in a single EC currency and control of national monetary policy by a European central bank. In addition, Maastricht gave treaty status to the "Community Charter of the Fundamental Social Rights of Workers," more commonly known as the Social Charter.

Unlike Thatcher, Major positioned himself as pro-Europe and was solicitous of his allies. But he stood his ground at Maastricht. Negotiating well, Major secured a crucial opt-out clause for Britain. The United Kingdom would not be bound by the Social Charter or by any single currency plans. Unfortunately for Major and the Conservatives, almost before he could enjoy his Maastricht victories, Major's integration strategy faced a nearly fatal setback.

In September 1992, the European Monetary System collapsed under the impact of downward pressures in the British economy and the strains of German unification. The prime minister's reputation was badly damaged, and the momentum for economic unity among EC countries was abruptly stalled. The Thatcherite anti-Maastricht hard core in the Conservative Party dug in against him on the key issues of economic and monetary union, thereby undermining his leadership and forcing him to squander his political capital on the lost cause of party unity on Europe. Major never recovered, and it took several years before plans for economic integration in the EU were put back on track. Remarkably, a single European policy (the ERM) led to Thatcher's downfall and politically haunted John Major throughout his premiership.

Developments in European integration present a formidable hurdle for Tony Blair (this will be discussed further in Section 5). Few in Britain find it easy to countenance a common currency in place of the pound sterling (the British currency), a symbol of empire and national autonomy. Britons are also extremely reluctant to lose direct control over monetary policy to a European central bank. But since Tony Blair's Britain wants to assume leadership in Europe and position itself on the cutting edge of globalization, Britain faces a significant dilemma over the euro. The political repercussions of economic and monetary considerations will help shape the challenges that New Labour, future governments, and the country face in the years ahead.

As our world of states theme suggests, a country's participation in today's global economic order diminishes national sovereign control, raising unsettling questions in even the most established democracies. Amid complicated pressures, both internal and external, can state institutions retain the capacity to administer policy effectively? How much do the growth of powerful bureaucracies at home and complex dependencies on international organizations such as the EU limit the ability of citizens to control policy ends? We turn to these questions in Section 3.

Section ❸ Governance and Policy-Making

An understanding of British governance begins with consideration of its constitution. Britain lacks a constitution in the usual sense, that is, a single authoritative text that carries special status and can be amended only by special procedures. Rather, the British constitution is a combination of statutory law (mainly Acts of Parliament), common law, convention, and authoritative interpretations. Although it is often said that Britain has an unwritten constitution, this is not accurate. It is probably best to say that "what distinguishes the British constitution from others is not that it is unwritten, but rather that it is part written and uncodified."[18]

In many areas the structure and principles of government have been accepted for so long that appeal to convention has enormous cultural force. Thus, widely agreed-upon rules of conduct and conventions, rather than law or American-style checks and balances, set the limits of government power. Most of the time these rules constrain officials from overstepping generally accepted boundaries and prevent any state institution from achieving undue power.

This reality underscores an important aspect of British government: *absolute* principles of government are few. At the same time, those that exist are fundamental to the organization of the state and central to governance, policy-making, and patterns of representation.

Organization of the State

What are the central organizing principles of the British state? First, the core constitutional principle of the British political system and cornerstone of the Westminster model is **parliamentary sovereignty.** Parliament can make or overturn any law; the executive, the judiciary, and the throne do not have any authority to restrict or rescind parliamentary action. Only Parliament can nullify or overturn its own legislation. In a classic **parliamentary democracy**, the prime minister is answerable to the House of Commons (the elected element of Parliament) and may be dismissed by it.

note the centrality of party — its leader becomes PM

Second, Britain has long been a **unitary state**. By contrast to the United States, where powers not delegated to the national government are reserved for the states, no powers are reserved constitutionally for sub-central units of government in the United Kingdom. However, the Labour government of Tony Blair has introduced a far-reaching program of constitutional reform that promises to create, for the first time, a quasi-federal system in Britain. If implemented, specified powers have been delegated (the British prefer to say "devolved") to legislative bodies in Scotland and Wales, and potentially in Northern Ireland. In addition, some powers will be redistributed from the Westminster Parliament to an authority governing London and, potentially, to regional assemblies as well.

Third, Britain operates within a system of **fusion of powers** at the national level: Parliament is the supreme legislative, executive, and judicial authority and includes the monarch as well as the House of Commons and the House of Lords. The fusion of legislature and executive is also expressed in the function and personnel of the cabinet. Whereas American presidents can direct or ignore their cabinets, which have no constitutionally mandated function, the British cabinet bears enormous constitutional responsibility. Through its collective decision-making, the cabinet—and not an independent prime minister—shapes, directs, and takes responsibility for government. Cabinet government stands in stark contrast to presidential government and is perhaps the most important feature, certainly the center, of Britain's system of government.

role of cabinet

Finally, sovereignty rests with the Queen-in-Parliament (the formal term for Parliament). Britain is a **constitutional monarchy**: the position of head of state passes by hereditary succession, but nearly all powers of the Crown must be exercised by the government or state officials. Taken together, parliamentary sovereignty, parliamentary democracy, and cabinet government form the core elements of the British or Westminster model of government, which many consider a model democracy and the first effective parliamentary democracy. The absence of legally enforceable limits to the exercise of power raises questions about the gap between democratic ideal and political reality in Britain. Can a willful prime minister overstep the generally agreed limits of the collective

no check on power (except by people)

no mention of sup. Court add

responsibility of the cabinet and achieve an undue concentration of power? How well has the British model of government stood the test of time—and radically changed circumstances? What are the political and constitutional implications of Blair's reform agenda?

These questions underscore the problems faced even by the most stable democracies. They also help identify important comparative themes, because the principles of the Westminster model were, with some modifications, adopted widely by former colonies ranging from Canada, Australia, and New Zealand to India, Jamaica, and Zimbabwe. So British success (or failure) in preserving citizens' control of their government has implications reaching well beyond the British Isles.

good for why study UK?

The Executive

The term *cabinet government* is useful in emphasizing the key functions the cabinet exercises: responsibility for policy-making, supreme control of government, and coordination of all government departments. However, the term does not capture the full range of executive institutions or the scale and complexity of operations. The executive reaches well beyond the cabinet. It extends from ministries (departments) and ministers to the civil service in one direction, and to Parliament (as we shall see in Section 4) in the other direction.

Cabinet Government

After a general election, the Crown invites the leader of the party that emerges from the election with control of a majority of seats in the House of Commons to form a government and serve as prime minister. The prime minister usually selects approximately two dozen ministers to constitute the cabinet. Among the most significant assignments are the Foreign Office (equivalent to an American secretary of state), the Home Office (Ministry of Justice), and the Chancellor of the Exchequer (a finance minister or a more powerful version of an American Treasury secretary).

The responsibilities of a cabinet minister are immense. "The Cabinet, as a collective body, is responsible for formulating the policy to be placed before Parliament and is also the supreme controlling and directing body of the entire executive branch," notes S. E. Finer. "Its decisions bind all Ministers and other officers in the conduct of their departmental business."[19] In contrast to the French Constitution, which prohibits a cabinet minister from serving in the legislature, British constitutional tradition *requires* overlapping membership between Parliament and cabinet. Unlike the informal status of the U.S. cabinet, its British counterpart enjoys considerable constitutional privilege and is a powerful institution with enormous responsibility for the political and administrative success of the government.

The cabinet system is a complex patchwork of conflicting obligations and potential divisions. Each cabinet member who is a departmental minister has responsibilities to the *ministry* that he or she must run; and, unless he or she is a member of the House of Lords, a cabinet member is also linked to a *constituency*, or electoral district (as an elected member of Parliament or MP), to the *party* (as a leader and, often, a member of its executive board), to the *prime minister* (as an appointee who shares in the duties of a plural executive), and to a *political tendency* within the party (as a leading proponent of a particular vision of government).

The cabinet room at 10 Downing Street (the prime minister's official residence) is a place of intrigue as well as deliberation. From the perspective of the prime minister, the cabinet may appear as loyal followers—or as ideological combatants, potential challengers for party leadership, and parochial advocates for pet programs that run counter to the overall objectives of the government. Against this potential for divisions, the convention of collective responsibility normally assures the continuity of government by unifying the cabinet on matters of policy. In principle, the prime minister must gain the support of a majority of the cabinet for a range of significant decisions, notably the budget and the legislative program.

The only other constitutionally mandated mechanism for checking the prime minister is a defeat on a vote of no confidence in the House of Commons (discussed in Section 4). Since this action is rare and politically dangerous, the cabinet's role in constraining the chief executive remains the only routine check on his or her power. Collective responsibility is therefore a crucial aspect of the Westminster model of democracy. Prime ministers, however, reserve the option to develop policies in cabinet committees, whose membership can be manipulated to ensure support, and then to present policy to the full cabinet with little chance for other ministers to challenge the results. In addition, the principle of collective responsibility requires that all ministers support any action taken in the name of the government, whether or not it was brought to cabinet. Does collective responsibility effectively constrain the power of prime ministers or does it enable the prime minister to paint "presidential" decisions with the veneer of collectivity?

A politician with strong ideological convictions and a leadership style to match, Thatcher often attempted to galvanize loyalists in cabinet and either marginalize or expel detractors. Therefore, controversial issues (such as the proposed reorganization of health provision in 1988–1989) were often decided by hand-picked cabinet committees or in combination with personal advisers and senior civil servants. In this way, Thatcher often avoided full cabinet scrutiny of critical policies. In the end, Thatcher's treatment of the cabinet helped galvanize the movement to unseat her as party leader and stretched British constitutional conventions.

Major returned to a more consultative approach, in keeping with the classic model of cabinet government. As one observer put it, "When John Major became Prime Minister it was as though he had read textbooks on British constitutional theory, had observed very closely the circumstances of Margaret Thatcher's downfall, and had come to the conclusion that he was going to do things differently—very differently."[20]

Blair, like Thatcher, has narrowed the scope of collective responsibility. Cabinet meetings are dull and perfunctory, debate is rare. Real decisions are taken in smaller gatherings by the same people who ran the election campaign: the prime minister, a few key cabinet members, and a handful of advisors. In a striking example of this process, the full cabinet had not yet met when the government announced the decision right after the election to free the Bank of England to set interest rates.

Alongside collective responsibility, members of the cabinet assume individual responsibility for personal or private misconduct and, more importantly, for administrative or political misjudgment. Responsibility is taken seriously: it means resignation. Since 1900, more than a hundred ministers have resigned, although far more often for personal misconduct or to avoid being fired than out of high political principle or to take responsibility for an error of judgment in their departments. One classic illustration of the latter (and its political use to insulate the prime minister), was the resignation of the foreign secretary, Lord Carrington, and two colleagues after the Argentine invasion of the disputed Falkland/Malvinas Islands in 1982 for failing to anticipate the attack.

pol. of ordinary (?)

On balance, cabinet government represents a durable and effective formula for governance. It is important to remember that the cabinet operates within a broader cabinet system (see Figure 3). Since the prime minister is the head of the cabinet, the PM's office helps develop policy, coordinates operations, and functions as liaison with the media, the party, interest groups, and Parliament. Both cabinet committees (comprised of ministers) and official committees (made up of civil servants) supplement the work of the cabinet. In addition, the treasury plays an important coordinating role through its budgetary control, while the cabinet office supports day-to-day operations. Leaders in both the Commons and the Lords, the whips, help smooth the passage of legislation sponsored by the government, which is more or less guaranteed a working majority.

Figure 3

The Cabinet System

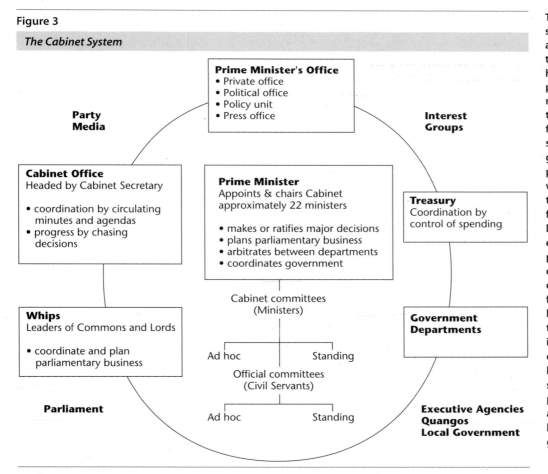

Prime Minister's Office
- Private office
- Political office
- Policy unit
- Press office

Party Media

Interest Groups

Cabinet Office
Headed by Cabinet Secretary

- coordination by circulating minutes and agendas
- progress by chasing decisions

Prime Minister
Appoints & chairs Cabinet approximately 22 ministers

- makes or ratifies major decisions
- plans parliamentary business
- arbitrates between departments
- coordinates government

Treasury
Coordination by control of spending

Cabinet committees
(Ministers)

Government Departments

Whips
Leaders of Commons and Lords

- coordinate and plan parliamentary business

Ad hoc   Standing

Official committees
(Civil Servants)

Parliament

Ad hoc   Standing

**Executive Agencies
Quangos
Local Government**

The cabinet is supported by a set of institutions that help formulate policy, coordinate operations, and facilitate the support for government policy. Acting within a context set by the fusion of legislature and executive, the prime minister enjoys a great opportunity for decisive leadership that is lacking in a system of checks and balances and separation of powers among the branches of government.

Source: Continuities and Change, Third Edition, by Dennis Kavanagh, p. 251. Copright © 1996 by Oxford University Press. Reprinted by permission.

The cabinet system ensures that there is no Washington-style gridlock (the inability of legislature and executive to agree on policy) in London! On the contrary, if there is a problem at the pinnacle of power in the U.K., it is the potential for excessive concentration of power by a prime minister who is prepared to manipulate cabinet and flout the conventions of collective responsibility.

Bureaucracy and Civil Service

Policy-making at 10 Downing Street may appear to be increasingly concentrated in the prime minister's hands. At the same time, when viewed from Whitehall (a street name referring to the London nerve center of the civil service), the executive may appear to be dominated by its vast administrative agencies. The range and complexity of state policy-making mean that in practice the cabinet's authority must be shared with a vast set of unelected officials.

Cabinet members have the formal title *secretary of state for X,* where X designates the ministry, such as Defense or Employment. A few have a special title such as Chancellor of the Exchequer. To help bridge the closely linked functions of policy-making and implementation of policy, each secretary has a few political assistants (appointed by the prime minister in consultation with the secretary). These *ministers of state* may take responsibility for specific policy areas and often assume some discretionary authority over policy. *Junior ministers* act as intermediaries with the nonpolitical bureaucracy of the civil service and may also assume responsibility for particular departmental duties.

How is the civil service organized? A very senior career civil servant, called a *permanent secretary*, has chief administrative responsibility for running a department. The permanent secretaries are assisted, in turn, by other senior civil servants, including deputy secretaries and undersecretaries (the top three grades of senior civil servants number some 650). There are approximately 75,000 senior executives a few rungs down from the level of interaction with ministers and junior ministers. In addition, the minister reaches into his or her department to appoint a *principal private secretary,* an up-and-coming civil servant, who assists the minister as gatekeeper and liaison with senior civil servants. In 1996, the total number of civil service personnel was just over 494,300, down from a high of 735,400 in 1979, a decline of one-third.

Successful policy requires the effective translation of policy goals into policy instruments. Since nearly all legislation is introduced on behalf of the government and as the policy directive of a ministry, civil servants do the work of developing legislation that is performed by committee staffers in the U.S. Congress. Civil servants, more than ministers, oversee the day-to-day operations of ministries and, despite a certain natural level of mutual mistrust, the two must work closely together. To the impartial, permanent, and anonymous civil servants, ministers are too political, unpredictable, and temporary—and they are tireless self-promoters who may neglect or misunderstand the needs of the ministry. To a conscientious minister, the permanent secretary may be protecting "his" or "her" department too strenuously from constitutionally proper oversight and direction. But without a sharp delineation between the responsibilities of ministers and civil servants, there is no choice but to execute policy together.

Civil servants are servants of the Crown, but they are not part of the government (taken in the more political sense, like "the administration" in common American usage). A change of government does not involve a change in departmental staffs. Civil servants are highly respected for their traditional anonymity and political neutrality, and for the technical expertise and continuity they contribute to policy-making. The structure and behavior of the British civil service is often considered a model of politically insulated, efficient administration, free of the partisanship, insider dealing, and corruption found in many bureaucracies, particularly in postcommunist, postauthoritarian, and postcolonial regimes. Nevertheless, the civil service has been assaulted from many directions. Since the early 1980s, the pace of change at Whitehall has been very fast, with governments looking to cut the size of the civil service, streamline its operations, and enhance its accountability to citizens.

As a result of this initiative (known as "new public management" or NPM), the civil service inherited by New Labour is very different from the civil service of thirty years ago. It has been downsized and given a new corporate structure (divided into over 120 separate executive agencies). Few at the top of these agencies (agency chief executives) are traditional career civil servants. More generally, a tradition of a career service, in which nearly all the most powerful posts were filled by those who entered the bureaucratic ranks in their twenties, is fading. Many top appointments are advertised and filled by "outsiders." The Blair government seems unlikely to reverse the NPM trends toward accountability, efficiency, and greater transparency in the operations of the executive bureaucracy. Potential constitutional changes such as devolution and the introduction of a Freedom of Information Act hold the promise of directly and indirectly reforming the civil service further.

Semipublic Agencies

Like other countries, Britain has institutionalized a set of administrative functions that expand the role of the state well beyond the traditional core executive functions and agencies. The ebb and flow of alternative visions of government in the postwar period—from collectivist consensus to Thatcherism to New Labour—have resulted in substantial changes in emphasis. We turn now to a brief discussion of "semipublic" agencies, entities sanctioned by the state but without direct democratic oversight.

Nationalized Industries. The nationalization of basic industries was a central objective of the Labour government's program in the immediate postwar period after World War II. Nationalization symbolized Labour's core socialist aspiration affirmed in the famous Clause IV of its party constitution ("to secure for the workers by hand or brain the full fruits of their industry . . . upon the basis of common ownership of the means of production, distribution and exchange . . ."). Between 1946 and 1949, the Bank of England was nationalized, and coal, iron and steel, gas and electricity supply, and the bulk of the transport sector became public corporations. By 1960, nationalized industries accounted for about 18 percent of total fixed investment, produced about one-tenth of the national income, and employed some 8 percent of the U.K. workforce.[21]

Replacing private entrepreneurs and acting through government-appointed boards of directors for each industry, the state now hired, bargained with, and fired workers; paid the bills; set pricing policies; and invested, planned, and presided over a vast industrial empire. Nationalization created state monopolies backed by public financing that could operate more effectively than the smaller undercapitalized firms they had replaced. The state takeover of industries was designed to ensure the cheap and reliable provision of essential fuel supplies and transport, facilitate a modicum of central coordination of personnel and investment planning, and improve productivity.

The nationalized industries have operated by principles that give all of the advantages and none of the risk to private capitalists—for example, "buy dear" (at a high price) from the private sector and "sell cheap." Private firms made a profit from selling materials and equipment and saw their costs of production drop with the steady and relatively cheap supply of basic fuel and energy, for example. During the 1970s and especially since Thatcher's rejection of the collectivist consensus in 1979, the boards of the nationalized industries have practiced increasingly hard-nosed strategies toward labor unions. The coal miners' strike of 1984–1985, the longest and most violent industrial dispute in postwar Britain, illustrates this approach. More generally, extensive privatization sharply reduced the scale and political significance of the public sector. During the eighteen years of Conservative government beginning in 1979, nearly a million workers transferred from public to private sector employment, and by 1995 the output of the nationalized sector was less than half the percentage of GDP it had been in 1975.

Before assuming leadership of the Labour Party, Blair argued that a revision of Clause IV was necessary to make it clear that the Labour Party has broken with its past. He reiterated that goal in his first speech as leader to the Party conference in October 1994 and, within months, a new Clause IV was in place that speaks to middle-class aspirations and rejects the notion that the capitalist market economy is immoral or inherently exploitative. For New Labour, a return to the program of public ownership of industry is unthinkable. Instead, when thinking of expanding state functions, we can look to a growing set of semipublic administrative organizations.

Nondepartmental Public Bodies. During the past thirty years, an increasing number of administrative functions have been transferred to quasi-nongovernmental organizations, better known as **quangos**. In Britain, there are three traditional kinds of nondepartmental public bodies: executive bodies, tribunals, and advisory bodies or agencies. Quangos have increasing policy influence and enjoy considerable administrative and political advantages. They take responsibility for specific functions and can combine governmental and private sector expertise. At the same time, ministers can distance themselves from controversial areas of policy, such as arms sales or race relations.

Despite Thatcher's attempts to reduce their number and scale back their operations by the early 1990s, a new generation of powerful, broadly defined, and well-funded quangos had replaced the smaller-scale quangos of the past. In 1990–1991 quangos were spending three times as much as they had in 1978–1979. The growth was particularly significant in locally appointed agencies, including bodies with responsibility for education, job training, health, and housing. By the late 1990s, there were some 6000 quangos, 90 percent operating at the local level. They were responsible for one-third of all public spending and staffed by approximately 50,000 people. Key areas of public policy previously under the authority of local governments are now controlled by quangos, which are nonelected bodies.

Some observers have expressed concern that the principle of democratic control is being compromised by the power of quangos, which are not accountable to the electorate. Some argue that the growth of local quangos has contributed to the centralization of power, as agencies appointed by ministers take over many functions of local government. Although critical of the "quango state" while in opposition, New Labour is probably no more likely to be successful in paring down the quasi-nongovernmental sector than was Thatcher. We will return later to consider local government in Britain, but we move now to a discussion of a set of formal institutions both within and outside the executive.

Other State Institutions

Although British public administration extends well beyond its traditional focus on finance or foreign affairs or law and order, these policy areas remain critical. In this section, we examine the military and police, the judiciary, and subnational government.

The Military and the Police

From the local bobby (a term for a local police officer derived from Sir Robert Peel, who set up London's metropolitan police force) to the most senior military officer, those involved in security and law enforcement have enjoyed a rare measure of popular support in Britain. Public opinion polls show that the army and the police rank first and second, respectively, among the institutions in which Britons have confidence. Constitutional tradition and professionalism distance the British police and military officers from politics—they harbor virtually no political ambitions and have traditionally steered clear of partisan involvement. Nevertheless, in recent decades both institutions have been placed in more politically controversial and exposed positions.

In the case of the military, British policy in the post-Cold War period remains focused on a gradually redefined set of NATO commitments. Still ranked among the top five military powers in the world, Britain retains a global presence, and the Thatcher and Major governments deployed forces in ways that enhanced their political positions and maximized Britain's global influence. In 1982, Britain soundly defeated Argentina in a war over the disputed Falkland/Malvinas islands in the South Atlantic. In the Persian Gulf War of 1991, Britain deployed a full armored division in the UN-sanctioned force arrayed against Iraq's Saddam Hussein. Under Blair's leadership, Britain was the sole participant alongside the United States in the aerial bombardment of Iraq in December 1998. Since the mid-1990s, the British have supported diplomatic efforts to stabilize the territories of the former Yugoslavia; in 1999 the U.K. strongly backed NATO's Kosovo campaign and pressed for ground troops.

The broad-based popularity of these missions must be measured, however, against the more controversial role of the military in the dispute in Northern Ireland. After a civil rights movement calling for Catholic political and economic equality helped provoke Protestant riots in the autumn of 1969, the British government sent troops to Northern Ireland. During the height of the "troubles," in a context set by paramilitary violence on all sides, the reputation of the army was tarnished by its use of techniques that violated civil liberties. The powers used by security forces to detain suspects were found to violate the European Convention of Human Rights. In addition, a set of extremely embarrassing decisions by the European Court of Justice on Human Rights (ECJHR) concerning Britain's interrogation procedures in Northern Ireland resulted in procedural changes in the British treatment of suspects. Subsequently, the court ruled that Britain unlawfully killed three IRA members in a 1988 action by undercover soldiers in Gibraltar. The British army was also subject to accusations that it was used as a partisan political instrument to repress Irish nationalism.

As for the police, which traditionally operate as independent local forces throughout the country, the period since the 1980s has witnessed growth in government control, centralization, and level of political use. The coal miners' strike of 1984-1985 raised significant questions about the political roles forced on the police (and, as we shall see, the judiciary) by the Thatcher government. In practice, police operated to an unprecedented—and perhaps unlawful—degree as a national force coordinated through Scotland Yard (London police headquarters). Police menaced strikers and hindered miners from participating in strike support activities. This partisan use of the police in an industrial dispute flew in the face of constitutional traditions and offended some police officers and officials. During the 1990s, concerns about police conduct have focused on police/community relations including race relations, corruption, and the interrogation and treatment of people held in custody. In particular, widespread criticism of the police for mishandling their investigation into the brutal 1993 racist killing of Stephen Lawrence in South London resulted in a scathing report by a commission of inquiry in 1999. The case raised basic questions about police attitudes toward ethnic minorities as well as their conduct in racially sensitive cases, and focused renewed attention on necessary reforms.

The entire criminal justice system, including the police and the judiciary, has received harsh scrutiny in recent years. In July 1993, the Royal Commission on Criminal Justice proposed 352 recommendations for overhauling criminal justice. The report left few satisfied and underscored growing concerns that problems abound.

New Labour has advocated expanding police-community partnerships and improving relations with ethnic minority groups. At the same time, it considers tough action on crime as part of its broader approach to community that places considerable emphasis on the responsibilites of individuals and citizens (**communitarianism**). In an interesting twist, in 1996 Blair dispatched to New York the person tapped to be home secretary in the future Labour government to study that city's success in reducing street crime. New Labour then adopted the "zero-tolerance" approach trumpeted by New York's Republican mayor, Rudolph Giuliani.

The Judiciary

The function of the British judiciary has been far more limited than that of its French, German, or U.S. counterparts. In Britain, the principle of parliamentary sovereignty has limited the role of the judiciary. Courts have no power to judge the constitutionality of legislative acts (**judicial review**); they can only determine whether policy directives or administrative acts violate common law or an act of Parliament.

Since it cannot rule on matters of constitutionality and is never called upon to set policy on controversial issues (such as a woman's right to abortion or the limits of affirmative action), the British judiciary is generally less politicized and influential than its American counterpart. In recent decades, however, governments have pulled the courts into political battles over the rights of local councils, the activities of police in urban riots, and the role of police and trade unions in industrial disputes. For example, in the 1984–1985 coal miners' strike, the courts interpreted the new Employment Act of 1982 very broadly and froze the entire assets of the miners' union. This decision helped tip the balance in the dispute toward the government. Also concerning the miners' strike, in a decision that confounded many, the Court of Appeal rejected an unusual application by the local police authority in Northumbria to compel the home secretary to withdraw instructions for the use of tear gas and plastic bullets to disperse the miners. At a stroke, the decision showed the new and controversial political role of the courts, advanced the centralized cabinet-level (hence, political) control over policing, and affirmed an ancient royal prerogative against the local police authorities.

Jurists have also participated in the wider political debate outside of court, as when they have headed royal commissions on the conduct of industrial relations, the struggle in Northern Ireland, and riots in Britain's inner cities. Some observers of British politics are concerned that governments have used judges in these ways to secure partisan ends, deflect criticism, and weaken the tradition of parliamentary scrutiny of government policy. Nevertheless, Sir Richard Scott's harsh report on his investigation into Britain's sales of military equipment to Iraq in the 1980s, for example, indicates that inquiries led by judges with a streak of independence can prove highly embarrassing to the government and raise important issues for public debate.

Subnational Government

Since the United Kingdom is a state comprised of distinct nations (England, Scotland, Wales, and Northern Ireland), the distribution of powers involves two levels below the central government: national government and local (municipal) government. Because the British political framework has traditionally been unitary, not federal, no formal powers devolved either to the nation within the U.K. or to subnational units (states or regions) as in the United States, India, or Germany. Initiatives undertaken by Blair's government promise far-reaching constitutional changes in the distribution of power between the U.K. government and sub-central national units. Constitutional reforms to create legislative bodies in Scotland and Wales and reconfigure the political arrangement in Northern Ireland will be discussed in Section 5. The discussion here will be limited to local government.

Although no powers have been constitutionally reserved to local governments, they historically had considerable autonomy in financial terms and discretion in implementing a host of social service and related policies. Before 1975, elected local governments set their own spending and taxation levels through the setting of *rates*, or local property taxes. In the context of increased fiscal pressures that followed the 1973 oil crisis, the Labour government introduced the first check on the fiscal autonomy of local councils by introducing *cash limits* (ceilings on spending) beginning in fiscal year 1976–1977. In 1980, the newly elected Thatcher government introduced the Local Government, Planning and Land Act, further tightening the fiscal constraints on local government. Finally, in 1982, the central government set a ceiling on local rates (a *rate cap*).

In this era of constraint, local councils tried a variety of experimental approaches. Conservative councils began to contract out (and thereby privatize) services to private enterprise. Labour councils pursued a range of socialist or progressive initiatives, including the promotion of local job opportunities, the creation of nuclear-free zones, the reduction of fares for public transportation, and the funding of community groups. The struggle between left-wing Labour councils and the right-wing Conservative government bent on reducing welfare provision and limiting local control over budgets pushed the role of local councils to the forefront of British political debate. The outright abolition of London's progressive and multiculturally oriented city government (the Greater London Council, or GLC) and several other metropolitan councils in March, 1986, completed the political onslaught on local autonomy.

Riots in several British cities in 1981 and 1985 and the much-vaunted Battle for London—the campaign of resistance to the GLC's abolition—provoked some of the most hard-edged debates about democracy in recent British history. Given the GLC's emphasis on ethnic minority cultural initiatives and its campaign for equal opportunity and political access, the struggle also highlighted the racial dimension of British politics.

In 1989, the Thatcher government introduced a poll tax, an equal per capita levy for local finance, to replace the age-old system of rates. This radical break with tradition, which shifted the burden of local taxes from property owners and businesses to individuals—and taxed rich and poor alike—was monumentally unpopular. The poll tax proved a tremendous political liability, maintained the local edge to national politics, and helped lead to Thatcher's departure. As in other areas of public policy, Major tried to depoliticize local government. He quickly replaced the poll tax with a new local tax linked to the value of properties, although he kept policies in place that centralized and controlled local finance.

Although much of New Labour's agenda concerning subcentral government is focused on the political role of nations within the U.K., devolution within England is also on the agenda. The Blair government's program includes the formation of Regional Development Agencies in 1999 and, in the long term, the introduction of regional assemblies. Interestingly, changes in the governance of London are on the fast track. New Labour has no plans to reconstitute the GLC or return to a city government the powers currently enjoyed by quangos and by London's boroughs. Nevertheless, plans are firmly in place for the formation of a citywide strategic authority with extensive powers and the direct election of an American-style mayor by 2000. In addition, New Labour has emphasized greater local democracy and accountability, although it appears genuinely ambivalent about decentralization with the loss of direction and control it entails.

The Policy-Making Process

As already discussed, parliamentary sovereignty is the core constitutional principle of the British political system. However, when it comes to policy-making and policy implementation, the focus is not on Westminster, but rather on Whitehall (the London street that once housed government ministries and whose name still connotes the world of ministers and civil servants). In many countries, such as Japan, India, and Nigeria, personal connections and informal networks play a large role in policy-making and implementation. How different is the British system?

The interaction between the Cabinet Secretary and his or her junior ministers and their counterparts among the career civil servants—notably the permanent secretary, deputy secretary, and undersecretary—reveals much about the policy-making process. Policy-making emerges primarily from within the executive—from the efforts of what is sometimes called the *partisan executive* (the ministers) and the *merit executive* (the career civil servants, who are duty-bound to turn policy goals into instruments, then implement the executive orders and Acts of Parliament that result).

Unlike the American system, in which policy-making is concentrated in Congressional committees and subcommittees, Parliament has little direct participation in policy-making. Britain preserves decision-making for the corridors of Whitehall. However, the policy-making process involves much more than just a collaboration between high-flying junior ministers and anonymous mandarins (a term originally referring to officials in Imperial China and used colloquially to describe traditional top career civil servants who are generalists steeped in the culture of Whitehall).

Decision-making is strongly influenced by *policy communities*, informal networks with extensive knowledge, access, and personal connections to those responsible for policy. In this "private, specialized, and invariably 'closed' world," civil servants, ministers, and members of the policy communities (sometimes referred to as *subgovernments*) trade expertise and mutual recognition of authority. This is the make-or-break context in which policy is made.

A cooperative style, even a coziness, develops as the ministry becomes an advocate for key players in its policy community, and as civil servants come perhaps to overidentify the public good with the advancement of policy within their area of responsibility. For example, some have accused the Ministry of Agriculture, Fisheries and Food of defending farmers and manufacturers in their effort to boost food prices and profits. In a similar vein, classic **patron-client relations** develop in which "sponsor departments" advance the interests of the sectors affected by their policies. This describes, for example, the relationship between the Department of Health and Social Security and the medical establishment for much of the postwar period. In the late 1980s, however, efforts by the Conservative government to introduce unpopular internal market reforms in health care broke the cooperative policy styles and sent doctors rushing into the Commons and the committee rooms to battle legislation they had been unable to rewrite or block through the normal functioning of their policy communities.

As will be discussed further in Section 4, the breakdown of the collectivist consensus transformed politics at many levels, from the policy-making process to the organization of interests and the broad dynamics of representation and political participation, to which we now turn.

Section ④ Representation and Participation

As discussed in Section 3, parliamentary sovereignty is the core constitutional principle defining the role of the legislature and, in a sense, the whole system of British government. No act of Parliament can be set aside by the executive or judiciary, nor is any Parliament bound by the actions of any previous Parliament. Nevertheless, in practice, the control exerted by the House of Commons (or Commons) is not unlimited. In this section, we investigate the powers and role of Parliament, both Commons and Lords, as well as the party system, elections, and contemporary currents in British political culture and identity. We also assess broader patterns of political participation linked to class, race, gender, region, nation, and ethnicity.

The Legislature

Is Parliament still as sovereign in practice as it remains in constitutional tradition? Clearly, it is not so powerful as it once was. From roughly the 1830s to the 1880s, it collaborated in the formulation of policy and members amended or rejected legislation on the floor of the House. Today the Commons does not so much legislate as assent to government legislation because (with rare exceptions) the governing party has a majority of the seats and requires no cross-party voting to pass bills.

Legislative proceedings are conducted according to time-honored customs and procedures. A law begins in draft form as a parliamentary bill. Although there are private bills that concern matters of individual or local interest, most bills are public bills sponsored by the government. The most important of these have generally passed through an elaborate process before they reach the floor of the House, where they undergo additional extensive scrutiny before proceeding to the Lords. The elaborate path followed by prospective legislation is described in the Institutional Intricacies Box: The Legislative Process.

The House of Commons

In constitutional terms, the House of Commons, the lower house of Parliament (with 659 members at the time of the 1997 election), exercises the main legislative power in Britain. Along with the two unelected elements of Parliament, the Crown and the House of Lords, the Commons has three main functions: (1) to pass laws, (2) to provide finance for the state by authorizing taxation, and (3) to review and scrutinize public administration and government policy.

In practical terms, the Commons has a very limited legislative function; nevertheless it serves a very important democratic function. It provides a highly visible arena for policy debate and the partisan collision of political world views. The House comes alive when opposition members challenge the government, spark debates over legislation, and question the actions of cabinet members. During *question time*, a regular weekly feature of Commons debate, ministers give oral replies to questions submitted in advance by MPs and offer off-the-cuff responses to follow-up questions and sarcastic asides (often to the merriment of all in attendance). A half-hour session each week is allotted to the prime minister's question time, when the prime minister and the leader of the opposition engage in highly charged verbal combat. The exchanges create extraordinary theater and can make and unmake careers: the ability to handle parliamentary debate with style and panache is considered a prerequisite for party leadership.

The high stakes and the flash of rhetorical skills bring drama to the historic chambers, but one crucial element of drama is nearly always missing: the outcome is seldom in doubt. The likelihood that the Commons will invoke its ultimate authority, to defeat a government, is very small. MPs from the governing party who consider rebelling against their leader (the prime minister) are understandably reluctant in a close and critical vote to force a general election—which would place their jobs in grave jeopardy. Only once since the defeat of Ramsay MacDonald's government in 1924 has a government been brought down by a defeat in the Commons (in 1979). Contemporary constitutional conventions provide a good deal of "wiggle room" for the government. It was once taken for granted that defeat of any significant motion or bill would automatically result in cabinet resignation or a

---

Institutional Intricacies: | **The Legislative Process**

To become law, bills must be introduced in the House of Commons and the House of Lords, although approval by the latter is not required. The procedure for developing and adopting a public bill is quite complex. The ideas for prospective legislation may come from political parties, pressure groups, think tanks, the prime minister's policy unit, or government departments. Prospective legislation is then normally drafted by civil servants, circulated within Whitehall, approved by the cabinet, and then refined by one of some thirty lawyers in the office of Parliamentary Counsel.*

According to tradition, in the House of Commons the bill usually comes to floor three times (referred to as *readings*). The bill is formally read upon introduction (the *first reading*), printed, distributed, debated in general terms, and after an interval (from a single day to several weeks), given a *second reading,* followed by a vote. The bill is then usually sent for detailed review to a standing committee of between sixteen and fifty members chosen to reflect the overall party balance in the House. It is then subjected to a report stage during which new amendments may be introduced. The *third reading* follows; normally, the bill is considered in final form (and voted on) without debate.

After the third reading, a bill passed in the House of Commons follows a parallel path in the House of Lords. There the bill is either accepted without change, amended, or rejected. According to custom, the House of Lords passes bills concerning taxation or budgetary matters without alteration, and can add technical and editorial amendments to other bills (which must be approved by the House of Commons) to add clarity in wording and precision in administration. After a bill has passed through all these stages, it is sent to the Crown for royal assent (approval by the queen or king, which is only a formality), after which it becomes law and is referred to as an Act of Parliament.

*See Dennis Kavanagh, *British Politics: Continuities and Change*, 3d ed. (Oxford: Oxford University Press, 1996), 282–288.

---

dissolution of Parliament. However, it is now likely that only defeat on a motion that explicitly refers to "confidence in Her Majesty's government" still mandates dissolution. For now, the balance of institutional power has shifted from Parliament to the governing party and the executive.

The House of Lords

The upper chamber of Parliament, the House of Lords (or Lords) is an unelected body that includes hereditary peers (nobility of the rank of duke, marquis, earl, viscount, or baron), life peers (appointed by the Crown on the recommendation of the prime minister), and law lords (appointed to assist the House in its judicial duties and who become life peers). The Lords also includes the archbishops of Canterbury and York and two dozen senior bishops of the Church of England. There are roughly 1200 members of the House of Lords, but there is no fixed number, and membership changes with the appointment of peers. Not surprisingly, the Conservatives have a considerable edge in the upper house with just over one-half of peers; Labour runs a distant second at roughly one-sixth. About one-third are *crossbenchers*, or independents.

The House of Lords is the final court of appeal for civil cases throughout Britain and for criminal cases in England, Wales, and Northern Ireland. This judicial role, performed by the Law Lords, drew international attention in 1998 and 1999 when a Spanish court attempted to extradite General Augusto Pinochet of Chile on charges of genocide, torture, and terrorism. In modern times, however, the Lords has served mainly as a chamber of revision, providing expertise in redrafting legislation. Although the Lords does not act as a serious impediment to the government, it can slow down legislation and encourage modifications. Since the 1970s, government "defeats" (adverse votes) have generated considerable interest and sometimes encouraged compromises. During the Thatcher years, the House of Lords took on a highly visible and surprisingly adversarial role, voting against the government 155 times. In 1994, the Lords forced the Major government to modify the Police and Magistrates' Courts bill, especially with reference to the powers of the Home Secretary to appoint members to local police authorities. Most dramatically, Lady Thatcher used the Lords as a forum for challenging the more conciliatory stance of the Major government toward Europe.

The House of Lords attracts a variety of opinions. Some MPs on the Labour left (and others) have persistently called for its abolition as an undemocratic body. Others view it, like the Crown, with a tolerant affection. In 1999, legislation was introduced to remove the right of hereditary lords to speak and vote, and a commission was founded to recommend a framework for the creation of a new second chamber.

Recent Reforms in Behavior and Structure

It is a sign of the contemporary decline of the Commons that constitutional commentators through the mid-1990s stressed the independence of the Lords. But the more significant development is the shift in power toward the executive and especially the cabinet: "Supposedly, Parliament, Lords no less than Commons, checks and controls the executive. In practice it is the other way around."[22] How significant are contemporary changes in the House? How far will they go to stem the tide in Parliament's much-heralded decline?

Behavioral Changes: Backbench Dissent. Since the 1970s, backbenchers (MPs of the governing party who have no governmental office and rank-and-file opposition members) are markedly less deferential. A backbench rebellion against the Major government's EU policy took a toll on the prestige of the prime minister and contributed to his historically low approval ratings. A resolute leader with a very large majority, Blair seems less likely to face significant rebellion from Labour MPs and, at the same time, is more able to tolerate it. Likely sources of division may include social welfare policy, the euro, the treatment of trade unions and related industrial policy. After Major's problems with backbench dissent, many commentators argued that weaker party discipline had become a permanent condition; but more evidence is necessary before we can be certain that the open challenges to

Major were more than merely a passing reflection of the exceptional divisions over Europe in the Conservative party.

Structural Changes: Parliamentary Committees. In addition to the standing committees that routinely review bills during legislative proceedings, in 1979 the Commons revived and extended the number and "remit" (i.e., responsibilities) of _select committees._ Select committees help Parliament exert control over the executive by examining specific policies or aspects of administration.

The most controversial select committees are "watchdog" committees that monitor the conduct of major departments and ministries. Select committees hold hearings, take written and oral testimony, and question senior civil servants and ministers. They then issue reports that often include strong policy recommendations at odds with government policy. As one side effect of the reform, the role of the civil service has been complicated. Traditionally, ministers take responsibility for policy and face scrutiny in Parliament. Tradition requires senior civil servants to testify on behalf of their ministers, but the more aggressive stance of select committees has, for the first time, pressed them to testify, in effect, _against_ their ministers, in cases of misconduct or poor judgment. As a result, the powerful norms of civil service secrecy have been compromised and the relationship with ministers disturbed.

On balance, the committees have been extremely energetic. Power is another issue, however, because the committees' direct influence on legislation and their ability to hold executive departments or the government accountable is limited. For the most part, when the committees have been effective it is because they have served to publicize and critically evaluate government policy. They serve as magnets to attract otherwise scattered criticisms and give them the visibility and prestige of a parliamentary audience.

Reform bodies have recommended that select committees be given greater resources and powers, perhaps including a role in confirming appointments and a capacity to compel the testimony of ministers. Radical changes in procedure, political culture, and tradition would be necessary to make select committees powerful watchdogs approximating the role of their counterparts in the U.S. Congress.

Political Parties and the Party System

Like the term *parliamentary sovereignty*, which conceals the reduced role of Parliament in legislation and the unmaking of governments, the term *two-party system*, which is commonly used to describe the British party system, is somewhat deceiving. It is true that since 1945, only leaders of the Labour or Conservative parties have served as prime ministers. From 1945 through the 1997 election, the Conservative Party won eight general elections and the Labour Party seven. It is also true that throughout the postwar period, these two parties have routinely divided some 90 percent of the seats in the House of Commons. But a variety of other parties—centrist, environmental, nationalist, and even neofascist—have complicated the picture of party competition. We discuss, in turn, the parties themselves and then recent patterns of electoral behavior.

The Labour Party

As one of the few European parties with origins outside electoral politics, the Labour Party was launched by trade union representatives and socialist societies in the last decade of the nineteenth century and formally took its name in 1906. From its inception in a Labour Representation Committee, supporters sought to advance working-class political representation and to further specific trade unionist demands. In the years preceding World War I, the party expanded its trade union affiliation but made only weak progress at the polls. Labour secured only 7.1 percent of the vote in 1910, but the radicalizing effects of the war and the expansion of the franchise in 1918 nearly tripled its base of support. In 1918, it received 22.2 percent, even with a shift of emphasis from the defense of trade union rights to explicitly socialist appeals. Its landslide 1945 victory promoted a party with deep working-class roots and a socialist ideology to major player status in British politics. At the same time, Labour began moderating its ideological appeal and broadening its electoral base.

Early in the postwar period, it was clear that Labour Party *fundamentalism*, which stressed state ownership of industry and workers' control of production, would take a back seat to a more moderate perspective that advocates the projects of the collectivist consensus (this shift was referred to by contemporaries as *revisionism* or *Labourism*). During the height of Labourism (roughly 1945 to the mid-1970s), party identification and electoral behavior displayed a strong correlation with occupation. In the 1950s and early 1960s, those not engaged in manual labor voted Conservative three times more commonly than they did Labour; more than two out of three manual workers, by contrast, voted Labour. During this period Britain conformed to one classic pattern of a Western European party system: a two-class/two-party system.

The period since the mid-1970s has been marked by significant changes in the party system and by a growing disaffection with even the moderate social democracy associated with the Keynesian Welfare State and Labourism. The party suffered from divisions between its trade unionist and parliamentary elements, constitutional wrangling over the power of trade unions to determine party policy at annual conferences, and disputes over how the leader (a potential prime minister) would be selected. In 1981, a centrist breakaway of leading Labour MPs further destabilized the party.

Divisions spilled over into foreign policy issues as well. Although generally internationalist, persistent voices within Labour challenged participation in the European Community on the grounds that EC policy would advance the interests of business over labor and damage the standard of living of working Britons. However, by the late 1980s, Labour began to look to the European Community as a means of resisting attacks on the principles of the welfare state at home. In particular, the adoption of the Social Charter to extend workers' rights and protections in 1989 helped turn Labour into a pro-EC party. On defense issues, there was a strong pacifist and an even stronger antinuclear sentiment within the party. Support for unilateral nuclear disarmament (the reduction and elimination of nuclear weapons systems with or without comparable developments on the Soviet side) was a decisive break with the national consensus on security policy, and contributed to the party's losses in 1983 and 1987; unilateralism was then scrapped.

The 1980s and 1990s have witnessed a period of relative harmony within the party, with moderate trade union and parliamentary leadership agreeing on major policy issues. Blair's immediate predecessors as party leaders—Neil Kinnock (who served from 1983 until Labour's defeat in the March 1992 election), and John Smith (who replaced Kinnock and served as leader until his death in May 1994)—helped pave the way for New Labour by abandoning socialism and taking the party in a new pragmatic direction. It seems clear that for the foreseeable future there will be no return to Labour fundamentalism. Labour has become a moderate left-of-center party in which ideology takes a back seat to performance. The challenges faced by New Labour will be discussed further in Section 5.

The Conservative Party

The pragmatism, flexibility, and organizational capabilities of the Conservative Party—a party which dates back to the eighteenth century—have made it one of the most successful and, at times, innovative center-right parties in Europe. In contrast to some leading conservative parties in Italy and Germany, it has been a secular party wholly committed to democratic principles, free of the association with fascism during World War II that tainted the others. Although it has fallen on hard times in recent years, it would be unwise to underestimate its potential as both an opposition and a governing party.

Although the association of the Conservative Party with the economic and social elite is unmistakable, it is also true that it was the Conservative government of Prime Minister Benjamin Disraeli (1874–1880) that midwifed the birth of the modern welfare state in Britain. The creation of a "long-lasting alliance between an upper-class leadership and a lower-class following"[23] made the Conservative Party a formidable player in British politics. Throughout the postwar period, it has also routinely (with some exceptions) provided the Tories, as Conservatives are colloquially called, with electoral support from about one-third or more of the manual working class. Even in Labour's landslide victory of 1997, 29 percent of manual workers voted Conservative.[24]

Several ideologies of governance have developed within the Conservative Party, and there is no consensus about their relative significance. Some scholars see a cleft in the party between hierarchical and paternalistic attitudes on one side and individualistic free-enterprise

traditions on the other. Others argue that the Conservative Party represents the interests of one class (the bourgeoisie or property-owning class) and not the nation as a whole; and ideological currents and factions within the party can be largely explained by the divisions of interest among different capitalist elements (for example, financial versus manufacturing interests or domestic versus internationalist interests). The analysis here, by contrast, tends to emphasize the shift, starting with Thatcher, away from the principles of the collectivist consensus that Labour and Conservative elites had shared for three decades.

Contemporary analysis of the Conservative Party must also emphasize the cost to the party of the internal divisions over Britain's role in the EU. The Tories have seldom if ever experienced divisions as serious as those over Europe in the 1990s. The bitter leadership contest that followed Major's resignation after the 1997 defeat only reinforced the impression of a party in turmoil. The new party leader, a centrist, William Hague, has his work cut out for him. The Conservatives remain divided between the "Eurosceptics," who reject further European integration, and those who support integration balanced by a firm regard for British sovereignty. In addition, despite party support for a unitary—not a federal—arrangement, the Conservatives under Hague must find credible positions on the constitutional reforms that are already in the pipeline. Finally, although economic and social policy divisions have been eclipsed by the clash over Europe, disagreements remain on social policy, industrial policy, and the running of the economy.

The Liberal Democrats and Other Parties

Since the 1980s a changing roster of centrist parties have posed a potentially significant threat to the two-party dominance of Conservative and Labour. Through the 1970s, the Liberal Party, a governing party in the pre–World War I period and thereafter the traditional centrist third party in Britain, was the only centrist challenger to the Labour and Conservative parties. In 1981, the Social Democratic Party (SDP), formed out of a split within the Labour Party. In the 1983 election the Alliance (an electoral arrangement of the Liberals and the SDP) gained a quarter of the vote. The strength of centrist parties in the mid-1980s led to expectations of a possible Alliance-led government (which did not occur), and observers of British politics began to talk about a party system with "four major national parties" (Conservative, Labour, Liberal, and SDP).[25] After the Conservative victory in 1987, the Liberal Party and most of the SDP merged to form the Social and Liberal Democratic Party (now called the Liberal Democrats, or the LD).

Under the leadership of Paddy Ashdown, the Liberal Democrats fought the 1992 election from the awkward stance of "equidistance" from the two major parties. After a disappointing result—17.8 percent of the vote and only 20 seats in the Commons—the party changed its position in 1994 and began working more closely with Labour. Most importantly, the two parties created a Joint Constitutional Committee that developed a degree of unity on proposals for constitutional reform. Many credit the Liberal Democrats with inspiring Blair's constitutional agenda. Nevertheless, under Ashdown's effective leadership, the Liberal Democrats preserved their independence in the 1997 election. Liberal Democrats targeted the seats where they had the greatest chance of victory, with impressive results. Although their share of the vote actually slipped slightly between 1992 and 1997 (from 17.8 to 16.8 percent), they won more than twice as many seats (46). Amidst a growing debate about the relationship between Labour and the Liberal Democrats, early in 1999 Ashdown unexpectedly announced his intention to resign as leader.

The appeal of smaller parties in Britain is constantly shifting. One party, the Greens (formed in 1973 by environmentalists, and the oldest Green Party in Europe) surprised everyone (themselves included) by achieving a 15 percent third-place showing in the June 1989 elections to the European Parliament (but winning no seats). With public opinion surveys ranking "pollution and the environment" as the third-most-common concern,[26] the major parties hustled to acquire a greenish hue. But the Green Party failed to capitalize on its 1989 showing. By the mid-1990s, party membership declined and environmental activists focused on a wide range of grassroots initiatives. In 1997, it ran only 95 candidates (down from 253 in 1992), with very little impact (it averaged only 1.4 percent in the constituencies it contested).

TOO MUCH VIOLENCE ON TELEVISION . . .

The internal fighting in the Conservative party over Europe haunted Thatcher and Major and presents a significant challenge for William Hague, the new party leader. This cartoon, which originally appeared in *The Times*, depicts the backstabbing on the Conservative front benches in the Commons. It suggests that Tory in-fighting echoes the findings of a publicized report on television violence. *Source:* © Peter Brookes/Times Newspaper.

The National Front (formed in 1967)—a far-right, neofascist, anti-immigrant party—won seats on local councils and entered candidates (unsuccessfully) for Parliament. After the National Front faded in the late 1970s, the British National Party (BNP), formed in 1983, emerged as the most visible far-right party. Concentrating its electoral strategy on impoverished inner-city constituencies, it ran 57 candidates who registered a meager 1.3 percent average share of the votes cast.

Another party, the Referendum Party, made a huge splash in 1997, although it may never surface again. Launched by a multimillionaire to exploit Tory divisions over Europe, the party attracted a great deal of attention by calling for a vaguely worded referendum that asked voters to choose between "a federal Europe" and a "return to an association of sovereign nations." Sporting a well-financed and splashy campaign, it ran 547 candidates, the most ever for a minor party, but none won. In addition to these center, environmental, far-right, and single-issue parties, Britain has several national parties, which are described below as part of our discussion of trends in electoral behavior.

Elections

British elections are exclusively for legislative posts. The prime minister is not elected as prime minister but as an MP from a single constituency (electoral district) averaging about 65,000 registered voters. Parliament has a maximum life of five years, with no fixed term. General elections are held after Parliament has been dissolved by the Crown at the request of the prime minister. However, for strategic political reasons the prime minister may ask the Crown to dissolve Parliament at any time. The ability to control the timing of elections is a tremendous political asset for the prime minister. This contrasts sharply with a presidential system, characteristic of the United States, with direct election of the chief executive and a fixed term of office.

Electoral System

Election for representatives in the Commons (who are called members of Parliament, or MPs) is by a "first past the post" (or winner-take-all) principle in each constituency. In this **single-member plurality system**, the candidate who receives the most votes is elected. There is no requirement of a majority and no element of proportional representation (a system in which each party is given a percentage of seats in a representative assembly roughly comparable to its percentage of the popular vote). Table 3 shows the results of the general elections from 1945 to 1997.

This "winner-take-all" electoral system tends to exaggerate the size of the victory of the largest party and reduce the influence of regionally dispersed lesser parties. Thus, in 1997, with 45 percent of the popular vote, Labour won 419 seats. With 17 percent of the vote, the Liberal Democrats, despite targeting their most winnable constituencies, won only 46 seats. Thus, Labour received fewer than three times as many votes as the Liberal Democrats, but won more than nine times as many seats. Such are the benefits to the victor of the "first past the post" system.

With a fairly stable two-and-a-half party system (Conservative, Labour, and center), the British electoral system tends toward stable single-party government. However, the electoral system raises questions about representation and fairness. The system reduces the competitiveness of smaller parties with diffuse pockets of support. In addition, the party and electoral systems have contributed to the creation of a parliament that has been a bastion of white men. The number of women and ethnic minorities holding seats has grown in recent elections, however. In 1992, sixty women were elected as MPs out of 650 seats (9.2 percent), an increase from forty-two members in 1987 (6.3 percent). Also in 1992, six ethnic minority candidates were elected, up from four in 1987, the first time since before World War II that Parliament included minority members. The 1997 election may represent a breakthough for women: the number of women MPs nearly doubled to a record 119 (18.1 percent). In addition, the number of black and Asian MPs rose to nine (1.4 percent). Despite the trend of increased representation of women and minorities, they remain very substantially under-represented in Parliament.

Trends in Electoral Behavior

Recent general elections have deepened geographic and regional fragmentation on the political map. British political scientist Ivor Crewe has referred to the emergence of *two* two-party systems:

1. Competition between the Conservative and Labour parties dominates contests in English urban and northern seats.
2. Conservative-center party competition dominates England's rural and southern seats.[27] In addition, a third two-party competition may be observed in Scotland, where Labour-national party competition dominates.

The national parties have challenged two-party dominance since the 1970s. The Scottish National Party (SNP) was founded in 1934, and its Welsh counterpart, the Plaid Cymru, in 1925. Coming in a distant second to Labour in Scotland in 1997, the SNP won 21.6 percent of the vote and six seats. With its greatest strength in agenda-setting on devolution, it is likely to play a vocal and potentially influential role in the ongoing processes of constitutional reform. The Plaid Cymru contested every seat in Wales in 1997, but won only four seats where Welsh is still spoken widely. Its experience is another illustration of the effects of the first-past-the-post system. With its support concentrated in districts where Welsh is spoken the most, the

Table 3

British General Elections, 1945–1997

		Percentage of popular vote						Seats in House of Commons					
	Turnout	Con.	Lab.	Lib.[a]	Nat.[b]	Other	Swing[c]	Con.	Lab.	Lib.	Nat.	Other	Government majority
1945	72.7	39.8	48.3	9.1	0.2	2.5	−12.2	213	393	12	0	22	146
1950	84.0	43.5	46.1	9.1	0.1	1.2	+3.0	299	315	9	0	2	5
1951	82.5	48.0	48.8	2.5	0.1	0.6	+0.9	321	295	6	0	3	17
1955	76.7	49.7	46.4	2.7	0.2	0.9	+2.1	345	277	6	0	2	60
1959	78.8	49.4	43.8	5.9	0.4	0.6	+1.2	365	258	6	0	1	100
1964	77.1	43.4	44.1	11.2	0.5	0.8	−3.2	304	317	9	0	0	4
1966	75.8	41.9	47.9	8.5	0.7	0.9	−2.7	253	363	12	0	2	95
1970	72.0	46.4	43.0	7.5	1.3	1.8	+4.7	330	288	6	1	5	30
Feb 1974	78.7	37.8	37.1	19.3	2.6	3.2	−1.4	297	301	14	9	14	−34[d]
Oct 1974	72.8	35.8	39.2	18.3	3.5	3.2	−2.1	277	319	13	14	12	3
1979	76.0	43.9	37.0	13.8	2.0	3.3	+5.2	339	269	11	4	12	43
1983	72.7	42.4	27.6	25.4	1.5	3.1	+4.0	397	209	23	4	17	144
1987	75.3	42.3	30.8	22.6	1.7	2.6	−1.7	376	229	22	6	17	102
1992	77.7	41.9	34.4	17.8	2.3	3.5	−2.0	336	271	20	7	17	21
1997	71.4	30.7	43.2	16.8	2.6	6.7	−10.0	165	419	46	10	18	179

[a] Liberal Party 1945–79; Liberal/Social Democrat Alliance 1983–87; Liberal Democrat Party 1992–97.

[b] Combined vote of Scottish National Party (SNP) and Welsh National Party (Plaid Cymru).

[c] "Swing" compares the results of each election with the results of previous election. It is calculated as the average of the winning major party's percentage point increase in its share of the vote and the losing major party's decrease in its percentage point share of the vote. In the table, a positive sign denotes a swing to the Conservatives, a negative sign a swing to Labour.

[d] Following the February 1974 election, the Labour party was 34 seats short of having an overall majority. It formed a minority government until it obtained a majority in the October 1974 election.

Source: *New Labour Triumphs: Britain at the Polls,* ed. Anthony King (Chatham, NJ: Chatham House, 1998), 249. Copyright © 1998 by Chatham House. Reprinted by permission.

Plaid Cymru won four seats despite polling a modest 9.9 percent. By contrast, with support more evenly spread, the Conservatives polled 19.4 percent in Wales and won no seats. With the Tories shut out in both Wales and Scotland in 1997, the prospects of a common two-party pattern of electoral competition throughout Britain are more remote than ever.

For now the winner-take-all electoral system has preserved two-party dominance in Parliamentary representation. But the popular vote tells a different story: between 1974 and 1997 the combined share of the popular vote for Conservative and Labour averaged under 75 percent. The British electoral system is more complicated than it seems at first glance. Some potentially significant subcurrents evident in Tony Blair's landslide 1997 election will be discussed further in Section 5.

Political Culture, Citizenship, and Identity

In their classic study of the ideals and values that shape political behavior, political scientists Gabriel Almond and Sidney Verba wrote that the civic (or political) culture in Britain was characterized by trust, deference to authority and competence, pragmatism, and the balance between acceptance of the rules of the game and disagreement over specific issues.[28] Many have considered these characteristics the model for active, informed, and stable democratic citizenship. Viewed retrospectively, the 1970s appear as a crucial turning point in British political culture and group identities. It is too early to be certain, but the electoral earthquake of 1997 may represent another critical shift in British politics and culture.

During the 1970s, the long years of economic decline culminated in an actual decline in the standard of living for many Britons. Also for many, the historic bonds of occupational and social class grew weaker. Union membership fell as jobs continued to be lost in the traditional manufacturing sectors. More damaging, unions lost popular support as they appeared to bully society, act undemocratically, and neglect the needs of an increasingly female and minority workforce. At the same time, a growing number of conservative think tanks and the powerful voice of mass-circulation newspapers—which are overwhelmingly conservative—worked hard to erode the fundamental beliefs of the Keynesian Welfare State. **New social movements** (such as feminism, antinuclear activism, and environmentalism) challenged basic tenets of British political culture. Identities based on race and ethnicity, gender, and sexual orientation gained significance. Thus, a combination of economic strains, ideological assaults, and social dislocations helped foster political fragmentation and, at the same time, a shift to the right in values and policy agendas.

Thatcher's ascent reflected these changes in political culture, identities, and values. It also put the full resources of the state and a bold and determined prime minister behind a sweeping agenda for change. As a leading British scholar put it, "Thatcher's objective was nothing less than a cultural revolution."[29] Although most observers agree that she fell considerably short of that aim, Thatcherism cut deep. It touched the cultural recesses of British society, recast political values, and redefined national identity.

To the extent that the Thatcherite worldview took hold (and the record is mixed), its new language and ethos helped transform the common sense of politics and redefined the political community. Monetarism (however modified) and the appeal to an enterprise culture of competitive market logic and entrepreneurial values fostered individualism and competition—winners and losers. It rejected collectivism, the redistribution of resources from rich to poor, and state responsibility for full employment. Thatcherism

considered individual property rights more important than the social rights claimed by all citizens in the welfare state.

In addition to her positive appeals to the enterprise culture, Thatcher's reform agenda included negative appeals. A review of Thatcher's first general election reveals the repoliticization of race. She promised tougher nationality legislation to restrict immigration, expressed sympathy for those who harbored "fear that [England] might be swamped" by nonwhite Commonwealth immigrants, and associated minorities with lawlessness. In a similar vein, during the 1984–1985 miners' strike, she denounced the miners as the "enemy within," comparing them to the external Argentine enemy during the Falklands/Malvinas war of 1982. Thatcher symbolically expelled some groups—ethnic minority communities and the unrepentant miners—from the national community. In this way, Thatcherism involved an attempt to redefine national identity by implicit appeals to a more secure, provincial, and unified Britain.

As political scientist Benedict Anderson observed, national identity involves the belief in an "imagined community" of belonging, shared fates, and affinities among millions of diverse and actually unconnected citizens.[30] Since the 1970s, the question of what constitutes "Britishness"—who is included and who is excluded from the national political community—has become increasingly vexed. The politicization of immigration in the 1979 election underscored the resentment white Britons felt toward minority communities who maintained their own religious beliefs and cultures. In defining themselves, some might say they were Pakistani or Jamaican or Muslim, but they didn't feel very British.

The 1970s also saw the emergence of a growing gap in the economic prospects of North (suffering industrial blight and high unemployment) and South (more prosperous and competitive). In addition, pressure for devolution and growing nationalist sentiment in Scotland and Wales fueled a center-versus-periphery division. Finally, working-class identity and politics were stigmatized as government sharply criticized the behavior of unions. The traditional values of "an honest day's work for an honest day's pay," resistance to cutbacks in wages or changes in work assignments, and solidarity among coworkers in industrial disputes were characterized as "rigidities" that reduced productivity and competitiveness.

Thus, the imagined community of Britain fragmented into smaller communities of class, nation, region, and ethnicity that existed side by side but not necessarily in amiable proximity. Can New Labour recreate a more cohesive political culture and foster a more inclusive sense of British identity? Unlike Thatcher, Blair is a conciliator and he has worked hard to revitalize a sense of community in Britain. The efforts of the Blair government to forge unity and build community and the obstacles it faces are discussed in Section 5.

Interests, Social Movements, and Protest

Given the two-party/two-class model that has traditionally dominated British politics, the most influential interests have been those linked to class and industrial interests. During the period of consensus that framed politics from the end of World War II until the 1970s, business interests and trade union organizations vied for influence over economic and social policy. Equally important, governments tried very hard, often without success, to gain the cooperation of these interests in the formulation and implementation of policy.

Throughout the postwar period until Thatcher's administration, British governments struggled to reduce the frequency and duration of strikes, constrain the political power of trade unions, and limit wage increases in both the public and private sectors. They tried two somewhat contradictory policy approaches. On the one hand, governments sought to restrict trade union rights by law (for example, by the 1972 Industrial Relations Act of the Heath government). On the other hand, they tried to expand the involvement of the national association of trade unions—the Trades Union Congress (TUC)—in the design and implementation of policy. Why not "turn the poacher into the gamekeeper" and involve trade union leaders in the enforcement of voluntary wage restraints? For example, the 1974–1979 Labour government negotiated a series of highly visible Social Contracts, initially with the TUC and subsequently with individual trade unions. When these agreements fell apart, strikes erupted in the 1978–1979 winter of discontent, lead-

ing to Thatcher's victory the following May. Labour and Conservative governments alike tried both approaches, with only fleeting success.

Under the Conservative leadership of Thatcher and Major, governments held class-based interests at arm's length and worked to curb their political and industrial power. A formidable combination of legislated constraints, trade union defeats in industrial disputes, and massive unemployment (particularly in the traditionally unionized manufacturing sectors) helped crystallize a pattern of decline in union membership, militancy, and power. Although Blair's reasons are different—he emphasizes the realities of the new global economic competition—he has done little to reverse the decline in union influence.

How has the arm's-length approach introduced by the Conservatives influenced the ability of business to advance its interests? Medium-scale manufacturing industries are organized politically through the Confederation of British Industry (CBI). In general, Thatcher remained aloof from interest pleading. As a result, organizations like the CBI that traditionally operated upon the executive developed closer relations with Parliament. In general, the work of interest groups and lobbyists in the Commons has increased considerably in recent years. Ironically, Blair's business partnership opens new doors both to middle-size industry and to larger transnational corporate interests and financial interests. The influence of the City of London (the capital's financial district) over economic policy remains considerable.

At the same time, social movements have changed the landscape of politics in Britain since the late 1960s. By contrast to the traditional interest-group-oriented social movements, the NSMs tend to be more fluidly organized and democratic, less oriented to immediate payoffs for their group, and more focused on fundamental questions about the values of society. For example, in the 1970s and 1980s, the women's peace movement protested Britain's participation in NATO's nuclear defense and organized a string of mass demonstrations. In general, following the NSM approach, the women's movement in Britain has remained decentralized and activist-oriented. It has been less involved than the American women's movement, for example, in legislative lobbying or coalition politics. The British feminist movement has emphasized consciousness raising, self-help, and life-style transformations. The movement has spawned dozens of action groups, ranging from health clinics to battered women's and rape crisis shelters, to feminist collectives and black women's groups, to networks of women in media, law, and other professions. More recently, women have confronted government over inadequate child care provisions and the difficulties posed for women's daily struggle to juggle the demands of work and family.

Simultaneously, the subcultures and countercultures of black Britain have been a vital source of NSM activity, often expressed in antiracist initiatives. "Rock Against Racism" concerts in the 1970s brought reggae and skinhead bands together in public resistance to the National Front; today, lower profile efforts are made to sensitize local councils to the cultural and material needs of ethnic minorities and to publicize their potential political clout. Efforts to secure improved housing have been a persistent focus of ethnic minority political mobilization. Like the women's movement, such movements are decentralized and culturally engaged. They are much less focused on legal challenges, legislation, or coalition building than comparable movements in the United States.

Since the 1970s, class-based interest bargaining has declined, while social movements based on ethnic and gender attachments have grown in significance. Quite powerful political subcurrents persist, despite the impressive support for Blair and New Labour.

Section ❺ British Politics in Transition

In the fall of 1994, cease-fire declarations made by the IRA and the Protestant paramilitary organizations renewed hope for a peace settlement in Northern Ireland. Then in a dramatic new development in early spring 1995, British Prime Minister John Major and Irish Prime Minister John Bruton jointly issued a Framework Agreement, inspiring mounting optimism about a political settlement. Although Major did what he could to secure public and parliamentary support, he lacked the necessary political capital to bring the historic initiative to fruition.

With his landslide victory, Blair had political capital to spend—and he chose to invest a chunk of it on peace in Northern Ireland. Blair arranged to meet Gerry Adams, president of Sinn Fein, the party in Northern Ireland with close ties to the IRA—and shook his hand. He was the first prime minister to meet a head of Sinn Fein since 1921. Blair later spoke of the "hand of history" on his shoulder.

Under deadline pressure imposed by Blair and the new Irish prime minister, Bertie Ahern, and 33 hours of round-the-clock talks, an agreement was reached on Good Friday, 1998. It specified elections for a Northern Ireland assembly in which Protestants and Catholics would share power, and the creation of a North-South Council to facilitate "all-Ireland" cooperation on matters such as economic development, agriculture, transportation, and the environment. Much was left unclear, for example, the details of how and when the IRA would give up its weapons, and questions about the release of prisoners affiliated with the paramilitary groups. It did not address the reform of the police force in Northern Ireland, which is overwhelmingly Protestant and partisan and does not enjoy the confidence of the Catholic community. Nevertheless, despite doubts about the fine print, in May 1998, both parts of Ireland voted "Yes" in a referendum to approve the peace agreement. It appeared that a new era was dawning in Northern Ireland.

Like the bombs that can shake peace efforts in the Middle East at any time, handshake or not, devastating bombs have exploded in Northern Ireland since the agreement. But the political resolve on all sides seems firm, and this time the violence has tended to bring the divided communities closer together in the cause of peace. Certainly Blair has the will to see the process through and he has shown considerable fortitude and political courage in the effort thus far.

There can be no greater political challenge for a British prime minister than peace in Northern Ireland.

Global Connection: *The Euro*

In May 1998, eleven EU countries, led by Germany, France, Italy, and Spain—but not including Britain—signed on to the single European currency, the euro. One month later, the European Central Bank was established, operating with considerable institutional and political independence, and charged primarily with maintaining price stability and advancing the economic policies of the Community. At the beginning of 1999, exchange rates were locked in, the euro became legal tender, and euro-based foreign exchange operations began. Already, without Britain's participation in the single currency, much of the action on trading floors in the City (London's financial center)

is conducted in euros. The conversion timetable calls for the introduction of euro bills and coins for everyday use on New Year's day, 2002, and the withdrawal of the legal status of national currencies six months later.

The introduction of the euro reflects the larger vision of creating a more fully integrated EU, or what many have called (some approvingly and some derisively) a "United States of Europe." More concretely, finanacial analysts point to increased trade, reduced transaction costs, and substantial savings on cross-border commerce. With a population larger than that of the United States and with a bigger GDP (even without further enlargement), an integrated Europe poses a formidable competitive challenge to the United States. In addition, many observers expect that monetary union will accelerate and make irreversible a tendency toward greater European political and foreign policy cooperation.

Sources: *The euro*, ed. Paul Temperton (Chichester: John Wiley & Sons, 1997); "Goodbye to All That?," *The European*, 27 April–3 May 1998, 5.

And, to be sure, Blair's initiative displays in full measure his willingness to find innovative solutions and provide decisive leadership. In that sense, it is a central part of his government's program. In addition, the troubles in Northern Ireland confirm the important proposition that unresolved tensions in state formation shape political agendas for generations. The "troubles" in Northern Ireland reflected enduring political tensions flowing from antagonistic collective identities, as differences in political power and economic privilege enflamed cultural (in this case, religious) divisions. Northern Ireland, however, is but one of a host of challenges facing Britain on Tony Blair's agenda; with the prospects of peace likely to be uncertain for years to come, Blair is unlikely to risk too much political capital in one place.

Political Challenges and Changing Agendas

In this section, we consider the most critical challenges facing Britain today in the context of each of our four themes. The chapter concludes with a discussion of the broader comparative implications of developments in Britain.

Britain and the European Union

From 1989 to 1997, the seemingly endless backbiting over the Social Charter and Maastricht in the Conservative Party sidetracked Thatcher and Major and cost them dearly in political terms. Britain's traumatic withdrawal from the ERM in 1992 stands as a warning that deeper European integration can be economically disruptive and politically dangerous. In the years ahead, Britain's decision whether, when, and under what conditions to join the single currency will almost certainly prove a serious challenge to New Labour's managerial skills and unity. (See Global Connection Box: The Euro.)

Thus far, the government has opted to play down the political significance of the euro. Blair and his followers have begun to make the case for the "yes" campaign that has already emerged, despite government assurances that the promised referendum on the euro will not be held until after the next general election. Despite some strong hints early in 1999 that the government will ultimately support entry, Foreign Secretary Robin Cook claims that "the high-water mark of European integration has already been reached"; Chancellor of the Exchequer Gordon Brown repeatedly assures listeners that the decision on entry into the single currency will be based on how high the euro scores on a series of economic tests.[31]

Most observers note, however, that the issues swirling around British participation in the single currency are profoundly political and that the tide of European integration is rising. In fact, the matter of Britain's participation in the euro seems likely to create significant political pressures for New Labour. Unofficially, key members of the government support British participation in the single currency and the decision to free the Bank of England from direct government control (See p. 43) was a very powerful indication that Blair and Brown intend to create the proper conditions for British entry. Although no decision has been made by the government to endorse the euro, the prospect of all but irreversible and comprehensive European integration has inspired significant resistance within New Labour and among the public. Polls in early 1999, after the launch of the euro, showed that the gap between supporters and opponents of the single currency had narrowed, but a solid majority of respondents were still against U.K. membership. One might add that the Conservative opposition will surely make it a leading campaign issue in the next election (expected in 2001 or 2002).

For those countries that have joined the euro club, the European Central Bank has acquired critical economic policy powers that have reduced national sovereign control. Participation holds significant consequences for price stability, and for the capacity of national governments to manipulate interest rates and exchange rates to cushion declines in demand and limit unemployment. In addition, the euro will create pressure for coordination of tax policies. Economic and monetary integration, therefore, has potentially quite significant repercussions for standards of living and distributional politics at home. Inevitably New Labour will have to face these issues, and the divisions that will almost certainly follow, head on. The euro will cast a long shadow over New Labour's strategies for *governing the economy* and perceptions about Blair's handling of the U.K. position on the euro are likely to have tremendous political repercussions for years to come.

In addition, U.K.–EU relations in general, and their acute focus on the single currency, underscore the importance of our *world of states* theme. In Chapter 1, we discussed the expectation that a middle-rank power, even in European terms, would encounter difficulty in managing the domestic impact of decisions by regional blocs, and here the British case is no exception. Britain is no longer a world power and cannot rival Germany or France in its influence on EU developments. "Euroscepticism" has all but crippled the Conservative party since the 1980s, and New Labour seems reticent, thus far, about committing itself to first-tier participation which would have required an early endorsement of the euro. The poorer countries in Europe, led by Spain, which worked very hard to be accepted as a charter member in the euro-club, see integration as an engine of prosperity and greater political influences. By contrast, uncertain about participating in a game it cannot dominate, Britain continues to pay the price of its ambivalence about Europe.

Constitutional Reform

Even in Britain, issues about democratic governance and citizen participation remain unresolved. Because the traditionally sacrosanct royal family has been rocked by scandal and improprieties, questions about the undemocratic underpinning of the British state are asked with greater urgency. "Why is the House of Commons not sovereign?" wondered one observer somewhat caustically. "Why does it have to share sovereignty with other, unelected institutions?"[32] Few reject the monarchy outright, but there is more grumbling than ever about the role and deportment of the Crown. When a fire at Windsor Castle brought the issue of royal finances to the fore in 1991, the cost to taxpayers of the expensive and battered monarchy was openly debated, and the Queen agreed to pay taxes "voluntarily" for the first time. In the mid-1990s, publicity surrounding the marital problems of Princess Diana and Prince Charles subjected the monarchy to intense criticism. In 1997, the initially cool and stand-offish reaction of the royal family to Diana's death alienated many Britons and created an unprecedented level of popular antipathy toward the Crown. Although Charles's increased informality and evident devotion to his sons helped improve his standing after Diana's death, questions about the role of the monarchy helped place on the agenda broader issues about citizen control over government and constitutional reform.

The balance of power among constitutionally critical institutions remains a major issue of contemporary political debate. One well-respected observer of the British constitution recently noted,

> The Commons is hobbled. It is constricted on one level by strong, oligopolistic political parties. On another, it is virtually neutered by a modern executive whose reach (vis-à-vis its own policy) far exceeds that of any other executive in the Western world.[33]

Add to these concerns the secrecy afforded the British government (there is no equivalent to a Freedom of Information Act) and the absence of an "entrenched" Bill of Rights (one that Parliament cannot override), and it seems appropriate to raise questions about the accountability of the British government to its citizens.

In fact, constitutional reform may become New Labour's most enduring legacy. The government's reform agenda is quite extensive. In addition to proposals for far-reaching reforms of the monarchy and Parliament, it promises to introduce a Freedom of Information Act and incorporate the European Convention on Human Rights into U.K. law. Moreover, the peace agreement in Northern Ireland (if implemented) and power-sharing arrangements between Westminster and local legislatures in Scotland and Wales promise dramatic changes. It is too early to be sure about the success of these reform initiatives but it is certain that the constitutional reform agenda is highly significant. The May 1999 elections to the Scottish and Welsh parliaments— which produced national parties as the main rival to Labour in both places—already introduced major changes.

The range and depth of New Labour's constitutional reform agenda represent a breathtaking illustration of a core premise of our democratic idea theme, that even long-standing democracies face pressures to narrow the gap between government and citizens. If the British feel themselves removed from day-to-day control over the affairs of government, they are hardly alone! And despite the questions Britons raise about the rigidities of their ancient institutional architecture,

others—in Nigeria, Russia, Japan, or even the United States—see the Westminster model as an enduring exemplar of representative democracy, stability, tolerance, and the virtues of a constitutional tradition that balances a competitive party system with effective central government.

Identities in Flux

Although the relatively small scale of the ethnic minority community limits the political impact of the most divisive issues concerning *collective identities*, it is probably in this area that rigidities in the British political system challenge tenets of democracy and tolerance most severely. Given Britain's single-member, simple-plurality electoral system and no proportional representation, minority representation in Parliament is very low and governments have been unresponsive to concerns about cultural isolation.

There are deep-seated social attitudes that no government can easily transform. Although immigration policy is no longer a hot-button issue, for white Britons, immigration still inspires fear of "multi-culturalism and cultural dilution" and conjures very negative and probably prejudiced reactions. According to a 1996 survey of social attitudes in Britain, about two-thirds of the respondents believed that the number of immigrants should be reduced, about one-half felt that immigrants take jobs away from those born in Britain, and approximately one quarter said that immigrants increase crime rates.[34]

How about other dimensions of collective identity? The situation is fluid. The electoral force of class identity has declined in Britain for the time being, as have the strike rates that signal working-class militancy. New Labour's efforts to develop a partnership with business and keep trade unions at arm's length may well compel the labor movement to go into "internal opposition" and challenge the government on industrial relations and economic policy. On the positive side, the economic vitality of the 1990s has created some pockets of renewal in the north of England and taken some of the edge off North-South divisions. In addition, the increased prospects of a political settlement in Northern Ireland offer the hope that discord over national identity may be reduced in a very profound way. More unsettling, the agreement in Northern

Ireland, the constitutional reforms in Scotland and Wales, and the processes of "Europeanization" all involve some weakening of the central authority of Westminster and Whitehall. Thus, British identity, which is already weakly felt, will lose some of its institutional security at the same time that European identity is pulling from above and regional, ethnic, and national identities are pulling from below.

British Politics in Comparative Perspective

For many reasons, both historical and contemporary, the British case represents a critical one in comparative terms, even though Britain is no longer a leading power. How well have three centuries of constitutional government and a culture of laissez-faire capitalism prepared Britain for a political and economic world it has fewer resources to control? Does Britain still offer a distinctive and appealing model of democracy? What are the lessons that may be drawn in time from Blair's New Labour—a modernizing politics that aspires to go beyond left and right?

Until the Asian financial crisis that began in 1997, it was an axiom of comparative politics that economic success required a style of economic governance that Britain lacks. Many argued that innovation and competitiveness in the new global economy required the strategic coordination of the economy by an interventionist state. Interestingly, however, the United Kingdom escaped the recession that plagued the rest of Europe for much of the 1990s, with six solid years of uninterrupted growth between 1992 and 1998, and it outperformed Germany throughout much of the 1980s and 1990s.

The reasons for Britain's success and its economic prospects for the future continue to fuel debate inside the U.K. and attract considerable attention elsewhere. Perhaps Britain has already reaped the competitive benefits of ending restrictive labor practices and attracting massive foreign investment looking for a European base with few restrictions—and it is time to introduce a German-style high-skill, high-wage, workforce and give it similar opportunities to participate in management. Or perhaps Britain's "less is more" approach to economic management, augmented by Tony Blair's business partnership, and welfare reforms that encourage active participation in the labor force, provides an important and timely alternative to the more state-centered and interventionist strategies of Germany, France, and Japan. Time will tell, and partisan debate will probably never end, but the British approach has gained favor in recent years. In many countries throughout the world, politicians are looking for an economic model that can sustain economic competitiveness while preserving individual liberties and improving the plight of the socially excluded. Tony Blair's "third way"—a political orientation that hopes to transcend left and right in favor of practical and effective policies—will be carefully watched and, if successful, widely emulated.

We began our analysis of British politics with Tony Blair's landslide victory, and return there now to consider some of the political implications that emerge from a review of the election results. Beyond the impressive size of Blair's victory, nothing about the May 1997 election was more clear than the unprecedented **volatility** of the electorate. In previous elections, commitment to party (partisan identification) and interests linked to occupation (class location) had largely determined the results. In 1997 attachments to party and class had far less influence. The most notable feature of today's electorate is its unpredictability. What are the consequences for government and for electoral politics if voters at each election feel totally free to choose whichever party they like? What variables, if any, have replaced the traditional influences on voting behavior?

It seems that Blair's success in transforming Labour into New Labour blunted the social basis of party identification. At the same time, the modernization agenda of New Labour resolutely emphasized fiscal responsibility over distributive politics. As a result, it seems that specific issues and the needs of voters mattered more than deep-seated attachments. People voted as consumers of policies: "Who will make it easier for me to find a good place to live or pay my mortgage, get the health care my family needs, best educate my children—and what role will the government play in underwriting or providing these goods?"

In addition, the British political scientist David Sanders has suggested that class and party identification may have been replaced by "the growth of alternative sources of identity—apart from class—that have no obvious attachment to the established political parties,"[35]

Current Challenges: *The Gender-Generation Gap* → *come back to this later on the course.*

The issue of a gender gap in voting behavior has long been a mainstay of British electoral studies. From 1945 to 1992, women were more likely than men to vote Conservative. In addition, since 1964 a "gender-generation" gap has become well established. The phenomenon was very clear in the 1992 election. Among younger voters (under 30 years old), women preferred Labour while men voted strongly for the Conservatives, producing a 14-point gender gap favoring Labour; among older voters (over 65 years old), women were far more inclined to vote Conservative than were their male counterparts, creating a gender gap of 18 points favoring the Conservatives.

What happened to the gender gap in the 1997 election? The modest all-generation gender gap that favored the Tories in 1992 (6 percent) was closed in 1997, as a greater percentage of women shifted away from the Conservatives (11 percent) than did men (8 percent). As a result, women and men recorded an identical 44 percent tally for Labour. The gender-generation gap continued, however, with younger women more pro-Labour than younger men, and the pattern reversing in the older generation. Moreover, one of the most striking features of the 1997 election was the generational dimension: the largest swing to Labour was among

Sources: Pippa Norris, *Electoral Change in Britain since 1945* (Oxford: Blackwell Publishers, 1997), 133–135; Joni Lovenkuski, "Gender Politics: A Breakthrough for Women?," *Parliamentary Affairs* 50, no. 4 (October 1997): 708–719.

those in the 18–29 age group (+18 percent), and among first-time voters; there was no swing to Labour among those over 65.

What are the implications of this overlay of gender and generational voting patterns? For one thing, it seems that a party's ability to recognize and satisfy the political agendas of women in Britain may offer big political dividends. Studies suggest, first, that issues at the top of the list of women's concerns (e.g., childcare, the rights and pay of part-time workers, equal pay, support for family care givers, domestic violence) do not feature strongly in the existing policy agendas of the political parties. Secondly, to the extent that women and men care about the same broadly defined issues, women often understand the issues differently than men, and express different priorities. For example, while men (and the three major parties) consider unemployment the central employment issue, women emphasize equal pay and pensions, access to childcare, and the rights of part-time workers. Thirdly, research indicates that distinct sets of issues concern different groups of women. For example, older women are most concerned about pensions and transportation. Due to the overrepresentation of women in lower-paid part-time jobs, working women express particular concern about the minimum wage and the treatment of part-time workers. Mothers find the level of child benefit more important than issues of tax cuts. Finally, younger women strongly support policies that would help them balance the responsibilities of work, family, and childcare.

including ethnicity, gender, and other increasingly important ways in which people define themselves. As the Current Challenges Box on the gender-generation gap suggests, gender presents the most interesting case for the electoral influence of alternative collective identities, as women link their voting decisions to a specific set of needs that vary by generation and material circumstances.

In 1997, Labour made a concerted effort to attract female voters and was handsomely rewarded. The unprecedented election of 119 women MPs and the appointment of a significant number of women onto the Labour front benches raised hopes that 1997

marked a critical breakthrough for women in British politics. Will the gender gap tilt toward Labour in 1997, driven by the interests and identities of young women, become a case of "easy come, easy go"? To a significant degree, Blair's dream to govern Britain for ten or even fifteen years may depend on New Labour's success in responding to the needs of younger women looking to balance work and family responsibilities.

Without the traditional constraints of partisan and class identities, voters can shift allegiances easily, like consumers, following short-term policy preferences or the most confidence-inspiring management team. If this process comes to accurately describe contemporary party competition in Britain, then the landslide victory in 1997 could become a startling defeat in 2001 or 2002 if Labour fails to satisfy the huge numbers of floating voters that appear to determine electoral results. Thus a partisan need for re-election inspires a greater challenge: to identify and satisfy the needs of voters and citizens as a way of restabilizing British electoral politics.

In this era of uncertain democratic transitions, divided leadership, and intense global pressures on economic competitiveness, Britain's response to contemporary challenges will be closely watched. These are tough times for national governments to maintain popular support and achieve desirable goals. Can an immensely popular and resolute leader who is riding a wave of economic prosperity in one of the most secure democracies govern effectively? If not, many will conclude that these tough times just got tougher.

Key Terms

free trade
hegemonic power
franchise
welfare state
Commonwealth
euro
gender gap
Westminster model
Keynesian
  demand management
Keynesianism
macroeconomic policy
industrial policy
monetarism
neo-liberalism
social security

parliamentary
  sovereignty
parliamentary
  democracy
unitary state
fusion of powers
constitutional monarchy
quangos
communitarianism
judicial review
patron-client relations
single-member plurality
  system
new social movements
volatility

Suggested Readings

Beer, Samuel H. *Britain Against Itself: The Political Contradictions of Collectivism*. New York: Norton, 1982.

Driver, Stephen, and Luke Martel. *New Labour: Politics After Thatcherism*. Cambridge: Polity Press, 1998.

Dunleavy, Patrick, et al. *Developments in British Politics 5*. New York: St. Martin's Press, 1997.

Giddens, Anthony. *The Third Way: The Renewal of Social Democracy*. Cambridge: Polity Press, 1998.

Gilroy, Paul. *'There Ain't No Black in the Union Jack': The Cultural Politics of Race and Nation*. Chicago: University of Chicago Press, 1991.

Hall, Peter A. *Governing the Economy: The Politics of State Intervention in Britain and France*. New York: Oxford University Press, 1986.

Hall, Stuart, and Martin Jacques, eds. *The Politics of Thatcherism*. London: Lawrence and Wishart, 1983.

Hobsbawm, E. J. *Industry and Empire*. Harmondsworth: Penguin/Pelican, 1983.

King, Anthony, et al. *New Labour Triumphs: Britain at the Polls*. Chatham, NJ: Chatham House Publishers, 1998.

Krieger, Joel. *British Politics in the Global Age. Can Social Democracy Survive?* New York: Oxford University Press, 1999.

Landes, David S. *The Unbound Prometheus: Technological Change and Industrial Development in Western Europe from 1750 to the Present*. Cambridge, England: Cambridge University Press, 1969.

Marsh, David, et al. *Postwar British Politics in Perspective*. Cambridge, England: Polity Press, 1999.

Marshall, Geoffrey. *Ministerial Responsibility*. Oxford, England: Oxford University Press, 1989.

Middlemas, Keith. *Politics in Industrial Society: The Experience of the British System since 1911*. London: Andre Deutsch, 1979.

Norris, Pippa. *Electoral Change in Britain since 1945*. Oxford, England: Blackwell Publishers, 1997.

Pierson, Paul. *Dismantling the Welfare State? Reagan, Thatcher, and the Politics of Retrenchment*. New York: Cambridge University Press, 1994.

Riddell, Peter. *The Thatcher Decade*. Oxford, England: Basil Blackwell, 1989.

Särlvik, Bo, and Ivor Crewe. *Decade of Dealignment: The Conservative Victory of 1979 and Electoral Trends in the 1970s*. Cambridge, England: Cambridge University Press, 1983.

Shaw, Eric. *The Labour Party since 1945*. Oxford, England: Blackwell Publishers, 1996.

Thompson, E. P. *The Making of the English Working Class*. New York: Vintage, 1966.

Endnotes

[1] See Anthony King, "The Night Itself," in *New Labour Triumphs: Britain at the Polls*, ed. Anthony King (Chatham, NJ: Chatham House, 1998), pp. 1–13. See also David Butler and Dennis Kavanagh, *The British General Election of 1997* (New York: St. Martin's Press, 1997), pp. 244–253.

[2] *Social Trends* 27, 1997 Ed., ed. Jenny Church (London: The Stationery Office), p. 28.

[3] Jeremy Black, *The Politics of Britain 1688–1800* (Manchester and New York: Manchester University Press, 1993), p. 6.

[4] E. J. Hobsbawm, *Industry and Empire* (Harmondsworth: Penguin/Pelican, 1983), pp. 29–31.

5 See Paul M. Kennedy, *The Rise and Fall of British Naval Mastery* (London and Atlantic Highlands, NJ: Ashfield Press, 1992), pp. 186–189.

6 Will Hutton, *The State We're In* (London: Jonathan Cape, 1995).

7 See Stephen Driver and Luke Martell, *New Labour Politics After Thatcherism* (Cambridge, England: Polity Press, 1998), pp. 32–73.

8 Michael Jones, *Marxism Today* (May 1980): 10.

9 Ivor Crewe, "Labor Force Changes, Working Class Decline, and the Labour Vote: Social and Electoral Trends in Postwar Britain," in *Labor Parties in Postindustrial Societies*, ed. Frances Fox Piven (New York: Oxford University Press, 1992), p. 34. See also David Marsh and R. A. W. Rhodes, "Implementing Thatcherism: Policy Change in the 1980s," *Parliamentary Affairs* 45, no. 1 (January 1992): 34–37.

10 Kenneth Newton, "Caring and Competence: The Long, Long Campaign," *Britain at the Polls 1992*, ed. Anthony King (Chatham, NJ: Chatham House, 1993), p. 147.

11 Peter Jenkins, "Thatcher's Britain," *Geopolitique* no. 31 (Autumn 1990): 14–15.

12 *Social Trends* 27, 1997 Ed. pp. 98–99.

13 Office of National Statistics Social Survey, *Living in Britain: Results from the 1995 General Household Survey* (London: The Stationery Office, 1997).

14 Stuart Hall, "The Question of Cultural Identity," in *Modernity and Its Futures*, ed. Stuart Hall, David Held, and Tony McGrew (Cambridge, England: Polity Press, 1992), p. 291.

15 Gail Lewis, "Black Women's Employment and the British Economy," in *Inside Babylon: The Caribbean Diaspora in Britain*, ed. Winston James and Clive Harris (London: Verso), pp. 73–96.

16 Bob Jessop, Kevin Bonnett, Simon Bromley, and Tom Ling, *Thatcherism* (Cambridge, England: Polity Press, 1988), p. 48.

17 Melanie Bien, "A Woman's Place Is in the Workplace—but Pay Her More," *The European*, 11–17 December, 1997, p. 35.

18 Philip Norton, *The British Polity*, 3d ed. (New York and London: Longman, 1994), p. 59. See Norton for a useful discussion of the sources of the British constitution.

19 S. E. Finer, *Five Constitutions* (Atlantic Highlands, NJ: Humanities Press, 1979), p. 52.

20 Anthony King, "Cabinet Co-ordination or Prime Ministerial Dominance? A Conflict of Three Principles of Cabinet Government," in *The Developing British Political System: The 1990s*, 3d ed., eds. Ian Budge and David McKay (London and New York: Longman, 1993), 63.

21 Simon Mohun, "Continuity and Change in State Economic Intervention," in *Restructuring Britain: Politics in Transition* (London: Sage, 1989), p. 73.

22 *The Economist*, November 5, 1983, p. 64.

23 Samuel H. Beer, *The British Political System* (New York: Random House, 1973), p. 157.

24 See David Sanders, "Voting and the Electorate," in *Developments in British Politics 5*, ed. Patrick Dunleavy, Andrew Gamble, Ian Holiday, and Gillian Peele (New York: St. Martin's Press, 1997), pp. 45–74.

25 Henry Drucker and Andrew Gamble, "The Party System," in *Developments in British Politics 2*, rev. ed., ed. Henry Drucker et al. (London: Macmillan, 1988), p. 60.

26 Market and Opinion Research International (MORI), *British Public Opinion* xiii, no. 6 (July 1990): 4.

27 Ivor Crewe, "Great Britain," in *Electoral Change in Western Democracies*, ed. I. Crewe and D. Denver (London: Croom Helm, 1985), p. 107.

28 Gabriel A. Almond and Sidney Verba, *The Civic Culture: Political Attitudes and Democracy in Five Nations* (Princeton, NJ: Princeton University Press, 1963); Almond and Verba, eds., *The Civic Culture Revisited* (Boston: Little, Brown, 1980); and Samuel H. Beer, *Britain Against Itself: The Political Contradiction of Collectivism* (New York: Norton, 1982), pp. 110–114.

29 Ivor Crewe, "The Thatcher Legacy," in *Britain at the Polls 1992*, ed. Anthony King et al. (Chatham, NJ: Chatham House, 1993), p. 18.

30 Bendict Anderson, *Imagined Communities*, rev. ed. (London and New York: Verso, 1991).

31 "Goodbye to All That?," *The European*, 27 April–3 May 1998, 5.

32 Stephen Haseler, "Britain's Ancien Regime," *Parliamentary Affairs* 40, no. 4 (October 1990): 418.

33 Ibid., p. 420.

34 Lizanne Dowds and Ken Young, "National Identity," in *British Social Attitudes: The 13th Report*, ed. Roger Jowell, John Curtice, Alsion Park, Lindsay Brook, and Katarina Thompson (Aldershot: Dartmouth Publishing Company, 1996), pp. 141–160.

35 David Sanders, "The New Electoral Battlefield," in *New Labour Triumphs: Britain at the Polls*, op. cit., p. 221.

CHAPTER 3
France

Mark Kesselman

French Republic

Land and Population

Capital	Paris	
Total Area (square miles)	210,026	(Slightly less than twice the size of Colorado)
Population	59 million	
Annual Average Population Growth Rate (1990–1997)	0.5%	
Urban Population	75%	
Ethnic Composition	French-born	93%
	Other European	3%
	North African	2%
	Other	2%
Major Language	French	
Religious Affiliation	Roman Catholic	76.3%
	Muslim	6.3%
	Protestants	2.9%
	Other	14.5%

Economy

Domestic Currency	French franc, euro; after January 1, 2002, euro	
Total GNP (US$)	$1.526 trillion	
GNP per capita (US$)	$26,052	
GNP per capita at purchasing power parity (US$)	$21,860	
GNP average annual growth rate (1996–1997)	2.3%	
GNP per capita average annual growth rate	1996–1997	1.9%
	1980–1995	1.4%
	1965–1980	3.7%
Income Gap: GDP per capita of (US$)	Richest 20% of population	$40,098
	Poorest 20% of population	$5359
Structure of Production (% of GDP)	Agriculture	2%
	Industry	27%
	Services	71%
Labor Force Distribution (% of total)	Agriculture	5%
	Industry	26%
	Services	69%
Exports as % of GDP	23%	
Imports as % of GDP	20%	
Electricity Consumption per capita (kwh)	7272	
CO_2 Emissions per capita (metric tons)	5900	

Society

Life Expectancy	Female	82.6
	Male	74.4
Doctors per 100,000 population	280	
Infant Mortality per 1000 live births	5.8	
Adult Literacy	99% (male and female)	

(although the UN estimates that 16.8% of people age 16–65 are functionally illiterate)

Access to Information and Communications (per 1000 population)	Radios	895
	Televisions	579
	Telephone Lines	590
	Personal Computers	134

Women in Government and Economy

Women in Parliament 10.9% (lower house) 5.9% (upper house)	
Women at Ministerial Level	7%
Women as % of Total Labor Force	44%
Female Business Administrators and Managers	9%
Female Professional and Technical Workers	41%

1998 Human Development Index ranking (out of 174 countries, 1 = highest)   14

Political Organization

Political System   Unitary republic

Regime History   Semipresidential system; popularly elected president, popularly elected parliament, and prime minister and government appointed by president and responsible to National Assembly.

Administrative Structure   Unitary, with 22 regions and 100 departments.

Executive   Dual executive: president (seven-year term); PM appointed by president, generally leader of majority coalition in National Assembly, and responsible to National Assembly.

Legislature   Bicameral: Senate (upper house) has power to delay legislation passed by lower house. National Assembly (lower house) can pass legislation and force government to resign by passing a censure motion.

Judiciary   A nine-member independent Constitutional Council named for nonrenewable nine-year terms; president of republic names three members, president of each house of parliament names three. They exercise right of judicial review.

Party System   Multiparty. Principal parties: Socialist Party (PS); Rally for the Republic (RPR), Union for French Democracy (UDF); minor parties: National Front (FN), Communist Party (PCF), and Green Party.

Section ❶ The Making of the Modern French State

Politics in Action

In every country, certain dates have particular importance. For the United States, it is July 4, 1776, the signing of the Declaration of Independence. For France July 12, 1998, has gained a position in the nation's collective consciousness as one of the most important dates in modern history. For on that day, France's soccer team, "les bleus," was crowned World Champions by winning the World Cup, the most important sports event in the world. (An estimated two billion people watched the broadcast of the final, pitting France against Brazil.)

As the game ended, the largest crowd since the Liberation of France from Nazi occupation in 1944 jammed the Champs Elysées (France's largest and most famous boulevard, which stretches majestically from the Tuileries Gardens to the Arc de Triomphe in central Paris). The celebration lasted through the night and for the next two days, running into the celebration traditionally held in France on July 14 to commemorate the storming of the Bastille prison in 1789—an event generally regarded as marking the beginning of the French Revolution.

France's World Cup Soccer Team. *Source:* Associated Press.

"So, the presence of blacks and Arabs doesn't upset you?"
"Not as long as they score goals." *Source:* Pancho, from *Le Monde*, July 2, 1998.

The heady atmosphere produced by France's victory marked a welcome contrast to the usual reports of high unemployment, political scandals, and debates about French national identity. At least for a moment, French citizens were able to visualize France as a country in the very first rank. For students of politics, one of the most noteworthy features of the event was the composition of the French team. National teams in the World Cup can recruit only citizens of that country. Among the players were Zinedine Zidane, whose parents are Algerian immigrants, Lilian Thuram, whose parents are from Guadeloupe, and Marcel Desailly, who hails from Ghana. Other players were of Armenian and Polish descent. Nothing could have better demonstrated that France is a country of immigrants. And nothing could have better discredited the vicious claim of the racist National Front party that immigrants pose a danger to France.

Leading French politicians sought to bask in the glory of the victory. Although President Jacques Chirac and Prime Minister Lionel Jospin are from opposing parties and are bitter opponents, they sat side by side at the World Cup final and presented a picture of blissful harmony as they embraced the winning team. Not surprisingly, following the victory, both men enjoyed a 15 percent surge in popularity in post-game polls.

Geographic Setting

France occupies a key position in Europe, bordering the Mediterranean Sea in the South and sharing borders with northern European countries (Belgium, Switzerland, and Germany) on the North and East, Spain in the Southwest, and Italy in the Southeast. France is Britain's closest continental neighbor; the two are separated by a mere 25-mile stretch of the English Channel and the construction of the Chunnel (the rail line under the channel) has brought the two countries even closer. France has quite secure natural borders of mountains and seas on all sides, save for the open plains of the Northeast. The flat, open terrain separating France from Germany enabled German forces to invade France three times in the nineteenth and twentieth centuries.

France is among the world's favored countries, thanks to its temperate climate, large and fertile land area, relatively low population density, and high standard of living. However, the country is poorly endowed in natural energy and mineral resources. France must import most of its petroleum, which is why the government has sponsored an intensive nuclear power program since the 1950s. France must also import most minerals, due to an initial scarcity of reserves and years of extensive exploitation. As a result, France must concentrate its efforts on producing high-value-added products to compete internationally.

With a population of over 58,000,000 inhabitants, France is one of the most populous countries in Western Europe, but its large size—221,000 square miles—makes its population density low. An unusual feature of French national territorial boundaries is that some overseas territories, such as the Caribbean islands of Guadeloupe and Martinique and the Pacific island of Réunion, are considered an integral part of the country. (They, therefore, have a fundamentally different status than colonies.) Their inhabitants are French citizens who enjoy full civil rights and liberties; for example, they elect their own representatives to the French legislature.

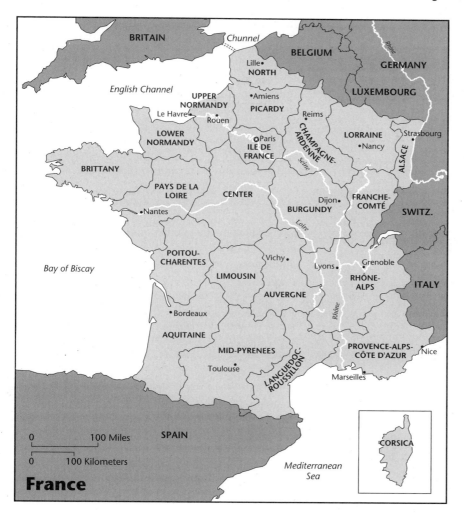

France's gross national product (GNP) of over $1 trillion and the per capita income of $20,000 make the country among the most affluent in the world. Most families own a television, a VCR, a telephone, and an automobile. One-half own their own home. France ranks fourteenth among the 174 nations in the world in overall quality of life, according to the 1998 United Nations Human Development Index.

France has a modern economy, and the bulk of the population works in the industrial and service sectors. However, agriculture continues to occupy a significant place in the economy and, because the country was predominantly rural until quite recently, it retains an even stronger place in the country's collective memory. Moreover, the proportion of French who live in rural areas and small towns is greater than for most other industrialized countries. No other French city comes close to rivaling Paris, the capital, in size and influence, and, other than Lyons and Marseilles—the next largest French cities—there are few large cities in France.

Critical Junctures

Creating Modern France

For five centuries at the beginning of the modern era,

the area that is now France was part of the Roman Empire. It was called *Gaul* by the Romans (the source of the term Gallic, sometimes used to describe the French). It took its current name from the Franks, a Germanic tribe that conquered the area in the fifth century A.D., with the breakup of the Roman Empire. The Merovingian dynasty ruled France for several centuries, when most of the population became Christian. It was succeeded by the Carolingian dynasty whose most noteworthy ruler, Charlemagne, briefly brought much of Western Europe under his control during the ninth century. Following Charlemagne's death, the empire disintegrated.

During the next two centuries, a succession of powerful French monarchs patiently and tenaciously sought to unify France against the fierce resistance of powerful provincial rulers. France was nearly overrun by the English during the Hundred Years' War (1337–1453). Joan of Arc, a simple peasant, finally led French forces to victory over the invading English army. Along with Charlemagne and a handful of other historic figures, she remains a symbol of intense national pride.

France flourished during the next several centuries, especially after Henri IV (who ruled from 1589–1610) ended fierce religious wars between Catholics and Huguenots (Protestants) when he issued the Edict of Nantes in 1598. The Edict granted Protestants limited religious toleration. In the sixteenth and seventeenth centuries, France and England competed for colonies in the Caribbean and North America. The rivalry between the two eventually ended with France's defeat, symbolized by the signing of the Treaty of Paris in 1763, when France accepted British domination in North America and India. (At a later period, France would engage in further colonial conquests in Africa and Asia.)

The seventeenth and early eighteenth centuries were the high point of French economic, military, and cultural influence throughout the world. France was the most affluent and powerful country in Europe, as suggested by the many exquisite chateaux (some of which still survive) throughout France built by monarchs and aristocrats. But France was also the artistic and scientific capital of Europe, home of the Enlightenment in the eighteenth century, the philosophical movement that emphasized the importance of using scientific reasoning to understand and change the world.

The Ancien Régime

French political life was shaped for centuries by the attempt of French monarchs to undermine local loyalties and foster uniform rules throughout the country. The powerful king Louis XIV (1643–1715) sponsored the creation of a relatively efficient state bureaucracy, separate from the Crown's personal domain and the feudal aristocracy. France began to be administered according to a legal-rational code in which standardized regulations were applied throughout the country. France was a pioneer in developing the absolutist state, which has shaped French development ever since.

The modernizing, absolutist state created by Louis XIV and other monarchs coexisted with an intricate and burdensome system of feudal privileges that the common people increasingly resented. Another target of popular discontent was the Catholic church, a large landowner, tax collector, and ally of the feudal authorities. This complex patchwork of institutions was later called the ***ancien régime***, or old regime. Furthermore, the monarchy collected taxes not only to finance a modern legal and administrative system but also to support the wasteful royal court at Versailles.

Worse, Louis XIV and his successor, Louis XV, accumulated massive state debts as they pursued a series of military adventures in Europe and colonial conquests overseas. For most of the period from the mid-seventeenth to the mid-eighteenth century, France was at war with her neighbors. As historian Simon Schama notes, "No other European power attempted to support both a major continental army and a transcontinental navy at the same time."[1] France had been the most powerful nation in Europe in the seventeenth century. In the eighteenth century, Britain was able to challenge France's preeminence, thanks to the economic advantages that Britain reaped from the Agricultural and Industrial Revolutions. France's stagnant economy could not generate the resources to compete with an increasingly productive England. As a result, the French monarchy had to borrow to maintain the economy so that by 1788, French state debt was so large that interest on past loans consumed over one-half of current state expenditures.[2] When Louis XVI was forced to try to raise taxes, which fell heavily on the common people, he sealed the fate of French monarchy.

The Two Faces of the French Revolution (1789–1815)

On July 14, 1789, an angry crowd burst through the gates of the Bastille prison and freed the prisoners, launching the French Revolution. This was soon followed by the toppling of the French monarchy and the entire *ancien régime* of nobility and feudal privileges. The First Republic was proclaimed in 1792. These momentous events marked the beginning of a new era in French and world history (see Critical Junctures in Modern French Political Development). France was the first European nation in which a **revolution** abolished the monarchy and established a **republic** based on the belief that all citizens, regardless of social

Critical Junctures in Modern French Political Development	
Until 1789	*Ancien régime* (Bourbon monarchy)
1789–1799	Revolutionary regimes
	Constituent Assembly, 1789–1791 (Declaration of Rights of Man, Aug. 26, 1789)
	Legislative, 1791
	Convention, 1792–1795: Monarchy abolished and First Republic established, 1792
	Directory, 1795–1799
1800–1814	Consulat and First Empire (Napoleon Bonaparte)
1814–1830	Restoration
1830–1848	July Monarchy
1848–1851	Second Republic
1852–1870	Second Empire (Louis Napoleon)
1870	Paris Commune
1870–1940	Third Republic
1940–1944	Vichy regime
1946–1958	Fourth Republic
1958–Present	Fifth Republic
1958–1969	Charles de Gaulle*
1969–1974	Georges Pompidou
1974–1981	Valéry Giscard d'Estaing
1981–1995	François Mitterrand
1995–	Jacques Chirac

*First president of the Fifth Republic

background, were equal before the law. It is difficult to overestimate the impact of the revolution on people's thinking. As historian Lynn Hunt observes:

> The chief accomplishment of the French Revolution was the institution of a dramatically new political culture. . . . The French Revolution may be said to represent the transition to political and social modernity, the first occasion when the people entered upon the historical stage to remake the political community.[3]

The revolution was at the same time a *national* revolution, which affirmed the people's right to choose their own political regime; an *international* revolution, which inspired national uprisings elsewhere in Europe and sought to expand French revolutionary values internationally (often through military means); a *liberal* revolution, which championed the value of individual liberty in the political and economic spheres; and a *democratic* revolution, which proclaimed that a nation's identity and the legitimacy of its government depend on all citizens having the right to participate in making key political decisions. These provocative ideas have since been diffused on a global level.

We should not idealize the traditions dating from this period. Although it proclaimed progressive values of liberty, equality, and fraternity, the revolutionary regime could be harsh toward its opponents. (At the extreme, during the Reign of Terror, the Revolution guillotined those found guilty by revolutionary tribunals.) Historian Joan Landes has analyzed how, despite some reforms responsive to women's demands (for example, short-lived divorce legislation), the revolutionary ferment was also quite hostile to women: "The [First] Republic was constructed against women, not just without them, and nineteenth-century Republicans did not actively counteract this masculinist heritage of republicanism."[4]

In other ways, too, the revolution left a complex legacy which was brilliantly analyzed in the nineteenth century by Alexis de Tocqueville, a French aristocrat. Tocqueville was the first to emphasize two quite opposite faces of the French Revolution: it both produced a rupture with the *ancien régime* and furthered the goal pursued by French monarchs of strengthening state institutions. In particular, many of the centralizing institutions created by Napoleon

Bonaparte, the popular general who seized power and proclaimed himself emperor in 1802, remain to this day. Napoleon established the system by which state-appointed officials called **prefects** administer localities and the *Conseil d'État* (State Council), which supervises the central administration. And he promulgated the Napoleonic Code of law, an elaborate legal framework.

Since Napoleon's defeat and exile in 1815, French politics has often revolved around the question of how to reconcile state autonomy—the state's independence from pressure from groups within society—with democratic participation and decision-making. Compared to some successful democracies, notably Britain, France has been less able to combine the two within a stable political regime. The French state successfully developed the capacity to regulate important as well as quite trivial areas of social life. For example, the Ministry of Education tightly controls the curriculum that is taught in all public schools; and, until quite recently, the Ministry of the Interior kept close watch on the names local governments assigned to city streets and vetoed proposed changes it disliked. But, while citizens often sought state help, they also resented its heavy hand and periodically took to the streets in opposition. The result was extensive political instability.

Many Regimes, Slow Industrialization (1815–1940)

France spent much of the nineteenth and early twentieth centuries digesting and debating the legacy of the Revolution. The succession of regimes and revolutions for more than a century after 1815 can be interpreted as varied attempts to combine state autonomy and direction with democratic participation and decision-making. The monarchy was restored to power in 1815 but was overthrown in a popular uprising in July 1830, which installed a distant royal cousin, Louis Philippe, as king. In 1848, another revolution produced yet another regime, the short-lived Second Republic. Napoleon III, the nephew of Napoleon Bonaparte, overthrew the republic after three years and proclaimed himself emperor. When France lost the Franco-Prussian war of 1870, the Second Empire was swept away by a revolutionary upheaval which produced the Paris Commune, a brief experiment in worker-governed democracy. The Commune was violently crushed after a few months, to be succeeded by the Third Republic, created in 1870 under the shadow of military defeat and civil war.

Despite the Third Republic's less-than-glorious origins and although it never commanded widespread support, it turned out to be France's most durable modern regime, lasting until 1940. (The second most durable regime is the current Fifth Republic, created in 1958.) The Third Republic was described, in a famous phrase by nineteenth-century sociologist Ernest Renan, as that regime "which divides us [French] least." The Third Republic was a parliamentary regime with two powerful legislative bodies (the Chamber of Deputies and Senate). Its institutions were designed to prevent decisive leadership, given the recent legacy of Napoleon III's illegal seizure of power and the ideologically fragmented state of French society. Yet the republic survived the terrible ordeal of World War I and held firm against extremist forces on the right during the 1920s and 1930s, when republics were crumbling in Germany, Italy, and Spain.

In sharp contrast with the dizzying pace at which regimes came and went, the rate of economic change in France during this period was quite gradual. In contrast to Germany, France chose economic stability over modernization.

There have been endless attempts to explain why France did not become an industrial leader in the nineteenth century. Although France began the century as the world's second most important economic power, fairly close to Britain in terms of economic output, by 1900 France trailed the United States, Great Britain, and Germany in industrial development. A large peasantry acted as a brake on industrialization, as did the shortage of key natural resources, notably coal, iron, and petroleum. Historians have also pointed to the relatively underdeveloped entrepreneurial spirit in France. Within the ranks of the middle class, professionals, administrators, and shopkeepers outnumbered industrial entrepreneurs. In general, French manufacturers excelled in sectors that did not fuel industrial expansion, notably, agricultural produce for local markets and custom-made luxury goods (silkweaving and porcelain), which did not lend themselves to mechanized production and for which mass markets did not exist.

Another factor inhibiting industrial development was the slow growth of the French population. In the middle of the nineteenth century, France was the second most populous nation in Europe (after Russia). However, although the British population more than tripled in the nineteenth century and the number of Germans more than doubled, France's population increased by less than one-half.[5] France had 15 percent of Europe's population in 1800, but only 8 percent in 1950.[6] Slow population growth meant smaller demand and less incentive for businesses to invest and increase productivity.

More important than technical or demographic factors was the role of the state. In Britain, the government removed restrictions on the free operation of market forces, and in Prussia (later Germany), Bismarck imposed industrialization from above. By contrast, the French state aimed to "maintain an equilibrium among industry, commerce, and agriculture and attempt[ed] to insulate France from the distress and upheaval that had struck other nations bent upon rapid economic advance."[7] France retained some of the highest tariff barriers in Western Europe in the nineteenth and early twentieth centuries. The purpose of this **protectionist** policy was to shield small producers—farmers, manufacturers, and artisans—from foreign competition. Economic historian Richard Kuisel observes that "rarely, if ever, did [the French state] act to promote economic expansion, plan development, or advance economic democracy."[8]

Yet the state did not confine its economic activity to purely protectionist purposes. In a tradition that dates back to Colbert, the finance minister of Louis XIV who directed the creation of the French merchant marine, the state sponsored a number of large-scale economic projects. For example, in the 1860s, under Napoleon III, the state consolidated several small railroad companies and organized an integrated national rail network; encouraged the formation of the Crédit Mobilier, an investment bank to finance railroad development; and guaranteed interest rates on the bonds sold to underwrite railroad construction.

Through much of the nineteenth century and well into the twentieth century, however, the state sought to preserve political stability rather than promote economic modernization. Slow economic growth did not prevent political conflict. But it did contribute to France's humiliating defeat by Germany in 1940.

Vichy, France (1940–1943) and the Fourth Republic (1946–1958)

World War II was one of the bleakest periods in French history. When France was overrun by Germany in 1940, the Third Republic collapsed and Marshall Pétain, an aging military hero, signed an armistice that divided France in two. The North was under direct German occupation; the South was controlled by a puppet regime, whose capital was at Vichy, presided over by Pétain. The Vichy government collaborated with the Nazi occupation by providing workers and supplies for the German war machine. It had the dubious distinction of being the only political regime in Western Europe that delivered Jews to the Nazis from areas not directly under German occupation. About 76,000 Jews, including 12,000 children, were sent to Nazi death camps. Vichy not only failed to protect foreign Jews who had fled to French soil for asylum but organized its own program of imprisoning French Jews and sending them to Nazi concentration camps.

Although the vast majority of French quietly accepted France's defeat and meekly complied with the Vichy government's directives, a small resistance movement developed within France. Charles de Gaulle, a prominent general in the Third Republic, publicly broke with Vichy and advocated armed opposition to the regime. He succeeded in assuming leadership over the communist, socialist, and progressive Catholic opposition forces and consolidated them into what became known as the *Resistance*. Although France contributed little to the Allied victory, de Gaulle's skillful actions enabled France to gain acceptance as a member of the victorious coalition and obtain one of the five permanent seats on the United Nations Security Council following the war.

To salvage French honor after World War II, de Gaulle helped create the myth of a broad and powerful Resistance movement against Pétain. In fact, the Vichy regime encountered little opposition and the Resistance was quite limited. Most French citizens, including the vast majority of civil servants, cooperated with the Vichy regime. It took fully half a century after the end of the war for a French president to apologize publicly, in the name of the state, for the crimes committed by the Vichy regime. Soon after his election in 1995, President Jacques Chirac declared, "Those dark hours will forever tarnish our history and are a disgrace to our past and to our tradition. We all know that the criminal madness of the occupying forces [the Nazis] was assisted by the French, that is, the French state."

In 1945, de Gaulle sought to sponsor a new regime which would avoid the errors that, in his view, had weakened France and contributed to its moral decline and defeat by Germany. He opposed the institutional design of the Third Republic, in which the executive was completely dependent on parliament. He proposed creating a regime in which the government was independent and powerful.

De Gaulle failed in this attempt. Having just overthrown the **authoritarian** Vichy regime, French citizens opposed the creation of a new republic with a strong executive. De Gaulle abruptly resigned as leader of the provisional regime that was drafting a new constitution and mounted an unsuccessful campaign against the new republic that resulted. The Constitution of the Fourth Republic was in fact very similar to that of the Third Republic.

The Fourth Republic, which survived for a dozen years, from 1946 to 1958, embodied an extreme form of parliamentary rule and a weak executive. The Constitution gave parliament a near-monopoly of power, which it exercised in a quite destructive fashion: governments were voted out of office an average of once every six months. This situation was due in part to the fact that many parties were represented in parliament because the National Assembly, the powerful lower house of parliament, was selected by proportional representation. As in the Third Republic, rapid shifts in party alliances, as well as a lack of discipline within parties, meant that governments lacked the cohesion and authority to make tough decisions and develop long-range policies. Although the Fourth Republic was often described as highly *unstable*, the situation might better be described as one of political *stalemate*.

Neither the Vichy regime nor the Fourth Republic satisfactorily combined state direction and democratic participation. By their opposite excesses, they underlined the need for devising a new constitutional framework that would promote stable, democratic rule.

Despite some important achievements, notably, setting France on the road to economic expansion and modernization, the Fourth Republic was unable to take decisive action in many important spheres. The regime was severely handicapped by the fact that powerful political forces, notably the Communist party and de Gaulle's political movement, were well represented in parliament and strongly opposed one government after another. The Fourth Republic's failure to crush the Algerian independence movement, which opposed French rule of the North African colony, provided de Gaulle with the opportunity to regain power. By threatening to lead a military rebellion against the republic, he pressured parliament to authorize him to scrap the Constitution and propose a new constitutional framework more to his liking. The Constitution of the Fifth Republic, drafted under his direction, provided for a vastly strengthened executive and a weakened parliament.

The Fifth Republic (1958 to the present)

The contrast between the Fourth and Fifth republics provides a textbook case of how institutions shape political life. The Fourth Republic could be described, unkindly but accurately, as an example of all talk and no action. On the other hand, the Fifth Republic created institutions in which leaders could act decisively but, at least in the early years, were hardly accountable to parliament or public opinion.

The history of the Fifth Republic is closely linked to the growth of the European Union (first known as the European Economic Community), which was created in 1957, a year before the birth of the Fifth Republic. The European Union (EU) helped to knit together historic rivals France and Germany, foster economic growth, and increase Europe's economic and political role internationally. The growing economic and political integration of Europe, thanks in significant measure to French leadership within the EU, represents a fundamental change after centuries of intense conflicts within Europe. The Fifth Republic reaped handsome benefits from the growth of the European Union.

Although de Gaulle became the first president of the Fifth Republic in the unsavory circumstances of a possible military intervention, he was able to command wide popular support. Resistance hero, commanding presence, and one of the political giants of the twentieth century, de Gaulle was able to persuade the French to support a regime in which democratic participation was strictly limited. He defended the new Constitution on the grounds that a parliamentary regime along the lines of the Fourth Republic or the British Westminster model was not appropriate for a country as divided as France. Although the new Constitution was approved by a large majority in a popular **referendum**, de Gaulle's high-handed governing style and the centralized institutions of the Fifth Republic eventually provoked widespread opposition. The most dramatic example was in May 1968, when students and workers engaged in the largest general strike in West European history. At the height of the May uprising, half of France's workers and a larger proportion of students were on strike. For weeks, workers and students occupied factories, offices, and universities, and the regime's survival hung in the balance. Although de Gaulle regained control of the situation, he was discredited and resigned from office the following year. In subsequent years, popular support for the Fifth Republic has gradually increased, in part because political institutions have become more responsive. (The functioning of political institutions is described in Sections 3 and 4.)

The Fifth Republic was severely tested once again in 1981. Until then, the same broad political coalition, representing **conservative** forces, had won every national election since 1958. In 1981, the Socialist Party candidate François Mitterrand was elected president, and in the parliamentary elections that followed his allies swamped the conservative coalition. Despite fears that the Fifth Republic would not be able to survive a **socialist** government, the institutions of the Fifth Republic proved highly successful at accommodating political alternation.

President Mitterrand's Socialist government sponsored one of the most ambitious reform agendas in modern French history that included changes which strengthened the autonomy of the judiciary, the media, and local governments. The centerpiece was a substantial increase in the number of industrial firms and financial institutions in the public sector. However, by seeking to extend the sphere of public control of the economy, France was swimming against the international economic and political tide. During the 1980s, the predominant tendency elsewhere in the industrialized world was to strengthen private market forces rather than extend public control. (Recall that Margaret Thatcher and Ronald Reagan were elected to leadership positions in Britain and the United States at nearly the same time that Mitterrand captured the French presidency.) When the Socialist experiment began to provoke an economic and financial crisis in 1983–1984, the government reluctantly decided to reverse course. Since then, French governments of left and right alike have generally pursued policies designed to strengthen market forces. As a result, the "ideological war" of left and right in France—which raged for centuries—has declined. Since the 1980s, frequent changes in the governing coalition have occurred, but there has been extensive continuity in economic policy.

Does the convergence between the major political parties of center-left and center-right mean the end of major political conflict in France? Not at all. Several new issues have emerged to divide the French electorate and challenge French political institutions.

"What!?? The president's a Socialist and the Eiffel Tower is still standing!??" "Incredible!"   *Source:* Courtesy Plantu, from *Le Monde*, May 1981.

France after the Millennium

No one event can be identified as a critical juncture as France began a new millennium. However, a cluster of developments produce the impression of political instability and even crisis within current French politics. One ingredient is the rapid-fire series of electoral shifts that have occurred. From 1986 to 1998, there were six presidential and parliamentary elections in France. In every one, control shifted from the ruling coalition to the opposition. For example, two years after electing conservative Jacques Chirac to the presidency, voters elected a Socialist parliamentary majority headed by Lionel Jospin. (Jospin became prime minister and shared power with a considerably weakened President Chirac.) Voters thus are quick to demonstrate their displeasure with the "ins"— although it does not take long for them to register their displeasure with the new ruling coalition! A second ingredient is that an endless series of political scandals has tarnished the reputation of many leading politicians, including party leaders, cabinet ministers, and the two most recent presidents (Mitterrand, president from 1981–1995, and Chirac, elected to a seven-year term in 1995). Third, a growing number of French citizens have turned against the major governing parties of both left and right, preferring to abstain or support fringe parties. Fourth, many scholars assert that underlying these changes is the fact that the French political system is unable to deal effectively with pressing social and economic challenges, involving record levels of unemployment, French participation in the European Union, and the meaning of French national identity in an era of globalization. To illustrate: the enthusiasm and national unity produced by the French victory in the 1998 World Cup was quickly followed by strikes and demonstrations, further political scandals, and other sour evidence of "politics as usual."

Themes and Implications

Historical Junctures and Political Themes

France in a World of States. France's relationship to Europe and other regions of the world, particularly Asia and Africa, has heavily shaped state formation. For over a century following Napoleon's defeat in 1815, the country displayed an isolationist orientation. For example, France erected high tariff barriers throughout the nineteenth century and the first half of the twentieth century to minimize international trade. Nevertheless, France participated aggressively in the new imperialism of the late nineteenth century, creating a new French empire in Southeast Asia, North and sub-Saharan Africa, and the Pacific.

France's relationship with Germany, against whom France fought three devastating wars, has weighed heavily on state development. The fact that the two countries developed cordial relations after the Second World War, in part thanks to the mutually beneficial expansion of the world economy, has provided France with a vastly increased measure of security. The alliance between the two countries has been vital in promoting closer European economic and political integration within the European Union. At the same time, France and Germany continue to compete, although these days it takes the form of economic rivalry between business firms rather than military confrontation.

No longer in the first rank militarily, France remains an important player on the world stage. For example, it is a major nuclear power and among the world's leading arms exporters. France has been an important participant in the Western alliance led by the United States. But in contrast to Britain and Germany, France has often been a gadfly to the United States. Under President de Gaulle's leadership, France withdrew from the military command structure of the North Atlantic Treaty Organization (NATO) in the 1960s and ordered U.S. troops stationed in France to leave. Similarly, when the United States launched air strikes against Iraq in 1998 because of President Saddam Hussein's refusal to allow access to UN weapons inspectors, France registered public opposition.

The French state has been a powerful, capable instrument that helped the country adapt to the challenges posed by global economic competition. In recent decades, the state skillfully promoted internationally acclaimed high-tech industrial projects, including high-speed rail (the TGV), leadership in the European consortium that developed an efficient wide-bodied airplane (the Airbus), an electronic telephone directory and data bank (the Minitel), and relatively safe and cheap nuclear power plants. The fact that the French state has played such a key role in nation-building and in economic and cultural development is why countless observers have noted, "No other nation in the world has as dense and passionate a relationship with the State as does France."[9] Yet France's **statist** tradition is under siege as a result of increased international economic integration and competition, highlighted by French participation in the EU, as well as ideological shifts and citizens' demands for more autonomy.

Governing the Economy.   Our discussion of France's statist tradition is useful in understanding the way that France organizes governance of the economy. In the period following World War II, the French pioneered in developing methods to steer and strengthen the private economy. As a result of planning, state loans and subsidies to private business, and crash programs to develop key economic sectors (for example, the steel industry), the French economy soared. However, state direction has created problems in an era when rapidly changing technology and economic globalization put a premium on flexibility. The French state can be compared to a stately ocean liner that can move powerfully once the direction has been set but has great difficulty changing course.

The Democratic Idea.   France has had an intense and complex relationship to the democratic idea. On the one hand, France's deeply rooted statist tradition is quite hostile to democratic participation and decision-making. On the other hand, France has been deeply attached to two quite different democratic currents. The first dates back to the eighteenth-century philosopher Jean-Jacques Rousseau. The theory of direct democracy inspired by Rousseau is hostile to political representation and intermediate associations, on the grounds that citizens should participate directly in political decisions, rather than merely choose leaders who monopolize political power.

A second powerful democratic current in French political culture fears direct democracy and stresses the value of representative democracy. Many opponents of de Gaulle criticized him for violating the representative democratic tradition and furthering *le pouvoir personnel*—"personal power." The parliamentary tradition opposes anything that smacks of direct democracy. It advocates instead delegating power to the people's elected representatives in parliament.

Despite their great differences, the two democratic traditions share with each other and with the statist tradition an important common feature, one that, until recently, could be considered a central pillar of French political culture. All three have traditionally opposed the concept of a written constitution, interpreted by an independent judiciary, that limits state power. The French have rarely viewed a constitution with the reverence many Americans feel toward the U.S. Constitution. And they have even more vehemently opposed an independent judiciary that limits the executive and legislature. A key change in French political culture since the 1970s has been the development of widespread support for the Constitution of the Fifth Republic and the right of the Constitutional Council to strike down governmental decisions as contrary to the Constitution.

France's democratic theory and institutions face important challenges in the current period. One problem stems from French participation in the European Union—which exhibits what has been dubbed a "democratic deficit," that is, too much administrative direction and too little democratic participation and representation. Another strain derives from the continuing difficulty of reconciling state autonomy and democratic participation within France. For example, as we shall analyze in Section 3, the French executive centralizes enormous powers and exhibits a relative lack of accountability. The kind of democratic deficit that many assert is a weakness of the European Union may also be said to characterize France's own political system.

The Politics of National and Collective Identities. French national identity has always been closely linked to state formation. The French Revolution championed the idea that anyone could become French if he or she accepted republican values. The French approach to citizenship and national identity encourages immigrants to become French citizens on condition that they accept dominant cultural and political values. Such an approach stresses that what binds people are shared political values rather than common racial or ethnic, that is, inherited, characteristics.

At the same time, the French have been strongly divided by social, economic, and cultural cleavages. There has long been a working-class subculture, closely linked to the powerful French Communist

Party (PCF), as well as a Catholic subculture, in which the Church played a key role. In recent decades, these subcultures have declined in importance. Occupational shifts, notably a drastic decline in blue-collar jobs and the rapid expansion of a white-collar service sector, have blurred class boundaries. During this period, the PCF has gone from being one of France's most powerful parties to a minor party. There has also been a dramatic decline in religious observance and the Catholic Church is no longer a powerful source of collective identity.

In the realm of collective identity, then, the legacy of the past weighs less heavily than in other areas. The whole issue of citizenship and collective identity has been complicated by economic difficulties and immigration. While class cleavages have declined, the relentless operation of market forces have created a large number of French who lead a precarious existence—for example, the long-term unemployed or those engaged in part-time or temporary work and often unable to afford decent housing. At the same time, many children whose parents were immigrants consider themselves fully French—but oppose dominant cultural norms. They have affirmed their pride in being Algerian and Muslim, demanded cultural autonomy and the right to be different in their dress, food, and religious practice.

French national identity is also jostled by French participation in the European Union and, more broadly, the opening of France's geographic and cultural horizons as a result of processes of globalization. Decisions affecting French citizens are increasingly made outside France—by officials in Brussels, Belgium, headquarters of the European Union, and by corporate executives and bankers in London, New York, and Tokyo. The French can no longer believe what was always to some extent a myth—that they lived in a self-contained world that they refer to (because of France's geographic boundaries) as the hexagon.

Implications for Comparative Politics

The study of French politics provides rich lessons for the study of comparative politics. France has continually tried to reshape its destiny by conscious political direction, and it provides a natural laboratory in which to test the importance of variations in institutional design. To illustrate: comparativists debate the impact of different kinds of electoral procedures on the character of political parties and on who gets elected. Since French electoral procedures have often changed in a brief period, it is possible to make fine-grained comparison of the impact of institutional variation.

At a more general level, the French have often looked to the state to achieve important economic and political goals. In countries without a statist tradition (for example, the United States and Britain), private groups rely to a greater extent on their own efforts. What can we learn from comparing the two approaches? What are the strengths and weaknesses of statism?

As we analyzed above, France also provides a fascinating case of a country that seeks to combine a strong state and strong democracy. The French do not believe that a state that acts vigorously need be undemocratic. In practice, however, combining the two is no easy matter. How successful is the French attempt? What can it teach groups elsewhere that are debating this issue?

As a leading participant in the EU, France provides students of comparative politics with an excellent case of a country seeking to forge close economic and political ties with its neighbors while retaining an important measure of autonomy. The EU is an extraordinary experiment in regional cooperation, but participation involves costs as well as benefits. What kinds of strains have been produced within France as a result of its membership in the EU? How effectively has France been able to shape EU institutions to maximize benefits for itself and other member countries?

Section ❷ Political Economy and Development

France is one of the world's leading economic powers. It has the fourth highest GNP, ranks fourth in terms of

world trade, and is the second largest importer and exporter of capital. A key to understanding the relative success of the French economy is the vigorous role played by the state.

State and Economy

During the early period of industrialization in Western Europe, the French state pursued a quite distinctive goal compared to Britain and the German states. Along with the United States, these nations were the world's leading economic powers in the nineteenth century. In Britain, the world's first industrialized power, the state sought to remove restrictions on the free operation of market forces. In Prussia (Germany after 1871), the state sponsored a crash program of industrialization. In France, the state directed whatever modernization occurred, for example, the construction of an extensive railroad network in the nineteenth century. But it generally sought to preserve traditional forces, notably, artisans, shopkeepers, and small-scale manufacturers, not foster economic modernization. This situation could last only so long as the state was able to protect France's economy and the nation from external threat. However, this became increasingly difficult and eventually proved impossible. The low point was reached when the Third Republic collapsed and Marshall Pétain signed an armistice with the Nazi regime that signified France's virtually total defeat.

The New French Revolution

When the Fourth Republic was created in 1946, influential groups concluded that the state had to seek economic modernization. At this time, a fundamental transformation occurred in the state's relationship to the economy. "After the war," economic historian Richard Kuisel observes, "what was distinctive about France was the compelling sense of relative economic backwardness. This impulse was the principal stimulus for economic renovation and set France apart from other countries."[10] Two scholars have described the postwar shift as "a new French Revolution. Although peaceful, this has been just as profound as that of 1789 because it has totally overhauled the moral foundations and social equilibrium of French society."[11]

The new French Revolution involved sweeping changes in the economy, society, and values. As a result of its long statist tradition, France was potentially well equipped to develop the institutional capacity to steer the economy. Kuisel describes the French state's approach as follows:

> France resembled other capitalist countries in developing an arsenal of institutions for managing the economy. . . . Yet France found its own way to perform these tasks. It lodged responsibility in new public institutions and staffed them with modernizers. It relied heavily on state intervention and planning. . . . The result was a Gallic style of economic management that blended state direction, corporatist bodies, and market forces.[12]

From guardian of the established order, the state became the sponsor of social and economic progress. It began to provide a wide array of cash transfers and social services, including family subsidies, day care facilities, old-age pensions, public health care, unemployment insurance, and public housing. The French welfare state eventually included the most extensive array of cradle-to-grave social programs of any country in the world.

Two key ingredients which enabled the state to undertake ambitious economic reforms were the development of mechanisms for planning and the personal leadership of Charles de Gaulle.

Planning. Soon after World War II, the French developed what they called **indicative planning**. A national Planning Commission, composed of civil servants appointed by the government, set national economic and social priorities for the next four or five years. The Planning Commission was assisted by modernization commissions, composed of public and private officials, which established targets for specific economic and social sectors. Successive plans sought to establish the maximum feasible rates of economic growth, proposed crash programs for development of specific industries and regions, and identified high-priority social goals such as educational targets. The state then used the plan as a basis for setting legislative and budgetary priorities. Perhaps more important than the specific goals that were pursued was that planning helped change France's political culture. The process of planning fostered the belief that change was to be welcomed, a sharp contrast to the past conservative pattern.

Planning developed broad support in part because it was not imposed in a heavy-handed fashion. In contrast to many of France's traditionally large, top-heavy bureaucracies, the planning agency was a small flexible agency, staffed by dynamic, young problem-solvers. French plans were guides to action, not legal directives, and were the product of an informal consensus among public and private officials. The planning process provided a way to share information and streamline economic decision-making.

The process did not represent interests equally. At its core, it encouraged the formation of a close alliance between the state and dynamic producer interests, especially large, technologically advanced firms seeking to compete in world markets. Small business, trade unions, and consumer interests were largely excluded. Critics charged, quite correctly, that planning was undemocratic because important decisions affecting France's future were made behind closed doors and important voices were excluded from the planning process.

Dirigisme under de Gaulle.   Planning began in the Fourth Republic, but the first steps were halting and uncertain. Vigorous leadership by the executive was needed to overcome conservative forces that opposed change. Such leadership was provided after 1958, when Charles de Gaulle, the most influential politician in twentieth-century French history, regained power and created the Fifth Republic.

De Gaulle was a complex, controversial, and contradictory figure. On the one hand, he was a faithful representative of traditional France, deeply attached to the values of order and hierarchy, all of which earned him the enmity of the Left. On the other hand, his personal leadership and the republic that he created provided the force to undermine traditional groups and restructure the French political economy.

General de Gaulle's return to power in 1958 ushered in a period of state-led industrialization and growth based on a distinctive pattern of indicative planning. The state bureaucracy expanded the scope of its activity and developed specific instruments to promote economic modernization. The state steered cheap credit toward favored sectors and firms, and in key industrial sectors encouraged the creation of large firms—they later came to be called "national champions." The French described the new relationship between the state and economy as *dirigiste* (directorial), which highlights the state's importance in steering the economy. Many key economic decisions were made in governmental ministries, especially the ministries of finance, economy, and industry, as well as the planning agency. The state thus stepped in to compensate for the relatively weak role played by private entrepreneurs.

Four key elements of the *dirigiste* approach can be identified. First, the French state engaged in intensive efforts to coordinate economic policy-making through the planning process, the government, the Ministry of Finance, and other agencies.

Second, the state used subsidies, loans, and tax write-offs to achieve its economic goals, such as industrial concentration, specialization in new fields, and technological innovation. For much of the postwar period, the state provided the bulk of capital for new investment, limited the outflow of French capital, created a host of parapublic banking institutions, and closely regulated private bank loans. The central aim was to provide "favored sectors with access to credit at subsidized rates."[13] The other side of the coin (given the lack of private sources of business credit) was that

---

Table 1

Average Growth Rates in Gross National Product, 1958–1973	
Japan	10.4%
France	5.5
Italy	5.3
West Germany	5.0
Belgium	4.9
Netherlands	4.2
Norway	4.2
Sweden	4.1
United States	4.1
United Kingdom	3.2

Students and workers unite in a mass demonstration on the Left Bank of Paris, May 27, 1968. *Source:* AP/Wide World Photos.

firms and sectors unable to obtain state financial assistance—in particular, traditional, inefficient firms—were doomed.

Third, the state developed plans to restructure specific sectors, including steel, machine tools, and paper products. The ministry of industry pressured medium-size industrial firms to merge in order to create national champions able to compete in world markets. Fourth, in some key sectors, the state created and managed entire new industries. Some of these state-created and managed firms were in the vanguard of technological progress throughout the world. In the French economic model, the state was chief economic player.

France's Economic Miracle

During the period labeled by one French economist "the thirty glorious years" (1945–1975), the planners and their allies were remarkably successful (see Table 1). The rate of French economic growth was among the highest of any European nation and second only to that of Japan—a striking contrast with the 1930s, when the French economy declined at the rate of over 1 percent annually.[14]

Economic growth made for higher living standards. The average French citizen's income nearly tripled between 1946 and 1962, producing a wholesale transformation of consumer patterns.[15] For example, between 1946 and 1962, the proportion of homes with running water more than doubled. The number of automobiles registered in France increased from under 5 million in 1959 to 14 million in 1973. The number of housing units built annually increased from 290,000 to 500,000 during the same period. In sum, after a century of economic stagnation, France leapfrogged into the twentieth century.

May 1968 and Beyond: Economic Crisis and Political Conflict

Despite the dramatic economic growth of the 1950s and 1960s, many resented the way that economic restructuring had been carried out. Political scientist Peter A. Hall identified a central dilemma in the planning process: "The reorganization of production to attain great[er] efficiency tends to intensify the social conflict that planning is also supposed to prevent."[16] The most dramatic evidence of the regime's fragility occurred in a massive wave of unrest and strikes in May 1968. The opposition movement was triggered by a variety of causes: government-imposed wage restraints, the reduction of trade union representation on the governing boards of the Social Security (public health) system, and the rapid expansion of higher education. (Universities were hastily constructed with inadequate provision of facilities and guidance for students.)

May 1968 was a massive movement of diverse groups united in their opposition to the way that a distant state was deciding their fate with little grassroots consultation or participation. Although the movement was overcome, it ushered in a period of intense labor mobilization. Strikes in the early 1970s were frequent and often involved highly militant tactics, such as seizing factories, sequestering managers, and even organizing production directly. Striking workers challenged harsh authority in the workplace, speedups in the pace of work, and technological innovations that increased workplace hazards. A rapid increase in female employment (see Figure 1), beginning in the early 1970s, also produced some important strikes when women protested against employers attempted to provide them with fewer benefits than men (see photo on p. 95).

As a result of their militance, workers gained increased rights and benefits, and the state and employers' associations sought to achieve stability by organizing collective bargaining at industrywide and national levels. But a political challenge from the Left, and widening economic crisis, thwarted these efforts.

In 1972, the two largest left-wing opposition parties, the Communist Party (PCF) and Socialist Party (reformed and renamed the Parti Socialiste in 1969), forged a coalition that seemed poised to gain power in the near future. The alliance, named the Union of the Left, advocated substantial economic and social changes, notably, increasing the number of state-owned banks and industrial firms, labor law reform, and increased social welfare spending.

Economic Instability

The Left's fortunes were further improved when severe economic strains in the 1970s tarnished the reputation

The expansion of women working outside the home.

Figure 1

Women in the Labor Force

Source: INSEE, in Louis Dim, *La Société française en tendances* (Paris: PUF, 1990), 108.

of the governing conservative coalition. First, as the substantial shift of workers out of agriculture and from rural to urban areas began to reach its limit, gains in productivity began to slow down. Further, France was badly damaged by international economic shocks. Heavily dependent on imported oil, France was squeezed when petroleum prices increased sharply in the 1970s. The restructuring of international capitalism in the 1970s damaged French industry in two ways. On the one hand, the newly developing nations, such as Taiwan, South Korea, and Brazil, began to out-compete France in such basic industrial sectors as textiles, steel, and shipbuilding. French firms not only began to be less competitive internationally but also lost substantial shares of the domestic market to foreign competition. Hundreds of thousands of jobs were eliminated in these three industries alone; for example, more than one-third of all steelworkers were permanently laid off. Entire regions were devastated.

On the other hand, the French economy was battered by technological advances achieved by other industrialized nations. France was too small to be a world leader in micro-electronics, bioengineering, and robotics, and U.S. and Japanese producers rapidly captured markets in these fields. Thus, at the very time that the country needed to increase exports in order to finance the increased costs of petroleum, French firms were losing export markets to the fastest-growing Third World nations, where wage costs were low, and importing high technology from advanced capitalist leaders.

The new trends provoked a crisis in the French model of development. The postwar approach was highly successful in sponsoring crash programs for industrial reconstruction and modernization. But in the new, more competitive world, it was necessary to adapt rapidly, decentralize economic decision making, and outcompete foreign firms. Success today is achieved by creative breakthroughs, not emulation. The inadequacy of the postwar approach was driven home when it was refurbished and extended by the Socialist government in the early 1980s—with very mixed results.

French Socialism in Practice—and Conservative Aftermath

After conservative governments failed to meet the economic challenges of the 1970s, the Left finally gained the chance to try. A new era began in 1981, when the Socialist and Communist parties gained power after twenty-three years in opposition. François Mitterrand soundly defeated incumbent President Valéry Giscard d'Estaing in the 1981 presidential election.

Mitterrand immediately dissolved the conservative-dominated National Assembly and called for new elections. Capitalizing on Mitterrand's popularity, the Socialist Party obtained an absolute majority of seats, giving the government a free hand to enact its reform proposals. The Socialist government sponsored a range of economic measures to revive the ailing economy, create jobs, and recapture domestic markets. The major reforms included:

- a hefty boost in social benefits, including increases in the minimum wage, family allowances, old-age pensions, rent subsidies, and state-mandated paid vacations, from four to five weeks each year
- the creation of public-sector employment
- a vigorous industrial policy, including state assistance to develop cutting-edge industrial technologies (such as biotech, telecommunications, and aerospace)
- a hefty expansion of **nationalization** in the industrial and banking sectors

On two previous occasions French governments had extended public control over the economy, the Socialist government of Léon Blum during the Popular Front of 1936–1938 and in 1946 after the end of World War II. In 1981–1983, the Socialist government went further. As a result of the nationalization measures, public sector firms accounted for 28 percent of gross domestic production (an increase of 7 percent), 23 percent of French exports (compared to the previous level of 11 percent), and 36 percent of investments (from 29 percent).[17] Thirteen of France's twenty largest industrial firms and virtually all banks were now in the public sector.

The Socialist approach was a radicalized version of the postwar *dirigiste* approach, supplemented by newly created mechanisms for increasing participation by rank-and-file workers and labor unions in economic decision-making. (For example, labor unions gained greater rights on the shop floor and at higher levels, and new channels were set up to provide for worker consultation.)

How successful was the Socialist program? On the one hand, many French citizens reaped significant benefits, and many of the newly nationalized firms, which were in financial difficulties when they were nationalized, were put on a firmer footing thanks to the infusion of government subsidies. But the program failed in one decisive respect: it did not revive economic growth, which was needed to create new jobs and generate the revenues for the added government spending. There were two reasons: first, French business executives and international investors were hostile to the government's policy orientation. Rather than investing in French industry, they exported capital abroad. Second, an international recession in the early 1980s meant that French firms had difficulty exporting their products whereas the benefits distributed by French government spending were often used to buy foreign imports. In brief, many of the benefits from the reforms were reaped by foreign firms.

Many of the Socialist reforms helped to modernize the French economy, society, and state in the long run. However, in the short run, the cost of the reforms provoked a severe economic crisis that drove France to the brink of bankruptcy. Budget deficits soared, international investors avoided France like the plague, and France's international currency reserves were rapidly exhausted. Something had to give—and fast.

The crisis cruelly demonstrated how limited was the margin of maneuver for a medium-rank power like France. Mitterrand's government was soon forced to choose between reversing its reformist course or adopting strong protectionist measures to shield France from international pressures. The latter strategy involved high risks, because it would provoke international isolation—especially since conservative-minded leaders held office in Washington, Bonn, and London at the time. After intense soul-searching, Mitterrand ordered a complete about-face in economic policy in 1983. The decision to turn back from radical statism was one of the most important made within the Fifth Republic, and it set France on a conservative course from which it has not departed since.

France's Neo-Liberal Modernization Strategy

Although the state has relaxed control over the economy, it maintains significant direct and indirect influence over market forces. Among the most important elements in economic policy orientation since 1983 are privatization, deregulation and liberalization, and economic policies in conformity with EU directives—what Peter Hall has dubbed "France's neo-liberal modernization strategy."[18]

Privatization.   In the early 1980s, the Socialists had undertaken an ambitious nationalization program. Part of their "right turn" in 1983 involved halting this process. Within a short time, the government began partially privatizing what had only recently been nationalized.

The trend toward **privatization** was pursued with great vigor by the conservative governments that governed in 1986–1988 and 1993–1997, and in more moderate fashion by the Socialist government elected in 1997. A large number of state-owned industrial firms, investment houses, and banks were sold to private investors. The sweeping change reflects an assumption—quite new to France—that the state should not own or direct firms that are in the competitive sector. An even more sweeping change involves firms in the transportation, power, and communications sectors, which were formerly considered public monopolies. Many, including Air France, France Télécom, and Eléctricité de France (the sprawling firm which supervises electric power generation and distribution), are in the process of being partially or wholly privatized. Some of France's most intense conflicts pits the government against workers in these firms who oppose the shift.

Although privatization apparently represents a total shift from public to private control, this appearance is misleading. First, the state granted a small number of large investors (with whom it has close relations) a controlling share in privatized firms in order to maintain informal state leverage and management stability. Second, the state often retained a considerable say in the management of the privatized firms because state-owned firms and banks (notably, the giant savings bank network which operates through the postal system) were usually part of the favored few investors (the "hard core," as they were called) who purchased controlling blocks of stock in the newly privatized firms. Third, state influence continued in an indirect way as a result of continuity in managerial ranks.

Many of France's largest firms, including the privatized firms, are directed by executives who are graduates of state-run elite schools to train civil servants. These graduates remain steeped in a statist tradition, are life-long members of state networks (the *grands corps*, described in Section 3), and move back and forth between positions in the public and private sectors. Thus, there remains a dense network of relations between the state and private business firms.

Most of the sales of newly created shares in the privatized firms were highly successful. Selling state-owned firms generated tens of hundreds of billions of francs in public revenues. Privatization also altered French social structure by substantially increasing the number of stockholders in France. The number of French citizens owning shares of stock increased from under two million to approximately eight million, which helped promote what conservative governments called "people's capitalism" in France.

Opponents of privatization—primarily on the Left of the political spectrum, and especially the Communist Party—charged that the process represented the sale of vital public assets at bargain-basement prices, and that the most affluent citizens were reaping the lion's share of the benefits. In some cases, employees of firms slated for privatization waged strikes to protest the change, on the grounds that their hard-won benefits—good wages and fringe benefits, job security, and rights to representation within the firm—would be in peril. In general, their fears were justified. Indeed, one of the forces driving privatization was the desire to cut costs by reducing jobs and employee benefits. Political leaders reasoned that it would be less damaging politically if benefits cutbacks were carried out by executives of private firms. These strikes, often in key sectors like transportation, have caused considerable disruption and political damage for the government.

Privatization has occurred in other European countries (including formerly communist countries in East and Central Europe). However, within West Europe, the move is especially noteworthy in France because it marks such a departure from the traditionally preeminent role of the state.

Deregulation and Liberalization. Before the shift away from *dirigisme* in 1983, the state exercised close supervision over the economy. State regulations defined technical standards, specified market share, set prices and terms of credit, and even determined where investments were permitted. Policymakers provided themselves and private firms with the space to pursue these policies by erecting stiff tariffs to shelter French producers. The state regulated labor markets to protect workers. It limited employers' freedom to schedule work-time and promote and fire workers. For example, employers were required to obtain administrative authorization to reduce the workforce for economic reasons, and to obtain such approval usually involved providing workers with significant benefits. For many matters, employers needed the approval not merely of one administrative authority but of administrators in a host of bureaus and ministries. In brief, the French economy often seemed to be strangled by kilometers of red tape.

Some state regulations were beneficial. Consumers benefited when the administration set high standards and rigorously enforced them. For example, the French transportation network had an enviable safety record, and workers benefited when state labor inspectors prevented arbitrary employer actions.

However, since 1983 there has been a strong trend toward **deregulation**. In many sectors, the state has loosened or eliminated restrictions on private enterprise. For example, employers no longer need to obtain administrative authorization to lay off workers, and they have greater freedom to schedule work in a flexible manner. Price controls have been largely eliminated.

Deregulation has been especially sweeping in the financial sector, where the elaborate framework of state supervision, subsidized loans, differential interests rates, and credit rationing has been substantially eliminated. Today, market forces, not Ministry of Finance officials, determine who should receive loans, how much, and at what interest rates. Private firms are forced to fend for themselves, both for better—since they are forced to be more efficient—and for worse— since loans are given according to strictly economic criteria, which may not take into account what is in the interest of society.

Deregulation has meant that French firms can no longer rely on tariffs, technical standards, and government policies to shield them from foreign

Global Connection: *France and the European Union*

France has been a charter member and one of the most powerful states in the European Union since it was founded in 1958. (The EU was originally known as the European Economic Community.) Before World War II, France had preferred isolation to international cooperation. But three devastating wars in less than a century between France and Germany taught both countries that there was no alternative but to cooperate. The EU has proved to be the most effective mechanism for fostering closer ties between the two countries and the other member states of the organization. (The number of members has steadily increased, from the original seven to thirteen at the end of the century.) Indeed, French and German support for the EU has been essential to the EU's success. The EU has gained great credit from having contributed to the vast increase in prosperity and political stability in Western Europe in the past decades. As a result of the EU's sponsorship of lower tariffs among member states, as well as other measures to liberalize trade and investment, France has developed extremely close economic relations with her West European neighbors. The EU has emerged as one of the three major economic regions in the world, along with North America and East Asia.

France has played a leading role within the EU from the beginning—although when Charles de Gaulle was president between 1958 and 1969, he did not hesitate to produce some notable crises to prevent the organization from limiting France's freedom of action! The two most powerful leaders of the EU have both been French—Jean Monnet, the first director of the organization (he came to be known as the Father of Europe), and Jacques Delors, president of the European Commission, the administrative directorate of the EU, from 1984 to 1994.

French participation in the EU has not been costless. Many French citizens fear that France's distinctive culture and identity are being blurred by membership in the EU. Some EU decisions have produced painful results for France, including economic austerity and the need to alter some government policies and decisions to conform with EU regulations.

The introduction of the euro in 1999 ushered in a new and even closer phase of economic integration. It resulted from a historically unprecedented decision by France and other members of the European Monetary Union (linked to the EU) to delegate key decisions over monetary policy to the newly created, independent European Central Bank. Will the outcome produce further gains—or economic hardship and a political backlash? Stay tuned.

competition. French businesses must now compete with foreign firms as never before both at home and abroad. In brief, the new policy stance relies heavily on market competition to achieve economic and technological modernization.

The Impact of the European Union.   France's participation in the EU has been a critical factor in strengthening the move toward a reduced role for the state in economic management (see Global Connection: France and the European Union). It was no coincidence that when Mitterrand abandoned more traditional Socialist goals in 1983, he turned toward revitalizing European integration. Some scholars assert that he exchanged the project of socialism within France—which proved unrealistic in any event, in part because of the existence of conservative governments elsewhere—for a European project.

The adoption of the Single European Act in 1987, the Maastricht Treaty in 1991, and the Stabilization Pact in 1997 tied France ever more tightly to its European neighbors. The Maastricht Treaty required member states to adopt austerity measures, called **convergence criteria**, in order to qualify for participation in a common European currency, the euro. States had to cut annual budget deficits to under 3 percent of the GDP (in the mid-1990s the French government deficit was nearly twice this amount), limit total public debt to under 60 percent of the GDP, and grant its central bank independence from its government so that it could pursue anti-inflationary economic policies.

The policy changes mandated by Maastricht often conflicted with traditional patterns of the French political economy. For example, the Banque de France, France's central bank, was traditionally under government control and regulated the banking industry and set interest rates in accordance with government policy. However, the government sponsored legislation in 1994 which considerably enhanced the independence of the Banque de France. Directors of the bank now are appointed for fixed terms of six years and cannot be dismissed under normal circumstances.

The adoption of a plan for European Monetary Union (EMU) in 1991 and the launching of the euro in 1999 were of central importance. The European Central Bank (ECB), comprised mostly of bankers, was set up in 1998 to control the euro for the eleven member states whose currencies will be replaced by the euro by 2002. Most members of the EU participated in launching the euro; the major exception was Britain (see Chapter 2).

The ECB has the authority to regulate interest rates, the euro's exchange rates, and the size of the money supply of member states in order to prevent inflation. Critics charge that this single-minded pursuit of price stability comes at the expense of other worthy goals, such as economic growth and job creation; and one of Prime Minister Jospin's aims was to persuade other governments in the EMU to give priority to economic expansion and job creation.

The goal of currency reform is to produce a vast unified economy. The eleven states have an economy as large as that of the United States: each accounted for about one-fifth of the world's total annual production. By creating a common currency, it became far easier for firms in the EU to invest and trade across borders of the member states. Presumably, this produces gains in efficiency which should provide benefits to all concerned. But the adoption of the euro, as well as other measures promoting greater economic integration, also involves costs for states and citizens. When states like France pool and delegate to EU officials power to regulate the currency, interest rates, and the exchange rate, state officials and citizens lose control over core elements of sovereignty. This restricts the arenas in which citizens and state officials can influence policy choices. The "democratic deficit" within the EU may signify reduced accountability by those who make key decisions affecting citizens' economic and social life.

Not surprisingly, the new policy initiatives encountered stiff popular resistance. French voters came within a hair of rejecting the 1991 referendum on the Maastricht Treaty. Even more dramatic was the reaction in 1995 when the government announced a program of austerity measures designed to qualify France for the launching of the euro. In 1995, conservative Prime Minister Alain Juppé, at President Chirac's direction, announced cutbacks in state social programs, including retirement benefits for railway workers, civil servants' salaries, and reimbursement for medical costs. Massive strikes by public sector workers (in varied sectors, including transportation, postal service, and schools) threatened the Juppé government's very existence (see Section 5). However, despite marginal differences among the economic policies of different governments since 1983, none has openly challenged the orientation chosen at that time.

The End of Dirigisme or Dirigiste Disengagement?

If the French have turned toward neo-liberalism, they have done so in a distinctively French manner. Political scientist Vivien Schmidt observes that France has not

> abandoned its statist model. . . . The state . . . remains embedded in French culture and embodied in its institutions, with change able to come only through the state, not against it. . . . Governments have not stopped seeking to guide business, albeit in more indirect ways . . . and they as always play a primary role in deciding the direction of economic growth and the shape and organization of economic activity, even as they engineer the retreat of the state.[19]

Schmidt calls the shift in France's political economy "*dirigiste* disengagement." In recent years, the state has supervised the retrenchment of industries like steel and shipbuilding, rather than their expansion, as occurred in the earlier period. It has steered the French economy toward integration within the EU and has shifted its efforts toward exerting influence on EU institutions. This is *dirigisme* of a different—and less overbearing—sort, but, for better or worse, statism is still alive and well in France.

Society and Economy

Relations between management and labor have been a problem that has traditionally hindered economic performance. Typically, French workers have gained benefits by protest at work and in the streets rather than by cooperating with their employers, as in Germany. It took the May 1968 uprising for labor unions to gain the right to organize plant-level locals. Until the Socialist government sponsored labor reforms in the early 1980s, including the obligation for French employers to bargain collectively over wages and hours, French workers did not enjoy benefits that workers in northern European nations had gained decades earlier. Because the labor movement has traditionally been quite weak, it was especially vulnerable during the recent period of economic crisis and restructuring. The French labor movement has suffered severe declines in membership, and less than 10 percent of the wage-earning population currently belongs to a labor union.

In part because of working-class pressure exercised in the streets and through political parties, French governments have enacted among the most extensive cradle-to-grave welfare state programs of any country in the world. State-provided and/or financed social services begin before birth, for pregnant women are entitled to free prenatal care. The Social Security system, as it is called in France, provides nearly free health care for all citizens, and the elderly enjoy a quite generous system of old-age pensions. French citizens have access to excellent low-cost public day care facilities—staffed by teachers with advanced training who receive good salaries. Checks are sent monthly to families with more than one child (a measure aimed at checking the declining birth rate).

Public education is excellent in France, and all students who pass a stiff high school graduation exam are entitled to virtually free university education. An extensive system of public housing and rent subsidies makes housing affordable for most citizens. Workers enjoy a minimum wage nearly double the level prevailing in the United States, five weeks of paid vacation annually, and additional training throughout their working lives financed by a tax on employers. There is an extensive system of unemployment insurance and benefits for retraining in the event of layoffs. A program created in 1988 provides minimum income for the long-term unemployed. In 1998, the Jospin government legislated a reduction in the legal work week to 35 hours in order to encourage job creation.

The French are fiercely attached to their system of extensive social protection and regard it as an alternative to the American market model, in which citizens are held responsible for their fate. In the American model, state services are meant only to provide the bare minimum for those who have failed to purchase services in the private market. In France, it is generally believed that the state should provide generous benefits on a universal basis—not only to the very poor. An American journalist described the French welfare state "as a global ideological rival" to the American social and economic pattern.[20]

Despite the state's provision of social services, free-market competition generates winners and losers in France as elsewhere. The French have coined the term "the social fracture" to describe the existence of a permanently excluded group of citizens—those without stable jobs, the long-term unemployed, the poor, and/or the homeless. The precise number of people at the bottom is hard to determine, but the number of homeless in France has been estimated at between 200,000 and 500,000; soup kitchens organized by nonprofit organizations serve 500,000 meals daily to the poor.[21] Nearly two million citizens receive grants under the minimum income program for the impoverished and long-term unemployed. Although the program was designed to help reintegrate this group into the French economy and society, few recipients of the grants have been able to find stable employment. Thus, France's prosperous economy and ample welfare state do not prevent large numbers of citizens from being excluded from full participation in French society. Although there have been fewer welfare cutbacks in France than in many countries, one finds the same tendency toward growing economic inequality. One result has been increased social unrest. In 1997, unemployed workers occupied many of France's unemployment offices, to the great embarrassment of the recently elected Socialist government of Lionel Jospin. Although the Jospin government proposed a package of measures to assist the unemployed and the excluded, it is unlikely they will succeed in solving the problem.

A related dilemma in recent years involves the rising costs of the welfare state. On one hand, the "Sécu" (as the system of health and retirement benefits is known) is among the most popular programs in France. Prior to 1995, not even conservative governments dared attack it frontally. However, the welfare state has become increasingly costly, due to rising medical costs, high levels of unemployment, a slowdown in birth rates (which means fewer active workers are available to contribute to finance welfare benefits), and a growing ratio of retired to younger workers. (For example, the proportion of elderly will double by 2050; currently, there are three French adults who work for every retired worker. In 2050, the ratio will drop to 1.5 workers for every retired worker.) At the same time, the government faces severe pressure to contain costs, as a result of international economic competition, citizen opposition to tax increases, and France's participation in the EU. These conflicting pressures have produced intense political controversy. Prime Minister Juppé's proposal for reorganizing the public health system in 1995, involving benefits cutbacks, was one cause of the extensive strikes that immobilized France at year's end and swept the conservative coalition from office in 1997. But the pressures to reduce state spending did not vanish. In 1998 Lionel Jospin, who led the Socialist coalition that ousted Juppé, was forced to impose an income ceiling for families receiving child care payments from the state. This signified a challenge to the principle of universal access to benefits and could narrow the coalition of those supporting these programs.

One of the key reasons for rising welfare costs is that so many French citizens cannot find a job. Thus, there are fewer workers who pay the taxes that support the welfare state and more citizens who are claimants for state benefits. Since the 1980s, France has experienced double-digit unemployment rates, among the highest of the industrialized nations. Youth, immigrants, and women are considerably more likely to be out of work. The Socialist government sponsored a plan in 1997 to create 700,000 jobs in the nonprofit and public sector for unemployed youth. For years, voters have consistently ranked unemployment the most important problem in France, and successive governments' inability to reduce unemployment has contributed to the frequent electoral gyrations of the recent period.

The centerpiece of the reform program sponsored by the Jospin government was a measure to create jobs by work sharing. Legislation taking effect in 2000 orders firms employing 20 or more workers to reduce the work week to 35 hours. The government reasoned that, to offset the shorter work week, employers would need to create additional jobs. Critics charged that the reform would simply increase France's wage costs and make its economy less competitive. Time will tell which side is correct.

France and the International Political Economy

France benefited for centuries from its relatively large size, ample natural resources, skilled workers, and a large internal market. By going it alone, the French economy performed remarkably well until the 1970s. France remains a major world economic power. But as global economic integration and competition have increased, France chose to pool its resources with other European countries within the framework of the European Union. France's position in the international political economy has become heavily influenced by its participation in the EU.

As described above, the Socialist reformist experiment of the early 1980s may have been France's last attempt to pursue solitary state-directed economic expansion. When the attempt failed, President Mitterrand proposed revitalizing Europe as an alternative project. The decade that followed witnessed an enormous expansion in the scope and intensity of European economic integration. France's economic fate has become intensely intertwined with that of Western Europe. For example, in the 1990s over 60 percent of its imports and exports were with other member states of the EU.

The style of economic governance in the EU is closer to that of Britain or Germany than France. EU regulations prohibit states from engaging in the kind of *dirigisme* that was the hallmark of the French state in the postwar period: for example, credit rationing, subsidies, and state ownership. As a result, France is forced to make greater adjustments in its style of economic management than is the case for other member countries of the EU.

Furthermore, EU membership has drawbacks. For example, in order to qualify for the euro membership in the EMU, member states were forced to make economic cutbacks in government spending—and this just when high levels of unemployment might have suggested the wisdom of increasing government programs to stimulate the economy. The intense public-sector strikes in France in the 1990s, as well as the political pendulum swings that have produced frequent electoral shifts, are a direct response to this situation.

Section ❸   Government and Policy-Making

Organization of the State

Despite the frequent changes of regimes in France in the past two centuries, three important underpinnings of the French state have remained nearly constant—at least, until recently. First, for centuries there was nearly universal agreement on the value of a unitary state. Since the French Revolution, subnational governments have been regarded as an administrative arm of the state based in Paris; their primary purpose is to help implement national policy. Although the French remain united on maintaining the unitary character of the state, an important change occurred in the 1980s when the Socialist government transferred substantial powers to local governments. A new spirit of local autonomy is evident.

Second, most French supported the long-established tradition of statism, reviewed in Sections 1 and 2, which claims that the state should play an active role in directing the society and economy. This tradition has also been challenged in recent years.

The third change involves limits on state action from within the state itself. Until recently, the French accorded relatively little importance to the principle of constitutional supremacy. It may be surprising to learn that a nation that emphasizes the importance of formalized legal codes and that, along with the United States, boasts the modern world's first written constitution, did not consider that the constitution should be scrupulously respected. French political practice reflected the view that representatives chosen by democratic elections should have a free hand to govern and not be hindered by constitutional or judicial restraint. Judges in France have traditionally enjoyed little autonomy and, indeed, have been considered part of the executive branch. This too has changed in the recent past. The Constitution of the Fifth Republic has come to be regarded as the authoritative source for allocating power among political institutions; the judiciary has gained the vital power to strike down legislation and executive decisions on the grounds that they violate the Constitution.

Principles of Constitutional Power

The Fifth Republic is usually described as a **semi-presidential system**, combining elements of presidential and parliamentary systems. In a wholly presidential system, as in the United States, the executive and the legislature are chosen separately and neither is answerable to the other. The legislature and executive have independent powers and neither controls the agenda of the other. Moreover, both institutions have fixed terms in office and neither the government nor the legislature can force the other to resign and face new elections.

In a parliamentary system, as in Britain, the executive and legislature are fused. The government is accountable to the parliament and must resign if the parliament passes a motion of no-confidence. At the same time, the government has substantial control over the parliamentary agenda and can dissolve the parliament, thereby provoking new elections.

In the Fifth Republic, both the president and parliament are popularly elected. The president is elected for a fixed term and can be removed only by impeachment. (For the president to be impeached in France, a text must be voted in identical terms by an absolute majority of both houses of parliament. The president's case is then judged by a High Court of Justice composed of twelve deputies and twelve senators elected from and by the two houses.) The government is appointed by the president but is answerable to parliament. As in parliamentary systems, the National Assembly (the more powerful house of parliament) can force the government to resign by voting a motion of no-confidence, what the French call a motion of censure.

Why is the Fifth Republic a *semi*-presidential system? The "semi" refers to the fact that in several respects, notably, the existence of a government that is responsible to parliament, the legislature and executive are not wholly separate, as they are in a "pure" presidential system. The system is called semi-presidential, not semi-parliamentary, because the executive dominates parliament, not the other way around. Whenever the political system of the Fifth Republic deviates from the purely parliamentary or the purely presidential model, the result is to strengthen the executive—primarily the president. The executive largely controls the parliamentary agenda and can dissolve parliament and provoke new elections. There is thus a *fusion* of executive and legislative powers characteristic of parliamentary regimes in a manner that strengthens the executive. But there is a *separation* of powers in that the National Assembly *cannot* pass a censure motion forcing the president to resign. The result is a particularly sharp imbalance between executive and legislature.

Despite criticism that the executive is unduly powerful, the Fifth Republic has become one of the most stable regimes in French history. One poll found that 61 percent of the French judged that political institutions have functioned well in the Fifth Republic. An overwhelming majority of 89 percent supported popular election of the president—a controversial innovation when it was introduced in 1962—and 91 percent approved of the constitutional provision that provides for the holding of a popular referendum.[22] For the first time in modern French history political conflicts are played out within a widely accepted institutional framework.

Since the beginning of the 1980s, the Fifth Republic has survived two important political challenges: first, a shift in political control (alternation) from one political coalition to another; and second, **cohabitation**, as it is called by the French, or power-sharing, which occurs when opposing coalitions control the presidency and parliament.

The first alternation in the history of the Fifth Republic occurred in 1981, when the conservative coalition that ruled since the beginning of the Fifth Republic was defeated by the Socialists. Since then,

alternation has become a normal feature of French political life.

For many years, the French judged that if opposing forces were to gain control of the executive and legislature (cohabitation), political stalemate or worse would occur. The unthinkable finally did occur in 1986. Five years after Mitterrand was elected president, parliamentary elections produced a conservative majority in the National Assembly and Mitterrand appointed Jacques Chirac, leader of the conservative forces, prime minister. The event proved to be the mouse that roared. The two found workable solutions to governing together and, despite a few tremors, the regime held firm. The first period of cohabitation ended in 1988, when Mitterrand was reelected president. He immediately dissolved the National Assembly and succeeded in sweeping a Socialist plurality into power. When a new period of cohabitation began in 1993, following a conservative victory in legislative elections that year, the rules of the game for such a situation were firmly in place.

Three reasons might be advanced to explain why political institutions have been able to overcome the challenges of alternation and cohabitation. First, the ideological distance between left and right had declined *prior* to these challenges. The gap further diminished after the Socialist government moderated its policies in 1983–1984. Second, the Constitutional Council (a court whose powers will be described below) has effectively maintained a balance (equilibrium) among institutions. Finally, public opinion polls suggested that most French citizens wanted political institutions to function normally. These developments signify a profound change in French political culture, involving a diminution of ideological intensity and the rise of a more moderate, pragmatic political style.

The Triple Executive

Besides Russia, France is the only major country with a semi-presidential system. In parliamentary regimes, the head of state—either a president or a monarch—exercises purely ceremonial duties, while the bulk of executive power is wielded by the head of government, who is responsible to parliament. In France, the president is not only the head of state but also enjoys substantial policy-making and executive power.

The president is far from all-powerful, however, since he (there has not yet been a woman president of France) shares executive and policy-making powers with the prime minister and the cabinet. Particularly during periods of cohabitation, the prime minister's constitutional powers sharply limit presidential leadership. Although the president names the prime minister and other members of the government, the National Assembly (the lower house of parliament) can force the government to resign by voting a motion of no-confidence. Thus, when the National Assembly is controlled by a majority hostile to the president—the situation during cohabitation—the president must bow to political realities and appoint a government that represents opposing political forces. In this situation, the government, not the president, controls most major policy decisions, although both the president and prime minister have important reasons to cooperate, despite their differences, since voters might punish both leaders if gridlock occurred.

To describe France as having a dual executive, as many do, obscures the power of the bureaucracy, a third key element of the executive. The bureaucracy is a large and sprawling organization that reaches far and wide to regulate French society. (See our discussion later in this section.) The three pillars of the executive provide the motor force of the French state.

The President

As long as both the executive and the legislature are controlled by the same party coalition, what we will term *united control*, the powers of the French president are immense. During cohabitation, what we will term *divided control* of the executive, the pendulum swings toward greater balance between president and prime minister. During periods of unified control, the president, who is elected for a seven-year term, combines the independent powers of the U.S. president—notably, command of the executive establishment and independence from legislative control—with the powers that accrue to the government in a parliamentary regime—namely, control over parliament's agenda and the ability to dissolve parliament and force new elections. Indeed, the government, under the president's direction, controls parliament more tightly than is the case in other parliamentary democracies. The

result is a greater degree of executive dominance than in virtually any other democratic nation.

The president occupies the office at the very top of this commanding edifice. The presidency has become so powerful for three reasons: (1) the towering personalities of Charles de Gaulle, the founder and first president of the Fifth Republic (who was president between 1958 and 1969), and François Mitterrand, the Socialist president who held office from 1981 to 1995; (2) the ample powers conferred on the office by the Constitution; (3) the political practices of the Fifth Republic.

Presidential personalities. Charles de Gaulle (1890–1970) was unquestionably the most influential French politician in the twentieth century. He first achieved prominence in leading the Resistance forces in France during World War II. De Gaulle shaped the political institutions of the Fifth Republic to provide strong nonpartisan leadership in order to enable France to exercise maximum power on the the world stage. As the first president of the Fifth Republic, de Gaulle set the precedent for a strong, active president and pursued policies that considerably increased France's economic and political position.

The two presidents after de Gaulle, Georges Pompidou and Valéry Giscard d'Estaing (both of whom were de Gaulle's political allies), were pale shadows of the Fifth Republic's first president. The next president to use presidential powers to the full was François Mitterrand. Mitterrand was a youthful leader in the Resistance during World War II and an ally of de Gaulle, but personal ambition soon divided the two. Mitterrand charged that de Gaulle had created a presidential office that would allow him to exercise power in an arbitrary and authoritarian manner. Mitterrand succeeded in remaking the Socialist Party into a major alternative to the Gaullist coalition and, in 1981, on his third try, he defeated the incumbent president, Giscard d'Estaing. Thus began Mitterrand's fourteen-year reign, the longest presidential term in the history of the Fifth Republic.

The supreme irony is that, as president, Mitterrand ruled in a manner strikingly similar to that of his archrival, de Gaulle. Many of the criticisms he had leveled at de Gaulle were applied to Mitterrand: He was solitary, capricious, and monarchical in his governing style. As he humorously remarked soon after taking office in 1981, "The institutions of the Fifth Republic weren't created with me in mind, but they suit me fine!" Under Mitterrand, the Left became fully integrated within the institutions of the Fifth Republic.

The Constitutional Presidency.   The Constitution of the Fifth Republic endows the president with the ceremonial powers of head of state. He is the fortunate occupant of the resplendent Elysée Palace in a fashionable section of Paris, he is the symbolic embodiment of the majestic French state, and he enjoys preeminence over the prime minister at international diplomatic gatherings.

The Constitution also grants the president important political powers that had belonged to the prime minister in the past, as well as new powers not exercised in previous republics. Thus, the president both symbolizes the unity and majesty of the state and actively participates in political decision-making.

The president, the only official chosen in a nationwide election, is elected for a term of seven years, a long period that in itself bolsters presidential power. (The office of vice president does not exist in France; if a president dies in office, a new election is held within a short time and the newly elected president begins a new seven-year term.) The system of direct election provides the president with powerful personal support and probably bolsters the legitimacy of the entire regime.

In order to be nominated for president, a candidate must obtain the signatures of hundreds of local elected officials throughout France. (Unlike the U.S. Constitution, there are no requirements regarding minimum age or the necessity to be a French citizen.) The requirement is not too demanding, however, and in all elections there are many candidates—usually more than five. In reality, only candidates nominated by the major political parties (see Section 4) stand any chance of winning.

A two-ballot system of election is used for presidential elections. To win on the first ballot, a candidate must obtain an absolute majority, that is, over 50 percent of those voting. If no candidate receives a majority, a runoff election is held between the two front-runners. Since many candidates compete, it is unlikely that any candidate will gain an absolute majority at the first ballot. Thus far there have been runoffs in all six presidential elections held by universal suffrage in the Fifth Republic.

Presidents are eligible for reelection without limit. President Giscard d'Estaing was seeking reelection in 1981 when he lost to François Mitterrand. Only Mitterrand served two full seven-year terms. Given the enormous powers of the presidential office, there are periodic proposals to amend the Constitution, either to reduce the presidential term to five years or limit presidents to a single seven-year term. Critics charge that it is undemocratic to elect someone to such a powerful office for such a long term without adequate mechanisms of accountability.

The Constitution grants the president vital political powers, including the right to:

- name the prime minister and approve the prime minister's choice of other cabinet officials, as well as name other high-ranking civil, military, and judicial officials.
- preside over meetings of the Council of Ministers (the government). Note that the president, not the prime minister, is charged with this responsibility.
- conduct foreign affairs, through the power to negotiate and ratify treaties, as well as to name French ambassadors and accredit foreign ambassadors to France.
- direct the armed forces, bolstered by a 1964 decree which grants the president exclusive control over France's nuclear forces.
- dissolve the National Assembly and call for new elections. However, if the president has dissolved the National Assembly, he cannot do so again for a year.
- appoint three of the nine members of the Constitutional Council, including its president, and refer bills passed by parliament to the Council to determine if they conform to the Constitution.

Four other constitutional grants of power further strengthen the president's position. Article 16 authorizes the president to assume emergency powers when, in his judgment, the institutions of the republic, the independence of the nation, the integrity of its territory, or the execution of France's international (treaty) commitments is threatened.

Article 89 authorizes the president, with the approval of the prime minister, to propose constitutional amendments. An amendment must be approved by a majority of both houses of parliament and ratified either by a national referendum or by a three-fifths vote of a congress composed of both houses of parliament. The amendment procedure has been used with increasing frequency in recent years.

Article 11, amended in 1995, authorizes the president to sponsor a national referendum to approve policy initiatives or reorganize political institutions, provided that the proposed change is first approved by the government. The use of the referendum in the Fifth Republic creates a direct link between the president and citizens, and thus represents a sharp break with French parliamentary traditions and practice.

However, because of the custom that a president whose referendum is defeated should resign, calling a referendum is a high-risk strategy. It is doubtful that future presidents will sponsor many referenda.

Presidential power is greatly bolstered by Article 5, which directs the president "to ensure, by his arbitration, the regular functioning of the governmental authorities, as well as the continuance of the State. He shall be the guarantor of national independence, of the integrity of the territory, and of respect for . . . agreements and treaties." Because the president is the sole official charged with arbitrating and guaranteeing national independence, the Constitution confers on the office enormous legitimacy and power over the state machinery.

The Political President.   The Constitution creates a powerful office on paper. However, to be effective, a president must translate formal powers into the actual exercise of influence.

The fact that the president is the only official to be elected by the entire nation sets the office apart. The democratic legitimacy conferred by electoral victory provides a powerful weapon that can be used in the president's combat with the opposition, and can also be useful in keeping the president's own political associates in line.

When the president shares party sympathies with the parties allied within the majority party coalition in the National Assembly, the president is able to name a loyal prime minister and government, and parliament will generally support the president's policies. This was the situation for the nearly three decades from the beginning of the Fifth Republic until 1986. However, the election in 1986 of a conservative parliamentary majority opposed to President Mitterrand represented a fundamental break in the previous pattern of presidential leadership. Since then, periods of cohabitation (1986–1988, 1993–1995, 1997 to present) have alternated with periods of united control.

De Gaulle and successive presidents have used their formal and informal powers to the hilt; the result has been to increase further presidential power. In addition to the constitutional power to designate prime ministers, presidents have successfully claimed the ability to dismiss them as well, thus making the government responsible not only to the National Assembly, as specified in the Constitution, but also to the president. Except during the periods of cohabitation, prime ministers have accepted the fact—nowhere specified in the Constitution—that they serve at the president's pleasure. Presidents have also assumed the power, formally delegated by the Constitution to the government, to develop policy and intervene in virtually any domain that they choose. (A reminder: the situation is very different during cohabitation.)

The Prime Minister and Government

If one referred only to the Constitution, one would be surprised that presidents have made the key policy decisions during most of the Fifth Republic. For the Constitution designates the government, not the president, as the preeminent policy-making institution. Article 20 states that the government "shall determine and direct the policy of the nation. It shall have at its disposal the administration and the armed forces." And Article 21 authorizes the prime minister to "direct the action of the government. He [the prime minister] is responsible for national defense. He assures the execution of the laws." Thus, when governments follow the president's lead, it is because of *political dynamics* rather than *constitutional directive*. In analyzing the policy-making process, it is essential to distinguish between those periods of united party control of the presidency and National Assembly, and periods of divided control.

The government (also known as the cabinet) is a collective body under the prime minister's direction. The Constitution directs the president to appoint the prime minister, who is usually leader of the major party in the dominant parliamentary coalition. The prime minister in turn nominates, and the president appoints, other cabinet ministers. Most cabinet ministers are powerful members of the coalition that controls parliament. (Given France's multiparty system, described in Section 4, it is highly unusual for one party to gain an absolute parliamentary majority. Therefore, the typical situation is that parties that are ideologically close join forces in order to command a majority of parliamentary seats.) Cabinet ministers direct government departments and propose specific policy initiatives which, after receiving the approval of the government and president, constitute the legislative and administrative agenda.

Although the president appoints the government, the Constitution specifies that the government is responsible only to the National Assembly. This means that a government is not constitutionally obliged to resign at the president's request. Only the National Assembly can force a government to resign, by voting a censure motion (a procedure we describe in the next section). Here is one of the important differences between periods of united versus divided party control. When there has been united party control, every prime minister has publicly affirmed the president's right to replace the prime minister and government.

The Constitution of the Fifth Republic is hopelessly confused regarding the respective powers of the president and government. Put differently, there is both a presidential and a parliamentary interpretation of the Constitution. The fact that the Constitution assigns some of the same key powers to *both* the president and prime minister contains the seeds of potential conflict when there is divided control.

Article 21 states that the prime minister is "responsible for national defense," but Article 15 designates the president as "commander of the armed forces" and directs him to preside over key military policy-making committees. Similarly, Article 21 makes the prime minister responsible for directing the government and ensuring the execution of the laws, and empowers the government to direct the bureaucracy; yet Article 5 mandates the president to ensure the regular functioning of governmental authorities and Article 9 directs him to preside over weekly meetings of the council of ministers (that is, the government)! Given this confusion, it is no wonder there was so much uncertainty about how cohabitation would function. However, once the first period of cohabitation began in 1986, political necessity quickly forced President Mitterrand and Prime Minister Chirac to reach an accommodation. Despite some dramatic confrontations, the process of governing was relatively stable and cohabitation became relatively routine when it again occurred in 1993 and 1997.

The prime minister and other government ministers have extensive staff assistance to help them develop policy proposals and direct the immense and far-flung bureaucracy. For example, the prime minister's office includes the general directorate of the public service, the general secretariat of the government, and the general secretariat of defense. By contrast, the president's personal staff numbers around 50 and the entire staff of the presidential office is 600–700. Thus, presidents can at best intervene only selectively to enforce their preeminence. Nonetheless, when the president leads the dominant parliamentary coalition, to which the prime minister and other cabinet ministers belong, there is no doubt about who ranks number one within the executive. During periods of united control, there has never been a major instance when the prime minister and government have not accepted presidential leadership. During periods of cohabitation, on the other hand, the president has little choice but to beat a dignified retreat from center stage and cultivate the image of a statesman presiding over France's longer-run destiny but not immersed in shaping the government's policy orientation.

The prime minister is the second most powerful position in the Fifth Republic. The Constitution specifies that the prime minister directs the bureaucracy and the government and has exclusive responsibility for issuing regulations, which have the force of law. Most prime ministers have been prominent politicians and the office is regarded as a stepping stone to the presidency. Thus far, two prime ministers—Georges Pompidou and Jacques Chirac—have become president.

During periods of united government, the prime minister's most unpleasant function is to serve as

Institutional Intricacies: *Of Presidents and Prime Ministers*

The relationship between the president and prime minister is of central importance in the Fifth Republic. There are two possible situations: (1) when the president and prime minister are political allies, and (2) the periods of cohabitation, when the two are political opponents. The first situation occurred from the beginning of the Fifth Republic in 1958 until 1986. During this long period, when the president enjoyed the support of a parliamentary majority, he was able to name a close political ally as prime minister. The result was undisputed presidential supremacy. Most of the time, presidents selected the prime minister from the ranks of leaders of the majority party coalition. Loyal prime ministers can provide the president with important political assets: parliamentary support for the government's policies, skill in gaining sympathetic media treatment, and experience in directing the state bureaucracy.

Nevertheless, even when the same political coalition controls the presidency and parliament, tensions between the prime minister and president are inevitable. Prime ministers are constantly tempted to stake out a position independent of the president in the hope that, one day, they will move from the Matignon (the prime minister's official residence) to the Elysée. In order to do so, a prime minister must be more than a presidential lapdog.

During cohabitation, the balance shifts from open displays of cooperation to open displays of rivalry. The president cannot expect the prime minister and parliament to support presidential initiatives. The president is now forced to assume the mantle of dignified and ceremonial head of state, while the prime minister assumes the responsibility—and risks—of policy leadership. The situation somewhat resembles that in parliamentary regimes—save that the French prime minister must also contend with the ever-present danger that the president may publicly criticize prime ministerial decisions (the parallel situation in Britain—that the queen would openly oppose the government—is unthinkable). When cohabitation in France occurred in 1986, following the election of a Conservative parliamentary majority, it lasted only briefly because the electoral calendar provided for a presidential election to be held within two years. Mitterrand won reelection that year, dissolved the National Assembly, and persuaded the electorate to produce a Socialist victory (thus ending divided control).

In 1997, the Socialists' victory in legislative elections occurred only two years into President Chirac's seven-year term. This meant that, unless parliament was dissolved before the normal expiration of its five-year term or President Chirac left office before his term expired in 2002, cohabitation would continue for five long years.

---

lightning rod to deflect criticism from the president (see Institutional Intricacies: Of Presidents and Prime Ministers). In general, prime ministers are expected to take responsibility for unpopular decisions and give the president credit for popular actions. As a result, prime ministers generally become increasingly unpopular and are replaced after two or three years in office. Political scientist Robert Elgie describes the thankless position of prime minister: "When things go well, the President often receives the credit. When things go badly, the Prime Minister usually takes the blame. If things go very badly and the President starts to be criticized, then the Prime Minister is replaced. If things go very well and the Prime Minister starts to be praised, then the Prime Minister is also replaced."[23]

The prime minister is responsible for leading the cabinet and assuring its cohesion, which requires him or her to arbitrate conflicts among cabinet ministers over policy and budget priorities. This is no easy matter, for the cabinet is always composed of a coalition of parties with divergent programs and interests. Moreover, it includes France's most prominent and ambitious politicians, who possess an autonomous power base. Thus far in the Fifth Republic, there has been one woman prime minister, Edith Cresson, who directed a Socialist government in 1992–1993.

As we have seen, the prime minister's role is especially important during periods of cohabitation, when he or she takes responsibility for policy formulation and implementation. Of course, this is the situation of prime ministers in parliamentary democracies—except that they do not have to contend with a popularly elected president from a different party coalition! The prime minister's task during cohabitation is to convey the impression of being fully in control so as to gain credit for any positive developments, yet to avoid prolonged confrontation with the president, for this would prove highly unpopular.

As with cabinets in most political systems, the French cabinet is not a forum for searching policy debate or collective decision-making. Cabinet meetings are occasions for announcing decisions made elsewhere and for fulfilling formalities required by the Constitution, such as approving nominations to high administrative positions. The most important policy decisions are made at a higher level—at the Elysée Palace or Matignon (official residence of the prime minister)—or by interministerial committees, which bring together ministers from several departments for a specific policy area. Interministerial committee meetings are smaller and more informal than full cabinet meetings and are headed by the president, prime minister, or their representatives. They are a forum for fuller discussion and decision-making.

The Bureaucracy: An Elite Within the Elite

The most prominent officials in the French state are found in the Elysée, the Matignon, and ornate government ministries scattered throughout Paris. The day-to-day work of the state, however, is performed by a veritable army of administrators who number 2 1/2 million—one for every 22 French citizens! Given France's long-standing *dirigiste* tradition, the bureaucracy has enormous influence over the country's social and economic life. The Fifth Republic bolstered the influence of the bureaucracy by confining parliament's legislative power and authorizing the bureaucracy, under the prime minister's direction, to issue legally binding regulations.

Key positions at the top of the bureaucracy, the sector on which we focus here, command great power. The bureaucracy offers among the most prestigious and powerful career possibilities in France. Having proper educational credentials is essential, since the top posts are reserved for graduates of selective educational institutions, called **grandes écoles**. Competition for admission to these schools is intense: of the over one million students enrolled in higher education at any given time, only 52,000 students are at a *grande école*. At the very top of the educational

pyramid are the handful of the most select *grandes écoles*, which admit about 3,000 students annually.[24]

Students who graduate at the top of their class at a *grande école*, especially the two most prestigious ones, the Ecole Nationale d'Administration and the Ecole Polytechnique, are admitted into an even more select fraternity: one of the **grands corps**, small, specialized, cohesive networks of civil servants. Membership in a *grand corps* is for life, and guarantees a fine salary, excellent position, and considerable power. Members of a *grand corps* leapfrog to the top of the bureaucracy at a remarkably young age. The *grands corps* have informally colonized key positions in leading ministries, meaning that positions in a given sector are reserved for members of a given *corps*. Recently, members of the *grands corps* have also gained top executive positions in large industrial firms and banks. And members of the *grands corps* are well placed to launch political careers, often running for parliament after compiling some administrative experience. Many members of the *grands corps* have become cabinet ministers, several became prime minister, and two—Valéry Giscard d'Estaing and Jacques Chirac—were elected president.

Among the many influential bureaucratic positions, particular mention should be made of what the French term a ministerial *cabinet*, that is, the personal staff advising a government minister. (In order to distinguish the *cabinet*, or personal staff, from the cabinet that is composed of government ministers, we italicize *cabinet* when referring to the former agency.) Members of a *cabinet* are not, strictly speaking, part of the bureaucracy (during the period they are serving in a *cabinet*). Rather, their job is to advise the minister on policy and partisan matters, and informally supervise the bureaucracy in the minister's name. French ministers have considerable power over the bureaucracy, thanks to the help provided by their *cabinets*.

Given the French state's retreat to a more modest role since the 1980s, one might have expected that the *grandes écoles* would decline in importance. But the schools have adapted well to the increased importance of the private sector. After several years of obligatory service in the state bureaucracy, many graduates now migrate to the private sector and obtain attractive positions in large banks and corporations. One study found that nearly half of all chief executives of France's 200 largest firms are graduates of the two top *grandes écoles*.[25]

But all is not well in the French administration. The retreat of the state has affected the morale and social position of civil servants. The increased power of the private sector, as well as the EU's increased role, signifies that the civil service is no longer larger than life. In the past the civil service was regarded as an impartial and nonpartisan instrument. However, once the Gaullist regime blurred the previously sharp boundaries between the civil service and the policy-making/political apparatus, with civil servants moving into high political office, the civil service's reputation for impartiality suffered.

Semipublic Agencies.   Since World War II, France has had an important array of public sector enterprises in basic industry, transportation, energy, telecommunications, and services. Further, the state controlled many investment decisions, both directly, through state-owned industrial firms, and indirectly, as a result of the credit policies of state-controlled banks and the ministry of finance. As discussed in Section 2, this sector was sharply reduced by the sale of state-owned enterprises beginning in the middle 1980s.

Other State Institutions

Army and Police

In all countries, the army and police are key executive agencies that provide the coercive force to enforce state decisions. In some countries, the armed forces play an important role in shaping policy and directing the state. In France, the army has traditionally played a minor role in politics. However, in some exceptional but important cases, the army has played a key role, most recently in 1958, when it helped topple the Fourth Republic and return de Gaulle to power.

The French army has traditionally been regarded as a pillar of the republic because it was a conscript army, that is, all French male youth were subject to the draft. The army was seen as a device for socializing French youth from diverse backgrounds. However, the French pattern seemed quite old-fashioned and costly in an age when mass armies involving draftees with relatively little training have been replaced elsewhere by professional armies. In 1996, President Chirac undertook a major break with the past when he ended conscription, cut back the army, and placed far greater emphasis on professional recruits.

For many years, France deployed its armed forces in its former colonies in Africa and the Pacific to protect repressive client regimes. In the process, France made a mockery of its proclaimed commitments to democracy and universal human rights. For example, an international human rights organization charged France with bolstering a regime in Rwanda that engaged in widespread genocide against the Tutsi population. Prime Minister Jospin announced that the government would no longer bolster dictators in Africa, and the downsizing of France's armed forces may contribute to the policy shift.

The police forces in France enjoy considerable freedom in carrying out their duties, far too much freedom, according to many. The "forces of order," as they are called in France, have a reputation for abusing power, including illegal surveillance, arbitrary actions, and even torture. Immigrants and French citizens from North Africa, black Africa, and the Caribbean are especially liable to be subject to identity checks, strip searches, and other indignities. The judiciary and high executive officials have rarely acted vigorously to restrain the police. At the same time, public opposition to arbitrary police activity has increased so that the situation may improve in the future.

The Judiciary and the Constitutional Council

Traditionally, the French judiciary had little autonomy and was considered an arm of the executive. In the past two decades, however, this has changed dramatically. Possibly no political institution in the Fifth Republic has gained more power than the Constitutional Council. As one study of the Council observes, "Originally an obscure institution conceived to play a marginal role in the Fifth Republic, the Constitutional Council has gradually moved toward the center stage of French politics and acquired the status of a major actor in the policy-making system."[26]

The nine members of the Council are named for staggered nine-year non-renewable terms by three important political officials (each of whom names three members of the Council): the president of the republic and the presidents of the two houses of parliament, the National Assembly and Senate. The president of the republic names the president of the Council. Those named to the Council are generally distinguished jurists, as well as somewhat elderly politicians who are considered not to be highly partisan. The first woman named to the Council was appointed only in 1992; a second was named in 1998. As with other institutions at the summit of the state, the Council is hardly representative of France's diverse socioeconomic groups.

Several changes in the Fifth Republic have increased the independence of the judiciary and promoted the idea that the government, including its highest officials, should be accountable to an independent judiciary. The most important changes include:

- broadening access to the Constitutional Council. At first, only the president of the republic and the presidents of the two houses of the legislature could bring cases to the Council. A constitutional amendment passed in 1974 authorized sixty deputies or sixty senators to bring suit. As a result, the Council is now asked to rule on most important legislation.
- broadening the Council's jurisdiction to include the power of judicial review, that is, the power to invalidate legislation that in its opinion violates the Constitution. This key change occurred as a result of the Council's skillful strategy in a key decision that it rendered. The decision proved popular and the precedent could be used in future cases. Although this development is unprecedented in French history, the Council now routinely exercises the sweeping power in a bold and continuous fashion. If the primary innovation of the Fifth Republic in the first years of the republic was to consolidate the dominance of the executive over the legislature, the primary development since then has been to consolidate the primacy of the Constitution, as interpreted by the Constitutional Council, over *both* the legislature and executive. The change has involved a substantial expansion of the powers of the Council and a greater equilibrium of powers within the regime.
- Transfer of the power to appoint judges from the executive to magistrates elected from among the rank of judges. This change required a constitutional amendment in 1993. The same amendment

created a new Court of Justice to try cases against government ministers accused of crimes committed while in office and in 1999 three former ministers were tried for alleged failure to safeguard the purity of France's supply of blood in the 1980s during the AIDS crisis.

State Council

The French administrative system includes a system of several dozen administrative courts, at the apex of which is the *Conseil d'Etat* (State Council), which hears cases brought by individuals alleging that administrative regulations violate their rights. The Council also advises the government in drafting new legislation. Although the government can overrule the Council, it rarely does so since the Council's opinions command great respect. (Members of the *Conseil d'Etat* are considered among the most powerful and prestigious *grands corps*.) The Council plays the role of watchdog on the executive, an especially important function in the French political system, where the executive has such great autonomy.

Economic and Social Council

The Economic and Social Council is a consultative body composed of representatives of various interests, including business, agriculture, labor unions, social-welfare organizations, and consumer groups, as well as leading citizens from cultural and scientific fields. Although the Council has issued some influential reports on matters pending in parliament, it is little known to most French citizens and has no formal legislative or administrative role and little political influence.

Subnational Government

Until the 1980s, responsibility for regulating local affairs was in the hands of field officers who represented national government departments—prefects, supervisors of civil engineering, financial officers, and so on. Locally elected municipal governments were quite weak and the local governmental structure was extremely fragmented: There are over 36,000 village and city governments in France, more than all the local governments in other major Western European countries combined.

The Socialist government's first major reform in 1981 was a fundamental overhaul of local government. State supervision of local governments was reduced, regional governments were created, and localities were authorized to levy taxes and engage in a wide range of activities. The decentralization reform is widely recognized as one of the Left's greatest achievements. As a result of the transfer of substantial taxing and spending authority, local governments became more autonomous and vibrant. For example, regional governments organized public transport facilities to reduce dependence on automobiles; local governments sponsored cultural activities to revitalize their areas. Although some major Left reforms were reversed when the Right regained power, decentralization has taken firm root and is popular among most French citizens, political parties, national politicians, and local officials.

The Policy-Making Process

Until 1986, the beginning of the first period of cohabitation, there was great unity of purpose and a nearly hierarchical chain of command linking the president, government, bureaucracy, and parliament. The president, often in consultation with the prime minister, formulated major policy initiatives. The government, assisted by the formidable bureaucracy, developed the detailed legislative proposals and administrative regulations for implementing policy. And the parliament generally approved the government's proposals (although, as we will see in the next section, the government could not take parliamentary approval for granted).

During periods of cohabitation, the policy-making process has been quite different. In such cases, the prime minister has had the dominant say in policy-making and the president has assumed a marginal role.

Divided control affects policy implementation less than policy formulation because cabinet ministers and their *cabinets* direct the process of implementation regardless of relations between the president and government, and also because bureaucratic agencies possess considerable autonomy in managing their own affairs. Although often forced to bargain with interest groups for their support in order to implement policy, the bureaucracy usually has the upper hand. However, one cannot predict the details of policy *outcomes* merely by knowing the content of policy *decisions*. The bureaucracy is itself often divided by competition among different ministries, and bureaucrats have expertise and power which can be used to protect their own and their agency's interests.

In France there are few opportunities for those outside government to influence executive decisions. The Constitution enshrines executive dominance at the expense of the legislature and popular participation. In particular, the Fifth Republic accords parliament precious little autonomy—a striking contrast to the British, German, and other parliamentary regimes.

Nonetheless, the executive is not all-powerful. First, electoral swings produce party alternation in office, which often results in policy shifts. Second, strikes, demonstrations, and other forms of protest have periodically erupted and influenced the direction of policy. Third, the Constitutional Council has gained an important role in the policy process. Finally, the freedom of the executive and the French state more generally have been increasingly limited by France's participation in the global economy, especially French membership in the EU. Jacques Delors, a French political leader who for years served as president of the Commission of the EU, claimed that about 80 percent of the legislation regulating French affairs now originates in Brussels, Belgium (the seat of the EU).

Section ❹ Representation and Participation

The Constitution of the Fifth Republic grants the executive an astonishing array of powers and severely limits popular participation, representation, and legislative autonomy. These arrangements were inspired by Charles de Gaulle, principal architect and first president of the Fifth Republic. De Gaulle believed

that political parties and parliament had overstepped their proper role in the Third and Fourth Republics. The Constitution of the Fifth Republic was designed to assure the independence of the executive and limit the influence of political parties, organized interests, and parliament.

For better or worse, de Gaulle did succeed in limiting parliament's influence. But the framework failed to prevent the proliferation of well-organized, centralized parties that he opposed. The irony is that the growth of strong parties has helped achieve the goals for which de Gaulle designed political institutions in the first place, notably, decisive leadership, extensive popular support, and political stability.

De Gaulle's decision to provide for popular election of the presidency has been the major factor in the development of strong parties. In order to maximize their chances of winning the all-important contest, parties had to become centralized, powerful organizations. Yet political parties have served better to facilitate strong executive leadership than to provide channels for expressing opposition to the executive. As a result, and especially given the absence of other effective means of representation, France's centuries-old tradition of popular protest against state authority persists. Political stability is constantly threatened by protest in streets, factories, and offices.

The Legislature

In the French political system, the operative assumption seems to be that parliament should be seen but not heard. In France's semi-presidential system, parliament lacks the autonomy and separation from the executive that legislatures enjoy in presidential systems; yet parliament cannot hold the executive accountable, as legislatures in parliamentary systems can. The French parliament provides a poor forum for important national debates, fails to adequately represent conflicting interests, and has proved a feeble mechanism for checking abuses of power. With that said, parliament does provide a means by which the government negotiates compromises within the majority coalition and parliament has gradually gained power since the early years of the Fifth Republic.

The French parliament is bicameral: The two chambers are the National Assembly and the Senate. Members of the National Assembly are known as deputies; members of the Senate are known as senators. Together, the two groups are known as members of parliament. In the Third and Fourth Republics, parliament was regarded as the sole voice of the sovereign people. Under the Fifth Republic, parliament is no longer the seat of sovereignty and has been stripped of many powers. The Constitution limits the areas within which parliament is authorized to act. At the same time, the executive is granted extensive powers independent of parliament, as well as numerous weapons to control parliamentary activity.

As reviewed in Section 3, the executive can choose to dissolve the National Assembly before its normal five-year term ends. The decision to dissolve is delegated to the president, but the prime minister and government are closely involved in the process. (The executive cannot dissolve the Senate, but, as described below, the Senate's powers are limited in any event.) When the executive dissolves the National Assembly, it cannot do so again for a year.

Article 34, which defines parliament's legislative jurisdiction, represented a minor revolution in French constitutional law. Rather than authorizing parliament to legislate in all areas except those it designates as off-limits, the Constitution enumerates areas in which parliament *is* authorized to legislate. Outside these constitutionally specified areas, the executive can issue legally binding regulations and decrees. Even within the areas of parliamentary competence, Article 38 authorizes the government to request parliament to delegate it the power to issue ordinances with the force of law. This may happen, for example, if the government wishes to save time, avoid extensive parliamentary debate, or limit unwelcome amendments.

Within the limited area of lawmaking, the Constitution grants the government extensive powers to control legislative activity. The government is mostly responsible for establishing the parliamentary agenda, and, as in other parliamentary regimes, most legislation coming before parliament is initiated by the government, not back benchers or the opposition.

The government's control over parliament's legislative and other activity is bolstered by some additional important measures. Under Article 44, the government can call for a single vote—known as the *vote bloquée* ("blocked vote," informally known as the package vote)—on all or a portion of a bill. The government can select which amendments will be included with the text. Governments have used—abused, according to the opposition—the package vote procedure to restrict debate on many key legislative texts.

The government can further curb parliament by calling for a confidence vote either on its overall policies (Article 49, clause 1) or on a specific piece of legislation (Article 49, clause 3). This provision applies only to the National Assembly, since the Senate cannot vote censure, that is, bring down a government. When the government declares a confidence vote, its motion is considered to have been approved—in the absence of a vote supporting the government—unless the National Assembly passes a censure motion within twenty-four hours.

The Constitution imposes an especially severe restriction for a censure motion to pass. An absolute majority of the National Assembly must vote in favor of censure. Thus, deputies who are absent or who abstain, in effect, count as supporting the government. The government uses these formidable weapons not only to check opponents but to keep in line deputies from its own coalition who might otherwise be tempted to oppose the government on a particular policy. When opposing the government might cause it to fall, in which case it might dissolve the Assembly and provoke new elections, the government's supporters are much more inclined to silence!

Deputies can also submit motions to censure the government on their own initiative. Such a motion must be signed by one-tenth of all deputies in the National Assembly. The procedure for passing this kind of censure motion is the same as that called by the government.

Given the fact that the government normally commands majority support in the National Assembly, it rarely has to worry about being forced to resign by a vote of censure. Although several censure motions are proposed every legislative session, only one has ever passed since the creation of the Fifth Republic.

In a recent analysis, political scientist John Huber has provided a subtle analysis of how the package vote and censure procedures serve an important and little-noticed purpose.[27] Whereas most observers have focused on how these measures are a weapon that the government can use to limit parliament's autonomy, Huber emphasizes their utility as a way for the government to promote binding agreements among the parties represented in the majority coalition. This approach takes its point of departure from the fact that the partners in a coalition are also rivals. In brief, the package vote and censure motion provide the prime minister with resources to negotiate and enforce agreements among his or her supporters.

Parliament has more limited control over the budgetary process than in other areas of legislative competence. Members of parliament are prohibited from introducing budget amendments that will raise expenditures or lower revenues. Further, parliament must approve the budget within seventy days after it has been submitted by the government or the government can enact it by decree (although this has never occurred in the Fifth Republic).

In some parliamentary systems, parliamentary committees or, as the French term them, commissions, play a vital role. But not in the Fifth Republic. There are six permanent commissions: foreign policy; finances and economy; defense; constitutional changes, legislation, and general administration; cultural, family, and social affairs; and production and exchange. (There may also be special commissions appointed to examine especially important legislation, as occurred regarding the Socialist government's nationalization reform in 1981.) Commissions are responsible for reviewing proposed legislation. Although they may propose important changes, the government can employ the constitutional powers described above to reject unwanted modifications. The Constitution also authorizes parliament to create commissions of inquiry to control the executive, but few have been created and they have proved quite ineffective.

In recent years, parliament has modestly increased its standing. When some powerful party leaders occupied the position of President of the National Assembly or Senate (roughly equivalent to the British speaker of the house), they have sponsored changes to provide members of parliament more opportunities to question cabinet ministers. Members of parliament have successfully exploited the right to amend government-sponsored bills. Parliament's informal power has further increased in two kinds of situations. First, rank-and-file deputies count for more when the government does not have a large majority in parliament, a frequent occurrence in recent years. Second, cohabitation has enlarged the possibility for parliamentary maneuvering. Although members of parliament often grumble at the restrictions under which they labor, there is little prospect that the present situation will be drastically changed, since it would require governments to voluntarily relinquish their power.

Unequal Bicameralism

The National Assembly is by far the more powerful chamber of parliament. Only the Assembly can censure the government, and it has the decisive role in passing legislation.

Most bills that receive serious parliamentary consideration are introduced by the government in either the National Assembly or Senate. After review and possible amendment by one of the six standing commissions, the bill is submitted to the full chamber for debate, further amendment, and vote. If a text is approved, it is considered by the second chamber.

If a bill is passed in identical form by the two chambers, it becomes law. If, however, the two houses vote different versions or the Senate rejects a text approved by the National Assembly, a joint commission from the two houses seeks to negotiate a compromise, which is again considered by both houses. The government can expedite this process and ask both houses to reconsider and approve an identical text. If all else fails, it can ask the National Assembly to override the Senate and, if the bill is approved by the National Assembly, it becomes law despite the Senate's opposition.

After a bill is passed, the Constitution authorizes the president of the republic, president of either chamber of the legislature, or 60 deputies or senators to request a review by the Constitutional Council. The Council can strike down those portions of a bill or the entire text that it judges to be in violation of the Constitution. If the Council has not been asked to rule within one month after a bill is passed, it becomes law and can never be reviewed by the Council.

Why would the National Assembly and Senate have different positions on a policy issue? One reason is that members of the two houses are elected by different procedures and represent different interests. Deputies, that is, members of the National Assembly, are chosen from single-member districts for five years (unless the government dissolves the chamber before the end of its normal term). There are currently 577 seats in the National Assembly; thus, there are 577

districts. A two-ballot procedure is used, similar to the one for presidential elections. A candidate must receive an absolute majority of the votes cast to be elected on the first ballot. (Elections are held on Sundays to encourage turnout.) If no candidate does—the usual situation—a runoff election is held the following week. Unlike the presidential election, in which only the two front-running candidates may compete at the runoff, any candidate receiving at least 12.5 percent of the votes can compete in the runoff. Typically, however, parties on the left and right negotiate alliances in which they agree to support the best-placed candidate from the alliance in each district. The result is that parties agree to withdraw less well-placed candidates in the coalition, even if they obtain over 12.5 percent of the vote. Parties entering into these agreements stand a much better chance of seeing their candidates elected. However, fringe parties, like the National Front, can exercise an important influence if many of their candidates clear the 12.5 percent threshold and refuse to withdraw in the runoff.

Since party alliances typically reflect the left-right divide, the system used to elect the National Assembly contributes to polarization within French politics. But the major effect of the system is to maximize the chances of a stable majority emerging in parliament, and it thereby bolsters political stability in the entire political system. This is why political scientist Jean Charlot claims that the two-ballot single district system "has proved . . . one of the most solid underpinnings of the Fifth Republic. The electoral law . . . weakens or even neutralizes the natural tendency of the French and their parties toward division."

By design, the two-ballot system penalizes small, isolated parties that cannot form agreements with major parties. The most dramatic case in recent years is that of the National Front (FN). In the 1997 parliamentary elections, the FN obtained 15 percent of the popular vote but, because its supporters were spread throughout France and the FN could not ally with a large party, it failed to elect a single deputy.

The procedure used to select senators means that the chamber is responsive to different interests. The 322 senators are chosen for nine-year terms by mayors and town councillors from each *département* (the 100 administrative districts into which mainland and overseas France is divided). (Twelve senators are elected by non-resident French citizens.) Rural interests are substantially over-represented: although one-quarter of the population lives in villages of under 1500, 40 percent of the local officials electing senators represent these communes (localities). The Senate is thus particularly zealous in defending the interests of small towns and villages.

Political Parties and the Party System

Ironically, the emergence of powerful political parties—the very factor that de Gaulle feared would nurture division, instability, and paralysis—has promoted political stability in the Fifth Republic They have done so by making possible stable leadership and political alternation in office. Popular support and political stability increase when elections represent a choice between alternative political coalitions. In recent years, however, the decline in ideological distance between the center-left and center-right has reduced the importance of the electoral outcome; many French citizens feel unrepresented by *both* of the two major alternatives. The result is a withdrawal of support for the major established parties, as described below.

Popular election of the president has produced *polarization* and "**presidentialization**" of the party system. Polarization describes the tendency for the electorate to divide into two camps as a result of the procedures used to elect the president. Presidentialization means that parties give priority, in terms of their program, internal organization, alliance strategy, and leadership, to winning the next presidential election. Parties are organized to be efficient electoral vehicles, and the process favors leaders who project an appealing image and perform well on television. The party shapes its program to capture the widest possible audience, which produces a tendency toward ideological moderation. As French parties have moved in this direction, some observers have described French politics as becoming "Americanized," for the emphasis on winning the presidential elections, the focus on candidates' personalities, and ideological centrism are major features of American politics.

Counterpressures, however, constantly challenge the trend toward polarization and presidentialization.

In particular, because the major parties neglect certain groups in their march toward the ideological center, opportunities have opened up for a variety of fringe parties. The result is a countertendency toward fragmentation within the party system. Splinter parties have performed especially well in elections to the European parliament and to municipal and regional councils, where the stakes are lower and representatives are chosen by proportional representation (PR). Since seats are allotted in PR according to the proportion of votes each party receives, there is less incentive for parties to ally or for voters to cast their ballot for large parties. Consequently, small parties generally fare better in elections held by PR.

In the past several decades, three major parties have vied for dominance, each of which has held top offices within the Fifth Republic. In addition, we review three smaller parties.

The Major Parties

The *Rassemblement pour la République (RPR)*. Parties on the right of the French political spectrum have traditionally been numerous and fragmented. Under de Gaulle's leadership, a new party was created, which—largely because of his popularity—dominated the Fifth Republic in the early years. The RPR, as it is presently known, never had a precise program. It was originally created to support de Gaulle's personal leadership and his somewhat vague program of championing France's national independence, providing strong political leadership within France, and modernizing French society and economy while retaining France's distinctive cultural heritage.

Beginning in the mid-1970s, the RPR slipped from first place. Jacques Chirac, who became leader in 1974, lost presidential bids in 1981 and 1988. The RPR temporarily regained its premier role in the Fifth Republic when Chirac won the 1995 presidential elections and named Alain Juppé, a close ally, as prime minister. Since the Conservative coalition had already won a swollen parliamentary majority in legislative elections in 1993, the Conservative sweep was complete. However, the victory celebration soon ended. When in late 1995 Juppé proposed cutbacks in social benefits (see Section 2), severe strikes shook the regime to its roots. Chirac tried to regain control by dissolving the National Assembly and calling new elections in 1997. But the attempt backfired, and the victory of the Socialist-led coalition led to another period of cohabitation, most likely for the remainder of Chirac's first term.

The social base of the RPR generally reflects its conservative orientation. Business executives, professionals, the highly educated, and the wealthy are more likely to favor either the RPR or the second conservative party which we review below. In the runoff ballot of the 1995 presidential election, 67 percent of respondents in a public opinion poll who identified themselves as well-off favored Chirac.

The *Union des Démocrates pour la France (UDF)*. Created in 1978, the UDF was an umbrella organization for several small Center-Right parties that opposed de Gaulle and the RPR. The party's major leader was Valéry Giscard d'Estaing, president from 1974 until his defeat in 1981.

There were good reasons at first to have two major Center-Right parties. The two differed sharply on many issues: the RPR strongly supported de Gaulle, the UDF opposed him; the UDF supported European integration, the RPR was divided on the issue; the RPR favored state direction of the economy, the UDF preferred free enterprise. But de Gaulle is long gone and disagreements over other issues do not so much pit the two parties against each other as divide them internally. Moreover, because of the polarizing logic of the French electoral system, the RPR and UDF usually join forces during most campaigns and they formed a coalition government after the 1986 and 1993 parliamentary elections.

For years, Jacques Chirac and Valéry Giscard d'Estaing remained political rivals and the parties remained distinct and often opposed organizations. The situation changed in 1995, when Chirac outmaneuvered Giscard in the campaign leading up to the presidential elections. When Chirac won the election itself and began a seven-year term, the aging Giscard began to withdraw from active political life. The UDF began to disintegrate, with a prominent leader of the UDF bolting to form a separate party. At the same time, the dividing line between the RPF and UDF became increasingly blurred. In 1998 the parties formed a joint grouping, the Alliance for France;

many speculate that they will eventually merge to form a single party.

The Socialist Party (PS). The PS is one of the major success stories in contemporary France. From a party of aging local politicians and schoolteachers in the Fourth and early Fifth Republics, it became the vanguard of a new France in 1981, when it swept presidential and parliamentary elections. Since 1981, the Socialist Party has been France's dominant political force. It has profoundly shaped present-day France by accepting the institutions of the Fifth Republic, changing its policy orientation, and undertaking a series of sweeping reforms.

Three factors explain the Socialist success. First, the Gaullist coalition that ruled the Fifth Republic became increasingly rigid and conservative. Second, the May 1968 protests exposed the weakness of the Gaullist coalition and its potential for defeat, especially if the PS could meld a coalition of the industrial working class with the new white-collar groups whose ranks were swelling by rapid economic expansion. Third, the PS was led since 1972 by François Mitterrand, who helped fashion the PS into a new breed of socialist party. Although it continued to advocate substantial reforms, it kept its distance from the working class and labor unions which enabled it to preserve policy flexibility.

The PS reached power in 1981 by advocating substantial, even radical, changes, and it sponsored a whirlwind of reforms in its first years in office. However, when President Mitterrand reluctantly decided on a dramatic about-face in 1983–1984, after the government encountered severe economic difficulties, French socialism lost its ideological bearings. By abandoning its reformist approach in 1983 and championing conservative policies, the Socialist movement seemed hopelessly confused.

As Mitterrand's long presidency drew to an end, his reputation was tarnished by a series of scandals involving his close personal associates and by revelations that, before becoming a Resistance leader during World War II, he was active in a far-right organization in the 1930s and had been awarded a decoration by the Vichy regime. The PS was further discredited by the fact that many PS leaders were accused of crimes ranging from abuse of power for personal enrichment

Leaders: *Lionel Jospin*

Prime Minister Lionel Jospin might be tempted to agree, "Yes, Virginia, there is a Santa Claus." For Jospin went from political has-been in the early 1990s to France's most powerful politician in 1997, in the process reviving the severely flagging fortunes of the Socialist Party, which he led for many years.

Unlike many French political leaders, Jospin may have succeeded in spite of—not because of—his public demeanor. Admittedly, he is a product of the French elite educational system—he graduated from the prestigious civil servant training school, the Ecole National d'Administration (described in Section 3). But unlike most top French politicians, he was not born into affluent circumstances. His father ran a school for delinquents near Paris and his mother was a midwife. Jospin has a quite down-to-earth, no-nonsense approach and does not excel in delivering polished speeches or making sparkling off-the-cuff remarks. For many years, he taught in a technical institute—an institution that occupies a lowly position in France's vast educational system. Yet these very qualities of simplicity and integrity have endeared him to millions of French citizens, tired of the revelations of dishonesty and deception that have tarnished the reputations of so many French politicians in the 1990s—from Presidents Mitterrand and Chirac on down.

Jospin worked his way up the political ranks by his close association with François Mitterrand. Jospin took over control of the Socialist Party when Mitterrand was elected president in 1981. While Socialist leaders were appointed to high ministerial office, Jospin plodded along managing the party's affairs. He was eventually appointed education minister in 1988. Jospin's fortunes declined along with those of the Socialist Party in the early 1990s and he retired from politics.

Everything changed for Jospin as the 1995 presidential elections approached. Everyone agreed that the Socialist Party stood no chance of winning. It was in part for this reason that Jacques Delors, a more prominent Socialist and former president of the EU Commission, who could have had the party's nomination for the asking, decided not to run. Jospin saw his chance. He won the nomination by beating another lackluster candidate in a party primary. The real shock was when Jospin emerged as a credible and attractive candidate in the presidential election. His appeal derived, in part, from his simple, direct manner, which struck a responsive chord with voters. Jospin promised to tell the truth—and voters believed him. Given a boost by a split between two major right-wing candidates, Jospin emerged as the frontrunner at the first ballot of the election and went on to score a respectable 47 percent in the runoff ballot against Jacques Chirac, the victorious candidate.

Jospin was launched—but he would have remained in the political wilderness were it not for the large strikes in late 1995 that led Chirac to dissolve parliament in 1997 in the hope of gaining a fresh electoral mandate. Jospin pulled off what was unthinkable a short time earlier: he led the Left forces to victory and was named prime minister.

Jospin is often compared to Britain's Tony Blair. The two became prime minister just a few months apart in 1997. Whereas Blair reached office on a platform promising a "New Labour" agenda (see Chapter 2), Jospin has maintained a commitment to traditional Socialist policies and values while accepting the scaled-back version that developed after the Socialist government's U-turn of 1983. Thus, Jospin represents a prudent mixture of the Socialist old and new. He praises the importance of the public sector, while he favors privatizing nationalized firms. He has defended the importance of public services, sponsored measures to stimulate job creation, and sought to preserve France's relatively extensive welfare state at the same time that he accepted the launching of the euro (with the accompanying obligation to maintain restrictive economic policies).

In his first years in office, Jospin's popularity remained at record levels, no mean feat given that Conservative president Jacques Chirac was constantly waiting to pounce on any mistakes Jospin might commit. One reason for his success was good luck, since an economic upturn in France and Western Europe in the late 1990s produced a modest spurt in French economic growth and employment. Another reason was that Jospin remained refreshingly simple and direct in approach, a welcome contrast to the wheeling and dealing that had become typical among French politicians. If he was no inspired visionary, he was highly successful in maintaining his reputation as a squeaky-clean administrator.

to running illegal money-laundering operations to finance the party. The low point was reached in 1993, when the PS was soundly defeated in parliamentary elections. Historian Donald Sassoon observed, "At the end of the Mitterrand experiment, the French Left appeared more devoid of ideas, hopes and support than it had been in its entire history."[28]

But the PS demonstrated remarkable resilience. PS candidate Lionel Jospin performed creditably in the 1995 presidential elections, coming in a close second in the runoff to Jacques Chirac. (The bulk of voters who reported themselves as having low income voted for Jospin.) Jospin led the party to victory in the 1997 parliamentary elections, enabling him to form a Socialist-led government (see Leaders: Lionel Jospin). Thus, the PS has controlled the presidency and/or the government ever since 1981, except for the brief period from 1995 to 1997. (During much of this time, however, it has had to share power with conservative parties.)

What explains the party's durable electoral success? For one thing, although its achievements fell far short of its ambitious goals, its policies have proved quite effective. It presided over a thorough overhaul of the French economy and played a leading role in strengthening European integration. Another major PS achievement was to broaden support for the Fifth Republic. Until 1981, conservative forces had exercised a monopoly of power. The PS demonstrated that the Left could gain high office and represent the interests of previously excluded groups. A final reason for PS success was the weakness of conservative forces, due to internal divisions between the two center-right parties, the fact that neither party had a leader able to rival François Mitterrand, and the defection of many conservative voters to the far-right National Front party (described below).

Small Parties

As the programs of the three major parties become increasingly alike, many voters believe that none of the major parties is responsive to their concerns. As a result, there is significant support for several small parties, whose combined forces are quite substantial. The result is relatively great fragmentation within the French party system.

The Communist Party (PCF).   From 1945 to the 1980s, the PCF was one of the largest political parties in France, commanding over 20 percent of the vote in elections in the postwar period. It presented itself as the heir to the French revolutionary tradition, proud of its close links both to the French working class—whose electoral support was key to the party's strong position—and to the Soviet Union. For much of this period, the PCF's stated goal was to replace France's capitalist system—which, it argued, was undemocratically organized and exploitative—by public ownership and control of the economy. This put the party on a collision course with other political parties and forces (save for small ultra-left groups).

Ever since its creation at the time of the Bolshevik Revolution, the PCF's internal organization, like that of orthodox Communist parties elsewhere, was based on the concept of democratic centralism. In practice, this meant that the distribution of power within the party was long on centralism and short on democracy. The party's top leaders, especially its secretary general and his closest associates in the secretariat, chose party officials and decided the party's general orientation. Critics in the party's ranks were quickly isolated and expelled from the party.

PCF support began to dwindle when it adapted too little and too late to the political, social, and economic modernization that began to transform France in the 1960s. Wave after wave of dissidents failed to persuade party leaders to reject the Soviet model, promote internal party democracy, and modernize the party's ideology and program. PCF electoral support fell to under 10 percent by the 1980s. Although it joined the PS in the governing coalition elected in 1981, it was a very junior partner, and it left the government in 1984 in protest against the Socialists' right turn.

Two other factors contributed to weakening the PCF. The party had close ties to France's largest trade union, the *Confédération Générale du Travail (CGT)*. But when workers began to desert the CGT in the 1970s, this weakened the PCF. Finally, the dismantling of the Soviet Union, a momentous change in world politics, left the PCF isolated and somewhat discredited. Many of the kinds of voters who would have supported the PCF in the past, especially workers, youth, and the less well educated, have drifted to the National Front, whose coarse opposition to established parties is appealing to those on the margin of French society. In brief, the party is a shadow of its once-mighty self and its decline has moved the entire political spectrum toward the right.

The PCF survived the disintegration of the Soviet Union and its leader, Robert Hue, won 9 percent of the vote in the 1995 presidential elections. The party retains an important base by running many local governments. The PCF allied with the PS and Green party to win the 1997 parliamentary elections, and two PCF leaders were named to the Jospin government.

The National Front (FN). The National Front has existed for decades, but its rapid rise in the 1980s was fueled by high unemployment, fears about increased crime, and the choice of a handy scapegoat—immigrant workers and their families.

The FN was one of the first openly racist political parties in Western Europe in the contemporary period. Its slogan of "France for the French" implies that immigrants, especially those who are not white, are not "truly" French. Although party leaders have engaged in anti-Semitic and anti-immigrant rhetoric across the board, their favorite targets are Arabs from Algeria, France's former North African colony. The FN advocates depriving immigrants of employment, social benefits, and education, and, if possible, deporting them. In the 1990s, the party broadened its program and increased its support by proposing simplistic solutions to other problems that trouble the French. It advocates authoritarian measures to deal with France's rising crime rate, and fiercely opposes European economic and political integration, which in its view fuels unemployment and dilutes French national identity.

FN leader Jean-Marie Le Pen, a dynamic, articulate orator, has powerfully contributed to the FN's success. In both the 1988 and 1995 presidential elections, Le Pen gained 15 percent of the first ballot vote, just behind the major candidates. In 1998, however, Le Pen was convicted of assaulting a political opponent and, under French law, was barred from holding public office for two years. The party was, therefore, deprived of its most popular leader for the 1999 elections to the European Parliament. One of Le Pen's close associates challenged him for party leadership.

In the conflict that followed, the party split and its future prospects suddenly dimmed.

The FN's popularity has posed a dilemma for the center-right: should it reject the FN outright or make concessions in a bid for its support? For example, in regional elections in 1998, three UDF leaders were expelled from the party when they accepted FN support to retain their seats as president of regional councils. When one of the three was later readmitted to the party, it caused a severe split within the UDF.

The FN took the lead among political parties in Western Europe in targeting ethnic minorities. (Parties in Austria, Denmark, and elsewhere later followed the FN's lead.) Morever, FN propaganda has borne fruit. In a 1998 poll, 40 percent of French respondents reported holding racist beliefs—twice as many as Germans or British. Despite the crisis within the FN in 1998, it has had a substantial impact on French politics. This is why political scientist James Shields claims that "The rise of a powerful extreme-right party in France is arguably the most important political development of the past fourteen years."[29]

The Greens (*les Verts*). While the major political parties have been quite indifferent to environmental issues, French citizens now rank ecology fourth in importance among their preoccupations.[30] The state's relative indifference to environmental concerns provided the potential for a green movement in France. For example, France has the largest nuclear power program in Western Europe. The state-controlled nuclear power and electric power agencies are often described as states within the state because of their isolation and overbearing approach, and the Greens first reached public notice by sponsoring antinuclear protests.

The Greens had been on the French political scene for years before achieving a major breakthrough in the 1989 European elections, gaining 10.6 percent of the vote. The Greens' breakthrough was linked to the "new look" that the party adopted in the late 1980s, which appealed to young, well-educated voters (who provide the bulk of support for the Greens). At this time, the party abandoned a leftist orientation and claimed that it was "neither right nor left"—but green.

To an even greater extent than other parties, the Greens have been divided by the personal ambitions

Table 2

Electoral Results, Elections to National Assembly, 1958–1997 (percentage of those voting)

	1958	1962	1967	1968	1973	1978	1981	1986	1988	1993	1997
Far-Left	2%	2%	2%	4%	3%	3%	1%	2%	0%	2%	2%
PCF	19	22	23	20	21	21	16	10	11	9	10
Socialist Party/ Left Radicals	23	21	19	17	22	25	38	32	38	21	26
Ecology	—	—	—	—	—	2	1	1	1	12	8
Center parties	15	15	18	10	16	{21	{19		{19	{19	{15
Center-Right	14	14	0	4	7						
UNR → RPR	18	32	38	44	24	23	21	{42	19	20	17
Far-Right	3	1	1	0	3	0	3	10	10	13	15
Abstentions	23	31	19	20	19	17	30	22	34	31	32

Note: Percentages of parties do not add to 100 because of minor-party candidates and rounding errors.

Sources: Françoise Dreyfus and François D'Arcy, *Les Institutions Politiques et Administratives de la France* (Paris: Economica, 1985), p. 54; *Le Monde*, March 18, 1986; "Les élections législatives," *Le Monde*, 1988; Ministry of the Interior, 1993, 1997.

of their leaders. In the 1993 parliamentary elections, the Greens split in part because of rivalry between two Green leaders. Nonetheless, the larger grouping of the Greens allied with the PS in the 1997 parliamentary elections and party leader Dominique Voynet was appointed minister of environment in the Jospin government.

Elections

French voters go to the polls nearly every year, to vote in a referendum or in elections for municipal, departmental, or regional councillor, deputy to the European Parliament or National Assembly, and president.

The decline of the Communist party means that, for the first time in two centuries, the far-left is not a major force in French politics (see Table 2). A key to its decline is the massive desertion of young voters, who traditionally were quite likely to vote for the Communist and other far-left parties. Whereas 37 percent of young voters supported the far-left in the late 1970s, 20 percent did so in the early 1980s, with a further sharp decline occurring later in the decade and continuing through the early 1990s.[31]

Some scholars describe the shift as the "normalization" of French politics, in that French political patterns increasingly resemble politics in northern Europe and the United States. One feature is the declining ideological distance between political parties, as a result of the PCF's decline and the PS's right turn. Another contributing factor has been the frequent alternation between parties of the center-left and center-right. Since 1974, there has been a change in the governing majority in every legislative election.

These changes represent a fundamental restructuring of the French party system and political life. Yet, rather than celebrating the new era as signifying political health, some scholars see it as a crisis of political representation and the party system. Four trends can be noted.

First, there has been a shift in support away from the major governing parties. The combined vote total of "peripheral" candidates in the 1995 presidential election was 38 percent; to this should be added the 3 percent of voters who deliberately spoiled their ballot papers at the first round (and thus whose vote wasn't counted), as well as some portion of the 22 percent of nonvoters. Thus, well over half the electorate chose not to support candidates from the "big three" parties.

Second, there has been increased volatility in voting patterns, as evidenced by greater vote switching among parties, suggesting a decline in party loyalty.

Third, the level of abstentions and deliberately spoiled ballots has increased, further evidence of citizens' discontent with the choices that parties offer them. Nearly 10 percent of voters cast a blank or spoiled ballot in the 1993 legislative elections; 5 percent did so in the 1995 presidential elections. As the major parties move closer together, citizens become skeptical that parties can make a difference, and fewer citizens bother to cast a useful ballot.

Finally, the standing of French political leaders has been damaged by a series of scandals, involving illegal campaign contributions, bribes and misuse of public office for private gain, and possible official misuse of power. For example, a former prime minister and two health ministers were tried in 1999 on charges that they were lax in safeguarding the blood supply against the AIDS virus. The result is that public trust in politicians has plummeted.

Political Culture, Citizenship, and Identity

French public opinion is divided, confused, and often angry. Economic problems, urban problems, and France's changing relation to the international order pose challenges that the ideologies, party organizations, and loyalties of the past seem unable to meet. The two most important examples are the decline of Marxism, along with the related decline of the PCF as well as an erosion of working-class self-identification; and a dramatic decline in Catholic religious observance, along with the weakening of the Catholic Church and the social networks that formerly promoted the Right's social cohesion.

Interests, Social Movements, and Protest

Most scholars agree that the overbearing French state has tended to limit possibilities for social movements as well as for private interests to organize and regulate their own affairs. The Fifth Republic reinforced this tendency by further strengthening the executive. Organized interests, however, do play a significant role. In some sectors, interest groups compete with each other. In others, the state provides for extensive consultation with private interests by creating advisory bodies on which they are represented.

There is a great variety of possible relations between administrative agencies and interest groups. At one extreme, the National Federation of Farmers'

Unions (FNSEA) exercises immense power. Its representatives serve on the administrative commissions that set levels of agricultural prices and subsidies. In some respects, it is difficult to distinguish where the bureaucracy ends and the FNSEA begins. Another powerful organization is the major organization of business executives. Trade associations and labor unions play an important part in administering the far-flung public health system as well as state-financed vocational training programs. Representatives of interest groups also serve on the Economic and Social Council (see Section 3).

At the other extreme, French labor unions are terribly weak (see Citizen Action: French Trade Unions). Unlike the FNSEA, which speaks with a single voice, labor unions are highly divided. There are four major trade unions that claim to represent workers throughout the economy, as well as independent unions in specific sectors (such as teachers) and a host of independent unions determined to keep their distance from the major confederations. For years, the labor movement could not persuade the state to legislate even minimal protection for union officials against arbitrary employer actions. Unions have had little say in formulating and implementing policies of direct concern to workers and unions. Under these conditions, they have typically been forced to express their demands by direct protest—a more dramatic, but often less effective, means than behind-the-scenes meetings with administrative officials.

Women, the largest "minority"—in reality a 51 percent majority—are highly under-represented in the French political system. There has never been a female president of the republic and only one prime minister—Edith Cresson, who served briefly under President Mitterrand and was the object of considerable ridicule, in part because of her gender. Whereas 11 percent of the deputies elected to the National Assembly in 1997 were women, women comprised 40 percent of the legislature in Sweden, 33 percent in Finland and Denmark, and 28 percent in the Netherlands. Women gained somewhat better representation in the Juppé and Jospin governments, and in 1998 Prime Minister Jospin's government proposed a constitutional amendment requiring that the electoral slates of political parties be composed equally of men and women.

Citizen Action: *French Trade Unions*

The character of the French trade union movement and its relationship to politics helps explain much about protest in France. In many industrialized democracies, such as Britain, Germany, and Japan, trade unions in specific sectors—for example, steel, transportation, teaching, the civil service—are allied in a central trade union confederation. As a consequence, organized labor speaks with relatively one voice. In addition, the central union confederation is usually allied with the country's major left-of-center political party—the Labour Party in Britain, Social Democratic Party in Germany, and the Socialist Party in Japan.

The situation is very different in France. Rather than one umbrella trade union confederation, there are four—as well as a number of other independent unions. Each confederation pursues its own economic and political agenda. The confederations compete with each other in recruiting members and in elections to representative bodies (called works councils) based in shopfloors and offices. Traditionally, divisions have been heightened because each confederation was loosely allied with a competing political party. The largest confederation was closely allied with the Communist Party, while other confederations had links to the Socialist and centrist parties. The confederations' ties to political political parties have weakened in recent years, but their rivalry with each other continues.

Since French labor does not speak with one voice but with many discordant voices, trade unions have relatively little direct influence in shaping public policy. Although the French trade union movement is among the oldest in the world, the rate of union membership has traditionally been among the lowest of the industrialized democracies. In the 1990s, with the downsizing of manufacturing which produced high levels of unemployment, the union movement suffered a further loss of members and power. Membership has sagged to under 10 percent of the labor force, a historic low in the postwar period.

This description suggests that, because of their small numbers, organizational and political divisions, and meager clout, unions are a weak force in French politics and society. And in "normal" times, French unions do indeed play a marginal role. But in times of crisis French unions gain strength because they are the only force with which employers and the state can negotiate in order to restore order.

During normal periods, French employers and the state are tempted to ignore unions and workers' interests on the assumption that unions are not a significant force. But occasionally workers' anger boils over to produce "abnormal" periods of direct protest—and trade unions use the currency of disruption to increase their bargaining power. When strikes and demonstrations shut down plants, firms, economic sectors, and even large regions or the entire country, employers and the state must court union leaders. Feverish all-night negotiations are held among management, government officials, and union leaders, which often produce settlements providing wage gains and institutional reforms. Whereupon the cycle of "normalcy" resumes, and unions retreat to a more marginal position—until the next explosion.

France may be said to be the home of modern feminist thought. Philosopher and novelist Simone de Beauvoir's *The Second Sex*, published after World War II, is a landmark in this regard, and in the 1960s and 1970s French feminist theorists contributed to reshaping literary studies throughout the world. However, although there is considerable gender inequality in France, women's movements, like many other social movements, have been relatively weak. State policy often has been unresponsive to women's concerns, partly as a result of their meager political representation. Contraception, for example, was ille-gal in France until 1967. Abortion was banned until 1974. A law outlawing sexual harassment was passed in 1992, but the scope of the legislation is limited to the attempt by supervisors at work to coerce sexual favors. The law ignores the possibility of harassment by those who are not hierarchical superiors, and the concept of a hostile working environment does not exist in French law. On the other hand, legislation outlawing the publication of sexist material, and France's extensive welfare state benefits, including public preschool facilities and health programs, serve women's interests.

Although Fifth Republic institutions were designed to discourage citizens from acting autonomously, they have not always succeeded. France has a long tradition of direct protest. Throughout the nineteenth century, regimes were toppled by mass opposition in the streets. More recently, the May 1968 uprising was "the nearest thing to a full-blown revolution ever experienced in an advanced industrial society," and a vivid reminder of how fragile political stability can be in France.[32] A repeat performance occurred in December 1995, when transportation workers brought Paris and other large cities grinding to a halt. (See Section 5.)

Although the number of strikes has declined in recent years as a result of high unemployment, the strikes that do occur are often highly militant and disruptive. Among the groups resorting to strikes and demonstrations in the 1990s were farmers, fishing interests, postal workers, teachers, high school students, truckers, taxi drivers, pilots, railway workers, health care workers, and immigrants and their offspring—to provide only a partial list! These diverse groups are united only by the angry claim that political institutions serve their interests poorly.

The Fifth Republic erected sturdy institutions to facilitate state action. But an adequate balance has not yet been struck between a strong state on the one hand and citizen participation and representation on the other. Thus, when specific challenges develop, as we review in Section 5, established channels do not provide an effective forum to debate and address problems.

Section ❺   French Politics in Transition

Political Challenges and Changing Agendas

What a distance separates French politics at the start of the new century from politics even a few years earlier. Political conflict in the 1970s and 1980s—as well as the major political parties—were arrayed quite neatly along a left-right ideological continuum linked to social class divisions. In the 1970s, attention was riveted on the rivalry between an alliance of the Communist and Socialist Parties and the conservative center-right parties. In the early 1980s, the reform initiatives of the Socialist government dominated the news. When the center-right coalition gained a parliamentary majority in 1986, its first priority was to roll back many of the reforms.

By the middle-1990s, however, the center-left and center-right were in quite close agreement on the major political priorities. All three major parties accepted France's mixed economy, consisting of the coexistence of a strong role for the state but also heavy reliance on private market forces. All three accepted that, for the sake of further European integration (notably, the launching of the euro), it was worth making unpleasant economic policy choices, including cutbacks in state spending—especially social spending—in order to reduce government deficits. This general policy orientation dated from the mid-1980s and had been pursued by Socialist and conservative governments for a decade. By the mid-1990s, then, it appeared that significant ideological controversy, at least among the major political parties, had ended.

Yet, in retrospect, the calm that prevailed was the calm before the storm. We review below a political challenge in 1995 that highlighted continuities and changes in France's political agenda—and the inadequacy of the existing system to confront that agenda.

The Strikes of December 1995: May 1968 Revisited?

In late 1995 France was rocked by a series of strikes and demonstrations whose extent and intensity recalled those of May 1968. An analysis of the strikes reveals the key elements of change that have recently occurred in France, elements of continuity, and the challenges that France is presently confronting.

Dashed Expectations: The 1995 Elections and Thereafter.   The extensive economic restructuring of France since 1983 has produced modernization for many industries but devastation for entire regions and sectors of the population. Since the Socialists' "turn" in 1983, governments of left and right had promoted the intensive modernization of French industry by a program of deregulation, privatization, high interest rates, and social retrenchment.

In the 1995 presidential election, the RPR candidate Jacques Chirac held out the hope that things could be different. As a respected journalist commented in a book about Chirac's campaign, "He was forced to adopt the strategy of an outsider, gambling that victory would go not to a candidate proposing continuity, but to the candidate who advocated change."[33] For the first time since the Socialist Party's U-turn of 1983, a candidate from one of the "big three" centrist parties challenged the consensus that there was no alternative but to pursue austerity policies. In a famous phrase during the campaign, Chirac declared, "the pay stub [i.e., decent wages] is not the enemy of employment." And when Chirac gained election, it was no surprise that, in his victory speech, he proclaimed, "Our battle has a name: the struggle against unemployment."

Chirac's strategy struck a responsive chord with voters. As Table 3 shows, unemployment ranks far above any other issue in citizens' concerns. But Chirac's campaign promises soon proved politically costly. Only months after he had raised expectations that things could be different, and that government policy would accord priority to reflation and social ends, he abruptly orchestrated an about-face. The need

---

Table 3

Citizens' Concerns

"Which of the following problems do you judge most pressing?"*

Welfare system	55%
Immigration	38
Reforming political institutions	8
Constructing Europe	30
French foreign and defense policy	10
The struggle against unemployment	92
Improving the moral level of public life	16
Reforming education	27
The struggle against exclusion	37

*Answers exceed 100% because those questioned could provide up to four responses.

Source: *Le Monde*, May 11, 1995.

---

to comply with the strict fiscal requirements of Maastricht collided with Chirac's electoral promises, and the promises lost. In a television interview in October, he announced that his initial optimism was misplaced.

Immediately after Chirac's interview, Prime Minister Juppé announced a series of major reforms, which—both in form and substance—represented virtually a declaration of war on labor unions, especially those in the public sector. Juppé proposed tightening requirements for civil servants' pensions and ending preferential retirement benefits for railway workers, electrical and gas workers, and postal workers. Juppé called for revamping the state-run railway system, including partial privatization, closing unprofitable sectors, and laying off workers. And he proposed to overhaul the Social Security (health care) system. His plan included tightening benefits and limiting future increase in expenditures; partially transferring control to parliament (that is, the government) from the previous system, in which unions had a major role; and modifying the system of financing health care by increasing the number of those taxed and creating a new tax which would apply to virtually all citizens. Further, he mandated financial austerity for universities, including cutbacks in hiring of new staff, as well as limiting new construction and maintenance. In addition, government ministers hinted that new reforms would soon follow, including the partial privatization of France Télécom, the sprawling state telecommunications agency, and increases in income taxes.

Reaction was swift. The railway workers were the first to announce a strike, continuing their tradition of militancy. (Although railway workers represent only 1 percent of all French wage earners, they account for one-fifth of all the work time lost due to strikes.) Other transport workers quickly followed their lead: Paris métro workers and bus drivers, public transport workers in other French cities, and air traffic controllers and Air France personnel. France was quickly brought to a halt, as gridlock and miles of traffic jams immobilized Paris and other large cities. Massive demonstrations brought out ever more participants, climaxing in a two-million strong demonstration on December 7. Soon, the postal system ground to a halt, garbage began to accumulate on city streets, schools closed, and power slowdowns occurred.

In face of this overwhelming and sustained opposition, Juppé retreated on some key points. In fact, the major reason that President Chirac dissolved parliament in 1997 and called for new elections was his gamble that a fresh electoral mandate would enable the Juppé government to sponsor further spending cutbacks. The costly result was to produce a Socialist parliamentary majority in 1997 and a Socialist government.

Although the strikes were of major significance in showing the depth of popular opposition to the dominant orientation of economic policy, they failed to alter that orientation in fundamental respects. The strikes revealed the continuing vitality of the French tradition of popular protest, and they highlighted the importance of French participation in the EU, both for shaping French policy and provoking popular opposition.

New Issues and Sources of Partisan Conflict: Economy and Identity

French politics has entered a new era. On the one hand, traditional ideological conflicts have waned, and established political parties have moved closer together. The center-left Socialist Party has drained much of the support that in the past made the PCF one of France's largest parties. The two major center-right parties uneasily coexist. Further, ideological struggles about how to organize the economy have given way to a kind of centrist, pragmatic managerialism, with widespread acceptance of a mixed economy consisting of state regulation and market competition. Political institutions surmounted some key challenges in the 1980s and, although the executive remains overbearing and there are inadequate channels for popular participation, somewhat greater balance has developed in the present period.

Yet, as we have seen, this appearance of stability may be deceptive and the democratic idea—and practice—are under stress. Established parties command ever smaller levels of support. Citizens are voting with their feet—by supporting dissident political parties or not voting at all. In brief, the established French political parties have been relatively unable to resolve two major issues: the economic challenge of assuring adequate standards of living for all French citizens and the cultural issue of French national identity. Each

is a difficult issue; in tandem, the two produce the major political challenge that confronts the French political system.

The Economy. Governments generally flourish when the economy flourishes—and are punished when the economy stagnates. The uneven performance of the French economy in the past several decades is a large part of the explanation for the political gyrations that have occurred. Although the economy has been considerably modernized and strengthened in the recent period, it has come at a heavy price, notably by high rates of unemployment and a large number of marginalized, excluded citizens. The temporary improvement in the economy in the late 1990s helped produce Prime Minister Jospin's exceptionally high poll standings, as did the Jospin government's sponsorship of assistance targeting youth, the excluded, and the long-term unemployed. But France's economic difficulties and associated social problems are too deeply rooted to be solved by simple legislation.

French economic difficulties are compounded by the French style of governing the economy. In the postwar period, the French excelled at state-directed promotion of large firms that produce projects for captive markets at home and abroad (the latter negotiated with foreign states), as well as at "crash programs" of industrial development (such as rail and road transport, aerospace, and telecommunications). In the current economic race, victory goes not to the large but to the flexible, and state direction may prove a handicap, not an advantage. Moreover, the cost of innovation in many new spheres now exceeds the capacity of a medium-size power such as France.

As in many countries, economic restructuring has produced social marginalization. In France, however, this situation has generated nationwide protest movements that have disrupted politics as usual. In 1997 jobless workers stormed unemployment insurance offices throughout France to demand increased benefits and greater government assistance in finding jobs. The conflict temporarily subsided when Prime Minister Jospin offered a carrot and a stick. The carrot consisted of a package of measures that targeted the long-term unemployed, as well as the mandated reduction of the work week to 35 hours. The stick was Jospin's order to the police to storm and evacuate the occupied offices. An economic uptick in 1998 helped reduce unemployment slightly, but deep problems persist, involving high levels of unemployment, a costly welfare state, and the budgetary constraints imposed by participation in the European Monetary Union.

"France for the French:" The Changing Politics of National and Collective Identity. France has traditionally attracted significant numbers of immigrants. Indeed, in 1930, there was a higher proportion of immigrants in France than in the United States, a country known as a major destination for emigrants.[34] In the past, tensions often ran high between native-born French and immigrants arriving from Poland, Italy, and Portugal, for example. But two factors in the recent past have intensified conflicts around the issue of immigration. The first involves cultural conflict and anxiety about France's national identity in an era of globalization. Sociologist Rogers Brubaker has emphasized the traditionally close link in France between nationhood, citizenship, and common cultural values.

> In the French tradition, the nation has been conceived in relation to the institutional and territorial frame of the state. . . . Yet while French nationhood is constituted by political unity, it is centrally expressed in the striving for cultural unity. Political inclusion has entailed cultural assimilation, for regional cultural minorities and immigrants alike."[35]

There have been intense conflicts in the current period over the right of immigrants and their children to obtain French nationality. In the 1990s, conservative governments scrapped France's traditional policy of granting automatic French citizenship to children of immigrants and required them to apply for citizenship. While the change was largely symbolic, in that all those who qualified were granted citizenship, critics charged that the new policy sent a signal that immigrants were not welcome members of the national community.

France's ailing economy is the second reason why the issues of immigration and cultural identity have assumed such importance. This, in turn, suggests that the twin issues of France's economic difficulties and its national identity are closely intertwined. For economic factors play an important role in inflaming opinion on the place of immigrants in French society. Immigrants were tolerated when they were needed to perform necessary jobs like building roads, homes, and automobiles. Recently, however, the shift to a service-based economy, as well as lagging economic growth, has reduced the number of unskilled and semiskilled jobs, and there is a surplus, not a shortage, of workers. The result is that, on the one hand, immigrants and their children are far more likely to be unemployed. On the other hand, recent immigrants prove a convenient target for native-born French living a precarious existence—and for politicians eager to reap political gains from the situation.

The major controversy over immigration centers on the status of the most recent wave of immigrants, who are mainly from North Africa. There are about four million Muslims in France, two million of whom are French citizens. Many arrived in France during the 1960s, mostly from Algeria, when there was a large demand for foreign workers willing to work for low wages on public works projects, and the French government helped organize the recruitment of workers from North Africa. Since the middle 1970s, with the onset of economic stagnation, successive governments have often used brutal means to stop the flow of new immigrants. (New immigration is now prohibited, save for families of already established immigrants and applicants for political asylum.) As a result, the number of new immigrants arriving yearly has fallen from 250,000–300,000 to 100,000–120,000.[36] (Note that issues of immigration and identity came to the fore *after* new immigration to France had slowed to a trickle.) The conspicuous presence of police carrying out identity checks in métro stations and elsewhere illustrates that the government seeks to demonstrate its determination to expel undocumented immigrants, that is, those who migrate to France without official authorization.

The Muslim community in France is quite diverse and divided—by country of origin, degree of religious observance, and generationally. Among the most politically active groups is the Beurs, that is, the roughly one million children of immigrant parents from North Africa. Although the Beurs have made energetic efforts to achieve social mobility (with women far more apt to succeed), Muslims in France are often considered second-class citizens and the object of widespread hostility. Every year, they are the object of numerous violent and racist attacks.

The explosive mix just described has stimulated the growth of new parties and movements. In the early 1980s, National Front leader Jean-Marie Le Pen failed to gain the modest number of signatures from local politicians to qualify as a presidential candidate. Ten years later, the National Front was the fourth largest party in France. The party's slogan of "France for the French" does not answer the question, "Who (and what) is French?" But its simplistic and racist approach has reshaped the structure of ideological conflict and public opinion. For example, many French citizens on the economic and social margin have been persuaded by the graffiti sprayed by the FN in prominent places: "3 million immigrants = 3 million unemployed," which falsely implies that immigrants cause unemployment.

The FN has polarized public opinion on the immigration issue and moved the center of political gravity in a conservative direction. In an attempt to undercut support for the National Front, governments of left and right have enacted harsh policies toward undocumented immigrants.

There has also been intense mobilization in support of the undocumented immigrants and against racism. On several occasions, undocumented immigrants have camped out in churches to dramatize their plight. The Jospin government was squeezed from both sides in 1998 when it sponsored legislation to review and regularize the situation of qualified undocumented immigrants. On the one hand, conservatives lambasted the government for being "soft" on immigrants. On the other hand, the government was severely criticized when the interior ministry rejected the claims of half the 150,000 applicants for regularization and announced that they would be deported. Leading French artists and intellectuals, led by four famous film makers, launched a movement of solidarity with the immigrants, opposing the government. The action was highly embarrassing to a Socialist government proudly proclaiming its commitment to human rights and humanist ideals.

The two examples described above are interrelated and together shape a new axis of political division in France, which pits those who are socially and economically excluded, along with their supporters, against the more economically and socially privileged. The social fracture, discussed in Section 2, does not correspond neatly to established party divisions or even the left-right dimension.

An important question on France's political agenda is how to preserve the welfare state, which provides fairly generous contributions that enable citizens to obtain high-quality childcare, medical care, education, and job training. The French pride themselves on resisting the American model in which access to these goods and services depends on one's income. The French regard these goods and services as a right of all citizens. But can this conception survive when unemployment is high, the proportion of the working population (which finances such programs) is declining, and EU treaty obligations impose heavy fiscal constraints?

How can the French adapt to the new complex global economy? Will France be able to maintain its favored position in a world of states? How can French national identity be refashioned in an era when the French values of liberty, quality, and fraternity have become more widely shared—and yet when groups within France have begun to reject the French model of cultural assimilation and seek to preserve their own cultural identities?

An official commission appointed to reflect on "The State and French Society in the Year 2000" asserted that, because of its traditional patterns, France has severe handicaps in confronting the future. It asked, "Will the road toward democratic maturity, within the context of the globalization of values and a reduced role for national states, be more arduous in France than in other nations?"[37] In light of the previous discussion, the answer seems quite obvious.

French Politics in Comparative Perspective

France has long provided an interesting case for comparative analysis because of its many attempts at state- and regime-making. By comparing the Fourth and Fifth Republics, we can study the impact of institutions on political outcomes. The same country was governed in two dramatically different ways within a short time. Unfortunately, the experiment teaches what to avoid as much as what to emulate. The Fourth

Republic demonstrated the pitfalls of a fragmented multiparty system with undisciplined parties, and a parliamentary regime with a weak executive. The Fifth Republic demonstrates the danger of an isolated and overly powerful executive. The Fifth Republic has taken halting steps toward developing more balanced institutions, including a larger role for the Constitutional Council, stronger local governments, and independent media. The results suggest that France's semi-presidential system may prove attractive to countries seeking lessons in political-institutional design.

On the level of political culture, France has prided itself on its universalist, yet distinctive, role in history, deriving from its revolutionary heritage of liberty, equality, and fraternity. But at the same time that they have become increasingly accepted, both within France and on a global scale, these values are less able to promote cohesion among French citizens. There is much to learn from how France adjusts to the process of abandoning its claims to being preeminent among the countries of the world. It is also useful to study how France seeks to reconcile a centralized state with democratic values, as well as how to meld presidential and parliamentary forms. Similarly, France is not alone in seeking to reconcile the conflicting claims of maintaining national cohesion in face of extensive internal diversity and increasing integration in the international economic and political system. More than thirty years after the youthful French protestors chanted in May 1968, "The struggle continues," the words have lost none of their relevance.

Key Terms

ancien régime	dirigiste
revolution	nationalization
republic	privatization
prefects	deregulation
protectionist	convergence criteria
authoritarian	semi-presidential system
referendum	
conservative	cohabitation
socialist	grandes écoles
statist	grands corps
indicative planning	presidentialization

Suggested Readings

Boy, Daniel, and Nonna Mayer, eds. *The French Voter Decides*. Ann Arbor: University of Michigan Press, 1994.

Brubaker, Rogers. *Citizenship and Nationhood in France and Germany*. Cambridge, MA: Harvard University Press, 1992.

Chapman, Herrick, Mark Kesselman, and Martin A. Schain, eds. *A Century of Organized Labor in France: A Union Movement for the Twenty-First Century?* New York: St. Martin's Press, 1998.

Daley, Anthony, ed. *The Mitterrand Era: Policy Alternatives and Political Mobilization in France*. New York: New York University Press, 1996.

Daley, Anthony. *Steel, State, and Labor: Mobilization and Adjustment in France*. Pittsburgh: University of Pittsburgh Press, 1996.

Duyvendak, Jan Willem. *The Power of Politics: New Social Movements in France*. Boulder, CO: Westview, 1995.

Friend, Julius W. *The Long Presidency: France in the Mitterrand Years, 1981–1995*. Boulder, CO: Westview, 1998.

Gaffney, John, and Lorna Milne, eds. *French Presidentialism and the Election of 1995*. Brookfield, VT: Ashgate, 1997.

Hall, Peter, Jack Hayward, and Howard Machin, eds. *Developments in French Politics 2*. New York: Macmillan, 1998.

Howell, Chris. *Regulating Labor: The State and Industrial Relations Reform in Postwar France*. Princeton, NJ: Princeton University Press, 1992.

Huber, John D. *Rationalizing Parliament: Legislative Institutions and Party Politics in France*. Cambridge, England: Cambridge University Press, 1996.

Ireland, Patrick. *The Policy Challenge of Ethnic Diversity: Immigrant Politics in France and Switzerland*. Cambridge, MA: Harvard University Press, 1994.

Keeler, John T. S., and Martin A. Schain, eds. *Chirac's Challenge: Liberalization, Europeanization, and Malaise in France*. New York: St. Martin's Press, 1996.

Levy, Jonah. *Tocqueville's Revenge: Dilemmas of Institutional Reform in Post-Dirigiste France*. Cambridge, MA: Harvard University Press, 1998.

Mazur, Amy G. *Gender Bias and the State: Symbolic Reform at Work in Fifth Republic France*. Pittsburgh: University of Pittsburgh Press, 1996.

Pierce, Roy. *Choosing the Chief: Presidential Elections in France and the United States*. Ann Arbor: University of Michigan Press, 1995.

Schmidt, Vivien A. *From State to Market? The Transformation of French Business and Government*. Cambridge, England: Cambridge University Press, 1996.

Simmons, Harvey G. *The French National Front: The Extremist Challenge to Democracy*. Boulder, CO: Westview, 1996.

Smith, W. Rand. *The Left's Dirty Job: The Politics of Industrial Restructuring in France and Spain*. Pittsburgh: University of Pittsburgh Press, 1998.

Stone, Alec. *The Birth of Judicial Politics in France*. New York: Oxford University Press, 1992.

Tiersky, Ronald. *France in the New Europe: Changing Yet Steadfast*. Belmont, CA: Wadsworth, 1994.

Tilly, Charles. *The Contentious French: Four Centuries of Popular Struggle*. Cambridge, MA: The Belknap Press of Harvard University Press, 1986.

Endnotes

[1] Simon Schama, *Citizens: A Chronicle of the French Revolution* (New York: Knopf, 1989), 62.

[2] Perry Anderson, *Lineages of the Absolutist State* (London: New Left Books, 1974), p. 111. This section also draws on Theda Skocpol, *States and Social Revolutions: A Comparative Analysis of France, Russia, and China* (New York: Cambridge University Press, 1979).

[3] Lynn Hunt, *Politics, Culture, and Class in the French Revolution* (Berkeley: University of California Press, 1984), pp. 15, 56.

[4] Joan B. Landes, *Women and the Public Sphere in the Age of the French Revolution* (Ithaca, NY: Cornell University Press, 1988), pp. 171–172.

[5] William H. Sewell, Jr., *Work and Revolution in France: The Language of Labor from the Old Regime to 1848* (Cambridge, England: Cambridge University Press, 1980), p. 199.

[6] Georges Dupeux, *La Société Française, 1789–1970* (Paris: Armand Colin, 1974), p. 10.

[7] Richard F. Kuisel, *Capitalism and the State in Modern France* (Cambridge, England: Cambridge University Press, 1981), p. 15.

[8] Ibid., p. 16.

[9] Laurence Ménière, ed., *Bilan de la France, 1981–1993* (Paris: Hachette, 1993), p. 12.

[10] Ibid., p. 277.

[11] Henri Mendras with Alistair Cole, *Social Change in Modern France: Towards a Cultural Anthropology of the Fifth Republic* (Cambridge, England: Cambridge University Press, 1991), 1.

[12] Kuisel, op. cit., p. 248.

[13] John G. Goodman, "Monetary Policy and Financial Deregulation in France," *French Politics and Society*. 10, no. 4 (Fall 1992); 32.

[14] Kuisel, op. cit., p. 264.

[15] William G. Andrews, "Introduction," *The Fifth Republic at Twenty*, ed. William E. Andrews and Stanley Hoffman (Albany: State University of New York, 1981), p. 4.

[16] Peter A. Hall, *Governing the Economy: The Politics of State Intervention in Britain and France* (New York: Oxford University Press, 1986), p. 163.

[17] Ménière, op. cit., p. 18.

[18] Peter A. Hall suggested this term to describe the economic policy followed by successive French governments since the mid-1980s. See his "From One Modernization Strategy to Another: The Character and Consequences of Recent Economic Policy in France," unpublished paper presented at the Tenth International Conference of Europeanists, Chicago, March 15, 1996.

[19] Vivien A. Schmidt, *From State to Market? The Transformation of French Business and Government* (Cambridge, Eng.: Cambridge University Press, 1996), p. 442.

[20] Roger Cohen, "Paris and Washington Speak Softly," *The International Herald Tribune*, October 20, 1997.

[21] See *Le Monde*, October 22–23, 1995; and Assayers-CGT, *Rapport sur la situation économique et sociale, 1994–95* (Montreuil: VO Editions, 1995), p. 9.

[22] Jean Charlot, *La Politique en France* (Paris: Livre de Poche, 1994), p. 27.

[23] Robert Elgie, *The Role of the Prime Minister in France, 1981–91* (New York: St. Martin's Press, 1993), p. 1.

[24] Ezra Suleiman, "Les élites de l'administration et de la politique dans la France de la Vᵉ République: homogénéité, puissance, permanence," in Ezra Suleiman and Henri Mendras, eds., *Le recrutement des élites en Europe* (Paris: La Découverte, 1995), p. 33.

[25] Michel Bauer and Bénédicte Bertin-Mourot, "La tyrannie du diplôme initial et la circulation des élites: la stabilité du modèle français," in ibid., p. 51.

[26] John T.S. Keeler and Alec Stone, "Judicial-Political Confrontation in Mitterrand's France: The Emergence of the Constitutional Council as a Major Actor in the Policy-Making Process," in *The Mitterrand Experiment: Continuity and Change in Modern France*, ed. George Ross, Stanley Hoffmann, and Sylvia Malzacher (New York: Oxford University Press, 1987), p. 176.

[27] John D. Huber, *Rationalizing Parliament: Legislative Institutions and Party Politics in France* (Cambridge, England: Cambridge University Press, 1996).

[28] Donald Sassoon, *One Hundred Years of Socialism: The West European Left in the Twentieth Century* (New York: The New Press, 1996), p. 571.

[29] James G. Shields, "Le Pen and the Progression of the Far-Right Vote in France," *French Politics and Society*. 13, no. 2 (Spring 1995); 37.

[30] Olivier Duhamel and Jérôme Jaffré, "Le mal-être de la gauche," in Duhamel and Jaffré, eds., *L'Etat de l'opinion, 1990* (Paris: Le Seuil, 1990); pp. 9–20.

[31] Charlot, op. cit., p. 159.

[32] Stephen Bernstein, "States and Unions: From Postwar Settlement to Contemporary Stalemate," in *The State in Capitalist Europe, A Casebook*, ed. Stephen Bernstein, David Held, and Joel Krieger (Winchester, MA: George Allen & Unwin, 1984), p. 64.

[33] Patrick Jarreau, *La France de Chirac* (Paris: Flammarion, 1995), p. 9.

[34] Patrick Weil, *La France et ses étrangers* (Paris: Gallimard, 1991), p. 28.

[35] Rogers Brubaker, *Citizenship and Nationhood in France and Germany* (Cambridge, MA: Harvard University Press, 1992), p. 1.

[36] Patrick Weil, "Immigration, nation et nationalité: regards comparatives et croisés," *Revue française de science politique*. 44 (April 1994): 308–326.

[37] Bernard Cazes, Fabrice Hatem, Paul Thibaud, "L'Etat et la société française en l'an 2000," *Esprit*, no. 165 (October 1990), p. 95.

CHAPTER 4

Germany

Christopher S. Allen

Federal Republic of Germany

Land and Population

Capital	Berlin
Total Area (square miles)	137,803 (slightly smaller than Montana)
Population	82 million
Annual Average Population Growth Rate (1990–1997)	0.5%
Urban Population	87%

Ethnic Composition

German	91.5%
Turkish	2.4%
Other	6.1%

Major Language	German

Religious Affiliation

Protestant	38.0%
Roman Catholic	34.0%
Muslim	1.7%
Unaffiliated or other	26.3%

Economy

Domestic Currency	German mark (DM), euro; after January 1, 2002, euro
Total GNP (US$)	$2.32 trillion
GNP per capita (US$)	$28,260
GNP per capita at purchasing power parity (US$)	$21,300

GNP average annual growth rate

1997	1.8%
1987–1997	1.5%

Income Gap: GDP per capita (of US$)

Richest 20% of population	$37,963
Poorest 20% of population	$6594

Structure of Production (% of GDP)

Agriculture	3%
Industry	41%
Services	56%

Labor Force Distribution (% of total)

Agriculture	1.1%
Industry	34.5%
Services	64.4%

Exports as % of GDP	23%
Imports as % of GDP	22%
Electricity Consumption per capita (kwh)	6615
CO_2 Emissions per capita (metric tons)	10,200

Society

Life Expectancy	Female	79.5
	Male	73
Doctors per 100,000 population		319
Infant Mortality per 1000 live births		5
Adult Literacy		99%

(although the UN estimates that 14.4% of people aged 16–65 are functionally illiterate)

Access to Information and Communications per 1000 population		
	Radios	944
	Televisions	550
	Telephone Lines	494
	Personal Computers	165

Women in Government and Economy

Women in Parliament 18.8% (lower house); 30.9% (upper house)	
Women at ministerial level	16%
Women as % of total labor force	42%
Female business administrators and managers	26%
Female professional and technical workers	49%
1998 Human Development Index ranking (out of 174 countries; 1 = highest)	19

Political Organization

Political System   Parliamentary democracy

Regime History   After Third Reich's defeat, Germany was partitioned and occupied by Allies in 1945. In 1949 the Federal Republic of Germany (FRG) was established in the west and the German Democratic Republic (GDR) was established in the east. The two German states unified in 1990.

Administrative Structure   Federal, with 16 states. Germany does not have sharp separation between levels of government.

Executive   Ceremonial president is the head of state, elected for a five-year term (with a two-term limit) by the Federal Convention. Chancellor is head of government and is a member of the *Bundestag* and a leader of the majority party or coalition.

Legislature   Bicameral. *Bundestag* (669 members at 1998 federal election) elected via dual ballot system combining single-member districts and proportional representation. Upper house (*Bundesrat*) comprises 69 members who are elected and appointed officials from the 16 states.

Judiciary   Autonomous and independent. The legal system has three levels: Federal High Court, which is the criminal-civil system; Special Constitutional Court, dealing with matters affecting Basic Law; and Administrative Court, consisting of Labor, Social Security, and Finance courts.

Party System   Multiparty. Major parties are Social Democratic Party (SPD), the Greens, Christian Democratic Union (CDU), Christian Social Union (CSU), Free Democratic Party (FDP), and Party of Democratic Socialism (PDS).

Section 1 The Making of the Modern German State

Politics in Action

Jubilant celebrations took place outside Social Democratic Party (SPD) and Green Party headquarters in Bonn on September 27, 1998: the two parties had unexpectedly won the 1998 elections and ushered in a "Red-Green" coalition for the first time in German history.

Green parties are no longer a political novelty. Concerned primarily with environmental protection, they sprang up in the 1980s and 1990s in all industrialized countries. Yet, until 1998, they were marginal parties attempting to challenge Social Democratic and Labor parties for support of the democratic left. The Greens are less concerned with working-class material issues than with "postmaterial" ones. Germany has the most famous Green party, but the Greens had an uneasy relationship with the Social Democrats until they formed their 1998 coalition. Green Party members come from disparate roots, but all share the belief that the SPD became too bureaucratic and unwilling to address the concerns of rank-and-file members during the 1970s and 1980s. Some Greens—ex-members of the SPD—resented the removal of left-wing activists from the civil service in the early 1970s under SPD chancellor Willy Brandt. Brandt later regretted this action and often referred to the Greens as the SPD's lost children. In part, this division and uneasiness between Reds (SPD) and Greens enabled Helmut Kohl to face far less formidable challenges from the Left during his sixteen years in power.

The Greens first obtained seats in the *Bundestag* in 1983 and repeated the feat in 1987. However, the party failed to attain seats in the 1990 election and faced political uncertainty in the immediate postunification period. Yet, by the mid-1990s, it found new support among the population. In the 1994 election the Green Party emerged as the third-largest party in the Federal Republic, receiving 7.3 percent of the vote while the traditional third party, the centrist Free Democratic Party (FDP), achieved only 6.9 percent. The 1998 elections again gave the Greens the edge over the FDP as the third-strongest party.

The relationship between the Greens and the SPD is important because it is the only possible electoral combination that excludes the right-aligned Christian Democrats. In time, however, if the eastern German former communist party, the Party of Democratic Socialism (PDS), is seen as a democratic party "like all the rest," it could also be a potential member of a left-leaning coalition.

The Red-Green coalition agreement in 1998 was unprecedented, since the two parties did not explicitly run as coalition partners, as did the SPD and FDP from the 1969 to the 1980 elections. Both SPD and Greens were wary of each other before the 1998 election. The Greens saw the SPD as too bureaucratic and wedded to a belief in economic growth without sufficient concern for ecological issues. In turn, most members of the SPD viewed the Greens as a rag-tag group pursuing alternative life-styles with little understanding of the responsibility required to govern the largest Western European country. The SPD also believed that the Greens underestimated how important material issues still were in a Germany with a 10 percent unemployment level. If anything, argued some in the SPD, more materialism, not less, was what the working class and the unemployed needed. Before 1998 there were several attempts to form a Red-Green coalition at the *Land* (state) level, the most long-lasting being the coalition in the state of Hesse, where Frankfurt is the largest city. This coalition fell apart on the issue of economic growth versus ecology. Many observers critical of the Left feel that the national coalition between the SPD and the Greens will eventually struggle with these sometimes incompatible goals.

Yet a state coalition is different from a national coalition. After a month of deliberations following the election, the new Red-Green coalition was sworn into office on October 27, 1998. The two parties quickly discovered during the course of their negotiations that their alliance was serious business. Squabbling among opposition parties is expected, but bickering among governing coalition partners is a blueprint for disaster—and a quick return to the opposition benches.

Coalition governments require the two parties to forge a specific and binding common program. The

SPD carried the largest weight in coalition negotiations, yet the Greens obtained a significant number of their primary demands. The coalition's first priority was overcoming Germany's high unemployment. Combining an aggressive job retraining program—in conjunction with Germany's famous apprenticeship system—with a tax cut aimed at poor and working-class families, the Red-Green government focused on increasing domestic economic demand as an engine of growth. As part of ecological or *qualitativ* economic growth, the coalition also instituted a higher fuel tax to encourage energy conservation and a long-term plan to phase out nuclear power plants. Among the other coalition planks were a commitment to increase equality between men and women both in the workplace and in society; a solidification of the German social state on sound financial principles; an explicit commitment to coordinate policy with its European

Union (EU) neighbors on major issues, such as reducing European-wide interest rates to spur economic growth; and a change in the immigration policies to allow easier attainment of German citizenship for foreigners.

Can advanced industrialized states combine a strong economy with environmental sensitivity and social solidarity? The Greens and the Social Democrats of Germany are providing a unique test case. Germany stands at a turning point that could lead in one of two directions. The first might see the new SPD-Green coalition lead to the consolidation of postwar successes in which the former East Germans achieve the material prosperity and democratic political culture of their western counterparts. This could help Germany to become the anchor in the expanding European Union as a partner, not a conqueror, of its neighbors. The second path would be much more dangerous. It could lead to a fractious governing coalition (as illustrated by the resignation of SPF leader Oskar Lafontaine from the cabinet in 1999), rising social conflict, weakened domestic institutions, and uncertain international relations.

Geographic Setting

Germany is located in central Europe and has been as much a western European nation as an eastern European one. It has a total area of 137,803 square miles (slightly smaller than the state of Montana). Its population of 82 million, comprising about 90 percent Germans, all of whom speak German as the primary language, is roughly evenly divided between Roman Catholics and Protestants. Germany has been relatively homogeneous ethnically; however, the presence of several million Turks in Germany, first drawn to the Federal Republic as *Gastarbeiter* (guest workers) in the 1960s, suggests that ethnic diversity will continue to grow. Furthermore, increased migration across borders by EU citizens will also decrease cultural homogeneity.

For a densely populated country, Germany has a surprisingly high 54 percent of its land in agricultural production. It is composed of large plains in northern Germany, a series of smaller mountain ranges in the center of the country, and the towering Alps to the south at the Austrian and Swiss borders. It has a

temperate climate with considerable cloud cover and precipitation throughout the year. For Germany, the absence of natural borders in the west and east has been an important geographic fact. For example, on the north it borders both the North and Baltic seas and the country of Denmark, but to the west, south, and east it has many neighbors: the Netherlands, Belgium, Luxembourg, France, Switzerland, Austria, the Czech Republic, and Poland. Conflicts and wars with its neighbors were a constant feature in Germany until the end of World War II.

Germany's lack of resources—aside from iron ore and coal deposits in the Ruhr and the Saarland—has shaped much of the country's history. Since the Industrial Revolution in the nineteenth century, many of Germany's external relationships, both commercial and military, have revolved around gaining access to resources not present within the national borders. Germany is divided into sixteen federal states (*Bundesländer*), many of which correspond to historic German kingdoms and principalities (e.g., Bavaria, Saxony, Hesse) or medieval trading cities (e.g., Hamburg, Bremen).

Critical Junctures

Nationalism and German Unification (1806–1871)

The first German state was the Holy Roman Empire, founded by Charlemagne in A.D. 800 (sometimes referred to as the First Reich). But this loose and fragmented "Reich" (empire) bore little resemblance to a modern nation-state. The empire was composed of as many as three hundred sovereign entities and included the territories of present-day Germany, Austria, and the Czech Republic.

Two main factors hindered German state formation: uncertain geographic boundaries and religious division.[1] Germany was divided by the Reformation into a mostly Protestant north and a mostly Roman Catholic south. With the emergence of a strong Prussian state in northeastern Germany in the eighteenth century, German affairs were constantly roiled by the struggle between Protestant Prussia and Catholic Austria, whose Habsburg rulers served as Holy Roman emperors.

The geographic and religious divisions caused the German language and German physical and cultural traits to define German national identity to a much greater extent than in other European states. From the Reformation to the early nineteenth century, intellectual and literary giants such as Martin Luther, Johann Wolfgang von Goethe, and Friedrich von Schiller created and defined German culture. For many Germans in the early nineteenth century, the lack of political unity stood in sharp contrast to the strong influence of German culture in literature and religion.

The victories of the French emperor Napoleon against Prussia and Austria brought an end to the Holy Roman Empire. Napoleon consolidated most of Germany outside Prussia and Austria into a confederation under his "protection." Defeat and occupation aroused strong German nationalist sentiment, and in 1813–1814 the Prussians led an alliance of German states in a "War of Liberation." After Napoleon's final defeat in 1815, the victorious allies created a new German Confederation, including both Prussia and Austria.

Prussian leaders, flush with military victory, were confident that their authoritarian leadership was best suited to an awakening German nation. In 1819 they launched a tariff union with neighboring German states that by 1834 encompassed almost all of the German Confederation except Austria, greatly expanding Prussian influence at Austria's expense. But free-market capitalism and democracy did not take root in the Prussian-dominated Germanic principalities. The outstanding features of Prussian rule were (1) a strong state deeply involved in economic affairs (an economic policy known as **mercantilism**), (2) the dominance of politics and the military by a reactionary group of noble landlords in eastern Prussia called *Junkers*, (3) a patriotic military, and (4) a political culture dominated by virtues such as honor, duty, and service to the state.

The European revolutions of 1848 sparked pro-democracy uprisings across Germany, including Berlin and Vienna, the Prussian and Austrian capitals. German rulers had to consent to the convening of an all-German assembly in Frankfurt to draft a constitution for a united democratic Germany. The effort at unification failed when the king of Prussia declined the offer to rule as a constitutional monarch; as he put it, he refused to "pick up a crown from the gutter." The revolutionary democratic movements in Germany and Austria were violently suppressed.

Germany would be united, instead, by a "revolution from above" led by Count Otto von Bismarck.[2] Bismarck became minister-president of Prussia in 1862. He was a *Junker* and reflected the values and authoritarian vision of his class. Bismarck realized that Prussia needed to industrialize and modernize its economy to compete with Britain, France, and the United States. He created an unlikely and nondemocratic coalition of rural *Junkers* from the northeast and iron industrialists of the Ruhr region in the northwest. It relied on a coalition of elites rather than on democratic working-class and peasant/farmer support, as had the French and American revolutions. Bismarck was contemptuous of democracy: "Not by speeches and majority votes are the great questions of the day decided—that was the great error of 1848 and 1849—but by blood and iron," he proclaimed.

Bismarck was as good as his word. He launched three short wars—against Denmark (1864), Austria (1866), and France (1870)—which culminated in the unification of Germany.[3] The so-called Second Reich—excluding Austria and with the king of Prussia as *Kaiser* (emperor), was proclaimed in 1871.

The Second Reich (1871–1918)

The Second Reich—a term not used at the time but only retrospectively in the twentieth century—was an authoritarian regime that was democratic in appearance only. Undemocratic forces (industrial and landed elites) controlled political and economic power. Bismarck's regime was symbolically democratic in that the "Iron Chancellor" allowed for universal male suffrage for the lower house (*Reichstag*) of the bicameral legislature, but real decision-making authority lay in the hands of the upper house (*Landtag*), whose members were either directly or indirectly appointed by Bismarck. In other words, the *Reichstag* could pass legislation, but there was little if any hope that it would become law.

The primary goal of the Second Reich was rapid industrialization, supported by state power and a powerful banking system geared to foster large-scale industrial investment rather than by the trial-and-error methods of free markets.[4] This path was so successful

Critical Junctures in Germany's Political Development

1871–1918	Unification, Second Reich
1919–1933	Weimar Republic
1933–1945	Third Reich
1939–1945	World War II
1945–1949	Occupation
1949	Founding of Federal Republic of Germany (FRG) and German Democratic Republic (GDR)
1955	West Germany joins NATO; East Germany joins Warsaw Pact
1957	West Germany cofounds European Economic Community
1990–Present	Unification; GDR incorporated into FRG

that Germany had become a leading industrial power by 1900. At the fore were such industries as coal, steel, railroads, dyes, chemicals, industrial electronics, and machine tools. The state emphasized the development of such heavy industries at the expense of those producing consumer goods. Lacking a strong domestic consumer-goods economy, Germany had to sell a substantial portion of what it produced on world markets.

Rapid transformation of a largely agrarian society in the 1850s to an industrial one by the turn of the twentieth century created widespread social dislocation and growing opposition to the conservative regime. A small middle class of professionals and small-business owners with rising expectations pressured the government to democratize and provide basic liberal (i.e., free-market) rights. Industrialization also promoted the growth of a manually skilled working class and the corresponding rise of a militant Social Democratic Party (*Sozialdemokratische Partei Deutschlands*). The Social Democrats' primary goals were economic rights in the workplace and democratization of the political system. The SPD was greatly influenced by the writings and the active participation of the founders of socialism, Karl Marx and Friedrich Engels, both of whom were German. Socialist philosophy argues that workers, who produce the goods and services in society, should receive a greater share of economic and political power. The SPD grew as fast as the pace of German industrialization.

As German chancellor from 1871–1890, Bismarck alternately persecuted and grudgingly tolerated the democratic and socialist opposition. He banned the Social Democratic Party yet created the first welfare state as a way to blunt the effects of rapid economic growth. Social welfare benefits included health insurance and the first forms of state-sponsored old-age pensions. This combination of welfare with political repression is sometimes referred to as Bismarck's iron fist in a velvet glove.

Bismarck also significantly influenced German political culture by creating a strong and centralized German state. The ***Kulturkampf*** (cultural struggle) he initiated was a prime example of Prussian and Protestant dominance. Essentially a movement against the Catholic church, it sought to remove educational and cultural institutions from the church and place them under the state. This action, which polarized the church and many Catholic Germans, left a powerful political legacy.

By 1900, Germany's primary economic problem was how to obtain the necessary raw materials and access to world markets for their finished goods in order to sustain rapid economic growth. Other than iron and coal deposits, Germany had few natural resources. Germany then embarked on an imperial adventure sometimes called "the scramble for Africa."[5] However, Germany was a latecomer on this continent, after Britain, France, Belgium, and the Netherlands, and was able to colonize only in resource-poor southwestern Africa. From 1871 until World War I, Germany tried and failed to extend its colonial and economic influence. This inflamed German nationalists and pushed German leaders to invest in the rapid development of a shipbuilding industry and a navy to secure German economic and geopolitical interests.

An undemocratic domestic political system, the lack of profitable colonies, an exposed geopolitical position in central Europe, and increasingly inflamed nationalism heightened Germany's aggression toward other nations and ultimately prompted it to help launch World War I in 1914.

German leaders expected the war to be brief and victorious. It turned into a protracted conflict, however, and cost Germany both its colonial possessions and its imperial social order. The Second Reich collapsed in November 1918, leaving a very weak foundation for the country's first attempt to establish a parliamentary democracy. The costs of defeat were substantial and fatally compromised Germany's first democratic regime, the Weimar Republic.

The Weimar Republic (1918–1933)

Kaiser Wilhelm II abdicated at the end of World War I, and the Weimar Republic (the constitution was drafted in that eastern German city) replaced the Second Reich. The SPD, the only remaining party not discredited by the failed war, found itself in charge of Germany's first democracy. Its first unwelcome task was to surrender to the Allies. The new government was a procedural democracy; it held regular elections and comprised multiple parties from the far left to the far right. Yet its fatal flaw was that the many right-wing political parties and social forces—as well as the Communists on the left—refused to accept the legitimacy of democratic government.

From the beginning, the SPD leadership was on shaky ground. Three fateful incidents ruthlessly undercut the legitimacy of the Weimar regime: (1) the SPD's foolish and panicked turn to the undemocratic military to "guarantee" order and stability in the first turbulent years of Weimar; (2) the steady drumbeat of accusations by right-wing forces that the government had "stabbed Germany in the back" by agreeing to onerous reparations payments to the Allies; and (3) the ruinous inflation of 1923, when the government was forced to print worthless Reichmarks to pay the war reparations imposed by the Allies on Germany.

Into this turmoil stepped Adolf Hitler, a little-known, Austrian-born former corporal in the German army, who became the leader of the Nazi Party in 1920. **Nazi** is a German acronym for National Socialist German Workers' Party. Taking advantage of a deepening economic crisis, the Nazis mobilized large segments of the population by preaching hatred of the left and of "inferior, non-Aryan races."

After the Great Depression spread to central Europe in 1931, Germany became even more unstable, with none of the major parties (Communists, Social Democrats, Catholic Center, Democrats, Liberals, Bavarian People's Party, Nationalists, Conservatives, or Nazis) able to win a majority or even form durable government coalitions. Frequent elections produced ever-shakier minority governments.

The Nazis relentlessly pressed for political power from a population that continued to underestimate Hitler's real intentions and viewed his hate-filled speeches as merely political rhetoric. The Nazis were rewarded in early 1933, when Hitler outmaneuvered Weimar's aging President Paul von Hindenburg, a World War I general, to become chancellor in a Nazi-Nationalist coalition government sworn in on January 30, 1933. Under the Weimar Constitution, as in many parliamentary systems, the head of state must choose the next head of government if no one party or coalition has received a majority of the seats. Once in power, the Nazis arranged for a fire at the *Reichstag* that they falsely blamed on the Communists. After Hindenburg issued emergency decrees that suspended free speech, free press, and other liberties, this enabled Hitler on March 23 to ram through the *Reichstag* the infamous Enabling Act. It gave sweeping powers to the Nazi-dominated cabinet, rendering the *Reichstag* irrelevant as a representative political body.

The Third Reich (1933–1945)

After the Nazis had obtained the chancellorship, establishing social control was their next major priority, and the initial step was banning political parties. Even civic institutions such as clubs, neighborhood organizations, and churches were subject to Nazi control, influence, or restrictions on independent action.

Ultimately, the Nazis employed propaganda and demagoguery in the absence of democratic opposition to mobilize large segments of the German population. Using mesmerizing speeches and a relentless propaganda ministry led by his aide Joseph Goebbels, Hitler exercised total control of political power and the media to reshape German politics to his party's vision. This vision allowed no opposition, not even within the party.

Initial Nazi domestic policy was concentrated in two major areas: (1) centralization of political power, and (2) the rebuilding of an economy devastated by the depression.of the early 1930s. The Nazis centralized all political authority in Berlin, removing any regional political autonomy. The main purpose of this

Hitler strides triumphantly through a phalanx of Nazi storm troopers (SA) in 1934. *Source:* © Ullstein Bilderdienst.

top-down system was to ensure that Nazi policy regarding the repression of political opposition and Jews and other minorities was carried out to the most minute detail.

The Nazis' economic program was also autocratic in design and implementation. Because free trade unions had been banned, both private and state-run industries forced workers, including slave laborers during World War II, to work long hours for little or no pay. The program emphasized heavier industries (coal, steel, chemicals, machine tools, and industrial electronics) that required massive investment from the large manufacturing cartels, the banking system, and the state itself. Although some segments of big business had initially feared Hitler before he took power, most of German industry eventually endorsed Nazi

economic policies. The Nazis also emphasized massive public works projects, such as building the Autobahn highway system, upgrading the railroad system, and constructing grandiose public buildings. Almost all favored Nazi industries had direct military application. Even the Autobahn was built more for easing military transport than for encouraging pleasure driving.

Hitler incited German nationalism by glorifying the warrior tradition in German folklore and exulting in imperial Germany's conquests in the nineteenth century. Touting a mythically glorious and racially pure German past, he made scapegoats out of homosexuals, ethnic minorities such as gypsies, and especially the Jews. Anti-Semitism proved a powerful political force that allowed Hitler to blame Germany's problems on an "external" international minority and to target them as enemies to be relentlessly persecuted and suppressed.

The Nazis refused to abide by the provisions of the Treaty of Versailles that the Weimar government had signed in 1919. Nazi Germany began producing armaments in large quantities and remilitarized the Rhineland. Hitler rejected the territorial divisions of World War I, claiming that a growing Germany needed increased space to live (*Lebensraum*) in eastern Europe. He ordered a forced union with Austria in March 1938 and the occupation of the German-speaking Sudetenland areas of Czechoslovakia in September 1938. The Third Reich's attack on Poland on September 1, 1939, finally precipitated World War II.

Hitler's grandiose visions of German world domination were dramatically heightened by the conquest of much of Europe in 1939 and 1940. In 1941 he turned his attention to the only continental power that stood in his way: the Soviet Union. Hitler assumed that the defeat of the USSR would happen as easily as his other conquests. Therefore, he embarked on a direct attack on the Soviet Union in the summer of 1941, violating the Nazi-Soviet Nonaggression Pact of 1939. The attack not only ended German military successes but also began the defeat of the Third Reich, a process that would grind on for almost four more years. Yet even as defeat loomed for Germany in May 1945, Hitler wanted the country totally destroyed rather than have it surrender "national honor."

The most heinous aspect of the Nazi regime was the systematic extermination of 6 million Jews and millions of other civilians in concentration camps. Hitler explicitly stated in his book *Mein Kampf* (*My Struggle*) that the Germans were the master race and all those of non-Aryan ethnicity, especially Jews, were inferior. The Nazis placed most of the extermination camps in occupied countries like Poland; the most infamous one in Germany was Dachau, just outside Munich.

A Divided Germany (1945–1990)

Germany was occupied by the victorious Allied powers from 1945 to 1949. As tensions grew between the Soviet Union and the other three Allied powers (Britain, France, and the United States) in the late 1940s, Germany became the dividing line between the two camps. The birth of a separate West Germany (Federal Republic of Germany—FRG) on May 23, 1949, and the transformation of the Soviet zone of occupation into communist East Germany (German Democratic Republic—GDR) on October 7, 1949, preempted any quick reunification.

During the years of occupation, German and Allied officials reduced the powers of the central state in domestic politics, which were partly assumed by regional governments. Although German sovereignty resumed in 1949, the Allies prevented the German military from obtaining legal independent status until the mid-1950s, after which time it was closely monitored and controlled by the North Atlantic Treaty Organization (NATO). German reformers also rebuilt the party system, helping to create parties with more broad-based interests and ideological considerations. The most significant political development was the merger in 1946 of Roman Catholic and Protestant interests into the Christian Democratic Party, as was not the case during the Weimar period, when the Catholics had their own separate party.

Nation-statehood was restored to the two Germanies in 1949, but neither Germany was fully sovereign. The FRG deferred to the United States in matters of international relations, as did the GDR to the Soviet Union. Neither of the two Germanies joined the Cold War's international alliances—NATO and the Warsaw Pact, respectively—until 1955. The United States and the USSR felt it was necessary to restrict their respective German client states, a condition that continued for decades. This constraint on the Federal Republic created an economic giant/political dwarf syndrome that began to change only in the 1990s.

With the founding of the FRG in 1949, a more stable, democratic form of government emerged in West Germany. The Federal Republic became a democracy, characterized by constitutional provisions for free elections, civil liberties, and individual rights, and an independent judiciary. Its main political institutions were a bicameral parliamentary system, a **Chancellor** (head of government), a President (head of state), a multiparty system, and an independent judiciary.

The Federal Republic's democratic system developed in four phases, three before unification in 1990 and one after. The first phase took place under chancellors Konrad Adenauer (1949–1963) and Ludwig Erhard (1963–1966), leaders of the newly formed Christian Democratic Union (CDU). This first phase saw the establishment of a new parliamentary regime, an extensive system of social welfare benefits, a politically regulated market economy, and the reestablishment of strong regional governments, which assumed responsibilities formerly handled by the central government.

The second phase was ushered in by the 1969 election, in which the Social Democratic Party became the dominant coalition partner, a position it retained until 1982. The Social Democrats' tenure was largely due to the strong leadership of chancellors Willy Brandt (1969–1974) and Helmut Schmidt (1974–1982). Brandt's tenure saw robust full employment and a large increase in social services, which were followed during the Schmidt years by moderate cutbacks in social services and increased unemployment in the recession-plagued late 1970s. As was not the case in many Western capitalist countries in the 1980s, West Germany's postwar welfare state retained many of its services and most of its public support.

The third phase (1982–1998) returned the Christian Democrats to power in the person of Chancellor Helmut Kohl, who formed a center-right coalition with the Free Democratic Party (FDP). The coalition enthusiastically embraced the concept of the single European market and pragmatically moved to reunite the East and West Germanies. The opposition (both the Social Democrats and the Greens) was slower to embrace either of these developments, to their political detriment.

The fourth phase (1998 to the present) produced the return of the Social Democrats with Chancellor Gerhard Schröder, this time allied with the leftist and environmentalist Green Party. It also coincided with the continued advancement of the European Union. This phase also saw the introduction of the new currency, the euro, and continued integration of the economies and polities of the major European nation-states.

These four phases established the viability of constitutional democracy in the Federal Republic, as the country maintained a firm commitment to parliamentary government and political stability. Forces on the democratic left (the Social Democrats and Greens as well as the trade unions) also advocate a more equal distribution of income. The government passed legislation requiring in-plant works councils and firmwide **co-determination** (trade union participation on company boards). For most of the post–World War II period, this rank-and-file democratic participation, often called **democratic corporatism**,[6] helped alleviate much of the social tension that had plagued Germany before 1945 (see Section 2).

In the meantime, the German Democratic Republic (a "people's democracy," in communist parlance) was established in Soviet-occupied East Germany in 1949. The GDR was a one-party state under the control of the communist party, which was known as the Socialist Unity Party (SED), or *Sozialistische Einheits Partei*. Although the state provided full employment, housing, and various social benefits to its citizens, it was a rigid, bureaucratic, Stalinist regime that tightly controlled economic and political life under the leadership of party chairmen Walter Ulbricht, Willi Stoph, and finally Eric Honnecker. East Germany assumed a universal consensus about the correctness of communism and suppressed public dissent as deviationist and undermining the true path of socialism. East Germans caught trying to flee to the West were subject to execution on the spot. In August 1961, East Germany erected the Berlin Wall to keep its citizens from fleeing to West Germany.

For more than forty years, the international role of the two Germanies was limited. Because of NATO's geopolitical restrictions, West German energies were focused instead on rebuilding the economy and pursuing European economic integration. East Germany was similarly restricted. While it became the strongest of the Warsaw Pact's economies, it also loyally toed the Soviet line in international affairs.

Unified Germany (1990 to the Present)

Germany's unification in 1990 took place rapidly, surprising West and East Germans alike. When the Berlin Wall was opened in November 1989, the two German states envisioned a slow process of increased contacts and cooperation while maintaining separate sovereign states for the short term. But the initial slow flow of East Germans moving West turned into a deluge.

Germans sing and dance on top of the Berlin Wall to celebrate the opening of East-West German boundaries in November 1989. *Source:* AP/Wide World Photos.

When a currency reform provided East Germans with valuable West German deutschemarks, it fueled the migration westward in the summer of 1990. After a referendum on unification and hurried negotiations in the late summer, the former East Germany was incorporated into the Federal Republic of Germany as five new West German states (*Länder*).

Formal unification took place in the fall of 1990 as Chancellor Kohl, the "unification Chancellor," won a strong reelection victory for his center-right Christian Democratic Union–Free Democratic Party coalition. The period of euphoria did not last, as the costs of unification placed increased stress on Germany's budget and democratic institutions. Incorporating the disadvantaged eastern region had an adverse impact on a wide range of public policies, including unemployment expenses, structural rebuilding funds, and the large tax increases necessary to pay for it all. The large number of unemployed in eastern Germany—approximately 20 percent, more than double the figure in the prosperous West—helped fuel scattered ultraright-wing political movements. They sought out foreigners (often Turks) as scapegoats, and there were several heinous incidents in the mid-1990s of vicious attacks on minority groups. Finally, the accelerating pace of European integration with its movement toward a common monetary policy, a European central bank, and a single currency in 1999 placed additional pressures on the Federal Republic. Many Germans wondered whether the anchor of stability represented by the redoubtable deutschemark (DM) and the inflation-fighting *Deutsche Bundesbank* (Central Bank) would begin to drift in the uncertain sea of the European Union.

Leaders: *Helmut Kohl*

During the early years of Helmut Kohl's six-teen-year (1982–1998) chancellorship, the CDU leader was roundly criticized as colorless, provincial, and lacking in vision. Following the urbane Helmut Schmidt was a difficult task for the career politician from the city of Ludwigshafen in the state of Rhineland-Palatinate. Unlike Schmidt, Kohl does not speak English in public and often seemed ill at ease at ceremonial functions. He is a physically robust man, who is said to typify to non-Germans the avuncular and *gemütlich* (jovial) characteristics that seem more appropriate for German travel posters than for a federal chancellor.

Kohl's most important domestic task during his long tenure—second only to Bismarck in length of service—was holding the governing coalition together. The FDP's critical swing position in the Federal Republic's political system as the CDU/CSU's small coalition partner often produced independent and high-profile politicians such as Otto Graf Lambsdorff and Hans-Dietrich Genscher. Managing that relationship was Kohl's most immediate responsibility. Not far behind was the management of the relationship with the CDU's sister party, the Bavarian-based CSU. For many years, until his death in 1988, the CSU was led by Franz-Josef Strauss, a larger-than-life figure and Kohl's rival for the CDU/CSU chancellorship in the elections of 1976 and 1980. Kohl handled this relationship carefully and purposefully, realizing that any disturbance could produce disaster for his leadership. Coalition meetings among Strauss, Kohl, and the former FDP leader Martin Bangemann—large men, all of them—were often characterized in the German press as the "Elephants' Waltz." However, Kohl saw that the culmination of such meetings always concluded with none of the elephants trampling any innocent bystanders, or each other. Coalitional political intricacies aside, former Chancellor Helmut Kohl's lasting legacy during his sixteen years in power lies in two areas: German unification and European integration.

The speed with which East Germany came apart after the fall of the Berlin Wall surprised everyone, not least Helmut Kohl. Acting quickly and pragmatically, Kohl seized the moment and defused tensions in 1989, then supervised German monetary transformation and political unification in 1990. Kohl can certainly be faulted for misjudging the economic and the political costs of German unification. In fact, his overestimation of the speed of eastern German transformation in the early 1990s was a critical factor in his electoral loss in 1998. However, his quick actions to integrate East Germany as five new *Länder*, when an independent, noncommunist East Germany proved unworkable in the spring and summer of 1990, helped alleviate what could have been a politically disastrous situation.

As an early enthusiast of European integration, Kohl realized the opportunity for Germany that a more formally united continent would present. In its relations with other states after World War II, Germany faced two different kinds of criticism. First was the fear of a too powerful Germany, a country that had run roughshod over its European neighbors for most of the first half of the twentieth century. Second was the opposite problem, the so-called economic giant/political dwarf syndrome in which Germany was accused of benefiting from a strong world economy for fifty years while taking on none of the political responsibility. The fact that these are mutually contradictory positions did not spare Germany from criticism. Yet, an integrated Europe promised the possibility of solving both problems simultaneously. Germany is and will remain the economic anchor of the EU, while Germany's membership in the EU will enable it to take on political responsibilities that it would be unable to assume on its own. Kohl realized this and was a firm advocate of any and all measures that would assist in a smooth, stable, and comprehensive EU.

As the 1998 election approached, Helmut Kohl felt confident that he would win reelection. He believed that German unification, despite its remaining challenges, and the European Union, in which Germany would play a leading role, would insure victory. The voters did not agree, handing the CDU-FDP coalition a resounding defeat in the September 27 elections. Successfully convincing Germans that a change was necessary, newly elected SPD Chancellor Gerhard Schröder—a generation younger than Kohl—entered into a coalition government with the Greens for the first time in the nation's history.

Significant, too, was the continued strong support for the former communist party in eastern Germany (over 20 percent) which enabled it to gain more than 5 percent of the total German vote. With almost 54 percent of the electorate voting for parties of the left, clearly a new era had arrived in Germany.

Themes and Implications

Historical Junctures and Political Themes

Germany's role in the world of states is contentious. For all states, military strength is a basic tool used to shape and consolidate. But in Germany the rise of militarism and a corresponding authoritarian political culture was exaggerated for several reasons. Germany's exposed position in the central plains of Europe encouraged military preparedness because any of its many neighbors could mount an attack with few constraints. Since various German-speaking lands lacked a solid democratic or liberal political culture before unification in 1871, Prussian militarism exerted a dominant influence over political and civic life. In other words, late unification accompanied by war created a state that caused tremendous fear among Germany's neighbors. The conduct of World War I and especially the Third Reich of the Nazis and World War II further intensified this fear. Although more than fifty years have passed since the end of World War II and although Germany's independent political actions are constrained by the European Union, many Europeans remain wary of Germany's international role.

The second theme, governing the economy, has been colored profoundly by Germany's late unification and the issue of state-building. Clearly, nation-states can promote economic growth more easily than can fragmented political entities. Delayed unification and industrialization in Germany prevented it from embarking on the race for empire and raw materials until the late nineteenth century. By the time Germany joined the global economy, it lagged behind Britain and France in industrializing and securing access to the natural resources of the developing world. Thus, pursuit of fast economic growth and an awakened sense of German nationalism in the late nineteenth

century produced an aggressive, acquisitive state in which economic and political needs overlapped. The fusion of state and economic power is what enabled Hitler to build the Third Reich. Consequently, post–World War II policymakers and political leaders desired to remove the state from actively governing the economy. Thus, the postwar period saw the development of *Modell Deutschland* (the German Model), a term often used to describe the Federal Republic of Germany's distinctive political/socioeconomic features, namely, coordinated banking and industrial relations; democratic participation by workers on the job; and extensive public-sector benefits.[7] This model was unlike either the free-market traditions of countries like the United States and Great Britain or the more state-centered policies of democracies like France and Japan. Rather, postwar Germany developed an organized capitalist model that placed primacy on coordination among private-sector actors to promote efficiency and competitiveness. As a counterweight to concentrated economic power, the Federal Republic also developed a strong labor movement that used democratic corporatism to participate in fundamental decisions often left only to management in other countries. This model has served Germany exceptionally well until the late 1990s, but its future is uncertain in the new era of the European Union. Whether previously successful German economic institutions will continue to function well in a unified Europe remains an open question.

The democratic idea, our third theme, is one that developed much later in Germany than in most other advanced industrialized countries. It was not until 1918 and the shaky Weimar Republic that Germany first attained democracy at all. Despite a formal democratic constitution, Weimar was a prisoner of forces bent on its destruction. Unlike stable multiparty political systems in other countries, the Weimar Republic was plagued by a sharp and increasing polarization of political parties. The constitution of the Federal Republic in 1949 was designed to overcome Weimar's shortcomings. A system of federalism, constitutional provisions to encourage the formation and maintenance of coalitions, and a streamlined political party system proved solid foundations for the new democracy. Electoral turnout of between 80 percent and 90 percent for almost all elections since 1949 suggests that Germans have embraced democracy, although skeptics argue that Germans are voting more out of duty than anything else.[8] However, four peaceful electoral regime changes in the past fifty years, in which both the government and the opposition functioned more smoothly than in most democratic regimes, may finally put to rest doubts about German democracy. The remaining uncertainty is how well and how quickly the democratic culture will penetrate former communist eastern Germany.

The fourth theme, the politics of collective identity, offers a unique look at the intersection of democracy and collectivity. More than in other democratic countries, German political institutions, social forces, and patterns of life emphasize collective action rather than the individualism characteristic of the United States. This should not imply that German citizens have less freedom compared to those in other developed democracies nor that there is no conflict in Germany. It means that political expression, both in the state and in civil society, revolves around group representation and cooperative spirit in public action. Certainly Germany's history from Prussian militarism through Nazism has led many observers to believe that collectivist impulses should be eradicated. However, to expect Germany to embrace an individualistic democracy like that of the United States with no deep history of this is misguided. Germany's development of a collective identity since 1945 has relied on a redefinition of Germany in a European context. For example, one of the first provisions of the SDP-Green coalition agreement was to alter Germany's restrictive immigration law to legitimize those who have lived in Germany for decades without citizenship. German collective identity is changing.

Implications for Comparative Politics

Why study Germany? Germany differs from other developed countries in substantial ways. First, Britain and France are unitary states, whereas Germany is a federal one. Second, Germany's later industrialization, like that of Japan, produced a strong though unbalanced economic growth until after World War II.

Combining nationalism and militarism in the late nineteenth and early twentieth centuries, Germany, like Japan, was feared by its neighbors, and with good reason. A third difference is Germany's delayed development of democratic forms of representation until the Weimar Republic, again sharing a similarity with Japan. Destroyed by the Third Reich, parliamentary democracy did not return until the founding of the Federal Republic in 1949. The most significant difference between Germany and other Western European states is, of course, the Nazi period and the destruction that the Third Reich wrought. Such concerns are somewhat allayed, however, by several factors: the general stability of Germany's postwar development, a stability supported by its alliance with Western industrialized states; the successful development of its democratic institutions; and a political economy characterized by a highly organized business community and active worker participation within a strong labor movement. The parallels with Japan continue here as well. Unification continues to present Germany with unique challenges. The economic, political, cultural, and physical strains of uniting two disparate societies have placed great stress on the Federal Republic's politics and institutions. Last, Germany's role in the European Union presents both opportunities and challenges to Germany and its neighbors. As the strongest European power, Germany has many economic and political advantages in integrating Europe. However, it must deal with the suspicions that its history has aroused among its neighbors and confront the question of whether its post–World War II political institutions, so well suited to Germany, will also fit its partners in the European Union.

Germany's significance for the study of comparative politics lies in several areas: the contrast between its nationalistic history and democratization in an integrating Europe; its unique form of organized capitalism that is neither state-led nor laissez-faire; its successful form of representative democracy that combines widespread participation and representation of the entire electorate in a stable parliamentary regime; and a politics of identity that builds on existing collectivities in an increasingly multifaceted political culture.

Section ❷   Political Economy and Development

Some suggest that to enjoy sustained economic growth, a state should have a balanced relationship among its various social and economic interests and between the means of production and exchange. The state should promote an independent economic strategy but work closely with influential economic sectors within society, including financial institutions, trade unions, and business elites, in order to make more informed decisions. According to this theory, neither state nor market interests should overpower the other. The Federal Republic of Germany comes close to approximating this model; Germany has taken a development path that emphasizes cooperative interaction between the state and a dense interest-group network made up of key social and economic participants. In this way, post–World War II Germany has avoided the imbalances that plague many nation-states, such as when powerful private interests—typically leaders from one sector of the economy—capture or dominate state policy, or when the state dominates or captures private interests. As we suggest later, the Federal Republic's unique form of organized capitalism combined with a social market economy have spared Germany an economic policy of unpredictable changes and boom or bust cycles.

State and Economy

Germany is an organized capitalist country—the world's third largest with one of the highest standards of living—in which the state plays a leading but not a directing role. Numerous powerful business organizations, some representing industry generally and others representing employers specifically, play significant coordinating roles. Rather than emphasizing individual entrepreneurship and small business as the defining characteristics of its economy, Germany has relied on an organized network of small and large businesses working together. In addition, the banking system and financial community are directly involved in private investment and engage in little of the financial speculation characteristic of Wall Street brokers. Their primary role is to provide long-term investments to support the internationally competitive manufacturing

industries that are the foundation of the economy. For example, unlike their U.S. counterparts, German banks are legally allowed to develop close financial ties with firms in other industries, including owning the stock of such firms, granting them long-term loans, having representatives on their boards of directors, and voting as stockholders or on behalf of third-party investors. The end result is private investment based on long-term relationships among familiar partners rather than the short-term deals common among banks, investors, and firms in the United States. Although the universal applicability of these practices has eroded somewhat in the face of globalization, deregulation, and Europeanization, the core principles of this arrangement remain.

The Role of the State before 1945

In the years before unification in 1871 many of Germany's regional governments played a strong role in promoting economic growth and development. They worked directly and indirectly with private economic interests, thus blurring distinctions between the state and the market.

The economic powers assumed by the modern states (*Länder*) of the Federal Republic after 1945 were also derived from their century-long involvement in promoting industrialization. The most common way to analyze industrial growth in Germany during the nineteenth century has been Alexander Gerschenkron's late industrialization thesis. He maintained that Germany's transformation from a quasi-feudal society to a highly industrialized one during the latter two-thirds of the nineteenth century was characterized by explicit coordination among big business, a powerful universal banking system (universal because banks, then as now, handle all financial transactions and were not segmented into savings and commercial branches, for example), and government. This progress has often been called rapid German industrialization, although a more accurate term might be rapid Prussian industrialization because it was Bismarck's vision and mobilization of Prussian interest groups that proved the dominant force.

Unlike Britain and the United States, Germany did not experience the kind of trial-and-error capitalism that characterized much of the early nineteenth century. By the time it was unified in 1871, Germany was forced to compete with a number of other countries that had already developed industrialized capitalist economies. German business and political elites realized that a gradual, small-firm-oriented economy would face ruinous competition from countries such as Britain, France, and the United States. To be competitive, the German state became a significant and powerful force in the German economy. This meant building on the foundations established by the formerly independent and autonomous states such as Prussia and Bavaria which became part of a united Germany in 1871.

The foundations for economic growth were established, and the most spectacular early leaps of industrial modernization happened, before Germany's unification in 1871. The creation of the customs union (*Zollverein*) in 1834 from eighteen independent states with a population of 23 million people propelled industrial modernization. This process was led by Prussia long before Bismarck was on the scene. Yet Bismarck became the dominant symbol for Prussia's hegemonic position in brokering the interests of grain-growing *Junkers* in the east with those of the coal and steel barons in the Ruhr. Bismarck used the development of the railroads[9] as a catalyst for this "marriage of iron and rye."[10] He astutely realized that although railroads were a primary consumer of coal and steel, they also provided an effective way to transport the *Junkers'* grain from the relatively isolated eastern part of Germany to market. The image of Prussian-led, rapid, state-enhanced industrial growth is important, but the opening of trade among these independent principalities did not dislodge the distinct patterns of modernization that the less powerful states had developed on their own. Small-scale agricultural production remained in many parts of the southern states, particularly in Bavaria, and small-scale craft production continued in Württemberg as well as in many other regions where feudal craft skills were adapted to the patterns of industrial modernization.

Because each state had different material needs and social circumstances, their regional governments may have done a more effective job of fulfilling needs than a central state could have done. Certainly, Bismarck's welfare-state measures brought economies of scale to those programs that needed to be implemented on a national basis. However, the strong role of the regional governments in meeting certain needs continued, especially during the Second Reich (1871–1918). Later, when the Weimar regime was succumbing to the Third Reich, regional governments tried unsuccessfully to resist the Nazi state's goal of massive centralization of policy.

During the Third Reich, between 1933 and 1945, the state worked hand-in-glove with German industry to suppress workers, employ slave labor, and produce military armaments. As a result, a number of leading industrialists, notably those of the Krupp steel works and the IG Farben chemical complex, were tried for war crimes after the Allied victory.

The Social Market Economy

Government economic policy is indirect and supportive rather than heavy-handed and overregulatory. Although the government sets broad guidelines, it encourages the formation of voluntary associations to coordinate negotiations among employers, banks, trade unions, and regional governments in order to reach the government's policy objectives. Its economic policy-making is flexible in two ways.

First, German regulation establishes a general framework for economic activity rather than detailed standards. The government sets rigorous but broad licensing and performance standards for most professions and industries. For example, German banks must possess greater capital reserves than internationally accepted minimums, and their officers must demonstrate competence to hold their positions to a semipublic institution, the Federal Bank Supervisory Office. Government policymakers believe that once their core requirements are met and their general objectives known, private actors can be trusted to achieve government goals without detailed regulation. Failure to uphold government standards can result in fines or, in some criminal cases, imprisonment. In contrast, the United States has no such core requirements but has issued many layers of detailed regulations in the wake of banking failures and abuses.

Second, among the major European economies, Germany has the smallest share of industry in national

---

Institutional Intricacies: *The Social Market Economy*

The Social Market Economy (*Sozialmarktwirtschaft*) is the term used to describe the set of economic policies in the post–World War II Federal Republic of Germany. Its intellectual origins derive from the economics department of the University of Freiburg during the 1920s and 1930s as well as from Christian social and economic teachings characteristic of the European Catholic church. The Social Market Economy is often considered the linchpin in the rapid economic growth of the Federal Republic during the 1950s and early 1960s, the period also known as the **Economic Miracle**. These social market principles continued to shape German economic policy during the 1970s, 1980s, and 1990s.

The Social Market Economy is sometimes referred to as simply a combination of a free-market economy with a considerable layer of social benefits, but this does not do justice to this concept. Its authors devised a set of economic policies that avoided the shortcomings of Nazism, communism, laissez-faire, and the post–World War II Keynesian policies. The Social Market Economy embeds the market system within a framework that mandates the cooperation of private and public institutions. The implementation of these policies generally produces an effective and stable set of economic outcomes agreeable to all parties. The Social Market Economy does not lie halfway between state and market but represents a qualitatively different approach.

The social component of the Social Market Economy is more far-reaching than social benefits programs elsewhere. For example, all employees receive six weeks' paid vacation plus numerous holidays and enjoy a broad spectrum of welfare state measures, including full health and dental coverage, free education through university or vocational school, subsidies for housing, and child allowances for all but the very rich. However, in the Federal Republic, benefits serve as more than just distributive income transfer devices. For example, two of the most important provisions, government savings subsidies to individuals and a comprehensive vocational education system, have direct and positive benefits for the competitiveness of the entire German economy.

---

government hands, but it allows state governments considerable power. This is called cooperative federalism, which delegates to the states (*Länder*) the administrative powers of laws and regulations passed at the federal level. Both characteristics are integral parts of Germany's Social Market Economy.

Postwar policymakers avoided a strong role for the state in the Federal Republic's economic life. Unlike the French and the Japanese states, which have intervened much more in the economy, the German state has evolved a careful balance between the public and private sectors. Rather than creating a state-versus-market standoff, the German public and private sectors have evolved a densely interpenetrated association. Germany has avoided the opposite pattern as well, namely, the antigovernment, free-market policies of Britain and the United States in the 1980s and 1990s.

In other words, the relationship between state and market in Germany is neither free-market nor state-dominant. Rather, the state sets clear general ground rules, acknowledged by the private sector, but then allows market forces to work relatively unimpeded within the general framework of government supervision. Since the time of the first postwar chancellor, Christian Democrat Konrad Adenauer, the Germans have referred to this approach as the **Social Market Economy** (*Sozialmarktwirtschaft*). Basically, the term refers to a system of capitalism in which fundamental social benefits are essential, not antagonistic, to the workings of the market. Among the social components of the German economy are health care, workers' rights, public transportation, and support for the arts. In some respects, these benefits are similar to those provided by the Japanese and French governments. However, the provision of some public benefits through organized private interests (the quasi-public "sickness funds" that provide for health insurance, for example) make the German Social Market Economy a blend of public and private actions that support and implement public policies. The Social Market Economy blurs state market distinctions in the hope of producing a socially responsible capitalism.

The social component of the Social Market Economy is unique to Germany. "Several programs such as savings subsidies and vocational education (see box on p. 150) contribute to the production of income. The former contributes to a stable pool of investment capital, while the latter helps create a deep pool of human capital that has enabled Germany to produce high quality goods throughout the postwar period."

The German system of framework regulation is best explained in the words of economist Wilhelm Röpke, one of the shapers of post–World War II economic policy:

> [Our program] consists of measures and institutions which impart to competition the framework, rules, and machinery of impartial supervision, which a competitive system needs as much as any game or match if it is not to degenerate into a vulgar brawl. A genuine, equitable, and smoothly functioning competitive system cannot in fact survive without a judicious moral and legal framework and without regular supervision of the conditions under which competition can take place pursuant to real efficiency principles. This presupposes mature economic discernment on the part of all responsible bodies and individuals and a strong impartial state.[11]

This system has enabled German economic policy to avoid the sharp lurches between laissez-faire freedom and state-led economic policy that have characterized Britain during the post–World War II period.

Germany today is a high-wage, high-welfare nation that has maintained its competitive world position far better than other advanced industrialized states since the oil crisis of 1973. Its success in combining strong competitiveness with high wages and social spending has surpassed even that of Japan. An emphasis on high skills in key export-oriented manufacturing industries is the specific path that German economic policy has taken to maintain its competitive position. An elaborate vocational education system combined with apprenticeship training underlies this

policy. It is implemented through the works councils elected by every worker in all German firms with five or more employees. This system of advanced skills training has enabled Germany to resist the siren song of the postindustrial service-sector-oriented world to which countries such as the United States and Britain have succumbed.

Relying extensively on this elaborate apprenticeship training program, Germany has maintained a competitive position in such traditional manufacturing industries as automobiles, chemicals, machine tools, and industrial electronics. By stressing the value that its highly skilled workforce adds to raw materials, Germany has resisted the claim that it must lower its wage costs to match those of newly industrializing countries. Germany's record suggests that a developed country can still compete in manufacturing by raising quality rather than by lowering wage costs. Despite a lack of natural resources, Germany maintains a trade surplus and still has a large working-class population that historically has spurned protectionism. With one in every three jobs devoted to exports (one in two, in the four manufacturing industries just mentioned), protectionism would be self-defeating for German unions. The skills of its workers help German industry overcome the costs of acquiring resources and paying high wages; in fact, German industry has emphasized that high quality and high productivity offset these costs. This enables their highly skilled blue-collar workers to drive expensive German automobiles and to enjoy six weeks of paid vacation per year. The last years of the Kohl era were a period of deep introspection questioning these previously effective, yet high-cost, practices. However, the Gerhard Schröder-led SPD-Green government pledged to maintain the core features of the *Sozialmarktwirtschaft*.

Germany's research and development strategy has enhanced these economic policies. Rather than push for specific new breakthroughs in exotic technologies or invent new products that might take years to commercialize, the strategy is to adapt existing technologies to traditional sectors and to refine already competitive sectors. This is the exact opposite of the United States' research and development strategy, for example. During the postwar years, this policy has enabled Germany to maintain a favorable balance of trade and a high degree of competitiveness. However,

German unification and European integration have forced German industry and policymakers to examine whether this model needs modification. Taking others' core discoveries and quickly applying them to production is a delicate task that requires coordinated policies among all producer groups. The primary challenge during the 1990s has been trying to institute West German policies among former GDR workers raised in a different industrial culture. One of the major planks in the 1998 SPD-Green coalition agreement was to increase funds for Germany's vocational education system, particularly in the five eastern states.

Other than the government, the German institution most responsible for shaping economic policy is the very independent *Bundesbank*. This institution is both a bankers' bank, in that it sets interest rates, and the agency that determines the amount of money in circulation. This second role proved especially contentious during the 1980s and early 1990s. The *Bundesbank* prefers low inflation, both because this is a traditional demand of all central bankers and because of Germany's history of ruinous inflation during the Weimar Republic. The relevance for economic policy is that when the government wishes to expand the economy by increasing spending or reducing taxes, the *Bundesbank* always prefers policies that favor monetary restrictions over fast economic growth. As a result, the government and the *Bundesbank* have disagreed on economic policy repeatedly in the years since unification.

This organized capitalist model is not considered a complete success by all Germans. Both the Greens, the environmental political party that first won *Bundestag* seats in 1983, and the free-market-oriented business sector feel that this pattern favors those that are inside the system (such as industry organizations, employer groups, and the banking community) and excludes those outside. Moreover, the Greens criticize many business policies as not being sufficiently protective of the environment. The primary complaint of the small-business sector is that the organized nature of large-firm-dominant capitalism is not sufficiently flexible in the creation of new products and industries. However, neither group has been able to dislodge the dominant position of German organized capitalism in the shaping of economic policy. Of course, with the

Greens as junior members of the Schröder government, previously unassailable government policies such as continued reliance on nuclear power and resistance to a rise in gasoline taxes for ecological purposes may give way.

Welfare Provision

Welfare policies can be described as the social part of the Social Market Economy. The Federal Republic's social welfare expenditures are consistent with historically generous West European standards. Although they are not as extensive as those in countries such as the Netherlands and Scandinavia, public services in the Federal Republic dwarf those in the United States. From housing subsidies to savings subsidies, health care, public transit, and the rebuilding of the destroyed cities and public infrastructure, the Federal Republic is still remarkably generous in its public spending. Even under the moderately conservative rule of the CDU-led Adenauer coalition during the 1950s and early 1960s, there was a strong commitment to providing adequate public services. This strategy recalls Bismarck's efforts to use public services to forestall radical demands in the late nineteenth century. For nondemocratic conservatives like Bismarck and for democratic conservatives like Adenauer, comprehensive welfare benefits were not philanthropic but a response to the demands of the Social Democratic Party and the trade unions. Thus, welfare in Germany has never been a gift but a negotiated settlement, often after periods of conflict between major social forces that have agreed to compromise.

The development of welfare services has been tremendously enhanced as well by the European Christian social tradition—a major force in the CDU/CSU coalition. Both Roman Catholic and Protestant churches advocate public spending for services as a responsibility of the strong for the welfare of the weak. Similarly, the unions' and the SPD's demands for increased public spending ensured that both the Left and the Right shared a commitment to public provision of social services throughout the Federal Republic's history.

During the mid-1970s, when unemployment grew from 1 or 2 percent to roughly 4 percent, and when some social welfare measures were capped (but not reduced), citizens of the Federal Republic spoke of the crisis of the welfare state. Yet non-German observers were hard-pressed to find indications of crisis. Clearly, contraction of substantial welfare-state benefits in no way approximated the cutbacks of the United States and Britain in the 1980s and 1990s.

In the 1980s continued high unemployment (by German standards) and the costs of support for workers who had depleted their benefits presented difficult dilemmas for the welfare state. German jobs tend to be highly paid, so employers have tried to avoid creating part-time jobs, preferring to wait to hire until the need for employees is sustainable. During times of recession, the number of new jobs created can be miniscule.

Current Strains on the Social Market Economy

Uncertain economic conditions in the early 1980s cost the Social Democratic Chancellor Helmut Schmidt his position. Yet even during his successor Helmut Kohl's sixteen-year tenure, the heady days of less than 1 percent unemployment never returned. Unemployment has not dropped below 6 percent since then. One persistent problem facing successive German governments has been shouldering the cost of sustaining the long-term unemployed through general welfare funds. More seriously, how could the Federal Republic's elaborate vocational education and apprenticeship system absorb all the new entrants into the labor market? This problem could have undermined one of the strengths of the German economy, the continued supply of skilled workers. Despite these threats in the mid-1980s, both the unemployment compensation system and the vocational education and apprenticeship system survived under the Kohl government. However, this issue resurfaced with the large increase in the unemployment rate following unification in 1990, particularly in the eastern German states.

In the early 1990s the idea of a smoothly functioning German economic juggernaut faltered. First, the Kohl government badly misjudged the costs of unification. In 1992, Kohl finally acknowledged that the successful integration of the eastern economy into the western one would cost much more and require a longer period of time than originally predicted. Second, the structural challenges that the German

A cynical western German view of money spent to rebuild eastern Germany. *Source: Frankfurter Allgemeine Zeitung.*

political economy faced in the mid-1990s were far more extensive than any the Federal Republic had experienced since the 1950s. The amount budgeted in the early 1990s for reconstruction of eastern Germany's infrastructure was approximately 20 percent of the entire budget. In addition, funds from private firms, regional governments, and other subsidies amounted to another DM 50 billion, yet even these huge sums were not enough to help smooth the assimilation process, and today a large gap in productivity levels exists between the two regions. Third, the western German democratic corporatist institutions—composed of employers and trade unions with a long history of cooperation—became difficult to transfer as a model to eastern Germany, since they had to be created from scratch. If present, they could have been effective mediating institutions to soften the costs of transition for eastern Germans. In their absence, the *Treuhand* (the government reconstruction agency) took the path of least resistance and simply privatized some 7,000 of the total of 11,000 firms that it had inherited from East Germany. One of the most significant costs of this transition from state to private ownership was high unemployment in the eastern sector. Some 1.2 million workers were officially unemployed, and in the early 1990s another 2 million enrolled in a government-subsidized short-term program combined with job training (this program's funds were slashed as part of an austerity budget).

The costs of the Social Market Economy, particularly during unification, stressed the upper limits of Germany's capacity to pay for them. Massive budget cuts became imperative by the early and mid-1990s. The completion of the EU's Single Market, the grand culmination of a post–Cold War spirit of German and European unity, have placed additional strains on the German government. Its alleged immediate benefit will likely only strengthen the trends toward decentralization and deregulation already begun in Western Europe. More significantly for the German regime, European union has begun to disturb the organized capitalism of its small and large businesses, which features an intricate, mutually reinforcing pattern of government and business self-regulation. In addition, the growing push for deregulation in European finance could threaten Germany's distinctive finance/manufacturing links, which depend on long-term relationships between the two parties, not on short-term deals.[12] Thus the trend toward Europeanization, on a path that challenges Germany's preeminent position, may be incompatible with the consensus-oriented and coordinated nature of Germany's political and social institutions.

Tensions have also flared up between former East and West Germans. The East German economy was strong by communist standards and provided jobs for virtually all adults who wanted one. But East German industry, as in most former communist countries, was inefficient by Western standards, and most firms were not able to survive the transition to capitalism. Among the most serious problems were overstaffing and inadequate quality control. Consequently, many easterners lost their jobs. For a time, they were generously supported by western subsidies, but recovery in the five new eastern states lagged much more than the Kohl government had anticipated. Easterners resented the slow pace of change and high unemployment, and western Germans were bitter about losing jobs to easterners and paying, through increased taxes, for the cleanup of the ecological and infrastructural disaster inherited from the former East German regime.

In short, the magnitude of the problems in eastern Germany threatened to overwhelm the institutional capacity to handle them. It certainly helped contribute to the defeat of Helmut Kohl's CDU/CSU-FDP center-right coalition government in 1998. Some pessimistic observers began to suggest that these stresses placed the German political economy in a precarious position. Germany's economic prowess has depended on certain manufacturing industries that produce eminently exportable goods but whose technologies must constantly be upgraded and whose labor costs continue to rise. Complicating the demands on Germany's economic institutions is the obligation to align Germany's economic policies with those of its European neighbors. The future of this model is examined more closely in Section 5.

Society and Economy

During the boom years of the mid-twentieth century, German economic growth provided a sound foundation for social development. The Social Market Economy of the Christian Democrats was augmented by governments led by Social Democrats from 1969 to 1982, when the supportive social programs of the 1950s and 1960s were extended and enhanced. This growth, with its corresponding social policies, helped Germany to avoid the kind of occupational and regional conflict common to many other countries. Germany is a prosperous country with a high standard of living, high savings rates, and a well-paid workforce. The strong role of trade unions and the consequent unwillingness of employers to confront workers on wage and workplace issues have minimized stratification of the society and the workplace. There is some stratification, however, within the labor force. The primary workplace fault line lies between the core of mostly male, high-skilled blue-collar workers in the largest competitive industries and less-skilled workers, often employed in smaller firms with lower wages and not always full-time work. A significant number of women and immigrants are among the less-skilled workers.

The most controversial issues for German society in the 1990s have been race and ethnicity, with profound implications for Germany's ideology and political culture. Racist attacks have forced Germans to confront the possibility that almost fifty years of democracy have not tamed the xenophobic aspects of Germany's political culture. The issue of ethnic minorities affected the economy and society during the 1980s and was exacerbated in the 1990s by unification and European integration. Nationalism, apparently, has not disappeared. East Germans were raised in a society that did not celebrate, or even value, toleration or dissent and in which official unemployment did not exist. East Germany was a closed society, as were most communist regimes, and many of its citizens had little contact with foreign nationals before 1989. In contrast, since the 1960s, West Germany has encouraged the migration of millions of guest workers (*Gastarbeiter*) from southern Europe. The Federal Republic has also provided generous provisions for those seeking political asylum, in an effort to overcome—to some degree at least—the legacy of Nazi persecution of non-Germans from 1933 to 1945.

The *Gastarbeiter* program originated after 1961 when the construction of the Berlin Wall caused a labor shortage because East Germans could no longer emigrate to the West. Thus, temporary workers were recruited from southern Europe with the stipulation that they would return to their native countries if there was an increase in unemployment. However, the economic boom lasted so long that by the time the economy did turn down in the mid-1970s, it was difficult for these so-called guests to return to homes in which they had not lived for a decade or more. And as semi-permanent residents, they were eligible for welfare benefits. These foreign workers produced heightened social strain in the 1970s and 1980s, at a time of increasing unemployment. Because German citizenship was not granted to the guest workers or their children, the problem remained unresolved. Although not as severe as in the Second Reich, the clash between German and *Gastarbeiter* cultures increased in intensity into the 1980s, particularly in areas where Turkish workers were highly concentrated. However, in a significant departure from past practice, the Schröder-led SPD-Green government made one of its first items of business the changing of the immigration law. The new government planned to adopt a much easier immigration policy allowing second- and third-generation *Gastarbeiter* to attain German citizenship or maintain dual citizenship.

Upon unification, when different ethnic minorities flooded into the former East and West Germanies, few former GDR citizens were able to respond positively. Instead of guaranteed lifetime employment, they faced a labor market that did not always supply enough jobs, one where structural unemployment idled up to 25 percent of the workforce. And they were expected to embrace completely and immediately a much more open and ethnically diverse society than they had ever known. Thus, immigrants and asylum seekers became the scapegoats for the lack of employment, and those Germans who were falling through the cracks of the welfare state were susceptible to racist propaganda blaming ethnic minorities for the rapid upheaval that had occurred.

Another important issue has been the role of women in German society. Until the late 1970s men traditionally dominated all positions of authority in management and the union movement. The union movement has made greater strides than management in expanding leadership opportunities for women, but men still hold the dominant positions in most unions. More than half of all German women entered the workforce by the late 1970s, but their participation plateaued at about 62 percent in the 1990s, while the male participation rate remained steady at 80 percent (see Table 1). Beyond the workplace, the differences between the laws of the former East and West Germanies have created a firestorm of controversy. In the East, women had made far greater social and economic progress than in the West, and both women and men had received generous government support for childcare and family leave. During the last Kohl government, one of the most heated debates concerned the cancellation of the more liberal East

Table 1

Labor Force Participation Rates (Ages 15–65)					
Year	1993	1994	1995	1996	1997
Male %	81.3	81.3	81.0	80.3	80.3
Female %	62.3	62.7	62.6	62.3	62.8

Source: Federal Statistical Office, Germany, 1998.

German policies toward women (including abortion) in favor of the more conservative and restrictive ones of the Federal Republic.

Germany and the International Political Economy

Germany's relationship to the regional and international political economy is shaped by two factors: the European Union (EU) and Germany's political role on the world stage.

The European Union

The EU was embraced by most Germans and by the political and industrial establishment, especially in the first few years after unification. As Europe's leading economic power, Germany has benefited greatly from European integration because its position of strength has been enhanced by wider market opportunities. Many actions and policies that might once have been viewed by its neighbors as German domination have become more acceptable when seen as Germany's active participation as a member of the larger European Union.

Several difficult issues confront Germany's international position at the turn of the century. One concern is whether successful German-specific institutional arrangements—such as its institutionalized system of worker (and union) participation in management, its tightly organized capitalism, and its elaborate system of apprenticeship training—will prove adaptable or durable in a wider European context. What works well for Germany may be derived from indigenous institutional, political, or cultural patterns that will not successfully transfer beyond the Federal Republic. Another concern involves Germany's political role on the world stage. After German unification and European integration, many observers in Europe, Japan, and North America assumed that Germany would take on greater political responsibility. However, indecision and inaction in world affairs by the Kohl regime in the 1990s suggested Germany's unwillingness or inability to assume the responsibilities of a world power. Examples of this inaction can be seen in the failure of leadership in areas such as the crisis in the former Yugoslavia and UN policy toward Iraq.

Kohl's initial inaction on the breakup of Yugoslavia paralyzed German (and European) foreign policy, but his later impulsive recognition of Slovenia and Croatia and acceptance of Bosnia's separatists was ill-considered. Other Western powers opposed Kohl's position, the effect of which encouraged the Serbs to respond with what became the violent disintegration of Yugoslavia.

If Germany were to assume stronger leadership, a united Europe might be able to develop a regionwide geopolitical policy. But leadership requires working with one's allies, not taking a position diametrically opposed to their interests. Successful future European coordination on strategic issues is closely tied to this question of leadership in the European Union. Whether the UN, NATO, or the European Union itself is to take military responsibility for Europe remains uncertain. This uncertainty is prolonged by Germany's own ambivalence about its international political role. In their defense, the Germans continue to stress the strains and huge costs of unification. However, great nations find ways to do extremely difficult things when it is convenient. Even under the sixteen-year Kohl regime, Germany had not developed the skills necessary to meet the obligations of political responsibility. However, Chancellor Gerhard Schröder has gone on record that Germany will assume a greater role in European political leadership.

Germany in the World

Other issues such as trade, economic competition with East Asia and North America, the introduction of the euro, and the general pace of economic integration remain major areas of concern, though less serious than the ones just discussed. Germany, as a goods-exporting nation, has always favored an open trading system. Management and unions realize that exports represent both profits and jobs and that seeking refuge in protectionism would be self-defeating. The Japanese economic threat receded in the mid-1990s, as the Japanese experienced the recession that had earlier beset Europe and North America. Germany's strategy to deal with the Japanese economic challenge differed from that of other Western nations. Instead of giving up older manufacturing industries in the face of Japanese competition, the Germans felt that these industries could remain competitive with a high-skill, high-value-added approach. This approach has largely succeeded and has given the German economy some breathing room as Japan struggled with its own recession and banking crisis.

As for how quickly European integration proceeds, countries that might consider emulating German institutions require not just strategies but also the means of implementing them. The lack of a cohesive European-wide institutional framework would severely hinder efforts to develop strategies appropriate to meeting the domestic and international challenges of European unification. Most other

European nations can identify their goals, namely, a highly skilled workforce able to compete in international markets on some basis other than a combination of low labor costs and high-tech production strategies. But whether they can or want to follow Germany's example remains to be seen, especially in light of recent German economic difficulty. Is Germany a model for other countries? The preoccupation of Germany with its immediate domestic issues and the German-specific nature of the institutions of its political economy have partially diminished the luster of German-style policies for the New Europe.

Section ❸   Governance and Policy-Making

The primary goals at the Federal Republic's founding in 1949 were to work toward eventual unification of the two Germanies and, more important, to avoid repeating the failure of the Weimar Republic. When unification was blocked indefinitely, the founders instituted the **Basic Law** (*Grundgesetz*) as a compromise. They preferred to wait until Germany could be reunited before using the term *constitution* (*Verfassung*). After unification in 1990, however, the term *Basic Law* has been retained because of its unqualified success.

Their other goal, insuring a lasting democratic order, presented a more complicated problem. Two fundamental institutional weaknesses had undermined the Weimar government: (1) provisions for emergency powers had enabled leaders to arbitrarily centralize authority and suspend democratic rights; and (2) the fragmentation of the political party system had prevented stable majorities from forming in the *Reichstag*. This second weakness, instability, encouraged the first, the use of emergency powers to break legislative deadlocks.

Organization of the State

The Basic Law Promoting Stability

Under Allied occupation guidance, the builders of the postwar government sought to inhibit centralized

power by establishing a federal system with significant powers for the states (*Länder*). It is paradoxical that a constitution that owes so much to the influence of foreign powers has proved so durable. Under the Basic Law of the Federal Republic, many functions that had formerly been centralized during the imperial, Weimar, and Nazi periods, such as the educational system, the police, and the radio networks, now became the responsibility of the states. Although the federal *Bundestag* (lower house) became the chief law-making body, the implementation of many laws fell to the state governments. Moreover, the state governments sent representatives to the *Bundesrat* (upper house), which was required to approve bills passed in the *Bundestag*.

There was little opposition from major actors within the Federal Republic to this shift from a centralized to a federal system. The Third Reich's arbitrary abuse of power had created strong sentiment for curbing the state's repressive capacities. In addition, political leaders, influenced by advisers from the United States, were inclined to support a federal system. Further, the development of a federal system was not a departure, but a return to form. Prior to the unification of Germany in 1871, the various regions of Germany had formed a decentralized political system with such autonomous institutions as banks, universities, vocational schools, and state administrative systems.

Several methods were used to surmount party fragmentation and the inability to form working majorities. The multiplicity of parties characteristic of the Weimar Republic was partly controlled by the **5 percent rule**: a political party had to receive at least 5 percent of the vote to obtain seats in the *Bundestag* or in state or municipal governments. Under the 5 percent rule, smaller parties tended to fade, with most of their members absorbed by the three major parties. However, the Green Party in the early 1980s and the former communist party of East Germany, reformed as the Party of Democratic Socialism, in the 1990s surpassed the threshold and appear likely to remain in the *Bundestag*.

The *Bundestag* is more likely to achieve working majorities than the Weimar government did for several other reasons. Since the interval between elections is set at four years except under unusual circumstances, governments have a fair opportunity to implement their programs and take responsibility for success or failure. The electoral system was also changed from an unstable proportional representation system under the Weimar government to a combination of proportional representation and single-member electoral districts. New constitutional provisions limited the possibility for the *Bundestag* to vote a government from office. Under the Weimar constitution, negative majorities often garnered enough votes to unseat the chancellor but were not united enough to install a replacement. In the Federal Republic, a **constructive vote of no confidence** is required, meaning that any action to vote out one chancellor simultaneously votes in another. In addition, the chancellor's powers are now more clearly defined. As the leader of the dominant party or coalition of parties, the chancellor now has control over the composition of the cabinet, so that the federal president is merely the ceremonial head of state. Under the Weimar Constitution the president could wield emergency powers. Hitler invoked this rule to manipulate the system under President Hindenburg in 1932 and 1933. In the Federal Republic the president has been stripped of such broad power.

The principles of the Federal Republic's government contained in the Basic Law give the nation a solid foundation, one that appeared capable of assimilating the five *Länder* of the former GDR when unification occurred in 1990. After surviving for almost fifty years, the Federal Republic has clearly attained its most important goals. However, in the 1990s, threats of neo-Nazi movements and racist violence surprised many observers who thought these sentiments had long since been purged from German politics. The political scientist Ralf Dahrendorf has stated in his book *Society and Democracy in Germany* that until the arrival of the Federal Republic, Germany had been a premodern country. From 1949 until unification it appeared much like other western industrialized countries. After unification in 1990, with the difficulties in integrating the two regimes and the uncertainties regarding European integration, some of the more pessimistic assumptions about a reformed, democratic Germany have been questioned. Yet, another successful democratic alternation of power, this time to the Red-Green coalition in 1998, the continued support for the democratized former communist party in the east, and the minuscule support for undemocratic right-wing parties suggests the durability of democracy in Germany.

Government Institutions

The German state is organized as a federal system, with sixteen states, each with considerable powers (see Figure 1 on p. 159). The states have the right to raise revenue independently as well as to own and operate firms, usually in partnership with private industry. As a parliamentary democracy, the German government resembles the parliamentary systems of Britain and Japan; namely, there is a fusion of powers in that the chancellor, the executive or head of government, is also the leader of the leading party (or coalition) in the *Bundestag*. This contrasts with the separation of powers system used in the United States, in which the president and cabinet officials cannot simultaneously serve in the Congress. Generally the executive dominates the legislative in the Federal Republic, but this authority derives from the chancellor's role as party leader and a high level of party discipline. Most members of the governing parties support the chancellor at all times, as their own positions depend on successful government. This loyalty diffuses the lone-ranger syndrome, so common in the U.S. House of Representatives and Senate, where individual members of Congress often act as independent political entrepreneurs.

The Federal Republic's legislature is bicameral, with the 669-member *Bundestag* as the lower house

Figure 1

Constitutional Structure of the German Federal Government

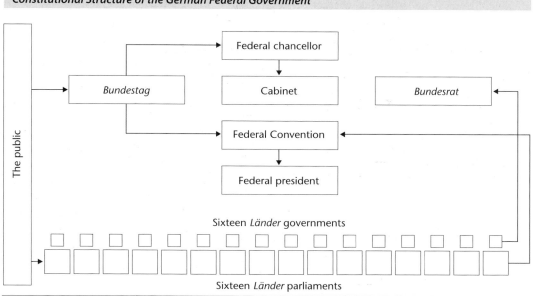

and the 69-member *Bundesrat* as the upper house. Unlike the U.S. Senate and the British House of Lords, the *Bundesrat* is composed of elected and appointed officials of the sixteen states. In this way, Germany's constitutional system allows more governmental overlap than countries that are unitary (France, Britain) or that have a sharp separation of powers within the federal government and between federal and state governments (United States). The *Bundestag* members are elected in a proportional representation system (see Section 4), and the leader of the major party, who is usually the leader of the largest party in a two- or three-party coalition, becomes chancellor. As in most parliamentary systems, the chancellor must maintain a majority for the government to survive, with the added provision (i.e., the constructive vote of no confidence) that the opposition must have a replacement ready to assume office.

The Executive

The division between the head of government (the chancellor) and the head of state (the president) is firmly established in the Federal Republic, with major political powers delegated to the chancellor. Responsibilities and obligations are clearly distinguished between the two offices. For example, the chancellor can be criticized for the government's policies without the criticism being perceived as an attack against the state itself. This division of power in the executive branch was essential to establish respect for the new West German state after Hitler assumed both offices as the *Führer*.

The German president is the head of state, a much weaker position than that of the chancellor. Like constitutional monarchs in Britain, for example, German presidents stand above the political fray, which means that their role is more ceremonial than political. Among the most common functions are signing treaties, presiding at formal state functions, and overseeing *Bundestag* protocols. German presidents are almost always semiretired politicians who are moderates within their respective parties and thus broadly acceptable to the electorate. However, if there were a political crisis affecting the chancellor, the president would remain as a caretaker of the political process, thus providing continuity in a time of national calamity. For example, should a parliamentary crisis arise and no candidate can command the support of an absolute majority of *Bundestag* members, the president can decide whether the country is to be governed by a minority administration under a chancellor elected by a plurality of deputies or whether new elections are to be called.[13] In July 1994, Roman Herzog was elected president by the Federal Convention (*Bundesversammlung*), an assembly of all *Bundestag* members and an equal number of delegates elected by the state legislatures according to the principle of proportional representation (the equivalent of an electoral college). The presidential term is five years, with a limit of two terms. Herzog replaced Richard von Weizsäcker, who had emphasized the moral role of the office, officially apologizing for Nazi war crimes. All Federal Presidents to date have been men—and all from the Rhineland—so when Herzog announced he would only serve one term, many Germans hoped that a woman might get a chance to serve in this post. Yet, in 1999 only men were nominated and Johannes Rau, the Social Democratic *Minister-Präsident* (Governor) of North Rhine–Westphalia was elected President in May.

The chancellor is elected by a majority of the members of the *Bundestag*. In practice, this means that the chancellor's ability to be a strong party leader (or leader of a coalition of parties) is essential to the government's success. A government is formed after a national election or, if the chancellor leaves office between elections, after a majority of the *Bundestag* has nominated a chancellor in a constructive vote of no confidence. The new leader consults with other party (and coalition) officials to make up the cabinet. These party leaders have considerable influence in determining which individuals receive ministries. In the event of a coalition government, party leaders often designate during the election campaign who will receive certain ministries. Negotiations on which policies a coalition will pursue can often become heated, so the choice of ministers for particular ministries is made on policy as well as personal grounds.

From their party or coalition, chancellors select members of the cabinet who can best carry out the duties of the executive branch. The most significant cabinet ministries are those of finance, economics, justice, interior, and foreign policy (the Foreign Ministry). Decision-making within the cabinet meetings is often pro forma, since many of the important deliberations are conducted beforehand. In many cases, chancellors rely on strong ministers in key posts, but some chancellors have taken ministerial responsibility themselves in key areas such as economics and foreign policy. Helmut Schmidt and Willy Brandt, respectively, fit this pattern. The economics and finance ministries always work closely with the *Bundesbank,* the powerful independent central bank.

Once the cabinet is formed, the chancellor has considerable authority to govern, thanks to the power of the Federal Chancellery (*Bundeskanzleramt*). This office is the "first among equals" of all the cabinet ministries, enabling the chancellor to oversee the entire government as well as mediate conflicts among the other ministries. It is a kind of superministry with wide-ranging powers in many areas.

The office of the chancellor (an office essentially equivalent to prime minister) has played a pivotal role in the Federal Republic. The clearly defined role of the chancellor within the federal framework has resulted in a far more effective office than was the case in the Weimar period. On the other hand, the chancellor's more limited role within the context of a federal system has constrained the ability of the central government to take sweeping action. To many Germans, the limitation of centralized executive power has been a welcome improvement.

Perhaps the most significant source of the chancellor's powers is a constitutional provision called the constructive vote of no confidence. To avoid the weakness of the cabinet governments of Weimar, the drafters of the Basic Law added a twist to common parliamentary practice in which a prime minister is brought down on a vote of no confidence. In most parliamentary democracies, if prime ministers lose such a vote, they must step down or call for new elections. In the Federal Republic, however, such a vote must be "constructive," meaning that a chancellor cannot be removed unless the *Bundestag* simultaneously elects a new chancellor (usually from one of the opposition parties). This constitutional provision strengthens the chancellor's power in at least two ways: (1) chancellors can more easily reconcile disputes among cabinet officials without threatening their own position; and (2) the opposition must come up with concrete and specific alternatives to the existing government, thus preventing confrontation for its own sake.

Chancellors also face significant limits on their power. As discussed in Section 4, the *Bundesrat* (upper house) must ratify all legislation passed in the *Bundestag* (lower house) unless overridden by a two-thirds vote. In addition, since the *Bundesrat* generally implements most legislation, chancellors have to consider the position of the upper house on most issues.

The Bureaucracy

An essential component of the executive is the national bureaucracy. In Germany it is very powerful and protected by long-standing civil service provisions. It is very difficult to fire or remove a bureaucrat. **Civil servants** maintain the conviction that their work is a profession, not just a job. During the Second and Third Reichs, German civil servants had a reputation for inflexibility and rigidity. Even though the bureaucracy is under democratic supervision today, there are certainly inefficiencies in the Federal Republic's public sector, just as there are in all public and private bureaucracies.

Surprisingly, only about 10 percent of civil servants are employed by the federal government, with the remainder employed by state and local governments. Today most civil servants either are graduates from major German universities or come from positions within the political parties. The federal bureaucrats are primarily policymakers who work closely with their ministries and the legislature. The bureaucrats at the state and local levels are the predominant agents of policy implementation because the states must administer most policies determined at the national level. This overlapping and coordinating of national, regional, and local bureaucracies is supported by the importance that Germans give to the provision of public services. The ongoing institutionalized relationship among the various levels of the bureaucracy has produced a more consistent and effective public policy than is found in other countries where federal and state governments are often at odds with one another.

Overlapping responsibilities on policy issues make it difficult to demarcate specifically the responsibility of federal institutions from the national to the

regional level, and from the regional to the local level. For example, the cities of Bremen and Hamburg, which have been members of the Hanseatic League specializing in foreign trade, remain city-states. Even today they have overlapping municipal and state governments. The recently unified Berlin city government fits into this category, too.

Renowned for being officious, rigid, and unfriendly, the German bureaucracy has won high, if grudging, respect from the population. It is generally seen as efficient, although sometimes arcane. Some bureaucrats, mostly top federal officials, are appointed on the basis of party affiliation; following the traditional German pattern of proportionality, all major political groupings are represented in the bureaucracy. However, in the 1970s the Social Democratic Brandt government attempted to purge the bureaucracy of suspected radicals by issuing the so-called Radicals Decree, a move that tarnished its reputation for impartiality and fairness. But the majority of civil servants are chosen on the basis of merit, with elaborate licensing and testing for those in the highest positions. German bureaucrats enjoy a well-deserved reputation for competence, especially when compared to the bureaucracies of most developed states.

Semipublic Institutions

Semipublic institutions are powerful, efficient, and responsible for much national policy-making. The most influential include the *Bundesbank,* the health insurance funds that administer the national health care system, and the vocational education system (which encompasses the apprenticeship training system). These are part of the integrated system of democratic corporatism in which national (and state) governments delegate certain policy-making authority to these institutions, which engage in continuous dialogue with all relevant participants in the policy community until appropriate policies are found.

In countries that had a guild system in the Middle Ages, such as Germany, an inclusionary, often corporatist, form of representation is common. Semipublic institutions combine aspects of both representation and implementation. German semipublic institutions differ greatly from pluralist representation in countries such as the United States, where interest groups

Citizen Action: *Co-Determination*

Co-determination is an institutional relationship between organized labor and business that gives labor movements the right to participate in major decisions that affect their firms and industries. Found in northern Europe, including the Netherlands and Scandinavia, but best known in the Federal Republic of Germany, co-determination (*Mitbestimmung*) allows representatives of workers and trade unions to obtain voting seats on the supervisory boards of directors of firms with 2000 or more employees.

German co-determination has two official forms, one for the coal and steel industries and one for all other industries. The former provides full parity for worker representatives in all decisions on the supervisory board, whereas the latter provides nearly full parity between worker and employer representatives because a representative of management always has the tie-breaking vote. Post–World War II roots of co-determination sprang from the anger of German workers toward the complicity of German industrialists with the Nazi war machine. This was especially true of the coal and steel barons; hence the full parity in those industries. The idea of placing workers and union representatives on the boards of directors of these firms was seen by many as a way to ensure accountability from German capitalism.

The laws governing co-determination, first passed in the early 1950s and expanded in the 1970s, reflect the powerful role of the trade unions in the politics of the Federal Republic. They give the workers—and indirectly their unions for those firms so organized—a form of institutionalized participation via membership on the supervisory boards of German firms. This participation, rather than making German firms uncompetitive, actually had the opposite effect. Workers and unions can comprehend, if not unilaterally determine, corporate decisions regarding investment and the introduction of new technologies. Co-determination has allowed German workers a broader and deeper knowledge of the goals and strategies of the firms for which they work.

But co-determination has not been conflict-free. In 1976, at the time of the broadening of some of the unions' powers, the Constitutional Court ruled that worker representatives could never attain majority representation on the supervisory board, since such a provision could compromise private property. Despite this residual tension, however, co-determination has provided substantial benefits to German business, workers, and the entire society. The most pressing challenge for co-determination in the future will be whether these German-specific institutional patterns will infiltrate their way into other European countries or whether they will be overtaken by European-wide labor relations policies that take other forms.

petition public authority for redress of grievances while keeping at arm's length from the implementation process. The corporatist interest groups are also very much intertwined with the Federal Republic's semipublic agencies, which are institutions crucial for the functioning of the German political economy. A gray area encompassing both public and private responsibilities, these institutions are an apparent seamless web that shapes, directs, implements, and diffuses German public policy.

In the late 1940s the idea of a strong central state in Germany was discredited for two reasons: the excesses of Nazism and the American occupation authorities' strong affinity for the private sector. West German authorities faced a dilemma. How would they rebuild society if a strong public sector role was prohibited? The answer was to create modern, democratic versions of those nineteenth-century institutions that blurred the differences between the public and private sectors. These institutions have played a crucial role in the German political economy, one that has long been unrecognized.

The political scientist Peter Katzenstein has written extensively about the semipublic agencies, calling them detached institutions.[14] He sees them as primarily mediating entities that reduce the influence of the central state. Katzenstein finds that they have tended to work best in areas of social and economic policy. Among the most important semipublic agencies are the Chambers of Industry, the Council of Economic Advisors (known colloquially as the Six Wise Men), and the institutions of worker participation (co-determination and the works councils). Even areas of the welfare system are semipublic because the distribution system for welfare benefits is often administered by organizations not officially part of the state bureaucracy. The most significant example of this are the **health insurance funds** (*Krankenkassen*), which bring all major health interests together to allocate costs and benefits via an elaborate system of consultation and group participation.

Another important set of semipublic institutions is the unions, which participate in industrial relations through the system known as co-determination (*Mitbestimmung*). This group of institutions is discussed here because co-determination legally gives workers opportunities to shape public policy.

Co-determination provides that workers, including union members, participate on the boards of directors of all medium and large firms, thus giving unions an inside look at the workings of the most powerful firms in the Federal Republic. Unions can thus understand, if not control, major corporate decisions on such issues as investment and application of technology. Based on laws passed in the early 1950s and expanded in the 1970s, co-determination gives workers (and unions) up to one-half of the seats on company boards. The unions' problem in challenging management positions on contentious issues is that (with the exception of the coal and steel industries) the laws also give management one additional, usually tie-breaking, vote.

Another uniquely German institution, the **works councils** (*Betriebsräte*), gives German workers access to the policy implementation process. In contrast to co-determination, which gives trade unions input outside the plant (i.e., on the board), the works councils represent workers inside the workplace and address shop-floor and plant-level affairs. The trade unions have historically addressed collective bargaining issues, whereas the works councils have concentrated on social and personnel matters. With the trend to more flexible workplaces in the late 1980s and through the 1990s, these lines of demarcation have become blurred.

The unions have clout on the boards because they are a countrywide, multi-industry organization representing a large number of diverse workers. The works councils, on the other hand, owe their primary allegiance to their local plants and firms. The distribution of power between these two bodies causes rivalries, periodic rifts, and competing spheres of interest. Despite an 85 percent overlap in personnel between unions and works councils, and despite a structural entanglement between these two major pillars of labor representation in the Federal Republic, these divisions can produce tensions among organized labor. A period of general flux and plant-related, management-imposed flexibility beginning in the middle and late 1980s exacerbated these tensions. However, the unions have successfully avoided the proliferation of any serious plant-level divisions among workers that might have eroded their stature in the German economy in the 1990s.

Other State Institutions

In addition to the institutions discussed so far, the military, the judiciary, and subnational governments are essential institutions for governance and policy-making.

The Military

From the eighteenth century (when it was the Prussian military) through World War II, the German military was powerful and aggressive. After World War II the German military was placed completely under civilian control and tightly circumscribed by law and treaty. The end of the Cold War has produced two other important changes in German military policy: the reduction in U.S. armed forces stationed in Germany, and payments made to Russia for removal of soldiers and matériel from the former East Germany.

Germany has a universal service arrangement requiring all citizens over the age of eighteen to perform one year of military or civilian service. In 1990, Germany had about 600,000 men and women in the military, but in 1994 the Federal Government fixed the figure at approximately 340,000. Germany spends 1.5 percent of its GDP on the military; in 1996 it spent DM 47.1 billion. Germany's armed forces have been legally proscribed from extranational activity, first by the Allied occupation and later by the German Basic Law. Under the provisions of the Basic Law, the German military is to be used only for defensive purposes within Europe, and then in coordination with NATO authorities. Only very limited military activity under tightly circumscribed approval (via NATO) has altered the general prohibition. German participation in the UN peacekeeping mission in Bosnia was one example, and agreeing to participate in opposition to Serbian aggression in Kosovo in 1998 was another.

Since World War II two generations of Germans have been educated to deemphasize the military and militarism as a solution to political problems. The irony is that it is now politically—and until recently, constitutionally—difficult for Germany to commit troops to regional conflicts, even under UN auspices. The dilemmas intensify when the issues of Bosnia, Serbia, and the catastrophe of the former Yugoslavia are considered. In opposition, the SPD and the Greens had argued that, because of the Third Reich's aggressive military expeditions to the east in World War II, it was impossible for the German military, either under UN or NATO auspices, to play a constructive role in Eastern Europe. Yet now in government, the SPD and the Greens face increased international pressure for Germany to play a leading role in European foreign policy.

The Judiciary

The German judiciary is an independent institution whose rulings are almost always consistent with accepted constitutional principles. Judges are appointed by federal or state governments, depending on the court, and are drawn from practitioners of the law, similar to the pattern in other countries. In 1996 there were 26,357 judges in Germany—20,999 male and 5,358 female. The German judiciary remains outside the political fray on most issues, although a ruling in 1993 limiting access to abortion for many women, in direct opposition to a more liberal law in East Germany, was a clear exception to the general pattern. The judiciary was also criticized in the 1990s for showing too much leniency toward perpetrators of racist violence.

The court system in the Federal Republic is three-pronged. One branch consists of the criminal-civil system, which has as its apex the Federal High Court. It is a unified rather than a federal system and tries to apply a consistent set of criteria to cases in the sixteen states. The Federal High Court reviews cases that have been appealed from the lower courts, including criminal and civil cases, disputes among the states, and matters that would be viewed in some countries as political, such as the abortion ruling.

The Special Constitutional Court deals with matters directly affecting the Basic Law. A postwar creation, it was founded to safeguard the new democratic order. Precisely because of the Nazis' abuses of the judiciary, the founders of West Germany added an additional layer to the judiciary, basically a judicial review, to ensure that the democratic order was maintained. The most notable decisions of the Constitutional Court in the 1950s were the banning of both the ultra-right Socialist Reich Party and the leftist Communist Party as forces hostile to the Basic Law. During the early 1970s when the so-called Radicals Decree was promulgated, the Constitutional Court ruled that several individuals who had lost their jobs were "enemies of the constitution." During the brief terrorist wave of the late 1970s, when several prominent individuals were kidnapped or killed by the ultra-radical Red Army Faction, this court was asked to pass judgment on the terrorists' actions. At that time, it sanctioned a wide, indiscriminate sweep for all those who might be supporters of the Red Army Faction. In a state that claimed to be an adherent of western-style liberalism, and in one ruled by the SPD-led government, such far-reaching action alarmed many who were concerned about individual freedoms and due process.

The **Administrative Court** is the third branch of the court system. Consisting of the Labor Court, the Social Security Court, and the Finance Court, the Administrative Court system has a much narrower jurisdiction than the other two branches. Because the state and its bureaucracy have such a prominent place in the lives of German citizens, this level of the court system acts as a check on the arbitrary power of the bureaucracy. Compared to Britain and France, where much public policy is determined by legislation, German public policy is more often determined by the administrative actions of the bureaucracy. Citizens can use these three courts to challenge bureaucratic decisions—for example, if authorities improperly take action with respect to labor, welfare, or tax policies.

The judiciary has always played a major role in German government because of the state's deep involvement in political and economic matters. But the worst abuses of the judiciary for political purposes came during the Nazi regime, when it was induced to make a wide range of antidemocratic, repressive, and even criminal decisions. Among these were banning non-Nazi parties, allowing the seizure of Jewish property, and sanctioning the deaths of millions.

The Federal Republic's founders were determined that the new judicial system would avoid these abuses. One of the first requirements was that the judiciary explicitly safeguard the democratic rights of individuals, groups, and political parties, stressing some of the individual freedoms that had long been associated with the American, British, and French legal systems. In fact, the Basic Law contains a more elaborate and explicit statement of individual rights than exists in either the U.S. Constitution or in British common law.

However, the Federal Republic's legal system differs from the common-law tradition of Britain, its former colonies, and the United States. The common-law, precedent-based system is characterized by adversarial relationships between contending parties, in which the judge (or the court itself) merely provides the arena for the struggle. In continental Europe, including France and Germany, the legal system is based on a codified legal system with roots in Roman law and the Napoleonic code.

In the Federal Republic, the judiciary is thus an active administrator of the law rather than solely an arbiter. Specifically, judges have a different relationship with the state and with the adjudication of cases. This judicial system relies on the concept of the "capacity of the state" (as the political sociologist Theda Skocpol terms it) to identify and implement certain important societal goals.[15] And if the task of the state is to create the laws to attain these goals, then the judiciary should safeguard their implementation. In both defining the meaning of very complex laws and in implementing their administration, German courts go considerably beyond those in the United States and Britain, which supposedly have avoided political decisions. The German courts' role in shaping policy has been most evident in the ruling on whether to allow the unions to obtain increased co-determination rights in 1976. The court allowed the unions to obtain near parity on the boards of directors but stated that full union parity with employers would compromise the right of private property.

In the 1990s the courts came under great pressure to resolve the intractable policy issues that unification and European integration brought about. As they were drawn deeper into the political thicket, their decisions came under increased scrutiny. Clandestine searches for terrorists in the late 1970s left many observers believing that the rights of citizens who were unaffiliated with any terrorist organizations had been compromised. Many critics wish that today's courts would show the same diligence and zeal in addressing the crimes of neo-Nazis as the courts did in the 1970s, when Germany was confronted with violence from small ultra-leftist groups. The courts' response to the violence of the 1990s has not been as resolute as in the 1970s.

Subnational Government

There are sixteen states in the Federal Republic, eleven of which composed the old West Germany and five the former East Germany. Among the best-known regions are Bavaria, the Rhineland including the industrial Ruhr River valley, the Black Forest area in the southwest, and the city-states of Hamburg and Bremen. Unlike the weakly developed regional governments of Britain and France, German state governments enjoy considerable autonomy and independent powers. Each state has a regional assembly (*Landtag*), which functions much like the *Bundestag* does at the federal level. The governor (*Minister-Präsident*) of each *Land* is the leader of the largest party (or coalition of parties) in the *Landtag* and forms a government in the *Landtag* in much the same way as does the chancellor in the *Bundestag*. Elections for each of the sixteen states are held on independent, staggered four-year cycles, which generally do not coincide with federal elections and only occasionally coincide with elections in other *Länder*. Like the semipublic institutions, subnational governments in Germany are powerful, important, and responsible for much national policy implementation.

Particularly significant is Germany's "marble-cake" federalism, the interaction among state and federal government that sees the former implement many of the laws passed by the latter. A good way to show how it works is to cite the example of **industrial policy** (*Ordnungspolitik*). Regional governments are much more active than the national government in planning and targeting economic policy and therefore have greater autonomy in administering industrial policy. Since the *Länder* are constituent states, they are able to develop their own regional versions of industrial policy. Because the different regions have different economic needs and industrial foundations, these powers are seen as legitimate and appropriate by most voters.

The state governments encourage banks to make direct investment and loans to stimulate industrial development. They also encourage cooperation among regional firms, many in the same industry, to spur international competition. This coordination avoids violation of the Cartel Law of 1957, Germany's principal antitrust law, because it does not impede domestic competition. State governments also invest heavily in vocational education to provide the skills needed for manufacturing high-quality goods, the core of the German economy. Organized business and organized labor have a direct role in shaping curricula to improve worker skills via the vocational education system. These *Land* governments have improved industrial adaptation by shaping the state's competitive framework rather than adopting a heavy-handed regulatory posture.

The states do not pursue identical economic policies, and there are various models of government involvement in economic policy. The specific patterns identified have included the organized yet flexible specialization of Baden-Württemberg, the late industrialization of Bavaria, and the managed decline and adjustment of North Rhine–Westphalia.

In the Federal Republic state politics are organized on the same political party basis as the national parties. This does not mean that national politics dominate local politics. However, the common party names and platforms at all levels let voters see the connection among local, regional, and national issues. Since parties adopt platforms for state and city elections, voters can see the ideological differences between parties and not be swayed solely by personalities. This does not mean that personalities do not play a role in

German regional politics. Rather, the German party system encourages national political figures to begin their careers at the local and state levels. Regional and local party members' careers are tied closely to the national, regional, and local levels of the party. Thus ideological and policy continuity across levels is rewarded. Some observers suggest that this connection in the Federal Republic among national, regional, and local politics may be one reason why voter turnout in German state elections far exceeds that of equivalent U.S. elections.

Local governments in the Federal Republic can raise revenues by owning enterprises, and many do. This has partly resulted from the historical patterns of public sector involvement in the economy but also from the assumption that these levels of government are the stewards of a collective public good. By operating art museums, theater companies, television and radio networks, recreational facilities, and housing complexes, and by providing various direct and indirect subsidies to citizens, local governments attempt to maintain the quality of life in modern society. Even during the recessions of the early 1980s and the early 1990s, there were remarkably few cutbacks in ownership of public enterprises or in these various types of social spending.

The Policy-Making Process

The chancellor and the cabinet have the principal responsibility for policy-making, but their power cannot be wielded in an arbitrary fashion. The policy-making process in Germany is largely consensus-based, with contentious issues usually extensively debated within various public, semipublic, and private institutions. Although the legislature has a general role in policy-making, the primary driving forces are the respective cabinet departments and the experts on whom they call.

Policy implementation is similarly diffuse. Along with corporatist interest groups and various semipublic organizations, the *Bundesrat* (upper house) also plays a significant role. Among the areas of policy most likely to be shaped by multiple actors are vocational education, welfare, health care, and worker participation. Germany's status as a federal state and one populated by a broad range of democratic corporatist groups and parapublic institutions means that policy implementation has many participants. Even in such areas as foreign and security policy, the federal cabinet departments sometimes rely on business interests in policy implementation. European Union policy is shaped by both national and regional governments as well as by private sector interests that use corporatist institutions to participate in the process.

Many observers do not understand exactly why and how institutions support the Federal Republic's economic policy-making process. The role that the various institutions have played in the process of flexible adaptation to competitive pressures has been substantial. It has enabled the German economy to outperform the economies of most other industrialized countries for most of the post–World War II period. At first glance, it seems such institutions are merely regulatory agencies that inhibit economic freedoms. A closer examination, however, reveals that German institutions regulate not the minute details, but the general framework. Because all economic actors are clear on the general parameters, German regulatory policy is remarkably free of the microregulations common in other countries. Moreover, many policies, especially in the banking and manufacturing industries, are reinforced by industry self-regulation that makes heavy-handed government intervention unnecessary.

What components of this policy-making process actually create economic policy? First of all, corporatism is a system and not just a collection of firms or discrete policies. In this system, business, labor, and the government work together from the outset of the process and develop consensual policy solutions to national, regional, state, and local issues. The Germans have spoken of their "social" (not "free") market economy because of the deeply entrenched belief that business must share in the responsibility to provide a stable order for the economy and indirectly for society.

German business, labor, and government support for the **framework regulations** has produced a system that often appears externally rigid but internally flexible (in the sense that large institutions and firms are often surprisingly flexible in adapting applied technologies to produce specialized goods). In short, this system regulates not the details, but the general rules of the game under which all actors must play.

Some would criticize such a system as being too cumbersome and inflexible. However, the Germans praise their system for generally producing agreement on major policy direction without major social dislocation. Once agreement has been informally worked out among all the major parties, it is easier to move forward with specific legislation. This process is generally less conflict-oriented than in Britain because the German parliamentary system takes steps to secure support from major interest groups.

This consensual system was challenged by the extraordinary nature of unification issues, which put this informal style of policy-making under tremendous pressure. Among the issues that proved most intractable are those of political asylum, racist violence, and scandals that tarnished the reputations of major public figures in the political system and in major interest groups. Moreover, for all of its system-maintaining advantages, the German consensual system contains a certain intolerance of dissent. Among examples are the party list system, the 5 percent threshold for party representation, and judicial banning of political parties. This helps to explain the protest from outside the parties that started in the 1960s and has continued on and off ever since.

Section ❹   Representation and Participation

In the aftermath of unification and European integration, Germany continues to strive for democratic participation that is both inclusive and representative. The nation still struggles with issues surrounding collective identities. Incorporating disparate political cultures (east and west, for example) when respect for dissent and dialogue is not deeply ingrained is a dilemma for any society. The key issue for Germany is how to develop a system of democratic participation that encompasses both extrainstitutional groups and organized political institutions.

The Legislature

The legislature occupies a prominent place in the political system, with both the lower house (*Bundestag*) and the upper house (*Bundesrat*) holding significant and wide-ranging powers. The Federal Republic is similar to other parliamentary regimes that have a fusion of power in which the executive branch derives directly from the legislative branch. In other words, there is not a sharply defined separation of powers between cabinet and legislature.

The process for choosing members of the two houses differs substantially. The *Bundestag* elects its members directly; voters choose both individual district representatives and the political parties that represent their interests. The *Bundesrat's* members, on the other hand, are officials who are elected or appointed to the regional (*Länder*) governments. Both branches of the legislature are broadly representative of the major interests in German society, although some interests such as business and labor are somewhat overrepresented whereas ecological and noneconomic interests are somewhat underrepresented.

The executive branch introduces legislation in accordance with the Basic Law, which requires that federal budget and tax legislation be initiated by the executive. Although most bills are initiated in the cabinet, this does not diminish the influence of *Bundestag* or *Bundesrat* members. In fact, because the chancellor is the leader of the major party or coalition of parties, no sharp division exists between the executive and legislative branches. There is generally strong consensus within parties and within coalitions about what legislation should be introduced. Parties and coalitions, which depend on party discipline to sustain majorities, place a high value on agreement regarding major legislation.

When the chancellor and the cabinet propose a bill, it is sent to a relevant *Bundestag* committee. Most of the committee deliberations take place privately so that the individual committee members can have considerable latitude to shape details of the legislation. The committees will call on their own expertise as well as that of relevant government ministries and testimony from pertinent interest groups. To some this may appear to be a kind of insiders' club, and to some degree it is. However, the committees generally call

on a wide range of groups, both pro and con, that are affected by the proposed legislation. By consulting the corporatist interest groups, a more consensus-oriented outcome is achieved. In contrast, legislative sessions in countries with a more pluralist (less inclusive) form of lobbying, such as Britain, tend to be contentious and less likely to produce agreement. Under pluralism it is relatively easy for groups to articulate issues; however, without a coordinated institutional structure, policy-making is more haphazard.

After emerging from committee, the bill has three readings in the *Bundestag*. The debate in the *Bundestag* often produces considerable criticism from the opposition and sharp defense by the governing parties. The primary purpose of the debate is to educate the public about the major issues of the bill. Following passage in the *Bundestag*, a bill must be approved by the *Bundesrat*, whose assent includes determining how a particular law will be implemented at the regional level. Finally, it must be signed by the federal president.

Most of the members of the national legislature are male, middle-class professionals, even in the supposedly working-class Social Democratic Party, which had a much greater proportion of blue-collar deputies in the 1950s. There were few women lawmakers until the 1980s and 1990s, when the Greens elected an increased number of female *Bundestag* members and women began to gain slots on the Social Democrats' electoral lists.[16] Fewer than 10 percent of *Bundestag* members were women through the 1983 election, but since 1987 the number of women has increased substantially, reaching more than 30 percent with the 1998 election (see Table 2). The addition of newer parties such as the worker-oriented ex-communist Party of Democratic Socialism (PDS) and the continued presence of the Greens with their counterculture life-styles have increased the variety of backgrounds among *Bundestag* members. In fact, the proportional representation system used in Germany increases the number of women and minorities elected to the *Bundestag*. Many parties, particularly the Social Democrats, the Greens, and the PDS, select candidates for their electoral lists based on gender and diversity.

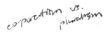

Table 2

Percentage of Women Members in the Bundestag													
Yr	'49	'53	'57	'61	'65	'69	'72	'76	'80	'83	'87	'90	'94	'98
%	6.8	8.8	9.2	8.3	6.9	6.6	5.8	7.3	8.5	9.8	15.4	20.5	26.3	30.2

Source: *Bundeszentrale für Politische Bildung*, 1998.

The Bundestag

The lower house of the legislature, the *Bundestag*, consists of 669 seats. This large number—increased by 175 members after unification—caused a strain on the facilities in Bonn. When the capital moved to Berlin in 1999 to the rebuilt *Reichstag*, all *Bundestag* members could finally be accommodated.

Bundestag members almost always vote with their parties. This party unity contributes to consistency in the parties' positions over the course of a four-year legislative period and enables the electorate to identify each party's stance on a range of issues. Consequently, all representatives in the *Bundestag* can be held accountable based on their support for their parties' positions. Party discipline, in turn, helps produce more stable governments.

The tradition of strong, unified parties in the *Bundestag* has some drawbacks. The hierarchy within parties relegates newer members to a comparatively long stint as backbenchers. Since the legislative agenda and key policy decisions are controlled by party elders and the Federal Chancellery, individual legislators have few opportunities to make an impact. Some of the most prominent national politicians preferred to serve their political apprenticeship in state or local government, where they would have more visibility. Chancellors Gerhard Schröder and Helmut Kohl took this route as governors of Lower Saxony and Rhineland Palatinate, respectively.

The Bundesrat

The *Bundesrat* has a different role than the U.S. Senate or the British House of Lords. The *Bundesrat* is the mechanism that makes the federal system work. It is responsible for the distribution of powers between national and state governments and grants to the states the rights to implement federal laws. It is the point of intersection for the national and the state governments and is made up of sixty-nine members from the sixteen state governments. Each state sends at least three representatives to the *Bundesrat*, depending on its population. States with more than 2 million residents have four votes, and states with more than 6 million people have five votes.

The political composition of the *Bundesrat* at any given time is determined by which parties are in power in the states. Each state delegation casts its votes on legislation in a bloc, reflecting the views of the majority party or coalition. Consequently, the party controlling the majority of state governments can have a significant effect on legislation passed in the *Bundestag*. And because state elections usually take place between *Bundestag* electoral periods, the *Bundesrat* majority can shift during the course of a *Bundestag* legislative period.

The *Bundesrat* must approve all amendments to the constitution as well as all laws that address the fundamental interests of the states, such as taxes, territorial integrity, and basic administrative functions. It exercises a **suspensive veto**; that is, if the *Bundesrat* votes against a bill, the *Bundestag* can override the *Bundesrat* by passing the measure again by a simple majority. If, however, a two-thirds majority of the *Bundesrat* votes against a bill, the *Bundestag* must pass it again by a two-thirds margin. In usual practice, the *Bundesrat* has not acted to obstruct. When the legislation is concurrent—that is, when the state and national governments share administrative responsibilities for implementing the particular policy—there is almost always easy agreement between the two houses. Also when a party or coalition achieves a stable majority in the *Bundestag*, it can overcome any possible obstruction by the *Bundesrat*.

The *Bundesrat* introduces comparatively little legislation, but its administrative responsibilities are considerable. Most of the members of the *Bundesrat* are also state government officials well experienced in the implementation of particular laws. Their expertise is frequently called upon in the committee hearings of the *Bundestag*, which are open to all *Bundesrat* members. This overlapping is a unique feature of the Federal Republic. Many U.S. observers make the mistake of equating German and U.S. federalism. However, Germany has a qualitatively different relationship between national and state governments. The Federal Republic avoids the jurisdictional problems that sometimes plague other decentralized federal countries because many of the laws passed in the *Bundestag* are implemented at the state level.

The *Bundesrat's* strong administrative role is a key component of the government. In different ways, this system avoids the shortcomings of both the fragmented legislative practices of the United States and the overly centralized policies of previous German governments. Because the *Bundesrat* is concerned with implementation, its role is more purposeful than that of the U.S. Congress, where laws that overlap or contradict previous legislation are frequently passed. For example, the *Bundesrat* coordinates the link between regional and national economic policies, vocational education systems, and a major television network (ARD). The *Bundesrat's* structure positions it close to the concerns and needs of the entire country and provides a forum for understanding how national legislation will affect each of the states.

Although the *Bundesrat* was originally envisioned to be more technocratic and less politically contentious than the popularly elected *Bundestag*, debates in the *Bundesrat* became strongly politicized beginning in the 1970s. The most common occurrence was the conflict that emerged when regional elections caused a change in control of the *Bundesrat*, especially when this change gave more influence to the party, or group of parties, that was in opposition to the *Bundestag*. For example, part of Helmut Kohl's difficulty in his last term (1994–1998) resulted from the Social Democrats' controlling a majority of state governments, where they occasionally blocked national legislation.

Political Parties and the Party System

Germany has often been called a **party democracy** because its parties are so important in shaping state policy. Its multiparty system has proved quite stable for most of the post–World War II period. Until the early 1980s, Germany had a "two-and-a-half" party system, composed of a moderate-left Social Democratic Party (SPD), a moderate-right Christian Democratic grouping (CDU in all of West Germany except Bavaria, where it is called the CSU), and a small centrist Free Democratic Party (FDP). The ideological distance between these parties was not great. The SPD broadened its base from its core working-class constituency to include more middle-class supporters beginning in the late 1950s. The CDU/CSU includes both Catholics (mostly from the Bavarian-based CSU) and Protestants. The FDP is liberal in the European sense and favors free-market solutions to economic problems and extensive personal freedoms for individuals. With only 5–10 percent of the vote, it is a pragmatic party and until 1998 usually chose to ally itself with one of the two larger parties to form a government. During their time as the only parties on the political landscape (1949–1983), these groups presided over a stable, growing economy and a broad public consensus on economic and social policies.

During the 1980s and 1990s, two new parties emerged to challenge the "two-and-a-half" major parties (see Table 3) and to complicate Germany's comparatively tidy political landscape: the Greens/*Bündnis '90*, generally of the left and favoring ecological, environmental, and peace issues; and the Party of Democratic Socialism (PDS), the former Communist Party of East Germany. Two other small right-wing parties, the Republicans (*Republikaner*) and the German Peoples Union (*Deutsche Volksunion*, DVU), also emerged. Much more conservative than the CDU/CSU, they emphasized nationalism and aggression toward immigrants and ethnic minorities. Neither of these two right-wing parties has yet won seats in the *Bundestag* because of the 5 percent rule. Both have exceeded 5 percent in regional elections, however, and have won seats in those bodies.

The Greens/*Bündnis '90* entered the political scene in 1979 and have won seats at national and regional levels ever since. The PDS is concentrated in the five states of the former East Germany, and while it has received as much as 25 percent of the vote in some regional and local elections, it draws well under the 5 percent mark in the states of the former West Germany.

Table 3

FRG Election Results, 1949–1998

Year	Voter Turnout (%)	Party	% of Vote	Government	Year	Voter Turnout (%)	Party	% of Vote	Government
1949	78.5	CDU/CSU	31.0	CDU/CSU-FDP	1980	88.6	CDU/CSU	44.5	SPD-FDP
		SPD	29.2				SPD	42.9	
		FDP	11.9				FDP	10.6	
		Others	27.8				Others	0.5	
1953	86.0	CDU/CSU	45.2	CDU/CSU-FDP	1983	89.1	CDU/CSU	48.8	CDU/CSU-FDP
		SPD	28.8				SPD	38.2	
		FDP	9.5				FDP	7.0	
		Others	16.7				Greens	5.6	
1957	87.8	CDU/CSU	50.2	CDU/CSU			Others	0.5	
		SPD	31.8		1987	84.3	CDU/CSU	44.3	CDU/CSU-FDP
		FDP	7.7				SPD	37.0	
		Others	10.3				FDP	9.1	
1961	87.8	CDU/CSU	45.3	CDU/CSU-FDP			Greens	8.3	
		SPD	36.2				Others	1.3	
		FDP	12.8		1990	78.0	CDU/CSU	43.8	CDU/CSU-FDP
		Others	5.7				SPD	33.5	
1965	86.8	CDU/CSU	47.6	CDU/CSU-SPD (Grand Coalition)			FDP	11.0	
		SPD	39.3				Greens	3.8	
		FDP	9.5				PDS	2.4	
		Others	3.6				Bündnis '90	1.2	
1969	86.7	CDU/CSU	46.1	SPD-FDP			Others	3.5	
		SPD	42.7		1994	79.0	CDU/CSU	41.5	CDU/CSU-FDP
		FDP	5.8				SPD	36.4	
		Others	5.4				FDP	6.9	
1972	86.0	SPD	45.8	SPD-FDP			Greens	7.3	
		CDU/CSU	44.9				PDS	4.4	
		FDP	9.5				Others	3.5	
		Others	16.7		1998	82.3	SPD	40.9	SPD-Greens
1976	90.7	CDU/CSU	48.2	SPD-FDP			CDU/CSU	35.1	
		SPD	42.6				Greens	6.7	
		FDP	7.9				FDP	6.2	
		Others	0.9				PDS	5.1	
							Others	6.0	

Source: German Information Center, 1990–1998.

The Social Democratic Party

As the leading party of the left in Germany, the *Sozialdemokratische Partei Deutschlands* (SPD) has had a long and durable history. The SPD was founded in 1875 in response to rapid industrialization, survived Bismarck's attempts in the 1880s to outlaw it, and grew to be the largest party in the *Reichstag* by 1912.[17] Following World War I, it became the leading party—but without a majority—of the Weimar Republic during its early years.

Despite strong influence in postwar Germany from 1945 to 1948, the SPD was only able to obtain about 30 percent of the popular vote from 1949 until the early 1960s. In an attempt to broaden its constituency, the SPD altered its party program at a 1959 party conference in Bad Godesberg. Deemphasizing its primary reliance on Marxism, its new goal was to broaden its base and become what the political scientist Otto Kirchheimer has called a "catchall party."[18] The SPD did not relinquish Marxism completely and continued to represent the working class, but it also began to seek and attract support from groups outside the traditional blue-collar working class. The Bad Godesberg conference transformed the SPD into a party similar to other western European social democratic parties.

The SPD finally took office as the leading member of a majority coalition—with the FDP—in 1969 and remained in power for thirteen years under chancellors Willy Brandt and Helmut Schmidt. The SPD brought to the coalition a concern for increased welfare and social spending,[19] partly because of pressure by left-wing extraparliamentary opposition groups as part of student demonstrations in 1968. The FDP brought its support for increased individual freedom of expression at a time when youths in all industrialized societies were seeking a greater voice. The principal factor

cementing these two dissimilar parties for such a long time was the strong performance of the economy. The coalition finally broke up in the early 1980s, when an economic recession prevented the increased social spending demanded by the SPD left wing.

During the 1980s and 1990s, when the SPD was out of power, it failed to formulate clear alternative policies to make itself attractive to its members, supporters, and voters. In 1998 the Kohl regime was exhausted and had overpromised the speed of transformation in eastern Germany. An effective campaign by Gerhard Schröder enabled the SPD to increase its share of the vote by 5 percent over 1994 and emerge as Germany's leading party (see Figure 2).

The Greens

The Green Party is a heterogeneous party that first drew support from several different constituencies in the early 1980s: urban-based **Citizens Action Groups**; environmental activists; farmers; antinuclear-power activists; the remnants of the peace movement; and small bands of Marxist-Leninists. After

Figure 2

Distribution of Seats in the Fourteenth Bundestag

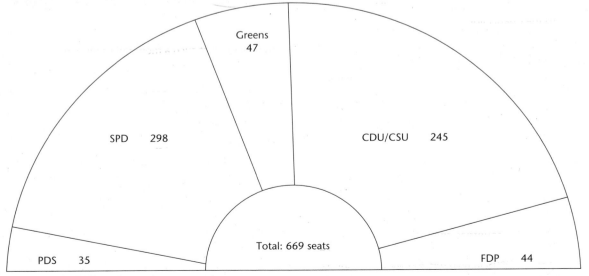

The Fourteenth German *Bundestag* was elected on September 27, 1998. At present, 669 deputies represent the Federal Republic of Germany's 60.1 million voters.

Leaders: *Gerhard Schröder*

Gerhard Schröder, the Chancellor of Germany elected in 1998, is the first German political leader truly of the postwar generation. Unlike his predecessor, Helmut Kohl, who was a teenager during World War II, Schröder was born at the war's cusp, in 1944, in the small Lower Saxony town of Rosenburg. He was, however, profoundly affected by the war in one sense; his father, a German soldier, was killed on the eastern front in Romania. As a young man, Gerhard Schröder had to work while he completed his education, serving a stint in a hardware store before completing the first phase of his university studies.

In his 20s, Schröder became active in Social Democratic party politics, belonging to the *Jungsozialisten* (Young Socialists), or *Jusos*, as they are known colloquially. He embraced Marxism—as did most *Jusos* at the time; this fact is not surprising given the Marxist roots of virtually all Social Democratic, Socialist, and Labor parties. Schröder then received his law degree from Göttingen University in 1976, and by then he had become an influential young politician in the SPD. He became a member of the *Bundestag* in 1980, and in 1990 was elected *Minister-Präsident* (Governor) of Lower Saxony. Even in his early years in public life, Schröder had high ambitions. One evening in Bonn in the 1980s, Schröder, who had taken perhaps an extra glass of wine or two, was walking past the gate to the Chancellor's office then occupied by Helmut Kohl; he put his hands on the gate and exclaimed: "I want to be in there!" Schröder's personal life is not without controversy; he has been married and divorced three times, and his present wife is number 4. During the 1998 campaign the youth wing of Helmut Kohl's CDU used a gag slogan urging voters to reject Schröder and the SPD, stating "three women can't be wrong."

During the 1998 election campaign Schröder was compared with British Prime Minister Tony Blair and with U.S. President Bill Clinton. Observers stressed one apparent thread that tied the three young (all are in their 40s or 50s) political leaders together. As heads of nominally left parties in their respective countries, they seemed to share an affinity for moving their parties toward more centrist positions. In fact, the SPD slogan for the 1998 campaign was "*die neue Mitte*" (the New Middle)

Source: AP/Wide World Photos.

suggesting just such a moderating tendency. Further contributing to this perception was the intention to award the powerful economics ministry to the free-market-oriented computer magnate Jost Stollman during Red-Green coalition negotiations.

Yet a funny thing happened on Schröder's way toward the center: German politics. Unlike Bill Clinton, who can often operate without regard to his own Democratic Party's concerns, or Tony Blair, who controls and shapes policy of his majority Labour Party, Gerhard Schröder is much more institutionally constrained. For one thing, the SPD is in coalition with another party, the Greens, and does not have a majority by itself. Just as important, though, is the institutional structure of the SPD, with its various factions and constituencies.

(continued on next page)

Leaders: *Gerhard Schröder* (continued)

The Green Party's position as an essential member of the coalition government meant that some of Schröder's overtures toward the center were challenged by Green concerns. The Greens' leader—and the coalition's foreign minister—Joschka Fischer drove hard bargains in insuring that many Green environmental positions would be part of the coalition agreement.

In addition, more leftist members of the SPD acted as a brake on some of Schröder's more centrist-leaning tendencies, especially Oskar Lafontaine, the chairman of the SPD and the coalition's finance minister until his final resignation in 1999. If Schröder is interested in supply-side measures such as reinvigorating the economy with technological innovation and increased flexibility, Lafontaine relied more on a demand-side approach such as increasing the number of jobs, decreasing inequality, and aiming tax cuts and social benefits toward the working class and the trade unions, the SPD's largest constituency. Lafontaine drove such a hard bargain that he persuaded Schröder to give more authority to the finance ministry, especially concerning EU affairs. Stollman—the computer magnate—balked at this power shift and withdrew his name as a candidate for economics minister. Yet this high-stakes gamble by Lafontaine cost him both the finance ministry and the SPD Chairmanship as Schröder forced him to resist from both posts in March 1999. Perhaps Schröder really did want to move to *"die Neue Mitte."*

Finally, one other indluence may have delayed Schröder's move toward the center: he was brought up by his widowed mother, and he retains a powerful commitment to maintaining a strong welfare state and a social benefits package that will sustain widows like his mother in their old age.

---

overcoming the 5-percent hurdle in the 1983 *Bundestag* elections, the Green Party went on to win seats in most subsequent state elections by stressing noneconomic quality-of-life issues. The electoral successes of this "anti-party party" generated a serious division within the party, between the *realos* (realists) and the *fundis* (fundamentalists). The *realos* believed it was important to enter political institutions to gain access to power; the *fundis* opposed any collaboration with existing parties, even if this meant sacrificing some of their goals.

The realists gained the upper hand, but there was no guarantee of long-term success for the Greens because all the other parties began to include environmental and qualitative issues in their party programs. Until the merger with the eastern German *Bündnis '90* in 1993, the Greens' position looked bleak. The squabbling between *fundis* and *realos* undercut the party's credibility among potential new voters. Its inability to develop positions to address the problems of unification made the party appear unwilling to deal with reality. The Greens' failure to motivate its own core constituency during the early 1990s greatly hampered the party. The unexpected death (by suicide) of a former party leader—the American-born Petra Kelly, a *fundi*—and the moderation of a current party leader (and foreign minister), Joschka Fischer, signaled the transformation of the Greens as a potential coalition partner.

The persistent ecological problems of the former East German states have presented the Greens a tremendous opportunity. After gaining over 6 percent of the vote in the 1994 and 1998 elections and becoming the junior coalition partner in the SPD-Green coalition, the party has a firm base, and it is likely to remain a permanent fixture in the German *Bundestag*.

The Christian Democrats

The Christian Democrats combine the Christian Democratic Union (CDU, in all *Länder* except Bavaria) and the Christian Social Union (CSU, the affiliated Bavarian grouping). Unlike the older parties (SPD and FDP) of the Federal Republic, the CDU/CSU was founded immediately after World War II, when most nonleftist parties worked to avoid the bickering and divisiveness of the Weimar period and establish a counterweight to the SPD. The CDU/CSU united Catholics and Protestants in one confessional

(Christian) party and served as a catchall party of the center-right.

Programmatically, the CDU/CSU stressed the Social Market Economy. This policy blended elements of European Catholic social concerns about the poor and workers with market economy concerns to create a program that was capitalist but with a paternalistic sense of social responsibility.[20] Under Chancellors Adenauer and Erhard, the Christian Democrats held political power for almost twenty years.

After the SPD and FDP established their center-left coalition in 1969, the CDU/CSU spent thirteen years as the opposition party. Returning to power in 1983 under the leadership of Helmut Kohl, the CDU/CSU with their FDP coalition partners continued their traditions of a moderate center-right regime and retained power through four elections until 1998. The twin legacies of the long Kohl regime are German unification and Germany's integration into the European Union, truly historic accomplishments.

The Free Democratic Party

The philosophy of the FDP comes closest to the individualistic ideals of British liberal and American libertarian parties. (It must be emphasized again that *liberal* is used in the European sense of an emphasis on the individual as opposed to an activist state tradition.) The FDP's major influence is its role as a swing party because it has allied with each of the two major parties (SPD and CDU/CSU) at different periods since 1949. Regularly holding the foreign and economics ministries in coalition with the Christian Democrats, the FDP's most notable leaders were Walter Scheel, Otto Graf Lambsdorff, and Hans-Dietrich Genscher.

The FDP's perspective encompasses two ideologies, broadly characterized here as economic liberalism and social liberalism. During the postwar period, the FDP relied on two philosophies to align itself with the two major political groupings, the CDU/CSU and the SPD. It remained in power until 1998, when the FDP was shut out of the cabinet for only the third time since 1949: the two previous occurrences were the CDU/CSU majority from 1957 to 1961 and the Grand Coalition from 1966 to 1969. For its strategy of co-governing with first one major party and then the

other, the FDP has occasionally been accused of lacking strong political convictions.

The Party of Democratic Socialism

The Party of Democratic Socialism (PDS), a new party concentrated in the former East Germany, has had a long and volatile history. It sprang from the Communist Party of Germany, which was founded after World War I. In the late 1940s the Communist Party flourished in the Soviet zone and under USSR acquiescence forced a merger with the Social Democrats in the east. The merged Communist/Socialist party was renamed the Socialist Unity Party (*Sozialistische Einheits Partei*, SED). It dominated all aspects of life in East Germany under the leadership of Walter Ulbricht, Willi Stoph, and Erik Honnecker, and was considered the most Stalinist and repressive regime in Eastern Europe.

With unification in 1990 reality confronted the SED. Under the leadership of the reformer Gregor Gysi, it quickly changed its name and showed considerable strength in the five states of the former East Germany. Throughout the 1990s the difficulties of unification helped to renew the strength of the PDS. It gained over 20 percent of the vote in the five new German states in both the 1994 and 1998 elections, and won seats in the *Bundestag* in three consecutive elections. In the mid-1990s it formed regional coalitions with the SPD in eastern Germany. Whether the PDS could ever be considered a potential coalition partner at the national level is uncertain. To some observers, the most interesting development is that the PDS is not a "communist" party any more. Rather, it has become a regionally based party beseeching the national government for greater resources. In this sense, it seems to be a left-wing eastern German version of the right-wing Bavaria-based CSU.

Elections

Germany's two-ballot electoral system has produced two significant outcomes. First, the proportional representation electoral system produces multiple parties that help reinforce the constitution's specific support for the parties as essential institutions in a democratic polity. Second, the 5 percent hurdle ensures that only parties with sufficient support attain seats in the *Bundestag*. This has helped Germany avoid the wild proliferation of parties that plagues some democracies, such as Italy and Israel, where coalition formation is extremely difficult.

The Germany parliamentary system represents a synthesis between the British and U.S. traditions of a single legislator representing one district and the European tradition of proportional representation in which the percentage of the vote is equal to the percentage of the parliamentary seats. Single-member district voting systems tend to produce a two-party system, and the Germans wanted to ensure that all major parties were represented, not just two. The German hybrid system, known as **personalized proportional representation**, requires citizens to cast two votes on each ballot: the first for an individual candidate, and the second for a list of national/regional candidates grouped by party affiliation (see Figure 3). This system has the effect of personalizing list voting because voters have their own representative but also can choose among several parties. To insure that only major parties are represented, only those that get 5 percent of the vote or that have three candidates who directly win individual seats can gain representation in the *Bundestag*.

Allocation of seats by party in the *Bundestag*, however, functions more like proportional representation. Specifically, the percentage of total seats won per party corresponds strongly with the party's percentage of the popular vote. For example, if a party's candidate wins a seat as an individual member, his or her party loses one seat from those won via list voting. In practice, most of the district seats are won by the two large parties, the Social Democrats and the Christian Democrats, because the district vote is winner-take-all. The smaller parties' representatives are almost always elected through the party lists. Thus, the list system creates stronger, more coherent parties.

One direct result of the party discipline is that the Federal Republic has high electoral participation (80 to 90 percent at the federal level). High electoral participation is strongly enhanced by clear party ideology. The newer parties—Greens and PDS—with similar kinds of ideological coherence, appear to confirm this. For nearly fifty years in the Federal Republic, voting participation rates matched or exceeded those in all other West European countries.

As Table 3 suggests, Germany has been a country without volatile electoral swings. There were three major periods of party dominance (plus the Grand Coalition) between 1949 and 1998:

CDU/CSU-FDP coalition (1949–1966)
Grand Coalition (CDU/CSU-SPD) interregnum (1966–1969)
SPD-FDP coalition (1969–1982)
CDU/CSU-FDP coalition (1982–1998)

Figure 3

1990 Bundestag Election Ballot

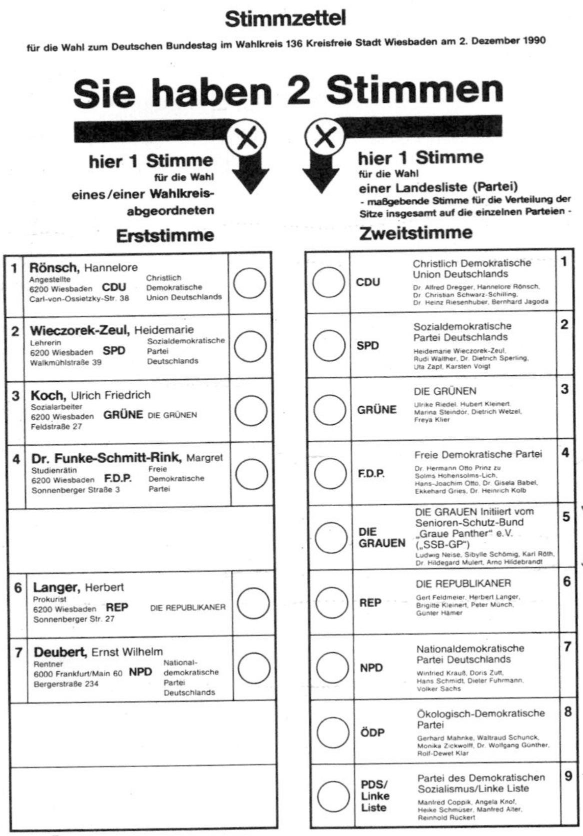
Stimmzettel

für die Wahl zum Deutschen Bundestag im Wahlkreis 136 Kreisfreie Stadt Wiesbaden am 2. Dezember 1990

Sie haben 2 Stimmen

hier 1 Stimme für die Wahl eines/einer Wahlkreis-abgeordneten — **Erststimme**		**hier 1 Stimme** für die Wahl einer Landesliste (Partei) - maßgebende Stimme für die Verteilung der Sitze insgesamt auf die einzelnen Parteien - — **Zweitstimme**	
1	**Rönsch,** Hannelore, Angestellte, 6200 Wiesbaden, Carl-von-Ossietzky-Str. 38 — **CDU** Christlich Demokratische Union Deutschlands	**CDU** Christlich Demokratische Union Deutschlands — Dr. Alfred Dregger, Hannelore Rönsch, Dr. Christian Schwarz-Schilling, Dr. Heinz Riesenhuber, Bernhard Jagoda	1
2	**Wieczorek-Zeul,** Heidemarie, Lehrerin, 6200 Wiesbaden, Walkmühlstraße 39 — **SPD** Sozialdemokratische Partei Deutschlands	**SPD** Sozialdemokratische Partei Deutschlands — Heidemarie Wieczorek-Zeul, Rudi Walther, Dr. Dietrich Sperling, Uta Zapf, Karsten Voigt	2
3	**Koch,** Ulrich Friedrich, Sozialarbeiter, 6200 Wiesbaden, Feldstraße 27 — **GRÜNE** DIE GRÜNEN	**GRÜNE** DIE GRÜNEN — Ulrike Riedel, Hubert Kleinert, Marina Steindor, Dietrich Wetzel, Freya Klier	3
4	**Dr. Funke-Schmitt-Rink,** Margret, Studienrätin, 6200 Wiesbaden, Sonnenberger Straße 3 — **F.D.P.** Freie Demokratische Partei	**F.D.P.** Freie Demokratische Partei — Dr. Hermann Otto Prinz zu Solms Hohensolms-Lich, Hans-Joachim Otto, Dr. Gisela Babel, Ekkehard Gries, Dr. Heinrich Kolb	4
		DIE GRAUEN DIE GRAUEN Initiiert vom Senioren-Schutz-Bund „Graue Panther" e.V. („SSB-GP") — Ludwig Neise, Sibylle Schömig, Karl Röth, Dr. Hildegard Mulert, Arno Hildebrandt	5
6	**Langer,** Herbert, Prokurist, 6200 Wiesbaden, Sonnenberger Str. 27 — **REP** DIE REPUBLIKANER	**REP** DIE REPUBLIKANER — Gert Feldmeier, Herbert Langer, Brigitte Kleinert, Peter Münch, Günter Hämer	6
7	**Deubert,** Ernst Wilhelm, Rentner, 6000 Frankfurt/Main 60, Bergerstraße 234 — **NPD** National-demokratische Partei Deutschlands	**NPD** Nationaldemokratische Partei Deutschlands — Winfried Krauß, Doris Zutt, Hans Schmidt, Dieter Fuhrmann, Volker Sachs	7
		ÖDP Ökologisch-Demokratische Partei — Gerhard Mahnke, Waltraud Schunck, Monika Zickwolff, Dr. Wolfgang Günther, Rolf-Dewet Klar	8
		PDS/Linke Liste Partei des Demokratischen Sozialismus/Linke Liste — Manfred Coppik, Angela Knof, Heike Schmüser, Manfred Alter, Reinhold Rückert	9

With their "first vote," voters from the Bonn electoral district can choose a candidate by name from the lefthand column. The "second vote" in the righthand column is cast for a party list at the federal level.

Germany has enjoyed relatively stable electoral allegiance, despite unification, European integration, and the introduction of two new parties in the *Bundestag* during the decade of the 1990s.

Political Culture, Citizenship, and Identity

With political parties representing such a broad ideological spectrum, there is wide-ranging political debate in Germany. This diversity is reflected in the media, where newspapers appeal to a broad range of political opinion. The major print media range from the mass-market tabloid *Bild Zeitung* (literally, picture newspaper) on the right, to conservative and liberal broadsheet newspapers such as *Die Welt* of Hamburg, the *Süddeutscher Zeitung* of Munich, and the *Frankfurter Allgemeine Zeitung*. The *Frankfurter Rundschau* is close to the SPD in its editorial positions, while the *TAZ* of Berlin is closest to the Greens. There is a wide variety of private TV cable channels, but the three main networks are public channels, and they are careful to provide a balance of major party positions. Until the late 1990s most public channels prohibited paid TV campaign commercials during the two-month electoral campaigns. Instead the networks present round-table discussions in which all parties participate. This approach has prevented the bigger and richer parties from buying a larger share of the popular vote, although some parties have begun advertising on private channels.

The wide range of public opinion has helped dispel the view that Germany's high voting turnout is due to a sense of duty and not to any real commitment to democracy. There is a strong participatory ethic among the democratic left, fostered by the many opportunities for participation at the workplace through co-determination and the works councils. Moreover, one of the primary appeals of the Greens has been their emphasis on **grassroots democracy**—that is, rank-and-file participation. The strength of the Greens, and now the PDS, has forced the traditional parties to focus on mobilizing their supporters and potential supporters. The arrival of the Greens and the PDS has also helped remove from German political culture some of the old stereotypes about the country's legendary preference for consensus, order, and stability.

Germany's educational system has also changed since the Federal Republic was created, particularly in terms of the socialization of German citizens. The catalyst was the student movement of the 1960s. At that time, the university system was elitist and restrictive and did not offer sufficient critical analysis of Germany's bloody twentieth-century history. Not only did the student mobilizations of the 1960s open up the educational system to a wider socioeconomic spectrum, they also caused many of the so-called '68 Generation (1968 was the year of the most significant demonstrations) to challenge their parents about attitudes shaped by the Nazi period and before. Even in the 1990s many critics of the German educational system argued that some of the older attitudes toward non-Germans remain and that the educational system should increase its efforts to build a tolerant citizenry.

Germany's Social Market Economy enjoys broad acceptance among Germans, with the possible exception of some Greens, the PDS, and the extreme right. The Social Market Economy provides benefits to almost all segments of the population, including public transit, subsidies for the arts, virtually free higher and vocational education, and a generous welfare state. Thus there is a general tolerance for a wide variety of political and artistic opinion and very little of the squabbling and acrimony over public funding of the arts that is common in some other countries.

The optimistic view that Germany has become a typical parliamentary democracy was challenged by anti-ethnic and anti-immigrant violence in the late 1980s and mid-1990s. The attacks on foreign immigrants, including families who had lived in Germany for more than thirty years, raised questions among some observers regarding the genuineness of German toleration. Given Germany's persecution of Jews and all non-Germans during the first half of the twentieth century, and the unimaginable horrors of the Holocaust, such concerns must be taken extremely seriously. Although Germany is not alone among industrialized nations in racist violence, its history brings German citizens the burden to confront and overcome any display of intolerance if it is to gain the world's respect as a decent nation.

The Schröder Red-Green government began to change the rules on citizenship, democracy, and participation in Germany. Until 1998, German citizenship was based on blood, on German ethnicity. Unlike many other European nations, Germany made it difficult for residents without native ethnicity to be naturalized, no matter how long they had lived in the country, and denied citizenship to the children of noncitizens born on native soil. On the other hand, ethnic Germans whose ancestors had not lived in Germany for centuries were allowed to enter Germany legally and to become citizens immediately. One of the first acts of the Schröder government was to allow expedited citizenship for long-time foreign residents.

Perhaps the most contentious citizenship/identity problem has surrounded the political asylum question. Following World War II, Germany passed one of the world's most liberal political asylum laws, in part to help atone for the Nazis' political repression of millions. With the end of the Cold War and the opening up of East European borders, the trickle of asylum-seekers turned into a flood. This influx drove the Kohl government to curtail drastically the right of political asylum, a step that put into question whether German democracy was as mature and well developed as it had claimed during the stable postwar period. Germany's commitment to democratic rights appeared to contain some new conditions, and many of them involved a definition of identity that looked remarkably insular in a Europe that was becoming more international.

Interests, Social Movements, and Protest

Germany remains a country of organized collectivities: major economic producer groups such as the BDI (Federal Association of German Industry), BDA (Federal Association of German Employers) and DGB (German Trade Union Confederation); political parties (in which real, participatory membership remains higher than in most other countries); and social groups. Germany has never been a country with a strong individualistic ethos. Occasionally individuals stand out in German politics amidst the powerful organized collectivities, but they are in the minority. In fact, the ascension of most individuals to political prominence in Germany owes as much to their skills in "working the organizations" as it does to individual initiative. Leaders such as Helmut Kohl, Gerhard Schröder, Joschka Fischer, and the late Petra Kelly obtained prominence by knowing how organizations

and institutions work and taking advantage of the system.

From the descriptions of organized business and organized labor in Section 3, it is clear that interest groups in Germany operate differently than they do in the United States and Britain. In the Federal Republic, interest groups are seen as having a societal role and responsibility that transcend the immediate interests of their members. Germany's codified legal system specifically allows private interests to perform public functions, albeit within a clearly specified general framework. Thus interest groups are seen as part of the fabric of society and are virtually permanent institutions. This view places a social premium on their adaptation and response to new issues. To speak of winners and losers in such an arrangement is to misunderstand the ability of existing interest groups to make incremental changes over time.

Strikes and demonstrations on a wide range of economic and noneconomic issues do occur, but they should be counted as evidence of success. Political institutions sometimes are mistakenly seen as fixed structures that are supposed to prevent or repress dissent. A more positive way to analyze such conflicts is to take a new institutionalist approach.[21] This theory argues that political organizations shape and adapt to social and political protest, and channel such action in ways that are not detrimental to democratic participation, but in fact represent its essence.

Rather than encouraging fractious competition, this system creates a framework within which interest groups can battle yet eventually come to an agreement on policy. Moreover, because they aggregate the interests of all members of their group, they often take a broader, less parochial view of problems and policy solutions. As part of the fabric of German society, interest groups have an institutional longevity that surpasses the duration of interest groups in most other industrialized countries. How does the German state mediate the relationship among interest groups? Peter Katzenstein observes that in the Federal Republic, "the state is not an actor but a series of relationships," and these relationships are solidified in what he has called "para-public institutions."[22] The para-publics encompass a wide variety of organizations, among which the most important are the *Bundesbank*, the institutions of co-determination, the labor courts, the social insurance funds, and the employment office. Under prevailing German public law, which is rooted in pre-1871 feudal traditions, they have been assigned the role of "independent governance by the representatives of social sectors at the behest of or under the general supervision of the state." In other words, German organizations, seen as mere interest groups in other countries, are combined with certain "quasi-government agencies" to fill a "para-public" role in the Federal Republic.

Other important groups include the Protestant and Catholic churches, the Jewish synagogues, the Farmers Association, the Association of Artisans, and the Federal Chamber of Physicians. Each of these groups has been tightly integrated into various para-public institutions to perform a range of essential social functions that in other countries might be performed by state agencies. These groups also act as the nation's conscience. One example is the vocal Jewish community's demand for reparations to be paid to Israel and to survivors of slave labor factories during World War II. A second is the demand by Turkish residents for Muslim education to accompany Christian teachings in the schools. These organizations assume a degree of social responsibility, via their roles in policy implementation, which goes beyond what political scientist Arnold Heidenheimer has called the "freewheeling competition of 'selfish' interest groups."[23] For example, through the state, the churches collect a church tax on all citizens born into either the Protestant or Roman Catholic churches. This provides the churches with a steady stream of income, assuring them institutional permanence while compelling them to play a major role in the provision of social welfare and aid to the families of foreign workers. The Farmers Association has been a pillar of support for both the FDP and the CDU/CSU and has for decades strongly influenced the agricultural ministry. It has also resisted the attempts by the European Union to lower direct subsidies paid to European farmers as part of the EU's common agricultural policy. The Association of Artisans is a major component of the the German Chamber of Commerce, to which all firms in Germany must belong, and the Chamber of Physicians has been intimately involved with the legislation and implementation of social and medical insurance.

These interest groups and the para-public agencies

limit social conflict by regular meetings and close coordination as part of a small-scale democratic corporatism. However, this system is subject to the same problems that have plagued corporatism in other, more centralized industrial societies such as Sweden and France; that is, it must express the concerns of member organizations, channel the conflicts, and recommend (and sometimes implement) public policy. If the system fails and conflicts are allowed to go unresolved, the effectiveness of the institutions is questioned and some elements of society may go unrepresented. A partial failure of certain interest groups and institutions led to a series of social movements during the 1960s and 1970s, particularly around university reform, wage negotiations, and foreign policy. The very existence of the Green Party in the 1980s and 1990s is a prime example of a movement that responded to the inability of existing institutions to address, mediate, and solve certain contentious issues.

Until recently, most conflicts and policy responses were encompassed within this system. Yet not all individuals found organizations to represent their interests. Germany's openness, new parties, and European integration place strains on German institutions. Those who are outside the organized groups fall into several categories. Political groups that fail to meet the 5 percent electoral threshold, such as the *Republikaner* and the German Peoples Union (DVU), belong in this category along with smaller right-wing groups. The substantial Turkish population, comprising 2.3 percent of Germany's inhabitants, might be included here until it obtains citizenship. Many Turks have resided in Germany for decades, but unlike workers from EU countries like Italy and Spain, Turkish residents have had few rights in Germany. Finally, the once-active leftist community of revolutionary Marxists still retains a small presence, mostly in large cities and university towns. Some of these left-wing parties contest elections, but they never get more than 1 percent of the vote.

Since the student mobilizations of the late 1960s, Germany has witnessed considerable protest and mobilization of social forces outside established channels. Among the most significant social forces in the postwar Federal Republic have been feminists, the peace movement, the antinuclear movement, and the peaceful, church-linked protests in East

Germany in 1989 that were a catalyst for the breakdown of the communist regime. All four groups, in different ways, challenged fundamental assumptions about German politics and highlighted the inability of the institutional structure to respond to their needs and issues. From opposition to a restrictive abortion law in the 1970s to demonstrations against the stationing of nuclear missiles on German soil in the 1980s, to regular protests against nuclear power plants since the 1970s, and to courageous challenges to communism, the spirit of direct action has animated German politics in ways that were not possible earlier.

The 1990s, however, witnessed less protest from the left than from the right. Illegal neo-Nazi groups were responsible for racist attacks. Significantly, all of these attacks by the right-wing fringe were met with spontaneous, peaceful marches of 200,000 to 500,000 people in various cities. This reaction suggests that social protest, as a part of an active democratic political discourse, has matured in the face of this new threat from the right. As stated at the beginning of this section, the challenge for German politics is to maintain a system of democratic participation that encompasses both extrainstitutional groups and specific organized political institutions in a way that enhances democracy rather than destroys it.

Section 5 German Politics in Transition

German politics is truly in transition. The unprecedented election of a Red-Green coalition in September 1998 promises to take German politics in a new direction after sixteen years of center-right government. However, this election also represented another stage of Germany's journey toward becoming a more "normal" country. After fifty years of democratic rule with high electoral participation and the alternation of power between right and left for the fourth time, perhaps German politics has finally matured.

Yet the legacy of two major events in the 1990s—celebration of unification and residual racial hatred in parts of Germany—causes a tempering of unalloyed enthusiasm for Germany's prospects for the next century. Is contemporary Germany best represented as a revitalized democracy, exemplified by the celebration and joy for increased freedoms unleashed by the destruction of the Berlin Wall? Or is Germany again becoming a place hostile to foreigners and any who do not appear German, as suggested by the firebombs thrown at a hostel housing immigrants? An accurate picture of contemporary German politics lies between these two extremes. Nevertheless, both represent aspects of modern Germany, and it remains a political challenge for the SPD-Green government—and for all German citizens—to cultivate the spirit of freedom while discouraging the outrages of xenophobia.

The path taken by German politics will be determined by the resolution of the four core themes identified in Section 1. The more optimistic direction would be continued integration of eastern Germany into the fabric of the Federal Republic as a whole; however, mutual suspicions between eastern and western Germans remain high. The former resent the so-called elbow society of the West, in which material goods appear high in the order of societal goals, while the latter resent the huge costs, and increased taxation, required to rebuild the eastern states. Yet successful economic, political, and social integration demands patience and a sound institutional foundation on the part of the government. Only with a sound and effective foundation of domestic polity will Germany be able to address successfully the larger issue of European integration.

The more pessimistic direction may mean a less than robust economy with consequent social tensions and conflict, possibly exacerbated by tensions within the Red-Green coalition. There are now five significant political parties in Germany's political landscape rather than the customary three. Can Germany's organized society and institutional political structure sustain the increased cooperation necessary to maintain a vibrant democracy? And what of Germany's economic giant/political dwarf syndrome? Can Germany assume the political responsibility that accompanied its economic stature? Do its European neighbors really want it to do so? And what of Germany's high-wage and welfare structure in the face of increased economic competition from lower-wage countries in East Asia and elsewhere? Will the introduction of the euro enable Germany to thrive, or will it undermine the previous strengths of the German economy? And what is the state of the German economy in the face of domestic structural challenges as well as globalization of the international economy and the uncharted territory of "Euroland," as those countries that have adopted the euro as their currency are called? Negative answers to any of these questions could compromise satisfactory outcomes for Germany and its neighbors.

Political Challenges and Changing Agendas

For many years Germany was presented as a model for other industrialized societies to emulate. But there have been significant changes in Germany since unification, and the *Modell Deutschland* of the 1970s and 1980s is less appropriate. Can Germany evolve peacefully and democratically in a region where increased integration will become more likely? The expansion of the EU in the 1990s has enabled more European citizens to live and work outside their home countries. What will happen to German collective identity given this fluidity and the change in German citizenship laws by the SPD-Green government? Can the elaborate and long-effective institutional structure that balances private and public interests be maintained? Will the EU augment or challenge Germany's position in Europe? Will these challenges threaten Germany's enviable position in the face of increased globalization of the world economy? The future of German politics depends on how the country addresses the four primary themes identified in this analysis of the Federal Republic: a state's position in the world of states, governing the economy, the democratic idea, and collective identities. For much of the post–World War II period Germany enjoyed a spiral of success that enabled it to confront these issues with confidence and resolve. For example, problems of collective identities were handled in a much less exclusionary way as women, non-native ethnic groups, and newer political parties and movements began to contribute to a stable and healthy diversity in German politics that had been lacking for most of the country's history. Democratic institutions effectively balanced participation and dissent, offsetting the country's turbulent and often racist

past by almost fifty years of a stable multiparty democracy. Even while Germany was governed by a moderate-conservative Christian Democratic party, it supported one of the most powerful and respected Social Democratic parties in the world. Germany's economic success has been significant and unique. The country is a stronghold of advanced capitalism yet supports an extensive state welfare program and mandates worker/trade union/works councils participation in managerial decision-making. These successes have helped Germany participate more effectively on the international scene. In the 1980s and 1990s, Germany has confidently—and with the support of its neighbors and allies—taken a leading role in European integration. It is firmly anchored in western Europe but is uniquely positioned to assist in the transition of the former communist central and eastern European states toward economic and political modernization.

However, close examination of these four major themes reveals that Germany's path is not yet certain. Can the country continue to succeed in all four areas, or will tensions and difficulties undermine its success and produce a period of economic, political, and social instability? In the area of collective identities, Germany faces many unresolved challenges. Turkish and other non-German guest workers remain essential to Germany's economy, and now some will be able to obtain German citizenship. The long-term acceptance of the opposition CDU/CSU—not to mention the smaller ultra-right parties—will likely be key to a fundamental change in the concept of "Who is a German?" The influx of refugees and asylum-seekers has placed great strains on German taxpayers and increased ethnic tensions. German nationalism, suppressed since the end of World War II, has shown some signs of resurgence. Two generations after the end of World War II, some younger Germans are asking what being German actually means. The change in citizenship laws will complicate this issue, for, although this search for identity can be healthy, its dark side is manifested by various extremist groups, which still preach exaggerated nationalism and hatred of foreigners and minorities. Such tendencies are fundamentally incompatible with Germany's playing a leading role in a unifying Europe.

Democracy in Germany appears well established after nearly fifty years of the Federal Republic. It features high voter turnout, a stable and responsible multiparty political system, and a healthy civic culture.[24] Many observers believe that broad-based participation is part of the fabric of German political life. The overriding challenge for Germany's political institutions is the assimilation of the five eastern states. Can eastern Germans who have lost jobs and benefits in the transition to capitalism understand that ethnic minorities are not the cause of their plight? Can tolerance and understanding develop while a right-wing fringe is preaching hatred and searching for scapegoats to blame for the costs of unification? Also, what is the legacy of a bureaucratic state that as recently as the 1970s, under a Social Democratic–led government, purged individuals who appeared to have radical tendencies? In other words, if social tensions continue to grow in the 1990s, how will the German state respond?

There is some reason for optimism. Eastern Germans have shown that they understand and practice democracy amazingly well. After years of authoritarian communist rule, for many East Germans dissent was not political participation, it was treason. However, the evolution of the PDS into an effective political party that articulates the interests of its voters offers considerable promise. In the 1998 elections the PDS was considered not suitable as a potential coalition partner because of its origins as a communist party. However, when the Greens first obtained seats in the *Bundestag* in 1983, observers—many of whom were SPD officials—refused to consider the Greens as a coalition partner. Yet fifteen years later, the Greens have joined the SPD in the first left-wing majority government in German history. The lesson to be learned from the Greens' transformation from a motley crew of *alternativen* to a governing coalition partner is that continued participation in democratic institutions can have positive results for both the party and the institutions. Rather than marginalizing dissent, the German practice of including parties that attain 5 percent of the vote enables these parties to represent their distinct constituencies. And by participating in the *Bundestag* in opposition, such parties convince others that they play by the same democratic rules as do other parties. In time, such a path may produce new "suitable" coalition partners.

Germany's approach to governing the economy was also challenged in the late 1990s. For many years the German economy was characterized as "high everything" in that it combined high-quality manufacturing with high wages, high fringe benefits, high worker participation, and high levels of vacation time (six weeks per year).[25] Since the first oil crisis in 1973, critical observers have insisted that such a system could not last in a competitive world economy. Nevertheless, the German economy has remained among the world's leaders. But the huge costs of unification, the globalization of the world economy, and the exaggerated emphasis on laissez-faire principles in many countries challenge the German model anew. Together they have caused many of the old criticisms about an extended, inflexible, and overburdened economy to surface again.

Pessimists began to suggest that the stresses of the 1990s placed the German political economy in a precarious position. This "anti–German Model" consisted of several related arguments.[26] First, Germany's economic prowess resided in manufacturing industries (such as automobiles and machine tools) whose goods were exportable but whose technologies were decidedly "low." As wage costs in these sectors continued to rise, German exports would inevitably be less competitive. Second, the costs of the Social Market Economy, particularly with unification, pressed on the upper limits of Germany's capacity to pay for them. In addition, economic tensions remained at the heart of conflict between former East and West Germans. While easterners resented the slow pace of change and high unemployment, western Germans were bitter about losing jobs to easterners and paying for the cleanup of the ecological and infrastructural disasters inherited from the former East German regime. The larger issue in this argument was that German economic strength has been predicated on specific "organized capitalist" institutions that worked well with traditional manufacturing industries. In a globalizing economy of service sector industries, software, telecommunications, and financial mobility, what happens to German organized capitalism?[27]

The primary economic task of the Red-Green coalition is to address the competitiveness issue and manage the transition to an economy that can confront the technological and globalizing pressures that German firms continue to face. The trend toward Europeanization may be incompatible with the consensus-oriented and coordinated nature of Germany's adjustment patterns. In fact, economic tensions within the SPD regarding stimulating economic policy caused the forced resignation of the left-leaning SPD finance minister, Oskar Lafontaine, five months after taking office. And as Europe becomes more open to the world economy, how well will Germany's "high everything" system be able to withstand increased global economic competition? The completion of the single market of the European Union has also complicated Germany's relationship with other states. Although the EU was supposedly the grand culmination of a post–Cold War spirit of European unity, it has proved more difficult to establish than first anticipated. Its manifestations in the late-1990s have only strengthened the trends toward decentralization and deregulation already under way in Western Europe rather than enhancing integration. More significantly for the German economy, such deregulatory tendencies, if spread throughout Europe, could potentially disturb the organized capitalism of Germany's small and large businesses. In addition, the apparent deregulation in European finance threatens Germany's distinctive finance/manufacturing links. The effects of introducing the euro are unknown. Adoption of the euro requires a European central bank, a common monetary policy of all eleven "Euroland" nations, and a common set of fiscal policies. In short, fundamental tools that in the past had defined sovereignty for nation-states will now be subject to European, not national, control. Germany has tried to model the European central bank after the *Bundesbank*—it is located in Frankfurt, not Paris or London—but the coordination of monetary and fiscal policies by the European Central Bank may not always be what German governments and German firms have come to expect.

Politically, can Germany emerge from its dwarf status and play a leadership role in integrating central and eastern European states into a wider European Union? As long as the Cold War prevailed, Germany had the luxury of deferring to the United States and NATO in foreign policy initiatives, yet the Cold War has been over for over ten years and Europe desperately needs clear and purposeful political leadership. With the passage of Helmut Kohl from the scene, the leaders of all the major European countries have been in office relatively briefly, so the opportunity for

leadership from one of this new generation of political leaders is there for the taking. Given their electoral strength and the positions of their countries, the two most likely candidates are Tony Blair and Gerhard Schröder.

One other similarity among the major European nations should not pass without mention, for it has significant implications for Germany in a world of states. Not only has Germany seen the election of a majority left-wing government for the first time in its history but all major European governments are currently led by left-of-center parties. This suggests the possibility of a European-wide political movement that could aggressively defend a "social" Europe and act as a brake on some of the ruthless and destabilizing free-market tendencies of a globalizing economy.

German Politics in Comparative Perspective

Germany offers important insights for comparative politics. First is the role of organized capitalism. *(1)* Germany offers a model for combining state and market in a way that is unique among advanced industrialized nations. Many models of political analysis choose to emphasize the distinctions between state and market. Debates about whether nationalized industries should be privatized, whether welfare should be reduced in favor of private charity, for example, are symptomatic of the conflict between state and market that animates the politics of most developed countries. Germany's organized capitalism, together with its Social Market Economy, has blurred the distinction between the public and private sectors. It has refused to see public policy as a stark choice between these two alternatives, preferring to emphasize policies in which the state and market work together. The German state pursues development plans that benefit from its cooperative interaction with a dense network of key social and economic participants. Despite Germany's prominence as a powerful, advanced industrialized economy, this model remains surprisingly understudied. Regardless of Germany's current economic challenges brought about by unification and the uncertain terrain of Europeanization, it remains a model worthy of comparative analysis.

The second insight concerns Germany's development as a collectivist democracy. In many developed *(2)* states, democracy is approached from the perspective of individual rights. Some scholars, following a formalized interpretation called rational choice, suggest that the base of politics is a series of individual choices, much as a consumer would choose to buy one product or another in a supermarket. Germany, on the other hand, has evolved a different model, which—while sometimes underplaying a more individualistic democracy—does offer insights for participation and representation in a complex society. German democracy has emphasized participation in *groups*. In other words, it has stressed the role of the individual not as a sole actor in isolation from the rest of society, but as a citizen in a wider set of communities, organizations, and parties that must find ways of cooperating if the nation-state is to maintain its democracy. It is clearly within this complex of policies that Germany is wrestling with its treatment of different groups within the Federal Republic.

Germany offers a third insight on the issues of tolerance and respect for civil rights for ethnic minorities. The Schröder government has modified Germany's immigration policies to allow long-time foreign workers to participate and make a meaningful contribution to German democracy. Can residual ethnic tensions—perhaps in response to this major change in immigration policy—be resolved in a way that enhances democracy rather than undermines it? Clearly, the issue of collective identities offers both powerful obstacles and rich opportunities to address one of the most crucial noneconomic issues that Germany faces at the dawn of a new century.

A fourth insight asks whether Germany can remake its political culture in the wake of a fascist past? Countries such as Japan, Italy, and Spain among developed states also bear watching on this point. Many have hoped that Germany's impressive democratic experience during the first fifty years of the Federal Republic has completely exorcised the ghosts of the Third Reich. But not all observers are certain. To what extent have the educational system, civil service, and the media addressed the Nazi past? To what extent do they bear some responsibility for the recent rise of right-wing violence? Have the reforms in the educational system since the 1960s provided a spirit

of critical discourse in the broad mainstream of society that can withstand right-wing rhetoric? Can judges effectively sentence those who abuse the civil rights of ethnic minorities? Will the news media continue to express a wide range of opinion and contribute to a healthy civic discourse? Or will strident, tabloid-style journalism stifle the more reasoned debate that any democracy must have to survive and flourish?

Fifth, what is the role of a middle-rank power as the potential leader of a regional world bloc of some 400 million people? To some extent this issue also confronts Japan, as it struggles to take on political responsibilities commensurate with its economic successes. In the late 1990s, Germany faced intense pressures from within its borders, such as conflict among ethnic groups, and from a complex mix of external influences. Germany's role as both a western and an eastern European power pulls at the country in different ways. Should the country emphasize the western-oriented EU and build a solid foundation with its NATO allies? Or should it turn eastward to step into the vacuum created by the demise and fragmentation of the former USSR? Can Germany's twentieth-century history allow either its western or eastern neighbors to let it play the geopolitical role that its low-profile postwar political status has only postponed? To some extent, the political cover of the EU will allow Germany to do more as the leading country in a powerful international organization than it ever could do as a sovereign nation-state with its unique political baggage.

Last, Germany's historical importance on the world political stage during the past 150 years means that understanding its transition is essential for comparative purposes. It was late to achieve political unity and late to industrialize. These two factors eventually helped produce a catastrophic first half of the twentieth century for Germany and the whole world. Yet the country's transition to a successful developed economy with an apparently solid democratic political system would seem to suggest that other countries, particularly those in the Third World, may be able to learn from the successes and failures of countries such as Germany as they also attempt to achieve economic growth and develop stable democracies.

Key Terms — 27

Gastarbeiter
(guest workers)
mercantilism
Junkers
Kulturkampf
Nazi
Chancellor
co-determination
democratic corporatism
liberal
Zollverein
Economic Miracle
Social Market Economy
Basic Law
5 percent rule
constructive vote of no
confidence
civil servants

overlapping
responsibilities
health insurance
funds
works councils
Administrative Court
industrial policy
framework
regulations
suspensive veto
party democracy
Citizens Action
Groups
personalized
proportional
representation
grassroots democracy

Suggested Readings

Braunthal, Gerard. *The Federation of German Industry in Politics*. Ithaca, N.Y.: Cornell University Press, 1965.
——. *Parties and Politics in Modern Germany*. Boulder, Colo.: Westview Press, 1996.
Craig, Gordon. *The Politics of the Prussian Army*. Oxford: Oxford University Press, 1955.
Dahrendorf, Ralf. *Society and Democracy in Germany*. Garden City, N.Y.: Anchor, 1969.
Deeg, Richard. *Finance Capital Unveiled: Banks and Economic Adjustment in Germany*. Ann Arbor: University of Michigan Press, 1998.
Eley, Geoff. *Reshaping the German Right: Radical Nationalism and Political Change after Bismarck*. New Haven, Conn.: Yale University Press, 1980.
Evans, Peter B., Dietrich Rueschemeyer, and Theda Skocpol, eds. *Bringing the State Back In*. Cambridge: Cambridge University Press, 1985.
Gerschenkron, Alexander. *Bread and Democracy in Germany*. 2d ed. Ithaca, N.Y.: Cornell University Press, 1989.
Hirschman, Albert O. *Exit, Voice, and Loyalty*. New Haven, Conn.: Yale University Press, 1970.
Inglehart, Ronald. *Culture Shift in Advanced Industrial Society*. Princeton, N.J.: Princeton University Press, 1990.
Katzenstein, Peter. *Policy and Politics in West Germany: The Growth of a Semi-Sovereign State*. Philadelphia: Temple University Press, 1987.
——. *Tamed Power: Germany in Europe*. Ithaca, N.Y.: Cornell University Press, 1997.

Kemp, Tom. *Industrialization in 19th Century Europe*. 2d ed. London: Longman, 1985.
Markovits, Andrei S., and Simon Reich. *The German Predicament: Memory and Power of the New Europe*. Ithaca, N.Y.: Cornell University Press, 1997.
Moore, Barrington. *Social Origins of Dictatorship and Democracy*. Boston: Beacon Press, 1965.
Piore, Michael, and Charles Sabel. *The Second Industrial Divide*. New York: Basic Books, 1984.
Rein, Taagepera, and Matthew Soberg Shugart. *Seats and Votes: The Effects and Determinants of Electoral Systems*. New Haven, Conn.: Yale University Press, 1989.
Röpke, Wilhelm. "The Guiding Principle of the Liberal Programme." In *Standard Texts on the Social Market Economy*, ed. H. F. Wünche. New York: Gustav Fischer Verlag, 1982.
Rueschemeyer, Dietrich, Evelyne Huber Stephens, and John D. Stephens. *Capitalist Development and Democracy*. Chicago: University of Chicago Press, 1992.
Schmitter, Philippe C., and Gerhard Lembruch, eds. *Trends Toward Corporatist Intermediation*. Beverly Hills, Calif.: Sage, 1979.
Shirer, William. *The Rise and Fall of the Third Reich*. New York: Simon and Schuster, 1960.
Steinmo, Sven, Kathleen Thelen, and Frank Longstreth, eds. *Structuring Politics: Historical Institutionalism in Historical Perspective*. New York: Cambridge University Press, 1992.
Tilly, Charles, ed. *The Formation of National States in Western Europe*. Princeton, N.J.: Princeton University Press, 1975.
Turner, Lowell, ed. *Negotiating the New Germany: Can Social Partnership Survive?* Ithaca, N.Y.: Cornell University Press, 1997.

Endnotes

[1] Charles Tilly, ed., *The Formation of National States in Western Europe* (Princeton, N.J.: Princeton University Press, 1975).

[2] Barrington Moore, *Social Origins of Dictatorship and Democracy* (Boston: Beacon Press, 1965).

[3] Gordon Craig, *The Politics of the Prussian Army* (Oxford: Oxford University Press, 1955).

[4] Tom Kemp, *Industrialization in 19th Century Europe*, 2d ed. (London: Longman, 1985).

[5] Geoffrey Barraclough, *An Introduction to Contemporary History* (Baltimore: Penguin, 1967).

[6] Philippe Schmitter and Gerhard Lembruch, eds., *Trends Toward Corporatist Intermediation* (Beverly Hills, Calif.: Sage, 1979).

[7] William E. Paterson and Gordon Smith, *The West German Model: Perspectives on a Stable State* (London: Cass, 1981).

[8] Ralf Dahrendorf, *Society and Democracy in Germany* (Garden City, N.Y.: Anchor, 1969).

[9] Colleen A. Dunlavy, "Political Structure, State Policy and Industrial Change: Early Railroad Policy in the United States and Prussia," in Sven Steinmo, Kathleen Thelen, and Frank Longstreth, eds., *Structuring Politics: Historical Institutionalism in Historical Perspective* (New York: Cambridge University Press, 1992), 114–154.

[10] Alexander Gerschenkron, *Bread and Democracy in Germany*, 2d ed. (Ithaca, N.Y.: Cornell University Press, 1989).

[11] Wilhelm Röpke, "The Guiding Principle of the Liberal Program," in H. F. Wünche, ed., *Standard Texts on the Social Market Economy* (New York: Gustav Fischer Verlag, 1982), 188.

[12] Richard Deeg, *Finance Capital Unveiled: Banks and Economic Adjustment in Germany* (Ann Arbor: University of Michigan Press, 1998).

[13] German Information Office, May 20, 1994.

[14] Peter Katzenstein, *Policy and Politics in West Germany: The Growth of a Semi-Sovereign State* (Philadelphia: Temple University Press, 1987).

[15] Peter B. Evans, Dietrich Rueschemeyer, and Theda Skocpol, *Bringing the State Back In* (Cambridge: Cambridge University Press, 1985).

[16] Frank Louis Rusciano, "Rethinking the Gender Gap: The Case of West German Elections," *Comparative Politics* 24, no. 3 (April 1992): 335–358.

[17] Carl E. Schorske, *German Social Democracy, 1905–1917: The Development of the Great Schism* (Cambridge, Mass.: Harvard University Press, 1983).

[18] Otto Kirchheimer, "The Transformation of the Western European Party System," in Roy C. Macridis, ed., *Comparative Politics: Notes and Readings*, 6th ed. (Chicago: Dorsey Press, 1986).

[19] Gerard Braunthal, *The German Social Democrats since 1969: A Party in Power and Opposition*, 2d ed. (Boulder, Colo.: Westview Press, 1994).

[20] Aline Kuntz, *The Bavarian CSU: A Case Study in Conservative Modernization*. Ph.D. Dissertation (Ithaca, N.Y.: Cornell University, 1987).

[21] Sven Steinmo, Kathleen Thelen, and Frank Longstreth, eds., *Structuring Politics: The New Institutionalism in Comparative Perspective* (New York: Cambridge University Press, 1992).

[22] Katzenstein, *Policy and Politics in West Germany*.

[23] Arnold J. Heidenheimer, *Comparative Public Policy: The Politics of Social Choice in America, Europe and Japan*, 3d ed. (New York: St. Martin's Press, 1990).

[24] Gabriel A. Almond and Sidney Verba, eds., *The Civic Culture Revisited* (Newbury Park, Calif.: Sage, 1989).

[25] Lowell Turner, ed., *Negotiating the New Germany: Can Social Partnership Survive?* (Ithaca, N.Y.: Cornell University Press, 1997).

[26] Gary Herrigel, "The Crisis in German Decentralized Production," *European Urban and Regional Studies* 3, no. 1 (1996): 33–52.

[27] Amy L. Fletcher and Christopher S. Allen, "Germany, the European Union, and the Politics of Global Telecommunications." Paper Presented at the Annual Meeting of the American Political Science Association, Boston, Mass., September 3–6, 1998.

CHAPTER 5

Japan

Shigeko N. Fukai
Haruhiro Fukui

Japan

Land and Population

Capital	Tokyo
Total Area (square miles)	145,845 (slightly smaller than California)
Population	125 million
Annual Average Population Growth Rate (1990–1997)	0.3%
Urban Population	78%
Ethnic Composition	Japanese 99.4%
	Other (mostly Korean) 0.6%
Major Language	Japanese
Religious Affiliation	Shinto and related religions 51.3%
	Buddhism 38.3%
	Christianity 1.2%
	Other 9.2%

Economy

Domestic Currency	Yen
Total GNP (US$)	$4.77 trillion
GNP per capita (US$)	$39,690
GNP per capita at purchasing power parity (US$)	$28,600
GNP average annual growth rate (1996–1997)	0.5%
GNP per capita average annual growth rate	1996–1997 0.2%
	1980–1995 2.7%
	1965–1980 5.1%
Income Gap:	Richest 20% of population
GDP per capita of (US$)	$38,738
	Poorest 20% of population $8987
Structure of Production (% of GDP)	Agriculture 2%
	Industry 38%
	Services 60%
Labor Force Distribution (% of total)	Agriculture 7%
	Industry 34%
	Services 59%
Exports as % of GDP	8.9%
Imports as % of GDP	7.6%
Electricity Consumption per capita (kwh)	7915
CO_2 Emissions per capita (metric tons)	9000

Society

Life Expectancy	Female	82.8
	Male	76.7
Doctors per 100,000 people		183
Infant Mortality (per 1000 live births)		4
Adult Literacy		99%

(although the UN estimates that 16.8% of people aged 16–65 are functionally illiterate)

Access to Information and Communications (per 1000 people)	Radios	916
	Televisions	619
	Telephone Lines	479
	Personal Computers	153

Women in Government and Economy

Women in parliament	4.8% (lower house) 17.1% (upper house)
Women at ministerial level	5.0%
Women as % of total labor force	41.0%
Female business administrators and managers	9.0%
Female professional and technical workers	43.0%
1998 Human Development Index ranking (out of 174 countries; 1 = highest)	8

Political Organization

Political System   Parliamentary democracy/Constitutional monarchy.

Regime History   Current constitution promulgated in 1946 and in effect since 1947.

Administrative Structure   Unitary state; 47 units of intermediate-level subnational government called prefectures and 3233 lower-level units (as of 1999) called city, town, or village.

Executive   Prime minister selected by legislature; a cabinet of about 20 ministers appointed by prime minister.

Legislature   Bicameral; the upper house (House of Councillors) has 252 members, 152 of whom are elected by single nontransferable vote from 47 multiple-seat prefecturewide districts and 100 by party-list proportional representation (PR) from the nation at large. Half of the members in each category are elected every three years for a six-year term. The lower house (House of Representatives) has 500 members, 300 of whom are elected from single-seat districts by plurality vote and 200 from 11 regions by party-list PR. Lower house members' normal term of service is four years, but the term may be shortened by the dissolution of the house.

Judiciary   Supreme Court has 15 judges appointed by the cabinet, except chief judge who is nominated by the cabinet and appointed by the emperor; all eligible to serve until 70 years of age, subject to popular review.

Party System   One-party dominant from the mid-1950s to early 1990s; competitive multiparty since. Principal parties: Liberal Democratic Party, Democratic Party of Japan, Clean Government Party, Liberal Party, Japan Communist Party, and Social Democratic Party.

Politics in Action

Japanese politics crossed a historic watershed in 1993. The Liberal Democratic Party (LDP), led by Prime Minister Kiichi Miyazawa, which had ruled the country continuously since the mid-1950s, lost the House of Representatives general election and yielded control of government to the opposition for the first time in thirty-eight years. The leading opposition party, the Japan Socialist Party (JSP), suffered even greater losses. The LDP won 223 of the 511 seats, compared with the 275 it had won in the general election of 1990, while the JSP won 70, compared with 136 in 1990. The other three parties that had been around since the 1960s, namely, the Democratic Socialist Party (DSP), the Clean Government Party (CGP), and the Japan Communist Party (JCP), neither gained nor lost any significant number of seats.

The big winners in the election were the three very young parties founded by LDP defectors less than a year-and-a-half before the general election. The Japan Renewal Party (JRP), the Japan New Party (JNP), and the New Party Harbinger (NPH) won, respectively, 55, 35, and 13, or a total of 103 seats, for the approximately 13 million votes they collected among them. Most of their votes and seats were taken from the LDP and JSP, which lost 118 seats and 13.6 million votes between them.

The 1993 general election brought to an end not only the LDP's stable one-party rule but also the party system installed in 1955—therefore known as the 1955 system—under which the JSP had been the LDP's main rival. The first coalition government formed in the wake of the general election did not include the LDP. Nor was it led by a JSP leader, but rather by the JNP leader Morihiro Hosokawa.

Geographic Setting

A group of islands lying off the eastern coast of Asia, Japan is a relatively small country prone to a host of recurrent natural disasters, such as earthquakes, typhoons, and tidal waves. The group comprises 6852 islands, all but four of which—Honshu, Hokkaido, Kyushu, and Shikoku—are less than 500 square miles in size each. The country is divided into forty-seven provinces, known as prefectures. With a territory of about 145,845 square miles, Japan is slightly smaller than California, slightly larger than Germany, and only about one twenty-fifth as large as China.

Japan is the eighth most populous country in the world, with about 125 million people. With about 130 people per square mile, it is the sixth most densely populated among countries with a population of 1 million or more. It is about twelve times as crowded as the United States, three times as crowded as France, one and a half times as crowded as Great Britain or Germany, marginally more than Belgium, and marginally less than the Netherlands. Slightly less than 80 percent of the Japanese today live in the urban areas within the boundaries of about seven hundred cities (each with a population of 50,000 or more), including twenty-three wards of Tokyo Metropolitan Prefecture.

Japan is very poorly endowed with natural resources, particularly coal, petroleum, metal ores, and timber. The only exception is water from normally plentiful rainfall that feeds the ubiquitous paddy fields and supplies the nation more rice than needed for immediate domestic consumption, at least for the present. Consequently Japan is unusually reliant on hydroelectric, nuclear, and thermal energy as well as on imports of oil from the Middle East. Indeed, Japan must import large quantities of most of the resources essential for modern industry from abroad.

Of Japan's smallish territory, only about 15 percent is arable, compared to more than 20 percent in the United States and Great Britain, and well over 30 percent in Germany, France, and Italy. Japanese farms cannot supply enough food (except rice) to feed the nation. Japan therefore ranks lowest, at about 60 percent in the mid-1990s, among the advanced industrial states in the degree of self-sufficiency in overall food supply. Modern Japan has been a natural trading state.

Japan's closest and most accessible neighbors are Korea, 30 miles west across the Sea of Japan, and China, some 500 miles west across the East China Sea. Ancient and medieval Japan imported enormous

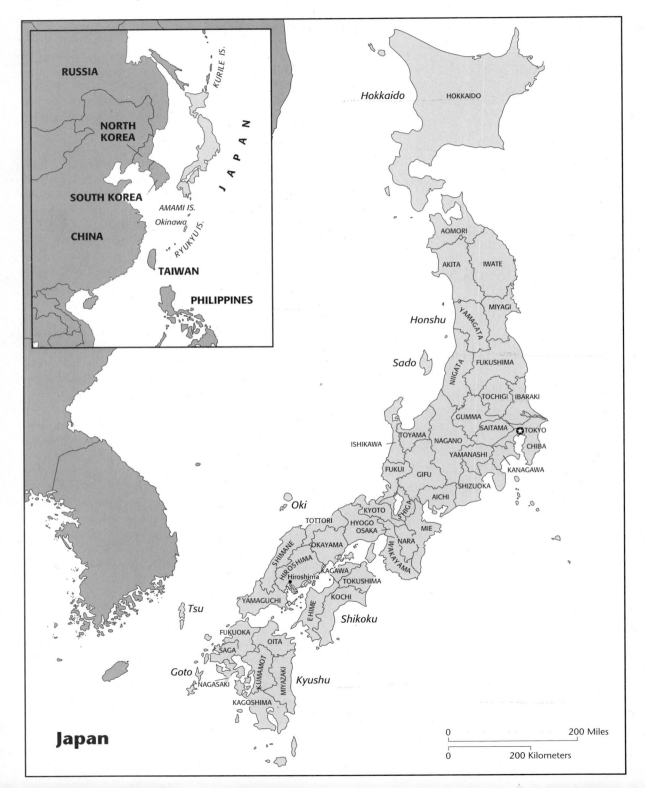

Japan

amounts not only of goods but also of science, technology, and culture—such as religions, rites, laws, letters, architecture, and fine arts—from both Korea and China. Medieval Japan also developed extensive trading and diplomatic relationships with many Southeast Asian states across the South China Sea, such as those in contemporary Indochina, Thailand, Malaysia, and Indonesia. Since the mid-nineteenth century, Japan has had extensive contacts—and sometimes conflict —with Russia to the north and, most important, the United States to the east across the wide Pacific Ocean.

The Asian and Pacific states remain Japan's most important partners economically, strategically, and culturally. Any serious issue in diplomatic or economic relations with one or another of them almost automatically becomes a serious issue in Japanese domestic politics. There is thus a very fine line between domestic and international politics in Japan.

Critical Junctures

Ancient and Medieval Japan

Japan was inhabited by tribes of hunters and gatherers as early as 2000 B.C. and possibly earlier. Surrounded by seas, the island domain's well-defined natural borders gave rise to a strong ethnic identity among its early inhabitants.

By the middle of the third century, a modest state had emerged. Broader control was established by a tribal chief who probably had ancestral roots in Korea and claimed to be a "heavenly king" descended from a mythical sun goddess. The early rulers of this small, insular state frequently sent diplomatic missions to Korea and the Chinese imperial court, which brought back products of an advanced culture—notably writing, religion, and architecture. An important example is the teachings of Confucius (Kong Fuzi), an ancient (551–479 B.C.) Chinese philosopher, about the moral foundations of political order and social harmony based on reverence for one's ancestors and submission to authority. Confucian ideas had a profound and enduring effect on Japanese society and politics. Buddhism, with its ancient origins in India, reached Japan via China and Korea in the middle of the sixth century. Thereafter, it thrived among Japan's rulers and people alike, although it divided into a number of

competing sects. Together with a native cult of nature and ancestor worship known as Shinto ("ways of the spirits"), Confucianism and Buddhism continue to shape everyday life in Japan today.

For more than fifteen centuries, Japan has remained a unified and independent state, except for several years of occupation after World War II. During the greater part of its classical period, up to the late twelfth century, Japan was ruled first by shifting coalitions of tribal groups, then by those claiming the title of heavenly emperor and their regents. The latter founded the world's longest surviving monarchy. During Japan's medieval era, which began in the late twelfth century, the monarchy yielded rule of the state to a succession of military leaders, or shoguns.[1] The most successful of these military leaders founded a durable dynasty known as the Tokugawa Shogunate.

The Tokugawa Shogunate (1603–1867)

Tokugawa Japan was a society where social classes were strictly segregated. Under its official classification system there were six classes—warriors (samurai), farmers, artisans, merchants, "filthy hordes," and "nonhumans"—although the last two categories were often lumped together as the "outcastes." There was also a minuscule class of nobles at the imperial court in Kyoto, which had long since lost all of its political power to the samurai. The court had survived as a traditional source of political legitimacy in a nation founded on the myth of the divine origin of its monarchs. Members of the various classes lived and worked separately, each within an officially demarcated neighborhood.

One type of class-based segregation that survived until after World War II is that imposed on Japan's outcastes.[2] With their origins in traditional class-based segregation, they were condemned to a pariah status associated with particular residential areas, known in recent times as "discriminated hamlets" or "unliberated hamlets," and types of work once regarded as unclean, such as disposing of carcasses and working with hides and leather. The Japanese caste system was not as complex as the Hindu caste system, but was very similar to systems found in early medieval Europe and especially in premodern and early modern China and Korea. As in China and Korea, the system has been legally abolished, but the prejudice it nurtured for centuries has not disappeared.

Under the influence of the Confucian doctrines that continued to order political and social relations in Tokugawa Japan, women were treated as inherently inferior and subordinate to men and were denied participation in public affairs even at the village level. In theory at least, though with considerable regional and class variations in practice, an adult woman's role was strictly within the family—as a faithful and obedient wife, a loving and caring mother, a selfless and hard-working housekeeper, and a dutiful daughter-in-law.[3] The ethnic, class, and gender divisions were enforced by the absolutist Tokugawa regime by the use or threat of physical force and the inculcation into the mind of the entire population of the Confucian principles of unquestioning deference to authority.

In Tokugawa Japan, the majority of those who belonged to the ruling warrior class, known as **bushi** or, more popularly, samurai, shared a well-defined sense of national identity. This group accounted for about 8 percent of the population, or about ten times the proportion of knights in medieval England or France. As a rule, boys from warrior-class families—and increasingly the sons of well-to-do merchant and farm families and even some girls—had access to primary school education. A few schools were funded by the central government and some 280 were funded by fief (regional) governments, but most—about 10,000, according to some estimates—were founded and taught by local intellectuals, such as members of samurai families, priests, and monks. In addition to reading, writing, and simple arithmetic, children were taught the idea of Japan as a nation separate from but equal to other nations. They were taught, above all, the Confucian principles of correct social order and proper personal behavior.[4]

Japan in the Meiji-Taisho Era (1867–1925)

The revolt that toppled the autocratic and isolationist Tokugawa regime in 1867, known as the Meiji Restoration, resulted partly from growing political tension within Japan caused by gradual but profound socioeconomic changes. It also resulted from rising pressure exerted by a number of Western powers to open and integrate the hermit nation into a rapidly expanding global economic system dominated by the Western powers. Most immediately, the revolution was brought about by the forced entry of a small flotilla of U.S. warships into Tokyo Bay in 1853 and 1854 in defiance of the centuries-old ban on the entry of unauthorized foreigners into Japanese territory.[5] The arrival of Commodore Matthew C. Perry's small squadron and the Shogun's capitulation to the demand from the U.S. government that Japan open its ports to American naval and merchant ships gave the Shogun's enemies an excuse to revolt against the military autocracy.

The young revolutionaries who overthrew the Tokugawa regime and founded modern Japan quickly consolidated their position as a new ruling clique consisting almost exclusively of men from four western domains. Leaders from Satsuma (contemporary Kagoshima Prefecture) and Choshu (contemporary Yamaguchi Prefecture) constituted the core of the ruling clique. They derived their legitimacy to govern the nation from their role as the official representatives of the emperor, whom they claimed to have restored to his long-lost position as Japan's ruler who was, as legend had it, descended from the divine founder of the nation and therefore divine himself. In the next half century, this oligarchy would spearhead a "revolution from above," which would transform the backward nation into one of the major industrial and military powers of the early twentieth century.

A prime goal of the Meiji state from the beginning was to renegotiate the "unequal treaties" that were concluded between Japan and a dozen Western powers in the last years of the Tokugawa Shogunate. These treaties contained two types of "unequal" clauses. One provided for "extraterritoriality," or the right of foreign diplomats to try citizens of their countries for offenses committed in Japanese territory. The other granted foreign governments the right to veto changes in Japanese tariff rates. After protracted and frustrating negotiations, the extraterritoriality provisions were eliminated by the last decade of the nineteenth century, and Japan regained control of its tariff policy by the first decade of the twentieth century.

Japan was no longer a nation isolated from the rapidly expanding world of modern capitalism. In fact, the opening of Japan was not only sudden but also complete. The new government not only let foreigners visit the country for diplomatic, commercial, and other purposes, it also sent Japanese nationals abroad, especially to the United States and Western Europe, to acquire the know-how and technology to modernize the nation as quickly as possible. To catch up with the most advanced and powerful nations of the late nineteenth and early twentieth centuries, Japan imported a wide array of Western institutions, ideas, and practices. For example, in 1871 a fifty-member mission was sent to the United States and Europe. Led by Senior Minister Tomomi Iwakura, the group spent eighteen months in a dozen different countries, visiting government offices and military academies, as well as shipyards, factories, banks, and chambers of commerce.[6] After their return to Japan in the summer of 1873, leading members of the group, such as Hirobumi Ito, who later became Japan's first prime minister, spearheaded Japan's drive to build a "rich nation, strong army," following in the footsteps of the Western powers.

Japanese society in this era was characterized by sharp economic, social, and political inequalities among its people. The countryside was in the grip of a small group of landlords who presided over a vast class of tenant farmers, while urban Japan was dominated by a handful of giant industrial and financial conglomerates, known as **zaibatsu**. The government bureaucracy, which acted as the primary agent of the ruling oligarchy, was dominated by graduates of a single government-funded and controlled university created as the incubator of able and obedient servants of the autocratic state. Despite the superficial Westernization of its political, social, and economic institutions, Meiji Japan was not fundamentally different from Tokugawa Japan, as far as the vast majority of Japanese people were concerned. The only significant difference was that they now had access to free and compulsory primary school education, which helped some of them climb out of the lower classes into the middle classes, though almost never into the upper classes.

In its effort to unite and mobilize the nation in a drive for military and economic parity with the Western powers, the Meiji government replaced the six-class system of the Tokugawa period with a three-class system. The warrior class was retained; the farmer, artisan, and merchant classes were consolidated into a single "commoner" class; and the outcaste classes were combined into a "new commoner" class. The change of names did not lead to a significant change in either the social status or the economic conditions of members of each class. Members of the "new commoner" class, in particular, continued to face open, systematic, and officially condoned discrimination and harassment until the early 1920s, when their leaders founded a national organization called the Leveling Society in obvious emulation of the Levelers' movement of mid-seventeenth-century England, which launched a vigorous campaign to attain equality for its members.

Conflicts arising from social divisions were kept under control before World War II by an ideology of national unity and cooperation, which was propagated through a centrally controlled education system and conformist mass media. The ideology focused the attention and energy of the nation on a drive to catch up with the Western powers.[7]

Meiji Japan imported not only economic models and cultural forms from abroad but political ideas as well. By the 1880s, Japanese translations of John Stuart Mill's *On Liberty* and Jean Jacques Rousseau's *The Social Contract* were published and widely read by Japanese intellectuals. And so were a dozen political treatises by Japanese authors that were either based on or inspired by Western writers' works. The spread of the democratic idea gave rise to a "freedom and people's rights" movement led by two proto-political parties. The Liberal Party espoused radical democracy in the spirit of the French Revolution, while the Reform Party advocated the moderate reformism associated with British political tradition. Led by former members of the early Meiji oligarchy who had left the government in a disagreement over policy issues, both parties called for adoption of parliamentary and other democratic institutions as the best means to mobilize the entire nation in pursuit of national goals. The oligarchic government responded to their call in 1889 by promulgating a constitution modeled after the Prussian prototype and instituting a bicameral legislature, the Imperial Diet, modeled after the British Parliament.

The 1889 constitution, or the Constitution of the Great Empire of Japan, however, merely formalized the governing role of the Meiji oligarchy. The charter guaranteed civil rights and freedoms to the emperor's subjects "subject to the limitations imposed by law" and required every law to be enacted with the consent of the Imperial Diet. The emperor retained the prerogative to sanction and promulgate all laws; open, close, and adjourn the Diet; and, in his capacity as the supreme commander of the armed forces, declare war, make peace, and conclude treaties.

In practice, the emperor's powers were delegated to his representatives, the ruling oligarchs. They dominated the powerful nonelective institutions of government, such as the Privy Council, the House of Peers, which was the upper chamber of the Imperial Diet, and above all, the civil and military services. The representatives of the emperor's subjects, on the other hand, spoke ineffectually through the only elective institution, the Diet's lower chamber, and a few legally recognized political parties. Lower house members could block legislation of which they did not approve, but the oligarchy could easily bully them into changing their minds or, if that did not work, they could simply have the emperor legislate by decree.

The lower chamber of the Imperial Diet did have some success in liberalizing and democratizing the regime in the era known as **Taisho Democracy** (1912–1926). As mentioned, Japan had proto-political parties in the 1870s, a decade and a half before the founding of the Diet.[8] During the Taisho Democracy period, two conservative parties—descendants of the Liberal and Reform parties now renamed, respectively, the Constitutional Party of Political Friends (Seiyukai) and the Constitutional Government Party (Kenseito)—alternately formed a government through electoral competition.[9]

The single most important political event of the Taisho Democracy period was the 1925 revision of the House of Representatives Election Law, better known as the Manhood Universal Suffrage Law. The event represented the culmination of a long and tortured campaign that had been launched in the last years of the nineteenth century but had gathered momentum in the "democratic '20s" following the end of World War I. The revision removed the restrictions on the grant of the vote to Japanese male adults based on the amounts of national taxes paid by them, although it did not extend the suffrage to adult women.

Taisho Democracy was short-lived, however. As

Japan's economy became mired in a protracted recession after World War I, then devastated by the Great Depression in the early 1930s, the advocates of democracy at home and peace abroad came under increasingly savage attack. Military and right-wing groups within and outside the civilian bureaucracy blamed the parties and party politicians for all of Japan's woes.

Japan under Military Rule and in War

The political power and influence of the military grew steadily throughout the Meiji-Taisho era, thanks mainly to the establishment of the Army General Staff Office in 1878 and the Naval General Staff Office in 1886. These offices were the institutional embodiments of the Meiji government's commitment to build a "rich nation, strong army" equal to the Western powers. They were invested with control over the armed forces, subject only to the will of the throne, placing the military beyond the control of the civilian government. The extraconstitutional status thus acquired eventually led the military to practice what amounted to its own diplomacy, often at cross-purposes with that of the civilian government, and to dominate decision-making on critical domestic and foreign policy issues.

Even more important were the Japanese victories in the 1894–1895 Sino-Japanese War and the 1904–1905 Russo-Japanese War. Accompanied by rapid growth of heavy industry, these wars marked the successful achievement of Meiji Japan's major goals, turning an economically underdeveloped and militarily vulnerable semifeudal nation into a burgeoning imperial power posed to expand into the neighboring territories. It was, however, not until the late 1920s that the military began seriously to seek to control the Japanese government and its policy.

The government led by Giichi Tanaka, an army general elected president of the Constitutional Party of Political Friends in 1925 and appointed prime minister in 1927, decided to try to bring northeastern China, known as Manchuria, under Japanese control to secure a regional market that absorbed 70 percent of Japan's exports at that time. Tanaka's policy encouraged Japanese army units in Manchuria to take matters into their own hands and expand their operations against local Chinese forces without prior authorization from the government in Tokyo.[10] One result was the assassination in 1928 of a Chinese warlord, Zhang Zuo Lin, an event that intensified the Chinese opposition to Japanese invasion.

The events in Manchuria provoked such intense international protest against and criticism of Japanese policy that Tanaka was forced to resign. He was succeeded by a liberal civilian, Osachi Hamaguchi. Under Hamaguchi's direction, Japan participated in the 1930 London Naval Disarmament Conference. It not only reaffirmed the agreement reached in Washington, D.C., in 1922 to limit the tonnage of its capital ships to 60 percent of those of the United States and Great Britain, but also newly agreed to limit the tonnage of its auxiliary ships to 70 percent of those of the other two naval powers. The acceptance of these limitations by the Japanese delegation to the conference caused an uproar among the military and right-wing groups at home and led to the assassination of Hamaguchi a few months later. Thereafter, the military steadily consolidated its control of the Japanese government with the emperor's acquiescence, if not explicit support. The military silenced its critics by propaganda, blackmail, and the use or threat of force.

While Hamaguchi's immediate successors were either civilians or moderate military leaders, they failed to control radical younger officers bent on conquering northeastern China and eventually the rest of China and Southeast Asia as a vast resource base for Japanese industry and armed forces. In an unsuccessful coup attempt in May 1932, a band of young naval officers attacked several government offices and fatally shot the prime minister. In a similar attempt in February 1936, army troops led by radical officers invaded a number of government offices, murdered the finance minister and several other government leaders, and occupied the central part of Tokyo for four days.[11] Neither action succeeded in immediately installing a military government, but both helped to intimidate and silence opponents of the military not only in the government but also in business circles, academia, and the mass media. The political parties were not only silenced but disbanded by 1941.

When the League of Nations condemned the Japanese invasion of northern China in 1933, the Japanese government, already under strong military and right-wing pressure, chose to withdraw from the League, an action followed by Nazi Germany later in the same year. As the international criticism of Japanese action in China intensified, Japan entered into an ostensibly anticommunist military alliance with Nazi Germany in 1936, which was joined by fascist Italy the following year. When the United States terminated its trade agreement with Japan in 1939, thus blocking Japan's access to a major source of petroleum and raw materials, the government in Tokyo decided to seek an alternative source of supplies in Southeast Asia. In July 1941, Japan moved its troops into French Indochina. This move, in turn, led Washington to freeze Japanese-owned assets in the United States and ban the sale of petroleum to Japan.

Faced with the prospect of exhausting its limited fuel supplies, the Japanese government, now led by General Hideki Tojo, made the fateful decision to start a war against the United States and its allies.[12] On December 7, 1941, Japanese naval air units executed a carefully planned attack on the major U.S. naval base at Pearl Harbor in Hawaii. The United States immediately declared war on Japan.

Japan enjoyed some notable successes at the outset of the war, but in less than a year began to lose one major battle after another. By late 1944, Japan's effort was reduced to a desperate defense of its major cities from increasingly frequent and destructive air raids by American bombers. In August 1945, Japan's resistance was brought to an end by the nearly total destruction of two major cities, Hiroshima and Nagasaki, by the first and only atomic bombs so far used in war. By then, virtually all major Japanese cities, including Tokyo, had been reduced to rubble by American bombing raids.

The Allied Occupation (1945–1952)

The Allied occupation of Japan that followed the end of World War II transformed a fundamentally autocratic state into a fundamentally democratic one.[13] The occupation, which lasted from 1945 to 1952, was formally a joint operation by the major victorious Allies, including the United States, Britain, the Soviet Union, and China. In practice, it was solely a U.S. operation, led by General Douglas

Department-store display of destruction resulting from dropping of atomic bomb on two Japanese cities.
Source: © Kitamura/Gamma Liaison.

MacArthur, **Supreme Commander for the Allied Powers (SCAP).**

During the first year and a half of the operation, SCAP made a determined effort to achieve its twin official goals, namely, complete demilitarization and democratization of Japan. The Japanese armed forces were swiftly dismantled, troops were demobilized, military production was halted, and wartime leaders were either arrested or purged. Almost as swiftly, Japanese workers' right to organize was recognized, women were given the vote for the first time, and many family-controlled conglomerates (*zaibatsu*) were dissolved. Virtually all other important political, legal, economic, and social institutions and practices were subjected to close scrutiny, and many were abolished for their alleged militaristic or antidemocratic tendencies.

By far the most important step taken for the democratization of Japan was the promulgation of a new constitution. Based on a draft prepared by a handful of American lawyers at General MacArthur's behest in 1946, and thereafter known as the MacArthur Constitution, the constitution was intended to legitimize and perpetuate the extensive occupation-sponsored reforms. It was a radically democratic and uniquely pacifist constitution. It bore the unmistakable marks of its American authorship in its overall tone and language, especially in the preamble.

The MacArthur Constitution relegated the emperor to a purely symbolic role while making the Japanese people the sovereign of the nation. It made all members of both chambers of the Diet directly elected by the people and elevated the Diet to the position of the nation's highest and sole law-making organ. In a provision unprecedented in the history of constitutions, the document forbade Japan to maintain any form of military power or engage in war as a means to settle international disputes. The spirit if not the letter of this provision has long since been violated by the creation in the early 1950s of the so-called **Self-Defense Forces (SDF)**, one of the largest and best-equipped military forces in the world today. But the pacifist spirit that the provision represents lives on in the minds of the majority of Japanese more than a half century later.

Contemporary Japan (1952 to the Present)

Party politics was also revived after the war, with SCAP's blessing and encouragement. The offspring of the prewar Party of Political Friends was renamed the Japan Liberal Party, despite its conservative ideology; it dominated Japanese politics for much of the occupation period. The Liberals' major rival was the Japan Socialist Party (JSP). The Socialists won a slim plurality in the Diet elections in 1947 and formed a coalition government with the descendant of the other prewar party, the Constitutional Government Party, now renamed the Japan Progressive Party but later the Democratic Party. The JSP-led coalition government lasted for a little over a year and a half before the Liberals returned to power and began to consolidate their hold on the Diet. The conservative domination of Japanese government became unassailable after the Liberals merged with the Democrats in 1955 to form the LDP.

The LDP held a majority or large plurality in the Diet, and thus nearly monopolistic control of the government, from 1955 to 1993. While there were no legal obstacles to the assumption of power by opposition parties, the LDP managed to win every Diet election, though not necessarily the majority of its seats. This prevented alternation of parties in office and led to the emergence of a stable **predominant-party regime**. The long era of LDP rule, however, was not uneventful. In fact, a major political crisis occurred in 1960 over the revision of the U.S.-Japan Mutual Security Treaty that had been concluded in 1952 at the end of the occupation.

Demonstrators against renewal of U.S.-Japanese Mutual Security Treaty in front of the Diet Building in Tokyo, May 1960. *Source:* AP/Wide World Photos.

The LDP government's proposal to revise the treaty but keep it in force provoked fierce opposition not only in the Diet but also in the streets of Tokyo and other major cities. Hundreds of thousands of protesters, led by JSP Diet members and leaders of the left-wing General Council of Trade Unions of Japan, or *Sohyo*, and the National Federation of Students' Self-Government Associations, or *Zengakuren*, marched against the treaty and Prime Minister Nobusuke Kishi's LDP government. They argued that the treaty would make Japan a permanent military ally of the United States and an enemy of both the People's Republic of China and the Soviet Union. Nonetheless, the government eventually railroaded the revised treaty through the Diet in defiance of the widespread public outcry. The new treaty was to remain in force for the next ten years, that is, until 1970, and thereafter be indefinitely renewable until denounced by either side.

The government's action caused such a violent public reaction with an anti-American tinge that President Eisenhower's scheduled official visit to Japan was canceled and Prime Minister Kishi and his cabinet resigned soon thereafter. On the other hand, the JSP, which led the protest movement, split amidst the turmoil, as a group of its more conservative Diet members formed a separate party, called the Democratic Socialist Party (DSP), in January 1960. The split caused considerable long-term damage not only to the JSP but also to its major ally, *Sohyo*, while helping their conservative rivals, namely, the DSP and, more important, the LDP among the parties and the Japanese Confederation of Labor, or *Domei*, among labor organizations.

The experience of the 1960 political crisis led Kishi's successors to avoid tackling controversial foreign and security policy issues and concentrate on economic issues. This change in the LDP's strategy ushered in an era of political stability and phenomenal economic growth. In the late 1960s and early 1970s, the Vietnam War rekindled the Japanese public opposition to the U.S.-Japan Mutual Security Treaty. By then, however, the attention of the Japanese public had turned to economic, rather than political or ideological issues. The year 1970 passed without a repetition of the political crisis of 1960.

The tendency of Japanese public and media attention to focus increasingly on economic issues became considerably more evident after the "oil shocks" of the 1970s. The first shock came in 1973 when the Organization of Petroleum Exporting Countries (OPEC) announced its decision to drastically raise the price of crude oil exported by its members and, in some cases, suspend the export altogether. The decision, intended to force all major industrial nations dependent upon Middle Eastern oil for their industries to support the Arab states in their protracted conflict with Israel, caused an immediate and widespread panic in Japan as well as in many other oil-importing nations, followed by a sharp economic downturn known as stagflation.

The second oil shock in 1979, caused by the revolution in Iran, did not have as dramatic and devastating an impact on the Japanese economy, thanks mainly to the effective energy-saving and storing measures that had been implemented after the first shock. The Japanese economy, however, has never regained the remarkable growth rates that it had experienced during the preceding two decades. Paradoxically, the economic difficulties did more damage to the opposition than to the ruling party; the LDP maintained its majority

position in the Diet through the 1980s, while the opposition, especially the JSP, failed to make headway.

The lackluster electoral performance of the socialist parties was due mainly to the weakening position of Japanese organized labor, particularly left-wing unions affiliated with *Sohyo*. The proportion of union members among Japanese workers steadily declined; from about 35 percent in 1970 to 30 percent in 1980, 25 percent in 1990, and 23 percent in 1997. *Sohyo* was the largest national federation of Japanese labor in 1960 but second to *Domei* by 1967. In 1987 a new national labor organization, the Japanese Trade Union Confederation, or *Rengo*, was formed under *Domei*'s leadership and *Sohyo* joined it two years later. This marked the end of the militant left-wing labor movement in Japan.

Japanese politics in the 1970s and 1980s were rocked by recurrent political scandals, in many of which top LDP leaders were implicated. In the Lockheed scandal of 1976, a former prime minister, Kakuei Tanaka, was charged with, and later found guilty of, accepting bribery from the Lockheed Corporation for his intervention in the purchase of Lockheed's planes by a Japanese airline. In the Recruit scandal of 1988, more than a dozen LDP leaders and senior bureaucrats were charged with receiving expensive bribes from the publisher of a job-information journal, although most were subsequently acquitted for the lack of evidence.

The scandals hurt the LDP's electoral performance, but not to the extent of threatening its control of government, until the country was hit by another sudden economic downturn in the early 1990s. Unlike the oil shocks of the 1970s, the new economic trouble was directly blamed on a series of wrong or unwise policies implemented by the government. They dated back to the Plaza Accord of 1985, in which the finance ministers and central bank governors of the five major economic powers, known as the G-5 for the Group of Five, agreed to collectively intervene in the foreign exchange market. Their purpose was to raise the relative values of the Japanese yen and the German mark so as to bring down that of the U.S. dollar and help the United States reduce its chronic and worsening trade deficits.

Worried that Japanese export-dependent industry would be hurt by the effects of the accord, the

Japanese government drastically reduced the Bank of Japan's discount rate in the next four years: from 5 percent to 3 percent in 1986 and 2.5 percent in 1987. The enormous amount of excess liquidity generated by these actions went mostly into speculative investments in the stock and real estate markets, sending the prices in both skyrocketing. This brought about a wild but short-lived boom, soon to be remembered as the "bubble economy."

The specter of a runaway inflation now scared the government into putting on the brakes by raising the central bank rate as drastically and abruptly as it had cut it in 1986: from 2.5 percent to 4.25 percent in 1989 and to 6 percent in 1990. These actions popped the bubble but also killed the engine of the Japanese economy, throwing it into a sudden recession. The government then reversed the gears again, cutting the discount rate back to 4.5 percent in 1991, 3.25 percent in 1992, 1.75 percent in 1993, 1 percent in 1995, and 0.5 percent in 1996. The latest reversal in the flip-flopping policy, however, failed to restart the engine.

For three and a half decades, from 1955 to 1990, Japan had been an "uncommon democracy" under the seemingly permanent rule by a powerful conservative party in a stable and cozy alliance with an even more powerful administrative bureaucracy. Such an image of the country was suddenly blown to pieces in the last decade of the twentieth century: Japan was no longer economically superdynamic nor politically superstable, while the once predominant LDP and the once prestigious national bureaucracy were now widely perceived both at home and abroad as bunches of bungling, and often corrupt, amateurs.

The first straw in the wind was the LDP's failure for the first time since the party's founding in 1955 to maintain its majority position in the House of Councillors, or the upper house, of Japan's bicameral parliament, or the National Diet, in 1989. This was followed by the LDP's even more dramatic defeat in the 1993 general election of the House of Representatives, or the lower house, and formation of two multiparty coalition governments without the LDP's participation and a third of the LDP and its long-time principal rival, the Social Democratic Party (SDP; until 1996 the Japan Socialist Party, JSP). The LDP regained enough strength, though still short of the majority, in the 1996 general election to form the

first single-party government in two and a half years. Neither the LDP nor the government, however, has since succeeded in changing its sullied public image.

The LDP's trouble and the resulting political instability were attributable to a combination of circumstances.[14] Particularly obvious and important among such circumstances was a widespread voter revolt caused by a series of corruption scandals involving many of the top LDP and government officials in the 1970s through the 1980s. The revolt led to the temporary ouster of the LDP from power, formation of self-avowed reformist governments, and enactment of several anticorruption laws. Another relevant and important circumstance was a sharp downturn that the Japanese economy experienced in the 1990s and the widely shared public perception of the government's inability to promptly and effectively deal with it. None of the reformist governments formed after the LDP's fall from power in 1993 succeeded in doing so in the next few years, thus only contributing to deepening the public disappointment, disillusion, and increasingly desperate search for an alternative government.

The continuing political instability and uncertainty in Japan has so far not directly threatened the basic strength and health of Japan's democratic political regime, established half a century ago in the wake of World War II. Combined with a protracted and worsening recession with no end in sight, however, the political stalemate and apparent leadership vacuum do threaten to drive the disillusioned electorate to rejection of the current constitutional form of Japanese government and democracy, if not either of government or democracy as such. As the twentieth century drew to its close, Japan appeared to stand at another hazardous political crossroads as it has done several times since it entered the modern world one and a half centuries ago.

Themes and Implications

Historical Junctures and Political Themes

As mentioned, Japan joined the modern world of states after two and a half centuries of self-imposed isolation and in a weak economic and military position, face-to-face with far more advanced and powerful Western states. This experience has strongly colored the Japanese perception of, and attitude toward, the rest of the world. To pre–World War II Japanese leaders, the world was divided between powerful, imperious, and self-aggrandizing states on the one hand and powerless, often conquered, and humiliated states on the other.

To survive in such a world, a state had to build strong armed forces and develop a highly productive industrial economy—Japan's policy during most of the prewar period—or secure the protection of a powerful ally—Japan's policy since World War II. The experiences during World War II, particularly the "atomic baptism," led most Japanese to abandon their faith in an independent military force as a way to ensure their national security in the age of nuclear weapons. The only alternative now was alliance, or at least cooperation, with other nations, particularly the most powerful. Contemporary Japan is thus an avowed internationalist state, but with a degree of realist, even fatalistic, cynicism in its view of international relations. This element of cynicism often makes the Japanese appear to the world, including their allies and trading partners, to be unreliable and even treacherous.

The entry into the modern world in the mid-nineteenth century also exposed the Japanese to the democratic idea. By the 1890s, Japan had become a constitutional monarchy with a partially elected parliament and vocal political parties. Its government was faced with a persistent popular demand for more democracy and popular participation in government. But pre–World War II Japan remained far more committed to rapid industrialization and military buildup than to democratization. Nor was it committed to social and economic justice and equality among its people. Prejudice and discrimination against descendants of the medieval outcaste classes, for example, continued until after World War II. So did the prejudice and discrimination against women.

Democracy became fully accepted both ideologically and institutionally in Japan only after 1945. Nonetheless, the experiment with democratic government in prewar Japan, however half-hearted and ultimately unsuccessful it may have been, helped the Japanese accept the idea of democracy and practice it with considerable skill and success in the postwar

period. This history and experience make democracy in contemporary Japan more durable and stable than in most other states outside of Western Europe, North America, and Oceania. Candidates and their supporters in Japanese elections may make liberal use of political contributions, as do their counterparts in the United States. But tampering with ballot boxes or refusing to accept the verdict of an election—practices commonplace in many developing nations—are virtually unheard of in Japan.

Meiji Japan developed an advanced industrial economy in a state that lacked both the natural resources and the modern technologies long thought to be essential for industrialization. The method involved extensive and systematic intervention by the state in the management of the national economy, later to be known as **industrial policy**. As discussed in Section 2, this approach was spectacularly successful in both prewar and postwar Japan, and was studied and copied by many other nations, especially those in East Asia. The approach, however, ceased to work as effectively in the global economy of the late twentieth century, as economic national boundaries virtually disappeared and the role of the state in the economy significantly declined. As the Asian markets for Japanese goods collapsed one by one starting in 1996, Japan found itself mired in a protracted recession that seemed to defy any industrial policy–based remedy.

The Japanese began to develop a sense of national identity early in their history—as early as the late seventh century. This was due partly to their nation's relatively high ethnic homogeneity, and partly to the deliberate construction and propagation of a nationalist ideology by its early rulers. Japan's insular position also helped by enabling its rulers in the Tokugawa period to pursue a radical isolationist policy for two and a half centuries. The early development of a national identity tended to suppress the growth of regional, communal, and class-based collective identities. Moreover, their own strong, well-defined national identity makes it difficult for many Japanese to understand and sympathize with other peoples of the world who lack, for a variety of reasons, such a strong national identity. This trait of traditional Japanese culture interferes with Japanese participation in the rapidly expanding arenas of global economy, culture, and politics.

Implications for Comparative Politics

Japan occupies an intermediate or borderline position among the states in the contemporary world in several senses. It is geographically and ethnically an Asian nation, but its political and economic development has more in common with those of many Western European nations. It was a late-developer in modernization and economic development relative to some Western nations, notably Britain and the United States, but an early-developer compared to most others. Once one of the most aggressive militarist nations, it is now one of the most pacifistic. Its intermediate position in these and other aspects makes Japan an exceptionally interesting and versatile case to be compared with either advanced Western industrial nations or newly industrialized or developing non-Western nations.

Japan's geographical, historical, and cultural attributes make it both sensible and interesting to compare Japanese politics—its past, present, and future—with those of other Asian nations, especially China, Taiwan, and North and South Korea in the Confucian cultural zone of Northeast Asia. Japan shares the "paddy culture" and has had close historical ties with most nations in Southeast Asia as well.

The evident physical and cultural similarities and affinities between Japan and these other East Asian nations encourage us to try to understand and explain differences between them through comparative analysis. The comparison involved in such an effort is known in the field of comparative studies as the "most similar nations design" or "Mill's method of difference".[15] Why, for example, did Japan begin to modernize its political system and social institutions and industrialize its economy so much earlier and apparently more successfully than the others, despite their physical and cultural similarities? Why has Japan experienced a stable one-party rule in a democratic system, while most others have experienced either stable but authoritarian government or unstable multiparty politics? Such questions will lead us to others, for example, Does the Japanese experience with modernization, industrialization, and democratization lend itself to meaningful reference, if not emulation, by other East Asian nations?

On the other hand, Japan's geographical, historical, and cultural attributes are markedly different from those of nations in Western Europe or North America. Yet, politics and economy in medieval and especially modern Japan share a number of important characteristics with some nations in the two regions. We may therefore investigate the causes of the similarities or parallels between nations that appear very different. This manner of investigation is known in the field as the "most dissimilar nations design" or "Mill's method of agreement." Why, for example, did the Japanese develop a national identity and unite the nation as early and as fast as, or even earlier and faster than, most Western European nations? Why did Japan succeed in modernizing its politics and society and industrializing its economy as quickly and as effectively as, if not more quickly and more effectively than, most nations in Western Europe and North America?

This line of inquiry leads us to try to explain in particular the similarities between modern Japan and modern Germany. Both entered the modern world about the same time in the nineteenth century, pursued rapid economic development, became major military powers by the early twentieth century, fought and lost World War II, were occupied and democratized by their wartime enemies, and returned to the postwar world as two of the most economically powerful and politically stable democracies. How can we explain these remarkable similarities? What lessons may we learn from the two nations' experiences?

Japan thus lends itself as naturally and provocatively as few other nations do to comparisons with nations in the two very different geographical regions and cultural zones of the world. The sections that follow suggest a number of specific aspects and dimensions of Japanese government and politics that invite comparisons with those of one or more nations in either region or both.

Section ❷   Political Economy and Development

Politics and economics seem to move in tandem, as if they were two sides of the same coin. That is the impression one gets from a glance at the history of modern Japan. To begin with, economic development was the first of Meiji Japan's two central objectives and commitments at its birth in the mid-nineteenth century, as suggested by its official slogan, "rich nation, strong army." Moreover, the pre–World War II Japanese state thrived in the subsequent decades, as long as its economy grew at a rapid and steady pace, until the end of World War I. As its economy fell into a serious and protracted slump in the wake of that war, the Japanese state began to face domestic political turmoil. The devastation of its economy by the worldwide depression a decade later set Japan on a course of increasingly harsh authoritarian rule at home and militarist expansionism abroad. The course led eventually to a fatal war with the United States and its allies.

Politics and economics in postwar Japan repeat the same story. The lesson learned the hard way led postwar Japan to abandon the "strong army" part of the earlier national agenda and concentrate on the "rich nation" part. This policy earned the nation an "economic miracle" and long political stability. The good times came to an end, however, as the economy turned into a bubble in a speculative frenzy; then the bubble burst in the last decade of the twentieth century. As the century approached its end, Japan appeared beset with deep political uncertainty and indecision.

It is thus hard to escape the conclusion that politics and economics in Japan are closely and presumably causally related to each other. The purpose of this section, then, is to look in some detail at how they actually interact, in what institutional and cultural contexts, and with what significant effects on the citizens' lives.

State and Economy

Wars and Japanese Economic Development

The rapid growth of the Japanese economy in the late 1950s through the early 1970s was known as an economic miracle. The impressive performance of the Japanese economy, however, did not begin after World War II; it had grown steadily by an average of 3 percent per year from the Meiji Restoration in 1867 through the early twentieth century, the growth rate accelerating to more than 5 percent in the 1930s.[16] On the eve of World War II, Japan was already one of the prewar world's fastest growing and most competitive economies.

The rapid growth of the Japanese economy was due to a combination of domestic factors, such as government policy, businessmen's entrepreneurial talent and initiative, and a hard-working, literate, and increasingly skilled workforce. International factors and circumstances, including wars, were also significant. The Sino-Japanese War (1894–1895) and the Russo-Japanese War (1904–1905) contributed to the growth of Japanese heavy industry, especially the munitions industry. World War I was a windfall for Japanese business. Taking advantage of the disruption of trade networks caused by the war, especially in Asia, Japanese textile, steel, machine tool, chemical, and shipping industries quickly expanded. The wartime boom brought Japan's trade balance into the black for the first time in the nation's history.[17]

The Korean War of the 1950s and the Vietnam War of the 1960s were also highly beneficial for Japan. Japanese factories were the main suppliers of the goods and services required by the U.S. military. The wartime "special procurement" triggered a series of long booms that became known as the Japanese miracle. By the time the wartime booms ended in the early 1970s, Japan had become the second-largest market economy in the world, a position it retains today.

Even World War II, which devastated Japan both physically and psychologically, was in a sense a blessing in disguise for its economy. The prewar Japanese economy had been hobbled with a structural problem that impeded growth and development, namely, the grossly uneven distribution of income and wealth. The poverty of the masses not only generated considerable social tension but also prevented the formation of a sufficiently large domestic market for Japan's own manufactures, not to mention imports from abroad. The Occupation-sponsored reforms rid the nation of the problem at one fell swoop by ending the domination of the *zaibatsu* and the landlords.

The reforms significantly reduced the concentration of wealth and power by dividing up the assets and control of the largest *zaibatsu* conglomerates into several new and independent firms, by unionizing a substantial portion of urban labor, and by redistributing most of the landlord-owned farmland among tenant farmers. Although the control of the giant conglomerates by members of their founding families came to an end, most of them survived and subsequently acquired even greater wealth and power. Well over half of Japan's urban workers were unionized by the end of the 1940s. The **land reform** reduced the tenant population from nearly 30 percent to about 5 percent of Japanese farmers.[18] This measure transformed an important source of prewar radicalism into one of the most reliable blocs of conservative voting in postwar Japan. Altogether, these changes vastly expanded Japan's middle class and its domestic consumer markets.

The demilitarization program, on the other hand, forced Japan not only to disarm but also to get out of the arms trade. This freed Japan from the heavy burden of military spending, which had swallowed up about one-third of the total budget in the early 1930s and three-quarters at the beginning of the war in the Pacific. Henceforth, Japan devoted its capital, labor, and technology almost exclusively to the production of goods and services for civilian consumption. This shift soon led to Japan's emergence as one of the most productive, competitive, and wealthiest powers in the postwar world.

The postwar Cold War, too, contributed to the Japanese economic miracle. U.S.-Soviet rivalry led to a dramatic shift in U.S. policy toward both Germany and Japan by 1948. Washington's primary objectives were no longer the total demilitarization and democratization of both occupied nations but their swift economic recovery and incorporation into the U.S.-led anticommunist bloc. After China fell to communist rule in 1949 and the Korean War broke out in 1950, Japan's new role as a key ally of the United States in Asia became even more evident. In this new role, Japan was granted privileged access to the export markets and advanced industrial technologies of the United States and its other allies. This helped Japan turn itself into a formidable export machine that was producing large trade surpluses by the mid-1960s.

From 1947 to 1951 the United States helped Japan rebuild its war-devastated economy by providing goods, including food, worth about $1.8 billion. The Occupation authorities also helped the Japanese government overcome postwar economic chaos, especially rampant inflation, by balancing the government budget, raising taxes, imposing price and wage freezes, and resuming limited foreign trade. After Japan regained its independence in 1952, the United States continued to help by opening its markets to Japanese exports and granting Japanese firms access to advanced industrial technology developed by U.S. firms. The United States supported Japan's admission to the United Nations, the International Monetary Fund (IMF), the World Bank, and the General Agreement on Tariffs and Trade (GATT). Membership in such international organizations helped Japan gain access to raw materials, merchandise and capital markets, and advanced industrial technology and scientific information.

Not surprisingly, the growth of the Japanese economy slowed down as the Cold War began to fade in the late 1970s and the early 1980s. Surging Japanese exports began to be viewed abroad as a serious threat to local industries, especially in the United States. Deprived of their former privileged position in U.S. markets, Japanese manufacturers faced increasingly intense competition not only abroad but also at home, as Japan's heavily protected markets were gradually forced open to foreign imports by rising international pressure. Under these changing circumstances, the annual growth rate of the Japanese economy fell from over 10 percent in the 1960s to about 4.5 percent in the 1970s and 1980s. Although it appeared to rebound in the late 1980s, this was largely a reflection of the hyperactive stock and real estate markets, which were in turn spurred by record low interest rates—a phenomenon called a bubble economy. When the bubble burst at the end of the decade, coinciding with the formal end of the Cold War, the Japanese economy slipped into a protracted recession with the growth rate dipping below zero by 1997 amidst a financial crisis of regional, and increasingly global, proportions. This spelled the end of the "economic miracle."

The State's Role

Japan's robust economic growth was a product not only of wars, to be sure. In addition to the contributions of astute and enterprising businessmen and of competent and industrious workers, the actions of government played a key role. The state was in fact a key actor in the development of the modern Japanese economy from the very beginning.

At the dawn of Japan's modern period after 1867, the Meiji state founded and operated munitions factories, mines, railroads, telegraph and telephone companies, and textile mills.[19] Within a decade and a half most of these businesses were sold at token prices to private entrepreneurs, some of whom subsequently emerged as heads of huge and powerful *zaibatsu* conglomerates. During the rest of the nineteenth century and especially the first forty years of the twentieth century, these formidable and increasingly transnational corporate empires dominated Japanese industry. The *zaibatsu* spearheaded the rapid expansion of the economy in cooperation with an ambitious, disciplined, and highly nationalistic state bureaucracy.[20] The bureaucracy provided a variety of incentives to *zaibatsu*-affiliated firms: direct subsidies, tax breaks, tariff protection, and the construction of roads, railroads, port facilities, and communications networks.

The state's role as the patron and protector of domestic industry continued after the Allied Occupation. In fact, no sooner had the occupation ended in 1952 than the Japanese government began to devise and implement policies and programs to jump-start the war-ravaged economy. Under what became known as industrial policy, the government provided investment funds, tax breaks, foreign exchange, and foreign technologies to specific strategic industries, including electric power, steel, transportation, and coal mining. Subsequently added to this package of special favors for the chosen industries was a system of informal government counsel known as **administrative guidance**. Such counsel often led to mergers and the formation of cartels, which gained significant advantages in competing with domestic rivals and foreign competitors.

Over the years, the benefits of industrial policy shifted to semiconductor, computer, aerospace, and other high-tech industries. The forms of government favors also changed. The new strategies included non-tariff barriers (NTBs) against foreign imports, public funds for corporate research and development projects, and joint public-private projects for development of cutting-edge technologies.[21] As Japan's gross national product (GNP) grew, and as its trade balance sheet began to show chronic surpluses after the mid-1960s, Japanese industrial policy in general and trade policy in particular began to draw increasingly vocal foreign criticism. By then many Japanese manufacturers and traders had grown strong enough to successfully compete in international markets without as much government help as before. These circumstances led to a gradual withdrawal of the Japanese state from the private sector of the economy. Nevertheless, the Japanese economy, especially its agricultural sector, remains far from completely open to foreign competition.

The hardest agricultural market for foreigners to enter was the huge (about 10 million tons per year) rice market. Until the early 1990s, Japanese governments had maintained a nearly total ban on the import of foreign rice in response to the politically powerful farmers. A sudden shortage caused by an exceptionally poor crop in 1993 led the Hosokawa government—the first non-LDP government, formed following the lower house election of that year—to permit the import of about 2 million tons of foreign rice. At the end of that same year, as part of the Uruguay Round of multilateral trade negotiations held under the auspices of the General Agreement on Tariffs and Trade (GATT), Japan agreed to gradually expand import quotas from 3 percent of domestic consumption in 1995 to 8 percent by 2000. The deal was made to avoid immediate replacement of the ban with a tariff and sold to the angry Japanese farmers with a sweetener of a little over ¥6 trillion (then about $60 billion) compensation or bribe money. At the end of 1998, however, the Japanese government decided, with the farmers' acquiescence, to replace the quotas with tariffs at prohibitive rates (about 1000 percent *ad valorem*) beginning in the spring of 1999.

The continuing protection of the domestic rice market is costing the Japanese government and consumers very dear. In the absence of foreign competition, Japanese farmers sell their rice at prices considerably higher than those in most other rice-producing countries. Moreover, under a system set up during World War II and still in place today, they sell more than a quarter of their rice to the government substantially *above* the market price, the government then sells it to rice dealers at the market price. In 1997, for example, the government paid farmers about $135 per 60 kilograms (about 132 pounds) of unhusked rice and spent an additional $75 for its transportation and storage, for a total of $210. It then sold the same amount of unhusked rice to government-appointed dealers for about $150. This transaction thus cost the government and taxpayers $60, or $1 per kilogram. Since about one and a half million tons of rice are estimated to have been distributed by the government in that year alone, Japanese taxpayers lost about $1.5 billion in indirect overpayments to farmers.

Japan's financial sector has been under particularly strong state control and protection. Administrative guidance has led the nation's major banks and securities firms to form among themselves networks of mutual cooperation and assistance. These have been backed by an implicit government commitment to bail out those in such serious trouble that the networks alone cannot rescue them. In other words, the state has assumed an implicit "lender of last resort" role in what has come to be known as the **convoy system**. The system has helped weak and internationally uncompetitive banks and securities firms survive and burden the Japanese economy in the long recession of the 1990s.

Society and Economy

The Private Sector

The private industrial sector of the Japanese economy is characterized by the interdependence and networking among a small number of giant firms on the one hand, and a vast number of small firms on the other. In the manufacturing sector more than 95 percent of nearly half a million firms are small businesses with less than one hundred employees per firm. On the other hand, most big businesses are affiliated with one or another of six huge business groups, known as *keiretsu*. Each *keiretsu* is composed of a major bank and several large manufacturing, trading, shipping, construction, and insurance companies. It is a group of firms of comparable size and capability that are horizontally linked with one another. There are also seventeen similar but smaller groups, including those built around the major automobile manufacturers, notably Toyota and Nissan. These are often called

keiretsu, but they are characterized more by vertical ties that link several large firms to numerous smaller ones. The latter serve as subcontractors to the former.

The Mitsubishi Group is a representative example of a horizontally organized *keiretsu*. Although it is a descendant of a pre–World War II *zaibatsu* group with the same name, today's Mitsubishi Group is no longer controlled by a single family. It is composed of about thirty formally independent, co-equal corporations whose presidents form an informal executive committee called the Friday Club, which, as its name suggests, meets once a week. Each of the member corporations is a leading firm in its own line of business.

By contrast, the Toyota Group, led by Toyota Motor Corporation, represents a vertically organized *keiretsu*. Under the automobile maker's direct control are a dozen large corporations, which maintain subcontracting relationships with about 250 small firms. In turn, many of these subcontractors hand down some of their work to even smaller firms. In other words, the Toyota Group is a huge pyramid made up of several hundred legally independent but operationally interdependent firms.

The subcontracting system provides small businesses with jobs and access both to markets and to some of the advanced technologies in the possession of the big businesses within their group. The big businesses benefit even more, since they can avoid keeping certain kinds of workers on their regular payroll by using subcontractors' employees on an as-needed basis. During an economic downturn, the big firms protect themselves by reducing orders placed with their subcontractors or by delaying payment for orders already filled.

Both types of *keiretsu* are now faced with the threat posed by rapidly increasing foreign direct investment, that is, acquisition of the shares of Japanese firms, including *keiretsu* members. As Japanese firms struggled to survive the hard times in the last decade of the twentieth century by restructuring themselves, many came under foreign firms' control through mergers and acquisitions. *Keiretsu* have not perished in the process, but ties among many of their members have been substantially loosened.

Small businesses in Japan hire large numbers of temporary and part-time workers, most of them women. Part-timers are paid, on average, far less than half as much per hour as regular employees. The wage differentials between regular employees (mostly male) and temporary and part-time employees (mostly female) help keep production costs down and profits up. This **dual-structure system**, or double-deck system, has also contributed to the international competitiveness of Japan's major export companies. Big firms pass on part of the savings to some of their regular employees in the form of job security and wages that rise with the length of service almost independently of employees' performance.

Women account for about 41 percent of Japan's labor force. Their ranks have grown in recent decades for several reasons. One is their rising educational level. In a little over one decade between 1985 and 1997, the rate of women high school graduates who go to college nearly doubled, from about 14 percent to 26 percent.[22] Women with college diplomas tend to work outside the home before, and increasingly after, getting married. Another reason is the diffusion of home appliances such as refrigerators and washing machines, which free housewives from many of the traditional housekeeping chores and permit them to seek part-time jobs. The downturn in the overall economic conditions since the 1970s, especially the significant deterioration in the 1990s, is still another reason. Many families find it increasingly hard to make both ends meet with one income. The growing number of women seeking jobs for additional income has been matched by the increasing need of service industries for low-paid temporary and part-time employees. In early 1997 about 42 percent of working women, compared to about 10 percent of working men, were either temporary or part-time employees. The ratio of the average woman worker's pay to the average man worker's in the manufacturing sector is the lowest among industrial nations: in 1995 it was 53 percent, compared to 68 percent in the United States, 79 percent in France, and 90 percent in Sweden.[23]

Another well-known characteristic of the Japanese economy is the close, and normally cooperative, relationships between labor unions and management. At the end of the 1980s several labor federations merged into a larger national organization known as the General Confederation of Japanese Labor, or *Rengo*. The merger was the result of the growing weakness of the labor movement. The proportion of unionized labor in Japan's industrial workforce had declined

Table 1

Income Distribution in Major Industrial Nations

| Nation | Data Year | Percent of Population with Income Level in | | |
		Bottom 30%	Middle 40%	Top 30%
Japan	1994	15.7	36.5	47.8
United States	1994	10.3	34.4	55.3
Britain	1995	12.2	33.8	54.0
Germany	1994	13.4	37.0	49.6
France	1989	12.1	36.7	51.2

Source: Copyright © 1998 by *New York Times*. Reprinted by permission.

from well over 50 percent in the late 1940s to less than half that figure by the end of the 1980s. In addition, leaders of many surviving unions had lost much of their control over the rank-and-file members' votes in elections. Moreover, union leaders, especially those of private-sector unions, became increasingly willing to cooperate with management and moderate their job-related demands. While many larger unions continue to participate in the annual wage negotiations coordinated by the national leadership, known as the **spring labor offensive**, the radicalism and militancy that once characterized labor's position in such negotiations have steadily diminished.

By the time Japan's economic miracle ended around 1990, it had become a nation virtually free of violent labor disputes and, more generally, free of a keen popular awareness of and interest in class divisions among its people. Thanks to a generally egalitarian pattern of income distribution in the society (see Table 1), most Japanese came to identify themselves as members of the middle class, i.e., as rich as most other Japanese. They believed they lived in a classless society. This popular perception, however, began to change in the late 1990s as the Japanese economy not only ceased to grow but actually shrank.

The State of the Economy and Society

Japanese workers earn wages comparable to those earned by most North American and Western European workers, though they are paid in a somewhat different way. The typical Japanese wage or salary consists of relatively low basic monthly pay, several allowances of variable amounts, and substantial semiannual bonuses. Allowances are paid, for example, for dependents, housing costs, and commuting costs, while the two bonuses, paid in midsummer and at year end, often amount to nearly half of the basic annual wage. Retirement benefits for most employees consist of lump-sum severance pay equal to about thirty-five months' pay and, if one satisfies the age and length-of-service requirements, a contribution-based pension. Many employees of large firms are provided with company-subsidized housing and the privilege of using company-owned recreational, sporting, and vacationing facilities.

In the last few decades of the twentieth century, Japan experienced significant economic and social changes as well. As its economy continued to grow through the 1970s, the demand for young and cheap labor continued to grow. But the birth and population growth rates began to level off in the mid-1950s and to decline in the mid-1970s. The result was a perennially tight labor market and low unemployment rate, conditions welcome to most Japanese citizens. In order to attract and keep skilled workers under such circumstances, many employers would guarantee such workers, explicitly or implicitly, security of employment until retirement at a certain age—usually the mid-50s. This practice was known, somewhat misleadingly, as a **lifetime employment** system.

These conditions, however, radically changed in the early 1990s as the Japanese economy plunged into a protracted recession. The hard times forced many firms to abandon the traditional practices of implicitly guaranteeing their employees job security until retirement and virtually automatic annual pay raises. Many firms began to pay their employees on the basis of performance ("merit") and retire or transfer them to lower-paying positions, often in subsidiary firms, at much younger ages than previously. As in the United States, increasing numbers of people of all ages started to work on a part-time, consulting, work-on-call, or work-at-home basis.

These changes caused considerable hardship, particularly because the Japanese social security system is relatively young and primitive compared to its counterparts in most Western European nations. Japan's publicly funded social security system developed very

slowly and haphazardly. A modest and partially government-funded health insurance program was created in the mid-1920s, which evolved into a national program for voluntary subscribers by the late 1930s. From then through World War II, several other programs, including workers' compensation, assistance to soldiers, protection of single-parent mothers and their children, and workers' pension insurance, were created. It was not until after World War II that the Japanese government made a systematic effort to provide a minimum level of social security for all citizens.

The development of a comprehensive national social security system was mandated by an article in the 1947 constitution: "In all spheres of life, the State shall use its endeavors for the promotion and extension of social welfare and security, and of public health." During the four decades following the Allied occupation, a number of state-sponsored and wholly or partially state-financed social security programs were established. But in the wake of the 1973 oil crisis, the government attempted to shift the major burden of financing the rapidly expanding social security system to the private sector.

This so-called Japanese-style welfare society approach failed to contain the growth of public or private welfare expenditures in subsequent years. Today, social security claims over 20 percent of the annual government budget (21 percent in 1997) and is the largest spending item, second only to interest payment on government bonds. The tax-financed pension, medical insurance, unemployment insurance, and workers' compensation programs provide virtually all Japanese citizens some social security benefits. However, given the extremely high cost of living in contemporary Japan, the amounts of the benefits are far from adequate to meet the needs of most citizens.

Like citizens in most other countries, Japanese pay both direct and indirect taxes. The former include income, corporate, inheritance, and land-value taxes; the latter include consumption (sales), alcohol, tobacco, petroleum, and stock-exchange taxes. A capital gains tax was introduced in 1989. The maximum rates of national and local income taxes are, as of 1997, 50 percent and 15 percent, respectively. The average Japanese taxpayer pays about 23 percent of his or her annual income in national and local taxes. This is only a little lower than the rate paid by the average U.S.

Current Challenges: *The Cost of Living in Japan*

Contemporary Japan is far from paradise on earth for most of its citizens. Housing conditions are generally poor, especially in big cities. The floor space of the average Japanese housing unit is roughly half the size of its U.S. counterpart, although not substantially smaller than the average unit in most European nations. In 1994, when the Japanese real estate market was nearly at the bottom of a long and deep depression, the average price of land in the average residential neighborhood in Tokyo, estimated by the purchasing power parity (PPP) method, was about ten times as high as in London, Paris, or Frankfurt, fifteen times as high as in San Francisco, and about thirty times as high as in New York. (The PPP method estimates the dollar value of the yen by comparing how much of what goods and services it can buy in Japan compared to how much of the same goods and services the dollar buys in the United States.) Public parks in Japanese cities are far more scarce and overcrowded than those in European or American cities. Tokyo, for example, has only about one-tenth as much park area per citizen as New York, Chicago, Los Angeles, or London.

Moreover, consumer prices in Japan are considerably higher than those in Europe or the United States. In 1994 the average prices of foods, clothing, home appliances, and most other consumer goods in Tokyo were about one-third higher than those in New York, Berlin, London, and Paris. As a result, average Japanese citizens, especially those in the nation's major cities, do not enjoy the standard of living that Japan's very high nominal GNP per person would suggest. For example, while Japan's $39,640 in 1995 was considerably higher than the United States' $26,980, the PPP estimate of Japan's per capita GNP was 82 percent of the U.S. per capita GNP. Growing awareness of the exceptionally high prices and generally inferior and deteriorating social and cultural environments, combined with a deepening concern about the current state of the economy, helped pave the way for the voter revolt of the late 1980s and 1990s.

---

taxpayer but considerably lower than that paid by the average Western European taxpayer. On the other hand, the average Japanese does not enjoy as many tax-supported social welfare benefits and public amenities as the average Western European does.

Japan and the International Political Economy

The Trading State

Since the Meiji Restoration of 1867 Japan's economic development has been based on a strategy of export-led industrialization. Japan's leaders pursued rapid industrialization initially by exporting relatively cheap products of labor-intensive industries, such as textiles, and then by exporting higher-value-added products of more capital-intensive industries, such as iron and steel, shipbuilding, and machinery. If implemented successfully, such a strategy makes it possible for a nation with few natural, financial, and technological resources and a small home market, such as

Meiji Japan, to industrialize by importing resources from abroad and paying for them with foreign exchange earned by exports. Since the 1960s a number of developing nations have successfully followed this strategy. The best-known examples are the newly industrializing countries in East Asia, including South Korea, Taiwan, and Singapore. By the early 1990s they had been joined by other Asian nations, such as Thailand, Malaysia, and Indonesia, as well as China.

For Japan, the export-led development strategy proved very successful until the end of the Cold War.[24] By the mid-1970s, Japan had emerged as an economic superpower, with the second largest GNP after the United States. By the mid-1990s, Japan was the leading official development aid (ODA) donor, the third largest source of foreign direct investments after the United States and Britain, and the third largest trader after the United States and Germany.

Nearly 90 percent of Japan's $443 billion exports in 1995 consisted of industrial and chemical goods, especially machinery and automobiles, while 40 percent of its $336 billion imports in the same year consisted of fuels, industrial raw materials, and food. Japan continues to import raw materials, turn them into industrial products, and sell them back to the world, often at large profits. As a result, Japan has chronic deficits in its trade balances with nations that export fuels, raw materials, and food, including most Middle Eastern nations, some South American nations such as Brazil and Chile, and Canada, Australia, and New Zealand. These deficits are more than made up for by chronic and larger surpluses in Japan's trade with the United States, some major European nations such as Germany and Britain, and, above all, most nations in Asia with the exception of China and Vietnam. In 1996, Japan's overall trade surplus amounted to about $62 billion.[25]

By far the largest of Japan's trading partners and also the largest contributor to Japan's overall trade surplus has been the United States (see Table 2). The U.S. contribution to Japan's trade surplus in 1996 was about $33 billion, or more than half of the total. Not surprisingly, Washington has repeatedly charged Tokyo with unfair trade practices of one kind or another, and the two governments have been engaged in trade disputes and negotiations for the last four decades.

In the 1950s, Japan was accused of adopting a protectionist policy of high tariffs on foreign manufactured goods. After tariffs were substantially lowered in the 1960s, the U.S. criticism shifted to a variety of **nontariff barriers**, such as import quotas, discriminatory application of safety and technical standards against imports, and a government procurement policy favoring domestic products.[26] In the 1980s, Japan was accused of creating and maintaining "structural impediments" to foreign imports and investments, including a complex domestic distribution system, collusive business practices among *keiretsu* companies, and exorbitant rents in metropolitan areas. According to U.S. critics, these practices made it virtually impossible for U.S. and other foreign companies to enter Japan's domestic markets and successfully compete with Japanese producers. Japanese companies have also been charged with engaging in "predatory" trade practices abroad, such as dumping (selling goods at prices lower than those charged at home).

The increasingly loud criticisms have left significant marks on Japan's economic policy in general and trade practices in particular. Over the years, Japan has become more sensitive and responsive to the criticisms, has removed or significantly reduced the tariff and nontariff import barriers, and has abandoned many of the "predatory" trade practices. By the mid-1980s there was growing realization among Japanese both within and outside the government that Japan, as a trade-dependent nation, not only had greatly benefited from the system of free trade that had been constructed largely at U.S. initiative and under Washington's leadership but could not continue to prosper without it. This realization has made them increasingly willing to abandon most of the protectionist policies and practices that had once served them well but had begun to hurt their long-term national interests.

Table 2

Japanese Trade with the World and the United States (US$ millions)

	1965	1970	1975	1980	1985	1990	1995
Exports to World	8,332	19,316	54,734	121,413	174,015	280,374	443,265
Imports from World	6,431	18,880	49,706	132,210	118,029	216,846	335,991
Balance with World	1,901	436	5,028	−10,797	55,986	63,528	107,274
Exports to U.S.	2,479	6,015	11,149	31,649	65,278	90,322	127,193
Imports from U.S.	2,366	5,565	11,608	24,448	25,793	52,369	64,039
Balance with U.S.	113	450	−459	7,201	39,485	37,953	63,154

Sources: Keizai kikakucho chosakyoku [Research Bureau, Economic Planning Agency], ed., *Keizai yoran (Heisei 6-nen ban)* [Economic handbook, 1994 edition] (Tokyo: Ministry of Finance Printing Office, 1994), 188–189, 192–193; Somucho tokeikyoku [Bureau of Statistics Management and Coordination Agency], ed., *Sekai no tokei* [*Statistics of the World*] (Tokyo: Ministry of Finance Printing Office, 1998), 202, 220–221.

Japan in International Organizations

Japan is a leading member of the United Nations and most of its specialized agencies, especially the International Monetary Fund (IMF) and the International Bank for Reconstruction and Development (the World Bank). It joined both organizations only a few months after the end of the Allied occupation in 1952. It is today the second largest subscriber to each organization's equity and operating funds after the United States—a position shared with Germany in the IMF. Since each of the five largest subscribers has the right to appoint its own representative on the board of executive directors, Japan effectively has a permanent seat on the boards of the World Bank and the IMF.

Japan joined the UN only in 1956, mainly because of the initial opposition of the Soviet Union to the admission of a major U.S. ally at the height of the Cold War. Japan is now the second largest contributor to the UN budget. Since the mid-1990s it has been seeking, so far unsuccessfully, a permanent seat on the Security Council.

Japan has been very active and visible in Asian and Pacific economic organizations. It is not only the largest contributor to the **Asian Development Bank (ADB)** but has provided all its past governors. It is a founding member and a major promoter of the **Asia Pacific Economic Cooperation (APEC)** forum and actively supports the **Association of Southeast Asian Nations (ASEAN)**. The Asia-Pacific region has been of special economic and strategic interest to Japan since the nineteenth century. The rising tide of regionalism around the world in recent years, highlighted by the creation of the European Union (EU) and the North American Free Trade Agreement (NAFTA), renews and reinforces Japan's interest in the regionalism in its own backyard.

Japan and the East Asian Financial Crisis of the Late 1990s

Several nations in East Asia plunged one after another into a sudden currency and banking crisis in the summer and fall of 1997. First to go was the Thai currency, the baht, the value of which relative to the dollar fell 16 percent in a single day in July, followed in rapid succession by the Philippine peso, the Malaysian ringgit, and the Indonesian rupiah. By the end of the year, the South Korean won had followed suit. Moreover, the crisis quickly grew into a wholesale economic and social crisis in each nation.

The main cause of the crisis was the burst of the financial bubble that had been blown up to the limit by speculative investments, mainly in local currencies, stocks, and real estate. The intensity of each crisis was magnified and the spread of its impact to other nations in the region accelerated by the peculiar character of the funds that had helped produce the bubble in the first place but now suddenly let it burst. These were highly mobile short-term funds managed by multinational investment firms based mostly in the United States and Western Europe for quick and high returns. Once the bubble was thought to have been blown up to the limit, the funds were quickly withdrawn from the local currency, stock, and real estate markets. The bubble burst, and a currency and banking crisis began.

As mentioned, Japan has been deeply involved with the politics and economies of its East Asian neighbors. As Japan's domestic economy stagnated in the 1990s following the burst of its own speculative bubble, Japanese direct investments in the region increased, particularly after 1994. The bulk of these investments went to the electrical, chemical, and transportation industries in the manufacturing sector and to financial and real estate businesses in the service sector. The regional economic crisis of 1997–1998 caused enormous losses for Japanese investors and traders as well as their American and European counterparts.

Seeing that it is in its own interest, as well as its Asian neighbors', to rebuild the ruined economies in the region as quickly as possible, Japan has been seeking an appropriate institutional means of doing so. For example, it has proposed to set up an Asian Monetary Fund with the bulk of the funds to be provided by Japan itself. The proposal has found widespread support among the nations in the region but strong resistance from the United States and the IMF, apparently based on concerns about the further consolidation of Japan's economic dominance in the region. Weakened by the decade-long recession at home but still regarded abroad as an economic superpower, Japan was groping for its proper role in the region at the end of the century.

Section ③ Governance and Policy-Making

Often cited as a typical strong state, contemporary Japan is governed by coalitions of ruling party members of the national legislature and national civil servants. The latter develop new policies and draft new bills to be debated and legislated by the former. The policies approved and laws enacted by legislators are then implemented by civil servants. In this process of governance and policy-making, civil servants, or bureaucrats, tend to lead, and legislators, or politicians, to follow, rather than the other way round. Policies and laws elicit diverse reactions from citizens and especially from organized special interests. Their reactions in turn lead bureaucrats and politicians to develop new policies and enact new laws. This section discusses various aspects of this cyclical process: its major participants, its cultural and institutional environment, and its significant consequences.

Organization of the State

Japan is a unitary state with forty-seven prefectures (provinces) that range from the entire island Hokkaido, a little larger than the state of Maine, to Kagawa, about two-thirds the size of Rhode Island. The prefectures are subdivided into 3233 municipalities (as of 1997), ranging from large cities like Yokohama, with about 3.3 million people, to half a dozen villages with no more than a few hundred inhabitants. The prefectures and municipalities are subordinate, both economically and politically, to the state and enjoy a much narrower range of decision-making power than their counterparts in a federal state.

Under the 1947 MacArthur Constitution, which remains in force, Japan is a constitutional monarchy and a parliamentary democracy, much like Britain or Sweden. In theory, the people are sovereign. The emperor is no longer considered to be divine; he is merely the symbol of the nation and of the unity of its people.

The Japanese people exercise their sovereign power through their elected representatives, who work at the national level through the highest organ of the state and its sole law-making body, the National Diet.

The Diet designates the prime minister who, in turn, appoints other members of the cabinet. By law, at least half of the cabinet positions must be filled by members of the Diet; in practice, all but a very few have been filled by ruling party members of the Diet. Laws enacted by the Diet are implemented by the executive branch of government, which is led by the cabinet and operates through a national civil service. The cabinet is constitutionally subordinate and collectively answerable to the Diet. The national civil service operates under the direction of the cabinet and is therefore indirectly answerable to the Diet.

The constitution invests the Diet with the power to enact laws, approve the government budget, ratify international treaties, and audit the financial transactions of the state. The Diet is bicameral, consisting of an upper chamber, the House of Councillors, and a lower chamber, the House of Representatives. Both houses consist exclusively of popularly elected members. The lower house is the larger and more powerful of the two, with the power to override the opposition of the upper house in votes on the budget and ratification of treaties. The Diet also has the power to investigate any matter of national concern, whereas the prime minister and the cabinet have the obligation to report to the Diet on the state of the nation and its foreign relations. In fulfilling this obligation, cabinet ministers regularly attend meetings of Diet committees and answer members' questions.

In theory, the prime minister and the cabinet ("the government") serve only as long as they have the confidence of the Diet. If the House of Representatives passes a motion of no confidence against a cabinet or refuses to pass a motion of confidence in a cabinet, the government must either dissolve the lower house within ten days or resign. This leads either to the formation of a new cabinet or to a new lower house general election. For example, in 1993 a motion of no confidence against an LDP cabinet passed with the support of a dissident LDP faction. This led to splits in the ruling party and the birth of two splinter parties, which in turn led to the LDP's historic defeat in the general election that followed and to the formation of the first non-LDP coalition government since 1955.

Leaders: *The Royal Family*

Emperor Akihito and Empress Michiko have three children, two sons and one daughter. Both sons, Crown Prince Naruhito and Prince Fumihito, studied at Oxford after graduating from a Japanese university, and both married commoners' daughters. The youngest child, Princess Sayako, also graduated from a Japanese university and visited both Britain and the United States. Prince Fumihito's marriage to his college sweetheart, Kiko Kawashima, in 1990 was the year's biggest media event in a country where the royal family remains an object of intense popular interest, though no longer of awe and reverence.

Crown Prince Naruhito's wedding in 1993 caused an even greater sensation, partly because the prince's apparent difficulty in finding a suitable and willing bride had been a hot topic in the tabloid press for several years and partly because the bride, Masako Owada, was a young diplomat who had studied at Harvard and Oxford as well as the University of Tokyo. Apart from the festivity of the occasion, the event also raised some constitutional and ideological issues. While few objected to the wedding itself, some objected to the government's financial and other involvement as a violation of the constitutional principle of the separation of state and religion. Others were disturbed by Owada's decision to give up her promising career, and her opportunity to help break the glass ceiling in a male-dominated profession, in favor of housekeeping in one of the most old-fashioned and rigidly controlled families in today's world. Still, opinion polls showed that an overwhelming majority of Japanese, young and old, approved of Owada's decision and hoped that she would use her new position as Japan's crown princess and future empress to reform and modernize the hidebound imperial institution at home and assist Japanese diplomacy abroad. So far these hopes have been dashed by the intransigent centuries-old tradition.

Constitutional theory notwithstanding, however, it is the cabinet rather than the Diet that has initiated most legislation and in effect made laws in the past. This has been largely because members of the Diet have virtually no legislative staffs of their own, whereas cabinet ministers, even though they have no more substantial staffs, enjoy much greater access to the staff and resources of the civil service. During the LDP's long one-party rule, civil servants drafted the majority of bills. Most of these bills then passed the Diet with the unanimous support of ruling party members. By comparison, bills introduced by individual Diet members, especially those sponsored by opposition members alone, were few in number and far less successful. Of the relatively few bills introduced by individual members during the period of LDP dominance, only those receiving nonpartisan support, and usually sponsored by a whole standing or ad hoc committee, enjoyed a good chance of passage.

The Japanese Monarchy and the Royal Family

Japan is the oldest surviving monarchy in the world. The present occupant of its Chrysanthemum Throne, Akihito, is the one hundred and twenty-fifth in an unbroken line of emperors and empresses, according to legend. His ancestors were Japan's actual rulers from the mid-sixth through the early tenth century and thereafter remained the nation's titular rulers until shortly after the end of World War II. Under the Meiji Constitution (1889–1947), the emperor was not only Japan's sovereign ruler but a demigod whose person was "sacred and inviolable." The MacArthur Constitution relegated the emperor to the status of a symbol of the Japanese state whose new sovereign was its people. Akihito's father, Hirohito (1901–1989), was thus the sovereign ruler of the Empire of Japan during the first half of his long reign (1926–1989) but a mere figurehead of the democratized Japan during the second half of his life.[27] The Japanese monarchy has survived both the devastating war and the far-reaching postwar reforms and continues to thrive.

Compared to his aloof and enigmatic father, who led Japan into and out of the disastrous war and whose role in that war remains controversial, Emperor Akihito is a far more modern and cosmopolitan monarch. An eleven-year-old boy at the war's end, he lived through the austere early postwar years as an impressionable young man, mingled freely with classmates from middle-class families, learned English from an American Quaker woman, and chose to marry a woman from a middle-class family (née Michiko Shoda). Nonetheless, the Japanese royal family remains sheltered and hidden from public view to a much greater extent than any of the Western European royal families. In this sense, the Japanese monarchy is an extraordinarily tradition-bound institution in the contemporary world.

Rigid adherence to the tradition of strict privacy and secrecy about all matters related to the imperial household has shielded the Japanese royal family from the constant and uncontrolled exposure in the mass media that has dogged British royalty in recent years. On the other hand, it has severely restricted the personal life of members of the royal family and their contact with people outside the small circle of family members and their close friends. The resulting isolation from the public is likely to erode genuine public interest in, if not curiosity about, the royal family and its role, especially among young people.

The Executive

The Cabinet

As suggested, the executive branch, led by the cabinet, has been the source of most legislative and administrative initiatives in Japan. Moreover, the long dominance of the Diet by a single party has made the executive branch much stronger than expected from the constitutional definition of its position and status relative to the Diet.

The cabinet is headed by a prime minister elected by the Diet. Each house separately elects a candidate for prime minister by a majority vote during a plenary session. If different candidates are elected by the two houses, the one elected by the lower house becomes prime minister. If no candidate wins an absolute majority, a runoff election is held between the top two candidates. Until the LDP's defeat in the 1993 general election, the Diet had consistently elected the leader (i.e., president) of the LDP as prime minister. The LDP's party rules provide for the selection of the party's president by ballot. In practice, however, LDP

presidents have been chosen as often by back-room negotiation among leaders of the several factions of LDP Diet members from among themselves. When an election was held, huge sums of money were spent by the factions to buy votes, directly or indirectly, for their own candidates.

Once elected, the Japanese prime minister has nearly absolute authority to appoint or dismiss any member of his cabinet. (While there is no legal restriction on the gender of the Japanese prime minister, no woman has ever held the office. One woman has served as the leader of a major party, the Social Democratic Party.) The appointment of members of an LDP cabinet has been dictated mainly by the prime minister's desire to maintain a balance of power among the several intraparty factions in order to preserve the unity of the party and prolong his own prime ministerial tenure. The three coalition cabinets that ruled the nation between August 1993 and January 1996, the first two of which did not include the LDP, were composed of representatives of the coalition parties chosen on the basis of the same principle of

Table 3

Cabinet Positions (September 1998)	
Prime Minister	Director-General of the Management and Coordination Agency
Deputy Prime Minister (optional)	
Minister of Justice	Director-General of the Hokkaido Development Agency
Minister of Foreign Affairs	
Minister of Finance	Director-General of the Defense Agency
Minister of Education	
Minister of Health and Welfare	Director-General of the Economic Planning Agency
Minister of Agriculture, Forestry, and Fisheries	Director-General of the Science and Technology Agency
Minister of International Trade and Industry	
Minister of Transportation	Director-General of the Environment Agency
Minister of Posts and Telecommunications	Director-General of the Okinawa Development Agency
Minister of Labor	
Minister of Construction	Director-General of the National Land Agency
Minister of Home Affairs	Chief Cabinet Secretary

balance among the several parties. In order to be appointed to a cabinet-level office in the Japanese government, one must have good standing—which simply means seniority, as a rule—in his or her faction or party but not necessarily special knowledge or experience in any particular policy area or areas. Cabinet positions as of 1998 are listed in Table 3 on p. 213.

The prime minister has the constitutional right to submit bills to the Diet in the name of the cabinet; report to the Diet on the state of the nation and its foreign relations; exercise control and supervision of the national civil service; approve or disapprove laws and cabinet orders; and in rare cases, suspend a cabinet member's constitutionally guaranteed immunity against a legal action during his or her tenure. The prime minister is also the nation's commander-in-chief under the Self-Defense Forces Law and has the power to declare a state of national emergency under the Police Law. If a prime minister resigns or otherwise ceases to hold his office, the cabinet as a whole must also resign.

The executive powers and responsibilities of the Japanese cabinet are wide-ranging. In addition to those common to the executive branch of government in most other industrial democracies, they include the following:

- Advising and taking responsibility for any of the emperor's actions that are of concern to the state (such as the promulgation of laws and international treaties, convocation of the Diet, dissolution of the House of Representatives, and receiving foreign ambassadors and ministers)
- Designating the chief justice of the Supreme Court, who is formally appointed by the emperor
- Appointing all other judges of the Supreme Court and those of the lower courts
- Calling the Diet into extraordinary session and the upper house into emergency session
- Approving expenditure of the state's reserve funds

Each member of the cabinet has the title of minister or director-general and is responsible for a particular ministry or one or more agencies. Agencies are generally newer and smaller than ministries. Some agencies, such as the Economic Planning, Environment, Science and Technology, and National Land, are represented in the cabinet by their own director-generals, but many are not. There are (as of 1999) twelve ministries and eight cabinet-rank agencies. Including the prime minister, the deputy prime minister, whose appointment is optional, and the chief cabinet secretary, the cabinet typically consists of twenty-two or twenty-three members. According to an administrative reform plan approved by the LDP government in 1997, consolidations will reduce the total number of ministries and agencies to roughly half that number by 2001. The change, however, is likely to be more cosmetic than substantive, leaving the functions and powers of the existing offices largely intact, albeit moved from one ministry or agency to another and often given new names.

While in theory a minister supervises the work of an entire ministry and a director-general that of one or more agencies, his or her supervisory power and responsibility are often more nominal than real. (Recent cabinets included one or two women.) This is largely because, as mentioned, ministers and director-generals are generally chosen not for their ability in a given policy area but on the basis of seniority in the ruling party or parties. Seniority is determined mainly by the number of times one has been reelected to the Diet. As a result, many cabinet members are inexperienced in the policy areas to which they are assigned and are at the mercy, rather than in command, of the career civil servants who are their subordinates.

Since every LDP faction and every coalition party has a long waiting list of candidates for cabinet posts, the prime minister is under constant pressure to replace incumbents with new people at short intervals. The result has been an average ministerial tenure of barely one year under the LDP and nine months under the three coalition cabinets formed since the LDP's fall from power in 1993. The short tenure denies cabinet members the time needed to learn the ropes of their ministry or agency, reinforcing their dependence on career bureaucrats for even routine ministerial duties, including answering legislators' questions in the Diet.

The National Bureaucracy

At the core of the contemporary Japanese state are half a dozen central government ministries and

Folks at the terminal stage of "portpolio." Ruling party politicians line up for cabinet positions, often getting into fights with each other. *Source:* Shin Yamada, *Asahi shinbun,* Tokyo.

agencies, each with more or less exclusive jurisdiction over a specific sector of the national economy, such as the ministries of Finance (MOF); International Trade and Industry (MITI); Construction (MOC); Transportation (MOT); Posts and Telecommunications (MPTC); and Agriculture, Forestry, and Fisheries (MAFF). Each ministry's or agency's mandate as defined by law and by practice includes both regulatory and protective powers over individuals, corporations, and other interested groups. The regulatory power is exercised mainly through the enforcement of legal and quasi-legal requirements for licenses, permits, or certificates for virtually any kind of activity with actual or potential effects on the public interest. The protective power is used to provide various types of public assistance to private citizens and groups, such as subsidies and tax exemptions for particular industries. Abuse of these powers was at the root of the pervasive political corruption that erupted

in periodic and sensational scandals in postwar as well as prewar Japan.

Japan's central government ministries and agencies are all very much alike, both in organization and behavior. Each is headed by a cabinet minister or director-general and consists of an administrative vice minister, one or two parliamentary vice ministers, a minister's secretariat, several staff bureaus, and several line bureaus, each subdivided into divisions and departments. The staff bureaus are concerned mainly with broad policy issues, while the line bureaus are responsible for implementation of specific policies and programs. All offices are headed and manned nearly exclusively by civil servants, although the parliamentary vice ministers are members of the Diet, that is, politicians.

For example, MITI's staff bureaus initiate and develop policy in the areas of international trade, international trade administration, industrial policy, and industrial location and environmental protection. MITI's line bureaus, on the other hand, are responsible for policy implementation in the areas of basic industries (for example, iron and steel, nonferrous metals, and chemicals), machinery and information industries (for example, industrial machinery, electronics, automobile, aircraft, and ordnance), and consumer industries (such as textiles, paper and pulp, ceramics, and home appliances).

MITI plays a central part in Japan's economic policy-making thanks chiefly to its control of a portion of **Fiscal Investment and Loan Program** (FILP) funds, known also as the nation's second budget.

As a result of the rapid turnover among ministers and director-generals, ministries and agencies are run in practice by their senior officials, the administrative vice minister, and one or two deputy vice ministers. These officials are career civil servants with many years of service in the same ministry or agency. A ministry or an agency is thus a bureaucracy with considerable autonomy and discretionary power of its own, particularly with regard to its internal organization and personnel decisions.

Ministerial autonomy often verges on ministerial chauvinism and can seriously interfere with cooperation between ministries. **Vertically divided administration** is thus a common characterization of the way the Japanese civil service operates. In the aftermath of

Institutional Intricacies: MITI and FILP

MITI, the Ministry of International Trade and Industry, is the best known, at least outside of Japan, of all the ministries as Japan's "economic general staff." It is, however, a relatively small ministry in terms of the amount of money it spends and the number of people it employs. In the mid-1990s, for example, its shares of the annual government budget and the central government employees were not much bigger than 1 percent and 1.5 percent, respectively. It ranked eighth in terms of the official budget and sixth in terms of personnel among the twelve ministries. MITI's much publicized clout is based mainly on its licensing and permit-giving authority, its skillful use of administrative guidance, and its large share of an unofficial government budget called the Fiscal Investment and Loan Program (FILP).

FILP has been Japan's "other" budget since the early 1950s, annually channeling huge amounts of funds from government-operated trust funds and pension, insurance, and postal savings programs into a variety of public works projects and selected areas of the private sector. The former includes highway construction and housing development, and the latter, high-tech industries, small businesses, and agriculture. The 1997 FILP budget was about ¥51.4 trillion, or just about two-thirds of the ¥77.4 trillion official budget. About one-fifth of the FILP funds were dispensed by MITI, giving the ministry a very large amount of discretionary power to intervene in and "administratively guide" the key industries.

the devastating earthquake that hit Kobe City in January 1995, ministerial egoism and parochialism were widely blamed for long delays, often with tragic consequences, in the Tokyo government's response. As an editorial writer of a national daily observed at that time, whenever disaster strikes, each government ministry and agency holds its own meetings, dispatches its own fact-finding teams, and implements its own relief measures, with little regard for what other ministries and agencies are doing.[28] The first priority is always coordination within each ministry or agency rather than cooperation with other ministries and agencies.

The cabinet usually meets twice a week, although the prime minister may call additional meetings on his own initiative or at the request of other members of his cabinet. The director-general of the Cabinet Legislation Bureau and two deputy chief cabinet secretaries are usually present at these meetings. However, most outstanding issues are settled in advance, at a meeting of administrative vice ministers, which is normally held the day before the cabinet meeting.

The power and prestige of the national civil service derive to an important extent from the unique position it occupies among the political institutions of contemporary Japan. Alone among prewar Japan's public institutions, the central government bureau-

cracy survived the occupation-sponsored postwar reforms virtually intact. The only notable casualty was the Home Ministry, which was divided into several smaller ministries and agencies. The national civil service actually became stronger after the reforms, which destroyed outright or drastically weakened other institutions and played the leading role in Japan's postwar recovery.

During most of the postwar period, institutional autonomy and discretionary power, combined with adequate though not exceptionally high pay and guaranteed job security gave Japan's national civil service enormous prestige. The prestige in turn attracted a large number of university graduates to the annual civil service entrance examinations and ensured that only the best performers were appointed to fast-track positions in the central ministries and agencies, especially the most prestigious among them, such as the Ministry of Finance (MOF), Ministry of International Trade and Industry (MITI), and Ministry of Foreign Affairs (MFA). As Japan grew richer, the attractiveness of careers in the private sector, especially in one of the conglomerate-affiliated giant corporations, rose rapidly, while the popularity of civil service careers declined. During the late 1980s the number of applicants taking the highest-level domestic service entrance examinations declined by nearly one-third. Still, the competition for fast-track jobs in the civil service remains stiff, and only about one out of fifteen applicants (and about one out of twenty-five in the highest-level diplomatic service examination) passes the examination.

By custom, though not by law, Japan's national civil servants retire at a relatively young age, usually about fifty-five, with fairly modest retirement benefits. This forces most retired civil servants to seek new jobs. Many find high-paying jobs in public or semipublic corporations or in the major private firms. This type of postretirement employment is known as ***amakudari***, or "descent from heaven." The "descent" is usually arranged in advance between the ministry or agency ("heaven") from which the official is retiring and one of the public, semipublic, or private enterprises with which the ministry has a close relationship. The Japanese civil service law forbids employment of a retired civil servant by a private enterprise that has had a close relationship in the recent past with the government office concerned. This restriction may be lifted at the National Personnel Authority's discretion, however, and has routinely been lifted for several dozens of retiring senior bureaucrats each year.

In 1995, Japan's national government employed about 1,173,000 people, or a little less than 2 percent of the employed workforce of about 64,570,000 people. The Japanese central government budget thus claimed a somewhat larger share of the nation's GDP than in Germany but less than in the United States or France and less than half as much as in Italy or Great Britain (see Figure 1). It is difficult to compare the efficiency of different nations' public bureaucracies, but it is probably reasonable to call Japan's relatively lean and thrifty. Its traditional image as a group of unselfish, public-minded, and incorruptible mandarins, however, was seriously compromised in the 1990s by a series of scandals in which senior officials were found guilty of bribery and other offenses. In one 1998 case, top officials of the Defense Agency winked at gross overcharges by some major contractors, allowing them to pay back only small portions of the overcharged amounts in exchange for their agreement to accommodate the agency's recent and prospective retirees in typical *amakudari* arrangements.

Figure 1

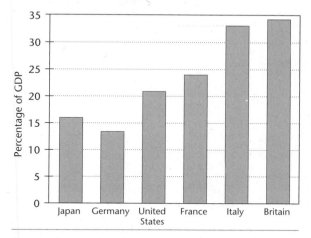

National Government Expenditures as Percentage of Gross Domestic Product, 1995

Source: International Department, Bank of Japan, *Comparative Economic and Financial Statistics: Japan and Other Major Countries 1997* (Tokyo: Bank of Japan, 1997), 109–110. Table 32.

Public and Semipublic Agencies

In 1997, Japan had about fifty active and forty inactive, virtually defunct, national public and semipublic enterprises. The active ones may be divided into three broad groups:

1. Nonprofit public financial institutions, including three government-owned banks (the Bank of Japan, the Japan Development Bank, and the Japan Export Import Bank) and about a dozen public funds and foundations. All receive their capital from the central government and make loans to organizations or individuals engaged in activities of public interest, such as small businesses, farm and fishing families, construction companies in the less developed regions of the country, home buyers, foreign governments (via the Japan Overseas Cooperation Fund), and foreign scholars (via the Japan Foundation). Their budgets and expenditures are subject to audit by the Diet.

2. Public corporations funded either by the central government or jointly by the central and local

governments. These are involved in large public works projects, such as development and conservation of natural resources, construction and management of highways, railroads, bridges, and airports.

3. Businesses that are wholly or partially supported by public funds. The activities of these businesses range from the development of nuclear reactors and space technologies to the construction and maintenance of sewage works and assistance to small businesses, livestock farmers, and mining companies.

The number of Japanese public and semipublic enterprises has been gradually declining for the past quarter century, a trend substantially accelerated in the 1980s by the global deregulation and privatization movement led by President Ronald Reagan in the United States and Prime Minister Margaret Thatcher in Britain. The movement gained considerable public support in Japan partly because many of Japan's public and semipublic enterprises were chronically in the red and required constant infusions of taxpayers' money. The Japanese National Railways (JNR) is a good example. Saddled with huge debts, JNR was on the verge of bankruptcy when it was privatized and divided into six private railroad companies in 1987. Nevertheless, many of the fifty or so survivors, notably the Japan Highways Corporation and the Housing and Urban Development Corporation, continue to let debts pile up to be picked up sooner or later by taxpayers.

Another important reason that many Japanese citizens are skeptical about public and semipublic enterprises is that they are believed to serve mainly as providers of lucrative "descent from heaven" postretirement employment for senior ministry bureaucrats. The practice gives senior civil servants an unfair advantage over others in the postretirement job market, such as most employees of private companies who retire at comparable ages. But since privatization means the elimination or downsizing of the targeted public and semipublic companies, it is opposed by many civil servants and has not gone very far. Japan is likely to remain home to dozens, if not hundreds, of public and semipublic enterprises for a long time to come.

Other State Institutions

The Military

Japan's military establishment was totally dismantled by the Allied occupation authorities after World War II. Article IX of the MacArthur Constitution renounces "war as a sovereign right of the nation" and declares that "land, sea and air forces, as well as other war potential, will never be maintained." In 1950 the outbreak of the Korean War led the Japanese government to launch a rearmament program at Washington's urging. Initially, a "police reserve force" was created, to avoid provoking controversy over its constitutionality. By 1954 this force had evolved into the Self-Defense Forces (SDF). In 1959 the Supreme Court ruled that Article IX allowed Japan to take necessary measures to defend itself as an independent nation. The SDF have since grown into very substantial armed forces.

More important in the long run is the gradual erosion, due in large measure to Washington's persistent pressure, of the Japanese antipathy to war and arms born of their harrowing experiences in World War II. Even the Socialist prime minister Tomiichi Murayama declared in his inaugural speech in the summer of 1994 that, contrary to his own party's long-standing policy, his government recognized the constitutionality of the Self-Defense Forces and supported the U.S.-Japan Mutual Security Treaty (see Section 1 pp. 189–201). So far, however, the majority of Japanese political leaders, like the majority of Japanese citizens, continue to oppose significant increases in the nation's defense budget or the troop levels of the Self-Defense Forces. Most remain highly ambivalent even about Japanese participation in U.N.-sponsored peacekeeping operations that involve the use of arms.

The Judiciary

The judicial branch of the Japanese government operates according to the rules and decisions of the Supreme Court and is theoretically free from interference by the other two branches of government or any private interest group. The Supreme Court consists of the chief judge and fourteen other judges. All judges are appointed by the cabinet, except the chief judge of

Institutional Intricacies: *Self-Defense Forces*

By the late 1990s the Japanese Self-Defense Forces were comparable in size and operational capability to the armed forces of most Western European nations and were supported by a budget of a comparable amount. This makes Japan by far the largest military spender in Asia. In 1995, Japan's $50 billion defense budget was more than 1.5 times China's, which was the second largest in Asia, more than 3.5 times South Korea's and Taiwan's, and nearly 10 times North Korea's. Even though Japan was spending only a little over 1 percent of its GDP on defense, $50 billion could buy very large amounts of advanced weapons and military technologies—a fact not lost on any of Japan's neighbors.

From Washington's point of view, on the other hand, Japan's defense spending has been too modest. In 1995 the United States spent nearly six times as much as Japan. Partly out of a growing frustration over the large and chronic trade deficits with Japan ($63 billion in 1995), U.S. leaders have continually demanded a larger defense effort by Tokyo, which they hoped would lead to increased Japanese purchases of American military products. Japan has partly responded to the U.S. demands by increasing its share of the maintenance costs of about 44,000 U.S. troops (as of early 1995) stationed at U.S. bases in Japan.

During the Persian Gulf War of 1991, Japan made a substantial financial contribution ($13 billion) to the efforts of the Coalition Forces, but no Japanese troops participated in their operations. In

Table A

Defense Expenditures, 1995

	US$ millions	Percent of GDP
Asia		
Japan	43,626	1.0
China	34,684	5.7
South Korea	15,168	3.3
Taiwan	13,295	4.9
North Korea	5,330	27.2
NATO		
United States	265,823	3.6
France	46,217	3.1
Germany	38,432	1.7
Great Britain	32,764	3.0
Italy	23,289	2.2

Source: From *The Military Balance 1997–98* by The International Institute for Strategic Studies. Copyright © 1996 by Oxford University Press. Reprinted by permission.

response to the criticism heard in many countries, especially the United States, that the Japanese would give money but would not risk the lives of their own citizens for any international cause, Japan has since dispatched some Self-Defense Forces personnel as well as civilians to trouble spots around the world, such as Cambodia and Mozambique. However, no Japanese troops have ever been stationed abroad since World War II.

the Supreme Court, who is nominated by the cabinet and appointed by the emperor. Supreme Court judges are subject to popular review and potential recall in the first House of Representatives election following their appointment, and every ten years thereafter. Otherwise, judges of all courts may serve until the mandatory retirement ages: seventy for judges on the Supreme Court and small claims courts, and sixty-five for all others. In the fifteen popular reviews of Supreme Court judges held through 1998, no judge received a negative vote from much more than 10 percent of the voters. The recall provision is thus no more than a ritual of no practical import.

The Supreme Court, eight higher (regional) courts, and fifty district (prefectural) courts are invested with and occasionally use the constitutional power of judicial review. But the Supreme Court has been extremely reluctant to do so and especially to declare an existing law unconstitutional. For example, lower courts have twice found the Self-Defense Forces in violation of the war-renouncing Article IX of the 1947 constitution—once in the late 1950s and again in the late 1970s. On each occasion, the Supreme Court reversed the lower court's verdict on the grounds that the issue was too political to be amenable to judicial review; this amounted to indirectly declaring the

Self-Defense Forces constitutional. During the half century of its existence up to 1998, the Supreme Court upheld lower court verdicts on the unconstitutionality of existing laws in only five cases, none of which involved a controversial political issue.

The passive posture of the Supreme Court helped sustain LDP domination of the Diet and the cabinet until the early 1990s. The court refused to order major changes in the boundaries of the nation's election districts to reflect the massive postwar population movement from the countryside to the cities. As a result, in 1993 voters in the most over-represented rural districts elected 2.8 times as many lower house members and 6.7 times as many upper house members *per voter* as their counterparts in the most under-represented urban districts. In that year the Supreme Court acknowledged, as it had done already in 1976, the unconstitutionality of such gross malapportionment, but it refused, as it had done on the previous occasion, to invalidate the results of the elections.

The reluctance of the Japanese Supreme Court to use its power of judicial review may be attributed to several factors. First, there is an influential legal opinion that holds that the judiciary should not intervene in highly political acts of the legislative or executive branches of government, which represent the people's will more directly than the judiciary. Second, Japan has a much weaker case law tradition than either the United States or Britain. This makes judges less inclined to challenge the constitutionality of new legislation on the basis of precedents. Third, most of the Supreme Court judges appointed by the LDP governments were conservative in their outlook and inclined to approve decisions made by the conservative party in power. Fourth, judicial passivity may reflect the traditional reluctance of the Japanese people to resort to litigation to settle disputes. Finally, Japan lacks a tradition of judicial review. Under the Meiji Constitution, the emperor was above the law and the courts did not have the power to deny the legality of any executive act taken in his name.

In 1997 a prefectural government made a donation to a Shinto shrine in Tokyo that houses Japan's war dead, including convicted World War II war criminals. The Supreme Court found the prefectural government's act to be in violation of the constitutional principle of the separation of government and religion.

Since the decision came in a suit brought by a group of concerned citizens against the prefectural government and did not concern the validity of an existing statute, it did not set a precedent in the practice of judicial review in Japan. Whether it was a sign of a turn to judicial activism among Supreme Court judges is yet to be seen.

Subnational Government

The Japanese prefecture and its subdivisions are under the extensive administrative and financial control of the central government and enjoy only a narrowly circumscribed range of decision-making authority. In this respect, Japan differs from most other industrial democracies except France.

The lopsided distribution of decision-making power is sustained by an equally lopsided division of taxing power. The central government collects nearly two-thirds of the taxes collected by all governments and provides the funds for nearly two-thirds of local governments' expenditures through extensive grants-in-aid and subsidies. Most of these programs and related local public works projects are planned as well as funded by the central government and merely administered by local governments. The scope of local discretion has somewhat expanded in recent years. In fact, some scholars argue that the relationship between the national and local governments in postwar Japan has been far less lopsided than widely believed.[29] Still, the findings and recommendations of an expert committee appointed by the central government in accordance with a 1995 law leave little room for doubt about the extremely limited scope of local autonomy under the existing system. The grossly skewed central-local relations are a major factor impeding the development of greater democracy in Japan. The system discourages citizens from participating in local government and politics, and makes the central government insensitive, even indifferent, to local interests and opinions.

The Policy-Making Process

The majority of bills passed by the Diet originate in the national civil service. When the LDP is in power, the draft bills are reviewed and approved by the party's Policy Research Council before being sent to the Diet. The council operates through seventeen standing committees, each corresponding to a government ministry or agency, and as of 1997, nearly one hundred ad hoc committees. Some of these ad hoc committees are concerned with broad, long-term policy issues, such as revision of the constitution, fiscal policy, and the educational system. Others deal with more specific issues, such as government assistance to depressed industries, treatment of foreign workers, and drug control. Their recommendations are presented to the executive committee of the Policy Research Council. If approved, these usually become LDP policies to be implemented through legislative actions of the Diet or administrative actions of the bureaucracy.

Most LDP policy committees are led by veteran Diet members who are experienced and knowledgeable in specific policy areas. Over the years, they have formed close personal relationships with senior civil servants and the leaders of special interest groups. These LDP legislative bosses, who form among themselves what are popularly known as *zoku* (tribes) work through informal policy-making networks with their bureaucratic and business allies. Such groups dominate policy-making in all major policy areas, including agriculture, construction, education, telecommunications, and transportation. Many of the bills drafted by bureaucrats and introduced in the Diet by an LDP cabinet originate in a tribe, as do many administrative measures implemented by a government ministry or agency.

Through such policy-making partnerships, or **iron triangles**, special interests are promoted by friendly politicians and bureaucrats, bureaucrats have their turfs protected and often extended by sympathetic politicians, and politicians have their campaign war chests filled with contributions from interest groups. LDP tribes are thus the principal actors in pork-barrel politics and the major sources of political corruption and scandals. As a result, many LDP policies are conservative and protectionist, their main purpose being to protect the well-organized, well-connected, and well-to-do special interests. Big businesses, small shop owners, farmers, realtors, builders, insurers, and doctors are all represented by their own tribes and protected against those who threaten their interests, whether they are Japanese consumers, insurance

policy holders, patients, foreign producers, exporters, or providers of various services.

This process and its consequences were dramatically illustrated by the evolution of the administrative reform campaign launched with great fanfare by Prime Minister Ryutaro Hashimoto and his LDP government in 1997. An interim report by a blue-ribbon panel chaired by the prime minister himself proposed to eliminate or consolidate all nonessential or redundant government offices. The proposal provoked ferocious opposition not only from the targeted ministries and agencies but also from their allied interest groups and "tribesmen" in the LDP and other parties' executive offices and policy board committees. In just a few weeks, the panel's original proposal was gutted of most of its substantive contents and Hashimoto's reform campaign was effectively over.

Hashimoto was by no means the first to call for reforming the bureaucracy. All three coalition governments that preceded him from 1993 to 1997 had promised thoroughgoing reform. But none had been able to deliver on their promises in the face of determined opposition by an assortment of iron triangles. The Japanese policy-making process thus remains—and is likely to remain for many years—basically as it was molded in the heyday of the LDP's one-party rule. Only the overwhelming pressure of public opinion, such as might be generated by a national economic or political crisis even more serious than the recession of the late 1990s, could break the resistance of the iron triangles to genuine reform.

As the term suggests, an iron triangle is characterized by strong solidarity among its members on the one hand and rivalry and competition with outsiders on the other. The policy-making process that revolves around dozens of such triangles is inevitably disjointed and incoherent. Decisions made by one triangle in one policy area are seldom coordinated with decisions made in another. The medley of policies that often run at cross-purposes are then passed by the Diet or announced as new government policies. As a result, there are numerous laws and regulations in contemporary Japan but few comprehensive, coherent, long-term policies.

Government by iron triangles and policy tribes was temporarily suspended during the rule of the eight-party coalition cabinet formed in the wake of the 1993 lower house election and led by the JNP leader, Morihiro Hosokawa. The fragmented policy-making system represented by the structure of the LDP Policy Research Council, which gave free rein to the party's policy tribes, was replaced by a much more centralized system under the new prime minister's direction. A Council of Representatives of the Coalition Parties composed of the secretary-generals of the eight parties now took command of decision-making on all important issues, leaving little room for the tribes' influence.[30]

The system was abandoned, however, in less than a year under the LDP-JSP-NPH coalition cabinet led by the JSP leader, Murayama. The secretary-generals' council was now replaced by eighteen "project teams" made up of Diet members of the three parties. The issues dealt with by these teams ranged from administrative reform and the protection of human rights to the celebration of the fiftieth anniversary of the end of World War II and aid to victims of environmental pollution. Few of these issues attracted the attention of special interest groups. Besides, a policy-coordinating committee composed of the policy board chairmen of the three parties was also installed.

Under this three-man committee, however, nineteen subcommittees nearly identical with the LDP's policy committees were set up and soon became new nests for the old iron triangles and policy tribes. Besides, these were now joined by a number of JSP Diet members, especially those tied to farm interests. It did not take very long for the old style of policy-making nurtured during the thirty-eight-year-long LDP rule to be back in fashion.

Section ❹ Representation and Participation

As in other democracies, politics in Japan is characterized by the representation of its citizens' interests and opinions in the conduct of the government and formulation of its policies. The official forums in which their interests and opinions are expressed and considered are the national and local legislatures. The official actors who represent them are the legislators, most of whom are affiliated with and supported by political parties. Citizens exercise a degree of control over the legislators' conduct and performance as their representatives through periodic elections. There are also other organizations and activities that express and represent citizens' interests and opinions outside the legislatures, such as interest groups and social movements. This section discusses the main features and problems of these organizations and activities in contemporary Japan.

The Legislature

Even during the period of LDP domination from the mid-1950s through the early 1990s, the Japanese national legislature played a central, indispensable role in the operation of democratic government as the most authoritative arena for public debates on important issues. The postwar constitution declares that the Diet is the highest and sole law-making organ of state. How the Diet is constituted and how it operates are therefore critical questions in assessing the current state and future prospects of democracy in Japan.

The House of Councillors, or the upper house of the bicameral Diet, currently has 252 seats. Upper house members have a fixed term of six years, but, as is the case with U.S. senators, their terms are staggered so that half of them are elected every three years. One hundred of them (fifty in each triennial upper house election) are elected by a party-list-based proportional representation (PR) method. Each qualified party—one that either has at least five current Diet seats or won at least 2 percent of the vote in the most recent Diet election or has at least ten candidates in the current election—submits a ranked list of its candidates to the election management committee in advance of the election. Votes are cast for parties, seats are allocated to parties in numbers proportionate to their shares of the total vote, and the seats given to each party are allocated to its candidates according to their rank on the party list.

The remaining 152 (76 in each upper house election) are elected from multiple-seat prefecturewide districts by a method known as single nontransferable vote (SNTV). Upper house members were originally expected to bring a broad, national perspective to parliamentary deliberations and be less influenced by parochial local interests than lower house members. In practice, however, this distinction has long been lost, and the two houses are virtually indistinguishable.

The House of Representatives, or the lower house, currently has 500 seats. The full term of office for its members is four years, but the actual term served by a member averages about two and a half years. This is because, unlike the upper house, the lower house may be dissolved by the cabinet when the house passes a motion of no confidence against the cabinet or refuses to pass a motion of confidence in the cabinet. In either case, the cabinet must choose either to resign or to dissolve the lower house and call a new election. The cabinet may voluntarily choose to dissolve the lower house at other times as well. The constitution gives the emperor the right to dissolve the lower house with the advice and consent of the cabinet; in fact, he cannot refuse such a request from the cabinet. The cabinet chooses to dissolve the lower house when it believes that the ruling party will win the general election.

A speaker and a vice speaker preside in the lower house; a president and a vice president preside in the upper house. Unlike their counterparts in the U.S. Congress, the presiding officers of the Japanese Diet are expected to be nonpartisan in discharging their duties. When a member of the Diet is elected to any of these four positions, the member nominally gives up his or her party affiliation and becomes an independent.

An ordinary session of the Diet sits for 150 days each year, beginning in December, subject to one or more extensions. An extraordinary session may be called at any time by the cabinet or by a quarter of the members of either house. As in the U.S. Congress, a good deal of business is conducted in the standing and ad hoc committees of each house. There are twenty lower house and seventeen upper house standing committees and, as of 1998, eight ad hoc committees in each house. The quorum for the plenary session and the meeting of a committee of either house is uniformly a simple majority. So is the number of votes required for the passage of a bill or a resolution by either house or its committee.

A bill may be first introduced in either house but must be considered and approved by both houses in order to become a law. In practice, an overwhelming majority of bills have been introduced first in the lower and later referred to the upper house. A bill may be introduced by the cabinet, the house, a committee of the house, or a member of the house. In all cases, it is first presented to the presiding officer of the house, then referred by him or her to an appropriate committee of the house for initial consideration, unless the introducer requests for special reasons that it be immediately sent to and considered by the entire house. A member's bill that does not require a budget appropriation must be co-signed by twenty or more lower house members or ten or more upper house members; one that requires a budget appropriation must be co-signed by fifty or more lower house or twenty or more upper house members.

A bill approved by a committee of either house is referred to and debated by the whole house, and, if approved, transmitted to the other house where the same process is repeated. A bill that has been approved by both houses, with or without amendments, is signed by the speaker of the lower house or the president of the upper house, whichever has approved it last, and presented to the emperor for promulgation. Promulgation is, however, purely a formality that does not entail the approval or endorsement of the bill by the emperor.

The lower house is the more powerful of the two houses of the Diet. First, if a bill has been approved by the lower house but disapproved by the upper house, it may still become a law by being passed again with a two-thirds majority in the lower house. Second, the annual government budget must be first introduced to the lower house and may be passed by that house alone, regardless of the upper house's action or opinion. Third, the lower house enjoys the same privilege in the ratification of international treaties.

Japanese Diet members normally vote strictly along party lines, unlike members of the U.S. Congress but as in most parliamentary democracies. In the 1950s and early 1960s the rigid enforcement of party discipline in Diet voting contributed to frequent confrontations between the LDP and the opposition, which sometimes led to fist fights on the floor of the Diet. By the mid-1960s, however, the opposition had given up such violent tactics in favor of delaying maneuvers such as repeated submissions of no-confidence motions against a cabinet. Since the early

1970s parliamentary battles between the ruling party and the opposition have become increasingly ritualized. The opposition first uses a boycott or other means to stall Diet proceedings and kill a government proposal, but eventually accepts a settlement mediated by the presiding officer of either house. The ruling party repays the opposition for its cooperation by making limited concessions.

Most Japanese legislators are men. While female voters' turnout has been consistently higher than male voters' in local elections since the late 1950s and in Diet elections since the early 1970s, there are few female legislators either at the national or local level.[31] Following the July 1998 upper house election, 43, or 17 percent, of the 252 members of that house and 24, or less than 5 percent, of the 500 lower-house members were women.

Women play a very limited role in Japan's national legislature, as they do in the executive and judicial branches of the national government and in prefectural and local governments. This is partly due to the traditional Japanese political culture that discourages women's participation in public affairs. More important, however, it is a consequence of the standard rules used in the selection of candidates in national and local elections by all major Japanese political parties. These rules give priority to incumbents, candidates chosen by the party's local branches, and candidates who are likely to win, roughly in this order. Nearly all incumbents are men and nearly all local branches of the major parties are under male politicians' control.

When an incumbent retires or dies, he or she is likely to be succeeded by his or her relative, typically a son, or a close aide. Thanks to the campaign organization and personal networks bequeathed by the predecessor, such a successor has significant advantage over rival candidates in terms of both the support of the local party branch and ability to win. As a result, many Diet members are now second-generation politicians. In the 1990s nearly a quarter of all lower house members and 40 percent of LDP lower house members belonged to this category. This makes Japan's parliament look more like a political club of the feudal period than a modern democratic institution.

In the Japanese Diet, as in the U.S. Congress, committee deliberations, where special interests and pressure groups can exert their influence most effectively, play the central part in the legislative process. By comparison, plenary sessions seldom lead to substantial changes in a bill. While in most Western democracies bills are read three or more times by the entire membership of a house, there is only one reading in the plenary session of the Japanese Diet. As a result, entrenched special interests represented by their own tribes and iron triangles in committee deliberations are likely to have their cases heard far more effectively than newer and less organized interests that are not so represented, such as those of urban residents, women, and youth.

The interests of the national civil service are also effectively represented in the work of Diet committees. Civil servants are in a position to interpret laws almost as they please by issuing administrative orders, which are supposed to help implement a law but often have the effect of modifying or even replacing it. Japanese laws tend to lack specific and detailed provisions, which gives bureaucrats wide discretion in interpreting them. As a result, bureaucratic interests, as well as special private interests, tend to prevail over those of the broader public.

Political Parties and the Party System

For nearly forty years from the mid-1950s, when the Liberal and Democratic parties merged, to the early 1990s, the LDP dominated the Diet. The party owed its success mainly to a booming economy, a generally satisfied electorate, and a divided and bickering opposition. By the late 1980s, however, a series of scandals began to take their toll. In 1993 the party became bitterly divided and fell from power. That event ushered in a period of uncertainty and instability in Japanese politics characterized by the rise and fall of parties new and old, as well as of cabinets, at short intervals (see Table 4).

At the end of the 1980s there were five parties regularly contesting Diet elections: the LDP, the Japan Socialist Party (JSP), the Clean Government Party (CGP), the Democratic Socialist Party (DSP), and the Japan Communist Party (JCP). The LDP, the JSP, and the JCP were descendants of prewar parties disbanded on the eve and revived in the wake of World War II. The DSP had been formed in 1960 by defectors from the JSP. The CGP was founded in 1964 as the political

Table 4

Number of Seats and Percent of Proportional Representation Vote, by Parties (1996 Lower House and 1998 Upper House Elections)

| | No. of Seats | | Percent of Vote | |
	1996	1998	1996	1998
Liberal Democratic Party	239	44 (103)	32.8	25.2
Japan Renewal Party	156	– –	28.0	–
Democratic Party of Japan	52	27 (47)	16.1	21.7
Japan Communist Party	26	15 (23)	13.1	14.6
Social Democratic Party	15	5 (13)	6.4	7.8
New Party Harbinger	2	0 (3)	1.0	1.4
Liberal Party	–	6 (12)	–	9.3
Clean Government Party	–	9 (22)	–	13.8
Other parties	1	0 (4)	2.6	6.1
Independents	9	20 (25)	–	–
Totals	500	126 (252)	100.0	99.9

Note: Numbers in parentheses for 1998 upper house seats are totals that include seats won in 1995.

Sources: *Asahi shinbun*, October 21, 1996, 1; October 21, 1996, evening ed., 3; July 13, 1998, 1, 4; July 14, 1998, 7.

arm of the national organization of lay members of the Buddhist sect, the Sokagakkai.

The LDP's defeat in the 1993 lower house election was triggered by a series of scandals, the LDP government's new tax and trade policies, and above all, the economic downturn. The voter revolt against the LDP was exploited by three new parties, the Japan New Party (JNP), the New Party Harbinger (NPH or Sakigake), and the Japan Renewal Party (JRP). The JNP had been founded in 1992 by a former LDP upper house member, while the NPH and the JRP were both formed by LDP defectors less than a month before the election.

In the following years, the LDP regained power while the other parties reorganized and renamed themselves. The JRP, JNP, CGP, and DSP merged into a New Frontier Party (NFP), later renamed the Liberal Party (LP); the CGP was revived by a group of its former members; the JSP was renamed the Social Democratic Party (SDP); defectors from the SDP and the NPH formed another new party, the Democratic Party of Japan (DPJ). The NPH disbanded following the 1998 upper house election. Only the JCP remained intact both in name and basic organizational structure.

At the end of 1998 there were thus six parties led by the LDP, little different from the situation a decade earlier (see Table 5).

As mentioned earlier, the LDP was formed in 1955 through the merger of two older conservative parties—the Liberal Party and the Democratic Party—which in turn had descended from prewar parties with their origins in the nineteenth century. The SDP (formerly JSP) evolved from a social democratic party founded in the mid-1920s. The JCP is a direct descendant of the prewar JCP, banned upon its founding in the wake of World War I and revived in 1945 when the party's leaders were released from jail on the orders of General MacArthur. The LDP draws its electoral and financial support mainly from the big- and small-business communities and farmer groups. The SDP is supported by public sector labor unions, and the JCP relies on small but loyal groups of urban workers and intellectuals. The CGP is sponsored by the lay group of a Buddhist sect founded by a thirteenth-century monk. The two newer parties, the DPJ and the LP, both draw the bulk of their support from former supporters of the LDP or SDP. Neither has yet built a well-defined and reliable base of electoral and financial support.

The LDP stands roughly at the right end and the JCP at the left end of an ideological spectrum, while the LP, DPJ, and SDP range right to left between them, roughly in that order. Japanese politics in general and party politics in particular have not been intensely ideological since the end of the Vietnam War in the mid-1970s and have become even less so since the end of the Cold War.

The JCP's official platform, which was revised most recently in 1985, continues to refer to Japanese monopoly capitalism and American imperialism. Nonetheless, the party now calls for the formation of a democratic coalition government in cooperation with conservative opposition parties and with the support of conservative but independent voters. The party has also abandoned its hostile attitude toward South Korea, and its leaders visit the country in defiance of North Korea's vociferous objections. In both its domestic and foreign policy, the present-day JCP is thus as pragmatic and politically astute as any other Japanese party. It is for that reason that its popularity at the polls has been steadily rising, earning it nine new seats in the 1998 upper house election and

Table 5

Japanese Political Parties, November 1998				
		Year	Diet Seats	
Ideology	Party Name	Founded	HR	HC
Right	Liberal Democratic Party (LDP)	1955	263	104
	Liberal Party (LP)	1997	35	12
Center	Democratic Party of Japan (DPJ)	1996	93	55
	Clean Government Party (CGP)	1964		24
	Clean Government Party/Reform Club (CGP/RC)	1964/1997	52	
	New Party Harbinger (NPH)	1993	2	0
Left	Social Democratic Party (SDP)	1955	14	14
	Japan Communist Party (JCP)	1945	26	23
Other groups			5	15
Independents			10	5
Totals			500	252

Note: HR = House of Representatives; HC = House of Councillors.

Source: *Asahi shinbun,* November 26, 1998, 2.

making it the third largest party in that house after the LDP and DPJ.

The LDP remains the largest party in the Diet. It suffers, however, from perennial factional divisions that militate against strong and stable party leadership. Since its birth in 1955 the party has been divided into several well-defined and deeply entrenched rival factions, each led by a veteran member. The boss and his followers are bound by patron-client relationships of mutual help and dependence. The boss helps his followers with campaign funds at election time and advocates their appointment to Diet, cabinet, and party offices. His followers reciprocate by pledging their support for the boss's actual or expected bid for the highest party office, the LDP presidency, which is, given the LDP's control of the Diet, virtually synonymous with Japan's premiership. A large factional following is therefore an essential asset for a boss with prime ministerial ambitions.

The LDP factions have evolved as intraparty campaign machines intent on promoting themselves at each other's expense. They influence the policy-making process indirectly by virtue of the fact that all important Diet, cabinet, and party offices are allocated on the basis of the standing of the factions in the party and members' standing in their own faction. In the early days of the LDP, the personal role of the faction boss was particularly great, and his death or

retirement often resulted in splits or disintegration of the faction. After the late 1970s, however, the five surviving factions became increasingly institutionalized, so that the departure of their bosses no longer threatened the groups' existence. Amid the complex party realignment process set off by the LDP's fall from power in 1993, all the factions declared themselves disbanded by the end of 1994. The declaration was, however, no more than a public relations gimmick, and the factions remained alive and active when the LDP returned to power in less than a year.

No other party except the SDP (formerly JSP) has ever been as seriously and chronically factionalized. The SDP has been host to intraparty factionalism as contentious as and, in some ways, more destructive than its counterpart in the LDP. While the LDP factions are concerned primarily with fund-raising and the distribution of government and party offices among its Diet members, the SDP factions have been primarily ideological and policy groups. Some advocate a more radical version of socialism than others; some favor a more hostile policy toward the Self-Defense Forces and the military alliance with the United States; some take a more critical attitude toward the middle-of-the-road parties; and so forth. The steady decline of the SDP's popularity may be attributed mainly to its inability to rally behind a leader or a leadership group and to part with its outdated Cold War–era ideological commitments. This inability has been a direct result of internal factional conflicts.

Elections

The House of Representatives election system was drastically changed in 1994. Under the old system, all lower house members, as well as some of the House of Councillors, were elected by the SNTV method that had been in effect in Japan since the mid-1920s but was very rare in national-level elections elsewhere. According to this method, two or more members are elected in each district but each voter casts a single ballot for a particular candidate, which may not be transferred to another candidate even of the same party. The candidates with the largest numbers of votes in each district win. At the time of the 1993 lower house election, Japan was divided into 129 lower house election districts, each of which elected between two and six members. Because many candidates (including candidates from the same party) would run for a seat in each district, it was possible to win a seat with as little as 10–15 percent of the vote. This system produced results very similar to those associated with a type of proportional representation, making it possible for smaller parties to win at least some seats.

The multimember district system forced candidates of the same party to compete by highlighting their qualifications and strengths in matters other than their views on policy issues. This tendency was particularly pronounced because all Japanese parties required their Diet members to support the party line on major policy issues. Under such circumstances, the most common way to win voters' support was to offer them a variety of constituency services, ranging from finding jobs for constituents or their children to lobbying for government subsidies for local firms. Constituency service activities were carried out primarily by the candidate's personal campaign organization, known as the *koenkai* (support association).

The *koenkai* mobilized local community groups, such as agricultural cooperatives and merchant associations, into solid blocs of voters for their candidates. It took enormous amounts of money and hard work to set up and maintain a *koenkai* organization, not so much to buy votes outright but to rent office space,

pay salaries, and finance constituency services. The funds were provided mainly by local and nonlocal businesses and business organizations. The LDP's long rule depended on the extensive and sturdy networks of patron-client relationships (**clientelism**) between party members, generous businessmen and business organizations, and *koenkai* organizations.

The LDP also owed its success to gross malapportionment that gave significant advantage to rural voters over urban voters. The malapportionment had its roots in a census taken right after World War II when Japan's major cities had been evacuated in the face of Allied air raids and the majority of Japanese were living in rural areas. This original apportionment has been only marginally adjusted to take account of the enormous population shifts from rural to urban areas that occurred in the next several decades. As a result, the LDP consistently championed farmers' interests and succeeded in turning rural Japan into a solid bloc of staunchly pro-LDP voters.

The systematic bias in the election system, and the "money politics" that was blamed for recurrent scandals involving top LDP leaders and business executives, raised serious doubts about the quality of democracy in Japan. Many Japanese critics, including some LDP leaders, were calling for reform for nearly a quarter century. The determined opposition of those who benefited from the status quo, however, had effectively blocked any meaningful change. The dramatic reversal in the electoral fortunes of the LDP in the early 1990s led at long last to some serious attacks on the decades-old problems.

In early 1994 four political reform bills were passed by the Diet in the hope that replacing the SNTV system with a combination of single-member district and proportional representation (PR) systems would help rid lower house elections of money politics. The existing 129 multimember districts that elected 511 lower house members were replaced with 300 single-member districts and eleven regional districts that would elect an additional 200 members by a party list–based PR method. In the first lower house election held under the new system in 1996, candidates were allowed to run simultaneously in both a single-member district and a PR district and could get elected by winning in one district while losing in the other. The LDP won 239 of the 500 seats, or 28 more than it had in the 511-seat house before the election. All the other parties except the JCP lost at least one and, in the SDP's case, as many as fifteen seats. In short, the reform had no significant immediate effect on the overall balance of power among the parties or on the general pattern of shift that had been seen before 1993.

The voter turnout in postwar Diet elections had fluctuated between about 68 and 77 percent in lower house elections and 57 and 75 percent in upper house elections until the late 1980s. In the 1990s, however, it fell steeply, from 73 percent in 1990 to 60 percent in 1996 in lower house elections and from 65 to 46 percent in upper house elections. In the latest upper house election of 1998, the turnout rate suddenly and unexpectedly rebounded to nearly 59 percent. Whether this was a freak event or marked a reversal of a long-term trend remains to be seen.

Political Culture, Citizenship, and Identity

As pointed out earlier, the Japanese are an ethnically and culturally homogeneous people with a well-developed sense of national identity. This sense was molded into a strong and aggressive nationalist ideology in prewar Japan, leading it to attempt to build a colonial empire in East Asia on the model of those created by European powers around the world. Japan's defeat in World War II put an end to the aggressive nationalist ideology and the dreams of empire. The strong sense of national identity, however, survived the war. The deep-rooted sense of belonging to an old and distinct nation sustained the efforts of the Japanese people to rebuild the war-ravaged economy and society and bring the nation back into a place in the sun.

At the heart of prewar Japanese national identity and nationalism was the quasi-Shinto cult of emperor worship. The cult inspired the drive to build a "rich nation, strong army" in the nineteenth century and an East Asian empire in the 1920s and 1930s. Either a secular religion or a substitute for a religion, the emperor cult had been fused with and nourished by another secular religion, Confucianism, which was imported from Korea by the fifth century. Confucianism, even more than Shinto or the quasi-Shinto emperor cult, has influenced and shaped the Japanese way of life, particularly attitudes toward the state, family, work, and education.

Religion has not been an important factor in modern Japanese politics or society. Most Japanese are nominally Buddhist and/or Shintoist, but their religious observance usually consists of visiting a shrine or temple on a festival day, hearing a Shinto priest intone at wedding ceremonies, or listening to a Buddhist monk's chant at a funeral service. The generally casual, often cavalier, attitude toward religion is reflected in the fact that many Japanese are not sure whether they are Buddhist or Shintoist and are in fact counted as both. For example, in 1995, when Japan's total population was about 125 million, there were more than 100 million Japanese Buddhists and nearly 65 million Shintoists. About 7 million Japanese belong to other, mostly newer, religions or cults, and there are nearly 1 million Christians.

Some Shinto and Buddhist organizations are politically active, usually as sponsors or supporters of conservative party (e.g., LDP) candidates in elections. One Buddhist organization, Sokagakkai (value-creation society), sponsors its own political party, the Komeito or Clean Government Party (CGP). The postwar Japanese constitution, like its U.S. model, provides for the separation of church (religion) and state (politics). This makes it theoretically impossible and practically very difficult for a religious organization such as Sokagakkai and its party to espouse an explicitly religious cause in an election or the national or local legislature.

The Japanese have built a society concerned nearly exclusively with matters of this world, such as economic success and material comfort. They enjoy the longest life expectancy at birth and one of the lowest infant mortality rates in the world. The enrollment rates of Japanese children in elementary and secondary schools are among the highest in the world. Virtually all Japanese families own a wide assortment of home appliances and electronic gadgets, such as color televisions, washing machines, vacuum cleaners, refrigerators, and automobiles.

Nonetheless, Japan remains a society with a Confucian fear of social conflict and a longing for order and harmony among and within all classes of people. In prewar Japan the Confucian ideology nurtured the idea of the unique nation ruled and protected by descendants of its original divine creator and to be revered by all its subjects as the source of their collective identity and the object of their boundless loyalty and devotion. In postwar Japan the nation as the object of personal loyalty has been largely replaced by a smaller organization or group, such as a firm; but the group-centered rather than individualistic view of life and society continues to prevail, with important political implications and consequences. For example, a company's management and labor union often jointly sponsor a particular candidate or slate of candidates in Diet or local elections.

The Japanese are among the best-educated people in the world. The six-year elementary and three-year lower secondary school education is compulsory, and virtually all children finish it. Moreover, over 95 percent of lower secondary school graduates go to three-year upper secondary schools, and over one-third of upper secondary school graduates go to two-year junior colleges or four-year universities. Schools are predominantly public, and private schools differ little from public schools in either organization or curriculum. All schools use very similar textbooks in all subject areas, thanks to the textbook certification system. All drafts of textbooks must be submitted to the Ministry of Education for inspection, often extensive revisions, and certification before they can be used in schools. This censorship system ensures that textbooks are generally consistent with the opinions, preferences, and prejudices of Ministry of Education inspectors. As a result, the history and social studies textbooks used in Japanese schools tend to avoid any controversial political issues. For example, they say little about the role of the emperor in the rise of Japanese imperialism, the constitutionality of the Self-Defense Forces, or the causes and consequences of Japanese trade protectionism. And, until 1997, they were silent on Japanese wartime atrocities, such as the attack on Chinese civilians known as the Rape of Nanjing.

The most important function of the school in contemporary Japan is to prepare students for entrance into either the job market or higher-level schools. Which school and, in particular, which university one attends largely determines what kind of job one will hold after graduation. Some universities are believed to prepare students better than others for the most prestigious companies or government agencies and therefore attract more and better-performing applicants to their entrance examinations. The preparatory mission common to all Japanese schools absorbs the bulk of their teachers' and students' time and energy, leaving little for acquiring knowledge for its own sake, learning to enjoy art, or developing critical faculties. On the other hand, the centralized and rigidly controlled educational system produces a literate, hardworking, and dedicated labor force.[32]

With a 99 percent literacy rate, contemporary Japan is also one of the most media-saturated societies. It has only about one-tenth as many daily newspapers as the United States and half as many as Germany, but many have far larger circulations than their U.S. or European counterparts. As a result, Japan boasts the highest total and per-person newspaper circulation among industrial nations. This is also true for books and magazines: some 43,000 new books per year, 3,000 monthly magazines, and 80 weekly magazines are published. Moreover, the average Japanese family owns two color televisions. The Japanese are thus exposed to a huge amount of media-purveyed information, although most of it is concerned with cultural and social news, such as sporting events, fashions, television personalities, and famous restaurants, not with political developments.

Japan's mainstream mass media are politically and socially conservative by American standards, due to the indirect but pervasive influence of the government and corporate management. Such influence is a function mainly of two characteristic features of the news business in contemporary Japan: the press club and the dependence on advertising. A press club consists of one or more reporters from each accredited member newspaper, television, and radio station. Each club is provided with rooms by the government or business it covers, and its members gather information mainly from the organization's official spokespersons. A reporter who seeks unofficial information risks losing good standing with the host organization and even club membership. The system thus works to suppress publication of news critical of government or corporate policy or deeds. In addition, since newspapers and privately owned television and radio stations depend on advertisements for a substantial portion of their income, they are reluctant to publish stories that could embarrass advertisers.

Interests, Social Movements, and Protest

Although Japan may appear politically conservative and quiescent—except at election time—it is not entirely free of political controversies. The constitutionality of rearmament and the Self-Defense Forces is one such issue; the constitutionality of official visits by government leaders, particularly cabinet members, to the Yasukuni Shrine is another. Public and elite opinion is so sharply and irreconcilably divided on both issues that they have been taken off the government's political agenda.

Environmental Issues

There are a number of other contentious issues in contemporary Japan. For example, the development and use of nuclear power by electric companies remains controversial in the only nation that has ever experienced the effects of an atomic bomb. The electric power industry and the LDP leadership have vigorously pushed the construction of nuclear reactors as an alternative to imported fuels, especially oil from the Middle East. Japan today is one of the world's major users of nuclear energy, with fifty reactors supplying about 30 percent of Japan's energy as of 1997. Still, a number of local communities and governments have vigorously opposed the construction of reactors in their own backyards. The opposition stiffened after the 1979 Three Mile Island accident in the United States and the 1986 Chernobyl disaster in the Soviet Union, forcing the suspension of construction plans and even the operation of some existing reactors at a number of sites around the country.

Rapid industrialization and urbanization have also given rise to intense conflicts over a number of other environmental issues. In fact, a series of extremely severe cases of industrial pollution in the 1950s and 1960s made Japan one of the world's best-known and most frequently cited victims of environmental hazards resulting from reckless industrialization. Cases include fatal mercury poisoning known as the **Minamata Disease**, which first occurred in Minamata City in southern Kyushu and later in northern Honshu, cadmium poisoning in central Honshu, and asthma in southwestern Honshu.

A set of stiff antipollution laws passed by the Diet in the early 1970s has helped prevent a recurrence of such devastating accidents. But citizens' concern about the continuing deterioration of the environment continues to spur battles in courtrooms and protests in the streets. Local citizens' opposition to noise, for example, often blocks or delays construction of new highways, railroads, and airports.

Violence and Terrorism

Most citizen protests are nonviolent and legal, but Japan is not free from violent conflicts. Most such conflicts involve extremist groups of either the left or the right who try to get their way by intimidating and occasionally attacking their opponents. At one end of the political spectrum are the student and youth groups known as the new left, including the Central Core, Revolutionary Marxists, and the Fourth International. The 10,200 or so members (as of 1997) of these groups have attacked symbols of authority in capitalist Japan, ranging from LDP headquarters and residences of members of the royal family to airports and nuclear power stations. Some engage in urban guerrilla actions using sophisticated time bombs and remote-controlled missiles, which often result in considerable property damage and occasionally human casualties. Their strength and effectiveness, however, have sharply declined in recent years, yielding to growing public hostility toward their extremist views and violent tactics and to their own internal conflicts.

The groups on the extreme right are far more numerous and better organized. There are about eight hundred rightist groups, with a combined membership of about 120,000. Most are vehemently chauvinist and anticommunist groups concerned—often more ostensibly than genuinely—about the future of the Japanese nation and its imperial tradition. Members of these groups have been involved in a series of shooting incidents targeting, for example, the mayor of Nagasaki City in 1990 for his remarks on the late Emperor Hirohito's responsibility for the last war, a former prime minister in 1994 for his remarks on the aggressive nature of Japan's role in World War II, and the JSP headquarters in 1995 for the party's support of a proposed antiwar resolution by the Diet.

In one of the most bizarre and frightening crimes committed in Japan in recent years, a cult group called Aum (from the Sanskrit magic word *Om*) released lethal doses of sarin gas to indiscriminately kill innocent citizens. The first attack occurred in June 1994 in a residential neighborhood in the central Japanese city of Matsumoto, killing 7 passersby and injuring about 150 others. Before the cult group was identified as the culprit, the second attack occurred inside subway trains in downtown Tokyo, killing 10 subway employees and passengers and injuring nearly 4,000 others. About two hundred members of the group were arrested, tried, and sentenced to prison. The motivation behind the crime is believed to have been the cult leader's personal grudge against society and the world.

Ethnic Minorities: Ainu, Outcastes, Koreans, and Immigrants

Belying its stereotype as a homogeneous society, contemporary Japan has some serious issues of collective identities to contend with, although they are neither as widespread nor as intense as those found in a number of other nations. Such issues are of great concern particularly to the numerically minuscule but increasingly vocal ethnic minority known as the Ainu, the much larger and far more vocal minority of former outcaste people, and Koreans and other resident foreigners.

The Ainu are descendants of the hunter-gatherers believed to have once inhabited the greater part of the northern half of the country. The traditional Ainu society had no concept of private property, and most of its communally owned land was taken by and distributed among new settlers from other regions of the country in a land "reform" undertaken by the Meiji government. The Ainu were left with only the land on which they lived in Japan's northernmost prefecture, Hokkaido. They were also forced to abandon hunting by government decree. Most Ainu quickly fell into extreme poverty. As the number of non-Ainu immigrants to Hokkaido grew, intermarriage increased. Today, about 25,000 Japanese are known to have some Ainu blood, but the number of full-blooded Ainu is estimated to be no more than a few hundred.

Since the Meiji period, the Ainu have ostensibly been protected by a "Law to Protect Former Natives of Hokkaido," but in practice little has been done to protect or help them. The Ainu community has long been afflicted with a high incidence of alcoholism, tuberculosis, and venereal disease. These problems, and the plight of the Ainu in general, were almost completely ignored by the Japanese government and public until the mid-1980s. When a prime minister thoughtlessly characterized Japan as a homogeneous nation, leaders of the Ainu community protested publicly. This led the prefectural government of Hokkaido to propose a new law to protect Ainu human rights, improve their social and economic condition, and preserve and promote their traditional culture. These efforts resulted in the enactment in 1997 of a new law popularly known as the Law to Promote Ainu Culture. The long-ignored problems of an important ethnic minority in the nation have been addressed at last. An Ainu scholar-author, Shigeru Kayano, ran as a candidate on the JSP proportional representation list in the 1992 upper house election and became the runner-up; two years later he filled a vacancy left by a deceased JSP member and became the first Ainu ever to serve in the Diet. He was instrumental in the enactment of the 1997 law.

The movement for the liberation of former outcaste people—descendants of those who had been forced to live in ghettos and work in occupations that were seen as unclean—and their residential neighborhoods picked up steam after World War II. In the 1970s a series of laws were passed to help "liberate" the approximately 4600 "discriminated hamlets" that still existed, mostly in the southwestern half of the country, and integrate the well over a million people who lived there into the broader national community. Considerable improvement has since been made in the economic conditions of former outcaste communities, but complete equality and integration into Japanese society, especially in areas such as employment and marriage, remain unfulfilled goals.

After the Meiji Restoration and especially after Japan annexed Korea in 1910, many Koreans began to migrate to Japan. Initially, they came to Japan voluntarily. By the 1930s, however, they were increasingly brought by force to work in some of the nation's most poorly equipped and accident-prone factories and mines. At the end of World War II more than 2 million Koreans were living in Japan. Most of them returned to South or North Korea, while a small minority acquired Japanese citizenship. About 650,000 Koreans currently live in Japan as resident aliens, some by choice but many because they are denied citizenship under the rules of Japanese immigration and naturalization policy.

There is substantial public support for allowing resident Koreans to vote and run as candidates in local legislative elections, though not in Diet elections. About 1,200 local legislatures, or well over one-third of the total, have adopted resolutions in favor of recognizing Korean residents' right to participate in local politics. The Supreme Court decided in 1995 that such a move would be constitutional. But the LDP and the Ministry of Home Affairs continue to oppose and have so far blocked the move.

The most important and difficult issue raised by ethnic minorities is not the physical hardships or material deprivations inflicted on them by deliberate government policy. In fact, many former outcaste communities have received generous financial assistance from both the national and local governments during the last three decades and today enjoy greatly improved community facilities, such as paved roads, well-equipped schools, public libraries, and community halls. Many Korean residents own successful businesses, mostly small enterprises such as restaurants and game parlors. The core problem facing the minorities in Japan is the social and cultural discrimination that they face, especially in employment and marriage.

Like many other advanced industrial societies, contemporary Japan has attracted many foreign workers, who often enter or stay in the country illegally. Nearly 300,000 foreign workers, mainly from Asia and the Middle East, were believed to be employed in Japan in the late 1990s, constituting the country's newest ethnic minority. Immigrants are a potential source of social tension over the issue of collective identities. They come to Japan in search of jobs, mostly menial, which pay much higher wages than they would be paid in their own countries. They are increasingly indispensable to many Japanese businesses suffering from chronic shortages of young and cheap workers. As in most high-wage industrial nations of North America and Western Europe, foreign workers are feared and resented by many Japanese, who see them as a threat to their own wages, pensions, free medical care, and even jobs in a period of recession. Unlike the situation in some European countries with much higher unemployment rates, no violent attacks on foreign workers by Japanese

citizens have been reported so far. The presence of a new ethnic minority nonetheless poses a particularly troubling problem to Japan, which has long prided itself on ethnic purity.

Women's Movement

Although there are very few women among Japanese legislators, senior bureaucrats, and judges, the movement to improve Japanese women's social and political status has a long history, dating back to the early part of the Meiji period. The movement had its origins in the democratic idea imported from the West at the time and was an important part of the "freedom and people's rights" movement in the 1880s. Japan's first major women's organization was the Tokyo Women's Temperance Union, founded in 1886, which campaigned mainly for the abolition of prostitution rather than alcohol. The Bluestocking Society, formed in 1911 by a group of younger women writers, attacked the traditional patriarchal family system and called for the expansion of educational and professional opportunities for women.

The Taisho Democracy era in the wake of World War I saw the birth of women's organizations more explicitly committed to achieving gender equality in politics. The Society of New Women founded in 1920 successfully lobbied the Imperial Diet to amend the Peace and Police Law, which prohibited women's participation in political parties and other political organizations. This was followed by the formation of Japan's first suffragist organization in 1924 and first openly socialist women's organization in 1929. In the 1930s, however, all these liberal women's organizations were disbanded and replaced by organizations promoting the traditional status and role of women as good homemakers, wives, and mothers.

The emancipation of women was one of the most important goals of the postwar reforms undertaken under the auspices of the occupation authorities. Japanese women were enfranchised for the first time and began to participate actively in politics as voters. Numerous women's organizations were founded, including the League of Japanese Women Voters, the Women's Democratic Club, and the Federation of Women's Organizations. Their presence and activities have helped to improve Japanese women's social status and political roles. As pointed out earlier, however, the actual participation of Japanese women in the nation's government and policy-making remains very limited.

Japan: A Classless Society?

Japanese society, under the Confucian view of the state as a big family where order and harmony prevail and everybody accepts his or her proper station, has never been hospitable to class-based identities. As Japan became increasingly affluent, what little class consciousness had developed among the working class during harder times steadily eroded. A high degree of social mobility contributed to the decline of class consciousness by blurring the boundaries between the classes. By the early 1970s about 90 percent of Japanese identified themselves as members of the middle class between the very rich and the very poor. Japan is often depicted as a classless society in which class distinctions have virtually disappeared in terms of income, wealth, consumption habits, lifestyles, levels of education, and basic values.

The emergence of the classless society has had an important political impact. In the mid-1950s slightly more than half of white-collar and blue-collar workers supported the JSP, while one-third supported the LDP; by the mid-1980s the ranks of JSP supporters had diminished to about one-fifth of the total, while the ranks of LDP supporters had increased to well over half. Business people and farmers have supported the LDP far more consistently. It is doubtful, however, that their partisanship results from class consciousness. It is more likely based on their personal and organizational involvement with the LDP and its Diet members. Class has been a weak basis for collective political action in contemporary Japan.

Apart from the sound trucks of various rightist groups, bedecked with the national flag and driven noisily around the streets of Tokyo and other major cities, today's Japan is still a politically quiet society whose citizens grumble privately rather than protest publicly.

Section 5   Japanese Politics in Transition

Japanese voters went to the polls in the summer of 1998 in a triennial upper house election. The LDP had returned to power in partnership with the JSP in the summer of 1994, after less than a year out of power. It had more fully returned to power in January 1996 by ditching the JSP and forming the first single-party government since 1993. On the eve of the 1998 upper house election, Prime Minister Ryutaro Hashimoto and other LDP leaders were hopeful that their party might win back the majority in the upper house that it had lost in 1989, so that the party could regain full control of the Diet and its business. The voters failed to cooperate: the LDP won 44 and the opposition 62 of the 126 contested seats. The LDP now had 103 seats, or 16 less than before, 23 short of the majority.

Blaming the stubborn recession for the electoral disaster, the Hashimoto cabinet resigned immediately and was succeeded by a new LDP cabinet led by Keizo Obuchi, the leader of the same LDP faction to which Hashimoto belonged. The passage of power from one leader of the largest LDP faction to another was consistent with the logic and tradition of LDP faction politics. The only innovation was the appointment as finance minister of the seventy-eight-year-old former prime minister, Kiichi Miyazawa, one of the few LDP politicians with some credentials in fiscal and banking policy. Judging by the magnitude of the LDP's defeat in the election, neither Obuchi nor Miyazawa represented the kind of change the voters wanted. Two months after the election, an Asahi newspaper poll found only 21 percent of the public approved of the new cabinet, the lowest level of support for any cabinet in a decade and even lower than the record low reached by Miyazawa's last cabinet in the spring of 1993. On the eve of a new century, Japan was a nation not only economically but also politically bruised and embittered.

Political Challenges and Changing Agendas

The main cause of the LDP's second electoral debacle in five years was obviously the prolonged and worsening recession and the widespread public perception that the Hashimoto government was incapable of fixing the problem. The problem was a combination of a prolonged recession caused by a bungled fiscal policy and a deepening banking crisis with its roots in the bubble economy of the 1980s. Amidst a continuing recession in 1997, the Hashimoto government had acted to dampen consumer spending by raising the consumption (sales) tax rate, pension premiums, and medical fees paid by patients covered by a public health insurance program, while simultaneously repealing temporary tax exemptions. The result was a further slide in the already record low growth rate of the Japanese economy.

Meanwhile, most of the nation's banks and finance companies were saddled with and gradually sinking under the weight of bad loans made to stock and real estate investors and speculators during the heyday of the bubble economy. By the end of 1997 many of the nation's largest banks and securities houses were already bankrupt or on the verge of bankruptcy. Their plight threatened to bankrupt not only their clients, particularly small businesses, and their depositors, including small savers, but the entire Japanese economy. Given the size and power of the contemporary Japanese economy, its collapse would have devastating impacts on the regional and global economies as well. Particularly serious would be the effects on the national economies in the Asia-Pacific region, many of which were already mired in banking crises caused by the bursting of their own bubble economies. Few doubted that the Japanese banking crisis had to be brought to an end, and quickly.

Opinion within Japan and the Japanese government was divided on two issues, however. How should the current crisis be dealt with in light of the chronic and worsening budget deficits and swelling public debt? More specifically, should the austerity policy initiated by the Hashimoto government in 1997 be continued or suspended in the face of the current crisis? Hashimoto and his cabinet flip-flopped on the issue and did too little too late to make a significant dent in either problem. The other issue was whether the bankrupt and near-bankrupt banks should be bailed out with taxpayers' money and, if so, on what conditions. The Hashimoto government and the LDP wanted to rescue at least the largest bank right away

"Ah, another bank bailout with taxpayers' money!" A fat banker receives a transfusion of "blood tax" from a taxpayer while comforted by the government in the guise of a nurse. *Source:* Isao Kojima, *Asahi shinbun*, Tokyo.

and virtually unconditionally, but the opposition balked, insisting on holding managers accountable for their mistakes, noting that bank managers and employees were among the highest paid in the nation. Divisions in public and media opinion reinforced the disagreement among the parties, contributing to the policy stalemate and inaction in the face of a deepening crisis.

Despite the sad state of its economy and the exasperating political stalemate, Japan remains an affluent and socially stable nation. Even after seven years of recession, its GNP (or GDP) per capita in 1998 was among the highest half dozen in the world. While Japan is rocked by heinous crimes from time to time, the frequency of such crimes is far lower than in any other advanced industrial nation—in 1995, less than half as high as in Britain, about one-fifth as high as in Germany, and less than one-eighth as high as in the United States. While the number of dropouts from elementary and lower middle school vastly increased in the 1990s—threefold at the elementary and twofold at the middle school level—they account for no more than about 1 percent and 3 percent, respectively, of the total number of students.

A problem of much greater concern is a dramatic demographic change, the graying of the population. Japan's current birth rate of about 10 per 1,000 is lower than that of any other nation with a substantial population, except Italy, Germany, Russia, and the Czech Republic. Japan is expected to have a higher percentage of citizens over sixty-five years of age by the year 2010 than any other advanced industrial nation. This must lead to a sharp rise in the cost of health care for old people and, at the same time, a significant fall in the number of younger and most productive workers, resulting in a general enfeeblement of the Japanese economy. These prospects worry both Japanese leaders and ordinary citizens and drive their efforts, so far unsuccessful, to reform and restructure the nation's economy, society, and politics.

In the area of foreign policy and relations, trade liberalization has been the most prominent and controversial issue both at home and abroad. Under rising foreign, especially U.S., pressure, both tariff and nontariff import restrictions have been gradually removed, and today's Japan is not significantly more protectionist than most other advanced industrial nations. The road toward freer Japanese markets, however, has been anything but smooth. When the quotas on imported beef and oranges were substantially enlarged in the 1980s, farmers fiercely opposed the decision and were quieted only by large amounts of compensation paid by the government, that is, by taxpayers. The determined opposition of farmers has kept Japan's 10-million-tons-per-year rice market virtually closed, despite the sustained pressure applied by the United States and other exporters. Given the state of the economy, further liberalization of agricultural imports—and of manufactured imports, for that matter—will be very difficult for the Japanese government and producers to accept. Trade disputes, often bitter enough to spill over into other issue areas such as mutual security, are likely to continue to plague Japan's relations with its trading partners, notably the United States and East Asian neighbors.

Japan faces another troubling international issue of considerable symbolic importance. Despite the dramatic change in its international status and role since World War II, Japan, along with its wartime allies, Germany and Italy, remains a pariah state in the text of the UN Charter. In 3 of its 111 articles, the Charter refers to these nations as enemy states, an expression Japan and the others have tried, so far in vain, to have expunged. Many Japanese support a larger role for Japan in the UN, especially a permanent seat on the Security Council. By the early 1990s, Japan had, in fact, begun to participate in an increasingly wide range of peacekeeping operations, in such places as Cambodia and Mozambique.

Japan's role in international politics remains, and must remain, limited under the terms of its pacifist constitution. While a vocal minority of Japanese citizens calls for a revision of the constitution, especially its war-renouncing article, the majority prefer to leave the original text of the document intact as a safeguard against involvement in another destructive war. In an April 1997 Asahi newspaper poll, 25 percent of the respondents thought the constitution should be revised immediately, 18 percent thought it should be revised sometime in the future, and 39 percent thought it should not be revised. When asked specifically about Article IX, 20 percent supported and 69 percent opposed its revision. Given the state of public sentiment, the Diet is unlikely to revise the MacArthur Constitution any time soon. Nor is Japan likely to play an international role of significant military nature in the foreseeable future.

In some important ways, however, Japanese values and attitudes are changing, if only gradually. Nationalism is not dead in today's Japan, but it has largely shed the bellicose racism and ethnocentrism that characterized its prewar variant. It is instructive in this regard to compare the way Japanese public agencies and private citizens treated foreigners, especially resident Koreans, in the aftermath of the great Tokyo earthquake of 1923 and the Kobe earthquake of 1995. In the former case, racist-inspired rumors led to a massacre of some 6,000 resident Koreans at the hands of both public officials and private citizens; in the latter case, Koreans thanked Japanese for treating every victim of the disaster equally regardless of his or her nationality or ethnicity. It is unlikely that Japanese nationalism will turn overtly racist or virulently xenophobic again in the ever smaller world of interdependent states.

Japanese Politics in Comparative Perspective

Japan is the only major non-Western advanced industrial state and the only non-Western member of the exclusive group of economically most powerful nations, the Group of Seven (G-7). Despite growing international concern about Japanese political and business leaders' ability to pull the nation out of the current economic troubles and continuing criticisms of some aspects of Japan's trade policy, there is still considerable confidence in the fundamental strength of its economy and democratic polity.

Japan thus presents a model of state-led development that worked successfully for more than a century but suddenly failed in the 1990s. This experience poses some obvious questions: Why did the model work for so long? Why did it seem to work more successfully in Japan than the rival model of market-led development in the earlier developed Western nations, notably Britain and the United States? Would the Japanese model work successfully in other non-Western, or even some Western, nations? Would it work successfully in other nations under certain domestic or international political or economic conditions but not under others? What conditions would facilitate or obstruct the application of the developmental state model?

Japanese society is also characterized by a number of distinctive cultural attributes, including high degrees of social cohesion and political stability, egalitarian income distribution, mass literacy, universal access to high-quality education, effective crime prevention, and a capable and dedicated government bureaucracy. Japan is a model of a non-Western nation that has succeeded in controlling the disruptive impact of modernization by preserving and utilizing many of its traditional cultural values and social institutions.

As the foregoing discussion has shown, many of the characteristics listed do not fit the Japan of today as well as the Japan of the 1970s or 1980s. The economic success of postwar Japan inspired many Asian nations. South Korea, Taiwan, and ASEAN members, such as Thailand, Malaysia, and Indonesia, are seen as having successfully adapted the developmental state model in modernizing their own economies. Like Japan, they used an assortment of government policies and institutions to facilitate human capital formation, high savings and investment rates, efficient resource allocation, and export expansion, leading to the rapid growth of their national economies. But today Japan is no longer a model of a successful miracle economy and polity.

Japan has often been cited as a model of so-called Asian-style democracy. The Western model of democratic government emphasizes active citizen participation in the affairs of the state, the role of independent political parties and interest groups, and the periodic alternation of power among competing political parties. The Japanese model, on the other hand, is said to rely on a passive and compliant citizenry and monopoly of power by one party or the government bureaucracy, at least during the early phase of development. Like Japan, most of its Asian neighbors tend to place far greater emphasis on economic growth and political stability than on citizen participation in government or the protection of political and human rights. This emphasis is particularly agreeable to those who believe in the Confucian ideal of an orderly, hierarchical, harmonious society governed by a wise and benevolent ruler with the support of a loyal and obedient citizenry. The model has often been used to justify repressive, authoritarian governments in many developing nations in contemporary Asia.

The state of Japanese politics and economy since the LDP's disastrous defeats in 1993 and 1998 calls into question the long-term viability of such a model of politics in contemporary Asia, not to mention democratic politics. Where there are deep economic, social, or ideological divisions in the population, democracy inevitably gives rise to political contention. Japan actually experienced intense political conflict during the formative period (1947–1960) of its postwar democracy. In fact, it took a major political crisis caused by a massive popular protest against the undemocratic and high-handed conduct of government in the 1960 revision of the U.S.-Japanese Mutual

Security Treaty to usher in the period of politics of compromise and consensus of the next three decades.

In other words, it took Japan a decade and a half of intense political conflict—and several more decades if one considers the struggle for democracy in prewar Japan—to learn to practice political democracy in peace. After the traumatic experience of 1960, the ruling LDP began to take the opposition's opinion and policies seriously and often to co-opt them. Many of the views and interests of organized labor, though not of unorganized workers or consumers, were incorporated into LDP programs through informal consultations and deals between the LDP and the opposition, if only to avert another political crisis.

Democracy thus did not get established in Japan in the absence of political conflict but rather in and through conflict, just as in Western Europe and the United States. The rupture of consensus and return of open conflict that led to the change of government in 1993 did not mean a breakdown of democracy in Japan. On the contrary, it reflected the strength and maturity of Japanese democracy by proving the ability of Japanese citizens to "throw the rascals out." Moreover, this changing of the guard gave the opposition an opportunity to learn how to govern and the LDP an opportunity to learn how to oppose within the framework of democratic government. While this first change of government in Japan in nearly forty years did not last long, it may have set an important precedent for the years to come, leading to a transition from a one-party-dominant system to an effective two-party or multiparty system.

The interruption of the LDP's perennial rule has helped make not only the LDP but all parties, and the Japanese government as a whole, more sensitive to public opinion and less beholden to special interests. For example, the coalition government formed in the wake of the 1993 general election was severely critical of the economic-growth-at-any-cost approach long followed by the LDP. In early 1994 the JSP minister of construction decided to review a controversial plan to build a dam on a river in central Japan that was home to a number of increasingly endangered native fishes. The plan had been approved by the LDP government in the early 1970s but was strongly opposed by local

fishermen and by virtually all environmentalist groups in the country. Later in 1994 the LDP-JSP-NPH coalition government led by a JSP prime minister decided to make a substantial cut in the growth rate of defense spending. It proposed a 0.9 percent increase over the previous year's budget, compared to a 1.9 percent increase approved by the LDP government in the 1993 budget. Japan appears poised to part with the one-party dominance model of democracy in favor of one more similar to the Western model in terms of responsiveness and accountability.

In one respect, however, Japan remains an uncommon nation. It continues to refuse to acquire a level of military power commensurate with its economic power. It remains a unique state with a constitution that renounces its right to maintain armed forces or to engage in belligerent international acts. In practice, Japan does maintain the Self-Defense Forces with a narrowly defined operational mandate and devotes a modest portion of its GNP to military spending. Most Japanese leaders and people have been happy to live with this imbalance between their nation's economic and military power. Despite the persistent pressure by Washington for Japan to embark on a more ambitious rearmament program, the Japanese have refused to risk repeating their prewar mistakes, continuing to affirm the pacifism that has become an integral part of their national identity.

The most important lesson one can learn from present-day Japan, then, is the way it has begun to adapt to the dramatic changes of the post–Cold War international system by changing some of the conventional rules of its politics. Many of its old policies and practices are being reviewed, formally or informally, and some have been abandoned or drastically modified, while new ones are being explored and developed. There is a good chance that Japan will negotiate this transition successfully and become a more robust democracy.

As the twenty-first century dawns, however, the first order of business for Japan is to find a way out of the current economic slump as quickly as possible, for the sake not only of the Japanese people but of many others in the Asia-Pacific region and, indeed, in the increasingly interdependent world.

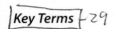 **Key Terms** — 29

- ✗ *bushi*
- ✗ *zaibatsu*
- Taisho Democracy
- Supreme Commander for the Allied Powers (SCAP)
- Self-Defense Forces (SDF)
- ✗ predominant-party regime
- ✗ *Sohyo*
- ✗ *Domei*
- ✗ *Rengo*
- industrial policy
- ✗ land reform
- administrative guidance
- convoy system
- *keiretsu*
- ✗ dual-structure system
- spring labor offensive
- lifetime employment
- nontariff barriers
- Asian Development Bank (ADB)
- Asia Pacific Economic Cooperation (APEC)
- Association of Southeast Asian Nations (ASEAN)
- ✗ Fiscal Investment and Loan Program (FILP)
- ✗ vertically divided administration
- *amakudari*
- *zoku*
- iron triangles
- *koenkai*
- clientelism
- Minamata Disease

Suggested Readings

Abe, Hitoshi, Muneyuki Shindo, and Sadafumi Kawato. *The Government and Politics of Japan*. Trans. James White. Tokyo: University of Tokyo Press, 1994.

Allinson, Gary D., and Yasunori Sone, eds. *Political Dynamics in Contemporary Japan*. Ithaca, N.Y.: Cornell University Press, 1993.

Barnhard, Michael A. *Japan Prepares for Total War: The Search for Economic Security, 1919–1941*. Ithaca, N.Y.: Cornell University Press, 1987.

Calder, Kent E. *Crisis and Compensation: Public Policy and Political Stability in Japan, 1949–1986*. Princeton, N.J.: Princeton University Press, 1988.

———. *Strategic Capitalism: Private Business and Public Purpose in Japanese Industrial Finance*. Princeton, N.J.: Princeton University Press, 1993.

Francks, Penelope. *Japanese Economic Development: Theory and Practice*. London: Routledge, 1992.

Fruin, W. Mark. *The Japanese Enterprise System: Competitive Strategies and Cooperative Structures*. Oxford: Clarendon Press, 1992.

Gluck, Carol. *Japan's Modern Myths: Ideology in the Late Meiji Period*. Princeton, N.J.: Princeton University Press, 1985.

Hall, John Whitney, et al., eds., *The Cambridge History of Japan*. 6 vols. Cambridge, U.K.: Cambridge University Press, 1988–1993.

Hayao, Kenji. *The Japanese Prime Minister and Public Policy*. Pittsburgh: University of Pittsburgh Press, 1993.

Ishida, Takeshi, and Ellis S. Krauss, eds. *Democracy in Japan*. Pittsburgh: University of Pittsburgh Press, 1989.

Johnson, Chalmers. *MITI and the Japanese Miracle: The Growth of Industrial Policy, 1925–1975*. Stanford, Calif.: Stanford University Press, 1982.

Kohno, Masaru. *Japan's Postwar Party Politics*. Princeton, N.J.: Princeton University Press, 1997.

Lincoln, Edward J. *Japan's New Global Role*. Washington, D.C.: Brookings Institution, 1993.

Lockwood, William W. *The Economic Development of Japan: Growth and Structural Change, 1868–1938*. Princeton, N.J.: Princeton University Press, 1954.

Miyashita, Kenichi, and David Russell. *Keiretsu: Inside the Hidden Japanese Conglomerates*. New York: McGraw-Hill, 1994.

Morikawa, Hidemasa. *Zaibatsu: The Rise and Fall of Family Enterprise Groups in Japan*. Tokyo: University of Tokyo Press, 1992.

Nakamura, Takafusa. *The Postwar Japanese Economy: Its Development and Structure, 1937–1994*. 2d ed. Trans. Jacqueline Kaminski. Tokyo: University of Tokyo Press, 1995.

Ramseyer, J. Mark, and Frances M. Rosenbluth. *The Politics of Oligarchy: Institutional Choice in Imperial Japan*. Cambridge, U.K.: Cambridge University Press, 1995.

Samuels, Richard J. *"Rich Nation, Strong Army": National Security and the Technological Transformation of Japan*. Ithaca, N.Y.: Cornell University Press, 1994.

Schlesinger, Jacob M. *Shadow Shogun: The Rise and Fall of Japan's Postwar Political Machine*. New York: Simon and Schuster, 1997.

Upham, Frank K. *Law and Social Change in Postwar Japan*. Cambridge, Mass.: Harvard University Press, 1987.

Endnotes

[1] George Sansom, *A History of Japan, 1334–1615* (Stanford, Calif.: Stanford University Press, 1961); A. L. Sadler, *A Short History of Japan* (Sydney: Angus and Robertson, 1963), Ch. 4–6.

[2] George De Vos and Hiroshi Wagatsuma, eds., *Japan's Invisible Race: Caste in Culture and Personality* (Berkeley: University of California Press, 1966); Frank K. Upham, *Law and Social Change in Postwar Japan* (Cambridge, Mass.: Harvard University Press, 1987), Ch. 3.

[3] Mikiso Hane, *Modern Japan: A Historical Survey* (Boulder, Colo.: Westview Press, 1986), 35–37.

[4] Ronald P. Dore, *Education in Tokugawa Japan* (London: Athlone, 1965).

[5] Alfred Tamarin, *Japan and the United States: Early Encounters 1791–1860* (London: Macmillan, 1970); Peter Booth Wiley, with Korogi Ichiro, *Yankees in the Land of the Gods: Commodore Perry and the Opening of Japan* (New York: Viking, 1990).

[6] W. G. Beasley, *Japan Encounters the Barbarian: Japanese Travellers in America and Europe* (New Haven, Conn.: Yale University Press, 1995), Ch. 9.

[7] Richard J. Samuels, *"Rich Nation, Strong Army": National Security and the Technological Transformation of Japan.* (Ithaca, N.Y.: Cornell University Press, 1994), Ch. 2.

[8] Robert A. Scalapino, *Democracy and the Party Movement in Prewar Japan* (Berkeley: University of California Press, 1962), Ch. 2–4.

[9] Peter Duus, *Party Rivalry and Political Change in Taisho Japan* (Cambridge, Mass.: Harvard University Press, 1968).

[10] Sadako N. Ogata, *Defiance in Manchuria: The Making of Japanese Foreign Policy, 1931–1932* (Berkeley: University of California Press, 1964), Pt. II.

[11] Ben-Ami Shillony, *Revolt in Japan: The Young Officers and the February 26, 1936 Incident* (Princeton, N.J.: Princeton University Press, 1973).

[12] Herbert Feis, *The Road to Pearl Harbor: The Coming of the War Between the United States and Japan* (Princeton, N.J.: Princeton University Press, 1950).

[13] Robert E. Ward and Sakamoto Yoshikazu, eds., *Democratizing Japan: The Allied Occupation* (Honolulu: University of Hawaii Press, 1987).

[14] Haruhiro Fukui and Shigeko N. Fukai, "The End of the Miracle: Japanese Politics in the Post–Cold War Era," in *The Rise of East Asia: Critical Visions of the Pacific Century,* ed. Mark T. Berger and Douglas A. Borer (New York: Routledge, 1997), 37–60.

[15] Charles C. Ragin, *The Comparative Method: Moving Beyond Qualitative and Quantitative Strategies* (Berkeley: University of California Press, 1987), Ch. 3; Adam Preworski and Henry Teune, *The Logic of Comparative Social Inquiry* (New York: Wiley-Interscience, 1970).

[16] Hugh Patrick and Henry Rosovsky, "Japan's Economic Performance: An Overview," in *Asia's New Giant: How the Japanese Economy Works,* ed. Hugh Patrick and Henry Rosovsky (Washington, D.C.: Brookings Institution, 1976), 7–9; Kazuo Yamaguchi, "Early Modern Economy (1868–1945)," in *Kodansha Encyclopedia of Japan,* vol. 2 (Tokyo: Kodansha Ltd., 1983), 151–154.

[17] William W. Lockwood, *The Economic Development of Japan: Growth and Structural Change, 1868–1938* (Princeton, N.J.: Princeton University Press, 1954), 38–39.

[18] Ronald P. Dore, *Land Reform in Japan* (London: Oxford University Press, 1959), 176, Table 9.

[19] Lockwood, *The Economic Development of Japan,* 14–15.

[20] Hidemasa Morikawa, *Zaibatsu: The Rise and Fall of Family Enterprise Groups in Japan* (Tokyo: University of Tokyo Press, 1992).

[21] Daniel I. Okimoto, *Between MITI and the Market: Japanese Industrial Policy for High Technology* (Stanford, Calif.: Stanford University Press, 1989), Ch. 2.

[22] Nihon fujin dantai rengokai [Japanese Federation of Women's Organizations], ed., *Fujin hakusho 1998* [*White Book on Women*] (Tokyo: Horupu shuppan, 1998), 297, Table 103.

[23] Nihon fujin dantai rengokai, *Fujin hakusho 1998,* 18, Fig. 2.

[24] Richard Rosecrance, *The Rise of the Trading State* (New York: Basic Books, 1986).

[25] Asahi shinbunsha, *Asahi nenkan 1998* [*Asahi Yearbook 1998*] (Tokyo: Asahi shinbunsha, 1998), 633.

[26] Stephen D. Cohen, *Cowboys and Samurai: Why the United States Is Losing the Industrial Battle and Why It Matters* (New York: HarperBusiness, 1991).

[27] Stephen S. Large, *Emperor Hirohito and Showa Japan: A Political Biography* (London: Routledge, 1992).

[28] Tadahiro Fujikawa, "Nature of Japanese Bureaucracy Hinders Ability to Conduct Coordinated Relief Effort," *Nikkei Weekly,* January 30, 1995, 7.

[29] Michio Muramatsu, *Local Power in the Japanese State,* trans. Betsey Sheiner and James White (Berkeley: University of California Press, 1997).

[30] Tomohito Shinoda, "Japan's Decision Making under the Coalition Governments," *Asian Survey* 38:7 (July 1998), 703–723.

[31] Haruhiro Fukui, "Japan," in *Passages to Power: Legislative Recruitment in Advanced Democracies,* ed. Pippa Norris (Cambridge, U.K.: Cambridge University Press, 1997), 106–108.

[32] Thomas P. Rohlen, *Japan's High Schools* (Berkeley: University of California Press, 1983). For an overview of contemporary Japanese school education, see Thomas P. Rohlen and Chris Björk, eds., *Education and Training in Japan,* 3 vols. (London: Routledge, 1998).

CHAPTER 6

India

Atul Kohli

Republic of India

Land and Population

Capital	New Delhi
Total Area (square miles)	1,222,559 (slightly more than one-third the size of the U.S.)
Population	961 million
Annual Average Population Growth Rate (1990–1997)	1.8%
Urban Population (% of total)	27%

Major Languages*		
	Hindi	38.77%
	Telugu	7.96%
	Bengali	7.56%
	Marathi	7.28%
	Tamil	6.56%
	Other	31.87%

Hindi is the main language, but English is the most important language for political, commercial, and other national-level communication.

Religious Affiliation		
	Hindu	80.3%
	Muslim	11.0%
	Christian	3.7%
	Sikh	2.0%
	Buddhist and other	3.0%

Economy

Domestic Currency	Rupee	
Total GNP (US$)	$373.9 billion	
GNP per capita (US$)	$390	
GNP per capita at purchasing power parity (US$)	$1650	
GNP average annual growth rate (1996–1997)		5.0%
GNP per capita average annual growth rate	1996–1997	3.2%
	1980–1995	3.2%
	1965–1980	1.5%
Income Gap: **GDP per capita (US$)**	Richest 20% of population $4288	
	Poorest 20% of population $907	
Structure of Production (% of GDP)	Agriculture	29%
	Industry	29%
	Services	41%
Labor Force Distribution (% of total)	Agriculture	64%
	Industry	16%
	Services	20%
Exports as % of GDP	12%	
Imports as % of GDP	15%	

Electricity Consumption per capita (kwh)	448
CO$_2$ Emissions per capita (metric tons)	1

Society

Life Expectancy	Female	61.8
	Male	61.4
Doctors per 100,000 people		48
Infant Mortality (per 1000 live births)		73
Adult Literacy	Female	37.7%
	Male	65.5%
Access to Information and Communications (per 1000 people)	Radios	81
	Televisions	61
	Telephone Lines	13
	Personal Computers	1.2

Women in Government and Economy	
Women in Parliament	2.6%
Women at ministerial level	4.0%
Women as % of total labor force	31.0%
Female business administrators and managers	2.0%
Female professional and technical workers	21.0%
1998 Human Development Index ranking (out of 174 countries; 1 = highest)	139

Political Organization

Political System   Parliamentary democracy and a federal republic.

Regime History   Current government formed by the Bharatiya Janata Party (BJP), under the leadership of Atal Behari Vajpayee.

Administrative Structure   Federal, with 26 state governments.

Executive   Prime minister, leader of the party with the most seats in the parliament.

Legislature   Bicameral, upper house elected indirectly and without much substantial power; lower house, the main house, with members elected from single-member districts, winner-take-all.

Judiciary   Independent constitutional court with appointed judges.

Party System   Multiparty system. Congress Party is dominant; major opposition parties include Bharatiya Janata Party (BJP), Janata Party, and the Communist Party of India, Marxist (CPM).

Politics in Action

On December 6, 1992, thousands of Hindus, encouraged by a leading opposition party, the Bharatiya Janata Party (BJP), stormed and destroyed an Islamic mosque in Ayodhya, India.

In May 1998, the BJP-led coalition government proclaimed that India was a nuclear power, since it had successfully detonated five underground nuclear explosions.

The tense, tumultuous, and bloody trek from Ayodhya to the nuclear bomb highlights the turbulent nature of Indian democracy at the end of the twentieth century. The Ayodhya incident was triggered by the electoral mobilization strategies of the Bharatiya Janata Party (BJP—Indian People's Party), a religious, nationalist party that had been courting the electoral and political support of **Hindus**, India's largest religious group at over 80 percent of the country's population. BJP leaders argued that the Islamic mosque at Ayodhya, a place of worship for India's **Muslims**, who constitute nearly 11 percent of India's population, had been built on the site that the BJP claimed was the birthplace of the Hindu god Rama. They wanted to replace the mosque with a Hindu temple. When the ruling party of that time, India's main centrist party, the Indian National Congress (or Congress Party), refused to allow demolition of the mosque, the BJP mobilized Hindus, including unemployed youth and small traders throughout India, in political protest. The political use of religious symbols touched a raw nerve in a multiethnic society in which religious conflict has a long history and in which stories and memories of communal hostility and suspicion are ever-present. After all, Indian independence in 1947 was achieved in an atmosphere of sectarian violence accompanying the dismemberment of the country into India and Pakistan. The ambivalent attitude of the Congress-led national government of that time in 1992 toward the growing Hindu mobilization highlights the challenge faced by Indian politics today. On the one hand, the government needed to protect India's minorities and maintain law and order, but on the other hand, the Congress Party was afraid of alienating the Hindu majority group, whose electoral support was crucial for winning future elections. As the national government hesitated, thousands of Hindus raged out of control and demolished the mosque at Ayodhya.

A crowd of Hindu fundamentalists listens to speeches by leaders around a disputed mosque in Ayodhya, a town in northern India, on December 6, 1992. The mosque was later torn down by belligerent volunteers, precipitating a major political crisis. *Source:* Reuters/ Bettmann.

The BJP's political mobilization using religious divisions was quite successful, culminating in its emergence as India's ruling party in March 1998 parlimentary elections. Shortly afterwards, in fulfillment of one of the BJP's electoral promises, the BJP-led coalition government gate-crashed the nuclear club, triggering a nuclear arms race in South Asia. Though the Indian government cited regional threats from China and Pakistan as the key reason, the decision to become a nuclear state can also be traced directly to the evolution of domestic politics of democracy in India since the late 1980s. The electoral mobilization along ethnic lines (religious, language, or caste) interacted with demands by the mobilized groups for more influence in an atmosphere of economic turmoil and poverty. The nuclear detonations provided a ready tool for mobilizing Indians under the slogan of national pride and turned popular attention away from the domestic woes of poverty and crises of government. By the end of May, India's archenemy and neighbor, Pakistan, had responded by testing its own bomb. Swift worldwide condemnation followed as economic and technology sanctions were imposed on both countries as punishment for the explosions. Over the course of 1998 tensions were managed through diplomatic channels organized by the United States and other Western powers.

The two incidents thus capture three important themes in contemporary Indian politics. First, political struggles in a relatively poor democracy are especially likely to be contentious. Given the multicultural nature of India, many of these struggles readily become ethnic conflicts; the lines of conflict are sometimes defined along religious affiliations, at other times, along language, caste, or territorial attachments. Second, attempts to satisfy the demands of the mobilized groups could lead to nationalistic and sometimes dangerous results, as witnessed by the decision to become overtly nuclear. And third, although growing conflicts often push Indian politics to the brink, for over half a century India's democracy has managed to somehow pull back, absorb the crises, and muddle through, albeit with a strained democratic system. The central dilemma for India is how a democratic government can simultaneously accommodate the demands of its diverse social groups and create a wealthier, egalitarian, and stable society.

Geographic Setting

India is a large, populous, and geographically and culturally diverse country. Its large size, at approximately 2,000 miles (3,200 kilometers) in both length and width, is rivaled in Asia only by China. And its rich geographic setting includes three diverse

Indian nuclear test, May 1998. *Source:* Baldev/Sygma.

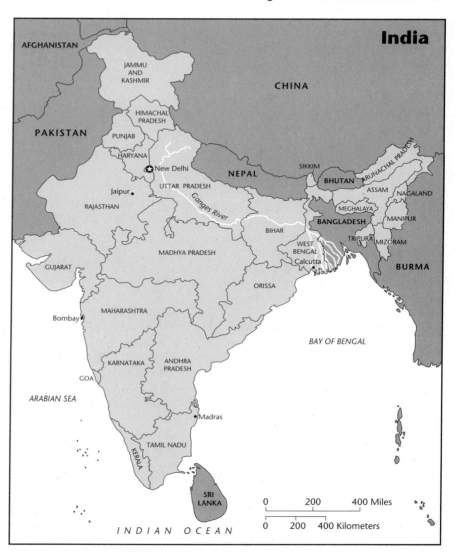

topographical zones (the mountainous northern zone, the basin formed by the Ganges river, and the peninsula of southern India) and a variety of climates (mountain climate in the northern mountain range; dry, hot weather in the arid, northern plateau; and subtropical climate in the south). Along with its neighbors Pakistan and Bangladesh, the region is physically isolated from the rest of Asia by the Himalayas to the north and the Indian Ocean to the east, south, and west. The northwest frontier is the only permeable frontier, and it is the route successive series of invaders and migrants have used to enter this region.

With a population of over 900 million (nearly the population of all African and Latin American countries combined), India is the second most populous country in the world, after its neighbor China. It is the world's largest democracy and the oldest democracy among the developing countries of Asia, Africa, and Latin America. India has functioned as a democracy with full adult suffrage since the late 1940s, when it emerged as a sovereign nation-state following the end of British colonial rule. The durability of Indian democracy is especially intriguing considering the diversity of Indian society. Some fourteen major languages and numerous dialects are spoken in India. Although Hinduism is the religion of four out of five Indians, people subscribing to nearly every one of the world's great religions live in India. These include many different ethnic groups, such as different, regionally concentrated tribal groups, as well as different religious minority groups such as Muslims, **Sikhs**, Jains, Buddhists and Christians. Furthermore, Indian society, especially the Hindu society, is divided into a myriad of castes. Although these are mainly occupation groups, they also tend to be closed social groups in the sense that people are born into, marry, and die within their caste.

Critical Junctures

India is among the most ancient civilizations of the world, dating back to the third millennium B.C. The Indian subcontinent, comprising Pakistan, India, and Bangladesh, has witnessed the rise and fall of many civilizations and empires. Only the most recent legacies that have shaped present-day politics are reviewed here. Of these, four are especially significant. First is the impact of nearly two hundred years of British colonial rule on the subcontinent from the mid-eighteenth to the mid-twentieth century, from which India and Pakistan emerged as sovereign states in 1947. Independent India inherited a relatively stagnant economy and a nationalist movement committed to bringing prosperity to a new nation. Second is the Nehru era (1947–1964), during which India developed a democratic and federal system of government and a planned economy. Third is the era of Indira Gandhi (1966–1984), under whom democratic politics became more populist and turbulent; her left-leaning rhetoric also failed to relieve India's considerable poverty. And fourth, in the 1990s, is the rise of opposition parties, most notably the BJP, more fragmented and fragile government coalitions, and the change in India's international role through its emergence as a nuclear power.

The Colonial Legacy (1757–1947)

Motivated by a combination of economic and political interests, the British started making inroads into the Indian subcontinent in the late seventeenth and early eighteenth centuries. Since 1526 large sections of the subcontinent had been ruled by the Mughal dynasty, who hailed from Central Asia and were Muslim by religion. As the power of the Mughal emperors declined in the eighteenth century, lesser princely contenders vied with one another for supremacy. In this environment the British East India Company—a large English trading organization with commercial interests in India and strong backing for its ventures from the British Crown—was able to play off one Indian prince against another, forming alliances with some, subduing others, and thus managing to enhance its control by a policy of divide and rule.

This informal empire was replaced in the mid-nineteenth century with a more formal one. After a major revolt by an alliance of Indian princes against growing British power—an incident known in Indian history as the Sepoy Rebellion or the Mutiny of 1857—the British Crown assumed the direct control of India. British rule over India from 1857 to 1947 left important legacies for the future of Indian politics. Like other colonies, India contributed to Britain's Industrial Revolution because it was a source of cheap raw materials and provided an outlet for both British manufactured goods and investment. Colonial rule in India also provided a model for subsequent British colonial ventures, for example, in Nigeria.

In order to consolidate their political and economic hold over India, the British entered into alliances with India's traditional ruling groups and eventually helped form a modern central government. The British created three main varieties of ruling arrangements within India. First, numerous small- to medium-sized states—as many as five hundred—covering an area equal to two-fifths of the subcontinent, continued to be ruled through the colonial period by traditional Indian princes, the **Maharajas**. In exchange for accepting British rule, these Indian princely states were allowed a relatively free hand within their realms. Second, in other parts of India, British indirect rule penetrated more deeply than in the princely states, for example, in the Bengal area with the introduction of modern educational institutions some educated Indians were incorporated into these government services. Unlike in some other colonies, especially those in Africa, the British in India helped create a relatively effective state structure. When India emerged from British rule in 1947, the new Indian state inherited, maintained, and expanded these colonial institutions. Since the civil, police, and armed services in contemporary India continue to be organized along the principles established by the British colonialists in the last century, it is fair to suggest that the roots of the modern Indian state can be traced back to their colonial origins.

The Nationalist Movement (1885–1947)

With the growth of commerce, education, and urban life, groups of urban, educated Indian elites, often of high caste origin, emerged as the new Indian "middle classes." They both observed and closely interacted with their colonial rulers and often felt slighted by their treatment as second-class citizens. Among these were early Hindu nationalists who believed that a reformed Hinduism could provide a basis for a new, modern India. Others were attracted to British liberal ideas and invoked these to seek greater equality with the British.

The two centuries of British colonial rule witnessed growing intellectual and cultural ferment in India. The British colonial rulers and traditional Indian elites had become allies of sorts, squeezing from the poor Indian peasantry resources that were simultaneously used to maintain the colonial bureaucratic state and to support the conspicuous life-styles of a parasitic landlord class. It was not long before Indian nationalists sought to oppose these arrangements, by founding the Indian National Congress (INC) in 1885. Its aim was to right the racial, cultural, and political wrongs of colonial rule.

In its early years, the INC was mainly a collection of Indian urban elites who periodically met and sent petitions to India's British rulers, invoking liberal principles of political equality and requesting greater Indian involvement in higher political offices. The British largely ignored these requests, and over time the requests turned into demands, pushing some angry

(currently Bihar, West Bengal, and Bangladesh). In these regions, the British transformed traditional Indian elites, who controlled much agricultural land, into legal landlords, the **zamindars**, in exchange for periodic payments to the colonial administration. Third, the British established direct rule in other parts of India, for example, in Bombay and the Madras presidencies (large areas around the cities of the same name), where British civil servants were directly responsible for collecting land taxes and for adjudicating law and order.

Although British rule in India took on a variety of forms, it seldom reached very deep into Indian society, especially in rural areas, which were organized into many relatively self-sufficient villages. Within villages, social life was further divided into religiously sanctioned caste groups, with some landowning castes dominating many other castes lower in the ritual hierarchy and occupational and income scales.

A semblance of coherence to British rule in India was achieved through the creation of a central government that could impose control over these various territories and indigenous authority structures. The British thus helped create an all-India civil service, police force, and army. Although at first only British nationals could serve in these institutions,

Leaders: *Mohandas Gandhi*

Born in 1869 in western India, Mohandas Gandhi studied law in London for two years and worked in Durban, South Africa, as a lawyer and an activist for twenty-one years before returning home to join the Indian nationalist movement. His work among the different communities in South Africa helped him to develop the political strategies of nonviolence, or *satyagraha* ("grasp of truth"). On his arrival in India in 1915, he set about transforming the Indian National Congress into a mass party by reaching out to the urban and rural poor, non-Hindu religious groups, and the scheduled castes, whom he called *Harijans*, or Children of God.

Following the British massacre of unarmed civilians gathered in protest in the Punjab (at the Jallianwala Bagh, a location well known in Indian history) in April 1919, Gandhi and Jawaharlal Nehru proposed a noncooperation movement. This required a boycott of British legal and educational institutions as well as British merchandise, for which were substituted indigenous, or *swadeshi*, varieties. (The image of Gandhi weaving his own cloth is familiar to many.) Gandhi believed that mass civil disobedience could succeed only if people were truly committed; the involvement of some Congress workers in a violent incident in 1922 greatly disturbed him, causing him to call off the noncooperation movement.

Gandhi was strongly opposed to the partition of India along religious lines in 1947, but because he had resigned from the Congress in 1934, his protests went unheard. Nevertheless, he dominated India's nationalist movement for more than two decades until he was assassinated in January 1948, five short months after India achieved its goal of self-rule, or *swaraj*. He is often referred to as the Mahatma, or "great soul."

Mahatma Gandhi, the leader of India's independence movement as he appeared at the head of a 200-mile march, staged in defiance of the statute establishing a government salt monopoly by the British colonial government in 1930. *Source:* UPI/Bettmann.

Indian elites into militancy and others into the nonviolent mobilization of the Indian masses.

World War I was an important turning point for Indian nationalists. After the war, as great European empires disintegrated, creating new sovereign states in Europe and the Middle East, the principle of self-determination for people who considered themselves a nation gained international respectability. The Russian revolution of 1917 also encouraged Indian nationalists because they interpreted it as a successful rising against imperialism.

The man most responsible for helping transform the INC from a narrow, elitist club to a mass nationalist movement was Mohandas Karamchand Gandhi, called Mahatma ("great soul") by his followers, one of the most influential and admirable leaders of the twentieth century. After becoming the leader of the INC in the 1920s, Gandhi successfully mobilized the Indian middle classes, as well as a segment of the Indian peasantry, into an anti-British movement that came to demand full sovereignty for India.

Three characteristics of the nationalist movement greatly influenced state-building and democracy in India. First, within what is now modern India, the INC succeeded in bringing together a wide variety of Indians in a relatively cohesive nationalist movement. Indians of different economic classes, castes, and ethnic backgrounds came to share some core political values. Because the INC became a powerful political organization committed to establishing an Indian nation, many conflicts could play themselves out within the INC as long as they did not threaten the cause of the Indian nation. The INC thus came to embody the principle of "unity within diversity," a principle that served India well in creating and maintaining a relatively stable political system.

Second, although a variety of Indians in their encounter with the British discovered what they had in common with each other—that is, their Indianness—they also recognized their differences, especially their different languages and their different gods. Even Hindus, India's majority population, are a highly diverse lot. There is no organized church in Hinduism; Hindus worship a variety of deities; and they are divided among themselves along different castes. As leaders of the INC sought to unite Indians against the British, some Indian groups became suspicious of other Indian groups. With much to gain by emphasizing the divisions among Indians, whenever the opportunity arose the British favored one group over another, thus contributing to growing divisiveness.

The most serious conflict was between Hindus and Muslims. A segment of the Indian Muslim elite refused to accept the leadership of Gandhi and the INC, demanded separate political rights for Muslims, and when the INC refused, demanded a separate Muslim state. The eventual division of the Indian subcontinent into the two states of India and Pakistan, and subsequent Hindu-Muslim hostilities within India (including those in the Indian state of Kashmir today), originated in the discovery of these differences.

And third, although the INC opposed British rule in India, it did so in a manner that was consistent with democratic norms. Many of the INC's prominent leaders, like Jawaharlal Nehru, were educated in England and were committed democrats. Gandhi's mobilizational style was also largely nonviolent. Moreover, the INC participated in limited elections allowed by the British, ran democratic governments with limited powers in various British Indian provinces, and elected its own leaders through internal elections within the INC. These pre-independence democratic tendencies were valuable assets for the subsequent success of democracy in India.

During the 1920s and 1930s, Gandhi, Nehru, and other leaders of the INC were increasingly successful in mobilizing Indians in an anti-British nationalist movement for India's independence. The more successful the movement became, the more the British had to either repress the INC or make concessions, and they tried both. However, World War II consumed Britain's energies so that the government could not simultaneously deal with a major European war and insurgent colonies. In order to gain Indian support for its war efforts, the British promised Indians greater independence following the war.

The Nehru Era (1947–1964)

India became a sovereign state in August 1947, when the British, weakened from World War II, decided to withdraw from the subcontinent. The resulting division of the subcontinent into two sovereign states—the Muslim state of Pakistan and the secular state of India—was a turbulent, bloody affair. Millions of Muslims rushed from India to Pakistan, and millions of Hindus fled the other way; over 10 million people migrated and nearly half a million died in communal violence. The euphoria of independence in India was thus tempered by the human tragedy that accompanied the subcontinent's partition.

Within India, Nehru, who was initially favored by Gandhi, emerged as the leader of the new nation. Soon thereafter Gandhi, who opposed the partition and later ardently defended Muslims within India, was assassinated by a Hindu fanatic. Nehru had become the uncontested leader of a new India, a position he maintained until his death in 1964. The years of Nehru's rule shaped the dominant patterns of India's future development.

Nehru's India had inherited an ambiguous legacy from the British rule: a relatively strong central government and a weak economy. Nehru, as a committed nationalist and social democrat, sought to strengthen India's independence and national power, on the one hand, and to improve its economy and the lives of the Indian poor, on the other. Nehru used the governmental machinery that India had inherited to accomplish these tasks.

At independence, India was confronted with major political problems, including a massive inflow of refugees, war with Pakistan over the disputed state of Kashmir, and the attempt to consolidate numerous Indian princely estates into a coherent national state. Concerned about India's capacity to deal with such problems, Nehru and other leaders, especially Vallabhai Patel, came to depend on and further strengthened the civil, police, and armed services that were a legacy of colonial rule. The strong state apparatuses facilitated India's political stability but also had other, less positive, long-term consequences. Most important, the new Indian state came to resemble the old British Indian state that Nehru and others had so vociferously opposed. The colonial state's tendency to favor traditional Indian elites, extract resources from Indian society, and maintain order within it was carried over into the post-independence era.

After independence, India adopted a democratic constitution and established a British-style democracy with full adult suffrage. Since political power now required winning elections, the INC had to transform itself from an opposition movement into a political party, the Congress Party. This it did quite successfully, by establishing a nationwide patronage system. Another important change in the decade following independence was the linguistic reorganization of states. As in the United States, the Indian constitution defines India as a federal system. The contentious political issue in the 1950s was the criterion by which Indian political groups could demand a state within the federal union. With Indians divided by the languages they speak, one obvious way to create a federal system was around language groups. Hindi is the most common indigenous language of India; however, most of India's Hindi speakers are concentrated in the north-central part of the country.

Those living in the south, east, and parts of the west are generally non-Hindi speakers. Concerned about domination by Hindi-speakers, many of these non-Hindi groups demanded a reorganization of the Indian union into linguistically defined states. Initially, Nehru resisted this demand, worried that linguistic states within a federation could turn secessionist and demand a sovereign country of their own. As demands for linguistic states mounted, especially from southern Indian groups, Nehru compromised in 1956, and the new Indian union was organized around fourteen linguistically defined states. Following subsequent changes, there are now twenty-three major states within India.

Major political changes instituted during the Nehru era put India firmly on a stable, democratic road. The powerful groups in the society—elite bureaucrats; wealthy landowners; entrepreneurs; and leaders of well-organized ethnic movements—were accommodated within the new system. However, the poor and the unorganized did not fare as well. While Nehru and the Congress Party continued to maintain a pro-poor, socialist rhetoric, their capacity to deliver on their promises was limited. This was not a serious political liability in the 1950s because the poor masses, mired in a centuries-old caste hierarchy, could not readily challenge elitist rule. Only in a few literate states such as Kerala were the poor organized, and they elected a communist state government.

Another legacy of the Nehru era is noteworthy. Jawaharlal Nehru was an internationalist who wanted India to play a global role. However, as Nehru was consolidating power in India, the Cold War was unfolding between the Soviet Union and the United States. Together with postcolonial leaders of Asia and Africa, Nehru initiated what became known as the nonaligned movement, which united those countries wishing to maintain a healthy distance from the two superpowers. India and many other developing countries viewed both Western capitalism and Soviet communism with suspicion. Under Nehru, India played a leadership role among other nonaligned developing countries while pursuing mixed economic policies at home that were neither fully capitalist nor fully socialist (see Section 2).

Leaders: *The Nehru-Gandhi Dynasty*

Jawaharlal Nehru

Jawaharlal Nehru was a staunch believer in liberal democratic principles. Along with Gandhi and others he was at the forefront of India's nationalist movement against the British. When India became independent in 1947, Nehru became prime minister as head of the Congress Party and retained that position until his death in 1964. During this period, he established India as a socialist, democratic, and secular state—in theory if not always in practice. On the international front, he helped found the nonaligned movement, a forum for expressing the interests and aspirations of developing countries that did not want to team with the United States or the Soviet Union during the Cold War.

Nehru attempted to set India on a rapid road to industrialization by establishing heavy industry. His efforts to effect redistribution of wealth through land reform were combined with an equally strong commitment to democratic and individual rights, such as the right to private property. Upon his death, India inherited a stable polity, a functioning democracy, and an economy characterized by a large public sector and an intricate pattern of state control over the private sector.

Indira Gandhi

Indira Gandhi became prime minister shortly after the death of her father, Jawaharlal Nehru, and dominated the Indian political scene until her assassination in 1984. Her years in power strengthened India's international position, but her domestic policies weakened the organizational structure of the Congress Party. Her tendencies toward centralization and the personalization of authority within the Congress and the concomitant use of populist rhetoric in electoral campaigns contributed to the erosion of the Congress Party. By presenting the regional conflict in the Punjab and problems with Pakistan as Hindu-Sikh and Hindu-Muslim problems, respectively, she contributed to further erosion of the party's secular base and to rising religious factionalism. Her decision to send troops into the holiest of the holy Sikh temples in Amritsar deeply alienated Sikhs, a small but important religious group in India. The ensuing bloodshed culminated in her assassination by one of her Sikh bodyguards in 1984. Her assassination ushered in a new generation of the Nehru-Gandhi dynasty, as her son Rajiv Gandhi served as prime minister until 1989.

The Indira Gandhi Era (1966–1984)

When Nehru died in 1964, the Congress Party was divided over the choice of a successor and hurriedly selected mild-mannered Lal Bahadur Shastri to be prime minister. When he died of a heart attack in 1966, the party elites found a compromise candidate in Nehru's daughter, Indira Gandhi. Two reasons favored her choice: (1) as Nehru's daughter, she would be helpful in elections; and (2) she was perceived by the Congress Party leaders as a weak woman who could be manipulated by competing factions within the party. They were right about the first point, but decisively wrong about the second.

As prime minister from 1966 to 1984, except for the brief period from 1977 to 1980, Indira Gandhi left several long-term legacies for contemporary Indian politics. First, Indian politics became not only more personal and populist but also more nationalist.

To bolster her popularity Indira Gandhi deliberately reignited Indian nationalism. During the late 1960s the Bengali-speaking eastern half of Pakistan, which was separated from its western half by nearly 1,000 miles of Indian territory, demanded sovereignty. As violence escalated within Pakistan and refugees from East Pakistan began pouring into India, Gandhi ordered Indian forces to intervene on the side of East Pakistan, which led to the creation of the sovereign state of Bangladesh. Because the United States sided with Pakistan in that conflict (and the Soviet Union backed India), Indira Gandhi was able to mobilize Indian nationalist sentiment against both Pakistan and the United States. This war-related victory added to her popularity. After losses in the 1967 national elections weakened many established Congress Party leaders, Indira Gandhi moved swiftly to consolidate her position. She pushed out the Congress Party leaders who opposed her, replaced them with those loyal to her, and created a new Congress Party in her own image. Subsequently, she depicted the old Congress elite as having stood for the status quo and having prevented her from helping the poor and implementing progressive policies. Gandhi's populist rhetoric won her immense popularity among India's poor. By 1971 she dominated Indian politics as much as Mahatma Gandhi or her father ever had, until her assassination in 1984.

A second legacy of Indira Gandhi's rule was the introduction of a top-down quality to India's political system. During the Nehru era, local elites had helped select higher political officeholders, but in the 1970s Gandhi appointed these same officeholders at both the national and regional levels. Although this strategy helped her consolidate her power rapidly, it led to such negative consequences for governing as growing centralization of decision-making in the nation's capital, Delhi, and the erosion of the legitimacy of local leaders.

A third important legacy of Indira Gandhi's rule was her failure to translate populist rhetoric into real gains for India's poor. She was neither able to redistribute agricultural land from large landowners to those who worked the land nor able to generate employment, provide welfare, or improve access to education and health for the really poor. The reasons for these failures are complex and controversial. Some analysts argue that she was never sincere in her commitment to the poor and that her populism was mainly a strategy for enhancing electoral popularity. But even if she had wanted to improve the lot of India's poor, she would have encountered many obstacles, given India's enormous numbers of poor, especially in relation to its wealth.

During Indira Gandhi's tenure, Indian politics became more and more turbulent. And this is a fourth legacy of her rule, with long-term significance. As her popularity soared, so did the opposition to her. The old Congress elite formed into a loosely knit but coherent opposition. They denounced Gandhi's populist political style, arguing that her government was corrupt and that India needed a total revolution to oust her from power and cleanse the government. This opposition, led by a credible follower of Mahatma Gandhi, Jai Prakash Narain, began organizing mass demonstrations and strikes to press its case. During 1974 the political situation in India became volatile, with the

opposition organizing general strikes and Indira Gandhi threatening massive state repression. When Narain called on the Indian armed forces to mutiny, Gandhi declared a national Emergency, suspended many democratic rights, and arrested most of the opposition leaders. This **Emergency** lasted nearly two years, the only period since 1947 when India was not a full democracy.

When the prime minister rescinded the Emergency and called for new national elections in 1977, she was rudely surprised. She was voted out of office, and for the first time since independence, a non-Congress government came to power. Various groups that had opposed Indira Gandhi joined together in a loosely and hastily organized party (the Janata Party) and won power. The party won because Indira Gandhi's authoritarian measures during the Emergency were unpopular but also because the Janata Party temporarily united India's fragmented opposition groups (a united opposition has a better chance of winning in India's electoral system). However, the Janata Party was a loose coalition, and soon after the elections top Janata leaders started bickering for positions. Factionalism at the top became so unwieldy that the Janata government collapsed, providing a new opportunity for Indira Gandhi to return to power in the 1980 parliamentary elections.

To summarize, a personal and populist political style, a more and more centralized, top-down political system, failure to implement antipoverty policies, and growing political turbulence were the most important legacies of Indira Gandhi's rule in the 1970s. Although much of this continued after she regained power in 1980, she slowly introduced two important sets of changes that have also had long-term significance. The first of these was in the realm of the economy. During the 1970s, India's industrial establishment grew relatively slowly for several reasons: the government was spending too much public money buying political support and not enough on investment; incomes of the poor were not improving and therefore demand for new products was limited; and excessive rules and regulations were counterproductive, both for domestic entrepreneurs and for integrating India into the world economy. With few means to rechannel government spending or to improve the spending capacity of the poor, Indira Gandhi started liberalizing the rules that governed India's economy.

The second important change concerns the strategy used to mobilize support for elections. Because poverty was not diminishing, it was clear that continuing appeals to poverty alleviation would not provide a successful electoral strategy. Moreover, economic policy was moving toward liberalization, whereas rapid progress toward poverty alleviation would have required greater government involvement. With the loss of populist promises as a strategy to win support, the prime minister needed a new appeal—at this point, religion returned to Indian politics. Since the 1950s, Nehru and Indira Gandhi had argued for socialism and secularism. In the early 1980s, however, Gandhi started experimenting with a different theme: using religious appeals to mobilize India's majority religious group, the Hindus. By introducing religion into politics the Congress Party itself sowed the seeds that grew into rising support for religious parties such as the BJP and thereby accelerated its own fall. Thus, religious conflicts reentered Indian politics in the early 1980s, as illustrated by the growing conflict between the Sikh religious minority, based in the Punjab, and the national government. During this conflict, Indian security forces attacked Sikh militants hiding inside the holiest of the Sikh shrines, the Golden Temple in the city of Amritsar. The resulting alienation of Sikhs from Indira Gandhi peaked with her assassination by one of her Sikh bodyguards in 1984.

India since Indira Gandhi (1984 to the Present)

With the death of Indira Gandhi, the tradition of powerful and populist prime ministers came to an end. Indian politics has been facing a crisis of governance because of three factors, all introduced during the Indira Gandhi era.

First, increasing factionalism and disintegration within the Congress Party; second, a similar scenario at the level of the central government because of the inability of other parties to fill the vacuum; and third, the rise of ethnic mobilization electoral strategies. Since 1984 only two governments, both Congress-led, have lasted their full terms, one led by Rajiv Gandhi from 1984 to 1989, and the second by Narasimha Rao from 1991 to 1996. Rao rode to victory on a sympathy vote in the aftermath of Rajiv Gandhi's assassination. The Congress Party split in May 1995 added to the

Table 1

Prime Ministers of India, 1947–1998

	Years in Office	Party
Jawaharlal Nehru	1947–1964	Congress
Lal Bahadur Shastri	1964–1966	Congress
Indira Gandhi	1966–1977	Congress
Morarji Desai	1977–1979	Janata
Charan Singh	1979–1980	Janata
Indira Gandhi	1980–1984	Congress
Rajiv Gandhi	1984–1989	Congress
V. P. Singh	1989–1990	Janata
Chandra Shekhar	1990–1991	Janata (Socialist)
Narasimha Rao	1991–1996	Congress
Atal Bihari Vajpayee	1996 (13 days)	BJP & allies
H. D. Deve Gowda	1996–1997	United Front
I. K. Gujral	1997–1998	United Front
Atal Bihari Vajpayee	1998–1999	BJP & allies

corrosion of party structures and vitality, a process set in motion by Indira Gandhi.

Second, at the level of the central government, the tendency for Indian elections to produce unstable and short-lived coalitions under leaders with little personal power or charisma has increased since 1996. The other parties have been able to fill the vacuum left by the Congress Party. Governments have alternated between the Congress, Janata, United Front, and BJP parties (see Table 1). The Congress Party's decline underlines deeper changes in Indian politics, namely, the decline of anticolonial nationalism, on the one hand, and the spread of power to many underprivileged groups, on the other. The United Front coalition represents mainly India's middle and lower castes. The BJP, by contrast, seeks to create a Hindu nationalist majority. None of these have come close to capturing a majority of the seats. The coalition governments from 1996 to 1998 were led by weak leaders of small parties and were provided with external support by the fractured Congress Party. The BJP government that came to power in 1998 was also a coalition; it lasted for only about a year.

Third, the religious factionalism that had been set in motion by Indira Gandhi's appeal to Hindus peaked during the Ayodhya episode, culminating in the victory of the BJP for a brief period in 1996 and again in 1998. Electoral mobilization strategies divided the country along ethnic lines and contributed to conflictual relationships in government and society. The BJP government initially appeared fragmented and weak as it sought to rule with a coalition of smaller, ideologically diverse parties. Even the brief nationalist resurgence among the populace, in the aftermath of the nuclear bomb testing in 1998, was not enough to unify the various religious, caste, and ethnic groups. In the late 1990s, mismanagement of the economy generated a popular backlash against the BJP. In elections held in November 1998 for seats in four state government assemblies, the BJP performed very badly, losing to the Congress Party in three states and to a regional party in the fourth state. Prior to the elections, soaring inflation had made basic commodities unaffordable to India's poor masses. The BJP government finally collapsed in April–May 1999 due to infighting among its coalition partners.

Whether any party or charismatic leader capable of unifying the country across the salient cleavages will emerge remains to be seen. (Attempts by Rajiv Gandhi's Italian-born widow, Sonia Gandhi, to knit together warring factions within the Congress Party bore fruit in the form of victory for the Congress Party in three states in the November 1998 elections.) Thus politics in India at the end of the 1990s is characterized by governments of precarious coalitions, weakened political institutions, and considerable political activism along ethnic lines. These developments have generated policies that range from limited action on the economic front to nationalist outbursts on the military front.

Themes and Implications

Historical Junctures and Political Themes

India in a World of States. India's domestic troubles both reflect and influence its changing status in the world of states. In an increasingly interdependent global political and economic system, the arrival of India as a nuclear power signaled the dawn of a new era, where simmering historical tensions over territories (such as Kashmir) will need to be managed very carefully. Today, India shares its borders with two nuclear powers, China and Pakistan, and has engaged in wars as well as periodic border skirmishes with them. With the end of the Cold War and the birth of a multipolar world, managing regional tensions poses problems. India and Pakistan have fought two wars, and tensions between them have been continually exploited by their politicians during domestic political crises. The challenge facing the Indian state is how to prevent domestic pressures from being translated into international belligerence. How will India's new role as a declared nuclear power change its international standing and influence its political and economic development? A very positive development in this regard was that India's and Pakistan's prime ministers made historic visits to each other's country in 1999. Nevertheless, shortly thereafter the two countries were again engaged in military conflict over Kashmir.

Governing the economy. The second theme is particularly important for India if it wants to fulfill its national and domestic ambitions. The historical junctures reveal a series of policies in the economic sphere that shifted from being protectionist to slowly and tentatively liberalizing the economy. Indian policymakers initially sought economic self-sufficiency through a policy of state-led industrialization focused on meeting the needs of its large internal market. This economic strategy had mixed results and did little to alleviate the country's terrible poverty. Like many other developing nations, India is having to adjust its economic strategy to meet the demands of increasingly competitive and interdependent global markets. But in a global environment that requires taking quick decisions and grasping ephemeral opportunities, the halting steps taken by Indian economic liberalizers have fallen short of expectations. How can India prevent its liberalization policy from being held hostage by entrenched elites? How can the policy-makers simultaneously provide for social benefits through well-aimed schemes that avoid clientalism and patronage, and pursue economic reforms? Will liberalization of India's state-controlled economy provide a basis for increased wealth in that poor country? These are among the most serious challenges that face Indian leaders and observers who are concerned about the future of this continent-sized, poor democracy.

The Democratic Idea. The democratic idea has been sustained in India for over half a century, barring a short period of authoritarianism in 1977–1979. India can boast of a vibrant and vigilant civil society, periodic elections, unfettered media, and relatively autonomous courts and bureaucracy. However, these institutions have been corroded over the years as a result of frequent interference from political leaders. Democracy in India has become increasingly participatory, as an elitist style gave way to a populist one under Indira Gandhi. Because the institutional capacity to implement antipoverty policies was missing, Indira Gandhi's radical posturing brought turbulence to Indian democracy, damaged the economy, and never provided real benefits to the poor. Since the late 1980s ethnic tensions have been exacerbated by electoral strategies deployed by most political parties. The challenge faced by India is how to balance an increasingly divided society with the demands of social, economic, and political citizenship demanded by democracy. Contemporary Indian politics poses major questions. For example, what political strategies can help create a successful and durable formula for appealing to a dominant identity and thereby winning elections? Has the appeal to religion provided such a formula? Then, if appeals to the dominant religion provide electoral dividends, what are the implications for India's religious minorities? Can India's democracy cope with numerous religious and other identity-based political conflicts especially when they turn violent? In recent years, brutal attacks have been directed against Muslims, Sikhs, and Christians. In other words, democracy and identity politics have become intricately linked, often in destructive fashion, in contemporary Indian politics.

The Politics of Collective Identity.   That there are intense conflicts around the issue of collective identity is not surprising in multicultural India. What is alarming is how mobilization of the electorate on ethnic grounds could corrode democratic values. Democracy, by its nature, provides a level playing field for a tussle between different interests and identities. But the victory of a Hindu nationalist party deepened regional and religious divisions and fundamentally changed the nature of Indian democracy. Thus India faces the challenge of reconciling domestic electoral strategies of ethnic mobilization to capture power with the demands of moderation demanded in the exercise of such power; and the challenge of coping with demands of multiethnic and multiclass groups and sustaining economic growth.

Implications for Comparative Politics

In this section, we examine some of the exceptional political features of the Indian state and discuss their significance for comparative politics.

First, India is poor and multiethnic, yet it is a democracy. Most Indians value their citizenship rights and, in spite of poverty and illiteracy, exercise them with vigor. In the face of expectations of modernization theorists who posited that democracy and economic growth were usually found together, India stands out as an exception. Indian history shows that at independence, the country was struggling to tackle problems of nation-building, poverty, poor human development indicators, and managing a transition to democracy. Against all odds, the country became and remains today a thriving and vibrant democracy, an achievement that seems even more striking when compared to the authoritarian fate of other newly independent British colonies in Asia and Africa.

Second, unlike other multiethnic states such as Yugoslavia or the former Soviet Union, which disintegrated with the advent of democracy, the Indian state has managed to remain cohesive and stable, albeit with a few frayed edges in Punjab, Kashmir, and Assam. Indian politics thus offers a case study of the tempering influence of democracy on ethnic cleavages. Contrast the exclusionist rhetoric of Hindu nationalism during the BJP's tenure as an opposition party with its rhetoric as India's ruling party. In an attempt to stabilize a fractious multiparty coalition government, the BJP was forced to put contentious religious issues such as the conflict at Ayodhya on a back burner.

Third, as home to nearly a billion people with diverse cultural, religious, and linguistic ties, Indian democracy offers an arena for testing and studying various theories and dilemmas of comparative politics. For instance, one dilemma in comparative politics is how multiethnic democracies can develop a coherent institutional system that gives representation to diverse interests without degenerating into authoritarianism or total collapse. The history of the

Congress Party until the Indira Gandhi era offers an example of how one party successfully managed to unite diverse and multiple ethnic identities under one umbrella.

Fourth, theorists dealing with recent transitions to democracy in Latin America and Eastern Europe have puzzled over the question of what constitutes a consolidated democracy and how one achieves such consolidation. Here, a comparison of India with Pakistan, which became authoritarian for much of its fifty-year existence, would help us evaluate the role of historical junctures, leaders, and their interaction with institutions. Moreover, the Indian experience with authoritarianism during the Emergency era in the late 1970s, and the resurgence of democratic norms when Indira Gandhi was voted out by an angry populace, shows the importance of democratic procedures such as elections in consolidating democracy. Indian politics shows that the practice of democratic procedures leads to the imbibing of democratic norms by people over a period of time.

Fifth, comparativists have focused on the dilemma of whether democracy and social equity can be achieved simultaneously in poor countries. The case of Kerala, a state in southern India, shows that such simultaneity is possible. Kerala's life expectancy of 72 years and infant mortality rate of 17 per 1,000 live births is on a par with several developed countries.

Thus, the preceding discussion of critical junctures in Indian history highlights the central challenge of contemporary Indian politics: how to establish a coherent, legitimate government while using the power of this government to facilitate economic growth and equitable distribution. The former requires forming durable electoral coalitions without exacerbating political passions and ethnic conflicts. The latter, in turn, requires careful implementation of policies that simultaneously help entrepreneurs produce goods and ensure a fair distribution of the growth in production. How India is coping with these contemporary challenges is discussed in subsequent sections.

Section ❷   Political Economy and Development

India at the time of independence was largely a poor, agricultural economy. Although it still has a very large agricultural sector and considerable poverty continues, India today also has a fairly substantial industrial base and a vibrant middle class. Since the introduction of economic liberalization policies under Narasimha Rao's Congress government in 1991, all Indian governments have listed the liberalization of India's economy as one of their priorities. Before discussing what liberalization entails, why it has become a main priority, and some of its implications for Indian politics, it is important to review the development of the Indian political economy.

State and Economy

The Economy under British Rule

The Indian economy during British rule remained inefficient and largely stagnant. The British did not colonize India to develop its economy; instead they ruled India for their own economic and political interests. An example of this is that their control enabled the British to sell their relatively cheap manufactured goods to Indians, with significant long-term economic consequences: indigenous manufacturing, especially of textiles, and a whole generation of Indian artisans were ruined by the forced opening of the Indian market to British goods. Another example is the agricultural sector. During the colonial period the Indian economy was largely agricultural, with hundreds of millions of poor peasants, living in thousands of small villages, tilling the land with primitive technology and producing at a fairly low level. The British, along with Indian landlords, extracted extensive resources from Indian agriculture, mainly in the form of land revenues, land taxes, and tributes from Indian princes. However, they only reinvested a small portion of this surplus into improving agricultural production. Most resources were squandered through conspicuous consumption by Indian princes and landlords or used to run the expensive colonial government. The result of this mismanagement of resources was that Indian agricultural productivity—that is, the amount of wheat, rice, or other products produced from one unit of land—mostly stagnated in the first half of the twentieth century. Agricultural productivity in India was considerably lower in 1950 than in Japan or even China.

Some industry developed under colonial rule, but its scope was limited. The British wanted to sell their own manufactured goods to India in exchange for Indian raw materials, and because the British economy was more advanced, it was difficult for Indians to establish manufacturing enterprises that could compete successfully. The British did not provide any real protection to Indian industry, and in any case most Indians were too poor to generate a substantial demand for industrial products. These factors made it difficult for Indians to enter manufacturing as viable competitors. The Indian economy at independence from Britain in 1947 was thus relatively stagnant, especially in agriculture, but also in industry.

The Economy after Independence

One of the central tasks facing Indian leaders after 1947 was to stimulate the growth of the sluggish economy. During Nehru's rule India adopted a model of development largely based on private property, although government ownership of firms and government guidance to private economic activity were considerable. Nehru created a powerful planning commission that, following the Soviet model, made five-year plans for the Indian economy, outlining the activities in which government investment would be concentrated. Unlike the plans in communist party-states, the Indian plans also indicated priority areas for private entrepreneurs, who remained a powerful force in the Indian economy.

The Indian government also levied high tariffs on imports, arguing that new Indian industries, so long disadvantaged under colonial rule, required protection from foreign competitors. The government tightly regulated the start-up and expansion of private industries under the presumption that the government was a better safeguard of the public interest than private entrepreneurs. This government-planned private economy achieved mixed results. It helped India create an impressive industrial base but did not do much to help the poor; and even the protected industries turned out to be quite inefficient by global standards.

Nationalist in temperament, Nehru and the Congress Party leaders were suspicious of involving foreign investors in India's economic development. If Indian investors were to be encouraged, however, they needed support from the government and protection from the more advanced foreign competitors. Indian government thus undertook a series of coordinated economic activities. It made significant public-sector investments to create such heavy industries as steel and cement; it protected Indian entrepreneurs from foreign competition; where possible, it further subsidized these producers; and finally, it created elaborate rules and regulations controlling the activities of private producers. As a result, India developed a substantial industrial base over the next few decades.

To improve India's agriculture, the Congress leaders promised to redistribute land from landowners to tenants. Their rationale was that such a move would simultaneously weaken the former supporters of colonial government and improve the incentives of those who till the land to increase production. Although some of the largest landowners were indeed eliminated in the early 1950s, poor tenants and agricultural laborers received very little land. Unlike the communist government in China, India's nationalist government had neither the will nor the capacity to undertake radical property redistribution. Instead, most of the land remained in the hands of medium- to large-sized landowners. Many of these became part of the Congress machine in the countryside. This development further weakened the Congress Party's capacity to side with the rural poor and diluted its socialist commitments to the point of ineffectiveness.

The failure of land reforms led to a new agricultural strategy in the late 1960s known as the **green revolution**. Instead of addressing land redistribution, this strategy sought to provide those who owned land with improved seeds and access to subsidized fertilizer. However, because irrigation was essential for this strategy to succeed, and because irrigation was only assured to larger farmers in some parts of India, the success of the green revolution was uneven. Production increased sharply in some parts of India, such as the Punjab, but in other regions the poorer farmers often got left behind. Nevertheless, India grows enough food to feed its population, even exporting some, and has avoided the worst scenarios of mass starvation and famines.

Between 1950 and 1980 the Indian government facilitated what is best described as **state-led economic development**. This development policy consisted of an expansion of the public sector, protection of the domestic sector from foreign competition, and rules and regulations to control private-sector activity—a policy most closely resembling the one followed by Brazil. The nationalist rulers hoped to strengthen India's international position by promoting self-sufficient industrialization. To a great extent the Indian government succeeded in achieving this goal. Even though it is a poor country, by 1980, India was a major industrial power that produced its own steel, airplanes, automobiles, chemicals, military hardware, and most consumer goods. On the agricultural side, although land reforms failed, a revised agricultural strategy improved food production.

This pattern of state-led development insulated the Indian economy from the dynamics of the global economy while allying the Indian state with its business and landowning classes. The strategy resulted in modest economic growth, not as impressive as that achieved in Brazil, Mexico, or the Republic of Korea (South Korea) but better than the performance of such African countries as Nigeria. The main beneficiaries of this economic growth were business classes, medium and large landowning farmers, and political and bureaucratic elites. A substantial urban middle class also developed during this phase.

There were also problems related to state-led development. First, given the lack of competition, much of this industry was inefficient by global standards. Second, the elaborate rules and regulations controlling private economic activity encouraged corruption, as entrepreneurs bribed bureaucrats to get around the rules. And third, the focus on heavy industry directed a substantial portion of new investment into buying machinery rather than creating jobs. In addition, poor tenant farmers and landless laborers failed to gain much from this pattern of growth. As a result, a large proportion of India's population—as much as 40 percent—did not share in the fruits of this growth. Also, since population continued to increase, the number of very poor people increased substantially during these decades.

A number of global and national changes moved India toward **economic liberalization**. Throughout the 1980s socialist models of development came under attack globally; India did not escape this worldwide trend. Within India, the political and economic elites were increasingly dissatisfied with India's relatively sluggish economic performance, especially in comparison to dynamic East Asian economies. For example, while India's economy during the 1970s grew at the rate of 3.4 percent per year, South Korea's grew at 9.6 percent. These new elites, less nationalist and socialist than their 1950s counterparts, interpreted India's slow economic growth as a product of too many governmental controls and of India's relative insulation from the global economy. India's business and industrial classes had grown during the intervening decades; now they increasingly found government intervention in the economy more of a hindrance than a help. Last, the elites were realizing that increased production would have to be sold to buyers abroad because India's poor did not have enough income to consume the new products.

Since 1984, but especially since 1991, Indian governments have been more or less committed to the liberalization of India's economy. Liberalization has both a domestic and an international component. The government has sought to dismantle its own controls over private-sector economic activities, especially in industry, and to improve the economic performance of the relatively large public sector. With respect to the global economy, the attempt was made to attract more foreign investment and to buy and sell more products from other countries, especially Western countries.

India's economy did relatively well during the 1980s—growing at nearly 5 percent per year—especially in comparison to the dismal performance of many debt-ridden Latin American and African economies, such as Brazil and Nigeria. Some of this improved performance resulted from the economic liberalization that integrated India more and more into the global economy. However, a large part of it was based on increased borrowing from abroad, which followed a shift away from a fairly conservative fiscal policy. An expansionary fiscal policy, largely funded by foreign loans, was harmful because India's exports to other countries did not grow very rapidly. For example, India's exports during the 1980s grew at approximately 6 percent per year in comparison to 12 percent per year for both South Korea and China. As a result, the need to pay back foreign loans put enormous pressure on the government toward the end of the decade. India was forced to borrow even more foreign currencies from such international agencies as the International Monetary Fund (IMF), which generally lend money only on condition that a government dismantles protectionist barriers and other forms of economic regulation. The Indian government entered into an agreement with the IMF in 1991 to further liberalize India's economy. This external pressure was the last of the forces that propelled India to shift its economic direction.

Despite these external and internal changes, the Indian government's efforts to liberalize the economy have not been consistent, perhaps because it is difficult to make sharp policy changes in India's large, cumbersome democracy. India's leaders are often worried about the impact these policy changes will have on their future electoral prospects. For example, the liberalization package involved reduction in government spending, but many groups in society who benefit from government spending reacted negatively to this planned reduction. So when Rao's government sought to reduce subsidies on fertilizer in 1992, farmers across India protested and the government made a hurried policy retreat. Other policy changes also affect specific groups adversely. Organized Indian labor, for example, reacted negatively to government plans to improve the efficiency of the public sector through privatization and increased private-sector competition, an effort likely to involve significant layoffs. In 1998 government efforts to increase private-sector participation in the insurance industry led to heavy protests by labor unions, thereby slowing down the process. This reaction has made the Indian government hesitant to sell public-sector companies to private buyers and has resulted in a slow privatization process, especially when compared to countries in Latin America or Eastern Europe. Even Indian business continued to resist certain aspects of the government's economic program, especially those parts aimed at encouraging foreign investors and foreign goods that Indian industrialists find threatening.

The liberalization program affects India's industry more directly than its agriculture. During the 1990s, India's agricultural production made steady and modest progress. Weather patterns, especially the timeliness of seasonal rains (the monsoons), continue to have significant bearing on Indian agriculture. Government policy also matters but has been of secondary importance. Agricultural production in India is dominated by medium- and small-sized peasant farmers. (Even the largest landowners in India are small by global standards; anyone who owns 40 to 50 acres of land is considered a large landowner.) The majority of the land is cultivated by farmers owning between 5 and 30 acres of land. Medium-sized and even some small farmers tend to use tenants or hired laborers to till the land. Scattered across different regions of India, millions of these peasant farmers are themselves divided by language and local culture, and even within the same region, they often belong to different castes, live in dispersed villages, and lack frequent communication with each other. As a result, India's peasant farmers cannot be readily organized as a distinct and cohesive national-level political force. When their political presence is felt at the national level, it is through indirect means. More often, landowning agriculturalists tend to be a powerful political force in state and local governments.

As a result of the green revolution, the largest landowning peasant farmers have become quite well-off in some states of India, notably the Punjab and Haryana. Increased wealth has also enabled these peasant farmers to become a political force. When the national government attempts to implement policies that may affect these groups adversely—as, for example, the removal of fertilizer subsidies—they express their opposition through mass protests and demonstrations. In this way, although they are not a well-organized political force, these peasant farmers can block the implementation of liberalizing policies that entail curtailing public expenditures. Moreover, because of their large numbers, most political leaders must consider the interests of these well-off peasants to attract their electoral support.

Below the national level, landowning peasant farmers play an influential political role in most Indian states, especially in the green revolution states. In some other states, the landowning peasant status tends to overlap with caste status; for example, in parts of Uttar Pradesh and Bihar, medium-sized agriculturalists are often members of the "backward castes," or a caste status that is intermediate, somewhere between the high-caste Brahmins and the lowly scheduled castes. This overlap between middle-level economic and middle-level caste positions strengthens the identity of members of this group, who often vote as a bloc and thus become a significant political force. For example, in the state elections held in Uttar Pradesh in 1993, the backward castes in alliance with the scheduled castes elected a state-level government from their numbers and thus temporarily displaced Brahmins and other elite castes from ruling positions.

Within India, governmental and bureaucratic elites, the business and industrial classes, and large and medium-sized landowning farmers are generally the privileged groups. Considering that India is a very poor country, many of these privileged groups are not that affluent by global standards. Moreover, these groups constitute India's ruling strata, and although there are differences and conflicts among them, for most purposes they manage to work together. They share many more interests and views with each other than they do with the bottom half of India's poor, the lower caste groups.

However, the BJP government that came to power in 1998 based much of its campaign on nationalist rhetoric. It gained support from those groups that feared liberalization, such as powerful Indian businesses whose monopolies were being threatened as well as public-sector employees who feared losing their jobs as a consequence of privatization. Once the BJP gained power, this rhetoric was toned down, though the extent of its commitment to liberalization still remains to be seen.

Social Welfare Policy

India's poor are a diverse, heterogeneous, and enormous social group constituting more than one-third of the population. Since independence, the percentage of poor has decreased from nearly two-thirds of the population to one-third. However, because of India's rapid population growth, this advance has not been sufficient to reduce the absolute number of poor, which increased from around 200 million in the 1950s to about 350 million by the late 1990s. The large number of poor has given India the sad distinction of having the largest concentration of poor people in the world. While nearly two-thirds of the Indian population live in rural areas, over three-fourths of the poor live in these areas. Moreover, though urban poverty only accounts for one-fourth of the poor population, the number of poor urban people, over 70 million, is staggering.

The truly poor of India tend to be the illiterate, women and children, and members of scheduled castes and tribes. They are often peasant farmers who own little land, agricultural tenants, landless laborers in villages, and those without regular jobs in cities who eke out a living on society's margins, often huddled into shantytowns or living on the streets of cities like Calcutta or Bombay. Although most of these poor remain politically unorganized, their political weight is felt in several ways. First, their sizable numbers impel many Indian politicians to adopt populist or socialist electoral platforms. Second, because many of the poor share a lower-caste status (especially within specific states), their group identity and united electoral behavior can have considerable impact on electoral outcomes. In some states, such as West Bengal and Kerala, there is a long history of radical politics; the poor in these states are well organized by communist or socialist parties, and they have periodically helped elect left-leaning governments. Third, the anger and frustration of the poor probably provides the raw material for many contemporary "movements of rage" within India. Although it is difficult to illustrate exactly how poverty leads the poor to participate in demonstrations, riots, or religious and other ethnic movements, the fact is that the participants in many incidents of political violence are the young and the poor.

The last point to be made in this discussion of the state and economy concerns government policies aimed at improving the lot of the poor. Over the years, Indian governments have tried different programs aimed at poverty alleviation, some of which have been successful, although most have not. Given the breadth of poverty in India, it is nearly impossible for any government to attempt a comprehensive welfare program. Redistribution of agricultural land to the poor was attempted but was mostly a failure compared to results in countries like China, where radical land redistribution was a key component of a successful assault on poverty. As a communist dictatorship, however, China could use government coercion to implement property redistribution. In some Indian states, such as West Bengal and Kerala, elected communist governments have also had some success in land redistribution. Overall, however, land reforms have proved to be nearly impossible in India's democracy.

India has very few Western-style welfare programs such as unemployment insurance, comprehensive public health programs, or guaranteed primary education. Some of these programs exist on paper but not in practice. The size of the welfare problem is considerable and would tax the resources of any government. No Indian government has ever attempted to provide universal primary education, although there has been considerable pressure from both Western and Indian observers to do so.

The one set of welfare-enhancing programs that has had modest success in India is public employment programs. These programs enable the national and state governments to allocate a portion of the public budget to such projects as the construction of roads or bridges, or the cleaning of agricultural waterways. Because the poor in villages are often unemployed for nearly half the year when there are no agriculture-related jobs, public employment programs become their off-season source of employment and income. Many surveys have demonstrated that such programs do help the poor, though the impact is not sufficient to improve their living conditions beyond the short run and the programs usually fail to reach the poorest. In the 1990s, however, under the impact of liberalization policies, government budgets came under considerable pressure, creating a squeeze on public investments, especially in such areas as public employment.

Society and Economy

Wealth and income present intense contrasts in Indian society. At the top are a small number of the incredibly affluent who have made their fortunes in basic business and industry. The personal wealth of the wealthiest of these—for example, Ambanis, Tatas, and Birlas, three of India's largest business houses—rivals the wealth of the richest business executives around the world. Below them, a much larger group, nearly 100 million Indians, are relatively well-off and have

the same standard of living as middle classes in many developed countries. By contrast, India's lower middle classes, some 500 million Indians, are mainly small farmers or urban workers, relatively poor by global standards; they barely eke out a living. And finally, at the bottom of the class structure are about 300 million people who are extremely poor and are concentrated mostly in India's thousands of villages as landless laborers or as the urban unemployed in shabby city slums.

Another aspect of Indian diversity is the contrast between primitive and sophisticated technologies of production. Low levels of literacy, poverty, and primitive technology characterize a good part of India's rural society. At the other end of the spectrum, India has a very sophisticated, technologically developed industrial sector that produces a variety of consumer products, military technologies, nuclear energy, and computers. For instance, the recent nuclear explosions were the culmination of years of scientific preparation.

So far the focus of this section has been on the state, social classes, and economy of India. In addition, the following issues need to be discussed to understand India's political economy: the growing size of the population; the status of women and children; the role of caste; and the role of intellectuals and the media in public life.

India's large population continues to grow at a relatively rapid pace. For better or for worse, it has been forecast that by 2005, India will become the largest country in the world, surpassing China. This suggests that India's population is growing at a faster rate than that of China. Since India already has more labor than it can use productively, rapid population growth hinders economic growth. Simply put, the more people there are, the more mouths there are to feed, and the more food and economic products must be produced to maintain people's standard of living, not to mention improve it.

Why should India's population continue to grow at such a rapid pace? The underlying causes are complex. The comparison with China again helps. The communist-led government of China has pursued very strict birth control policies—one child per family—since the late 1970s. In part, coercion was used to implement these policies, which did succeed in bringing down birthrates. India's democratic government, by contrast, has found it difficult to implement population control. Rates of population growth in some Indian states have slowed. For example, by 1995 the national rate of population growth was around 2 percent per year, while the rate in Kerala was 1.4 percent, close to that of China in the early 1990s. This statistic has important implications; it suggests that government coercion is not necessary to control population growth rates. What helped Kerala was one of the highest literacy rates, especially female literacy rates, in India. Whereas the national average female literacy rate in India is around 37 percent (the rate for males is around 65 percent), Kerala's female literacy rate is 87 percent. Since literate women are more likely to marry later, have more options in the workforce, have greater power in personal relationships, and use birth control, female literacy may be responsible for decreasing population growth in states like Kerala. If true, an important policy implication is that the education of women plays a significant role in bringing down the rates of population growth in countries like India.

India is one of the few countries in the world that has a lower percentage of females than males. This statistic is representative of the status of women in India. Despite the facts that India had a female prime minister, that about 10 percent of parliament members are women compared to just over 5 percent of the U.S. Congress, and that women have entered most professional jobs, the plight of the majority of Indian women is a dismal one. Indian society favors boys over girls, as evidenced in all social indicators from lower female literacy and nutrition rates to lower survival of female versus male infants. The favoring of males over females is reinforced through traditions, including the dowry system (the Hindu custom of giving the groom and his family a dowry, some form of assets, at the time of a daughter's wedding). These traditions, deeply rooted and slow to change, confine the majority of Indian women, particularly poor women, to a life of fewer opportunities than those available to men.

India also has the world's largest population of child labor. Children are employed widely, not only in agricultural labor but also in such urban enterprises as match-making and rug-weaving factories and selling tea or sweets at train stations. This is a problem, not only because children often work long hours under difficult conditions and at low wages, but because it deprives a segment of the population of an opportunity to develop through education and thus advance upward. The issue of child labor is closely related to India's failure to provide universal primary education. If school-age children were required to be in school, they could not be readily employed as full-time laborers. Many Indian elites argue that in their poor country, compulsory primary education is an unaffordable luxury. However, this argument is not very persuasive; many poor African countries have higher rates of primary school enrollments than does India. The more likely obstacle to universal primary education is India's caste system. Many upper-caste elites do not see lower-caste children as potentially their equals, and do not consider the issue of educating lower-caste children a priority. The deep-rooted cultural inequalities of India thus lock children into wage labor and out of schools. Child labor is directly linked to poverty and survival, since many poor families see larger numbers of children as a form of insurance. Yet, for most poor families, a larger family also means not being able to invest in each child's education and depending on their children's labor for survival. Thus child labor and poverty reinforce each other.

Caste issues pervade many other aspects of India's political and economic life. Not only does caste affect nearly all aspects of social life—social interactions, marriages, choice of occupation, social status, and political behavior—but it influences India's economy as well. First, by assigning people to specific occupations, it impedes the free movement of labor and talent. Although the link between caste and occupation has been weakening in India, especially in urban areas, it is nevertheless a very important principle on which employment is organized. And to the extent that caste inhibits the free movement of labor, it is an economic deficit for Indian society. Second, in the political arena, caste is a powerful force around which political groups and voting blocs coalesce. Although this is discussed in detail in Section 4, two side effects of this general tendency need to be mentioned here. Because caste is usually a local category, to a large extent Indian politics takes on a local and segmented quality. Related to this, caste cuts across class, making

---

Institutional Intricacies: *The Caste System*

Originally derived from the Portuguese word *castas*, today the word *caste* inevitably evokes images of a rigid hierarchy that characterizes Indian society. In reality, however, castes are less immutable and timeless categories than suggested by the popular image.

Historically, the **caste system** compartmentalized and ranked the Hindu population of the Indian subcontinent through rules governing various aspects of daily life, such as eating, marriage, and prayer. Sanctioned by religion, the hierarchy of caste is based on a conception of the world as divided into realms of purity and impurity. Each hereditary and endogamous group (that is, a group into which one is born and within which one marries) constitutes a *jati*, which is itself organized by *varna*, or shades of color. The four main varna are the **Brahmin**, or priestly, caste; the *Kshatriya*, or warrior

and royal, caste; the *Vaishyas*, or trading, caste; and the *Shudra*, or artisan, caste. Each of these *varna* is divided into many *jatis* that often approximate occupational groups (such as potters, barbers, and carpenters). Those who were not considered to be members of organized Hindu society—because they lived in forests and on hills rather than in towns and villages, or were involved in "unclean" occupations such as sweepers and leather workers—were labeled **untouchables**, outcastes, or **scheduled castes**.

Because each *jati* is often concentrated in a particular region, it is sometimes possible to change one's *varna* when one moves to a different part of the country by changing one's name or adopting the social customs of higher castes, for example, giving up eating meat. Some flexibility within the rigidity of the system has contributed to its survival across the centuries.

---

it difficult for labor, business, and other economic classes in India to act in a politically cohesive manner. Third, Indian government often uses caste as a basis for **reservations**, the Indian version of affirmative action. The government reserves some jobs, admissions into universities, and similar privileges for members of specific underprivileged castes. This has become a highly contentious issue in Indian politics. And last, those who suffer the most in India's caste system are those at the bottom of the caste hierarchy, namely, the untouchables. Nearly 10 percent of India's population, or some 90 million people, is categorized by the Indian census as belonging to the scheduled castes. Notwithstanding considerable government efforts, the social stigma suffered by members of this group runs deep in India. Because many untouchables are also poor, they suffer doubly: poverty and social ostracism lead to a lack of dignity.

A variety of social injustices abound in India's political economy. Nevertheless, it is important to note that there is widespread recognition of these injustices within India and that they are widely discussed and debated. India is a free and democratic country with a lively public culture. Although it is plagued by poverty, India has a significant middle class, many members of which are highly educated

and politically active. India's media, especially its newspapers and magazines, are as free as any in the world. They endlessly debate what is wrong with India and its politicians, and thus maintain the pressure for public action. This combination of a vocal intellectual stratum and a free press is a cherished one in India's democracy; its role, as well as the potential for the organization of the poor, sustains hope that pressures to address challenging social problems will be maintained within India.

India and the International Political Economy

After a prolonged colonial experience, nationalist India in the 1950s shunned economic links with the outside world. Although India pursued an active foreign policy as a leader of the **nonaligned bloc**, it was defensive in its economic contacts. A prolonged and successful nationalist movement helps explain both the urge within India to play a global political role and the urge to protect its economy from foreign influence. As mentioned earlier, India's political and economic elites favored protectionism in trade and sought to limit foreign investment. Although three decades of this policy helped generate an industrial base and domestic capitalism within India, at the same time several new problems arose. The subsequent efforts to liberalize and reintegrate the Indian economy into the world economy were in part aimed at dealing with such nagging problems. And these efforts have also run into some obstacles.

During the three decades of relatively autarkic development, powerful groups emerged that now have vested interests in maintaining the old order. To illustrate, many bureaucrats abused the system of government controls over private economic activities by accepting bribes to issue government licenses to start private businesses. Indian industry was often relatively inefficient because neither cheaper foreign goods nor foreign investors were readily allowed into India. Moreover, organized labor, especially in government-controlled factories, had a stake in maintaining inefficient factories because they offered a greater number of jobs. These well-entrenched groups resisted liberalization and threatened to throw their political weight behind opposition parties, making the ruling government hesitant to undertake any decisive policy shift.

The other significant component of India's performance in the international political economy concerns its regional context. India is a giant among the South Asian countries of Pakistan, Bangladesh, Sri Lanka, Nepal, and Bhutan, though its northern neighbor is an even bigger and more powerful giant, the People's Republic of China. Since 1947, India has experienced a fair amount of regional conflict: a war with China in 1962; three wars with Pakistan, the last of which was fought in 1971 and precipitated the break-up of Pakistan into the two states of Pakistan and Bangladesh; a military intervention into strife-torn Sri

Figure 1

Exports of India and Its Trading Partners, 1980 and 1997

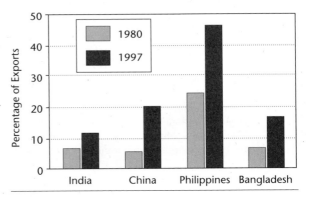

Source: World Development Report 1998/99 (Washington D.C.: World Bank, 1998).

Lanka in the 1980s; and on-and-off troubled relations with Nepal. The net effect is that India has not developed extensive economic interactions with its neighbors. Figure 1 compares exports as a percent of GNP for India and its major trading partners; India's export quantity and rate of growth are relatively low. As nations increasingly look to their neighbors for trade and investment, the pressure on India and its neighbors to put aside their mutual conflicts for increased economic contact is likely to grow. Some move in this direction was already evident in the first half of the 1990s, especially toward China, but there is still a long way to go before South Asia develops an integrated zone of economic activity.

Section ③ Governance and Policy-Making

During the last decades of the twentieth century, some of India's essential political institutions, such as political parties, the federal system, the bureaucracy, and the judiciary, did not function very effectively, partly because of the demands from India's diverse political groups. However, this ineffectiveness also resulted from the actions of India's top political leaders who,

when threatened, sought to block access that challengers might have to powerful positions. This is one reason why India's important political party, the Congress, stopped conducting internal party elections for selecting party officers. Also, leaders below the national level, especially at the state level, tend now to be appointed from above rather than elected from below. Loyal rather than competent party members have similarly been favored for appointments in the bureaucracy and the judiciary. Such developments have contributed to the growing ineffectiveness of some of India's most important political institutions, further complicating the task of governing India's complex society.

Organization of the State

India is a democratic republic with a parliamentary and a federal system of government. The constitution adopted in 1950 created this system, and although there have been many profound changes since then in the distribution and the use of power, the basic character of India's political system has remained unchanged. Moreover, for much of this period India has been a stable, democratic country with universal suffrage and periodic elections at all levels—local, provincial, and national. This continuity and democratic stability are remarkable among developing countries. Note the contrast with such other countries as Brazil and Nigeria. To simplify a complex reality, the main explanation for this stability is that Indian democracy has accommodated many new power challenges while successfully repressing the most difficult ones. India's democratic institutions, though always under pressure, have achieved considerable resilience and established their authority to mobilize sufficient coercion to contain the most serious political threats.

India's constitution is a lengthy and, in contrast to the British one on which it is modeled, a written document that is periodically amended by legislation. Among its special features, three are worth noting. First, unlike many constitutions, the Indian constitution directs the Indian government to promote social and economic equality and justice. The constitution thus goes beyond stipulating formal procedures of decision-making and allocating powers among political institutions, and outlines the goals of politics and of the state. Although the impact of these constitutional provisions on government policies is limited, the provisions ensure that issues of welfare and social justice cannot be ignored. Second, the Indian constitution, similar to the U.S. constitution, provides for freedom of religion and makes India a secular state. This was an especially controversial issue in Indian politics

during the late 1990s because the ruling BJP was committed to establishing Hinduism as a state-sanctioned religion. And third, the Indian constitution allows for the temporary suspension of many democratic rights under conditions of emergency. These provisions were used, somewhat understandably, during wars with Pakistan or China. But they were also invoked, more disturbingly, to deal with internal political threats, most dramatically during the national Emergency from 1975 to 1977, when a politically vulnerable Indira Gandhi suspended many democratic rights and imprisoned her leading political opponents.

India's federal system of twenty-six states and several other special political units is relatively centralized. The central government controls the most essential government functions such as defense, foreign policy, taxation and public expenditures, and economic planning, especially industrial planning. State governments formally control such policy areas as agriculture, education, and law and order within the states. Because they are heavily dependent on the central government for funds in these policy areas, however, the power of the states is limited.

India's social, economic, and political diversity provides a challenging context within which to comprehend the functioning of Indian democracy. India is a parliamentary democracy designed on the British model. The parliament—in India known as the **Lok Sabha**, or House of the People—is the most significant political body. The leader of the political party with the most seats in the *Lok Sabha* becomes the prime minister, who nominates a cabinet, mostly from the ranks of the other elected members to parliament. The prime minister and the cabinet, along with permanent civil servants, control much of the government's daily functioning. The prime minister is the linchpin of the system because effective power is concentrated in that office, where most of the country's important policies originate. By contrast, the office of the president is largely ceremonial. In periodic national elections, 544 members of the *Lok Sabha*, the lower house of the bicameral parliament, are elected. The *Lok Sabha* is much more politically significant than the **Rajya Sabha**, the upper house. The prime minister governs with the help of the cabinet, which periodically meets to discuss important issues, including any new legislation that is likely to be initiated.

Individually, these cabinet members are the heads of various ministries—for example, Foreign Affairs or Industry—that direct the daily work of the government and make up the permanent bureaucracy.

The Executive

The President and the Prime Minister

The president is the official head of the state and is elected indirectly every five years by an electoral college, using a complex formula that ultimately involves elected representatives from both the national and state governments. In most circumstances, the president acts on the advice of the prime minister and is thus not a very powerful political figure in India. The presidency is a ceremonial office, symbolizing the unity of the country, and is supposedly above partisan politics. Under exceptional circumstances, however, especially when the selection of a prime minister becomes a complex issue, the president can play an important political role. For example, in the 1998 election there was a "hung parliament" with no party gaining a clear majority. The president then requested the party with the largest percentage of votes, the BJP, to show that it could muster enough allies to form a government.

The prime minister and the cabinet are the most powerful political figures in India. Because they represent the majority party in parliament, the passage of a bill is not always as complicated a process as it can be in a presidential system, especially one with a divided government. The prime minister and the cabinet also head various ministries, so that after legislation is passed, they oversee its implementation. In practice, the permanent bureaucracy, especially the senior and middle-level bureaucrats, are truly responsible for policy implementation. Nevertheless, as in most parliamentary systems, such as those in Britain, Germany, and Japan, there is considerable overlap in India between the executive and the legislative branches of the government, creating a greater degree of centralization of power than at first seems evident.

The issue of who will become the prime minister has been a rather dramatic and initially infrequent issue in India's political life. Between 1947 and 1984, except for a few brief interludes, India had only two prime ministers: Nehru and Indira Gandhi (see Table 1). This is nearly unique among democracies; it underlines the powerful hold that the Nehru-Gandhi family had on India's political imagination, including the imagination of poor, illiterate Indians. Since then, however, there has been a more rapid turnover. Rajiv Gandhi, Indira Gandhi's son, succeeded his mother after her assassination in 1984. When he lost power four years later, there were two attempts to form non-Congress governments under the leadership of V. P. Singh and Chandra Shekhar. Factionalism within the loose coalitions that constituted these non-Congress governments broke out, however, and curtailed these attempts. As Rajiv Gandhi campaigned in a bid to return to power, he too was assassinated. Subsequently, the Congress Party returned to power in 1990 with Narasimha Rao as prime minister. While this Congress victory lasted six years, it was followed by a thirteen-day BJP government under the prime ministership of A. B. Vajpayee and two short-lived United Front prime ministerships under H. D. Deve Gowda and I. K. Gujral. In 1998 the BJP returned to power, with Vajpayee again prime minister. The BJP government's term in office again turned out to be short-lived because of internal factionalism.

The method of selecting a prime minister in India is fairly complex. The original choice of Nehru was a natural one, given his prominent position in the nationalist movement. The choice of Indira Gandhi was less obvious. She was chosen to head the Congress Party by a group of prominent, second-tier party leaders. Her choice reflected several considerations, the most important of which was her national name recognition and its ability to attract the popular vote. Although the process of passing power from a father to a daughter may appear rather feudal—to some extent it is—there is valid electoral rationale for such a choice in India. A similar logic prevailed when Rajiv Gandhi was chosen by party elites to succeed his mother. Rajiv Gandhi benefited from the wave of sympathy generated by his mother's assassination, and he led the Congress Party back to power in 1984 with a handsome electoral majority.

Following Rajiv Gandhi's assassination, the Nehru-Gandhi family line appeared to have reached an end, since Rajiv Gandhi was married to an Italian, Sonia Gandhi, and their children were too young to enter politics. In 1991, Narasimha Rao was brought back as an "elder statesman," nonthreatening and acceptable to competing factions within the Congress Party. He was the first prime minister from the south of India; all the previous heads of state had been from the north. Both subsequent United Front prime ministers, Gowda and Gujral, were compromise candidates who lacked the personality and power to manage their disparate coalitions. In 1998 the Congress Party attempted to resurrect its fortunes by choosing Sonia Gandhi to head their party. This effort appeared quixotic initially. However, the BJP's nationalist appeal faded in 1998 as bread-and-butter issues became politically salient. The Sonia Gandhi–led Congress stepped into this vacuum, opening the possibility that the political rule of the Nehru-Gandhi family may continue.

The Cabinet

The prime minister chooses the cabinet, mostly from among the party's elected members to parliament. Seniority, competence, and personal loyalty are the top criteria that any prime minister takes into account when choosing the cabinet ministers. Regional and caste representation at the highest level of government must also be considered. During Indira Gandhi's rule, personal loyalty was critical in the choice of senior ministers. Rajiv Gandhi, by contrast, put a high premium on competence, which unfortunately he equated with youth and technical skills at the expense of political experience. Since Vajpayee was able to form a government only with the help of many smaller parties, the heads of these parties had to be accommodated, producing an eclectic, disparate cabinet. Given his party's narrow power base, Vajpayee was less free than his Congress Party predecessors to select a personally loyal cabinet. Rather, he needed to include all those with power in one region or another of India, while taking into account issues of competence and the demand for representation by different castes, as well as ensuring that potential challengers are either coopted or kept at bay.

The Bureaucracy

The prime minister and cabinet ministers run the government in close collaboration with senior civil servants. Each senior minister oversees what is often a sprawling bureaucracy, staffed by some very competent, overworked, senior civil servants and by many not so competent, underworked, lowly bureaucrats, well known for taking long tea breaks while they stare at stacks of unopened files.

Because political leaders come and go, whereas senior civil servants stay, many civil servants possess a storehouse of knowledge and expertise that makes them very powerful. The higher-level civil servants in India reach their positions after considerable experience within the government. They enter the service, formally known as the **Indian Administrative Service** (IAS), at a relatively young age, usually in their early twenties, by passing a very competitive general exam. Some of India's most talented young men and women were attracted to the IAS during the 1950s and the 1960s, reflecting the prestige that service in national government used to enjoy in Indian society. This attraction of the IAS has declined, however, and many talented young people now also go into engineering or business administration, or if possible, leave the country for better opportunities abroad. Government services have become tainted as areas of corruption have developed and the level of professionalism within the IAS has eroded, mainly because politicians prefer loyalty over merit and seniority when making promotions. Nevertheless, the IAS continues to recruit very talented young people, many of whom mature into dedicated senior civil servants and who still constitute the backbone of the Indian government.

The IAS produces India's elite bureaucrats, those who occupy a critical but relatively thin layer at the top of India's sprawling bureaucracy. The competence of these elite bureaucrats is a central reason why India is moderately well governed. Below the IAS, unfortunately, the level of talent and professionalism drops rather sharply. Within each ministry at the national level, and in many parallel substructures at the state level, the bureaucracy in India is infamous for corruption and inefficiency. These problems contribute to the gap that exists in India between good policies made at the top and their poor implementation at the local level.

Other State Institutions

The Military and the Police

The Indian military, with more than a million well-trained and armed people, is a highly professional organization that enjoys the respect of Indian society. Unlike the militaries in many other developing countries—say, Brazil and Nigeria—the Indian military has never intervened directly in politics. This has to do with the fact that India is a relatively well-functioning democracy, and with the character of the Indian military. Over the years the continuity of constitutional, electoral politics and a relatively apolitical military have come to reinforce and strengthen each other. Civilian politicians provide ample resources to the armed forces and, for the most part, let them function as a professional organization. The armed forces, in turn, obey the orders of democratically elected leaders, and although they lobby to preserve their own interests, for the most part they stay out of the normal tumble of democratic politics.

Since the 1970s two factors have weakened this well-institutionalized separation of politics and military. First, during Indira Gandhi's rule, loyalty to political leaders became the key criterion for securing top military jobs. This policy tended to politicize the military and narrow the separation between politics and military. Second, there were growing political problems in India, especially regional and ethnic demands for secession (see Section 4). As these demands became more intense in some states, notably in Kashmir, and as those making the demands armed themselves, occasionally with the help of India's often hostile neighbor Pakistan, the Indian government called in the armed forces. However, soldiers are not trained to resolve political problems; rather, they are trained to use force to secure compliance from reluctant political actors. As a result, not only have democratic norms and human rights been violated in India, but the distance between politics and the military has narrowed further.

A similar trend toward politicization and deprofessionalization has occurred in India's sprawling police services, but with a difference. The Indian police organization was never as professionalized as the Indian armed forces, and the police services in India come under the jurisdiction, not of the central government, but of various state governments. Because state governments are generally less well run than the national government, the cumulative impact is that the Indian police are no longer apolitical civil servants. State-level politicians regularly interfere in police personnel issues, and police officers in turn regularly oblige the politicians who help them. The problem is especially serious at lower levels, where police officials interact with members of society. The image of the average police officer in most of India is not positive. The police are rightly viewed as easily bribed and often allied with criminals or politicians. In some states, such as Bihar and Uttar Pradesh, police often take sides in local conflicts instead of acting as neutral arbiters or enforcers of laws. Thus they tilt the power balance in favor of dominant social groups such as landowners or upper castes or the majority religious community, the Hindus.

In addition to the regular armed forces and the state-level police forces, there are paramilitary forces of nearly half a million men. These troops are organized under various names and are controlled by the national government. As Indian politics became more turbulent in the 1980s, these paramilitary forces steadily increased; their expansion reflects the Indian government's growing concern with maintaining internal law and order. But because the national government calls on the regular armed forces only as a last resort in the management of internal conflicts and because the state-level police forces are not very reliable, these paramilitary forces are viewed as a way to maintain order, albeit a very expensive solution. A large, sprawling, and relatively ineffective police service continues to remain a problematic presence in Indian society. Also, as terrorists or "freedom fighters" have become better armed, especially in Kashmir, paramilitary forces have proven inadequate to contain them.

The Judiciary

An independent judiciary is another component of India's state system. But unlike in Britain where the judiciary's role is limited by parliamentary sovereignty, Indian courts are haunted by a fundamental contradiction embedded in the Indian Constitution

Institutional Intricacies: *The Executive Versus the Judiciary*

Over the years, the Supreme Court has clashed head-to-head with the parliament as a result of the contradiction between principles of parliamentary sovereignty and judicial review that is embedded in India's constitution. For instance, during the early years of independence, the courts overturned state government laws to redistribute land from landlords (zamindars), saying that the laws violated the zamindars' fundamental rights. In retaliation, the parliament passed the first of a series of amendments to the constitution to protect the executive's authority to promote land redistribution. But matters did not end there. The Supreme Court responded by passing a judgment stating that the parliament did not have the power to abrogate the fundamental rights. In 1970 the court also invalidated the bank nationalization bill and a presidential order abolishing privy purses (including titles and privileges of former rulers of India's princely states).

In retaliation, the parliament passed a series of amendments that undercut the Supreme Court's rulings, thus moving the power balance toward parliamentary sovereignty. The Supreme Court responded that the court still reserved for itself the discretion to reject any constitutional amendments passed by parliament on the grounds that the amendments could not change the constitution's "basic structure". During the Emergency period, the parliament passed yet another amendment that limited the Supreme Court's judicial review to procedural issues. The Janata government in the post–Emergency era, however, reversed these changes, thus reintroducing the tension between the executive and judiciary.

Since the 1980s the courts have increasingly functioned as a bulwark for citizens by protecting their civil liberties from state coercion. For instance, since 1993 it has enforced a policy of compensating victims of violence while in police custody. In 1985, the Supreme Court upheld a verdict finding two people guilty of dowry murder and sentenced them to life imprisonment. In the mid-1980s the Supreme Court clashed with parliament on its interpretation of personal law, now referred to as the Shah Bano case. In India, in keeping with a secular ethos, personal law falls under the purview of religion, although an individual can choose secular alternatives. However, this recourse is circumscribed: a woman married under religious law cannot seek divorce or alimony under secular law. Neither Muslim nor Hindu personal law entitles women to alimony. The British colonial government had passed a law entitling destitute divorced women to maintenance by their husbands. Shah Bano, a destitute 75-year-old woman abandoned and later divorced by her husband, filed for maintenance under this law. The Supreme Court upheld Shah Bano's right to maintenance on the grounds that secular laws transcended personal law (religious law). The parliament, succumbing to pressures from religious leaders, passed a bill excluding Muslim women from the purview of secular laws.

The battle between the executive and the judiciary has taken a toll on the autonomy of the courts. The judiciary has been affected by the general malaise of institutional decay that has affected Indian politics over the years. The backlog of cases has grown phenomenally, while expeditious judgment of cases has declined dramatically.

between the principles of parliamentary sovereignty and judicial review. Over the years, the judiciary and the parliament have clashed, with the former trying to preserve the constitution's basic structure and the latter asserting its rights to amend the constitution. The judiciary comprises an apex court at the national level, high courts in states, and lower courts in districts.

The apex institution is the Supreme Court, comprising a chief justice and seventeen other judges, appointed by the president, but as in most matters of political significance in India, only on the advice of the prime minister. Once appointed, the judges cannot be removed from the bench until retirement at age sixty-five. The caseload on the Supreme Court, as on much of the Indian legal system, is extremely heavy, with a significant backlog. The main political role of the Supreme Court is to ensure that legislation conforms with the intent of the constitution. Because the Indian constitution is very detailed, the need for interpretation is not as great as in many other countries.

Nevertheless, there are real conflicts, both within the constitution and in India's political landscape, that often need to be adjudicated by the Supreme Court.

For example, the constitution simultaneously protects private property and urges the government to pursue social justice. Indian leaders have often promulgated socialist legislation such as requiring the redistribution of agricultural land. Legislation of this nature is necessarily considered by the Supreme Court because it potentially violates the right to private property. Many Supreme Court cases have involved the conflict between socialistically inclined legislation and basic constitutional rights. Cases involving other politically significant issues—for instance, rights of religious minorities such as Muslims and the rights of women in society—also periodically reach the Supreme Court for decisions.

Like many other Indian political institutions, the Supreme Court lost much of its autonomy in the 1980s and 1990s. The process began during Indira Gandhi's rule when she argued that the court was too conservative and an obstacle to her socialist program. To remedy this shortcoming, she appointed many pliant judges, including the chief justice. The Supreme Court itself more or less complied with her wishes during the two years of Emergency (1975–1977), when the political and civil rights of many Indians were violated. Unfortunately, this episode cost the Supreme Court considerable prestige as a neutral arbiter in India's state system. No such dramatic instance of a politicized Supreme Court has recurred since the late 1970s. Nevertheless, India's highest court, although still a political institution of some significance, is by no means as independent an institution as the founders of India's state system may have intended. However, that the Supreme Court still functions as a bulwark of sorts for citizens against state invasiveness is evident from many landmark judgments in defense of civil rights.

Subnational Government

Under its federal system, the balance of power between the central and state governments in India varies according to time and place. In general, the more popular the central government and the prime minister, the more the states feel obligated to the central government. During Nehru's, and especially during Indira Gandhi's rule, the states were often quite constrained. By contrast, a weaker central government, as for example the BJP-led alliance that took office in 1998, enlarges the room for state governments to maneuver. When state governments are run by political parties other than the national ruling party—and this is often true in contemporary India—there is considerable scope for central-state conflict. For example, a popular communist government in West Bengal has often disagreed with the national government in New Delhi, charging it with discriminatory treatment in the allocation of finances and other centrally controlled resources.

Below the national government, many different parties govern India's twenty-six states. The federal system allows for this political diversity, though not without political conflict between the central and state governments. Political power at state levels is held by the leader of the party with a majority of parliament seats. These leaders formulate policies that are implemented by a permanent bureaucracy. The quality of government below the national level is often poor, contributing to flaring regional and ethnic conflicts.

While the political parties at the national and the state levels may differ, the formal structure of the state governments parallels that of the national government. The chief minister of each state heads the state government; the office of the chief minister of a state thus parallels the office of the prime minister nationally. The chief minister is the leader of the majority party (or the party with most seats) in the lower house of the state legislature. As the prime minister does, the chief minister appoints cabinet ministers who head various ministries staffed by a state-level, permanent bureaucracy. In lieu of a president, each state has a governor, appointed by the national president. The governors, like the president, are supposed to serve on the advice of the chief minister, but in practice, they often become politically powerful, especially in states where the national government is at odds with the state government or where state governments are unstable. The governors can dismiss elected state governments and proclaim temporary presidential rule if they determine state governments to be ineffective. When this happens, the elected government is dissolved and the state is governed from New Delhi until fresh elections are called and a new government is elected. Although intended to be a sensible constitutional option, this provision has unfortunately often been used by an intrusive national government to achieve political ends in one state or another. For example, following the Ayodhya incident described in Section 1, the Supreme Court ruled that the BJP had acted illegally, a decision that allowed Narasimha Rao to dismiss four state governments governed by the BJP. When new elections were held in these four states in November 1993, the BJP returned to power in only one of the four states, contributing to long-term acrimony between the BJP and the Congress Party.

The power struggle between the central government and the states is an ongoing one. With many Indian states inhabited by people who share different histories and cultures, including language, and with political parties in power in the national government that differ from those in the states, the central-state conflicts become multidimensional, couched in the rhetoric of relative jurisdictions but fueled by substantial political and ethnic conflicts. Note that despite the formal division of power between the central and state governments, India's central government is really quite powerful.

Below state governments are district, city, and village governments. In 1992 the government added an amendment to the constitution that created the legal framework for all states to implement the Panchayat Raj (local self-government) Institutions, though models were allowed to differ between states. The primary role of the **panchayats** was envisioned as being in the areas of development, planning, and implementation of programs for economic development and social justice. While it is still too early to judge the effectiveness of these institutions, the establishment of the panchayats was an attempt to create greater local involvement in government and a direct effort to improve the quality of local governance. Given India's size, it is not surprising that the specific forms, quality of personnel, and effectiveness of these local governments vary greatly. Usually, however, most local governments have both elected and bureaucratic personnel. None of these subgovernments is a policy-making body; instead, policy is made at the national and state levels and these lower levels are responsible for implementation. Thus considerable resources pass through these institutions, and even though local governments seldom enjoy formal discretion over how these resources are allocated, there is ample room for misuse. Local political elites, bureaucrats, and other local "big men" often collude as they decide the location of projects, who gets a contract, or who gets jobs on public projects, ensuring themselves a healthy share of the public money. This is why many local governments in India tend to be corrupt and ineffective. There are some exceptions. In the state of West Bengal, a reform-oriented, leftist government helped improve the functioning of local governments. But for the most part, local governments in India languish and waste resources. City streets are not kept clean; potholes do not get filled; irrigation canals do not get desilted; wells are located in the backyards of village "big men"; and rural schools are so poorly built that they leak as soon as the monsoons start.

The Policy-Making Process

Major policies in India are made at the highest level of government, in New Delhi, the nation's capital. As mentioned earlier, the prime minister and the senior cabinet ministers are generally responsible for initiating new policies and related legislation. Behind the scenes, senior civil servants in each ministry, as well as in such specific cross-ministry offices as the prime minister's secretariat or the planning commission, play a critical role in identifying problems, synthesizing available data, and presenting alternative solutions and their implications to political leaders. After decisions have been made at the highest level, many of them require new legislation. Since the prime minister usually has a clear majority in the parliament, passage of most legislation is assured in India, except in extremely controversial areas. Rather, the real policy drama in India occurs during the early process, when major bills are under consideration, and then during the process of implementation. To understand these processes, one must understand how interests get organized and find representation.

Examples of several specific policies will help clarify these issues. First, consider economic liberalization policies. These policies represented a major economic change, and they were decided at the highest level of government, involving only a handful of senior ministers and bureaucrats. To reach these decisions, however, a fairly complex set of political activities took place. For example, the decision-makers needed to consult some of the most important interest groups, such as associations of Indian businessmen or representatives of multinational organizations like the World Bank or the IMF. Others, including those who might be adversely affected, needed to be heard; organized labor, for example, might call a one-day general strike (it actually did) to warn the government that any attempt to privatize the public sector would meet considerable resistance. Newspapers, magazines, and intellectuals also expressed their support or opposition publicly. Then political parties got into the act. Members of the ruling party, the Congress in this case, did not necessarily support the political thinking of their own leaders at the early stage; rather, they worried about the political implications of policies, both for intraparty power struggles and for future elections. Opposition parties, in turn, worried about the interests of their constituencies and adopted a more or less principled stand toward the new policies under consideration—that is, for, against, or somewhere in between. All of these pulls and pushes modified the policy that the government eventually adopted.

After policies have been adopted, their implementation is far from assured. Again, continuing with the liberalization example, some aspects of the new policy package proved easier to implement than others. Changing the exchange rate (the value of the Indian rupee in relation to such currencies as the U.S. dollar) was relatively easy to implement because both the policy decision and its implementation require the actions of only a handful of politicians and bureaucrats. By contrast, the attempts to simplify the procedures for Indian or foreign business executives to create new business enterprises proved more complicated. Implementation of such policies involves layers of bureaucrats, most of whom at one time benefited from the control they exercised over entrepreneurs. When forced to relinquish this control, many of them dragged their feet and, where possible, sabotaged the newly simplified procedures.

Another example is the policies aimed at improving the standard of living for the Indian poor. Since the 1960s the national government has attempted to redistribute agricultural land and provide public works programs to help India's rural poor. The national government set the broad outlines for land reforms and allocated funds for public works programs; but because both of these measures primarily influence rural and agricultural life within the jurisdiction of state governments, further refinement of these policies, as well as their implementation, was left to the states. State governments vary, both in terms of the class coalitions and political parties that rule within them and in terms of the quality of their bureaucracies. The result is that the implementation of antipoverty policies within India has been quite uneven.

Land redistribution involves taking land from well-off, powerful landlords and redistributing it to poor tenants or agricultural laborers. This is a highly controversial process, requiring some combination of forceful actions by state governments and the organization of the poor beneficiaries. Generally, attempts at land redistribution have been relatively unsuccessful in most Indian states because the interests of landowning classes are well-represented and state-level bureaucrats often have close links to these landowning groups. Partial exceptions to these trends are found in the states of Kerala and West Bengal, where communist state governments and the well-organized poor have made some progress in land reform.

Attempts to generate extra employment for the rural poor through public works projects (such as road construction and canal cleaning) have been somewhat more successful than land redistribution policies because they do not involve any direct confiscation of property. The main issues in the implementation of these policies are the quality of projects chosen, whether they target the poor, and how honestly they are completed. Because the quality of local governments in implementing national policies varies, although rarely is it very high, considerable resources assigned to poverty alleviation programs have been wasted. Public works policies have been most effectively implemented in the states of Maharashtra and West Bengal, where there is considerable political pressure from caste or class politics, and in some southern states, where the quality of local bureaucracy is somewhat better.

To review, the policy-making process in India, though relatively centralized, takes into account various interests and frequently produces well-developed policies. By contrast, the process of implementation is quite decentralized and relatively ineffective. What often start out as sound policy ideas and positive inten-tions do not always come to fruition, both because policies are diluted as they get redefined at the state level and because of lackluster implementation.

Section ❹ Representation and Participation

Over the years, India has become a participatory democracy, as previously excluded social groups such as the poor, the landless, and backward castes entered the political arena and used their influence to shape the political process. In the early years of independence, the Congress Party mobilized most groups. However, in recent years there has been a proliferation of political parties that have appealed to the Indian masses on ethnic grounds (particularly caste and religion), a trend initiated by Indira Gandhi. Simultaneously, the adoption of the democratic idea in the institutional sphere led to an explosion of social movements in civil society. Poor women have marched on the streets of Andhra Pradesh demanding prohibition of the sale of liquor (because of the economic toll it inflicts and its role in domestic violence), while in Maharashtra poor tribals have protested their displacement by the construction of large dams. The democratic idea is so insidious that today thousands of nongovernmental organizations function in the country representing causes ranging from welfare issues to environment to human rights. Some social movements have transformed themselves into political parties, while others have remained defiant of the system.

The Legislature

A good place to begin the discussion of representation and participation in a democracy is with the legislature, one arena in which diverse groups seek representation. As mentioned in Section 3, the Indian parliament consists of a two-house legislature, the *Rajya Sabha* and the *Lok Sabha*. The *Lok Sabha* at the national level and the various legislative assemblies at the state level provide such arenas in India. With considerable overlap between the executive and the legislative branches of government, legislative bodies do not have a direct or significant role in policy-making.

Nevertheless, election to a legislature is still much sought after in India, for two reasons. First, because a prime minister or a chief minister of a state needs the support of a majority in the legislature to acquire and maintain a position of leadership, legislatures hold a significant place in the pyramid of power. Second, those who become members of this power structure, although unable to influence policies directly, achieve considerable status, personal access to resources, and influence over allocations of government monies and contracts within their constituencies.

Elections to the *Lok Sabha* are supposed to be held at least every five years but, as in other parliamentary systems, the prime minister may choose to call elections earlier. India is currently divided into 544 electoral districts of roughly equal population, each of which elects and sends one representative to the national parliament. Those who contest elections generally contest them as nominees of one of the major political parties; that is, they contest them on a party ticket, with the support of one of the parties. Elections in India are won or lost mainly by parties, especially by party leaders, so most legislators are beholden to party leaders for securing a party ticket. Success in elections, therefore, does not depend on an independent power base but on a party whose leader—or, occasionally, whose programs—appeals to the populace. When these victorious legislators reach the *Lok Sabha*, they often fall in line with the goals of the party leadership, especially if the leadership is strong (in other words, has proven its capacity to appeal to voters).

The main business of the *Lok Sabha* is to pass new legislation as well as to debate the pros and cons of government actions. Most new legislation is introduced by the government, although there are opportunities for independent members to introduce bills. After the political and bureaucratic elite introduce new legislation, as in most parliamentary systems, the new bills are formally announced and then assigned to parliamentary committees for detailed study and discussion. The committees report the bills back to the *Lok Sabha* for debate, amendments, and preliminary votes. Then the bills go to the *Rajya Sabha*, the upper house. Most members of the *Rajya Sabha* are elected indirectly by state legislatures. This is not a very powerful body in India; it mostly accepts bills that have been passed by the *Lok Sabha*. After any final modifications by the *Rajya Sabha*, the bills come back for a third reading, after which they are finally voted on in both houses and eventually forwarded to the president for approval.

To understand why the *Lok Sabha* in India does not play a significant independent role in policy-making, keep in mind that (1) new legislation is generally introduced by a small group of government leaders; (2) most legislators, especially those belonging to the Congress Party, feel politically beholden to party leaders; and (3) all parties use party whips to ensure voting along party lines. One unfortunate implication of parliament's relative ineffectiveness is that its social composition does not have direct policy consequences. In other words, whether members of parliament are business executives or workers, men or women, members of upper or lower castes, is not likely to lead to dramatic policy shifts within India. The policy-making process is relatively centralized, and various interest groups influence it through channels other than the legislature. Nevertheless, dramatic shifts in social composition are bound to influence policy, and even if marginal shifts have little impact on policy, many groups in society derive satisfaction from having one of their own in the parliament.

The typical member of parliament in India tends to be a male university graduate between forty and sixty years of age. Over the years, there have been changes in the social composition along some criteria but not others. For example, an average legislator in the 1950s was likely to be a man of urban background, often a lawyer and a member of the higher castes. However, nearly half the members of parliament now come from rural areas, and many have agricultural backgrounds. Members of the middle castes (the so-called backward castes) are also well represented today. These changes reflect some of the broad shifts in the distribution of power in Indian society. By contrast, the proportion of women and of poor, lower-caste individuals in the parliament remains low.

Political Parties and the Party System

Political parties and elections are areas where much of the real drama of Indian politics occurs. Parties in control of a majority of seats in the national or state parliaments form the national or state governments and control government resources. Parties thus devote substantial political energy to contesting and winning elections. Since independence, the party system has evolved from one dominated by the Congress Party to one in which the party's role has been significantly challenged (see Table 2).

What began as nearly a one-party system has evolved into a real multiparty system, with three main

Table 2

Major Party Election Results

	1991		1996		1998	
	% of Popular Vote	Seats	% of Popular Vote	Seats	% of Popular Vote	Seats
Congress (I)	37.3	225	29	143	25.4	140
BJP & Allies	19.9	119	24	193	36.2	250
Janata	10.8	55	Joined with United Front		Joined with United Front	
United Front	—	—	31	180	20.9	98
Communists[a]	—	48	Joined with United Front		Joined with United Front	

[a] Includes both the CPM and the CPI.

Source: *India Today*, July 15, 1991, 40–55, *Economic Times* Web site; and *India Today*, March 16, 1998.

political tendencies: centrist, center-left and center-right. Within this framework there are at least four potentially significant national parties and many regional parties competing for power. The four parties with significant national presence are the Congress (I); the Janata Party; the BJP; and the Communist Party of India (Marxist), or the CPM. Whereas the CPM is a left-leaning party and the BJP is a religious, right-leaning one, both Congress (I) and the Janata are more or less centrist parties. During the 1996 elections the Janata Party joined forces with the CPM and other smaller parties to form the United Front and has been able to form two short-lived left-leaning governments.

The Congress Party

The Congress (I), usually referred to as the Congress, was India's premier political party until the 1990s. Many aspects of the Congress have already been discussed because it is impossible to analyze Indian politics without referring to the role of the Congress Party. To briefly summarize, the Indian National Congress, under the leadership of Mahatma Gandhi, Nehru, and others, spearheaded India's nationalist movement during the 1920s and 1930s. After independence, the Congress Party needed the electoral support of a majority of Indians, most of whom were poor, low-caste village dwellers. Because they were new to the democratic system, most of these underprivileged, uneducated poor citizens tended in the early years to follow the political lead of village "big men"—local influential people in villages and often men of high caste and means. The Congress Party thus built its electoral network by establishing a patronage system with such "big men" across India; the "big men" would mobilize electoral support for the Congress Party during elections and, once in power, the Congress Party would channel government resources to them further enhancing their local position and assuring their support. This patronage system (some call it machine politics) worked quite well for the Congress Party for nearly two decades. Even when electorally successful, however, this strategy bequeathed internal contradictions to the INC. The great, pro-poor Congress Party of India, with a socialist shell, came to be internally dominated by high-caste, wealthy Indians.

By the early 1950s, with Nehru at its helm, Congress was the unquestioned ruling party of India. Over the years, especially since the mid-1960s, this hegemony came to be challenged. By the time Indira Gandhi assumed power in 1966, India's old Congress Party had begun to lose its political sway and anti-colonial nationalism was fading. The spread of democratic politics had mobilized many poor, lower-caste citizens who depended less and less on village "big men" for political guidance. As a result, numerous regional parties started challenging Congress's monopoly on power. Weather-related food shortages in the mid-1960s also hurt the Congress Party in the 1967 elections.

Indira Gandhi sought to reverse the decline in Congress's electoral popularity through mobilizing India's vast majority, the poor, by promising "alleviation of poverty" as the core of her political program. This promise struck a popular chord, propelling Indira Gandhi to the top of India's political pyramid. Her personal success, however, came at a cost to the Congress Party. The old Congress split into two parties, with one branch, the Congress (O), dying and leaving the other, Congress (I)—the "I" standing for Indira—to inherit the position of the old undivided Congress. Nevertheless, the Congress Party formed the governments from independence to 1989, with only one interlude during which the Janata Party formed the government, during 1977–1980. Since 1989 the government has been formed by the Janata (1989–1991), the United Front (1996–1998), and the BJP (1998), with Congress heading the government from 1991 to 1996.

Prior to Indira Gandhi's prime ministership, rank-and-file party members elected the lowest-level Congress Party officers, who in turn elected the officers at higher levels of the party organization, up to the position of the party leader, who was the prime minister. In effect, the prime minister was elected from below and by the party. Indira Gandhi reversed this bottom-up party structure. She gained immense personal popularity by populist appeals to the masses and subsequently created a top-down party in which party officers were appointed by the leaders. With some modifications, including some limited internal party elections, this is basically how the contemporary Congress Party is organized. The top-down structure enables the leaders to control the party, but it is a major liability when grassroots support is necessary. As the nation's oldest party, the Congress continues to attract substantial electoral support. However, if this support ever declined sharply, most likely the party rank-and-file would demand its reorganization.

Whereas Congress during the 1970s had a left-of-center, pro-poor political platform, beginning in 1984 it moved toward the ideological center under Rajiv Gandhi. (See Section 2 for the reasons behind this shift.) Today the current Congress Party tilts to right-of-center, championing issues of economic efficiency, business interests, and limited government spending over the rights of the poor and the working people, and over social questions of health, education, and welfare.

As a nationalist party, the Congress Party is intimately associated with the stability of the Indian nation and the state in Indian political culture. Irrespective of its economic program, therefore, the Congress has always attracted support from diverse social groups: rich and poor, upper and lower castes, Hindus and Muslims, northerners and southerners. Nevertheless, elections in the 1990s indicate that the Congress has lost some of its traditional constituencies among the poor, lower castes, and such minorities as Muslims.

The Janata Party

The Janata Party, India's other centrist party, formed short-lived national governments in 1977, 1989, and together with other parties through the United Front in 1996 and 1997. The Janata Party, however, is not so much a political party as an umbrella for various parties and factions who move in and out depending on political circumstances. The Janata Party was created in 1977 when several smaller parties, who opposed Indira Gandhi's Emergency, hurriedly united to contest her and, much to their own surprise, won the national elections. This loose coalition lasted only for a little over two years, when conflicting leadership ambitions tore apart the fragile veneer of a party.

During the late 1980s the Janata Party enjoyed another brief term as a national government under the leadership of a breakaway Congress leader, V. P. Singh, who championed himself as an honest native son battling the corrupt and Westernized Rajiv Gandhi. Gandhi had been tainted by the Bofors scandal, so-called because the Swedish arms manufacturing company Bofors apparently bribed senior Congress officials in Rajiv Gandhi's government to obtain a lucrative arms contract. With these appeals, the Janata Party won enough seats in the national parliament to form a minority government in 1989. Once again factionalism overwhelmed any attempt at a stable government, and this second attempt with a non–Congress-led government collapsed after a little over two years. This brought about national elections in 1991; Rajiv Gandhi was assassinated during a campaign rally and Narasimha Rao was elected. Since then, the Janata Party has been able to survive only under the umbrella of the United Front, which is a collection of smaller parties, including the CPM.

The Janata Party has a very weak organizational structure and lacks a distinctive, coherent political platform. To distinguish itself from the Congress, it claims that it is more Gandhian—a reference to the decentralized, village-oriented vision of Mahatma Gandhi for modern India—more rural-oriented, and less pro-Brahmin. Although most of its efforts at political self-definition have not been very successful, while in power V. P. Singh undertook one major policy initiative that identified the Janata Party with a progressive cause. This was the acceptance of the Mandal Commission's recommendations that India's backward castes—generally, the middle, rural castes who constitute a near majority in the Indian countryside—be provided substantial reservations (or reserved access) in government jobs and educational institutions. The acceptance of this recommendation produced a nationwide outburst of riots and violence, led by members of upper castes who felt threatened. The uproar eventually contributed to the downfall of V. P. Singh's government. Nevertheless, the acceptance of "Mandal" by V. P. Singh associated the Janata Party with the interests of the backward castes. How strongly backward castes will continue to identify with the Janata in the future is unknown. For now, the Janata Party is viewed, especially in north-central India, as a party of small, rural agriculturalists who generally fall somewhere in the middle of the rigid caste hierarchy between Brahmins and the untouchables.

The Bharatiya Janata Party

The major new political party in contemporary India is the Bharatiya Janata party (BJP). Although formally constituted only in the early 1980s, the party is a direct descendant of the Jana Sangh party that entered the Indian political scene in 1951. The BJP is a right-leaning, Hindu-nationalist party, the first major party to mobilize explicitly on the basis of religious identity; it is also exclusionary in its appeals to Hindu identity that vilify Muslims. In comparison to both the Congress and the Janata, the BJP is better organized; it has disciplined party members, who after a prolonged apprenticeship become party cadres, and the authority lines within the party are relatively clear and well respected.

The party is closely affiliated with many related political organizations, the most significant of which is the Rashtriya Sevak Sangh (Association for National Service), the RSS. Most BJP leaders were at one time members of the RSS, which recruits young people (especially educated youth in urban areas) and involves them in a fairly disciplined set of cultural activities, including the study of a chauvinistic reinterpretation of India's "great Hindu past." These young people, uniformed in khaki shorts and shirts, can often be seen in Indian cities doing group exercises in the mornings and evenings and singing songs glorifying India's Sanskritic civilization (Sanskrit is the classical language in which some of the ancient Hindu scriptures are written). Recalling the pursuits of right-wing fascist groups of interwar Europe, the activities of these youth groups—seemingly no more than an appeal to cultural pride—dismay many non-Hindu minorities and Indian liberals, who fear the havoc that cultural pride can produce, as for example in Nazi Germany.

Those traditionally attracted to the Jana Sangh and the BJP were mainly urban, lower-middle-class groups, especially small traders and commercial groups. As long as this was its main source of support, the BJP remained a minor actor on the Indian political scene. Since the mid-1980s, however, the BJP appreciably widened its base of support by appealing to Hindu nationalism, especially in north-central India. The decline in the Congress Party's popularity created a vacuum that the BJP was well positioned to fill.

Moreover, the BJP found in Indian Muslims a convenient scapegoat for the frustrations of various social groups and successfully mobilized Hindus in an attempt to create a religiously oriented political force where none had existed before. The electoral success of the BJP in 1989 and 1991 and its formation of the government in 1998 underscore the party's rapid rise to power. BJP's early efforts resulted in its ruling four states from 1991 to 1993, though it lost power in three of the four in 1993. However, during the 1998 parliamentary elections the BJP scored a major success by being the party with the largest number of seats and thus being able to head the national government. There are many poor or otherwise frustrated social groups in India whose anger is available for political mobilization. Whether the BJP will succeed in continuing to tap this anger in the longer term cannot be predicted. What can be said is that democracy and large pockets of social frustration provide a combustible mix that will continue to generate unexpected outcomes in Indian politics.

The Communist Party

The fourth major political party is the Communist Party of India (Marxist), or CPM. The CPM is an offshoot of the Communist Party of India (CPI), which was formed during the colonial period and has existed nearly as long as the Congress Party. Though the contemporary CPM has a national presence—that is, it nearly always elects representatives to the *Lok Sabha*—its political base is concentrated in two of India's states, West Bengal and Kerala. These states have often been ruled by the CPM, and they often elect *Lok Sabha* members who run on a CPM ticket.

The CPM is a disciplined party, with party cadres and a hierarchical authority structure. Other than its name and internal organization, however, there is nothing communist about the CPM; rather it is a social democratic party like the British Labour Party or the German Social Democratic Party. The CPM accepts the framework of democracy, regularly participates in elections, and often wins them in West Bengal and Kerala. In these two states, the CPM enjoys the support of the lower-middle and lower classes, both factory workers and poorer peasants. Within the national parliament, CPM members often strongly criticize government policies that are likely to hurt the poor. On occasion the CPM joins with other parties against the BJP, as it did in the 1996 elections by joining the United Front. Where the CPM runs state governments, for example in West Bengal and Kerala, it has provided a relatively honest and stable administration. It has also pursued a moderate but effective reform program, ensuring the rights of agricultural tenants (such as preventing their evictions), providing services to those living in shantytowns, and encouraging public investments in rural areas.

Elections

The four major parties, along with several other minor parties, periodically compete for the votes of the Indian electorate. Elections in India are a colossal event. Nearly 500 million people are eligible to vote and close to 300 million actually do so. The turnout rate in the 1990s has been over 60 percent, considerably higher than in the United States. The level of technology used both in campaigning and in the conduct of elections is fairly low. Television plays an increasingly important role, but much campaigning still involves face-to-face contact between politicians and the electorate. Senior leaders fly around the country, making speeches to millions of potential supporters at political rallies held in tiny villages and district towns. Lesser politicians and thousands of their party supporters travel the dusty streets, blaring music and political messages from loudspeakers mounted on their vehicles.

Given the high rate of illiteracy, pictures of party symbols are critical: for example, a hand for the Congress (I); a lotus for the BJP; a hammer and sickle for the CPM. The way many voters signify their vote for a candidate in the polling booth is to put their thumb mark on one of these symbols. During the campaign, therefore, party representatives work very hard to associate certain individuals and election platforms with specific symbols. A typical election slogan, for example, is, "Vote for the hammer and sickle because they stand for the rights of the working people."

India's electoral system, like the British system, is a first-past-the-post system. A number of candidates compete in an electoral district; the candidate who has the most votes wins. For example, if the Congress candidate wins the most votes, say 35 percent of the vote from a district, and the candidates of other parties split the remaining votes, the Congress candidate is victorious. This system privileges the major political parties. It also generates considerable pressure for opposition parties to collaborate as a single voice against the government. In practice, however, given the differences between opposition parties and the considerable clash of leadership ambitions, many parties compete, enabling the candidates of the larger party to squeeze by as winners.

Political Culture, Citizenship, and Identity

The only generalization that can be made about Indian political culture is that, in such a large and culturally diverse country, no single set of cultural traits is shared by the entire population. Nevertheless, three important tendencies—or habits of mind, produced by repeated practice—are worth noting. These political cultural traits reflect India's hybrid political style, as a rigid, hierarchical, and village-oriented old civilization adapts itself to modern socioeconomic changes, especially to democratic politics.

Village women wait in line to get voting slips at a polling station in a village in India's Orissa state, March 7, 1995. *Source:* Reuters/Bettmann.

The members of India's political elite often have difficulty working and cooperating with each other, so a factionalized elite is a well-known characteristic of Indian politics. The roots of such behavior are complex, reflecting India's fragmented social structure; this style of politics by now seems deeply ingrained in India. Although some important exceptions exist, generally the personal political ambitions of Indian leaders prevent them from pursuing such collective goals as forming cohesive political parties, running a stable government, or focusing on problems of national development. In contrast to many East Asian countries, where the norms of consensus are powerful and political negotiation is often conducted behind closed doors, politics in India veer toward the other extreme, with open disagreements and conflicts the norm.

India's political and public spheres of activity are not sharply divided from personal and private spheres of activity. India is not unique in this; it is an issue in most developing countries and, in some respects, given its long history of a nationalist movement and its well-established civil service, India has a much better developed sense of the public sphere than, say, many African countries. Nevertheless, the idea that a public office is not a legitimate means for personal enrichment or for furthering the interests of family members or of personal associates is not yet fully accepted in India. One important result is a fairly widespread misuse of public resources for personal gain, or more directly, widespread corruption in political life.

The third political cultural tendency that deserves mention concerns fragmentation of political life in India. Indian society is highly segmented. Different regions have different languages and cultures; within regions, villages are poorly connected with each other; and within villages, different castes often live in isolation from one another. As this segmented and localized society has been drawn into democratic politics, the results have often been unexpected. For example, there is an expectation in democratic politics that those sharing similar interests will unite politically to pursue collective interests. Following this logic, one might expect the poor in India to come together politically to make collective demands on the state. However, the habits of mind in India have inhibited any such group formation based on class. Instead,

politics is often fragmented along caste lines, but even caste grievances tend to remain local rather than accumulate nationally or even regionally. Some observers of India find this segmented quality of Indian politics a blessing because it localizes problems, facilitating political stability, but others find it a curse because it stymies the possibility of pursuing reforms to improve the lot of the poorest members of Indian society.

Democracy is relatively well established in India. Most Indians value their citizenship rights and, in spite of poverty and illiteracy, exercise them with vigor. One of the four core themes of this book is the power of the democratic idea. This can certainly be applied to India. However, the spread of democratic politics can simultaneously fuel political conflicts. In India, the spread of democracy is undermining many of India's political givens, including some of the most rigid hierarchies, and has begun to produce new political patterns.

The most significant of these recent developments concerns identity politics, whereby the dynamics of democratic politics mobilizes latent identities to produce powerful collective identities. Region, language, religion, and caste all help Indians define who they are and, as a result, help them categorize "we" and "they" in political associations and conflicts. Such differences have generated political cleavages in India, underlining the importance and yet the malleability of collective identities, for example, the Hindu-Muslim conflict at the time of independence. Some of these identity conflicts remained dormant when Nehru's secular nationalism and Indira Gandhi's poor-versus-rich cleavage defined the core political issues. In the 1980s and 1990s, however, with the relative decline of the Congress Party, and with developments in communications and transportation making people more aware of each other's differences, identity-based political conflicts have mushroomed in India. Two of the more significant conflicts deserve mention.

First, caste conflicts, though usually confined to local and regional politics, have taken on a national dimension in recent years, for example, the acceptance of the Mandal Commission recommendations by the former prime minister V. P. Singh. These recommendations were meant to benefit India's backward castes, who are numerically significant and who tend to be rural agriculturalists by occupation and somewhere in the middle of the caste hierarchy. Groups of backward castes had made a political mark in many states, but prior to "Mandal," they were seldom a cohesive factor in national politics. In all probability, V. P. Singh, by approving the Mandal recommendations, hoped to create a powerful support base out of these disparate groups. However, the move backfired. The threatened upper castes reacted sharply with demonstrations, riots, and political violence. Not only did this disruption contribute to the downfall of V. P. Singh's government but it also converted the conflict between castes from a local and regional issue to a divisive national issue.

The second identity-based political conflict that has reemerged in recent years has pitched Indian Hindus and Muslims against each other. Tensions between these religious communities go back several centuries to when Muslim rulers from Central Asia established the Moghul dynasty in India. Stories and memories of the relative greatness of one community over the other, or of atrocities and injustices unleashed on one community by the other, abound in India's popular culture. For the most part, these legends fan low-level, latent hostilities that do not prevent peaceful coexistence. However, political circumstances, especially political machinations by ambitious leaders, can unleash these latent tendencies and instigate overt conflict. This is what has happened since the mid-1980s as the BJP has whipped up anti-Muslim sentiments in an effort to unite disparate Hindu groups into a political force. The resulting victimization of Muslims in acts of political violence, including destruction of life, property, and places of worship, illustrates the dangers of identity-based political passions.

Interests, Social Movements, and Protest

India's democracy is an active one. At any time, numerous groups are demanding a greater share of wealth, status, or power from a state or the national government. How business and other elite groups influence government has been discussed. In addition, organized labor is politically active in India, but labor unions are politically fragmented. Instead of the familiar model of one factory/one union, within one factory in India competing unions can be organized by different political parties. Above the factory level,

several labor organizations compete for labor's support. While unions can bring considerable pressure to bear on both management and politicians, for the most part they are not well-organized on the national level. The government generally stays out of labor-management conflicts. India's industrial relations are thus closer to the pluralist model practiced in Anglo-American countries than to the corporatist model, say, of Mexico. The political energies of unions are channeled into frequent local battles involving strikes, demonstrations, and a peculiarly Indian protest technique called *gherao*, "encirclement." Labor groups using *gherao* will encircle a member of management and not let him go—sometimes for days—until management meets their demands. Labor politics in India is thus active but not coherent.

Except for big business groups and unionized labor, many demand groups unite for a specific purpose and then disband. For example, the better-off peasantry periodically organize at the state or national level to demand higher support prices for agricultural products or increased subsidies for inputs such as fertilizer. Groups formed around caste and religion are also very active in Indian politics. Such political activities demonstrate the health of Indian democracy but highlight a central tension in it: How can government simultaneously accommodate multiple demands and yet facilitate a coherent program for national development?

There are several active women's movements in India, especially in urban areas but also in rural settings. They bring together educated, middle-class women and, at other times, poor women. The movements composed of middle-class women tend to be more durable because they usually aim to alter deeply held attitudes, whereas others are likely to raise a protest against an immediate specific injustice like a rape or a dowry death (a murder or suicide because of a perceived inadequate marriage dowry) or against the unrestricted sale of alcohol, which is viewed as responsible for alcoholism among husbands.

A number of environmental movements also exist. These are often led by educated, urban environmentalists who mobilize victims of development projects. For example, the movement against deforestation, called the Chipko movement, has been fairly successful. Also, a very large project sponsored by the World Bank—construction of a dam over the river

Narmada—aroused protestors, who said the construction would cause environmental problems, including the displacement of thousands of families. The protest was sufficient to cause the World Bank to rescind its support, but the Indian government is still pursuing the project.

A variety of poor people's movements flourish. Most tend to be local and short-lived, but they can mobilize quickly and have considerable political impact. For example, a variety of "tribal" groups, often ethnically distinct, live in remote areas, tend to be very poor, and are categorized as tribals because the government chooses to label them as such. Many of these groups organize political protest, demanding a greater share of public resources, preservation of the meager resources they control, or the like. India's untouchable castes also organize politically to protest caste injustices. In some states, like Bihar, such movements have become very violent, with various caste groups arming themselves in private armies. At times, issues of caste, tribe, and poverty overlap to produce a highly volatile mix. In the southern state of Andhra Pradesh, for example, poor tribals have been organized by armed revolutionaries who hang village landlords and other perceived exploiters to achieve a measure of local justice. Even though such protests are violently suppressed by police intervention, their proliferation illustrates the considerable activism and dissatisfaction in India's political society.

To review, political participation in India has over the years broadened in scope and deepened in intensity. As more groups demand a share of power, it can be suggested that forces of democratization in India have spread wide and deep. A single-party system dominated by the Congress Party has slowly been supplanted by a multiparty system of parties on the left and the right. Similarly, old hierarchies of caste have eroded in Indian society; upper castes cannot readily control the political behavior of those below them. The result is that many groups in society increasingly feel empowered and hope to translate this new consciousness and sense of efficacy into material gains by influencing government policies. The challenge for any government in India is how to respond to these growing demands; the dilemma is how to promote economic efficiency and growth while channeling resources to these newly empowered groups.

Section 5   Indian Politics in Transition

Between 1996 and 1998 India had four national governments (see Table 1). All were minority governments, requiring a variety of coalition arrangements to survive. The BJP government that came to power in 1998 lost a vote of confidence in the *Lok Sabha* in May 1999. The government resigned, necessitating yet another election. As these developments demonstrate, India desperately needs a stable, majority government to meet its enduring challenges.

Political Challenges and Changing Agendas

Because India is a large developing country and a democracy, a study of Indian politics sheds light on more general issues of comparative politics. In this chapter, India's development has been examined in light of four comparative themes. As a large country with a legitimate government and sizable armed forces, India is not readily influenced by external forces. For example, India tested nuclear bombs in 1998 and successfully withstood international condemnation and sanctions. However, in an increasingly interdependent global economic context, as seen in the 1997 East Asian economic crisis, India is no longer invulnerable to global pressures. An examination of the sequence of events in the aftermath of the nuclear tests in India will clarify the interdependent dynamic of the world of states.

The nuclear tests of May 1998 opened a Pandora's box of intensified geopolitical rivalry in Asia and the risk of future copycat attempts in other volatile regions of the world. The focus of international (particularly U.S.) diplomacy shifted from punitive economic and technological sanctions to seeking a universal nonproliferation agreement. India cannot ignore its dependence on other states for economic and technological support, and the rest of the world cannot ignore the implications of India's nuclear outing. The Vajpayee and the Clinton administrations engaged in several rounds of delicate arms control talks; efforts were made to persuade India to sign the Comprehensive Test Ban Treaty (CTBT) and the Nuclear Non-Proliferation Treaty (NPT) in exchange for completely lifting U.S. sanctions. India opposed the NPT on the grounds that it was unfair to nonnuclear countries because it did not establish a procedure for eventual phaseout of nuclear weapons by the nuclear powers. The United States also urged India to exercise restraint on its nuclear weapons and missiles programs, while New Delhi insisted on its right to minimum nuclear deterrence. In late 1998, India announced its intention to sign the Comprehensive Test Ban Treaty if talks with the United States ended successfully and also signaled its willingness to join other nuclear control groups.

Thus one major political challenge for India is how to negotiate with the rest of the world, particularly the United States, on its emergence as a nuclear weapons state. How will India combine its new nuclear power status with responsible use of such weapons? How will it negotiate with its nuclear neighbors, Pakistan and China, to ensure that South Asia does not set off a nuclear disaster? In February 1999, during a historic visit to Pakistan by the Indian prime minister, both countries agreed to continue their declared nuclear moratoriums on further nuclear tests. How India confronts challenges on the nuclear front is closely tied to its success on the economic front and management of rising ethnic tensions.

Comparativists debate how well an economy is governed. India's economic experience is neither a clear success nor a clear failure. If many African countries have done rather poorly economically and many East Asian countries (prior to 1997) have had dramatic successes, India falls somewhere in the middle. Three conditions may explain this outcome. First may be the nature and the quality of the government for promoting economic growth. In this, India has been fortunate to have enjoyed relatively good government since independence: its democratic system is mostly open and stable; its most powerful political leaders are public-spirited; and its upper bureaucracy is well trained and competent. These positive attributes truly stand out when India is compared to such African countries as Nigeria. The second condition concerns India's strategy for economic development. As noted previously, India in the 1950s chose to insulate its economy from global forces, limiting the role of trade and foreign investment and emphasizing the role of government in promoting self-sufficiency in heavy industry and in agriculture. The positive impact of this strategy was that India now produces enough food to feed its large and growing population while it simultaneously produces a vast range of industrial goods. This strategy, however, was not without costs. The protective atmosphere reduced competition to the extent that most of India's manufactured goods are produced rather inefficiently by global standards. The additional economic growth that might have come from competing effectively in the global markets and by selling its products abroad was sacrificed. India also gave up another area of potential economic growth by discouraging foreign investment. And last, during the phase of protective industrialization, India did little to alleviate its staggering poverty: land redistribution failed, job creation by heavy industries was minimal, and investment in the education and health of the poor was minuscule in relation to the magnitude of the problem. The poor also became a drag on economic growth because they were unable to buy goods and stimulate demand for increased production and because an uneducated and unhealthy labor force is not a productive labor force.

A stable government and an emphasis on self-sufficiency have promoted modest economic growth in India; higher rates of growth, however, have been difficult to achieve without greater links to the outside world and with the staggering numbers of poor people. This leads to the third condition regarding India's middling political economy: it concerns the emerging trends. India's continuing economic weakness has made it more vulnerable to global forces. The country's economic crisis in the early 1990s during the Gulf War exposed its vulnerability and prompted a shift toward a more open economy. This trend reflects a growing confidence and an awareness that sustained higher rates of growth necessitate such a shift. Meanwhile, the continuation of staggering levels of poverty in India is a disturbing problem. If India is to achieve sustained levels of high economic growth, the

Indian government must address the issues of literacy, health, and welfare for the poor, enabling them to join the economy as truly productive participants. The challenge faced by Indian politicians is to reconcile the demands of promoting an efficient economy with those of winning elections. The latter involves encouraging an expansion of government programs and subsidies to discontented groups, while the former calls for austerity. Restricting government's role conflicts with implementing distributive or populist programs; opening the national economy to foreign economic actors and products is likely to aggravate nationalist sentiments.

Some comparative scholars suggest that the widespread desire of citizens to exercise some control over their government is a potent force encouraging democracy. This assumption is clearly illustrated in Indian political trends. Even though democracy was introduced to India by its elites, the democratic tendency has permeated society, helping democracy put down firm roots in India. A clear example supporting this view was India's experience with Emergency rule, when Indira Gandhi curtailed democratic freedoms from 1975 to 1977. In the next election, in 1977, Indian citizens decisively voted Indira Gandhi out of power, registering their preference for democratic rule. Moreover, although India is challenged with numerous strains and stresses, no widespread anti-democratic movement exists. On the contrary, most Indians value democracy and use its institutions to advance their claims, at times even excessively.

India also provides a rich case for studying a fourth area of comparative interest, namely, the growing political impact of ethnic identities. Mobilized ethnic groups seeking access to state power and state-controlled economic resources are a basic component of the contemporary Indian political scene. Caste, language, and religion all provide identities around which political mobilization can be galvanized. Identification with a group, in turn, is further heightened by the democratic context, in which parties and leaders freely choose to manipulate such symbols. When studying Indian politics, it is difficult to separate interest- and identity-based politics. For example, caste struggles in India are simultaneously struggles for identity, for power, and for wealth. Identity politics in India is likely to be characterized by two trends: considerable political

ferment, with a variety of dissatisfied groups making demands on parties and governments; and pressure on political parties to broaden their electoral appeal to disadvantaged groups, especially those belonging to the middle and lower strata, many of whom are very poor. India's political leaders will thus continue to experience pressures to expand their support base by promising economic improvements or by manipulating nationalist symbols. Under what conditions will such political forces engage in constructive rather than destructive actions? Will democracy succeed in merely tempering the effect of such forces, or will it in the long run promote a positive channelling of identity politics?

Indian Politics in Comparative Perspective

By the twenty-first century, India will surpass China as the most populous country in the world. How such a country is governed will remain an issue of considerable significance, not only for the billion people residing within India's boundaries but also for India's neighbors and the world. A democratic and prosperous India could be a stabilizing force. A turbulent India, driven by ethnic and class turmoil, and with a collapsing authority structure, could have profound negative consequences, not just for Indians, but globally. In this concluding section, we first examine the implications of the study of India for comparative politics, and then assess how Indian politics and its economy will influence developments in a regional and global context.

Comparativists debate whether democracy or authoritarianism is better for economic growth. In the past, India did not compare well with the success stories of East Asian and Chinese authoritarian-led countries. The collapse in the late 1990s of several East Asian economies and the subsequent rise of instability within those societies makes a study of Indian democracy more relevant to understanding the institutional and cultural factors underpinning economic stability in the long run.

Another theme has been to assess the implications of establishing democracy in multiethnic societies. The rising tide of nationalism and the break-up of the Soviet Union and Yugoslavia, among others, has prompted closer examination of how and why India continues to exist as a cohesive entity. By studying India's history, particularly the post-1947 period, comparativists could explore questions of how cleavages of caste, religion, and language in India balance one another and cancel the most destructive elements in each.

Comparativists have also puzzled about the conditions under which multiple and contradictory interests could be harnessed within a democratic setup to generate positive economic and distributional outcomes. Here, the variable performance of the different regions in India could serve as a laboratory. For instance, two communist-ruled states, Kerala and West Bengal, have (to a certain extent) engaged in land redistribution policies. An examination of factors such as the role of the mobilizing parties and the interaction between the landless poor and the entrenched landed elite could provide answers. Another question engaging comparativists is whether success in providing education and welfare inevitably leads to success in the economic sphere. Again, the case of Kerala provides pointers for further research. Kerala scores high on human development indicators such as literacy and health, but paradoxically the state has not performed well on the economic front.

What are the international and domestic challenges faced by India at the dawn of the twenty-first century? How will India cope with its new-found status as a nuclear power? How can India prevent further escalation of conflict in the region that could end in a nuclear conflagration? A worst-case scenario would be a conventional war with Pakistan that could escalate into a nuclear war. Domestically, both countries are currently wracked with ethnic tensions and weak central governments. In an attempt to hold on to power, the leaders of each country could try to divert attention toward a national security threat from its neighbor, a ploy that has been used effectively in the past by politicians in both countries. The past history of three wars between India and Pakistan, the simmering tensions over Kashmir, and the fear of a decisive first strike could prompt a nuclear strike. The challenge for India is to establish a stable relationship with its nuclear neighbors, Pakistan and China, that would eschew proliferation of its nuclear and ballistic missiles arsenals and engage in constructive diplomatic and economic cooperation. India's history of wars with both countries is not an encouraging starting point, but the engagement of Western powers in gen-

erating a dialogue between these countries is a portent for the future. The visit to Pakistan by the Indian prime minister in 1999, the first visit in ten years and only the third ever, provides grounds for optimism. Whether such overtures will result in fruitful negotiations on Kashmir and on economic cooperation in the region remains to be seen. Answers to these questions depend heavily on developments in the sphere of domestic politics.

The history of fifty years of democracy in India has been a double-edged sword. Winning elections involves attracting votes. While avoiding authoritarianism, the practice of democracy, particularly electoral politics, has worsened ethnic animosities between Hindus and Muslims, upper caste and lower caste, and north and south. With the spread of democracy, many dissatisfied groups are finding their voices and becoming politically mobilized. The challenge for Indian politics is how to repair the divide within a democratic framework. The results of the November 1998 elections to the state government assemblies provides a more optimistic scenario. Despite the BJP-led central government's nuclear achievements, voters opted for the Congress party in three of the four states, and for a regional party in the fourth state. Current voter emphasis on good governance and sound economic management rather than on religious or nationalistic issues might transform electoral platforms in the twenty-first century. In any case, Indian politics will continue to tread a shaky path, as witnessed by the intensification of communal tensions marked by the macabre killing of a Christian missionary and his two young sons in Orissa in January 1999 by Hindu fundamentalists, as well as other attacks on Christians in scattered regions. Will India be able to manage its domestic tensions and enlarge social, political, and economic rights for its citizens?

Another challenge for India is how to combine its global ambitions of becoming a strong power with its program for economic liberalization. The increasing interdependence of global economies as manifested in global effects of the 1997 East Asian crisis and the dependence of developing countries on investor confidence and external aid should not be underestimated. While India was protected from the East Asian debacle because of the partially closed nature of its economy, the country nevertheless suffered economic blows in the aftermath of becoming nuclear in the form of frozen aid programs worth billions. In addition, a decrease in foreign direct investment followed from the loss of investor confidence as a result of the downgrading of India's credit rating. The economic woes engendered by the sanctions were accentuated by the BJP government's lack of progress on the economic liberalization front. Instead of opening up sectors such as insurance and consumer goods in an attempt to further integrate the Indian economy with the rest of the world, the BJP has so far continued to champion the protection of Indian businesses from global competitors. The Indian case embodies the tensions inherent in combining democracy with economic liberalization. Political parties in India face pressures to expand their support base by promoting contradictory economic improvements or by manipulating nationalist symbols. But simultaneously, these promises clash with the task of economic liberalization. The challenge faced by governments in India is how to combine the task of economic liberalization with the conflicting demands of electoral politics. Can India afford to take halting steps toward transformation of its economy? If the economic problems are not addressed swiftly and effectively, the world will be confronted by an India that is poor, ethnically mobilized, and controlling a formidable nuclear arsenal. This would compromise not just the regional but also global security.

How India reconciles its national political ambitions, domestic political demands for greater economic redistribution, and global pressures for an efficient economy will affect India's influence on regional and global trends. Will India be able to capitalize on some of its positive achievements such as the long-standing democratic ethos framed by functioning institutions, a vibrant civil society and media, and a growing middle class imbued with the desire to succeed economically? Or will India be chained down by increasingly belligerent ethnic cleavages resulting in, at best, inaction on all fronts and, at worst, total disintegration of the country? If the Congress Party is able to remobilize its old "umbrella party" constituency (such as Muslims, backward castes, and others) under Sonia Gandhi, we might see a return to the era of one-party rule in India. However, if current trends are any indication, the stage seems set for a scenario of two-party rule, with

either a BJP-led or a Congress-led coalition ruling at the center. There also seems to be some room for optimism with regard to voter needs and interests on the international and domestic fronts. For instance, during the February 1999 Vajpayee visit to Pakistan, some public opinion polls showed that an overwhelming number of people in India and Pakistan wanted improved relations between the two countries. On the domestic side, the preoccupation of voters with economic management, law and order, and other governance issues was evident from the results of the 1998 assembly elections. Of course, balancing the demands of simultaneously achieving equity and efficiency generates its own problems. The study and understanding of evolving political trends in India will remain matters of continuing significance.

Key Terms

Hindus	caste system
Muslims	Brahmin
Sikhs	untouchables
Maharajas	scheduled castes
zamindars	nonaligned bloc
Emergency	*Lok Sabha*
green revolution	*Rajya Sabha*
state-led economic development	Indian Administrative Service
economic liberalization	panchayats
reservations	

Suggested Readings

Bardhan, Pranab. *The Political Economy of Development in India.* New Delhi: Oxford University Press, 1984.

Bayly, C. A. *The New Cambridge History of India: Indian Society and the Making of the British Empire.* Vol. 2, no. 1. Cambridge: Cambridge University Press, 1988.

Brass, Paul R. *The New Cambridge History of India: The Politics of India Since Independence.* Vol. 4, no. 1. Cambridge: Cambridge University Press, 1990.

Carras, Mary C. *Indira Gandhi: In the Crucible of Leadership.* Boston: Beacon Press, 1979.

Chatterjee, Partha, ed. *State Politics in India.* Themes in Politics Series. Vol. 1. New Delhi: Oxford University Press, 1997.

Cohen, Stephen P. *The Indian Army: Its Contribution to the Development of a Nation.* Berkeley: University of California Press, 1971.

Dreze and Sen Amartya, eds. *Economic Development and Social Opportunity.* New Delhi: Oxford University Press, 1995.

Frankel, Francine. *India's Political Economy, 1947–1977.* Princeton, N.J.: Princeton University Press, 1978.

Gopal, Sarvepalli. *Jawaharlal Nehru: A Biography.* Vols. 2 and 3. New Delhi: Oxford University Press, 1984.

Graham, Bruce. *Hindu Nationalism and Indian Politics.* Cambridge: Cambridge University Press, 1990.

Hardgrave, Robert L., Jr., and Stanley A. Kochanek. *India: Government and Politics in a Developing Nation.* 4th ed. New York: Harcourt Brace Jovanovich, 1986.

Jaffrelot, Christophe. *The Hindu Nationalist Movement and Indian Politics, 1925 to the 1990s: Strategies on Identity Building, Implantation and Mobilization.* New York: Columbia University Press, 1996.

Jalan, Bimal. *India's Economic Crisis: The Way Ahead.* New Delhi: Oxford University Press, 1991.

Kohli, Atul. *The State and Poverty in India: The Politics of Reform.* Cambridge: Cambridge University Press, 1987.

——. *Democracy and Discontent: India's Growing Crisis of Governability.* Cambridge: Cambridge University Press, 1991.

Misra, B. B. *Government and Bureaucracy in India: 1947–1976.* New Delhi: Oxford University Press, 1986.

Nayar, Baldev Raj. *India's Mixed Economy.* Bombay: Popular Prakashan, 1989.

Rothermund, Dietmar. *An Economic History of India: From Pre-Colonial Times to 1986.* London: Croom Helm, 1988.

Rudolph, Lloyd, and Susanne Rudolph. *In Pursuit of Lakshmi: The Political Economy of the Indian State.* Chicago: Chicago University Press, 1987.

Sarkar, Sumit. *Modern India: 1885 to 1947.* Madras: Macmillan, 1983.

Weiner, Myron. *The Indian Paradox: Essays in Indian Politics.* New Delhi: Sage Publications, 1989.

——. *The Child and the State in India.* Princeton, N.J.: Princeton University Press, 1992.

CHAPTER 7

United States

Louis DeSipio

United States of America

Land and Population

Capital	Washington, D.C.
Total Area (square miles)	3,787,403 (about one-half the size of Russia)
Population	270 million
Annual Average Population Growth Rate (1990–1997)	1.0%
Urban Population	79%

Ethnic Composition		
	Non-Hispanic White	72.1%
	Non-Hispanic Black	12.1%
	Hispanic	11.4%
	Asian and Pacific Islander	3.7%
	American Indian and Eskimo	0.7%

Major Languages	English
	Spanish (spoken by approximately 8 percent of households)

Religious Affiliation		
	Protestant	57.9%
	Roman Catholic	21.0%
	Other Christian	6.4%
	Jewish	2.1%
	Muslim	1.9%
	Nonreligious	8.7%
	Other	2.0%

Economy

Domestic Currency	U.S. dollar	
Total GNP (US$)	$8.110 trillion	
GNP per capita (US$)	$28,600	
GNP per capita at purchasing power parity (US$)	$28,600	
GNP average annual growth rate	1996–1997	3.8%
GNP per capita average annual growth rate	1996–1997	2.9%
	1980–1995	1.5%
	1965–1980	1.8%
Income Gap: GDP per capita (of US$)	Richest 20% of population $51,705	
	Poorest 20% of population $5800	
Structure of Production (% of GDP)	Agriculture	2%
	Industry	26%
	Services	72%
Labor Force Distribution (% of total)	Agriculture	3%
	Industry	26%
	Services	71%
Exports as % of GDP	11%	
Imports as % of GDP	13%	
Electricity Consumption per capita (kwh)	12,660	

CO_2 Emissions per capita (metric tons)	20,500

Society

Life Expectancy	Female	79.6
	Male	72.9

Doctors per 100,000 population		245
Infant Mortality (per 1000 live births)		6
Adult Literacy		97%

(although the UN estimates that 20.7% of people aged 16–65 are functionally illiterate)

Access to Information and Communications per 1000 people	Radios	2122
	Televisions	776
	Telephone Lines	626
	Personal Computers	328

Women in Government and Economy

Women in Congress	13.3% (House) 9% (Senate)
Women at ministerial (cabinet) level	28.5%
Women as % of total labor force	45.0%
Female business administrators and managers	43.0%
Female professional and technical workers	53.0%
1998 Human Development Index ranking (out of 174 countries; 1 = highest)	4

Political Organization

Political System   Presidential system

Regime History   Representative democracy, usually dated from the signing of the Declaration of Independence (1776) or the Constitution (1787).

Administrative Structure   Federalism, with powers shared between the national government and the fifty state governments; separation of powers at the level of the national government among legislative, executive, and judicial branches.

Executive   President, "directly" elected (with Electoral College that officially elects president and vice president) for four-year term; cabinet is advisory group selected by president to aid in decision-making but with no formal authority.

Legislature   Bicameral. Congress composed of a lower house (House of Representatives) of 435 members serving two-year terms and an upper house (Senate) of 100 members (two from each state) serving six-year terms; elected in single-member districts (or, in the case of the Senate, states) by simple plurality.

Judiciary   Supreme Court with nine justices nominated by president and confirmed by Senate, with life tenure; has specified original and appellate jurisdiction and exercises the power of judicial review (can declare acts of the legislature and executive unconstitutional and therefore null and void).

Party System   Essentially two-party system (Republican and Democrat), with relatively weak and fractionalized parties; more than in most representative democracies, the personal following of candidates remains very important.

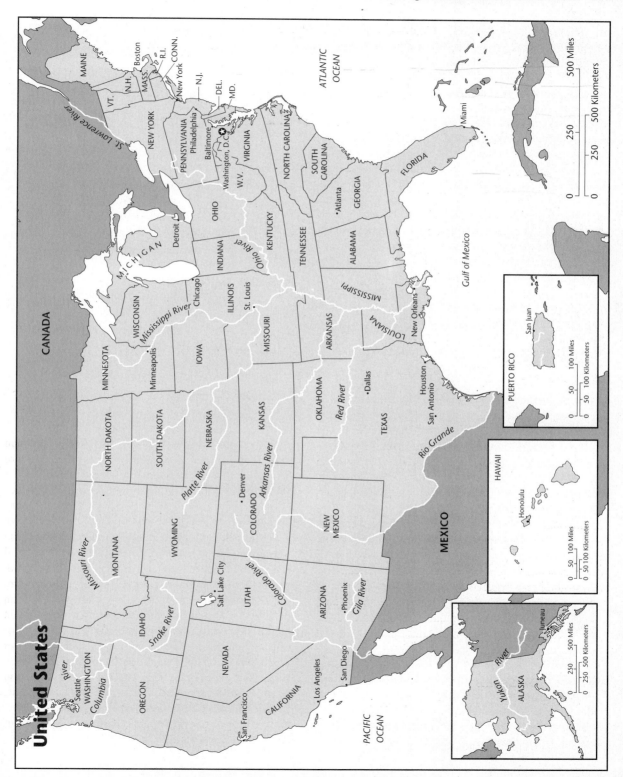

United States

CANADA

St. Lawrence River

MAINE
N.H.
VT.
MASS.   Boston
R.I.
CONN.
New York
N.J.
DEL.
MD.

NEW YORK
PENNSYLVANIA
Philadelphia
Baltimore
Washington, D.C.
W.V.
VIRGINIA
NORTH CAROLINA
SOUTH CAROLINA

ATLANTIC OCEAN

MICHIGAN
Detroit
OHIO
INDIANA
Ohio River
KENTUCKY
TENNESSEE
GEORGIA
Atlanta
FLORIDA
Miami

WISCONSIN
Chicago
ILLINOIS
Mississippi River
St. Louis
MISSOURI
ALABAMA
MISSISSIPPI
LOUISIANA
New Orleans

MINNESOTA
Minneapolis
IOWA
ARKANSAS
Houston
San Antonio

NORTH DAKOTA
SOUTH DAKOTA
NEBRASKA
KANSAS
OKLAHOMA
Red River
Dallas
TEXAS
Rio Grande

Platte River
Arkansas River
Denver
COLORADO
NEW MEXICO

Missouri River
MONTANA
WYOMING
Salt Lake City
UTAH
Colorado River
ARIZONA
Phoenix
Gila River

IDAHO
Snake River
NEVADA

Seattle
WASHINGTON
Columbia River
OREGON
San Francisco
CALIFORNIA
Los Angeles
San Diego

PACIFIC OCEAN

MEXICO

Gulf of Mexico

500 Miles
250
0
500 Kilometers
250
0

PUERTO RICO
San Juan
100 Miles
50
0
100 Kilometers
50
0

HAWAII
Honolulu
100 Miles
50
0
100 Kilometers
50 0

ALASKA
Juneau
Yukon River
500 Miles
250
0
500 Kilometers
250
0

migration, particularly from Europe, caused the nation's population to double and double again.

European colonization led to the eventual unification of the territory that became the United States under one government and the expansion of that territory from the Atlantic Ocean to the Pacific Ocean. This process began in the early 1500s, but reached its peak in the nineteenth century when rapid population expansion was reinforced by an imperialist national ideology ("**manifest destiny**") to push the westward boundary of the nation from the Appalachians to the Pacific. The indigenous residents of the western territories were pushed aside in the process of expansion. The United States experimented with colonialism at the turn of the twentieth century, leading to the annexation of Hawaii, Guam, and Puerto Rico.

The United States faces little challenge to its territorial boundaries today. While some in Puerto Rico seek independence, most want either a continuation of commonwealth or statehood.

Critical Junctures

The critical junctures in U.S. political history appear at points when mass discontent becomes sufficiently organized to alter governing institutions. Although these are ongoing in U.S. political history, four are explored here. These are the period from the beginning of the American Revolution through the ratification of the U.S. Constitution; the Civil War and Reconstruction; the New Deal; and a contemporary period that begins with California's passage of Proposition 13, a state initiative to limit property taxes, in 1978. The outcomes of these eras of mass discontent are not necessarily those envisioned by the initial proponents of the changes. Each of these periods, however, proved central to development of the modern American nation.

The Revolutionary Era (1773–1789)

The American Revolution was sparked by mass and elite discontent with British colonial rule that resulted in the signing of the **Declaration of Independence** on July 4, 1776. The Revolution itself was only the beginning of a process of creating a new form of government. Mass interests wanted to keep government

---

Critical Junctures in U.S. Political Development

1776	Independence from Great Britain declared.
1788	U.S. Constitution replaces Articles of Confederation.
1803	Supreme Court establishes judicial review in *Marbury v. Madison.*
1803	Louisiana Purchase.
1830s	Mass political parties emerge, and electorate expands to include a majority of white men.
1861–1865	U.S. Civil War.
1865–1876	Reconstruction era. The United States establishes but fails to guarantee voting rights for freed slaves.
1896	Voter turnout in elections begins century-long decline.
1933–1940	The New Deal responds to the economic distress of the Great Depression.
1941–1945	U.S. participates in World War II.
1964	Tonkin Gulf Resolution authorizes military actions in Vietnam.
1974	Richard Nixon resigns the presidency in the face of certain impeachment.
1978	California passes Proposition 13.
1996	Federal government ends the guarantee of social welfare programs to the poor established during the New Deal.
1998–1999	U.S. House of Representatives impeaches and the U.S. Senate acquits President Clinton.

---

close to home, in each colony, and wanted each colony to have autonomy from the others. Elite interests advocated a national government with control over foreign policy and the ability to establish national rules for commerce.

Mass interests won this battle initially. From 1777 to 1788 the **Articles of Confederation** governed the nation. The Articles' weaknesses allowed elite interests to gain support for their replacement with the **Constitution**. The Constitution maintained most power with the states but granted the federal (or national) government authority over commerce and foreign and military policy. It also provided the federal government with a source of financing independent of the states.

The Civil War and Reconstruction (1861–1876)

The second critical juncture in U.S. political history was the Civil War. While the morality of slavery convulsed the nation prior to the war, the war itself began over the question of whether the states or the national government should be dominant. Despite the seeming resolution of this question during the Revolutionary era, many states still believed they could nullify actions of the federal government. The Civil War resolved this issue in favor of the indivisibility of the union.

As part of the process of establishing full citizenship for the freed slaves after the war, Congress revisited the question of individual liberties and citizenship for the first time since the Revolutionary era. It established several important principles in the Fourteenth Amendment to the Constitution (1868) that shape citizenship today. First, it extended the protections of the Bill of Rights to cover actions by states as well as the federal government (the courts slowed the implementation of this provision). Second, it extended citizenship to all persons born in the United States. This made U.S. citizens of freed slaves but also guaranteed that children of the tens of millions of immigrants who migrated after 1868 would become U.S. citizens. Without this constitutional protection, the children of immigrants could have formed a legal underclass—denied citizenship but with no real tie to a foreign land. This kind of excluded status characterized the children of immigrants to Germany until the late 1990s. Third, Congress sought to establish some federal regulation of voting and to grant the vote to African Americans (these provisions were strengthened in the Fifteenth Amendment, ratified in 1870). Failure of the federal government to continue to enforce black voting rights meant that African Americans could not routinely exercise the vote until the passage of the Voting Rights Act in 1965.

The New Deal Era (1933–1940)

The third critical juncture in U.S. political development was the New Deal, which came in response to the economic crisis of the Great Depression. During this period of crisis, the federal government tapped its constitutional powers to regulate commerce to vastly expand federal regulation of business (which had begun tentatively around the turn of the century with antitrust legislation). The federal government also established assistance programs for targeted groups, such as Social Security to provide benefits to the elderly who had worked, or housing programs to provide housing for the working poor. These programs, which had traditionally been understood as being within the purview of the states to the extent that they existed at all, expanded dramatically in the fifty years after the New Deal. The legislative and judicial battles to establish such policies are direct outcomes of the New Deal.

This juncture also saw the federal government assert dominance over the states in delivering services to the people. Equally important, it saw the presidency assert dominance over the Congress. The U.S. president during the New Deal era, Franklin D. Roosevelt, found powers that no previous president had exercised and dramatically changed the office of the presidency.

Contesting the Size and Scope of Government (1978 to the Present)

The fourth critical juncture is ongoing today. The era began with the passage of Proposition 13 by California voters in 1978. California, like a handful of other states, allows citizens to propose ballot initiatives—legislation that appears on the state ballot. If passed by the voters, it cannot be reversed by the legislature. This is one of the few forms of direct democracy in the U.S. system.

Proposition 13 limited the size of property taxes that local governments in California could raise to keep up with the needs of expanding government.[2] The dissatisfaction expressed by Californians with the cost and scope of government, and efforts to limit them, soon spread to other states. The passage of Proposition 13, then, began an era that continues today in which many citizens reject the expansion of government and its role in citizens' lives that began with the New Deal.

Popular discontent in the contemporary era is not limited to taxes; it also focuses on the scope of government. This same period saw popular mobilization to reshape government's involvement in "value" issues. This era saw the emergence of pro- and anti-abortion movements, advocates of "traditional" values and movements of people (such as feminists, gay men, and lesbians) who oppose their exclusion from such agendas, and fundamentalist religious movements. Each group seeks to use the government to protect its interests, while condemning government for allegedly promoting the interests of groups with alternative positions on the same issues. As will be evident in the discussion of the constitutional structure of American government and its policy-making institutions, the U.S. government offers individuals and groups with differing positions the opportunity to influence policy in different (governmental) arenas. As a result, U.S. governing institutions cannot directly resolve conflicts over value issues.

Themes and Implications

Historical Junctures and Political Themes

The conflict between the president and Congress exemplified by the impeachment process, the centralization of federal power in the twentieth century, and the growing opposition to the cost and scope of government represent ongoing themes in U.S. politics. These are not quickly or easily resolved in the United States because the Constitution slowed resolution of such conflicts by creating a system of federalism and separation of powers (see Section 3). When the Constitution was drafted in 1787, its framers were wary of allowing the federal government to intervene too readily in matters of individual liberties or states' prerogatives, so they created a governing system with multiple powers.

In the modern world the United States may be at a disadvantage with such a system relative to other governing systems that can react more quickly and decisively to societal needs and that can change leadership when leaders lose support from the legislature. In parliamentary systems, even when they are burdened by the compromises necessary to maintain coalition governments, a prime minister can exercise power in a way that a U.S. president or Congress can never expect to do. When a prime minister loses the support of his or her party on key issues, elections are called. In the United States elections are held on a regular cycle, and the presidency and Congress have come to be routinely controlled (since 1968) by the two major

opposing parties. In addition to the differences between the parliamentary and the presidential systems, U.S. federalism (division of governing responsibilities between the national government and the states) further slows government action.

The tensions inherent in a system designed to impede governmental action are seen in each of the cross-national themes explored in this book—the world of states, governing the economy, the democratic idea, and the politics of collective identities.

Until the New Deal era and World War II, the United States pursued a contradictory policy toward the rest of the world of states. It sought isolation from international politics but unfettered access to international markets. World War II changed the first of these stances, at least at elite levels (see Section 2): the United States sought to shape international relations through multilateral organizations and military force. It designed the multilateral organizations so that it could have a disproportionate voice (for example, in the United Nations Security Council). The United States used military force to contain communism around the world. The nation's experience in Vietnam dampened its interest in military involvement abroad (the citizenry would not support such activities for long), but it did maintain its new internationalism. With the decline of communism and the end of the Cold War, this post-war internationalism has declined somewhat, and some now call for a reduced role of the U.S. government in the world of states. This decline in interest in the U.S. role in the world among some in U.S. society reflects the fact that foreign policy has never been central to the evolution of U.S. politics and governance. Because the founders designed the Constitution to impede government, both proponents and opponents of an active U.S. role in the world can find a forum to represent their views.

The U.S. government and the states have sought to manage the economy by building domestic manufacturing and exploiting the nation's natural resources while interfering little in the conduct of business (see Section 2). Thus, the United States has governed the economy only selectively. To build industry and exploit resources, the government built roads and other infrastructure, educated citizens, and opened its borders to guarantee a workforce. It also sought access to international markets. Only in exceptional circumstances has it limited the operations of business through antitrust regulation. Yet, its ability to continue to promote the nation's commerce is today limited by the challenge to the size and scope of government.

③ The democratic idea inspired the American Revolution and all subsequent efforts to secure and increase freedom and liberty. The democratic idea in the U.S. context was one of an indirect, representative democracy with checks on democratically elected leaders. The emergence of a strong national government after the New Deal era meant that national coalitions could often focus their demands on a single government. The decline in mediating institutions that can channel these demands reduces the ability of individual citizens to influence the national government (see Section 4).

④ A continuing challenge in U.S. governance is the politics of collective identities. As a nation of immigrants, the United States must unite immigrants and descendants of immigrants from Europe, Africa, Latin America, and Asia with the established U.S. population. Previous waves of immigrants experienced only one to two generations of political and societal exclusion based on their differences from the larger society. Whether today's immigrants experience the same relatively rapid acculturation remains an open question. Preliminary evidence indicates that the process may be even quicker for immigrants with skills and education but slower for those without these. National economic decline or the rise of a virulent anti-immigrant sentiment could slow or stop the acculturation process. Despite the acculturation of previous waves of immigrants and their children, the United States has never fully remedied its longest-lasting difference in collective identities with full economic and political incorporation of African Americans.

Implications for Comparative Politics

Scholars of U.S. politics have always had to come to terms with the idea of American exceptionalism, the idea that the United States is unique and cannot easily be compared to other nations. In several respects, the United States *could* be considered exceptional. As indicated, its geography and natural resources offer it an advantage that few nations can match. Its experience with mass representative democracy is longer than other nations. It has been able to expand the citizenry beyond the descendants of the original members. And, finally, U.S. society has been much less divided by class than have the societies of other states.[3]

The United States has influenced other nations both because of its success and because it sometimes imposes its experiences on others. The U.S. Constitution, for all of its limitations, has served as the model for the constitutions of many newly independent nations. Some form of separation of powers (see Section 3) has become the norm in democratic states. Similarly, district-based and single-member-plurality electoral systems (see Section 4) have been widely adapted to reduce conflict in multiethnic states, of which the United States was the first large-scale example. Through its active role in multilateral institutions such as the United Nations (UN) and international financial institutions such as the International Monetary Fund (IMF), the United States also attempts to impose its will on other nations. Thus, for all of its strengths and weaknesses, it is necessary to know about the U.S. experience to understand more fully the shape of modern democracies throughout the world.

Section ❷ Political Economy and Development

State and Economy

When national leaders present the accomplishments of the United States, they often hold its economy up as an example both of what the nation offers to the world and what it offers to its citizens. By governing the economy less, the United States allows the private economy to thrive. In the simplified version of this story, the private sector is the engine of national growth, and this private sector is most successful when left alone by government. Economic success, then, is tied to the **free market**—the absence of government regulation and the opportunity for entrepreneurs to build the nation's economy.

Relative to other advanced democracies, the U.S. economy is much less regulated. The U.S. government has traditionally taken a **laissez-faire** attitude toward economic actors. This absence of regulation allowed for the creation and expansion of many new types of production that subsequently spread throughout the world, such as the assembly line early in the twentieth century, industrialized agriculture at mid-century, and Internet commerce at its end.

The Constitution reserves for the federal government authority to control interstate commerce. As a result, state and local governments—those most knowledgeable about business or consumer interests in their areas—are limited in their ability to shape the economy. The effects can be both beneficial (small-group needs can be protected and abuses of power reined in more easily by local oversight than by a large federal bureaucracy), and detrimental (vocal interest groups can "hijack" economic or legal matters to the disadvantage of the general public). When states have tried to regulate commerce, their efforts have been ruled unconstitutional by the Supreme Court (over time, states have established the ability to regulate workplace conditions as part of their police powers or of jurisdiction over public health and safety).

With the exception of agriculture and some defense-related industries, the size of various sectors of the economy are almost entirely the result of the free market. The federal government does try to incubate some new industrial sectors, but it primarily uses grants to private agencies—often universities—to accomplish this end. This stimulation of new economic activity makes up a very small share of the nation's gross national product. The United States also occasionally supports ailing industries. While these account for more in terms of federal expenditures than does stimulation for new industries, political support for propping up ailing industries usually dies quickly. With limited government intervention, the shape of the economy is determined almost entirely by market forces.

Agriculture is something of an exception to this pattern. Since the New Deal, the federal government has guaranteed minimum prices for most agricultural commodities and has sought to protect agriculture by paying farmers to leave some soil fallow. It has also considerably reduced the costs of production and risks associated with agriculture by providing subsidized crop insurance, subsidies for canals and aqueducts to transport water, and flood control projects. It has also subsidized the sale of U.S. agricultural products abroad. In the 1990s the federal government began to move away from the guarantees of minimum prices for crops, although it continued to provide funds to sell U.S. crops abroad.

The federal government has also limited its own ability to regulate the economy. With the formation of the **Federal Reserve Board** in 1913, for example, it removed control of the money supply from the democratic process. Today, unelected leaders on the Federal Reserve Board, many with ties to the banking industry, control the volume of money in the economy and the key interest rates that determine rates at which private lenders lend. Further, the United States has not regulated the flow of capital, which has allowed many large U.S.-based firms to evolve over time into multinational corporations and hence remove themselves from much U.S. government regulation.

While the United States has taken a more laissez-faire approach to its economy than have other advanced democracies, it is important to recognize that from the nation's earliest days, the federal government has promoted agriculture and industry, spurred exports, and (more recently) sought to stabilize the domestic and international economy. These promotional efforts included tariffs, which sought to disadvantage products that competed with U.S. manufactures; roads and canals, so that U.S.-produced goods could be brought to market cheaply and quickly; the distribution of federally owned lands in the West to individuals and to railroads, so that the land could contribute to national economic activity; and large-scale immigration, so that capital would have people to produce and consume goods (see Section 3).

These efforts to promote U.S. industry often came at the expense of individual citizens, who are less able to organize and make demands of government. Tariffs, for example, kept prices high for domestic consumers; and the enhanced road system and consequent cheap transportation forced native producers to compete in a world economy where their locally produced goods might be more expensive than the same goods produced elsewhere in the United States or abroad.

Through much of the nation's history, the United States used its diplomatic and military resources to maintain markets for U.S.-produced commodities and manufactures abroad. During the nineteenth century, as industry and agriculture geared up to produce for mass markets domestically and abroad, the United States entered into bilateral trading agreements to sell its natural resources, agricultural produce, and manufactured products abroad. The U.S. military protected this commerce. Today, the United States uses its position in the world economy to open markets, to provide loans for nations facing economic distress, and to protect some U.S.-produced goods from foreign competition. In sum, despite national rhetoric to the contrary, the United States has consistently promoted economic development, though not by regulating production or spurring specific industries.

The government, here federal and state government, regulate aspects of the economy and employer-labor relations. Beginning in 1890 the United States enacted antitrust legislation that gave it ability to break up large businesses that could, by the nature of their size, control an entire market. These antitrust powers have been used sparingly, in the oil industry early in the century and in the long-distance telephone and computer industries more recently. Antitrust legislation gives the government a power that is very much at odds with a laissez-faire ideology.

Finally, in the twentieth century, the U.S. government took on new responsibilities to protect citizens and to tax businesses, in part, to provide government-mandated services for workers. The government also expanded regulation of workplace safety, pension systems, and other worker-management relations issues that limit the ability of industry to operate in a free market relative to its workforce (see Section 3).

The public sector has traditionally been smaller in the United States than in other advanced democracies. Nevertheless, the U.S. government and the states conduct activities that many believe could be better conducted by the private sector. The federal government operates hospitals for veterans (through the Veteran's Administration), provides water and electrical power to Appalachian states (through the Tennessee Valley Authority), manages lands in the West and Alaska (through the Department of Interior), and runs the civilian air traffic control system (through the Federal Aviation Administration). Some localities own local electric and gas utilities and provide trash service

(though in most places these services are privately owned). There has never been a U.S. national airline in the United States, but roads have traditionally been built and maintained by the state and federal governments.

The federal government has privatized some activities in recent years. The postal service, for example, became a semi-independent corporation in 1970. The federal government is now trying to end subsidies for the semi-independent passenger rail corporation (Amtrak) that it inherited when the company's private-sector owners went bankrupt.

Often left out of the story of the development of the U.S. economy is the role of its natural resources and the environment. The nation's territory is unique. While not the largest country, it is the most diverse in terms of natural resources and environments, stretching from tropical to arctic. The territory includes arable land that can produce more than enough year-round for the domestic market as well as for extensive exports. These lands have not been subject to invasion for much of the nation's history. Land has become increasingly concentrated in a few hands, but for much of the nation's history, it was held in small plots tilled at least in part by the owners. This tradition of equitable land distribution (encouraged by government policies in the nineteenth century that distributed small plots to resident landholders) dampened the class tensions that appeared in societies with entrenched landholding elites.

The United States has also been advantaged in terms of trade. It has protected ports and navigable rivers, and few enemies that can challenge U.S. control over these transportation resources. For over a century, it was able to expand trade while not investing in a large standing military to defend its trade routes.

Society and Economy

The United States adheres more strictly to its laissez-faire ideology in terms of the outcomes of the economic system. The distribution of income and wealth is much more unequal in the United States than in other advanced democracies. In 1997, for example, the richest fifth of families earned approximately 49 percent of the nation's income. The poorest fifth, on the other hand, earned just 4 percent of the income.

Figure 1

Immigration to the United States, 1821–1996

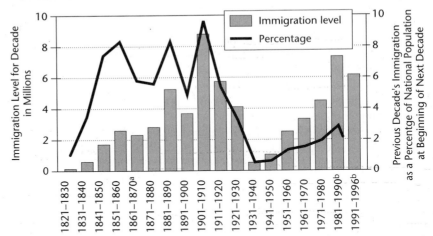

a Until 1867, the federal government recorded as immigrants only people who arrived at seaports.

b These figures include recipients of legalization under the Immigration Reform and Control Act of 1986 who immigrated to the United States prior to 1982 but were recorded as having entered in the year in which they received permanent residence.

Source: Adapted from DeSipio, Louis and Rodolfo O. de la Garza,1998. *Making Americans/ Remaking America: Immigration and Immigrant Policy* (Boulder, Colo.: Westview Press), Table 2.1.

The nation has always tolerated these conditions and sees them as an incentive for people at the lower end of the economic spectrum. Wealth and income have become more skewed since 1980, a phenomenon that has not been an issue of national concern.

The vast gap between rich and poor in the United States might well have led to the emergence of class-based political movements, but immigration policy—which also promoted economic development—focused workers' attention away from class and toward cultural differences that reduced the salience of class divisions in U.S. society.

Agriculture and industry could not have grown in the United States without the importation of this immigrant labor. With only a few exceptions, the nation has sought to remedy labor shortages with policies that encouraged migration. Today, the United States is one of just four countries that allow large-scale migration of those who do not already have a cultural tie to the receiving nation. The others share a colonial history with the United States—Canada, Australia, and New Zealand. Contemporary immigra-

tion to the United States numbers approximately 800,000 people annually, who immigrate under the provisions of the law to a permanent status that allows for eventual eligibility for U.S. citizenship. Another 300,000 migrate without legal status each year.[4] Migration at this level adds about 4 percent to the U.S. population each decade (see Figure 1).

Although the United States tolerates the unequal distribution of income and wealth, it has in the twentieth century intervened directly in the free market to establish protections for workers and, to a lesser degree, to guarantee the welfare of the most disadvantaged in the society. The programs for workers, which are primarily **distributive policies**, receive much more public support than do programs to assist the poor, which are primarily **redistributive policies**. Distributive policies allocate resources into an area that policymakers perceive needs to be promoted without a significant impact on income or wealth distribution. Redistributive policies, on the other hand, take resources from one person or group in society and allocate them to a different, more disadvantaged group in the society. It should be noted that most worker benefits, such as health insurance, child care, and pensions are provided by private employers, if they are provided at all, but are regulated by the government.

Best known among the federal programs aimed toward workers is Social Security, which taxes workers and their employers to pay for benefits for retired workers (and nonworker spouses). In the past, retirees almost always received more than they had paid into the system (a form of intergenerational redistribution), but it will take some reform to guarantee that this pattern continues when today's workers reach retirement age. The government also established a minimum wage and a bureaucratic mechanism to enforce this wage. Some states and localities established higher minimum wages than the federal minimum wage. In addition to Social Security retirement benefits and the minimum wage, the federal government has established a health insurance program for elderly retirees and their nonworking spouses (Medicare), paid for by workers and their employers; programs to provide financial and health care assistance for disabled workers (through Social Security); and insurance for private pension plans (paid for by employers).

The states also regulate worker-employer relations through unemployment insurance and insurance against workplace injuries. These programs, unlike the federal programs, are paid for entirely by the employer. Benefits and eligibility requirements vary dramatically by state.

Beginning in the 1930s the United States also established social welfare programs to assist the economically disadvantaged. As one would expect in a system organized around the free market, these programs have never been as broad-based or as socially accepted as in other economies. These programs, which expanded in the 1960s and 1970s and were restructured in 1996, provided food, health care, housing assistance, some job training, and some cash assistance to the poor. The states administered these programs with a combination of federal and state funds, established benefit levels, and were responsible for moving recipients off the programs. Eligibility and benefit levels varied dramatically from state to state. Prior to 1996 there was a federal guarantee of some

food and cash assistance for everyone who met eligibility thresholds.

This guarantee disappeared in 1996 with the passage of comprehensive welfare reform. After 1996 recipients were limited in the duration of their eligibility, and states were entrusted with developing programs to train recipients for work and to get them jobs. Some states have taken these responsibilities seriously and others have not. It is too early to judge the success of these reforms, though all observers acknowledge that they have been helped considerably by the strength of the U.S. economy in the late 1990s. That said, the states have not yet faced the point where they must end welfare eligibility for large numbers of recipients. Although enacted separately from the 1996 welfare reform, the federal government also reduced the availability of federally managed housing for the poor and expanded subsidies for the poor to secure housing in the private market.

The United States and the International Political Economy

Since colonial times the United States has been linked to world trade. By the late twentieth century, the United States had vastly expanded its role to international finance and was an importer of goods produced abroad (often in low-wage countries that could produce goods less expensively than U.S. factories) as well as an exporter of agricultural products.

After World War II, the United States reversed its traditional isolationism in international politics to take a leading role in the regulation of the international economy. The increasing interdependence of global economies was the result, in part, of conscious efforts by world leaders at the end of World War II, through the Bretton Woods Agreement, to establish and fund multinational lending institutions. These were to provide loans and grants to developing economies in exchange for their agreement to reduce government regulation of their economies and open their domestic markets to internationally produced goods. Chief among these institutions were the World Bank and the International Monetary Fund. Since their establishment in the 1940s they have been supplemented by a network of international lending and regulatory agencies and regional trading agreements. The Group of Seven (G-7), for example, conducts annual meetings of the leaders of the seven largest economies (the United States, Japan, Germany, Britain, France, Italy, and Canada). The United States is also part of regional trading networks, such as the North American Free Trade Agreement (NAFTA) with Canada and Mexico.

The U.S. government plays a central role in the international political economy. It achieves this through its domination of international lending agencies and regional defense and trade organizations. Although these international organizations reflect a desire by policymakers to address some international financial issues multilaterally (at least with the other advanced democracies), these efforts are ultimately limited by domestic politics. Some in Congress and a significant minority of the citizenry oppose U.S. involvement in multilateral organizations. Thus, while presidents may promote an international agenda, Congress often limits the funding for international organizations. The United States then appears to many outside of the country as a hesitant and sometimes resentful economic leader.

In recent years, another multilateral institution has emerged that can potentially challenge U.S. economic dominance. The European Union (EU) is much more than a trading alliance. The EU is an organization of fifteen European nations with growing international influence. On January 1, 1999, most EU members entered into a currency union (not included were Britain, Denmark, Greece, and Sweden). As the euro, the common currency, comes into widespread use, the dollar will face its first challenge in many years as the world's dominant trading currency.

In addition to contributing to multilateral institutions, the United States funds binational international lending through such agencies as the Export-Import Bank and the Overseas Private Investment Corporation. These agencies make loans to countries and private businesses to purchase goods and services from U.S.-owned businesses. The United States also provides grants and loans to allies to further U.S.

strategic and foreign policy objectives or for humanitarian reasons.

The new role of the United States in multilateral economic and defense organizations and the growth in bilateral aid reflects a change in the nation's approach to its role in the world economy. The United States has slowly, grudgingly, adapted to a world where it can no longer rest on its exceptionalism or simply assert its central role. Its economy and the larger society feel the effects of economic changes abroad. Thus, the U.S. government and, more slowly, the American people have seen their problems and needs from a global perspective. This incorporation into the larger world is certainly not complete. The separation of powers between the executive and legislative branches, and the local constituencies of members of Congress, ensures continuing resistance to this new international role.

With the decline in Asian economies starting in 1997, the role of the United States in the international economy may be tested in coming years in a way that it has not been since the formation of the multilateral organizations after World War II. The strength of these organizations is inherently limited by the increasing presence of multinational corporations that are able to transfer capital and production across national boundaries with little control by governments. While this change in the political economy is a political problem that all countries will face in the twenty-first century, the United States is and will be central to this problem. As the domestic U.S. economy is increasingly shaped by these international forces, U.S. citizens will demand economic stability from their government. The U.S. government was designed to be weak (see Section 3), so it will not easily be able to respond. The seeming lack of response will lead to strengthened calls by some in U.S. society to isolate the United States from the regulation of the international economy that it has helped shape. If these voices become dominant, the United States may find itself at odds with the international organizations that it helped create and that promote U.S. trade internationally.

Section ❸   Governance and Policy-Making

Organization of the State

The governing document of the United States is the Constitution. It was drafted in 1787 and ratified by the necessary nine states the following year (all thirteen colonies had ratified it by 1790). The Constitution was not the first governing document of the United States. It was preceded by the Articles of Confederation, which concentrated most power in the states. The revision of the Articles—the Constitution—established a central government that was independent of the states but left the states most of their pre-existing powers (particularly **police powers** and public safety, the most common area of interaction between citizens and government). Although it had limited powers, the new U.S. government exercised powers over commerce and foreign policy that were denied to the states.

Understanding two principles is necessary to understand American constitutional government: federalism and separation of powers. **Federalism** is the division of authority between multiple levels of government. In the case of the United States, the division is between the federal and state governments. **Separation of powers** is an effort to set government against itself by vesting separate branches with independent powers so that any one branch cannot permanently dominate the others.

Federalism and separation of powers were necessary compromises to guarantee the ratification of the Constitution. They should not, however, be viewed simply as compromises. On the contrary, they reflect a conscious desire by the constitutional framers to limit the federal government's ability to control citizens' lives. To limit what they perceived of as inevitable tyranny, the framers designed a system that set each part of government against all the other parts. Although the potential for tyranny remained, the framers hoped that the individual ambitions of the members of each branch of government would cause each branch to fight efforts by other branches to undermine individual liberties.[5]

Federalism and separation of powers have a consequence that could not be fully anticipated by the framers of the Constitution. That is, U.S. government is designed to be inefficient. Since each part of government is set against all others, policymaking is difficult. Inefficiencies can be partly overcome through extragovernmental mediating institutions such as political parties, but no single leader or branch of government can unequivocally dominate policymaking as the prime minister can in a parliamentary system, for example.

Federalism is the existence of multiple sovereigns. A citizen of the United States is simultaneously a citizen of the nation and of one of the states. Each citizen has responsibilities to each of these sovereigns and can be held accountable to the laws of each. Over the nation's two-hundred-year history, the balance of power between the two principal sovereigns has shifted, with the federal government gaining power relative to the states, but to this day, states remain responsible for many parts of citizens' lives and act in these areas independently of the federal government.

Over time, many powers traditionally reserved to the states have shifted to the federal government. The period of the most rapid of these shifts was the New Deal, when the federal government tapped its commerce-regulation powers to create a wide range of programs to address the economic and social needs of the people.

The second organizing principle of American government is separation of powers. While each of the states has adopted some form of separation of powers, its purest form exists at the federal level. Each of the three branches of the federal government—the executive, the legislature (see Section 4), and the judiciary—shares in the responsibilities of governing and has some oversight over the other two branches. In order to enact a law, for example, Congress (the legislative branch) must pass the law and the president (the executive branch) must sign it. The president can block the action of Congress by vetoing the law. Congress can override the president's veto through a two-thirds vote in both houses of Congress. The courts (the judicial branch) can review the constitutionality of laws passed by Congress and signed by the president. Congress and the states acting in unison, however, can reverse a Supreme Court ruling on the constitutionality of a law by passing a constitutional amendment by a two-thirds vote that is subsequently ratified by three-quarters of the states. The Senate (the legislative branch) must ratify senior appointments to the executive branch, including members of the cabinet, as well as judges. The president nominates these judges, and Congress sets their salaries and much of their jurisdiction (except in constitutional matters). In sum, separation of powers allows each branch to limit the others and prevents any one branch from carrying out its responsibilities without the others' cooperation. It also allows a phenomenon unanticipated by the framers of the Constitution—divided government—in which different political parties control the executive and legislative branches of government. Since 1968 divided government has been the norm. Both modern presidential impeachments took place during, and were facilitated by, divided government.

Federalism and separation of powers create a complexity in U.S. government that cannot be found in other advanced democracies. This complexity encourages an ongoing competition for political power that is reflected in the battle between the president and Congress over impeachment, but more regularly in battles over policy. The states traditionally played a greater role in these battles but are relatively less important late in the twentieth century than they were before the 1930s.

The Executive

The Presidency

The American presidency has grown dramatically in power since the nation's first days. The president, who is indirectly elected, serves a fixed four-year term. Since a Constitutional amendment ratified in 1951, the president has been limited to two terms. The president is both head of state and head of government. The roots of presidential power are found in these roles more than in the powers delegated to the presidency in the Constitution.

Through much of the political history of the United States, the president was not at the center of the federal government. Quite the contrary, the Constitution established Congress as the central branch of government and relegated the president to a much more poorly defined role whose primary responsibilities are administering programs designed and funded by Congress. Although twentieth-century presidents have found new powers and exercised powers unimaginable to earlier presidents, the structural weaknesses of the presidency remain.

The president is the commander-in-chief of the military, may grant pardons, make treaties (with the approval of two-thirds of the Senate), and make senior appointments to the executive branch and to judicial posts (again with Congressional concurrence). The president is required to provide an annual state of the union report to Congress and may call Congress into session. Finally, the president manages the bureaucracy, which at the time of the Constitution's ratification was small but has subsequently grown in size and responsibility. Thus, in terms of formal powers the president is far weaker than Congress.

With one exception, presidents until the turn of the twentieth century did not add considerably to the delegated powers. Instead, nineteenth-century presidents largely served as clerks to the will of Congress. During the war of 1812, for example, Congress directed battle strategy. The exception among nineteenth-century presidents was Abraham Lincoln, who dominated Congress during the Civil War. His example was one that twentieth-century presidents followed. He became a national leader and was able to establish his own power base in the citizenry. He realized that each member of Congress depended on a local constituency (a district or state) and was able to label as being local or sectional in its interests. He established the president as the only truly national leader (an important position during the Civil War). Lincoln had an advantage in being commander in chief during wartime; however the foundation of his power was not the military but his connection to the people.

In the twentieth century, presidents discovered that they had a previously untapped resource. Beginning with Theodore Roosevelt, they used the office of the president as a bully pulpit to speak to the nation and propose public policies that met national needs. No member of Congress or the Senate could claim a similar national constituency.

Later in the twentieth century, presidents found a new power. As the role of the federal government expanded, they managed a much larger federal bureaucracy that provided goods and services used by nearly all citizens. Thus, a program like Social Security connects almost all citizens to the executive branch. Beginning with the New Deal, presidents proposed programs that expanded the federal bureaucracy and, consequently, the connection between the people and the president.

Finally, twentieth-century presidents learned an important lesson from the experience of Abraham Lincoln. The president has an authority over the military that places the office at the center of policy-making in military and international affairs. This centrality is particularly evident in times of war or conditions perceived as warlike and when immediate decisions may have to be made, such as in an era with nuclear weapons. Thus, in the period from World War II to the collapse of the Soviet Union, the presidency was empowered by the widely perceived need for a single decision-maker.

Although the presidency has gained powers in the twentieth century, the office remains structurally weak. The period of presidential dominance in the period after World War II appears to be coming to an end. As discussed later, the bureaucracy is a weak link on which to build institutional power. Congress has significant powers to shape it.

To date, all presidents have been men, all have been white, and all but one—John F. Kennedy—have been Protestant. While being a former general was once a stepping stone to the presidency, in today's politics having served as a governor works to a candidate's advantage. Despite a common assumption, only four vice presidents have been elected to the presidency immediately at the end of their terms. It is more common for vice presidents to move to the presidency upon the death (or, in one case, the resignation) of the president.

The Cabinet and the Bureaucracy

To manage the U.S. government, the president appoints (and the Senate confirms) senior administrators to key executive branch departments. The chief officers at each of the core departments make up the president's cabinet. These senior officers include heads of prominent departments such as the Secretary of State, the Attorney General, and the Secretary of Defense as well as lesser-known officials such as the Secretary of Veterans' Affairs. Contrary to the case in parliamentary systems, the U.S. cabinet has no legal standing, and presidents frequently use it only at a symbolic level. The president is also free to extend membership to other senior appointed officials (such as the U.S. Ambassador to the United Nations), so the number of cabinet members fluctuates from administration to administration.

The senior officers of the executive branch agencies manage a workforce of approximately 1.7 million civil servants (the bureaucracy). Although formally part of the executive branch, the bureaucracy must also be responsive to Congress. Under certain circumstances, it operates independently of both elective branches and, rarely, under the direction of the courts. The presidential appointees establish broad policy objectives and propose budgets that can expand or contract the responsibilities of executive branch offices. Congress must approve these budgets, and it uses this financial oversight to encourage bureaucrats to behave as their Congressional monitors wish.

Arguably, the inability of either Congress or the President to fully control the bureaucracy should give it an independence. While this may be true in the case of policy areas that are of little interest to the elected branches, the bureaucracy as a rule does not have the resources to collect information and shape the laws that guide their operations. Interest groups have steadily filled this informational role, but the information comes at a cost. Bureaucracies often develop symbiotic relations with the interests that they should be regulating. The interest groups have more access to Congress and can shape the operations of the regulatory agencies. Thus, without an independent source of authority, the bureaucracy is dependent not just on the elected branches but also on interest groups.

Other State Institutions

Besides the presidency and the Congress (see Section 4, "The Legislature"), three other institutions are central to the operation of U.S. government—the military, the judiciary, and state and local governments.

The Military

The United States Army, Navy, and Air Force are made up of approximately 1.5 million individuals.

The president is commander in chief of the U.S. military, but on a day-to-day basis, the forces serve under the command of a nonpolitical officers' corps made up primarily of graduates of the nation's military academies who have risen through the ranks.

Because of the unique geographical advantages of the United States, the military has had to dedicate few of its resources to defending U.S. territory. In the nineteenth century its primary responsibilities were to defend U.S. shipping on the high seas and to colonize the West. In the twentieth century U.S. troops have seen more service abroad. Beginning with the new U.S. geopolitical role after World War II, the U.S. military was given new responsibilities to support U.S. multilateral and regional defense agreements.

With the increased expectations for the military came increased reliance on defense technologies. U.S. nuclear weapons, intelligence technologies, and space-based defense technologies as well as the maintenance of conventional weaponry and troop support have significantly raised the cost of maintaining the military. This has led to ongoing national debates about the cost of the military and whether defense resources should be expended for technology or for troops. Industries have emerged to provide goods and services to the military. Proposals to cut defense spending often face opposition from these industries.

The Judiciary

Of the three branches of federal government, the courts are the most poorly defined in the Constitution. Initially, it was unclear what check the courts had on other branches of government. Equally important, the courts were quite dependent on the president, who appointed judges, and on Congress, which approved the nomination of judges and set the jurisdictional authority for the courts. The early days of the federal courts confirmed this weakness. In the Judiciary Act of 1789, Congress created a Supreme Court and a network of lower federal courts—thirteen district courts and three circuit courts.

In 1803 the Supreme Court established the foundation for a more substantial role in federal policymaking. It ruled in *Marbury v. Madison* that the courts inherently had the right to review the constitutionality of the laws. This ruling, though used rarely in the nineteenth century, gave the judiciary a central place in the system of checks and balances.

The judicial branch, however, remained weaker than the other branches. In addition to Congress's ability to establish court jurisdiction in nonconstitutional cases and the president's ability to fill the courts with people of his choosing, the courts have other weaknesses. They must rely on the executive branch to enforce their decisions. Enforcement proves particularly difficult when the court's rulings are not in line with public opinion, such as when the courts ruled that organized prayer did not belong in the public schools or that busing should be used as a tool to accomplish racial integration in the schools. The courts' own rules have also limited their powers. Traditionally, the courts limit standing—the ability to bring suits—to those who are *individually* affected by some action of government.

Beginning in the second half of the twentieth century, the federal courts gained power relative to the other branches of government. In part, this was accomplished by expanding the rules of standing and by maintaining longer jurisdiction over cases as a tool to establish limited enforcement abilities. More important, they became a venue for individuals and groups in society whose interests were neglected by the democratically elected institutions but who could make claims based on constitutional guarantees. African Americans, for example, received favorable rulings from federal courts before Congress and the president responded to their demands. Similarly, courts expanded protections to federal prisoners in the 1960s and 1970s (before reversing themselves). The courts also gained relative power because of the expansion of federal regulatory policy. Unclear laws and regulations, often requiring technical expertise to implement, placed the courts at the center of many policy debates. So, while the courts are the weakest of the three branches of the federal government, their responsibilities and powers have grown considerably in the twentieth century.

Subnational Government

State governments serve as an important part of government in the United States. Their responsibilities include providing services to people more directly than does the federal government. Most important among these is education, which has always been a state and local responsibility in the United States. Until the New Deal era, state and local governments served as the primary point of interaction between the citizenry and the government.

States and localities continue to serve a critical function in contemporary U.S. governance. They are able to experiment with new policies. If a policy fails in a single state, the cost is much lower than if the entire nation had undertaken a new policy that eventually failed. Successes in one state, on the other hand, can be copied in others or nationally. For example, Wisconsin experimented with welfare reform in the early 1990s before the federal government changed national welfare laws in 1996. In the Wisconsin experiment, the state limited the amount of time that a household could receive welfare benefits, particularly Aid to Families with Dependent Children (AFDC), which provided food subsidies to households with incomes below designated levels. In exchange, Wisconsin dedicated additional resources to training welfare recipients for work and to finding them jobs (though none were guaranteed). Wisconsin also lowered (AFDC) benefits for welfare recipients who moved to Wisconsin from states with lower benefits. Policymakers outside of Wisconsin saw the Wisconsin reforms as a success and implemented similar (though more draconian) reforms nationally. Had these reforms not been perceived to be successful in Wisconsin, they would not have become the model for federal welfare reform, and the cost of experimentation would have been confined to Wisconsin. Even after the implementation of this reform, Wisconsin spends far more than many other states on social welfare programs.

In addition to state governments, citizens pay taxes to and receive services from an array of local governments that include such entities as counties, cities, districts for special services such as water and fire protection, and townships. These local entities have a different relationship to the states, however, than do states to the federal government. The local entities are creations of the state and can be altered or eliminated by the state. Thus, they have no independent constitutional standing (and are not a form of federalism).

Local governments are, nevertheless, very important in the system of American governance. They provide many of the direct services that the citizenry gets from the government. Most important among these is public education which has traditionally been the responsibility of local governments. Because states and localities have different resources (often based on local property taxes) and different visions of the responsibilities of government, people in the United States can receive vastly different versions of the same government service depending simply on where they live. Again, education provides an example. Property tax-poor areas can spend just a few thousand dollars per year educating students while property tax-rich areas can spend $15 to $20,000 per student. Some states try to equalize education spending within the state while others see disparities this great within the state.

The Policy-Making Process

Separation of powers and constitutional limits on each branch of government create a federal policy-making process with no clear starting or ending point. Instead, citizens and organized interests have multiple points of entry and can contest outcomes through multiple venues. There is little centralization of policy-making except in a few areas where there is consensus among national leaders. Without centralization, policies often conflict with each other (for example, the United States currently subsidizes tobacco cultivation but seeks to hamper tobacco companies from selling cigarettes through high taxes, health warnings, and limits on advertising). Federalism further complicates policy-making. Each of the states sets policy in many areas, and states often have contradictory policies. State policy-making institutions are often used strategically to shape the debate around an issue or to influence other states or the federal government. In sum, policy advocates have many venues in which to propose new policies or change existing policies—Congressional committees, individual members of Congress, executive branch regulatory agencies, state governments, and, in some states, direct ballot initiatives.

With so many entrance points, there are equally many points at which policies can be blocked. Once Congress passes a law, executive branch agencies must issue **regulations** to explain specifically how the law will be implemented. Subtle changes can be inserted as part of this process. On controversial issues, cabinet secretaries and other senior appointees set policy for the writing of regulations. Laws that must be implemented by several agencies raise a possible role for the cabinet, but recent presidents have not used the cabinet as a whole to structure policy-making in this way.

Further, people or interest groups who feel disadvantaged by the regulations can contest regulations in the courts. Or they can contest the law itself, if the assertion can be made that the law is unconstitutional or conflicts with another law or with state government responsibilities. Once a policy is in place, it can be opposed or undermined by creating a competing policy in another agency or at the state level.

The Constitution gives no guidance about the origins and outcomes of policy initiatives. The president is directed to present an annual report to Congress on the state of the nation. Over time, this has evolved into an organized set of policy proposals. In the absence of presidential leadership in policy-making, Congress partially filled the void. Enumerated powers in the Constitution direct Congress to take action in specific policy areas, such as setting tax policy, establishing a post office, and building public roads. Once Congress established committees to increase its efficiency (see Section 4), these committees offered venues for discussion of narrow policy areas of importance to society. These committees, however, are not mandated in the Constitution and are changed to reflect the policy needs of each era. Thus, while presidents can propose policies (and implement them) only Congress has the ability to deliberate about policy.

The courts have long provided a forum for debating the outcome of policy decisions but have rarely initiated policies on their own. Beginning in the 1970s, however, some federal courts experimented with initiating policy as a way of maintaining jurisdiction in cases brought before them. These efforts, such as court-mandated busing of public school students to achieve racial integration, spurred much national controversy and caused the judiciary to decline in public opinion. Today, the courts are much more likely to block or reshape policies than initiate them.

Since there is no clear starting point for initiating policies, individual citizens have great difficulty when they seek to advocate a new policy. Into this void have come extragovernmental institutions, some with narrow interests and some promoting collective interests. Prominent or wealthy individuals or groups can get Congress's or the president's attention through campaign contributions and other types of influence in support for their candidacies and the causes they support.

Mediating institutions have also emerged to represent mass interests. Political parties, organized on a mass basis in the 1830s, organize citizen demands and channel them to political leaders. The parties balance the needs of various interests in society and come as close as any group in the society to presenting comprehensive policy proposals (often summarized in the parties' platforms). Group-based interests also organize to make narrow demands. Veterans are an early example of a group in society that made a group-specific demand on federal policy-making. In the twentieth century, as both federal and state governments began to implement more widespread distributive and redistributive policies, more organized interest groups appeared. These interest groups have become the dominant form of mediating institution in U.S. politics (see Section 4). Unlike political parties, however, interest groups represent only a single issue or group, or narrowly related issues. Thus, the complexity of policy-making in the United States has created an equally complex structure of making demands.

Section ❹ Representation and Participation

The Legislature

Of the three branches in the federal government, the founders envisioned that Congress would be at the center and would be the most powerful. They concentrated the most important powers in it and were most explicit about its responsibilities. For most of the nation's history, their expectations for the powers of Congress have been met.

One of the most important compromises of the Constitutional Convention involved the structure of Congress. States with large populations wanted seats in the national legislature to be allocated based on population. Small states feared they would be at a disadvantage under this system and wanted each state to have equal representation. The compromise was a **bicameral** system with two houses, one allocated by population—the House of Representatives—and the other with equal representation for each state—the Senate. This compromise has remained largely uncontested for the past two hundred years despite the growing gap in population between large and small states. Today, for example, the 454,000 residents of Wyoming elect two senators, the same number elected by the more than 30 million residents of California.

These two legislative bodies are structured differently. The House has 435 members (a number that has been fixed since 1910) and is designed to be more responsive to the popular will. Terms are short (two years) and the districts are smaller than Senate seats except in the smallest states. After 1990 the average House seat had 650,000 constituents and will continue to grow. The Senate has only 100 members and is designed to be more deliberative, with six-year terms.

Membership in Congress is slightly more diverse than the people who have held the presidency, though most members of Congress are white male Protestants. In the 1990s approximately 12 percent of officeholders were women, 9 percent were African American, 4 percent were Latino, and 0.5 percent were Asian American. Most members of Congress, regardless of gender, race, or ethnicity, are highly educated professionals. Lawyer is the most common profession.

The two central powers of Congress are legislation and oversight. For a bill to become law, it must be passed in the same form by both the House and the Senate, and signed by the president. Equally important, Congress has the ability to monitor the implementation of laws that it passes. Since it continues to control the appropriation of funds for programs each year (all government spending must begin with an **appropriations** bill in the House of Representatives), Congress can oversee programs being administered by the executive branch and shape their implementation, either through allocations of money or by rewriting the law.

Congress has organized itself to increase its efficiency. Discussion and debate takes place in committees and subcommittees. The committee system permits each member to specialize in some area. Committees are organized topically, and members often seek to serve on committees that are of particular interest to their constituencies—for instance, a member of Congress from a rural area may seek to serve on the Agriculture Committee. All members seek to serve on committees that have broad oversight of a wide range of government activities, such as the Appropriations Committee through which all spending bills must pass. Specialization allows each member to have some influence while not requiring that he or she know the substance of all facets of government.

For a bill to become law, it must be reviewed by the committee and subcommittee that has responsibility for the substantive area that it covers. When a member proposes a bill, it is referred to committee based on the subject matter of the legislation and usually never gets any further. In each session, only relatively few bills are given hearings before a subcommittee or committee. The House and Senate leadership (the Speaker of the House, the Senate Majority Leader, and committee chairs) are central to deciding which bills receive hearings. If the bill is able to receive support from the committee, it must then be debated by the body as a whole. In the House, this may never occur, as that institution has another roadblock—the Rules Committee—that determines what can be debated on the floor and under what terms. Only in the Senate can debate be unlimited (though even it can be limited by a vote of sixty senators). These hierarchical structures strengthen the powers granted to the House and the Senate in the Constitution because they allow Congress to act efficiently and to use its powers to investigate federal programs, even though it does not administer these programs. As a result, Congress places itself in the center of the policy-making process. When Woodrow Wilson, in his years as a political scientist before he ran for president, studied U.S. government, he saw Congress as the central branch of government and the committee system as the central organizational tool of Congress.[6] Although Congressional power has waned somewhat in the late twentieth century, it remains the foremost branch of American government.

Congress did not sit idly by as the president gained power in the twentieth century. It passed legislation to undermine presidential power. Equally important, Congress applied its traditional authority to investigate federal programs to the president. Beginning with

Watergate (the Nixon administration scandals in which Nixon and his aides used the institutions of the federal government to investigate and intimidate Nixon's political opponents), Congress directly investigated presidents. Congress also created a legal structure—the independent counsel—whereby the executive branch is forced to investigate itself. These investigations weaken the connection between the presidency and the people (regardless of the specific charges being investigated or the outcome of the investigation). Investigations of Presidents Nixon and Clinton to determine charges for impeachment can be seen in terms of congressional efforts to weaken not just the presidents as individuals but the presidency as an office.

Political Parties and the Party System

Electoral politics in the United States is organized around two political parties. The roots of two-party politics can be found both in the nation's political culture and in the legal structures that govern elections. Today, the two major parties are the Democrats and the Republicans. The Democrats can trace their origins to the 1800 election, while the Republicans first appeared in 1856. Despite the fact that today's parties have consistently competed against each other in each of the past thirty-six presidential elections, the coalitions that support them (and which they, in turn, serve) have changed continually.

Today, the Republicans depend on a coalition of upper-income voters, moral and religious conservatives, small-business owners, and evangelical Christians. They receive more support from men than from women and are strongest in the South and the Mountain West. The Republicans have tried to make inroads in minority communities but have been largely unsuccessful with the exception of Cuban Americans and some Asian American groups (see Table 1). Some Republican candidates, particularly the governors of Texas and Florida, have been successful at reaching out to Hispanic people, but for Republicans to do so on a wider scale would alienate some core Republican constituencies.[7] No comparable Republican outreach efforts have been made to African Americans.

The Republican Party tends to have fewer registrants than do the Democrats; approximately 35 percent of registered voters are Democrats, 30 percent

Table 1

1998 Congressional Vote, by Race and Ethnicity

	Percent of Total Vote		Percent Change Republican
	Democrats	Republicans	Voting 1996–1998
White	42%	55%	+1
Black	88	11	−7
Hispanic	59	35	+9
Asian	54	42	−11

Source: Voter News Service, published in *USA Today,* November 4, 1998.

are Republicans, and 35 percent are Independent. The Republicans, nevertheless, have been the dominant party at the presidential level since 1968 and have controlled both houses of Congress since the 1994 election. After the 1998 election they controlled governorships in thirty-one states.

The contemporary Democratic coalition includes urban populations, the elderly, racial and ethnic minorities, owners of export-oriented businesses, unionized labor, and increasingly, working women. Though diminished, this coalition formed in the 1930s in response to New Deal programs promoted by President Franklin D. Roosevelt, a Democrat. Today's Democrats are strongest in urban areas, in the Northeast, and on the West coast. The Democrats have maintained a steady dominance over the Republicans in terms of registration, but their supporters (often the poor, the less educated, and the young) are less likely to turn out on election day.

The Democrats were less successful than the Republicans in recruiting new members during the last two decades of the twentieth century. Internal conflicts in the Democratic Party in the 1970s and 1980s limited its ability to present a cohesive message and reach out to new constituencies. These conflicts—particularly disputes over the size and scope of government, over affirmative action (programs designed to redress past discrimination against racial and ethnic minorities and women) and other race-sensitive programs, and over taxation and the deficit—subsided during the Clinton presidency but may return after he leaves office.

Internal conflict, however, is growing in the contemporary Republican Party. Moral conservatives and

American political parties are not ideologically rigid. Instead, they borrow programs and positions from each other in order to build winning coalitions. *Source:* Smith for *The Las Vegas Sun*, reprinted in *The Washington Post National Weekly Edition*, August 17, 1998.

fiscal conservatives each want the party to focus on their interests and jettison the others' issues as a way of expanding the party's base of support.

These party divisions—in the Democratic Party in the 1970s and 1980s and in the Republican Party in the 1990s—lead to speculation that new parties might emerge. The political culture of the United States limits the likelihood that a faction of one of the parties (such as the religious right from the Republicans) will break off and form a party that competes in elec-

tion after election. Instead, two coalitional parties are the norm.

Electoral law reinforces this situation. Most U.S. elections are conducted under a **single-member plurality (SMP) system**. The candidate who wins the most votes wins the election, and only one person is elected from each district. One common variant is a single-member majoritarian system, in which a candidate must win a majority of votes cast (used primarily in the South as a tool to reduce the likelihood of African Americans getting elected when the white vote divides). SMP elections reward coalitional parties and diminish opportunities for single-issue parties. Broad coalitional parties can contest a seat election after election, while smaller parties are likely to dissolve after a number of defeats. Finally, since the existing parties have written the electoral laws in each of the states (the laws vary dramatically from state to state), they have made it difficult for new parties to get on the ballot.

Geography reinforces the difficulty faced by small and single-issue parties in an SMP system. There are more than 600,000 elected offices in the United States. To compete regularly in even a small percentage of these, a party must have a national presence and a national infrastructure.

Thus, it is unlikely that a new major party will emerge in the United States. Much more than in countries with proportional representation, the electoral law in the United States limits the ability of new parties to emerge and, if they do, to survive. Both the political culture and the geography of the United States, however, make this unlikely to occur. The heterogeneity of the U.S. population and the range of regional needs and interests advantages a system that forces coalitions prior to elections, as does a system with just two political parties. The Constitution-driven inefficiency of U.S. government would become all the more dramatic if multiple parties (rather than two that must, by their nature, be coalitions) were competing in legislatures to shape outcomes.

Elections

The United States takes pride in its long practice of democracy. As an example of its commitment to democratic norms, it points to the frequency of elections and the range of offices filled through elections. As is not the case in parliamentary systems, these elections are conducted on a regular schedule—presidential elections every four years, Senate elections every six years, House of Representatives elections every two years. States and localities set the terms of state and local offices, but almost all have fixed terms (local judicial offices in some states are the rare exception). General elections for federal offices are held the first Tuesday after the first Monday in November. States

and localities establish dates for primary elections and for general elections for nonfederal offices. Thus, while elections are regularly scheduled, there are frequently multiple elections in the same year.

Fundamental to understanding U.S. elections is federalism. States set the rules for conducting elections and for who can participate. When the nation was founded, this authority was almost complete, since the Constitution said little about elections. At the nation's founding most states limited electoral participation to white male landholders. By the 1830s many states reduced or eliminated the property-holding requirement, in part in response to the emergence of competitive political parties that sought to build their memberships.

Further expansion of the U.S. electorate required the intervention of the federal government and amendment of the Constitution. The first of the efforts to nationalize electoral rules was initially a failure. This was the effort to extend the franchise to African Americans after the Civil War through the Fourteenth and Fifteenth Amendments. More successful was the Nineteenth Amendment, ratified in 1920, which extended the vote to women.[8] The Civil War amendments finally had an impact with the passage of the Voting Rights Act (VRA) in 1965, which secured African Americans access to the ballot box. In 1975, Congress extended the VRA to other ethnic and racial groups who had previously seen their right to vote abridged based on their origin or ancestry—Hispanics, Asian Americans, Native Americans, and Alaskan Natives. The Twenty-sixth Amendment gave the vote to all citizens between the ages of 18 and 20 in 1971.

States continue to be able to regulate individual participation in elections through their control of the registration process. This process prescreens potential voters to make sure that they meet the state's requirements for voting, usually residence in the state and the jurisdiction for a set amount of time and the absence of felony convictions. While this may appear minimal and necessary to prevent voter fraud such as an individual's voting multiple times in the same election, the requirement to register in advance of the election prevents many from being able to vote.[9] In 1993, Congress sought to expand opportunities for registration by requiring the distribution of voter registration materials at certain state agencies such as

Institutional Intricacies: *The Electoral College*

Most Americans would be very surprised to find out that even if they vote and they are in the majority, they do not elect the president or the vice president. Instead, the president and vice president are elected by the Electoral College, which in turn is elected by the voters on election day.

The framers of the Constitution designed the Electoral College to act as a check on the passions of the citizenry. Like the indirect election of Senators by state legislatures that survived until 1913, the Electoral College was a device to place community leaders between voters and the selection of leaders. Senators are now elected directly, but the Electoral College remains. Although it would be illegal in many states, and would violate two hundred years of custom, this largely unknown body could potentially impose its views and select a presidential candidate other than the one chosen by the people.

On election day, voters actually vote for a slate of electors who are pledged to vote for a particular candidate. The number of electors in a state is equal to the state's number of Representatives plus its two Senators. The District of Columbia also has three electors, although it has no voting representation in Congress. To win, a candidate must earn half the total number plus one, or 270 at present, of the Electoral College votes.

The electors, who are not named on the ballot, are selected by the state parties and, in some cases, by the candidates. They are usually state party leaders who are named as an honor for past service. As a result, they are very likely to support the candidate to whom they are pledged when the electors meet in each state capital early in December. Most states also require (by law) that an elector vote for the candidate to whom he or she is pledged. But there are examples, as recently as the 1988 election, where electors did not vote for their pledged candidate.

Such "faithless" electors have not affected the outcome of any election so far. What would happen in a close election if a handful of electors did not vote for the candidate to whom they were pledged? Congress, under the Constitution, would have to count their votes as reported. Thus, in this hypothetical close election, a few stray electors could deny the winner a majority by voting for a third candidate. This would throw the election into the House of Representatives. Or, in a more unlikely scenario, the electors could vote for the losing candidate and give him or her the ultimate victory in the Electoral College.

Even without violating state laws or custom, the Electoral College system can make a winner out of the person who places second in the popular vote. All but two states award electoral votes on a winner-take-all basis (this practice maximizes the influence of their voters and increases the likelihood that candidates will campaign in that state; no large state is likely to sacrifice this practice unless all do). Thus, the candidate who receives the most votes in these winner-take-all states wins all of the state's Electoral College votes. In races with three or more serious candidates, these votes can be awarded to candidates who received far less than a majority of the state's votes.

In a close election, a candidate could win less than a plurality of votes but still win the presidency. By winning small victories in key states, this losing candidate could win a majority of the Electoral College votes. This scenario almost occurred in 1976 when Jimmy Carter defeated Gerald Ford. Ford carried several large (and Electoral College vote-rich states) by very narrow margins. Carter won many smaller states by large margins, raising his popular vote total over that of Ford. Had Ford won the Electoral College vote while losing the popular vote, the nation would have suddenly learned the consequence of its indirect system of electing the president.

---

motor vehicle offices (hence "motor voter" legislation). While not as sweeping in impact as the VRA, "motor voter" was a continuing effort to nationalize the rules for voting.

There is a second consequence of federalism on U.S. elections. The responsibility for holding elec-

tions, for deciding which nonfederal offices are filled through elections, and how long nonfederal office-holders will serve before again having to be elected is the responsibility of the states and, if the states delegate the power, to localities. Thus, a local office that is elected in one state could be appointed in another. Terms for state and local offices, such as governors, vary. Elections are held at different points throughout the year. In states that have primary elections to determine who each party's candidate should be, the primary can be just a month before the general election or as many as ten months before.

What are the consequences of this system of elections? At a minimum, it leads to confusion and burnout among potential voters. Many voters are unaware of elections that are not held on the same schedule as national elections (with the general election in November). Others who are aware become overloaded with electoral responsibilities in jurisdictions that have frequent elections and so choose not to participate in local races.

One result of this decentralized system with a legacy of group-based exclusion is that increasing numbers of citizens do not vote. In the late 1800s, for example, turnout in national elections often exceeded 80 percent of those eligible to vote, and the poor participated at rates comparable to the rich. In 1996, on the other hand, turnout in the presidential election dropped below 50 percent. In state and local races, turnouts in the range of 10 to 20 percent are the norm. Perhaps more important, turnout varies dramatically among different groups in society. The poor are less likely to vote than the rich, the young less likely than the old, and the less educated less likely than the more educated.[10] Since blacks and Hispanics are more likely to be poor and less likely to have high levels of formal education, they are less likely to vote than are whites. Hence, political institutions are less likely to hear their demands and respond to their needs.

These class- and age-driven differences in participation are not entirely the result of federalism and variation in the rules for individual participation and the conduct of elections. Declining party competitiveness also plays a role. Nevertheless, it is important to observe that the steady elimination of formal group-based exclusion has been replaced by the informal exclusion of the majority of some groups, such as African Americans and Hispanics. Thus, despite the expansion of the electorate to almost all adults, the nation has yet to live up to its democratic ideals; many adults continue not to participate.

This declining participation should not obscure the dramatic changes in leadership and issues addressed that result from elections. The 1994 elections saw an unprecedented increase in Republican members of the House of Representatives that allowed Republicans to take control of the House for the first time in forty years. Republicans also took control of the Senate in that year and were able to pass legislation that dramatically changed the nation's welfare system and slowed the growth of the federal government. In 1998, Democrats unexpectedly gained seats in the sixth year of a presidential term by a member of their party. This gain in representation in the House of Representatives in the sixth year of a presidential term was the first such gain since 1822. The long-term consequences of this victory cannot be gauged at this writing, but, at a minimum, it exerted some influence on the Senate's acquittal of President Clinton of impeachment charges and led the Speaker of the House, Representative Newt Gingrich, to resign his speakership and his seat in the House.

Political Culture, Citizenship, and Identity

The United States is a large nation with distinct regional cultures, ongoing immigration leading to distinct languages and cultures, class divisions, and a history of denying many Americans their civil rights. Despite these cleavages, however, the United States has maintained almost from its first days a set of core political values that have served to unify the majority of the citizenry. These values are liberty, equality, and democracy.

Liberty, as it is used in discussions of U.S. political culture, refers to liberty *from* restrictions imposed by government. A tangible form of this notion of liberty appears in the **Bill of Rights**, the first ten Amendments to the Constitution, which provide for the rights of free speech, free assembly, free practice of religion, and the absence of cruel and unusual punishment. Support for liberty takes a second form—support for economic liberty and free enterprise. Property rights and contract rights, for example, are protected at several places in the Constitution. Further, Congress, not the states, is empowered to regulate commerce.

Clearly, these liberties are not mutually exclusive. Protections of the Bill of Rights often conflict with each other. Economic liberties reward some in the society at the cost of economic opportunities for others. Nevertheless, the idea that citizens should be free to pursue their beliefs and their economic objectives with only limited government interference has been a unifying element in U.S. political culture.

Equality is the second unifying American political value. In the Declaration of Independence, it is "self-evident" that "all men are created equal." Nevertheless, at various times in the nation's history, women, Native Americans, African Americans, Mexican Americans, Chinese Americans and Japanese Americans, and immigrants have been excluded from membership in the polity and, consequently, from access to this equality. But each of the excluded groups—such as African Americans during the civil rights movement—has used the widespread belief in equality to organize and demand that the nation live up to its ideals.

It is important to observe what this belief in equality is not. The equality that has long been sought is equality of opportunity, not equality of result such as that sought in the communist states. There is support for the notion that people should have an equal opportunity to compete for economic rewards, not that they should end up at the same point.

The final unifying value is democracy. Throughout the nation's history, there has been a belief that government is legitimate only to the degree that it reflects the popular will. As with the notion of equality, the pool of citizens whose voices should be heard has changed over time, from white male property-holders at the time of the founding to most citizen adults today (convicted felons are excluded from the franchise in many states). Nevertheless, excluded populations have continually sought to influence the polity.

These values are still at the heart of contemporary political debates. Leaders have marshaled these values throughout the nation's history to reduce potential cleavages in U.S. society. Since the United States cannot look to a common ethnicity of its people (as, for example, Germany can), to a sovereign with a historical tie to the citizenry (as in a monarchy), or to a purported common religion or ideology among its citizens (as does Iran or Cuba), the belief in these values has been used to unify the diverse peoples of the United States.[11] Voluntary membership based on belief in this creed, then, serves to unify the disparate peoples of the United States.

Interests, Social Movements, and Protest

In the United States political participation has long included activities other than elections and party politics. In the nation's story about its origins, protest proves central; the Revolution was spurred by acts of civil disobedience such as the Boston Tea Party. Similarly protest and social movements repeatedly forced the nation to live up to its democratic ideals. From the woman suffrage movement of the nineteenth century to the civil rights movement of the 1950s and 1960s, people defined as being outside of the democratic community organized to demand that they be included. The success of these movements was enhanced by their ability to tap the political values discussed in the previous section.

These protest movements have also been able to tap the willingness of Americans to become involved in collective action. First chronicled by a visitor from France in the 1830s, Alexis de Tocqueville, this volunteerism and civic involvement has long been identified as stronger in the U.S. democracy than in other advanced democracies.

In recent years, however, observers of U.S. politics have noted a decline in this pattern of rich civic involvement. Although social movements remain (the Christian Coalition would be a successful example from contemporary politics), they have become much more driven by elites than their predecessors. At the same time, voluntarism and civic involvement have declined and the likelihood of participation has followed the patterns of voting, with the more educated, wealthier, and older generally more likely to volunteer and be civically engaged.[12] Protest, of course, remains as an option for people who feel neglected by the political order. The decline in social movements and other ways to organize the politically marginalized (such as labor unions), however, has shifted the focus of protest from organized collective actions to more isolated and, often, violent protests—such as the 1995 bombing of the federal building in Oklahoma City—that fail to build more support for the demands of the people organizing the protest. Militia movements—organizations of individuals willing to take up arms to defend their own notion of U.S. political values and the Constitution, for example—represent the concerns of some in today's society, but few support their activities.

Citizen Action: *The Christian Coalition*

Social movements are much less common in late-twentieth century U.S. politics than in previous eras. Bucking this trend, however, is the Christian Coalition, an organization of social and religious conservatives that has been remarkably successful in recruiting members, influencing elections, and shaping public policy debates. Its many successes and, more important, the limits it faces, offer a portrait of the reasons that social movements are in decline in contemporary U.S. politics.

The Christian Coalition first appeared as a group of Protestant church-based activists who became involved in Republican Party politics in the 1980s in support of Ronald Reagan. In 1988 the minister and religious broadcaster Pat Robertson ran for the Republican presidential nomination and tried to build this diffuse electorate into a cohesive voting block. Although unsuccessful in his candidacy, Robertson formed the Christian Coalition in 1989 to institutionalize what he had tried to accomplish in his own candidacy. Seeing great potential for this group to influence electoral politics (particularly Republican Party politics) and public policy, Robertson created the coalition as a tax-exempt organization that would not directly involve itself in electoral politics but would inform its members so that they could be more effective voters (following the model of contemporary interest groups). To run the day-to-day operations of the Christian Coalition, Robertson hired a Republican campaign professional, Ralph Reed.

The Christian Coalition asserts that people of faith have a right and a responsibility to be involved in the world around them. Their involvement is shaped around an agenda of eight propositions, including strengthening the family, protecting innocent human life, easing the tax burden on families, and defending the institution of marriage. In order to promote this agenda, the Christian Coalition developed a grassroots network of more than 2000 local affiliates and, at its peak, 2 million members. These affiliates link individual members to a lobbying staff in Washington and many state capitals. The Christian Coalition seeks to influence elections by publishing voter guides that compare the positions of candidates for office on the propositions of the Christian Coalition agenda and to influence public policy by sending action alerts, postcards, and e-mail to their members prior to key legislative votes. The organization maintains a tax-exempt status by not endorsing candidates or parties, or promoting specific legislative outcomes.

The Christian Coalition can be seen as a successful modern social movement. It has built a network of previously unempowered individuals around a set of issues that the political parties and the institutions of government either could not or would not touch. It successfully prompted its members to elect candidates to office and to promote specific issues so that the organization could continue to add new members. Further, it provided the resource most needed in contemporary politics—money. By its own estimate (which probably overstates the actual level of contributions), its members donated $26 million to the organization in 1996, much of which was used to produce the candidate guides and issue alerts.

Yet, the structure of the organization demonstrates that social movements can no longer rely simply on mass participation. The Christian Coalition is driven by elites, unlike social movements of earlier days, which were driven by mass participation. Pat Robertson formed the organization, and Ralph Reed applied the techniques of the modern political campaign to the cause of social and religious conservatism. A professional staff manages the dissemination of information. There is a cost in this elite focus; leaders become more important than the members, and the organization's issue focus is personalized. When Reed left the organization after the 1996 elections, many expected it to decline in influence. Reed, however, alienated many in the organization while he was director because he was willing to compromise on some issues to increase the prominence of the organization (and, arguably, himself).

A second difference with social movements of earlier eras has to do with money. The Christian Coalition's impact is felt not just because it mobilized 2 million people but because it has the resources to produce voter guides and to maintain the extensive affiliate network. Money, then, spread its success. Previous social movements relied on the commitment of their members and their labor, not on their financial contributions.

Despite its successes in the late 1980s and early 1990s in creating an organization of dues-paying members, the Christian Coalition has begun to show evidence of declining as precipitously as have previous social movements. Its core activists have been absorbed by the Republican Party. Its core issues have been absorbed in the Republican agenda, though in somewhat diluted form. Its membership is declining. Social movements, even modern high-technology social movements, require too much of their members to survive for long unless they merge with one of the political parties. Although some Christian Coalition issues and activists have been absorbed by the Republican Party, they cannot become fully absorbed because many Republicans who are economic conservatives do not share its beliefs or would not give priority to the Christian Coalition's moral conservatism.

The twentieth century has seen the rise of a new form of organized political activity—the **interest group**. Like political parties and candidates for office, these organizations try to influence the outcome of public policy by influencing policymakers. They differ, however, in that they are usually organized to influence a single issue or a tightly related group of issues. Also unlike social movements, they rely on money and professional staff rather than on committed volunteers.[13] Interest groups increased in prominence as the federal and state governments increasingly implemented distributive and redistributive policies. Beginning in the 1970s, a specialized form of interest group—the **Political Action Committee (PAC)**—appeared to evade restrictions on corporate and organized labor financial contributions to political candidates and political parties.

Interests groups are so numerous in contemporary U.S. politics that it is not possible to even venture a guess as to their number. To show their diversity, however, it is important to realize that they include national organizations, such as the National Rifle Association, as well as local groups, such as associations of library patrons who seek to influence city council appropriations. They include mass organizations, such as the American Association of Retired Persons, which claims to represent the interests of more than 30 million people over the age of fifty, and very narrow interests, such as oil producers seeking to defend tax protections for their industry.

Although interest groups and PACs are now much more common than social movements in U.S. politics, they do not replace one key function traditionally fulfilled by the social movements, which seek to establish accountability between citizens and government. Interest groups by definition are organized to protect the needs of a cohesive group in the society and to make demands that government allocate resources in a way that benefits the interests of that group. Thus, they tend to include as members people who already receive rewards from government or are seeking new benefits. Their membership, then, tends to include more socially, financially, and educationally advantaged members of U.S. society. There is no place in the network of interest groups for individuals who are outside of the democratic community or whose voices are ignored by the polity. The key role that social movements and protest have played in U.S. politics is being replaced by a more elite and more government-focused form of political organization. This is not to say that social movements and collective protest will not reappear in the future, but such a reappearance would require that the insider-focused strategy employed by interest groups could no longer ensure the outcomes that their members seek from government.

Section ⑤   United States Politics in Transition

Political Challenges and Changing Agendas

The United States today faces some familiar and some new challenges that result from the nation's new place in the world of states. Primary among the continuing challenges is the need to live up to its own definition of the democratic idea and to balance this idea of representative government elected through mass participation with the economic outcomes that result from its laissez-faire approach to governing the economy. As it has throughout its history, the United States must address these challenges with a system of government that was designed to impede the actions of government and a citizenry that expects much of government but frequently does not trust it to serve popular needs.

Although challenges to achieve the democratic idea are not new to U.S. political life, the circumstances in which they are debated are new for several reasons. Most important, the United States has assumed a relatively new role and set of responsibilities in the world of states, at least new as far as the past fifty years. U.S. governing institutions must now respond not just to their own people but more broadly to an international political order that is increasingly interconnected and seeks rapid responses to political and economic crises. The institutions of the U.S. government reduce the likelihood of quick responses. They are reinforced by a citizenry that, for the most part, cares little about foreign policy (except when war threatens) and that has little respect, and sometimes open animosity, for multinational political and economic institutions such as the UN and the IMF. Despite the citizenry's continued focus on domestic concerns, U.S. jobs and national economic well-being are increasingly connected to international markets. Over time, many in the United States may come to resent this economic integration (as is already evidenced in the political rhetoric of commentator and presidential candidate Patrick Buchanan).[14]

Economics is not the only role that the United States plays in the world of states. Its military and its bilateral and multilateral defense arrangements guarantee that the U.S. military will have a global presence. Again, this represents a substantial change from the nation's historical role prior to World War II. Although the citizenry has demonstrated a willingness to pay the financial cost of a global military, it has been much less willing to sacrifice the lives of members of the military. As a result, U.S. leaders must continually balance their military objectives and responsibilities to allies and international organizations with an inability to commit U.S. forces to conflicts that might lead to substantial casualties.

In addition to its economic and military roles in the world of states, the United States exports its culture and language throughout the world. Certainly, this process contributes to economic development in the United States, but, equally important, it places the United States at the center of an increasingly homogenizing international culture. The process also can generate hostile reactions in defense of national and local cultures.

The substantial changes in the U.S. linkages to the world of states have not been matched by equally dramatic changes in the U.S. role in governing the economy. The laissez-faire governance that has characterized the nation from its earliest days continues in the modern era. The United States tolerates income and wealth disparities greater than those of other advanced democracies. Equally important, business is less regulated and less taxed in the United States than in other democracies. Few in the polity contest this system of economic regulation.

Since the Great Depression, the United States has seen an expansion of redistributive programs to assist the poor. Beginning with Proposition 13 and coming

to fruition with the 1996 Welfare Reform legislation, however, the nation has reduced its commitment to assisting the poor. While some programs will undoubtedly survive, the current pattern indicates that the United States will not develop targeted programs to assist citizens in need that come anywhere close to those of other advanced democracies. Distributive programs targeted to the middle class—such as Social Security, Medicare, and college student loans—have also been implemented in the twentieth century. These have much more support among voters and will be harder to undermine, even if they challenge traditional laissez-faire approaches to the U.S. role in governing the economy.

Regardless of whether the focus is domestic or international policy, the U.S. government faces a challenge to its sense of its own democratic idea that is more dramatic than that faced by other advanced democracies. Fewer Americans are choosing to participate in the electoral politics of the nation. Turnout in the 1996 presidential election was lower in percentage terms than in any national election since the 1920s (just after women had been granted the right to vote, but before they voted in large numbers). Official turnout rates for 1996 indicated that less than half of eligible adults turned out to vote. Turnout in nonpresidential-year elections is even lower. Approximately 38 percent of voters turned out in 1998 for those. As has been indicated, participation is not spread evenly across the population. Older, more affluent, and more educated citizens are much more likely to turn out than are the young, the less educated, and the poor. Thus, elected representatives are simultaneously receiving less guidance from a more narrow subset of the people. Contributing to this process is the increasing cost of campaigns in the United States and the burdensome need to raise ever-increasing sums of money.

The breadth of nonelectoral politics is also narrowing. Previous study of the United States found rich networks of community-based organizations, voluntary organizations, and other forms of nonelectoral political activity. Community politics in the United States, however, began to decline in the 1950s (roughly the same time when electoral turnout began to decline) and appears to be at record lows today.

This decline in electoral and nonelectoral politics magnifies a final dilemma that the United States faces as it looks to the future. The politics of collective identities has always been central to U.S. politics because the nation has through much of its history been a recipient of large numbers of immigrants. Each wave of immigrants has differed from its predecessors in terms of culture and religion. These differences forced the nation to redefine itself in order to live up to its democratic idea. The "old" group of each era also perceived the "new" group as a threat to the political values of the nation. Today, Asian and Hispanic immigrants are perceived as a challenge by the descendants of European immigrants who populated the nation before large-scale immigration of these groups began in 1965.[15] These political fears lead to periodic spasms of anti-immigrant rhetoric that disappear rapidly when it becomes evident that the new wave of immigrants has adopted the political values of the nation (in the long run, cultural differences are more tolerated).

The United States has experienced a long period of sustained high levels of immigration since 1965. The absence of strong political parties, mediating institutions, and nonelectoral community politics may dampen the political integration of these immigrants and their children. The preliminary evidence is that naturalization rates are increasing but that naturalized citizens vote and participate in other forms of politics at lower levels than comparably situated U.S.-born citizens. If these patterns continue, the nation faces a risk that has not come to pass in its long history of high levels of immigration. Specifically, contemporary immigrants and their children may not be represented in the political order.

In the past, the weaknesses of the U.S. constitutional system could be overcome in part through institutional arrangements and mediating institutions. In terms of institutions, Congress dominated the executive until the New Deal era, after which the president dominated Congress until the Watergate scandal. This institutional dominance reflected the framers' intent through the Depression and after, at least in terms of the dominance of one branch. It is unclear that the framers envisioned a system where two, and occasionally all three, branches of government would compete for dominance and where the Congress and the presidency would be controlled by different political parties.

Mediating institutions also played a role in the past that they are incapable of addressing today. Once they formed as mass institutions in the 1830s, the parties served a necessary role in unifying popular opinion and forcing elite compromise. Today, parties are in decline and have been replaced by a distinct type of mediating institution that does not seek compromise across issues and instead promotes narrow interests. Interest groups connect the citizenry to political institutions, as did parties, but the purpose of this connection is to advance a narrow agenda.

Thus, the United States faces the challenges that it has faced throughout its history, and continues to be limited by a governing system that seeks to inhibit government activity. In the past, it has been able to overcome these challenges through active citizen participation, often channeled through mediating institutions and the mobilization of new groups to active political participation. With citizen participation in decline (or becoming more selective) and mediating institutions less broad-based, the nation is more poorly situated to face challenges. This difficulty in governing will only become more pronounced if impeachments become the norm. As the United States is now centrally positioned in the international economic and political order, its ability to overcome challenges has implications not just for the people of the United States, but for people throughout the world.

United States Politics in Comparative Perspective

From the perspective of the study of comparative politics, the United States may well remain something of an enigma. Its size, wealth, unique experiences with immigration, history of political isolation from the world, and reliance on separation of powers and federalism do not have clear parallels among the other advanced democracies. This distinctness comes through perhaps most clearly in the way the nation engages its international political responsibilities. While the president has traditionally directed the scope of U.S. foreign policy, Congress, as it reasserts power relative to the president, will likely play an increasing role. Members of Congress, who represent narrow geographic districts and who are more directly connected to mass interests, are less likely to take an internationalist perspective than is the president. When Congress speaks on international issues, it is often with multiple voices, including some that oppose U.S. involvement in multilateral organizations. This conflict over control and direction of foreign policy has become more evident since the end of the Cold War.

The impacts of these structural and institutional weaknesses of U.S. government are not limited to the American people. The United States plays a dominant role in the world economy as well as a central political role in international organizations. Thus, the inefficiencies and multiple entry points into U.S. policy-making shape the ability of the United States to respond to crises and to develop coherent long-term policies in conjunction with its allies. In 1998, for example, as the world economy declined, the president, with the support of the Chair of the Federal Reserve, proposed that the United States increase its contribution to the IMF by $18 billion so that the IMF could expand its ability to provide short-term loans to Asian and Latin American countries. Congress initially balked at this request for several reasons, none of which were apparent to the United States' allies. Some opposed the new appropriations because of concerns about international organizations in general, reflecting the tradition of isolationism. Others sought to block presidential initiatives, in general, because of the president's political weaknesses. Still others, likely the majority of those who opposed the initiative, thought that they could bargain with the president to earn his support for initiatives that they sought to pass. While the power of intransigence and horse trading makes a great deal of sense to analysts of U.S. politics, analysts abroad cannot so easily understand the United States' seeming failure to act in time of a crisis. Eventually, Congress passed the added IMF appropriation.

In sum, despite its central role in the international economic system and in multilateral organizations, the United States often remains reluctant to embrace fully the international system that it helped shape. This hesitancy appears despite the active role of U.S. economic interests abroad and the importance of international trade to the U.S. economy. Although the United States has assumed many new international economic and security responsibilities since World War II and does not hesitate to impose its will abroad when it perceives its security threatened, it is sometimes unwilling to play by the rules that these international organizations create. Thus, despite its central role in the world of states, the United States is sometimes a hesitant leader.

Key Terms

manifest destiny
Declaration of Independence
Articles of Confederation
Constitution
free market
laissez-faire
Federal Reserve Board
distributive policies
redistributive policies
police powers (301)
federalism (301)
separation of powers (301)

divided government (302)
Marbury v. Madison
checks and balances (304)
regulations (305)
bicameral
appropriations
Watergate
single-member plurality (SMP) system
Bill of Rights
interest group
Political Action Committee (PAC)

Suggested Readings

Amar, Akhil Reed. *The Bill of Rights: Creation and Reconstruction.* New Haven, Conn.: Yale University Press, 1998.

Deering, Christopher J., and Steven S. Smith. *Committees in Congress.* 3d ed. Washington, D.C.: Congressional Quarterly Books, 1997.

DeSipio, Louis. *Counting on the Latino Vote: Latinos as a New Electorate.* Charlottesville: University Press of Virginia, 1996.

Elkins, Stanley, and Eric McKitrick. *The Age of Federalism.* New York: Oxford University Press, 1993.

The Federalist Papers. Edited by Clinton Rossiter. New York, Mentor, 1961.

Fenno, Jr., Richard F. *Home Style: House Members in Their Districts.* Glenview, Ill.: Scott, Foresman, 1978.

Greider, William. *Who Will Tell the People? The Betrayal of American Democracy.* New York: Simon and Schuster, 1962.

Hartz, Louis. *The Liberal Tradition in America.* New York: Harvest/HBJ, 1955.

Levinson, Sanford. *Constitutional Faith.* Princeton, N.J.: Princeton University Press, 1988.

Lowi, Theodore J. *The End of Liberalism: The Second Republic of the United States.* 2d ed. New York: Norton, 1979.

Schrag, Peter. *Paradise Lost: California's Experience, America's Future.* New York: New Press, 1998.

Sniderman, Paul, and Thomas Piazza. *The Scar of Race.* Cambridge, Mass.: Harvard University Press, 1993.

Teixeira, Ruy A. *The Disappearing American Voter.* Washington, D.C.: Brookings Institution, 1992.

Tulis, Jeffrey A. *The Rhetorical Presidency.* Princeton, N.J.: Princeton University Press, 1988.

Verba, Sidney, Kay Lehman Schlozman, and Henry Brady. *Voice and Equality: Civic Voluntarism in American Politics.* Cambridge, Mass.: Harvard University Press, 1995.

Wilson, Woodrow. *Congressional Government: A Study in American Politics.* Baltimore: Johns Hopkins University Press, 1885.

Wolfinger, Raymond, and Steven Rosenstone. *Who Votes?* New Haven, Conn.: Yale University Press, 1980.

Endnotes

[1] U.S. Bureau of the Census, *Statistical Abstract of the United States 1993* (Washington, D.C.: U.S. Bureau of the Census, 1993), Table 1374.

[2] Peter Schrag, *Paradise Lost: California's Experience, America's Future* (New York: New Press, 1998).

[3] Louis Hartz, *The Liberal Tradition in America* (New York: Harvest/HBJ, 1955).

[4] U.S. Immigration and Naturalization Service, *1996 Statistical Yearbook of the Immigration and Naturalization Service* (Springfield, Va.: National Technical Information Service, 1997).

[5] See *The Federalist Papers,* ed. Clinton Rossiter (New York: Mentor, 1961), particularly Federalists 10 and 51.

[6] Woodrow Wilson, *Congressional Government: A Study in American Politics* (Baltimore: Johns Hopkins University Press, 1885).

[7] Louis DeSipio, *Counting on the Latino Vote: Latinos as a New Electorate* (Charlottesville: University Press of Virginia, 1996).

[8] Kristi Andersen, *After Suffrage: Women in Partisan and Electoral Politics Before the New Deal* (Chicago: University of Chicago Press, 1996).

[9] Ruy A. Teixeira, *The Disappearing American Voter* (Washington, D.C.: Brookings Institution, 1992).

[10] Raymond Wolfinger and Steven Rosenstone, *Who Votes?* (New Haven, Conn.: Yale University Press, 1980).

[11] Sanford Levinson, *Constitutional Faith.* (Princeton, N.J.: Princeton University Press, 1988).

[12] Sidney Verba, Kay Lehman Schlozman, and Henry Brady. *Voice and Equality: Civic Voluntarism in American Politics* (Cambridge, Mass.: Harvard University Press, 1995).

[13] Theodore J. Lowi, *The End of Liberalism: The Second Republic of the United States,* 2d ed. (New York: Norton, 1979).

[14] William Greider, *Who Will Tell the People? The Betrayal of American Democracy* (New York: Simon and Schuster, 1992).

[15] Louis DeSipio and Rodolfo O. de la Garza. *Making Americans/Remaking America: Immigration and Immigrant Policy* (Boulder, Colo.: Westview Press, 1998).

CHAPTER 8

Brazil

Al Montero

Federative Republic of Brazil

Land and Population

Capital	Brasilia	
Total Area (square miles)	3,286,500 (slightly smaller than the U.S.)	
Population	164 million	
Annual Average Population Growth Rate (1990–1997)	1.4%	
Urban Population	80%	
Ethnic Composition	White	54.4%
	Mulatto and Mestizo	40.1%
	Black and Black/Amerindian	4.9%
	Asian	0.5%
	Amerindian	0.1%
Major Language	Portuguese	
Religious Affiliation	Catholic	74.3%
	Protestant	22.5%
	Other	2.3%

Economy

Domestic Currency	Cruzeiro real	
Total GNP (US$)	$773.4 billion	
GNP per capita (US$)	$4720	
GNP per capita at purchasing power parity (US$)	$6240	
GNP average annual growth rate (1996–1997)		2.4%
GNP per capita average annual growth rate	1996–1997	1.1%
	1980–1995	–0.4%
	1965–1980	6.3%
Income Gap:	Richest 20% of population	
GDP per capita (US$)	$18,563	
	Poorest 20% of population	
	$578	
Structure of Production (% of GDP)	Agriculture	14%
	Industry	37%
	Services	49%
Labor Force Distribution (% of total)	Agriculture	23%
	Industry	23%
	Services	54%
Exports as % of GDP	7%	
Imports as % of GDP	8%	
Electricity Consumption per capita (kwh)	1954	
CO_2 Emissions per capita (metric tons)	1.6	

Society

Life Expectancy	Female	70.7
	Male	62.8
Doctors per 100,000 people		134
Infant Mortality per 1000 live births		44
Adult Literacy	Female	82.2%
	Male	83.3%
Access to Information and Communications (per 1000 people)	Radios	399
	Televisions	278
	Telephone Lines	75
	Personal Computers	13
Women in Government and Economy		
Seats in Parliament held by Women		6.7%
Women at Ministerial Level		4.0%
Women as % of Total Labor Force		35.0%
Female Business Administrators and Managers		17.0%
Female Professional and Technical Workers		63.0%
1998 Human Development Index ranking (out of 174 countries; 1 = highest)		62

Political Organization

Political System Federal republic, presidential with separation of powers.

Regime History Democratic since 1946 with periods of military authoritarianism, especially 1964–1985.

Administrative Structure Federal, with 26 states plus the Federal District, which also functions as a state. Subnational legislatures are unicameral. State governments have multiple secretariats, the major ones commonly being economy, planning, and infrastructure. The states are divided into municipalities (over 5,000), with mayors and councillors directly elected.

Executive President, vice president, and cabinet. The president and vice president are directly elected by universal suffrage in a two-round runoff election for four-year terms.

Legislature Bicameral: The Senate is made up of three senators from each state and from the Federal District, elected by plurality vote for an eight-year term; the Chamber of Deputies consists of representatives from each state and from the Federal District, elected by proportional vote for a four-year term.

Judiciary Supreme Court, High Tribunal of Justice, regional courts, labor courts, electoral courts, military courts, and state courts. Judiciary has financial and administrative autonomy. Judges are nominated for life.

Party System Multiparty system including several parties of the right, center-left, and left. Elections are by open-list proportional representation. There is no restriction on the creation and merging of political parties.

Section ❶ The Making of the Modern Brazilian State

Politics in Action

In May 1997 thousands of Brazilians gathered outside the stock exchange in Rio de Janeiro while hundreds more collected inside the building. All were waiting for the beginning of an auction of Companhia Vale do Rio Doce (CVRD), the mining conglomerate, and Brazil's largest public firm. The sale of Vale, as the company is known, was the latest in a series of **privatization** moves that began in the early 1990s with the sale of Brazil's steel mills, fertilizer firms, and utilities companies. Fifty-two state enterprises had been sold; now it was Vale's turn. However, for the Brazilians gathered outside the stock exchange, the sale of Vale meant much more: a cherished piece of Brazil's past was being lost to the faceless market. Vale represented memories of the Brazilian economy that blossomed in the post–World War II era with ambitious industrialization projects led by large public firms. Now all of that was under attack by "greedy capitalists" intent on exploiting the patrimony of the Brazilian people for personal gain. For the students, workers, and professionals who joined to protest the sale of the mining giant, it was too much to take. Minutes before the auction gavel fell, tempers flared. The angry crowd pushed against police barricades. Some threw punches, while others were hurled to the floor and trampled. Many would leave with bloodied faces, but the painful defeat was felt by all. The old Brazil was dead.

For those inside the stock exchange, the sale of Vale meant the birth of a new Brazil. By agreeing to privatize one of the most recognizable symbols of Brazilian industry, the country's leaders were embracing the importance of the market in modernizing Brazil. Despite its past successes, the state could no longer guarantee Vale or any industrial firm the resources needed to become competitive in global markets. By putting Vale up for sale, Brazil's political leadership was guaranteeing that the firm would have a future. The new owners of Vale were young Brazilian industrialists and bankers as well as international investors, including U.S. firms such as NationsBank and the financier George Soros. Unlike most Brazilian firms, which are family-owned, the new Vale would be owned by shareholders and operated by professional administrators, much like major U.S. and European multinational firms. Nothing less would befit the world's largest exporter of iron ore. The new Vale was emblematic of the new Brazil: modern, competitive, and linked to global markets.

Although opponents were thwarted in their attempts to stop the sale, the opposition to the auctioning of Vale revealed aspects of the new Brazil. Only a week before the sale, opponents had filed 135 separate lawsuits in state courts to halt the privatization. In response, squads of lawyers for the National Development Bank, the federal agency responsible for organizing the sale of Vale, had traveled to the far corners of Brazil to defeat each and every lawsuit. Yet the absence of a centralized and hierarchical system for adjudicating the dispute highlighted both the weakness of democratic institutions in Brazil and the difficulty of ruling over such a large, decentralized political order. The new Brazil is a relatively young democracy, and like Russia and India, it is big and complicated.

Geographic Setting

Brazil's size is only the most obvious characteristic of this country of 164 million people. In land surface, Brazil is larger than the continental United States and occupies two-thirds of South America. It borders all the other countries of South America except Ecuador and Chile. Because of the expansion of the coffee economy in São Paulo state during the nineteenth century and the growth of an industrial economy during the twentieth century, Brazil's largest cities are concentrated in the southern and southeastern regions. More than 15 million inhabitants live in Greater São Paulo alone. This density contrasts with the northern, sparsely populated rain forest regions of the Amazon. Generally, however, Brazil's 18.2 inhabitants per square kilometer means that the country is more sparsely populated than the United States.

The physical geography of Brazil is impressively diverse, including thick rain forest in the Amazon valley, large lowland swamps known as the *pantanal*

323

Brazil

in the central western states, and vast expanses of badlands known as the *sertão* in the north and northeast. The country is rich in natural resources and arable land. The Amazon has an abundance of tropical fruit and minerals; the central and southern regions provide most of the country's iron ore and coal; off- and onshore sources of petroleum in Rio de Janeiro and the northeast coastline are also significant. Brazil's farmlands are particularly fertile, including large soy-producing areas in the central savannahs called the *cerrados*, coffee areas of the Paraíba Valley near Rio de Janeiro and in São Paulo, and sugar and other agriculture along the narrow stretch off the northeast coast called the *litoral*. While the Amazon's climate is wet and the *sertão* is dry, the agricultural areas of the central, southeastern, and southern regions are temperate.

Centuries of voluntary and involuntary immigra-

tion of Europeans and Africans contributed to the emergence of an ethnically mixed society. Combinations of Europeans, Africans, and Indians produced hundreds of distinct colors of people. Although this complexity makes any classification scheme precarious, the National Brazilian Institute of Geography and Statistics (IBGE) claims that 57 percent of the population is white, 37 percent is *pardo* (brown or mulatto), 6 percent is black, and 0.6 percent is Asian.[1] These numbers probably ignore people of mixed race, from indigenous and white parents, who are known as *mestizos* but are sometimes classified erroneously as being white or *pardo*. The indigenous people, who live in the vast Amazon basin and once numbered in the millions, were largely decimated by colonization and modernization. Their number is usually estimated at 250,000, but they occupy over 8.5 million square kilometers, 11 percent of the total area of Brazil.[2] The Asian population is dominated by people of Japanese descent who immigrated to the southeastern states and particularly São Paulo after 1925. Numbering over 2 million, São Paulo's community of Japanese descendants is the largest such grouping outside of Japan.

Like other ethnically plural societies such as India, Mexico, Nigeria, Russia, Iran, and the United States, Brazil is a unique blend of distinct cultural influences. Unlike the people of India, Iran, and Nigeria, however, Brazilians are not greatly divided over religious differences. Roman Catholicism was imposed by Portuguese colonial rule, then reinforced by immigration from Catholic Italy, Spain, and Portugal at the end of the nineteenth century. In recent years, evangelical Protestants have made inroads and now compose about 11 percent of the population. Afro-Brazilian religions represent an older, and far more difficult to measure, tendency with religious practices that often mix Catholic and African traditions but are sometimes practiced independently. Indigenous religions and traditions are also part of the cultural landscape. More than religion, the dominance of Portuguese as the language of the land has served to keep this large country united.

Because of its size, large population, large internal market for foreign and domestic industry, and dominance over a majority of the rain forests in the Amazon (the so-called green lung of the planet), Brazil possesses resources that could make it a global superpower. Yet Brazil is also a poor country that struggles to provide for its own people out of its impressive abundance of natural resources. Brazilian governments have often contended with this paradox by entertaining ideas for agrarian reform to break up a very concentrated system of land tenure. All such attempts at distribution have been limited by the priorities of industrial development.

Addressing the immense social problems of this big country requires administering its considerable resources with foresight. Unfortunately, Brazil's potential has often fallen victim to the political baggage from its past.

Critical Junctures

The Brazilian Empire (1822–1889)

Europeans first arrived in Brazil in 1500 with the expedition led by Pedro Alvares Cabral. Unlike the other countries of Latin America, Brazil was a Portuguese colony, not a Spanish one. As a result, Brazil was

---

Critical Junctures in Brazil's Political Development

1822   Dom Pedro I declares himself emperor of Brazil, peacefully ending three hundred years of Portuguese colonial rule.

1824   Constitution drafted.

1888   Abolition of slavery.

1889   Dom Pedro II, who assumed throne in 1840, is forced into exile; landowning elites establish an oligarchical republic.

1891   A new constitution establishes a directly elected president.

1930   Getúlio Vargas gains power after a coup led by military and political leaders. His period of dictatorship (1937–1945) is known as the New State.

1945   Vargas calls for general elections. General Eurico Dutra of the Social Democratic Party wins.

1950   Vargas is elected president. Scandals precipitate his suicide in 1954.

1956   Juscelino Kubitschek becomes president.

1960   Jânio Quadros becomes president.

1961   Quadros resigns. João Goulart gains presidency despite an attempted military coup.

1964   A military coup places power in the hands of successive authoritarian regimes.

1985   *Diretas Já!*, a mass mobilization campaign, calls for direct elections.

1985   Vice presidential candidate José Sarney becomes president upon the sudden death of elected president Tancredo Neves.

1988   A new constitution grants new social and political rights.

1989   Fernando Collor is elected president.

1992   Collor is impeached; vice president Itamar Franco assumes presidency.

1994   Fernando Henrique Cardoso is elected president after his Real Plan controls inflation.

1998   Cardoso is reelected in the midst of a growing financial crisis.

spared the devastatingly violent wars of independence that afflicted other Latin American states, including Mexico. Violence, however, played a prominent role in Brazil's conquest and development as indigenous peoples and African slaves were mistreated and killed, or died of diseases. Ninety-five percent of the Tupis, the dominant ethnic group of the Atlantic Forest were ravaged in the first decades of the conquest.

In 1808, when Napoleon Bonaparte invaded Spain and Portugal, the Portuguese king, João VI, and his court escaped to Brazil. After the defeat of Napoleon, Dom João returned to Portugal to reclaim his throne. But he left his son, Dom Pedro, behind in Rio de Janeiro as prince regent. In September 1822, Dom Pedro declared Brazil independent and took the new title of Emperor of Brazil. In 1824 a constitution was drafted, making Brazil the only constitutional monarchy in the Americas. In 1840, Dom Pedro I's son, Dom Pedro II, assumed the throne.

The Brazilian empire's chief concern was keeping control of the country's large, mostly unexplored territory. Complicating this task was the divisive issue of slavery, upon which Brazil's plantation economy depended. The solution was to centralize authority in the emperor, who acted as a **moderating power** (*poder moderador*), mediating conflicts among the executive, legislative, and judicial branches of government and powerful landowning elites. This centralization of authority provided a contrast with the other postcolonial Latin American states, which suffered numerous conflicts among territorially dispersed strongmen called *caudillos*. Brazil avoided the rise of figures such as Mexico's arch-strongman, Porfirio Díaz.

The importance of the national slave economy had a direct effect on the centralization of power. In 1819 there were 1.1 million slaves, corresponding to 30 percent of the population. British pressure during mid-century to end the international slave trade led the Brazilian imperial state to take a strong international position in favor of slavery. The regional **oligarchy** was far too fragmented politically and geographically to present a unified front to Britain's influence. Instead, the landed oligarchy relied on the central government to confront international opposition to slavery. This reaffirmed the authority of the central state.

The constitutional empire marked the birth of Brazilian liberal institutions. In contrast with its neighbors, the country enjoyed several features of a functioning representative democracy: regularity of elections, the alternation of parties in power, and scrupulous observation of the constitution. In substance, however, liberal institutions only regulated political competition among the rural, oligarchical elites, reflecting the interests of a privileged minority and not the larger Brazilian population. The social reality of the country was an agrarian and illiterate slave society governed by a cosmopolitan elite that mimicked European civilization.

The Old Republic (1889–1930)

The next critical juncture in Brazilian history occurred in 1889 with the peaceful demise of the empire and the emergence of an oligarchical republic commanded by landowning elites. Many causes led to the end of the empire. The institutions of slavery and the monarchy were topics of heated debate among landowners, politicians, and commercial elites. The international pressures of abolitionists to end slavery resulted in the freeing of slaves over sixty years of age and children of slaves not yet born. Socioeconomic changes also paved the way for abolition. The dynamic coffee economy concentrated in the state of São Paulo had grown impressively since the 1830s. Unlike the plantation sugar economy of the northeast, coffee did not require the use of slave labor, which was prohibitively expensive. Under sustained pressure by the coffee elite, all slaves were freed in 1888. By this time, too, liberal political values in opposition to the centralization of political authority had taken root among the coffee oligarchy.

The Old Republic (1889–1930) consolidated the political rise of the coffee oligarchy and a small urban industrial class and commercial elite linked to the coffee trade. By the end of the nineteenth century, coffee had become the main economic commodity, with Brazil supplying most of the world's demand. Railroads linked coffee growers and markets from the rural areas of São Paulo with the urban commercial elites of Rio de Janeiro and contributed further to the development of the central southern region. These structural changes in the economy accentuated the political influence of coffee elites.

The constitution of 1891, which was inspired by the U.S. model, established a directly elected president as the head of government, guaranteed the separation of church and state, and expanded the franchise to include all literate males (about 3.5 percent of the population before 1930). The **legitimacy** of the republican political system was established on governing principles that, although limited to a privileged few, were no longer determined by the hereditary rights of the emperor. Power was decentralized to the states, which gained greater authority to formulate policy, spend money, levy taxes, and maintain their own militias.

Although the republican elite went further than the empire's elite in expressing liberal ideas in the constitution, to the majority of Brazilians republican liberalism was a sham. Most Brazilians continued to reside in rural areas, where the landed oligarchy vigorously suppressed dissent. As in the southern United States, landed elites manipulated local political activity. The colonels, as these elites were called in Brazil, assumed extensive extralegal authority to gather their poor workers and "vote them" (use their votes to guarantee the election of officials favored by the local colonels). This process became widely known as *coronelismo*.

The ties that developed between the patron (the landowner) and the client (the peasant) during the Old Republic became the basis of modern Brazilian politics. In return for protection and occasional favors, the client did the bidding of the patron. As urbanization and the growth of the state's administrative and bureaucratic agencies proceeded, the process of trading favors and demanding action was transformed and became known as **clientelism**. *Coronelismo* in rural areas and clientelism in urban areas were extended to the politics of the national state. In this way, the state was dominated by **patrimonialism**—the injection of private interests into public policy-making. Pervasive corruption, graft, and outright bribery developed as means of reinforcing patrimonialism.

In contrast to the centralization of power during the empire, the Old Republic consecrated the power of local elites. Perhaps at no time in Brazilian political history was the **politics of the governors** as blatant as it was during the years of the Old Republic. Regional elites, mainly from the coffee and cattle regions, dominated national politics. Three states in particular emerged as key players: São Paulo (coffee), Minas Gerais (coffee and ranching), and Rio Grande do Sul (ranching). These states profoundly influenced economic policy-making and the choice of presidential candidates. The presidency alternated almost on a regular basis between São Paulo and Minas Gerais. The pattern was so obvious that this period of Brazilian political history is popularly referred to as the rule of *café com leite* ("coffee with milk"), reflecting the dominance of the São Paulo coffee and Minas Gerais cattle elites.

Brazilian society became more complex with the arrival of large numbers of European and Asian immigrant laborers after the end of the slave trade in 1851. From 1881 to 1930 almost 4 million Italian, Portuguese, Spanish, and German immigrants entered the country.[3] From 1925 onward, Japan subsidized Japanese immigration. Between 1931 and 1940, the Japanese were the second largest group of immigrants to enter Brazil. Despite the diversity of the immigration experience, immigrants tended to settle in the richer southern half of Brazil. In 1920, 93.4 percent of all foreigners lived in the central, southern, and southeastern regions. Fifty-two percent of all foreign residents in the country lived in the state of São Paulo. European immigrants with socialist and radical trade union backgrounds were the first organizers of the Brazilian labor movement during the Old Republic and often provided leadership in the newly formed trade unions.

The upsurge in European immigration and the beginnings of industrialization paved the way for an expansion of the middle class. Artisans, professionals, politicians, civil servants, and military officers emerged as important actors during the early twentieth century. Their increasing influence in Brazilian politics severely threatened the political monopoly of the rural oligarchy and its clientelistic order.

The 1930 Revolution

The Great Depression of the 1930s upset the economic and political base of the Old Republic. As world demand for coffee plummeted, the coffee and ranch elites faced their worst crisis. Worker demonstrations and a resurgent Brazilian Communist Party

Leaders: *Getúlio Dornelles Vargas*

Getúlio Dornelles Vargas came from a wealthy family in the cattle-rich southernmost state of Rio Grande do Sul. Vargas' youth was marked by political divisions within his family between federalists and republicans, conflicts that separated Brazilians during the Old Republic and particularly in Rio Grande do Sul, which had a strong regional identity. Political violence, which was common in the state's history, also affected Vargas' upbringing. His two brothers were each accused of killing rivals, one at the military school in Minas Gerais that Getúlio attended with one of his older siblings. After a brief stint in the military, Vargas attended law school in Porto Alegre, where he excelled as an orator. Like many in his generation, Vargas' university education was incomplete. He supplemented his studies by reading many foreign books.

After graduating in 1907, he began his political career as a district attorney. Later he served as majority leader in the state senate. In 1923, Vargas was elected federal deputy for Rio Grande do Sul, and in 1924 he became leader of his state's delegation in the Chamber of Deputies. In 1926, Vargas made another political career change when he was named finance minister for the Washington Luis administration (1926–1930). He served for a year before winning the governorship of his home state. Never an ideologue, Vargas embraced a highly pragmatic style of governing that made him one of Brazil's most popular politicians by the end of the 1920s.

Vargas' powerful political position as governor of Rio Grande do Sul catapulted him into national prominence in 1929. The international economic crisis compelled several regional economic oligarchies to unite in opposition to the coffee and financial policies of the government. The states, including the state of São Paulo, divided their support between two candidates for the presidency:

Getúlio Vargas as president in 1952.
Source: Photoworld/FPG.

one, Julio Prestes, supported by President Luis, and the other, Vargas, head of the opposition. The two states of Minas Gerais and Rio Grande do Sul voted as a bloc in favor of Vargas, but he lost the 1930 election. Immediately after this loss, a conspiracy among discontented military and political leaders led to the coup of October 1930, which installed Vargas in power.

No other figure in Brazilian political history affected the country as much as Getúlio Vargas. His New State launched a series of reforms that established the terms on which Brazilian society would be linked to the state for decades. Even today, his political legacy continues in the form of state agencies and laws protecting workers.

Source: For more on Vargas' life, see Robert M. Levine, *Father of the Poor? Vargas and His Era* (New York: Cambridge University Press, 1998).

challenged the legitimacy of the Old Republic. Among the ranks of discontented political elites a figure emerged who would change the shape of Brazilian politics for the rest of the century—Getúlio Vargas.

After a disputed presidential campaign in 1930, Vargas came to power as the head of a new "revolutionary" government. Vargas moved swiftly to crush middle-class and popular dissent. He built a political coalition around a new economic project of industrialization led by the central government and based on central state resources. In contrast to the Old Republic, Vargas insisted on controlling the regional governments by replacing all governors (except in Minas Gerais) with hand-picked allies (*interventores*). Once again, the center of gravity of Brazilian politics swung back to the national state.

Under the Old Republic, calls for rights by workers and middle-class professionals had been treated as issues for the police to resolve with force. By contrast, Vargas believed he could win the support of these groups by answering their demands in a controlled way. They would be allowed to participate in the new political order but only if they mobilized within state-created and state-regulated unions and associations.

This model of government was **state corporatism**. State corporatism refers to a method of organizing societal actors in state-sponsored associations. It rejects the idea of competition among social groups by having the state arbitrate all conflicts. For instance, when workers requested increases in their wages, state agencies would determine to what extent such demands were answered and how business would pay for them.[4]

By 1937, Vargas had achieved a position of virtually uncontested power. From such a vantage point, he implemented a series of reforms whose influence is still felt. During the next eight years, Vargas consolidated his state corporatist paradigm with labor codes, the establishment of public firms to produce strategic commodities such as steel and oil, and paternalistic social policies. Packaged with nationalist fervor, these policies were collectively called the **New State** (*Estado Novo*).

The New State was decidedly authoritarian. Vargas, who was called *pai do povo* ("father of the people"), could not be upstaged by competing political images and organizations. Parties and congressional politicians became mere onlookers. Brazilian society would be linked directly to the state and to Vargas as the state's primary agent. Vargas expressed the illegitimacy of representative bodies this way: "From now on there are to be no middlemen between the president and the people." One of the key thinkers of the New State put it even more clearly: "The new regime can have only one party, namely that of the state, which is at the same time the party of the nation."

Although the New State's constitution had fascist overtones, Vargas' policies were as much inspired by the New Deal of U.S. President Franklin D. Roosevelt as by fascist Italy or Nazi Germany.[5] The new regime expanded the existing rudimentary social insurance and pension programs into a broad welfare and health care system for urban workers. Although unemployment insurance was not envisaged by the new laws, workers were provided with insurance against occupational accidents, illness, and death. Vargas created a Ministry of Labor and labor courts to regulate and solve conflicts between employers and labor.

In the New State, the military became an ever more important institution in Brazilian politics. The armed forces experienced marked improvements in armament production and recruitment. Professional standards of promotion, conduct, and the use of force were codified in the establishment of the Superior War College (*Escola Superior de Guerra*). The military even developed new doctrines to justify the use of public funds to own and operate industries seen as essential to the nation's security. The ideology of the military regimes that dominated Brazil from 1964 to 1985 emerged directly from these earlier experiences.[6]

The Populist Republic (1945–1964)

The ever-growing mobilization of segments of the working and middle classes as well as U.S. diplomatic pressure forced Vargas, in 1943, to call for full democratic elections to be held in December 1945. Three political parties emerged to contest the election: the Social Democratic Party (PSD), the Brazilian Labor Party (PTB), and the National Democratic Union Party (UDN). The PSD was a collection of *Estado Novo* supporters and members of clientelist political machines across the country. The PTB was created by Vargas to mobilize members of the official labor unions. The PSD and the PTB, which operated in alliance, were both dependent upon the state. The UDN, on the other hand, brought together the various regional, anti-Vargas forces, which advocated a return to the liberal constitutionalism of the Old Republic. The UDN continued to support the role of the state in promoting economic development, however. By October 1945, the bitterness of the campaign led the military to force Vargas' resignation, two months before the general election.

The turn to democracy in 1945 fell far short of breaking with the past. The new president, Eurico Dutra of the PSD, was one of the architects of the New State. Although the new 1946 constitution provided for periodic elections, state corporatism continued in full force. The most important economic and social policies of the country were still decided by Brazil's far-flung state bureaucracy, not by the national legislature.

Populism, not democracy, became the defining characteristic of the new political order. In Brazil, the terms *populist* and *populism* refer to politicians, programs, or movements that seek to expand citizenship to previously disenfranchised sectors of society in return for political support. Populist governments tend to grant benefits to guarantee support, but they discourage lower-class groups from creating autonomous organizations. Populist leaders, around whom personality cults often form, were successful in Brazil and other Latin American countries in generating mass support among urban working and middle classes (and sometimes rural groups) through the provision of social insurance, health care, and wage hikes. Yet in no way were these leaders directly representative or accountable to their constituencies.

Populism was Vargas' most important tool after his elected return to the presidency in 1950 with PSD and PTB support. Brazilian workers supported his return because he promised to increase the minimum wage, improve the social insurance system, and provide subsidies for public transportation and basic foodstuffs. However, many of these promises were threatened by economic problems in the early 1950s as inflation increased and wages eroded. Opposition politicians charged that Vargas was no longer able to assure Brazil's development and that, if given a chance, he would impose another dictatorship on the country.[7] Already politically vulnerable, Vargas was soon swept up in a bizarre scandal involving the attempted assassination of a popular journalist. The crisis drove Vargas to take his own life on August 24, 1954.

Under Vargas' democratic successor, Juscelino Kubitschek (1956–1960), the economic picture improved. Brazilian industry expanded tremendously in the 1950s. Kubitschek was a master of political symbolism and **nationalism**. His administration promoted images of a new and bigger Brazil, capable of generating "fifty years of development in five." Chief among these symbols of the new Brazil was Kubitschek's decision to move the country's capital from Rio de Janeiro to a planned city called Brasília. The building of this utopian city served to divert attention from the country's economic and social problems. It also acted as a political symbol to rally support among Brazil's business class for Kubitschek's developmentalist policies.[8]

The weak point in Brazil's political economic order was the country's incoherent party system. After Kubitschek's term ended, a populist anti-party maverick, Jânio Quadros, won the presidency in 1960 because of fragmented party identities and unstable partisan alliances.[9] Economic bad times returned as inflation soared and growth slowed. Then, without much explanation, Quadros resigned, elevating João Goulart, Vargas' former minister of labor and Quadros' acting vice president, to the presidency.

Goulart embarked on an ill-fated campaign for structural reforms, mainly of the educational system and the federal administration, and a progressive agrarian policy. Meanwhile, Brazilian politics were becoming more polarized into right and left. New political actors burst onto the scene: peasant league movements, students, and professional organizations. Protests, strikes, and illegal seizures of land by poor Brazilians heightened ideological tensions. Goulart was severely hindered in responding to these problems by a congress that was almost perpetually stalemated in partisan bickering.[10] Finally industrial and landowning elites came down firmly against Goulart's reforms. Right-wing organizations flooded the streets of the main capital with anti-Goulart demonstrators. Convinced that the situation was out of control and that Goulart would soon resort to extraconstitutional measures, the military intervened in 1964, putting an end to Brazil's experiment with democratic populism.

Brazil's capital, Brasília. The planned city was designed by the world-famous Brazilian architect Oscar Niemeyer.
Source: Georges Holton.

The Rise of Bureaucratic Authoritarianism (1964–1985)

The military government that came to power in 1964 installed what the Argentine sociologist Guillermo O'Donnell has termed **bureaucratic authoritarianism**, or BA.[11] BA regimes are authoritarian regimes that emerge in response to severe economic crises and that are led by the armed forces and key civilian allies, most notably professional economists, engineers, and administrators. Repression in Brazilian BA varied from combinations of mild forms that constricted civil rights and other political freedoms and harsher forms that included wholesale censorship of the press through institutional acts, torture of civilians, and imprisonment without trial. The first and the last two military rulers, Castelo Branco (1964–1967), Ernesto Geisel (1974–1979), and João Figueiredo (1979–1985) presented less violent forms of authoritarianism, whereas the rule of Artur Costa e Silva and of Emilio Médici (1968–1974) encompassed the worst forms of physical repression.

Initially the military government envisioned a quick return to civilian rule and even allowed, in a limited form, the continuation of democratic institutions. Although purged in 1964 of perceived enemies of the military, the national congress continued to function afterwards and direct elections for federal legislators (but not the president or state governors) were held at regular intervals. In November 1965 the military abolished all existing political parties and replaced them with only two: the National Alliance for Renovation, or ARENA, and the Brazilian Democratic Movement, or MDB. ARENA was the military government's party, and MDB was the "official" party of the opposition. Although previous party labels were discarded, former members of the three major parties joined one of the two new parties. The most important party affiliations in ARENA belonged to former UDN and PSD members, while many PTB members flocked to MDB. Even though the two parties did not operate until Castelo Branco left office in March 1967, the military hoped that the reform would give the bureaucratic-authoritarian regime a level of democratic legitimacy.[12]

Although these democratic institutions were more than pro forma, their powers were severely limited. The military government used institutional decrees to legislate the most important matters, thereby stopping the congress from having an important say. Few civilian politicians could speak out directly against the military for fear of being removed from office.

In economic policy, the military reinforced the previous pattern of state interventionism. The government actively promoted **state-led development** by creating hundreds of state corporations and investing millions in established public firms such as Vale. Under military leadership, Brazil implemented one of the most successful economic development programs in the Third World. Often called the Brazilian miracle, these programs demonstrated that, like France, Germany, and Japan, a developing country could create its own economic miracle.

The Transition to Democracy and the First Civilian Governments (1974–1998)

After the oil crisis of 1973 set off a wave of inflation around the world, the economy began to falter. Increasing criticism from Brazilian business led Geisel and Figueiredo to embrace a gradual process of democratization.[13] Initially, these leaders envisioned only a liberalizing, or "opening" (*abertura*), of the regime that would allow civilian politicians to contest for political office. As was the case with Gorbachev's *glasnost*, however, control over the process of liberalization gradually slipped from their hands and was captured by organizations within civil society. In 1974 the opposition party, the MDB, stunned the military government by increasing its representation in the Senate from 18 to 30 percent and in the Chamber of Deputies from 22 to 44 percent. These numbers did not give the MDB a majority, but the party did capture a majority in both chambers of the state legislatures in

the most important industrialized southern and south-eastern states.[14]

Abertura accelerated in the following years. The opposition made successive electoral gains and used them to get concessions from the government. The most important of these concessions was the reestablishment of direct elections for governors in 1982, political amnesty for dissidents, the elimination of the government's power to oust legislators from political office, and the restoration of political rights to those who had previously lost them. The gubernatorial elections of November 1982 sealed the fate of promilitary candidates. Opposition gubernatorial candidates won landslide victories, capturing the most developed states—Minas Gerais, São Paulo, and Rio de Janeiro. The process of liberalizing the authoritarian regime was now irreversible.

The military, which wanted to maintain as much control over the succession process as possible, preferred to have the next president selected within a restricted electoral college. In 1983 mass mobilization campaigns seeking the right to directly elect the next president got off the ground. The *Diretas Já!* ("Direct Elections Now!") movement, which comprised an array of social movements, opposition politicians, and labor unions,[15] expanded in size and influence in 1984. Their rallies exerted tremendous pressure on the military at a moment when the question of who would succeed General Figueiredo was not clear. The military's fight to keep the 1984 elections indirect alienated civilian supporters of the generals, many of whom broke with the regime and backed an alliance (the Liberal Front) with Tancredo Neves, the candidate of the opposition PMDB, or Party of the MDB. Neves' victory in 1984, however, was short-lived. His sudden death on the eve of his inauguration meant that Vice President José Sarney became the first civilian president of Brazil since 1964.

The bizarre sequence of events that led to Sarney's presidency was a keen disappointment to those who had hoped for a clean break with the authoritarian past. Labor unions in particular distrusted Sarney as a former political hack of the military. Such divisions weakened Sarney's government. He became embroiled in conflicts with unions, business organizations, the Catholic church, and international financial institutions. More important, his administration failed to reform the old authoritarian modes of policy-making, including corporatist institutions and military prerogatives over civilian government.

A chance for fundamental change appeared in 1987 when the national Constituent Assembly met to draft a new constitution. Given the earlier success of the opposition governors in 1982, state political machines became important players in the game of constitution writing. The state governments petitioned for the devolution of new authority to tax and spend. Labor groups also exerted influence through their lobbying organization. Workers demanded constitutional protection of their right to strike and called for an extension of the right to public employees who were heretofore prohibited from engaging in such activism. The constitution also granted workers the right to create their own unions without authorization from the Ministry of Labor.[16] As a whole, the constitution guaranteed a rich array of social and political rights, yet it also left vestiges from the corporatist past, including protection of public firms in petroleum and telecommunications from foreign investment and privatization.

The other primary issue of the day was inflation. Soon after Sarney's rise to power, annual rates of inflation began to skyrocket. The government invoked several stabilization plans to stop the explosion of prices but to no avail. By the presidential elections of 1989, the first since the 1960s to be held as direct elections for that post, Brazilian society was calling for a political leader who would remedy runaway inflation and remove corrupt and authoritarian politicians from positions of power.

Rising from political obscurity, an ex-governor from Alagoas, a small state in the poor northeast, Fernando Collor de Mello, became president. Collor and his small party, the Party of National Reconstruction (PRN), had fought a grueling campaign against the popular left-wing labor leader and head of the Workers' Party (*Partido dos Trabalhadores,* or PT), Luiz Inácio "Lula" da Silva. To counteract Lula's appeal among the Brazilian people, Collor's campaign rhetoric appealed to the poor, to the *descamisados* ("shirtless ones"), who were attracted by his attacks against politicians and the social problems caused by bureaucratic inefficiency. As a skillful campaigner on television, Collor convinced Brazilians that he could "kill inflation with one shot" and get rid of the "maharajahs"—corrupt public servants who collected massive salaries but did little.

The Collor presidency was itself a critical juncture as the government's economic team began the privatization of state enterprises, deregulation of the economy, and the reversal of decades of policies that had kept Brazil's markets closed to the world. Yet Collor failed to solve the nagging problem of inflation and, ironically, he was soon accused of bribery and influence peddling and was impeached in September 1992; an ignominious end for the first directly elected president since the 1960s.

Collor's impeachment brought to the presidency Itamar Franco, a well-known politician in Minas Gerais who was less well known at the national level as Collor's vice president. Despite a high level of uncertainty during Franco's first year, including rumors of a military coup that was allegedly in the works, his government provided an important stabilizing role. Perhaps his most important decision was to support his Minister of Finance, Fernando Henrique Cardoso, a sociologist and senator from São Paulo, in a plan to conquer inflation. In July 1994, Cardoso implemented a plan to fight inflation, the Real Plan, which succeeded. Monthly inflation fell from 26 percent to 2.82 percent in October 1994 (see Section 2).

Cardoso rode the success of the Real Plan to the Brazilian presidency, beating out Lula of the PT in 1994 and again in 1998 to become the first Brazilian president in modern times to be reelected. After his inauguration in January 1995, Cardoso proved adept at keeping inflation low and in consolidating some of the structural reforms of the economy, many that had been initiated by Collor. As the tale of Vale suggests, privatization has moved forward. Other reforms, however, remain stuck in congress, including crucial reforms of the pension system. Brazil's budget and trade deficits increased, requiring the government to finance the shortfall with short- and medium-term debt. As in Mexico in 1994, these conditions caused foreign investors to abandon the Brazilian market, leading to billions of dollars in capital flight. Financial crisis in Asia and Russia worsened the crisis in 1998 and 1999. Even Cardoso's reelection in October 1998 could not stop Brazil from becoming the latest casualty in a widening global financial crisis.

Themes and Implications

Historical Junctures and Political Themes

The state has played a central role in the story of modern Brazilian politics. In the world of states, both international and domestic factors have influenced the Brazilian state's structure, capacity, and relations with society. During the days of the empire, international opposition to slavery forced powerful oligarchs to turn to the state for protection. The coffee and ranch economies that provided the material base for the power of the Old Republic were intricately tied to Brazil's economic role in the world. Even the *Estado Novo*, with its drive to organize society, was affected by the events outside Brazil. The defeat of fascism in Europe helped turn the New State's authoritarian project into a populist-democratic one. The return to democracy during the 1980s was also part of a larger, global experience, as authoritarian regimes gave way all over Latin America, eastern Europe, southern Europe, and the Soviet Union.

Within Brazil, the state adjusted to changes in the distribution of power, the rise of new, politically active social classes, and the requirements of development. In the federal state, power shifted regularly between the central and subnational governments. From the centralizing, moderating power of the Brazilian emperor Dom Pedro II and the state corporatist *Estado Novo* of Getúlio Vargas, to the decentralized, power-sharing exchange of *café com leite*, the swings of the pendulum between center and local punctuated many of the critical junctures of Brazilian politics. In recent decades, the pendulum has swung between the centralization of political power required by bureaucratic authoritarianism and the liberalization (and decentralization) of power involved in the transition to democracy.

The inclusion of new political actors such as the working and middle classes reshaped the Brazilian state during the twentieth century. The state corporatism of Vargas' New State provided mechanisms for mobilizing and organizing workers and professionals. Populist democracy later provided these social segments protection from unsafe working environments, the effects of eroding wages, and the prohibitive expense of health care. Public firms such as Vale

employed hundreds of thousands of Brazilians and dramatically altered the development possibilities of the country. Now these policies have come under attack by reformists both within the government and in the international financial institutions that believe their reform requires another round of state restructuring, this time with a generous dose of market-oriented criteria. Privatization, deregulation, economic liberalization, and the reform of public employment and pension programs are dramatically altering the role of the Brazilian state and its relations with society.

As for Brazil's distinctive approach to governing the economy, no one should discount the legacies of state-led development in the country's history. During the twentieth century, Brazil was transformed from a predominately agrarian economy into an industrialized economy. To some extent, markets and foreign investment played key roles in this process, but the state also provided crucial financial, technical, and political support that made this great transformation possible. As a result, Brazil's position in the global system of production and exchange was fundamentally guided by politics.

Nonetheless, the growth produced by state-led development was poorly distributed. Social problems that emerged from this unequal model of development are at the heart of the country's ongoing struggles with democracy. For many Brazilians living in poverty, it was not clear what benefits the return to democracy had produced.

Regarding the democratic idea, Brazil certainly has the institutions of a democracy, but in many ways these rules remain incomplete. Decades of patrimonialism, populism, and corporatism have eroded democratic institutions. Brazilian politicians can switch parties with few impediments, for example. As a result, Brazilian political parties are extremely weak. Personal appeals and demagoguery tend to produce positive returns in Brazilian electoral politics. The reign of these **personalist politicians** is exemplified by the initial popularity of Collor. Once in power, Brazilian politicians often ignore the people who elected them. Clientelist relations, favoritism, nepotism, and outright bribery produce rewards for politicians but leave little for constituencies.

Yet even with these enduring shortcomings in democracy, Brazilians continue to prefer this form of government. The appeal of democracy is based, in part, on their negative memories of the repression they suffered under the authoritarian regime and the military's poor management of the economy. More important, Brazilians impute positive values to the improved access to decision-making processes that democracy gives them. Thousands of new political groups, social movements, civic networks, and economic associations have emerged in recent years. The Brazilian state is highly decentralized into twenty-six states, a federal district, and over 5,000 municipalities. Each of these centers of power has become a locus of demand-making by citizens and policy-making by elites. Under these circumstances, centralized rule following the model of the New State or the bureaucratic authoritarian period is impossible today and, in any case, seems undesirable to most Brazilians.

Collective identities remain uncertain in Brazil, even though Brazilians are now more commonly linked through their place in the democratic order. The question Who are the Brazilians? has always been a vexing one, no less so now that Brazil's borders are becoming obsolete in a world of heavy flows of international commerce, finance, and ideas. One common response to the question is that the symbols of the Brazilian nation continue to tie Brazilians together: carnival, soccer, *samba*, and *bossa nova*. Yet even as these symbols have become more prevalent, they have also lost some of their meaning because of commercialization and export as part of a tourist-attracting image of Brazil. Catholicism is a less unifying force today as pentecostalism and evangelism have eaten into the Church's membership. Women have improved both their social position and their political awareness as gender-based organizations have become a more important resource of civil society. Yet even here, Brazil remains an extremely patriarchal society where women are expected to balance motherhood and other traditional roles in the household while they are pressured by economic need to produce additional income.

Perhaps race, more than any other form of identity, remains the most tricky issue in Brazilian politics and society. Racial identity continues to divide Brazilians, but not in the clear-cut manner it does blacks and whites in the United States. These categories are more fluid in Brazil. Racial mixing has been accompanied by ideas of integration, not the segregation that helped to mobilize blacks in the United States during the 1960s. Perhaps it is the fuzziness in Brazilian race relations that undercuts the political mobilization of blacks.

Like race, class continues to separate Brazilians. Economic reforms and the erosion of populist redistribution have only caused social gaps to widen further, making Brazil a highly fragmented society. Although it is one of the world's ten wealthiest economies, with a gross domestic product over US$500 billion, that wealth is poorly distributed. Like India, Brazil's social indicators such as income distribution, infant mortality, and nutrition consistently rank near the bottom in the world of states. Income disparities mirror racial differences as the poor are represented by mostly blacks and mulattoes. The rich are almost invariably white. The poverty of the north and northeast also contrasts with the more industrialized and prosperous southeastern and southern states.

Implications for Comparative Politics

As a large, politically decentralized, and socially fragmented polity, Brazil presents several extraordinary challenges to the study of comparative politics. First, the Brazilian state is an anomaly. It has been both highly centralized and decentralized during different periods of its history. In each of these periods, the state produced lasting political legacies that have both strengthened and weakened its capacity for promoting development, democracy, and social distribution. Although political centralization has been an important factor in making the French state strong, decentralized states such as the U.S. and German federations have also proven to be successful formulas for government. The Brazilian case is a laboratory for evaluating which approach is likely to be more successful in other large, highly decentralized states in the developing world, such as Russia, China, and India.

While the complexity of the Brazilian state represents one problem area, the weakness of the country's democratic institutions suggests another, perhaps more troubling, concern. Along with Russia, Brazil demonstrates how the lack of coherent party systems and electoral institutions can endanger democracy. In contrast to the highly organized polity of Germany and the strength of parties in parliamentary democracies like the United Kingdom and Japan, Brazil's experience highlights how anemic representative institutions can weaken democracy.

Paradoxically, as Brazil developed economically and made its way back to democracy in the 1980s, it also became a more socially unequal country. Established democracies like India and transitional democracies like Mexico and Russia have also experienced the reality that democratization does not improve distribution of wealth. Yet the longest established democracies in our study—the United States, Britain, France, Germany, and Japan—are also the richest and, by and large, the countries where wealth is most equally distributed. Brazil and India, therefore, are a bit of a puzzle: if democracy and social development are intricately linked, shouldn't the distribution of wealth be getting better, not worse, in these two countries?

Finally, the complex divisions afflicting Brazilians' collective identities challenge all attempts to address the country's problems. Yet, even today, Brazilians and outside observers continue to treat the country as a singular unit. In this regard, Brazil presents a puzzle for theories about collective identities: How has such a socially fragmented society remained a coherent whole for so long?

Section ② Political Economy and Development

Brazilian politics have always been shaped by the country's quest for economic and social development. Two processes in particular have left enduring legacies: the pattern of state intervention in the domestic market and the effects of external economic change. Historically these two factors have influenced each other. External economic crises—world depressions, fluctuations in the price of exported goods such as coffee, upsurges in the prices of imported goods— have compelled the Brazilian state to intervene in the domestic economy, through protection, subsidies, and even the production of goods that were previously imported. In turn, policies aimed at promoting the industrial growth of the country have made Brazil one of the newly industrialized countries of the world, alongside states such as Mexico, Taiwan, South Korea, and Indonesia.

In order to clarify how political and economic development have been intertwined in Brazil, this section explores the state-led model of development; considers how the domestic effects of the state-led model and its reform generated enormous social costs; and discusses the international capitalist forces that shaped domestic economic policy and society.

State and Economy

Like that of its Latin American neighbors, Brazil's early economic development was based on **export-led growth**, that is, on the export of agricultural products such as sugar, cotton, coffee, and for a short time in the early 1900s, rubber. Throughout most of the nineteenth century, coffee emerged as the engine of growth in the Brazilian economy. By the time of the Old Republic, a strong demand for Brazilian coffee in Europe and North America gave the country a virtual monopoly in the global market. Cotton, sugar, and cereals continued to be important export products, too, but they were secondary to coffee. By 1919 coffee composed 56 percent of Brazil's total exports. Only five years later, that figure had jumped to 75 percent.[17]

The dominance of coffee ensured that the Old Republic would keep Brazil active in the world market. That meant that the state had only a minimal role in promoting the export-led economy, which functioned so well that money generated by coffee provided a reservoir of capital to build railroads, power stations, and other infrastructure. These investments, in turn, spurred the growth of some light industries, mostly in textiles, footwear, and clothing.

The Brazilian state's role in the economy became far more **interventionist** during the 1930s when the Great Depression caused international demand for coffee decline. As exports fell, imports of manufactured goods also declined. The coffee export sector had created demand for these goods among the urban population in the decades before the Great

Depression.[18] Therefore as the coffee economy declined, incentives to boost domestic industrial production to substitute for previously imported manufactures increased.

During the 1930s, Brazil's economy pursued **import substitution industrialization** (ISI), a model of development that promoted domestic industrial production of previously imported manufactured goods. By 1937 this policy, which relied heavily on state intervention, became a major pillar of Vargas' New State. At first, large doses of state intervention were not necessary. The initial phase of ISI—the so-called light, or easy, phase—focused on manufactured products that required little capital or sophisticated technology. Most of these industries, such as textiles and food processing, were labor-intensive and therefore created jobs. Although these conditions did not require large infusions of state capital, the New State provided limited subsidies and tariff protection to nascent ISI sectors.

At the end of World War II, new ideas about Third World development came to be adopted by various international agencies. The new goal was to "deepen" the ISI model by promoting heavy industry and capital-intensive production. In Brazil, as in Argentina, Mexico, and India, a new generation of state **technocrats**—experts in economic development—took an active role in designing new policies. Inspired by the texts of the United Nations Economic Commission for Latin America (ECLA), these technocrats targeted particular industrial sectors as strategic.[19] Then, through the use of industrial policies including planning, subsidies, and financial support, state agencies promoted the quick growth of these sectors.

Brazil was the epitome of ECLA-style **developmentalism**, the ideology and practice of state-sponsored growth, during the 1950s in Latin America. More than any other Latin American state, the Brazilian state was organizationally capable of implementing industrial policies to deepen ISI. New bureaucratic structures, such as a national development bank and national public firms, were created during the first and second Vargas governments. Petrobrás, the state oil firm, quickly became a model of what the Brazilian state wanted to become—a state that could produce as well as regulate. The producer state promoted private investment by extracting and distributing raw materials for domestic industries at prices well below the international market level. These lower prices were in effect subsidies to domestic industry. In this way, subsidized steel and subsidized credit from the national development bank fueled domestic industrialization. Other firms linked to sectors of the economy receiving these supports would benefit in a chain reaction.

Although growth rates achieved impressive levels during the 1950s and early 1960s and even higher levels in the 1970s (see Table 1 below), it was during this period that the first serious contradictions of ISI emerged.[20] Protection fostered noncompetitive, inefficient production because it removed incentives for competition. Although industries grew, they did so by depending too heavily on public subsidies. ISI also became import-intensive. Businesses used subsidized finance to import technology and machinery. The government helped these firms by overvaluing the currency to make import prices cheaper. This overvaluation of the currency hurt export earnings, which were necessary to pay for imports. As a result, the export sector could not supply the state with much-needed revenues to sustain growth, prompting the government to print money, which in turn led to inflation. Under the Goulart government (1961–1964), the economy's capacity to import and export dwindled, and stagnation set in. The economic crisis that soon followed contributed to the coup of 1964 and Goulart's fall.

The rise of the military governments in 1964 did not mean either the end of ISI or its continued deepening. The state retained its role as the main planner

Table 1

GDP Growth Rates, 1940–1997	
Year	GDP Growth Rate
1940–1950	5.6%
1950–1960	6.1
1960–1970	5.4
1970–1980	12.4
1980–1990	1.5
1990–1997	2.1

Source: Brazilian Institute of Geography and Statistics (IBGE), *Anuario Estatístico Brasileiro* (Rio de Janeiro: IBGE, various years).

Table 2

Sector Composition of the GDP, 1970–1990

Year	Agriculture	Industry	Services
1970	11.55%	35.87%	52.59%
1980	10.16	40.99	48.84
1990	9.26	34.20	56.54

Source: Werner Baer, *The Brazilian Economy: Growth and Development*, 4th ed. (New York: Praeger, 1994), 382–383. Copyright © 1995 by Werner Baer. Reprinted by permission of Greenwood Publishing Group, Inc. All rights reserved.

and coordinator of domestic industry, but its functions and the political structures that would manage developmental policy changed under military rule.

From 1964 to 1985 the state continued to promote industrialization, especially the production of consumer durable goods such as automobiles, televisions, refrigerators, and machinery for the domestic market. Domestic entrepreneurs relied on the transfer of technology from foreign investors, particularly after 1970, when they collaborated with multinational firms to produce pharmaceuticals and later computers. Table 2 highlights the important contribution of industry to the Brazilian GDP.

Para-statals, also known as public or state firms, played an important role in the military's development model. Large-scale projects in shipbuilding, mining, steel, oil, bauxite, and aluminum were financed and managed by bureaucratic agencies and state firms. These projects often operated in conjunction with larger development plans designed to attract domestic and foreign entrepreneurs. Peter Evans, an American political economist, insightfully characterized these complex relations among the state, foreign investors, and domestic capitalists as a "triple alliance."[21] The state, however, remained the dominant partner.

In the 1970s, Brazil's military leaders realized that the deepening of ISI could not rely on domestic capital alone. In order to finance the huge public expenditures of national industrial policy, the military turned to international financial markets, particularly private investment markets in North America and Europe. The military also began to emphasize primary exports such as coffee, iron ore, cereals, and other agricultural products. Policies designed to increase agricultural

productivity and technological modernization that had already been implemented in the first years of military rule were expanded. Agriculture began to be integrated with industrial production.

The export of agricultural surplus and the sale of food products in the internal market were facilitated by a growing agribusiness sector. Spurred on by state subsidies, agribusiness supplied new resources and management for inefficient agricultural subsectors. Agricultural production in the agribusiness sector employed heavy machinery and advanced technologies that increased the size of the average yield. One of the most unusual agribusiness ventures occurred in the 1970s when the military government introduced a plan to use sugarcane alcohol as a fuel source. Northeast agribusiness boomed during these years as the sugar economy became tied to the dynamic industrial economy of the southern and southeastern regions.

The Environmental Costs of State-Led Growth

The impressive growth of industry and agriculture was concentrated in the central and southern regions of Brazil. Centers of growth in the states of São Paulo, Minas Gerais, Rio de Janeiro, and Rio Grande do Sul became the locomotives of the country's development and sites of environmental degradation. As capital-intensive industries became more common in Brazil, ecologically destructive technologies were used without much regulation. Before the mid-1970s, Brazilian policymakers were unconcerned with the emission of toxic waste into the ground at major industrial zones, air pollution in overgrown urban areas, or pesticide and chemical fertilizer use in agricultural regions. Industrial growth was simply more important.

The environmental costs of these attitudes became clear in the 1970s. Guanabara Bay and the Paraiba do Sul River basin, both in Rio de Janeiro state, were brought to the brink of biological death. Urban pollution in São Paulo devastated the Tietê River, which runs through the city, making it no better than a toxic waste dump in some areas and threatening the health of millions. By far the worst tragedy was in Cubatão, an industrial city 60 kilometers east of metropolitan São Paulo. There, petrochemical industries and steel mills wreaked havoc on the environment, pumping 1 million kilograms of pollutants into the surrounding ecological system each day. The conditions in the residential area of Cubatão became so bad that by 1981 one city council member reported that he had not seen a star in twenty years.[22] Thousands reported becoming afflicted with tuberculosis, pneumonia, bronchitis, emphysema, asthma, and cancer. Forty of every thousand babies in Cubatão were stillborn.

Big development projects reached the forests of the Amazon River basin in the 1970s with Vale do Rio Doce's Carajás mining work in the Eastern Amazon. This and other industrial projects threatened the tropical forests, as did cattle ranching, timber extraction, and slash and burn agriculture by poor farmers, a practice that allowed frequent rains to leech nutrients from the soil and prevent the return of tropical habitats. By the 1980s it was clear that the primary result of these practices was the deforestation of the Amazon.

Brazil's worsening environmental problems received official attention after 1972, when the United Nations held its Conference on the Human Environment. Soon afterwards, Brazil created an environmental secretariat, and in 1981 the government established a National Environmental Council (CONAMA), which included officials from national and state government and representatives from business, professional, and environmental groups. State governments also established their own environmental agencies and passed important legislation.[23] In 1975, São Paulo passed a comprehensive antipollution law. The cleanup of Cubatão began in 1983.

Partly as a result of the return to democracy in 1984, new environmental movements within and outside of Brazil began to influence official and public opinion on the costs of resource degradation. Much attention was brought to these problems when the Brazilian government successfully persuaded the United Nations to hold its Conference on the Environment, a follow-up to the 1972 conference, in Rio de Janeiro in 1992. Thousands of delegates and hundreds of **nongovernmental organizations** gathered in Rio to discuss global environmental problems that were virtually all present in Brazil. By that time, numerous environmental organizations were already active in Brazilian politics.[24]

Despite the attention the Rio conference brought to the issue, rates of deforestation, pollution, and resource degradation fell only briefly after 1992, and

have since returned to historically high levels. Brazilian business has shown only passing interest in the use of clean technologies because of their expense. In the third international UN conference on the environment, held in Kyoto, Japan, in 1997, Brazil was joined by the rest of the developing world in deflecting the finger of blame for ecological problems. However, it did play an important diplomatic role toward the end of the conference by supporting a U.S.-backed clean development fund. Nevertheless, Brazil currently lags behind its neighbor Argentina, which in November 1998 became the first developing country to adopt binding targets for controlling emissions of industrial waste gases.

The Fiscal System

In developed countries such as the United States, Germany, France, and Britain, governments can use tax policy to punish polluters. In Brazil, however, tax collection has been notoriously weak, making this a less useful instrument to regulate business or individuals. Tax evasion has been a chronic problem. The military governments attempted to change that through a constitutional reform in 1967 that created new taxes, made the federal government better able to collect taxes, and centralized fiscal policy and the control of revenues. However, because one of the military's primary objectives was to stimulate private savings and to increase capital formation, the new tax systems allowed for numerous costly exemptions and transfers of budgetary resources to private firms and to the upper and middle classes. As a result, the Brazilian tax system became more regressive by shifting the tax burden onto the middle and working classes.

As the Brazilian economy became more complex, new opportunities for evading taxes emerged. An **informal economy** of small firms, domestic enterprises, street vendors, and unregistered employees proliferated, virtually outside the domain of the taxable economy. In some cases, these enterprises acquired substantial size, accounting for distribution of everything from artisans' goods to professional services. Legally registered companies began to subcontract unregistered professionals to render services beyond the reach of the tax system. Although reliable information is lacking, economists estimate that the informal economy represents close to half of Brazil's GDP (about US$300 billion) and employs about 30–45 million people.

Other problems developed for the tax system after the transition to democracy. The new constitution of 1988 decentralized the fiscal structure by allowing the states and municipalities to expand their collection of taxes and to receive larger transfers of funds from Brasília. Significant gaps emerged in tax collection responsibilities and public spending as a result of these changes. Although the central state spent less than it collected in taxes between 1960 and 1994, Brazil's 5000 municipal governments spent several times more than they collected. Subnational governments also gained more discretion over spending. More than 90 percent of funds transferred from the federal government to the states went unearmarked, so state governments could use these monies for their own purposes.

New reforms during the Collor administration began to reverse some of the adverse effects of fiscal decentralization and the weak tax system. In the 1980s the state governments, which held almost half of Brazil's total debt, continued to roll over their debt with federal outlays and failed to cut expenditures. In the early 1990s federal threats to cut off debt servicing and close down profligate regional banks owned by the state governments put an end to this unsustainable practice. Other reforms shifted some of the tax burden onto business, which helped to increase tax receipts to 25 percent of GDP.[25]

The Cardoso administration had some success in recovering federal tax revenues and reducing the fiscal distortions produced by Brazil's federal structure. Tax evasion declined as the federal tax collection agency was expanded and its surveillance powers enhanced. Legislation in 1994 allowed the federal government to employ more discretion over transfers of funds constitutionally earmarked for the state and municipal governments. That allowed the federal government to exert some leverage on state governments to control their spending. Brasília also shifted more spending responsibilities in health care, housing, and social policy to subnational governments. That has allowed the federal government to reduce its own spending and control how the states spend their resources. Such stopgap measures reined in public spending. Despite these efforts, high levels of capital flight and the threat by governors opposed to Cardoso's reforms to default on their debt payments to the federal government, led to a widening financial crisis in early 1999. These problems compelled the president to threaten recalcitrant states by freezing their share of federal funds, leading to a serious intergovernmental conflict.

The Problem of Inflation

Inflation deserves special mention in Brazil, for in no other country, with the possible exception of Germany, has this phenomenon had such a lasting impact on a country's politics. In Brazil inflation accompanied state-led development, especially after 1974. Through various types of controls, the Brazilian state, business, and unions all attempted to govern prices, interest rates, and wages. Such manipulation distorted the value of goods and services, and facilitated inflation. With the return to democracy after 1985, successive governments attempted to control inflation. All of these "stabilization" packages proved unable to sustain the fiscal and monetary discipline necessary for their success, leading to an economic deterioration and four-digit inflation. Figure 1 illustrates this terrible track record.

Figure 1

Annual Rates of Inflation, 1989–1996

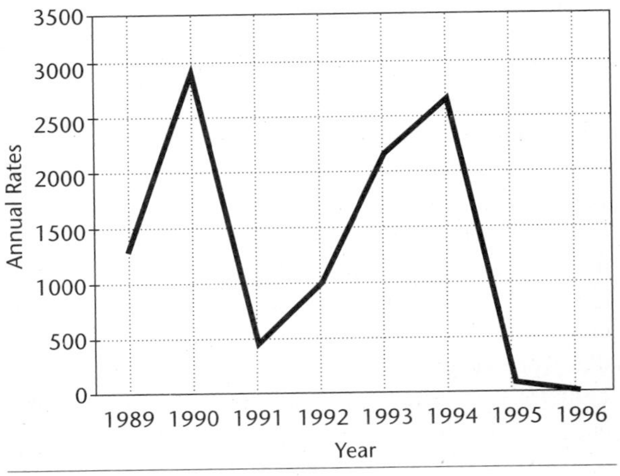

Source: Fundação Getúlio Vargas, *A Economia Brasileira em Gráficos* (Rio de Janeiro: FGV, 1996), 24.

Sarney initially promised to produce "Japanese growth with Swiss inflation." His Cruzado Plan (1986) used a mix of price controls and some fiscal restraint to arrest sharp upsurges in prices for an eight-month period. But inflation eventually returned and became worse. Collor took a more direct approach to the problem. Through another stabilization "shock," the Collor Plan in 1990, the government froze all savings accounts. Inflation fell, but by early 1991 it was back.

The failures of the previous plans prompted the Ministry of Finance under the Itamar Franco government to avoid wage and price freezes or other shock policies. Instead the government attacked inflation through budget cuts, tax increases, curbs on tax evasion, and attempts to stabilize the currency by indexing it to the U.S. dollar, all elements of the *Plano Real* (Real Plan) launched in July 1994. The plan, which successfully curbed inflation, was the brainchild of Franco's Minister of Finance, Fernando Henrique Cardoso, who became president in late 1994.

Like its predecessors, the Real Plan changed the name of the national currency in an attempt to eliminate the memory of inflation. But its most important feature was unique to it. The Real Plan attempted to anchor the real, the new currency, in a unit of real value (URV), which was itself indexed to the U.S. dollar. Unlike a similar plan in Argentina, the Real Plan did not fix the real to the dollar strictly but allowed it to float within bands, thus achieving more flexibility in the exchange rate.

Paradoxically, the Real Plan's formula for success proved to be a source of weakness. Soon after the Mexican peso crisis of December 1994, Central Bank managers in Brasília became convinced that the real was overvalued, just as the peso had been before its crash. Overvaluation made exports more expensive abroad, raised the costs of production, and made imports cheaper. Brazil's trade deficit rose by more than 140 percent after 1995, threatening to scare away foreign investors.[26] Despite dire predictions, though, Brazil's large foreign reserves (US$75 billion in mid-1998) kept investors confident in the economy, although turmoil in Asian financial markets led to the bleeding of these foreign reserves at $1 billion a day during October 1998. Improvements in tax collection, an influx of foreign investment, modest growth, and

repeated attempts by the Cardoso administration to close the trade deficit by limiting imports and removing taxes on exports, helped to keep the real's value stable. Yet high interest rates, escalating public debt, the inability to rein in spending, and monetary instability in Asia and Russia continued to threaten the real's stability. Signs of hope emerged in November 1998 when the IMF negotiated a US$42 billion bailout agreement with Brazil in order to keep the economy from sinking further into financial upheaval. These efforts proved unsuccessful. In January 1999, Itamar Franco, the ex-president and the newly elected governor of Minas Gerais, threatened his former Minister of Finance with a moratorium on the state government's debt to Brasília. The threat led to an upsurge in capital flight (US$6 billion in the first 14 days of 1999) as investors lost confidence in Cardoso's government. Central Bank president, Gustavo Franco, one of the Real Plan's chief defenders, resigned abruptly. The new president, Francisco Lopes announced a "controlled" devaluation of 8 percent. Within just two days, pressures on the real forced the government to abandon the Real Plan's exchange rate regime altogether. The real was forced to float, causing it to decline in value by more than 50 percent against the dollar. The devaluation generated renewed fears of inflation and refocused attention on the need to contain public sector spending.

Society and Economy

Brazil's astounding levels of industrialization during the 1950s, 1960s, and 1970s had lasting effects on the urban population. In 1950, 35 percent of the population lived in urban areas. By 1980 that number had increased to 68 percent. During the same period, employment in industry jumped from 14 percent to 24 percent, while employment in agriculture declined from 60 percent to 30 percent. Import substitution had created these jobs by expanding the domestic market. ISI led to a jump in the size of both the working class and the middle class. Service sector professionals like lawyers, doctors, and private teachers soon found clients as the domestic consumer market grew along with the working class.

Nevertheless, the number of jobs created in the industrial sector did not begin to absorb the huge number of unemployed Brazilians. Many of the new jobs required skilled and semiskilled specialized labor. Metallurgy, automobile production, and mining did not provide many opportunities for the large numbers of unskilled workers in the Brazilian labor market. In the late 1980s and 1990s even skilled workers faced losing their jobs because of intense industrial restructuring. From 1990 to 1996 manufacturing jobs fell by 38.1 percent and unemployment in metropolitan areas rose above 18 percent.[27] Service sector employment increased but not enough to make up for industrial job losses. These jobs also paid less and offered fewer protections from arbitrary dismissal.

Industrialization also failed to eradicate the racial inequalities inherited from slavery. Despite the impressive industrial development of Brazil, Afro-Brazilians continued to make less than their white colleagues and had fewer opportunities for upward mobility. According to one study, nonwhite men and women in Brazil have made real gains in their income because of improvements in education and occupation, but the gap separating nonwhite income from white income remains significant.[28] On average, blacks make 41 percent and mulattoes make 47 percent of what whites make.

Women constitute 28 percent of the economically active population in Brazil and they continue to enter the labor market in record numbers. Working women typically have more years of schooling than men and are better prepared to meet the demands of an increasingly technological economy. Despite such developments, women receive lower salaries than men employed at the same job. Women make 57 percent of what men make. Afro-Brazilian women, who are doubly disadvantaged by race and gender, are in a particularly precarious situation. Many are employed in underpaid and menial jobs, particularly as domestic servants, 90 percent of whom are black women. Mulatto women receive 46 percent of what white men make, and black women take in only 40 percent of what white men make.

The Welfare System

In a country of startling social inequalities, welfare policy plays a remarkably minor role in the lives of most Brazilians. Although welfare and education expenditures currently constitute about 11 percent of the GDP, among the highest levels in the world, the money has not improved Brazil's mediocre welfare state. Unlike the systems in Britain, France, Germany, and Japan, Brazil's welfare system has not reduced the high level of poverty or helped the majority of the poor. Vast sectors of the population, deprived of finance, titles, and jobs, remain totally outside the reach of welfare services.

Brazil supports a public school system as well as a health, retirement, and social assistance system that includes funds for unemployment relief. Salaried workers are entitled to benefits such as health care, workmen's compensation, retirement pensions, paid vacations, and overtime pay. Yet only an estimated 15 percent of the Brazilian population qualify for these benefits. Workers in the informal sector, who are normally undocumented, cannot collect welfare since technically the federal government does not consider them employed. Corruption, clientelism, and outright waste make the welfare system incapable of delivering benefits to the people that need them the most.[29]

Part of the problem is that more people need welfare than actually contribute to the welfare state. Today only half of the 70 million people who are economically active contribute to the welfare system. In the last eleven years, while the population doubled, the number of retired people multiplied elevenfold, adding to the roster of those depending on public welfare spending. In 1995 the welfare system received US$3.5 billion *less* than was needed to pay the retirement pensions of the 15.2 million inactive workers and 3 million new beneficiaries.

During the military period, changes to the welfare system produced additional distortions. Since the days of the New State, workers employed by a firm for ten years or more were guaranteed generous severance benefits. The military replaced these guarantees with a social insurance fund that prorated inferior benefits to the years of employment. The military expanded protection to several sectors of employment that previously had been outside the welfare system: rural workers, domestic workers, and professionals. But the chief beneficiaries of the new system continued to be public employees (including politicians and members of the military). Compared to total benefit payments of US$35.2 billion to 15 million inactive workers in the private sector, inactive public sector workers, who number 404,000, received $10.5 billion during the 1990s. That means that the average retired or unemployed civil servant received $2,188 monthly as compared to an average of $194 for private workers.

As in Margaret Thatcher's Britain, fundamental welfare reform in Brazil came with the rise of a new political figure. Fernando Collor began to dismantle the welfare system soon after his election to the presidency. The funding and quality of welfare services deteriorated to levels never seen in contemporary Brazilian history. Federal funds for health care fell 50 percent. In 1988 the federal welfare system devoted 25 percent of its revenues to health care; in 1990 that number was only 15 percent. In 1993 *no funds* were allocated. At present, the subnational governments have been left to take up the slack, with differing results throughout Brazil.

The combination of distortions in the distribution of welfare benefits and unavoidable social pressure to expand outlays to the poor caused the Cardoso administration to step up efforts to reduce tax evasion and reform the public pension system. Private employers and state companies (among the worst offenders) were increasingly obligated by federal authorities to pay their share of social welfare contributions. As in the United States, France, South America, and Chile, the debate over welfare has begun to revolve around the issue of completely or partly privatizing the system. The experiences these other countries have with such ideas may influence Brazil's choices, but the final response will depend upon whether state agencies and political parties can refrain from employing welfare as a means of clientelism.

Agrarian Reform

The restructuring of the rural economy in the 1960s and 1970s altered the rural social structure. The growing role of agribusiness created jobs for some segments of the rural working class while it crowded out small landowners. After 1964 various state welfare programs were launched in the agricultural sector: retirement policies for low-income producers, pension plans for rural workers, and financial support to community rural associations. These policies played a prominent role in breaking landowners' political and economic control of the rural population. During the 1970s and 1980s rural workers were organized into rural unions that received welfare transfers from the state—medical plans, job security, and protection of wages against inflation.

Land ownership in Brazil remains concentrated in the hands of only 1 percent of the landowning class. The arable land held by this small group of owners (about 58,000) is equal to the size of Venezuela and Colombia combined. Over 3 million other farmers survive on only 2 percent of the country's land. An additional 4.5 million Brazilians are farm laborers or squatters who own no land. In the 1980s and 1990s several landless peasant movements grabbed headlines by sanctioning illegal land invasions and coming to blows with rural landowners and police. Among the most important of these groups, the Landless Workers' Movement (*Movimento dos Sem-Terra*, or MST) attracted the most attention by seizing some 1.38 million acres of land.

The Cardoso administration responded to these problems by expropriating some unproductive estates and settling 186,000 families on them. Substantial sums were set aside to provide financial support and the placement of additional rural families. However, these efforts fell far short of providing a lasting solution to rural poverty. Brazil continues to lack true agrarian reform.

Any serious effort to address rural poverty will affect urban poverty. Through rural to urban migration, the landless poor have swelled the rings of poverty that surround Brazil's major cities. During the 1950s and 1960s the growth of industry in the south and southeast enticed millions to migrate to the states of São Paulo, Minas Gerais, and Rio de Janeiro in the hopes of finding new economic opportunities. The rapidity of rural to urban migration was striking. In the 1960s over 13.8 million people (about 36 percent of the rural population in 1960) migrated to the cities of the south and southeast. In 1970, 17 million (approximately 42.2 percent of the rural population in 1970) moved from the countryside to the city. It took migrations in the United States eight decades to reach the same level of migrants as went from rural to urban areas in Brazil during the 1960s and 1970s. By the early 1980s, 68 percent of Brazil's population was living in urban areas. Between 1960 and 1980 rural to

Favelas **in Rio de Janeiro.** *Source:* © Marc Valdecantos.

urban migration accounted for 58 percent of urban population growth.

The flood of migrants to urban areas and the growth of urban populations created terrible social problems. The pressures on Brazilian cities for basic services such as sanitation, education, and transportation soon overwhelmed the budgets of municipalities and state governments. Poor people were left to their own devices. Squatters soon took government land, settling on the outskirts of the major cities. Millions of these *descamisados* ("shirtless ones") built "homes" out of cardboard, wood from dumps, and blocks of mortar and brick. Huge shanty towns called *favelas* sprang up around cities like Rio and São Paulo.

Regional disparities in income worsened during this period. The military governments addressed this problem by transferring revenues from the industrialized south and southeast to the poor north and northeast, where many of their supporters were based. The federal government subsidized communication and transportation in the poorer regions and created new state agencies to implement regional developmental projects. These policies had mixed results. The contribution of poor regions to the gross domestic product increased. The growth rate of the central and western regions was spurred on by agribusiness activities, mineral exploration, and financial services. The economic gap between regions narrowed, but social and income disparties within the underdeveloped regions increased.[30] Industrialization in the poorer regions was capital-intensive and therefore labor-saving but not job-creating. Only the most skilled workers in these regions benefited from these changes. Poor agricultural management, ecological destruction, the murder of native Brazilians, and corruption all weakened the distributive effect of these policies.

Today, the northern and northeastern regions remain much poorer than those in the south and southeast. Whereas 15 percent of the population in the southeast subsists under the poverty line, more than 50 percent of the inhabitants of the northeast are below that marker. The life expectancy of a northeasterner—fifty-eight years—is nine years below that of a resident of São Paulo state (sixty-seven years) and fifteen years below that of a resident of Rio Grande do Sul (seventy-three years).[31]

The shrinking labor market for unskilled workers, the rapidity of rural to urban migration, and the regional disparities that add to poverty have all worked against the equalization of income distribution in Brazil. Compared with other developing countries, including Mexico and India, Brazil has the worst structure of income distribution in the world (see Table 3 on p. 345).

Brazil and the International Political Economy

As the financing needs of state-led industrialization outstripped the resources of the national development bank and domestic bankers, the deepening of ISI required Brazil to pursue international sources of credit. During the late 1960s and the 1970s private lenders were eager to provide loans to Brazil and other

Table 3

Brazilian Income Distribution in Comparative Perspective

Country	Year	Percent of Total Income Received by			
		10% Richest	20% Richest	40% Poorest	20% Poorest
Peru	1994	34.3%	50.4%	14.1%	4.9%
China	1995	30.9	47.5	15.3	5.5
United States	1994	28.5	45.2	15.3	4.8
India	1994	25.0	39.3	22.2	4.1
France	1989	24.9	40.1	19.9	7.2
Britain	1986	24.7	39.8	19.9	7.1
Brazil	1995	47.9	64.2	8.2	2.5
Chile	1994	46.1	61.0	10.1	3.5
Mexico	1992	39.2	55.3	11.9	4.1
Germany	1989	22.6	37.1	22.5	9.0
Poland	1992	22.1	36.6	23.1	9.3

Source: World Bank, *World Development Report 1998/99* (Washington, D.C.: World Bank, 1998), 198–199.

fast-growing countries. As a result, Brazil became the largest single debtor country in the developing world. Figure 2 (on p. 346) illustrates the tremendous growth of foreign debt.

External events had a hand in creating and then managing Brazil's external debt. By the end of the 1970s the world economy had been hit with two oil price shocks that sent inflation rates soaring in the United States and other industrialized countries. Many of these countries also held Brazilian debt. As the central banks in Europe and the Federal Reserve in the United States ratcheted interest rates upward to force prices back down, Brazil's interest payments grew precipitously.[32]

After Mexico declared a moratorium on interest payments in 1982, private investors began to shun Brazil and other Latin American debtors. During the 1980s, the so-called Lost Decade of slow growth and debt crisis, the International Monetary Fund and the World Bank became important suppliers of badly needed credit. But only debtors who promised to take concrete steps to reduce inflation, open their domestic markets to foreign competition, promote exports, and privatize state industries were eligible for help.

Brazil, along with Argentina and Peru, rejected these conditions. The Sarney government refused to implement the free-market policies demanded by the international financial institutions. In 1987 his government took the ultimate gamble in resisting creditors by declaring a moratorium on debt repayment, a move that sent a signal to investors that Brazil would control its own reform agenda on its own terms. The moratorium, however, did not last. It was lifted a few months later under intense pressure from the international financial community. Opposition to the moratorium within the country was also great among the business community, which feared such aggressive action would scare away foreign investors and ruin the country's already tattered credit rating.

Collor reversed course. He agreed to put Brazil on the path of free-market policies—partly in response to pressure from international creditors and partly in recognition that Sarney's alternative policies had failed. The Collor administration invoked both macroeconomic reforms to bring down inflation and reduce balance-of-payments deficits and "structural adjustment" policies to liberalize the domestic market, privatize state enterprises, and deregulate the economy. Although Collor's anti-inflation plans failed, his structural reforms provided a crucial catalyst for freeing up the economy from layers of bureaucratic red tape and inefficiency. These domestic changes were

Figure 2

Growth of Public, External Debt for Select Years, 1973–1996

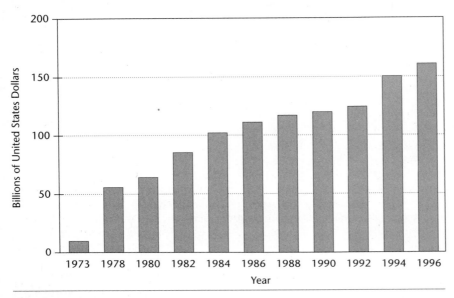

Sources: Inter-American Development Bank, *Economic and Social Progress in Latin America, 1988 Report* (Washington, D.C.: IADB, 1988), 580; *Economic and Social Progress in Latin America, 1997 Report* (Washington, D.C.: IADB, 1997), 256.

reflected externally as Collor began to normalize relations between Brazil and the multilateral agencies, especially the IMF.

The liberalization of markets opened Brazilian industry to higher degrees of foreign competition. As a result, the competitiveness of domestic firms has emerged as a core problem. Brazilian industrial productivity reached its lowest levels in 1992, when, on a list of fifty countries, Brazil was ranked just ahead of Pakistan, which was last. One 1997 study showed that the overall productivity of Brazilian industry runs at only 27 percent of the U.S. level.[33] Although productivity levels improved by 7 percent after 1992, inherent inefficiencies caused by poor infrastructure, untrained labor, and lack of access to technology and capital continue to create obstacles to higher growth. The average Brazilian worker has only six years of schooling, half as much as the average worker in Japan or the United States. These problems undermine the rationale of IMF-style free-market policies, since

they suggest that free markets alone cannot guarantee the country's growth.

How Brazil will fare in an increasingly interconnected and competitive global marketplace will also depend on its external political relations. During the 1980s, Brazil engaged in numerous conflicts with the United States over steel exports (one of Brazil's most export-competitive industries), computer hardware, and patent protection for multinational companies operating in Brazil. Washington threatened to slap protective tariffs on Brazilian products in retaliation. The political climate changed during the Bush and Clinton administrations, when international free-trade accords, such as the North American Free Trade Agreement (NAFTA), received the support of both Washington and most Latin American governments. During the Summit of the Americas in Miami in December 1994, the leaders of the United States, Central America, the Caribbean (except Cuba), and South America agreed to form a Free Trade Area of

Global Connection: **MERCOSUL**

After several years of negotiating the Treaty of Asunción, Brazil, Argentina, Paraguay, and Uruguay inaugurated MERCOSUL, a regional common-market group, in January 1995. Under MERCOSUL (Mercosur in Spanish), Brazil and its trade partners agreed to gradually reduce tariffs on imports from signatories until 2006, when the 10,000 items that make up the tariff listings of all four countries must conform to a common external tariff (CET) regime.

During the negotiations over the Treaty of Asunción between March 26, 1991, and MERCOSUL's inauguration, trade among the partners increased from 8 to 20 percent, making the case for a subhemispheric common market stronger. After a rough start due to the Mexican peso crisis, the signatories reaffirmed their commitment to forge the common market. Efforts to gradually remove tariff protections and nontariff protections such as regulations that slow down the flow of trade, proceeded with few disruptions.

At the center of MERCOSUL's evolution is the long list of products that the CET targets. However, the signatories are allowed to exclude up to 300 items (399 in Paraguay) as exceptions to the CET. The partners also agreed to numerous dispute-resolution mechanisms to avoid conflicts that might threaten the free-trade group.

Source: Lia Valls Pereira, "Tratado de Assunção: Resultados e Perspectivas," in *Mercosul: Perspectivas da Integração*, ed. Antônio Salazar P. Brandão and Lia Valls Pereira (Rio de Janeiro: Fundação Getúlio Vargas, 1996), 11.

MERCOSUL is only the latest in a list of common-market schemes in Latin America. In 1960 the Latin American Association of Free Trade (ALALC) initiated a process for forming a common market in twelve years. Although this goal was unfulfilled because of persistent differences among the group's members, intraregional trade increased from 7.7 percent in 1960 to 13.8 percent in 1980. Subhemispheric common-market groups unconnected to ALALC also emerged as the Andean Group in 1969 (Bolivia, Colombia, Ecuador, and Venezuela) and the Central American Common Market in 1960 (Costa Rica, Guatemala, El Salvador, Honduras, and Nicaragua). ALALC was replaced in 1980 with the Latin American Integration Association (ALADI). Unlike ALALC's mission of forming a common market, ALADI's goal was to foster the formation of preferential trade agreements among subhemispheric groups. These efforts received their most important boost soon after the Bush Administration delivered its Enterprise for the Americas Initiative (EAI) in 1990, a plan of lofty goals for hemispheric economic integration. Soon after the EAI was announced, the existing regional groups and a new wave of other groups formed preferential organizations. Besides MERCOSUL, the most important of these was the North American Free Trade Agreement (NAFTA), initiated on January 1, 1994.

Like its predecessors, MERCOSUL was a product and a cause of increased commercial integration among its signatories. Since its creation, MERCOSUL has contributed to a threefold increase in trade among its signatories.

the Americas (FTAA) by the year 2005. At present, Brazil belongs to its own subhemispheric group, the Market of the South (MERCOSUL).

Brazil's degree of commitment to the international free-trade system will depend on the endurance of the country's domestic reform agenda. If inflation threatens to return, Brazil's leaders have already shown that they would be willing to sacrifice MERCOSUL and other commitments to free trade. For example, an attempt to stave off growing trade deficits that threatened the Real Plan in 1995 forced Brazilian policymakers to increase tariffs on imported automobiles from 32 percent to 70 percent, an act that immediately angered Argentina. Although such disagreements are regularly resolved through MERCOSUL's dispute resolution mechanisms, a larger crisis could push Brazil to sacrifice these commitments on the altar of inflation control.

Section ③   Governance and Policy-Making

Organization of the State

The institutions of the Brazilian state have changed significantly since independence. Even so, a number of institutional legacies have endured and continue to shape Brazilian politics today. The most important is the centralization of state authority in the executive. Paradoxically, though, a second legacy is the decentralized federal structure of the Brazilian state. The constitution of 1988 attempted to construct a new democratic order but left these contradictory tendencies in place. The president retained the authority to legislate on social and economic matters, but new powers governing the implementation of these policies were devolved to the state and municipal governments.

As a result, the 1988 constitution was simultaneously the focus of much hope and intense attack. It was to be the governing document for the new democracy, but it became an instrument used to confound political and economic reform. As a product of political horse-trading, it failed to provide a coherent vision of how institutions should be structured and what functions they should have. The separation of powers remains ill-defined in Brazil. Instead, ad hoc and stopgap arrangements continue to determine the boundaries of official authority, while informal relations and understandings play a major role in the interpretation of law.

Some generalizations about the organization of the Brazilian state can be made. First, the church and state are officially separated. The Catholic Church never controlled any portion of the state apparatus or directly influenced national politics as it did in other Catholic countries, including Spain. This does not mean, however, that the Catholic Church plays no role in Brazilian politics (see Section 4).

Second, Brazil has a presidential system of government. The directly elected president is the head of state, head of government, and commander in chief of the armed forces. The Brazilian state has traditionally placed vast power in the hands of the executive. Although the executive is one of three branches of government (the legislature and the judiciary being the other two), Brazilian presidents have traditionally

been less bound by judicial and legislative constraints than their European or North American counterparts. Brazilian constitutions have granted the executive more discretion than the other branches in enforcing laws or in making policy. The legislature and the judiciary historically have played secondary roles.

The Brazilian state does not have the checks and balances of the United States government system. It differs also from the semipresidentialism of France, in which the president, although dominant over the legislature and judiciary, faces broader constraints in the possibility of having to work with a hostile parliamentary majority. Although the French prime minister is appointed by the executive and is not elected by the legislature, as in other parliamentary systems, he or she is chosen from the party with the majority of elected representatives in parliament, which is not necessarily the president's party. Moreover, the French party system is more organized and less fragmented than its counterpart in Brazil, making the legislature more efficient and capable of checking executive actions.

In Brazil the executive and the bureaucracy manage most of the policy-making and implementation functions of government. Both the federal legislature and the state governments look to the presidency and, in economic matters, to the minister of the economy, for leadership on policy. The key agencies of the economic bureaucracy, including the ministers of the economy, planning, the president of the central bank, and the head of the national development bank, have more discretion over the details of policy than the president. Although some Brazilian presidents have delegated less to bureaucratic agencies, recent presidents have had little choice but to delegate, given the growing complexity of economic and social policy. Ultimate authority, however, remains in the hands of the president, who may replace his ministers.

Although the Brazilian president remains the dominant player among the three branches of government, the powers of the legislature and the judiciary are becoming more formidable. After the transition to democratic rule in 1985, these institutions have become critical to democracy. The 1988 constitution gave many oversight functions to the legislature and judiciary so that much presidential discretion in economic and social policy is now subject to approval by either the legislature or the judiciary or both. This gives these branches of government some independence and leverage over the presidency, although this power is not often employed effectively. Centralizing traditions are still strong in Brazil, making the obstacles to the deconcentration of executive power enormous.

A third generalization that may be offered on the Brazilian state is that it is decentralized. Like Germany, India, and the United States, the Brazilian state has a federal structure. The country's twenty-six states are divided into 5000 municipal governments. Most of the country's presidents have relied on subnational bases of power to stay in office. The presidents of the Old Republic and even Getúlio Vargas counted on the support of local clientelist political machines led by self-interested governors and mayors.

With the transition to democracy, these "barons of the federation," as one study calls them, became a crucial source of political support for legislators as well as presidents.[34] By controlling indispensable reservoirs of patronage through their powers of appointment and spending, governors and even some mayors can wield extraordinary influence. In recent years, some of the harsher elements of reform legislation have been jettisoned to mollify this subnational constituency.

Seen as a whole, political decentralization, which was accelerated with the constitution of 1988, has further fragmented the Brazilian polity. At the same time, however, some subnational governments have become an important source of innovative policy-making. Average Brazilian citizens have more access to their municipal and state governments than they do to their federal representatives, which suggests that decentralization may eventually strengthen democracy by making political elites more accountable to their local constituencies.

The Executive

A majority of delegates to the 1987 National Constituent Assembly that drafted the new democratic constitution favored the creation of a parliamentary system. President Sarney, who did not want to see his powers reduced, used his support among the governors to lobby against the parliamentary option.

The best he could do was force the members of the assembly to defer the issue to a plebiscite in 1993. Yet the plebiscite, envisioned by the constitution's framers as the climactic event that would determine Brazil's political structure, ended by giving a stamp of approval to the existing presidential system. With virtually no experience in parliamentary politics, Brazilians opted for presidentialism.

Why is there no parliamentarism in Brazil? For many Brazilians, governmental effectiveness has historically been identified with presidential supremacy. For the poor and for organized sectors such as workers and professionals, the presidency has always been the focus of their demands for improvements in living conditions and wages. As for the armed forces, few generals could imagine being led by a prime minister and a legislature. Although not a constitutional requirement, all Brazilian presidents, and most elected officials, have been men.

In 1993 widespread suspicion of legislative politics was fanned by the argument of the campaign to retain presidentialism that the parliamentary option was little more than a trick to "take the right to vote away from the people." The concept of a parliamentary system that would allow a prime minister to be elected by legislative elites and not directly by the citizenry seemed contrary to what Brazilians had fought for during the long struggle for democracy. Brazilians did not want to lose the ultimate check on the presidency: direct elections by voters every four years. This principle has become even more important as the Cardoso presidency gained the constitutional right to allow the president to run for a second term. Popular elections will now present a crucial test for presidents wishing to pursue their agendas for another four years.

If parliamentary government seemed a far-off goal, rules designed to rein in the power of the federal executive still found their way into the 1988 constitution. In part as a reaction to the extreme centralization of executive authority during military rule, the delegates restored some of the congressional prerogatives that had existed prior to 1964 and granted new ones. The congress gained oversight over economic policy and the right of consultation on executive appointments. Executive decrees—which allowed the president to legislate directly—were abolished. In their place "emergency measures" were established, which preserved the president's power to legislate for thirty days, at the end of which congress can pass or reject the new law. President Collor used emergency measures to install his anti-inflation plans, but they had to survive a two-thirds vote of both houses of the congress. Finally, the 1988 constitution limited the president to a single term, a provision common to Latin American constitutions. In 1997, however, Cardoso succeeded in passing a constitutional amendment through congress that removed the no-reelect rule, allowing him and twenty-two governors to run again in 1998.

Despite these new constraints, Brazilian presidents were still able to use emergency measures with considerable success because of the sad state of the economy. Given such crisis conditions, how could congress deny the president the right to railroad through much-needed reform legislation? Some presidents articulated such arguments with great frequency. Collor, for example, severely abused these powers. In his first year in office, Collor handed down 150 emergency measures. Technically, this meant that the country experienced a crisis situation every forty-eight hours.[35] Worse still, the Supreme Tribunal, the highest court in Brazil, did little to curb this obvious abuse of constitutional authority by the president. The use of presidential discretionary power has only reinforced the powers of the executive to legislate. Over 80 percent of all legislation originates in the executive branch.

The president also retains extremely valuable powers of appointment over the huge Brazilian bureaucracy, particularly at the ministerial level. The Brazilian president retains broad powers to select and dismiss close associates. The president selects ministers for the armed forces according to the merit system prevailing in their respective branches. For most other positions, the president usually appoints ministers from groups of his longtime cronies and collaborators or from any of the existing parties. Although these appointees are not as cohesive a group as the presidential *camarillas* in Mexico, this comparison serves to illustrate the importance of personal ties to the president in Brazil. Under the 1988 constitution, the president must negotiate with congress and some powerful groups (e.g., business associations, labor unions, bar associations) over certain positions in the cabinet, mainly those responsible for economic policy-making. Even so, the power of appointments in Brazil continues to be a source of great influence.

Among the chief cabinet posts, the ministries of Economy (also called Finance during certain administrations) and Planning have had extraordinary influence. Since the beginning of the military governments, the Ministry of Economy has had more authority than any other executive agency of the state. These powers were heightened as a result of the economic problems of the 1980s and the reform agenda of the 1990s. Thanks to their control of the federal budget and the details of economic policy, recent ministers of the economy have had levels of authority typical of a prime minister in a parliamentary system. The success of Cardoso in the 1994 presidential campaign was due in large part to his effective performance as Itamar Franco's Minister of Economy.

The Bureaucracy: State and Semipublic Firms

Bureaucratic agencies and public firms have played key roles in Brazilian economic and political development during the twentieth century. After 1940 the state created a large number of new agencies and public enterprises. Many of these entities were allowed to accumulate their own debt and plan development projects without undue influence from the central ministries or politicians. Public firms became a key part of the triple alliance of state, foreign, and domestic capital that governed the state-led model of development. Yet it was the state that dominated this alliance. By 1981 ten of the top twenty-five enterprises in Brazil were owned by the federal government and eight others were owned by state governments. Public expenditures as a share of GDP increased from 16 percent in 1947 to more than 32 percent in 1969, far higher than in any other Latin American country, except socialist Cuba.[36]

Much of this spending (and the huge debt that financed it) was concentrated on development projects, many of gigantic proportions. Key examples include the world's largest hydroelectric plant, Itaipú; Petrobrás' petroleum processing centers; steel mills such as the gargantuan National Steel Company in Volta Redonda, Rio de Janeiro; and Vale do Rio Doce, a public firm with interests in sectors as diverse as mining, transport, paper, and textiles. Under the last three military governments (Médici, Geisel, and Figueiredo), dozens of other projects were completed, including the Trans-Amazonian highway, the Tucuruí hydroelectric plants, the Açominas metallurgy park, and the National Nuclear Reactor Program. These and hundreds of other, more modest, projects accounted for much of the country's industrial production. On the eve of the debt crisis in 1982, the top thirty-three projects, including those just listed, absorbed US$88 billion in external debt, employed 1.5 million people, and added $47 billion to the GDP.

Managing the planning and finance of these projects required enormous skill. Several public agencies were responsible, but the National Bank for Economic and Social Development (*Banco Nacional de Desenvolvimento Economico e Social*, or BNDES), stands out as an important coordinator. Founded by Vargas in the early 1950s, the BNDES played a key role in channeling public funds to industrial projects. Among the bank's greatest achievements was the creation of an automobile sector based on subsidized public steel, foreign assemblers such as Ford, General Motors, and Volkswagen, and domestic suppliers of parts and labor. Under President Juscelino Kubitschek, the BNDES implemented an industrial policy in automobiles called the Plan of Goals (*Plano de Metas*), which coordinated domestic and international resources to create the largest automobile industry in Latin America.[37]

The experience of the BNDES demonstrated that despite Brazil's clientelist legacies, the Brazilian bureaucracy could function effectively. Meritocratic advancement and professional recruitment granted these agencies some autonomy from political manipulation. Such agencies were considered islands of efficiency in a state apparatus characterized by patronage and corruption.[38]

Other state and semipublic firms, however, were rife with clientelism. Civilian and military leaders often appointed their supporters as the heads of these enterprises, positions with quite generous salary and retirement packages. Many public firm managers took advantage of their positions to dole out government contracts to associates and even to their own companies in the private sector.

The fiscal crisis of the 1980s had put severe strains on the entire economic bureaucracy, but some things failed to change. The 1988 constitution did not alter significantly the concentration of power in the economic bureaucracy that made developmentalism with clientelism possible. In fact, the new constitution reinforced certain bureaucratic monopolies by codifying them as rights. For example, the state's control over petroleum, natural gas, the exploration of minerals, nuclear energy, and telecommunications was protected constitutionally. These sectors could not be privatized—much less sold to foreign governments or multinational companies.

What the writers of the new constitution did do in response to the fiscal crisis was place new restraints on the activity of state-directed industries. The fiscal independence of state firms was curtailed with restrictions on the amount of debt they could incur. The constitution imposed additional obstacles to the creation of public firms, including the requirement that congress approve any new state enterprises proposed by the executive branch.

Some of the constitutional protections of the public firms lasted only a few years. After his election in 1989, Fernando Collor began a sweeping reform of Brazil's public bureaucracy, beginning with the privatization of large public firms in steel, chemicals, and mining. In 1990 his government launched the National Destatization Program (*Programa Nacional de Destatização*, PND). Under the PND, more than US$20 billion in public firms was sold ($8.5 billion in the steel sector alone). Although the program slowed under the Franco administration, the sell-offs of the steel firms were completed. The Cardoso administration went even further. The government convinced the congress to amend the constitution to remove the public monopoly on petroleum refining, telecommunications, and infrastructure, making these sectors available for auction. Electricity distribution, cellular phone bands, and the octopuslike structure of Vale were put up for privatization. In 1998 much of the public telecommunication sector was privatized, bringing in about $25 billion.

Paradoxically, the agency at the center of the privatization process in Brazil is the BNDES, the agency most responsible for developmentalism. Faced with the fiscal crisis of the 1980s, BNDES' managers adopted a new perspective of the state's role in the economy. Instead of targeting industries and spending large sums to promote them, BNDES' new mission was to provide financing to productivity-enhancing investments such as new technology and labor retraining, outlays that promise to make both soon-to-be-privatized and already-privatized firms more competitive in international markets.[39] As a result, the economic bureaucracy in Brazil continues to play a crucial role in the country's development.

The Military and the Police

The military is another significant arm of the state. Like many other South American militaries, the Brazilian armed forces retain a substantial degree of independence from civilian presidents and legislators. Brazil has suffered numerous coups; those in 1930 and 1964 were critical junctures, while others brought in caretaker governments that eventually ceded to civilian rule. Although the military's grip on power was never as tight as in Nigeria during the Abacha regime, the generals have maintained influence in Brazilian politics, blocking policies they do not like and lobbying on behalf of those they favor.

The military's participation in Brazilian politics became more defined following the transition to democracy. The armed forces were successful in keeping broad prerogatives to "guarantee internal order" and to play a "tutelary role" in civilian government. During the Sarney administration, members of the armed forces retained cabinet-level rank in areas of importance to the military, such as the ministries of the armed forces and the nuclear program. Military officers also kept middle- and lower-level positions in public firms and bureaucratic agencies. Most important, the armed forces were successful in obtaining amnesty for human rights abuses committed during the preceding authoritarian regime.

In an effort to professionalize the armed forces and keep them in the barracks, the Collor government slashed the military budget and replaced the top generals with officers who had few or no connections to the authoritarian regime and were committed to civilian leadership. Collor's reforms were helped by the decline of the country's arms industry, which, during the 1980s, lost key markets for ordinance, tanks, and guns in the Middle East. These industries had previously supplied capital and armaments to the Brazilian armed forces, keeping them autonomous from civilian control. The collapse and, in some cases, privatization of these military industries gave civilians more control over the generals.[40] The geographic isolation of the Brazilian arms industry in one area of São Paulo state and increasing conflicts over the marketability of expensive weapons systems favored by the armed forces weakened the military's lobbies in Brasília, further eroding the generals' ability to defend their interests.[41]

Police enforcement primarily falls into the domain of the state governments. The state police consists of two forces: the civil police force, which acts as an investigative unit and is not completely uniformed, and the uniformed military police force, which maintains order. The military police are not formally under the command of the military; the constitution stipulates that in the event of a national emergency they can be called to perform active military service. Like the military, the military police are governed by a separate judicial system.

Despite official oversight of police authorities, in practice the military and civil police forces in many cities of the northeast, in São Paulo, and in Rio de Janeiro often act extrajudicially. Cases of arbitrary detention, torture, corruption, and systematic killings by Brazilian police have received much international attention. Human rights investigations have found that off-duty police officers are regularly hired by merchants and assorted thugs to kill street urchins whom they accuse of thievery. One study in Rio de Janeiro between 1993 and 1996 showed that police officers preferred the use of deadly force, shooting to kill rather than to disable.[42] The majority of victims were shot in the shoulders or the head; in 40 of the 697 cases, the victims were shot in the back of the head in gangland, execution style. Most astonishingly, the victims were mostly young black men and boys and had no criminal records whatsoever. Other studies have shown that at least 10 percent of the homicides in Rio de Janeiro are committed by the police. In São Paulo, police violence is just as bad. In 1992 alone, the São Paulo police killed 1,470 people, accounting for one-third of all homicides in the state.[43]

The federal police force is a small unit of approximately 3000 people. It operates as a combined U.S. Federal Bureau of Investigation, Secret Service,

Drug Enforcement Agency, and Immigration and Naturalization Service. Under the authority of the executive the federal police are responsible for providing security to public officials, cracking down on drug rings, administering customs regulations, and investigating federal crimes. The demands placed on this single agency have caused some Brazilian politicians to propose that the federal police be split up into more specialized units, as in the U.S. system.

Other State Institutions

The Judiciary

The Brazilian judiciary is composed of a network of state courts, with jurisdiction over state matters; and a federal court system, not unlike the one in the United States, which maintains jurisdiction over federal crimes. A supreme court (the Supreme Federal Tribunal), similar in jurisdiction to the U.S. Supreme Court but lacking authority over the other branches of government, acts as the final arbiter of court cases. It is composed of eleven justices, each appointed by the president and confirmed by an absolute majority of the Senate. A Superior Court of Justice with thirty-three sitting justices operates under the Supreme Federal Tribunal as an appeals court. Matters requiring interpretation of the constitution go to the Supreme Federal Tribunal. The military maintains its own court system. All judges in the Brazilian judicial system serve for life.

The judiciary is designed to adjudicate political conflicts as well as civil and social conflicts. The Electoral Supreme Tribunal (*Tribunal Supremo Electoral*, TSE) has exclusive responsibility for the organization and oversight of all issues related to voting. The seven-member TSE is composed of three justices elected from the members of the Supreme Federal Tribunal; two from the Superior Court of Justice; and two nominated by the president from a group of six attorneys of notable quality that are selected by the Supreme Federal Tribunal. The seven justices on the TSE have the power to investigate charges of political bias by public employees, to file criminal charges against persons violating electoral laws, and to scrutinize and validate electoral results. In addition to these constitutional provisions, under

electoral law and its own regulations the TSE monitors the legal compliance of electoral campaigns and executive neutrality in campaigns. The integrity of the tribunal in the conduct of elections has remained very high, making fraud a relatively rare thing in national elections. The TSE is assisted in this process by a system of regional electoral courts, which oversee local elections.

As in the rest of Latin America, penal codes govern the powers of judges. This makes the judiciary less flexible than its North American counterparts, which operate on case law, but it provides a more effective barrier against "judicial activism"—the tendency of the courts to render broad interpretations of the law.

Since the 1940s the judicial branch of government in Brazil has in theory been highly independent from the executive. In practice, especially under authoritarian rule, the judiciary has been dictated to by the executive branch. President Collor exercised sweeping executive powers without much judicial review. The Supreme Federal Tribunal was viewed as ceding significant extraconstitutional authority by not challenging Collor's rule by fiat. A year after Collor's anti-inflation asset freeze, some of the country's most renowned jurists decided to oppose further blockage of financial assets on the grounds that it was unconstitutional. Although their opposition came late, it began a national debate that continues to this day about the president's "emergency measures." Even so, Cardoso continues to rely heavily upon these discretionary powers.

In recent years, the judiciary has been severely criticized for its perceived unresponsiveness to Brazil's social problems and the persistent corruption in the lower courts. These problems are particularly apparent in rural areas, where impoverished defendants are often denied the right to a fair trial by powerful landowners, who have undue influence over judges and procedures. Children are especially victimized, as courts have refused to hear cases prosecuting those who profit from child prostitution, pornography, and the killing of street urchins.

Prosecuting the police for their misdeeds is exceedingly difficult. In the state of Rio de Janeiro, between January 1996 and July 1997, 68 percent of cases in military court involving the police were retired without a hearing because of insufficient evidence (which is often destroyed by the police) or because of the police's favorite excuse, that the defendant was injured or killed "while resisting arrest." Although federal legislation in 1996 granted civil courts jurisdiction over such matters, paradoxically the power to investigate these crimes was left in the hands of the police.

The Supreme Tribunal's reluctance to act on these matters leaves little hope for change in the short term. Judicial reform has thus far focused upon speeding up the Supreme Tribunal's judicial review functions, avoiding the trickier question of restructuring the judiciary to eliminate corruption.

Restructuring of the judiciary will continue to get attention as the 1988 constitution is revised. Proposals for reform include subjecting judges to external control through periodic elections. Members of the judiciary deeply resent and fear such a prospect. They argue that it would push the institution into the kind of partisanship that has marred policy debates on key social and political issues. Others consider that it is the structure of the judiciary and its approach to interpreting and implementing laws that are the central obstacles to accomplishing policy goals. Like the Brazilian bureaucracy, the judiciary has a complex structure, with multiple jurisdictions at different levels of government. The problems inherent in this complex network of adjudication were made clear during the privatization of Vale when opposition groups in different states and jurisdictions were able to use the local courts to create numerous obstacles to the sale. Attempts to reform the judiciary, most notably in 1997, have been severely limited by jurisdictional conflicts.

Subnational Government

The structure of subnational politics in Brazil is not unlike that of other federal systems throughout the world. Each state government consists of a governor; his chief advisers, who also usually lead key secretariats such as economy and planning; and a unicameral legislature, which is often dominated by the supporters of the governor. Governors are elected to four-year terms and, under the 1997 amendment of the 1988 constitution, they may run for another term.

State and municipal governments wield tremendous influence in Brazilian politics. Since the days of

the Old Republic, governors and mayors have been essential sources of support for presidents and federal legislators. This "politics of the governors" expanded with the transition to democracy. The fact that the 1982 elections created the first opportunity since the inauguration of the military regime for Brazilians to elect their governors directly made these subnational politicians crucial standard-bearers of the transition. It lent legitimacy to the governors' campaign to decentralize fiscal resources in the form of taxes and federal transfers. For the "barons of the federation," decentralization was nothing less than part of the democratization process.

The 1988 constitution provided much of what the governors and mayors wanted. First the states and municipalities were promised a larger share of tax revenues. At the same time, however, the governors and mayors were successful in deflecting Brasília's attempts to devolve additional spending responsibilities to subnational government, particularly in the areas of education, health, and infrastructure. The governors also proved successful in protecting state banks from a major overhaul, which was greatly needed given that these financial institutions continued to fund irresponsible subnational spending by accumulating huge debts that the federal government agreed to roll over.

During the Collor administration, the federal government began to regain much of the fiscal authority it had lost to the states and municipalities. The Central Bank made good on its threats to intervene in bankrupt state banks and privatize them. The federal government also refused to roll over state debt without a promise of reform, including the privatization of money-losing utility companies. The Cardoso administration required states and municipalities to finance a larger share of social spending, including education and health care. At the same time, new legislation empowered Brasília to claim more discretionary authority over fiscal transfers and tax revenues that had previously been devolved to subnational governments.

Despite these efforts, Brazilian presidents must continue to negotiate the terms of reform with governors as much as with the congress. Because they can now run for reelection, the governors and their political machines will represent an even more consistent element in national politics. The October 1998 elections proved the staying power of incumbent governors as fifteen of the twenty-two incumbents who ran were reelected, a turnover rate well below the high levels in the legislature (see Section 4).

Although most subnational politics are still preoccupied with the distribution of political favors in return for fiscal rewards, certain governors and mayors have devised innovative solutions to Brazil's social and economic problems. One recent study of the state of Ceará in the poor northern region has demonstrated that even the most underdeveloped subnational governments can produce important policies to promote industrial investment, employment, and social services.[44] Such an example is a useful reminder that not all states and municipalities are the same in a federal system. Much depends on the interests and quality of political and bureaucratic leadership.

The Policy-Making Process

Even though policy-making continues to be fluid and ambiguous in Brazil, certain domains of policy are clearly demarcated. Foreign policy, for example, is exclusively within the purview of the executive branch. Political parties and the congress in general still have only inconsistent power over investment policies. As most legislation originates in the executive branch, bureaucratic agencies have retained command over the details of social and economic policies.

The process of making policy in Brazil can be characterized by one common quality: the tendency of clientelism to inject itself at every stage, from formulation and decision-making to implementation. Even when policies are formulated without the undue influence of societal and political actors, implementation is often obstructed or distorted by clientelism. Again, as noted, exceptions exist, but they are only that—exceptions.[45]

Complex formal and informal networks linking the political executive, key agencies of the bureaucracy, and private interests tend to be the chief players in clientelist circles. One of Cardoso's contributions to sociology before he became involved in Brazilian politics was his characterization of these clientelistic networks as **bureaucratic rings**. For Cardoso, the Brazilian state is highly permeable, fragmented, and therefore easily colonized by private interests that make alliances with midlevel bureaucratic officers. By shaping public policy to benefit these interests, bureaucrats gain the promise of future employment in the private sector. While in positions of responsibility, bureaucratic rings are ardent defenders of their own interests. Because they are entrenched and well connected throughout the Brazilian bureaucracy, few policies can be implemented without the resources and support of the most powerful bureaucratic rings.

One example of the role of bureaucratic rings is the creation of large development projects. The politics surrounding these decisions were often intense. Governors and mayors wanted lucrative public projects to be placed in their jurisdiction; private contractors yearned for the state's business; and politicians positioned themselves for all the attendant kickbacks, political and pecuniary.[46] Although the days of huge development projects are over, the public sector still formulates policy and allocates resources under the influence of bureaucratic rings.

Among the key sources of influence external to the state is organized business. Unlike business associations in some Asian and West European countries, Brazilian business groups have remained independent of corporatist ties to the state. There is no Brazilian version of the French agricultural association FNSEA or the para-public institutions of the Federal Republic of Germany. Business associations have also remained aloof from political parties. Brazil has nothing akin to Mexico's PAN, a party that claims to represent a large portion of the business class. That does not mean, however, that Brazilian business interests are not organized. Lobbying by Brazilian entrepreneurs is common, and their participation in bureaucratic rings is legendary. Few major economic policies are passed without the input of the Federation of São Paulo Industries (*Federação das Industrias do Estado de São Paulo,* or FIESP). Other business groups, some that have broken off from FIESP, continue to defend their interests energetically as Brazil reforms its economy.

The country's labor confederations and unions have had less consistent access to policy-making. Although unions were once directly organized and manipulated by the corporatist state, they gained autonomy in the late 1970s and the 1980s. From then on they sought leverage over policy-making through outside channels, such as the link between the *Central*

Única dos Trabalhadores (CUT, Workers' Singular Peak Association) and Lula da Silva's Workers' Party. Attempts to bring labor formally into direct negotiations with business and the state have failed. Shortly after assuming power, Sarney initiated talks among business, government, and representatives of the major labor federations. These talks quickly broke down. Widening cleavages within the Brazilian union movement tended to split sectors of organized labor, causing some segments to refuse to be bound by any agreement. Later, during the Collor administration, a second attempt at tripartite negotiation emerged in the form of "sectoral chambers" in the São Paulo automotive sector. These talks produced some noteworthy accords, but the chambers did not last because of opposition from the Ministry of Economy and other agencies. These experiences contrast sharply with the legacy of codetermination in Germany and other formulas for maintaining collective bargaining with state mediation in West European countries.

Policy implementation is also highly politicized. Debate and lobbying do not stop in Brazil once laws are enacted. Policy implementation is a subject of perpetual bargaining. One popular phrase—*o jeito brasileiro* ("the Brazilian way")—captures this aspect of Brazilian politics.[47] The Brazilian way is to scoff at the law and find a way around it. If one wants to get something without really paying for it, one asks for a *jeito*. Paradoxically, *jeito* can be the source of great efficiency in Brazilian society, but it carries a heavy price in that the rule of law is not respected. Therefore, reform of the policy-making process in Brazil will require more than restrictions on clientelism and legislative and judicial oversight of suspected bureaucratic rings. It will require a shift in thinking about the role of law in Brazilian society.

Section ❹ Representation and Participation

Because of urbanization and modernization of the economy, the Brazilian electorate grew impressively after 1945. Improved literacy and efforts by political parties to expand voter registration helped to increase the number of citizens eligible to vote. Voting rights were granted in 1981 to anyone eighteen or older (but not illiterates) and in 1988 to anyone over sixteen. As a result of these changes, the percentage of the total population eligible to vote increased from 16.2 percent in 1945 to 60 percent in 1994. The Brazilian electorate stands at 106 million, 78.5 percent of which turned out for the presidential election in October 1998.

The expansion of the Brazilian electorate coincided with the proliferation of political organizations and movements dedicated to marshaling popular support. Mass appeal became an important element in campaigns and political alliances. With the return to democracy in the 1980s, newly independent labor unions and special-interest organizations emerged, making new alliances in civil society possible.

Nevertheless, the richness of political organization was restrained by the legacies of state-centered structures of social control. Despite the transition to democracy, state corporatism continued to govern important segments of the Brazilian polity. Some political parties and many of the new social movements and political organizations that helped end the military government lacked staying power. Clientelism continued to fragment the legislature and weaken other democratic institutions.

The Legislature

The national legislature (594 members) is bicameral, consisting of an upper house, the Senate, and a lower house, the Chamber of Deputies. Each state and the federal district elects three senators, for a total of eighty-one. Senators are elected by simple majority. Senators serve for eight-year terms and may be reelected without limits. Two-thirds of the Senate is elected at one time and four years later the remaining one-third is elected. For example, in the elections of 1994, two-thirds of the Senate was renewed. In 1998 the remaining one-third was renewed. Senatorial elections are held concurrently with those for the Chamber of Deputies, which places all of its seats up for election after each four-year cycle. Federal deputies may be reelected without limits. The number of members in the Chamber of Deputies is, in theory, proportional to the population of each state and the federal district. Each state is allowed a minimum of eight and a maximum of seventy deputies, regardless of population. In 1998 there were 513 deputies.

Both houses of the legislature have equal authority to make laws. In all cases, one chamber acts as a revisor of legislation passed by the other. Bills go back and forth between houses without going through a conference committee of the two chambers, as is the case in the United States. Once the bill is passed by both houses, the president may sign it into law, reject it as a whole, or reject it in part. The legislature can override a presidential veto with a majority of the vote in both houses during a joint session. Constitutional amendments must survive two three-fifths votes in each house of congress. Amendments may also be passed with an absolute majority in a special unicameral constituent assembly proposed by the president and created by both houses of congress. The Senate retains authority to try the president and other top officials, including the vice president and key ministers and justices, for impeachable offenses. The Senate also has the power to approve appointments to high offices, including justices of the high courts, heads of diplomatic missions, and the directors of the Central Bank.

The formula for determining the proportionality of population to representatives is distorted by complex constitutional rules that favor the most sparsely populated states. As these states are the most numerous in the federal system, they tend to be overrepresented in the legislature. For example, between 1990 and 1994, the northern region had 4.85 percent of the voters but elected 11.33 percent of the deputies, while the southeastern region had 46 percent of the electorate but only 33.59 percent of the seats. Only 40 percent of the population elects a majority of the Chamber of Deputies. The least populated states are also the poorest and most rural in Brazil. Typically, they have been political bases for conservative landowning interests and, more recently, agribusiness. After 1964 the military cultivated support among conservative rural groups by granting statehood to sparsely populated territories in the north and northeast, reinforcing their overrepresentation in the Chamber. These precedents continued into the democratic period and largely explain why conservative landowners and

agribusiness elites maintain positions of great influence in the Brazilian congress.

In contrast to the presidency, the Brazilian legislature has rarely played a dominant role in the country's politics. In part, that is due to the ability of the president to impose policy through corporatism and populism. However, the congress must accept some of the blame. Many senators and deputies are more interested in cultivating and dispensing patronage than in representing and being accountable to the voters. As a result, representatives have never organized their parties or large segments of the population in support of national policy. Only the rarest of exceptions exist to this rule of Brazilian congressional politics.

Legislators view their service primarily as a means to enhance their own income with generous public pensions and through kickbacks earned in the dispensing of political favors. Election to the federal legislature is often used as a stepping stone to even more lucrative posts.[48] After the presidency, the governorships of the industrialized states are the most coveted positions. Appointment to head any of the premier ministries and state firms also ranks high, since these are choice positions from which to distribute and receive favors. Although many members of congress are independently wealthy, most come from the middle or upper middle class and therefore have much to gain in the economics of public administration.

The congress has largely failed to use the expanded powers granted by the 1988 constitution. Lack of a quorum to vote is a frequent problem, and recently acquired powers have provided greater opportunities for some legislators to practice corruption and backroom dealing, conditions that have helped to break down party loyalties and reinforce the self-serving nature of congressional politics. The many deficiencies of the Brazilian legislature were magnified in the mid-1990s by several corruption scandals. In the most serious case, a handful of senators and deputies were accused of embezzling from the national treasury.

One response to legislative corruption has been the use of parliamentary commissions of inquiry to review cases of malfeasance by elected officials. Although these temporary committees have demonstrated some influence, most notably the parliamentary commission of inquiry that investigated Collor and recommended his impeachment, they have not always produced results. The temporary committees work alongside sixteen permanent legislative committees that treat issues as diverse as taxation and human rights. These committees, however, are not nearly as strong as the major committees in the U.S. Congress. Due to the self-interested focus of Brazilian politicians and the related weakness of political parties, legislative committees, both temporary and permanent, often fail to get to the end of an investigation or to find solutions to persistent dilemmas in policy.

Public opinion about the federal congress reflects its weakness and irrelevance to the key issues facing Brazil. In a 1996 survey by the JB-Vox Populi organization, the national congress received a mere 17 percent approval rating, the second lowest rank among the thirteen institutions listed in the poll. Only municipal government in the largest cities received a lower score.[49]

Political Parties and the Party System

The Brazilian political party system is one of the most mercurial in the world. Party names, party affiliations, and the structure of party alliances are constantly in flux. This is nothing new in Brazilian political history. Like many of the country's current problems, party instability stretches back to the New State of Getúlio Vargas and the centralization of politics in the Brazilian state. State corporatism and populism were hostile to the development of independent party organizations. Political parties, when they did emerge, were created by state managers. Populist redistribution reinforced these tendencies, as workers and the middle class became accustomed to asking what they would receive from a politician in return for support. Except for members of the Communist Party and other extreme organizations, Brazilian voters did not develop a strong sense of political identity linked to established parties. Personalist loyalties and the distribution of goods and services were more important.

Many of the traditional weaknesses of the party system were reinforced after the transition to democracy, making parties even more anemic. The rules governing the party system made it easier for politicians to switch parties, virtually at will. One of the most important observers of Brazilian democracy, Scott Mainwaring, found that the 559 representatives of the 1987–1991 legislature had belonged to an average of over three parties per politician.[50] Politicians switched parties to increase their access to patronage. Other rules of the electoral system created incentives for politicians to ignore the importance of party labels. Brazil's experience with **proportional representation** (PR), which is used to elect federal and state deputies, is particularly important in this regard.

Brazil's mix of presidentialism and multiparty democracy creates other problems for the country's system of representation. Given the political fragmentation of the legislature and the weakness of the party system, presidents are unable to maintain majority alliances in congress, a requirement for stability in a multiparty system. In parliamentary systems, the party in power has an absolute majority or stands at the head of an alliance of parties that compose a majority. As a result, the ruling party or alliance can implement a programmatic approach to legislation. By contrast, in Brazil, the president has never been able to maintain a supraparty alliance in congress. More often, Brazilian presidents have attempted to govern above parties, dispensing favors to key congressional politicians to get legislation approved. Alternatively, presidents have not been shy about railroading reform through congress by using their discretionary authorities. As Timothy Power, a scholar of presidential authority in Brazil, has noted, "The [presidential] pen is mightier than the congress."[51]

In the midst of Brazil's confusing party system, a number of political organizations have emerged over the last few years. These parties can be defined ideologically, although discrete categories are often not possible. Significant distinctions exist among the country's political parties.

Political parties on the right currently defend neoliberal economic policies designed to shrink the size of the public sector. They support the reduction and partial privatization of the welfare state. A majority advocate a liberal trade policy and MERCOSUL, but a substantial minority press for protectionism and the continuation of subsidies, particularly in agriculture. No party of the right has yet emerged as a solid defender of neoliberal restructuring of the economy. On constitutional reform, right-wing parties are fairly united in favor of curtailing the number and range of social rights protecting welfare entitlements and

Institutional Intricacies: *Proportional Representation*

Proportional representation was first introduced in Brazil in 1932 and was later reaffirmed by the military governments. Unlike Mexico, Britain, and the United States, but like many of the European parliamentary democracies, Brazil is divided into electoral districts that choose more than one representative. The ability to choose more than one representative means that a broader range of voices may be heard in elected offices.

Minority parties can make alliances to pass the threshold of votes needed to achieve representation. Proportional representation may be based on either a closed-list or an open-list system. In a closed-list PR, the party selects the order of politicians, and voters cannot cross party lines. Since voters are effectively choosing the party that best represents them, this system encourages party loyalty among both the electorate and individual politicians. In an open-list PR system, the voters have more discretion and can cross party lines. Brazil's PR system is open-list. Voters cast single ballots either for a party label, which adds to the party's total for determining representation, or for individuals. No names appear on Brazilian ballots, so voters must write in their choices.

Electoral districts for the election of state and federal deputies are entire states in Brazil. In any given election, there may be between six and seventy federal deputies and from twelve to eighty-four state deputies running for office. With few limits on how many individuals and parties may run in the same electoral district, crowded fields discourage party loyalty and emphasize the personal qualities of candidates, who must stand out in the minds of voters. Party affiliations do little to reduce the confusion of the average Brazilian voter as he or she is confronted with dozens of names for each position. Worse still, the open-list PR system creates incentives for politicians to ignore party labels, since voters can cross party lines with ease. That even leads to politicians from the same party running against each other for the same position within a district.

Open-list proportional representation explains why there are so many parties in Brazil. With so much emphasis on the personal qualities of politicians, ambitious individuals can ignore the established party hierarchies while achieving elected office. They need only create their own parties or form alliances to get on the ballot and gain enough votes to qualify for representation. As a result, Brazil has the most fragmented party system in Latin America and one of the most fragmented in the world.

As if the open-list PR system were not distorting enough, Brazilian electoral law also allows incumbents to keep their party affiliation and remain on the ballot for the next election. This provision strips political parties of any control over their members: an incumbent may ignore the party's interests while in office but still must be kept on the ballot during the next contest.

Brazil's electoral system differs from other open-list proportional representation systems in that state, not national, parties select legislative candidates. In most cases, Brazilian governors exert tremendous influence over who can be elected. This further weakens national party leaders, who remain beholden to governors who can reward them with supportive nominees or rivals.

Source: Scott Mainwaring, "Brazil: Weak Parties, Feckless Democracy," in *Building Democratic Institutions: Party Systems in Latin America*, ed. Scott Mainwaring and Timothy R. Scully (Stanford, Calif., Stanford University Press, 1995), 375.

workers; they also advocate electoral reform—specifically, the establishment of a majority or mixed, rather than purely proportional, district voting system.

A loose set of conservative parties currently struggles for the mantle of the right. In front of the pack is the PFL (Party of the Liberal Front), the second largest party in the Senate and the largest party in the Chamber. Many wildcard parties, with low to moderate levels of representation in congress, ally themselves with right-wing and center-right parties or advocate right-wing issues: the Brazilian Labor Party (PTB), the Progressive Party (PPB), and the Liberal Party (PL) are examples. Various microparties also compose the right-wing side of the ideological spectrum, including the Party of National Reconstruction (PRN), the neofascist Party of the Reorganization of

Citizen Action: *The Workers' Party*

The creation of the Workers' Party (PT) was a remarkable innovation in Brazilian history. The PT was founded in the early 1980s by workers who had defied the military government and engaged in strikes in São Paulo's metalworking and automobile industries in 1978 and 1979. Although the PT began with a working-class message and leftist platform, its identity broadened during the 1980s and early 1990s. The party and its leader, Luiz Inácio "Lula" da Silva, increasingly campaigned for the support of the middle class, the rural and urban poor, and even segments of business and the upper classes. Unlike previous populist parties in Brazil, the PT aimed both to bring previously excluded groups into the political arena and to change the status quo substantively.

Lula da Silva ran for the presidency three times, in 1989, 1994, and 1998. In 1989 he qualified for, but lost, the runoff to Collor. In 1994 and 1998, he was beaten during the first turn by Cardoso. In 1998, the PT forged an electoral alliance with Leonel Brizola's PDT as well as with the PSB, PC do B, and the PCB. Despite a unified leftist ticket, da Silva captured 31.7 percent of the vote to Fernando Henrique Cardoso's 53.1 percent.

As Margaret Keck, an American scholar of the PT, argues, the Workers' Party was a novel development because it sought to represent the interests of workers and the poor. This had never before been attempted by a political organization that operated independently from the state. The PT also tries to be an internally democratic party. Its leaders respect the views of grassroots organizers and ensure that their voices are heard in the party's decision-making.

Luiz Inácio "Lula" da Silva, founder of the Workers' Party. *Source:* © Jornal do Brasil, August 19, 1998, Alexandre Sassaki.

˙Source: Margaret Keck, *The Workers' Party and Democratization in Brazil*. (New Haven, Conn.: Yale University Press, 1992), 219–220.

the National Order (PRONA), the Christian Social Party (PSC), the Democratic Social Party (PDS—no relation to the Vargas-era PDS; successor to the military's ARENA party), and the Christian Democratic Party (PDC). In 1993 the PDS and PDC merged to form the Reformist Progressive Party (PPR), which joined the Progressive Party (PP) in September 1995 to form the PPB.

The largest party in the Senate and the third largest in the Chamber, PMDB (Party of the Brazilian Democratic Movement—a descendant of the old MDB), and the second largest party in the Chamber and third largest in the Senate, PSDB (the Brazilian Social Democratic Party—originally an offshoot of the PMDB; Cardoso's party through 1999), dominate the center and center-left segment of the ideological spectrum. These two parties are ideologically diverse. Segments of these parties identify with the positions that define the political right or the political left.

Political parties on the left advocate reducing

Table 4

Party Representation in Congress, 1999

| Chamber of Deputies | | Senate | |
Party	Percent of Vote	Party	Percent of Vote
PFL	20%	PMDB	33%
PSDB	19	PFL	23
PMDB	16	PSDB	20
PPB	12	PT	9
PT	12	PDT	5
PTB	6	PPB	4
PDT	5	PSB	4
PSB	4	PTB	1
Other	6	PPS	1

deficits and inflation, but also maintaining the public sector in public hands and improving the welfare state. Left-oriented parties want to expand the state's role in promoting and protecting domestic industry. On constitutional reform, they support the social rights guaranteed by the 1988 constitution.

On the left, the most important party continues to be the Workers' Party (PT). Since 1985 the PT has occupied much of the left's political space, marginalizing already peripheral parties such as the Brazilian Socialist Party (PSB), the Brazilian Communist Party (PCB—renamed the Popular Socialist Party, or PPS, in 1992), the Communist Party of Brazil (PC do B), and the Green Party (PV). The Democratic Labor Party (PDT), a populist organization led by Leonel Brizola, the ex-governor of Rio de Janeiro, advocates Vargas-era nationalism and state-led development. In the elections of October 1998, this party formed an alliance with the PT at the national level. The PPS is led by Ciro Gomes, a former finance minister under the Itamar Franco presidency and a former governor of Ceará. Gomes ran for president in 1998, garnering third place with 10.97 percent of the vote.

As might be expected, the proliferation of political parties has only added to the incoherence of legislative politics. Currently, no party has more than 33 percent of the seats in either house of congress. As Table 4 shows, Cardoso's multiparty alliance of the PSDB-PFL-PTB-PPB controls 57 percent of the vote in the lower house and 48 percent in the upper house. However, because of

party switching and clientelism, the loyalty of these "progovernment" parties to the administration is remarkably soft. Consistency of support is difficult to maintain as turnover in the Chamber is high, with 50–60 percent of the members being replaced with each election. This reality has reinforced the common claim of the executive to be the only source of political order in the Brazilian democratic system.

The results of the October 1998 elections produced mounting recriminations among the leftist parties that a divided opposition was ineffectual. Conservative parties remained suspicious of Cardoso's social reform agenda while center-left forces considered alternatives to right-wing support. Discussions have focused on the possibility of consolidating Brazil's political parties into a three- or four-party left-center-right structure. Brizola has suggested a fusion of the PT and the PDT, which might include an alliance with other parties of the left. The PFL will likely support their leader, Antônio Carlos Magalhães, in his run for the presidency in 2002. Along with alliance partners in the PPB and PTB, this coalition would form a formidable conservative bloc of 209 deputies. The center-left might attempt to make new alliances by rejoining the PMDB with its dissident wing, now the PSDB. A more ambitious plan would be a broader center-left coalition led by PPS leader Ciro Gomes that would unite the PT-PDT merger with the PPS, the PSB, and the most progressive elements of the PMDB and PSDB.

Figure 3

Major Parties in the Chamber of Deputies and Their Percentages of the Vote, 1999 Congress

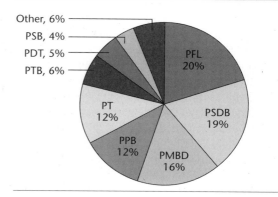

Source: Data from final TSE rally.

Figure 4

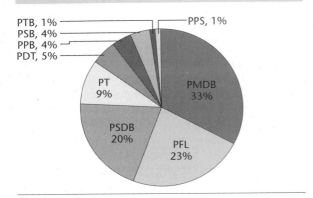

Major Parties in the Senate and Their Percentage of the Vote, 1999 Congress

Source: Data from final TSE rally.

Elections

Contests for public office in Brazil are dominated by the rules of proportional representation (PR). Everything from federal legislative to municipal council positions is distributed on the basis of several mathematical calculations to assure proportionality among political parties. Generally, the number of seats obtained by each party is determined by multiplying the ratio between party and total votes by the total number of seats.

In addition to its effects on the party system, open-list PR rules distort democratic representation in other ways. Given the multiplicity of parties, the unbalanced apportionment of seats among the states, and the sheer size of some electoral districts, candidates often have few incentives to be accountable to their constituency. In states with hundreds of candidates running in oversized electoral districts, the votes obtained by successful candidates are often scattered, limiting the accountability of those elected. In less populated states, there are more seats and parties per voter; the electoral and party quotients are lower. As a result, candidates often alter their legal place of residence immediately before an election in order to run for a safer seat, further compounding the lack of accountability. Electoral laws are highly permissive regarding the candidate's change of residence. For example, ex-president Sarney, realizing that he would

not be eligible to run for a Senate seat in his home state, successfully changed his residence only a few months before the 1990 elections.

As in all modern nations, the media play a key role in Brazilian political campaigns. With the *abertura*, political parties gained the right to air electoral propaganda on radio and television. All radio stations and TV channels are required to broadcast, at no charge, two hours of party programming each day during a campaign season. The parties are entitled to an amount of time on the air proportional to their number of votes in the previous election. Some candidates have no more than a few seconds to present themselves and their platform to the public.

In recent years' elections, particularly presidential contests, have become touchstones of the country's progress in building democracy. Although the president was elected indirectly in 1984 and the eventual president, José Sarney (PMDB and PFL), had not been selected to be president in the first place, this first election set Brazil on the path to democracy. More important was the contest of 1989, which gave Brazilians their first opportunity to elect the president directly. Collor's (PRN) selection became an important precedent that further strengthened Brazilian democracy. Ironically, his impeachment two years later also promoted democracy, because it reinforceed the rule of law and enhanced the oversight functions of the congress. Fernando Henrique Cardoso's election in 1994 and reelection in 1998 repeated and reinforced the 1989 precedent of direct elections for the presidency. Although elections cannot guarantee democracy, recent contests have shown how far Brazilian democracy has come in little over a decade.

Seen from the perspective of average Brazilians, however, the situation is a bit more complex. Although most Brazilians are suspicious of authoritarianism and wary of the return of the military or any other form of dictatorship, they seem to be disappointed with the results of democracy. The weakness of political parties, coupled with the persistence of clientelism, has only discouraged average Brazilians with their country's politics. In one study reported by Scott Mainwaring, Brazilians were asked to classify their interest in politics: 14 percent of the respondents said they had a lot of interest, 22.3 percent said they had moderate interest, 17.8 percent said they had little interest, and 45 percent said they had no interest.[52] Brazilians are increasingly disengaging from electoral politics, and that can only bode ill for the country's democracy.

Political Culture, Citizenship, and Identity

The notion of national identity describes a sense of national community that goes beyond mere allegiance to a state, to a set of economic interests, regional loyalties, or kinship affiliations. The cultivation of a national identity occurs through a process of nation-building during which a set of national symbols, cultural terms and images, and shared myths consolidate around historical experiences that define the loyalties of a group of people.

Several developments made Brazilian nation-building possible. Unlike nation formation in culturally, linguistically, and geographically diverse Western Europe, Africa, and Asia, Brazil enjoyed a homogeneous linguistic and colonial experience. As a result, Brazilian history largely avoided the ethnic conflicts that have become obstacles to nation-building in

Eastern Europe, Nigeria, and India. Immigrants added their ideas and value systems at the turn of the century, but they brought no compelling identities that could substitute for an overarching national consciousness. Regional secessionist movements were scarce in Brazilian history and were short-lived experiences when they did emerge in the twentieth century.

Despite Brazil's rich ethnic makeup, racial identities in Brazil have seldom been the basis for political action. In part, this was the result of the historical myth that the country was racially mixed. Therefore, a singular racial consciousness emerged around the spurious idea that Brazil was a racial democracy. Even in the face of severe economic and political oppression of native peoples, Afro-Brazilians, and Asians, the myth of racial democracy has endured in the national consciousness. As a result, the unique contributions of different ethnic groups were not appreciated.

Brazilian literature, political discourse, and history textbooks reinforced the myth of racial democracy. For example, the famous Brazilian historian Gilberto Freyre in his book *The Masters and the Slaves,* described the evolution of social relations among

Carnival in Brazil, the world's largest floor show, is also an insightful exhibition of allegories and popular myths about the country, its people, and their culture. *Source:* Reuters/Bettmann.

blacks and whites since colonial times, but he treated the underlying reality of racial conflict as an issue of secondary importance.[53] For such intellectuals, miscegenation had diminished racial differences and made conflict unlikely. This thinking buttressed the false belief that prejudice and discrimination were lacking among whites, blacks, Indians, and mulattoes.

Like the myth of racial democracy, the major collective political identities in Brazilian history have sought to hide or negate the real conflicts in society. For example, the symbols and images of political nationalism tended to boost the quasi-utopian visions of the country's future development. Developmentalists under democratic leaders such as Kubitschek and the military governments espoused the optimism that "Brazil is the country of the future." Even in the face of severe fiscal, social, and political problems, Brazilians continue to have faith in their country, even when their confidence in their politicians and democratic institutions has been shaken.

Both the persistence of optimistic myths about the country and an almost angry disengagement from politics are reflections of a weak system of political socialization. Given the dominance of corporatism and populism in twentieth-century Brazilian politics, and the current crisis in these forms of mobilizing popular support, Brazilians lack avenues for becoming more involved in politics. The weakness of political parties is one problem. But an underfunded primary and secondary educational system and the less-than-critical role of the media leave most Brazilians without the resources to become more politically aware. Brazil's illiteracy rate of 16.7 percent remains one of the highest in Latin America and is a key obstacle to mobilizing the electorate. The frenetic nature of political change in Brazil has confused the citizenry, further breaking down whatever continuous political identities might emerge. Perhaps the ultimate reflection of these distressing tendencies is the cynical joke among Brazilians that "Brazil is the country of the future *and will always be.*"

The political sentiments of Brazilian society are actually quite static because most Brazilians feel powerless to change their fates. Brazilians have always considered liberal democratic institutions, particularly individual rights, as artificial or irrelevant. Although this view may appear cynical, it is a deeply ingrained notion in Brazilian political culture. Since the end of the nineteenth century, Brazilians have made a distinction between the "legal" Brazil and the "real" Brazil. The former involves the formal laws of the country; the latter refers to what actually occurs. A prime example was the turn-of-the-century liberal democracy, which concealed the patronage-ridden interior of Brazilian politics. Brazilian intellectuals developed the phrase *para ingles ver* ("for the English to see") to describe the notion that liberal democracy had been implanted to impress foreign observers, hiding the fact that the real politics would be conducted behind the scenes. As Brazil struggles to balance the interests of foreign investors with those of its own people, many Brazilians continue to believe that much of the politics they observe is really "for the English to see."

One of the key outcomes of the sense of powerlessness among the majority of Brazilians was the belief that the state should organize society. This idea helped to justify both the Vargas dictatorship in 1937 and the military rule that followed the coup of 1964. The primacy of the state manifested itself in Brazilian political culture. The notion that the state had a duty to provide for its citizens' welfare placed the state at the center of the Brazilian polity and the president at the center of the state. It should be clear, based on this analysis, that both society and the state in Brazil developed a set of core ideas that favored the establishment of a strong central government with an overbearing presidentialism. These ideas were not just imposed on Brazilians by savvy politicians; they were the product of many decades of social and political conflict.

During the redemocratization process, new trends in Brazilian political culture emerged. Most segments of Brazilian society came to embrace "modernization with democracy," even if they would later raise doubts about its benefits. The Catholic Church played an important role in promoting democracy. During the transition, a number of Catholic political organizations and movements aided by the Church organized popular opposition to the military governments. After the transition, archbishops of the Catholic Church helped assemble testimonials of torture victims. The publication of these depositions in the book *Nunca Mais* (*Never Again*) fueled condemnation of the authoritarian past. In this way, an establishment that had previously been associated with social conservatism and political oppression became a mobilizer of popular opposition to authoritarianism.

Another trend that developed during and after the transition to democracy was the growth of a profound distrust of the state. Brazilians began to doubt the ability of the state to find solutions to the country's economic and social problems. Business groups assailed the failures of state-led development, while labor unions claimed that corporatist management of industrial relations could not satisfy the interests of workers. As a result, Brazilians became increasingly receptive to fringe voices that promised to eradicate the previous economic-political order. By 1989 most Brazilians were willing to trust a little-known politician, Fernando Collor, who told the electorate what they wanted to hear. Collor swore to go to war against indolent state employees, corrupt politicians, and inefficient state enterprises. The results were, at least in part, disastrous. By ceding their authority to an untested figure like Collor, Brazilians failed one of the most important tests of democracy: assuring that elected officials will be accountable to the electorate. In the end, anti-statism proved hostile to democracy.

A third trend in Brazilian political culture can be seen among the most elite segments of society. Soon after the transition to democracy, many journalists, economists, politicians, intellectuals, and entrepreneurs began to embrace the notion that national institutions could be adjusted incrementally to strengthen democracy and promote economic growth. Constitutional, administrative, and economic reform became priorities of politicians such as Fernando Henrique Cardoso.

For average Brazilians, the dynamics of institutional tinkering are virtually unintelligible. The electorate must feel substantial change, primarily in their pocketbooks. Cardoso was able to deliver in 1994 when his Real Plan reduced inflation and increased the buying power of most Brazilians. That success gave Cardoso the popular support he needed to become president and launch an array of institutional reforms. In 1998, facing another presidential contest, Cardoso struggled to convince voters that his government of technocrats had the answers to the country's problems. With his reforms stuck in congress, Cardoso had difficulty backing up his claim to deserve a second term. Economic growth began to stall, raising fears that Cardoso's reforms had run their course

and were beginning to erode. Despite these problems, he was reelected, but he continued to struggle with congress on the reform agenda.

The task of selling even the most complex sets of policies to a population with weak political socialization and poor general education has become central to gaining and maintaining political power in Brazil. That has placed a premium on the adept management of the media, particularly radio and television.

The Brazilian media are free to criticize the government, and most of the broadcast businesses are privately owned. Although there is significant government influence over the resources necessary for media production and the advertising revenue from government campaigns, there is no overt government censorship, and freedom of the press is widely and constitutionally proclaimed. Government officials must engage in a complex dance of symbols and words to attract the attention of the private media and cast the most appealing image to a distrustful electorate.

The largest media organizations are owned by a small group of conglomerates. The Globo network is Brazil's preeminent media empire and one of the five largest television networks in the world. It has been formidable in shaping public opinion; some believe it played a prominent role in Collor's election in 1989. Conglomerates like Globo have played favorites in the past and no doubt will continue to do so. In return, the media giants expect licensing concessions from their political friends.

The media's independence from government interference varies. The print media are generally less restrained than the broadcast media in criticizing politicians and governments. Though television newscasts, which attract millions of viewers, continuously cover events embarrassing to the government or criticize government policies, the majority of viewers hear woefully little information on how and why political decisions are made, why one policy is favored over another, and the ultimate results. Domestic broadcast news coverage in Brazil is often merely the broadcasting of official government versions.

Interests, Social Movements, and Protest

Despite the growing disengagement of most Brazilians from politics and the country's legacy of state corporatism, autonomous collective interests have been able to take positions of importance in the political landscape. The previously mentioned role of business lobbies, rural protest movements, and labor unions, particularly those linked to the Workers' Party, are all examples of how Brazilian civil society has been able to break through the vise of state corporatism and social control.

As noted, the Catholic Church was actively engaged in organizing grassroots movements during and after the transition to democracy. After the profound changes in Catholic doctrine brought about by the Second Vatican Council in the early 1960s, the Church in Brazil became more active in advocating social and political reform. The Brazilian Church, through the National Conference of Brazilian Bishops (CNBB), produced an array of projects to improve literacy, stimulate political awareness, and improve the working and living conditions of the poor. Although some conservative segments of the Brazilian Church reacted violently against the Church's "messing in politics," the CNBB pressed on.

One well-known outcome of these changes was the development of liberation theology, a doctrine which argued that religion had to free people from both their sins and social injustice at the same time. In Brazil this thinking was associated with the Franciscan theologian Leonardo Boff. During the *abertura,* this doctrinal shift sought to relate theology to Brazilian reality by having priests become directly involved in improving the lot of poor Brazilians by defending their social and political needs.[54] By organizing community-based movements to press for improved sanitation, clean water, basic education, and most important, freedom from oppression, Catholic groups mobilized millions of citizens. Among the Brazilian Church's most notable accomplishments was the development of an agrarian reform council in the 1970s, the Pastoral Land Commission. The commission called for the extension of land tenure to poor peasants. The Brazilian Church also created ecclesiastical community movements (CEBs) to improve conditions in the *favelas.*

In the mid-1970s, Brazil witnessed a historic awakening of social and political organization: grassroots popular movements; new forms of trade unionism; neighborhood movements; professional associations of doctors, lawyers, and journalists; entrepreneurial associations; and middle-class organizations. At the same time, a host of nongovernmental organizations (NGOs) became more active in Brazil, for example, Amnesty International, Greenpeace, and native Brazilian rights groups. Domestic groups active in these areas increasingly turned to the NGOs for resources and information, adding an international dimension to what was previously an issue of domestic politics.

Women's organizations played a significant role in popular urban social movements during the 1970s. By the 1980s women were participating in and leading popular initiatives on a wide variety of issues related to employment and the provision of basic services. Many of these organizations enlisted the support of political parties and trade unions in battles over women's wages, birth control, rape, and violence in the home. Although practically absent in employers' organizations, women are highly active in urban unions. Out of the country's 5324 urban unions, 14.8 percent have elected women directors. Fewer women are leaders of rural unions (6.6 percent), but they compose 78 percent of active membership. In recent years, Brazilian women have created over 3000 organizations to address their issues. Included in this total are special police stations (*delegacias de defesa da mulher,* DDMs) dedicated to addressing crimes against women. The DDMs have emerged in major Brazilian cities and particularly in São Paulo, where their performance has been highly rated.

Women's groups have seen their power increase as more women have joined the workforce; 39 percent of women now work outside the home. That figure is higher than in Mexico (22 percent) and Argentina (33 percent). More than 20 percent of Brazilian families are supported exclusively by women. The share of domestic servants in the female workforce has declined from 32 percent to 20 percent over the last ten years, suggesting that traditional roles for women have not absorbed the increase in the female workforce.

Despite women's improved economic and social importance, progress on women's issues is slow. On average, women earn only 57 percent of what men make. Only 7 percent of women with university degrees earn more than twenty times the minimum wage (about $75 per month), as compared to 28 percent of men. Thirty-four percent of illiterate women earn the minimum wage or less, versus 5 percent of illiterate males.

In contrast to the progress of women's movements, a politically significant organization to address racial discrimination has not emerged. This fact is especially surprising because Brazil is one of the world's most racially mixed countries. Only during the 1940s did some public officials and academics acknowledge that prejudice existed against blacks. At that time, the problems of race were equated with the problems of class. Given the absence of legally sanctioned discrimination since the abolition of slavery in 1889, prejudice came to be viewed as class-based, not race-based. Attacking class inequality was thus considered a way to address prejudice against blacks. This belief seemed plausible because most poor Brazilians are either *pardo* (mulatto) or black. But it might be just as logical to suggest that they are poor because they are black. In any case, the relationship between race and class in Brazil is just as ambiguous as it is in the United States and other multiethnic societies.

Some analysts believe that a gradual and peaceful evolution of race relations is possible. Others argue that, as a consequence of white domination, blacks lack the collective identity and political organization necessary to put race relations on the political agenda. Both sides seem to agree, however, that although poverty and color are significantly correlated, overt confrontation among races is uncommon. Ironically, this may explain why no serious national discussion of race relations has ever emerged in Brazil.

On the other hand, the rights of Brazil's indigenous peoples, the Indians of the Amazon, remain at the center of the debate on the country's most pressing social problems. Over the past half century, the development of the Amazon has directly threatened the cultures and lives of Indians. For example, members of the Ianomami, a tribe with one of the largest reserves in Brazil, are frequently murdered by miners so they can gain access to mines in Indian territory. Many such massacres have occurred in territories legally provided by the central state to the Ianomami. During the military government, the national Indian agency,

FUNAI, turned a blind eye to such abuses with its claim that indigenous cultures represented "ethnic cysts to be excised from the body politic."[55] With the *abertura,* many environmental NGOs defended the human rights of indigenous people as part of their campaign to defend the Amazon and its people. The end of military rule and the economic crisis of the 1980s slowed down the exploitation of the Amazon.

The 1988 constitution recognized the rights of indigenous peoples for the first time, creating large reserves for tribes like the Ianomami. Yet these protections were eroded when President Cardoso, under pressure by landowning conservative allies from the northeast, implemented a policy to allow private interests to make claims on over half of all indigenous lands. Miners, loggers, and land developers invade native lands, often with destructive consequences for the ecology and for indigenous people. Allied against these interests are members of the Workers' Party, a coalition of indigenous groups known as COIAB, and church-based missionary organizations. The Kayapó and their resistance to large-scale development projects in the Amazon are a key example of how environmental, labor, and indigenous issues are melding together to form a powerful grassroots campaign. Members of the Kayapó tribe have been successful in politically disrupting damming and mining projects through mass media campaigns.[56] Their struggle continues, but without more federal protection Amazonian Indians will continue to be threatened.

The sprouting of movements, associations, and interest groups may seem impressive, but they represent specific constituencies. Most Brazilians do not bother to participate in parties, movements, and unions because the basic functions of government such as security, justice, education, and health care simply do not reach most Brazilians. When confronted with immediate deprivations, many Brazilians avoid organized and peaceful political action, often taking to the streets in sporadic riots. Such events demonstrate that many Brazilians feel they have only two choices in the face of unresponsive political and state organizations: violent protest or passivity.

Section ⑤ Brazilian Politics in Transition

Political Challenges and Changing Agendas

As the financial and monetary crisis that began in Asia in late 1997 continued to scare foreign investors throughout the developing world, Fernando Henrique Cardoso appeared on a Cable News Network business show in December. The Brazilian president proclaimed his country a safe place for foreign money, a stable and growth-oriented economy sure to maintain itself immune from the quagmire in Asia. To scholars of Brazil, Cardoso's CNN appearance seemed paradoxical. Here was an avowed social democrat, an old theorist of leftist sociology, pitching his country to international investors. They noted that Cardoso made no mention of his country's worsening social problems, its disparities in income, land tenure, and access to basic social and educational services. For many Brazilians on the left, Cardoso's comments were a ruthless betrayal of shared principles.

From a comparative perspective, we might interpret Cardoso's CNN interview in very different terms. Cardosa's remarks become more understandable when we consider the dilemmas connected to our theme of governing the economy. Much like other leaders of developing countries, Cardoso needs to preserve a stable domestic economy attractive to foreign investors, who are likely to turn to other countries at the first signs of instability. Not surprisingly, then, on CNN the president talked up his economic policy and downplayed the political and social negatives of investing money in Brazil. Rather than a betrayal of his social democratic principles, Cardoso's pitch could be seen as a pragmatic attempt to turn a necessity into a virtue.

At the same time, there are serious costs to Cardoso's strategy of reforming the Brazilian political and economic structure in order to become more competitive in global markets. The Brazilian president has had to embrace the very mechanisms of clientelism that he once so thoroughly criticized to build a political alliance of the center-right. Given a weak party system and constitutional requirements that all amendments survive two majority votes of 60 percent in both houses of congress, clientelism has become Cardoso's most powerful mechanism for cultivating support. Only with the support of conservative and probusiness groups, who maintain a majority of votes in both houses of congress, does Cardoso believe he will have the wherewithal to implement the constitutional, administrative, and social security reforms needed to restructure the economy.

This strategy has created serious paradoxes for the Brazilian president. Rather than strengthen Brazil's weak political parties and fragmented legislature, Cardoso's tactics have reinforced the factors that make the country's democratic institutions anemic. By kowtowing to clientelistic interests, Cardoso's administration has put on hold reforms to the electoral and party system. In the process, members of his own party, the Brazilian Social Democratic Party (PSDB), have rebuked the president for cultivating support from other parties, particularly the conservative Liberal Front Party (PFL), and sometimes hurting his own social democrats in congressional and gubernatorial contests. By wooing many conservative interests, mostly in the north and northeast regions, Cardoso has strengthened groups that oppose significant agrarian reform, income distribution, and improvements in social services. Most important, his strategy has depended on increased spending, financed with public debt at high interest. The result has been a soaring deficit and public debt. The devaluation of the real in early 1999 will only add to these problems and perhaps bring inflation back.

Despite the heady rhetoric of Cardoso's 1994 presidential campaign and the rising expectations of long-frustrated social democrats inside and outside Brazil, the new president has offered little in the way of changing Brazilian politics for the long haul. Cardoso has made only token progress on the country's persisting social inequalities. The Real Plan reduced the eroding effect of mega-inflation on the incomes of the poor, boosting consumption for millions of Brazilians. But other policies have been less effective. Economic liberalization has caused thousands of Brazilian firms to shave their labor costs, putting hundreds of thousands of Brazilians out of work. As urban unemployment has increased, so has urban violence and crime. The government distributed more land to poor people in rural areas, but these efforts have failed to make a dent in Brazil's concentrated system of land tenure. Education and health reform have received only lip service from the administration.

Both the fiscal and the environmental limits to Brazil's economic development have been stretched almost to their breaking points. Even without a significant downturn in the global economy, the fate of the Brazilian economy is being threatened by the state's burgeoning indebtedness, the inability to cut public spending, and the social and ecological costs of the maldistribution of income and the abuse of natural resources. The tendency to see solutions to Brazil's economic problems in terms of promoting exports and enlarging the economy only deepens these problems. Considering that many of Brazil's exports are still extractive (e.g., iron ore, lumber) these recommendations place ever more pressure on the country's ecology. The quality of life of most Brazilians can only suffer as a result.

The challenges facing Brazil and the way that the country's political leaders have chosen to deal with them are similar to experiences elsewhere. The Brazilian state lacks the resources to promote development as it did during the days of Vargas, Kubitschek, and military rule. As the needs of the Brazilian citizenry grow, the state appears less capable, and political leaders less willing, to respond. With the advent of the Real Plan, the priorities have been to attract foreign capital, boost export earnings, and favor the highest bidders in the privatization of public firms. The developmentalist state lives on only in some BNDES policies. Like former state-led industrializers India, Mexico, and France, Brazil has turned in the neoliberal direction, limiting the state's role in the economy. This shift in the state's organization reminds us of the importance of our theme highlighting critical junctures in state formation.

In contrast to the corporatist and populist role of the state, the moderating power in Brazilian history, the central state has today become a far more passive agent in society. Brazilian workers no longer negotiate labor issues with state mediation, as they still do in Germany. Instead, labor unions, when they are capable, negotiate directly with business. In most cases,

given high urban unemployment, the interests of business usually prevail. Urban workers receive little or no compensation from the state when they suffer layoffs or reductions in their salaries and workplace benefits. Most rural workers, the millions in the informal sector, and minorities are in an even more precarious position as they lack the few benefits and protections enjoyed by salaried, urban workers. The weakness of the judiciary, the abusive use of police authority, and the tendency to vigilantism and class conflict in poor, rural areas reinforce the anemia of a civil society that increasingly discounts its role in politics.

In this context, Brazilian democracy has suffered greatly, the importance of which we highlighted in our theme of the democratic challenge. The poor feel doubly divorced from politics, as they are both socially and politically disenfranchised from a process they view as unresponsive to their needs. Over time, this sense of disengagement has turned into open doubt about the utility of democracy itself. Stories of official corruption and the popular assumption that a politician's priority is his or her own pocketbook reinforce the idea that representatives are unaccountable to their constituencies. The weakness of political party loyalties and the fragmentation of interests compound the problem of accountability. By contrast, much stronger democracies such as Germany, the United States, France, and Britain rely on well-defined rules that force political leaders to be accountable to other branches of government and to their own constituencies. Brazil's example has shown how difficult it is to embrace the democratic idea without these structures.

While some of Brazil's problems are unique, many take the same form they do elsewhere. Like all other major economies in the world, Brazil's is well integrated into the global economy. Despite the country's current problems with monetary stability and debt, Brazil is one of the world's key platforms for agricultural production and manufacturing. Brazil's share of the world market in iron ore, textiles, footwear, steel, machine parts, and autos makes it an important hub in the multinational production of several industrial products. Brazil is a crucial supplier of raw materials as well as a large market for multinational producers. As such, it has advantages few other developing countries enjoy. That also means, however, that Brazilian firms and workers (not to mention the public sector itself) must be able to adapt to greater competition from abroad and the needs of foreign capital. Given the speed with which technology outpaces itself, the pressure to train workers, boost productivity, and enhance research and development has grown tremendously. Brazil is struggling just to keep pace with globalization.

As globalization and democratization have made Brazilian politics less predictable, older questions about what it means to be Brazilian have reemerged. Brazil highlights the point made in the discussion of our theme on political identities in the Introduction that political identities are often reshaped in changed circumstances. What it means to be Brazilian has become a more complex question given the way that Brazil, like the rest of the world, has been bombarded by foreign consumer images. Democracy has given ordinary Brazilians more of a voice, and they have used it to forge their own understandings, but mostly on local issues, not at the national level. Women, nongovernmental organizations, Catholics, pentecostals, blacks, landless peasants, and residents of *favelas* have all organized in recent years around social and cultural issues. On the one hand, these movements have placed additional pressure on an already weakened state to deliver goods and services. On the other hand, these groups have supplied alternatives to the state by providing their own systems of social and cultural support. As the domain of the state in other countries is constrained by the need to compete in the global economy, space is created for nonstate actors to provide goods and services that were previously produced by the state. What is missing in all of this is a sense of the "national question." How are all these disparate groups linked? Do they have a common, national interest? If they are increasingly disconnected, then the proliferation of social movements and organizations is only a symptom of the wider disengagement from the state and political society already being practiced by most Brazilians.

Brazilian Politics in Comparative Perspective

The most important lesson that Brazil offers for the broader study of comparative politics is that frag-

mented polities threaten democracy, social development, and nation-building. The Brazilian political order is fragmented on several levels. The central state is fragmented by conflicts between the executive and the legislature, divided alliances and self-interested politicians in the congress, decentralized government, and an indecisive judiciary with a complicated structure and an uncertain mission. Political parties are fragmented by clientelism and electoral rules that create incentives for politicians and voters to ignore party labels. Finally, civil society itself is fragmented into numerous, often conflictual, organizations, interest groups, professional associations, social movements, churches, and most important, social classes and ethnic identities.

In some societies that are similarly fragmented, such as the United States and India, institutions have proven successful in bridging the gaps between individualistic pursuits and the demand of the people for good government. Rich systems of social organization and reciprocity that are linked to the state through political parties, parliaments, and even informal associations help to strengthen democracy in these countries. Where these systems are faulty, as they are in Brazil, fragmentation reinforces the weakness of the state and the society.

Recent Brazilian politics show that a weak state deepens the citizenry's sense that all politics is corrupt. Although corruption is present in all polities to some degree, it does not by itself produce the angry disengagement from politics that has emerged in Brazil. Much more is wrong with the Brazilian political order. Police brutality, judicial incompetence, and the inability of bureaucratic agencies to respond to social demands have just as powerful an effect in legitimizing civil disengagement.

This only reinforces the importance of creating systems of accountability to reduce the corruption, police abuse, and bureaucratic incompetence that have given rise to these doubts. Unfortunately, the English word *accountability* has no counterpart in either Portuguese or Spanish. Given Brazil's (and Latin America's) long history of oligarchical rule and social exclusion, the notion of making elites accountable to the people is so alien that the languages of the region lack the required vocabulary. Systems of accountability must be built from the ground up; they must be

Weyland, Kurt. *Democracy Without Equity: Failures of Reform in Brazil.* Pittsburgh: University of Pittsburgh Press, 1996.

Endnotes

[1] IBGE (Instituto Brasileiro de Geografia e Estatística), *PNAD—Síntese do Indicadores da Pesquisa Básica da PNAD de 1981 a 1989* (Rio de Janeiro: IBGE, 1990). For more on Brazil's multiclassification system, see George Reid Andrews, *Blacks and Whites in São Paulo, Brazil, 1888–1988* (Madison: University of Wisconsin Press, 1991).

[2] See Bertha K. Becker and Claudio A. G. Egler, *Brazil: A New Regional Power in the World Economy: A Regional Geography* (New York: Cambridge University Press, 1992), 5, and Terence Turner, "Brazil: Indigenous Rights vs. Neoliberalism," *Dissent* Summer (1996), 67.

[3] For an analysis of immigration during this period, see Douglas Graham and Thomas Merrick, *Population and Economic Development in Brazil—1800 to the Present* (Baltimore: Johns Hopkins University Press, 1979).

[4] For a complete treatment of state corporatism in Brazil during this period, see Ruth Berins Collier and David Collier, *Shaping the Political Arena: Critical Junctures, the Labor Movement, and Regime Dynamics in Latin America* (Princeton, N.J.: Princeton University Press, 1991), 169–195.

[5] Robert M. Levine, *Father of the Poor? Vargas and His Era,* (New York: Cambridge University Press, 1998), 8–9.

[6] For an analysis of this "new professionalism," see Alfred Stepan, *The Military in Politics: Changing Patterns in Brazil* (Princeton, N.J.: Princeton University Press, 1971).

[7] Thomas E. Skidmore, *Politics in Brazil, 1930–1964: An Experiment in Democracy* (New York: Oxford University Press, 1967), 101.

[8] Ibid.

[9] Maria do Carmo Campello de Souza, *Estado e Partidos Políticos no Brasil (1930 a 1964)* (São Paulo: Editora Alfa-Omega, 1975).

[10] Youseff Cohen, "The Heresthetics of Coup Making," *Comparative Political Studies* 24; no. 3 (October 1991), 348–355.

[11] Guillermo O'Donnell, *Modernization and Bureaucratic-Authoritarianism: Studies in South American Politics* (Berkeley: Institute of International Studies, University of California, 1973).

[12] Thomas E. Skidmore, *The Politics of Military Rule in Brazil 1964–85* (New York: Oxford University Press, 1988), 49.

[13] Leigh A. Payne, *Brazilian Industrialists and Democratic Change* (Baltimore: Johns Hopkins University Press, 1994), Ch. 4.

[14] For an analysis of these critical elections, see Bolivar Lamounier, "Authoritarian Brazil Revisited: The Impact of Elections on the *Abertura,*" in *Democratizing Brazil: Problems of Transition and Consolidation,* ed. Alfred Stepan (New York: Oxford University Press, 1989), and Kurt von Mettenheim, *The Brazilian Voter: Mass Politics in Democratic Transition, 1974–1986* (Pittsburgh: University of Pittsburgh Press, 1995), 101–103.

[15] Margaret Keck, *The Workers' Party and Democratization in Brazil* (New Haven, Conn.: Yale University Press, 1992), 219–220.

[16] Margaret Keck, "The New Unionism in the Brazilian Transition," in *Democratizing Brazil: Problems of Transition and Consolidation,* ed. Alfred Stepan (New York: Oxford University Press, 1989), 284.

[17] See Celso Furtado, *The Economic Growth of Brazil: A Survey from Colonial to Modern Times* (Berkeley: University of California Press, 1963).

[18] For a description of how the coffee export complex created incentives for the substitution of manufactured imports with domestic production, see Bertha K. Becker and Claudio A. G. Egler, *Brazil: A New Regional Power in the World Economy: A Regional Geography,* 45.

[19] For a more complete treatment of how developmentalist ideas cultivated in ECLA affected policy choices in Brazil, see Kathryn Sikkink, *Ideas and Institutions: Developmentalism in Brazil and Argentina* (Ithaca, N.Y.: Cornell University Press, 1991).

[20] More complete treatment of the ISI experience can be found in Albert O. Hirschman, *A Bias for Hope: Essays on Development and Latin America* (New Haven, Conn.: Yale University Press, 1971).

[21] Peter B. Evans, *Dependent Development: The Alliance of Multinational, State, and Local Capital in Brazil* (Princeton, N.J.: Princeton University Press, 1979).

[22] These and other examples of ecological destruction are analyzed in Werner Baer and Charles C. Mueller, "Environmental Aspects of Brazil's Development," in *The Brazilian Economy: Growth and Development,* 4th ed. Werner Baer (New York: Praeger, 1995).

[23] For more on state environmental efforts, see Barry Ames and Margaret E. Keck, "The Politics of Sustainable Development: Environmental Policy Making in Four Brazilian States," *Journal of Interamerican Studies and World Affairs* 39, no. 4 (Winter 1998–99).

[24] Kathryn Hochstetler, "The Evolution of the Brazilian Environmental Movement and Its Political Roles," in *The New Politics of Inequality in Latin America: Rethinking Participation and Representation,* ed. Douglas Chalmers, Carlos M. Vilas, Katherine R. Hite, Scott B. Martin, Kerianne Piester, and Monique Segarra (New York: Oxford University Press, 1997).

25 Alfred P. Montero, "Devolving Democracy? Political Decentralization and the New Brazilian Federalism," in *Democratic Brazil: Actors, Institutions, and Processes,* ed. Peter R. Kingstone and Timothy J. Power (Pittsburgh: University of Pittsburgh Press, forthcoming).

26 Alfred P. Montero, "Getting Real About the Brazilian Real Plan," *Hemisphere* (February 1997).

27 William C. Smith and Nizar Messari, "Democracy and Reform in Cardoso's Brazil: Caught Between Clientelism and Global Markets?" *The North-South Agenda Papers* 33 (September 1998).

28 Peggy A. Lovell, "Race, Gender, and Development in Brazil," *Latin American Research Review* 29, no. 3 (1994).

29 Kurt Weyland, *Democracy Without Equity: Failures of Reform in Brazil* (Pittsburgh: University of Pittsburgh Press, 1996).

30 Wilson Cano, "Concentración, desconcentración y descentralización en Brasil," in *Territorios en Transformación: Análisis y Propuestas,* ed. José Luis Curbelo, Francisco Alburquerque, Carlos A. de Mattos and Juan Ramón Cuadrado (Madrid: Fondo Europeo de Desarrollo Regional, 1994).

31 Leonardo Guimarães Neto, "Desigualdades Regionais e Federalismo," in *Desigualdades Regionais e Desenvolvimento,* ed. Rui de Britto Álvares Affonso and Pedro Luiz Barros Silva (São Paulo: FUNDAP, 1995).

32 Jeffry A. Frieden, *Debt, Development, and Democracy: Modern Political Economy and Latin America, 1965–1985* (Princeton, N.J.: Princeton University Press, 1991), 54–65.

33 Diana Jean Schemo, "The ABC's of Business in Brazil," *New York Times* July 16, 1998, B1, 7.

34 Fernando Luiz Abrúcio, *Os Barões da Federação: O Poder dos Governadores no Brasil Pós-Autoritário.* Unpublished master's thesis, Universidade de São Paulo, 1994.

35 Timothy J. Power, "Politicized Democracy: Competition, Institutions, and 'Civic Fatigue' in Brazil," *Journal of Interamerican Studies and World Affairs* 33, no. 3 (Fall 1991).

36 Thomas J. Trebat, *Brasil's State-Owned Enterprises: A Case Study of the State as Entrepreneur* (New York: Cambridge University Press, 1983).

37 Helen Shapiro, *Engines of Growth: The State and Transnational Auto Companies in Brazil* (New York: Cambridge University Press, 1994).

38 Peter B. Evans, "Predatory, Developmental, and Other Apparatuses: A Comparative Political Economy Perspective on the Third World State," *Sociological Forum* 4, no. 4 (1989).

39 Alfred P. Montero, "State Interests and the New Industrial Policy in Brazil: The Case of the Privatization of Steel, 1990–1994," *Journal of Interamerican Studies and World Affairs* 40, no. 3 (Fall 1998).

40 Carlos H. Acuña and William C. Smith, "The Politics of Arms Production and the Arms Race among the New Democracies of Argentina, Brazil, and Chile," in *Security, Democracy, and Development in U.S.-Latin American Relations,* ed. Lars Schoultz, William C. Smith, and Augusto Varas (New Brunswick, N. J.: Transaction Publishers, 1994).

41 Wendy Hunter, *Eroding Military Influence in Brazil: Politicians Against Soldiers* (Chapel Hill: University of North Carolina Press, 1997).

42 Paulo Sérgio Pinheiro, "Popular Responses to State-Sponsored Violence in Brazil," in *The New Politics of Inequality in Latin America: Rethinking Participation and Representation,* ed. Douglas Chalmers, Carlos M. Vilas, Katherine R. Hite, Scott B. Martin, Kerianne Piester, and Monique Segarra (New York: Oxford University Press, 1997).

43 Human Rights Watch, *Police Brutality in Urban Brazil* (New York: Human Rights Watch, 1997), 13.

44 Judith Tendler, *Good Government in the Tropics* (Baltimore: Johns Hopkins University Press, 1997).

45 For a study of how these exceptions have emerged in Brazil, see Barbara Geddes, *Politician's Dilemma: Building State Capacity in Latin America* (Berkeley: University of California Press, 1994).

46 Ben Ross Schneider, *Politics Within the State: Elite Bureaucrats and Industrial Policy in Authoritarian Brazil* (Pittsburgh: University of Pittsburgh Press, 1991).

47 Lívia Neves de H. Barbosa, "The Brazilian Jeitinho: An Exercise in National Identity," in *The Brazilian Puzzle: Culture on the Borderlands of the Western World,* ed. David J. Hess and Roberto A. DaMatta (New York: Columbia University Press, 1995).

48 Barry Ames, "Electoral Strategy under Open-List Proportional Representation," *American Journal of Political Science* 39, no. 2 (May 1995).

49 Juan J. Linz and Alfred Stepan, *Problems of Democratic Transition and Consolidation: Southern Europe, South America, and Post-Communist Europe* (Baltimore: Johns Hopkins University Press, 1996), Ch. 11.

50 Scott Mainwaring, "Brazilian Party Underdevelopment in Comparative Perspective," *Political Science Quarterly* 107 (1993).

51 Timothy J. Power, "The Pen is Mightier than the Congress: Presidential Decree Power in Brazil," in *Executive Decree Authority: Calling Out the Tanks or Just Filling Out the Forms?*, ed. John M. Carey and Mathew S. Shugart (New York: Cambridge University Press, 1998).

52 Scott Mainwaring, "Brazilian Party Underdevelopment in Comparative Perspective," 692.

53 See especially Gilberto Freyre, *The Mansions and the Shanties: The Making of Modern Brazil* (New York: Knopf, 1963), Ch. 12.

[54] Ralph Della Cava, "The 'People's Church,' the Vatican, and *Abertura,"* in *Democratizing Brazil: Problems of Transition and Consolidation,* ed. Alfred Stepan (New York: Oxford University Press, 1989).

[55] Terence Turner, "Brazil: Indigenous Rights vs. Meoliberalism," 67.

[56] William H. Fisher, "Megadevelopment, Environmentalism, and Resistance: The Institutional Context of Kayapó Indigenous Politics in Central Brazil," *Human Organization* 53, no. 3 (1994).

CHAPTER 9

Mexico

Merilee S. Grindle

United Mexican States

Land and Population

Capital	Mexico City
Total Area (square miles)	756,066 (about three times the size of Texas)
Population	98.5 million
Annual Average Population Growth Rate (1990–1997)	1.8%
Urban Population	74%

Ethnic Composition

Mestizo (Amerindian-Spanish)	60%
Amerindian	30%
White	9%
Other	1%

Major Languages

Spanish	94.1%
Indigenous Languages	5.9%
Other languages not significant	

Religious Affiliation

Roman Catholic	89%
Protestant	6%
Other and none	5%

Economy

Domestic Currency	Peso
Total GNP (US$)	$348.6 billion
GNP per capita (US$)	$3680
GNP per capita at purchasing power parity (US$)	$8120
GNP average annual growth rate (1996–1997)	8%

GNP per capita average annual growth rate

1996–1997	6.2%
1980–1995	–0.9%
1965–1980	3.6%

Income Gap: GDP per capita (US$)

Richest 20% of population	$19,383
Poorest 20% of population	$1437

Structure of Production (% of GDP)

Agriculture	8%
Industry	26%
Services	67%

Labor Force Distribution (% of total)

Agriculture	28%
Industry	24%
Services	48%

Exports as % of GDP	25%
Imports as % of GDP	22%
Electricity Consumption per capita (kwh)	1646

CO_2 Emissions per capita (metric tons)	3.9

Society

Life Expectancy

Female	75.1
Male	69.2

Doctors per 100,000 people	107
Infant Mortality per 1000 live births	27

Adult Literacy

Female	87.4%
Male	91.8%

Access to Information and Communications (per 1000 population)

Radios	263
Televisions	192
Telephone Lines	96
Personal Computers	26

Women in Government and Economy

Seats in Parliament held by Women	17.4% (upper house)
	14.8% (lower house)
Women at ministerial level	14.0%
Women as % of total labor force	32.0%
Female business administrators and managers	20.0%
Female professional and technical workers	45.0%
1998 Human Development Index ranking (out of 174 countries, 1 = highest)	49

Political Organization

Political System   Federal republic.

Regime History   Current form of government since 1917.

Administrative Structure   Federal with 31 states and a federal district.

Executive   President, elected by direct election with a six-year term of office; reelection not permitted.

Legislature   Bicameral; upper and lower house elections held every three years. There are 128 senators, 4 from each state, elected for six years to serve in the upper house. Three senators from each state are elected by simple majority vote, the fourth is assigned to the largest minority party. Five hundred deputies are elected every three years to serve in the lower house: 300 are elected by simple majority, 200 by proportional representation.

Judiciary   Independent Supreme Court with 21 justices and 5 auxiliary judges.

Party System   Multiparty system, with the Institutional Revolutionary Party (PRI) dominating elections after 1929; other important parties are the National Action Party (PAN) and the Democratic Revolutionary Party (PRD).

Politics in Action

On March 23, 1994, presidential candidate Luis Donaldo Colosio finished a campaign speech in the northern border city of Tijuana. Then, as he struggled through the noisy crowd greeting his supporters, an unknown assailant approached quickly, drew a gun, and shot Colosio in the head and torso. The candidate for Mexico's highest office died a few hours later.

The assassination of Colosio, the candidate of the Institutional Revolutionary Party (PRI, pronounced "pree"), which had governed the country without interruption since 1929, shocked Mexico's 90 million citizens and shook its political elite deeply. Not since 1923, when a military revolt threatened presidential elections, had there been such uncertainty about who would lead the government for the next six years. Not since 1928, when president-elect Alvaro Obregón was assassinated, had a politician bound for the highest office met with violent death. Not since 1929, when the PRI was founded, had there been such fear that the political elite was so divided that overt violence, not accommodation and compromise, might be used to resolve disputes.

President Carlos Salinas de Gortari moved quickly to appoint a new candidate. He chose Ernesto Zedillo, Colosio's campaign manager, one-time Minister of Education, and former Minister of Planning and Budgeting, who had never held an elected office. Zedillo was another economic planner in a line of U.S.-educated technocrats who had governed the PRI (and therefore the nation) since 1982, seeking to reform the party from within. Many Mexicans were convinced that the assassination was part of a conspiracy involving party "dinosaurs," political hard-liners who opposed any kind of democratic transformation.

Although the self-confessed "lone gunman" was jailed, the ensuing investigation raised concerns about a possible conspiracy involving party and law enforcement officials as well as drug cartels. Rumors circulated about a cover-up scandal. Eventually, skepticism about the integrity of the inquiry was so great that President Salinas called for a new investigation.

At this point, little remains known about what exactly happened in Tijuana and why.

Despite the public's widespread disillusionment with the political system, Ernesto Zedillo easily won election in August 1994. Many Mexicans feared the prospect of violence and instability caused by political change more than they feared politics as usual. It is a sentiment eloquently expressed in Mexico with a saying, "Better to have the bad that you know than the good that you don't." Some citizens, having spent all their lives under the PRI, remembered the party's triumphs of decades past and continued to support it with a sense of national pride.

Yet great changes were already under way. Increasingly during the 1980s and 1990s, many Mexicans openly questioned the right of the PRI to monopolize political power. They organized to press for fairer elections and more responsive public officials. They demanded the right of opposition parties to compete for power on an equal basis with the PRI. They argued that the president had too much power and that the PRI was riddled with corruption.

At the same time, the government introduced major policy changes that affected virtually every aspect of the country's economy. Reformers wanted Mexico to have a market-oriented economic system to replace one in which the state played a major role in guiding the process of development. They wanted to see the country's industry and agriculture thrive in a competitive global market. However, the new policies, together with a series of economic crises, affected many people adversely. Incomes fell, businesses went bankrupt, jobs were lost, and government services were cut back.

Political and economic dissatisfaction surge today in part because of painful inequalities among social classes in the country. For elites, the opportunities of globalization have provided unprecedented wealth and a cosmopolitan life-style that spans the continent. At the same time, indicators of malnutrition are rising in the general population. The public education and health systems struggle with minimal resources to meet the demands of the poor. In the countryside,

Mexico

0 —————— 300 Miles

0 —————— 300 Kilometers

modern commercial farmers prosper as the country's large peasant population faces increasing poverty. Many citizens feel that the government must become more representative and responsive to their needs, and that an overhaul of the political system is essential.

As a result, the assassination of Colosio drew attention to ongoing and interrelated challenges of Mexico's development:

Govt Qs for Mexico's Future

- Would a country with a long tradition of authoritarian government be able to move toward the more open and democratic political system being demanded by its citizens?
- Would a country that had long sought economic development through government activism and the growth of a domestic market be able to compete effectively in a competitive and market-driven global economy?

- Would a country long noted for severe inequalities between the rich and the poor be capable of providing better living standards for its growing population?

Geographic Setting   – 3 neighbors

Mexico is one of the most geographically diverse countries in the world, encompassing snow-capped volcanoes, coastal plains, high plateaus, fertile valleys, rain forest, and desert within an area slightly less than three times the size of Texas. To the north, it shares a 2000-mile-long border with the United States; to the south, a 600-mile-long border with Guatemala and a 160-mile-long border with Belize.

Two imposing mountain ranges run the length of Mexico, the Sierra Madre Occidental to the west and the Sierra Madre Oriental to the east. As a result, the country is noted for its peaks, plateaus, and valleys that produce an astonishing number of microclimates and a rich diversity of plants and animals. Mexico's varied geography has historically made communication and transportation between regions difficult, and infrastructure expensive. The mountainous areas tend to limit large-scale commercial agriculture to irrigated fields in the northern part of the country, while the central and southern regions produce a wide variety of crops on small farms. Soil erosion and desertification are major problems because of the steep terrain and unpredictable rainfall in many areas. The country is rich in oil, silver, and other natural resources but has long struggled to manage those resources wisely.

The human landscape is equally dramatic. With over 98.5 million inhabitants, Mexico is among the world's ten most populated countries—the second-largest nation in Latin America after Portuguese-speaking Brazil, and the largest Spanish-speaking nation in the world. Sixty percent of the population are *mestizos*, or people of mixed Amerindian and Spanish descent. Another thirty percent are all or mostly **Amerindian**, while the rest are Caucasian or have other backgrounds. Official figures report that about 8 percent of the population speaks an indigenous language, the largest **indigenous groups** being the various Maya in the south and Náhuatl in the central regions, with well over a million speakers each. Other important groups like the Zapotec, Mixtec, Otomi, Purépecha, and the Tarahumara number in the tens of thousands. However, there are dozens and perhaps hundreds of smaller linguistic and social groups throughout the country. Although Mexicans pride themselves on their Amerindian heritage, problems of racism and classism run deep, and there is a great deal of ambivalence about issues of "Indian-ness."

Mexico was transformed from a largely rural to a largely urban country in the second half of the twentieth century, with approximately 74 percent of the population now living in urban areas. Meanwhile, Mexico City has become one of the world's largest cities with about 18 million inhabitants. Population growth has slowed to about 1.8 percent, but society continues to adjust to the baby boom of the 1970s and early 1980s as these 15–30-year-olds enter a competitive job market and form families during a housing crunch.

Migration both within and beyond Mexico's borders has become a major issue. Greater economic opportunities in the industrial cities of the north lead many men and women to seek work there in the *maquiladoras*, or assembly industries. Border cities like Tijuana and Cuidad Juárez have experienced tremendous growth in the last fifteen years. Many job-seekers continue on to the United States, lured by a larger job market and higher wages. The problem repeats itself in reverse on Mexico's southern border, with many thousands of Central Americans looking for better prospects in Mexico and beyond.

Critical Junctures

Mexicans are deeply affected by the legacies of their collective past, particularly the central formative event in the country's modern history, the Revolution of 1910. Mexico experienced the first great social

Critical Junctures in Mexico's Political Development

1810–1821	War of independence from Spain.
1876–1911	Dictatorship of Porfirio Díaz.
1910–1921	Mexican Revolution.
1917	Mexican Constitution.
1929	Plutarco Elías Calles founds PRI.
1934–1940	Presidency of Lázaro Cárdenas; entrenchment of corporatist state.
1968	Massacre of Tlaltelolco; 200 students are killed.
1978–1982	State-led development reaches peak with petroleum boom and bust.
1982	Market reformers come to power in PRI.
1988	Carlos Salinas elected amid charges of fraud.
1989	First governorship won by an opposition party.
1994	NAFTA goes into effect; uprising in Chiapas; Colosio assassinated.
1996	Four largest political parties agree on electoral reform.
1997	Opposition parties advance nationwide; PRI loses absolute majority in congress for first time in its history.

Global Connection: *Conquest or Encounter?*

The year 1519, when the Spanish conqueror Hernán Cortés arrived on the shores of the Yucatán Peninsula, is often considered the starting point of Mexican political history. But the Spanish explorers did not set off across an uninhabited land waiting to be excavated for gold and silver. Instead, the land that was to become New Spain and then Mexico was home to extensive and complex indigenous civilizations that were advanced in agriculture, architecture, and political and economic organization—civilizations that were already over a thousand years old. The Mayans of the Yucatán and the Toltecs of the central highlands had reached high levels of development long before the arrival of the Europeans. By 1519 diverse groups had fallen under the power of the militaristic Aztec Empire, which extended throughout what is today central and southern Mexico.

The encounter between the Europeans and these indigenous civilizations was marked by bloodshed and violence. The great Aztec city of Tenochtitlán—the site of Mexico City today—was captured and largely destroyed by the Spanish conquerors in 1521. Cortés and the colonial masters who came after him subjected indigenous groups to forced labor, robbed them of gold, silver, and land, and introduced flora and fauna from Europe that destroyed long-existing aqueducts and irrigation systems. They also brought alien forms of property rights and authority relationships, a religion that viewed indigenous practices as the devil's work, and an economy based on mining and cattle—all of which soon overwhelmed existing structures of social and economic organization. Within a century,

wars, savage exploitation at the hands of the Spaniards, and the introduction of European diseases reduced the indigenous population from an estimated 25 million to 1 million or less. The Indian population took three hundred years just to stop decreasing after the disaster of the Conquest.

Even so, the Spanish never constituted more than a small percentage of the total population, and massive racial mixing between the Indians, Europeans, and to a lesser extent Africans, produced a new *raza*, or *mestizo* race. This unique process remains at once a source of pride and conflict for Mexicans today. What does it mean to be Mexican? Is one the conquered or the conqueror? While celebrating Amerindian achievements in food, culture, the arts, and ancient civilization, middle-class Mexico has the contradictory sense that to be "Indian" nowadays is to be against progress, backwards, even barbaric. Many Amerindians are stigmatized by mainstream society if they speak a native dialect. But perhaps the situation is changing, with the upsurge of indigenist movements from both the grassroots and the international level striving to promote ethnic pride, defend rights, and foster the teaching of Indian languages.

The collision of two worlds resonates in current national philosophical and political debates. Is Mexico a Western society? Is it colonial or modern? Third or First World? South or North? Is the United States an ally or a conqueror? Perhaps most important, many Mexicans at once welcome and fear full integration into the global economy, asking themselves: Is globalization the new Conquest?

---

revolution of the twentieth century, a conflict that lasted for more than a decade and claimed the lives of as many as 2 million people. Some died in violent confrontations, but the majority lost their lives through the massive destruction, dislocation, and famine caused by the shifting and sporadic nature of the conflict. The revolution was fought by a variety of forces for a variety of reasons, which made the consolidation of power that followed as significant as the revolution itself. The institutions and symbols of the current political regime emerged from these complex conflicts.

Independence and Instability (1810–1876)

Spain ruled Mexico for three centuries, administering a vast economic, political, and religious empire in the interests of the imperial country, its kings, and its representatives in North America. Colonial policy was designed to extract wealth from New Spain and to limit the possibilities for Spaniards in the New World to benefit from agriculture, commerce, or industry without at the same time benefiting Spain. It was also designed to ensure commitment to the Roman Catholic religion.

In 1810, however, a parish priest in central Mexico named Miguel Hidalgo issued a rallying cry to a group assembled in a parish church in the town of Dolores. He called for an end to Spanish misrule. At the head of a motley band of rebels, he began the first of a series of wars of independence that pitted rebels against the Spanish crown for eleven years. Despite the fact that independence from Spain was recognized in 1821, Mexico struggled to create a stable and legitimate government for decades thereafter.

Liberals and conservatives, federalists and centralists, those who sought to expand the power of the church and those who sought to curtail it, and those who wanted a republic and those who wanted a monarchy were all engaged in the battle for Mexico's soul during the nineteenth century. Between 1833 and 1855, thirty-six presidential administrations came to power. During this disorganized period, Mexico lost half its territory to the United States.

Mexico's northern territory of Texas proclaimed and then won independence in a war ending in 1836. The Lone Star Republic was annexed to the United States by Congress in 1845, and claims on Mexican territory north of the Rio Grande were increasingly heard from Washington. On the basis of a very dubious claim that Mexico had invaded U.S. territory, the United States declared war on its southern neighbor. The war was first fought along what was later to become the border between the two countries and then, in 1847, the U.S. army invaded the port city of Veracruz. Causing considerable loss of civilian lives, this army marched toward Mexico City and the final battle at Chapultepec Castle. An 1848 treaty gave the United States title to what later became the states of Texas, New Mexico, Utah, Nevada, Arizona, California, and part of Colorado for about $18 million, leaving a legacy of deep resentment about U.S. imperialism.

Throughout this period, liberals and conservatives continued their struggle to resolve issues of political and economic order and, in particular, the power of the Catholic Church. The constitution of 1857 incorporated many of the goals of the liberals, such as republican government, a bill of rights, abolition of slavery, and limitations on the economic and political power of the church. Benito Juárez, who occupied the presidency on three separate occasions, continues to be revered in Mexico today as an early proponent of open and republican government.

The constitution of 1857 did not guarantee stability, however. In 1861, Spain, Great Britain, and France occupied the coastal town of Veracruz to collect customs claims from the government, providing the French army an opportunity to march on Mexico City and establish the government of Emperor Maximilian and Empress Carlota (1864–1867). Conservatives and Catholic loyalists welcomed this respite from the liberals. But Juárez was back in office in 1867, spearheading reforms in economic, social, and political arenas as well as building up the institutions of a new national government.

Over the next few years, a popular retired general named Porfirio Díaz became increasingly dissatisfied with the tedious new rule of law and criticized what he saw to be a "lot of politics" and "little action." After several failed attempts to win and then take the presidency, he finally succeeded in 1876. His dictatorship lasted thirty-four years and was at first welcomed by many because it brought sustained stability to the country.

The Porfiriato (1876–1911)

When Díaz took power, Mexico had been experiencing decades of political and economic turmoil. Díaz imposed a highly centralized authoritarian system to create political order and economic progress. In time, he relied increasingly on a small clique of advisers, known as *científicos* (scientists), who wanted to adopt European technologies and values to modernize the country, forcefully if necessary. Deeply disdainful of the vast majority of the country's population, Díaz and the *científicos* encouraged foreign investment and amassed huge fortunes, which they used to support lavish life-styles and to copy the latest European styles. During this period, known as the Porfiriato, this small elite monopolized political power and reserved lucrative economic investments for themselves and their allies. Economic and political opportunities were closed off for new generations of middle- and upper-class Mexicans, who became increasingly sensitive to the greed of the Porfirians and their own lack of opportunities.

In 1914, Pancho Villa (right) met with Emiliano Zapata in Mexico City to discuss the revolution and their separate goals for its outcome. *Source:* Freck/Odyssey, Chicago.

The Revolution of 1910 and the Sonoran Dynasty (1910–1934)

In 1910 conflict broke out as a new generation of reformers sought to end the dictatorship. Díaz had pledged himself to an open election for president, and in 1910, Francisco I. Madero, a landowner from the northern state of Coahuila, presented himself as a candidate. The slogan "Effective Suffrage, No Reelection" summed up the reformers' goals in creating opportunities for a new class of politically ambitious citizens to move into positions of power. When this opposition swelled, Díaz decided against having an election and tried to clamp down. But it was too late. Madero—who was later assassinated—became president of a distintegrating country.

At the same time that middle-class reformers struggled to displace Díaz, a peasant revolt that focused on land claims erupted in the central and southern states of the country. This revolt had roots in legislation that made it easy for wealthy landowners and ranchers to claim the lands of peasant villagers. Encouraged by the weakening of the old regime and driven to desperation by increasing landlessness, villagers armed themselves and joined forces under a variety of local leaders. The most famous of these was Emiliano Zapata, who amassed a peasant army from Morelos, a state in southern Mexico. Peasant battalions swept through the countryside and grew in numbers; women as well as men flocked to fight under Zapata and other revolutionary leaders. Zapata's Plan de Ayala, first announced in 1911 and agreed to at a national meeting of revolutionary leaders in 1915, became the cornerstone of the radical agrarian reform that would be incorporated into the constitution of 1917.

In the northern part of the country, Francisco (Pancho) Villa rallied his own army of workers, small farmers, and ranch hands. He presented a major challenge to the national army, now under the leadership of Venustiano Carranza, who had inherited Madero's middle-class reformist movement and eventually became president. Villa's forces recognized no law but that of their chief and combined military maneuvers with banditry, looting, and warlordism in the territories under their control.

The constitution of 1917 was forged out of this diverse and often conflicting set of interests. It established a formal set of political institutions and guaranteed a range of progressive social and economic rights to citizens—agrarian reform, social security, the right to organize in unions, a minimum wage, an eight-hour work day, profit sharing for workers, and universal secular education. One thing it did not do, it should be noted, is provide suffrage for women, which was granted for local elections in 1953 and for national elections in 1958. In an effort to limit the power of foreign investors, the constitution declared that only Mexican citizens or the government could own land or rights to water and other natural resources. It also contained numerous articles that severely limited the power of the Roman Catholic Church, long a target of liberals who wanted Mexico to be a secular state. The signing of the document signaled the formal end of the revolution and the intent of the contending parties to form a new political regime. Despite such noble sentiments, violence continued as competing leaders sought to assert power and displace their rivals. Political assassinations were common through the 1920s, as were regional skirmishes among local warlords. Zapata, Villa, Carranza, and General Obregón were all assassinated, the last two while president.

Despite this violence, power was gradually consolidated in the hands of a group of revolutionary leaders from the north of the country. Known as the Sonoran Dynasty, after their home state of Sonora, these leaders were committed to a capitalist model of economic development. During the 1920s they skillfully outmaneuvered those who wished to see a socialist economy rise from the ashes of civil war. Eventually, one of the Sonorans—Plutarco Elías Calles—emerged as the *jefe máximo*, or supreme leader. Elected president in 1924, Calles managed to select and dominate his presidential successors from 1929 to 1934. The consolidation of power under his control was accompanied by extreme **anticlericalism**, which eventually resulted in warfare between conservative leaders of the Catholic Church and their followers, and the government.

In 1929, Calles brought together many of the most powerful contenders for leadership, including many regional warlords, to create a political party. The bargain he offered was simple. Contenders for power would accommodate each others' interests in the expectation of even greater power and spoils. Despite name changes in 1939 and 1946, the party they created exists to this day—the PRI. For the next sixty-five years, Calles's bargain was effective in ensuring a tradition of nonviolent conflict resolution among elites and the uninterrupted rule of the PRI in national politics.

Although the revolution was complex and the interests contending for power in its aftermath were numerous, there were five clear results of this protracted conflict. First, the power of traditional rural landowners was undercut. In the years after the revolution, wealthy elites would again emerge in rural areas, but they would never again be so powerful in national politics, nor could their power be so unchecked in local areas. Second, the power of the Catholic Church at the national level was firmly destroyed. While the church remained important in many parts of the country, it no longer participated openly in national political debates. Third, the power of foreign investors was severely limited; prior to the revolution, foreign investors owned much of the country's land as well as many of its railroads, mines, and factories. Henceforth, a clear sense of Mexican nationalism would shape economic policy-making.

Fourth, a new political elite consolidated power and agreed to resolve conflicts through accommodation and bargaining rather than violence. And fifth, the new constitution and the new party laid the basis for a strong central government that could assert its power over the agricultural, industrial, and social development of the country. Modern Mexican government and the country's economic development were profoundly affected by these accomplishments.

Lázaro Cárdenas, Agrarian Reform, and the Workers (1934–1940)

In 1934, Plutarco Calles handpicked Lázaro Cárdenas, a revolutionary general and state governor, as his successor to the presidency. He fully anticipated that Cárdenas would go along with Calles's behind-the-scenes management of the country and continue the economic policies of the postrevolutionary coalition. To his great surprise, Cárdenas executed a virtual coup that established his own supremacy and sent Calles packing to the United States for an "extended vacation."[1] Even more unexpectedly, Cárdenas mobilized peasants and workers in pursuit of the more radical goals of the 1910 revolution. He encouraged peasant syndicates to petition for land and claim rights promised in the constitution of 1917. He eventually superintended the distribution of more than 17 million hectares of land (1 hectare = 2.471 acres). Most of these lands were distributed in the form of *ejidos* (collective land grants) to peasant groups who would be responsible for them. *Ejidatarios* (members of the *ejido*) became one of the most enduring bases of support for the government because of the redistribution of lands that was so forcefully pursued in the 1930s. Cárdenas also encouraged workers to form unions and demand higher wages and better working conditions. He established his nationalist credentials when he nationalized the petroleum industry in 1938, wresting it from U.S. and British investors.

During the Cárdenas years from 1934 to 1940, the bulk of the Mexican population was incorporated into the political system. Organizations of peasants, workers, middle-class groups, and the military were added to the party, and the voices of the poor majority were heard within the councils of government, reducing the risk that they would become radicalized outside them.

Mexican presidential candidates are expected to campaign hard, traveling to remote locations, making rousing campaign speeches, and meeting with citizens of humble origins. Here, presidential candidate Ernesto Zedillo is on the campaign trail in 1994. *Source:* AP/Wide World Photos.

In addition, the Cárdenas years witnessed a great expansion of the role of the state as the government set up a powerful investment bank to encourage industrialization, provided credit to agriculture, and invested in infrastructure.

Lázaro Cárdenas continues to be a national hero to Mexicans, who look back on his presidency as a period when government was clearly committed to improving the welfare of the country's poor. His other legacy was to institutionalize patterns of political succession and presidential behavior that continue to set standards for Mexico's leaders. He campaigned extensively, even though he was not seriously challenged by other candidates, and his campaign travel took him to remote villages and regions, where he listened to the demands and complaints of humble people. Cárdenas served a single six-year term, called a *sexenio*, and relinquished full political power to the new president, Manuel Avila Camacho. Cárdenas's conduct in office created hallowed traditions that subsequent PRI presidents have all observed.

The Politics of Development (1940–1994)

Although Cárdenas had directed a radical reshuffling of political power in the country, his successors were able to use the institutions he created to counteract his reforms. Ambitious local and regional party leaders and leaders of peasants' and workers' groups began to use their organizations as pawns in exchange for political favors. Gradually, the PRI developed a huge patronage machine, providing union and *ejido* leaders with jobs, opportunities for corruption, land, and other benefits in return for delivering their followers' political support. Extensive chains of personal relationships based on the exchange of favors allowed the party to amass far-reaching political control and limit opportunities for organizing independently of the PRI. These exchange relationships, known as **clientelism**, became the cement that built loyalty to the PRI and the political system.

This kind of political control translated into the capacity of post-Cárdenas presidents to reorient the country's development away from the egalitarian social goals of the 1930s toward a development strategy in which the state actively encouraged industrialization and the accumulation of wealth. Initially, industrialization created jobs and made available a wide range of basic consumer goods to Mexico's burgeoning population. Growth rates were high during the 1940s, 1950s, and 1960s, and Mexicans flocked to the cities to take advantage of the jobs created in the manufacturing and construction industries. By the 1960s, however, industrial development policies were no longer generating rapid growth and could not keep pace with the rapidly rising demand for jobs.

The country's economy was in deep crisis by the mid-1970s. Just as policymakers began to take actions to correct the problems, however, vast new amounts of oil were discovered in the Gulf of Mexico. Soon, rapid economic growth was refueled by extensive public investment programs in virtually every sector of the economy. Based on the promise of petroleum wealth, the government and private businesses borrowed huge amounts of capital from foreign lenders who were, of course, eager to do business with a country that had so much oil. Unfortunately for Mexico, however, international petroleum prices plunged sharply in 1981. Almost overnight, there was no more credit to be had and much less money from petroleum to pay for economic expansion or the interest on the debts incurred in preceding years. Mexico plunged into a deep economic crisis that affected many countries around the world.

In fact, this crisis helped two presidents, Miguel de la Madrid (1982–1988) and Carlos Salinas (1988–1994), introduce the first major reversal of the country's development strategy since the 1940s. New policies were put in place to limit the government's role in the economy and to make it easier for Mexican producers to export their goods. This period clearly marked the beginning of a new effort to become more important in international economic affairs. In 1993, by signing the North American Free Trade Agreement (NAFTA), which commits Mexico, the United States, and Canada to eliminating trade barriers among them, Mexico's policymakers signaled the extent to which they envisioned the future prosperity of their country as tied to that of its two neighbors to the north. Efforts to increase trade and investment to Latin American, European, and Asian countries also emphasized Mexico's new commitment to competitiveness in a global economy. The economic reforms of the 1980s and 1990s were a turning point for the country's development, even though they left unresolved issues of democratic and social reform, and meant that Mexico's future development would be closely tied to conditions in the international economy. A major economic crisis at the end of 1994, in which billions of dollars of foreign investment fled the country, was indicative of this new international vulnerability. The

administraton of Ernesto Zedillo (1994–2000) struggled to recover from this crisis.

Rifts and Openings (1994 to the Present)

For the Mexican government, 1994 was not an auspicious year. On January 1 a guerrilla movement called the Zapatista National Liberation Front (EZLN) seized four towns in the southern state of Chiapas. The group demanded land, democracy, indigenous rights, and an immediate repeal of NAFTA. Many citizens throughout the country openly supported the aims of the rebels, pointing out that the movement brought to light the reality of two very different Mexicos: those Mexicans who marched forward confidently into the twenty-first century with wealth and influence, and those who were getting left behind because of poverty and repression. The government and the military were criticized for inaction and human rights abuse in the state.

Following close on the heels of the rebellion came the Colosio assassination in March. The murder opened wide rifts within the PRI and unleashed a flood of speculation and distrust among the citizenry. Fear of violence helped provide the PRI with strong support in the August 1994 elections, although the secretary-general of the PRI, José Francisco Ruiz Massieu, was assassinated the following month. But the year's crowning inglorious event came in the form of economic meltdown in December, just three weeks after Zedillo took office. A severely overvalued peso led to a currency crisis and devaluation. This, coupled with tremendous government debt from the year's rampant public spending to soothe Chiapas and other impoverished areas, led to a financial emergency, loss of confidence, and massive amounts of money leaving the country. The peso lost half of its value against the dollar within a few short days, and the government lacked the funds to pay its obligations. Suddenly, Mexico's status among nations seemed dubious once more, and the country felt betrayed by outgoing President Salinas, convinced that he had patched together a shaky house of cards only long enough to get himself out of office.

The economy shrank by 6.2 percent in 1995, inflation soared, taxes rose while wages were frozen, and the bank system collapsed. The United States orchestrated a 50-billion-dollar bailout, $20 billion of

Citizen Action: **Rebellion in Chiapas**

In the months after January 1994 indigenous women set out daily for the tourist-laden zones of central Mexico City to sell handmade dolls. These dolls, dressed in brightly colored costumes, also sported black ski masks. They represented a symbolic connection to the rebels of the Zapatista National Liberation Front (EZLN) in the southern state of Chiapas, who wore ski masks to avoid identification by the government. Images of the ideological leader and public spokesman of the Zapatista movement, Subcomandante Marcos, also appeared throughout the country, and people of diverse ethnic, class, and political backgrounds began expressing support for the goals of the rebels.

The rebellion by some 2000 members of the EZLN broke out on January 1, 1994, the day that NAFTA went into effect. The Zapatista army captured four towns in the state of Chiapas, including the city of San Cristobal de las Casas, a popular tourist destination. The EZLN demanded "jobs, land, housing, food, health, education, independence, freedom, democracy, justice and peace."* The peasant army also called on the government to repeal NAFTA. These demands and the progress of the rebellion were immediately transmitted throughout Mexico and around the globe by domestic and international media as camera crews and reporters flocked to this remote, poverty-stricken state.

The EZLN's call for an end to exploitation at the hands of voracious landowners and corrupt bosses of the PRI, as well as for social services and citizenship rights, resonated deeply throughout the country. Soon, a broad spectrum of local, regional, professional, and human rights groups took up the banner of the Chiapas rebels and called on the government to open the political system to more just and democratic elections, decision-making processes, and policies. By calling in the army to suppress armed peasants, most of whom were Mayan Indians, and to retake the four towns by force, the government only increased sympathy for the marginalized, impoverished indigenous groups. The Chiapas rebellion symbolized for many the reality of Mexico's political, economic, and social inequalities.

The Zapatistas were not seeking to overthrow the Mexican political system. They believed, however, that the system created and maintained by the PRI had become very much like the dictatorship of Porfirio Díaz, toppled in the Revolution of 1910. They were united in their demand that indigenous groups throughout Mexico be granted fair treatment and the means to escape their poverty and powerlessness. They resorted to violence because they believed the government would not otherwise pay attention to their demands.

The Zapatista rebellion presented a major challenge to Mexico's image of political stability. It had a profound effect on the election of 1994, as competing political parties and candidates sought to identify with rebel demands for indigenous rights, economic justice, and honest elections. The rebels rejected a peace treaty that would have promoted the electoral fortunes of the PRI, arguing instead for increased space for political debate and dialogue. The government spent over $200 million on social programs and infrastructure projects in the state in the months leading up to the election, a 44 percent increase over what had been budgeted. Just weeks before the elections, however, the EZLN hosted a National Democratic Convention of a large number of groups committed to pressuring the government for fundamental political reform.

The rebels insisted that economic assistance alone would not solve the problems in the southern part of the country. They pointed to the deeper causes of injustice—namely, concentration of wealth in the hands of a brutal local elite and monopolization of power by a government that valued stability and compromise with local elites above all else.

In the aftermath of the rebellion, Mexican officials sought to erase the impression that the insurgency was an Indian uprising. They pointed out that many indigenous groups rejected the EZLN. Yet major indigenous organizations across Mexico and elsewhere in Latin America expressed solidarity with the Chiapas rebels and with the decision to take up arms. While some argued that the Chiapas rebellion was a local phenomenon and an isolated set of incidents, others predicted the spread of the Mexican example of armed uprisings by indigenous groups. The roots of such insurrections are in economic and social exploitation, they argued, not in specific ethnic identities. A stalemate still existed five years later: talks broke down, foreign observers were expelled, and accusations of human rights violations by the government were on the rise.

*As cited in Neil Harvey, *Rebellion in Chiapas: Rural Reforms, Campesino Radicalism, and the Limits to Salinismo* (San Diego: Center for U.S.-Mexican Studies, University of California, 1994), 1.

which came directly from the U.S. Treasury. Faced with limited options, Zedillo implemented a severe and unpopular economic austerity program, which restored financial stability over the next two years.

In the meantime, a second guerilla movement came to light, called the Popular Revolutionary Army (EPR), which was far more mysterious, less ideological, and more committed to violence than the Zapatistas. Considered terrorist by the government, the movement claimed to have operatives throughout the country and took responsibility for several destructive actions. Also in 1996, Raúl Salinas, brother of the former president, was indicted on charges of masterminding the murder of Ruiz Massieu as well as illicit enrichment and money-laundering.

These shocks provoked widespread disillusionment and frustration with the political system. Many citizens, especially in urban areas, decided that there was no longer any reason to support the PRI. Since 1994 opposition parties have become much more organized, experienced at governance, and effective at challenging the PRI nationwide. Buoyed by a 1996 electoral reform agreed upon by the four largest parties (PRI, PAN, PRD, and PT [Partido del Trabajo—Worker's Party]), important gains were made by the opposition in the July 1997 elections. For the first time in modern Mexican history, the PRI lost its absolute majority in the Chamber of Deputies. Since then, the congress has shown increasing dynamism as a counterbalance to the presidency, blocking executive decisions, demanding unrestricted information, and initiating new legislation. In addition, opposition parties have won important governorships and mayorships; it is estimated that more than half of Mexico is now governed by the opposition on the state or local level.

Mexicans seem to have increasing faith in the electoral process, but the biggest test of all remains: the presidency. Many citizens believe that Mexico will not be a truly democratic country until an opposition candidate sits in the presidential palace.

Themes and Implications

Historical Junctures and Political Themes

The modern Mexican state emerged out of a popular revolution that proclaimed goals of democratic government, social justice, and nationalism. In the chaotic years after the revolution, the state created conditions for political and social peace. By incorporating peasants and workers into party and government institutions and providing benefits to low-income groups during the 1930s, it became widely accepted as legitimate. In encouraging considerable economic growth in the years after 1940, it also encouraged belief in its ability to provide material improvements in the quality of life of large portions of the population. These factors worked together to create a strong state capable of guiding economic and political life in the country.

In its external relations, Mexico has always prided itself on ideological independence from the world's "great powers." Its large population, cultural richness, political stability, and front-line position in regard to the United States has prompted Mexico to consider itself a natural leader of Latin America and the developing world in general. However, the reforms of the 1980s and 1990s, especially NAFTA, have caused great concern among many citizens, who perceive that the government is accepting a position of political, cultural, and economic subordination to the United States.

Mexico has enjoyed considerable economic advancement since the 1940s, although a number of other developing countries have been equally or more successful in generating sustained economic growth and improving standards of living. In the 1990s it acquired aspirations to be considered one of the newly industrializing countries of the world, similar in stature to countries such as South Korea, Malaysia, and Taiwan. It was certainly facing up to many of the problems of the more advanced industrial nations—trying to achieve international competitiveness for its products, dealing with problems of air and water pollution, and managing the growth of its megacities. The decision to promote a free-trade agreement with its northern neighbors clearly indicated the government's recognition of the need to secure Mexico a place in the global economy.

However, the crises of 1994 and 1995 shook Mexico's confidence in its ability to achieve this goal on its own terms and highlighted conflict between a market-oriented development strategy and the country's philosophical tradition of a strong and protective state. The larger questions of whether a new development strategy can generate growth, whether Mexican products can find profitable markets overseas, whether investors can create extensive job opportunities for millions of unemployed and part-time workers, and whether the country can maintain the confidence of those investors over the longer term continue to challenge the country.

In many ways, the Revolution of 1910 could be interpreted as a struggle between collective identities that had remained latent during the Porfiriato. Its resolution, through the creation of the PRI and the notion of a strong state, represented the victory of the *mestizos* as a group, curtailing the colonial power of the Roman Catholic Church and Western-style elites as well as resubmerging the demands of justice and autonomy for the indigenous poor. The PRI was very successful at replacing the traditional politics of collective identities with the politics of a **corporatist state**, meaning that interest groups became an institutionalized part of state structure.

Despite the fact that many citizens remained marginal to full participation in the country's economic, political, and social life, most Mexicans agreed, at least until the 1980s, that the state was legitimate and nationalist. This does not mean that Mexican society was unorganized or passive. Indeed, many Mexicans were actively involved in local community organizations, religious activities, unions, and public interest groups. But traditionally, the scope for challenging the government, for insisting on basic civil rights, or for demanding an open and responsive government was very limited. Nor did Mexico's strong state mean that the government was openly repressive or brutal. On the contrary, officials in the government and the party generally worked hard to find ways to resolve conflicts peacefully, and they maintained the belief that the state represents the aspirations of all Mexicans. In fact, most Mexicans pursued their daily lives without feeling directly threatened by the power of the state. The norm in Mexico's state-society relationship has been peaceful resolution of conflict and behind-the-scenes accommodation of conflicting interests.

With frustrations mounting in the 1980s and 1990s because of economic crises and the incapacity of government to respond to civilian demands, the traditional politics of collective identities began to strongly surface once more. Ethnic groups, religious groups,

community movements, private business, and regionalism have all emerged as important forces, and it remains to be seen how the current transformation of the Mexican political scene will accommodate them.

The revolution resolved the conflict between the democratic idea and Mexico's centralized, authoritarian tradition in much the same way it dealt with the conflict among collective identities: through corporatism. The country opted not for true democracy but for representation through government-mediated organizations within a corporatist state. This development increased state power in relation to civil society. The state took the lead in defining goals for the country's development and, through the school system, the party, and the media, inculcated a broad sense of its legitimate right to set such goals. In addition, the state had extensive resources at its disposal to control or co-opt dissent and to purchase political loyalty. The PRI was an essential channel through which material goods, jobs, the distribution of land, and the allocation of development projects flowed to increase popular support for the system or to buy off opposition to it. Citizens wishing to have greater input into national decision-making faced an uphill battle.

By the 1980s, however, cracks began to appear in the traditional ways in which Mexican citizens interacted with the government. As the PRI began to lose its capacity to control political activities, and as civic groups increasingly insisted on their right to remain independent from the PRI and the government, the terms for the state-society relationship were clearly in need of redefinition. Through the formation of private interest groups and organized social movements, civil society increasingly pressured government to be more responsive, fair, democratic, and effective. The administration of President Zedillo signaled its willingness to cede political power to successful opposition parties in fair elections, with the electoral reform of 1996 and the elections of 1997 being particularly significant steps in the emergence of a true multiparty system. As more citizens found themselves governed by different parties, they seemed to gain confidence that democracy can succeed in Mexico. Of course, many groups benefit from the corporatist system and do not want it to change. Mexico's future stability depends on how well the government can accommodate these conflicting interests while, at the same time, transforming political institutions and providing economic opportunities to a largely poor population.

Implications for Comparative Politics

The Mexican political system is unique among developing countries in the extent to which it has managed to institutionalize and maintain civilian political authority for a very long time. In a world of developing nations, wracked by political turmoil, military coups, and regime changes, this regime has established enduring institutions of governance and conditions for political stability. Other countries have sought to emulate the Mexican model of stability

based on an alliance between a dominant party and a strong development-oriented state, but rarely have governments had the legitimacy to appropriate all facets of social life as in Mexico. The regime's revolutionary heritage as well as its ability to maintain a sense of national identity are important factors in accounting for its political continuity.

Currently, Mexico represents a nation attempting to undergo significant political change without violence, to transform itself from a corporatist state to a truly democratic one for the first time in its long history. At the same time, it struggles to resolve the conflicts of development through an integration with its North American neighbors that it hopes will improve the quality of life of its citizens.

Section ❷   Political Economy and Development

Mexico has been categorized as a relatively prosperous developing country, along with countries such as Argentina, Portugal, South Korea, and Venezuela.[2] It has made significant strides in industrialization, which accounts for about 26 percent of the country's gross domestic product (GDP). Agriculture contributes about 8 percent to GDP, and services contribute some 67 percent. This structure is very similar to the economic profiles of Brazil, New Zealand, and Hungary. But, unlike those countries, Mexico is oil-rich. The government-owned petroleum industry is a ready source of revenue and foreign exchange, but it is also extremely vulnerable to changes in international oil prices.

Mexico's industrial and petroleum-based economy means a higher per capita income than in most other developing countries. If income were spread evenly among all Mexicans, each would receive $3680 annually—far more than the per capita incomes of India ($390), China ($860), and Nigeria ($269) but considerably less than those of Britain ($20,710), France ($26,052), and Germany ($28,260).[3] Of course, income is not spread evenly. Mexico suffers from great inequalities in how wealth is distributed, and poverty continues to be a grim reality for millions of Mexicans. The way Mexico promotes economic growth and industrialization is important in explaining

why widespread poverty has persisted and why political power has not been more equitably distributed.

State and Economy

During the years of the Porfiriato (1876–1911), the country began to produce some textiles, footwear, glassware, paper, beer, tiles, furniture, and other simple products. At that time, however, policymakers were convinced that Mexico could grow rich by exporting its raw materials to more economically advanced countries. Their efforts to attract domestic and international investment encouraged a major boom in the production and export of products such as henequin (for making rope), coffee, cacao (cocoa beans), cattle, silver, and gold. Soon, the country had become so attractive to foreign investors that large amounts of land, the country's petroleum, its railroad network, and its mining wealth were largely controlled by foreigners. Nationalist reaction against the power of these foreign interests played a significant role in the tensions that produced the Revolution of 1910.

In the new Mexican state, this nationalism combined with a sense of social justice inspired by popular revolutionary leaders such as Zapata. Mexicans widely shared the idea that the state had the responsibility to generate wealth for all its citizens. In addition, it was thought that only the state was powerful enough to mobilize the resources and stimulate the development necessary to overcome the destruction of the revolution. As a result, the country adopted a strategy in which the government guided the process of industrial and agricultural development and set the political conditions for its success. Often referred to as **state capitalism,** this development strategy relied heavily on government actions to encourage private investment and to lower risks for private entrepreneurs.

In the twenty years following the revolution, many of those concerned about the country's development became convinced that economic growth would not occur unless Mexico could industrialize more fully. They argued that reliance on exports of agricultural products, minerals, and petroleum—called the agro-export model—forced the country to import manufactured goods which, over the long term, would always cost more than what was earned from exports. Critics of the agro-export model of development also argued that prices of primary products shifted greatly from one year to the next. Countries that produced them were doomed to repeat boom/bust cycles as their domestic economies reflected sharp fluctuations in international prices for the goods they exported. Mexico, they believed, should begin to manufacture the goods that it was currently importing.

Import Substitution and Its Consequences

Between 1940 and 1982, Mexico pursued a form of state capitalism and a model of industrialization known as import substitution, or **import substituting industrialization (ISI).** Like Brazil and other Latin American countries during the period, the government promoted industrialization by encouraging domestic and international investment, providing credit and tax incentives to industrialists, maintaining low rates of inflation, and keeping wage demands low through subsidized transportation, housing, and health care for workers. It also fostered industrialization by establishing state-owned steel mills, electric power generators, ports, and petroleum production. Between 1940 and 1970, over 40 percent of all fixed capital investment came from the government. These policies had considerable success. Initially, the country produced mainly simple products like shoes, clothing, and processed foods. But by the 1960s and 1970s it was also producing consumer durables (refrigerators, automobiles, trucks), intermediate goods (steel, petrochemicals, and other products used in the manufacturing process), and capital goods (heavy machinery to produce manufactures).

Mexican agriculture was also affected by this drive to industrialize. With the massive agrarian reform of the 1930s (see Section 1), the *ejido* had become an important structure in the rural economy, accounting for half the cultivated area of the country and 51 percent of the value of agricultural production by 1940. After Cárdenas left office, however, government policymakers moved rapidly away from the economic development of the *ejidos*. They became committed instead to developing a strong, entrepreneurial private sector in agriculture. For them, "the development of private agriculture would be the 'foundation of industrial greatness.'"[4] They wanted agriculture to provide foodstuffs for the growing cities, raw materials for industry, and foreign exchange from exports. To encourage these goals, the government invested in transportation networks, irrigation projects, and agricultural storage facilities. It provided extension services and invested in research. It encouraged imports of technology to improve output and mechanize production. Since policymakers believed that modern commercial farmers would respond more to these investments and services than would peasants on small plots of land, the government provided most of its assistance to large landowners.

The government's encouragement of industry and agriculture set the country on a three-decade path of sustained growth. Between 1940 and 1950, gross domestic product grew at an annual average of 6.7 percent, while manufacturing increased at an average of 8.1 percent. In the following two decades, GDP growth rates remained impressive and manufacturing growth continued to outpace overall growth in the economy. In the 1950s manufacturing achieved an average of 7.3 percent growth annually; in the 1960s, 10.1 percent annually. Agricultural production grew rapidly as new areas were brought under cultivation and green revolution technology (scientifically improved seeds, fertilizers, and pesticides) was extensively adopted on large farms. These were years of great optimism as foreign investment increased, the

Table 1

Mexican Development, 1940–1990						
	1940	*1950*	*1960*	*1970*	*1980*	*1990*
Population (thousands)	19,815	26,282	38,020	52,771	70,416	88,598
Life expectancy[a] (years)	—	51.6	58.6	62.6	67.4	68.9
Infant mortality[a] (per 1,000 live births)	—	—	86.3	70.9	49.9	42.6
Illiteracy (% of population age 15 and over)	—	42.5	34.5	25.0	16.0	12.7
Urban population (% of total)	—	—	50.7	59.0	66.4	72.6
Economically active population in agriculture (% of total)	—	58.3	55.1	44.0	36.6	22.0
	1940–1950	*1950–1960*	*1960–1970*	*1970–1980*	*1980–1990*	
GDP growth rate (average annual percent)	6.7	5.8	7.6	6.7	1.6	
Per capita GDP growth rate	—	—	3.7	3.7	−0.7	

[a]Five-year average.

Sources: *Statistical Abstract for Latin America* (United Nations, Economic Commission for Latin America); Roger Hansen, *The Politics of Mexican Development* (Baltimore, Md.: Johns Hopkins University Press, 1971); *Statistical Bulletin of the OAS.*

middle class grew larger, and indicators for health and welfare steadily improved. Between 1940 and 1970, Mexico City grew from a modest-sized city of a million and a half people to a major metropolis of over 8 million inhabitants. Even the poorest Mexicans believed that their lives were improving. Table 1 presents data that summarize a number of advancements during this period. So impressive was Mexico's economic performance that it was referred to internationally as the Mexican Miracle, paralleling Germany's *Wirtschaftswunder* and Japan's Economic Miracle.

U.S. private investment was an important source of capital for the country's effort to industrialize; in the twenty years after 1950, it grew at an average of over 11 percent a year. In 1962 the United States accounted for 85 percent of all foreign investment in Mexico. Moreover, two-thirds of Mexico's imports typically came from the United States, while it regularly sent two-thirds of its exports there. Mexican policymakers increasingly saw the closeness and size of

the U.S. economy as a significant threat, and many policy initiatives—restricting foreign investment in industries considered important to national development and seeking to diversify trade relationships with other countries, for example—were undertaken to lessen the country's dependence on the United States.

While the government took the lead in encouraging industrialization, it was not long before a group of domestic entrepreneurs developed a special relationship with the state. Government policies protected their products through high tariffs or special licensing requirements, limiting imports of competing goods. Business elites in Mexico received subsidized credit to invest in equipment and plants; they benefited from cheap, subsidized energy; and they rarely had to pay taxes. Additionally, inflation was kept in check and the government helped ensure a supply of cheap labor by providing workers' housing, transportation, and medical coverage.

Through the impact of such policies, an elite of protected businesses emerged as powerful players in national politics. In the 1940s and 1950s they strengthened a set of industry-related interest groups that worked to promote and sustain favorable policies. With this organizational base, groups like the chambers of industry, commerce, and banking began to play increasingly important roles in government policy-making. They were able to veto efforts by the government to cut back on their benefits and to lobby for even more advantages. The government remained the source of most policy initiatives, but generally it was not able to move far in the face of opposition from those who benefited most from its policies. Perhaps just as important, business elites became adept at side-stepping government regulations, paying bribes to acquire licenses, credit, permits, and exemptions, and working out deals with officials on a one-to-one basis.

Workers also became more important players in national politics. As mentioned in Section 1, widespread unionization occurred under President Cárdenas, and workers won many rights that had been promised in the constitution of 1917. Cárdenas organized the unions into the National Confederation of Workers, the CTM, which became the most powerful official voice of organized labor within the PRI. The policy changes initiated in the 1940s, however, made the unions more dependent on the government for benefits and protection; the government also limited the right to strike. Wage standards were set through active annual negotiation between the CTM and the government, with employer groups largely sitting on the sidelines. Despite the fact that unions were closely controlled, organized workers continued to be an elite within the country's working classes. Union membership meant job security and important benefits such as housing subsidies and health care for families. These factors helped compensate for the lack of democracy within the labor movement. Moreover, labor leaders had privileged access to the country's political leadership and benefited personally from their control over jobs, contracts, and working conditions. In return, they guaranteed labor peace.[5]

In agriculture, those who benefited from government policies and services were primarily farmers who had enough land and economic resources to irrigate and mechanize and who had the capacity to make technological improvements in their farming methods and crops. By the 1950s a group of large, commercially oriented farmers had emerged to dominate the agricultural economy.[6] They, like their urban counterparts in business, became rich and powerful. Industrialization also created a powerful class of government officials. Many abused their power to dispense jobs, licenses, and permits for a variety of activities, public works projects, and government investments by selling such favors in return for *mordidas* (bites, or bribes) or political support. They also became firm supporters of the continuation of government policies that provided them with special advantages.

There were significant costs to this pattern of economic and political development. Most important, government policies eventually limited the potential for further growth.[7] Industrialists who received extensive subsidies and benefits from government had few incentives to produce efficiently. High tariffs kept out foreign competition, further reducing incentives for efficiency or quality in production. Importing technology to support industrialization eventually became a drain on the country's foreign exchange. In addition, the costs of providing benefits to workers increased beyond the capacity of the government to generate revenue, especially because tax rates were kept extremely low as a further incentive to investors. Mexico's tax rates, in fact, were among the lowest in the world, and opportunities to avoid payment were extensive. Eventually, the ISI strategy became less effective in generating new jobs as industrialists moved from investing in labor-intensive industries such as processed foods and textiles to capital-intensive industries such as automobiles, refrigerators, and heavy equipment. As a result, cities began to fill up with underemployed and unemployed workers.

Moreover, as the economy grew, and with it the power of industrial, agricultural, and urban interests, many were left behind. The ranks of the urban poor grew steadily, particularly from the 1960s on. Mexico developed a sizable **informal sector**—workers who produced or sold goods and services at the margin of the economic system and who faced extreme insecurity. By 1970 a large proportion of Mexico City's population was living in inner-city tenements or squatter settlements surrounding the city.[8]

Also left behind in the country's development after 1940 were the country's peasant farmers. Their lands were often the least fertile, plot sizes were minuscule, and access to markets was impeded by poor transportation and exploitive middlemen who trucked products to markets for exorbitant fees. The 1940s and 1950s were important years for increasing the gap between commercial agriculture, largely centered in the north and northwestern regions of the country, where much of Mexico's political elite originated, and subsistence agriculture, largely made up of small private farmers and *ejidatarios* who lived in central and southern parts of the country. Farming in the *ejido* communities, where land was held communally, was particularly difficult. Because *ejido* land could not be sold or (until the early 1980s) rented, *ejidatarios* could not borrow money from private banks because they had nothing to pledge as collateral if they defaulted on their payments. Government banks provided credit, but usually only to those who had political connections. The government invested little in small infrastructure projects throughout the 1960s, and because the *ejidatarios* did not have individual title to their land, they had little incentive to provide their own infrastructure. Agricultural research and extension focused on the large-farm sector. Since prices for basic foodstuffs were controlled, the *ejidos* saw little advantage to investing in farming. Not surprisingly, the *ejido* sector consistently reported low productivity.

Increasing disparities in rural and urban incomes, coupled with high population growth rates, contributed to the emergence of rural guerrilla movements and student protests in the mid- and late 1960s. The government was particularly alarmed in 1968, when a student movement openly challenged the government on the eve of the Olympic games being hosted by Mexico City. Moreover, by the early 1970s, it was becoming evident that the size of the population, growing at a rate of some 3.5 percent a year, and the structure of income distribution were impeding further industrial development. The domestic market was limited by poverty; many Mexicans could not afford the sophisticated manufactured products the country would need to produce in order to keep growing under the import substitution model.

Mexican governments hoped that industrialization would free the economy from excessive dependence on the industrialized world, and particularly on the United States, making the country less subject to abrupt swings in the prices for primary commodities. Industrialization, however, highlighted new vulnerabilities. Advanced manufacturing processes required ever more foreign investment and imported technology. Concern grew about powerful multinational companies, which had invested heavily in the country in the 1960s, and so did the need to spend scarce foreign exchange for foreign technology. By the late 1960s the country was unable to meet domestic demand for basic foodstuffs and was forced to import increasingly large quantities of food, costing the government precious foreign exchange that it could have used for better purposes. By the 1970s some policymakers had become convinced that industrialization had actually *increased* the country's dependence on advanced industrial countries and particularly on the United States.

Sowing the Oil and Reaping a Crisis

In the early 1970s, Mexico faced the threat of social crisis brought on by rural poverty, chaotic urbanization, high population growth, and the questioning of political legitimacy. The government responded by increasing investment in infrastructure and public industry, regulating the flow of foreign capital, and increasing social spending. The government was spending much more than it generated, causing the public internal debt to grow rapidly and requiring heavy borrowing abroad. Between 1971 and 1976 inflation rose from an annual average of 5.3 percent to almost 16 percent and the foreign debt more than tripled. In response to mounting evidence that current policies could not be sustained, the government devalued the peso in 1976 and signed a stabilization agreement with the International Monetary Fund (IMF) to reduce government spending, increase tax collection, and control inflation. Little progress was made in changing the existing set of policies, however, because just as the seriousness of the economic situation was being recognized, vast new finds of oil were reported.

Between 1978 and 1982, Mexico was transformed into a major oil exporter. As international oil prices rose rapidly—from US$13.30 per barrel in 1978 to $33.20 per barrel in 1981—so did the country's fortunes, along with those of other oil-rich countries such as Nigeria, Iran, Indonesia, and Venezuela. The administration of President José López Portillo

(1976–1982) embarked on a policy to "sow the oil" in the economy and "administer the abundance," with vast investment projects in virtually all sectors and major new initiatives to reduce poverty and deal with declining agricultural productivity. Oil revenues paid for much of this expansion, but the foreign debt also mounted as both public and private sectors borrowed heavily to finance investments and lavish consumer spending. Mexico, like many other countries, was able to borrow extensively because international financial markets were flush with so-called **petrodollars**, money not only generated but also anticipated by the oil boom.

In 1982, Mexico's foreign debt was US$86 billion and the exchange rate was seriously overvalued, making the peso and Mexican products more expensive on the world market. Oil accounted for 77.2 percent of the country's exports, causing the economy to be extremely vulnerable to changes in oil prices. And change they did. In 1983 global overproduction brought the international price for Mexican petroleum down to $26.3 a barrel. Revenues from exports declined dramatically. At the same time, the United States tightened its monetary policy, and access to foreign credit dried up. Wealthy Mexicans responded by sending vast amounts of capital out of the country just as the country's international creditors were demanding repayment on their loans. In August 1982 the government announced that the country could not pay the interest on its foreign debt, triggering a crisis that reverberated around the world.

The impact of these conditions on the Mexican economy was devastating. GDP growth in 1982 was −0.6 percent and fell to −4.2 percent the following year. New policy measures were put in place by the administration of Miguel de la Madrid (1982–1988) to deal with the economic crisis, but they were repeatedly overtaken by escalating inflation, financial-sector panic, depleted foreign reserves, severe trade imbalances, and debt renegotiations. In 1986 petroleum prices dropped to $12 a barrel.

The economic crisis had several important implications for structures of power and privilege in Mexico. First, faith in the import substitution policy was destroyed. The crisis convinced even the most diehard believer that import substitution created inefficiencies in production, failed to generate sufficient

employment, cost the government far too much in subsidies, and increased dependency on industrialized countries. By the mid-1980s, few policymakers or informed citizens argued strongly for the traditional highly interventionist state or for its protectionist and social welfare role.

In addition, the power of interest groups and their ability to influence government policy declined. Prolonged economic crisis hit the business sector particularly hard. When the economy stagnated, declined, and failed to recover rapidly, private debts could not be repaid, inflation and unemployment reduced demand, government subsidies were repeatedly cut back, and most public investment plans were put on hold. The inevitable result was the failure of many Mexican companies. Bankruptcy and recession exacted their toll on the fortunes of even large entrepreneurs. As economic hardship affected their members, traditional business organizations lost their ability to put strong pressure on the government.

Similarly, the country's relatively privileged unions lost much of their bargaining power with government over the issues of wages and protection. Union leaders emphasized the need for peace and order to help the nation get through tough times, while inflation and job loss focused many of the country's workers on putting food on the table. A shift in employment from the formal to the informal sector further fragmented what had once been the most powerful sector of the PRI. Cuts in government subsidies for public transportation, food, electricity, and gasoline created new hardships for workers. The combination of these factors weakened the capacity of labor to resist policy changes that affected the benefits they received.

New voices emerged to demand that the government alter its policies. During the recession years of the 1980s, wages lost between 40 and 50 percent of their value, increasingly large numbers of people became unemployed, inflation cut deeply into middle-class incomes, and budgets for health and education services were severely cut back. Mexico's citizens demanded that the government do something to address the hardship. During the 1980s a wide variety of interests began to organize outside the PRI. Massive earthquakes in Mexico City in September 1985 proved to be a watershed for Mexican society. Severely disappointed by the government's failure to respond to the problems created by death, destruction, disorientation, and homelessness, hundreds of communities organized rescue efforts, soup kitchens, shelter, and rehabilitation initiatives. A surging sense of political empowerment developed, as groups long accustomed to dependence on government learned that they could solve their problems better without government than with it.[9]

In addition, the PRI was challenged by the increased popularity of opposition political parties, one of them headed by Cuauhtémoc Cárdenas, the son of the country's most revered president, Lázaro Cárdenas. The elections of 1988 became a focus for protest against the economic dislocation caused by the crisis and the political powerlessness that most citizens felt. Carlos Salinas, the PRI candidate, received a bare majority of 50.7 percent, but opposition parties claimed widespread electoral fraud.

New Strategies and Emerging Democratic Institutions

Demands on the Salinas administration to deal with the economic and political crisis were extensive. At the same time, the weakening of the old centers of political power provided it with a major opportunity to reorient the country's strategy for economic development. The government took advantage of this opportunity. Between 1988 and 1994, the dependent relationship between industry and government was weakened when new free-market policies were put in place. Decreasing regulation was an important part of this restructuring of state-economy relationships. Deregulation gave the private sector more freedom to pursue economic activities and less reason to seek special favors from government. A number of large government industries, such as the telephone company, the banking sector, the national airlines, and steel and sugar mills, were reorganized and sold to private investors. A constitutional revision made it possible for *ejidatarios* to become owners of individual plots of land; this made them less dependent on government but more vulnerable to losing their land. In addition, financial-sector reform, such as changing laws about banking and establishing a stock exchange, encouraged the emergence of new banks and brokerage and insurance firms.

Salinas pursued, and Zedillo continued, an overhaul of the federal system and the way government agencies work together. Called the New Federalism, it is an attempt to give power and budgetary responsibilities to state and local governments, which are historically very weak in Mexico. Beginning with pilot programs in education and health, the presidents hoped through this decentralization to make government more responsive to citizens and more effective. In addition, federal agencies began to be broken down into regional bureaus, which work more closely with lower levels of government. In the past, nearly all important government functions were carried out by federal government offices located in Mexico City. Additionally, the central bank became independent from the government in 1994, though exchange rates are still determined by the Finance Ministry.

Among the most far-reaching initiatives carried out by the Salinas administration was the North American Free Trade Agreement (NAFTA) with Canada and the United States. This agreement created the basis for gradual introduction of free trade among the three countries. These changes were a major reversal of import substitution and economic intervention that had marked government policies in the past. However, the liberalization of the Mexican economy and opening up its markets to foreign competition increased the vulnerability of the country to changes in international economic conditions. These factors, as well as mismanaged economic policies, led to a major economic crisis for the country at the end of 1994 and profound recession in 1995. Since then, exports have increased tremendously because of the cheapness of the peso internationally, government finances look steady, and GDP has risen by 5.2 percent in 1996, 7 percent in 1997, and over 4 percent in 1998. Foreign investment has also recuperated, reaching record levels in 1997.[10]

In political matters, a series of electoral reforms culminated in 1996 with the creation of an independent election board composed of private citizens, as well as constitutional amendments regarding campaign fairness. Election funds are mostly public, with private expenditures limited. There are also procedures for auditing the political parties. As mentioned previously, elections have become much more hotly contested.

Leaders: *Carlos Salinas de Gortari*

No other man in the modern era of Mexico has inspired as much hope or hatred as former president Carlos Salinas de Gortari (1988–1994). Born in Mexico City in 1948 to a politically prominent family, he attended the National Autonomous University and later earned a Ph.D. in political economy from Harvard University. During his *sexenio*, Mexico aspired to leave behind the twin phantoms of backwardness and unrealized economic potential to join the ranks of developed nations.

He originally rose to prominence after 1982 during a terrible economic crisis that gave market reformers a chance to control the PRI. Called technocrats for their advanced degrees and detached attitude toward traditional politics, this group began to deregulate the economy and weaken powerful interest groups. At the end of the *sexenio*, the outgoing president, Miguel de la Madrid, thought that Minister of Budgeting and Planning Salinas would be the most likely to continue these changes. He appointed him the PRI's candidate for president.

But years of crisis had left the country tired and bitter, and the presidential race was tight. The PRI emerged from a mysterious computer failure on election night with a tight victory. The popular opposition candidate, Cuauhtémoc Cárdenas, claimed that only blatant fraud had prevented him from winning, and many observers agreed.

But once he became president, Salinas worked hard to regain legitimacy. He created a new Ministry for Social Development and implemented a Solidarity program that directed vast resources to infrastructure projects in local communities. Some citizens complained that it was controlled by PRI groups and used for political ends, but most praised the program. Salinas began to talk about the power that Mexico had to take charge of its own development and destiny.

He confronted opponents forcefully, jailing corrupt union bosses and smothering the opposition. His government undertook sweeping administrative reforms and privatized numerous state-owned industries, and the economy began to improve markedly in the early 1990s. He also projected a strong international presence and gained worldwide recognition, promoting his administration's environmental efforts at the Earth Summit in Rio de Janeiro in 1992, for example.

Perhaps most important, he spoke of Mexico as a great nation, ready to take its place at the table of advanced industrial society. New currency was issued, without the "zeros" of past inflation. Instead of three thousand pesos equaling one U.S. dollar, three pesos equaled one dollar. With a strong currency, controlled inflation, and increasing free trade, Mexicans had more purchasing power than ever before. But his greatest project was NAFTA. Salinas promoted a free-trade agreement with the United States more than any other single person, and his negotiations were so successful that Canada decided to join. The culmination of his efforts went into effect on January 1, 1994, the same day that everything began to unravel.

With an uprising in Chiapas, the assassinations of Colosio and Ruiz Massieu, widespread spending by the PRI, rumors of rampant drug mafias, and increasing suspicions falling on him and his associates, Salinas left office. No sooner had he done so than the currency collapsed and the country entered a sudden and sharp state of economic emergency. Overnight, he became a popular villian. Masks of his face, some with diabolical horns, sold on street corners. Shortly thereafter, his brother was found to have millions of dollars in Swiss banks and was indicted in the murder of Ruiz Massieu. After a widely ridiculed hunger strike to protest the accusations against him, Carlos Salinas left the country in unofficial exile. Since then, the PRI itself has declared him an outcast.

However, although he left office at the end of 1994, Salinas continues to cast a long shadow over Mexican politics. Newspaper articles report his activities and movements (first in Ireland, then in Cuba), and speculate on his motives. In response, he says that the future will vindicate him and his policies, and that he would like to return to Mexico.

Society and Economy

Mexico's economic development has had a significant impact on social conditions in the country. Overall, the standard of living has improved markedly since the 1940s. Rates of infant mortality, literacy, and life expectancy have steadily improved. Provision of health and education services expanded until government cutbacks on social expenditures in the early 1980s. Among the most important consequences of economic growth was the development of a large middle class, most of whom live in Mexico's numerous large cities. By the 1980s a third or more of Mexican households could claim a middle-class life-style, that is, steady income, secure food and shelter, access to decent education and health services, a car, some disposable income and savings, and some security that their children would be able to experience happy and healthy lives.

These achievements reflect well on the ability of the economy to increase social well-being in the country. However, the impressive economic growth through the early 1970s and between 1978 and 1982 could have produced greater social progress. In terms of standard indicators of social development—infant mortality, literacy, and life expectancy—Mexico fell behind a number of Latin American countries that grew less rapidly but provided more effectively for their populations. Costa Rica, Colombia, Argentina, Chile, and Uruguay had less overall growth but greater social development in the period after 1940. These countries paid more attention to the distribution of the benefits of growth than did Mexico. Moreover, in its pursuit of rapid industrialization, Mexico City has become one of the most congested and polluted cities in the world. In some rural areas, oil exploitation has left devastating environmental damage, destroying the life-styles and opportunities of *ejidatarios* and small farmers.

Mexico's economic development has also resulted in a widening gap between the wealthy and the poor and among different regions in the country. Although the poor are better off than they were in the early days of the country's drive toward industrialization, they are worse off when compared to middle- and upper-income groups. In 1950 the bottom 40 percent of the country's households accounted for about 14 percent of total personal income, while the top 30 percent had 60 percent of total income.[11] In 1992, it is estimated, the bottom 40 percent accounted for about 11 percent of income, while the top 30 percent shared 69 percent.[12] As in the United States, the rich are growing richer and the poor are growing poorer.

Among the poorest are those in rural areas who have little or no access to productive land and those in urban areas who do not have steady jobs. Harsh conditions in the countryside have fueled a half-century of migration to the cities. Nevertheless, some 23 million Mexicans continue to live in rural areas, many of them in deep poverty. Many of them work for substandard wages and migrate seasonally to search for jobs in order to sustain their families. Traditionally, those who crossed the border to the United States, legally and illegally, in search of jobs came from depressed rural areas. Increasingly, however, they come from urban areas.

Among those rural inhabitants with access to land, almost half have five hectares (1 hectare = 2.471 acres) or less. Almost all of this land is unirrigated and dependent on erratic rainfall. The land is often bleached of nutrients as a result of centuries of cultivation, population pressure, and erosion. Many families have land that is insufficient to provide even for their subsistence. The crops grown on such farms, primarily corn and beans, are poor people's crops and do not bring high prices in the markets. To improve production, peasant farmers would have to buy fertilizer, improved seeds, and insecticides, and they would have to find ways to irrigate their plots. But they generally have no money to purchase these supplies or invest in irrigation. In many areas, farm production provides as few as twenty to one hundred days of employment each year. Not surprisingly, underemployment is high in rural Mexico, as are rates of seasonal migration. It is also not surprising to learn that the incidence of disease, malnutrition, and illiteracy is much higher in Mexico's rural areas than in urban areas. When the rebels in Chiapas called for jobs, land, education, and health facilities, they were clearly reflecting the realities of life in much of the country.

Poverty has a regional dimension in Mexico. The northern areas of the country are significantly better off than the southern and central areas. Much of the regional distribution of poverty is related to conditions

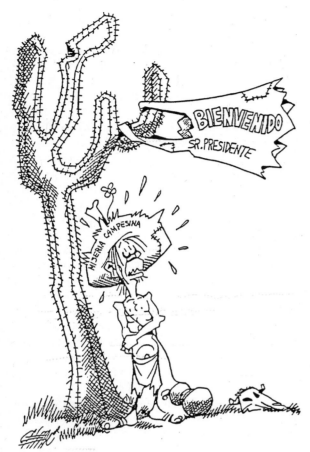

A farmer with a hat labeled "rural misery" hangs his overalls on a cactus: "Welcome, Mr. President." Among those who have benefited least from the government's development policies are the rural poor. *Source: Ausencias y Presencias Gente de Ayer y Hoy en su Tinta: Problematica Politica, Social, Vista por un Cartoonista Potosino* by Luis Chessal, Unversidad Autonoma de San Luis Potosi, Mexico, 1984.

in the agricultural sector. In the north, large commercial farms grow fruits, vegetables, and grains for export using modern technologies. The U.S. border, the principal destination of agricultural products, is close at hand, and transportation networks are extensive and generally in good condition. Moreover, industrial cities such as Monterrey and Tijuana provide steady jobs for skilled and unskilled labor. Along the border, a rapidly growing band of manufac-turing and assembly plants, called *maquiladoras*, has provided numerous jobs, particularly for young women who are seeking some escape from the burdens of rural life or the constraints of traditional family life.

In the southern and central regions of the country, however, the population is denser, the land poorer, and the number of *ejidatarios* eking out subsistence is greater. Transportation is often difficult, and during parts of the year, some areas may even be inaccessible because of heavy rains and flooding. In addition, most of Mexico's remaining indigenous groups live in the southern regions, often in very remote areas where they have been forgotten by government programs and exploited by regional bosses for generations. The conditions that spurred the Chiapas rebellion are found throughout the southern states.

The economic crisis of the 1980s had an impact on social conditions in the country. Wages declined by about half and unemployment soared as businesses collapsed and the government laid off workers in public offices. The informal sector expanded rapidly. Here, people eke out a living by hawking chewing gum, umbrellas, sponges, candy, shoelaces, mirrors, and a variety of other items in the street, jumping in front of cars at stoplights to wash windshields and sell newspapers, producing and repairing cheap consumer goods such as shoes and clothing, and selling services on a daily or hourly basis. While the informal sector provides important goods and services, conditions of work are often dangerous and insecurity about where the next peso will come from is endemic.

The economic crisis of the 1980s also reduced the quality and availability of social services. Expenditures on education and health declined after 1982 as the government imposed austerity measures. Salaries of primary school teachers declined by 34 percent between 1983 and 1988, and many worked second and even third jobs in order to make ends meet. Per capita health expenditures declined from a high of about 150 pesos in 1980 to under 90 pesos in 1990. Hospitals, clinics, and schools were left in dis-repair, and obtaining equipment and supplies became almost impossible. Although indicators of mortality did not rise during this troubled decade, the incidence of diseases associated with poverty—malnutrition, cholera, anemia, and dysentery—increased. The diet of most Mexicans became less rich in protein as they ate less meat and drank less milk. The crisis began to ease in the early 1990s, however, and many came to believe that conditions would improve for the poor. The government began investing in social services. Then, in late 1994, a new economic crisis emerged, marking 1995 with rapidly rising levels of unemployment and austerity measures that severely limited investments.

Although macroeconomic indicators have rebounded since then and large businesses look to grow, wages remain low for the majority of workers while taxes have increased. Subsidies on basic goods like tortillas, water, and gas have been lowered or eliminated, making the cost of living rise steeply for the poor and the working class.

Mexico and the International Political Economy

The crisis that began in 1982 clearly indicated that a policy of encouraging more Mexican exports and opening markets to foreign goods was essential. In the years after 1982 the government relaxed restrictions on the ability of foreigners to own property, reduced and eliminated tariffs, and did away with most of the import licenses. Foreign investment was courted in the hope of increasing the manufacture of goods for export. The government also introduced a series of incentives to encourage the private sector to produce goods for export. In 1986, Mexico joined the General Agreement on Tariffs and Trade (GATT), a multilateral agreement that attempts to promote freer trade among countries.

The government's effort to pursue a more outward-oriented development strategy culminated in the ratification of NAFTA in 1993, with gradual implementation beginning on January 1, 1994. This agreement is important to Mexico. In 1996, 83.9 percent of the country's exports were sent to the United States and 75.5 percent of its imports came from that country. The next most active trading country with Mexico was Japan, which received only 1.7 percent of its exports and accounted for only 4.6 percent of its imports.[13] Access to the U.S. market is thus essential to Mexico and to domestic and foreign investors. NAFTA

signaled a new period in U.S.-Mexican relations by making closer integration of the two economies a certainty. To date, trade between Mexico, Canada, and the United States has increased along with foreign direct investment.

Additionally, NAFTA contains two "parallel agreements" regarding the environment and labor that were negotiated in order to pass the treaty in the U.S. Congress. These documents created trinational institutions to cooperate and mediate on these issues to prevent potentially damaging side effects from the free trade. They have not been terribly active, however, and it is unknown what positive effect, if any, they are having.

NAFTA also entails risks for Mexico. Domestic producers worry about competition from U.S. firms. Farmers worry that Mexican crops cannot compete effectively with those grown in the United States; for example, peasant producers of corn and beans have been hard hit by lower-priced U.S.-grown grains. In addition, many people believe that embracing free trade with Canada and the United States indicated a loss of sovereignty and that Mexico's economic situation would now be much more vulnerable to the ebb and flow of economic conditions in the U.S. economy.

The incorporation of Mexico into NAFTA introduced novelties in economic and political relationships. During negotiations, new international political alliances developed. Environmental groups from the United States sought support in Mexico and Canada for fighting the agreement, and labor groups also looked across both borders for allies in opposing new trade relations. Environmental and labor groups united around concerns that Mexico would not enforce environmental protection and fair labor legislation. Some business interests allied across countries in supporting the agreement, anticipating opportunities for larger markets, cheaper labor, or richer sources of raw materials. For Mexico, which has traditionally feared the power of the United States in its domestic affairs, internationalization of political and economic relationships poses particularly difficult problems of adjustment.

On the other hand, the United States, newly aware of the importance of the Mexican economy to its own economic growth and concerned about instability on its southern border, hammered together a US$50 billion economic assistance program composed of U.S., European, and IMF commitments to support its neighbor when crisis struck in 1994. The Mexican government imposed a new stabilization package that contained austerity measures, higher interest rates, and limits on wages. By 1998, Mexico had remarkably paid off all of its obligations to the United States. When a similar crisis affected the economies of many Asian countries in 1997 and then spread throughout the globe, Mexico may have been partly shielded by its close relationship with the U.S. economy, which was enjoying a period of peak performance.

Socially, the expansion of modern means of communication has stripped Mexico of some of the secrecy that traditionally surrounded government decision-making, electoral processes, and efforts to deal with political dissent. More than before, the 1980s and 1990s focused international attention on the country. The Internet and e-mail, along with lower international telephone rates, have all played strong roles in increasing information flow across borders. The government could no longer respond to events such as the peasant rebellion in Chiapas, alleged electoral fraud, or the management of exchange rates without considering how such actions would be perceived in Tokyo, Frankfurt, Ottawa, London, or Washington.

Section ❸ Governance and Policy-Making

Mexico is a federal republic, though the state and local governments have held few resources and a limited sphere of action when compared with the national level. The nation's government can be characterized as a strong presidential system. Historically, the executive branch was the only true operative branch of government, while the legislative and judiciary followed the executive's lead and were considered "rubber stamp" bodies. Like Japan, India, and Sweden at different moments, Mexico has had a predominant party, the PRI, in power for an extended period of time. Though it has always been nominally democratic, Mexico has often been characterized as authoritarian and corporatist. Interestingly enough, all of these characterizations have been changing since the end of the 1980s, with great efforts being made by the government and civil society to reinvigorate the nation's laws and institutions and make the country fully democratic in practice.

Organization of the State

According to the supreme law of the land, the constitution of 1917, Mexico's political institutions resemble those of the United States. There are three branches of government, and a set of checks and balances limits the power of each. The congress is composed of the Senate and the Chamber of Deputies. One hundred twenty-eight senators are elected, four from each of the country's thirty-one states and an additional four from the federal district (capital). Five hundred deputies are elected from 300 electoral districts, 300 by simple majority vote and 200 by proportional representation. States and local governments are also elected. The president, governors, and senators are elected for six years, and deputies and municipal officials are elected for three.

In practice, the Mexican system is very different from that of the United States. The constitution is a very long document that is easily amended, especially when compared to that of the United States. It lays out the structure of government and guarantees a wide range of human rights, including familiar ones such as freedom of speech and protection of the law, but also economic and social rights such as the right to a job and the right to health care. The political system is highly centralized and presidentialist. It is making a series of pragmatic adjustments to pressures for greater democracy and electoral honesty, but it still has a way to go before it is fully democratic. Its policy-making processes are also very distinct from those in the United States, even though the constitutional arrangement of powers is superficially similar.

The Executive

The President and the Cabinet

"The political sun rises and sets every six years on the presidency."[14] This statement by an observer of

Mexican politics suggests the importance of the presidency to the political system. In residence at Los Pinos, the Mexican presidency is the central institution in a centralized system of governance and policy-making. In the past, the incumbent president always selected who would run as the PRI's next presidential candidate, appointed officials to all positions of power in the government and the PRI, and often named the PRI candidates, who almost automatically won elections as governors, senators, deputies, and local officials. The president continues to set the broad outlines of policy for the administration and has numerous resources to ensure that those policy preferences are adopted. Until the mid-1970s, Mexican presidents were considered above criticism in national politics and revered as symbols of national progress and well-being. While economic and political events of the 1980s and 1990s diminished presidential prestige, the extent of presidential power remains impressive.

Mexican presidents have a set of formal powers that allows them to initiate legislation, lead in foreign policy, create government agencies, make policy by decree or through administrative regulations and procedures, and appoint a wide range of public officials. More important, informal powers provide them with the capacity to centralize control in the executive. As head of the PRI, the president manages a vast patronage machine for filling positions at all levels of government and the party, and initiates legislation and policies that were, until recently, routinely approved by the congress.

To date, the PRI presidential candidate has always been male and almost always a member of the outgoing president's cabinet. In past years, several had been Minister of the Interior, the person responsible for maintaining law and order. This was true of Miguel Alemán (1946–1952), Adolfo Ruiz Cortines (1952–1958), Gustavo Díaz Ordaz (1964–1970), and Luis Echeverría (1970–1976). With the expansion of the government's role in economic development, candidates in the 1970s and 1980s were selected from the ministries that manage the economy. José López Portillo (1976–1982) had been Minister of Finance, and Miguel de la Madrid (1982–1988) and Carlos Salinas (1988–1994) had served as Minister of Budgeting and Planning. The selection of Luis Donaldo Colosio, who had been Minister of Social Development and Welfare, was thought by political observers to signal renewed concern with problems of social development. When Colosio was assassinated, the selection of Ernesto Zedillo, who had first been Minister of Budgeting and Planning and then Minister of Education, was interpreted as an ongoing concern with social problems of the country and as an effort to maintain the policies of economic liberalization that Salinas had introduced.

Candidates since the mid-1970s have spent more of their careers in Mexico City and have tended to be trained in economics and public management rather than in the traditional field of law. Presidents since López Portillo have had postgraduate training at elite institutions in the United States. Miguel de la Madrid held a master's degree in public administration from Harvard; Carlos Salinas received a Ph.D. degree in political economy and government from Harvard; Luis Colosio studied for a Ph.D. degree in economics from the University of Pennsylvania; and Ernesto Zedillo had a Ph.D. degree in economics from Yale. Some have argued that because of their urban and elite backgrounds recent presidents have lost touch not only with the masses but also with the traditional politicians of the PRI, who have their roots in regional, labor, or rural politics. By the 1980s a topic of great debate in political circles was the extent to which a divide between *políticos* and *técnicos* (technocrats) had emerged within the national political elite. Among the old guard of the PRI, there was open skepticism about the ability of young technocrats like Carlos Salinas and Ernesto Zedillo to manage political conditions in the country. During the presidential campaign of 1994, considerable efforts were made to stress the more humble beginnings of Colosio and Zedillo and the fact that they had had to work hard to get an education.

Once elected, the president moves quickly to name a cabinet. Generally, he selects as his closest advisers those with whom he has worked over the years as he has risen to political prominence. He may also use cabinet posts to make certain he has a broad coalition of support; in this regard, he may appoint people with close ties to the labor movement, or to business interests, or to some of the regional strongholds of the party. Only in rare exceptions have they not been active members of the PRI. Few women have been selected for ministry-level posts—there are a handful of examples in recent administrations—and thus far only in those agencies that have limited influence over decision-making, like Tourism, Ecology, and Foreign Relations.

The president fills numerous high-level positions, which allows him to provide policy direction and keep tabs on what is occurring throughout the government and the party. The president uses his appointment power to build a team of like-minded officials in the government and ensure their loyalty to him. In turn, high-level appointees fill many jobs in their organizations. Like the president, they use this patronage power to put together personally loyal teams of officials whose career advancement is tied to their own political fate. These officials, in turn, build their own teams, and so on down through middle levels in the bureaucracy.

The beginning of each administration is therefore characterized by extensive turnover of positions, although many of the newly appointed officials served in other positions in prior administrations. This giant patronage system has the potential to be extremely inefficient. Indeed, little happens in government in the year prior to an election as officials bide their time or jockey for positions in the next administration, or in the year following an election as newly appointed officials learn the ropes and assemble their teams. Nevertheless, when a president has set clear goals and expects high performance from his personally chosen officials, these people in turn must expect good performance from their staffs if they are to produce for the president. In many situations, then, the patronage system results in the potential for increased presidential leadership and effective performance, at least at high levels in government. Many middle- and high-level officials hope that their performance will be noticed by their minister, especially if that person has the potential to be selected as the PRI's presidential candidate. If this should happen, they could expect to be appointed to a higher-level office in the next administration. This system, however, assumes that the PRI will continue to win elections.

Mexican presidents, though powerful, are not omnipotent. They, must, for example, abide by a deeply held constitutional norm—fully adhered to since 1940— to step down at the end of their term, and they must honor the political norm to step out of the political limelight to allow the successor to assume full presidential leadership. In addition, several factors tend to limit the extent of presidential discretion. Mexican presidents in the past have always been "creatures of the system," selected because they have proved themselves adept at understanding and playing by the existing rules. Through their careers in politics or government, they became familiar with the range of interest groups in the country and demonstrated a willingness to compromise on policy and political issues so that these interests would not unduly challenge the government. They also proved themselves to be skillful in the fierce bureaucratic politics that surround career advancement and in guessing about who the next PRI candidate for president was likely to be. In addition, presidents must demonstrate their loyalty to the myths and symbols of Mexican nationalism, such as the indigenous roots of much of its culture, the agrarian origins of the revolution, commitment to social justice, and sovereignty in international affairs. If, in the future, Mexico should elect a president who is not from the PRI, an important question will be whether these traditions will continue to hold true.

In the 1990s, President Zedillo relinquished a number of the traditional powers of the presidency, favoring instead a larger role for checks and balances in government. He announced, for example, that he would not select his PRI successor. In doing so, however, he created considerable conflict and tension as other institutions had to take on unaccustomed roles and as politicians sought to fill the void left by the "abandonment" of presidential power.

The Bureaucracy

Mexico's executive branch is large and powerful. Almost a million and a half people work in the federal bureaucracy, most of them in Mexico City. An additional million work in the national education system, and yet another million work for the large number of state-owned industries and semiautonomous agencies of the government. State and local governments employ over 600,000 people. Pay scales are usually low, and in the past the number of people filling lower-level positions such as drivers and messengers and clerical and maintenance jobs far exceeded the demand for them. In the 1980s austerity measures cut down on some of this overstaffing.

Officials at lower levels in the bureaucracy are unionized and protected by legislation that gives them job security and a range of benefits. At middle and upper levels, most officials are called confidence employees; that is, they serve as long as their bosses have confidence in them. These are the officials who are personally appointed by their superiors at the outset of an administration. Their modest salaries are compensated for by the prospect of career mobility and by the significant power that they can have over public events. For aspiring young professionals, a career in government is often attractive because of the challenge of dealing with important problems on a daily basis and being part of the process of finding solutions. Some employees also benefit from opportunities to take bribes or use insider information to promote private business deals.

The Para-Statal Sector

The **para-statal sector**—composed of semiautonomous or autonomous government agencies, many of which produce goods and services—has been extremely large and powerful in Mexico. Because the government provided significant support for the development of the economy as part of its post-1940 development strategy, it engaged in numerous activities that in other countries are carried out by the private sector. Thus, until the Salinas administration (1988–1994), the country's largest steel mill was state-owned, as were the largest fertilizer producer, sugar mills, and airlines. In addition, the national electricity board still produces energy and supplies at subsidized prices to industries. The petroleum company, PEMEX, grew to enormous proportions in the 1970s and 1980s under the impact of the oil boom. NAFIN, a state investment corporation, provides a significant percentage of all investment capital in the country. At one point, a state marketing board called CONASUPO was responsible for the importation and purchase of the country's supply of basic staples, and in the 1970s it played a major role in distributing food, credit, and farm implements in rural areas.

The para-statal sector was significantly trimmed by the economic policy reforms of the 1980s and 1990s. In 1970 there were 391 para-statal organizations in Mexico. By 1982 their number had grown to 1155, in part because of the expansion of government activities under presidents Echeverría and López Portillo and in part because of the nationalization of private banks in 1982. In the 1980s and 1990s concerted efforts were made to privatize many of these industries, including the telephone company, the national airline, and the nationalized banks. By 1994 only 215 state-owned industries remained and efforts continued to sell or liquidate many of them.

Other State Institutions

The Military

Mexico is one of only a few countries in the developing world that have successfully depoliticized the military. Much of the credit for this process belongs to Plutarco Calles, Lázaro Cárdenas, and subsequent presidents who introduced the rotation of regional commands so that generals could not build up regional bases of power. In addition, postrevolutionary leaders made an implicit bargain with the military leaders by providing them with opportunities to engage in business so that they did not look to political power as a way of gaining economic power. After 1946 the military no longer had institutional representation within the PRI and became marginalized from the centers of power.

The military has been called in from time to time to deal with domestic unrest—in rural areas in the 1960s, in Mexico City and other cities to repress student protest movements in 1968, in 1988 in the arrest of a powerful labor leader, in 1989 to break a labor strike, in 1990 to deal with protest over electoral fraud, in Chiapas beginning in late 1994, and to manage the Mexico City police in 1997. The military was also called in to deal with the aftermath of the earthquake in Mexico City in 1985, but its inadequate response to the emergency did little to enhance its reputation in the eyes of the public. In recent years, the military has been heavily involved in efforts to combat drug trafficking, and rumors abound about deals struck between military officials and drug barons. Such fears were confirmed when General Jesus Gutierrez Rebollo, the head of the anti-drug task force, was arrested in February 1997 on accusations of protecting a drug lord.

Whenever the military is called in to resolve domestic conflicts, some Mexicans become concerned that the institution is becoming politicized and may come to play a larger role in political decision-making. From time to time, rumors of preparations for a coup are heard, as during financial panics in the 1980s and in the aftermath of Colosio's assassination. Thus far, such fears have not been realized, and many believe that as long as civilian administrations are able to maintain the country's tradition of stability, the military will not intervene directly in politics.

The Judiciary

Unlike Anglo-American law systems, Mexico's law derives from the Roman/Napoleonic tradition and is highly formalized and explicit. The constitution of 1917 is a lengthy document that has been amended many times and contains references to a wide range of civil rights, including, for example, items as broad as the right to a healthy environment. Regulatory agencies can also create rules and regulations regarding material under their jurisdiction; this is considered administrative law. Because Mexican law tends to be explicit and definable, and because there are no punitive damages, there are few lawsuits. One important exception to this is the *amparo*, whereby citizens may ask for a writ of protection claiming that their constitutional rights have been violated by specific government actions or laws. Each citizen who wants an *amparo* must present a separate case.

There are federal and state courts in Mexico. The federal system is composed of the Supreme Court, which decides the most important cases in the country; circuit courts, which take cases on appeal; and district courts, which is where all cases enter the system. Supreme Court justices are nominated by the president and approved by the Senate. Since most of the important laws in Mexico are federal, state courts have played a subordinate role. However, this is changing. As Mexican states become more independent from the federal government, state law has been experiencing tremendous growth. In addition, there are many important specialized federal courts, such as labor courts, military courts, and electoral courts.

Like other political institutions in Mexico, the judiciary was for many decades politically, though not constitutionally, subordinate in the presidential system. The courts occasionally slowed the actions of government by issuing *amparos*; however, in almost every case in which the power of government or the president was at stake, the courts ruled on the side of the government. The administration of Ernesto Zedillo has tried to change this by emphasizing the rule of law over that of powerful individuals. Increasing interest in human rights issues by citizens' groups and the media has added pressure to the courts to play a stronger role in protecting basic freedoms. Citizens and the government are increasingly resorting to the courts as a primary weapon against sticky problems like corruption and police abuse. President Zedillo's refusal to interfere with the courts' judgments has also strengthened the judiciary.

Subnational Government

As with many other aspects of the Mexican political system, regional and local government in Mexico is quite different from what is described in the constitution. Mexico has a federal system, and each state has its own constitution, executive, unicameral legislature, and judiciary. Municipalities (equivalent to U.S. counties) are governed by popularly elected mayors and councils. But state and municipal governments are poor and are subordinate to Mexico City economically and politically. Most of the funds they command are transferred to them from the central government, and they have little legal or administrative capacity to raise their own revenue.

States and localities suffer greatly from the lack of well-trained and well-paid public officials. As at the national level, many jobs are distributed as political patronage, but even officials who are motivated to be responsive to local needs are generally ill-equipped to do so. Several presidents have sought to decentralize public-sector activities to the state level, but most such initiatives have sought to decentralize central government functions rather than delegate powers to subordinate levels of government. For example, in the early 1970s regional headquarters of the national Ministry of Agriculture were established in the states rather than improving the capacities and responsibilities of the state-level ministries of agriculture. A similar effort to decentralize the Ministry of Health was undertaken in the early 1980s. In a break with this tradition, the Salinas administration delegated powers over education to state ministries of education. Interestingly, many governors resisted this initiative because it meant that they would have to deal with the powerful teachers' union and because they lacked the administrative capacity to handle such a large and complex responsibility. They were also worried that they would be unable to acquire the budgetary resources necessary to carry out their new responsibilities.

There are exceptions to this picture of regional and local government impoverishment and lack of capacity. State governments in the north of the country, such as Nuevo Leon, have been more responsive to local needs and better able to administer public services. In such states, local municipalities have become famous for the extent to which they differ from the norm in most of Mexico. Monterrey, in Nuevo Leon, for example, has a reputation for efficient and forward-looking city government. Much of this local capacity can be credited to a regional political tradition that has stressed independence from—and even hostility to—Mexico City and the PRI. In these cases entrepreneurial groups and private citizens have often invested time and resources in local government.

Until 1988 all governors were from the PRI, although many believe that only electoral fraud kept two governorships out of the hands of an opposition party in 1986. Finally, in 1989, a non-PRI governor assumed power in Baja California Norte—an important first. As of February 1999 opposition parties had won seven more gubernatorial elections, some in large and important states. Also, municipalities have increasingly been the focus of authentic party competition. As opposition parties came to control these levels of government, they were challenged to improve services such as police protection, garbage collection, sanitation, and education. PRI-dominated governments have also tried to improve their performance because they are threatened by the possibility of losing elections.

The Policy-Making Process

The Mexican system is enormously dependent on the quality of its leadership and presidential understanding of how economic and social policies can affect the development of the country. As indicated throughout this chapter, the *sexenio* is an extremely important fact of political life in Mexico. New presidents introduce extensive change in positions within the government and the PRI. They are able to bring in "their" people who, in turn, build teams of "their" people within ministries, agencies, and party networks. This generally provides the president with a group of high- and middle-level officials who share a general orientation toward public policy and who are highly motivated to carry out his goals. They also believe that, in doing so, they enhance their chances for upward political mobility. In such a context, it is likely for changes in public policies to be introduced every six years, creating innovation, discontinuity, or both.

Policy initiative is routinely taken by the central ministries in direct response to the president's policy priorities. Ministries headed by the most likely presidential candidates and staffed by people closest to the president are the ones that respond with greatest zeal to the president's lead. Ministries awarded to groups or interests that are important to the PRI's coalition may be more resistant to presidential preferences that might have negative consequences for those interests.

Once the newly appointed officials are in office, the president is in a position to set and carry out important policy measures. Together with the bureaucracy, the president is the focal point of policy formulation and political management. Until 1997 the legislature always had a PRI majority and acted as a "rubber stamp" body on presidentially sponsored legislation. Since then, the congress has proven to be a more active policymaker, blocking legislation, forcing its negotiation, and introducing its own bills.

The extent of change is usually limited by the resources the government has and by elite support for such changes. Presidential skills in negotiating, managing the opposition, using the media to acquire public support, and maneuvering within the bureaucracy can be important for ensuring that his program is fully endorsed. Under extraordinary conditions such as the deep and sustained economic and political crisis faced by Carlos Salinas, it is even possible to reverse national development strategies. Ernesto Zedillo's administration was marked by considerable conflict with disaffected elements in the PRI and many questioned the president's political skills and ability to build support for his agenda.

Significant limits on presidential power also occur when policy is being implemented. In fact, in areas as diverse as the regulation of working conditions, antipollution laws, tax collection, election monitoring, and health care in remote rural areas, Mexico has extremely advanced legislation on the books. Yet the persistence of unsafe factory conditions, pollution in Mexico City, tax evasion, election fraud, and poor health care suggests that legislation is not translated into practice. At times, policies are not implemented because public officials at the lower levels disagree with the policies or make deals with affected interests so they can benefit personally. This is the case, for example, with taxes that remain uncollected because individuals or corporations bribe officials to overlook them. In other cases, lower-level officials may lack the capacity or skills to implement some policies, such as those directed toward improving education or rural development services. For whatever reasons, Mexican presidents cannot always deliver on their intentions. Traditionally, they have been above criticism when this has occurred because of the willingness of Mexican citizens to blame lower-level officials for such "slippage." However, exempting the president from responsibility for what does or does not occur during his watch became much less common in the 1980s and 1990s.

Section ④ Representation and Participation

How do citizen interests get represented in Mexican politics, given the high degree of centralization, presidentialism, and, until recently, PRI domination? Is it possible for ordinary citizens to make demands on government and to influence public policy? In fact, Mexico achieved more than seventy years of relatively peaceful political interactions in part because the political system offered some channels for representation and participation. Through its long history, the political system emphasized compromise among contending elites, behind-the-scenes conflict resolution, and distribution of political rewards to those willing to play by the formal and informal rules of the game. It has also responded, if reluctantly and defensively, to demands for change.

Often, citizens are best able to interact with the government through a variety of informal means rather than through the formal processes of elections, campaigns, and interest-group lobbying. Interacting with government through the personal and informal mechanisms of clientelism usually means that the government retains the upper hand in deciding which interests to respond to and which to ignore. For many interests, this has meant "incorporation without power."[15] Increasingly, however, Mexican citizens are organizing to alter this situation.

The Legislature

Students in the United States are frequently asked to study complex charts explaining how a bill becomes a law, because the formal process of lawmaking affects the content of legislation. In Mexico, while there are formal rules that prescribe such a process, studying them would not be useful for understanding how the legislature worked for most of its history. Mexico's two-chamber legislature—the Senate and the Chamber of Deputies—was dominated by the PRI for almost sixty years. Because of the overwhelming presence of this political party, opposition to presidential initiatives was rarely heard. To the extent that representatives did not agree with policies they were asked to approve, they counted on the fact that policy implementation was flexible and allowed for after-the-fact bending of the rules or disregard of measures that were harmful to important interests.

The PRI's grip on the legislature was broken in 1988. The growing strength of opposition parties, combined with legislation that provided for greater representation of minority parties in the congress, led to the election of 240 opposition deputies that year. After that, when presidential legislation was sent to the chamber, the opposition challenged the tradition of legislative passivity and insisted on real debate about issues. Because the Salinas administration introduced major reforms, some of which required constitutional amendments in order to be implemented, some initiatives were not brought to congress, slowing down the reform process. In other cases, the president pursued policy initiatives through decree laws and administrative measures rather than submitting them to the legislature where they might be questioned. The two-thirds PRI majority was returned in 1991—amid allegations of voter fraud—and presidentialism was reasserted. Nevertheless, the strong presence of opposition parties continued to encourage debate as the PRI delegates were challenged to defend proposed legislation. The 1994 elections returned a clear PRI majority of 300 deputies and 64 senators, but in 1997 the PRI lost this majority when 261 deputies (of a total of 500) and 51 senators (of a total of 128) were elected from opposition parties. For the first time in its history, the PRI did not have an absolute majority in the Chamber of Deputies.

Because important policy decisions were not made—only approved—in congress until 1997, interest groups did not pay much attention to the deputies or senators or to the process of legislation. Groups wishing to influence policy preferred to focus their attentions on the president and the executive branch.

As a genuine multiparty system begins to emerge, the Mexican congress has become a more important forum for a variety of political voices and points of view. PRI candidates are facing more competitive elections in many locales, and the number of "safe seats" for party stalwarts is declining. As the congress increases in importance as a place where legislation is debated and shaped, interest groups will begin to pay it greater attention and focus more of their lobbying activities on it.

Representation in congress seems to have diversified somewhat since the end of the 1980s. In 1998 women held 14.2 percent of all seats which, though paltry, compared favorably with 11.2 percent in the United States.[16] Some representatives also emerged from the ranks of community activists who had participated in activities such as the urban popular movements.

Political Parties and the Party System

The PRI

Mexico's Institutional Revolutionary Party, the PRI, was founded by a coalition of political elites who agreed that it was preferable to work out their conflicts within an overarching structure of compromise than to continue to resort to violence. In the 1930s the PRI incorporated a wide array of popular interests,

becoming a mass-based party that drew support from all classes in the population. Its principal activities were—and continue to be—generating support for the government, organizing the electorate to vote for its candidates, and distributing jobs and development resources in return for loyalty to the system.

Until the 1990s party organization was based largely on the corporate representation of class interests. Labor was represented within party councils by the National Confederation of Labor (CTM), which includes industry-based unions at local, regional, and national levels. Peasants were represented by the National Confederation of Peasants (CNC), an organization of *ejido* and peasant unions and regional syndicates. The so-called popular sector, comprising small businesses, community-based groups, and public employees, had less internal cohesion but was represented by the National Confederation of Popular Organizations (CNOP). Of the three, the CTM was consistently the best organized and most powerful.

Within these corporate structures, the PRI functioned through extended networks that distributed public resources—particularly jobs, land, development projects, and access to public services—to lower-level activists who controlled votes at the local level. This informal clientelist organization forms multiple chains of patron-client interaction that culminate at the highest level of political decision-making within the PRI and the office of the president. In this system, those with ambitions to public office or to positions within the PRI put together networks of supporters from above (patrons), to whom they deliver votes, and supporters from below (clients), who trade allegiance for access to public resources. Traditionally, the PRI's strongest support has come from the countryside, where *ejidatarios* and other peasants have been the most grateful for and dependent on rewards of land or jobs. As the country has become more urbanized, the support base provided by rural communities has remained important to the PRI but less so in terms of overall electoral support.

For well over half a century, this system worked extremely well. PRI candidates won by overwhelming majorities until the 1980s (see Figure 1 on p. 410). Of course, electoral fraud and the ability to distribute government largesse are central explanations for these numbers, but they also attest to an extremely

Figure 1

PRI Support in Congressional Elections, 1946–1997

a Percentage base includes annulled votes and those cast for nonregistered candidates.

Source: For 1946–1988: Juan Molinar Horcasitas, *El tiempo de la legitimidad: Elecciones, autoritarismo y democracia en México* (México, D.F.: Cal y Arena, 1991). For 1991: Secretaría Nacional de Estudios, Partido Acción Nacional, *Análisis del Proceso Federal Electoral 1994*, 1995. For 1994: Instituto Federal Electoral, *Estadística de las Elecciones Federales de 1994, Compendio de Resultados*, México, D.F., 1995. For 1997: http://www.ife.org.mx/wwworge/tablas/mrent.htm.

well-organized party. Although the PRI became much weaker in the 1980s and 1990s, it was still the only political party that could boast a network of constituency organizations in virtually every village and urban community in the country. Through the patron-client networks, it continues to provide means for people of humble origin, especially those living far from the center of political power, to interact with the political system in ways that allow them some access to benefits, however meager. Its vast political machinery also allows it to monitor events, even in remote areas.

Within the PRI, power was centralized, and the sector organizations (the CTM, the CNC, and the CNOP) responded primarily to elites at the top of the political pyramid rather than to member interests. Over time, the corporate interest-group organizations, particularly the CTM and the CNC, became widely identified with corruption, bossism, centralized control, and lack of effective participation. By the 1980s the PRI was facing increasing difficulties because of the way in which such characteristics limited effective representation of interests. New generations of voters were less beholden to patronage-style politics and much more willing to question the party's dominance. When the administrations of de la Madrid, Salinas, and Zedillo imposed harsh austerity measures, the PRI was held responsible for the resulting losses in incomes and benefits. Simultaneously, as the government cut back sharply on public-sector jobs and services, the PRI had far fewer resources to distribute to maintain its traditional bases of support. Moreover, it began to suffer from increasing internal dissension between the old guard and those who wanted to reform the party. In the aftermath of the election of

Table 2

Voting in Presidential Elections, 1934–1994

Year	Votes for PRI Candidate[a] %	Votes for PAN Candidate %	Votes for All Others[b] %	Turnout (% Voters Among Eligible Adults)[c]
1934	98.2	—	1.8	53.6
1940	93.9	—	6.1	57.5
1946	77.9	—	22.1	42.6
1952	74.3	7.8	17.9	57.9
1958	90.4	9.4	0.2	49.4
1964	88.8	11.1	0.1	54.1
1970	83.3	13.9	1.4	63.9
1976[d]	93.6	—	1.2	29.6
1982	71.0	15.7	9.4	66.1
1988	50.7	16.8	32.5[e]	49.4[f]
1994	50.1	26.7	23.2	77.16

[a]From 1958 through 1982, includes votes cast for the Partido Popular Socialista (PPS) and the Partido Auténtico de la Revolutión Mexicana (PARM), both of which regularly endorsed the PRI's presidential candidate. In 1988, they supported opposition candidate Cuauhtémoc Cárdenas.

[b]Excludes annulled votes; includes votes for candidates of nonregistered parties.

[c]Eligible population base for 1934 through 1952 includes all males ages 20 and over (legal voting age: 21 years). Both men and women ages 20 and over are included in the base for 1958 and 1964 (women received the franchise in 1958). The base for 1970–1988 includes all males and females ages 18 and over (the legal voting age was lowered to 18, effective 1970).

[d]The PRI candidate, José López Portillo, ran virtually unopposed because the PAN failed to nominate a candidate. The only other significant candidate was Valentín Campa, representing the Communist Party, which was not legally registered to participate in the 1976 election. More than 5 percent of the votes were annulled.

[e]Includes 31.1 percent officially tabulated for Cuauhtémoc Cárdenas.

[f]Estimated using data from the Federal Electoral Commission. However, the commission itself has released two different figures for the number of eligible voters in 1988. Using the commission's larger estimate of eligible population, the turnout would be 44.9 percent.

Source: From *Comparative Politics Today: A World View*, 4th ed. by Gabriel Almond and G. Bingham Powell, Jr. Copyright ©1988. Reprinted by permission of Addison-Wesley Educational Publishers, Inc. For 1994, Insituto Federal Electoral, *Estadística de las Elecciones Federales de 1994, Compendio de Resultados*, México, D.F., 1995.

1994, these tensions resulted in open conflict between the modernizers and the so-called dinosaurs. Most significantly, many of the groups that became politically active during the 1980s fiercely resisted traditional methods of control used by the party.

Until the elections of 1988, there was no question that the PRI candidate would be elected president. Victories recording 85–95 percent of the total vote for the PRI were the norm (see Table 2 above). In 1988 and in 1994, however, PRI candidates were challenged by parties to the right and left, and outcomes were hotly contested by the opposition, which claimed fraudulent electoral practices. In 1994, Zedillo won primarily because the opposition was not well organized and failed to present a program beyond opposition to the PRI. Presidents Salinas and Zedillo also distanced themselves from the party during their administrations, giving the first clear signals in PRI history that there was a distinction between the party and the government.

As the PRI faced greater competition from other parties and continued to suffer from declining popularity, efforts were made to restructure and reform it. The

Table 3

Support for the PRI by Type of Congressional District (percentage of total vote)

Districts	1979	1982	1985	1988	1991	1994	1997	Average 1979–1997
Federal District (Mexico City)	46.7	48.3	42.6	27.3	46.2	39.5	23.1	39.1[a]
Other Urban[b]	53.4	56.2	51.1	34.3				
Mixed[c]	67.9	66.2	59.2	46.4				
Rural[d]	83.5	80.9	77.3	61.3				

[a]Average for the 1979–1997 period.

[b]Urban districts are those in which 90 percent or more of the population lives in communities of 50,000 or more inhabitants. Total number: 40 in the Federal District and 56 in other urban areas.

[c]Districts in which more than 50 percent but less than 90 percent of the population live in communities of 50,000 or more inhabitants. Total number: 44.

[d]Districts in which less than 50 percent of the population live in communities of 50,000 inhabitants. Total number: 160.

Sources: For 1979–1988: Juan Molinar Horcasitas, *El tiempo de la legitimidad; Comparative Politics Today: A World View*, 4th ed. by Gabriel Almond and G. Bingham Powell, Jr. Copyright © 1988. Reprinted by permission of Addison-Wesley Educational Publishers, Inc. For 1991, Eduardo Castellanos Hernández, *Formas de Gobierno y Sistemas Electorales en México.* Published by Centro de Investigación Científica "Ing. Jorge L. Tamayo", A. C., 1995. For 1994, Instituto Federal Electoral, *Estadística de las Elecciones Federales de 1994, Compendio de Resultados*, México, D.F., 1995. For 1997, http://www.ife.org.mx/wwworge/tablas/mrent.htm.

CNOP was replaced by the UNE (Citizens in Movement), which sought to incorporate a wide array of non-class-based citizen and neighborhood movements. In 1990 membership rules were altered to allow individuals and groups not identified with its corporate-sector organizations to join. In addition, regional party organizations gained representation at the national level. Party conventions were introduced in an effort to democratize the internal workings of the party, while some states and localities began to hold primaries to select PRI candidates—a significant departure from the old system of selection by party bosses. Efforts were made to undercut regional bosses who had been closely allied with the patron-client system of the past. To give the appearance of a modern party system, electoral reforms introduced by the López Portillo, de la Madrid, Salinas, and Zedillo administrations made it easier for opposition parties to contest elections and win seats in the legislature. In 1990 an electoral commission was created to regulate campaigns and elections, and in 1996 it became fully independent from the government. Parties receive funding from government and have assured access to the media.

The PRI continues to face a difficult future. The Mexican electorate is now predominantly urban. Voters are younger, better educated, and more middle-class than in the days of the PRI's greatest success—the 1940s, 1950s, and 1960s. In 1990 only 27 percent of the population lived in rural areas, while 32 percent of the population lived in cities of 1 million or more; 25 percent of the population lived in Mexico City, which has become one of the world's largest megacities. The 1988 elections demonstrated the relevance of these demographic conditions for the PRI when only 27.3 percent of the population of Mexico City voted for the PRI candidate and only 34.3 percent of the population in other urban areas supported him. While rural support for the party had remained strong, it had also clearly diminished since the 1970s (see Table 3).

The PAN

Several opposition parties compete in elections. The National Action Party, or PAN, is among the oldest. Founded in 1939 to represent business interests opposed to the centralization and anticlericalism of the PRI, its strength is centered in northern states where the tradition of resistance to Mexico City is strong. The PAN has traditionally campaigned on a platform endorsing greater regional autonomy, less government intervention in the economy, reduced regulation of business, clean and fair elections, rapprochement with the Catholic Church, and support for private and religious education.

In the past, the PAN was usually able to elect 9–10 percent of all deputies to the national congress and to capture control of a few municipal governments. Then, in the early 1980s, and especially after President López Portillo nationalized the banks, opposition to centralism and statism grew more popular. The PAN began to develop greater capacity to contest elections at higher levels of government. In particular, the party gained popularity among urban middle-class voters, won elections in several provincial cities, and came close to winning governorships in two states. In 1988 it captured 16.8 percent of the vote for president, 101 Chamber of Deputies seats, and one Senate seat. The following year, it won the governorship of the state of Baja California Norte. For the first time since the PRI was founded, the dominant party did not control all governorships in the country. In the 1994 elections, PAN's candidate, Diego Fernández de Cevallos, garnered 26 percent of the presidential vote and the party won 119 seats in the Chamber of Deputies and 25 in the Senate. In 1997 it managed to win 121 seats in the Chamber and 33 in the Senate. In closely watched elections during the administration of Ernesto Zedillo, the PAN won the governorships of several large and important states. It is widely recognized for its organizational effectiveness, and its strong base of support in the north of the country.

The PRD

Another significant challenge has come from the Democratic Revolutionary Party, or PRD, a populist and nationalist alternative to the PRI. Its candidate in the 1988 and 1994 elections was Cuauhtémoc Cárdenas, the son of Mexico's most famous and revered president. He was a PRI insider until party leaders virtually ejected him for demanding internal reform of the party and a platform emphasizing social justice. In the 1988 elections Cárdenas was officially credited with winning 31.1 percent of the vote, and the party captured 139 seats in the Chamber of Deputies. He benefited from massive political defection from the PRI and garnered support from workers disaffected with the boss-dominated unions as well as peasants who remembered his father's concern for

agrarian reform and investment in the poor. Mexico City gave him 50.4 percent of the vote, which also represented some middle-class support.

Even while the votes were being counted, the party began to denounce widespread electoral fraud and claim that Cárdenas would have won an honest election. The PRD challenged a number of vote counts in the courts and walked out of Salinas' inaugural speech. Considerable public opinion supported the party's challenge. In the aftermath of the 1988 elections, then, it seemed that the PRD was a strong contender to become Mexico's second most powerful party. It was expected to have a real chance in future years to challenge the PRI's "right" to the presidency.

However, in the years leading up to the 1994 elections, the party was plagued by internal divisions over its platform, leadership, organizational structure, and election strategy. By 1994 it still lagged far behind the PRI in establishing and maintaining the local constituency organizations needed to mobilize votes and monitor the election process. In addition, the PRD found it difficult to define an appropriate left-of-center alternative to the market-oriented policies carried out by the government. While the claims that such policies ignored the need for social justice were popular, policies to respond to poverty that did not imply a return to unpopular government intervention were difficult to devise. In the aftermath of the Colosio assassination, citizens also became more alarmed about violence, and some were concerned that the level of political rivalry represented by the PRD threatened the country's long-term political stability. In the 1994 elections Cárdenas won only 17 percent of the votes; the PRD elected 71 deputies and 8 senators.

But thanks to the government's continued unpopular economic policies and the leadership of a successful grassroots mobilizer named Andres Manuel Lopez Obrador, who was elected to head the party in 1996, the PRD began to stage a remarkable turnaround. Factional bickering was controlled and organizational discipline increased. In addition, the PRD proved successful in moving beyond its regional stronghold and established itself as a truly national party. In 1997 the party increased its share of seats to 125 in the Chamber of Deputies and 13 in the Senate. Most important, Cárdenas became the first popularly elected mayor of Mexico City. This provided him and the party with a critically important opportunity to demonstrate their ability to govern, not to mention a potential platform for the presidential elections of 2000. By February 1999, the PRD had managed to shed some of its reputation as a "one-horse show" and had won two governorships, with the PRI under question for fraud in a third.

Elections

Each of these three political parties draws voters from a wide and overlapping spectrum of the electorate. Nevertheless, a typical voter for the PRI is likely to be from a rural area or small town, to have less education, and to be older and poorer than voters for the other parties. A typical voter for the PAN is likely to be from a northern state, to live in an urban area, to be a middle-class professional, to have a comfortable life-style, and to have a high school or even a university education. A typical voter for the PRD is likely to be young, to be a political activist, to have an elementary or high school education, to live in one of the central states, and to live in a small town or an urban area.

As we have seen, the support base for the PRI is the most vulnerable to economic changes occurring in the country. Voting for opposition parties is an urban phenomenon, and Mexico continues to urbanize at the rate of 3 percent per year. This means that, in order to stay competitive, the PRI will have to garner more support from urban areas. It must also be able to appeal to younger voters, especially the large numbers who are attracted to the PRD and the PAN. The cost of acquiring such support, however, may be willingness to democratize its internal decision-making processes and to desist from blatant acts of electoral fraud.

Elections are becoming more competitive in Mexico. The government is also under tremendous pressure to make them fairer. In the 1990s, laws to limit campaign spending and campaign contributions and to mandate greater media coverage of opposition parties and candidates were part of the response to the demand to "level the playing field" between the PRI and the other parties. Voter registration was reformed to ensure that fraud would be more detectable. Election monitoring was also strengthened and another reform increased the chances for opposition parties to win representation in the Senate. In the 1994 elections, however, citizens continued to be skeptical about the honesty of elections. An opinion poll carried out during the first week of June 1994 indicated that only 50.4 percent of respondents were "confident that the upcoming presidential election [would] be clean."[17] In fact, the elections were credited with having been among the fairest in history, and midterm and subsequent congressional elections reinforced the impression that electoral fraud is on the wane in many areas. Some state and local elections continue to be questioned, especially in rural areas in the south, where local PRI bosses remain powerful. For example, many citizens could not believe that the PRI had swept the 1997 congressional elections in the state of Chiapas, where opposition to the government is so strong that it generated a guerrilla movement.

Political Culture, Citizenship, and Identity

Most citizens in Mexico demonstrate overall commitment to the system while expressing considerable criticism—and often cynicism—about how it works and how equitable it is. A survey of almost any *ejido*, for example, will uncover lengthy local histories of how *ejidatarios* have been mistreated, "given the runaround" by bureaucratic organizations, and cheated by local, regional, and national leaders of the CNC, the PRI, and government agencies. The survey will reveal deep commitment to the country's heroes, the president, and the institutions of government along with anger, distrust, frustration, and biting jokes told at the expense of the rich and powerful.

Most Mexicans have a deep familiarity with how the political system works and the ways in which they might be able to extract benefits from it. They understand the informal rules of the game in Mexican politics that have helped keep the system in place despite extensive inequalities in economic and political power.

Clientelism, or the exchange of favors among people of different status or degrees of power, extends from the very top of the political system to the most remote and poverty-stricken villages. It is a form of participation in the sense that many people, even the poorest, are able to interact with public officials and get something out of the political system. This kind of participation emphasizes how limited resources, such as access to health care, can be distributed in a way that provides maximum political payoff. This informal system is a fundamental reason why many Mexicans continue to vote for the PRI.

However, new ways of interacting with government are emerging, and they coexist along with the clientelistic style of the past. An increasing number of citizens are seeking to negotiate with the government on the basis of citizenship rights, not relationships. The movements that emerged in the 1980s sought to form broad but loose coalitions with other organizations and attempted to identify and work with reform-oriented public officials. Their suspicion of traditional political organizations such as the PRI or the CNC and the CTM also carried over to suspicion of close alliances with the PAN and the PRD.

As politics and elections become more open and competitive, the roles of public opinion and the mass media are also becoming more important. In the past, public opinion polling was often contaminated by the dominance of the PRI, and some polling organizations were even subsidized by the party or the government. Increasingly, however, even the PRI and the government are interested in objective information and analysis of public opinion. These data have influenced the content and timing of government decisions and the development of strategies in election campaigns. In 1994 politicians, citizens, and political activists closely followed the popularity polls for the three major candidates for president, and party officials monitored how the image of their contender could be molded to capture higher voter approval ratings.

Since extensive public opinion polling is comparatively new in Mexico, it is difficult to assess how attitudes toward the regime have changed over time. Surveys taken in the 1980s and 1990s indicate that confidence in the regime fell extensively during the 1980s but rebounded somewhat in the 1990s. Fewer Mexicans claim a party preference today than in the past, and the percentage of citizens who identify with the PRI has fallen sharply. According to one analyst, "The average Mexican regards participation in electoral campaigns, attendance at rallies, voting, and affiliation with political parties as ritualistic activities. He or she believes that engaging in such activities may be necessary to extract benefits from the system,

but they have little effect on the shape of public policy or the selection of public officials."[18]

The media play an important role in public opinion formation in Mexico. In the past, it was not easy for newspapers, magazines, or radio and television stations to be openly opposed to the government. For many years, the government used access to newsprint, which it controlled, to reward sympathetic news coverage and penalize coverage it considered hostile. In addition, the government subsidized the salaries of some reporters, and politically ambitious public and PRI officials paid stipends to those who covered their activities sympathetically. A considerable amount of the revenue of newspapers and other media organizations came from advertising placed by the government. Each of these mechanisms was used to encourage positive reporting of government activities, strong endorsement of presidential initiatives, and quashing of stories that reflected ill on the party or the government, all without resorting to outright government control of the media.

As with other aspects of Mexican politics, the media are also in a period of transition, enjoying a "spring" of greater independence and diversity of opinion. There are currently several major television networks in the country, and many citizens have access to CNN and other global networks. The number of newspapers is expanding, as is their circulation, and news magazines such as *Nexos* and *Proceso* play the same role in Mexico that *Time* and *Newsweek* do in the United States. Citizens in Mexico today clearly hear a much wider range of opinion and much greater reporting of opposition to government and the PRI than at any time previously.

Interests, Social Movements, and Protest

As has been noted, clientelism is a way for individuals to acquire benefits from a system that is controlled from the top. The Mexican system also responds to broader groups of citizens through pragmatic **accommodation** to their interests. This is one important reason why political tensions among major interests have rarely escalated into the kind of serious conflict that can threaten stability. Where open conflict has occurred, it has generally been met with efforts to find some kind of compromise solution, even in cases in which the government has repressed opposition. Accommodation serves to respond to interests as diverse as business, labor, and rebellious students.

Accommodation has been particularly apparent in response to the interests of business. Mexico's development strategy encouraged the growth of wealthy elites in commerce, finance, industry, and agriculture (see Section 2). Although these elites were the primary beneficiaries of the country's development, they were never incorporated into the PRI. Instead, they represent themselves through a set of business-focused interest groups and through personal relationships with influential officials. Through these networks, business organizations and individuals have long sought policies that are favorable to their interests.

Labor has been similarly accommodated within the system. Wage levels for unionized workers grew fairly consistently between 1940 and 1982, when the economic crisis caused a significant drop in wages. At the same time, labor interests were attended to in terms of concrete benefits and limitations on the rights of employers to discipline or dismiss workers. Labor union leaders controlled their rank-and-file in the interest of their own power to negotiate with government but, at the same time, they sought benefits for workers who continued to provide support for the PRI. The power of the union bosses is declining, in part because the unions are weaker than in the past, and in part because union members are demanding greater democratization.

Accommodation is often coupled with **co-optation** as a means of incorporating dissidents into the system so that they do not threaten its continuity. In 1968, for example, students protesting against authoritarianism and the failure to address poverty and inequity challenged the government just prior to the opening of the Olympic games. The government responded with force—in one instance killing several hundred students in Mexico City—sparking even greater animosity. When Luis Echeverría became president in 1970, he recruited large numbers of the student activists into his administration. He also dramatically increased spending on social services, putting many of the young people to work in expanding antipoverty programs in the countryside and in urban slums. Through these actions, a generation of political and social activists was incorporated into the

system and there was some accommodation to their concerns.

Despite the strong and controlling role of the PRI in Mexico's political history, the country also has a tradition of civic organizations that operate at community and local levels with considerable independence from politics. Local village improvement societies, religious organizations, sports clubs, and parents' organizations are widespread. Many of their activities are not explicitly political, although they may have political implications in that they encourage individuals to work together to find solutions to problems or organize around common interests. Other organizational experiences are more explicitly political. The student movement of 1968 provided evidence that civic society in Mexico had the potential to contest the power of the state. The emergence of independent unionism in the 1970s was another indication of renewed willingness to question the right of the state to stifle the voices of dissent and the emergence of demands for greater equity and participation.

The economic crisis of 1982 combined with this civic tradition to heighten demands for assistance from the government. In October 1983 as many as 2 million people participated in a civic strike to call attention to the crisis and demand a forceful government response. A less successful strike in June 1984 made the same point to the government. In urban areas, citizen groups demanded land rights in squatter settlements, as well as housing, infrastructure, and urban services, as rights of citizenship rather than as a reward for loyalty to the PRI. In the aftermath of the 1985 earthquake, citizen groups became especially dynamic in demanding that government respond to the needs of citizens without reference to their history of party loyalty. Residents of Mexico City demanded that the government let them decide how to rebuild and relocate their neighborhoods and choose who would serve as mayor and represent them.[19] Many also became active in groups that share concerns about quality-of-life issues such as clean air and safe neighborhoods.

In rural areas, peasant organizations also demanded greater independence from government and the leaders of the PRI and the CNC in the 1980s.[20] In addition to greater access to land, they also

Citizen Action: *Urban Popular Movements*

In October 1968 hundreds of students and working-class people took to the streets of Mexico City to protest high unemployment and the authoritarianism of the government. What began as a peaceful rally in Tlatelolco Plaza ended in a tragedy when government troops opened fire on the crowd and killed an estimated two hundred people.

The political activism of the students heralded the birth of urban popular movements in Mexico. The massacre in Tlatelolco became a symbol of a government that was unwilling or unable to respond to citizen demands for economic and political equity. The protest movements sparked by the events of 1968 sought to transcend class boundaries and unite voices around a range of urban issues, from housing shortages to inadequate urban services to lack of land to government centralization in decision-making. Such social movements forged new channels for poor and middle-class urban residents to express their needs. They also generated forums for demanding democratic government that the traditional political system was not providing. In May 1980 the first national congress of urban movements was held in Monterrey in northern Mexico.

Urban popular movements, referring to activities of low- and modest-income (popular) groups, gained renewed vitality in the 1980s. When the economic crisis resulted in drastic reductions of social welfare spending and city services, working- and middle-class neighborhoods forged new coalitions and greatly expanded the national discussion of urban problems. The Mexico City earthquake of 1985 encouraged the formation of unprecedented numbers of grassroots movements in response to the slow and poorly managed relief efforts of the government. Turning to each other, earthquake victims organized to provide shelter, food, and relocation. The elections of 1988 and 1994 provided these groups with significant opportunities to press parties and candidates to respond to their needs. They insisted on their rights to organize and protest without fear of repression or co-optation by the government or the PRI. As the opposition parties expanded rapidly, some leaders of urban movements enrolled as candidates.

Urban popular movements bring citizens together around needs and ideals that cut across class boundaries. Neighborhood improvement, the environment, local self-government, economic development, feminism, and professional identity have been among the factors that have forged links among these groups. As such identities have been strengthened, the need of the political system to negotiate and bargain with a more independent citizenry has increased. Urban popular movements have helped transform political culture on the most local level—one reason the PRI has become less certain that it can maintain its hold on political power in the future.

demanded better prices for the crops they produced, access to markets and credit, development of better infrastructure, and the provision of better education and health services. They began to form alliances with other groups. For example, in the Yucatán peninsula in the late 1970s and 1980s, PEMEX's exploration and production of oil caused massive ecological damage and was carried out with complete disregard for the rights of local *ejidatarios*. Environmental groups joined peasant organizations and student activists in protesting against PEMEX. Since 1994 the rebels in Chiapas have become a focal point for broad alliances of those concerned about the rights of indigenous groups (ethnic minorities) and rural poverty. Indigenous groups have also emerged to demand that

government be responsive to their needs and respectful of their traditions.

A variety of groups have also organized around middle-class and urban issues. In Mexico City, community groups and broader citizen alliances have been active in calling attention to the disastrous levels of air, water, and noise pollution in the capital. Women, with a strong cultural role as caretakers of the home, have begun to mobilize in urban areas around demands for equal pay, legal equality, and opportunities in business traditionally denied them.[21] Religious groups, both Catholic and Protestant, have begun to demand greater government attention to problems of poverty and inequity as well as more government tolerance of religious education and religious practices.

Mexicans demonstrate for better housing in Mexico City's central plaza. *Source:* Freck/Odyssey, Chicago.

In the early 1990s the government's own Solidarity social development program—which many critics claim was a ploy by President Salinas to win back respect for his government after the flawed elections of 1988—helped organize thousands of grassroots organizations and possibly contributed to a trend in broader mobilization independent of the PRI clientelist networks.[22] In 1997 unprecedented numbers of citizens volunteered their time to civic associations that observed the vote to assure, ballot box by ballot box, that the votes were counted accurately. Where this occurred, mostly in urban areas, there were few accusations of fraud.

Civic society in Mexico is becoming more pluralist and less easily controlled. There is broader scope for legitimate protest, opposition, and dissent from government. In predicting change for the future, however, it is important to remember that Mexico has achieved over seventy years of relative stability because its political system offered some channels for representation and participation, despite a high degree of centralization, presidentialism, and PRI domination. It has responded—if reluctantly, slowly, and defensively—to demands for political and policy change and has emphasized compromise, accommodation, and piecemeal distribution of political rewards in order to keep the political peace. Today, Mexicans are engaged in an increasingly open discussion about how to transform the political system rather than how to overthrow it.

Section **5**   Mexican Politics in Transition

Political Challenges and Changing Agendas

When U.S. President Bill Clinton visited Mexico in May 1997, his hosts hoped to show him the richness of Mexican culture and tradition. They brought him two hours outside of Mexico City to a small city called Tlaxcala, in the center of a strongly Nahuátl Indian region. An open-air ceremony had been set up to receive local townspeople so that Clinton could meet everyday citizens face-to-face. Mexican reporters observed the proceedings with some shock even to themselves. There was the expected folklore show for the visitor's benefit, with brightly colored costumes, typical dances, and mariachis, but looking around at the crowd, one could see villagers who came down out of the hills dressed in sparkling white sneakers, impeccable T-shirts with logos, and neatly fitted baseball caps. Any question one would have about the possibility of integrating of these two very different societies was pushed aside—the people already lived it. Posturing by both governments regarding boundaries and nationhood suddenly seemed moot.

This story illustrates a world of increasing interdependence between countries, where nation-states struggle to redefine the meaning of politics. Doubly so, Mexico must confront the evolving nature of its domestic state as well as its international position in terms of relationships with its neighbors. Many Mexicans see NAFTA as the beginning of closer integration with trading partners in Latin America, Asia, and Europe. For all countries, economic integration raises issues of national sovereignty and identity. Mexicans define themselves in part through a set of historical events, symbols, and myths that focus on the country's troubled relationship with the "Colossus of the North." Among numerous national heroes and martyrs are those who distinguished themselves in confrontations with the United States. The myths of the Revolution of 1910 emphasize the uniqueness of the country in terms of its opposition to the capitalists and militarists of the northern country. In the 1970s, Mexicans were encouraged to see themselves as leading Third World countries arguing for increased bargaining positions vis-à-vis the industrialized countries of the north. This view stands in strong contrast to more recent perspectives touting the benefits of an internationally oriented economy, and the undeniable reality of information, culture, money, and people flowing back and forth across borders.

The sense of national identity is affected by international migration. Of particular importance in the Mexican case is labor migration. Every year, large numbers of Mexicans enter the United States as workers to stay for a season, a few years, or settle down permanently. Many return to their towns and villages with new values and new views of the world. Most continue to believe that Mexican culture is preferable to American culture, which they see as excessively materialistic and violent. While they believe that Mexico is a better place to nurture strong family life and values, they are nevertheless strongly influenced by United States mass culture, including popular music, movies, television programs, fast food, and consumer goods.

The future of Mexican politics will be significantly shaped by the ability of the regime to govern the economy. Currently, Mexico's population of 98 million is a young one, with about half under the age of sixteen. The rate of population increase has slowed considerably since the early 1970s and is now growing at less than 2 percent per year. Nevertheless, high birthrates in earlier decades mean that the labor force is growing faster than the population. According to some estimates, 1 million new jobs need to be created every year just to keep up with increasing demand. The demand for jobs for new entrants into the labor market, of course, must be added to existing demand from large numbers of unemployed and underemployed people. Some estimates suggest that as much as one-quarter to one-third of the labor force falls into these categories.

New development policies need to be designed with employment creation in mind. Demand for urban jobs will be particularly strong because of changes in property rights on agricultural lands. In the past, the stipulation that *ejidatarios* could maintain claim to *ejido* plots only if they cultivated them two out of three years kept many of them, even those with the smallest and least productive land, in the countryside. Under legislation introduced by the Salinas administration, many of these peasants are likely to sell or abandon their land and migrate to urban areas in search of jobs.

The inability of the Mexican economy to create enough jobs pushes many Mexicans to seek work in the United States. Extensive migration to the United States has been occurring since the 1880s, when Mexican workers were recruited to help build railroads. In the 1920s and between 1942 and 1964, Mexico and the United States concluded a number of bilateral agreements to provide workers to help the United States meet labor shortages. When such programs ended, a greater proportion of the labor migrants crossed the border into the United States illegally. Differences in wage levels—as high as 13 to 1 during the 1980s—and the jobs lost during the Mexican economic crisis added to the number of workers seeking employment in the United States. The U.S. Congress passed stiff legislation to contain illegal immigration in 1986, but it has been largely ineffective. The difference in wages between the two countries will persist for a long time, which implies that so will migration. In fact, the militarization of the border and the increasing danger of crossing leads more illegal immigrants to settle down permanently in the U.S. rather than risk more trips.

There is disagreement about how to respond to the economic challenges the country faces. Much of the debate surrounds the question of what integration into a competitive international economy really means. For some, it represents the final abandonment of Mexico's sovereignty. For others, it is the basis on which future prosperity must be built. Those who are critical of the market-based, outward-oriented development strategy are concerned about its impact on workers, peasants, and national identities. They argue that the state has abandoned its responsibilities to protect the poor from shortcomings of the market and to provide for their basic needs. They believe that U.S. and Canadian investors have come to Mexico only to find low-wage labor for industrial empires located elsewhere. They see little benefit in further industrial development based on importation of foreign-made parts, their assembly in Mexico, and their export to other markets. This kind of development, they argue, has been prevalent in the *maquiladoras*, or assembly industries, located along the U.S.-Mexico border.

Those who favor closer integration with Canada and the United States acknowledge that some foreign investment does not promote technological advances or move the workforce into higher-paying and more skilled jobs. They emphasize, however, that most investment will occur because the country has a relatively well-educated population, the capacity to absorb modern technology, and a large internal market for industrial goods.

Mexico provides a testing ground for the democratic idea in a state with authoritarian traditions. Although the youth of the population, its increasing education level, and its concentration in urban areas are working against the continued dominance of the PRI, the party continues to have great leverage to set the terms for the interaction of state and civil society. The party has access to extensive resources for buying political support, and its operatives are skilled in the arts of electoral manipulation, even fraud. There is an ongoing struggle for the "soul" of the PRI between those who would like it to become more modern and democratic and those who fear such a path because the party would inevitably lose some of its power.

If the modernizers are successful, their changes will increase the likelihood that the PAN or the PRD will install a president in Los Pinos in the near future. For many party loyalists, this outcome is almost unimaginable. The modernizers retort that the failure to become more democratic will doom the party to loss of legitimacy and push the opposition to violent tactics in an effort to acquire access to power. They believe that the only way the PRI can continue to be relevant to the country's future is to accept more democratic processes and win elections in ways that are accepted as fair by most citizens. It is not yet clear, however, whether their commitment to democracy is strong enough to enable the modernizers to step down from the presidency gracefully should an election go against them. This untested commitment stands in sharp contrast to

the commitment of the old guard to hold onto power by whatever means necessary.

More important than internal debate, however, are the large numbers of Mexico's citizens pressuring its political system to become open and democratic, to allow political opposition, and to ensure that public officials can be held accountable for their actions. The democratic ideas of citizen rights to free speech and assembly, free and fair elections, and responsive government are major reasons why the power of the PRI is under attack by so many in Mexico.

The continuing centralization of the Mexican government is one of the critical issues. Countries around the globe increasingly recognize that the solutions to many policy problems lie at regional and local levels. Issues such as how to ensure that children are receiving a high-quality education, how to relieve chronic and massive traffic congestion, how to dispose of garbage in ways that do not threaten public health, and how to reduce air and water pollution require state and municipal governments that have money, authority, and capable public officials—precisely the conditions that only a very few regional and local governments in Mexico have had.

The complexity of contemporary problems and the inability of a single, centralized government to deal with them all at once make the politics of collective identities more important. The pressure for change in Mexico and many other countries is accelerating as modern technology increases the extent to which people in one country are aware of what is occurring in others and the degree to which citizens are able to communicate their concerns and interests among themselves and to the government. However, the ability of citizen groups and opposition parties in Mexico to resist manipulation by the government and to sustain pressure on the regime over an extended period remains untested. The formation of a strong civil society capable of articulating its interests and ensuring that government is responsive to its needs is the other side of political reform.

Human and social development in a country make such a functioning civil society possible. Improving social conditions is an important challenge for Mexico. While elites enjoy the benefits of sumptuous life-styles, education at the best U.S. universities for their children, and luxury travel to the capitals of the world, large numbers of Mexicans remain ill-educated, poorly served with health care, and distant from the security of knowing that their basic needs for food, shelter, and employment can be met. The Chiapas rebellion of 1994 made the social agenda a topic of everyday conversation by reminding Mexicans that some people lived in appalling conditions with little hope for the future. Indeed, the average length of schooling is still under five years nationwide, and only about half of the eligible students are enrolled in secondary school.

What to do about these conditions is debated. As in the United States, some argue that economic growth and expanded employment will resolve the major problems of poverty in the country. They believe that prosperity, tied to Mexico's economic future internationally, will benefit everyone in the long run. For this to occur, however, they insist that education will have to be improved and made more appropriate for developing a well-educated workforce. They also believe that improved education will come about when local communities have more control over schools and curriculum and when parents have more choice between public and private education for their children. From their perspective, the solution to poverty and injustice is fairly clear—more and better jobs and improved education.

For those critical of the development path on which Mexico embarked in the 1980s and 1990s, the problems of poverty and inequity are more complex. Solutions involve understanding the diverse causes of poverty, including not only lack of jobs and poor education but also exploitation, geographical isolation, discriminatory laws and practices, and families disrupted by migration, urbanization, and the tensions of modern life. Citizens must define the role of government in providing social welfare. In the past, Mexicans looked to government for such benefits, but their provision was deeply flawed by inefficiency and political manipulation. The government and the PRI consistently used access to social services as a means to increase their political control and limit the capacity of citizens to demand equitable treatment. Thus, while many continue to believe that it is the responsibility of government to ensure that citizens are well educated, healthy, and able to make the most of their potential, the populace is deeply suspicious of the government's capacity to provide such conditions fairly and effi-

ciently. Decentralization, local control, and active community organizations might provide an answer to how public goods such as social services and basic infrastructure could be provided more effectively.

Mexican Politics in Comparative Perspective

Mexico faces many of the same challenges that beset other countries—creating equitable and effective democratic government, becoming integrated into a global economy, and responding to complex social problems. Indeed, these were precisely the challenges that the United States faced in the 1990s, along with India, Nigeria, China, Japan, Germany, and others. Like these other countries, Mexico confronts these challenges within the context of a unique historical and institutional evolution. The legacies of its past, the tensions of the present, and the innovations of the future will no doubt evolve in ways that continue to be uniquely Mexican.

What will the future bring? How much will the pressures for change and the potential loss of national identity affect the nature of the political system? In 1980 few people could have predicted the extensive economic policy reforms and pressures for democracy that Mexico faced in the next ten years. Many still cannot believe them and are fighting them. But it is important to remember that Mexico has a long tradition of relatively strong institutions. It is not a country that will easily slip into sustained political instability. A tradition of constitutional government, a strong presidency, a political system that has incorporated a wide range of interests, a weak tradition of military involvement in politics, and a strong sense of national identity—these are among the factors that need to be considered in predicting the political consequences of democratization, economic integration, and greater social equality.

Mexico represents a pivotal case for the hemisphere. If it can successfully bridge the gap between its past and its future and move from centralization to effective local governance, from regional vulnerability to global dependability, and from the control of the few to the participation of the many, then the rest of the Americas will surely look to follow in its footsteps. Its success or failure will have serious implications for future patterns of global integration.

Key Terms

mestizos

Amerindian

indigenous groups

maquiladoras

anticlericalism

ejidos

ejidatarios

sexenio

clientelism

corporatist state

state capitalism

import substituting
   industrialization

informal sector

petrodollars

para-statal sector

accommodation

co-optation

Suggested Readings

Baer, M. Delal, and Sidney Weintraub. *The NAFTA Debate: Grappling with Unconventional Trade Issues.* Boulder, Colo.: Lynne Rienner, 1994.

Bailey, John. *Governing Mexico: The Statecraft of Crisis Management.* New York: St. Martin's Press, 1988.

Collier, Ruth Berins. *The Contradictory Alliance: State-Labor Relations and Regime Change in Mexico.* Berkeley: University of California Press, 1992.

Cook, Maria Lorena, Kevin J. Middlebrook, and Juan Molinar, eds. *The Politics of Economic Restructuring in Mexico.* San Diego: Center for U.S.-Mexican Studies, University of California, 1994.

Cornelius, Wayne A. "Nation-Building, Participation, and Distribution: The Politics of Social Reform under Cárdenas." In *Crisis, Choice, and Change: Historical Studies of Political Development*, ed. Gabriel A. Almond, Scott Flanagan, and Robert J. Mundt. Boston: Little, Brown, 1973.

Cornelius, Wayne A., and Philip Martin. *The Uncertain Connection: Free Trade and Mexico-U.S. Migration.* San Diego: Center for U.S.-Mexican Studies, University of California, 1993.

Cornelius, Wayne A., Ann L. Craig, and Jonathan Fox, eds. *Transforming State-Society Relations in Mexico: The National Solidarity Strategy.* San Diego: Center for U.S.-Mexican Studies, University of California, 1994.

Cornelius, Wayne A., Judith Gentleman, and Peter H. Smith, eds. *Mexico's Alternative Political Futures.* San Diego: Center for U.S.-Mexican Studies, University of California, 1989.

Eckstein, Susan, ed. *Power and Popular Protest: Latin American Social Movements.* Berkeley: University of California Press, 1989.

Foweraker, Joe, and Ann L. Craig, eds. *Popular Movements and Political Change in Mexico.* Boulder, Colo.: Lynne Rienner, 1990.

Grindle, Merilee S. *Bureaucrats, Politicians, and Peasants in Mexico: A Case Study in Public Policy.* Berkeley: University of California Press, 1977.

———. *Challenging the State: Crisis and Innovation in Latin America and Africa.* London: Cambridge University Press, 1995.

Hamilton, Nora. *The Limits of State Autonomy: Post-Revolutionary Mexico.* Princeton, N.J.: Princeton University Press, 1982.

Hansen, Roger. *The Politics of Mexican Development.* Baltimore: Johns Hopkins University Press, 1971.

Lustig, Nora. *Mexico: The Remaking of an Economy.* Washington, D.C.: Brookings Institution, 1992.

Meyer, Michael C., and William L. Sherman. *The Course of Mexican History.* 5th ed. New York: Oxford University Press, 1995.

Mumme, Stephen, C. Richard Bath, and Valerie J. Assetto. "Political Development and Environmental Policy in Mexico." *Latin American Research Review* 23, no. 1 (1988).

Paz, Octavio. *The Labyrinth of Solitude: Life and Thought in Mexico.* New York: Grove Press, 1961.

Purcell, Susan Kaufman, and Luis Rubio, eds. *Mexico under Zedillo.* Boulder, Colo.: Lynne Rienner, 1998.

Roett, Riordan, ed. *The Challenge of Institutional Reform in Mexico.* Boulder, Colo.: Lynne Rienner, 1994.

Ronfeldt, David, ed. *The Modern Mexican Military: A Reassessment.* San Diego: Center for U.S.-Mexican Studies, University of California, 1984.

Smith, Peter. *Labyrinths of Power: Political Recruitment in Twentieth-Century Mexico.* Princeton, N.J.: Princeton University Press, 1979.

Suárez-Orozco, Marcelo, ed. *Crossings: Mexican Immigration in Interdisciplinary Perspective.* Cambridge, Mass.: Harvard University Press, 1998.

Womack, John, Jr. *Zapata and the Mexican Revolution.* New York: Vintage Books, 1968.

———. *Rebellion in Chiapas. An Historical Reader.* New York, New Press, 1999.

Endnotes

[1] An excellent history of this event is presented in Wayne A. Cornelius, "Nation-Building, Participation, and Distribution: The Politics of Social Reform under Cárdenas," in *Crisis, Choice and Change: Historical Studies of Political Development*. ed. Gabriel A. Almond, Scott Flanagan, and Robert J. Mundt. (Boston: Little, Brown, 1973).

[2] World Bank, *World Development Report, 1994* (New York: Oxford University Press, 1994).

[3] World Bank, *World Development Report, 1997* (New York: Oxford University Press, 1997).

[4] Merilee S. Grindle, *State and Countryside: Development Policy and Agrarian Politics in Latin America* (Baltimore: Johns Hopkins University Press, 1986), 63, quoting President Avila Camacho (1940–1946).

[5] Kevin J. Middlebrook, ed., *Unions, Workers, and the State in Mexico* (San Diego: Center for U.S.-Mexican Studies, University of California, 1991).

[6] Grindle, *State and Countryside*, pp. 79–111.

[7] For a description of this process, see Carlos Bazdresch and Santiago Levy, "Populism and Economic Policy in Mexico," in *The Macroeconomics of Populism in Latin America*, ed. Rudiger Dornbusch and Sebastian Edwards (Chicago: University of Chicago Press, 1991), 72.

[8] For an assessment of the mounting problems of Mexico City and efforts to deal with them, see Diane E. Davis, *Urban Leviathan: Mexico City in the Twentieth Century* (Philadelphia: Temple University Press, 1994).

[9] Joe Foweraker and Ann L. Craig, eds., *Popular Movements and Political Change in Mexico* (Boulder, Colo.: Lynne Rienner, 1989).

[10] The Economist Intelligence Unit. Country Profile, Mexico. 1998–1999.

[11] Roger Hansen, *The Politics of Mexican Development,* (Baltimore: Johns Hopkins University Press, 1971), 75.

[12] Guillermo Trejo and Claudio Jones, "Political Dilemmas of Welfare Reform: Poverty and Inequality in Mexico," in *Mexico under Zedillo*, ed. Susan Kaufman Purcell and Luis Rubio (Boulder, Colo.: Lynne Rienner, 1998), 70.

[13] The Economist Intelligence Unit. Country Profile, Mexico. 1998–1999.

[14] Frank Brandenburg, *The Making of Modern Mexico* (Englewood Cliffs, N.J.: Prentice Hall, 1964), 141.

[15] Daniel Levy and Gabriel Székely, *Mexico: Paradoxes of Stability and Change* (Boulder, Colo.: Westview Press, 1983), 100.

[16] United Nations Development Programme, Human Development Report, 1997.

[17] *El Norte de Monterrey/Reforma* Opinion Poll on Mexico's Presidential Race, June 1–6, 1994.

[18] Wayne A. Cornelius and Ann L. Craig, "Politics in Mexico," in *Comparative Politics Today*, ed. Gabriel Almond and G. Bingham Powell, 5th ed. (Boston: Scott Foresman & Co., 1992), 502.

[19] Susan Eckstein, ed., *Power and Popular Protest: Latin American Social Movements* (Berkeley: University of California Press, 1989).

[20] Jonathan Fox and Gustavo Gordillo, "Between State and Market: The Campesinos' Quest for Autonomy," in *Mexico's Alternative Political Futures*, ed. Wayne A. Cornelius, Judith Gentleman, and Peter H. Smith (San Diego: Center for U.S.-Mexican Studies, University of California, 1989).

[21] Foweraker and Craig, *Popular Movements and Political Change in Mexico.*

[22] Wayne A. Cornelius, Ann L. Craig, and Jonathan Fox, eds., *Transforming State-Society Relations in Mexico: The National Solidarity Strategy* (San Diego: Center for U.S.-Mexican Studies, University of California, 1994).

CHAPTER 10

Russia

Joan DeBardeleben

Russian Federation

Land and Population

Capital	Moscow
Total Area (square miles)	6,592,800 (slightly less than 1.8 times the size of U.S.)
Population	147 million
Annual Average Population Growth Rate (1990–1997)	–0.1%
Urban Population	77%
Ethnic Composition	Russian 81.5%
	Tatar 3.8%
	Ukrainian 3.0%
	Chuvash 1.2%
	Bashkir 0.9%
	Byelorussian 0.8%
	Moldavian 0.7%
	Other 8.1%
Major Language	Russian
Religious Affiliation	Russian Orthodox 16.3%
	Muslim 10.0%
	Protestant 0.9%
	Jewish 0.4%
	Roman Catholic 0.3%
	Other/nonreligious 72.1%

Economy

Domestic Currency	Ruble
Total GNP (US$)	$403.5 billion
GNP per capita (US$)	$2740
GNP per capita at purchasing power parity (US$)	$4190
GNP average annual growth rate (1996–1997)	–1.4%
GNP per capita average annual growth rate	1996–1997 –1.5%
	1980–1995 –3.3%
Income Gap:	Richest 20% of population
GDP per capita (US$)	$12,804
	Poorest 20% of population $881
Structure of Production (% of GDP)	Agriculture 7%
	Industry 38%
	Services 55%
Labor Force Distribution (% of total)	Agriculture 14%
	Industry 42%
	Services 45%
Exports as % of GDP	22%
Imports as % of GDP	22%

Society

Life Expectancy (1995)	Female	71.7
	Male	58.3
Doctors per 100,000 people		380
Infant Mortality per 1000 live births		20
Adult Literacy		99%
Access to Information and Communications (per 1000 people)	Radios	340
	Televisions	280
	Telephone Lines	170
	Personal Computers	18

Women in Government and Economy

Seats in National Legislature held by Women	10.2% lower house
	0.6% upper house
Women at Ministerial Level	2.4%
Women as % of Total Labor Force	8.0%
Female Business Administrators and Managers	Not available
Female Professional and Technical Workers	Not available
1998 Human Development Index ranking (out of 174 countries; 1 = highest)	72

Political Organization

Political System   Federal state, semipresidental system.

Regime History   Re-formed as an independent state with the collapse of communist rule in December 1991; current constitution since December 1993.

Administrative Structure   Federal system with 89 subnational governments including 21 republics, 55 provinces (*oblast', krai*), 11 autonomous districts or regions (*okrugs* or autonomous *oblast'*), and 2 cities of federal status.

Executive   Dual executive (president and prime minister). Direct election of president; prime minister appointed by the president with the approval of the lower house of the parliament (State Duma).

Legislature   Bicameral. Upper house (Federation Council) made up of heads of regional executive and representative organs. Lower house (State Duma) chosen by direct election, with half of the 450 deputies chosen through a proportional representation system and half from single-member constituencies. Powers include proposal and approval of legislation, approval of presidential appointees.

Judiciary   Independent constitutional court with 19 justices, nominated by the president and approved by the Federation Council, holding 12-year terms with possible renewal.

Party System   Fragmented multiparty system with changing party names and coalitions.

Section ❶ The Making of the Modern Russian State

Politics in Action

In late summer 1998 a visitor to Russia would have observed a disturbing sight. Hundreds of Russians, young and old, were lined up outside the country's many banks wishing to withdraw rubles or dollars from their accounts. Nearby, shop shelves, which just weeks earlier had been stacked with supplies of imported Western food, were nearly empty. As the Russian ruble lost two-thirds of its value against the U.S. dollar within a period of two weeks, some banks closed their doors and others allowed their clients to withdraw only small amounts of the devalued rubles which they had deposited over the previous years and months. Business accounts were also frozen, forcing some firms to lay off employees and in some cases to close their doors. Underlying the crisis was the Russian government's inability to pay its many creditors. The pyramid of state debt that had fed the government budget had finally collapsed. Many Russian banks, holders of the Russian government's short-term bonds, were facing imminent bankruptcy, and with the Russian government itself in default, bailouts were unlikely. The government began to print more of the increasingly valueless rubles, threatening to undermine the ruble's value further and thus intensify the underlying financial crisis.

The collapse of the Russian ruble in the fall of 1998 triggered a political crisis, which raised new questions about the government's commitment to radical market reform that was proclaimed following the collapse of the USSR in late 1991. President Yeltsin asked the prime minister, Sergei Kiriyenko, to resign, even though he had been in office for only four months. The Communist-dominated parliament (the Duma) refused to confirm Yeltsin's nominee to fill the post. Finally Yeltsin offered a compromise candidate, Evgenii Primakov, the foreign minister and former adviser to the Soviet Union's last Communist leader, Mikhail Gorbachev. It appeared that the appointment of Primakov and his cabinet might mark a crucial shift in Russia's direction; the new government showed every sign of slowing the pace of reform and seeking a more moderate path of transition. However, Yeltsin's decision

to remove Primakov from the post just eight months later reopened the question of Russia's direction. Sergei Stepashin was approved as new prime minister in May 1999 and was voicing support for a renewed commitment to a more assertive policy of market reform.

Many observers have described Russia as being in transition. The events of late 1998 raised the question, transition to what? Although some had expected the economic transition to lead to the gradual, if painful, emergence of a market economy, it now seemed likely that the country might fall prey to a new spiral of economic decline and disorder. Political instability also rose. Could Russia produce a sustainable democracy in the midst of economic turmoil? Would the country hold together at all, or would economic decline feed regional separatism, mimicking the process that a few years earlier had pulled the Soviet Union apart? Russia could hardly move back to the Communist system, which had been rejected in 1991, but the path forward was less clear than ever. The new government installed in September 1998 represented a mish-mash of political tendencies that reflected the confusion of Russia's political landscape and future.

Geographic Setting

In December 1991 the Soviet Union ceased to exist. Each of the fifteen newly independent states that emerged in early 1992 began the process of forming a new political entity. In this section we focus on the Russian Federation, the most important of these fifteen successor states. With a population of just over 147 million, Russia is the largest European country both in population and size, and in terms of territory the largest country in the world, spanning ten time zones. Russia underwent a period of rapid industrialization and urbanization in the Soviet period; only 18 percent of the population lived in rural areas in 1917, rising to 73 percent in 1989. Despite its vast expanses, only 8 percent of Russia's land is arable, while 45 percent is forested.[1] Russia is rich in natural resources, which are generally concentrated in the vast regions of Western Siberia and the Russian north, far from

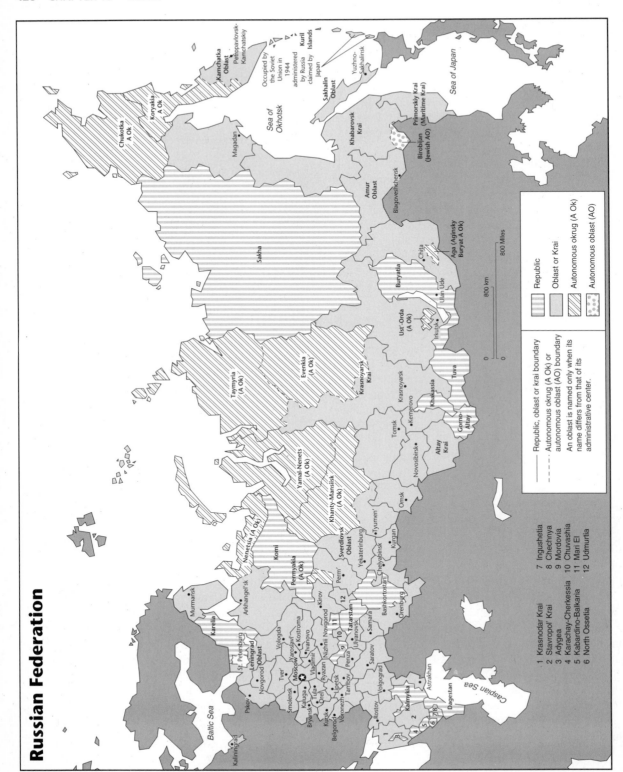

Russian Federation

Republic, oblast or krai boundary
Autonomous okrug (A Ok) or autonomous oblast (AO) boundary

An oblast is named only when its name differs from that of its administrative center.

Republic
Oblast or Krai
Autonomous okrug (A Ok)
Autonomous oblast (AO)

1 Krasnodar Krai
2 Stavropol' Krai
3 Adygea
4 Karachay-Cherkessia
5 Kabardino-Balkaria
6 North Ossetia
7 Ingushetia
8 Chechnya
9 Mordovia
10 Chuvashia
11 Mari El
12 Udmurtia

0   800 km
0   800 Miles

Moscow, the Russian capital. Russia's wealth includes deposits of oil, natural gas, mineral resources (including gold and diamonds), and extensive forest land.

Before the Communists took power in 1917, the Russian Empire extended east to the Pacific, south to the Caucasus mountains and the Muslim areas of Central Asia, north to the Arctic Circle, and west into present-day Ukraine, eastern Poland, and the Baltic states. Unlike the empires of Western Europe with their far-flung colonial possessions, Russia's empire bordered its historic core. With its unprotected location between Europe and Asia, Russia had been repeatedly invaded and challenged for centuries. This exposure to outside intrusion encouraged an expansionist mentality among the leadership; some historians argue that this factor, combined with Russia's harsh climate, encouraged Russia's rulers to craft a centralizing and autocratic state.[2]

With the formation of the Soviet Union after World War I, the Russian Republic continued to form the core of the new multiethnic state. Russia's ethnic diversity and geographic scope have always made it a hard country to govern. In the contemporary period, although only one of Russia's republics (Chechnya, in the Caucasus region) has attempted outright secession from the Russian Federation, other regions have asserted their autonomy in a manner that has challenged the authority of the Russian state. Russia also faces pockets of instability and regional warfare on several of its borders, most notably in the Central Asian countries of Tadzhikistan and Afghanistan, and in the countries of Georgia and Armenia located on Russia's southern border in the Caucasus region. On the west, Russia's neighbors include the newly independent states of Ukraine, Belarus, Estonia, Latvia, and Lithuania as well as the formerly allied country of Poland. Several of Russia's neighbors to the west have unambiguously embraced a European identity, with policies directed toward joining Western institutions such as the European Union and the North Atlantic Treaty Organization (NATO). Former Soviet allies, Poland, Hungary, and the Czech Republic were admitted to NATO in March 1999. Russia's identity is more ambiguous. Some have described the country as Eurasian, reflecting the impact of Asian and European cultural influences. Efforts to unite most of the former Soviet republics in the Commonwealth of Independent States, which was formed at the time of the Soviet collapse in December 1991, have produced few concrete results. In December 1998 a set of accords was signed by Russia and Belarus pointing in the direction of a possible economic and political union of the two countries.

Critical Junctures

The Decline of the Russian Tsarist State

Until the revolution of 1917, Russia was ruled through an autocratic system headed by the tsar, the Russian monarch and emperor. The historian Richard Pipes explains that before 1917, Russia had a **patrimonial state**, that is, a state that not only ruled the country but owned the land as well.[3] Serfdom was an economic and agricultural system that tied the majority of the population (peasants) to the nobles whose land they worked. The serfs had been emancipated by the tsar in 1861 as a part of his effort to modernize Russia, to make her militarily competitive with the West, and thus to retain her status as a world power. Emancipation freed the peasants from bondage to the nobility but did not destroy the traditional communal peasant organization in the countryside, the *mir*. Most peasants remained bound to the *mir*, which was collectively responsible for paying the state redemption payments for forty-nine years. Thus individual peasant farming did not develop in Russia on a significant scale.

A Russian bourgeoisie, or entrepreneurial class, also failed to emerge in Russia as it had in Western Europe. The key impetus for industrialization came from the state itself and from injections of foreign (especially French, English, German, and Belgian) capital in the form of joint-stock companies and foreign debt incurred by the tsarist government. The dominant role of state and foreign capital was accompanied by the emergence of large factories alongside small private workshops. Trade unions were illegal until 1906, and even then their activities were carefully controlled. Under these conditions, worker discontent grew, culminating in the revolution of 1905, which involved widespread strikes in the cities and rural uprisings. Despite some transient reforms, the tsarist regime was able to retain control through increasing repression until its collapse in 1917.

The Bolshevik Revolution and the Establishment of Soviet Power (1917–1929)

In 1917, at the height of World War I, two revolutions occurred in Russia. The March revolution threw out the tsar (Nicholas II) and installed a moderate provisional government. In November that government was overthrown by the Bolsheviks, a part of the Russian Social Democratic Labor Party led by Vladimir Lenin. This second revolution marked a major turning point in the history of Russia. Instead of trying to imitate Western European patterns, the Bolsheviks applied a dramatically different blueprint for economic, social, and political development.

The Bolsheviks were Marxists who believed their revolution reflected the political interests of a particular social class, namely the proletariat (working class). Most of the revolutionary leaders, however, were not themselves workers but were from the more educated and privileged strata, commonly referred to as the intelligentsia. But in 1917 the Bolsheviks' slogan "Land, Peace, and Bread" appealed both to the working class and to the discontented peasantry, which made up over 80 percent of Russia's population. With his keen political sense, Lenin was able to grasp the strategy and the proper moment for his party to seize state power.

The Bolsheviks formed a tightly organized political party based on their own understanding of democracy. Their strategy was founded on the notions of **democratic centralism** and vanguardism, concepts that differed significantly from the liberal democratic notions of Western countries. Democratic centralism mandated a hierarchical party structure in which party leaders were elected from below with freedom of discussion until a decision was taken, but strict discipline was required in implementing party policy. In time, the centralizing elements of democratic centralism took precedence over the democratic elements, as the party tried to insulate itself first from informers of the tsarist forces and later from both real and imagined threats to the new regime. The concept of a **vanguard party** governed the Bolsheviks' (and later the Communist Party's) relations with broader social forces: party leaders claimed that they understood the interests of the working people better than the people did themselves. It was democracy "for the people," not "by the people." In time, this philosophy was used to rationalize virtually all actions of the Communist Party and the state it dominated. Neither democratic centralism nor vanguardism emphasized democratic procedures or accountability of the leaders to the public. Rather, these concepts focused on achieving a "correct" political outcome that would reflect the "true" interests of the working class, as defined by the leaders of the Communist Party.

Once in power, the Bolsheviks formed a new government, which in 1922 brought the formation of the first Communist party-state, the Union of Soviet Socialist Republics (USSR), henceforth referred to as the Soviet Union. The four republics (the Russian, Transcaucasian, Ukrainian, and Belorussian Republics) that formed the initial union were joined by additional republics after 1922. In the early years, the Bolsheviks felt compelled to take extraordinary measures to ensure the survival of the regime. The initial challenge was an extended Civil War (1918–1921) for control of the countryside and outlying regions. The Bolsheviks introduced War Communism to ensure the supply of materials necessary for the war effort. The state took control of key economic sectors and forcibly requisitioned grain from the peasants. Political controls also increased: the Cheka, the security arm of the regime, was strengthened, and restrictions were placed on other political groups, including other socialist parties.

By 1921 the leadership recognized the political costs of War Communism. The peasants resented the forced requisitioning of grain and the policy stymied initiative. With the New Economic Policy (1921–1928) concessions were made to this group. Once in-kind taxes were paid, peasants were allowed to sell their product in the free market. In other sectors of the economy, private enterprise and trade were also revived. The state, however, retained control of large-scale industry and experimented with state control of the arts and culture.

Gradually throughout the 1920s the authoritarian elements of Bolshevik thinking eclipsed the democratic elements. Lacking a democratic tradition and bolstered by the vanguard ideology of the party, the Bolshevik leaders engaged in internecine struggles following Lenin's death in 1924. These conflicts culminated in the rise of Joseph Stalin and the arrest or exile of prominent party figures such as Leon Trotsky and Nikolai Bukharin. By 1929 all opposition, even within the party itself, had been eliminated. Sacrifices of democratic procedure were justified in the name of protecting class interests.

The Bolshevik revolution also initiated a period of international isolation for the new state. To fulfill their promise of peace, the new rulers had to cede important chunks of territory to Germany under the Brest-Litovsk Treaty (1918). Only the defeat of Germany by Russia's former allies (the United States, Britain, and France) reversed some of these concessions. However, these countries were hardly pleased with internal developments in Russia. Not only did the Bolshevik revolution bring expropriation of foreign holdings and Russia's withdrawal from the Allied powers' war effort, it also represented the first successful challenge to the capitalist order. As a result, the former allies sent material aid and troops to oppose the new Bolshevik government during the Civil War.

Lenin had hoped that successful working-class revolutions in Germany and other Western countries would bolster the fledgling Soviet regime and bring it tangible aid. When this did not occur, however, the Soviet leaders had to rely on their country's own resources to build a viable economic structure. In 1923, Stalin announced the goal of building "socialism in one country." This policy defined Soviet state interests as synonymous with the promotion of socialism. It simultaneously set the Soviet Union on a course of economic isolation from the larger world of states. To survive in such isolation, the new Soviet leader, Joseph Stalin, pursued a policy of rapid industrialization and increased political control.

The Stalin Revolution (1929–1953)

Beginning in 1929 until Joseph Stalin's death in 1953, the Soviet Union faced another critical juncture. During this time, Stalin consolidated his power as Soviet leader by establishing the basic characteristics of the Soviet regime that substantially endured until the collapse of the Communist system in 1991. Russia's problems since 1991 reflect the difficulties of extracting Russia from the Stalinist system.

The Stalin revolution brought changes to virtually every aspect of Soviet life. The result was an interconnected system of economic, political, and ideological power. Under Stalin, the state became the engine for rapid economic development, with state ownership and control of virtually all economic assets (land, factories, housing, and stores). By 1935 over 90 percent of agricultural land had been taken from the peasants and made into state or collective farms. This **collectivization** campaign was justified as a means of preventing the emergence of a new capitalist class in the countryside, but it actually targeted the peasantry as a whole, leading to widespread famine and loss of life. Those who resisted were arrested or exiled to Siberia. In the industrial sector, a program of rapid industrialization favored the heavy industries (steel mills, hydroelectric dams, machine building); production of consumer goods was neglected. Economic control was exercised through a complex but inefficient system of central economic planning, in which the state planning committee (Gosplan) set production targets for every enterprise in the country. The industrialization campaign was accompanied by social upheaval. People were uprooted from their traditional lives in the countryside and catapulted into the rhythm of urban industrial life. There were dramatic changes in the cultural and social spheres as well. Media censorship and state control of the arts stymied creativity as well as political opposition. The party/state became the authoritative source of truth, so anyone deviating from the authorized interpretation could be charged with treason.

In the early 1920s the Communist Party was the only political party permitted to function; and by the early 1930s opposition or dissent within the party itself had been eliminated. Gradually the party became subject to the personal whims of Stalin and his secret police. Party bodies ceased to meet on a regular basis, and they no longer made important political decisions. Party ranks were periodically cleansed of potential opponents, and previous party leaders as well as citizens from many walks of life were violently purged (arrested, sentenced to labor camps, sometimes executed). Overall, an estimated 5 percent of the Soviet population was arrested at one point or another under the Stalinist system, usually for no apparent cause. Social groups lost all autonomy. People could not form independent political organizations, and public discussion about controversial issues was prohibited. The arbitrary and unpredictable terror of the 1930s left a legacy of fear. Only among trusted friends and family members did people dare to express their true views. Forms of resistance, when they occurred, were evasive rather than active: peasants killed their livestock to avoid giving it over to collective farms; laborers worked inefficiently and absenteeism was high; in some cases, citizens simply refused to vote for the single candidate offered in the elections.

The Stalinist model has often been labeled **totalitarian**, a term used to describe political systems in which the state seeks to penetrate all aspects of public

and private life through an integrated system of ideological, economic, and political control.[4] Mechanisms to achieve this included complete control of the mass media, state ownership of the economy, an atmosphere of fear created by an arbitrary exercise of power by the secret police, and mobilization of the population to participate in a range of organizations and activities controlled from above. The term *totalitarian* was coined not only to describe Stalinist Russia but also to demonstrate its similarities to Nazi Germany. In reality, however, the scope of state control in the Stalinist period was less complete than the concept of totalitarianism suggests.

Isolation of the Soviet citizen from interaction with the outside world was a key tool of Stalinist control. Foreign news broadcasts were jammed, travel abroad was highly restricted, and contacts with foreigners brought citizens under suspicion. The economy was also highly autarkic, that is, isolated from interaction with the international economic system. Although this policy shielded Soviet society from the effects of the Great Depression of the 1930s that shook the capitalist world (indeed the decade of the 1930s was a period of rapid economic growth in the Soviet Union), it also allowed an inefficient system of production to survive in the USSR. Protected from foreign competition, the economy failed to keep up with the rapid pace of economic and technological transformation in the West.

In 1941, Nazi Germany invaded the Soviet Union, and Stalin had little choice but to join the Allied powers. World War II had a profound impact on the outlook of an entire generation of Soviet citizens. Soviet propaganda dubbed it the Great Patriotic War, evoking images of Russian nationalism rather than of socialist internationalism—the sacrifices and heroism of the war period remained a powerful symbol of Soviet pride and unity until the collapse of Communist power. The period was marked by support for traditional family values and by a greater tolerance for religious institutions, whose support Stalin sought for the war effort. Among the social corollaries of the war effort were a declining birthrate and a long-lasting gender imbalance, as a result of high wartime casualties for men. The war also affected certain minority ethnic groups that were accused of collaborating with the enemy during the war effort and were deported to areas farther east in the USSR. These included Germans, Crimean Tatars, and peoples of the northern Caucasus regions such as the Chechens, Ingush, and Karachai-Balkar. Their later rehabilitation and resettlement caused renewed disruption and conflict, contributing to the ethnic conflicts of the post-Soviet period. In sum, the war experience had a long-lasting influence on the development of postwar political elites, on demographic patterns in the country, and on ethnic relations.

The Soviet Union was a major force in the defeat of the Axis powers in Europe. After the war, the other Allied powers allowed the Soviet Union to absorb new territories into the USSR itself (these became the Soviet republics of Latvia, Lithuania, Estonia, Moldavia, and portions of western Ukraine), and they implicitly granted the USSR free rein to shape the postwar governments and economies in eastern Germany, Poland, Hungary, Czechoslovakia, Yugoslavia, Bulgaria, and Romania. Western offers to include parts of the region in the Marshall Plan were rejected under pressure from the USSR. With Soviet support, local communist parties gained control of all of these countries; only in Yugoslavia were indigenous communist forces sufficiently strong to gain power largely on their own and thus later to assert their independence from Moscow.

Following World War II, the features of Soviet communism were largely replicated in those areas newly integrated into the USSR and in the countries of Eastern Europe. The Soviet Union tried to isolate its satellites in Eastern Europe from the West and to tighten their economic and political integration with the USSR. The Council for Mutual Economic Assistance (CMEA) and the Warsaw Treaty Organization (a military alliance) were formed for this purpose. With its developed industrial economy, its military stature bolstered in World War II, and its growing sphere of regional control, the USSR emerged as a global superpower. But the enlarged Soviet bloc still remained insulated from the larger world of states. Some countries within the Soviet bloc, however, had strong historic links to Western Europe (especially Czechoslovakia, Poland, and Hungary), and in these areas, domestic resistance to Soviet dominance forced some alterations or deviations from the Soviet model. Over time, these countries served not only as geographic buffers to direct Western influence on the USSR but also as conduits for such influence. In the more Westernized Baltic republics of the USSR itself, the population firmly resisted assimilation to Soviet rule and eventually spearheaded the disintegration of the Soviet Union in the late 1980s.

Attempts at De-Stalinization

Stalin's death in 1953 triggered another critical juncture in Soviet politics. Even the Soviet elite realized that Stalin's system of terror could be sustained only at great cost to the development of the country. The terror stymied initiative and participation; and the unpredictability of Stalinist rule inhibited the rational formulation of policy. The period from Stalin's death until the mid-1980s saw a regularization and stabilization of Soviet politics. Terror abated, but political controls remained in place, and efforts to isolate Soviet citizens from foreign influences continued.

Nikita Khrushchev, who succeeded Stalin as the party leader from 1955 until his removal in 1964, embarked on a bold policy of de-Stalinization. Although his specific policies were only minimally successful, he initiated a thaw in political and cultural life, an approach that planted the seeds that ultimately undermined the Stalinist system. Khrushchev rejected terror as an instrument of political control. According to Khrushchev, the party still embodied the positive Leninist values that had inspired the 1917 revolution —namely, the construction of an egalitarian and democratic socialist society that would protect the true interests of the working population. Khrushchev revived the Communist Party as a vital political institution able to exercise political, economic, and cultural authority. The secret police (KGB) was subordinated to party authority, and party meetings were resumed on a regular basis. However, internal party structures remained highly centralized and elections were uncontested. In the cultural sphere, Khrushchev allowed sporadic liberalization, with the publication in the official media of some literature critical of the Stalinist system.

Leonid Brezhnev, Khrushchev's successor who headed the party from October 1964 until his death in 1982, partially reversed the de-Stalinization efforts of the 1950s and early 1960s. Controls were tightened again in the cultural sphere. Individuals who expressed dissenting views (members of the so-called dissident movement) through underground publishing or publication abroad, were harassed, arrested, or exiled. However, unlike in the Stalinist period, the political repression was predictable; people knew when they were transgressing permitted limits of criticism. In short, forms of political control came to resemble those typical of other authoritarian regimes. The Brezhnev regime could be described as primarily bureaucratic and conservative, seeking to maintain existing power structures rather than to introduce new ones.

During the Brezhnev era, a **tacit social contract** with the population governed state-society relations.[5] In exchange for political compliance, the population enjoyed job security; a lax work environment; low prices for basic goods, housing, and transport; free social services (medical care, recreational services); and minimal interference in personal life. Wages of the worst-off citizens (especially agricultural and industrial workers) were increased relative to those of the more educated and better-off portions of the population. For its part, the intelligentsia (historically Russia's social conscience and critic) was allowed more freedom to discuss publicly issues that were not of crucial importance to the regime.

Nonetheless, from the late 1970s, an aging political leadership was increasingly ineffective at addressing the mounting problems facing Soviet society.

Economic growth rates declined and improvements in the standard of living were minimal (see Table 1). Many consumer goods were still in short supply, and quality was often mediocre. As the economy stagnated, opportunities for upward career mobility declined. To maintain the Soviet Union's superpower status and competitive position in the arms race, resources were diverted to the military sector, gutting the capacity of the consumer and agricultural spheres to satisfy popular expectations. Russia's rich natural wealth was squandered, and the costs of exploiting new resource deposits (mostly in Siberia) soared. High pollution levels lowered the quality of life and health in terms of morbidity and declining life expectancy. At the same time, liberalization in some Eastern European states and the telecommunications revolution made it increasingly difficult to shield the population from exposure to Western life-styles and ideas. Among a certain critical portion of the population, aspirations were rising just as the capacity of the system to fulfill them was declining. It was in this context that the next critical transition occurred.

Perestroika and Glasnost (1985–1991)

Mikhail Gorbachev took office as Communist Party leader in March 1985, at the relatively young age of fifty-three. Gorbachev hoped to reform the system in

Table 1

Provision of Urban and Rural Population with Various Goods at the End of the Year (total items per 1,000 persons)

	1970	1975	1980	1985	1989	1994
Clocks	1193	1319	1523	1580	1647	2032
Televisions	143	215	249	293	316	380
Cameras	77	77	91	102	102	124
Refrigerators and freezers	89	178	252	275	276	309
Bicycles and mopeds	145	156	144	165	176	179
Sewing machines	161	178	190	190	185	176
Washing machines	141	189	205	205	216	265
Tape recorders	21	46	73	110	150	205
Radio sets	199	230	250	289	285	340

Source: DeBardeleben, Joan, *Russian Politics in Transition,* Second Edition. Copyright 1997 by Houghton Mifflin Company. Reprinted with permission.

order to spur economic growth and political renewal, but without undermining Communist Party rule or its basic ideological precepts.

Four important concepts formed the basis of Gorbachev's reform program—*perestroika, glasnost, demokratizatsiia,* and "New Thinking." **Perestroika** (restructuring) involved decentralization and rationalization of the economic structure to enable individual enterprises (firms) to increase efficiency and take initiative. The central planning system was not to be disbanded but reformed. To counteract the resistance of entrenched central bureaucracies, Gorbachev enlisted the support of the intelligentsia, who benefited from his policy of *glasnost.* **Glasnost** (openness) involved relaxing controls on public debate, the airing of diverse viewpoints, and the publication of previously prohibited literature. **Demokratizatsiia** (Gorbachev's conception of democratization) was an effort to increase the responsiveness of political organs to public sentiment, both within and outside of the party. *Demokratizatsiia* did not endorse all components of Western liberal democracy, but it did place greater emphasis on procedural elements (competitive elections, a **law-based state**, freer political expression) than did the traditional Leninist approach. Thus it implicitly challenged both democratic centralism and vanguardism; it represented movement toward a conception of democracy "by the people" rather than simply "for the people." Finally, "New Thinking" in foreign policy involved a rethinking of international power in nonmilitary terms; it emphasized the search for cooperation rather than confrontation with the West.[6] Gorbachev advocated integration of the USSR into the world of states and the global economy. Rather than depicting the relationship between the Soviet Union and the West as one of ideological competition and class struggle, Gorbachev emphasized the common challenges facing East and West, such as the cost and hazards of the arms race and environmental degradation.

Gorbachev's policies triggered a fundamental change in the relationship between state and society in the USSR. Citizens pursued their interests and beliefs through a variety of newly created organizations at the national and local levels. These included ethnonationalist movements, environmental groups, groups for the rehabilitation of Stalinist victims, charitable groups, new or reformed professional organizations,

political clubs, and many others. The existence of these groups implicitly challenged the Communist Party's monopoly of power. Splits also developed within the Communist Party. Gorbachev tried to utilize these diverse strains to revitalize the party by encouraging competitive elections within the organization. A new party program was proposed to reflect the values of the reform agenda. By March 1990 pressures from within and outside the party forced the Supreme Soviet (the Soviet parliament) to rescind Article 6 of the Soviet constitution, which provided the basis for single-party rule. Embryonic political parties challenged the Communist Party's monopoly of political control. In the spring of 1989 the first contested elections since the 1920s were held for positions in the Soviet parliament. These were followed by elections at the republic and local levels in 1990, which, in some cases, put leaders in power who pushed for increased republic and regional autonomy.

The most divisive issues facing Gorbachev were economic policy and demands for republic autonomy. The Soviet Union was made up of fifteen **union republics**, each formed on the basis of an ethnic or national group, as only 50.8 percent of the Soviet population was ethnically Russian in 1989. In several of these union republics, popular front organizations formed, sometimes supported by a portion of the local Communist leadership. First in the three Baltic republics (Latvia, Lithuania, and Estonia), then in other union republics (particularly Ukraine, Georgia, Armenia, Moldova [formerly Moldavia], and Russia itself) demands for national autonomy and, in some cases, for secession from the USSR were put forth. Gorbachev's efforts to bring consensus on a new federal system for the fifteen union republics failed, as popular support and elite self-interest took on an irreversible momentum, resulting in a "separatism mania."

Gorbachev's economic policies failed as well. They involved half-measures that sent contradictory messages to enterprise directors, producing a drop in output and national income and undermining established patterns that had kept the Soviet economy functioning, albeit inefficiently. Gorbachev hesitated to adopt a comprehensive program of economic transformation, because any such program would have caused immediate economic dislocations. But Gorbachev's failure to act decisively also resulted in an economic downturn that intensified as *perestroika* progressed. Money was issued with nothing to back it, so that too much money was chasing too few goods. Most prices were still subject to state control, so shortages of even basic goods were common. The economic decline reinforced demands by union republics for economic autonomy even as central policy appeared to shackle any real improvement. To protect themselves, regions and union republics began to restrict exports to other regions, despite planning mandates. "Separatism mania" was accompanied by "the war of laws," as regional officials openly defied central directives. Whereas previously the state had been able to enforce the basic outlines of its political and economic strategy, now its ability to implement its policies was rapidly declining. In response, Gorbachev issued numerous decrees; their number increased as their efficacy declined.

Gorbachev achieved his greatest success in the foreign policy sphere. Just as his domestic support was plummeting in late 1990 and early 1991, he was awarded the Nobel Peace Prize, reflecting his esteemed international stature. Under the guidance of his "New Thinking," the military buildup in the USSR was halted, important arms control agreements were ratified, and many controls on international contacts were lifted. In 1989, Gorbachev refused to prop up unpopular communist governments in the East European countries. First in Hungary and Poland, then in the German Democratic Republic (East Germany) and Czechoslovakia, pressure from below pushed the communist parties out of power, and a process of democratization and market reform ensued. More gradual transformations occurred in Bulgaria and Romania. Politicians in both East and West declared the Cold War over. To Gorbachev's dismay the liberation of Eastern Europe fed the process of disintegration in the Soviet Union itself.

Collapse of the USSR and the Emergence of the Russian Federation (1991 to the Present)

On August 19, 1991, a coalition of conservative figures attempted a coup d'état, temporarily removing Gorbachev from the leadership post to stop the reform initiative and prevent the collapse of the USSR. The failed coup proved to be the death knell of the Soviet system. While Gorbachev was held captive at his summer house (*dacha*), Boris Yeltsin, the popularly elected president of the Russian Republic, climbed atop a tank loyal to the reform leadership and rallied opposition to the attempted coup. Yeltsin declared himself the true champion of democratic values and Russian national interest. The Soviet Union collapsed at the end of 1991 when Yeltsin joined the leaders of Ukraine and Belorussia (later renamed Belarus) to declare the formation of a loosely structured entity, called the Commonwealth of Independent States, to replace the Soviet Union. In December 1991, the Russian Federation stepped out as an independent country in the world of states. Its independent status (along with that of the other fourteen former union republics of the USSR) was quickly recognized by the major world powers.

Yeltsin proclaimed his commitment to Western-style democracy and market economic reform, but that program proved hard to implement. The attempt to pursue market reform and democratization simultaneously produced deep tensions. The market reform produced severe and unpopular economic repercussions, as traditional economic patterns were disrupted. The Russian parliament elected in 1990 was leery of embracing the radical economic reform, partly for fear of the social consequences and partly because it might undermine traditional patterns of political power. The president relied heavily on the power of decree to try to implement his program, raising questions about the democratic nature of the new regime. The conflict erupted violently during debate surrounding creation of a new Russian constitution. The failure to achieve a consensus among the political elite, particularly between the executive and legislative branches of the government, led to a bloody showdown in October 1993, after Yeltsin disbanded what he considered to be an obstructive parliament and laid siege to its premises, the Russian White House. The president mandated new elections and a constitutional referendum in December 1993. The constitution, adopted by a narrow margin of voters, put in place a set of institutions marked by a powerful president and a weak parliament.

The new Russian state was undermined by high levels of corruption, which also permeated the government's efforts to privatize former state enterprises. The government's economic reform program failed

Leaders: *Boris Nikolaevich Yeltsin*

On February 1, 1931, Boris Yeltsin was born to a working-class family in a village in the Russian province of Sverdlovsk located in the Ural Mountains. Like so many men of his generation who later rose to top Communist Party posts, his education was technical, in the field of construction. His early jobs were as foreman, engineer, supervisor, and finally director of a large construction combine. Yeltsin joined the Communist Party of the Soviet Union in 1961, and in 1968 he took on full-time work in the regional party organization. Over the next ten years he rose to higher positions in Sverdlovsk *oblast*, first as party secretary for industry and finally as head of the regional party in 1976. In 1981, Yeltsin became a member of the Central Committee of the CPSU and moved onto the national stage.

Because of Yeltsin's reputation as an energetic figure not tainted by corruption, Mikhail Gorbachev drafted Yeltsin into his leadership team in 1985. Yeltsin's first important post in Moscow was as head of the Moscow party organization. Gorbachev also selected Yeltsin to be a nonvoting member of the USSR's top party organ, the Politburo.

Yeltsin soon gained a reputation as an outspoken critic of party privilege. He became a popular figure in Moscow, as he mingled with average Russians on city streets and public transport. In 1987 party conservatives launched an attack on Yeltsin for his outspoken positions; Gorbachev did not come to his defense. Yeltsin was removed from the Politburo and from his post as Moscow party leader in 1988; he was demoted to a position in the construction sector of the Soviet government. At the party conference in June 1988, Yeltsin defended his position in proceedings that were televised across the USSR. Yeltsin's popular support soared as the public saw him single-handedly taking on the party establishment.

Rivalry between Gorbachev and Yeltsin formed a backdrop for the dramatic events that led to the collapse of the Soviet Union in December 1991. Yeltsin represented a radical reform path, while Gorbachev supported gradualism. Yeltsin established his political base within the Russian Republic; thus Russia's self-assertion within the USSR was also a way for Yeltsin to secure his own position. Under his guidance on June 8, 1990, the Russian Republic declared sovereignty (not a declaration of independence, but an assertion of the right of the Russian Republic to set its own policy). One month later, Yeltsin resigned his party membership. On June 12, 1991, Yeltsin was elected president of the Russian Republic by direct popular vote, establishing his legitimacy as a spokesman for democratization and Russian independence.

During the attempted coup d'état by party conservatives in August 1991, Yeltsin reinforced his popularity and democratic credentials by taking a firm stand against the plotters while Gorbachev remained captive at his *dacha* in the Crimea. Yeltsin's defiance gave him a decisive advantage in the competition with Gorbachev and laid the groundwork for the December 1991 dissolution of the USSR engineered by Yeltsin (representing Russia) and the leaders of Ukraine and Belorussia. In an unusual turn of events, the rivalry between Yeltsin and Gorbachev, as well as between their differing approaches to reform, was decided through the disbanding of the country Gorbachev headed.

In 1992, Yeltsin embarked on the difficult task of implementing his radical reform policy in the newly independent Russian Federation. Economic crisis, rising corruption and crime, and a decline of state authority ensued. Yeltsin's popularity plummeted. His reputation as a democratic reformer was marred by his use of force against the Russian parliament in 1993 and in the Chechnya war in 1994–1996. Although Yeltsin's campaign team managed to orchestrate an electoral victory in 1996, Yeltsin's day was past. Plagued by poor health and failed policies, Yeltsin could hope only to serve out his presidential term and groom a successor. How history will view Yeltsin is hard to say. On the one hand, it was he who led Russia to independence, oversaw the final collapse of the USSR, and undertook Russia's brash experiment with market reform and democratization. On the other hand, it is as yet unknown whether the experiment will yield positive results.

The White House, seat of the Russian parliament, burns while under assault from troops loyal to President Yeltsin during the confrontation in October 1993. *Source:* AP/Wide World Photos.

to produce an effective market economy but instead generated a confusing and disorderly system of quasi-market relations that often left workers without wages for months on end. The crisis of August/ September 1998 was but the culmination of this failed reform process. Yeltsin's repeated reshuffling of the government beginning April 1998 reflected the difficulties of finding a leadership team and government policy that could set Russia on a more successful economic and political course.

Themes and Implications

Historical Junctures and Political Themes

The main assets Russia possessed as independence dawned were a widespread rejection of the Communist past, hope for a better future, and broad international support for the new regime. By 1999 these resources were nearly exhausted.

The stature of the newly independent Russia in the world of states and the initial support offered by the international community to Russia's reform agenda were replaced by skepticism. Initial expectations were dashed; the hoped-for transition to democratic and market structures compatible with Western norms faltered. At the same time, the Russian leadership and population had to accept their country's status as a failed superpower. National humiliation intensified the bitter reality of economic decline. The Russian government repeatedly sought Western aid and accepted sometimes harsh conditions in exchange. Resentment of Western involvement reinforced anti-Western tendencies within Russia. The air attack carried out by the newly expanded North Atlantic Treaty Organization (NATO) in early 1999 against Yugoslavia reinforced these sentiments, as many Russians viewed NATO's actions as an assertion of power against a historically close Slavic nation. These concerns, combined with the chaotic state of the economy and polity, raised concerns about Russia's management of its nuclear arsenal.

On the economic front, the situation in Russia was arguably worse in late 1998 than at any time in the last several decades. The Yeltsin leadership was not successful in governing the economy, as the country emerged from its Communist past. The failed promises of Yeltsin's policy have elicited a growing skepticism toward the Western economic model and the processes of global integration that accompany it. While nostalgia for the stability of the Soviet period surfaces frequently in contemporary Russia, few want to revive the highly centralized structures of the Communist period.

The problem is that Russia has not been able to define a third path for itself, that is, an economic model that suits Russian conditions and history better than the Western market model but that still allows the benefits of integration into the global economy.

Russians also associate their declining standard of living with the introduction of democratic institutions, and to some extent this has elicited skepticism toward the democratic idea itself. The country is governed by popularly elected institutions, but the public has become increasingly cynical about their ability to solve any of the problems facing Russia. The process itself also seems suspect, since political deal-making is apparently not responsive to popular sentiments but rather to hidden cartels of elite interests. For many Russians, Soviet institutions, while not democratic, had the advantage of providing a predictable and stable economic and political environment. The public's association of democracy with economic decline may provide fertile ground for a populist leader to introduce a strongly nationalist agenda, possibly utilizing authoritarian means.

Finally, Russians are engaged in trying to define new forms of collective identity. With the collapse of Marxist-Leninism, both individuals and groups must find new foundations for political and social values. This has, for some, meant a revival of religious values or ethnic identity. In some cases, separatist tendencies have emerged; the attempt of one of Russia's regions, the Republic of Chechnya, to secede from the Russian Federation beginning in 1991 provides the most dramatic example of how division over collective identity can engender political instability and conflict. Other aspects of identity are also being reconsidered. Social class, a linchpin of Soviet ideology, needs to be redefined if it is to serve as a basis of identification and group solidarity. The importance of economic factors in defining identity is likely to increase in future years.

Implications for Comparative Politics

Many countries in the world today are undergoing a process of transition from some sort of authoritarian regime to democratic political structures. The Russian experience is, however, unique in many respects. Indigenous political traditions and political culture influence the nature of political change in any country. In Russia's case one of the most important factors is the tradition of the patrimonial state of tsarist times, which extended into the Soviet period. In addition, the intertwined character of politics, economics, and ideology in the Soviet Union has made democratization and economic reform difficult to realize. Altering the political structures has necessitated dismantling the entire foundation of the former Soviet system. In effect, four transition processes were begun at once:

- The attempted democratization of the political system, including the introduction of competitive elections and competing political parties
- Dismantling state dominance of the economy through privatization, the release of prices from state control, and the end of guaranteed employment
- A search for new forms of collective identity to replace those provided by the old Communist ideology
- A process of economic integration into the world of states and exposure to ideas and goods from the Western world

Whereas other democratizing countries may have undergone one or two of these transitions simultaneously, several of the post-Communist states, including Russia, have tried to tackle all four of them at once. Thus, the stakes and the stress are high. Through the study of Russia, we can explore some of the fundamental issues that are involved in the formation of political institutions, identities, and decision-making processes. As one analyst of Russia has suggested, Russia is building "democracy from scratch."[7] The search for methods to structure political conflict, build political legitimacy, and resolve policy problems is posed in a very stark form in the Russian case. There are few political precedents or examples for Russians to follow from their own history. The Russian case also allows us to examine how political and economic factors interact. For example, the Communist elites had no private wealth to fall back on, so many relied on corrupt or illegal methods to maintain former privileges after Communism collapsed. Citizens, confronted with economic decline and an uncertain future, may be susceptible to nationalist appeals, demagogues, or antidemocratic movements. Examining these strong linkages between political and economic forces in Russia may provide insights for understanding other political settings.

Section ❷ Political Economy and Development

Imagine a Russian bureaucrat traveling to London and observing that traffic there is less chaotic than in Moscow. The official concludes that Russia should adopt the English system and have people drive on the left-hand side of the road. Back in Moscow, traffic officials agree it is worth a try. But fearing public outrage, they first order only professional drivers (trucks and buses) to switch; ordinary drivers would be given time to adapt.[8] Well, you can imagine the result.

Some experts on post-Communist economies liken the dangers of half-reform to the lesson of this anecdote. However, turning a highly centralized economy into a decentralized market structure is more complicated than reforming traffic patterns, and certainly has broader social and political consequences. The truth is that none of the so-called experts really know how to do it; and the politicians face a far more complex task than the economic experts do. They not only need to know what to do but also how to get others to comply. Meanwhile, large segments of the Russian economy appear to be in chaos. Is this the consequence of a flawed reform program? Has reform been too slow or too fast? Who are the winners and losers so far? In this section we examine the sequence of the present economic crisis and the nature of Russia's economic system as it is now developing, as well as social and international aspects of the economic changes.

State and Economy

As noted in Section 1, the tsarist state played the leading role in Russia's economic development until the Bolshevik revolution. The economic structures put in place in the 1930s, after the abandonment of the New Economic Policy, also strengthened the dominant role of the state. The basic features of that system were retained until the early 1990s. Therefore, to understand the dilemma of economic transformation in Russia, it is necessary to be familiar with some Soviet economic practices and their social implications.

The Soviet Economic System

Under the Soviet command economy, land, factories, and all other important economic assets belonged to the state. Powerful state ministries oversaw the various sectors of the economy, such as machine-building, light industry, and agriculture. Each was a large, hierarchically structured bureaucracy that extended down to the individual enterprises (firms). Gosplan (the state planning committee) was responsible for working out one-year and five-year economic plans to be implemented through the ministries. The one-year plans were operational, providing specific instructions as to what should be produced, by whom, and in what quantities. Although the plans had the force of law, they were frequently too ambitious to be fulfilled. In the agricultural sector, the state farm was the equivalent of the industrial enterprise. Some peasants worked on collective farms, which theoretically were collectively run and owned by the peasants themselves. In practice the collective farms were included in the state plan and operated in much the same way as state farms, although collective farm workers did not receive all of the same social benefits as state farm workers. Even after the collectivization campaign of 1929–1933, peasants were permitted to till small individual private plots that were not included in the state planning system yet provided families with food and supplementary income from sales at the peasant markets in the city. In the 1980s these plots accounted for about 25 percent of total agricultural output, but only about 1.5 percent of total agricultural land. These were not, however, small, free-standing farms, because peasants needed resources from the state sector (equipment, seeds, fertilizers) to operate them. The peasant looked to the state or collective farm for a steady income, access to supplies, and social benefits.

Prices were centrally controlled—they were set by the state and did not rise when demand was high and supplies were limited, as in a market economy. Only in the peasant markets and the illegal black market did prices fluctuate in response to conditions of shortage or surplus. Enterprises were to meet state-set production targets and were not motivated by the need to turn a profit. Therefore, producers had neither the incentive nor the resources to increase production of goods in short supply or to respond to consumer demands. Retail stores piled up stocks of unwanted goods while goods in high demand (even some basic ones) were often unavailable. For the average citizen, the shortages meant waiting in line, even for basic items. Both individuals and enterprises snatched up what they could, squirreling it away for trade or later use.

Environmental quality deteriorated under Soviet rule. Environmental protection was a low priority. Marxist-Leninist ideology saw technology as capable of mastering nature and counteracting any negative effects. Thus, large nature-transforming projects (hydroelectric dams, huge factory complexes) were glorified as symbols of Soviet power. At the same time, priority industries (metallurgy, machine-building, chemicals, energy production) were highly polluting. On paper, Soviet standards for industrial emissions were often impressive, but they were not enforced, partly because they were unrealistically ambitious. Inadequate technological safeguards and an insufficient regulatory structure led to the disastrous nuclear accident at Chernobyl (in Ukraine) in 1986, which contaminated immense areas of agricultural land in Ukraine and Belorussia (now Belarus). In highly polluted regions, the incidence of respiratory and other ailments was visibly higher; high nitrate levels and other contaminants in food, resulting from excessive use of chemical fertilizers and pesticides, were present in many areas of the USSR.

By the 1970s easily accessible deposits of natural resources in the western part of the country approached depletion. To deal with this, Soviet leaders gave priority to development of northern Siberia to permit exploitation of valuable deposits of oil, natural gas, and precious metals located there, resources that also served as valuable export commodities. However, Siberian development proved to be complicated and expensive. Costs were increased by permafrost conditions, transport distances, and the necessity of paying higher wages to attract workers. Technology was insufficient to deal with many problems, resulting in a massive waste of resources and serious environmental problems, such as oil pipeline leaks.

Russian Reform Efforts

During the years of Gorbachev's *perestroika*, efforts to reform the economic system were halting and

contradictory. Gorbachev was unwilling to give up the state's role in assuring full employment; this constraint necessitated maintaining other elements of state control. The result was declining economic performance, increasing regionalism, and an uncertain economic environment.

Following the collapse of the Soviet Union in December 1991, Yeltsin, along with advisers such as deputy prime ministers Yegor Gaidar and Gennady Burbulis, immediately endorsed radical **market reform**, sometimes referred to as **shock therapy** because of the radical rupture it implies. This commitment marked a great change in the broad sweep of Russian and Soviet history, a distinctive turn away from the patrimonial state that characterized the tsarist and Soviet periods. The basic notion underlying the government's reform policy was to free prices from state control and to take ownership of economic assets away from the state and place them in private hands. In this way, decision-making about production and distribution of goods would be turned over to new private owners, who would be forced to respond to consumer demand. Enterprises would no longer receive state subsidies; they would be responsible for their own success or failure. Only certain key sectors of the economy were to remain largely under state control, including transport, defense, health care, education, culture, communications, research, and certain portions of the energy sector. Some of these were to be privatized in later stages of the process. The changes were to be rapid and thorough, thus jolting the Russian economy into a new mode of operation. By definition, this strategy involved a breakdown of the tacit social contract. Shock therapy would inevitably throw parts of the economy into a downward spin; it was hoped that recovery would be relatively quick. The success of the policy would depend on instituting measures to stabilize the monetary system, especially strict controls on the emission of rubles by the state bank and on state budget expenditures. The final goal of the policy was to create a Western-type market economy, integrated into the global economic system and capable of producing domestic prosperity.

Yeltsin quickly took steps to implement the economic reform. In January 1992 price controls on most goods were loosened or lifted entirely. The result was a period of high inflation, reaching 1354 percent in

1992. In the early 1990s inflation was fueled by a soft monetary policy pursued by the State Bank of the USSR and later the Central Bank of Russia; money was printed with nothing tangible to back it up. Real wages, on average, declined by an estimated 50 percent between late 1991 and January 1993. Under pressure from the International Monetary Fund the emission of money was restricted in the period 1995–1998. Inflation fell to 6.4 percent for the twelve months ending June 1998, before the financial crisis later that year pumped it up again.[9]

By 1999 it was apparent that the government's reform program had failed to achieve its goals. Russia was in the grip of a severe depression and financial crisis. Although the exact extent of the decline is hard to specify (economic statistics are unreliable and official figures may misstate actual levels of production), some estimates indicate that in 1998 gross domestic product was only 54 percent of the 1989 level. Industrial production had slipped to less than half of the 1990 level. After registering the first slim growth of GDP in 1997 (0.8 percent, according to Russian figures), the economy slipped again in 1998, falling back 5 percent from 1997 (see Table 2). Some sectors, such as machine-building, light industry, construction

materials, and wood products have suffered the most. Many enterprises have lost their old customers and suppliers. Transport systems have sometimes been ruptured, or costs of transport are too high. The depression feeds on itself; declining capacity in one sector deprives other sectors of buyers or suppliers. Consumer purchasing power also dropped with the decline in real wages. The economy shows high levels of interenterprise debt and payment arrears. Firms are unable to pay their suppliers, so that in February 1998 over half of credits issued between enterprises were reported as overdue. Overdue tax payments were growing even faster than debt arrears to suppliers.

Under these conditions, barter arrangements, often involving intertwined linkages of several enterprises or organizations, have become common. At the same time, **capital flight**, in which money is removed from the country and deposited in foreign accounts or assets, deprived the domestic economy of an estimated 3 percent of GDP in 1995–1996. Diverse methods of laundering money to avoid taxes and extract a profit from the remaining state-owned entities are also common; the decentralized but organized network of crime and corruption is widely referred to as the **mafia**. Some government officials, the police, and operators abroad

Table 2

Economic Indicators for the Russian Federation (percent change from previous year, unless otherwise indicated)

	1991	1992	1993	1994	1995	1996	1997	1998 (est.)
Economic growth[a]	−5.0%	−14.5%	−8.7%	12.6%	−4.0%	−3.5%	0.8%	−5.0%
Industrial production	−8.0%	−18.8%	−16.2%	−22.8%	4.7%	−6.5%	0.3%	−5.0%
Agricultural production	−3.7%	−9.0%	−4.0%	−12.0%	−8.0%	−9.0%	0.1%	−9.0%
Consumer price inflation[b]	93%	1526%	875%	307%	197%	48%	15%	27%
Rubles per one U.S. dollar[c]	169	415	1247	3550	4640	5560	5960	20.990
Population (in millions, Jan. 1)	148.3	148.9	148.7	148.4	148.3	148.0	147.8	147.2
Unemployment rate (average)[d]	0.0%	4.8%	5.5%	7.5%	8.8%	9.3%	10.7%	11.6%

[a]Growth in real domestic product (controlled for inflation).
[b]Average for the year.
[c]At year end. Figures for 1998 are in new redenominated rubles, where one new ruble = 1,000 old rubles. The redenomination occurred in January 1998.
[d]According to the definition of the International Labor Organization in the year indicated.

Source: European Bank for Reconstruction and Development, *Transition report 1997: Enterprise performance and growth* (London, 1997), 223; Economist Intelligence Unit, *EIU Country Report: Russia, 4th Quarter, 1998*, 5, 18; World Bank Data (obtained from the Web site at *www.worldbank.org*): *PlanEcon Report*, vol. XIV (no. 45–46, Jan. 15, 1999), 6; *Obzor ekonomicheskoi politiki v Rossii za 1997 god* (Survey of the economic policy of Russia for 1997) (Moscow: Bureau of Economic Analysis, 1998), 391.

Russians doubt their banks. Sign reads:"Quiet! An operation is under way." *Source:* Aleksandr Evtyshenko, *Izvestiia*, September 5, 1998.

are all part of this illegal network. In the first half of the 1990s its existence fueled a rising crime rate, which has remained high; rich foreigners and Russian bankers are particular targets, as are Russian journalists who expose crime and mafia operations.

The financial crisis that hit Russia in late summer 1998 was fueled by a structure of **pyramid debt**, in which the government successively took on new loans at progressively higher rates of interest in order to pay off existing debts. With low and falling tax revenues, in 1993 the Russian government began to issue short-term obligations (GKOs) to generate revenue to pay its creditors. The government had to offer higher interest rates on each new set of GKOs in order to find lenders. Because the revenues the government acquired through GKOs were utilized, in large part, to

pay interest on debt, they did not generate any usable income for the government. By August 1998 the Russian government's inability to meet its financial obligations produced a financial crisis that reverberated throughout the entire financial structure of the country and extended to international markets. Following a sharp upturn in 1996–1997, the Russian stock market lost over 90 percent of its value by August 1998. In early September the Ministry of Finance failed to meet its obligations to both domestic and international lenders. Russian commercial banks that held previously lucrative GKOs were threatened with bankruptcy. The government was finally forced to allow a radical devaluation of the Russian ruble. In January 1999 the exchange rate was twenty-two rubles to one U.S. dollar compared to the precrisis level of about six to one. The crash of the ruble meant that prices of imported food items and durable goods rose dramatically, placing them out of reach of most Russian consumers. Banks limited withdrawals of rubles and foreign currency from personal and commercial accounts, forcing many small businesses to close and leading some foreign investors to draw back. Those who had benefited from the previous reform process, namely, the new Russian middle class and the region of Moscow, were most immediately affected, but over time the effects spread to the population as a whole.

Regional conflicts have also been fueled by the reform process and its failures. Regions rich in natural resources have demanded more economic autonomy, and some have resisted transferring tax funds to the federal authorities. Regions making demands have often won concessions, leading other areas to claim unfair treatment and press for similar privileges. The financial crisis of 1998 reinforced regionalism. As foreign imports declined, some regional governments put restrictions on the export of agricultural produce to other parts of Russia to assure that food supplies would be adequate for the local population.

Privatization was a key component of the economic reform package, pursued under the leadership of the minister of privatization, Anatoly Chubais. This policy involved the privatization of already existing state firms as well as the encouragement of new private enterprises. While many small private businesses have sprung up since 1991, their survival has been made difficult by high and complicated taxes as well by the poor infrastructure (transport, banking, communications). With the breakdown of the Soviet distribution system, trade became a lucrative business and the area in which the many successful private enterprises operate. These include not only thousands of small kiosks operating on city streets but behind-the-scenes middlemen who buy up stocks of goods and resell them at inflated prices. Through use of contacts, savvy, and bribes, some of these "businessmen" are able to accumulate huge profits and deposit them in banks abroad; other small entrepreneurs barely scrape by. Less common is the entrepreneur who invests the profits in a factory that produces tangible products, for this is a more risky venture.

An important part of the government's policy involved an effort to quickly privatize the state sector. **Spontaneous privatization** had occurred in some state-owned enterprises in the late 1980s and early 1990s; existing managers or ministry bureaucrats transformed promising enterprises into private entities without a clear legal framework for doing so. This permitted former elites to appropriate state property for private benefit. In 1992 a privatization law went into effect, providing a legal context for the process. By early 1994 an estimated 80 percent of medium-sized and large state enterprises in the designated sectors of the economy had been transformed into **joint-stock companies**.[10] Ownership of such companies is in the hands of shareholders, each of whom owns a portion of the firm's value. Shareholders may be individuals, Russian or foreign businesses, other organizations (e.g., trade unions or professional organizations), or state organs.

As part of the government's privatization plan, in November 1992 each citizen of Russia (including children) was issued a **privatization voucher** with a nominal value of 10,000 rubles (at that time equivalent to about ten U.S. dollars). These vouchers could be used to buy shares in enterprises undergoing privatization, to sell for cash, or to invest through newly formed investment funds that handled investment choices for voucher holders. In 1993 auctions selling shares in some state enterprises occurred in which these investment funds played an active role. Some workers bought shares in their own enterprises, a practice encouraged by the law on privatization and

by enterprise managers. Many people were confused about how to use the vouchers and viewed them as primarily symbolic, representing the government's attempt to convince citizens that they were getting a share of the people's property.

The law on privatization mandated that most large state enterprises be transformed into joint-stock companies. An important issue was how to distribute shares between present workers and managers ("insiders"), on the one hand, and outside buyers, on the other. The law established various options for the formation of joint-stock companies, each involving a different scheme for the portion of insider and public shares. The most popular option gave managers and workers of the enterprise the right to acquire a controlling packet (51 percent) of the enterprise shares at virtually symbolic prices, in part through the use of privatization vouchers. Remaining shares were temporarily held by a state agency or sold at voucher auctions. This path resulted in **insider privatization**, that is, placing the majority of enterprise shares (and thus effective control of the enterprise) in the hands of those who work there.

Many consider insider privatization an obstacle to reform. Because managers need worker support to gain the majority of shares for the work collective, they have been reluctant to take radical measures that might alienate the workforce and lead to labor conflict. Many of the old managers do not have the necessary skills to restructure enterprise operations effectively. Because shareholder rights are weakly exercised, some managers have been able to extract personal profit from enterprise operations rather than investing available funds to improve production. Despite passage of a bankruptcy law in 1992, most unprofitable enterprises have not been forced to close.

A second phase of privatization, **money-based privatization**, began in 1994. At that time firms could sell remaining shares for cash or investment guarantees. State-owned shares in already privatized companies could be sold through auctions, a potential way to generate revenue for the state. However, money-based privatization has gone much more slowly than expected. Many enterprises are pink elephants—technology is backward and the production profile unpromising without massive infusions of capital for restructuring.

In agriculture, large joint-stock companies and

Figure 1

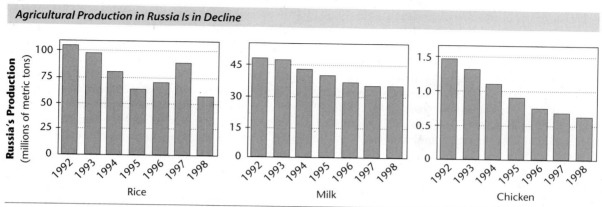

Agricultural Production in Russia Is in Decline

associations of individual households also formed on the basis of former state and collective farms. As in industry, these privatized companies operate inefficiently. Agricultural production declined throughout the 1990s, and there was a particularly bad harvest in 1998 because of severe heat and drought in the summer months (see Figure 1 above). In 1997 the numbers of livestock (cattle, sheep, goats, and pigs) were about half their 1993 level. Foreign food imports (including meat and a whole range of processed goods) also undercut domestic producers, contributing to a downward spiral in investment and production in the agricultural sector. In 1996 food and agricultural products constituted 25 percent of imports from countries outside the former Soviet Union.[11] "Dumping" and the sale of expired or nearly expired Western products have been points of grievance for Russian agricultural producers. However, with ruble devaluation of 1998, imports of Western commodities, including food products, were sharply reduced. Over time, this situation could make domestic producers more competitive and help to revive Russia's agricultural sector.

Peasants have generally been reluctant to begin individual private farming and to give up the minimal security offered by employment in the state sector or in the new joint-stock farms. Several presidential decrees and legal enactments laid a partial groundwork for land privatization, but these have been slow in bringing real changes. For example, the 1994

Russian Agrarian Reform Law established a framework for allowing collective and state farms to redistribute land and equipment to present employees, and a 1996 presidential decree granted owners of shares in agricultural joint-stock companies broader and clearer rights in disposing of their property. The Russian legislature, the Duma, has resisted measures to support private sales of land, and in many cases the legal rights granted by the various enactments have not been assertively exercised by the rural population. In early 1996 the estimated 250,000 private farms accounted for less than 5 percent of agricultural output, while another 40 million people owned *dachas*, small private plots or vegetable gardens, which accounted for about 43 percent. In 1995, 60,000 farms went bankrupt.[12]

Technical problems hinder rural transformation: poor roads, transport, and storage facilities; overuse of chemical fertilizers and pesticides; and outdated equipment. Individual farmers have even fewer resources to resolve these problems than the state. Ineffective marketing structures for produce from both small and large farms have allowed middlemen—speculators—to extract excessive profits. In some cases, agricultural producers must pay off the local mafia to gain access to lucrative market outlets. Both private farmers and the new joint-stock farms are subject to the uncertainties of the market and the weather. A "scissors" effect has also adversely affected the ability of farms to generate investment funds. The prices of manufactured goods, farm equipment, and energy increased faster than those of agricultural products, correcting for the distorted price structure of the Soviet period. This has made it difficult for agricultural producers to improve their operations. As a result, direct state subsidies have been maintained. In 1996 these amounted to over 5 billion dollars, making them roughly equal to all wages and salaries paid to Russian agricultural workers.

Following the financial crisis of late 1998, the new prime minister, Evgenii Primakov, asserted his continuing commitment to market reform. However, measures proposed by the new government indicated a likely retreat. These included the generous emission of rubles, reassertion of state control of some central sectors of the economy, possible renationalization of key enterprises, and increasing control over foreign currency exchanges. Primakov's removal in May 1999 and his replacement by a new prime minister, Sergei Stepashin, raised expectations that the more assertive reform program pursued before Primakov's appointment might be reinstated. Stepashin committed himself to improved tax collection, prevention of capital flight, and the pursuit of economic stabilization and restructuring measures demanded by international lenders such as the World Bank and the International Monetary Fund.

Society and Economy

Soviet Social Policy

The Soviet system did allow the leadership to establish priorities; they were defined by the political elites with little input from society. Military production was one policy priority; the best resources went to this sector. At the same time, through control of production and distribution, the state was able to establish social priorities, which provided the basis for the tacit social contract discussed in Section 1.

In this context, low-cost access to essential goods and services was made a policy goal; housing, transport, food supplies, cafeterias in the workplace, children's clothing, books, cultural facilities, vacation facilities were all heavily subsidized by the state. As in China today, citizens received many of these benefits through their place of employment, thus making the Soviet workplace a social as well as an economic institution. In many cases, however, even basic necessities were in short supply. Housing is a prime example. Housing was generally allocated through local state organs, trade unions, or the workplace; there was no open housing market because most housing was state-owned, in the form of high-rise apartment buildings in cities or developments constructed under Soviet rule. Often young couples and their children had to share a small apartment with parents; people would often wait years for housing, a factor that restricted geographical mobility.

A basic social safety net was provided by the Soviet government. Health care was free, even if its quality was at times dubious; sometimes under-the-table payments prompted better-quality service. Although the number of physicians per capita was among the highest in the world, health care expenditure by the Soviet government, as a proportion of national income, was lower than in most Western countries.[13] Nonetheless, considerable gains were made over the decades in reducing infant mortality rates and the incidence of infectious diseases. Alcoholism and health damage due to environmental pollution were significant problems in the Soviet period. Despite a commitment to equal treatment, regional differences characterized Soviet health care: rural areas and the less developed non-Russian union republics (especially in Central Asia) fell behind.

Under Soviet rule, mass education was emphasized; within the first decades after the revolution virtually all segments of the population were provided access to primary and secondary schooling. The Soviet system did not allow private schools or private higher educational institutions (although private tutoring did go on), and the state provided education free of charge, with state stipends provided to university students. Following graduation, university graduates were assigned to particular jobs (sometimes in remote places) for a brief period as payment for the free education provided by the state. In theory, the educational system was structured to provide training and knowledge to meet society's needs. In practice, the state found it difficult to match educational training to society's needs; therefore, many people were employed in jobs below their skill levels or in positions that did not match their formal training.

Job security was a core element of the tacit social contract—only in exceptional cases could an enterprise fire an employee. Participation in the labor market was high: almost all able-bodied adults, men and women, participated in the workforce. People were usually permitted to seek employment for themselves rather than be assigned to a particular enterprise. Restrictions on labor mobility were generally the result of housing shortages or of difficulties in gaining residency permits for desirable locations such as Moscow. An irony of the system was that labor in many sectors was in constant short supply, reflecting the inefficient use of the workforce. Labor productivity was low, by international standards, and work discipline weak: drunkenness and absenteeism were common. A Soviet saying of the time captured this element of the tacit social contract: "We pretend to work, they pretend to pay us." Whereas the lax work atmosphere reduced the likelihood and frequency of labor conflicts, it also kept production inefficient.

Wage rates were centrally set; however, enterprise managers could make adjustments through reclassification of jobs to attract employees with needed skills. Pay rates in dangerous occupations or in difficult climatic conditions (such as in parts of Siberia) were set higher to attract labor. Another feature of the system was the relatively low level of inequality. As a matter of state policy, wage differentials between the best- and worst-paid were lower than in most Western economies. Because land and factories were state-owned, individuals could not accumulate wealth in the form of real estate, stocks, or ownership of factories. Any privileges that did exist were modest by Western standards. Political elites did have access to scarce goods, higher-quality health care, travel, and vacation homes, but these privileges were hidden from public view.

Other state benefits included the right to maternity leave (partially paid), child benefits, and disability pensions. Unemployment compensation, a mainstay of Western social protection systems, did not exist because the state was committed to a full-employment policy. The retirement age was fifty-five for women and sixty for men, although in the early 1980s about one-third of the elderly continued to work after retirement age. Modest pensions were guaranteed by the state, assuring a stable but minimal standard of living for retirement.

Economic Reform and Russian Society

Social and economic patterns from the Soviet system helped define potential bases of collective identity, expectations about state policy, and grievances against authority in the new Russia. A market economy involves less direct state involvement in securing the types of social welfare that Russians had come to expect, and budget constraints have produced cutbacks in state welfare programs at a time when there is a growing need for them. Pensions have decreased buying power, and state services to deal with increasing problems of homelessness and poverty are inadequate. Tuition fees for postsecondary education are more common, and high-quality health care also requires payment. The cost of medicine is beyond the reach of many citizens. Benefits provided through the workplace have also been cut back, because many enterprises are close to bankruptcy and even viable businesses face pressures to reduce costs and increase productivity.

Some groups have suffered more from the reform process than others, including children, pensioners, and the disabled. The number of homeless and beggars has skyrocketed, especially in large cities like Moscow, a magnet for displaced persons and refugees from war zones on Russia's perimeter. Alongside the "new poor" are the "new rich," probably less than 2–3 percent of the population, who enjoy a standard of living luxurious even by Western standards. These people, many of them multimillionaires with Western bank accounts, were able to take advantage of the privatization process to gain positions in lucrative sectors like banking, finance, oil, and gas. Between these two extremes, the mass of the Soviet population itself is affected by growing differentials in income. Dramatic declines in income have affected those without easily marketable skills, including unskilled laborers in low-priority sectors of the economy and people working in areas of public service such as education. Wage rates are highest for skilled workers in the natural resource sectors (e.g., oil and gas) and in new sectors such as banking and finance. Individuals who have marketable skills (e.g., accounting, knowledge of English or German) have also benefited. These growing income differentials are becoming more visible, but many Russians view them as illegitimate, a sign of corruption rather than of hard work and initiative.

Surveys indicate that in 1998 the majority of Russians were pessimistic about their economic future. Among the most troubling issues were delays in payment of wages and pensions. By May 1998 the equivalent of about 10.3 billion U.S. dollars were owed to Russian workers of privatized firms and state organizations.[14] Employees of state "budget" agencies (including the military) are affected by the government's inability to collect taxes. Privatized enterprises often have insufficient business (and thus inadequate income) to pay employees, but the managers may be reluctant to fire workers, particularly those with specialized skills who would be hard to replace if business revived. In many cases, workers continue to come to work despite the fact that they have not been paid. Many individuals have two to three jobs just to make ends meet. Increasingly, strikes and protests have erupted in response to the situation. In the spring of 1998 miners blocked railway arteries in an effort to force the government to provide payment to their

firms, which would allow wages to be issued. Promises were made, but in many cases the workers did not receive their back pay, fueling further discontent. Teachers and transport workers have also gone on strike. Most workers blame the government rather than the managers of their own firms for wage delays. However, there are growing suspicions that enterprise managers are siphoning off profits to build extravagant homes or to feed foreign bank accounts while employees are left to suffer.

Unemployment, an expected side effect of the shock therapy, has proven difficult to measure. Based on methods utilized by the International Labor Organization, unemployment showed a surprisingly low rate of 9 percent of the economically active population in 1997. According to the Russian State Statistical Service, by December 1998 it was at 12 percent. But these figures hide short-term layoffs, workers still employed but only sporadically paid, or people shifted to partial employment. Thus, the unemployment rate seems artificially low because it does not reflect unpaid wages, unpaid leaves, and other stratagems that enterprise managers have utilized to keep workers on their rolls. On the other hand, some employment in the shadow economy goes unreported.

Promises, promises. "Your mother is here with your salary!" Russian politicians make repeated promises that back wages will be paid, and citizens often feel powerless when these promises are not kept. *Source:* Nikolai Kincharov (Volgograd), *Izvestiia,* August 14, 1998, 5.

In some cases, economic strains have reinforced ethnic and national cleavages. Levels of unemployment are particularly high in some regions, including some republics and regions with high ethnic minority populations, such as Dagestan, Ingushetia, and other republics in the northern Caucasus; the nearby republic of Kalmykia; and Tuva and Buryatia in eastern Siberia.[15] Aboriginal groups in Russia's far north have suffered particularly adverse effects of the economic decline. Northern regions depend on the maintenance of a fragile transport and communications system for deliveries of basic necessities such as fuel and food. The financial crisis of late 1998 disrupted these services, undermining the standard of living and forcing the evacuation of several northern settlements. Other ethnic groups, such as the Tatars, have sought greater economic autonomy for their regions to permit them to take advantage of potential profits from natural resource wealth located in their regions.

Women suffer many of the same hardships now that they did in the Soviet period. They continue to carry the bulk of domestic responsibilities, including shopping, cooking, housework, and childcare. In addition to shouldering domestic responsibilities, most women feel compelled to work outside the home to help make ends meet. Childcare facilities still exist in some enterprises and neighborhoods, but these services have been cut back. Many women take advantage of the permitted three-year maternity leave, which is only partially paid. Fathers play a relatively small role in child-raising; many women must rely on grandparents to help out. Employers are sometimes reluctant to hire women of child-bearing age who have certain rights to maternity leave that employers may view as disruptive or expensive to fulfill. Some data suggest, however, that while women are more likely to register with unemployment offices and take longer to find new jobs, levels of actual unemployment are fairly equal for men and women.[16]

The birthrate in Russia is declining, falling from 16.6 births per 1,000 people in 1985 to an annual rate of only 9.3 in 1995.[17] This pattern has affected almost all industrialized countries, but in Russia the excessive demands placed on women by the dual burden of home and workplace have reinforced it. In addition, many couples are reluctant to have children because of daily hardships, rising costs, the declining standard of living,

and continuing housing shortages—a line of thinking that reflects a dangerous demoralization of public life. Today, contraceptive devices and sanitary products are more widely available than in the past, but the former are expensive if they are of reliable quality (usually Western imports). Women continue to rely on abortion as a primary means of birth control, even though unsanitary conditions and insufficient regulation sometimes result in infertility, infection, or even death. Since 1992 the death rate has exceeded the birthrate; the decline in population has been tempered only by the immigration of ethnic Russians from other former Soviet republics. Life expectancy for Soviet men fell from 64 years in 1964–1965 to just over 58 years in 1995, and from 74 to just below 72 for women.[18] These demographic trends are a striking example of the social costs of the economic transformation.

Russian Political Culture and Economic Change

Alongside more objective factors, culture affects processes of economic change. Particular aspects of Russian political culture that may inhibit adaptation to a market economy include a weak tradition of individual entrepreneurship, a widespread commitment to egalitarian values, and a reliance on relations of personal trust rather than on legal contracts. An insistence on legally binding contracts may be interpreted as an expression of distrust. Profit, as a measure of success, is less important to many Russians than is maintaining support for the work collective; thus, firing redundant workers may be an unpalatable approach. Also, economic competitiveness may be sacrificed if it collides with personal loyalty accorded to long-term associates or partners. Selection of business partners or recruitment of personnel may be strongly influenced by personal contacts and relationships rather than by merit.

Victor Zaslavsky suggests that Soviet socialism also contributed to the specific culture that underlies Russia's business and work environment.[19] He characterizes the "state-dependent worker" as one who displays "acts of work avoidance rather than self-discipline and productivity, a general disdain for work in all state-managed economic sectors, a specific disinclination to risk personal initiatives." The state-dependent worker values security over achievement. However, when offered appropriate incentives, employees of Western firms in Russia tend to operate at high levels of efficiency and, after a period of time, to adopt work habits rewarded by the employing organization.

Younger Russians are more able to adapt to the new economic conditions than their elders. They are also more supportive of the market transition and are more oriented toward maximizing self-interest and demonstrating initiative. Thus, generational change is an important factor in understanding Russia's economic development. On the other hand, a significant portion of Russians of all age groups still seem to question many of the values underlying the market reform process. They may prefer an economy that is less profit-driven, which places more emphasis on equality and the collective good but at the same time is somewhat less efficient and productive. Survey data suggest that although Russians support the idea of democracy and appreciate the freedom they have gained since the collapse of communism, they are much less enamored with the basic notions underlying the capitalist economic system.[20]

Russia and the International Economy

Right up to the end of the Soviet period, the economy remained relatively isolated from outside influences. Most of the USSR's trade (53 percent of imports, 51 percent of exports, in 1984) was carried out with the countries of Eastern Europe.[21] The ruble, the Soviet currency, was nonconvertible, meaning that its exchange rate was set by the state (at various levels for various types of exchange) and did not fluctuate freely in response to economic forces. Furthermore, the ruble could not legally be taken out of the country. All foreign trade was channeled through central state organs, so individual enterprises had neither the possibility nor the incentive to seek external markets. Accounts in Western currencies (so-called hard currency) were under state control. Russia's rich natural resource base, particularly oil and gas, provided an important source of hard currency income and, in Soviet times, insulated the country from incurring a large hard-currency debt.

Gorbachev sought to integrate the USSR more fully into the global economy by reducing international tensions, encouraging foreign investment, and reducing barriers to foreign contacts. The new Russia has pursued this policy even more aggressively. One long-term goal has been to achieve convertibility of the ruble, a policy that should eventually increase domestic confidence in the currency. Since 1992 the ruble has been freely convertible in Russia; since 1996 it is convertible for foreign trade operations, but only for some international investment purposes. Intervention by the Russian Central Bank succeeded in maintaining relative stability in the ruble's value at an artificially high level within a defined exchange rate corridor, until August 1998 when the financial crisis led to de facto devaluation. In the face of Russia's financial and economic uncertainty, some businesses and even individuals prefer to keep their monetary assets in U.S. dollars or German marks.

Given Russia's dire economic situation, its political leaders have courted Western economic assistance. This has been a much debated topic in the West, and several governments, most notably Germany, have made fairly generous commitments of aid, mostly in the form of repayable credits. Assistance programs include training programs to help government officials, individual entrepreneurs, and social organizations adapt to the new challenges of market reform. The World Bank, the International Monetary Fund, and the European Union have contributed economic assistance, although it has often come with strings attached. For example, release of money from a ruble stabilization fund established by the IMF is contingent on Russia's pursuing a strict policy of fiscal and monetary control and lifting remaining price controls. The Russian government has had some difficulties in meeting these conditions, and thus the funds have been released intermittently and often in limited amounts. By the end of 1998 the Russian government owed international lenders US$160 billion (of which nearly $100 billion was inherited from the Soviet period); Russian banks and companies owed $54 billion. After the August 1998 crisis, however, the Russian government effectively defaulted first on the ruble-denominated short-term debt and then on the former Soviet debt. Debt service payments for 1999 alone amounted to $17.5 billion, much of which will not be paid.[22]

Russia has also had problems attracting foreign investment. Although a large number of foreign-Russian joint ventures are legally registered, many are not operational. Most operate in the trade, tourism, or natural resource sectors, with fewer entering central areas of production. Continued uncertainty and instability regarding government policy toward joint ventures has reduced business confidence, particularly since August 1998.

Russia's position in the international political economy remains undetermined. With a highly skilled workforce and an advanced technological base in certain (especially military) sectors, Russia has many of the ingredients necessary to be a competitive and powerful force in the global economy. However, efforts to convert former military production facilities to civilian uses have so far had only limited success. Export of weapons and military equipment, including to disreputable countries such as Iraq, has been a tempting alternative but one that has engendered international concern and criticism. If the decline in Russia's industrial capacity continues, Russia will be forced to rely even more on the export of natural resources (and foreign investment in those sectors) for hard currency income, making the country highly sensitive to fluctuations in raw material demand from the developed industrial nations. Declines in commodity prices (e.g., oil and gas exports), such as occurred in

1997–1998, make the Russian economy vulnerable to economic developments over which it has no control. At the same time, its wealth in natural resources has given Russia advantages over its neighbors because expensive imports are not needed to supply industry with energy and basic raw materials. Russia can now demand hard currency payment for the export of oil and gas to other former Soviet Union republics, although they are often unable to pay, leading to conflicts over debt payment and energy shortages in these countries. Russia has already been able to use these exports as a way to gain trade concessions and political leverage with Ukraine, Belarus, and the Baltic states. Gas and petroleum are thus important resources in the regional balance of power.

Ultimately, Russia's position in the global economy will depend on the ability of the country's leadership to construct a politically viable approach to domestic economic problems. If that endeavor fails, Russia's leaders may again be tempted to try to isolate the country from the global economy. But the clock cannot be turned back to the days of economic isolation that characterized the Soviet period. Any attempt to do so would likely make the country an outpost of poverty and backwardness.

Section ❸ Governance and Policy-Making

Like everything else in Russia, the organization of the state has undergone dramatic change since 1985. In 1985, Russia was a union republic in a nominally federal Soviet Union; now Russia is an independent state with its own constitution and political institutions. In 1985 state organs had to answer to the Communist Party, the only political party that was permitted to function. Now the executive organs of the state are dominant, and political parties play a secondary role. Finally, in the Soviet period the head of state was the leader of the Communist Party, whereas now he is a powerful popularly elected president. Many critics feel, however, that Russia's new constitutional structure gives too much power to the president and the state's executive bodies, enabling a possible revival of a semiauthoritarian system.

Organization of the State

Soviet Political Institutions

Prior to examining present political processes, a brief review of the Soviet state is in order. As noted, before Gorbachev's reforms, top organs of the Communist Party of the Soviet Union (CPSU) dominated the state. The CPSU was a hierarchical structure in which lower party bodies elected delegates to higher party organs, but these elections were uncontested, and top organs determined candidates for lower party posts.

The Politburo, the top party organ, considered all important policy issues and was the real decision-making center. A larger body, the Central Committee, represented the broader political elite, including regional party leaders and representatives of various economic and social interests. The bureaucracy of the Communist Party, under the party Secretariat, was answerable to the Central Committee. In the late 1970s an estimated 1500 employees worked in the central party bureaucracy, and some 10,000 at lower levels.

Alongside the CPSU were Soviet state structures. These institutions formally resembled state structures of Western parliamentary systems, but they had little decision-making authority. The party made policy, while state institutions implemented it. The state bureaucracy, which was considerably larger than the party bureaucracy, had day-to-day responsibility in both the economic and political spheres but operated in subordination to the party's directives. People holding high state positions were appointed through the *nomenklatura* system, a mechanism that allowed the CPSU to fill key posts with politically reliable individuals. The head of the CPSU was also the head of state, and members of the Council of Ministers (the cabinet) were chosen by the party. The Supreme Soviet, the parliament, was a rubber-stamp body; its members were directly elected by the population, but the single candidate who ran in each district was chosen by higher CPSU organs (but was not necessarily a party member).

In theory, the Soviet state was governed by a constitution; the last Soviet constitution was adopted in 1977. However, in practice, the constitution was of symbolic rather than operational importance, since many of its principles were ignored. The constitution provided for legislative, executive, and judicial organs, but the concept of separation of powers was considered inapplicable to Soviet society. Because the CPSU claimed to represent the interests of society as a whole, artificial controls over its exercise of authority were considered unnecessary. With the power of appointment firmly under party control, it made little sense to speak of legislative or judicial independence. When the constitution was violated (as it frequently was), the courts had no independent authority to protect its provisions. "Telephone justice" occurred in political cases, where judges would receive instructions from the party (by phone, in some cases).

The Soviet Union was designated a federal system; that is, according to the constitution, certain powers were granted to the fifteen union republics (which have since become independent states). However, this was "phony federalism," since all aspects of life were overseen by a highly centralized Communist Party. Within the Russian Republic, now the Russian Federation, there were a number of so-called **autonomous republics**, each formed around a core non-Russian population group residing within Russia's borders (see map in Section 1). In the Soviet period, these autonomous republics were granted certain constitutional rights, which were largely unrealized in practice. In addition to the autonomous republics, the Russian Republic was divided into regional administrative units, the *oblasts* and *krai*, which had no ethnic basis. So-called autonomous regions (*okrugs*) and autonomous districts also existed; like the autonomous republics these were ethnically based but had more limited formal powers.

Gorbachev began a process of radical institutional change through the introduction of competitive elections, increased political pluralism, reduced Communist Party dominance, a revitalized legislative branch of government, and renegotiation of the terms of Soviet federalism. Although Gorbachev retained his post as general secretary of the CPSU until August 1991, by March 1990 the locus of political leadership was shifting to the Soviet state, to assure a broader base of political legitimacy and support. Gorbachev also tried to bring the constitution into harmony with political reality, and many constitutional amendments were adopted that altered existing political institutions. Together, these changes slowly moved the political system slowly and unsurely in a direction resembling the liberal democratic systems of the West. But the legacy of Soviet political institutions and practices continued to affect the nature of the political processes during this transition period.

The failed coup d'état of August 1991 precipitated the USSR's collapse and ushered in even more radical political changes in the newly independent Russian Federation. Incremental changes in the political institutions of the Russian republic itself began before the Russian Federation achieved independence in December 1991. A new post of president was created for the Russian republic and on June 12, 1991, Boris Yeltsin was elected by direct popular vote as its first incumbent. This election gave Yeltsin a base of popular legitimacy during his first years in the leadership post. Once Russia became an independent state, it quickly became clear that the existing institutional structures were not functioning well, so an entirely redrafted Russian constitution would be needed. A crucial turning point was the adoption by referendum of a new Russian constitution in December 1993.

Russian Political Institutions

The Russian constitution, adopted by referendum in December 1993, has survived the five year mark, indicating that it has provided at least a moderately effective framework for governance. Based on Western principles, such as separation of powers, a competitive electoral system, and judicial independence, it represents a radical departure from the Soviet period (see Figure 2 below). The constitution establishes a semipresidential system, formally resembling the French system but with stronger executive power. The president is the head of state, and the prime minister, appointed by the president but approved by the lower house of the parliament (the Duma), is the head of government. The president's nominee for prime minister need not be a member of parliament, and the president and the parliament are chosen in completely separate electoral procedures (see Section 4). The bicameral legislature has a weak position compared to

Figure 2

Political Institutions of the Russian Federation (R.F.), December 1993 to the Present.

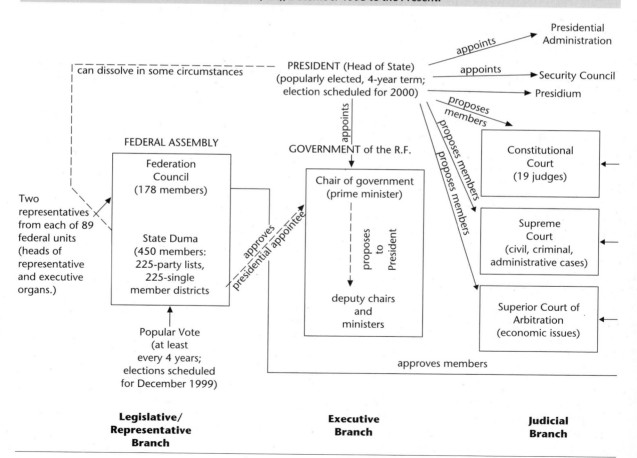

the executive branch, and the president enjoys extensive powers of presidential decree. The judiciary, including a Constitutional Court, has considerable independence from the other branches of government. As its name denotes, the Russian Federation has a federal system, with 89 constituent units of various sizes and types. While these units are formally equal, as a result of the Soviet legacy and differences in natural resource endowment they in fact enjoy varying levels of autonomy in diverse aspects of the policy process.

The Russian constitution was adopted in 1993 under contentious political conditions, and many of its basic elements continue to be the subject of intense political debate. Two of the most important issues involve the balance of power between the legislative and executive branches, and the nature of Russian federalism. Although the constitution defines political institutions in both spheres, many of the provisions are unclear. The document is difficult to amend, so revisions to the constitutional order would need to be built on a broad base of political support or instituted by extralegal measures. In the face of Russia's financial and political crisis of late 1998, discussion of proposed amendments took on renewed vigor. These included the possibility of reintroducing the post of vice president, measures to reduce presidential power and boost parliamentary authority, reconfiguration of the federal system, and revisions to the parliamentary electoral system. In October 1998, President Yeltsin announced that a constitutional panel would be convened to consider the various proposed amendments.

The Executive

The Russian constitution places primary power in the hands of the president, who is much more than a figurehead (in contrast to Germany's). In fact, Russia has a dual executive, since the prime minister holds executive authority as the head of government. This existence of the dual executive can, at times, raise doubts about who is actually in control. With Yeltsin's continuing health problems in 1998 and 1999, power seemed to reside with the prime minister, but this was most likely a temporary anomaly.

The president is elected directly by the population every four years, and no individual may serve more than two terms. The first election for the Russian

presidency was held in June 1991, before Russia achieved independent statehood and before the new Russian constitution was adopted. Boris Yeltsin was the victor. In 1996 the first presidential elections under Russia's new constitution were carried out. Despite Yeltsin's low popularity in early 1996, he waged a successful election campaign, with the help of Western campaign advisers, by defining the choice as one between reform or a return to communism (see Section 4). Following his reelection, Yeltsin's health declined further and his political rating remained low. In September 1997 only about 8 percent of the population listed Yeltsin among politicians they trusted, down from 11 percent in late 1996 (see Figure 3, p. 455).[23]

Because so much power resides in the office of the president, the decline in President Yeltsin's health contributed to Russia's crisis conditions. Impeachment of the president is a complicated process involving the Duma, the Federation Council, the Supreme Court, and the Constitutional Court. If the president dies in office or becomes incapacitated, the post is filled by the prime minister until new presidential elections can be held. In late 1998 discussion arose of reinstating the post of vice president, a position omitted from the new constitution because President Yeltsin felt betrayed when Vice President Rutskoi opposed his 1993 siege of the Russian parliament. If Yeltsin remains in office for his full term, presidential elections would occur in mid-2000.

One of the president's most important powers is the authority to issue decrees, which frequently address contentious issues such as privatization, salaries of state workers, the running of the economy, electoral arrangements, and anticrime measures. Presidential decrees have the force of law until formal legislation is passed, so decrees can fill a policy vacuum in addressing immediate issues. In other cases, the president has used decrees in political battles with the parliament. Failing to get parliamentary approval for his initiatives, the president has issued decrees; and presidential decrees sometimes contradict parliamentary decisions. Policy-making by decree can also allow the president to ignore the parliament entirely. For example, the president's decision to launch the offensive in Chechnya was not brought before either house of parliament, despite strong objections from a broad range of political groups.

Figure 3

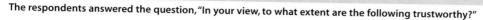

Level of Trust in Various Institutions in Russia (September 1997)

The respondents answered the question, "In your view, to what extent are the following trustworthy?"

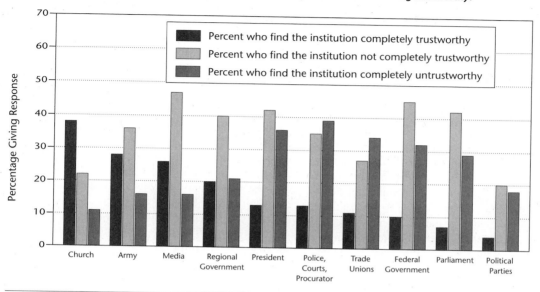

Source: Data from Russian Centre for Public Opinion Research (VTsIOM), *Ekonomicheskie i sotsial'nye peremeny: monitoring obshchestvennogo mneniia* (*Economic and Social Change: The Monitoring of Public Opinion*), no. 32 (Nov.-Dec. 1997), 64–65.

The president has other powers, including the right to call a state of emergency, impose martial law, grant pardons, call referendums, and temporarily suspend actions of other state organs if he deems them to contradict the constitution or federal laws. Some of these actions must be confirmed by other state organs (for example the upper house of the parliament, the Federation Council); however, the constitution is vague on how disputes over such actions are to be resolved. The president is commander in chief of the armed forces and heads the Security Council, which is in charge of security matters broadly conceived. He conducts affairs of state with other nations.

The Russian government consists of the prime minister, deputy prime ministers, and federal ministers. Although the president's choice of prime minister must be approved by the lower house of the parliament (see Section 4, pgs. 463–475), other ministers do not require parliamentary approval. They are recommended to the president by the prime minister, who also presents to the president his proposals for the structure of the executive branch. Like the president, the government can issue resolutions and directives, which the president may override if he deems them to contradict federal laws, presidential decrees, or the constitution. The government proposes the budget, proposes legislation (as does the president), and acts to ensure implementation of a unified state policy in areas such as economic policy, culture, education, defense, security, and protection of civil rights. The actual day-to-day work of drafting policy documents on major social and economic issues happens largely within the executive branch of government. Without disciplined parties in Russia, and none that effectively link the executive and the legislative branches (as would exist in a "normal" parliamentary system), governmental proposals often face resistance in the parliament.

The National Bureaucracy

The new Russian state inherited a large bureaucratic apparatus from the Soviet state. Since market reform reduced the role of the state in economic management, a decrease in the size of the bureaucracy was widely expected. But, despite proclaimed intentions, efforts to downsize the executive bureaucratic apparatus have been only partially successful. Many agencies have been reorganized, often more than once. New ones have been formed, bodies have been renamed, and personnel have been shifted from one office to another. During periods of restructuring, some agencies stopped functioning. In the face of the financial and political crisis in autumn 1998, five new ministries, five state committees, and two new federal services were created, while three ministries were abolished. All of these changes provided opportunities for political appointments. In addition, a new structure to advise the president, the government Presidium, was created, including selected regional leaders, key government ministers, the head of the Russian Academy of Sciences, and the head of the Central Bank.

Reorganization of the state's bureaucracy results not only from restructuring of the economy; top leaders also use reorganizations to place their clients and allies in key positions in the new agencies and to weaken political opponents. **Patron-client networks**, which were important in the Soviet period, continue to play a key role. These linkages are similar to "old boys' networks" in the West (and they most often involve men in the Russian case); they underscore the importance of personal career ties between individuals as they rise in bureaucratic or political structures. The patron-client networks are more complex and less transparent now than they were in the Soviet period, but equally important. With the collapse of the *nomenklatura* system and the absence of a functioning system of civil service appointments, politicians and government officials look to people they know and trust as they staff their organizations.

Along with the state bureaucracy is the presidential administration, that is, the personal staff of the president, which is estimated at around 1,800 people. The president also uses consultants from outside formal government structures to advise his staff on particular issues.

Other State Institutions

The Military

The Soviet military ranked as one of the largest and most powerful forces in the world, second only to that of the United States and justifying the country's designation as a superpower. But despite its privileged position in the Soviet economic structure, the military has not played a direct political role in Russian and Soviet politics. The Communist Party controlled military appointments in the Soviet period and gave preferential treatment to the military sector. At times, the military did assert its interests in conflicts between civilian leaders (for example, it was a contributing factor in Khrushchev's downfall in 1964), and the military was almost always represented in the top decision-making body of the party, the Politburo. In the late 1980s several developments led observers to wonder whether the Soviet (and later the Russian) military might begin to intervene more actively in civilian political affairs. First, the threatened break-up of the USSR and the loss of superpower status alarmed most military officers. Second, several specific issues were of great concern in military circles. These included conflict between Ukraine and Russia over control of the Black Sea fleet; disputes over control of the nuclear arsenal located in former Soviet republics outside Russia; wars in neighboring countries; removal of Soviet (now Russian) troops from formerly allied states; and the status of Russians (including military personnel) living in former Soviet republics. Alongside these issues, both Gorbachev and Yeltsin oversaw a reduction in military expenditures.

Despite these tensions, thus far the military establishment has not directly intervened in civilian political affairs. During the August 1991 coup attempt, troops remained loyal to Yeltsin and Gorbachev even though the Minister of Defense was among the coup plotters; there were no orders to fire on Soviet citizens who took to the streets in defense of the government. In October 1993, despite some apparent hesitancy in military circles, military units defended the government's position, but this time they fired on civilian protesters, shocking the country. Prior to the 1996 presidential election, Yeltsin wooed the military with promotions and military decorations. An indication of increasing politicization of the military occurred during the national elections of 1995 and 1996. The military sponsored some 120 candidates in the parliamentary elections, and several prominent military officers or former officers figured in the leadership of electoral blocs and parties. Aleksandr Lebed, former commander of Russia's 14th Army, has become a visible political figure as governor of one of Russia's larger federal units (Krasnoyarsk *krai* in Siberia) and appears to be positioning himself to run in the presidential election scheduled for the year 2000.

Tension has characterized many aspects of President Yeltsin's relationship with the military. In May 1997, Yeltsin removed the Minister of Defense, Igor Rodionov, for his resistance to further budget cuts and his failure to undertake restructuring of the military consistent with the government's downsizing of the budget. His successor, Igor Sergeyev, has been more cooperative. In March 1998 downsizing plans included the discharge of 300,000 officers (who by law, must be provided with housing), accompanied by cutbacks in troops to reach a target of 1.2 million by the year 2000 (from 1.5 million in 1998 and 2.5 million in the early 1990s). The dismal performance of the military in the Chechnya offensive and resistance by some field commanders to carrying out orders raised serious questions about the reliability of the command structure and the possibility of splits within military ranks on a regional basis.[24] Reports of deteriorating conditions in some Russian nuclear arsenals raised international concerns about nuclear security. The situation of military personnel, from the highest officers to rank-and-file soldiers, has deteriorated dramatically. Salaries have often been unpaid for months, inadequate living quarters and food supplies have sometimes left troops to fend for themselves, and military personnel suffer from reduced public respect following the Chechnya debacle. Russian concerns over NATO's military actions in the Kosovo crisis of 1999 produced pressure for a reversal in military downsizing and suggested a possible increase in the military budget.

The Judiciary

Concepts such as judicial independence and the rule of law were poorly understood both in prerevolutionary Russia and in the Soviet era. Gorbachev, however, emphasized the importance of constructing a law-based state, and he took several measures to make laws conform more closely with political practice. Notions of judicial independence and due process were widely accepted during this period; however, implementing them has been a difficult and not wholly successful endeavor. Russia continues to operate on the basis of the European civil law, rather than British common law, tradition.

In Russia, a Constitutional Court was formed in 1991. Its decisions were binding, and in several cases even the president had to bow to its authority. One controversial decision involved overriding Yeltsin's decree banning the further operation of the Communist Party. The court ruled that while the central structure of the old Communist Party of the Soviet Union could be outlawed, the state could not ban local communist organizations. In 1992 and 1993 both the executive and legislative branches looked to the court to adjudicate disputes between them. But Yeltsin suspended the Constitutional Court after its chief justice announced that the court considered Yeltsin's dissolution of the Supreme Soviet to be unconstitutional. Yeltsin's suspension of the court's activities was itself unconstitutional, but no institution remained to make a judgment on the issue. The ideal of rule of law was, in practice, suspended until the new constitution went into effect following the December 1993 referendum. Both the national parliament and the Constitutional Court had been struck down by the president's actions, removing any semblance of separation of powers, judicial oversight, or rule of law.

The Russian constitution of December 1993 again provides for a Constitutional Court with the power to adjudicate disputes on the constitutionality of federal and regional laws, as well as jurisdictional disputes between various political institutions. Justices are nominated by the president and approved by the Federation Council, a procedure that produced a stalemate, since some of Yeltsin's nominees were considered to be political appointments. As a result, the court did not become functional until 1995. Among the justices are political figures, lawyers, legal scholars, and judges. Since 1995 the court has hesitated to take contentious positions on several controversial issues relating to executive-legislative and center-periphery relations. The court has also been cautious in confronting the executive branch, on which it depends to enforce its decisions. It remains to be seen whether the present law will provide a workable framework for the operation of the court; if not, then the system will be devoid of a mechanism for the judicial resolution of constitutional conflicts. The outcome of this issue may be a good test of how firmly the rule of law has penetrated Russia's political culture and system.

Alongside the Constitutional Court is an extensive system of lower and appellate courts, with the Supreme Court at the pinnacle. These courts hear ordinary civil and criminal cases. In 1995 a system of commercial courts was also formed to hear cases dealing with issues related to privatization, taxes, and other commercial activities. Supreme Court judges are approved by the Federation Council after nomination by the president, and the constitution also grants the president power to appoint judges at other levels. In practice, methods of judicial selection vary, since executive authorities in some regions appoint judges anyway.[25] Measures to shield judges from political pressures include criminal prosecution for attempting to influence a judge and protections from arbitrary dismissal and criminal prosecution. Low judicial salaries draw qualified personnel away, lowering the overall quality of judicial decision-making.

Subnational Government

The collapse of the Soviet Union was precipitated by the demands of some union republics for more autonomy and then independence. After the Russian Federation became an independent state, the problem of constructing a viable federal structure resurfaced. The Russian Federation inherited a complex structure of regional subunits from the Soviet period. Between 1991 and 1993 negotiations between the central government and the various regions led to the establishment of a federal structure that includes 89 units. These include 21 republics, 49 *oblasts*, 6 *krai*, 10 autonomous *okrugs*, 1 autonomous *oblast*, and 2 cities with federal status (St. Petersburg and Moscow). While all of these 89 federal units are given equal status by the constitution, in fact they are treated differently (and not always equally). The republics form a somewhat special category. In the Soviet period they held the status of autonomous republics or autonomous *oblasts* because of the presence of a significant national minority group within their borders. For example, the Tatars formed 48.5 percent of the population of the Republic of Tatarstan in 1989 (when the last census was taken), the Yakuts formed one-third of the population of Yakutia (now the Republic of Sakha), and the Chechen and Ingush formed 70 percent of the Republic of Chechnya at that time. The republics tend to be in peripheral areas of the Russian Federation (except for Tatarstan and Bashkortostan, which lie in the center of the country). Many of the republics, particularly in Siberia, are rich in natural resources, and an issue of dispute with the federal government has been control of these resources and the revenue they generate. Because of their previous status and their resource wealth, the republics generally have more autonomy than other units of the federation. They may declare a second state language (in addition to Russian) and may adopt their own constitutions. These documents may not contradict the federal constitution, but some provisions in fact do so. Since 1994 individual treaties have been negotiated between the federal government and several of Russia's republics, outlining the jurisdiction of each level of government. In contrast to this approach, the Republic of Chechnya declared independence from the Russian Federation in 1991. The central government rejected the claim, leading to a protracted and costly civil war.

The de facto privileges granted to the republics have drawn protests from leaders of some of Russia's other regions—the *oblasts*, *krais*, and *okrugs*. In the mid-1990s several of these subnational units demanded that special agreements or treaties be concluded with the federal government, like those concluded with republics. This ad hoc approach has produced **asymmetrical federalism**, because it provides different regions with varying privileges rather than imposing a uniform division of powers between the federal and subnational levels of government. The result has been an escalation of demands for regional privilege and a drop in the perceived fairness of central policy. In general, the central government's limited capacity to govern has allowed subnational authorities to assume more power. Specific areas of conflict involve control of valuable resources, ownership of property or factories, division of tax revenues, responsibility for social welfare programs (which the center wishes

Current Challenges: *The Chechnya Crisis*

Despite its small size and population (estimated at 600,000 in 1994), the break-away republic of Chechnya holds an important position on Russia's southern border. The republic is widely perceived as a safe haven for criminal elements that operate in Russia. The Russian leadership also feared that Chechnya's example might embolden other republics to pursue outright independence. These concerns motivated Russia to send troops into Chechnya on December 11, 1994, fueling a regional civil war.

The desire for independence has deep roots in Chechnya. Prior to its incorporation into the Russian Empire in 1859 and again after the Bolshevik revolution in 1917, local forces fought to maintain Chechnya's independence. In 1924, Chechnya was made part of the USSR, and in 1934 it was joined with an adjacent region, Ingushetia, to form a single autonomous republic within the Soviet Union. During World War II, following an anti-Soviet uprising, Stalin deported hundreds of Chechens to Soviet Central Asia.

Taking advantage of the ongoing political upheaval in the USSR, in October 1991 the newly elected president of the republic, Dzhokar Dudaev, declared Chechnya's independence from Russia. In 1992, Checheno-Ingushetia was offically recognized by the Russian government as two separate republics. Following the split, Chechen leaders continued to pursue independence, a claim rejected by the Russian government. At the same time, internal political conflicts began to emerge in Chechnya. In 1993 the Chechen parliament voted to impeach Dudaev, who proceeded to dissolve the parliament. An opposition Provisional Council was formed in August 1994. Fighting then broke out between government (proindependence) and opposition forces.

Intervention by Russian military forces in December 1994 evoked criticism within the Russian Federation and its leadership circles. Some opposed the intervention completely, favoring a political solution; others were primarily critical of the ineffective manner in which the war effort was carried out. The campaign was poorly organized and internal dissension within the army and security forces demoralized the troops. Civilians in Chechnya and the surrounding regions suffered at the hands of both sides. On June 14, 1995, Chechen fighters took control of a city (Budennovsk) in the adjacent Russian province of Stavropol and held some 1,500 hostages in a local hospital. An attempt by Russian forces to storm the hospital led to the escape of only 150 of the hostages, while others were killed. In January 1996 another hostage-taking in the adjacent republic of Dagestan again took the conflict beyond Chechnya's borders.

The unpopular war became an important issue in the 1996 presidential campaign and threatened to undermine Yeltsin's already fragile support. In late May 1996, a cease-fire agreement was signed, and in June, Yeltsin decreed the beginning of troop withdrawals. Apparently these steps were sufficient to prevent the issue from undermining Yeltsin's reelection prospects, but they were not sufficient to stop the war, as skirmishes continued. One reason for the failure of Yeltsin's efforts was that the future status of Chechnya was not resolved.

In August 1996, Aleksandr Lebed, drafted by Yeltsin as Secretary of Russia's Security Council, took the leadership role in new peace efforts. In September 1996 an agreement with the rebels was again signed. The joint declaration put off a decision on Chechnya's status for five years; in so doing, it left the door open for Chechnya to reassert its claim for national independence. Ironically, many of the Russian politicians who had been the most vocal critics of the war now attacked the concessions contained in the agreement Lebed had fashioned. On October 17, 1996, Yeltsin dismissed Lebed from his government posts, charging that he was planning a coup.

On January 27, 1997, an election was held for the president of the Republic of Chechnya. Observers generally considered the vote to be fair, with 79 percent of the eligible population participating. In a race involving thirteen candidates, Asian Mashkhadov received 59 percent of the vote. Relative to other leading candidates, Mashkhadov is considered to be a moderate. However, he publicly supports Chechnya's independence drive and has refused to take his seat representing Chechnya in Russia's Federation Council. The situation in the republic continues to be unstable, as opposition forces periodically try to undermine Mashkhadov's government. Meanwhile, the republic's final status remains undecided.

Adapted from Joan DeBardeleben, *Russian Politics in Transition*, 2nd ed. (Boston: Houghton Mifflin Co., 1997), pp. 146–148.

to transfer to the regions), provision of central subsidies for local enterprises or industrial restructuring, and issues of regional equalization.

After the events of October 1993, Yeltsin issued a decree reaffirming his right to appoint governors of the *oblasts*, *krais*, and *okrugs*. (Heads of the republics have generally been popularly elected.) At that time Yeltsin also ordered that the existing local and regional representative bodies be disbanded because he viewed them as conservative holdovers from the Soviet period. New elections to most regional councils were held between December 1993 and early 1995 (on the basis of a presidential decree). In many of these elections, the refashioned Communist Party did better than expected. Yeltsin endeavored to postpone new elections until 1997 (after the 1996 presidential elections), but after protests and appeals to regional courts, he backed down. On the basis of a new federation law, new elections were carried out in 1996 and 1997. As the result of a political compromise in late 1995, the Russian president also agreed that all governors should be popularly elected no later than the end of 1996. These changes have given executive authorities at the regional level more political independence; they are responsible neither to the president nor to local legislative bodies. The president continues to appoint presidential representatives at the regional level. These serve as a liaison between the president and the region but do not have any actual decision-making authority. The president may also suspend acts of executive organs of regional governments until the courts make a ruling, if he deems them to contradict the constitution or federal laws, or the basic rights and freedoms of citizens.

In August 1995 a law on local self-government was adopted that provided a broad framework for local government (at the city or rural district level). This law was supplemented by the adoption of regional laws and statutes. The law requires that representative organs at the local level be popularly elected. State (executive) authority at the local level is separate from the representative organs; thus local administrators are not answerable to these bodies. Local governments remain dependent on budgetary transfers from higher levels, since they have limited possibilities for generating local tax revenue. Ambiguities in the law about issues such as control of municipal and state property, the division of authority between the levels of government, and taxation authority have led to maneuvering between political authorities at various levels of government, a situation that has encouraged corruption and irregularities.[26]

Case studies of politics in particular regions have become an important avenue for understanding Russian politics; these studies reveal that there is immense diversity among regions. In regions such as Moscow and Nizhnii Novgorod *oblast*, reformist governments have tried to push market reform and privatization forward assertively. In other regions old structures of political power have remained largely intact. In addition, differences between rich regions (such as Moscow and the oil/gas regions of Siberia) and poor regions (those with archaic industrial structures, weak infrastructure, or a poor natural resource base) have increased dramatically. Local and regional governments have been saddled with new responsibilities for social welfare, but they do not usually have adequate financial resources to handle them, even though they are permitted to collect certain types of taxes and receive a portion of other tax income. Regional and local governments continue to lobby for special treatment or central support to deal with their problems; budgetary issues are negotiated by regional officials and officials of the Russian Finance Ministry.

The Policy-Making Process

Policy-making occurs through both formal and informal mechanisms. The Russian constitution lays the ground rules for the adoption of legislation, one formal mechanism of policy-making. Legislation can be proposed by the federal government, the president, regional legislatures, individual parliamentary deputies, and, in some cases, the Constitutional Court and other judicial bodies. Various organizations may be involved in the drafting of legislation, including the State Legal Office (part of the presidential administration), parliamentary staff, and a special office within the federal government responsible for drafting economic legislation. Often, expert consultants are drawn into the process, and much informal lobbying occurs, involving regional, industrial, and sectoral interests, but this takes place in a much less structured way than in many Western countries. Sometimes the government, deputies, or parliamentary factions offer competing drafts of laws, leading to protracted and complicated bargaining. In order for a bill to become law, it must be approved by both houses of the parliament and signed by the president. If the president vetoes the bill, it must be passed again in the same wording by a two-thirds majority of both houses of parliament in order to override the veto (see Section 4). Budgetary proposals can be put forth only by the government, and they usually elicit sharp controversy in the parliament since proposed budget reductions affect key interests such as regional and local governments, the military, trade unions, enterprise directors, and other government agencies.

Many policy proclamations are made through presidential or governmental decrees, without formal consultation with the legislative branch. This decision-making process is much less visible and may involve closed-door bargaining rather than an open process of debate and consultation. Since October 1994 the Security Council has taken on increasing prominence as a consultative organ for the president. The formation of the Presidium in September 1998 appeared to be an effort to widen the scope of participants in these high-level consultations. In some ways these elite consultative bodies resemble the old CPSU Politburo, which operated at the top of the political structure in the Soviet period. The exclusion of the public and even most parliamentary deputies from involvement in this aspect of policy-making means that presidential decrees often elicit strong criticism and cynicism from other parts of the political elite.

Informal groupings also have an important indirect impact on policy-making. A prominent example is the industrialist lobby, which represents managerial interests of some of Russia's large privatized industries. Business magnates have been able to exert behind-the-scenes influence to gain benefits in the privatization of lucrative firms in sectors such as oil, media, and transport. A striking example is Boris Berezovsky, the founder of a powerful company (LogoVAZ) that owns interests in the media, banking, oil, and car-dealership sectors. Berezovsky managed to gain control of the management of large enterprises in these sectors early in the privatization process and also to gain political influence through back-room dealing as well as campaign contributions. In late

1996 (after the 1996 presidential election), Yeltsin appointed Berezovsky deputy head of the Security Council, only to remove him in November 1997. Berezovsky was made executive secretary of the Commonwealth of Independent States in April 1998 (generally considered a position with lesser influence). A strong network of patron-client relations influences many appointments and demotions, but it is not always possible to unravel the political linkages that govern them. In almost all cases, informal participation in policy-making does not extend to representatives of more broadly based citizens' groups. Policy-making remains the nearly exclusive domain of the elite and the experts.

One difficulty in comprehending the Russian policy process is its ad hoc nature. Even though political leaders mouth support for the rule of law and universalistic values, in practice particular accommodations are made for specific regions, institutions, or groups. At the same time, many significant legislative enactments have been recorded since 1991, including laws on local self-government, political associations and parties, voluntary associations, and electoral procedures and guarantees, as well as a new civil code. These laws, if effectively implemented, may serve to reinforce norms of democratic practice and citizen rights.

An even greater problem than policy-making is the inefficacy of policy implementation. Under Communist rule, the party's control over political appointments and promotions enforced at least some degree of conformity to central mandates. Now the fragmented and decentralized nature of political power gives even the executive branch few resources to ensure compliance. Referring to Russia's authoritarian past, a popular saying suggests that "the severity of Russia's laws is compensated by the laxity of their implementation." Russians have come to expect slippage during implementation, and they routinely develop strategies to circumvent regulations that obstruct their goals. The current Russian government has faced massive tax evasion, avoidance of military conscription, and circumvention of a wide variety of regulations in spheres ranging from environmental protection to export of foreign currency. Furthermore, at the regional and republic levels, in many instances local political authorities consciously and overtly

Citizen Action: *Political Jokes*

Soviet citizens liked to tell jokes about their political leaders. This was one of the few forms of political commentary in the Soviet period. Here are two jokes told about Brezhnev:

The foreign minister of the USSR, Andrei Gromyko, on returning to the USSR from a diplomatic visit to the United States, told the Communist Party leader Leonid Brezhnev that in the United States, applicants for government jobs are required to take a test. "Here is an example of a question," he said. "Who is my father's son but not me?"

Brezhnev hesitated and replied, "I don't know."

Gromyko said, "Well, it's my brother,"

The next day Brezhnev was talking with fellow Politburo member Nikolai Podgorny. He repeated Gromyko's story and asked Podgorny the same question: "Who is my father's son but not me?"

Podogrny hesitated and replied, "Your brother."

Brezhnev looked surprised and exclaimed, "No, it's Gromyko's brother!"

***

On Red Square in Moscow, a man shouts: "Brezhnev is an idiot!"

The militia seizes the man and puts him under arrest. He is sentenced on two charges: He is given fifteen days for hooliganism, and fifteen years for revealing a state secret.

***

In the late 1990s, a rash of new political jokes appeared, again a form of political commentary. Here are some examples of the new Russian political humor.

The Russian Duma receives a draft of a new constitution consisting of two items, Thou shalt not kill and Thou shalt not steal. Parliamentary speaker Gennady Seleznev calls an urgent press briefing: "We have now begun work on drafting amendments," he says.

President Yeltsin addresses the nation: "For years we have stood on the threshold of the abyss. Now, fellow countrymen, we have taken a great step forward."

***

A young man enters a bank and approaches the teller. He inquires, "I want to open an account. Whom should I see?" The teller replies: "A psychiatrist."

***

A Russian riddle: What's the difference between a pessimist and an optimist? Answer: A pessimist thinks things are as bad as they can get. An optimist thinks things can get worse.

Another riddle: What's the difference between a dollar and a ruble? Answer: Exactly one dollar.

Source: DeBardeleben, Joan, *Russian Politics in Transition*, Second Edition. Copyright 1997 by Houghton Mifflin Company. Reprinted with permission.

---

have chosen to ignore federal laws or decrees, realizing that little can be done to enforce them. Pervasive corruption also hinders enforcement of policy decisions. Special payments or favors are commonly received for issuing licenses, legal documents, or access to other goods and services needed to carry out economic activities. The mafia demands payoffs and protection money not only from private businesses but also from state organizations or public officials. In other cases, selective enforcement is used as a means of political pressure and even control. Violation of some regulations or laws can almost always be found

to justify punitive measures if political authorities desire them. Reasons for the selective enforcement of policy decisions are often hidden from public scrutiny, particularly if they concern the disposition of former state property, granting of special privileges or contracts, or other lucrative ventures.

The legal and extralegal forces that affect political decision-making in Russia sometimes produce contradictory policies that remain largely unenforceable. In the next section, we explore some of the social foundations for the disarray that plagues the political process.

Section ❹ Representation and Participation

Gorbachev's policies brought a dramatic change in the relationship between state and society. The communist political system was driven by an impetus to control society; out of this stifling environment, *glasnost* sparked new public and private initiatives. Most restrictions on the formation of social organizations were lifted and a large number of independent groups appeared. Observers in the late 1980s began suggesting that **civil society** was emerging, that is, an autonomous sphere of social life that could act on but was not dependent on the state.

Despite these hopeful beginnings, the ability of the Russian public to affect government seems relatively limited. Cynicism, resignation, and apathy are on the rise, leading many people to retreat into private life much as they did in the Communist period. On the other hand, unconventional forms of political protest, such as hunger strikes, sit-ins, and obstruction of transport, are more frequent. By examining mechanisms for political expression, we can better understand this aspect of Russian life.

The Legislature

The Russian legislature, the Federal Assembly, came into being after the parliamentary elections of December 12, 1993, when the referendum ratifying the new Russian constitution was also approved. Its upper house, the Federation Council, represents Russia's constituent federal units. The lower house, the State Duma, has 450 members and represents the people through direct popular vote for candidates and parties. This body was named after the short-lived assembly formed by the tsar following the revolution of 1905 and thus emphasizes continuity with the Russian (rather than the Soviet) tradition. The first Federal Assembly served only a two-year term. Subsequent elections to the State Duma are normally to occur every four years: the second set of parliamentary elections occurred in December 1995, and the third set in 1999. In some special circumstances earlier elections can be called. Within the Duma, factions unite deputies from the same or allied parties. The Duma also has a number of standing committees,

made up of members from the various factions, to review legislation. The Speaker of the State Duma is elected by the body and usually represents the strongest political faction, which was the Communist Party after the 1995 elections. Deputies to the Duma, as well as to the other house of the parliament, are granted immunity from criminal prosecution.

Compared to the Communist period, deputies in the representative bodies reflect less fully the demographic characteristics of the population at large. For example, in 1984, 33 percent of the members of the Supreme Soviet were women. The State Duma, by contrast, had only 46 female deputies (10 percent) in 1995.[27] At the regional level, a large number of deputies are individuals who hold executive positions at the local level or who are managers of enterprises. Data from early 1995 indicate that less than 1 percent were workers,[28] whereas in 1979 manual workers constituted 35 percent of the membership of the Supreme Soviet and over 40 percent of regional soviets. It is important to remember that the implicit demographic quotas that the CPSU enforced in the Soviet period were primarily symbolic, since the Supreme Soviet was largely powerless. On the other hand, the underrepresentation of women in the present Duma indicates the extent to which politics is considered a male domain in the Russian Federation.

The upper house of the Federal Assembly, the Federation Council, represents Russia's 89 regions and republics. It serves a function analogous to the German *Bundesrat*. It includes two delegates from each federal unit. In 1993 they were directly elected by the population, but since 1995 they are the head of the executive branch of the region (the governor) and the head of the legislative branch. Therefore, regional elections continually affect the composition of the body. Because they also hold leading regional posts, members have limited time to devote to their duties in the Federation Council. Due to its method of selection, the Federation Council provides a formal venue for the expression of regional concerns, and injects issues of center-regional relations into the federal political arena. The governors try to use their positions on the Federation Council to gain perks for their regions; this

President Boris Yeltsin talks with Russian Orthodox Church Patriarch Alexy II, second of left, Prime Minister Yevgeny Primakov and Presidential Chief of Staff Nikolai Bordyuzha, second of right at the Barvikha Sanitarium near Moscow on February 1, 1999. Yeltsin was in Barvikha recuperating form a stomach ulcer. *Source:* © Laski Diffusion/Gamma Liaison.

tightens the web of intrigue in negotiations between the federal and regional governments. Governors can also gain national prominence through the Federation Council. Most deputies do not belong to a political party group, so party factions play no significant role, as they do in the Duma. However, the interests of the various regions represented in the Federation Council are highly diverse.

The constitution grants parliament powers in the legislative and budgetary areas, but if conflict exists with the president or government these powers can be exercised effectively only if the body operates with a high degree of unity. In practice, parliamentary powers can often be overridden by the president through mechanisms such as the veto of legislation. To override the veto, two-thirds of the members of the Federal Assembly must support the original wording of the bill. Each house of parliament has the authority to confirm certain presidential appointees, in addition to the prime minister. For example, the State Duma

confirms the chair of the Central Bank of Russia and the Federation Council confirms federal judges. In some cases, failure to approve the president's nominees has produced stalemate or prevented certain offices from functioning for a period of time.

Because presidential and parliamentary elections are entirely separate from one another in Russia, conflict between the president and the legislative branch has been frequent, since the president's supporters do not necessarily control the Federal Assembly. Following electoral rebuffs in the 1993 and 1995 parliamentary elections, Yeltsin confronted a parliament that obstructed many of his policies, but the parliament did not have the power or unity to offer a constructive alternative. The prime minister, who heads the government of Russia, is nominated by the president, but his appointment requires approval of the lower house of the parliament, the Duma, producing another point of potential conflict between the two branches of government. If the Duma rejects the president's nominee three times, the president must dissolve the Duma, appoint an interim prime minister, and call new parliamentary elections. The Duma can issue a vote of no confidence in an existing government (that is, the prime minister and cabinet), but it must be repeated twice and if it is successful, the president can call new parliamentary elections while remaining in office himself. Given this structure, a recalcitrant parliament could vote itself out of existence by attempting to resist the president's choice for prime minister. In fact, the parliament, dominated by opposition forces, has never voted the government out of office through no-confidence votes, despite several attempts, and the body exercised little influence over the appointment of the prime minister before 1998. Victor Chernomyrdin, who held that post from late 1992 until early 1998, had a weak political base in the parliament, but the parliament acquiesced to his appointment until early 1998, when Yeltsin himself removed Chernomyrdin from the post. Following a brief interregnum under reform prime minister Sergei Kirienko, Yeltsin renominated Chernomyrdin for the post. The financial crisis of August 1998 provoked the communist-dominated parliament to use its muscle to reject the nomination and insist on the appointment of a figure closer to their own position. On September 11, 1998, Evgenii Primakov was approved as prime minister. Primakov took first steps in this direction by including in his government individuals representing a wide spectrum of political forces. In May 1999 Yeltsin removed him from the post and nominated as his successor a little known figure, Sergei Stepashin, the minister of the interior. To the surprise of many observers, the Duma quickly approved Stepashin's appointment, who vowed to put in place a government of "technocrats" that would continue the economic reform process.

Society's ability to affect particular policy decisions through the legislative process is minimal. First, the parliament itself has limited power compared to the executive branch. Second, the blocs and parties in the parliament are isolated from the public at large and suffer low levels of popular respect. Many of the mechanisms that link parties and parliaments to citizens in Western democracies do not exist in Russia: interest associations to lobby the parliament are weak; party membership is low; and the internal decision-making structures of parties are generally elite-dominated. The fragmentation of the party system makes parties themselves weak institutions for influencing policy. Third, public hearings on controversial issues are rare. Nonetheless, through the parliament, Russian citizens have had the opportunity to select deputies in truly competitive elections, and politicians may, to some degree, take note of the election results.

Political Parties and the Party System

The most important political change that occurred with the collapse of Communism was the shift from a single-party system to a multiparty system. In the Communist party-state, the CPSU not only dominated state organs but oversaw all social institutions such as the mass media, trade unions, youth groups, educational institutions, and professional associations. It defined the official ideology for the country, set the parameters for state censorship, and, through the *nomenklatura* system, ensured that loyal personnel occupied all important offices. Approximately 10 percent of adults in the Soviet Union were party members, but there were no effective mechanisms to assure accountability of the party leadership to its members. Because the CPSU did not have to compete for political office, it was a party of a special kind, whose authority could not be openly questioned.

National competitive elections were held for the first time in the USSR in 1989, but political parties were not formal participants in Russia until the 1993 elections. Since then a confusing array of political organizations has run candidates in elections. These include not only political parties but also political and socioeconomic movements as well as coalitions of several parties or movements. (In this section all of these electoral groupings are called parties, even though some are registered as movements or other types of political organizations.)

Russian political parties have some peculiarities when compared to their Western counterparts. First, they generally form around and are associated with a prominent individual. For example, the Yabloko group was named after its founding leaders, Grigorii Yavlinsky, Vladimir Lukin, and Yuri Boldeyev. Even after the latter two left the association, the name stuck. (The word *yabloko*, "apple," is easy for voters to remember.) In anticipation of the 1999 parliamentary elections, prominent political figures such as Aleksandr Lebed and Moscow's mayor, Yuri Luzhkov, formed new

Table 3

December 1995 Parliamentary Elections[a]

Party or Block	Leader(s)	Popular Vote in 1993 Elections[b]	Comments	Percent in Dec. 1995 Vote[b] (seats won)	Seats from Single-Member Districts	Total Seats in Duma[c]
Liberal/Reform						
Russia's Democratic Choice/United Democrats	Yegor Gaidar (former prime minister; supported shock therapy)	15.4%[d]	Coalition included part of former Russia's Choice; party of former prime minister	3.9	9	9
Yabloko	Grigory Yavlinsky (an economist)	7.8%	Wanted to accelerate economic reform; slogan was "Dignity, Order, Justice"	6.9 (31)	14	45
Party of Workers' Self-Government	Svyatislav Fyodorov (eye surgeon, business leader)	—	Supported market reform, with employee ownership	4.0	1	1
Centrist						
Our Home Is Russia	Viktor Chernomyrdin (prime minister at the time of both elections)	—	Support from the cabinet, some regional governors; prime minister's party; included leader of former Democratic Party of Russia	10.1 (45)	10	55
Women of Russia	Yekaterina Lakhova	8.1%	Concerned about family, women's issues	4.6	3	3
Communist/Socialist						
Communist Party of the Russian Federation	Gennady Zyuganov	12.4%	Favored price regulation; wanted government of national salvation	22.3 (99)	58	157
Communist–Working Russia–For the Soviet Union	Viktor Anpilov	—	Radical communist; critical of the "revisionism" of the CPRF	4.5	1	1
Agrarian Party	Mikhail Lapshin	7.9%	Close to Communist Party	3.8	20	20
Power to the People	Nikolai Ryzhkov (former prime minister under Gorbachev)	—	Opposed to incumbent government; favored "prognosis planning"	1.6	9	9
Nationalist/"Patriotic"						
Liberal Democratic Party	Vladimir Zhirinovsky	22.8%	Favored a strong Russian state	11.2 (50)	1	51
Congress of Russian Communities	Yuri Skokov (former secretary of the Security Council); Aleksandr Lebed (army general)	—	Moderate nationalist; support from some heads of republics, in the military, veterans	4.3	5	5

[a]Figures may not add up to 100 percent or to the total numbers of deputies because votes for very small parties and for independents are excluded.

[b]Percentage of the total popular vote the party or bloc received on the proportional representation portion of the ballot in December 1993 and December 1995. A dash indicates that the party or bloc was not included on that ballot or did not win a significant portion of the vote. Number in parentheses for 1995 is number of deputy seats won from the PR lists.

[c]Included here are the number of seats won in the proportional representation races as well as the number won in the single-member district races.

[d]Participated in the 1993 elections as "Russia's Choice."

Source: DeBardeleben, Joan, *Russian Politics in Transition*, Second Edition. Copyright 1997 by Houghton Mifflin Company. Reprinted with permission.

parties or movements, which are distinguished primarily by who leads them. The 1993 and 1995 ballots listed not only the names of the blocs and parties but also of their leaders (see Table 3 on p. 466). The importance of individual leaders has increased political fragmentation, because groups with similar programs often split along lines of personal loyalties; political figures may also resist forming coalitions with potential allies because this could compromise personal political power.

Unlike most parties in the West, most Russian parties do not have a firm social base or stable constituency. Many Russians are hesitant to join a political party. Some recall their unhappy experience with the CPSU. Others simply distrust politics and politicians. Furthermore, other than the Communist Party of the Russian Federation (CPRF), Russian parties are young, so deep-rooted political identifications are absent. Finally, many citizens do not have a clear conception of their own interests or how parties might represent them. In this context, image-making is as important as programmatic positions, so parties appeal to transient voter sentiments. If the situation in the country stabilizes, the interests of particular groups (for example, blue-collar workers, business entrepreneurs, or groups based on age, gender, or region) may take a more central role in the formation of parties.

Despite the personalistic nature of party politics, some key cleavages do help explain the political spectrum. A major cleavage relates to economic policy. Nearly all parties and electoral groupings mouth support for the market transition, but those on the communist/socialist end of the spectrum are markedly muted in their enthusiasm. They support renationalization of some firms, continued state subsidies, more extensive social welfare policies, and limits on foreign economic investment. At the other end of the spectrum are liberal/reform groupings, which support rapid market reform, including privatization, free prices, limited government spending, and reduced emission of rubles by the Central Bank. This group includes Yeltsin and his political allies.

Parties and blocs are also divided on noneconomic issues, particularly those involving national identity and Westernization. The nationalist/"patriotic" parties emphasize the defense of Russian interests vis-à-vis the West. They opposed the inclusion of Poland, Hungary, and other former Soviet allies into the North Atlantic Treaty Organization (NATO). They also favor a strong military establishment, protection from foreign economic influence, and reconstitution of some former Soviet republics into a larger federation. Liberal/reform parties, on the other hand, strongly support the integration of Russia into the global market and the adoption of Western economic and political principles, positions that go along with their general support for radical market reform.

Because of the primacy of both the economic and identity cleavages, one can conceive of the Russian party spectrum as being divided into three ideological groupings:

- The traditional left, represented by the CPRF, the Agrarian Party, and other smaller communist/socialist formations
- The liberal/reform forces, which support Western-type market reform and political norms
- The nationalist/"patriotic" forces, which are not primarily concerned with economic issues but emphasize concerns of national identity

These three groupings overlap in interesting ways, since, for example, the CPRF has nationalist elements in its platform. One puzzling feature of the Russian party spectrum is the absence of a strong social democratic party of the West European variety, which would fall between the communist and liberal/reform ends of the spectrum. Centrist parties try to straddle the three groupings, but they have not been successful in gaining much popular support. Despite the weakness of the political center, the CPRF and the leading nationalist/"patriotic" parties have acted throughout as a loyal opposition, that is, they have not challenged the structure of the political system but have chosen to work within it.

The Russian Left: The Communist Party of the Russian Federation

By far the strongest parliamentary party after the 1995 elections was the Communist Party of the Russian Federation (CPRF), which won over one-third of the seats in the State Duma. The CPRF is the clearest successor of the old CPSU, although it is formally a new entity. Many former members and leaders of the CPSU have joined other parties or left politics, so that the present leadership of the CPRF is new. Gennady Zyuganov has been the party leader since the first congress of the CPRF in March 1993. The party won about 12 percent of the popular party-list vote in 1993 and 22 percent in 1995. The party won 157 of the 450 seats in the State Duma.

The party contains a variety of ideological tendencies, some more orthodox communist than others. Strong elements of Russian nationalism are evident in the party program. The CPRF supported the defense of the White House against the Yeltsin siege in 1993 and has consistently criticized Yeltsin's economic reform program and often blocked legislation, such as the right to buy and sell land, which the reformers view as crucial. Nonetheless, the party accepts substantial elements of the market reform package, favoring a combination of state and private ownership. Primary among the party's concerns are the social costs of the reform process. Thus it has supported state subsidies for industry to ensure timely payment of wages and prevent enterprise bankruptcies. Some critics have questioned the commitment of the party leadership to democratic governance, and there was speculation in 1996 about whether the party would have reverted to authoritarianism had Zyuganov won the presidential race. The party's detractors see its leaders as opportunistic rather than as true democrats, but others point out that communist governors in some of Russia's regions have become less ideological and more pragmatic once in power.

Support for the party is especially strong among older Russians, the economically disadvantaged, and rural residents. The party is no longer credible as a vanguard organization representing the working class. Instead it appears to represent those who have adapted less successfully to the radical and uncertain changes that have occurred since the collapse of the Communist state as well as some individuals who remain committed to socialist ideals.

Yabloko and Other Liberal/Reform Parties

More than any other grouping in the political spectrum, the liberal/reform parties have found it hard to build a stable and unified electoral base. These groups espouse a commitment to traditional liberal values, such as limited interference of the state in economic affairs, support for free-market principles, and the protection of individual rights and liberties. Four parties or blocs running on a promarket reform plank won seats in the Duma in the 1993 elections, the most prominent being Russia's Democratic Choice, headed by Yegor Gaidar, and Yabloko, headed by Grigorii Yavlinsky. In 1995 several liberal/reform parties split the vote, and only the Yabloko group amassed more than the necessary 5 percent of the national vote to win deputies through the party-list vote. Support for Gaidar's party fell from just over 15 percent of the party-list vote in 1993 to under 4 percent in 1995, despite efforts to broaden the coalition. Support for liberal/reform parties generally is stronger among the young, the more highly educated, urban dwellers, and the well-off.

As the election results indicate, Yabloko has enjoyed the most success among the liberal/reform parties. An economist who became well-known for his role in fashioning an economic program for the important region of Nizhnii Novgorod, Yavlinsky has been a consistent critic of the government, albeit a supporter of Western-style democratization and market reform. He charged the Yeltsin regime with being insufficiently democratic in its methods, citing the siege of the Russian White House in 1993, the attack on Chechnya, and the strong powers granted to the president in the new Russian constitution. On the economic front, Yavlinsky represents a softer version of market reform. These positions may explain his more consistent following, for he has not been blamed for the failures associated with the government's version of market reform. Yavlinsky has sustained relatively consistent support, but from a relatively narrow constituency, especially in educated circles.

Liberal/reform parties more closely associated with the government lack a clear and attractive leader. Yeltsin has refused to associate himself with any political party. Gaidar, Yeltsin's first prime minister and an architect of Yeltsin's shock therapy program, was not able to win the trust of the population in the face of the economic sacrifices required by the government's policies. Many citizens consider him to be out of touch with Russian reality and too closely linked to the Western economic advisers whose policies he endorsed. The former governor of Nizhnii Novgorod *oblast*, Boris Nemtsov, who was drafted to the federal government as deputy prime minister in 1997 at the age of thirty-seven, represents another possible leader of the liberal/reform group, as does Sergei Kirienko, who served as prime minister for about four months in 1998.

Another obstacle faced by the liberal/reform forces has been their inability to form a unified coalition. Several parties running on a liberal/reform platform split the vote in 1995, reducing their representation in the State Duma. On November 21, 1998, the brutal murder by contract killers of the liberal/reform politician and Duma member Galina Starovoitova (one of Russia's most prominent female politicians) resulted in renewed efforts to form a united political bloc. This involved prominent leaders such as Gaidar, Chubais, and Nemtsov. However, Yavlinsky refused to participate because he did not want to be associated with the unpopular policies of these formerly establishment politicians. Other liberal/reform leaders, such as Kirienko also left their options open rather than openly endorsing the initiative.

The liberal/reform parties have been blamed for Russia's economic and national decline. A survey conducted in late 1995 found that 58 percent of respondents associated the use of the word *democracy* in Russia with negative developments such as confusion, chaos, lawlessness, criminality, or poverty. Only 20 percent had positive associations with the word, such as freedom, freedom of speech, and free elections.[29] The tarnished image of Russian democracy also affects the so-called democrats who lead the liberal/reform parties.

Nationalist/"Patriotic" Parties

To the surprise of many observers, the Liberal Democratic Party of Russia (LDPR), headed by Vladimir Zhirinovsky, got the strongest support on the party ballot in 1993, winning almost 23 percent of the vote; this declined to 11 percent in 1995. Neither liberal nor particularly democratic in its platform, the party might more properly be characterized as nationalist and populist. Its populism is based on Zhirinovsky's personal charismatic appeal. Many Russians believe he "speaks our language," while others radically oppose his provocative style and nationalist rhetoric. Democratic procedures and accountability are not well developed within the party. Surveys indicate that Zhirinovsky's support has been especially strong among working-class men and military personnel. Concern with the breakdown of law and order seems to rank high among the priorities of Zhirinovsky supporters.

In his speeches, Zhirinovsky has openly appealed to the anti-Western sentiments that have grown in the wake of Russia's decline from superpower status and the government's perceived groveling for Western economic aid. The party has supported revival of an expanded Russian state to include Ukraine, Belarus, and possibly other neighboring areas. Zhirinovsky was one of the few prominent political figures who supported the government's offensive in Chechnya. The reaction to Zhirinovsky in the West and in Russia's "near abroad" (that is, the former Soviet republics) has been one of alarm. Some view him as a fascist and see certain analogies between Russia's present plight and Germany's following World War I, preceding Hitler's rise to power.

By the late 1990s support for Zhirinovsky had weakened. His extreme political rhetoric and sometimes uncivilized public demeanor alienated many Russians. In addition, leaders of other parties took up "patriotic" themes. Zyuganov of the CPRF included nationalist elements in his appeals; even Yeltsin emphasized the defense of Russian national interests in his speeches after Zhirinovsky's strong showing in 1993. In addition, Aleksandr Lebed, a retired army general, took on greater prominence as a spokesman for "patriotic" sentiments. Lebed ran third in the 1996 presidential race and served as head of the Security Council for a period in 1996 after his defeat. In 1997 he was elected governor of the large Siberian province Krasnoyarsk *krai*, an area that has suffered economic decline due in part to the collapse of the military industrial sector there. In 1998 he formed his own political movement, the Honor and Homeland Movement, which may serve as a vehicle for participation in the upcoming parliamentary and presidential elections.

Centrist Parties

The strongest centrist bloc until late 1998 was Our Home Is Russia, led by Viktor Chernomyrdin, the Russian prime minister from late 1992 until early 1998. In the 1995 election this bloc represented an important part of the political and economic establishment, including many government ministers and governors of some important Russian regions. But it won about 10 percent of the party-list vote in 1995, a dismally poor showing to serve as a basis for governance. The party's platform emphasized support for

Leaders: *Yuri Luzhkov*

Yuri Luzhkov represents a transitional generation in Russian politics. Born in Moscow in 1936, Luzhkov came to adulthood in the Khrushchev years. Unlike Yeltsin and Gorbachev (who were born just a few years earlier), he never held a high party office in the Soviet period, although he did work in the Soviet state structure. He made his career in industry after graduating from the Gubkin Institute of the Oil, Gas, and Chemical Industries (Moscow). Luzhkov served in the Ministry of the Chemical Industry until the advent of *perestroika*, when he moved to a position in the Moscow city administration.

The first free elections for mayor of Moscow took place in June 1991. Luzhkov ran for vice mayor on a ticket with Gavriil Popov, a popular reform politician. The team won, and when Popov resigned as mayor in June 1992, Luzhkov took over. He was reelected with 89 percent of the vote in 1996. Elections to the Moscow city Duma, held in 1993 and again in 1997, produced a body supportive of Luzhkov's policies.

Luzhkov has proven to be a popular leader who is given credit for the blossoming of the Russian capital city as a center of business and finance with a strong city government. Important aspects of the city's infrastructure, such as the extensive and widely used Moscow subway system, the highway circling the metropolis, and city streets, have been well maintained or even upgraded. An active retail trade sector gives Muscovites access to a wide range of foreign and domestic products. Impressive construction projects have been undertaken, including the reconstruction of the nineteenth-century Christ the Savior Church (destroyed by Stalin in 1931).

Moscow's 850th anniversary, celebrated in 1997, provided Luzhkov with the perfect occasion to give the city an expensive facelift and to draw attention to the city's cultural wealth and contemporary stature.

As mayor of Moscow, Luzhkov has combined elements of market economics and state control. With Yeltsin's support, Moscow was permitted to retain exceptional control over the privatization process in the city, while elsewhere in Russia federal legislation granted less power to local authorities. Because of the special leeway given to the Moscow government, Luzhkov's team was able to retain a strong influence in key sectors such as real estate, media, communications, and banking. The city administration also brought in revenue by selling select properties to chosen buyers, and through a network of business connections, the Moscow mayor has been able to direct the city's development. The result has been an image of prosperity and growth. Still, many Western observers feel that corruption and mafia connections have played an important role in maintaining the political balance Luzhkov has engineered.

Luzhkov's image as a man who can govern Moscow with a firm hand while encouraging entrepreneurship and private initiative contributes to his popularity both inside and outside of Moscow. This makes him a leading contender in the presidential elections to be held in the year 2000. Luzhkov's Fatherland movement, which espouses a centrist policy combining market economics with a strong state role, portrays its leader as a successful politician and manager who can bring to the rest of Russia the achievements he is credited with in Moscow.

the program of the Chernomyrdin government. With Chernomyrdin's removal as prime minister and the discrediting of his policies in 1998, the already weak political base of the party suffered further. Chernomyrdin proved to be an uncharismatic leader, too closely associated with the oil and gas industry to make him an appealing alternative to the public. In April 1999 Yeltsin appointed Chernomyrdin as Russia's special envoy to Yugoslavia in the context of the Kosovo conflict. Chernomyrdin, when he took on a leading role

in efforts to broker a peace agreement between NATO forces and Yugoslavian president Slobovan Milosevic, took on renewed political prominence.

Another centrist movement, Fatherland, was formed by Moscow mayor Yuri Luzhkov and held its founding congress in December 1998. A vehicle for Luzkhov's presidential bid, the party also registered to run candidates in the 1999 parliamentary elections. The leader of this centrist movement tries to appeal to a broad spectrum of voters by supporting a strong state, market economics, social policy, and "patriotic" themes such as a strong defense sector and restoration of Russia's role as a global power. The party's platform is likely to prove less important than the personal appeal of Luzhkov. Although he is associated with Moscow, a capital city whose privileges many regional residents and elites resent, his apparent success in modernizing the city has given him an image of being an effective leader. The prime minister from September 1998 to May 1999, Evgenii Primakov, is also a centrist and could prove to be a viable leader for a centrist party formation, but at this point his larger political intentions are still unclear.

Another centrist party, Women of Russia, had a surprisingly good showing in the 1993 elections, when it won 8 percent of the party-list vote. The party was formed in 1993 on the basis of an alliance of women's groups, most prominently the Union of Women of Russia, a renamed version of an official organization of women formed by the Soviet regime. Its program emphasizes social welfare issues. The party's success in the 1993 vote put twenty-three women in the Duma, otherwise dominated by men. But in 1995, Women of Russia won only 4.6 percent of the party-list vote, below the 5 percent threshold needed to win seats from this part of the ballot in the parliament. Possible explanations for the decline include limited campaign funds, minimal media coverage of the party during the electoral campaign, the failure of the party to make its positions clear, and the fact that centrist parties generally did poorly in 1995.[30]

Elections

In the post-Communist period, elections seem to be a constant phenomenon in Russia. With its mixed presidential/parliamentary system, electoral contests for the two branches of government are completely separate from one another. There are also regular elections at the regional and local levels. The initial euphoria with the competitive electoral structure has been replaced by a high degree of voter fatigue. While voter turnout for federal contests has been respectable (about 65 percent for the 1995 Duma elections and around 70 percent for the second round of the 1996 presidential election), it has at times fallen below the required minimum of 25 or 50 percent of eligible voters in some regional and local contests, necessitating

repeat balloting. National elections receive extensive media coverage, and campaign activities begin as long as a year in advance of the contest. The widespread use of polling firms by candidates and parties to assess public opinion and devise campaign strategies has made political consulting a big business. In the 1996 presidential race, U.S. campaign advisers were instrumental in fashioning Yeltsin's victory.

The electoral system for the Duma resembles the one used for election of the German *Bundestag*, that is, it combines **proportional representation** with winner-take-all districts. Half of the 450 deputies are selected on the basis of nationwide party lists; any party gaining 5 percent of the national vote is entitled to a proportional share of these 225 deputies in the State Duma. A large percentage of voters have chosen small parties that do not win the 5 percent needed to cross the threshold, so these citizens, in effect, are not represented through that part of the balloting. Voters are also given the explicit option of voting against all candidates or parties. In 1993 about 4 percent of voters took this option. The remaining 225 deputies are elected in winner-take-all races in single-member districts; these races usually involve local notables. Although a majority of candidates who won in single-member districts in 1995 were associated with particular parties or blocs, many were not. Some of these independent candidates join party factions once in the parliament.

The impact of the electoral system on party fragmentation is ambiguous. Because Russian parties and electoral blocs are so fluid and politics is so personalized, proportional representation may both increase *and* decrease party fragmentation. Proportional representation gives parties a role in drawing up the candidate lists and the 5 percent threshold for representation does, to some extent, encourage the formation of electoral coalitions. On the other hand, proportional representation allows fairly small parties to gain representation in the Duma and may discourage broader coalitions. The winner-take-all races may not bolster the chances of large parties as much as they do in established democracies because well-known local figures may win in these races without being associated with a particular party or bloc. The final balance of forces in the parliament is determined by the combined result of the party-list vote and the single-member district votes. Experience with the Russian electoral system to this point suggests that it has been somewhat effective in holding down the number of parties gaining representation.

In both the 1993 and 1995 parliamentary elections, forces opposing the government came out ahead, signaling broad public concern about the social consequences of the government's economic policy. In 1993, Zhirinovsky's nationalist party led the pack; in 1995 the Communists (CPFR) finished at the top, with a strong enough position to be able frequently to form a majority coalition in the Duma. Despite the electoral rebuff, Yeltsin kept Viktor Chernomyrdin as prime minister after both elections, leaving the impression that parliamentary elections had little impact on governance.

Despite the poor showing of the government forces in the parliamentary elections, Yeltsin scored a personal victory in the presidential election of 1996. Under the Russian constitution, presidential elections are held every four years. If no candidate receives a majority of the votes in the first round, a runoff election is held between the two top contenders. Eleven candidates stood in the first round of the presidential election on June 16, 1996. Yeltsin won 35 percent of the vote, compared to 32 percent for Zyuganov, followed by 15 percent for Lebed. In the second round, on July 3, Yeltsin's share rose to 54 percent, compared to 40 percent for Zyuganov, making Yeltsin the clear victor. Nearly 5 percent of voters selected the option "against both candidates." Despite Yeltsin's declining popularity, many Russians feared further upheavals if Zyuganov won and reversed the course Yeltsin had laid out. Following the presidential elections, candidates associated with the CPRF won several gubernatorial races, giving the party significant regional bases of power. If Yeltsin carries out his full term of office, the next presidential election will be in 2000. The runup to this election involves a period of heightened political activity in Russia, particularly since Yeltsin has pledged not to seek reelection. The outcome of that election could profoundly affect the further trajectory of Russian political development. The peaceful democratic transfer of power to Yeltsin's successor would also be a sign that the new political institutions are providing a viable framework for the resolution of political conflicts.

Political Culture, Citizenship, and Identity

Political culture can be a source of great continuity in the face of radical upheavals in the social and political spheres. Indeed, in many ways, attitudes toward government that prevailed in the tsarist period seem to have endured with remarkable tenacity. These include acceptance of a wide scope of state activity; a tradition of oligarchic or one-man leadership; support for economic egalitarianism; collectivist values; a tendency to utopian thinking; a simultaneous attraction to order and to anarchy; and the desire for an authoritative source of truth. While depictions of political culture often oversimplify and therefore should be viewed with caution, they capture some of the distinctiveness of political orientations in particular countries. The Soviet regime embodied many of the traditional Russian values, but Soviet authorities also glorified science, technology, industrialization, and urbanization—values superimposed on the traditional way of life of the largely rural population. When Communism collapsed, Soviet ideology was discredited, and the government embraced political and economic values from the West. Many citizens and intellectuals rejected this "imported" culture. A crisis of identity resulted for both elites and average citizens. What does it mean to be Russian, and on what basis should Russia's political society and structures be built? As Russians ponder these issues, those who study the country wonder, is Russian political culture compatible or in conflict with Western norms of liberal democracy and market economics? Can Russian political culture generate its own variant of democracy and economic prosperity, distinct from both the Soviet and the Western models?

One way to study political culture is to examine evidence from public opinion surveys. Such surveys suggest that there is considerable support for liberal democratic values such as competitive elections, an independent judiciary, a free press, and basic civil liberties. One survey carried out in late 1995 and early 1996 found that 80 percent of the respondents supported the introduction of democracy in Russia and only about one-third felt that democracy is a foreign idea not suited to Russia. Other surveys suggest that Russians favor a strong state and strong leaders who can maintain order, but not an authoritarian government.[31] Present political arrangements and government policy might, therefore, be seen to contradict many Russian cultural preferences. The state is weak and unable to fulfill many of its traditional roles in maintaining order and welfare; economic inequality has increased dramatically, as marketization encourages individual rather than collective values; and there is no authoritative source of truth. It is therefore not surprising that there is considerable popular discontent with the way government and the economy are functioning.

Another dimension of the search for identity relates to what it means to be Russian. The Russian language has two words for "Russian"—*russkii*, which refers to an ethnicity, and *Rossiiskii*, a broader concept referring to people of various ethnic backgrounds included in Russia as a political entity. In the USSR just over 50 percent of the population was ethnically Russian. Since most of the major ethnic minorities now reside in independent states, the Russian Federation is considerably more homogeneous ethnically than was the USSR: 80 percent Russian and 20 percent a variety of non-Russian groups. The largest minority is the Tatars, a traditionally Muslim group residing primarily in Tatarstan, a republic of Russia. Other significant minorities are the Bashkirs; various indigenous peoples of the Russian north; the many Muslim groups in the northern Caucasus region; and ethnic groups (e.g., Ukrainians, Armenians) of other former Soviet republics. At the same time, some 25 million ethnic Russians reside outside of the Russian Federation in other former Soviet republics.

Given this situation, it is significant whether one considers Russianness to be defined by ethnicity or by citizenship. In 1998 a Communist State Duma deputy made public anti-Semitic statements, eliciting a heated discussion about political tolerance. Liberal/reform politicians wished to strip the deputy of immunity and bring legal action against him. Observers worried that crisis conditions might incite increasing racial and ethnic tension. Muslim groups from Russia's southern regions have also been the target of ethnic stereotyping. In addition, refugee flows from some of the war-torn regions of the Transcaucasus (Georgia, Azerbaijan, and neighboring regions of southern Russia such as Chechnya and Ingushetia) have heightened national tensions. Individuals from these regions

play an important role in Russia's trade sector and are viewed by many Russians as speculators and crooks.

Religion has long played a role in shaping Russian identity. Today the Russian Orthodox Church appeals to many citizens who are looking for a replacement for the discredited values of the Communist system. Russia is experiencing a revival of religious practice as residents of many localities have focused on reconstructing or refurbishing churches, some of which were used for other purposes during the Soviet period. Religion has not, however, become a defining cleavage in the Russian political landscape. The government of President Yeltsin has supported the revival of Russian Orthodoxy as a basis of national identity. A controversial law passed in 1997 made it harder for new religious groups to organize themselves; the law was directed primarily at Western proselytizers. Human rights advocates and foreign observers protested strongly, again raising questions about the depth of Russia's commitment to liberal democratic values.

In the Soviet period, the mass media, the educational system, and a variety of other social institutions played a key role in propagating the party's political values. Now, students are presented with a wider range of views, and the print media represent a broad spectrum of political opinion. Opposition newspapers publish sometimes scathing criticisms of the government. Nonetheless, restrictions on the ability of the press and other mass media to function freely still exist. First, financial constraints make their existence precarious. Many Russians cannot afford to buy newspapers regularly; therefore readership has declined dramatically since Soviet times. A second factor affecting the ability of the press to give fair and complete coverage is the mafia. As already noted, courageous journalists have been a particular target of organized crime. Third, powerful financial interests exert influence over the media to sway public opinion, particularly during election campaigns. For example, Boris Berezovsky has close links to the managers of Russia's most popular television network, ORT, through a network of business linkages. Politicians are concerned to receive favorable media coverage and therefore may be subject to pressures from the financial interests that control important media outlets. Finally, the government itself has exerted pressure on the media to present issues favorably, although this pressure has rarely taken the form of overt censorship, as occurred after the October 1993 events. But both the national and regional governments still pressure editors to limit the publication of highly critical viewpoints, and in the extreme case some editors have been forcibly removed from their posts. Because the major newspapers receive financial subsidies from the government, pressure can be exerted in this way as well as through government taxation policy.

The electronic media are even more subject to political pressure. The costs and limited availability of the technology needed to run television stations allow the state to to maintain effective control over this sector. Russian television has generally given favorable coverage to the government's positions, and in some cases debate has been overtly restricted. The continued political interference in media affairs is but one example of the difficult process involved in transforming political culture.

Interests, Social Movements, and Protest

In the late 1980s *glasnost* produced an outburst of public activity, involving the formation of a wide variety of political and social movements. In recent years, economic decline has dampened political activism. Citizens are preoccupied with personal economic survival, many times holding three or four jobs to make ends meet. This leaves little time for participation in political and societal organizations. Political and social organizations also face financial problems and are often unable to hire staff or to support basic organizational needs. In this environment, the most successful interest associations have been those formed by better-off elements of society (such as new business entrepreneurs), by officials, by associations like the Siberian Union, representing particular regions, or by groups receiving funding from international or foreign agencies. A main thrust of Western humanitarian assistance to Russia has been support for nongovernmental organizations. Most of this aid, however, comes with strings attached. For example, some Western organizations require particular attention to gender equality, an issue that is of less priority to many Russians.

Dozens and usually hundreds of political and social organizations exist in every region of Russia, alongside a large number of nationwide organizations representing the interests of children, veterans, women, environmental advocates, pensioners, the disabled, and cultural interests. Other groups are professional unions, sports clubs, trade unions, and organizations concerned with various aspects of social welfare. Most locally based interest associations have small staffs and rely for support on local government, grants from international organizations, contracts for work carried out, and commercial activities. Organizations generally must register with local authorities, and some develop such close relationships with the local administration as to possibly undermine their independence. Many groups are successors to Soviet-era associations, such as the trade union organizations and nature protection societies. Others are closely linked to international organizations, such as the YMCA and the Rotary Club, or receive assistance from international organizations such as the Soros Foundation, the Save the Children Federation, or TACIS (run by the European Union). Many try to influence state policy, such as the Committee of Soldiers' Mothers of Russia, the Socio-Ecological Union, the "Chernobyl" Union, and the Society of Veterans. Others, such as hobby clubs or sports associations, bring together people with common interests or problems.

Environmental activism was particularly important in the late 1980s as *glasnost* increased public knowledge of pollution. The fate of the environmental movements in the 1990s is a paradigm for interest representation in general. Groups that in the late 1980s sometimes gained enough public support to force the temporary closure of polluting industries are less successful today because people fear the loss of jobs more than the effects of pollution. Nonetheless, numerous environmental organizations exist throughout the country, some operating under the national umbrella of the Socio-Ecological Union. Greenpeace, an international environmental organization, has a Russian affiliate, and ecological parties have run, albeit unsuccessfully, in both parliamentary elections.

Labor issues have been another focus of public attention. The official trade unions established under Soviet rule have survived under the title Federation of Independent Trade Unions (FITU), although they are no longer an arm of the government or the Communist Party. Still the largest union in Russia, FITU, has lost the confidence of large parts of the workforce. In some sectors, such as the coal industry, new independent trade unions have formed, mainly at the local level. Labor actions have become an important form of social protest, including spontaneous strikes, transport blockades, and even hunger strikes. The main grievance is late payment of wages. In mid-1998 coal miners in Siberia and the Donetsk area of European Russia blocked railway arteries to protest late wage payment. Later that year, teachers from various regions of the country participated in protest actions against wage delays; in the city of Ulyanovsk a hunger strike led to the death of one teacher. Immediate concessions are often offered in response to such protests, but the underlying problems are rarely addressed. These cases illustrate the helplessness felt by many citizens; the use of nontraditional forms of protest is a radical and desperate attempt to gain the attention of domestic and international authorities. In other cases, current economic insecurity inhibits workers from protesting too assertively for fear of losing their jobs.

It may well be, however, that class conflict, along with pressures for regional autonomy, will generate the most pronounced collective identities as Russia enters the twenty-first century. The present economic crisis continues to reinforce and make more visible the cleavages between various economic strata and regions. Perhaps the collapse of Soviet Communism will usher in a renewed phase of social class conflict played out on the weak scaffolding of capitalism that the reformers have tried to construct. At this moment, however, one cannot say that civil society has really formed in Russia, except perhaps among elements of the intelligentsia. Whatever forms of collective identity have emerged, social forces do not, at this point, easily find avenues to exert constructive and organized influence on state activity. As Russian citizens awaken to political awareness, they seem to waver between activism and apathy, and the political system sways from near anarchy to renewed authoritarianism.

Section ⑤ Russian Politics in Transition

Political Challenges and Changing Agendas

In August 1991, in the face of the attempted coup d'état against the last Soviet leader, Mikhail Gorbachev, crowds in Moscow toppled a prominent statue of Felix Dzerzhinsky, the first head of the Bolshevik Security Service. Dzerzhinsky symbolized the arbitrary and oppressive nature of the Soviet regime. Seven years later, in December 1998, the Russian Federation legislature, the State Duma, passed a resolution providing that the monument be restored. The position was strongly supported by deputies from the Communist faction and its allies. The fact that Russia's democratically elected assembly supported the move raised concerns both in Russia and abroad. What did this gesture mean? Did it simply reflect nostalgia for a time when the state maintained authority? Or did it express support for a revival of Communist rule? Did it indicate that people were willing to accept state repression if it brought economic stability? Furthermore, to what degree did the Duma's

action enjoy broad public support?

None of these questions is easy to answer, nor is it possible to predict what awaits Russia. Certainly prospects looked gloomier as the new millennium approached than they did ten years earlier. When the first edition of this book was published in 1996, five possible scenarios for Russia's future were presented:

- A stable progression toward marketization and democratization
- The gradual introduction of "soft authoritarianism," involving some restrictions of personal freedom and independent political activity under the guise of a benevolent dictatorship
- A return to a more extreme authoritarianism of a quasi-fascist or communist variety
- The disintegration of Russia into regional fiefdoms or de facto individual states
- Economic decline, civil war, and military expansionism.[32]

Now, just a few years later, the more pessimistic outcomes seem more likely.

Russia in the World of States

In the international sphere, Russia's flirtation with Westernization in the early 1990s produced ambiguous results. In the face of economic decline, Russia can no longer claim superpower status but is in the constant position of requesting international assistance, most recently humanitarian aid to address the food crisis in the winter of 1998–1999 and rescheduling of its foreign debt. Major military-industrial facilities also have suffered cutbacks in production since the end of the Cold War, as conversion of former military production and research facilities to civilian uses has been slow to achieve success.[33] Talented and previously pampered nuclear scientists are now un- or underemployed. Western governments have supported programs to ensure that they are not tempted by offers of employment by unfriendly governments, such as Iraq.

Russia's protests against unpalatable international developments such as NATO expansion, the "Desert Fox" operation against Iraq in December 1998, and NATO's bombing of Yugoslavia in 1999 reveal Moscow's underlying resentment against Western dominance as well as the country's relative powerlessness in affecting global developments. With a weakened military structure and economy, Russia can do little more than issue verbal protests. The West's recognition that Russia's involvement was crucial to finding a diplomatic solution to the Kosovo crisis in 1999 did give Russia an important international role. But many Russian citizens saw NATO's attack on Yugoslavia as reflective of a new world order in which Russia was marginalized and could act only at the behest of Western institutions.

Governing the Economy

The Primakov government's short tenure did restore a certain stability to the economy following the 1998 financial crisis, but its removal and replacement by a new government in May 1999 posed the possibility of yet another change in direction. The new government, under Sergei Stepashin, appeared poised to reactivate the market reform agenda but challenges facing it included the threat of renewed inflation and Western hesitancy in committing new investment and assistance funds in the face of Russia's continuing inability to meet its debt obligations. At the same time, peripheral regions of Russia are confronted with the worst economic crisis in recent memory, as some northern areas have had to be evacuated in the face of fuel and food shortages. Russia might be compelled to rely ever more on arms exports and raw material exports to support its faltering economy, but lack of investment funds could possibly hamper even these sectors. Some analysts, however, see a ray of hope in the devaluation of the ruble and Russia's sobering realization that salvation will not come through outside assistance. The ruble's falling value means decreased reliance on Western imports (as they become too expensive); this opens the opportunity for struggling Russian producers to become competitive again on the Russian domestic market. This path would require a savvy government policy to support economic producers and sectors that have reasonable prospects for success. This in turn would assume at least a minimally effective governing structure, able to collect taxes and control corruption.

The Democratic Idea

Russia's attempted democratization has been formally successful, but marred by corruption, the power of big money, and the limited accountability of its leaders. The political structures put in place by the 1993 constitution have provided inadequate mechanisms for the public to express its interests. These structures have not produced the strong and effective government most Russians desire, nor have they permitted people to feel that their interests are being considered. The continual conflict between the executive and legislative branches has sometimes led to deadlock and has made it difficult for Russians to believe that elections actually affect political outcomes. The result has been a high level of cynicism about democracy in Russia, about the motives of politicians, and about the trustworthiness of institutions. The growth of regionalism is another specter that haunts Russia. While Chechnya has been the only case of an overt attempt at secession, other regions have resisted central authority in taxation, trade, and economic policy. A continuation of economic decline is likely to reinforce these trends. The progression of political liberalization and democratization may be called into further question in some regions.

At the same time, it is difficult to conceive that the freedoms that have been exercised since 1986 could be easily withdrawn. Russians value the personal freedom they have gained since the collapse of Communism. Expanding contacts with the West have made increasingly broad circles aware of the benefits of civic participation, even if the Russian system does not yet realize these potentials. This new social context would make a return to full-blown authoritarianism difficult.

The Politics of Collective Identities

Despite changes in social consciousness, the formation of new political identities remains unfinished business. In the Soviet period, the state-imposed homogeneity of interests and political repression hindered the formation of diverse interest associations. Now other obstacles prevail. Most people are preoccupied by the struggle to make ends meet; they have no time or energy to forge new forms of collective action to address underlying problems. Under such circumstances, the appeal to nationalism and other basic sentiments can be powerful. Charismatic leaders may attempt to mobilize these sentiments with populist appeals based on extreme political agendas. The weakness of Russian intermediary organizations (interest groups, political parties or associations) means that politicians can more easily appeal directly to emotions because people are not members of groups that help them evaluate the politicians' claims. These conditions are fertile ground for authoritarian outcomes. On the other hand, the high level of education and increasing exposure to international media may work in the opposite direction. Exposure to alternative political systems and cultures may make people more critical of their own political system and seek opportunities to change it. A significant portion of the intelligentsia and some political elites provide potential leaders for this democratic subculture.

Russia remains in what seems to be an extended period of transition. Radical upheavals have been frequent over the past century, which provides some solace to Russians, as they see their current conditions in continuity rather than in contrast to the past. History has been hard on Russians, but somehow the country has always muddled through. In the early 1990s, Russians frequently hoped for "normal conditions," that is, an escape from the uncertainty, insecurity, and political controls of the past. That "normality" seems a distant hope now, but Russians seem to have a capability to adapt to change and uncertainty that North Americans find at once alluring, puzzling, and disturbing.

Russian Politics in Comparative Perspective

Many countries in the world today are undergoing a process of transition from some sort of authoritarian regime to a more democratic political structure. The Russian experience is, however, unique in many regards. First, indigenous political traditions and political culture influence the nature of political change in any country. Other unique features of the Russian situation, compared to other systems attempting democratization, are a more direct inheritance of the former Communist system.

The Soviet Union was described by many historians as a totalitarian system in which the Communist party-state extended its control to encompass the basic values and private lives of its citizens. A corollary was the total integration of economics, politics, and ideology. The state was the owner of virtually all economic assets and nearly all citizens were employees of the state. The Communist Party, which controlled state structures, claimed a monopoly on the truth and tried to direct all of the major institutions of political socialization (schools, public organizations, the arts, and media). To maintain this system of control, society and economy were artificially isolated from the outside world.

The way in which politics, economics, and ideology were intertwined in the Soviet period has profoundly affected the nature of political change in all of the former Soviet republics and generally has made the democratization process more difficult. Altering the political structures has required dismantling the entire foundation of the Soviet system. In effect, four transition processes were begun at once: (1) liberalization and then attempted democratization of the political system; (2) dismantling state dominance of the economy; (3) a search for new forms of collective identity to replace those provided by the old Communist ideology; and (4) a process of economic integration into the world of states and exposure to ideas and goods from the West.

Whereas other countries seeking to democratize may have tackled one or two of these transitions simultaneously, several post-Communist states, including Russia, have tried to do all four at once. This has made the stakes and the stress very high. The old political elites had no private wealth to fall back on, and many turned to corrupt or illegal methods to maintain their former privileges. Individuals, confronted with economic decline and an uncertain future, may be susceptible to nationalist appeals, demagogic leaders, or antidemocratic movements. Value disorientation and confusion may affect large portions of the population, as the larger environment appears chaotic and unpredictable.

Another important factor should be mentioned here. Unlike developing countries currently experiencing democratization and economic transformation, Russia is a highly industrialized country with a skilled and educated workforce. While this offers advantages, this high level of development is associated with a host of contemporary problems: a heavily damaged natural environment; obsolescent industries; entrenched bureaucratic structures; a nuclear arsenal that must be monitored and controlled; and a public that expects the state to provide a stable system of social welfare. Unlike modernizing elites in the developing world, Russian leaders must first deconstruct existing modern structures before constructing new ones. This process of deconstruction almost inevitably involves at least a temporary decline in economic performance and a rise in unemployment. For example, inefficient or highly polluting factories may need to be closed; the military-industrial complex has been cut back or converted to other uses; and the state has reduced social benefits. These problems, in turn, make it more difficult for the state to manage the domestic and international challenges it confronts.

How is Russia faring compared to some of the other post-Communist systems, which faced many of these same challenges? The nations of Eastern Europe and the former Soviet Union were all subjected to a similar system of economic, political, and ideological power during the period of Communist rule. Some were under Communist rule for a shorter period of time, but most parts of the Soviet Union shared with Russia more than seven decades of the Communist party-state. Despite the efforts of the Soviet leadership to establish conformity throughout the region, national differences did emerge. The countries of Eastern Europe had a history of closer ties and greater cultural exposure to Western Europe; ideas of liberalism, private property, and individualism were less foreign to citizens in countries such as Czechoslovakia, East Germany, and Hungary than in regions farther east, including Russia. The Roman Catholic Church in Poland provided a focal point for national identity, and Poland's historical antipathy to Russia produced a stronger resistance to the imposition of the Soviet model than in other Slavic countries of the region. Such cultural, geopolitical, and historical differences affected the shape that communist rule took in the various countries.

In Poland collectivization of agriculture never succeeded, and communist rule took a softer form; in Hungary a form of quasi-market reform began to emerge in 1968; and in Czechoslovakia in 1968 a dramatic attempt to build "socialism with a human face" emerged from within the Communist Party elite itself and suffered defeat only at the hands of Soviet troops. Centuries of Ottoman rule in Yugoslavia and Bulgaria produced yet a different cultural mosaic, and in several countries problems with ethnic minorities created unique tensions, even if their open expression was, for the most part, suppressed under communist rule.

Within the Soviet Union, too, there was considerable variation among the union republics. The Baltic republics of Latvia, Lithuania, and Estonia took a more experimental approach in many spheres of activity and had a more Western European atmosphere; at the other extreme, the Central Asian republics retained aspects of traditional Muslim culture, preserved the extended family structure, and maintained within the construct of the Communist Party a greater prominence for links rooted in the clan system indigenous to the region. Only in Russia and Yugoslavia (as well as in China and Cuba) was communism largely an indigenous phenomenon rather than a pattern imposed by an outside force. In many ways Russia's culture helped to define the character of the communist system that it imposed throughout its sphere of influence.

All fifteen countries that gained independence after the collapse of the Soviet Union as well as the countries of Eastern Europe have experienced the collapse of the communist system of power since 1989.

Global Connection: *Western Aid to Russia*

With the collapse of the Iron Curtain, Western governments and international agencies were poised to help build market economies and democratic political structures in the former Communist countries of Central Europe and the former Soviet Union. To some extent the goals of this aid were self-interested: market economies would be more accessible to Western firms seeking external markets and profitable investment opportunities. Promotion of democratization was linked to a view that the West had won the Cold War, and democratic countries were considered likely to be more cooperative and peaceful neighbors and partners.

International aid has many sources. Between 1991 and 1997 about 60 percent of assistance to Russia came from individual countries, most notably Germany, followed by the United States, and the United Kingdom. Other significant donors have included Norway, Canada, France, Japan, Italy, and Sweden. Much of this aid has taken the form of programs to provide training and know-how in areas such as nuclear safety, legislative drafting, health care management, support for private entrepreneurs, encouragement of nongovernmental organizations, and development of the housing sector. Critics point out that a certain portion of such aid is expended in the donor country to pay consultants and training specialists' salaries that would be considered exorbitant in the recipient country. Also, it is often difficult to measure the direct impact of aid programs, although most assistance agencies try to do so. The most important effects may be unmeasurable, in the form of long-term changes in attitudes or exposure to alternative models for social or economic undertakings. Some assistance programs have involved humanitarian or food aid, investment funds, and repayable credits. Alongside such bilateral aid programs, international organizations also have provided assistance, most often in the form of repayable credits. The most important of these agencies are the following;

The International Monetary Fund The IMF was founded in 1944 and is probably the most influential international agency in Russia. Its mandate is to oversee the international monetary system and help maintain stability in exchanges between its 182 member countries, which can draw on the fund's resources. By 1998 Russia had an outstanding debt to the IMF of $2.8 billion, funds issued to Russia as short- and medium-term credits to help stabilize the ruble and Russia's internal and external monetary balance. The dispersal of these funds has been contingent on the fulfillment of certain conditions by the Russian government, particularly maintenance of noninflationary fiscal and monetary policies. These policies, in turn, have necessitated cutbacks in social services and subsidies to troubled economic sectors. Through conditions on its loans, the IMF has been able to influence the direction of the Russian reform program. (For more information, see the Web site at http://www.imf.org.)

The World Bank Also founded in 1944, the World Bank has as its purpose to promote and finance economic development in the world's poorer countries. After World War II this involved assistance in financing reconstruction in war-torn Europe. The agency is an investment bank with 180 member countries. Through its International Bank for Reconstruction and Development (IBRD), the World Bank has provided loans to support development programs in Russia in sectors such as agriculture, environment, energy, and social welfare. (See the Web site at http://www.worldbank.org.)

The European Bank for Reconstruction and Development The EBRD, formed in 1991, promotes the development of market economies in post-Communist countries by supporting privatization and entrepreneurship as well as developing infrastructure for production. EBRD provides loans, guarantees, and supports equity investments. (See the Web site at http://www.ebrd.com.)

The European Union initiated the TACIS program in 1991 as a vehicle for providing grants to finance the transfer of know-how to Russia and other countries in the former Soviet Union. In 1998 the TACIS budget provided for 112.2 million European currency units in grants to the region. (See the Web site at http://www.europa.eu.int/comm/dg1a/tacis.)

Despite the broad scope of assistance programs, aid to Russia in 1994 represented only 0.6 percent of gross domestic product and was at a level of US$12 per capita. Compared to the Marshall Plan, which assisted the reconstruction of Europe after World War II, this is an extremely modest contribution. Many Russians feel that Western assistance efforts have not made a noticeable difference. Some Russian politicians criticize organizations like the IMF for forcing a development strategy on Russia that has produced only economic crisis and decline. Following the financial crisis of August 1998, many assistance agencies undertook a review of their approaches to development assistance for Russia, a process that may well lead to an overall decline in its size. One positive effect of this may be to encourage Russia to seek solutions based on its own resources and capacities rather than on outside support.

Given the diversity of nations that were subject to the communist system, it is not surprising that paths of extrication from communist rule should also vary widely. How has Russia fared in the post-Communist period compared to these other countries? We can in sum say, "not the best, but not the worst either." All of the post-Communist states have shared common problems, but the elites have responded in different ways, and differences in traditional cultures and the particular nature of the communist system in each country have affected its present condition.

Russia has almost certainly suffered more severe economic dislocations than most of the countries of Eastern Europe (with the clear exception of Yugoslavia). Poland has pursued the most radical variant of the shock therapy approach, and it appears that its strategy has been the most successful in terms of gross economic indicators. However, huge differentials in income and high unemployment rates have been costs of the approach. Russia's attempt to implement the radical reform strategy has been less successful than Poland's because state institutions have been weaker, internal political opposition has been more successful in moderating economic policy, and indigenous culture is probably less conducive to market structures.

Russia has not fared so badly compared to neighbors like Ukraine, Belarus, and most of the Central Asian states. In Belarus and the Central Asian states democratization has not taken hold. In all of these countries the leaders have embraced market reform with considerably less commitment than the Russian government. Russia's recent financial crisis has had reverberations in Ukraine and Belarus, intensifying their economic problems. Because Russia possesses rich deposits of natural resources (including energy resources), it has been able to cope with the ruptured economic ties resulting from the collapse of the Soviet Union better than some of the less well endowed states. In addition, Ukraine and particularly Belarus are still suffering from the severe economic and health effects of the accident at the Chernobyl nuclear power plant, and the Central Asian states confront the disastrous effects of Soviet-imposed emphasis on cotton production and associated environmental degradation (Aral Sea crisis). Russia (along with Ukraine) has been the focal point of international economic assistance because of its large nuclear arse-

nal, its size, and its geopolitical importance. Although this aid has been insufficient to make the government's overall reform program successful, other parts of the former Soviet Union (with the likely exception of the Baltic states) have received even less international assistance, despite their weaker economic position.

In the political sphere, virtually all of the post-Communist states claim to be pursuing some form of democratization, but in some cases this is more in name than in practice, particularly in Central Asia and parts of the Transcaucasian area. Belarus has a distinctively authoritarian government. In all of the post-Communist states, the attempt to construct democratic political institutions has been characterized by repeated political crises, weak representation of popular interests, executive-legislative conflict, faltering efforts at constitutional revision, and corruption. These features are more marked in the more eastern countries. This may be the result of cultural differences between Russia and its more Europeanized western neighbors (particularly, Poland, eastern Germany, the Czech Republic, and Hungary) as well as of the shorter period of Communist Party rule in Eastern Europe, the Baltics, and some of the western portions of the former USSR (where the Communist Party took power only after World War II). The cultural and geographical proximity of Eastern Europe to the West has also meant less ambivalence on the part of the population and elite toward Western notions of political democracy.

In Russia, on the other hand, there is considerable skepticism about adopting the Western model of political development, and those political elites who mouth Western values have to a large degree not understood or internalized them. The question might be asked whether the patrimonial, collectivist, and egalitarian thrust of Russian culture, as well as some features of the cultures of Central Asia, Ukraine, and Belarus, are really compatible with Western economic and political ideas. Although the concept of democracy has a certain appeal in the region (partly because it has been associated with Western affluence), to much of the population in these countries it means, above all, personal freedom rather than support for notions of political accountability, rule of law, or the civic role of the citizen.

Even though Russian politics have been highly contentious and the government operates at very low levels of efficacy and legitimacy, with the exception of the Chechnya conflict Russia has escaped major domestic violence and civil war, unlike Yugoslavia, Armenia, Azerbaijan, Georgia, Moldova, and the Central Asian state of Tadzhikistan. For all their problems, Russian politicians have conducted themselves in a relatively civil manner, and Yeltsin himself has rarely appealed to exclusivist definitions of Russian identity. Citizenship rights for all ethnic groups have been maintained, and state-sponsored racism is largely absent. Some opposition figures have not been so restrained in their political rhetoric, but the Yeltsin government can be credited with avoiding marginalization of any major social groups.

Russia will undoubtedly continue to be a key regional force in Europe and Asia. Its vast geographical expanse, rich resource base, large and highly skilled population, and the legacy of Soviet rule will assure this. Yet its former allies in Central Europe, especially the Czech Republic, Hungary, Poland, and to some degree the Baltic states, are gradually drifting into the orbit of Western Europe, both economically and politically. They are seeking, and to a degree have already achieved, closer economic and political ties to the European Union; their identity is increasingly defined by those ties. This could potentially leave Russia isolated and increasingly resentful of the loss of stature in both the regional and international world of states. A rising sense of national humiliation could well make Russia a less tractable, more pugnacious force.

On Russia's eastern side, the former Central Asian republics (Turkmenistan, Uzbekistan, Tadzhikistan, and Kyrgystan) are being courted by the Middle Eastern states with whom they share linguistic, cultural, and religious ties. Here the pattern of economic and political transformation will be affected by traditions and cultures (including Islam) that play only a minimal role in the Christianized areas of the former Soviet bloc. And yet in many ways these regions, along with Kazakhstan, retain strong links to Russia, rooted in decades of economic and political interdependence. The states in the middle (Russia, Ukraine, Belarus, Moldova, Bulgaria, Romania) still lie between East and West. Here, efforts to adapt a Western European model of economy and polity have at times seemed tortured and incongruous with indigenous traditions and aspirations. The tradition of a strong state and weak society has not been reversed; cultural tendencies to egalitarianism, state paternalism, clientelistic networks, and communalism conflict with efforts to adopt Western market structures and legal regimes. And yet exposure to Western life-styles, affluence, and legal norms has instilled expectations and hopes, particularly in educated circles, for a more prosperous life-style, less encumbered by the bureaucratic control of the state. The global nature of politics and economics has made impossible the type of isolation that provided a bulwark for the legitimacy of the Soviet state for many decades. These states that lie between Western Europe and Asia will likely continue to be torn between conflicting values and international pressures, with Russia both a feared but influential model (either to emulate or reject) for the neighboring countries.

Will Russia be able to find a place for itself in the world of states that meets the expectations of its educated and sophisticated population? On the eve of the twenty-first century prospects look dim. But one thing is certain. Russia will continue to be an important factor by virtue of its size and its nuclear arsenal. If Russia's experiment of combining market reform and democratization gradually achieves success, then this may inspire movement in this direction in other countries like China. If it fails, this may demoralize democratic movements elsewhere and lead to an increase in regional instability.

Key Terms

patrimonial state
mir
democratic centralism
vanguard party
collectivization
totalitarian
tacit social contract
perestroika
glasnost
demokratizatsiia
law-based state
union republics
market reform
shock therapy
capital flight
mafia

pyramid debt
spontaneous
    privatization
joint-stock companies
privatization voucher
insider privatization
money-based
    privatization
autonomous republics
oblasts
krai
okrugs
patron-client networks
asymmetrical federalism
civil society
proportional
    representation

Suggested Readings

Blasi, R. Joseph, Maya Kroumova, and Douglas Kruse. *Kremlin Capitalism: The Privatization of the Russian Economy.* Ithaca, N.Y.: Cornell University Press, 1997.

Bova, Russell. "Political Dynamics of the Post-Communist Transition: A Comparative Perspective." In *Post-Communist Studies and Political Science: Methodology and Empirical Theory in Sovietology,* ed. Frederic J. Fleron, Jr., and Erik P. Hoffman, 239–263. Boulder, Colo.: Westview Press, 1993.

Buckley, Mary, ed. *Post-Soviet Women: From the Baltics to Central Asia.* Cambridge: Cambridge University Press, 1997.

Cohen, Stephen. *Rethinking the Soviet Experience: Politics and History Since 1917.* New York: Oxford University Press, 1985.

Cook, Linda J. *The Soviet Social Contract and Why It Failed.* Cambridge, Mass.: Harvard University Press, 1993.

DeBardeleben, Joan, and John Hannigan, eds. *Environmental Security and Quality after Communism.* Boulder, Colo.: Westview Press, 1995.

Eckstein, Harry, Frederic J. Fleron, Jr., Erik P. Hoffman, William M. Reisinger. *Can Democracy Take Root in Russia? Explorations in State-Society Relations.* Lanham, Md.: Rowman & Littlefield, 1998.

Fish, M. Steven, *Democracy from Scratch: Opposition and Regime in the New Russian Revolution.* Princeton, N.J.: Princeton University Press, 1995.

Friedgut, Theodore H., and Jeffrey W. Hahn, eds. *Local Power and Post-Soviet Politics.* Armonk, N.Y.: M. E. Sharpe, 1994.

Getty, J. Arch. *Origins of the Great Purges: The Soviet Communist Party Reconsidered.* Cambridge: Cambridge University Press, 1985.

Hajda, Lubomyr, and Mark Beissinger, eds. *The Nationalities Factor in Soviet Politics and Society.* Boulder, Colo.: Westview Press, 1990.

Handelman, Stephen. *Comrade Criminal: Russia's New Mafiya.* New Haven, Conn.: Yale University Press, 1995.

Hanson, Philip, "What Sort of Capitalism Is Developing in Russia," *Communist Economies and Economic Transformation* 9, no. 1 (1997), 27–42.

Herspring, Dale R. *Russian Civil-Military Relations.* Bloomington: Indiana University Press, 1996.

Hough, Jerry, and Merle Fainsod. *How the Soviet Union Is Governed.* Cambridge, Mass.: Harvard University Press, 1979.

Lewin, Moshe. *The Gorbachev Phenomenon: A Historical Interpretation.* Berkeley: University of California Press, 1991.

Marsh, Rosalind, ed. *Women in Russia and Ukraine.* Cambridge: Cambridge University Press, 1996.

Millar, James R., and Sharon L. Wolchik. *The Social Legacy of Communism.* New York: Woodrow Wilson Center Press, 1994.

Pipes, Richard. *Russia Under the Old Regime.* London: Widenfelt & Nicolson, 1974.

Pryde, Philip R., ed. *Environmental Resources and Constraints in the Former Soviet Republics.* Boulder, Colo.: Westview Press, 1995.

Smith, Gordon B. *Reforming the Russian Legal System.* Cambridge: Cambridge University Press, 1996.

Stavrakis, Peter J., Joan DeBardeleben, and J. L. Black. *Beyond the Monolith: The Emergence of Regionalism in Post-Soviet Russia.* Washington: Wilson Centre Press and Johns Hopkins Press, 1997.

Stoner-Weiss, Kathryn. *Local Heroes.* Princeton, N.J.: Princeton University Press, 1997.

Tucker, Robert C. *Stalin in Power: The Revolution from Above, 1928–1941.* New York: Norton, 1990.

White, Stephen. *After Gorbachev.* 4th ed. Cambridge: Cambridge University Press, 1993.

White, Stephen, Richard Rose, and Ian McAllister, *How Russia Votes.* Chatham, N.J.: Chatham House, 1997.

Wyman, Matthew. *Public Opinion in Post-Communist Russia.* London: Macmillan, 1996.

Web sites

Web site of the European Internet Network provides links to many other Web sites on Russia. www.russiatoday.com

Web site of the Center for Russian and East European Studies of the University of Pittsburgh provides many additional scholarly and government resources. www.ucis.pitt.edu/reesweb

Web site "Friends and Partners" was established by citizens of the United States and Russia "to promote better understanding between the people of our countries" and provides many interesting links. www.friends-partners.org/friends/index/html

Web site of Radio Free Europe/Radio Liberty provides a news service with the latest developments in Russia. www.rferl.org/newsline/

Endnotes

[1] Gosudarstvennyi komitet Rossiiskoi Federatsii po Statistike (State Statistical Committee of the Russian Federation), *Regiony Rossii: informatsionno-statisticheskii sbornik (Regions of Russia: information-statitistical collection),* vol. 1 (Moscow, 1997), 381, 615; and Central Intelligence Agency, *World Factbook 1997,* available on the World Wide Web at http://www.odci.gov/cia/publications/factbook/rs.html.

[2] Richard Pipes, *Russia Under the Old Regime* (London: Widenfelt & Nicolson, 1974).

[3] Pipes, 22–24.

[4] Carl J. Friedrich and Zbigniew K. Brzezinski, *Totalitarian Dictatorship and Autocracy* (Cambridge, Mass.: Harvard University Press, 1965).

[5] Peter Hauslohner, "Politics Before Gorbachev: De-Stalinization and the Roots of Reform," in *The Soviet System in Crisis: A Reader of Western and Soviet Views*, ed. Alexander Dallin and Gail W. Lapidus (Boulder, Colo.: Westview Press, 1991), 37–63.

[6] Mikhail Gorbachev, *Perestroika: New Thinking for Our Country and the World* (New York: Harper, 1987).

[7] M. Steven Fish, *Democracy from Scratch: Opposition and Regime in the New Russian Revolution* (Princeton, N.J.: Princeton University Press, 1995).

[8] Adapted from Marshall I. Goldman, "Gorbachev and Economic Reform," *Foreign Affairs* (Fall 1985): 64.

[9] Data in this and the following paragraphs are from the following sources: The Economist Intelligence Unit, *EIU Country Report: Russia, 1st Quarter 1998*, 47; *2d Quarter 1998*, 33; *3d Quarter 1998*, 31; and The Economist Intelligence Unit, *EIU Country Profile: Russia, 1998–99*, 37, 44; European Bank for Reconstruction and Development (EBRD), *Transition Report 1997* (London, 1997), 15; EBRD, *Transition Update 1998* (London, 1998).

[10] Radio Free Europe/Radio Liberty Daily Report (distributed by electronic mail), April 8, 1994, and May 17, 1994 (report by Keith Bush).

[11] The Economist Intelligence Unit, *EIU Country Profile: Russia, 1998–1999*, 45, 46.

[12] Data in this and the following paragraph are from Vasily Shchurov, *Trud*, March 13, 1996, 1; Vladimir Popov, *A Russian Puzzle: What Makes the Russian Economic Transformation a Special Case*, Research for Action 29 (Helsinki: World Institute for Development Economics Research (WIDER), The United Nations University, 1996), 35–36.

[13] See David Lane, *Soviet Society under Perestroika*, rev. ed. (London: Routledge, 1992), 357–361.

[14] The Economist Intelligence Unit, *EIU Country Report: Russia, 3d Quarter 1998*, 33.

[15] *Regiony Rossii*, vol. 1, 440–442.

[16] Sarah Ashwin and Elaine Bowers, "Do Russian Women Want to Work?" in *Post-Soviet Women: From the Baltics to Central Asia*, ed. Mary Buckley (Cambridge: Cambridge University Press, 1997), 23.

[17] *Regiony Rossii*, vol. 1, 393.

[18] *Regiony Rossii*, vol. 1, 405.

[19] Victor Zaslavsky, "From Redistribution to Marketization: Social and Attitudinal Change in Post-Soviet Russia," in *The New Russia: Troubled Transformation*, ed. Gail W. Lapidus (Boulder, Colo.: Westview Press, 1994), 125.

[20] Joan DeBardeleben, "Attitudes Toward Privatization in Russia," *Europe-Asia Studies*, 51, no. 3 (1999) 447–465.

[21] Figures adapted from The Economist Intelligence Unit, *EIU Quarterly Economic Review of the USSR, 1985 Annual Supplement*, 20.

[22] The Economist Intelligence Unit, *EIU Country Profile: Russia, 1998–99*, 49; *Nezavisimaia gazeta—Politekonomiia* (monthly supplement), no. 19 (December 1998), 3.

[23] Russian Centre for Public Opinion Research (VTsIOM), *Ekonomicheskie i sotsial'nye peremeny: monitoring obshchestvennogo mneniia (Economic and Social Change: The Monitoring of Public Opinion)*, no. 26 (Nov.-Dec. 1996), 55, and no. 32 (Nov.-Dec. 1997), 58.

[24] See Benjamin S. Lambeth, "Russia's Wounded Military," *Foreign Affairs* (March/April 1995): 86–98.

[25] Eugene Huskey, "Russian Judicial Reform after Communism," in *Reforming Justice in Russia, 1864–1996: Power, Culture, and the Limits of Legal Order*, ed. Peter H. Solomon, Jr., (Armonk, N.Y.: M. E. Sharpe, 1997), 336–337.

[26] Peter Kirkow, "Local Self-government in Russia: Awakening from Slumber," *Europe-Asia Studies* 49, no. 1 (1997), 43–58.

[27] Fond razvitiia parlamentarizma v Rossii, *Federal'noe sobranie: Sovet Federatsii, Gosudarstvennaia Duma, Spravochnik* (The Federal Assembly, Council of the Federation, State Duma, *Handbook*) (Moscow, 1996), 125; data from the Soviet period is from David Lane, *State and Politics in the USSR* (Oxford: Blackwell, 1985), 184–185.

[28] Darrell Slider, "Elections to Russia's Regional Assemblies," *Post-Soviet Affairs* 12, no. 3 (1996), 244.

[29] Jon Pammett, "Elections and Democracy in Russia," *Communist and Post-Communist Studies*, vol. 32, no. 1 (1999).

[30] Mary Buckley, "Adaptation of the Soviet Women's Committee: Deputies' Voices from "Women of Russia," in *Post-Soviet Women: From the Baltics to Central Asia*, ed. Mary Buckley (Cambridge: Cambridge University Press, 1997), 158, 163, 180.

[31] Pammett, "Elections and Democracy in Russia"; William M. Reisinger, Arthur H. Miller, Vicki L. Hesli, and Kristen Hill Maher, "Political Values in Russia, Ukraine, and Lithuania: Sources and Implications," *British Journal of Political Science* 24 (1994), 183–223.

[32] Joan DeBardeleben, "Russia," in *Comparative Politics at the Crossroads*, ed. Mark Kesselman, Joel Krieger, and William A. Joseph (Lexington, Mass.: D.C. Heath, 1996), 355–357.

[33] See Michael R. Gordon, "Hard Times for Russia's Nuclear Centers," *New York Times*, November 18, 1998, A1, A18.

CHAPTER 11

China

William A. Joseph

People's Republic of China

Land and Population

Capital	Beijing
Total Area (square miles)	3,696,100 (slightly larger than the U.S.)
Population	1.2 billion
Annual Average Population Growth Rate (1990–1997)	1.1%
Urban Population	32%
Ethnic Composition	Han (Chinese) 92%
	Other 8%
Major Languages	Chinese (various dialects)
Religious Affiliation	Officially atheist, though many people practice traditional folk and other religions
	Taoist, Buddhist, Muslim 2%–3%
	Christian 1.0%

Economy

Domestic Currency	Renminbi ("people's currency"), also called yuan
Total GNP (US$)	$1.055 trillion
GNP per capita (US$)	$860
GNP per capita at purchasing power parity (US$)	$3570
GNP average annual growth rate (1996–1997)	8.9%
GNP per capita average annual growth rate	1996–1997 7.8%
	1980–1995 8.6%
	1965–1980 4.1%
Income Gap:	Richest 20% of population
GDP per capita (US$)	$5114
	Poorest 20% of population
	$772
Structure of Production (% of GDP)	Agriculture 18.7%
	Industry 49.2%
	Services 32.1%
Labor Force Distribution (% of total)	Agriculture 72%
	Industry 15%
	Services 13%
Exports as % of GDP	21%
Imports as % of GDP	19%

(handwritten: Lvs.US - 3% Gem-1% UK-2% Mex zero 87-?%)

Society

Life Expectancy	Female	71.3
	Male	67.3
Doctors per 100,000 people		115
Infant Mortality per 1000 live births		38
Adult Literacy	Female	72.7%
	Male	89.9%
Access to Information and Communications (per 1000 people)	Radios	185
	Televisions	247
	Telephone Lines	34
	Personal Computers	2.1

Women in Government and Economy

Seats in national legislature held by women	21.8%
Women at ministerial level	6.0%
Women as % of total labor force	45.0%
Female business administrators and managers	11.6%
Female professional and technical workers	45.1%
1998 Human Development Index ranking (out of 174 countries, 1 = highest)	106

These data do not include Hong Kong.

Political Organization

Political System   Communist party-state; officially, a people's democratic dictatorship.

Regime History   Established in 1949 after the victory of the Chinese Communist Party (CCP) in the Chinese civil war.

Administrative Structure   Unitary system with 22 provinces, 5 autonomous regions, 4 centrally administered municipalities, and 1 Special Adminstrative Region (Hong Kong).

Executive   Premier (head of government) and president (head of state) formally elected by legislature, but only with approval of CCP leadership; the head of the CCP, the general secretary, is in effect the country's chief executive.

Legislature   Unicameral National People's Congress; delegates elected indirectly from lower-level people's congresses for five-year terms. Largely a "rubber stamp" body for Communist Party policies, although in recent years has become somewhat more assertive.

Judiciary   A nationwide system of people's courts, which is constitutionally independent but, in fact, largely under the control of the CCP; a Supreme People's Court supervises the country's judicial system and is formally responsible to the National People's Congress, which also elects the court's president.

Party System   A one-party system, although in addition to the ruling Chinese Communist Party, there are eight politically insignificant "democratic" parties.

Politics in Action

In June 1998, U.S. President Bill Clinton was greeted by China's president and Communist Party leader, Jiang Zemin, in Tiananmen Square in Beijing. Clinton was the first U.S. president to visit the People's Republic of China (PRC) since Chinese troops had used brutal force to remove pro-democracy demonstrators from that same square nearly a decade earlier. Some Americans and human rights groups were highly critical of Clinton's decision to be received just steps from where hundreds of civilians were massacred on the orders of China's leaders.

The 1989 demonstrations had begun in April when university students gathered in Tiananmen ("Gate of Heavenly Peace") to protest widespread official corruption and to demand that the Chinese Communist Party (CCP) allow more democracy in China. The protesters had been emboldened by the fact that the Chinese people had, for the past decade, been experiencing greater economic freedom than at any time since the Communists had come to power in 1949. The students now wanted to extend the process of reform into the realm of government and politics.

Throughout that spring, the demonstrations grew, and at one point more than a million people from all walks of life gathered in and around Tiananmen. For several months, the CCP, constrained by internal divisions about how to handle the protests and intensive international media coverage, did little other than engage in some threatening rhetoric to dissuade the demonstrators.

But China's leaders ran out of patience and the troops were ordered in during the very early morning hours of June 4. One protester who survived the assault described what happened when he and others joined hands on the outskirts of the square to form a human barricade to halt the army's advance:

> Then, without warning, the troops opened fire on us. People cursed, screamed and ran. In no time, seventy or eighty people had collapsed all around me. Blood spattered all over, staining my clothes.[1]

Student demonstrators erected a statue called the "Goddess of Democracy" in Beijing's Tiananmen Square in late May 1989 to symbolize their demands for greater political freedom in China. In the background is an official portrait of former Chinese Communist Party leader, Mao Zedong. Chinese troops toppled and destroyed the statue after they occupied the square on June 4, 1989, a process that also resulted in the death of many protesters.
Source: AP/Wide World Photos.

By the time dawn broke in Beijing, Tiananmen Square had indeed been cleared, but with a death toll that has still not been revealed. In the days that followed, thousands of Chinese citizens were arrested for their role in the demonstrations in Beijing and other cities, and there were several well-publicized executions of people charged with sabotage during the protests.

The order to move with deadly force against the students and their supporters was made by a handful of party elders, including Deng Xiaoping, who at that time was China's most powerful leader and the mastermind of the country's remarkable record of economic reform and success. The massacre was meant to send an unmistakable message that no political challenge to the Chinese Communist Party would be tolerated and all necessary means would be used to suppress any opposition.

The crushing of the Tiananmen demonstrations was one of the late twentieth century's most tragic political events, and it still casts a dark shadow over China's domestic politics as well as over U.S.-China relations. At a joint press conference with Jiang Zemin during the 1998 summit, President Clinton raised the issue of Tiananmen, saying that "the American people believe that the use of force and the tragic loss of life was wrong." Jiang Zemin's response made it clear that the Chinese Communist Party had not changed its views: "With regard to the political disturbances [in 1989]," Jiang said, "had the Chinese government not taken the resolute measures then we could not have enjoyed the stability that we are enjoying today."[2]

The People's Republic of China is one of only a few countries in the world that is still a **Communist party-state**, a political system in which the ruling Communist Party holds a monopoly on political power, claims the right to lead or control all government and social institutions, and proclaims allegiance (at least officially) to the ideology of **Marxism-Leninism**. China has experienced many changes since the Tiananmen tragedy, including further economic and social liberalization and even some political relaxation. But the CCP maintains a tight grip on power and rejects any meaningful movement toward democracy.

The rift between an oppressive party-state and an increasingly assertive society, which led to the shedding of blood in Tiananmen in 1989, remains deep and ominous. Yet, as the Chinese economy and society have become freer and more open to the outside world, the pressures for political change have also grown stronger.

Official attitudes about the Tiananmen demonstrations are one barometer of the potential for political change in China. As long as the Chinese authorities continue to insist that the protests were a "counter-revolutionary rebellion," the prospects for democratization will remain dim. But a willingness on the part of the CCP to set the historical record straight—or even to provide an honest accounting of how many people were killed—would be a significant political change that could be a step on the road to democracy.

Geographic Setting

The People's Republic of China is located in the eastern part of mainland Asia at the heart of one of the world's most strategically important and volatile regions. It shares land borders with more than a dozen countries, including Russia, India, Pakistan, Vietnam, and the Democratic People's Republic of Korea (North Korea) and is a relatively short distance by sea from Japan, the Philippines, and Indonesia. China, which had largely assumed its present geographic identity by the eighteenth century, is slightly bigger than the United States in land area, making it the third largest country in the world, after Russia and Canada.

The PRC is bounded on all sides by imposing physical barriers: the sea to the east, mountains to the north, south, and west (including the world's largest, Mt. Everest), deserts, vast grasslands, and dense forests in various parts of the north, and tropical rain forests to the south. In traditional times, these barriers isolated China from extensive contact with other peoples and contributed to the country's sense of itself as the "Middle Kingdom" (which is how the Chinese word for China, *zhongguo*, is translated) that lay not only at the physical but also at the political and moral center of its known world.

Administratively, the PRC is made up of twenty-two provinces, five **autonomous regions**, and four centrally administered cities (including the capital, Beijing), and one Special Administrative Region (Hong Kong). The sparsely populated but territorially vast western part of the country is mostly mountains, deserts, and high plateaus. The northeast, which is much like the U.S. plains states in terms of weather and topography, is both a wheat-growing area and China's industrial heartland. Southern China has a much warmer, and in places even semitropical climate, which allows year-round agriculture and

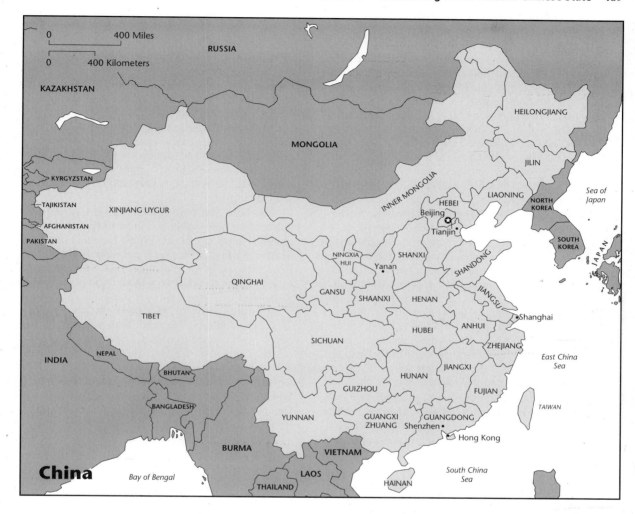

intensive rice cultivation. The country is very rich in natural resources, particularly coal and petroleum (including significant, but untapped on- and off-shore reserves) and is considered to have the world's greatest potential for hydroelectric power.

Although China and the United States are roughly equal in geographic size, China's population of 1.2 billion—by far the world's largest—is five times greater. But only about 10 percent of China's land is usable for agriculture. From a global perspective, China has a little over 20 percent of the world's population but only 7 percent of the world's arable land. The precarious balance between people and the land needed to feed them has been a dilemma for China for

centuries and remains one of the government's major concerns.

Industrialization and urbanization have expanded significantly in recent years. The PRC now has more than thirty cities of a million or more—the three largest being Shanghai (14 million), Beijing (12.5 million), and Tianjin (9.5 million). In 1997 the former British colony of Hong Kong, one of the world's great commercial centers (population 6.1 million), became part of the People's Republic of China. Nevertheless, about 70 percent of China's people still live and work in rural areas. The countryside has played—and continues to play—a very important role in China's political development.

Background: **A Very Brief Chinese Lesson**

Chinese is spoken by more people than any other language in the world. Yet Chinese really comprises many dialects, some of which are so different from one another that they are mutually incomprehensible and are often considered separate languages. Two of the major Chinese dialects are Mandarin, which is the form of Chinese spoken mainly in the northern part of the country, and Cantonese, which is spoken in the south.

But people who speak different Chinese dialects share the same written language. In other words, Mandarin and Cantonese speakers cannot understand each other in face-to-face conversations or over the telephone, but they can communicate by letter. This is because written Chinese is made up of characters rather than phonetic letters. These characters, which have evolved over time from symbolic pictures, depict meanings more than sounds, so that speakers of various Chinese dialects may pronounce the same character very differently. There are more than 40,000 different Chinese characters, although basic literacy requires knowledge of about 4000 because most of the characters are ancient and have fallen out of common usage.

Chinese does not have an alphabet; both the meaning and the pronunciation of Chinese characters can only be learned by memorization. Like many of the world's other languages—including Arabic, Greek, Hebrew, Japanese, and Russian—that do not use the Roman alphabet on which English is based, Chinese characters must be romanized, or transliterated, if English speakers are to have any idea of how to pronounce them. The most common way of romanizing Chinese is the *pinyin* ("spell sounds") system used in the People's Republic of China and by the United Nations. But because linguists have differed about how best to approximate distinctive Chinese sounds using Roman letters, there are still several alternative methods of romanizing Chinese.

This book and most other English-language publications now use the *pinyin* romanization for Chinese names, places, and phrases. In most cases, a word in *pinyin* is pronounced as it looks. However, there are a few letters that appear in Chinese words in this chapter for which a pronunciation guide may be helpful:

- *z* is pronouced "dz" (e.g., President Jiang Zemin)
- *x* is pronounced "sh" (e.g., Deng Xiaoping)
- *q* is pronounced "ch" (e.g., Emperor Qin)
- *zh* is pronounced "j" (e.g., Zhongguo, the Chinese word for China)

One other important point: In China (as in Japan and Korea), the family name, or surname (for instance, Deng), comes *before* the personal, or given, name (for instance, Xiaoping). Some people interpret this as a reflection of the priority given to the family or the group over the individual in East Asian culture.

China's population is highly concentrated along the eastern seaboard and in the most agriculturally fertile areas around the country's three great rivers, the Yellow River, the Yangzi (Yangtze) and the West River. The vast majority (92 percent) of China's citizens are ethnically Chinese (referred to as the Han people, after one of China's earliest dynasties). The remaining 8 percent is made up of more than fifty ethnic minorities, who differ from the Han in several major ways, including race, language, culture, and religion. Most of these minority peoples live in the country's geopolitically vital border regions, including Tibet. This makes the often uneasy and sometimes hostile relationship between China's minority peoples and the central government in Beijing a critical issue in Chinese politics today.

Critical Junctures

The People's Republic of China was founded in 1949. But understanding the critical junctures in the making of the modern Chinese state requires that we go back much further into China's political history. Broadly considered, that history can be divided into three periods: the imperial period (221 B.C.–A.D. 1911), during which China was ruled by a series of dynasties and emperors; the relatively brief and unstable republican period (1912–1949), when a weak central government was plagued by civil war and foreign invasion; and the communist period that takes us from the military and political triumph of the Chinese Communist Party and the founding of the People's Republic of China in 1949 to the present.

From Empire to Republic (221 B.C.–A.D. 1911)

Modern China is heir to one of the world's oldest cultural and political traditions. The roots of Chinese culture date back more than 4,000 years, and the Chinese empire first took political shape in 221 B.C., when a number of small kingdoms were unified under the Emperor Qin, who laid the foundation of an imperial system that lasted for more than twenty centuries until its overthrow in 1911. During those many centuries, China was ruled by more than a dozen different dynasties and experienced extensive geographic expansion and dramatic political, economic, social, and cultural development. Nevertheless, many of the core features of the imperial system remained remarkably consistent over time.

There are several reasons why the Chinese empire survived for such a long time. First, imperial China developed a sophisticated and effective system of national government long before the strong monarchical states of Europe took form in the seventeenth century. At the pinnacle of this government was an all-powerful emperor and a small group of advisers and ministers in the capital. But the most distinctive feature of the Chinese political tradition was the civil service branch made up of scholar-officials (mandarins) chosen through a rigorous and highly selective examination process and stationed throughout the empire.

Second, the traditional Chinese economy was a source of great strength to the empire. Chinese farmers pioneered some of the premodern world's most productive agricultural techniques, including irrigation and multicropping. Commerce, transport, and handicraft industries were also highly developed for the times. Urbanization expanded in China much sooner than it did in Europe, and Westerners, like Marco Polo, who journeyed to China as early as the thirteenth century were amazed by the grandeur of the Middle Kingdom's cities.

Third, the structure of traditional Chinese society, especially in the million or more small villages that were its foundation, gave the imperial system great staying power. The vast majority of the population was made up of peasants who were subordinated to a tiny landlord class that dominated life on the local level. The most powerful of the landlord families—the gentry—had close ties to the imperial civil service and helped the imperial officials extend their reach down to the very basic level of Chinese society by carrying out many government functions, such as collecting taxes.

Fourth, the traditional order was supported by the enduring influence in Chinese society of **Confucianism**. This philosophy, based on the teachings of Confucius (c. 551–479 B.C.), stresses the importance of the group over the individual, deference to one's elders and superiors, and the need to maintain social harmony. Confucianism did contain a teaching—the "Mandate of Heaven"—that an unjust ruler could be overthrown by the people, and Chinese history is full of rebellions against emperors who were judged to have lost the heavenly mandate. Nevertheless, Confucianism was basically a conservative philosophy that justified and preserved an autocratic state, a patriarchal culture, and a stratified society.

Finally, the Chinese imperial system endured because, throughout most of its history, China was the dominant political, military, and cultural force in its known world. Foreign influences or peoples that could not be repelled, such as Buddhism from India or invaders from Mongolia (who conquered China in 1279), were absorbed, or sinicized, by Chinese culture. China's power and relative geographic isolation contributed to a pervasive feeling among the Chinese that all non-Chinese were barbarians and that the Middle Kingdom could meet any challenge from outside without altering its basic way of life.

But in the late eighteenth and early nineteenth centuries, China experienced a population explosion and economic stagnation, along with a significant rise in official corruption and exploitation of the peasants by both landlords and the government. Social unrest culminated in the Taiping Rebellion (1850–1864), a massive revolt that took 20 million lives and nearly toppled the dynasty.

In the meantime, the West, which had surged far ahead of China in industrial development and military technology, was pressing China to expand its trade. China showed little interest in such overtures and tried to limit the activities of Westerners in China. But Europe, most notably Britain, in the midst of its era of mercantile and colonial expansion, used its military supremacy to compel China to engage in "free" trade with the West. China's efforts to stop Britain from selling opium in China led to military conflict between the two countries. After suffering a humiliating defeat in the Opium War (1839–1842), China was literally forced to open its borders to foreign merchants, missionaries, and diplomats on terms dictated by Britain and other Western powers. China lost control of significant pieces of its territory to foreigners (including Hong Kong) and important sectors of the Chinese economy fell into foreign hands.

There were many efforts to revive or reform the dynasty in the late nineteenth and early twentieth centuries. But political power in China remained largely in the hands of staunch conservatives who resisted change. As a result, when change came, it came in the form of a revolution in 1911, which brought an end to the 2000-year-old imperial system.

Warlords, Nationalists, and Communists (1912–1949)

The Republic of China was founded on January 1, 1912, with Dr. Sun Yat-sen, then China's best-known revolutionary and founder of its first political party, as president. However, the Western-educated Sun was not able to hold onto power, and China soon fell into a lengthy period of conflict and disintegration. Although the republic continued to exist in name, different parts of the country were controlled by military leaders known as warlords. Sun set about organizing another revolution to defeat the warlords and reunify the country under his Nationalist Party (the *Guomindang*).

In 1921 the Chinese Communist Party (CCP) was established by a few intellectuals who had become disenchanted with the derailing of the republican movement and with continuing foreign intervention in China's government and economy. They had been inspired by the Bolshevik triumph in Russia in 1917 and by the anti-imperialism of the newly founded Soviet Union to look for more radical solutions to China's problems. In 1924 the small Communist Party, acting on Soviet advice, joined with Sun Yat-sen's Nationalists to fight the warlords. After some initial successes, this alliance came to a tragic end in 1927 when Chiang Kai-shek, a military leader who had become the head of the Nationalist Party after Sun's death in 1925, turned against his coalition part-

Critical Junctures in Modern China's Political Development

1911	Revolution led by Sun Yat-sen overthrows 2000-year-old imperial system and establishes the Republic of China.
1912	Sun Yat-sen founds the Nationalist Party (*Guomindang*) to oppose warlords who have seized power in the new republic.
1921	Chinese Communist Party (CCP) founded.
1927	Civil war between Nationalists (led by Chiang Kai-shek) and Communists begins.
1934	Mao Zedong becomes leader of the CCP.
1937	Japan invades China, marking the start of World War II in Asia.
1949	Chinese Communists win the civil war and establish the People's Republic of China.
1958–1960	Great Leap Forward
1966–1976	Great Proletarian Cultural Revolution
1976	Mao Zedong dies.
1978	Deng Xiaoping becomes China's paramount leader and launches economic reforms.
1989	Tiananmen massacre; Deng promotes Jiang Zemin to become head of the Chinese Communist Party.
1997	Deng Xiaoping dies.

ners and ordered a bloody suppression that nearly wiped out the Communists. Chiang then proceeded to unify the Republic of China under his personal rule largely by striking an accommodation with some of the country's most powerful remaining warlords.

Ironically, the defeat of the CCP created the conditions for the eventual triumph of the man who would lead the party to nationwide victory. Mao Zedong, who had been one of the junior founders of the Communist Party, strongly advocated paying more attention to China's suffering peasants as a potential source of support. "In a very short time," he wrote in 1927, "several hundred million peasants will rise like a mighty storm, like a hurricane, a force so swift and violent that no power, however great, will be able to hold it back."[3] Mao's views grew out of his own peasant background and his investigations of spontaneous peasant uprisings against oppressive rural conditions.

However, his assessment was at odds with the orthodox Marxist-Leninist belief that a Communist-led revolution in China had to be based in the cities and rely on the support of the country's then minuscule industrial **proletariat**.

But after the suppression of the CCP by the Nationalists, the Communists had no choice but to retreat to the countryside, where Mao's strategy of peasant revolution gradually gained support in the party. In 1934–1935 the party undertook its fabled Long March, an epic journey of 6000 miles through some of China's roughest terrain, to escape attacks by Chiang's forces. At the end of the Long March, the CCP established a base in Yanan, a remote rural area in northwestern China.

In Yanan, Mao consolidated his political and ideological leadership of the Chinese Communist Party (through sometimes repressive means) and was elected party chairman in 1943, a position he held until his death in 1976. He also guided the effort to generate peasant support for the Communists through policies such as land reform and party-led quasi-democratic self-government, in which peasants were given a direct role in running village affairs.[4] At the same time, the Republic of China, under Chiang Kai-shek, became a right-wing dictatorship closely allied with big business, foreign interests, and the rural elite. Although the Nationalists did have some success in promoting economic modernization, the legitimacy of Chiang's government was severely undermined by corruption, mismanagement, and repression.

The course of the Chinese civil war between Nationalists and Communists was profoundly shaped by the Japanese invasion of China in 1937. Japan's assault pushed the Nationalist government deep into China's southwest and effectively eliminated it as an active combatant against Japanese aggression. In contrast, the CCP base in Yanan was on the front line against Japan's troops in northern China, and Mao and the Communists successfully mobilized the peasants to use **guerrilla warfare** to fight the invaders. By the end of World War II in 1945, the CCP had vastly expanded its membership and controlled much of the countryside in north China, while the Nationalists were isolated and unpopular with many Chinese.

The civil war resumed in earnest shortly after the Japanese surrender. Without any significant support from the Soviet Union, Communist forces won a decisive and surprisingly quick victory over the U.S.-backed Nationalists, who were forced to retreat to the island of Taiwan, 90 miles off the Chinese coast. On October 1, 1949, Mao Zedong stood on a rostrum in Tiananmen near the entrance to the former imperial palace in Beijing and declared the founding of the People's Republic of China.

Mao in Power (1949–1976)

The Chinese Communist Party came to power on the crest of an enormous wave of popular support because of its members' reputation as social reformers and patriotic fighters. In the early years of its rule, the CCP achieved some notable successes in rebuilding China's war-torn economy and restoring political order. Although most foreign-owned firms and many large businesses were taken over by the government, the PRC's economy in the early 1950s was a mix of state and private ownership. The CCP established firm control over China's new political system, but meaningful participation by noncommunists was also allowed.

Chairman Mao and the CCP also quickly turned their attention to some of the country's most glaring social problems. For instance, a massive **land reform** campaign redistributed property from the rich to the poor and increased productivity in the countryside. Highly successful drives eliminated opium addiction and prostitution from the cities, and a national law greatly enhanced the legal status of women in the family and allowed many women to free themselves from unhappy arranged marriages. Although the CCP did not hesitate to use violence to achieve its objectives and silence opponents, the party gained considerable legitimacy because of its popular and successful policies during these years.

In 1953–1957, the PRC implemented the first of its Soviet-style five-year plans. The complete **nationalization** of industry and **collectivization** of agriculture carried out as part of this plan were decisive steps away from the mixed state-private economy and toward **socialism**.

But Mao was particularly troubled by the persistence of inequalities in China, especially those caused by the First Five-Year Plan's emphasis on industrial and urban development and relative neglect of the countryside. In response, he launched the **Great Leap Forward** (1958–1960), a utopian effort to accelerate the country's economic development while making China into a radically egalitarian communist society. The Great Leap's objectives were to be reached by relying on the sheer labor and willpower of workers, peasants, and party activists rather than on the bureaucrats and intellectuals who had previously guided economic policy. Industry and agriculture were reorganized in ways that assumed people would work harder for communist goals than for monetary rewards.

The Great Leap was a great flop and turned into "one of the most extreme, bizarre, and eventually catastrophic episodes in twentieth-century political history."[5] In the rural areas, irrational policies, wasted resources, poor management, and the lack of labor incentives combined with bad weather to produce a famine that claimed between 20 and 30 million lives. An industrial depression soon followed the collapse of agriculture, causing a terrible setback to China's economic development.

In the early 1960s, Mao took a less active role in day-to-day decision-making. Two of China's other top leaders at the time, Liu Shaoqi and Deng Xiaoping, took charge of efforts to revive the economy using policies that combined the careful planning of the First Five-Year Plan with some market-oriented policies to stimulate production, particularly in agriculture.

This strategy revived the Chinese economy, but once again Mao found himself profoundly unhappy with the consequences of China's development. By the mid-1960s the chairman had concluded that the policies of Liu and Deng had led to a resurgence of bureaucratism and inequality that were threatening his revolutionary goals for China.

The result was the **Great Proletarian Cultural Revolution** (1966–1976), an ideological crusade launched by Mao to jolt China back toward his vision of socialism. Like the Great Leap Forward, the Cultural Revolution was a campaign of mass mobilization and utopian idealism, but its methods were much more violent and its main objective was the political purification of the party and the nation through class struggle, not accelerated economic development. Using his unmatched political clout

and **charisma**, Mao put together a potent coalition of radical party leaders, loyal military officers, and student and worker rebels to purge anyone thought to be guilty of revisionism, that is, betrayal of his version of Marxism-Leninism known as Mao Zedong Thought.

In the movement's first phase (1966–1969), 20 million or so high school and college students responded to Mao's pronouncement, "It is right to rebel!" by forming organizations called the Red Guards. They went on a rampage across the country, destroying countless priceless historical artifacts considered to be remnants of the imperial or capitalist past and, most tragically, harassing, torturing, and killing people accused of being class enemies. The Red Guards' reign of terror particularly targeted intellectuals, officials, and their families.

During the next phase of the Cultural Revolution (1969–1971), Mao used the People's Liberation Army (PLA) to restore political order. The army stopped the violence of the Red Guards, and millions of the young rebels were sent for several years to live and work in the countryside, where they were supposed to be reeducated by the peasants. The military's influence in politics was ended after some of its leaders allegedly attempted an abortive coup to seize power from Mao.

The final phase of the Cultural Revolution (1972–1976) involved intense conflict between radical leaders, who wanted the CCP to continue its emphasis on class struggle, and a more moderate group, who believed that the country needed to focus on economic development. These factions were locked in a dispute over who would succeed Mao as party chairman. Mao died in September 1976, and a month later the power struggle was settled when a coalition of the moderate leaders masterminded the arrest of their radical rivals, the so-called Gang of Four, which included Mao's wife and a leading radical, Jiang Qing.

The arrest of the Gang (who were sentenced to long prison terms) and the subsequent removal from power of many of their followers marked the end of the decade-long Cultural Revolution. Mao's last effort to steer China toward his vision of a communist utopia had claimed at least a half million lives, brought the nation to the brink of civil war, and led to a period of prolonged economic stagnation.

Deng Xiaoping and the Transformation of Chinese Communism (1976 to the Present)

China's first post-Mao leaders restored to office many of the veteran officials who had been purged by the radicals, including Deng Xiaoping. By 1978, Deng had clearly become the most powerful member of the CCP leadership. He remained so for nearly two decades even though he never occupied the formal top positions in either the party or the government, making sure instead that those posts were held by loyal lieutenants. Deng achieved this preeminence by skillful political maneuvering, through his close personal connections to many key party and military figures, and because he was widely regarded as the leader best able to repair the damage done to China by the Cultural Revolution.

Deng lost little time in using his newly consolidated political power to put China on a path of dramatic economic reform that transformed the nation. Deng's reforms were a profound break with the Maoist past. State control of the economy was significantly reduced, and market forces were allowed to play an increasingly important role. Agriculture was decollectivized and the management of farm production was turned over to individual families. Private businesses were encouraged in both city and countryside. The Chinese economy was opened to unprecedented levels of foreign investment and international trade soared.

On the cultural front, Chinese artists and writers saw the shackles of party dogma that had bound them for decades greatly loosened. Deng took major steps to revitalize China's government by bringing in younger, better-educated officials.

The results of Deng's initiatives were, by any measure, astounding. After decades of stagnation, the Chinese economy experienced unprecedented growth throughout the 1980s. The winds of freedom and openness seemed to be blowing through every sector of life in China. Deng was named *Time* magazine's "Man of the Year" in 1979 and 1986 in recognition of the boldness and success of his efforts to change China (see Figure 1).

These charts show dramatically how the Chinese economy has been transformed by the market reforms that were first introduced by Deng Xiaoping in 1978.

Figure 1

The Economic Transformation of Post-Mao China

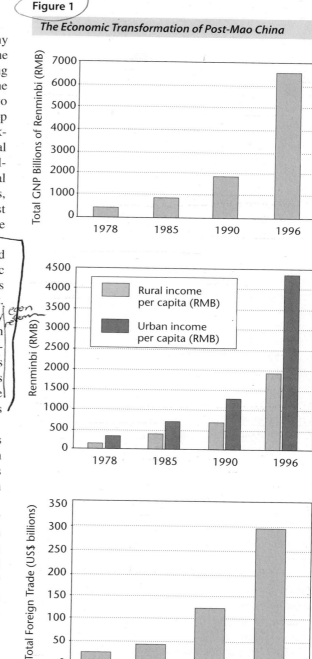

Source: *China Statistical Yearbook 1997* (Beijing: China Statistical Publishing House, 1998).

FREE MARKETS NOT PEOPLE!

DENG

WASSERMAN
© '92 BOSTON GLOBE
DIST. BY L.A. TIMES SYNDICATE

This cartoon captures the contradiction between economic reform and political repression that characterized China under the leadership of Deng Xiaoping. *Source:* © 1992, *The Boston Globe*. Distributed by Los Angeles Times Syndicate. Reprinted with permission.

Then came June 4, 1989, and the massacre near Tiananmen Square. There were a number of reasons why large-scale demonstrations erupted in Beijing and several other Chinese cities that spring, including discontent over skyrocketing inflation and widespread official corruption as well as a desire, especially among students and intellectuals, for more democracy. The brutal crushing of the Tiananmen protests was a shocking reminder that, for all the economic changes that had taken place under Deng Xiaoping, politics in China were to remain subject to strict regulation by the CCP.

Following the Tiananmen crackdown, China went through a few years of intensified political repression and economic retrenchment. But in early 1992, Deng Xiaoping took some bold steps to accelerate the reform of the economy. He did so largely because he hoped it would help the PRC avoid a collapse of the communist system such as had occurred just the year before in the Soviet Union. Since then, the Chinese economy has continued to become both more market-ized and more internationalized and has continued its record of spectacular growth and modernization.

Another important consequence of the 1989 Tiananmen crisis was the replacement as head of the Chinese Communist Party of one Deng protégé, Zhao Ziyang, by another, Jiang Zemin. Zhao was ousted because he was considered too sympathetic to the student demonstrators, while Jiang was promoted from his previous post as CCP chief in Shanghai because of his firm but relatively bloodless handling of similar protests in that city. Although Deng remained the power behind the throne for several years, he gradually turned over greater authority to Jiang, who in addition to his positions as general secretary of the CCP and chair of the powerful Central Military Commission became president of the People's Republic of China in 1993. When Deng Xiaoping died in February 1997, Jiang was fairly secure in his position as China's top leader. By the time he hosted President Bill Clinton at the Beijing summit in June 1998, Jiang Zemin had proven himself to be a capable leader committed to continuing, even deepening, the process of economic reform begun by Deng Xiaoping. Despite some signs of political relaxation in the late 1990s, Jiang also appeared determined to maintain the rule of the Chinese Communist Party. Dissidents who even indirectly challenged the authority of the CCP were sentenced to harsh prison terms, and writers considered too critical of party policy were silenced.

It will take several years before it is clear what, if any, special mark Jiang Zemin will make on Chinese politics. But he does represent a new kind of leader for the PRC. Unlike Deng or Mao, Jiang Zemin is not a professional revolutionary. Although they turned out to have very different ideas about how China should develop, Deng and Mao both made their whole careers in the inner sanctums of the Chinese Communist Party. In contrast, Jiang, although a member of the party since 1946, was trained as an engineer and served as a technical expert and bureaucrat in factories and government ministries before becoming mayor (and later party leader) of Shanghai in 1985. In this sense, the passing of power from Deng Xiaoping to Jiang Zemin in 1997 was a critical juncture in the political history of the People's Republic of China.

Themes and Implications

Historical Junctures and Political Themes

The World of States. The making of the modern Chinese state has been profoundly influenced at several critical points by China's encounters with other countries. The end of the Middle Kingdom's relative isolation from the non-Asian world and the conflict with the militarily superior West in the nineteenth century was a major factor in the collapse of the imperial system in 1911. Anger over European and U.S. treatment of China, admiration for the Russian revolution, and the invasion of China by Japan in the 1930s all played a role in propelling the Chinese Communist Party to power in 1949.

American hostility to the new Communist regime in Beijing helped push the People's Republic of China into an alliance with the Soviet Union and follow the Soviet model of development in the early 1950s. But Mao's disapproval of the direction in which Soviet Communist leaders were taking their country greatly influenced his decisions to launch both the Great Leap Forward in 1958 and the Cultural Revolution in 1966. In the early 1970s, Mao approved the beginnings of **détente** with the United States in response to what he saw as a growing and more immediate threat to China from the Soviet Union. The relationship between China and the United States deepened throughout the 1970s and paved the way for the marketization and globalization of the Chinese economy under Deng Xiaoping.

When the People's Republic was founded, China was in a relatively weak position in the international system. For more than a century, its destiny had been shaped by incursions and influences from abroad that it could do little to control. Mao made many tragic and terrible blunders, but one of his great achievements was to build a strong state able to affirm and defend its sovereignty. China's international stature has increased as its economic and military power have grown in recent decades. Though still a poor country by many per capita measures, the sheer size of its economy makes the PRC an economic powerhouse whose import and export policies have an important impact on many other countries. China is a nuclear power with the world's largest conventional military force; it is an active and influential member of nearly all international organizations, including the United Nations, where it sits as one of the five permanent members of the Security Council. Clearly, China has become one of the major players on the global scene.

Governing the Economy. Economic issues were central to the revolutionary process that led to the founding of the People's Republic. The Western powers were primarily motivated by the lure of the China market in their aggressive policies toward the Chinese empire in the nineteenth century. Chiang Kai-shek's Nationalist government lost popular support partly because of its mismanagement of the economy and inability to control corruption. Mass poverty and terrible inequality fueled the Chinese revolution and led millions of peasants and workers to back the Communist Party in the civil war.

The history of the PRC is largely the story of experimentation with a series of very different economic systems: a Soviet-style planning system in the early 1950s; the radical egalitarianism of the Maoist model; and Deng Xiaoping's market-oriented policies. Ideological disputes within the CCP over which of these development strategies China should follow were the main cause of the ferocious political struggles, such as the Cultural Revolution, that have so often wracked the country. Deng's bold reforms were, in large measure, motivated by his hope that improved living standards would restore the legitimacy of the CCP, which had been badly tarnished by the economic failings of the Maoist era. The remarkable successes of those reforms have helped sustain the CCP in power at a time when most other communist regimes have disappeared. Continuing China's economic progress will be one of the most important challenges facing Jiang Zemin and China's other leaders.

The Democratic Idea.   Jiang and the CCP also face major political challenges, especially the challenge of the democratic idea, which has had a troubled history in twentieth-century China. The revolution of 1911, which overthrew the imperial system and established the Republic of China under Sun Yat-sen, was the culmination of the first effort to establish a Chinese government in which citizens would have more say. But the combination of warlordism, civil war, world war, and Chiang Kai-shek's sharp turn toward dictatorship undermined any real progress toward democracy. Any hope that the democratic idea might take root in the early years of Communist rule in China was violently dispelled by the building of a one-party Communist state and Mao's unrelenting campaigns against alleged enemies of his revolution. The Deng Xiaoping era brought much greater economic, social, and cultural freedom for the Chinese people, but time and again the CCP acted to strangle the stirrings of the democratic idea, most brutally in Tiananmen Square in 1989.

The Politics of Collective Identity.   Because of its long history and high degree of cultural homogeneity, China has a very strong sense of national identity. Memories of past humiliations and suffering at the hands of foreigners still influence the international relations of the PRC. For example, Beijing's insistence that Britain return Hong Kong to Chinese control in 1997 was largely fueled by the desire to redress what it saw as one of the most blatant injustices of China's defeat in the Opium War of the mid-nineteenth century. And China believes that Japan should apologize more fully for atrocities committed by the Japanese army during World War II before the two Asian powers can have completely cordial diplomatic relations. As faith in **communism** has weakened, party leaders have increasingly turned to nationalism as a means to rally the Chinese people behind their government.

China's cultural homogeneity has also saved it from the kind of ethnic or religious violence that has plagued so many countries in the modern world. The exception to this has been in the border regions of the country, where there is a large concentration of minority peoples, particularly in Tibet and the Muslim areas of China's northwest (see Section 4).

China did experience a particularly vicious and destructive kind of identity politics during the Maoist era. Although landlords and capitalists had lost their private property and economic power by the mid-1950s, Mao continued to promote class struggle that pitted workers, peasants, and loyal party activists against "capitalist roaders" and other alleged counter-revolutionaries. When he took over in the late 1970s, Deng Xiaoping called for an end to such divisive class struggles and proclaimed an era of social harmony in which the whole nation could concentrate its energies on the overarching goals of modernization and economic development. But Deng's reforms led to new (or renewed) cleavages in Chinese society, including glaring inequalities between those who have profited handsomely from the marketization of the economy and those who have done less well or even been disadvantaged by the changes. These inequalities could become the basis of class, regional, or other kinds of identity-based conflicts that severely test the economic and political management skills of China's leaders.

Implications for Comparative Politics

For the student of comparative politics, China is a particularly important and interesting case. First, the PRC can be compared with other Communist party-states with which it shares or has shared many political and ideological features. From this perspective, China raises intriguing questions. Why has China's Communist party-state so far proven more durable than that of the Soviet Union and nearly all other similar regimes? By what combination of reform and repression has the Chinese Communist Party held onto power? What signs are there that it is likely to continue to be able to do so for the foreseeable future? What signs suggest that Communist rule in China may be coming to an end? Studying Chinese politics is important for understanding the past, present, and future of a type of political system—the Communist party-state—that has had a major impact on the modern world.

Second, China can fruitfully be compared with other developing nations that face similar economic and political challenges. Although the PRC is still very

Table 1

	Purchasing Power Parity GNP per Capita (US$)	GNP Growth Rate (%)	Life Expectancy at Birth (years)	Infant Mortality (per 1000 live births)	Adult Literacy (%)
China	3570	8.9	69	38	82
Brazil	6240	2.4	67	44	83
India	1650	5.0	62	73	52
Iran	5530	3.2	70	32	72
Mexico	3680	8.0	72	27	90
Nigeria	880	4.2	51	114	57

China's Development in Comparative Perspective

Note: All figures are for 1995–1997.

Sources: World Bank; United Nations.

much part of the Third World as measured by the average standard of living of its population, its record of growth in the 1980s and 1990s has been far better than most of the world's other developing countries. Furthermore, educational and health levels of the Chinese people are quite good when compared with many other countries at a similar level of economic development, for example, India and Nigeria (see Table 1). How has China achieved such relative success in its quest for economic development? On the other hand, while most of the Third World has gone through a wave of democratization in recent decades, China remains a one-party dictatorship. How and why has China resisted the wave of democracy? What does the experience of other developing countries say about how economic modernization might influence the prospects for democracy in China?

Napoleon Bonaparte, emperor of France in the early nineteenth century, is said to have remarked, "Let China sleep. For when China wakes, it will shake the world."[6] China has awakened, and given its geographic size, vast resources, huge population, surging economic strength, and formidable military might, the People's Republic will certainly be among the world's great powers in the future.

Section ❷   Political Economy and Development

The growth of China's economy since Deng Xiaoping began his market-oriented reforms in the late 1970s has been called "one of the century's greatest economic miracles," which has, in turn, led to "one of the biggest improvements in human welfare anywhere at any time."[7] Such superlatives seem justified in describing overall economic growth rates that have averaged about 10 percent per year for nearly two decades while most of the world's other economies were growing much more slowly. During the same period, the average income of the Chinese people quadrupled, and although there are still many very poor people in China, more than 200 million have been lifted from living in absolute poverty to a level where they have a minimally adequate supply of food, clothing, and shelter.

China's economic miracle has involved much more than growth in gross domestic product and personal income. There has also been a profound transformation of the very nature of economic life in the PRC from what it had been during the Maoist era.

State and Economy

The Maoist Economy

When the CCP came to power in 1949, the Chinese economy was suffering from the devastating effects of more than a hundred years of rebellion, invasion, civil war, and bad government. The first urgent task of China's new Communist rulers was the stabilization and revival of the economy. Although a lot of property was seized from wealthy landowners, rich industrialists, and foreign companies, much private ownership and many aspects of capitalism were allowed to continue in order to gain support for the government and get the economy going again.

Once production had been restored, the party turned its attention to building socialism in China by following the Soviet model of economic development. The essence of this model was a **command economy**, in which the state owns or controls most economic resources and economic activity is driven by government planning and commands rather than by market forces.

The command economy in China was at its height during the First Five-Year Plan of 1953–1957, when the government took control of the production and distribution of nearly all goods and services. The First Five-Year Plan yielded some impressive economic results, but it also created huge bureaucracies and new inequalities, especially between the heavily favored industrial cities and the investment-starved rural areas. These trends led Mao and his radical supporters to try to build a distinctive Chinese road to socialism that would be less bureaucratic and more egalitarian than the Soviet model. Both the Great Leap Forward and the Cultural Revolution embodied this Maoist approach to economic development.

In the Great Leap, more than a million backyard furnaces were set up throughout the country to prove that steel could be produced by peasants in every village, not just in a few huge modern factories in the cities. In the Cultural Revolution, highly participatory revolutionary committees, controlled by workers and party activists, replaced the Soviet-style system of letting managers run industrial enterprises. Both of these Maoist experiments were less than successful. The backyard furnaces yielded great quantities of useless steel and squandered precious resources, while the revolutionary committees led many factories to pay more attention to politics than production.

The economic legacy of Maoism is a mixed one. One the one hand, Mao's utopian experiments had very serious negative effects on the ability of the PRC to embark on a path of sustained economic development. The relentless suppression of any kind of economic activity thought to be a "capitalist weed" and the denial of opportunities to accumulate personal wealth meant that most people had little incentive to work hard. Furthermore, for all of its radical rhetoric, the Maoist strategy of development never really broke decisively with many of the basic precepts of the command system, including government domination of the economy. Bureaucratic interference, poor management, and ill-conceived projects led to wasted resources of truly staggering proportions. Overall, China's economic growth rates, especially in agriculture, barely kept pace with population increases during the Mao years, with the result that the standard of living for most Chinese rose very little between the late 1950s and Mao's death in 1976.

On the other hand, under Mao, the PRC "did accomplish, in however flawed a fashion, the initial phase of industrialization of the Chinese economy, creating a substantial industrial and technological base that simply had not existed before."[8] The state, as part of its socialist commitment to promote equality and reduce poverty, also assigned a high priority to building schools and medical clinics throughout the country. By the end of the Mao era, the people of China were much healthier and more literate than they had been in the early 1950s, and they were doing considerably better in terms of health and education than were people in most other developing countries, where government took little initiative to address such issues.

China Goes to Market

After he came to power in 1978, Deng Xiaoping took China in a direction far different from Mao's and any that had ever been followed by a Communist party-state anywhere. By the early 1960s, Deng had come to the conclusion that China needed less politics and ideology and more economic development. Deng's pragmatic views on how to promote development were captured in his famous 1962 statement, "It doesn't matter whether a cat is white or black, as long as it catches mice."[9] He meant that China should not be overly concerned about whether a particular policy was socialist or capitalist if it in fact helped the economy. Of course, Deng also believed that the economic cat should be kept on the party's political leash.

Deng knew that drastic action was needed to get the Chinese economy moving after the Cultural Revolution and to adapt China's socialist system to the realities of an increasingly interdependent and competitive modern world. He spearheaded a program of far-reaching reforms that, in the course of less than a decade, literally remade the Chinese economy, touched nearly every aspect of life in the PRC, and redefined the very nature of socialism in China. Deng referred to his economic reform program as China's second revolution, comparing it in importance to the first revolution, which had brought the Communists to power in 1949.[10] The upshot of these reforms was to greatly reduce (though not eliminate) the role of government commands while allowing market mechanisms to operate in increasingly large areas of the economy. Under Deng's leadership, China moved toward a mixed economic system that was based partly on socialist planning and partly on the capitalist free market.

Deng declared that the PRC had a socialist market economy. This may sound like a contradiction in terms, since a market economy is usually associated with capitalism. The idea of a socialist market economy can be seen as mere ideological window-dressing to allow the introduction of capitalism into a country still ruled by the Communist Party. But from the official CCP perspective, the term conveys the facts that China's economy now combines elements of both socialism and capitalism and also (in theory at least) that the market remains subordinate to government planning and party leadership, which will prevent too much capitalist-like exploitation and inequality.

Deng's reforms involved a significant degree of **decentralization** in the economy. Authority for making economic decisions passed from bureaucrats to individual families, factory managers, and private entrepreneurs, all of them presumably motivated by the desire to make more money. Most prices are set according to supply and demand, as in a capitalist economy, rather than by administrative decree, and in many sectors of the economy decisions about what to produce and how to produce it are no longer dictated by the state.

The Chinese government now encourages private and foreign ownership of factories and businesses. In many areas of the economy, government monopolies have given way to fierce competition between state-owned and non-state-owned firms. For example, the government-run national airline, which was the country's only airline until 1985, now competes with more than two dozen foreign and domestic carriers. Several government-approved stock markets, which sell shares in enterprises to private individuals, have been established, and many more unauthorized ones have sprung up around the country.

There are still more than 100,000 state-owned enterprises, which employ more than 100 million workers. These enterprises produce a large share of China's total industrial output and continue to dominate critical sectors of the economy, such as the production of steel and petroleum. But the role of the state sector is diminishing as private industries and so-called collective enterprises (which are usually run by combinations of local governments and private entrepreneurs) are expanding at a much faster rate (see Figure 2 on page 502). Even the government firms have been made more responsive to market forces. Under the command economy, state-owned industries had to turn over all profits to the government and were bailed out by state banks if they ran into financial difficulty, so there was little incentive to work hard or operate efficiently. Now a company pays a set tax on any profits, with the remainder available to be used as bonuses for the workers and managers and for investment in the factory.

Nevertheless, the majority of state-owned enterprises are still overstaffed and inefficiently run firms with outdated machinery. They remain a huge drain on the country's banking system and hinder modernization of key sectors of the Chinese economy. Threats to shut down the worst of them have never been seriously implemented because of the government's fear of the political consequences of tens of millions of unemployed workers. In late 1997, President Jiang Zemin made state-enterprise reform one of the government's top priorities. He unveiled plans to move ahead with bankruptcies of unprofitable firms and partially privatize what remains of the government-run sector of the economy.

These charts show how the share of China's total industrial output that comes from state-owned enterprises has declined sharply since Deng Xiaoping began to reform the PRC economy in 1978. The category "Collective" consists mostly of rural township and village enterprises (TVEs), which are owned by local governments but operate according to the market rather than by state planning. "Private" refers to industries owned by individuals, and "Other" includes foreign-owned enterprises and various kinds of mixed ownership.

Figure 2

China's Industrial Output by Ownership Type

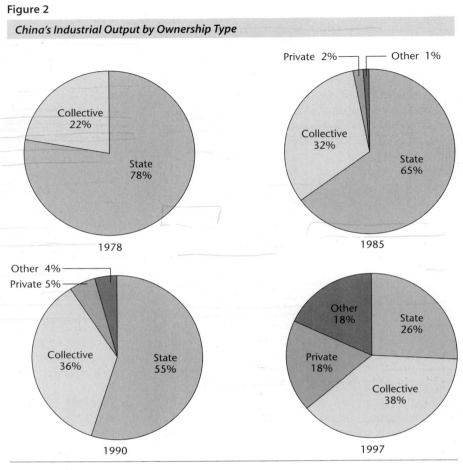

1978

Collective 22%

State 78%

1985

Private 2% — Other 1%

Collective 32%

State 65%

1990

Other 4%
Private 5%

Collective 36%

State 55%

1997

Other 18%

State 26%

Private 18%

Collective 38%

Source: China Statistical Yearbook 1997.

The economic results of China's move to the market have been phenomenal. As noted, the PRC has become one of the fastest-growing economies in the world and is likely to remain so for some time, given the financial crisis that struck much of the rest of East Asia in the late 1990s. China's gross national product (GNP) per capita (that is, the total output of the economy divided by the total population) grew at an average rate of 8.6 percent per year from 1980 to 1995. By way of comparison, the per capita GNP of the United States grew at only 1.5 percent per year during the same period, India's at 3.2 percent, and Brazil's at −0.4 percent. A booming economy and rapidly rising

incomes unleashed a consumer revolution in the PRC. To cite just one example, in the late 1970s, hardly anyone owned a television; now more than 90 percent of urban households have a color TV and nearly as many rural families have at least a black-and-white set.

The success of the reforms can be attributed largely to the reduction of bureaucratic and political interference in the economy and to the increased motivation to work hard created by the enormous expansion of opportunities for individuals, families, and businesses to earn, keep, and spend money.

Still, the PRC economy is only half-reformed. Central planning has been refined, not abandoned, and

This picture, taken in Shanghai in the early 1990s, graphically captures how the modern and the traditional exist side-by-side in China. It also shows how the market-style reforms introduced by Deng Xiaoping have greatly increased disparities in wealth, a problem that could lead to growing social and political tensions in the future. *Source:* Dan Habib/Impact Visuals.

national and local bureaucrats still exercise a great deal of control over the production and distribution of goods, resources, and services. The extent of private property is still restricted, while unproductive state enterprises continue to exert a considerable drag on key economic sectors. And even though the market reforms have gained substantial momentum that would be very hard to reverse, the Communist Party continues to wield the power to decide what direction economic reforms will take and whether they will continue. In other words, bureaucracy, politics, and ideology continue to tilt the balance of economic power in China decisively toward the party-state.

Remaking the Chinese Countryside

The economic changes in China have been particularly striking in the countryside, where over 900 million people still live and work.

One of the first major efforts launched by the CCP after it came to power in 1949 was a land reform campaign that confiscated the property of landlords and redistributed it as private holdings to the poorer peasants. But by the mid-1950s, as part of the transition to socialism, China's peasants had been reorganized into collective farms made up of about 250 families each. The land now belonged to the collective, and production and labor were directed by local officials working in coordination with the state plan. Individuals were paid according to how much they worked on the collective land, while most crops and other farm products had to be sold to the state at low fixed prices. During the Great Leap Forward, the collective farms were merged into gigantic **people's communes** with several thousand families. Although the size of the communes was scaled back following failure of the Leap, the commune system remained as the foundation of the rural economy throughout the rest of the Maoist period.

The system of collectivized agriculture proved to be one of the weakest links in China's command economy. The communes were able to deliver improved social services to the people in the countryside, and they undertook some large-scale construction projects (especially irrigation) that were of great benefit to rural areas. But many of the communes were poorly managed, and peasants often saw little reason to work hard, since much of the fruits of their labor went into the communal pot or to the state. Agricultural production and rural living standards were essentially stagnant from 1957 to 1977.

The first changes in the organization of agriculture in post-Mao China came from the spontaneous actions of local leaders who were looking for ways to boost production. They moved to curtail the powers of the commune and to allow peasants more leeway in planting and selling their crops. In the early 1980s, Deng Xiaoping used his newly won political power to support this trend and moved to "bury the Maoist model once and for all" in the countryside by the "massive dismemberment of the basic features of the former collectivized system."[11] The communes were replaced by a **household responsibility system**, which is still in effect today. In this system, farmland is contracted out to individual families who take full charge of the production and marketing of crops—functions that were previously tightly controlled by the commune. After paying government taxes and contract fees to the village, which still owns the land, the family is largely free to consume or sell what it produces. Families can now sign contracts for thirty years or more, but there has been no move to privatize agriculture fully by actually selling the land to individual families.

The freeing of the rural economy from the constraints of the communal system led to a sharp increase in agricultural productivity. In the 1980s agricultural production grew at the rate of about 6 percent a year, but it slowed considerably in the 1990s. This growth has greatly improved the living standards of China's rural families and provided the raw materials needed to support the country's efforts to modernize industrial production and feed the growing urban population.

But nothing has contributed more to the remaking of the Chinese countryside than the spread of a rural industrial and commercial revolution that, in speed and scope, is unprecedented in the history of the modern world. Although the foundations of rural industrialization were laid during the Maoist period, **township and village enterprises** (TVEs) expanded enormously under Deng's reforms. These rural factories and businesses, which vary greatly in size, are generally owned and run by local government and private entrepreneurs. Although they are called collective enterprises, TVEs operate outside of the state plan, make their own decisions about all aspects of the business process, and are responsible for their profits and losses. TVEs are the fastest-growing sector of the Chinese economy, produce 80 percent of the nation's clothes, and account for about 40 percent of China's total industrial output. They can be found in nearly every part of the country and employ over 130 million people. Although many people have moved from the countryside to the cities in search of better economic opportunities, the number of migrants would be much higher if the TVEs had not been able to absorb so much surplus rural labor.

The transformation of the Chinese countryside has not been without serious problems. Local officials who run TVEs "often behave more like business tycoons than public servants" and pay more attention to making money for themselves than to their civic duties.[12] Peasants have protested, sometimes violently, against high taxes, corrupt local officials, and delays in payments for agricultural products purchased by the government. There have also been concerns about China's ability to produce enough food to feed its big population. Now that the state no longer commands farmers to give priority to the production of grain and other essential foods, they often choose to raise more lucrative cash crops such as flowers and vegetables. In fact, China has recently had to import fairly large quantities of grain.

The social services safety net provided for China's rural dwellers by the communes has all but disappeared with the return to household-based farming. Many rural clinics and schools closed once government financial support was eliminated. The availability of health care, educational opportunities, disability pay, and retirement funds now depends on the relative wealth of families and villages, which has led to very large gaps between the prosperous and the poor areas of the country. Economic factors, such as the need for larger families in situations where income is dependent on household labor, have also contributed

Current Challenges: China's One-Child Policy

While he was in power, Mao Zedong did not see a reduction of China's population growth rate as an important national priority. On the contrary, he viewed vast amounts of human labor and the revolutionary enthusiasm of the masses as precious national resources. As a result, little was done to promote family planning in China during most of the Maoist era.

By the early 1970s, China's population had reached over 800 million, and because of greatly improved health conditions, it was growing at about 2.8 percent per year. This meant that the number of people in China would double in just twenty-five years, which would put a great strain on the country's resources. Cutting the birthrate came to be seen as a major prerequisite to modernization and economic development. Under Deng Xiaoping, the Chinese government implemented a stringent population control policy that has used various means to encourage or even force couples to have only a single child. These means have included intensive media campaigns lauding the virtues and benefits of small families, the monitoring of contraceptive use and women's fertility cycles by workplace medics or local doctors, positive incentives such as more land or preferred housing for couples with only one child, and negative sanctions such as fines or demotions for those who violate the policy.

The one-child campaign, the growing and modernizing economy, and a comparatively strong record in improving education and employment opportunities for women all played a role in the reduction of the population growth rate to 0.9 percent per year in the late 1990s. This figure is very low for a country at China's level of economic development. India, for example, has also had some success in promoting family planning, but its annual population growth rate is 1.6 percent, while Nigeria's is 2.9 percent. These might not seem like big differences, but consider this: At these respective growth rates, it will take seventy-eight years for China's population to double, whereas India's population will double in forty-four years and Nigeria's in twenty-four years.

There have, however, been some very serious problems with China's population policy. The compulsory, intrusive nature of China's family-planning program and the extensive use of abortion as a major means of birth control has led to some international criticism, criticism that Beijing has rejected as interference in its domestic affairs.

Farmers have evaded the one-child policy—for example, by not registering births—because the return to household-based agriculture has made the quantity of labor an important ingredient in family income. The still widespread belief that male children will contribute more to the family economically and that a male heir is necessary to carry on the family line causes some rural families to take drastic steps to make sure that they have a son. Female infanticide and the abandonment of female babies have increased dramatically, and the availability of ultrasound technology has led to a large number of sex-selective abortions of female fetuses. As a result, China has an unusual gender balance: Normally, 105 boys are born for every 100 girls, but in some parts of China the ratio is as high as 117 boys for every 100 girls. As a result, there are tens of thousands of "missing girls" in China's under-30 population.

In response to rural resistance and international pressures, the Chinese government has relaxed its population policies somewhat. Rural couples are now often allowed to have two children. In the cities, where there has been more voluntary compliance with the policy because of higher incomes and limited living space, the one-child policy is still basically in effect.

---

to peasant efforts to circumvent China's controversial one-child population control policy.

The Political Impact of Economic Reform

Efforts to transform the economy through market-style policies have had an important impact on China's domestic politics. First, both Deng Xiaoping and Jiang Zemin have faced opposition from other party leaders who believe that China has moved too fast and too far toward a market economy. The strongest opposition has come from "conservatives" in the Communist Party who do not want the party-state to give up so much control over the economy or society. There has also been "leftist" opposition from those who believe that the party is paying too little attention to politics and ideology, and has strayed too far from its socialist commitment to equality. Both conservatives and leftists blame the appearance of democratic ideas on the spread of capitalist influences at home and from abroad. Deng Xiaoping was able to beat back such challenges, and Jiang Zemin's emergence as Deng's clear successor put power in the hands of a leader strongly committed to continuing economic reform. But a major economic setback or widespread political turmoil could lead to a resurgence of antireform elements in the party.

Second, the decentralization of economic decision-making, which was such an important factor in the success of Deng's reforms, has greatly increased the autonomy of provincial and local governments. Some observers have even spoken of the appearance of "economic warlordism" in China as regions compete with one another by erecting tariff and other trade barriers between provinces. Some local governments defy or ignore the central government by, for example, evading taxes or undertaking massive construction projects without consulting Beijing. Such seepage of economic and political power from the central to the local levels poses serious questions about the ability of the national government to maintain control in the country.

Finally, China's economic transformation has brought far-reaching social change to the country, creating new pressures on the political system and new challenges to the Communist Party. The party wants the Chinese people to believe that economic growth depends on the political stability that only continuing party leadership can provide. CCP leaders hope that growing prosperity will leave most people satisfied with the Communist Party and reduce demands for political change. But economic reform has created many groups—entrepreneurs, professionals, middle-class consumers, the hundreds of thousands of Chinese students who have studied abroad—that must be allowed free rein if the party wants to sustain the economic boom. In time, these and other emerging groups are likely to press their claims for a more independent political voice and confront the regime with some fundamental questions about the nature of Communist power in China. Another challenge to the party may come from Hong Kong, the former British colony that became a Special Administrative Region of the People's Republic of China in July 1997.

China's government wants to take full advantage of Hong Kong's economic dynamism but is more wary of the free press, independent judiciary, and respect for civil liberties that developed under British rule.

Society and Economy

Market reform and modernization of the Chinese economy has created a more diverse and open society. People are much freer to choose careers, travel about the country (or even abroad), practice their religious beliefs, buy private homes, join nonpolitical associations, and engage in a wide range of other activities that were prohibited or severely restricted during the Maoist era. But economic change has also caused serious social problems. There has been a sharp increase in crime, prostitution, and drug use; although such problems are still far less prevalent in China than in many other countries, they are serious enough to be a growing concern for national and local authorities.

Economic reform has also brought significant changes in China's basic system of social welfare. The Maoist economy was characterized by what was called the **iron rice bowl**. As in other command economies such as the Soviet Union, this meant that employment, a certain standard of living (albeit, a low one), and basic cradle-to-grave benefits were guaranteed to most of the urban and rural labor force. In the cities the workplace was more than just a place to work and earn a salary; it also provided its employees with housing, health care, daycare, and other services.

China's economic reformers believe that such guarantees led to poor work motivation and excessive costs for the government and enterprises, and have implemented policies designed to break the iron rice bowl. Income and employment are now no longer guaranteed but are more directly tied to individual effort. Workers in state enterprises still have rather generous health and pension plans, but employees in the rapidly expanding semiprivate and private sectors usually have few benefits.

The breaking of the iron rice bowl has increased productivity and motivated people to work harder in order to earn more money. But it has also led to a dramatic increase in unemployment, which is estimated to be as high as 20 percent of the total labor force. Labor unrest, including strikes, slowdowns,

Current Challenges: *Hong Kong—From China to Britain and Back Again*

Hong Kong became a British colony in three stages during the nineteenth century as a result of what the Chinese call the "unequal treaties" imposed under military and diplomatic pressure from the West. Two parts of Hong Kong were ceded permanently to Britain in 1842 and 1860, respectively, but the largest part of the tiny territory was given to Britain with a ninety-nine year lease in 1898. It was the anticipated expiration of that lease that set in motion negotiations between London and Beijing in the 1980s over the future status of Hong Kong. In December 1984 a joint declaration was signed by the two countries in which Britain agreed to return all of Hong Kong to Chinese sovereignty on July 1, 1997. On that date, Hong Kong became a Special Administrative Region (SAR) of the People's Republic of China.

Britain ruled Hong Kong in a traditional, if benevolent, colonial fashion. A governor sent from London presided over a colonial administration in which foreigners rather than the local people exercised most of the power. There was a free press, a fair and effective legal system, and other important features of a democratic system. In the last years of British rule, there were efforts to appoint more Hong Kong Chinese to higher administrative positions and expand the scope of elections in choosing some members of the colony's executive and representative bodies. The British, who controlled Hong Kong for over a century, were criticized for taking steps toward democratization only on the eve of their departure from the colony. They allowed only a small number of Hong Kong residents to emigrate to the United Kingdom before the start of Chinese rule.

Hong Kong flourished economically under the free-market policies of the British and became one of the world's great centers of international trade and finance. Hong Kong has the highest standard of living in Asia outside of Japan and Singapore. At the same time, Hong Kong is characterized by extremes of wealth and poverty. China pledged to preserve Hong Kong's capitalist system for at least fifty years

after 1997. Because of the growing integration of the economies of Hong Kong and southern China, the PRC has a strong motivation not to do anything that might destroy the area's economic dynamism.

Although the PRC took over full control of Hong Kong's foreign policy and has stationed some troops of the People's Liberation Army in Hong Kong, Beijing has generally fulfilled its promise that the Special Administrative Region will have a high degree of political as well as economic autonomy. Civil liberties, the independence of the judiciary, and freedom of the press have been maintained.

However, the PRC has made sure that it keeps a grip on political power in Hong Kong. The SAR is headed by a chief executive, Tung Chee-hwa, a very wealthy businessman appointed by the PRC, and PRC-approved civil servants wield enormous authority in the government. China dissolved the legislature that had been elected prior to the start of Chinese rule and replaced it with a body filled with pro-Beijing members. In May 1998 democratic parties critical or at least skeptical of the Chinese Communist Party won nearly three-quarters of the twenty legislative seats up for election, although the remainder of the sixty-member legislature is chosen by an indirect process that strongly favors pro-China candidates. All in all, the SAR government is responsible to Beijing and ultimately subject to its authority, leading some residents and politicians who favor democracy in Hong Kong to worry that British colonialism has only been replaced by Chinese authoritarianism.

Hong Kong

Land Area (sq. miles)	401.5 (about six times the size of Washington, D.C.)
Population	6.5 million
Ethnic Composition	Chinese, 95%; other, 5%
GNP (US$)	$164 billion
GNP per capita (US$)	$26,000
Life Expectancy	Male, 76; Female, 82
Infant Mortality (per 1000 live births)	5
Literacy	93%

demonstrations, and sit-ins, was on the rise in the late 1990s. In the past the CCP has not dealt gently with protesting workers: the army was ordered to crush the 1989 Tiananmen demonstrations partly because party

leaders were alarmed by the large number of workers who had joined the protests under the banner of an unauthorized union. If inefficient state-owned firms are shut down or downsized as the current leadership has promised, another 30 million workers could lose their jobs. The best hope for dealing with this situation is if the economy continues to grow fast enough to create jobs for displaced workers. Otherwise unemployment and labor unrest could be a political time bomb for the Communist party-state.

Market reforms have also opened China's cities to a flood of rural migrants. After the agricultural communes were disbanded in the early 1980s, many of the peasants who were not needed in the fields found work in the rapidly expanding township and village enterprises. But many others, no longer constrained by the strict limits on internal population movement enforced in the Mao era, headed to the urban areas to look for jobs. The more than 100 million people who make up this so-called floating population are mostly employed in very low-paying temporary jobs such as unskilled construction work—that is when they can find any work at all. These migrants are putting increased pressure on urban housing and social services, and their presence in Chinese cities could become politically destabilizing if they find their aspirations thwarted by a stalled economy or if they are treated too roughly or unfairly by local governments, who often see them as intruders.

China's economic boom has also created enormous opportunities for corruption. In a country in transition from a command to a market economy, officials still control many resources and still have power over many economic transactions from which there are large profits to be made. Bribes are common in the heavily bureaucratized and highly personalized system. Because the rule of law is often weaker than personal connections (called *guanxi* in Chinese), nepotism and cronyism are rampant. In a major speech in the fall of 1997, President Jiang Zemin acknowledged, "The fight against corruption is a grave political struggle vital to the very existence of the Party and the state. . . . If corruption cannot be punished effectively, our Party will lose the support and confidence of the people."[13] The government has repeatedly launched well-publicized campaigns against official graft. Thousands of officials have been fired or jailed including the former mayor of Beijing, and some people have even been executed for particularly massive embezzlement. But this has done little to stem the widespread feeling that the use of official power for private economic gain pervades the political system from top to bottom.

The benefits of economic growth have spread throughout most of China. But there has also been a growth in various kinds of inequality—a contradiction for a country led by a Communist Party that still claims to believe in socialist ideals. Maoist China was never as egalitarian as its rhetoric led many people to believe, but various policies did limit the extent of inequality between people and parts of the country. China's market reforms and economic boom have created sharp class differences, generally benefited people who live in the cities more than those in the countryside, and caused a widening gap between the richer coastal regions and poorer inland areas.

Gender inequalities also appear to have increased in some ways since the 1980s. The situation of women in China has improved enormously since 1949 in terms of social status, legal rights, employment, and education. Women have also benefited from the improved living standards and expanded economic opportunities that the reforms have brought. But the trend toward marketization has not benefited men and women equally. In the countryside, only male heads of households may sign contracts for land, and therefore men dominate household economic life. This is true despite the fact that farm labor has become increasingly feminized as many men move to jobs in rural industry or migrate to the cities. Economic and cultural pressures have also led to an alarming suicide rate (the world's highest) among rural women. Although nine out of ten urban Chinese women work (giving China one of the highest female urban labor participation rates in the world), the market reforms have "strengthened and in some cases reconstructed the sexual division of labor, keeping urban women in a transient, lower-paid, and subordinate position in the workforce."[14] Sixty percent of China's unemployed—and 70 percent of its illiterates—are women.

Finally, the momentous economic changes in China have had serious environmental consequences. China's environment suffered greatly under the old command system, but ecological damage has gotten worse in the profit-at-any-cost atmosphere of the market reforms. Industrial expansion is fueled primarily by the use of highly polluting coal, which has made the air in China's cities and even many rural areas among the dirtiest in the world. Soil erosion, the loss of arable land, and deforestation are serious problems for the countryside. The dumping of garbage and toxic wastes goes virtually unregulated, and it is estimated that 80 percent of China's rivers are badly polluted. The government has enacted some policies to protect the environment and increase environmental spending. However, "as is the case in most developing countries, the quest for economic development has superseded concern over environmental pollution."[15]

Dealing with some of the negative social consequences of China's market reforms and economic growth is one of the main challenges facing the government of the PRC. The ability of labor, women's, or environmental movements to get these social issues on the political agenda remains limited by the party's tight control of political life and restrictions on the formation of autonomous interest groups in China (see Section 4).

China and the International Political Economy

Deng Xiaoping's program for transforming the Chinese economy rested on two pillars: the market-oriented reform of the domestic economy and the policy of opening China to the outside world. The extensive internationalization of the Chinese economy that has taken place in recent decades contrasts sharply with the semi-isolationist policy of economic self-reliance pursued by Mao Zedong.

In 1978, when Deng came to power, China was not a major trading nation. Total foreign trade was about US$20 billion (about 10 percent of GDP), and foreign investment in China was minuscule, as the stagnant economy and heavy-handed bureaucracy were not attractive to potential investors from abroad.

In the early 1980s, China embarked on a strategy of using trade as an important component of its drive for economic development, following in some ways the model of export-led growth pioneered by Japan and newly industrializing countries such as the Republic of Korea (South Korea). The essence of this model is to use low-wage domestic labor to produce goods that are in demand internationally and then to use the earnings from the sale of those goods to finance the modernization of the economy.

In 1997 foreign trade totaled more than US$300 billion (about 40 percent of GDP), making China the tenth largest trading nation in the world. China exports mainly clothing, fabrics, shoes, toys, and some light industrial goods, and imports mostly machinery, technology, and raw materials needed to support modernization. Despite having large domestic sources of petroleum and significant untapped reserves, China became a net importer of oil for the first time in 1993 because of the huge energy demands of its economic boom.

Most of China's trade is in East Asia, particularly with Japan, South Korea, and Taiwan. The financial crisis that hit that part of the world in the late 1990s caused a sharp drop in the rate of growth of Chinese exports (from 27 percent in 1997 to 0.5 percent in 1998) and raised concerns about the long-run viability of economic development that is so heavily dependent on foreign trade.

The United States has become one of the PRC's major trading partners (12 percent of imports and 17 percent of exports in 1995), and by the late 1990s the U.S. trade deficit with China had reached over US$50 billion per year, the second highest after Japan's. The growing trade imbalance increased tensions in U.S.-China relations, especially over the issue of restricted access to China's domestic market for U.S. goods and the violation of U.S. copyrights by Chinese firms that produce compact discs, video recordings, and computer software.

Foreign investment in China has also skyrocketed. Since 1978 about US$180 billion in foreign capital has been invested in or pledged to 240,000 different PRC enterprises. These enterprises range from small factories producing toys and clothing for export to large firms producing goods and services for the Chinese market, like Coca-Cola, Jeeps, and McDonalds.

Many of these foreign ventures are located in Special Economic Zones (SEZs) set aside by the government to attract overseas investors through incentives such as tax breaks, modern infrastructure, and the promise of less bureaucratic red tape. The SEZs are even more free-wheeling and faster-growing than the Chinese economy as a whole and have also become hotbeds of speculation, corruption, and crime. The largest SEZ, Shenzhen (near Hong Kong), has been

Current Challenges: *The Republic of China on Taiwan*

Despite the founding of the People's Republic of China on the Chinese mainland in October 1949, the Republic of China (ROC) under Chiang Kai-shek and the Nationalist Party continued to function on Taiwan. The Chinese Communists would very likely have taken over Taiwan at the end of the civil war if the United States had not intervened to protect the island. The U.S. government, alarmed by the outbreak of the Korean War in 1950, saw the defense of the Nationalist government on Taiwan as part of the effort to stop the further expansion of communism in Asia.

When Chiang Kai-shek and his supporters fled to Taiwan in 1949, the island was already firmly under the control of Nationalists, who had killed or arrested many of their opponents on Taiwan in the aftermath of a popular uprising in February 1947. The harsh dictatorship imposed by Chiang's Nationalists deepened the sharp divide between the "mainlanders," who had come over to escape the Communists, and the native Taiwanese majority, whose ancestors had first settled on the island centuries before and who spoke a distinctive Chinese dialect.

Economically, Taiwan prospered under Chiang Kai-shek's rule. With large amounts of U.S. aid and advice, the Nationalist government sponsored a highly successful and peaceful program of land reform and rural development, attracted extensive foreign investment, and encouraged an export-led strategy of economic growth that made Taiwan a model newly industrializing country by the 1970s. The government also invested heavily in the modernization of Taiwan's roads and ports, and promoted policies that have given the island health and education levels that are among the best in the world and a standard of living that is among the highest in Asia.

Political change, however, came slowly to Taiwan. After his death in 1975, Chiang Kai-shek was succeeded as president by his son, Chiang Ching-kuo, who most people expected would continue the repressive political policies of his father. Instead, the younger Chiang permitted some opposition and dissent, and gave important government and party positions previously dominated by mainlanders to Taiwanese. When he died in 1988, the presidency of

the republic passed to the Taiwanese vice president, Lee Teng-hui, who also became head of the Nationalist Party. Under President Lee, Taiwan continued to make great progress toward democratization. The laws used to imprison dissidents were revoked, the media are free of all censorship, and there are open multiparty elections for all local and islandwide positions. In presidential elections in 1996, Lee Teng-hui won 54 percent of the vote in a hotly contested four-way race, reflecting both the new openness of the political system and the credit that Taiwan's voters give the Nationalist Party for the island's progress.

The most contentious political issue in Taiwan is whether the island should continue to aspire to reunification with the mainland or declare its independence as a separate Republic of Taiwan. Advocating Taiwanese independence used to be a treasonous act, often resulting in a long prison term. The fact that this issue can now be openly debated shows that Taiwan's political transformation in recent decades has been as dramatic as its economic development.

Since the early 1980s, Taiwan and the People's Republic of China have developed extensive, if indirect, economic relations with each other, and millions of people from Taiwan have gone to the mainland to do business, visit relatives, or just sightsee. The governments of the PRC and ROC, though still technically in a state of war with each other, have engaged in some negotiations about possible reunification, but the two sides remain far apart because of their vastly differing political, economic, and social systems.

Taiwan

Land Area (sq. miles)	13,895 (about one-third the size of Virginia)
Population	22 million
Ethnic Composition	Taiwanese 84%, mainland Chinese 14%, aborigine 2%
GDP (US$)	$315 billion
GDP per capita (US$)	$14,700
Life Expectancy	Male, 74; Female, 81
Infant Mortality (per 1000 live births)	7
Literacy	86%

transformed in less than twenty years from a nondescript border town of 70,000 people into China's most modern city, with a population of over 2 million.

The growing economic integration of southern China, including Hong Kong, and Taiwan has led to the emergence of what is called Greater China. In this informal, emerging economic community, China provides inexpensive labor while Hong Kong and Taiwan provide capital, know-how, and technology. Extensive investment has also poured into the region from the far-flung community of overseas Chinese, who live in North America, Western Europe, and elsewhere. Many observers believe that Greater China is well on its way to becoming a powerhouse in the world economy.

China has emerged from the relative isolation of the Cultural Revolution period to become an active and important player in international politics. In 1971 the People's Republic took over China's seat in the United Nations. Prior to that, the UN, acting in accordance with the wishes and veto power of the United States, had recognized the Nationalist-led Republic of China as the legitimate government of all of China, even though it controlled only the island of Taiwan after 1949. The PRC is one of the five permanent members of the UN Security Council, and it acts there (and in the General Assembly and other UN-affiliated organizations) in a manner that reflects its dual status as both a major power and a developing nation.

In many international forums, the PRC serves as a strong advocate of what it sees as Third World interests. At the 1992 United Nations Conference on the Environment and Development in Rio de Janeiro, China took the position that the developed nations bore the "main responsibility for global environmental degradation" and that since the Industrial Revolution they "have exploited the environment without heeding the consequences of their actions."[16] The PRC argued that it was unfair to ask the world's poorer nations to sacrifice economic growth for environmental reasons and called on the developed nations to take the lead in making the sacrifices necessary to halt pollution.

Human rights became a sore point in relations between China and the United States after the Tiananmen massacre, when some members of the U.S. Congress wanted to impose restrictions on U.S.-China trade because of political repression in China. They argued that the United States should revoke China's most-favored-nation (MFN) status, an agreement between trading partners that guarantees each will extend to the other the same favorable terms (for instance, low tariffs on imports) that it grants to any other country. However, many Americans believed that restrictions on U.S.-China trade would harm U.S. business and consumer interests, dampen Chinese economic growth, and hurt those in China, such as private entrepreneurs, who might become a force for democratization in the future. This was the position adopted by both the Bush and Clinton administrations, and China's MFN status has been repeatedly renewed since Tiananmen, with only minor and easily fulfilled human rights conditions attached.

In response, China has challenged Western nations on the issue of human rights. The PRC vehemently rejects foreign criticism of its human rights record. It sees such criticism as interference in China's internal affairs, based on a narrow and ethnocentric definition of rights. A view of rights that stresses individual liberties above all else, they argue, is inappropriate to cultures like China's, which emphasize social needs and responsibilities. China contends that the "right to subsistence" as measured by economic growth and decent health and education standards, is the most basic human right and that on this score the PRC has done remarkably well compared to many nations. It points to homelessness, a high crime rate, and racism in the United States as human rights violations that invalidate U.S. criticism of the policies of other nations.

The sale of weapons by China to other Third World nations has also become a point of contention in China's relations with the United States and other developed countries. The PRC has become a major international weapons dealer in the post–Cold War era, though it still ranks well behind Russia, the United States, Britain, and France in terms of total arms sales. China has been criticized for selling weapons to countries involved in conflicts with the West, such as Iran and Iraq, and for providing advanced missile technology to potential nuclear powers like Pakistan. China argues that the West's position on international arms sales is self-serving, although the PRC has agreed to abide by international conventions regulating weapons transfers.

China has an important but somewhat contradictory position in the international system. On the one hand, its low level of economic and technological development compared to the industrialized countries makes it very much a part of the Third World. On the other hand, the total output and rapid expansion of its economy, its vast resource base (including its population), and its military strength make the PRC a superpower—or at least a potential superpower—among nations. In the years ahead, China is certain to become an even more active participant on the world scene. At the same time, international influences are likely to play an increasingly important role in China's economic and political development.

Section ❸ Governance and Policy-Making

The People's Republic of China is one of the world's few remaining Communist party-states, and by far the most important in terms of size and power. The basic political organization of the PRC, like that of the Soviet Union before its collapse in 1991, reflects the defining characteristics of this very distinctive type of system. These include Communist domination of all government and social institutions, the existence of an official state ideology, and the repression of any opposition to the party. The Chinese Communist Party claims that only it can govern in the best interests of the entire nation and therefore has a right to exercise the "leading role" throughout Chinese society. Although China has moved sharply toward a market economy in recent decades, the CCP still asserts that it is building socialism with the ultimate objective of creating an egalitarian and classless communist society.

Organization of the State

"The force at the core leading our cause forward is the Chinese Communist Party," observed Mao Zedong in a speech given in 1954 at the opening session of China's legislature, the National People's Congress, which according to the constitution adopted at that meeting, was the "highest organ of state power" in the People's Republic.[17] Mao's statement was a blunt reminder that the party was in charge of the national legislature and all other government organizations.

This same line was the very first entry in "The Little Red Book," the bible of Mao quotes used by the Red Guards who ransacked the country in the name of ideological purity during the Cultural Revolution. Although many party members became targets of the Cultural Revolution, the prominence of this quotation reflected the fact that, even at the height of the movement's near anarchy, Mao and his supporters never intended to call into question the primacy of Communist Party rule in China.

Similarly, Deng Xiaoping, despite embracing extensive economic liberalization, remained unshakably committed to the preservation of Communist rule in China after he came to power in 1978. In a speech in 1979 (a decade before Tiananmen), Deng rejected calls for more democracy and clearly spelled out his views on the role of the CCP in the Chinese political system:

> In the China of today we can never dispense with leadership by the Party and extol the spontaneity of the masses. Party leadership, of course, is not infallible and the problem of how the Party can maintain close links with the masses and exercise correct and effective leadership is still one that we must seriously study and try to solve. But this can never be made a pretext for demanding the weakening or liquidation of the Party's leadership.[18]

Despite the many fundamental changes that have taken place since the Maoist era, "Party leadership" remains an unchangeable principle of political life in China, and the nation's rulers still claim allegiance to communist ideology. Any analysis of governance and policy-making in China must begin with the ideology and power of the Communist Party.

Communist ideology in China is referred to as Marxism-Leninism–Mao Zedong Thought. The core of this ideology is said to be based on universal truths in the works of the founding fathers of communism, including Marx's critique of capitalism and his definitions of socialism and communism and Lenin's theories on party organization and leadership. Mao's contributions to the ideology come from his adaptation of Marxism-Leninism to China's particular historical circumstances, including its economic underdevelopment and largely peasant society. In 1997 the CCP added Deng Xiaoping Theory to its official ideology to reflect the late leader's role in justifying a self-proclaimed socialist country's use of market forces to promote economic development.

Most people in China have lost faith in communist ideology because of the Communist Party's erratic and repressive leadership over the last several decades. Many party members (about 58 million as of 1998) join more for career advancement than because of ideological commitment. There are also numerous other sources of beliefs and values in society, such as the family and religion. But Marxism-Leninism–Mao Zedong Thought–Deng Xiaoping Theory provides the framework for governance and policy-making and sets the boundaries for what, in the party's view, is permissible in politics.

The underlying political and ideological principles of party-state organization are clearly laid out in China's current constitution.[19] The preamble refers explicitly to "the leadership of the Communist Party of China and the guidance of Marxism-Leninism–Mao Zedong Thought." Article 1 defines the PRC as "a socialist state under the people's democratic dictatorship" and declares that "disruption of the socialist system by any organization or individual is prohibited." Such provisions imply that the Chinese "people"— implicitly defined as those who support socialism— enjoy democratic rights and privileges; but the Chinese constitution also gives the CCP the authority to exercise dictatorship over any person or organization that it believes is opposed to socialism and the party.

The People's Republic of China has had several governing documents since its founding in 1949, including four very different constitutions (1954, 1975, 1978, and 1982). These documents have only marginally had the force of law. Rather, constitutional change (from amendments to total replacement) has reflected the shifting political winds in China. The character and content of the document in force at any given time bears the ideological stamp of the prevailing party leadership. For example, in 1993 the current PRC constitution (adopted in 1982) was amended to replace references to the superiority of central planning and state ownership with phrases more consistent with economic reform, including the statement (Article 15) that China "practices a socialist market economy."

The constitution of the People's Republic specifies the structures and powers of subnational levels of government, including the country's provinces, autonomous regions, and centrally administered cities. But China is not a federal system (like Brazil, Germany, India, Nigeria, and the United States), in which subnational governments have considerable policy-making autonomy. Provincial and local authorities operate "under the unified leadership of the central authorities" (Article 3), which makes China a **unitary state** (like Britain, France, and Japan), in which the national government exercises a high degree of control over other levels of government.

The Executive

The government of the People's Republic of China is organizationally and functionally distinct from the Chinese Communist Party. For example, the PRC executive consists of both a premier (prime minister) and a president, whereas the CCP is headed by a general secretary. But there is no alternation of parties in power in China, and the Communist Party controls all government organizations and personnel. Therefore real executive power in the Chinese political system lies in the top leaders and organizations of the CCP. The government essentially acts as the administrative agency for carrying out and enforcing policies made by the party. Nevertheless, to fully understand governance and policy-making in China, it is necessary to look at both the Chinese Communist Party and the government of the People's Republic of China and the relationship between the two.

The Chinese Communist Party

The constitution of the Chinese Communist Party (which is a separate document from the constitution of the PRC) specifies in great detail local and national party structures and functions, the distribution of authority among party organizations, the requirements for joining the party, the behavior expected of members, and procedures for dealing with infractions of

Table 2

Who's Who in Beijing: China's Top Party and State Leaders Since 1949		
Leader	*Highest Position Held*	*Comment*
Mao Zedong (1893–1976)	CCP Chairman (1943–1976) PRC President (1949–1959) Military Commission Chair (1949–1976)	Became effective leader of the CCP in 1934–1935 during the Long March. Formally elected Chairman of the Politburo in 1943.
Liu Shaoqi (1898–1969)	PRC President[a] (1959–1968) CCP Vice Chairman (1949–1968)	Purged as a "capitalist roader" during the Cultural Revolution. Died in prison.
Zhou Enlai (1898–1976)	PRC Premier (1949–1976) PRC Foreign Minister (1949–1958)	Longtime Mao ally, but a moderating influence during the Cultural Revolution. Architect of détente with U.S. in early 1970s.
Lin Biao (1907–1971)	CCP Vice Chairman (1958–1971) PRC Vice Premier (1954–1971) PRC Defense Minister (1959–1971)	One of Mao's strongest supporters in the Cultural Revolution. Allegedly killed in plane crash after failure of attempted coup against Mao.
Hua Guofeng (1920–)	PRC Premier (1976–1980) CCP Chairman (1976–1981) Military Commission Chair (1976–1981)	Became CCP Chairman after Mao's death and purge of Gang of Four. Removed from power by Deng Xiaoping, who saw him as too much of a Maoist.
Deng Xiaoping (1904–1997)	PRC Vice Premier (1952–1966;1973–1976; 1977–1980) CCP Vice Chairman (1975–1976; 1977–1987) Military Commission Chair (1981–1989)	Purged twice during Cultural Revolution. Retired from all official posts by 1989, but remained China's most powerful leader for most of the 1990s.
Hu Yaobang (1915–1989)	CCP Chairman[b] (1981–1982) CCP General Secretary[b] (1982–1987)	Protégé of Deng. Ousted for favoring too much political reform. His death in 1989 helped touch off the Tiananmen demonstrations.
Zhao Ziyang (1919–)	PRC Premier (1980–1988) CCP General Secretary (1987–1989)	Another Deng protégé. Ousted for being too sympathetic to pro-democracy demonstrators during Tiananmen crisis.
Li Xiannian (1909–1992)	PRC President (1983–1988)	Veteran party leader rewarded with ceremonial post at end of career. Became PRC's first president since 1968.
Yang Shangkun (1907–1998)	PRC President (1988–1993)	Veteran military officer and Deng supporter.
Jiang Zemin (1926–)	CCP General Secretary (1989–) PRC President (1993–) Military Commission Chair (1989–)	Former Shanghai mayor and party leader promoted by Deng as a safe choice to carry out his policies after Tiananmen crisis. Consolidated his own power after Deng's death in 1997.
Li Peng (1928–)	PRC Premier (1988–1998) Chair, National People's Congress (1998–)	One of China's most conservative leaders. Widely held responsible for Tiananmen crackdown.
Zhu Rongji (1928–)	PRC Premier (1998–)	Committed reformer credited with effective management of the Chinese economy.

[a]The position of PRC president was vacant from 1968 to 1983.
[b]The position of CCP chairman was abolished in 1982 and replaced by the general secretary as the party's top position.
Note: All the listed leaders were also members of the Standing Committee of the CCP Politburo, the party's most powerful decision-making body.

party rules. But such details do not negate the fact that individual power, factional maneuvering, and personal connections are ultimately more important than formal constitutional arrangements for understanding how the party works.

For example, Deng Xiaoping, who was indisputably the most powerful individual in China from 1978 until he became physically incapacitated before his death in 1997, never occupied any of the top executive offices in the party or the government (see Table 2 on page 514). His highest formal positions during these years were vice chairman of the CCP (1977–1987), vice premier of the People's Republic (1977–1980), and chairman of the party's military commission (1978–1989), a post that made him the commander in chief of China's armed forces. By the early 1990s, Deng had resigned from all his formal positions other than that of president of China's bridge association, reflecting his continuing enjoyment of a card game he learned while a student in France in the 1920s. Although he no longer played an active role in day-to-day governance, he was still consulted about important policy matters, and no major decision was made without his approval. In the Chinese media, he was regularly referred to as China's "paramount leader" and the "chief architect" of the nation's economic boom. The sources of Deng's immense power came from informal factors, such as his seniority as one of the founding leaders of the regime, his deep personal connections to other influential political and military leaders, and his longtime advocacy of now widely supported ideas about how China should develop into a strong and modern nation.

By the late 1990s, most of the elderly men (including Deng) who had wielded great informal authority in post-Mao China were dead. Despite the persisting strong influence of personal ties in Chinese politics, the formal structures of power have assumed greater importance for understanding who has the power and how decisions are made.

According to the CCP constitution, the "highest leading bodies" of the party are the National Party Congress and the Central Committee (see Figure 3). But its infrequent meetings (every five years) and large size (more than 2000 delegates) means that the role of the Congress in the party is more symbolic than

Figure 3

Organization of the Chinese Communist Party

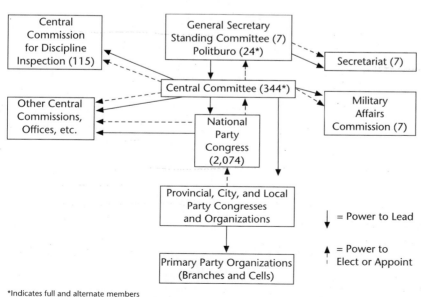

*Indicates full and alternate members

Numbers in parentheses refer to the number of members as of the late 1990s.

substantive. The essential function of the National Party Congress is to approve decisions already made by the top leaders and provide a showcase for the party's current policies. For example, the party congress that convened in the fall of 1997 was a highly orchestrated validation of Jiang Zemin's consolidation of power as Deng Xiaoping's successor.

The Central Committee is the next level up in the pyramid of party power. It has about 190 full and 150 alternate members (consisting of party leaders from around the country) and meets annually for about a week. It is elected by the National Party Congress by secret ballot, and there is some choice of candidates. Contending party factions may jockey to win seats, but the overall composition of the Central Committee is closely controlled by the top leaders to ensure compliance with their policies. The Central Committee elected in late 1997 continued a trend toward promoting younger and better-educated party members who are strong supporters of economic reform.

The Central Committee directs party affairs when the National Party Congress is not in session, but its size and relatively short and infrequent meetings (called plenums) greatly limit its effectiveness. However, Central Committee plenums and occasional informal work conferences do represent significant gatherings of the party elite, which can be a very important arena of political maneuvering and decision-making.

The most powerful political organizations in the Communist party-state are the two small "executive" bodies at the very top of the CCP's structure: the Politburo (or Political Bureau) and its even more exclusive Standing Committee. These bodies are elected by the Central Committee from among its own members under carefully controlled conditions. In the late 1990s, the Politburo had twenty-four members (including two alternates) and the Standing Committee—the formal apex of power in the CCP—had seven. Each member of the Standing Committee has executive responsibility for a particular area of policy, for example, economic affairs, national security, and foreign policy. People who study Chinese politics scrutinize the membership of the Politburo and Standing Committee for clues about leadership priorities, the balance of power among party factions, and the relative influence of different groups in policy-making.

The Politburo and Standing Committee are not responsible to the Central Committee or any other institution in any meaningful sense. The workings of these organizations are shrouded in secrecy. Their meetings are rarely announced and most of their work goes on, and many of the top leaders live, in a high-security compound adjacent to the former imperial palace near Tiananmen Square in Beijing. Their most important meetings are held every year in August, when they gather in exclusive villas at the seashore.

Power in the Chinese Communist Party is highly concentrated in the hands of the few individuals who control the highest party organizations and have little accountability to the general party membership. Prior to 1982 the top position in the party was the chairman of the Politburo's Standing Committee, which was occupied by Mao Zedong (hence Chairman Mao) for more than three decades until his death in 1976. The title of chairman was abolished in 1982 to symbolize a break with Mao's highly personalistic and often arbitrary style of leadership. Since then the party's chief executive has been the general secretary, who presides over the Politburo and the Standing Committee, a position which has been held since 1989 by Jiang Zemin. Although Jiang emerged in the early post-Deng era as China's most powerful individual, he does not have the personal clout or charisma of either Deng or Mao and therefore governs as part of a collective leadership that includes his fellow members on the Standing Committee and Politburo.

Two other party organizations deserve brief mention. The Secretariat (currently seven members) manages the day-to-day work of the Politburo and Standing Committee and coordinates the party's complex and far-flung structure. The Secretariat has considerable authority in organizational and personnel matters but is not a center of political or policy-making power, although it is important that anyone who aspires to the top leadership of the party have strong supporters on the Secretariat.

The Central Commission for Discipline Inspection is responsible for monitoring the compliance of party members with the CCP constitution and other rules. It has the power to investigate and recommend punishment (including expulsion from the party) for violations of party discipline, and it may turn its findings over to judicial authorities if it thinks criminal proceedings are warranted. The commission has been used as a vehicle against thousands of party members accused of corruption, but it has also been used to enforce adherence to the party line and to punish, for example, those who supported the Tiananmen demonstrations.

Below the national level, the CCP has a hierarchy of local party organizations in provinces, cities, and counties, each headed by a party committee. There are also more than 3 million primary party organizations, called branches and cells, which are found in workplaces, schools, urban neighborhoods, rural towns, villages, and army units. Local and primary organizations extend party control throughout Chinese society and are designed to ensure the subordination of each level of party organization to the next-higher level and ultimately to the central party authorities in Beijing.

The National Government

Government authority in China is formally vested in a system of people's congresses, which begins with a National People's Congress at the top and continues in hierarchically arranged levels down through provincial people's congresses, municipal people's congresses, rural township people's congresses, and so on (see Figure 4). In theory, these congresses (the legislative branch) are empowered to supervise the work of the "people's governments" (the executive branch) at the various levels of the system, but in reality, government executives (such as cabinet ministers, provincial governors, and mayors) are ultimately subject to party authority rather than to the people's congresses. Unlike the parallel system of *party* congresses, the *people's* congresses are supposed to represent *all* of the citizens at the relevant level, not just the minority who are members of the CCP. Like the party congresses, the people's congresses play a politically limited, but symbolically important, role in policy-making.

The National People's Congress elects the president and vice president of China. But there is only one candidate, chosen by the Communist Party, for each office. The president's term is concurrent with that of the congress (five years), and he is limited to two

Figure 4

Organization of the Government of the People's Republic of China

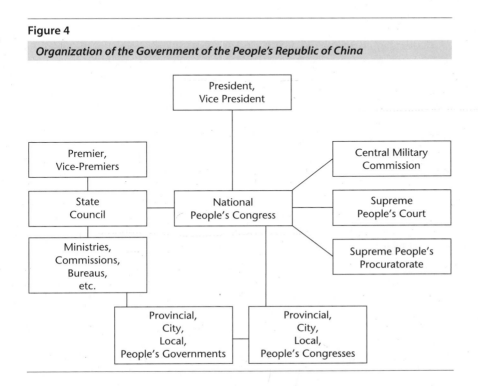

consecutive terms. Citizens must be forty-five or older to be eligible to serve as president. The position is largely ceremonial, though a senior party leader has always held it. As China's head of state, the president is important in greeting and negotiating with other world leaders. Jiang Zemin, who is also the general secretary of the CCP, was elected to a second term as China's president in 1998.

The premier is the head of the government and has considerable authority over the bureaucracy and policy implementation. The premier is formally appointed by the president with the approval of the National People's Congress. But, in reality, the Communist Party decides who will serve as premier, and that post has always been held by a member of the party's most powerful body, the Standing Committee. Like the president, the premier may serve only two five-year terms. Zhu Rongji, who became the PRC's premier in 1998, is a strong supporter of market reform and is widely credited with having dealt successfully with a number of serious economic problems (including skyrocketing inflation) that China faced in the mid-1990s while he was the vice-premier in charge of the economy.

The Bureaucracy

The premier directs the State Council, constitutionally "the highest organ of state administration" (Article 85). The State Council, which, in theory, is appointed by the National People's Congress, functions like the cabinet in a parliamentary system and is made up of the premier, the vice-premiers, the heads of government ministries or their equivalents, a secretary-general (who manages the day-to-day work of the council), and a few other top officials called state councillors.

The size of the State Council varies as ministries and commissions are created, merged, or disbanded to meet changing policy needs. At times, it has included more than one hundred ministerial-level officials, but in the late 1990s there were forty ministries and commissions (with plans to cut the number to twenty-nine), reflecting the decreased role of central planning and the administrative streamlining undertaken to make the government more efficient. The ministers and councillors run either functionally specific departments, such as the Ministry of Public Health, or organizations with more comprehensive responsibili-

ties, such as the powerful State Economic and Trade Commission. Beneath the State Council is an array of support staffs, research offices, and other bureaucratic agencies charged with policy implementation.

Government administration in the PRC is based on the principle of **dual rule**, which was adapted from the Soviet political system. Dual rule means that government organizations below the national level are under both the *vertical* supervision of the next higher level of government and the *horizontal* supervision of the Communist Party at their own level. For example, the organization in charge of education in one of China's provinces would be subject to both administrative supervision by the Ministry of Education in Beijing and to political control by the province's CCP committee. Such a system leads to complex and sometimes conflicting lines of authority within the Chinese bureaucracy. It also reinforces two key aspects of governance and policy-making in the PRC: centralization and party domination.

Since the 1980s government administration in China has become increasingly decentralized as the role of central planning has been reduced and more power has been given to provincial and local authorities, particularly in economic matters. Efforts have also been made to reduce party interference in administrative work. For example, the top party leader in a province (the party secretary) is no longer allowed to serve simultaneously as the province's governor, its chief administrator (although the governor is always a CCP member). Despite such reforms, government administration remains a top-down system that is subordinate to the power of the Communist Party.

China's bureaucracy is immense in size and expansive in the scope of its reach throughout the country. The total number of **cadres**—people in positions of authority who are paid by the government or party—in the PRC is in the range of 30 million. Of these, around 8 million work directly for the government or the CCP. The remainder occupy key posts in economic enterprises (e.g., factory directors); schools (e.g., principals); and scientific, cultural, and other state-run institutions. Not all party members are cadres; in fact, most party members are just "ordinary" workers, farmers, teachers, and so on. And not all cadres are party members, though party cadres ultimately have power over nonparty cadres.

During the Maoist years, cadre recruitment and promotion standards often gave strong preference to people with good ideological credentials ("reds") over those who may have been more professionally qualified ("experts"), which seriously compromised the ability of the bureaucracy to do its job well. The balance has now clearly shifted to the experts, and there is much greater emphasis on having better-educated and more technically proficient personnel staffing the government bureaucracy. Economic reform has made a technocratically oriented bureaucracy an essential part of the policy process in China. In 1998 the government also announced plans to cut the number of cadres directly on the state payroll in half (to 4 million) in order to promote efficiency and save money.

One of the most important administrative reforms of the post-Mao era—and one that is quite unprecedented in a Communist party-state—has been the implementation of measures to limit how long officials can stay in their jobs. Depending on their position, both government and party cadres must now retire between the ages of 60 and 70. A two-term limit has been set for all officials. In 1998, Premier Li Peng became the first top leader of the People's Republic to leave office at the end of a constitutionally specified term limit. But exceptions are still sometimes made for core leaders such as Jiang Zemin (born in 1926), who has nonetheless pledged to retire at the end of his current terms as president and General Secretary in 2003.

Other State Institutions

The Military and the Police

China's People's Liberation Army (PLA), which encompasses all of the country's ground, air, and naval armed services, is the world's largest military force, with about 3 million active personnel, although plans were announced in 1998 to cut this by a half million. The PLA also has a formal reserve of another million or so and a backup people's militia of around 12 million, which could be mobilized in the event of war, although the level of training and weaponry available to the militia are generally minimal. There is a draft in China, and Article 55 of the constitution says, "It is the honorable duty of citizens of the People's Republic of China to perform military service and join the militia in accordance with the law."

The Chinese military is, in fact, small in relation to China's total population. In the mid-1990s the PRC had 2.4 military personnel per 1000 population, far less than the U.S. ratio of 6.2 per 1000. China said that it spent US$10 billion on defense in 1998, which would be only about 4 percent of U.S. military spending in that year. Many analysts think that the PRC vastly understates its defense budget and estimate that it is really closer to three times the official figures; still, China devotes a much smaller part of its annual government spending to defense than does the United States.

The military has never held formal political power in the PRC, but it has been a very important influence on politics and policy. Ever since the days of the revolution and the civil war, there have been close ties between the political and military leaders of the CCP, with many top leaders (such as Mao and Deng) serving in both political and military capacities. One of the most famous quotes from Chairman Mao's writings, "Political power grows out of the barrel of a gun," conveyed his belief that the party needed strong military backing in order to win and keep power. However, the often overlooked second half of the quote, "Our principle is that the party commands the gun, and the gun must never be allowed to command the party,"[20] made the equally important point that the military had to be kept under civilian (that is, CCP) control. Although there have been a few periods when the role of the military in Chinese politics appeared to be particularly strong (such as during the Cultural Revolution), the party has always been able to keep the "gun" under its firm command.

The PLA assumed a prominent political role during the Tiananmen crisis in 1989, when the army was ordered to recapture the square from the demonstrators and did so with brutal force. While some senior PLA officers opposed the intervention, in the end they ordered the troops in because the Chinese military "is a disciplined, professional army that takes orders from the Party leadership."[21] The massacre greatly harmed the image of the PLA in the eyes of the Chinese public, who previously had a high regard for the military because of its incorruptibility and record of dedicated service to the nation.

The PLA continues to play an important, if muted, role in Chinese politics. Military support remains a crucial factor in the factional struggles that still figure prominently in inner-party politics. Deng Xiaoping's long-standing personal ties to many very senior PLA officers were critical to his success in defeating the efforts of conservative party leaders to slow down economic reform. Jiang Zemin, who has no such ties and lacks any military experience, has paid close attention to building political bridges to the PLA by supporting increased defense spending (13 percent in 1998) and promoting generals who are loyal to him. Although there are no military officers on the party's most elite body, the Standing Committee, two out of the twenty-four members of the Politburo are generals and PLA representatives make up over 20 percent of the full members of the Central Committee.

Chinese Communist leaders have long been divided over the issue of what kind of armed forces the People's Republic of China needed. Mao was a strong advocate of equality between rank-and-file soldiers and officers, the use of guerrilla tactics ("people's war") even in modern warfare, the importance of ideological education within the military, and of the extensive use of the PLA in nonmilitary tasks such as the construction of public works projects and the training of citizen paramedics ("barefoot doctors"). Some of China's foremost military leaders believed just as strongly that the PLA ought to emphasize the discipline, professionalism, and modernization needed to defend the nation. Under Deng Xiaoping and Jiang Zemin, the military leadership has been able to keep politics and ideology in the armed forces to a minimum and focus on making the PLA an effective, modern fighting force. But the PLA remains not only an institution committed to the national defense but also an instrument for keeping the CCP in power.

The key organizations in charge of the Chinese armed forces are the party's Military Affairs Commission and state's Central Military Commission. On paper, these appear to be two distinct organizations, but, in fact, they overlap entirely in membership and function. The chair of the state Military Commission is "elected" by the National People's Congress and is, in effect, the commander in chief of the PLA. This position is always held by a top party leader, for example, by Deng Xiaoping from 1977 to 1989 and since then by Jiang Zemin. The Communist Party extends its control of the PLA through a system of party committees and political officers who are attached to all military units.

Beginning in the 1980s, the PLA climbed on the economic reform bandwagon in order to supplement its official budget by converting a number of its military factories to the production of consumer goods such as refrigerators and motorcycles; running hotels and even discos; and opening up some of its secret facilities to foreign tourists. At one point it was estimated that the PLA was running more than 15,000 nonmilitary enterprises at home and abroad with over US$10 billion in revenues. In 1998 the government, concerned about both corruption and the need for the military to concentrate on its defense responsibilities, ordered the PLA to sell off many of its commercial ventures.

China's police apparatus consists of several different organizations. The Ministry of State Security is responsible for combating espionage and gathering intelligence both at home and abroad. The Ministry of Public Security is responsible for the maintenance of law and order, the investigation of crimes, and the surveillance of Chinese citizens and foreigners in China suspected of being a threat to the state. A one-million strong "People's Armed Police" guards public officials and buildings and is used to quell serious public disturbances, including worker or peasant unrest. The local branches of these various security organizations are under the command of central authorities in Beijing. So, in effect, China has a national police force stationed throughout the country. There are also local police forces, but they do little more than supervise traffic.

Public security bureaus have the authority to detain indefinitely people suspected of committing a crime without making a formal charge and can use administrative sanctions, that is, penalties imposed outside the court system, to levy fines or sentence detainees to up to three years in reformatories or prisons or to be supervised under a kind of house arrest. For people convicted of serious crimes, including political ones, the Ministry of Public Security maintains an extensive system of labor reform camps. These camps, noted for their harsh conditions and remote locations, are estimated to have millions of prisoners. They have become a contentious issue in

U.S.-China relations because of claims that they use political prisoners as slave labor to produce millions of dollars worth of products (such as toys) that are then exported to U.S. and other foreign markets. China has agreed to curtail the export of prison-produced goods, but it maintains that productive work by prison inmates (common in many countries, including the United States) helps to rehabilitate prisoners and is an important and legitimate part of the penal system.

The Judiciary

China has a four-tiered "people's court" system reaching from a Supreme People's Court down through higher, intermediate, and basic people's courts located at the various administrative levels of the state. The Supreme People's Court supervises the work of lower courts and the application of the country's laws, but it hears few cases and does not exercise judicial review over government policies. A nationwide organization called the "people's procuratorate" serves in the courts as both public prosecutor and public defender and also has investigatory functions in criminal cases. Citizen mediation committees based in urban neighborhoods and rural villages also play an important role in the judicial process by settling a large majority of civil cases out of court.

China's judicial system came under attack as a bastion of elitism and revisionism during the Cultural Revolution. The formal legal system pretty much ceased to operate during that period, and many of its functions were taken over by political or police organizations, which often acted arbitrarily in making arrests or administering punishments.

In recent decades, the legal system of the PRC has been revitalized. More than 100,000 judges and lawyers have been trained (some have even been sent abroad for legal education), and legal advisory offices have been established throughout the country to provide citizens and organizations with advice and assistance in dealing with the courts. Many laws and regulations have been enacted, including new criminal and civil codes, in the effort to regularize the legal system. In 1997 the government revoked a vaguely worded law against "counterrevolutionary crimes," which had given the authorities broad powers to detain political dissidents.

In recent years, there has been an enormous surge in the number of lawsuits filed (and often won) by people against businesses, local officials, and government agencies. Chinese courts can provide a real avenue of redress to the public for a wide range of nonpolitical grievances, including loss of property, consumer fraud, and even unjust detention by the police.

The criminal justice system works swiftly and harshly. Great faith is placed in the ability of an official investigation to find the facts of a case, and the outcome of cases that actually do come to trial is pretty much predetermined. In 1997 there was a conviction rate of 99.65 percent for all criminal cases that came to trial. Prison terms are long and subject only to cursory appeal. A variety of offenses in addition to murder—including, in some cases, rape and particularly serious cases of embezzlement and other "economic crimes"—are subject to capital punishment, which is carried out within days of sentencing. Hundreds, perhaps thousands, of people have been executed during the periodic government-sponsored anticrime campaigns, and China has been harshly criticized by human rights organizations such as Amnesty International for its extensive use of the death penalty.

Although the Chinese constitution speaks of judicial independence, China's courts and other legal bodies remain under rigorous party control. The appointment of judicial personnel is subject to party approval, and the CCP can and does bend the law to serve its interests. Recent legal reforms in China have been undertaken because China's leaders know that economic development requires detailed laws, professional judicial personnel, predictable legal processes, and binding documents such as contracts. Like other government institutions, the judicial system is meant to serve—or at least not challenge—the rule of the Communist Party. The scope of legality—the areas of society regulated by the legal system rather than by the whims of officials or personal connections—has widened greatly in the post-Mao era. China has, by and large, become a country where there is rule *by* law, in which the CCP uses the law to carry out its policies and enforce its rule. But it is still far from having established the rule *of* law, in which everyone, including the CCP, is accountable and subject to the law.

Subnational Government

There are four main layers of formal state structure beneath the central government in China: provinces (and autonomous regions), cities, counties, and rural towns. Each of these levels has a representative local people's congress that meets infrequently and briefly, and plays a limited role in managing local affairs.

Day-to-day administration at each subnational level is carried out by a local people's government, which consists of an executive (for instance, a provincial governor or city mayor), various functional bureaus, and judicial organs. According to China's constitution, the work of a local government is to be supervised by the local people's congress. But, in fact, the principle of dual rule makes local officials accountable more to higher levels of state administration and party organizations than to the local congresses.

Economic reform has led to a decentralization of decision-making. Provinces, cities, counties, and towns are now encouraged to take more initiative in promoting economic development in their areas. As a result, local governments are becoming increasingly vigorous in pursuing their own interests. Nevertheless, the central government still retains the power to intervene in local affairs when and where it wants. This power of the central authorities derives not only from their ability to set binding national priorities but also from their control over the military and the police, critical energy sources, and the construction of major infrastructure projects.

Beneath the formal layers of state administration are China's 900,000 rural villages, which are home to the large majority of the country's population. These villages are technically self-governing and are not formally responsible to a higher level of state authority. In recent years, village leaders and representative assemblies have been directly and competitively elected by local residents (see Section 4), which has brought an important degree of democracy to village government. Nevertheless, the most powerful person in Chinese villages is still the local Communist Party leader, who remains responsible to and under the supervision of higher-level CCP organizations.

The Policy-Making Process

At the height of Mao's power, many analysts described the policy process in China as a Mao-in-command system, in which the Chairman and a few of his closest associates made all major decisions and passed them along to be implemented by obedient party and government cadres. The Cultural Revolution led many scholars to conclude that policy-making in China was best understood as a result of factional and ideological struggles within the Chinese political elite. More recently, emphasis has shifted to analyzing the importance of bureaucratic actors and institutions in the policy process. Policy-making in the PRC is still seen as being very undemocratic. But rather than portraying it as simply a matter of the top party leaders' issuing orders, a new model of "fragmented authoritarianism" sees policy outcomes as the result of conflict, competition, and bargaining among party and government organizations at various levels of the system.[22]

Nevertheless, control of the policy process at all levels still rests with the Chinese Communist Party. The Communist Party makes policy and the government bureaucracy (headed by the premier and the State Council) implements it. Government policies and laws in China are formally enacted and in some ways significantly shaped by nonparty bodies such as the State Council and the National People's Congress. But the key decisions behind those policies and laws are made only by the Communist Party. Furthermore, public debate, media scrutiny, and the influence of organized interest groups play almost no role in the policy process in the Communist party-state.

The CCP uses a weblike system of organizational controls to make sure that the government bureaucracy complies with the party's will. For example, almost all key government officials are also party members and therefore subject to party discipline. The CCP also exercises control over the policy process through party organizations that parallel government agencies at all levels of the system. For example, each provincial government works under the watchful eye of a provincial party committee. In addition, through its committees, branches, and cells, the CCP maintains an effective presence inside every government organization.

Another means by which the Chinese Communist Party exercises control over the policy process is through the use of a cadre list, or as it was known in the Soviet Union, the *nomenklatura* system. The cadre list covers millions of positions in the government and elsewhere (including newspapers, hospitals, banks, and trade unions). Any personnel decision involving appointment, promotion, transfer, or dismissal that affects a position on this list must be approved by the party's organization department, whether or not the official involved is a party member. In recent years, the growth of nonstate sectors of the economy and administrative streamlining have led to a reduction in the number of positions directly subject to party approval. Nevertheless, the cadre list is still one of the major instruments by which the CCP tries to "ensure that leading institutions throughout the country will exercise only the autonomy granted to them by the party."[23]

Through these various mechanisms, the Chinese Communist Party not only supervises but has often taken over the work of the government. In recent years, there has been much talk about drawing a sharper distinction between party and government functions and bringing more nonparty experts into the policy loop. While some limited action has been taken, party domination remains a central feature of the policy process in China.

No account of policy-making or implementation in China is complete without noting the importance of *guanxi* ("connections"), the personal relationships and mutual obligations based on family, friendship, school, military, professional, or other ties. The notion of *guanxi* has its roots in Confucian culture and has long been an important part of political, social, and economic life in China. *Guanxi* still count mightily in the highly personalized world of elite politics within the CCP where policy is made. They are also basic facts of life within the Chinese bureaucracy, where personal ties are often the key to getting things done. Depending on how they are used, *guanxi* can either help cut red tape and increase efficiency or bolster organizational rigidity and feed corruption.

In sum, the power of the Communist Party—particularly the nearly unchecked power of the top twenty-five or thirty leaders—is at the heart of governance and policy-making in China. Party domination, however, does not mean that the system "operates in a monolithic way"; in fact, the system "wriggles with politics"[24] of many kinds, formal and informal. In order to get a complete picture of the policy process in China, it is important to look at how various influences, including ideology, factional struggles, bureaucratic interests, and personal connections shape the decisions made by the Communist Party leadership.

Section ❹ Representation and Participation

The Chinese Communist Party describes the government of the People's Republic as a **socialist democracy**, which it claims is superior to democracy in a capitalist country. From the CCP's point of view, the unequal division of private property and wealth profoundly influences politics in a capitalist country like the United States. The government of China under the leadership of the CCP, the argument goes, serves all the people, not just the privileged few. The official CCP view is that the party "has no interests of its own and rules solely in the interests of the nation and the people. It follows that rule by the party's leaders is rule in the people's interest and by definition democratic."[25] Unlike the social democracy of some Western European

political parties, such as the British Labour Party and the French Socialist Party, which is rooted in a commitment to competitive politics and political pluralism, China's socialist democracy is based on the unchallengeable leadership of the Chinese Communist Party.

Representation and participation play important roles in China's socialist democracy. There are legislative bodies, elections, and organizations like labor unions and student associations, all of which are meant to provide citizens with ways of influencing public policy-making and the selection of government leaders. But such mechanisms of popular input are strictly controlled by the CCP and are bound by the party's continuing insistence that all politics and policies in the country uphold the Four Cardinal Principles first laid down by Deng Xiaoping in 1979: the socialist road, the people's democratic dictatorship, the leadership of the Communist Party, and the ideology of Marxism-Leninism–Mao Zedong Thought. In essence, then, representation other than that guided by the CCP is regarded as unnecessary or marginal. Participation other than that sanctioned by and supportive of the party is seen as subversive.

The Legislature

Legislatures in Communist party-states have often been described as "rubber stamp" bodies. This implies that their main function is to give policies made by the party the appearance of being approved by representatives of the people. They may have some influence in important, though routine, state business (such as the formulation of the national budget), but such legislatures have very little substantive power when it comes to critical issues and in no way provide a check on the authority of the party.

The label "rubber stamp" may be a bit extreme to describe China's legislature, the National People's Congress (NPC), but it does convey the fact that the CCP closely monitors every aspect of the NPC's operations to ensure that it is in compliance with party policy. Nevertheless, the NPC is a very visible part of the Chinese political system, and it is important to understand its structure and function and to gauge whether the legislature could become an active force for democratization in China.

The Chinese constitution grants the National People's Congress (see Figure 4) the power to enact and amend the country's laws, approve and monitor the state budget, and declare and end war. It is also empowered to elect (and recall) the president and vice president of the PRC, the chair of the Central Military Commission (the commander in chief of the armed forces), the head of China's Supreme Court, and the Procurator-General (something like the U.S. Attorney General). It also has final approval over the selection of the premier and members of the State Council. These powers make China's legislature the most powerful branch of the government, with supervisory authority over the executive and judicial branches. The official Chinese view is that this is a very

democratic system because it vests supreme power in the branch of government most closely connected to the people, but in fact these powers are exercised only in the manner allowed by the Communist Party.

The National People's Congress is a unicameral legislature. It is elected for a five-year term and meets annually for only about two weeks. Deputies to the NPC are not full-time legislators but remain in their regular jobs and home areas except for the brief time when the Congress is in session. One of their responsibilities is to make regular "inspection tours" of their local areas. The Chinese government sees this as another advantage of the system because it allows deputies to stay in touch with their constituents and keeps them from becoming professional politicians.

The precise size of the NPC is set by law prior to each five-year electoral cycle. The NPC that was elected to serve from 1998 to 2002 consisted of just under 3000 deputies, which makes it the largest legislative body in the world. All the delegates, except those who represent the People's Liberation Army, are chosen on a geographic basis from China's various provinces, autonomous regions, and major municipalities. About 70 percent of the deputies elected to the currently serving congress are members of the Chinese Communist Party, with the others either belonging to one of China's few noncommunist political parties or having no party affiliation.

Rather than emphasizing the party affiliation of NPC deputies, the Chinese government stresses their occupational and social backgrounds in order to show that the legislature represents people from all walks of life. For example, workers and farmers made up about 20 percent of the deputies elected in 1998; intellectuals and professionals made up another 20 percent; government and party cadres accounted for a little more than a third; and the remainder consisted of representatives of other occupational categories, such as military personnel and entrepreneurs. Women made up 22 percent of the deputies. The average age of the deputies was 52 years, and 81 percent had at least a college education. The constitution guarantees that all minority groups have representation in the National People's Congress, and about 14 percent of the deputies elected in 1998 were ethnic minorities.

The annual sessions of the NPC are hailed with great fanfare in the Chinese press as an example of

Current Challenges: *The Three Gorges Dam*

The Three Gorges dam, which is being built on the Yangzi (Yangtze) River in China's Hubei province, will be the largest dam (over 600 feet high) and hydroelectric generating plant (84 billion kilowatt-hours per year) in the world when it is completed in the year 2009. The current budget for the project is US$11 billion, but some estimates that take inflation into account foresee huge cost overruns and put the total at around $70 billion.

Proponents of the dam argue that the project is needed to meet the huge energy demands of economic development in central and southwestern China, and that hydroelectric power is much preferable to the polluting coal that is currently China's major energy source. It will also make it possible for large ships to navigate the Yangzi deep into China's interior, and thus help promote domestic commerce and foreign trade. They also say that the dam will help to control the river's periodic lethal floods, which have killed more than 300,000 people in this century alone. In the summer of 1998 about 2,000 people died, 14 million were made homeless, and another 240 million people (one-quarter of China's population) in the Yangzi river basin were affected directly or indirectly by severe flooding.

Opponents of the Three Gorges dam see the project as an environmental, human, and political nightmare. The dam will submerge some of China's most stunning scenery, along with thousands of hectares of fertile cropland, rice paddies, and orchards. Many experts also believe that it will threaten several endangered species, including the rare Chinese river dolphin. Hundreds of historical sites will be inundated, some containing artifacts more than 10,000 years old. More than 1.3 million people will have to be relocated from the villages and towns that will end up under the 400-mile-long artificial lake (longer than Lake Superior) created by the dam. Although the Chinese government is compensating and assisting those who need to move, critics of the project say that most of those who relocate will probably, in the long run, be poorer than before they moved. There are also serious questions about the dam's safety in the earthquake-prone region, about whether the project's energy output will ever justify the huge cost, and even about whether it will solve or make worse the flooding situation along the Yangzi.

Opponents of Three Gorges also point out the completely undemocratic way in which the project was planned and implemented. The Chinese government, and especially former Premier Li Peng (who is a Soviet-trained hydroelectric engineer), has made the Three Gorges project into a symbol of Chinese modernization and nationalism, and the authorities have attempted to silence people who have spoken out against the dam. Critics of the project have been purged from their party and state offices, and others have been forced into exile. The media are allowed to carry only positive assessments of the project. A collection of essays by scientists, journalists, and intellectuals opposed to the dam was banned in China shortly after its publication in 1989. Citizen-based environmental groups are only now beginning to emerge in China but do not dare to seriously challenge a state-backed megaproject such as the Three Gorges dam.

The fact that even under such repressive circumstances one-third of the National People's Congress voted against the final authorization for the Three Gorges project in 1992 or abstained from voting shows just how much doubt about the dam there must be in China. But, given the current political situation, there is little reason to believe that such doubt can be expressed in open public debate or could deter the Chinese government from moving ahead with the project.

---

socialist democracy at work. During these sessions, deputies discuss and decide on legislation introduced by the premier and the State Council. Deputies may also make motions and suggestions to the congress, which are sometimes enacted into law. In recent years, important legislation has included major criminal and civil law statutes, laws governing foreign investment in China, and environmental regulations.

Most of the work of the NPC is routine, such as attending committee meetings or listening to long reports by officials. Legislation and other motions are generally passed by an overwhelming majority. But some debate and dissent do occur. For example, in 1992 about a third of the NPC deputies either voted against construction of the ecologically controversial Three Gorges dam project or abstained from voting. On rare occasions, government legislative initiatives have even been defeated. But all NPC proceedings are subject to party scrutiny. The congress never debates politically sensitive issues, and deputies, even though their right to speak and vote freely is protected by constitutional immunity, would be in serious political jeopardy if their actions were seen as a challenge to the principle of party leadership.

The CCP monitors the elections process to make sure that no outright dissidents are elected as NPC deputies, and the most important leadership positions in the NPC are on the CCP's cadre list, which means that they can only be filled by people who have the party's approval. The party's top bodies decide behind closed doors who will get which government position. This is followed by a more or less pro forma nomination and election process within the NPC, although some deputies do vote against or abstain from voting for party-endorsed nominees. For example, in 1998, 11 percent of the deputies did not vote for the official (and only) nominee to become chair of the congress (equivalent perhaps to the U.S. Speaker of the House of Representatives), Li Peng, the former premier whom many people despise because of his key role in the decision to crush the 1989 Tiananmen demonstrations. Such protest votes may signal a somewhat more independent attitude on the part of some NPC deputies, but they do not yet add up to meaningful opposition to party-designated candidates.

Still, as economics has replaced ideology as the main priority of China's leaders, the NPC has become a much more important and lively part of the Chinese political system than it was during the Mao era. Many NPC deputies are now chosen because of their ability to contribute to China's modernization rather than simply on the basis of political loyalty; therefore, some of them have become a bit more assertive in expressing their opinions on various issues.

Political Parties and the Party System

China is often called a one-party system because the country's politics are so thoroughly dominated by the Chinese Communist Party. In fact, China has eight political parties in addition to the CCP, but these parties neither challenge the basic policies of the CCP nor play a significant part in running the government.

The Chinese Communist Party

At the time of the National Party Congress in 1997, the CCP had about 58 million members. The party has grown steadily since it came to power in 1949, when it had just under 4.5 million members.

The Chinese Communist Party is the largest political party in the world in terms of total formal membership. But, as with all other former and current ruling communist parties, its members make up only a small minority of the country's population. CCP members are now only about 5 percent of China's population, or about 8 percent of those over eighteen, the minimum age for joining the party.

From the viewpoint of the CCP, the small percentage of Communists in Chinese society reflects the vanguard status and role of the party. Only those who are judged to be fully committed to the ideals of communism and who are willing to devote a great deal of time and energy to party affairs may join, and the process is long and arduous. Those admitted swear allegiance to the party and vow to "fight for communism throughout my life, be ready at all times to sacrifice my all for the party and the people, and never betray the people" (Article 6 of the CCP constitution).

The economic reforms begun by Deng Xiaoping paved the way for a milestone transition in the backgrounds of party members. During the Maoist era, "revolutionary cadres," whose careers depended on political loyalty and ideological purity, led the CCP at all levels; recruitment strongly favored the working classes and discriminated against intellectuals and other professionals. The CCP is now increasingly led by "party technocrats," people with higher-level technical training who have made their careers by climbing the ladder of the party-state bureaucracy. For example, all seven members of the party's current Standing Committee have academic and professional backgrounds in technical fields, and five of them (including General Secretary–President Jiang Zemin and Premier Zhu Rongji) were trained as engineers.

The social composition of the CCP's membership has also changed considerably in recent decades. In the mid-1950s peasants made up nearly 70 percent of party membership, and although they are still the largest single group in the party, less than 40 percent of party members now come from the peasantry. Factory workers account for less than 20 percent of party membership. The fastest growing membership category consists of officials, intellectuals, technicians, and other professionals, who together constitute about 30 percent of party membership. The remainder is made up of various groups, including military personnel, retired persons, and service workers. Women make up less than 20 percent of the CCP as a whole and only 4 percent of the Central Committee elected in 1998. One of the two alternate members of the Politburo is a woman (Wu Yi, who is also a senior government official and former minister of foreign trade). There are no female full members of the Politburo or its Standing Committee. The only woman ever to be a member of one of these elite bodies was Jiang Qing, the wife of Chairman Mao Zedong, who rose to power during the Cultural Revolution and was purged shortly after Mao's death in 1976.

Despite the party's tarnished image since Tiananmen and what many Chinese feel is the increasing irrelevance of communist ideology to their lives and the nation's future, the party's Youth League membership grew by 10.5 million between 1993 and 1998 (to a total of 68 million) and the CCP recruits between 1 and 2 million new members each year. Some join because they believe in communist ideals, but most are probably motivated more by opportunism than by idealism. Party membership provides unparalleled access to influence and resources, especially given the current quasi-market nature of China's economy, and being a party member is still a prerequisite for advancement in many careers in China.

China's Noncommunist Parties

The eight noncommunist political parties in the PRC are referred to as the democratic parties, a designation meant to signify the role they play in representing different interests in the political process and to lend some credibility to China's claim that it is a kind of democracy. Each democratic party draws its member-

ship from a particular group in Chinese society. For example, the China Democratic League consists mostly of intellectuals, whereas the China Democratic National Construction Association draws members mainly from the business world.

The democratic parties have a total membership of less than half a million and operate within what the preamble to the PRC constitution calls "a system of multiparty cooperation and political consultation under the leadership of the Communist Party." The noncommunist parties do not contest for power or challenge CCP policy. Their function is to provide advice to the CCP and generate support within their particular constituencies for CCP policies. Individual members of the parties may assume important government positions. But organizationally these parties are relatively insignificant and function as little more than "a loyal non-opposition."[26]

The main forum through which the noncommunist parties express their views on national policy is the Chinese People's Political Consultative Conference (CPPCC). This body meets in full session once a year for about two weeks at the same time as the National People's Congress (NPC), which CPPCC members attend as nonvoting deputies. Most of the leading figures in the 1998 CPPCC (approximately 2100 from various spheres of national life, such as education, business and the arts) were noncommunists. But all the delegates were chosen through a process supervised by the CCP, and a high-ranking party leader heads the CPPCC itself. CPPCC delegates sometimes speak out about national problems like corruption or the environment, but they do not express serious dissent from the party line on any matter. The severe prison sentences given to the activists who tried to establish a new, independent China Democratic Party in 1998 showed just how determined China's leaders are to prevent the formation of any political organization not subservient to the CCP.

Elections

Elections in the PRC are basically mechanisms to give the party-state greater legitimacy by allowing large numbers of citizens to participate in the political process under very controlled circumstances. The CCP has what amounts to effective veto power over all candidates for office. It controls the commissions that run elections, and it reviews draft lists of proposed candidates to weed out those it finds politically objectionable. But the CCP rarely has to exercise its veto power over nominations or elections because very few people dare to oppose the party openly.

China has both direct and indirect elections. In direct elections, all eligible citizens vote for candidates for offices in a particular government body. For example, all the voters in a rural county would vote for the deputies to serve at the county-level people's congress. In indirect elections, higher-level bodies are elected by lower-level bodies rather than by the voters at large. For example, deputies to the National People's Congress are elected by the provincial-level people's congresses, which, in turn, have been elected by county- or city-level people's congresses. All elections above the county level are indirect; there are no direct elections at the provincial or national levels.

Turnout for direct elections is heavy, usually over 90 percent of the eligible electorate. All citizens over the age of eighteen have the right to vote, except those who (as the Chinese constitution puts it) have been "deprived of political rights according to law" (Article 34). This latter category may include the mentally ill, convicted criminals, and political prisoners.

For several decades after the founding of the PRC only one candidate stood for each office, so the only choice facing voters was to approve or abstain. Since the early 1980s many direct and indirect elections have had multiple candidates for each slot, with the winner chosen by secret ballot. The nomination process has also become more open. Any group of more than ten voters can nominate candidates for an election. Most candidates in direct elections are now nominated by the voters, and there have been a significant number of cases where independent candidates have defeated official nominees, though even independent candidates are basically approved by the CCP.

The most significant progress toward true democratic representation and participation in China has occurred in the rural villages. Laws implemented since the late 1980s have provided for directly elected village representative assemblies and the election, rather than the appointment from above, of village officials. These are, for the most part, multicandidate, secret-ballot elections, though still carried out under the watchful eye of the CCP. The village assemblies are usually made up of one representative from every ten or so households and meet at least once every few months. Although the local Communist Party committee is still the most powerful organization in China's villages, these assemblies do have considerable authority over local economic matters and exercise some supervision over local officials. The direct election of local leaders has also given village people the opportunity to oust corrupt or ineffective officials. By 1999 about 60 percent of China's villages had held such contests, and there were some very tentative experiments to expand democratic elections in a few rural townships, the lowest formal level of state government in China.

Recent electoral reform has certainly increased popular representation and participation in China's government. But elections in the PRC still do not give citizens a means by which they can exercise effective control over the party officials and organizations that have the real power in China's political system. The CCP has repeatedly rejected calls from both domestic and foreign critics for freer and more extensive elections. They argue that multiparty elections would not work well in China because of the country's low level of educational and economic development and its relatively poor communications system. They also express the fear that more democracy might plunge the country into chaos, perhaps even civil war. Obviously, they also have reason to be apprehensive about the consequences of truly democratic elections for the party's hold on power. In a major speech in December 1998 marking twenty years of economic reform, President Jiang Zemin stated bluntly, "The model of the West's political system should not be copied." He vowed that China would adhere to a system of socialist democracy in which "the Communist Party, being the ruling party . . . , leads and supports the people in controlling and exercising the power to manage the country."[27]

Political Culture, Citizenship, and Identity

From Communism to Consumerism

Since the PRC's founding in 1949 its official political culture has been based on communist ideology, and the party-state has made extensive efforts to make people's political attitudes and behavior conform to the currently prevailing version of Marxism-Leninism. But this ideology has gone through severe crises and profound changes during the turbulent decades of Communist rule, which has left its future in China seriously in doubt.

During the Maoist era, Mao Zedong Thought was hailed as holding the answer to all of China's problems in domestic and foreign policy. By the mid-1970s, however, the debacles of the Mao years had greatly tarnished the appeal of communism in China.

After Deng Xiaoping came to power in 1978, he set about trying not only to restore the legitimacy of the Communist Party through economic reforms but also to revive communist ideology. As a first step, Mao's contributions to China and Mao Zedong Thought were reevaluated. There was no complete repudiation of Mao as there had been of Stalin in the Soviet Union in the 1950s, but Mao was judged to have made serious mistakes as well as great contributions. Those parts of Mao Zedong Thought, such as his views on the importance of maintaining a close relationship between communist officials and the people (the "mass line"), were considered useful in maintaining Communist rule. Parts considered outmoded or counterproductive, such as the emphasis on class struggle, were jettisoned.

Toward the end of 1997 the CCP amended the party constitution to add "Deng Xiaoping Theory" to its official ideology. Deng's theories, which are often referred to under the rubric of "Building Socialism with Chinese characteristics," emphasized that China is a relatively poor country in the "primary stage of socialism" and therefore must use any means possible—even capitalist ones—to develop the economy. But Deng, like Mao, believed that only the Communist Party can lead China in this quest for development. In essence, Deng Xiaoping Theory is an ideological rationale for the combination of economic liberalization and party dictatorship that characterizes contemporary China.

The CCP still tries to keep communist ideology viable and visible by continued efforts to influence public opinion and socialization—for instance, by controlling the media and overseeing the educational system. Although China's media are much livelier and more open than during the Maoist period, there is no true freedom of the press. Reduced political control of the media has, to a large extent, meant only the freedom to publish more entertainment news, human interest stories, and local coverage. Media sources that stray beyond the proscribed boundaries are shut down; television and radio are entirely state-controlled. Internet access is growing fast in the PRC, especially among university students and intellectuals. The government, worried about the potentially subversive influence of e-mail and Web pages from abroad, has found it difficult to control the flow of electronic information as tightly as it would like, although, in another sign of the times, the government of the PRC has set up its own Internet site (http://www.chinanews.org).

Schools are one of the main institutions through which all states instill political values in their citizens. Educational opportunities have expanded enormously in China since 1949. Today, primary school enrollment is close to 100 percent of the age-eligible (6–11) population, which helps to explain why China has such a high literacy rate (80 percent) for such a relatively poor country. However, enrollment rates drop sharply after primary school. Only about half of those between the ages of 12 and 17 are in secondary school (compared to about 90 percent in the United States), and only about 2 percent of the age-eligible population is in some type of college (compared to about 75 percent in the U.S.). Obviously, China is going to have to expand secondary and college education if its goals for economic modernization are to be met. At the same time, a more educated population could pose a potential threat to a regime intent on maintaining tight political control over its citizens.

In Mao's China, students at all levels spent a considerable amount of time studying politics and working in fields or factories, and teaching materials were often overlaid with a heavy dose of political propaganda. Today politics is a minor part of the curriculum as students are urged to gain the skills and knowledge they need to further their own careers and help China modernize. Yet schools are by no means centers of critical or independent thinking, and teachers and students are still closely monitored for political reliability. More than 80 percent of China's youth between the ages of 7 and 14 belongs to the Young Pioneers, an organization designed to promote good social behavior, patriotism, and loyalty to the party among school children. However, the party's efforts to keep socialist values alive in China do not appear to be meeting with much success, and public confidence in the party and in communist ideology is very low.

Alternative sources of socialization are growing in importance, although these do not often take expressly political forms because of the threat of repression. In the countryside, there has been a resurgence of traditional customs and organizations. Peasants have replaced portraits of Mao and other Communist heroes with statues of folk gods and ancestor worship tablets, and the influence of extended kinship groups such as clans often outweighs the formal authority of the party in the villages. In the cities, popular culture, including gigantic rock concerts, shapes youth attitudes much more profoundly than do party messages about socialism. Throughout China, consumerism and the desire for economic gain rather than communist ideals of self-sacrifice and the common good, provide the principal motivation for much personal and social behavior. And religions of various kinds, once ferociously repressed by the Maoist party-state, are attracting an increasing (though still small) number of Chinese adherents. Buddhist temples, Christian churches, and other places of worship operate more freely than they have in decades. However, the Chinese Catholic Church is prohibited from recognizing the authority of the Vatican, and clergy of any religion who are considered to be a political threat are still imprisoned.

Citizenship and National Identity

The PRC constitution grants citizens extensive rights, including political rights, such as freedom of speech and assembly, and economic rights, such as the right to work and the right to health care and education. The constitution also proclaims, "Women in the People's Republic of China enjoy equal rights with men in all spheres of life, political, economic, cultural and social, including family life" (Article 48).

The constitution also specifies the duties of China's citizens, including the duty to work, perform military service, pay taxes, and practice family planning. In addition, there are more general duties, such as "the duty to safeguard the security, honor and

interests of the motherland" (Article 54). Such duties are vague enough to allow the authorities great leeway in interpretation and enforcement.

There is even an article in the Chinese constitution that has been cited by party leaders as giving precedence to the duties expected of citizens over those articles that grant them rights such as freedom of speech and assembly. Article 51 states that in exercising their freedoms and rights, citizens of the PRC "may not infringe upon the interests of the state, of society and of the collective, or upon the lawful freedoms and rights of other citizens." This provision gives the party-state constitutional grounds for suppressing dissent and opposition.

China in the late 1990s was going through a profound and uncertain transformation in its national identity. CCP leaders realize that most citizens view communist ideology as irrelevant to their lives. Therefore the CCP has turned increasingly to nationalism to rally the country. The official media now put considerable emphasis on the greatness and antiquity of Chinese culture, with the not-so-subtle message that it is time for the Chinese nation to reclaim its rightful place in the world order. The government also does all it can to get political capital out of China's recent economic progress, its impressive performances in international sports competitions, and the return of Hong Kong to Chinese sovereignty in 1997. Some observers have expressed concern that such officially promoted nationalist sentiments could lead to a more aggressive foreign and military policy, particularly toward areas such as the potentially oil-rich South China Sea, where the PRC's historical territorial claims conflict with those of other countries like Vietnam and the Philippines.

China's Non-Chinese Citizens

China's ethnic minorities number more than 90 million, or about 8 percent of the total population of the PRC. There are fifty-five officially recognized minority groups in China, ranging in size from over 15 million (the Zhuang of southwest China) to about 2000 (the Lloba in the far west of the country). There are about 20 million Muslims spread among several different ethnic groups. Most of these minorities have come under the rule of China through the territorial expansion of the Chinese state over many centuries rather than through migration into China.

China's minority peoples are highly concentrated in the five autonomous regions of Guangxi, Inner Mongolia, Ningxia, Tibet, and Xinjiang, although only in the latter two do minority groups actually outnumber ethnic Chinese. These five regions are sparsely populated, yet they occupy about 60 percent of the total land area of the PRC. Some of these minority areas are resource-rich, and most are located in strategic border areas of the country, including the borders with Vietnam, India, and Russia.

The Chinese constitution grants autonomous areas the right of self-government in certain matters, such as cultural affairs, but their autonomy is, in fact, very limited, and the minority regions are kept firmly under the control of the national government. Minority peoples are given more latitude to develop their local economies as they see fit, religious freedom is generally respected, and the use of minority languages in the media and literature is encouraged, as is bilingual education. In order to keep the already small minority populations from dwindling further, China's stringent family planning policy is applied much more loosely among minorities, who are often allowed to have two or more children per couple rather than the one child that is the prescribed limit for most Chinese.

The constitution also specifies that chairs of people's congresses and the administrative heads of autonomous areas must be members of the minority nationalities in that area. There has also been a concerted effort to recruit and promote minority cadres to run local governments in autonomous areas.

The impact of these positive political trends is, however, tempered by the fact that there are very few minorities in the upper echelons of the party and military leadership. Furthermore, even in minority areas, the most powerful individual, the head of the regional or local Communist Party, is likely to be Chinese. Also despite significant progress in modernizing the economies of the minority regions, these areas remain among the poorest in China.

The most extensive ethnic conflict in China has occurred in Tibet, which has been under what is essentially Chinese military occupation since the early 1950s. There has also been increasing unrest in areas where some of China's 20 million Muslims live.

Several clashes with Islamic separatists have caused the Chinese government to worry that pan-Islamic sentiments and activities may spread to western China from Afghanistan, Pakistan, and the Central Asian states that were once part of the former Soviet Union.

China's minority population is relatively small and geographically isolated, and where ethnic unrest has occurred, it has been limited, sporadic, and easily quelled. Therefore, the PRC has not had the kind of intense identity-based conflict experienced by countries with more pervasive religious and ethnic differences, such as India and Nigeria. But it is very likely that in the future both domestic and international forces will cause identity issues to become more visible and volatile on China's national political agenda.

Interests, Social Movements, and Protest

The formal structures of the Chinese political system are designed more to extend state control of political life than to facilitate citizen participation in politics. Therefore, people make extensive use of their personal connections based on kinship, friendship, and other ties (*guanxi*) to help ease their contacts with the bureaucrats and party officials who wield such enormous power over so many aspects of their lives. Patron-client politics is also pervasive at the local level in China, as it is in many developing countries where ordinary people have little access to the official channels of power. For example, a village leader (the patron) may help farmers (the clients) avoid paying some taxes by reporting false production statistics in exchange for their support to keep him in office. Such clientelism can be an important way for local communities to resist state policies that they see as harmful to their interests.

Organized interest groups and social movements that are truly independent of party-state authority are not permitted to influence the political process in any significant way. Rather, the party-state tries to preempt the formation of autonomous groups and movements through the use of official "mass organizations." These organizations provide a means for interest groups to express their views on policy matters within strict limits. The charters of these organizations place them explicitly under the leadership of the CCP; however, they appear to be gaining influence

Current Challenges: *Tibet and China*

Tibet is located in the far west of China on the border with India, Burma, Nepal, and Bhutan. It is a large area (about 470,000 square miles, which is nearly 13 percent of China's total area) and is ringed by some of the world's highest mountains, including the Himalayas and Mt. Everest. Tibet has a population of only about 2 million people, 95 percent of whom are Tibetans, who are ethnically, linguistically, and culturally distinct from the Chinese. Another 2.5 million ethnic Tibetans live elsewhere in China, mostly in provinces near Tibet.

In the thirteenth century, Tibet became a theocracy in which absolute power was held by a Buddhist priest, called the Dalai Lama, who ruled the country with the help of other clergy and the aristocracy. Traditional Tibetan society was sharply divided between the tiny ruling class and the common people, most of whom were serfs living and working under difficult and often brutal conditions.

Tibet became subordinate to China in the early eighteenth century, although the Dalai Lama and other Tibetan officials continued to govern the country. After the collapse of China's imperial system in 1911, Tibet achieved de facto independence. However, Britain, which saw Tibet in the context of its extensive colonial rule in South Asia, exercised considerable influence in Tibetan affairs.

Shortly after coming to power, the Chinese Communists made known their intention to end foreign intervention in Tibet, which they, like previous Chinese governments, considered to be part of China. In 1951 the Dalai Lama, rather than face a full-scale military assault, agreed to the peaceful incorporation of Tibet into the People's Republic of China. Although some Chinese troops and officials were sent to Tibet, the Dalai Lama remained in a position of symbolic authority for much of the 1950s. In 1959 a widespread revolt against Chinese rule led to the invasion of Tibet by the People's Liberation Army; the Dalai Lama and over 50,000 of his supporters fled to exile in India, and Chinese rule was even more firmly established. In 1965 the Tibetan Autonomous Region was officially formed, but Chinese political and military officials have kept a firm grip on power in Tibet.

During the Maoist era, traditional Tibetan culture was suppressed by the Chinese authorities. Since the late 1970s, Buddhist temples and monasteries have been allowed to reopen and Tibetans have gained a significant degree of cultural freedom; the Chinese government has also increased its investment in Tibet's economic development. However, China still considers talk of Tibetan political independence to be treason, and Chinese troops have violently crushed several anti-China demonstrations in Lhasa, the capital of Tibet.

The current Dalai Lama is very active internationally in promoting the cause of independence for Tibet. In 1989 he was awarded the Nobel Peace Prize, and in 1991 he met at the White House with President George Bush and addressed the U.S. Congress, much to the displeasure of the Chinese government. In 1997 the Dalai Lama met with President Bill Clinton, and in 1999 the U.S. State Department appointed a special Coordinator for Tibetan Issues, which China saw as further proof of U.S. support for Tibetan independence. There have been some inconclusive talks between the Dalai Lama and Chinese officials about the conditions under which he might return to Tibet in some capacity. But the two sides appear far from any agreement, and tensions between Tibetans and Chinese in Tibet remain high and potentially explosive.

---

in the policy process as China's leadership tries to enlist broad support for its development goals.

China has many mass organizations formed around social or occupational categories, with a total membership in the hundreds of millions. Two of the most important mass organizations are the All-China Federation of Trade Unions, to which most Chinese factory workers belong, and the All-China Women's Federation, which is the only national organization representing the interests of women in general. Both of these federations are top-down, party-controlled organizations, and neither constitute an independent political voice for the groups they are supposed to represent. But they do sometimes act as an effective lobby in promoting the nonpolitical interests of their constituencies. For example, the Trade Union

Federation has pushed for legislation to reduce the standard work week from six to five days, while the Women's Federation has become a strong advocate for women on issues ranging from domestic violence to economic rights.

The reform era has led to the spread of **nongovernmental organizations** (NGOs) less directly subordinate to the CCP than the traditional mass organizations. There is an enormous variety of such NGOs, including environmental organizations, charitable foundations, and professional associations such as the China Political Science Association and the All-China Women's Entrepreneurs Association. These nongovernmental organizations have considerable latitude to operate within their functional areas of expertise without direct party interference if they steer clear of politics and don't challenge official policies. For example, environmental groups cannot openly oppose the Three Gorges project. All NGOs are supposed to register with the government, and organizations that would represent interests that the party-state does not recognize as legitimate, such as human rights or homosexuality, would not be given official permission to operate. In recent years, however, many thousands of unofficial grassroots organizations have formed to represent the interests of their members, but they run the risk of being shut down if they do anything to displease the authorities.

The various government bodies and other organizations discussed in this section should not be dismissed as entirely irrelevant to politics and policy-making in the PRC. Although they remain subordinate to the CCP, the National People's Congress, the Chinese People's Political Consultative Conference, the democratic parties, the mass organizations, and the NGOs do "provide important access points between the Party and the organized masses, which allow the voicing of special interests in ways that do not threaten Party hegemony and yet pressure the shaping of policy."[28]

Mechanisms of Social Control

While China has certainly loosened up politically since the days of Mao Zedong, the party's control mechanisms still penetrate to the basic levels of society and serve the CCP's aim of preventing the formation of groups or movements that could challenge its authority. In the rural areas, the small-scale, close-knit nature of the village facilitates control by the local party and security organizations. But the major means of control used by the party-state in urban China, called the unit (or *danwei*) system, is more complex. In the cities, almost everyone belongs to a unit, usually their place of work.

The unit is the center of economic, social, and political life for most urban residents. People depend on their units for jobs, income, and promotion, and larger units (like state-owned industries) may also provide housing, medical clinics, cafeterias, daycare centers, recreational facilities, and the like. The unit is also the citizen's basic point of contact with the formal political system. People vote in their workplace. If they belong to the party, they vote through the CCP branch in their unit; if there is a national campaign in progress, it is publicized through the unit. For example, compliance with the national family-planning policy is usually monitored through a woman's work unit.

The unit holds meetings to discuss the official line on important policies or events. The personnel departments of units also keep a political dossier on every employee. The dossier contains a detailed record of the political activities and attitudes of the employee and his or her immediate family members, and if a person changes jobs, the dossier moves, too. In these and other ways, the unit acts as a check on political dissidents.

Residents' committees are another instrument of control in every urban neighborhood. These citizen organizations, which are often staffed by retired persons, housewives, or others not attached to a work unit, effectively extend the unofficial reach of the party-state down to the most basic level of urban society. The committees address neighborhood concerns like crime prevention and sanitation, but they also keep a semiofficial eye on who is doing what in the neighborhood. Suspicious doings are reported to the Public Security Bureau for further investigation. Foreign journalists in China have often found it difficult to meet with Chinese citizens in their homes because of the surveillance of the residents' committees.

As Chinese society continues to change because of the impact of economic reform, these control mechanisms are weakening. The growth of private and semiprivate enterprises, increasing labor and residential mobility, and new forms of association (such as discos and coffeehouses) and communication (for example, cell phones, e-mail, fax machines, and TV satellite dishes) are just some of the factors that are making it much harder for the party-state to monitor citizens as closely as it has in the past.

Protest and the Party-State

The Tiananmen massacre of 1989 showed the limits of protest in China. The leadership was particularly alarmed at signs that a number of grassroots organizations, such as the Beijing Federation of Autonomous Student Unions and the Beijing Workers' Autonomous Union, were emerging from the protests. The success of Solidarity, the independent Polish workers' movement, in challenging the power of the communist party in Poland in the 1980s was much in the minds of China's leaders as they watched the Tiananmen protests unfold. Massive repression was their way of letting it be known that the "Polish disease" would not be allowed to spread to China and that neither open political protest nor the formation of autonomous interest groups would be tolerated.

There have been no significant political demonstrations in China since 1989, and pro-democracy groups have been driven deep underground. Known dissidents are continuously watched, harassed, imprisoned—and recently and more benevolently—expelled from the country.

But repression has not put an end to all forms of protest in the PRC. As mentioned previously, ethnic protests occur sporadically on China's periphery. Labor unrest has also been growing, with reports of thousands of strikes and other actions in recent years.

There have been large demonstrations at state-owned factories, where workers are angry about the ending of the iron rice bowl system of lifetime employment and guaranteed salaries. Workers at some foreign-owned enterprises have gone on strike to protest unsafe working conditions or low wages. Such actions have remained limited in scope and duration, so the government has usually not cracked down on the protesters and has, on occasion, actually pressured the employers to meet the workers' demands.

There have also been significant protests in China's countryside, especially in poorer inland provinces. Farmers have attacked local officials and rioted over high taxes and extralegal fees, corruption, and the government's failure to pay on time for agricultural products purchased by the state. These protests have remain localized and have focused on farmers' immediate material concerns, not on grand-scale issues like democracy. Nevertheless, if the countryside is left too far behind in the process of economic development, rural discontent could spread and translate into more generalized anger against the regime.

The political situation in China at the beginning of the twenty-first century presents a rather contradictory picture. Although people are freer in many ways than they have been in decades, repression can still be intense, and open political dissent is almost nonexistent. But there are many signs that the Chinese Communist Party is losing some of its ability to control the movements and associations of its citizens and can no longer easily limit access to information and ideas from abroad. Some forms of protest also appear to be increasing and, in some places, may come to pose a serious challenge to the authority of the party-state.

Section ❺ Chinese Politics in Transition

Political Challenges and Changing Agendas

Scenes from the Chinese Countryside

The economic and political circumstances of China's vast rural population differ dramatically depending on where in the countryside you look.[29]

Daqiuzhuang, Hebei Province   This village is perhaps the most prosperous place in all of China, with a per capita income (US$24,000 in the mid-1990s) nearly equal to that of the United States. Many villagers drive Mercedes-Benzes and other luxury cars, and all live in modern brick two-story houses—an unheard-of level of comfort for most Chinese. Although it is clearly still a rural area, the source of the village's wealth is industry, not agriculture. It has more than two hundred enterprises and tens of millions of dollars' worth of foreign investment. In addition to the 4000 or so now-rich native residents, many of whom hold managerial positions, there are several thousand less well-off—some would say exploited—workers from elsewhere in China who provide most of the labor for the factories. Although several of its former leaders were jailed on corruption and other criminal charges in 1993, the economic fortunes of Daqiuzhuang have continued to soar.

Qibailong, Guangxi Zhuang Autonomous Region
This rural town is located in one of the areas known as China's Third World, where persistent poverty rather than growing prosperity is still the common lot in life. There are no luxury cars here; most peasant families have a total income of less than US$50 a year. Many of the children are hungry and half-naked, and most of the houses are little more than poorly constructed huts. Education, professional health care, and other social services are minimal or nonexistent. There is no industry, and the land barely supports those who work it. Tens of millions of Chinese peasants in villages like Qibailong remain mired in poverty and have benefited little from the country's economic boom.

Daolin, Hunan Province In January 1999 thousands of angry farmers marched on the township government headquarters to protest excessive taxes and the gross corruption of local officials. One farmer was killed and dozens injured when the police used clubs and tear gas to disperse the crowd. Shortly afterwards, nine people suspected of being ringleaders of the protests were arrested. The demonstrations had been spurred by a grassroots organization called Volunteers for Publicity of Policies and Regulations, formed to bring attention to local violations of a national law that limits taxes on farmers to 5 percent of their income. In many parts of rural China, villagers are subject to a wide range of arbitrary fees; there are charges for slaughtering pigs, for sending kids to school, for permits to get married or to have a baby, for registering land, and for outhouse renovations—to name just a few. As a result of such local fees, Daolin's farmers were paying double the legal tax rate—which for people with an annual per capita income of only US$170 was quite a burden. And people were even more

furious because the extra fees often went to support the "wining and dining" of township bureaucrats rather than for worthy local projects.

Beiwang, Hebei Province This village of 2500 people recently elected its first representative assembly to supervise the work of local government officials. One of the first decisions made by the forty representatives was to reassign the contracts for tending the village's 3000 pear trees. After the rural communes were disbanded in the 1980s, each of the five hundred or so families in the village was given six trees to look after under the new household responsibility system. The assembly, however, decided that it would be better to reassign the trees to a very small number of families who would care for them in a more efficient and productive manner. The local Communist Party branch objected to this on the grounds that the village might lose much of the revenue that it earned from signing contracts with many households, which was used to pay for various public works projects such as road maintenance. The party was probably also concerned about the ideological implications of a less egalitarian distribution of the village's trees and the income derived from them. Nevertheless, assembly representatives were able to generate strong support from their constituents for their proposal, and the party branch allowed the trees to be recontracted to just eleven households. In a short time, pear production zoomed. The new system proved to be economically beneficial not only to the few families who looked after the trees but also to the village as a whole because of the government's share of the increased profits.

The varied scenes just described make several important points about Chinese politics today. First, they remind us of the central role that China's rural areas will play in the nation's future. Most Chinese still live in the countryside, and China's political and economic fate will be greatly influenced by what goes on there.

These scenes also reflect the diversity of the Chinese countryside: prosperity and poverty, mass protests and peaceful politics. It is very hard to generalize about such a vast and varied nation by looking at what is going on in only one small part of the country.

Although China has become more industrialized and urbanized in recent decades, most Chinese people still live in rural areas, and many of them still earn their living through fairly traditional agricultural labor. In general, rural incomes are less than half those of the urban areas. *Source:* AP/Wide World Photos.

The scene from Beiwang reminds us that in China, as in other countries, not all politics involves matters of national or international significance. For many, perhaps most, Chinese, who looks after the village pear trees matters more than what goes on in the inner sanctums of the Communist Party or the outcomes of U.S.-China presidential summits. The victory of the Beiwang representative assembly on the pear tree issue shows that sometimes, even in a one-party state, the people prevail against the government and democracy works on the local level—as long as the basic principle of party leadership is not challenged.

The Qibailong and Daolin scenes reflect the trouble that is brewing in parts of the Chinese countryside. No one would deny the astonishing improvement in living standards throughout most of rural China brought about since the 1980s by decollectivization and industrialization. But huge pockets of severe poverty persist, especially in inland regions like Guangxi that are far removed from the more prosperous coastal regions. Most of rural China falls somewhere between the conspicuous wealth of Daqiuzhuang and the extreme poverty of Qibailong. In the in-between areas like Daolin the combination of new hopes brought about by economic improvements and the anger caused by blatant corruption, growing inequalities, stagnating incomes, and other frustrations may prove to be politically explosive. Economic reform has yielded a better life and higher hopes for

most of China's peasants. The CCP now faces the challenge of having to satisfy those hopes or risk the wrath of a social group that for decades has been the bedrock of the party's support.

Economic Management and Political Legitimacy

The problems of China's rural areas are part of a larger challenge facing the country's leadership, namely, how to sustain and effectively manage the economic growth on which the CCP's legitimacy as China's ruling party is now largely based. The party is gambling that solid economic performance will literally buy it legitimacy in the eyes of the Chinese people and that most people will care little about democracy if their material lives continue to improve.

A serious economic crisis could raise questions about the future viability of communist rule in China. If the economy were to falter in a way that gravely affected the livelihood or dashed the expectations of a large segment of the population, the potential for social unrest and political upheaval would increase immeasurably. The party would be left with nothing but sheer coercion to sustain itself in power.

Despite the overall success of reform, the CCP faces a number of challenges in governing the economy that will affect the party's political fortunes. Failure to keep inequality under control, especially between city and countryside, or to continue providing opportunities for advancement for the less well-off could become a source of social instability and a liability for a political party that still espouses a commitment to socialist goals. The considerable autonomy gained by provinces and localities as a result of the decentralization of economic decision-making has fostered a growing regionalism that poses a potentially serious threat to the political control of the central government. Corruption, which affects the lives of most people more directly than does political repression, has become so blatant and widespread that it is probably the single most corrosive force eating away at the legitimacy of the Chinese Communist Party.

The reforms begun by Deng Xiaoping have unquestionably spurred national economic growth and improved the material well-being of most Chinese. However, there are deep doubts about the ability of the CCP to continue to manage the economy effectively because of its reluctance to make even more fundamental changes, such as extending the market reforms to sectors of the economy that remain under state control, like banking and the production of steel and oil. However, it is in just such crucial areas of the economy that the Chinese Communist Party has found it most difficult to pull back. This difficulty stems partly from entrenched bureaucratic interests in government ministries that do not want to give up control of their bailiwicks. It also comes from the political opposition of ideological conservatives in the party leadership who are very reluctant to allow the dismantling of the last strongholds of the socialist command economy. Even those committed to reform are fearful of the political consequences of laying off millions of workers from state-owned factories. But if China's leaders choose not to make these hard policy choices, the country is unlikely to be able to sustain its remarkable economic growth, which could have even more severe repercussions for the CCP's ability to continue governing the country.

China and the Democratic Idea

China in the 1990s evolved toward a system of what has been called Market-Leninism, a combination of increasing economic openness and continuing political rigidity under the leadership of a ruling party that

adheres to a remodeled version of communist ideology.[30] The major political challenges now facing the CCP and the country emerge from the sharpening contradictions and tensions of this hybrid system.

In the short run, the CCP's gamble that the country's economic boom would divert the attention of most Chinese from politics to profits has paid off. Continuing repression has also contributed to political calm in China since the Tiananmen crisis. However, as the people of China become more secure economically, better educated, and more aware of the outside world through access to modern media and telecommunications, they are likely to become politically less quiescent. Specific groups created or influenced by the course of economic development could become the source of pressures for political change. The rapidly expanding class of private entrepreneurs may want political clout to match their economic wealth; the intellectuals and specialists whose knowledge and skills are needed for the country's modernization drive may become more outspoken about the lack of political freedom; and the many Chinese citizens who travel or study abroad may find the political gap between China and the world's growing number of democracies to be increasingly intolerable. As China becomes more integrated with the global economy, the pressures from abroad for political change will also increase.

Maoist policies successfully eliminated any sphere of independent activity in China that might pose a challenge to the CCP's political domination. But economic reform and modernization over the last few decades in the PRC has led to the growth of **civil society**—a sphere of public life and citizen association truly autonomous from party-state control, which, if allowed to thrive and expand, could provide fertile soil for future democratization. The development of such a civil society, for example, among workers in Poland and intellectuals in Czechoslovakia, played an important role in the collapse of communism in East-Central Europe in the late 1980s by weakening the critical underpinnings of party-state control of society.

The Tiananmen demonstrations of 1989 reflected the stirrings of civil society in post-Mao China. One of the most remarkable things about Tiananmen was the way in which divergent groups, including students, workers, journalists, and entrepreneurs, joined the demonstrations to express their various dissatis-factions with the Communist Party. The viciousness of the Tiananmen crackdown revealed the CCP's deter-mination to crush civil society before it could seri-ously challenge Communist authority.

But civil society in China has begun to stir again. Continuing economic modernization and social liber-alization have led to the appearance of a multitude of unregistered grassroots organizations, such as those representing the interests of rural migrants in some of China's cities, which have become "a boiling pot [that's] difficult for Beijing to keep the lid on."[31] Similarly, a surprisingly wide-ranging discussion about the merits of democracy that took place in aca-demic journals and conferences in the late 1990s was a sign that intellectuals were once more testing the waters of what was possible to advocate in the way of fundamental political reform. And in the spring of 1999, more than 10,000 Chinese followers of a charis-matic martial arts and meditation master staged a peaceful protest in front of Communist Party head-quarters in Beijing against government efforts to stifle their movement.

At some point, the leaders of the Chinese Communist Party will face the fundamental dilemma of whether to accommodate or—as they have done so often in the past—repress organizations and ideas that grow outside of its control. On the one hand, accom-modation would require making some very basic changes in the Chinese political system, namely, less party control and more meaningful citizen representa-tion and participation. The party would have to modify or abandon its claim to an exclusive "leading role" in Chinese society, something that no commu-nist party has been able to do and still retain power. On the other hand, continued repression would strike at the heart of some of the groups and processes that are vital to the country's economic dynamism. This would have terrible costs for China and could also spell political trouble for the CCP.

The Future of Democracy

There are reasons to be both optimistic and pes-simistic about the future of the democratic idea in China.[32] On the negative side, China's long history of bureaucratic and authoritarian rule in both traditional

and modern forms and the hierarchical values of still-influential Confucian culture seem to be mighty coun-terweights to democracy. And even though its political legitimacy may be weak and some aspects of its social control have broken down, the coercive power of China's Communist party-state remains formidable.

China's status as a developing nation with a low general standard of living, large areas of extreme poverty, and poor communications also imposes some impediments to democratization. Neither are all seg-ments of the population equally receptive to calls for democracy. The appeal of democratic values is most apparent among intellectuals and urban residents, who still constitute a minority of the population. A large majority of the Chinese people are likely apathetic about national politics (preferring to focus on their immediate economic concerns) or fearful of the vio-lence and chaos that radical political change might unleash.

On the positive side, the impressive successes of democratization in Taiwan in the 1990s, including free and fair multiparty elections from the local level up to the presidency, strongly suggests that the values, insti-tutions, and process of democracy are not incompati-ble with Chinese culture. And, though it is still a rela-tively poor, developing country, China has a higher literacy rate, more extensive industrialization and urbanization, and less inequality (though there are some worrisome trends here) than most countries at its level of economic development—all of which are conditions widely seen by social scientists as favor-able to democracy.

Despite the CCP's continuing tight hold on power, there have been a number of significant political changes in China under Deng Xiaoping and Jiang Zemin that could be planting the seeds of democracy. They are the decentralization of political and eco-nomic power to local governments; the setting of a mandatory retirement age and term limits for all offi-cials; the coming to power of younger, better educated, and more worldly leaders; the increasingly important role of the National People's Congress in the policy-making process; the introduction of competitive elec-tions in rural villages; the spread of semiautonomous nongovernmental organizations; the strengthening and partial depoliticization of the legal system; tolerance of a much wider range of artistic, cultural, and religious expression; and the important freedom (unheard of in the Mao era) for individuals to be apolitical.

Furthermore, the spread of democracy around the globe in the last decades of the twentieth century has created an international trend that will be increasingly difficult for China's leaders to resist. The PRC has become a major player in the world of states, and its government must be more responsive to international opinion in order to continue the country's deepening integration with the global economy and growing diplomatic stature.

But the future of the democratic idea in China is far from certain, and bleaker outcomes are also possible. There are still very powerful hard-liners in the CCP who could come to power, particularly if the economy falters, and who could reimpose ideological orthodoxy and resist efforts to weaken the party's control of political life. A serious foreign policy crisis or an outbreak of widespread social disorder could provoke a military coup in the name of national security.

There are also circumstances that could lead China to experience various kinds of identity-based and other conflicts that would undermine the prospects for democracy. The sharp class differences that have emerged along with growing national prosperity have the potential to spill into political violence, especially if groups such as impoverished farmers or urban migrants lose hope that their rising expectations for a better life will be met. Serious disputes within the leadership or between the party and the people over the nation's future could lead to civil war, while economic troubles might propel a splintering of China into regional blocs only nominally loyal to Beijing. If the central government should be paralyzed by a power struggle or seriously weakened for any other reason, separatist movements in Tibet and other minority areas could gain momentum and alter the political map of the PRC. But the unifying power of Chinese culture makes it unlikely that China will experience the kind of extreme national fragmentation that occurred in the former Soviet Union or ethnic warfare like that in the former Yugoslavia.

Chinese Politics in Comparative Perspective

As mentioned in Section 1, it is particularly useful to compare politics in China with the politics of other nations from two perspectives. First, the People's Republic of China can be compared with other communist party-states with which it shares or has shared many political characteristics. Second, China can be compared with other Third World nations that face similar challenges of economic and political development.

China as a Communist Party-State

Why has the Chinese Communist party-state so far proven more durable than other regimes of its type? The PRC's successful economic restructuring and the rising living standard of most Chinese people have saved the CCP from the kinds of economic crises that greatly weakened other communist systems.

The nature of the revolution that first brought the CCP to power also provides some clues about why communism has survived in China. The Chinese Communists came to power through an indigenous revolution and did not depend on foreign support for their victory. This is very different from the situation in most of East-Central Europe, where the Soviet Red Army helped to install and maintain communist regimes, which never quite shed the image of having been imposed from the outside. Furthermore, because of their success as social reformers and patriotic fighters against the Japanese, the Chinese Communists were able to build a much larger and broader base of support, especially among the peasantry, than the Soviet Communists, who came to power much more quickly through a rapid, largely urban revolution. Therefore, even though repression and corruption may be harming the popularity of the CCP, among some segments of the population the party still has a deep reservoir of historical legitimacy.

But China also has many things in common with other communist party-states, including the basic features of what is often called its totalitarian political system. **Totalitarianism** (a term also applied to fascist regimes such as Nazi Germany) describes a system in which the ruling party prohibits all forms of meaningful political opposition and dissent, insists on obedience to a single state-determined ideology, and enforces its rule through coercion and terror. Such regimes also seek to bring all spheres of public activity (including the economy and culture) and many spheres of its citizens' private lives under the *total* control of the party-state in the effort to modernize the country and, indeed, to transform human nature.

Totalitarian systems like those in China under Mao and in the Soviet Union under Stalin are different in several important ways from authoritarian dictatorships like the military governments that have ruled Nigeria and Brazil. Both totalitarian and authoritarian regimes suppress opposition and dissent, often quite brutally, but authoritarian governments do not attempt to control or penetrate society in as thorough a manner as do totalitarian states. Authoritarian governments generally allow a large "zone of indifference" in society where citizens are free to pursue their interests (such as in religion or the arts) without state interference as long as they steer clear of sensitive political issues.

The case of China sheds interesting comparative light on the nature of change in totalitarian systems. Partly because of their inflexibility, totalitarian regimes in Russia and Eastern Europe collapsed quickly and thoroughly, to be replaced by democracies—or at least efforts to democratize. The CCP appears to be trying to save Communist rule in China by abandoning or at least moderating some of its totalitarian features.

In order to promote economic development, the CCP has relaxed its grip on many areas of life, resulting in a relatively large apolitical "zone of indifference." The PRC under Deng Xiaoping evolved from Maoist totalitarianism toward a less intrusive, but still dictatorial, "consultative authoritarian regime" that "increasingly recognizes the need to obtain information, advice, and support from key sectors of the population, but insists on suppressing dissent . . . and maintaining ultimate political power in the hands of the Party."[33] Thus, China may be going through a type of post-totalitarian transition that is characterized by bold economic reforms but leads to another form of dictatorship rather than to democracy.

China as a Third World State

The record of Communist rule in China raises important issues about the role of the state in economic development. It also raises interesting comparative questions about the complex relationship between economic and political change in the Third World.

When the Chinese Communist Party came to power in 1949, China was a desperately poor country, with an economy devastated by a century of civil strife and world war. The nation had also been torn apart politically and socially, and was in a weak and subordinate position in the post–World War II international order. Measured against this starting point, the People's Republic of China has made remarkable progress in improving its citizens' living standards and quality of life. The Communist Party has also enhanced China's global role and international prestige. It has built a strong state that not only has the capacity to control and repress its people but can also carry out most of the necessary functions of a modern government from running schools to delivering the mail.

Why has China been more successful than many other developing nations in meeting some of the major challenges of development? Many Third World states serve narrow class or foreign interests more than the national interest, and corrupt political leaders are a drain on development rather than a stimulus. The result is that governments of Third World countries often become defenders of a status quo built on extensive poverty and inequality rather than agents of needed fundamental change.

In contrast, the PRC's rulers have been quite successful in creating what social scientists call a **developmental state**, in which political leaders effectively use government power and public policy to promote economic growth. The Chinese Communist Party has not hesitated to use force to achieve its ends, but it has also been unflinching in pursuit of China's national development and unafraid to undertake radical change to do so. The Chinese developmental state under Deng Xiaoping and now Jiang Zemin certainly has serious economic and social problems, but the policies of market reform and opening the country to the international market made China one of the world's great economic success stories in the last decades of the twentieth century.

While much of the Third World seems to be heading toward democracy without development (or at least very slow development), China seems to be following the reverse course of very fast development without democracy. There is a sharp and disturbing contrast between the harsh political rule of the CCP and its remarkable accomplishments in improving the material lives of the Chinese people. This contrast is at the heart of what one journalist has called the "riddle of China" today. The government of the PRC, he notes, "fights leprosy as aggressively as it attacks dissent. It inoculates infants with the same fervor with which it arrests its critics. Partly as a result, a baby born in Shanghai now has a longer life expectancy than a baby born in New York City."[34] This "riddle" makes it difficult to settle on a clear evaluation of the overall record of Communist rule in China today. It also makes it hard to predict the future of the Chinese Communist Party, since the regime's economic achievements could provide it with a source of legitimacy and support that may help keep the CCP in power despite its serious political shortcomings.

The CCP's tough stance on political reform is, in part, based on its desire for self-preservation. But in keeping firm control on political life while allowing the country to open up in other important ways, the Chinese Communist Party also believes it is wisely following the model of development pioneered by the newly industrializing countries (NICs) of East Asia such as South Korea, Taiwan, and Singapore.

The lesson that the CCP draws from the NICs' experiences is that only a strong government can provide the political stability and social peace required for rapid economic growth. According to this view, democracy—with its open debates about national priorities, political parties contesting for power, and interest groups squabbling over how to divide the economic pie—is a recipe for chaos, particularly in a huge and relatively poor country. Chinese leaders point out that democracy has not often been conducive to successful economic development in the Third World. In India, for example, a democratic but weak government has been unable to respond effectively to internal ethnic strife and has been thwarted by entrenched interests in its efforts to alleviate poverty.

But another of the lessons from the East Asian NICs, one that most Chinese leaders have been reluctant to acknowledge so far, is that economic development, social modernization, and global integration also create powerful pressures for political change from below and abroad. In both Taiwan and South Korea, authoritarian governments that had presided over economic miracles in the 1960s and 1970s were forced to give way to democratic forces in the 1980s and 1990s. The dynamic expansion and transformation of the Chinese economy suggest that the PRC is in the early stages of a period of growth and modernization that may eventually lead it to NIC status.

However, in terms of the extent of industrialization, per capita income, and the strength of the middle and professional classes, China's economic development is still far below the level at which democracy succeeded in Taiwan and South Korea. It is also important to remember that "authoritarian governments in East Asia pursued market-driven economic growth for decades without relaxing their hold on political power."[35] Nevertheless, economic reform in China has already created groups and processes, interests and ideas that are likely to become sources of pressure for more and faster political change; and the experience of the NICs and other developing countries suggests that such pressures are likely to intensify as the economy and society continue to modernize. Therefore, at some point in the not-too-distant future, the Chinese Communist Party may again face the challenge of the democratic idea. How China's new generation of leaders responds to this challenge is perhaps the most important and uncertain question about Chinese politics as we enter the twenty-first century.

Key Terms

Communist party-state
Marxism-Leninism
autonomous regions
Confucianism
proletariat
legitimacy
guerrilla warfare
land reform
nationalization
collectivization
socialism
Great Leap Forward
Great Proletarian
    Cultural Revolution
charisma
détente
communism
command economy
decentralization
people's communes
household responsibility
    system
township and village
    enterprises
iron rice bowl
guanxi
unitary state
dual rule
cadres
nomenklatura
socialist democracy
nongovernmental
    organizations
danwei
civil society
totalitarianism
developmental state

Suggested Readings

Baum, Richard. *Burying Mao: Chinese Politics in the Era of Deng Xiaoping*. Princeton, N.J.: Princeton University Press, 1994.

Blecher, Marc J. *China Against the Tides: Restructuring Through Revolution, Radicalism, and Reform*. London: Pinter, 1997.

Brugger, Bill, and Stephen Reglar. *Politics, Economy, and Society in Contemporary China*. Stanford, Calif.: Stanford University Press, 1994.

Calhoun, Craig. *Neither Gods Nor Emperors: Students and the Struggle for Democracy in China*. Berkeley: University of California Press, 1994.

Chang, Jung. *Wild Swans: Three Daughters of China*. New York: Simon and Schuster, 1991.

Davin, Dalia. *Mao Zedong*. Herndon, Va.: International Publishers Marketing, 1998.

Fairbank, John King, and Merle Goldman. *China: A New History*. Cambridge, Mass.: Harvard University Press, 1998.

Gao Yuan. *Born Red: A Chronicle of the Cultural Revolution*. Stanford, Calif.: Stanford University Press, 1987.

Gilley, Bruce. *Tiger on the Brink: Jiang Zemin and China's New Elite*. Berkeley: University of California Press, 1998.

Gilmartin, Christina, Gail Hershatter, Lisa Rofel, and Tyrene White, eds. *Engendering China: Women, Culture, and the State*. Cambridge, Mass.: Harvard University Press, 1994.

Goldman, Merle. *Sowing the Seeds of Democracy in China: Political Reform in the Deng Xiaoping Era*. Cambridge, Mass.: Harvard University Press, 1994.

Goodman, David S.G., and Gerald Segal, eds. *China Rising: Nationalism and Interdependence*. London: Routledge, 1997.

Harding, Harry. *China's Second Revolution: Reform after Mao*. Washington, D.C.: Brookings Institution, 1987.

Joseph, William A., ed. *China Briefing: The Contradictions of Change*. Armonk, N.Y.: M. E. Sharpe, 1997.

Kristof, Nicolas D., and Sheryl WuDunn. *China Wakes: The Struggle for the Soul of a Rising Power*. New York: Time Books, 1994.

Lieberthal, Kenneth. *Governing China: From Revolution Through Reform*. New York: Norton, 1995.

MacFarquhar, Roderick, ed. *The Politics of China, 1949–1989*. Cambridge: Cambridge University Press, 1993.

Mackerras, Colin. *China's Minorities: Integration and Modernization in the Twentieth Century*. New York: Oxford University Press, 1994.

Meisner, Maurice. *Mao's China and After: A History of the People's Republic*. 3d ed. New York: Free Press, 1999.

Nathan, Andrew J., and Robert S. Ross. *The Great Wall and the Empty Fortress: China's Search for Security*. New York: Norton, 1997.

Naughton, Barry. *Growing Out of the Plan: Chinese Economic Reform, 1978–1993*. Cambridge: Cambridge University Press, 1995.

Oi, Jean. *Rural China Takes Off: The Institutional Foundations of Economic Reform*. Berkeley: University of California Press, 1999.

Perry, Elizabeth J. *Shanghai on Strike: The Politics of Chinese Labor*. Stanford, Calif.: Stanford University Press, 1995

Schell, Orville. *Mandate of Heaven: A New Generation of Entrepreneurs, Dissidents, Bohemians, and Technocrats Lay Claim to China's Future*. New York: Simon and Schuster, 1994.

Schell, Orville, and David Shambaugh, eds. *The China Reader: The Reform Era*. New York: Vintage Books, 1999.

Shambaugh, David, ed. *Deng Xiaoping: Portrait of a Chinese Statesman*. New York: Oxford University Press, 1995.

Spence, Jonathan D., and Annping Chin. *The Chinese Century: A Photographic History of the Last Hundred Years*. New York: Random House, 1996.

Starr, John Bryan. *Understanding China: A Guide to China's Economy, History, and Political Structure*. New York: Hill and Wang, 1997.

White, Gordon. *Riding the Tiger: The Politics of Economic Reform in Post-Mao China*. Stanford, Calif.: Stanford University Press, 1993.

Zweig, David. *Freeing China's Farmers: Rural Restructuring in the Reform Era*. Armonk, NY: M. E. Sharpe, 1997.

Endnotes

[1] Wu Ming (pseud.), "I Witnessed the Beijing Massacre," cited in Timothy Brook, *Quelling the People: The Military Suppression of the Beijing Democracy Movement* (New York: Oxford University Press, 1992), 129.

[2] *New York Times*, June 28, 1998.

[3] Mao Zedong, "Report on an Investigation of the Peasant Movement in Hunan," March 1927, in *Selected Readings from the Works of Mao Tsetung* (Beijing: Foreign Languages Press, 1971), 24.

[4] Brantly Womack, "The Party and the People: Revolutionary and Post-Revolutionary Politics in China and Vietnam," *World Politics* 39, no. 4 (July 1987): 479–507.

[5] David Bachman, *Bureaucracy, Economy, and Leadership in China: The Institutional Origins of the Great Leap Forward* (Cambridge: Cambridge University Press, 1991), 2.

[6] See, for example, "When China Wakes," *The Economist*, November 28, 1992; and Nicholas D. Kristof and Sheryl WuDunn, *China Wakes: The Struggle for the Soul of a Rising Power* (New York: Time Books, 1994).

[7] "When China Wakes," *The Economist*, November 28, 1992, pp. 3, 15.

[8] Barry Naughton, "The Pattern and Legacy of Economic Growth in the Mao Era," in *Perspectives on Modern China: Four Anniversaries*, ed. Kenneth Lieberthal, et al., (Armonk, N.Y.: M. E. Sharpe, 1991), 250.

[9] Deng Xiaoping first expressed his "cat theory" in 1962 in a speech entitled "Restore Agricultural Production" in the aftermath of the failure and famine of the Great Leap Forward. In the original speech, he actually quoted an old peasant proverb that refers to a "yellow cat or a black cat," but it is most often rendered "white cat or black cat." See *Selected Works of Deng Xiaoping (1938–1965)* (Beijing: Foreign Languages Press, 1992), 293.

[10] Deng Xiaoping, "Reform Is China's Second Revolution," March 28, 1985, in *Selected Works of Deng Xiaoping (1982–1992)* (Beijing: Foreign Languages Press, 1994), 119–120.

[11] Kathleen Hartford, "Socialist Agriculture Is Dead; Long Live Socialist Agriculture! Organizational Transformation in Rural China," in *The Political Economy of Reform in Post-Mao China*, ed. Elizabeth J. Perry and Christine P. W. Wong. Harvard Contemporary China Series Vol. 2. (Cambridge, Mass.: Council on East Asian Studies, Harvard University, 1985), 55.

[12] Christine P. W. Wong, "China's Economy: The Limits of Gradualist Reform," in *China Briefing, 1994*, ed. William A. Joseph (Boulder, Colo.: Westview Press), 50.

[13] Jiang Zemin, "Hold High the Great Banner of Deng Xiaoping Theory for an All-round Advancement of the Cause of Building Socialism with Chinese Characteristics to the 21st Century," *Beijing Review*, 40, no. 40 (October 6–12, 1997): 32.

[14] Emily Honig and Gail Herschatter, *Personal Voices: Chinese Women in the 1980s* (Stanford, Calif.: Stanford University Press, 1988), 337.

[15] Baruch Boxer, "China's Environment: Issues and Economic Implications," in Joint Economic Committee of Congress, *China's Economic Dilemmas in the 1990s: The Problems of Reform, Modernization, and Interdependence*, vol. 1 (Washington, D.C.: Government Printing Office, 1991), 306–307.

[16] "Environment and Development: A World Issue," *Beijing Review* 35, no. 23 (June 8–14, 1992): 20.

[17] Mao Zedong, "Strive to Build a Great Socialist Country," September 15, 1954, in *Selected Works of Mao Tsetung*, vol. 5 (Beijing: Foreign Languages Press, 1977), 149.

[18] "Uphold the Four Cardinal Principles," March 30, 1979, in *Selected Works of Deng Xiaoping (1977–1982)*, (Beijing: Foreign Languages Press, 1984), 178.

[19] The full text of the constitution of the People's Republic of China can be found in James C. F. Wang, *Contemporary Chinese Politics: An Introduction*, 6th ed. (Upper Saddle River, N.J.: Prentice Hall, 1999), 373–398. A text of the constitution of the Chinese Communist Party can also be found in Wang, 399–424.

[20] Mao Zedong, "Problems of War and Strategy," November 6, 1938, in *Selected Works of Mao Tsetung*, vol. 2 (Beijing: Foreign Languages Press, 1972), 224.

[21] Ellis Joffe, "The Chinese Army: Coping with the Consequences of Tiananmen," in *China Briefing, 1991*, ed. William A. Joseph (Boulder, Colo.: Westview Press, 1992), 42.

[22] Kenneth Lieberthal and David Michael Lampton, eds., *Bureaucracy, Politics, and Decision-Making in Post-Mao China* (Berkeley: University of California Press, 1992).

[23] John P. Burns, *The Chinese Communist Party's Nomenklatura System: A Documentary Study of Party Control of Leadership Selection, 1979–1984* (Armonk, N.Y.: M. E. Sharpe, 1989), ix–x.

[24] Gordon White, *Riding the Tiger: The Politics of Economic Reform in Post-Mao China* (Palo Alto, Calif.: Stanford University Press, 1993), 20.

[25] Andrew J. Nathan, *Chinese Democracy* (Berkeley: University of California Press, 1985), 124.

[26] James D. Seymour, *China's Satellite Parties* (Armonk, N.Y.: M. E. Sharpe, 1987), 87.

[27] BBC Summary of World Broadcasts, December 21, 1998, FE/3415/G; a summary of Jiang's speech is reported in *New York Times*, December 19, 1998, p. A6.

[28] James R. Townsend and Brantly Womack, *Politics in China*, 3d ed. (Boston: Little, Brown, 1986), 271.

[29] The following scenes are extrapolated from Nicholas D. Kristof and Sheryl WuDunn, *China Wakes: The Struggle for the Soul of a Rising Power* (New York: Times Books, 1994); Andrew Higgens, "Corrupt Village Regains Its Glory," *The Guardian* (London), November 24, 1995, p. 15; Agence France Presse English Wire Service, "Peasants Surviving on Less than 20 Dollars a Year," China News Digest–Global (on-line service), February 19, 1994; Erik Eckholm, "Heated Protests by Its Farmers Trouble Beijing," *New York Times*, February 1, 1999, pp. A1, A12; Susan V. Lawrence, "Democracy, Chinese-Style: Village Representative Assemblies," *Australian Journal of Chinese Affairs*, no. 32 (July 1994): 61–68.

[30] Nicholas D. Kristof, "China Sees 'Market-Leninism' as Way to Future," *New York Times*, September 6, 1993, pp. 1, 5.

[31] Jude Howell, cited in Matt Forney, "Voice of the People," *Far Eastern Economic Review*, May 7, 1998, p. 10.

[32] Many of the points in this section are based on Martin King Whyte, "Prospects for Democratization in China," *Problems of Communism* (May–June 1992): 58–69; Michel Oksenberg, "Will China Democratize? Confronting a Classic Dilemma," *Journal of Democracy* 9, no. 1 (January 1998), 27–34; and Minxin Pei, "Is China Democratizing?" *Foreign Affairs* 77, no. 1 (January–February 1998), 68–82.

[33] Harry Harding, *China's Second Revolution: Reform after Mao* (Washington, D.C.: Brookings Institution, 1987), 200.

[34] Nicholas D. Kristof, "Riddle of China: Repression as Standard of Living Soars," *New York Times*, September 7, 1993, pp. A1, A10.

[35] Nicholas Lardy, "Is China Different? The Fate of Its Economic Reform," in *The Crisis of Leninism and the Decline of the Left*, ed. Daniel Chirot (Seattle: University of Washington Press, 1991), 147.

CHAPTER 12

Nigeria

Richard Joseph
Peter Lewis
Darren Kew
Scott Taylor

Federal Republic of Nigeria

Land and Population

Capital	Abuja*	
Total Area (square miles)	356,669 (more than twice the size of California)	
Population	118 million	
Annual Average Population Growth Rate (1990–1997)	2.9%	
Age Structure	under 15	45.6%
	15–29	25.7%
	30–44	15.7%
	45–59	8.5%
	60–74	3.8%
	75 and over	0.7%
Urban Population	41%	
Ethno-Linguistic Composition	Hausa-Fulani	32%
	Yoruba	21%
	Igbo	18%
	Ibibio	6%
	Various dialects	14%
	Other	8%
Official Language	English	
Religious Affiliation	Muslim	50%
	Christian	40%
	Indigenous	10%

Economy

Domestic Currency	Naira	
Total GNP (US$)	$30.7 billion	
GNP per capita (US$)	$260	
GNP per capita at purchasing power parity (US$)	$880	
GNP average annual growth rate (1996–1997)		4.2%
GNP per capita average annual growth rate	1996–1997	1.2%
	1980–1995	−0.8%
	1965–1980	4.2%
Income Gap:	Richest 20% of population	
GDP per capita (US$)	$3796	
	Poorest 20% of population	
	$308	
Structure of Production (% of GDP)	Agriculture	28%
	Industry	53%
	Services	18%
Labor Force Distribution (% of total)	Agriculture	43%
	Industry	7%
	Services	50%
Exports as % of GDP	19%	
Imports as % of GDP	44%	

Society

Life Expectancy	Female 53.0	Male 49.8
Doctors per 100,000 population		21
Infant Mortality per 1000 live births		114

*On 12 December 1991 the capital was officially moved from Lagos to Abuja; many government offices remain in Lagos pending completion of facilities in Abuja

Adult Literacy	Female	47.3%
	Male	67.3%
Access to Information and Communications (per 1000 population)	Radios	197
	Televisions	38
	Telephones	4
	Personal Computers	Data Not Available for Nigeria
Women in Government and Economy		
Seats in Parliament held by Women		N/A
Women at Ministerial level		4.0%
Women as % of total labor force		36.0%
Female Business Administrators and Managers		6.0%
Female Professional and Technical Workers		26.0%
1998 Human Development Index ranking (out of 174 countries, 1 = highest)		142

Political Organization

Political System   Military dictatorship (until May 1999)

Regime History   A military regime led by General Abdulsalami Abubakar assumed power after the death of General Sani Abacha in June 1998. This military regime is the fourth since 1983, interrupted only by the 3-month unelected civilian regime of Ernest Shonekan in 1993.

Administrative Structure   Power has been centralized within the military governing body and the Provisional Ruling Council (PRC). However, a system of 36 federal states, plus the Federal Capital Territory (FCT) in Abuja, also exists. Since May 1999, the presidential system resembles that of the U.S.

Executive   Retired General Olusegun Obasanjo was elected president in February 1999 and began a four-year term in May 1999.

Legislature   A bicameral civilian legislature was elected in February 1999. The 109 senators were elected on the basis of equal representation: three from each state, and one from the FCT. The 360 members of the House of Representatives were elected from single-member districts.

Judiciary   The Nigerian judicial system resembles that of the U.S. with a network of local and district courts as well as state-level courts. The state-level judiciaries are subordinate to the Federal Court of Appeal and the Supreme Court of Nigeria, which consists of 15 appointed associate justices and the chief justice. Every state of the federation can also opt to establish a system of Islamic law (shari'a) courts for cases involving only Muslims in customary disputes (divorce, property, etc.); the secular courts, however, retain supreme jurisdiction at the federal level if any conflict arises over which system to use. Most Nigerian states feature such courts, which share a Federal Shari'a Court of Appeal in Abuja. All levels of the judiciary have been subject to manipulation and corruption by the military regimes.

Party System   Three parties were registered by the Nigerian electoral commission in December 1998: the Alliance for Democracy (AD), All People's Party (APP), and People's Democratic Party (PDP). PDP won the presidency, majorities in both houses of the National Assembly, and control of many of the governorships, state assemblies, and local governments.

Section ❶ The Making of the Modern Nigerian State

Politics in Action

On June 7, 1998, General Sani Abacha, Nigeria's most brutal and corrupt dictator, was poised to have himself declared president. He had orchestrated a three-year sham transition program to mask his own plans to remain in power. In the process, he stalled the economy and stole billions of dollars in oil revenue; murdered, imprisoned, or drove his opponents into exile; and made Nigeria an international pariah.

Then, on June 8, 1998, he suddenly died.

Many southern Nigerians filled the streets of Lagos and other cities to celebrate—until the military announced that another northerner, General Abubakar, was taking charge. Many northerners expressed quiet relief at Abacha's passing but feared a possible backlash from a southern military leader—until Abubakar was sworn in. Although Nigeria has developed well beyond the point in the 1950s when its leaders saw it as a mere geographic expression, the development of national consciousness and character has often progressed *in spite of* the nation's political direction. Many Nigerians intermarry across ethnic and religious lines, share common traditions like chewing kola nuts with friends, work—often their whole lives—and invest in cities outside their ethnic homelands, and unite in support of their national sports teams. Yet when talk turns to politics, southern Nigerians will complain of northern domination of the government, Igbos will claim that Yorubas cannot be trusted for their "betrayal" of Biafra during the civil war, Christians will complain that Muslims want an Islamic fundamentalist state, and so on. Forces of both integration and dissolution are evident throughout the country's independent history, with one or the other being most prevalent at any moment.

Nigeria offers, within a single case, characteristics that identify Africa. These opposing forces are rooted in the constant struggle in Nigeria between **authoritarian** and democratic governance, the push for development and the persistence of underdevelopment, the burden of public corruption and the pressure for accountability. Nigeria, like all African countries, has sought to create a viable nation-state out of the social incoherence created by the borders imposed during the colonial era. Over two hundred and fifty competing nationalities—or ethnic groups, largely defined by language differences—in Nigeria have repeatedly clashed over economic and political resources. All these factors combine to produce the political entity known as Nigeria with a very low level of popular **legitimacy** and **accountability** and an increasing inability to meet the most basic needs of its citizens. The country therefore provides a crucible in which to examine questions of democracy and authoritarianism, the pressures and management of ethnic conflict, and economic underdevelopment brought about both by colonial oppression and independent Nigeria's mismanagement of its vast resources.

Much about Nigeria is controversial. Since gaining independence from British colonial rule in 1960, Nigeria has undergone several political transitions, from democratic governments to autocratic regimes, both military and civilian, and from one military regime to another. After nearly four decades as an independent nation, Nigeria has yet to witness an orderly and constitutional transition from one democratic regime to another. It has experienced six successful coups (most recently in November 1993) and many unsuccessful attempted coups, and it was torn by three years of civil war that claimed over one hundred thousand military, and over a million civilian, casualties. Against this background, Nigeria today remains essentially an **unfinished state** characterized by instabilities and uncertainties.

Another critical turning point was reached in 1999 as a military government transferred power to civilians for the third time. Whether the country is moving toward an increasingly authoritarian future and greater underdevelopment, or toward the achievement of democracy and sustainable growth, remains unresolved.

The saying, "As Nigeria goes, so goes the rest of sub-Saharan Africa" may again be relevant. With a population of 110 million, Nigeria is by far the largest country in Africa and among the ten most populous countries in the world. About one out of every five

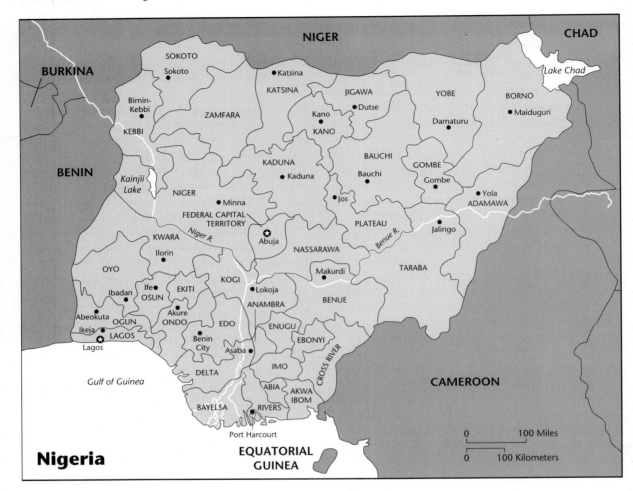

Nigeria

black Africans is a Nigerian. Unlike most other countries on the continent, Nigeria has the human and material resources to overcome the vicious cycle of poverty and **autocracy**. Hopes for this breakthrough for four decades of independent rule have been regularly frustrated, however. If Nigeria, with its vast resources, cannot succeed in breaking this cycle, what does that mean for the rest of sub-Saharan Africa?

Geographic Setting

Nigeria's 110 million people, inhabiting 356,668 square miles, live in the most populous nation in Africa. A center of West African regional trade, culture, and military strength, Nigeria is bordered by four countries: Benin, Niger, Chad, and Cameroon, and by the Gulf of Guinea in the Atlantic Ocean to the south. The modern-day country of Nigeria, however, like nearly all the contemporary states in Africa, is not even a century old.

Nigeria was a British colony from 1914 until its independence on October 1, 1960, although foreign domination of much of the territory had actually begun in the mid-nineteenth century. Britain first ruled northern and southern Nigeria as two separate colonies. Nigeria's identity took its final geographic form (at least in terms of its *external* borders) in 1914 following Britain's amalgamation of its Northern and Southern Protectorates.

Nigeria's location in West Africa, its size, and its oil-producing status have made it a hub of regional activity. In terms of demography and political economy, Nigeria overwhelms the other fifteen countries in West Africa, with a population equivalent to 57 percent of the region's total. Moreover, Nigeria's GNP typically represents more than two-thirds of the total GNP for the entire subregion. Not surprisingly, therefore, Nigeria has been a recipient of migrant labor from the region, and has engaged in recent years in peacekeeping missions, which has involved armed intervention in countries such as Liberia and Sierra Leone. However, Nigerian instability and the succession of military governments have also been a source of instability and uncertainty in the wider region.

Nigeria's ethnic map can be divided into six inexact areas or zones. The northwest (or "core North") is dominated by Nigeria's largest ethnic group, the Hausa-Fulani, two formerly separate groups that over the past century have largely merged. The northeast has minority groups, the largest of which is the Kanuri. Both regions in the north are predominantly Muslim. A large swath of territory stretching across the center of the country, called the Middle Belt, is also home to a wide range of minority groups of both Muslim and Christian identification. The southwest (referred to as the Western Region in the First Republic) is dominated by the country's second largest ethnic group, the Yoruba, who are approximately 40 percent Muslim, 40 percent Christian (primarily Protestant), and 20 percent practitioners of Yoruba indigenous beliefs. The southeast (which formed the hub of the First Republic's Eastern Region) is the homeland of the Igbo, Nigeria's third largest group, who are primarily Roman Catholic, although Protestant evangelical movements have recently been popular. Between the Yoruba and the Igbo regions of the south is the southern minority zone, which stretches across the Niger Delta areas and east along the coast as far as Cameroon.

Critical Junctures

A number of critical junctures helped shape the character of the Nigerian state, and illustrate the difficult path that the country has taken during the past century. This path features influences from the precolonial period, British colonialism, the alternation of military and civilian rule after independence, and the post-1980 economic collapse, precipitated by Nigeria's political corruption and overreliance on its petroleum industry.

The Precolonial Period (800–1860)

State Formation   Much of Nigeria's precolonial history before A.D. 1000 was reconstructed from oral histories because, with few exceptions, a literate culture evolved much later. In contrast to the peoples of the forest belt to the south, the more open terrain in the north, with its need for irrigation, encouraged the early growth of centralized states. Such states from the eighth century included Kanem-Bornu in the northeast and the Hausa states in the west. The more prominent Hausa states that included walled cities were Kano, Katsina, Zazzau (also called Zaria), Rano, Daura, Gobir, and Biram. Still another attempt at state formation led to the emergence of Jukun kingdom; however, by the end of the seventeenth century, the Jukun became a tributary state of the Bornu empire.

A major element that shaped the course of events in the savanna areas of the north was trade across the Sahara Desert with northern Africa. Trade brought material benefits as well as Arabic education and Islam, which gradually replaced traditional, spiritual, political, and social practices in what is now northern Nigeria. In 1808 the Fulani, who came from lands west of modern Nigeria through holy war (**jihad**), established an Islamic empire, the Sokoto Caliphate. Portions of the region to the south, the Middle Belt, were able to repel the jihad and preserve their independence and religious diversity. The Sokoto Caliphate used Islam and a common language, Hausa, to forge unity out of the disparate groups in the north. The Fulani empire held sway until British colonial authority was imposed on northern Nigeria by 1900.

Toward the southern edge of the savanna lived such groups as the Tiv, whose political organizations seldom extended beyond the village level. Within such societies, politics was generally conducted along lineage and kinship lines. Political authority was diffused rather than centralized. Considering their loose political structures, it is not surprising that they were later described by Western contacts as "stateless societies." Under colonialism, these societies escaped

Critical Junctures in Modern Nigeria's Political Development

1960	Independence. Nigeria consists of three regions under a Westminster parliamentary model. **Abubakar Tafawa Balewa**, a northerner, is the first prime minister.
January 1966	Civilian government deposed in coup. **General Aguiyi Ironsi**, an Igbo, becomes head of state.
July 1966	Countercoup led by **General Yakubu Gowon**, an Anga from the Middle Belt, with aid from northern groups.
1967–1970	Biafran civil war.
July 1975	Military coup deposes Gowon; led by **General Murtala Muhammed**, a northerner.
February 1976	Murtala Muhammed assassinated in failed coup led by Middle Belt minorities. Muhammed's second-in-command, **General Olusegun Obasanjo**, a Yoruba, assumes power.
September 1978	New constitution completed, marking the adoption of the U.S. presidential model in a federation with 19 states.
October 1979	Elections held. A majority in both houses is won by NPN, led by Northern/Hausa-Fulani groups. **Alhaji Shehu Shagari** is elected Nigeria's first executive president.
December 1983	Military coup led by **General Muhammadu Buhari**, a northerner.
August 1985	Buhari is overthrown by **General Ibrahim B. Babangida**, a Middle-Belt Muslim, in a palace coup. Babangida promises a return to democracy by 1990, a date he delays five times before being forced from office.
June 12, 1993	**Moshood Abiola** wins presidential elections, but Babangida annuls the election 11 days later.
August 1993	Babangida installs **Ernest Shonekan** as "interim civilian president" until new presidential elections could be held later that autumn.
November 1993	Defense Minister **General Sani Abacha** seizes power in a coup.
July–Sept. 1994	Pro-democracy strike by the major oil union, NUPENG, cuts Nigeria's oil production by an estimated 25 percent. Sympathy strikes ensue, followed by arrests of political and civic leaders.
October 1995	General Abacha announces a three-year transition to civilian rule.
November 1995	Ogoni-rights activists Ken Saro-Wiwa and eight others hung. Nigeria is suspended from the Commonwealth.
June 1998	General Abacha dies; succeeded by **General Abdulsalami Abubakar**, a Middle-Belt Muslim from Babangida's hometown.
July–August 1998	Abubakar releases nearly all political prisoners and installs a new transition program. Parties are allowed to form unhindered.
February 1999	Former head of state **Olusegun Obasanjo** and his party, the PDP, sweep the Presidential and National Assembly elections, adding to their majority control of state and local government seats.
May 1999	Obasanjo sworn in as president; the federation now contains 36 states.

much of the upheaval experienced by the centralized states and retained much of their autonomy.

The development of collective identities was equally complex in what is today southern Nigeria. Groups included the highly centralized empires and kingdoms of Oyo and Ife (now identified with the Yoruba), Benin to the west, the fragmentary, **acephalous societies** to the east (now identified with the Igbo), and the trading city-states of the Niger Delta and its hinterland.

Precolonial Polities and Societies. *Source:* K. Michael Barbour, Julius Oguntoyinbo, J.O.C. Onyemelukwe, and James C. Nwafor, *Nigeria in Maps* (New York: Africana Publishing Company, 1982), 37.

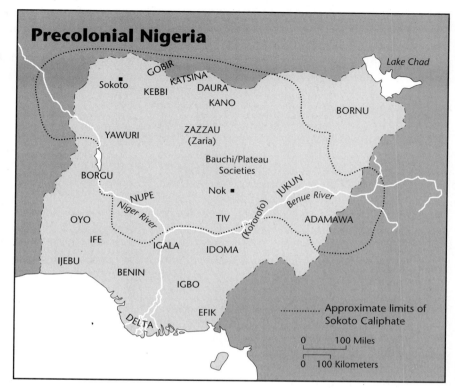

Contact with Europeans along the coast and the hinterland generated social conflicts and tensions, and provoked the subsequent loss of autonomy for these polities. External factors led to the eventual disintegration of the Oyo empire in the early nineteenth century through attacks from the Dahomey kingdom to the west (now in the neighboring country of Benin) and Islamic jihadists from the Fulani empire to the north.

The Emergence of the Democratic Idea   Several precolonial societies had democratic elements that scholars speculate might have led to more open and participatory polities had they not been stymied by colonialism. Among the Yoruba and Igbo communities, in particular, an important feature of governance was the doctrine of *accountability*: rulers could not disregard the views and interests of the governed or they would risk revocation of that consent and loss of their positions. Another element was *representation*, defined less in terms of procedures for selecting leaders than in terms of the representativeness of those who

governed, to ensure that the ruler and ruled adhered to culturally mandated principles and obligations.

Among the shared traits of many precolonial African societies were tales of origin that traced their political communities to a particular god, heaven, or mythical ancestor. The pervasive role of religion in the theory and practice of governance ensured that the use of social power was legitimized by divine and supernatural forces. Thus, many precolonial African political systems were theocratic and absolutist in their demand for loyalty, yet these theocratic elements provided important limits to the exercise of power. These limits were further strengthened by additional social structures such as councils of chiefs, secret societies, warrior bands, and age-grade associations. "Use-of-power" contracts in which the people could invoke ancestral spirits against a ruler who had abused his authority were not uncommon in precolonial societies. Moreover, the rights of both the ruler and the ruled were defined in communal rather than personal terms. The survival of the individual and the ruler therefore depended on the survival of the community. Not surprisingly, crimes against society often received more severe punishment than crimes against the individual.

Modes of participation in decision-making in precolonial societies also reflected aspects of the democratic idea. For example, popular discussions preceded public policy decisions in the acephalous societies of the Middle Belt as well as among the Igbos in the east. The age-based system of rule often meant that popular discussions occurred in councils of elders and similar institutions, thereby conferring on older persons greater powers to influence decisions. The southern empires and kingdoms featured what was essentially a constitutional monarch whose authority depended on the council of chiefs, the deities, and various corporate bodies that could articulate public views.

Among the Islamic communities of the north, political society was highly structured in line with Islamic principles established in the Qur'an. Leadership structures were considerably more hierarchical than those of the south, dominated by a few educated elites in positions of authority. In addition, although some of the pre-Islamic indigenous beliefs showed deference to important women spirit leaders, women were consigned to a subordinate position in systems of governance. The Islamic Fulani empire was a confederation in which the rulers, **emirs**, owed allegiance to the sultan, who was the temporal and spiritual head of the empire. The sultan's powers, in turn, were circumscribed by the obligation to observe the principles of Islam in fulfilling his duties.

Colonial Rule and Its Impact (1860–1960)

Competition for trade and empire drove the European imperial powers into Africa after 1860. During the colonial period Nigeria's resources were extracted, and its people exploited as cheap labor, to further the growth of British society and defray administrative costs of the British Empire. Colonialism left its imprint on all aspects of Nigeria's existence, bequeathing a British political system that was inappropriate in many respects.

Where centralized monarchies existed, particularly in the north, the British ruled indirectly, allowing traditional structures to persist subsidiary to the British governor and a small administrative apparatus.

Where more nearly democratic societies existed, particularly in the Igbo east, the colonialists strengthened the authority of traditional chiefs and kings and appointed **warrant chiefs**, weakening the rulers' accountability to the ruled and restricting or barring indigenous popular participation. Colonial regimes used these policies across Africa, upsetting older traditions that had checked the powers of rulers in many precolonial African polities.

By empowering certain individuals and groups and weakening others, the British left a heritage of harsh authoritarian domination that persists today. They instilled the idea that there were two sets of rules: one for political leaders and another for the citizenry. This dual standard left a conflicted democratic idea: formal democratic institutions dependent upon an authoritarian political culture. Colonialism also contributed to strengthening the collective identities of Nigeria's multiple ethnic groups by fostering competition among them, primarily among the three largest: the Hausa-Fulani, the Yoruba, and the Igbo.

Foundations of Nigeria's Political Economy The colonial experience helped shape the character of the Nigerian state in relation to the international capitalist system. Nigeria first entered the modern international economy as a colonial territory and had to operate within terms designed by more dominant and experienced members of the international system. Nigeria has since found it difficult to overcome its colonial political economy, structured by the British to export primary products.

Moreover, the concept of the state introduced into the colony was a set of administrative, legal, and coercive systems whose overriding purpose was to restructure relationships within and between civil society and public authority in order to subordinate the local economy to European capitalism. The Nigerian colonial state was conceived and fashioned as **interventionist**, in which the state intrudes into the major sectors of the economy and society. It was unhindered in the pursuit of its economic objectives, in contrast to the British state, where political freedoms and market capitalism limited state action.

The principal goals of the colonial enterprise were to maintain tight control over the Nigerian economy and the flow of resources from the colonies to Britain.

Of secondary concern was the creation of an economic environment driven by free markets and private enterprise. Nigeria's interventionist state went deep into the management of the economy, tightly controlling and frequently establishing significant ownership positions in areas as diverse as agriculture, banking, commerce, manufacturing, transportation, mining, education, health, and employment. The problems caused by such massive state intervention in Nigeria have continued to plague it since the pattern was first established in the colonial era.

Impact of Colonialism on Democratic Ideas
Colonialism introduced a cultural dualism—a clash of customs, values, and political systems—between the traditions of precolonial society and the dictates of the West. Traditional cultural traits, which had ensured accountability in society, were partly replaced with the ideas of individualism. The religious beliefs of traditional society, particularly as they pertained to governance and accountability, were also altered by colonialism and its Christian god, who was not directly concerned with issues of daily governance as were the deities of traditional beliefs. The marginalization of traditional norms and rulers early in the colonial regime caused a weakening of the indigenous basis for the accountability of rulers and the social responsibility of the governed as well as of age-old checks on abuse of office.

Colonial rule left Nigeria with the machinery of parliamentary democracy following the Westminster model but socialized the local population to be passive subjects rather than responsive participants. Even as colonial rule sought to implant democracy in principle, in practice it was a form of military rule that bequeathed an authoritarian legacy to independent Nigeria.

This dualism led to the development of two public realms to which individuals belonged: the communal realm, in which people are identified by ethnic or subethnic groups (Igbo, Tiv, Yoruba, etc.) and the civic realm under the colonial administration and its imposed institutions, in which citizenship was universal.[1] Both realms fed on each other, though the communal realm was often stronger in certain respects than the civic realm. For the populace, questions as to how one's citizenship is defined and to which group

one owes primary loyalty are unresolved. For those in government, questions persist about whose interests should be served at any given time, the national or the parochial? Because they saw the advent of the colonial civic realm and the colonial state as an alien, exploitative force, Nigerians tend to view its postcolonial successor as the realm from which rights must be extracted and from which duties and taxes must be withheld (see Section 4).

As colonial powers did elsewhere in Africa, Britain had to build a support system of Nigerians to incorporate into the management structure of the colony in order to limit the drain on the empire's overtaxed resources. These individuals were carefully selected from the traditional elite and rulers who were willing to work with the colonial government under a system of governance known as **indirect rule**. An indigenous bureaucracy was trained primarily in the south, where Christianity and Western education penetrated. In the north, where more developed, hierarchical political structures were already present and the British had significantly less penetration, they utilized indigenous structures and left intact the emirate authorities and Islamic institutions of the region.

Colonialism thus had profoundly different effects on the northern and southern regions. The south experienced both the benefits and burdens of colonial occupation. The proximity of Lagos, Calabar, and their regions to the Atlantic Ocean made them important hubs for trade and shipping activity, around which the British built the necessary infrastructure—schools, roads, ports, and the like—and a large African civil service in order to facilitate colonialism. Northern Nigeria, which was administered with less direct contact from British personnel, received few of these benefits. The north was remote from the shipping capitals of the south and possessed fewer resources of interest to the colonialists. Moreover, indirect rule largely preserved the north's traditional administration. A pattern of uneven development resulted, with the south enjoying the basis for a modern economy and exposure to democratic institutions, and the north remaining largely agricultural and monarchical. These disparities between northern and southern Nigeria would haunt the country well after independence.

Nigeria in 1955: Divided into Three Federated Regions. The administrative division of Nigeria into three regions later became the basis for ethnoregional conflicts. (Note: At the time of independence, the southeastern part of the country, which had been governed as a trust territory, opted to become part of independent Cameroon; two northern trust territories opted to become part of independent Nigeria.) *Source:* K. Michael Barbour, Julius Oguntoyinbo, J.O.C. Onyemelukwe, and James C. Nwafor, *Nigeria in Maps* (New York: Africana Publishing Company, 1982), 39.

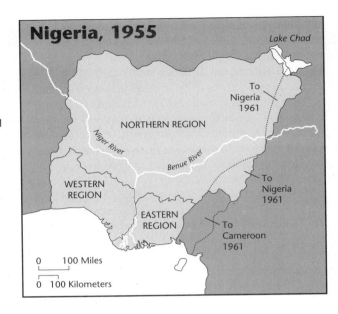

Ethnic Politics under Colonialism   Based on the British example, leaders of the anticolonial movement came to regard control of the state as a means to pursue personal and group interests rather than collective, national interests. Thus the three largest ethnic groups—Hausa-Fulani, Igbo, and Yoruba, which together compose approximately 65 percent of Nigeria's population—have dominated the political process since the British began to prepare Nigeria for independence in the 1940s. Ironically, these group identities did not exist in their contemporary forms in the precolonial era and were clearly delineated only in the context of colonial rule to manage the colony and establish administrative areas. Further, if the indigenous groups were pitted against one another, no unified threat of opposition to British authority would emerge. By providing resources to some groups, such as missionary education and lower-level civil service jobs, while depriving other groups, an environment of envy and mistrust was fostered.

Reinforced by colonial authorities and championed by local educated elites, Nigerian ethnic groups began to propound tales of origin that provided the bases for wider self-definition and a more exclusivist identity and heritage. Indigenous elites were able to rally followers based on notions of common identity. The self-declared representatives for these groups mobilized popular support, then constantly lobbied and challenged the colonial administration. Extensive attempts were made to develop standardized and written forms of the languages and histories of these groups where few had existed previously.

The early ethnic-based associations were initially concerned with nonpolitical issues: promoting mutual aid for housing and education as well as sponsoring cultural events. With the encouragement of ambitious leaders, however, these groups took on a more political character. As the prospects for independence increased, indigenous elites began to divide along ethnic lines because the appeal to ethnic identities was an effective means of mobilizing support. Pan-ethnic cultural groups formed and subsequently served as the nuclei for two of the parties that succeeded the colonial regime after independence, namely, the Northern People's Congress, or NPC, in the north, and the Action Group, or AG, in the west. In the case of the National Council of Nigeria and the Cameroons (NCNC) in the east, the Igbo State Union took over effective control of the party.

As independence approached, the British began to make provisions to bring Nigerians into the administration of the country, and Nigeria became a federation of three regions in 1954. Each of the federated units soon fell under the domination of one ethnic group and one party. The Northern Region came under the control of the NPC, associated with and dominated by Hausa-Fulani elites. In the southern half of the country, the Western Region was controlled by the AG, which was controlled by the elites of the Yoruba group. The Igbo, the numerically dominant group in the Eastern Region, were closely associated with the NCNC, which became the ruling party there. Thus the distinctive and often divisive ethnic and regional characteristics of modern Nigeria were reinforced during the transition to independence.

In a celebrated statement made in 1947, one of the first generation of Nigerian political leaders, Chief Obafemi Awolowo of the Action Group, argued that "Nigeria is not a nation. It is a mere geographical expression. There are no 'Nigerians' in the same sense as there are 'English,' 'Welsh,' or 'French.' The word 'Nigerian' is merely a distinctive appellation to distinguish those who live within the boundaries of Nigeria from those who do not."[2] Influential leaders like Awolowo helped entrench the belief that Nigeria was a mere "geographical expression" and made the task of governing an independent Nigeria as a unified nation all the more difficult.

The First Republic (1960–1966)

The British handed over Nigeria in 1960 to a civilian parliamentary government. Nigerians adopted the British Westminster model at the federal and regional levels, in which the chief executive—the prime minister—was chosen by the majority party. Northerners came to dominate the federal government by virtue of their greater population, based on the 1952–1953 census. The ruling coalition for the first two years, ostensibly an alliance between the predominantly Igbo NCNC and the Hausa-Fulani-dominated NPC, quickly turned into a northern-only coalition when the NPC achieved an outright majority in the legislature. Having benefited less from the positive economic, educational, and infrastructural aspects of colonialism, the northerners who dominated the First Republic set out to redistribute resources in their own direction. This NPC policy of "northernization" brought them into direct conflict with their southern counterparts, particularly the Yoruba-based Action Group and later with the Igbo-dominated NCNC as well.

When an AG internal conflict led to a political crisis in the Western regional assembly in 1962, the NPC-led national government seized the opportunity to declare a state of emergency in the West. The NPC government used the pretext of the crisis to marginalize AG's leader, Chief Awolowo, eventually trying and convicting him on questionable charges of treason, for which he served a prison sentence from 1962 to 1966. By most accounts, Awolowo's trial and subsequent detention were based more on the desire to silence a political rival than on legal procedures, for which the NPC, with support from the NCNC and an anti-Awolowo faction of the AG, showed little regard. This early lack of respect for the rule of law set a significant precedent for Nigerian politics.

The NPC-led national government was now in a position to subdivide the Western (largely Yoruba) Region into West and Midwest, diluting Yoruba political power. Violence escalated among the Yoruba factions in the West as the NPC-dominated government engaged in other acts of political corruption. A fraudulent census, falsified ballots, and violence against and intimidation of supporters and candidates alike assured the NPC a tarnished victory in 1965.

Rivalries intensified as the NPC sat atop an absolute majority in the federal parliament with no need for its former coalition partner, the NCNC. NCNC leader Nnamdi Azikiwe, who was also president in the First Republic (then a largely symbolic position), and Tafawa Balewa, the NPC prime minister, separately approached the military to ensure that, if it came to conflict, they could count on its loyalty. Thus, "in the struggle for personal survival both men, perhaps inadvertently, made the armed forces aware that they had a political role to play."[3]

Civil War and Military Rule (1966–1979)

Essentially offered by the civilian leaders a chance to settle the political struggle, a group of largely Igbo officers instead seized power in January 1966. Aguiyi Ironsi, also an Igbo, became head of state by dint of being the highest ranking officer rather than a coup plotter. His announced aim was to end violence in the Western Region and to stop political corruption and abuses by the northern-dominated government by centralizing the state apparatus, replacing the federation with a unitary state. Although Ironsi claimed to be multiethnic in his perspective, other Nigerians, particularly northerners, were deeply suspicious of his revocation of federalism and the fact that several northerners were killed in the coup, including Tafawa Balewa and the premier of the Northern Region, Ahmadu Bello. Countercoup plotting began almost immediately. A second coup in July 1966 killed General Ironsi and brought Yakubu Gowon, a Middle Belt Christian, to power as a consensus head of state among the non-Igbo coup plotters.

Because many northern officials had been killed in the initial coup, a tremendous backlash against Igbos throughout Nigeria flared throughout 1966, even after the second coup. Igbo migrant laborers were persecuted in the north, and many fled to their "home" region in the east. By 1967 the predominantly Igbo population of eastern Nigeria attempted to secede and form its own independent nation, called Biafra. The secessionists wanted to break free from Nigeria, believing that the north, by virtue of its greater numbers, would permanently lock the other regions out of power. Moreover, since the northern region was less developed economically and educationally than the East and West, many Igbos feared that the country's progress would continue to be hampered by northern dominance of the federal government. General Gowon built a military-led government of national unity in what remained of Nigeria (the North and West), and after a bloody three-year war of attrition and starvation tactics defeated Biafra by January 1970. The conflict exacted a heavy toll on Nigeria's populace, including an estimated 2 million deaths.

After the war, Gowon presided over national reconciliation with the mostly Igbo separatists, which proceeded fairly smoothly with the aid of growing oil revenues. He also oversaw an increase in the armed forces from about 10,000 men in 1966 to nearly 250,000. Senior officers reaped the benefits of the global oil boom in 1973–1974, and corruption was widespread. Influenced by the unwillingness of the military elite to relinquish power and the spoils of office, Gowon opted to postpone a return to civilian rule, which he had pledged originally to complete by 1976. He was overthrown in 1975 by Murtala Muhammed, who promptly reactivated the transition program.

General Olusegun Obasanjo was the Nigerian head of state who supervised the transition to civilian rule from 1976 to 1979. In 1995 he was arrested and convicted in a secret trial in connection with an alleged attempt to overthrow the regime of General Abacha. After his release, he won the presidency in 1999 as a candidate for the PDP. *Source:* Reuters/Bettmann.

Through its extensive and unrestrained use of the coup d'état, the highly politicized Nigerian military has often justified its takeover and stay in power as a corrective for civilian government corruption. Following the first coup in 1966, the centralized planning of the civil war economy, and federal control of petroleum revenues after the war, the central government became much more powerful than the states. Thus, access to and control of this source of wealth and power spurred even greater corruption in the unaccountable military than among their civilian predecessors. Murtala Muhammed claimed a commitment to the restoration of democracy, but he was assassinated in 1976. General Olusegun Obasanjo, Muhammed's second-in-command who took power after the assassination, peacefully ceded power to an elected civilian government in 1979. After his detention from 1995 to 1998 for allegedly plotting a coup against General Abacha, Obasanjo once again became central in Nigerian politics as victor of the 1999 presidential elections.

The Second and Third Republics, and Military Rule (1979 to the Present)

The president of the Second Republic, Alhaji Shehu Shagari, and his ruling National Party of Nigeria, NPN (the northern successor party to the First Republic's NPC), did little to assuage the mistrust between the various parts of the federation. Shagari's government was perceived as a defender of northern interests, and it failed to stem the increase in bribery, smuggling, and the diversion of government proceeds from petroleum production. The most flagrant acts of corruption in the Second Republic, however, were the methods employed by the NPN to "win" its 1983 reelection bid. Voter registration was falsified, names were added to the register in some constituencies and mysteriously deleted in the south. During the election itself, massive fraud was committed on ballots and in polling stations. When it was over, the NPN had won an implausible thirteen of (then) nineteen state governorships and overwhelming majorities in the House and Senate elections. In a multiple-candidate race, Shagari won reelection with an equally implausible 47 percent of the vote. Led by Major General Muhammadu Buhari, the military seized power just a few months later, in December 1983.

When General Buhari refused to pledge a rapid return to civilian rule, his popular support wavered, and in August 1985 General Ibrahim Babangida seized power. Although Babangida announced a program of transition to democratic rule as one of his first acts as the new head of state, he and his colleagues engaged in an elaborate set of stalling techniques in order to extend their tenure in office. What promised to be the dawn of a Third Republic ended in betrayal

when Babangida annulled the presidential election of June 12, 1993, which should have preceded a full withdrawal of the military from the political scene. In stark contrast to all prior elections since independence, the 1993 election was widely acclaimed as free and fair, apparently won by a southern businessman, Chief Moshood Abiola. The annulment provoked an angry reaction from a population weary of postponed transitions, military rule, and deception. Babangida could not withstand the pressure to resign, but he did manage to handpick his successor, Ernest Shonekan, and a civilian caretaker government.

Following the pattern set by his predecessors, General Sani Abacha seized power in November 1993 from Shonekan. Abacha, who had held top military positions in both the Buhari and Babangida regimes, seized the reins of power from the ineffectual Shonekan. Shonekan's government, never regarded as legitimate after Babangida installed it in August 1993, was vulnerable to increasing agitation from both civilian and military ranks. As head of state, General Abacha prolonged the now established tradition of military dominance and combined increased repression with frequent public commitments to restore constitutional democracy. Like Babangida, Abacha announced a new program of transition to civilian rule and regularly delayed the steps in its implementation. Only Abacha's sudden death in June 1998 saved the country from certain crisis, as his scheme to orchestrate the outcome of the transition to produce his own "election" as president became clearer. General Abdulsalami Abubakar, Abacha's successor, in his first broadcast to the nation, announced his intention to return power to civilians. Within two months, Abubakar had established a new transition program with a prompt handover promised in May 1999 to its election victors, Obasanjo and the People's Democratic Party. Nigeria's penchant for such transitions is discussed in Section 4.

Themes and Implications

Historical Junctures and Political Themes

Nigeria's adoption of a federal arrangement has been a strategy to ensure unity in diversity by building a coherent nation-state out of over two hundred

General Sani Abacha, a prominent member of Nigerian military regimes since December 1983, took over the government in November 1993, disbanded all elective institutions, and suppressed opposition forces. His death in June 1998 was celebrated in the streets; he and his close supporters looted billions of U.S. dollars from the nation's coffers. *Source:* AP/Wide World Photos.

and fifty different nationalities and blending the precolonial, traditional democratic values with modern accountable government. In reality, however, and as a consequence of many years of colonial and military rule, a *unitary* system has emerged in a federal guise; it is a system with an all-powerful center surrounded by weak and economically insolvent states.

Another consequence of military rule, whose roots must be traced to the colonial era, is the relative overdevelopment of the executive arm at all levels of government—federal, state, and local—at the expense of weak legislative and judicial institutions. Executive superiority, a key feature of the colonial era, has been strengthened by each period of military rule. This unchecked executive power has encouraged a web of patron-client networks that sap the economy of vitality, prevent accountability, and undermine the rule of law.

The dominance of the executive has also ensured that the vitality of institutions and processes crucial to a democratic system—elections, electoral institutions, an independent judiciary, and a free press— is in constant jeopardy. The result: a spate of electoral failures and cycles of civil and political instability culminating in periodic military coups.

Nigeria in the World of States: Oil Dependence and Decline Although Nigeria enjoys economic and military power within the West African region, on a global level Nigeria has become increasingly marginalized. Resource-rich, Nigeria has long been regarded as a potential political and economic giant of Africa. Yet the World Bank lists Nigeria among the poorest 20 percent of the countries of the world, with a GDP per capita of just US$269. Instead of independent growth, today Nigeria depends on dwindling oil revenues, sparse external loans, and aid, a victim of its leaders' bad policies and poor management. Owing to underinvestment in and neglect of agriculture, in the mid-1960s Nigeria moved from self-sufficiency in the production of basic foodstuffs to heavy dependence on imports of those goods less than twenty years later. Nigeria's total reliance on oil as a source of foreign earnings has made it vulnerable to price fluctuations in that market.

Nigerian politicians are infamous for their corruption. In order to win elections, they incur great debts to pay off supporters, so once in office they seek a return on their campaign "investments." With the constant danger of a military coup looming, they also seek to enrich themselves while their time in office remains. *Source: The Guardian* (Lagos), August 28, 1998.

Nigeria is increasingly vulnerable and weakened within the world of states. The inclusion of Nigeria on the U.S. government's list of countries making insufficient efforts to combat the illegal drug trade, and the fact that Nigeria is a way station for international drug trafficking to the United States, has intensified its isolation. Nigerian sponsorship of international commercial fraud has also gravely harmed its reputation. Until the arrival of the Abubakar regime in June 1998, Nigeria was a prominent target of international action to curb widespread human rights abuses.

Nigeria's Fragile "Collective" Identity   Given the potential explosiveness of ethnic conflict, efforts by both the Babangida and Abacha regimes to manipulate ethnoregional fears and to set different sections of the country against one another as part of their survival strategies have had tragic consequences. Thus, almost three decades after the Biafran civil war, Nigeria often seems as divided as it was in the prelude to that conflict. Fears of another civil war rose during the mid-1990s.

Nigeria's experience with alternating forms of government indicates that **clientelism**, corruption, and authoritarian governing structures hinder economic potential. Clientelism is the practice by which a particular group receives disproportionate policy benefits or political favors from a political patron, usually at the expense of the larger society. In Nigeria patrons are often linked to clients by ethnic, religious, or other cultural ties, and these ties have generally benefited only a small elite. Clientelism tends to undermine social trust and political stability, which are necessary conditions for economic growth.

Ruling elites, whether military or civilian, have used state power to redistribute wealth in their own favor rather than for the creation of new wealth and investment in productive assets that would benefit the country as a whole. The abuse of state power through corrupt and clientelist actions has perverted federalism into a means to distribute "the national cake" to explicitly ethnic clients rather than using federalism to mitigate conflict. The ethnic basis of political power, compounded by corruption, is inherently unstable, often opening the door for a military seizure of power. The politicization of the military leaves regimes vulnerable to countercoups from within their own ranks; thus the alternation of Nigerian governments continues to be a threat.

Implications for Comparative Politics

Nigeria remains the oldest surviving federation in Africa. At a time when other federations are dissolving, whether peacefully as in the former Czechoslovakia or violently as in the former Yugoslavia, Nigeria manages to maintain its fragile unity. That unity has come under increasing stress, and a major challenge is ensuring that Nigeria does not go the way of Yugoslavia. One fact is certain: Military dominance and northern dependence on revenues generated in the south preclude a peaceful dissolution of the federation. Nigeria's multiethnic, multireligious, multiclass, and multiregional nature make it an especially valuable case for the study of social cleavages in conflict and cooperation.

Nigeria's failure to sustain democracy and economic development also renders it an important case for the study of resource competition and the perils of corruption, and its experience demonstrates the interrelationship between democracy and development. Democracy and development also depend on other factors, including leadership, mass culture, the level of institutional autonomy, and the external economic climate. A long-standing debate among scholars of comparative politics suggests that authoritarian regimes—because they lack legislative opposition and can force uncomfortable changes on society without fear of electoral reaction—are better able to accelerate economic growth and development. More recent research has shown, however, that democracies are no less likely to foster economic development and, in fact, may even establish predictable norms and further respect for property rights, both essential for economic development. The history of independent Nigeria shows that a combination of authoritarian government and widespread corruption have thwarted sustained development. Moreover, the Nigerian experience points to the need to pursue, with conviction, both economic and political liberalization. The latter process would open up society to democratic tendencies, while the former would provide the material bases (across a wider spectrum of society) for democratic consolidation.

At this stage, whether Nigeria will return to the path of autocracy, underdevelopment, and fragmentation, or turn to a course of democratic renewal and vigorous national construction, is uncertain. In the following sections we explore these issues and evaluate how they may shape Nigerian politics in the years ahead.

Section ❷ Political Economy and Development

Politics and economics have become so inseparable in Nigeria one cannot be seriously addressed without discussing the other. Section 2 explores the domestic and international contexts of Nigeria's political economy, and the role of the state and how it has intervened in Nigeria's economy. This active role of the state is consistent with the legacy established by the colonial regime, as discussed in Section 1.

State and Economy

The state plays the central role in Nigeria in making decisions about the extraction, deployment, and regulation of scarce economic resources. As individuals, groups, and communities jostle for control of, or access to, the state, economic and social life has become overpoliticized. The state has evolved beyond being a regulator and licenser, as it is in laissez-faire, less interventionist economies like Hong Kong. Although access to the state and its leaders confers economic advantages in most societies, it does so even more in developing countries. In Nigeria, the state is perceived as the greatest economic resource.

At the international level, the state has remained weak and dependent on Western industrial and financial interests four decades after Nigeria became a full-fledged member of the international community. The country suffers from an increasing debt burden. In addition, Nigeria is dependent on the developed industrial economies for finance capital, production and information technologies, and basic consumer items and raw materials. Nigeria strives to provide leadership at the continental (African) and subregional (West African) levels. Most of its policy and intellectual elites support this self-image.

In the period since independence, state intrusion into the economy and society has been strengthened by the control over **rents** accruing from agricultural, then petroleum, exports. The exigencies of the civil war and the consequences of prolonged military rule contributed to the centralized and intrusive approach to economic affairs. At the same time, the state has become a theater of struggles for ascendancy among groups and interests in civil society. To that extent, the state simultaneously affects and reflects forces in the political economy.

Origins of Economic Decline

In the colonial and immediate postcolonial periods, Nigeria's economy was centered on agricultural production for domestic consumption as well as for export.[4] Peasant producers were "induced" by the colonial state to produce primary export commodities—cocoa in the west, palm oil in the east, and ground nuts and cotton in the north—through direct taxation, forced cultivation, and the presence of European agricultural firms. Despite the emphasis on exports, Nigeria was self-sufficient in food production at the time of independence. Vital to this effort was small-scale local production of sorghum and maize in the north and cassava and yams in the south. Some rice and wheat were also produced. It was not until later in the 1960s that emphasis shifted to the

development of nonfood export crops through large-scale enterprises.

Near-exclusive state attention to large-scale, non-food production meant that small farmers were left out and received scant government support. Predictably, food production suffered, and food imports were stepped up to meet the increasing needs of a burgeoning population. Nevertheless, agriculture was the central component of the national economy. Michael Watts points to a combination of three factors that effectively undermined the Nigerian agricultural sector. The first was the Biafran war (1967–1970), which drastically reduced palm oil production in the east, where the war was concentrated. Second, severe drought in 1969 produced a famine in 1972–1974. Finally, the development of the petroleum industry caused a total shift in economic focus from agriculture (in terms of both labor and capital investment) into petroleum production. In contrast, agricultural export production plummeted from 80 percent of exports in 1960 to just 2 percent by 1980. To compensate for widening food shortfalls, food imports exploded by 700 percent between 1970 and 1978.[5]

With revenue from oil, Nigeria greatly increased its expenditures on education, defense, and infrastructure throughout the 1970s. The university system was expanded, roads and ports were built, and industrial and office buildings were constructed. Imports of capital goods and raw materials required to support this expansion rose by over 700 percent between 1971 and 1979. Similarly, imports of consumer goods also rose dramatically (600 percent) in the same period, as an increasingly wealthy Nigerian elite developed a taste for expensive imported goods.[6] By 1978 the Nigerian government had outspent its revenues and could no longer finance many of its ambitious projects; consequently, the government was forced to borrow money to make up the deficit, causing debt levels to accelerate rapidly.

The acceleration in oil wealth was mirrored by a corresponding increase in graft. Many public officials became very wealthy by setting up joint ventures with foreign oil companies. Other officials simply stole public funds for their own benefit. According to Watts, "Throughout the 1970s, enormous but inestimable amounts of money capital mysteriously appeared in private European bank accounts (estimated to be

Institutional Intricacies: **Corruption in Nigeria**

Corrupt government and private-sector practices occur in all countries. The motivations to do so are as specific as the individuals involved, yet greed and the desire for quick funds are certainly universal. Developing states, however, are particularly susceptible to corruption for a number of reasons. First, political institutions are often weak, which means that they are unable to implement essential national policies that conflict with the interests of specific groups or personal goals. Second, in the absence of strong institutions, personal ties predominate. As a consequence, people may find their immediate interests are better served through their ethnic grouping or religious institution and thus may place the demands of their family, ethnic kin, or religious group above the functioning of the public or private institution within which they work. Loyalty to a public or private institution is thus often subverted by considerations of personal connections and status.

Economic decline also contributes to corruption. In Nigeria, between 1980 and 1998, per capita incomes dropped 75 percent and the value of the naira fell from one naira to almost two U.S. dollars, to ninety naira to one U. S. dollar. Funds for most public works projects and social services such as health and education dried up, and competition for what remained became fierce. Corruption among elites became a way of life, while for poorly paid state employees it became a means of survival.

Consider, for example, that a bureaucrat in the Ministry of Works and Housing has a contract to award to a construction company to build a public housing project. He (or, more recently, she) probably has his immediate family to support, as well as his extended family and friends in his home village expecting him to contribute to household expenses. He hears stories from his friends about the huge sums of money stolen by the heads of state and their immediate subordinates, yet the government has not paid his agency's salaries in over four months—salaries that have not kept pace with the exorbitant rate of inflation. All the firms bidding for the contract promise to inflate the costs to the government for their work by 50 percent or more and pass half of that money secretly back to the bureaucrat for receiving the contract. At the height of postindependence optimism in the 1960s, many Nigerians avoided such temptations. Over time and with the massive influx of profits from the oil boom, however, increasing numbers succumbed to corruption.

When oil revenues began to pour into the country in the early 1970s, massive profits began to flow through the offices of military brass and senior-level bureaucrats. Some of these individuals, each involved in the personal networks described above, diverted a portion of these profits for themselves. When civilians came to power under the Second Republic in 1979, the number of people with access to oil revenues expanded, and a bonanza of inflated contracts, bogus public projects, and other scams proliferated. General Buhari justified his successful coup in 1983 in part to stamp out this massive corruption, and he did so temporarily—at the expense of civil liberties, which he severely curbed. Nonetheless, Buhari and his second-in-command General Idiagbon are still remembered by many Nigerians as the sort of "strong-handed" leaders that Nigeria needs to fight corruption.

Yet the notion that the military was any less corrupt than the civilians was dashed by the unprecedented avarice of Generals Babangida and Abacha. In the shadow of these massively corrupt military strongmen stands the average Nigerian, trying to eke out some semblance of a life in a land of growing poverty. Lacking jobs with adequate salaries or security, Nigeria's large university-educated population tries to emigrate to the United States or Europe, or turns to commercial fraud scams (known as "419"). Some individuals have turned to smuggling heroin, so that by 1998, Nigeria had become the largest transit point for that narcotic into the United States. Most Nigerians, however, never engage in such conduct. They work two or three jobs, sell food or small products by the roadside, carry jugs of fuel for miles on their heads to sell in neighboring countries, or do whatever else they can to sustain their families.

between $5 and $7 billion), and the level of bureaucratic malfeasance was simply staggering."[7] The economic downturn of the 1980s created even greater incentives for government corruption, and the Babangida and later the Abacha administrations became infamous for avarice. By 1992 reporters uncovered World Bank allegations that Babangida had "diverted" at least US$2 billion of a $3 billion windfall during the Gulf crisis of 1990–1991. Two years later, a Nigerian government commission reported that some $12.2 billion had been diverted to "special" accounts between 1988 and 1993.

General Abacha continued this looting spree to the point that he was willing to bring the country to its knees to make a profit. Within three years of seizing power, he allowed all of Nigeria's oil refineries to collapse, forcing this giant oil-exporting country into the absurd situation of having to import refined petroleum. Shamelessly, Abacha's family members and friends, who essentially served as fronts for him, monopolized the contracts to import this fuel in 1997.

In sum, the oil boom was a double-edged sword for Nigeria. On one hand, it has generated tremendous income; on the other, it has become a source of external dependence and has badly skewed the Nigerian economy. Nigeria has relied on oil for over 90 percent of its export earnings since the early 1970s. In that time, the industry has accounted for about three-quarters of *all* government revenues, as shown in Table 1. Frenzied, ill-managed industrial and infrastructural expansion under both military and civilian regimes, combined with the neglect of the agricultural sector during the oil boom years, further weakened the Nigerian economy. As a result, the Nigerian economy was unable to absorb the sharp fall in world oil prices after 1981 and found itself in crisis.

From 1985 to the Present: Deepening Economic Crisis and the Search for Solutions

Structural Adjustment The year 1985 marked a turning point for the Nigerian state and economy. It ushered in Ibrahim Babangida's eight-year rule and revealed the precarious condition of the Nigerian economy. Within a year of wresting power from General Buhari in August 1985, the Babangida regime developed an economic **structural adjustment program** (SAP) with the active support of the World Bank and IMF (also referred to as the **international financial institutions,** or IFIs). The decision to embark on SAP was made against a background of increasing economic constraints arising from a combination of factors: the continued dependence of the economy on oil exports, a growing debt burden, **balance of payments** difficulties, and lack of fiscal discipline.

The Nigerian SAP contains provisions that are similar to most economic reform programs that have been instituted in Africa and elsewhere. It had three broad objectives: first, to restructure and diversify the economy to reduce dependence on oil and on various imports; second, to achieve fiscal discipline and balance of payments viability by curtailing government spending to reduce budget deficits and the rising debt; and third, to embark on the **privatization** of state-owned enterprises (para-statals). In the decade since SAPs came into widespread use in Africa, their success has been mixed. The length of time allotted to such programs has usually been extended because of the failure of Africa's economies to respond quickly to the shock treatment.

African governments and their publics in general have resisted SAPs and IFI intervention for two reasons. First, states do not relish the prospect of ceding important aspects of their economic sovereignty to international institutions. Second, the austerity that results from such programs, although intended and predicted to be a short-term consequence, can be destabilizing to governments and populations alike. However, because they are dependent on lenders for continued support, most African governments have complied with the demands of multilateral creditors. Besides, other creditors (including private banks or foreign governments) often will not consent to provide additional monies in the absence of an agreement with the IFIs.

Federal control of earnings from oil and other mining rights enabled the state to increase its involvement in direct production. Beginning in the 1970s, the state created a number of para-statals (state-owned enterprises) and acquired large shares in major banks and other financial institutions, manufacturing, and construction companies. This practice has ensured that the state remains the biggest employer as well as the most important source of revenue, even for the private sector. By the 1980s the public service bureaucracy in Nigeria had swollen to over 3 million employees (most employed by the federal and state governments), representing more than 60 percent of employment in the modern sector of the economy.

The share of the private sector in the economy has actually fallen in recent years. According to one analysis, private-sector investment across the economy was approximately 45 percent during the first national development plan (1962–1968). By contrast, the fifth

Table1

Oil Sector Statistics, 1970–1998

	Annual Output (million barrels)	Average Price Index	Oil Exports as Percent of Total Exports	Government Oil Revenue (Naira millions)	Percent of Total Revenue
1970	396	37	58	166	26
1971	559	43	74	510	44
1972	643	40	82	767	54
1973	750	39	83	1,016	60
1974	823	162	93	3,726	82
1975	651	109	93	4,271	77
1976	756	115	94	5,365	79
1977	761	115	93	6,081	76
1978	692	100	89	4,556	62
1979	840	237	93	8,881	81
1980	753	220	96	12,353	81
1981	525	225	97	8,563	70
1982	470	212	99	7,814	66
1983	451	200	96	7,253	69
1984	508	190	97	8,268	74
1985	544	180	97	10,915	75
1986	534	75	94	8,107	66
1987	464	90	93	19,027	76
1988	507	60	91	20,934	77
1989	614	87	95	41,334	82
1990	–	125	–	–	–
1991	–	80	–	–	–
1992	714	79	98	164,078	86
1993	720	62	91	162,102	84
1994	733	70	85	160,192	79
1995	705	65	95	244,902	53
1996	783	95	95	266,000	51
1997	803	85	95	250,000[a]	80
1998[a]	700	62	90	248,500	70

[a]Projected.

Sources: Output is from *Petroleum Economist* (1970–1989); price index and exports are from IMF, *International Financial Statistics* (1970–1984) and from Central Bank of Nigeria, *Annual Reports* (1985–1989); revenues are from Central Bank of Nigeria, *Annual Reports* (various years). From Tom Forrest, *Politics and Economic Development in Nigeria.* (Boulder: Westview Press, 1993), 134. 1990s statistics are from the Nigerian Federal Office of Statistics, *Annual Abstract of Statistics: 1997 Edition*, from the 1998 IMF *Annual Report*, and from *Report of the Vision 2010 Committee: Main Report* (Abuja: Federal Government of Nigeria, September 1997). Compilation and some calculations by Darren Kew.

Global Connection: **Structural Adjustment Programs**

The solutions to Nigeria's economic woes depend, in the first instance, on its own people and government, but assistance must also come from outside its borders. In addition to bilateral (country-to-country) assistance, multilateral economic institutions are a key source of loans, grants, and other forms of development aid. Two multilateral institutions that have become familiar players on the African economic scene are the International Monetary Fund (IMF) and the World Bank. These international financial institutions, or IFIs, were established following World War II to provide short-term credit facilities to facilitate growth and expansion of trade and longer-term financing packages, respectively, to rebuild the countries of war-torn Europe. Today, the functions of the IFIs have adapted and expanded to meet contemporary needs, including efforts to stabilize and restructure faltering economies. One area of emphasis by the IFIs, particularly among African countries, is the structural adjustment program (SAP).

Assistance from the World Bank and the IMF comes with many strings attached. These rigorous programs, which are intended to reduce government intervention and to develop free markets, call for immediate austerity measures by recipient governments. SAPs generally begin with currency devaluation and tariff reductions. These actions are followed by measures aimed at reducing budget deficits, restructuring of the public sector (particularly employment practices), privatizing state-owned enterprises, agricultural reform (especially raising producer prices), and the reduction of consumer subsidies on staple foods. The social and economic hardships of these programs, particularly in the short term, can be severe. SAPs result in considerable economic—and frequently social—dislocation; dramatic price increases in foodstuffs and fuel, plus rising unemployment, are seldom popular with the general population.

At Babangida's insistence, Nigeria's SAP was developed and deployed in 1986 independently of the IMF and the World Bank. The program was, however, endorsed by the IFIs, making Nigeria eligible to receive disbursements of funds from the IMF and the Bank and to reschedule US$33 billion of external debt with the Paris and London clubs of lenders. Ironically, Nigeria's SAP was in many regards more rigorous than an initial program designed by the IMF. Like SAPs elsewhere, the Nigerian program was designed to encourage economic liberalism and promote private enterprise in place of a reliance on state-owned enterprises and public intervention. The logic was that competition leads to more efficient products and markets. Recovery among Africa's struggling economies has, however, been limited. Africa's economic problems are deeply entrenched; although an economy may be stabilized relatively quickly, comprehensive *structural* adjustment takes considerably longer. Thus far, Nigeria's SAP—in part because of the popular reaction to austerity measures, continued corruption in its implementation, and the complicating factor of unstable military rule—has failed to revitalize the Nigerian economy. The final years of the Babangida administration (1985–1993) saw a marked slippage in the reform program, and the Abacha regime continued that trend. Abacha did enact a number of liberal economic policies in 1995 and 1996 that lowered inflation, stabilized the exchange rate, and fostered mild GDP growth, but by 1997 these achievements had been squandered. General Abubakar pledged to return to a liberal economic agenda, including the privatization of the major government para-statals.

national development plan (1981–1985) anticipated just a 14 percent contribution from the private sector.[8] That is, funding for the plan was to be provided mainly by the government. Attempts in the 1970s to widen Nigerian participation in business life and reduce the foreign presence enhanced state involvement because government had to take over shares and businesses when local bids proved inadequate.

The stated goal of Nigerian governments since the mid-1980s has been to reduce unproductive investments in the public sector, improve the sector's efficiency, and promote the growth of the private sector. Privatization, one of the most substantial aspects of economic liberalization, means that state-owned businesses would be sold to private (nonstate) investors, either domestic or foreign. The benefits of

Current Challenges: *Vision 2010*

In the early 1990s, concerned with the nation's economic decline, a number of the larger Nigerian businesses and key multinational corporations decided to pursue new initiatives. With the appointment as head of state in August 1993 of Ernest Shonekan, who was the former chairman of West Africa's largest local corporation, UAC, these businesses sensed an opportunity to alter the course of Nigeria's economic policies. With Shonekan's involvement, they arranged the first Economic Summit, a high-profile conference that advocated numerous policies to move Nigeria toward becoming an "emerging market" that could attract foreign investment along the lines of the high-performing states in Asia.

Shortly after the first Economic Summit, however, General Abacha took control and continued the ruinous economic approach of Babangida's later years. The Economic Summit, meanwhile, continued to meet annually. After his flawed 1994 budget sent the Nigerian economy into a tailspin, Abacha was ready to listen to the Summit participants. He accepted several of their recommendations, and by 1996 the economy began to make modest gains. Therefore, when key members of the Summit proposed *Vision 2010,* General Abacha seized the opportunity and endorsed it in September 1996.

Vision 2010 relies on a model of strategic planning that begins with a "visioning" process that identifies key corporate goals and the paths of action to realize these goals. The process brings together key stakeholders and "implementers" who are expected to bring goals to fruition. Malaysia and other developing countries successfully employed this model in the 1980s to devise blueprints for development. As part of the "visioning" process, the government adopts a package of business-promoting economic reforms, while business pledges to work toward certain growth targets consistent with governmental priorities in employment,

taxation, community investment, and the like. General Abacha's estimation of the potential of *Vision 2010* was so great that he quickly increased its scope beyond its initial economic intentions. Committees were set up to develop plans for Nigeria's sports teams, interethnic relations, media development, and even for civil-military relations under the expected democratic rule. Along with government and business leaders, key figures were invited to participate from nearly all sectors of society, including the press, nongovernmental organizations, youth groups, market women's associations, and others. Government-owned media followed *Vision 2010*'s pronouncements with great fanfare, while the private media reviewed them with a healthy dose of skepticism regarding Abacha's intentions and the elitist nature of the exercise.

In September 1997, on schedule, the *Vision 2010* executive committee presented its final report. Its four volumes painted a surprisingly candid picture of where Nigeria stood, and recommended how the country could transform itself into a strong emerging-market democracy by 2010. The recommendations called for, in part: restoring democratic rule, restructuring and professionalizing the military, lowering the population growth rate, rebuilding education, meaningful privatization, diversifying the export base beyond oil, supporting intellectual property rights, and central bank autonomy.

Whatever its merits, *Vision 2010* was imperiled because of its association with Abacha. After Abacha's death in 1998, General Abubakar (who had earlier participated in the formulation of *Vision 2010*) announced that his administration endorsed the *Vision 2010* recommendations. He pledged to implement the initial economic policy reforms, including privatization, before leaving office in May 1999. Business leaders remain generally enthusiastic, but what relationship they will enjoy with the new civilian government, and whether the key proposals of *Vision 2010* will be retained following the resumption of competitive multiparty politics, are uncertain.

Source: *Vision 2010 Final Report*, September 1997.

privatization are threefold: (1) revenue is generated for the state when the enterprise is sold; (2) there is a substantial reduction in state expenditure because the state is no longer financing the operation of money-losing operations; and (3) there is an implicit assumption that the private sector can run businesses more efficiently than the government sector. However, privatization typically results in job loss: a private company cannot afford to maintain a bloated payroll if it hopes to survive. The government is often reluctant to swell the ranks of the unemployed and to confront the consequent political opposition that such actions usually provoke.

Nevertheless, central to Nigeria's economic adjustment program is the commercialization and privatization of state enterprises. Government has successfully divested itself of shares in such areas as banking and finance, but has proceeded slowly regarding most of the key para-statals. Moreover, individuals in public office or with access to the state have been able to invest in privatized companies at insider prices. Much of the Nigerian economy therefore remains as interventionist and centralized as ever.

Expectations that deregulation would encourage investment in manufacturing by both Nigerians and foreign interests have not been fulfilled. The healthy annual growth rate in gross domestic investment of 14.7 percent between 1965 and 1980 dropped precipitously—10.2 percent annually from 1980 to 1990. For potential foreign investors, uncertainties about Nigeria's future have discouraged long-term investment. Meanwhile, new investors are hesitant to risk significant capital in an environment characterized by political and social instability, a weak economic adjustment program, and unpredictable military regimes. On a domestic level, Nigerian entrepreneurs have found that trading and government contracting offer more attractive and quicker yields than manufacturing. The service sector, as a consequence, grew between 1980 and 1990 whereas manufacturing and industry actually declined.

Economic Planning   Beginning in 1946, when the colonial administration announced a ten-year plan for development and welfare, national plans have been prepared by ministries of finance, economic development, and planning. Five-year plans were the norm from 1962 through 1985, when their scope was extended to fifteen years. The national plan, however, has not been an effective management tool. The reason for this disparity is the absence of an effective database for planning as well as a great lack of discipline in plan implementation. The state strives to

control and dictate the pace and direction of economic development but lacks the tools and political will to deliver on its obligations. Nigerian and foreign business leaders revived dialogue on economic direction in 1996 with the *Vision 2010* process. *Vision 2010*, however, was vastly different from past plans in that it was a business-led initiative that government later adopted and contributed to as an equal partner. *Vision 2010* also sought to scale back government's excessive role in the economy, in the hope of increasing market efficiency and reducing competition for control of the state.

Although *Vision 2010* eventually may provide a basis for reform, many problems must still be overcome in the economy: low investment, low capacity utilization, unreliable distribution, stifling corruption, and overregulation. Average annual GDP growth rates have been negative in several years since the early 1980s. Consumption and investment have also recorded negative growth (see Table 2).

Table 2

Selected Economic Indicators, 1980–1998

	Real GDP (Naira billions) (1993 = 100)	GDP (% Growth)	Manufacturing Capacity Utilization (%)[a]	Inflation Rate (%)
1980	96.2	5.5	70.1	9.9
1985	68.9	9.4	37.1	5.5
1990	90.3	8.1	40.3	7.4
1991	94.6	4.8	42.0	13.0
1992	97.4	3.0	41.8	44.6
1993	100.0	2.7	37.2	57.2
1994	101.0	1.3	30.4	57.0
1995	103.5	2.2	29.3	72.8
1996	106.9	3.3	32.5	29.3
1997	111.1	3.9	–	8.5
1998	113.3	2.0	–	9.0
1976–1986		–1.3		
1987–1997		1.6		

[a]Manufacturing capacity utilization is the average (across the economy) percentage of full production capabilities at which manufacturers are producing.

Sources: *Report of the Vision 2010 Committee: Main Report* (Abuja: Federal Government of Nigeria, September 1997); World Bank, "Nigeria at a Glance," 1998 (http://www.worldbank.org/); the 1998 IMF *Annual Report*.

Exacerbating Nigeria's economic decline is its heavy foreign debt. The total amount owed to foreign governments and international commercial banks exceeded US$28 billion by the end of 1996—ten times the total government budget for that year. Total debt service as a percentage of exported goods and services jumped fivefold, from 4.2 percent in 1980 to 37.4 percent in 1996. This means that of every dollar Nigeria earns from its exports, 37 cents must theoretically go to service the national debt. Such a level of debt servicing cannot, obviously, be met with more debt. Nigeria, once considered a country likely to achieve self-sustaining growth, now ranks among the more debt-distressed countries in the developing world. It cannot earn enough from the export of goods to service its foreign debt and also meet the basic needs of the population (see Table 3).

Social Welfare   Given the continued decline in its economic performance since the early 1970s, it is not surprising that Nigeria's social welfare has suffered greatly as well. Since 1986 there has been a marked deterioration in the quantity and quality of social services, complicated by a marked decline in household incomes (see Table 4). The SAP program, with its emphasis on austerity and the reduction of state expenditures, has forced cutbacks in spending on social welfare.

Economic austerity and stagnation have hurt vulnerable groups such as the urban and rural poor, women, the young, and the elderly. Indeed, Nigeria performs poorly in meeting basic needs: life expectancy is barely above fifty years, and infant mortality is estimated at more than 90 deaths per 1000 live births. Nigeria's provision of basic education is also inadequate. Moreover, Nigeria has failed to develop a national social security system, such as that found in the United States and elsewhere. There has also been a general tendency for growth in public social spending to lag behind growth in the economy. Much of the resulting gap has traditionally been filled by culturally based networks of extended families. The scant social spending that does exist is often manipulated for partisan political purposes by both civilian and military governments. Public spending on housing, for example, represents less than 1 percent of the federal budget and is often diverted to meet the needs of the military.

Table 3

Nigeria's Total External Debt (US$ millions; current prices and exchange rates)

1975–1979	1980	1981	1982	1983
3,304	8,934	12,136	12,954	18,540
1984	1985	1986	1987	1988
18,537	19,551	24,043	31,193	31,947
1989	1994	1995	1996	1997
32,832	34,000	35,010	33,442	32,906

Nigeria's Debt Compared to Its Earnings:

	1976	1986	1996	1997
Total Debt/GDP	3.7	109.9	72.0	63.1
Total Debt Service/Exports	3.7	28.4	15.2	15.9
Present Value of Debt/GDP	–	–	63.3	–
Present Value of Debt/Exports	–	–	178.6	–

Sources: UNDP, World Bank, *African Development Indicators* (Washington, D.C.: World Bank, 1992), 159; UNDP, *1998 Human Development Report*; World Bank, "Nigeria at a Glance," 1998 (http://www.worldbank.org/); the 1998 IMF *Annual Report*.

The provision of health care and other social services—water, education, food, and shelter—remain woefully inadequate in both urban and rural areas. Rural areas are doubly burdened by their relative isolation because of poor roads, transportation, telecommunication facilities, and sparse electrical power. In all parts of Nigeria, health care facilities lack equipment, drugs, and doctors. Although the national leadership gives lip service to the importance of social welfare in general, health care has been accorded a low priority in Nigeria's national development plans, especially when compared with expenditure on the military.

Society and Economy

The Nigerian state, and especially the central government, controls access to capital resources. As a result, the state has become the major focus for competition among ethnic, regional, religious, and class groups. In such an environment, elite members of these groups become "conflict generators" rather than "con-

Table 4

Index of Real Household Incomes of Key Groups, 1980/81–1986/87, 1996 (Rural self-employed in 1980/81 = 100)

	1980/81	1981/82	1982/83	1983/84	1984/85	1985/86	1986/87	1996[a]
Rural self-employed	100	103	95	86	73	74	65	27
Rural wage earners	178	160	147	135	92	95	84	48
All rural households	105	107	99	89	74	84	74	28
Urban self-employed	150	124	106	94	69	69	61	41
Urban wage earners	203	177	164	140	101	101	90	55
All urban households	166	142	129	109	80	80	71	45

[a]Estimated, based on 1980/81 figures adjusted for a 73% drop in per capita GDP from 1980 to 1996. The FOS lists annual household incomes for 1996 as US$75 (N 6,349) for urban households and US$57 (N 4,820) for rural households, suggesting that the gap between urban and rural households is actually 19% closer than our estimate.

Sources: National Integrated Survey of Households (NISH), Federal Office of Statistics (FOS) consumer price data, and World Bank estimates. As found in Paul Collier, *An Analysis of the Nigerian Labour Market*, Development Economics Department Discussion Paper (Washington, D.C.: World Bank, 1986). From Tom Forrest, *Politics and Economic Development in Nigeria* (Boulder: Westview Press, 1993), 214. 1996 data from FOS, *Annual Abstract of Statistics: 1997 Edition*, 80.

flict managers."[9] Furthermore, a partial explanation for the failure of economic strategies can be found within Nigerian society itself—a complex mix of contending, often hostile, ethnic, religious, and regional constituencies.

Ethnic and Religious Cleavages

Nigeria's ethnic relations have generated tensions that sap the country's economy of much-needed vitality. Competition among the three largest groups is centered on access to national economic and political resources. The dominance of the Hausa-Fulani, Igbo, and Yoruba in the country's national life, and the conflicts among political elites from these groups, flow over into economic affairs as policy decisions are often made less on their merits and more on how they impact perceptions of group strength.

Religious cleavages have also affected economic and social stability. Some of the federation's states in the far north are populated mainly by Muslims, whereas others, particularly in the middle and eastern parts of the south, are predominantly Christian. The imagery in popular (and often academic) discourse often simplifies the more complex reality by juxtaposing a so-called Christian south with a Muslim north (the Yoruba people in the southwest, for example, are almost equally divided between Muslims and Christians and with many adherents of Yoruba traditional beliefs).

A combination of inept government actions—or outright manipulation—and a worldwide upsurge in Islamic and Christian assertion have heightened conflicts between adherents. Christians have perceived the northern-dominated federal government as being pro-Islam in its management and distribution of scarce resources as well as in its policy decisions. Christians fear that government actions are jeopardizing the secular nature of the state and putting the country on the path to an Islamic theocracy. In response, Muslims have questioned the secular nature of the Nigerian state. Muslims insist that colonial rule, under the tutelage of the church-state of England, created a state more Christian than secular in Nigeria, and one that is unable to provide a positive environment for the observance of Islam. The consequence of these disputes throughout the 1980s and 1990s was a series of clashes along religious lines in various parts of the country, often accompanied by extensive loss of life.

Further complicating matters, the 1980s witnessed an increase in social disturbances associated mainly with the extremist fringes of Islamic groups in some parts of the north. The decline in the Nigerian economy also contributed to the rise of fundamentalism. As elsewhere in the world, Islamic leaders have increasingly blamed secular governments for the rise in poverty and social dislocation. In northern Nigeria, disputes over economic issues have sometimes escalated into physical attacks on Christians and members of southern ethnic groups residing in the north. Occasionally, religious revivalism among some of the various Christian sects has provoked violent protests by Muslims.

Poverty and social dislocation have yet to promote a militant religious movement in the Christian south, but evangelical Christian churches swept across the region in the 1990s. Offering music, dancing, community, and even instant miracles (especially in regard to fertility, relationships, and finances), these churches have sprouted in nearly every neighborhood where Christians are to be found. Although they do have an umbrella national organization, the evangelicals have yet to solidify into a coherent political force. Their social influence, however, has been unmistakable, as nearly every public figure peppers his pronouncements with religious references. The evangelical churches augment the more established denominations, including Anglicans, Roman Catholics, and Methodists.

Based on general perceptions that the south fears "northern political domination—the tyranny of population," while the north fears a "southern tyranny of skills,"[10] it is often argued that the north must continue to control political power at the central government level—through military or civilian means—so as to neutralize the south's perceived advantages. Such attitudes came into the open during the Babangida regime, which was perceived as a northern-dominated administration and willing to manipulate Nigeria's ethnic divisions more than any of his predecessors.

General Abacha's Provisional Ruling Council (PRC) tilted overwhelmingly in favor of northerners, specifically Hausa-Fulani, in its membership. Any appearance of regional representation in the council was shattered in August 1994 when Abacha replaced most of the non-northern senior military staffers. The December 1997 arrest of deputy head of state (nominally the second-highest position of power in the country) General Oladipo Diya for allegedly plotting a coup along with a dozen other generals and senior staff—all but one of whom were Yoruba—confirmed southern fears of a northern bias in the PRC. Meanwhile, numerous attacks were perpetrated against prominent southern civilians, particularly

Yoruba, and many suspected government complicity. The Abacha government also closed universities and detained a number of activists, particularly in the south.

But it is not only Yoruba groups that were adversely affected by Abacha's rule. The Ogoni, Ijaw, and other southern minorities, who are heavily represented among oil industry workers, were brutalized by military and police forces when they protested against the regime. The Ogoni in particular were well-organized through the Movement for the Survival of the Ogoni People (MOSOP), under the leadership of internationally renowned writer and environmentalist Ken Saro-Wiwa. MOSOP effectively blended its claims for **self-determination**, which in this case meant increased local political autonomy and national political representation, with concerns over oil industry pollution in the Niger Delta—primarily on the part of global oil giant Royal Dutch/Shell—as a platform to forge alliances with international environmental and human rights organizations.

This alliance became an active force in 1994, when Saro-Wiwa was arrested on trumped-up charges along with eight other Ogoni activists. Their kangaroo trial by a military tribunal brought pleas for clemency from international human rights organizations, as well as from South African President Nelson Mandela, U.S. President Bill Clinton, and other world leaders. Ignoring such pleas, the government executed Saro-Wiwa and his compatriots in November 1995. International condemnation followed: Nigeria was suspended from the Commonwealth (an international organization composed of former British colonies) within days, and a subsequent UN mission of inquiry in 1996 declared the hangings illegal, not only under international standards of jurisprudence but also under Nigeria's own system of laws.

Rejecting many of the harsher tactics of his predecessors, General Abubakar introduced a transition program in 1998 for a rapid return to democracy, in part to mitigate the intense ethnic and religious tensions. He also partly adjusted the ethnic balance in the PRC to allow greater southern representation. Yet the political space and freedoms restored by Abubakar released the pent-up ethnic tensions aggravated by Abacha and Babangida, a situation that bodes poorly for hopes of ethnic accommodation in the new civilian regime.

In an August 1998 meeting, Yoruba leaders largely agreed to forgo the late M.K.O. Abiola's 1993 presidential mandate and to participate in the Abubakar transition program, but only after a lengthy debate over calls for secession or for a confederal Nigeria. A number of leaders also threatened that the Yoruba would go their own way if Nigeria's next president was not from their region. Key Igbo leaders made similar calls for an Igbo president, while Hausa-Fulani politicians stressed the view that democracy means majoritarianism—meaning that their more numerous population should ensure a president from the north.

Meanwhile, youths from the Niger Delta minorities, primarily the Ijaw, occupied Shell and Chevron facilities in September and October 1998 to protest their group's perceived marginalization. In light of the oil companies' vital importance to the Nigerian government, they have recently become the favorite targets of Delta protests. Their operations were shut down or occupied several times in 1997 and 1998 as Ijaw and Itsekeri youths fought over control of their common local government.

Nigerian political and business elites have also demonstrated a propensity toward accentuating sectional cleavages. Culture or ethnicity is used to fragment rather than to integrate the country, with grave consequences for the economy and society. These divisive practices overshadow certain positive aspects of sectional identities. For example, associations based on ethnic and religious affinities often serve as vehicles for mobilizing savings, investment, and production, such as informal credit associations. In addition, professional associations—composed of lawyers, doctors, journalists, business and trade groups, academics, trade unions, or students' organizations—played a prominent role in the anticolonial struggle. These groups, which form the core of civil society, have continued to provide a vehicle for political expression while also reflecting the divisive pressures of Nigeria's cultural pluralism. It should benoted, however, that the most political of these groups traditionally have been dominated by men. Although women form a vital part of the economic sector, they have only recently begun to emerge as a major social force in Nigeria.

Gender Differences

Although the Land Use Act of 1978 stated that all land in Nigeria is ultimately owned by the government, land tenure in Nigeria is still governed by traditional practice, which is basically patriarchal. Despite the fact that women, especially from the south and Middle Belt areas, have traditionally dominated agricultural production and form the bulk of agricultural producers, they are generally prevented from owning land, which remains the major means of production. Trading, in which women feature prominently, is also controlled in many areas by traditional chiefs and local government councillors, who are overwhelmingly male.

Women have not succeeded in transforming their economic importance into political clout, but important strides are being made in this direction. Their past inability and current struggle to achieve direct access to state power is a reflection of several factors. Women's associations have tended to be elitist, urban-based, and mainly concerned with issues of trade, welfare, and religion. The few that did have a more political orientation have been largely token appendages of the male-dominated political parties or instruments of the government. An example of the latter was the "Better Life Program" directed by the wife of Babangida, and its successor, the "Family Support Program," directed by Abacha's wife. Women are grossly underrepresented at all levels of the governmental system.

Reflecting their historical economic and educational advantages, women's interest organizations sprouted in southern Nigeria earlier than in the north. Although these groups initially focused on generally nonpolitical issues surrounding women's health and children, organizations like Women in Nigeria began to form in the 1980s with explicit political goals, such as getting more women into government and making more money available for education.

By the 1990s northern women had become nearly as active as southerners in founding nongovernmental organizations (NGOs). As in the south, northern women's NGOs at first focused on nonpolitical issues, but by the end of the decade explicitly political organizations such as the 100 Women Groups, which sought to elect one hundred women to every level of government, emerged. Northern groups also showed tremendous creativity in using Islam to support their activities, which was very important considering that tenets of the religion have been regularly used by Nigerian men to justify women's subordinate status. Women's groups in general have been much more dynamic than male-dominated NGOs—nearly all of which are entirely dependent on foreign or government funding—in developing income-generating projects to make their organizations and the women they assist increasingly self-reliant.

Nigeria and the International Political Economy

In the years since independence, Nigeria has been active in the Organization of African Unity (OAU), the Commonwealth, the Nonaligned Movement, and the United Nations. In recent years, Nigeria played a major role in reorienting the focus of the Nonaligned Movement toward issues of economic development and cooperation. In bodies such as the OAU and the UN, Nigeria generally took firm positions to promote decolonization and the development of the Third World, and against the apartheid regime in South Africa. Unfortunately, this international goodwill was largely squandered by the Abacha regime, and, ironically, the democratic government of South Africa became one of its leading critics. President Nelson Mandela, himself a former political prisoner, was prominent among world leaders calling for the immediate release of Moshood Abiola. South Africa was the first country General Abubakar visited shortly after taking office in order to patch the relationships frayed under his predecessor.

Nigeria and the Regional Political Economy

Nigeria has aspired to be a regional leader in Africa. These aspirations have not been dampened by its declining position in the global political economy. Nigeria was a major actor in the formation in 1975 of the **Economic Community of West African States** (ECOWAS) and has carried a disproportionately high financial and administrative burden for keeping that troubled organization afloat. Nigeria has also been the largest contributor of troops to the West African peacekeeping force, the ECOWAS Monitoring Group (known as ECOMOG). Under

Nigerian direction, the ECOWAS countries dispatched ECOMOG troops to Liberia in August 1990 to restore order and to prevent the Liberian civil war from destabilizing the subregion. In July 1997 the election of a national governing committee under the former warlord Charles Taylor was an ambiguous outcome of these efforts. Ironically, despite military dictatorship at home, Nigerian ECOMOG forces invaded Sierra Leone in May 1997 to restore its democratically elected government—a move generally endorsed by the international community. These forces have been drawn more deeply into the conflict as the former Sierra Leonean military junta has formed alliances with rural rebel militias and counterattacked.

Because it is the largest economy in the West African subregion, Nigeria has been a magnet for illegal immigration. At the height of the 1970s oil boom, many West African laborers, most of them from Ghana, migrated to Nigeria in search of employment. When the oil-based expansion ceased and jobs became scarce, Nigeria sought to protect its own workers by expelling thousands of West Africans in 1983 and 1985.

On balance, ECOWAS has not accomplished its goal of economic integration. The region is riven by jealousies and rivalries among French- and English-speaking blocs. Each of these blocs maintains closer ties to its former colonial masters economically and culturally than with each other. As a result, formal-sector trade (that which pays taxes and ends up in GDP calculations, and usually derives from the activity of well-established businesses and manufacturers) within ECOWAS has been disappointing. The informal sector (petty trade, services, and smuggling) across West African borders, however, is estimated to be enormous, with Nigerian traders its driving force. A number of analysts estimate that the Nigerian informal sector can be valued at a figure approximately 20 percent the size of the entire Nigerian GDP—much of which is earned through cross-border trade. That trade is all the more important because it provides income to 70 percent of Nigerians, the poorer majority.

Nigeria and the Political Economy of the West

Nigeria's global influence peaked in the 1970s at the height of the oil boom. Shortly after the 1973–1974 global oil crisis, Nigeria's oil wealth was perceived by the Nigerian elite largely as a source of strength. In 1975, for example, Nigeria was selling about 30 percent of its oil to the United States[11] and was able to apply pressure to the administration of President Gerald Ford in a dispute over Angola. By the 1980s, however, the global oil market had become a buyer's market. Thereafter, it became clear that Nigeria's dependence on oil was a source of weakness, not strength. In addition to its dependence on oil revenues, Nigeria was dependent on Western technology and Western industrial expertise for exploration and extraction of its oil reserves.

Nigeria is listed very close to the bottom of the United Nations' Human Development Index (HDI), 142 out of 174, behind India and Haiti. Gross national product (GDP) per capita in 1996 was US$269, less than 2 percent of which was recorded as public expenditures on education and health. These figures compare unfavorably with the $860 per capita GNP for China and $390 per capita for India. On the basis of its per capita GDP, the Nigerian economy is the nineteenth poorest in the world in a 1997 World Bank ranking. For comparative purposes, the same study ranks Ghana as thirty-first poorest and India twenty-seventh.

The depth of this international weakness became clear with the adoption of structural adjustment in the mid-1980s. Given the enormousness of the economic crisis, Nigeria was compelled to seek IMF/World Bank support to improve its balance of payments and facilitate economic restructuring and debt rescheduling, and had to accept direction from foreign agencies for the first time since gaining independence. The annual budget proposals of the federal government and its various accounts have been subject to scrutiny by these institutions.

The link between internal and external (in this case, Western) factors in Nigeria's political economy is best reflected in the interplay of forces that eventually drove General Babangida from power on August 26, 1993, following his nullification of the June 12 presidential election. Pro-democracy groups were strengthened in their anti-Babangida campaign by the pressure from external donors and creditors, especially the United States, Britain, and the European Union.

Relations with these foreign powers deteriorated steadily after the 1993 election annulment. In July 1993 the United States announced plans to suspend commercial military sales to Nigeria and canceled all but humanitarian aid. In July 1994 the U.S. House of Representatives passed a resolution condemning human rights abuses and advocating the restoration of democracy, and the following year an economic sanctions bill was introduced in the Senate. Germany and Britain issued similar pronouncements. Nigeria nonetheless avoided severe sanctions from the international community because of its size, high-grade petroleum reserves, and the significant presence of foreign oil companies in the country. Pressure on their home governments by U.S. and European multinationals, especially oil companies alongside a group of well-paid Abacha lobbyists, ensured that severe economic sanctions on Nigeria were never imposed.

International pressure is often limited in what it can achieve. Nigeria's global leverage stems directly from oil. It remains a highly visible and powerful member of OPEC, selling on average 2 million barrels of petroleum daily and contributing approximately 8 percent to United States oil imports. Babangida and Abacha presided over an economy in which the leading European countries such as Britain, France, and Germany each had over US$1 billion in investments. Nigeria's oil wealth and its great economic potential have tempered the resolve of Western nations for combating human rights and other abuses, notably during the Abacha period from 1993 to 1998.

The government of General Abacha was far less sensitive to international pressure than its predecessors. Limited economic sanctions and the growing threat of more severe measures had little influence on the regime. Abacha at first decided unilaterally to stop implementing key features of the structural adjustment program. When the economy plummeted in 1994 as a result of this decision, the government instituted minor economic reforms that lowered inflation and increased GDP growth in 1995 and 1996. By 1997, however, these gains were erased as massive official corruption locked the nation in recession. Abacha and his cronies allowed Nigeria's already dysfunctional petroleum refineries to collapse, forcing this oil-exporting OPEC nation to import fuel—through contractors connected to Abacha. Transport prices doubled overnight, as did the price of food and most other goods. Further, in an ostensible effort to

Despite being sub-Saharan Africa's largest crude oil exporter, Nigeria faces chronic fuel shortages. General Abacha allowed the nation's four refineries to collapse, forcing the country into the absurd situation of importing fuel—through middlemen who gave enormous kickbacks to Abacha and his family. *Source:* Jay Oguntuwase-Asope, *The Guardian* (Lagos), August 12, 1998.

combat inflation, but more likely to cover up the billions his cabal was siphoning from the budget, Abacha withheld all appropriations to government agencies, except portions of the military, for the first seven months of 1997. Given the large role of the government in the economy, activity all but ground to a halt.

General Abubakar's release of most political prisoners and his regime's new transition program in 1998 quickly won back much of the international standing lost under Abacha. His promise to implement the economic reforms recommended by the *Vision 2010* committee, much of which President-elect Obasanjo pledged to continue, also won praise from businesses and renewed attention from some international investors.

Section ③ Governance and Policy-Making

The rough edges of what has been called the unfinished Nigerian state can be seen in its institutions of governance and policy-making. What seemed like an endless political transition under the Babangida and Abacha regimes was rushed through in less than a year by their successor, Abdulsalami Abubakar. A prolonged rambling process, followed over fourteen years, followed by a rushed one, makes it more difficult to characterize the institutions of governance in Nigeria than in other countries. With that in mind, an account is presented of how these institutions functioned in Nigeria historically, how Nigerians hoped they would perform, and how they have operated in practice.

Organization of the State

The National Question and Constitutional Governance

After four decades of independence, Nigerians are still debating the basic political structures of the country, who will rule and how, and even if the country should remain united. They call this fundamental governance issue the "national question": How is the country to be governed given its great diversity? What should be the institutional form of the government? How can all sections of the country work in harmony and none feel excluded or dominated by the others? Nigerian leaders have attempted to answer these questions in various ways. Since the creation of Nigeria by the British, one path has been reliance on the Anglo-American tradition of rule by law rather than by individuals. Another path has been military guidance. None have succeeded, so Nigeria has stumbled along, recently under some hybrid of these two tendencies. As a consequence, Nigeria has produced many constitutions but has yet to entrench constitutionalism.

Since the amalgamation of northern and southern Nigeria in1914, the country has introduced, or nearly inaugurated, nine constitutions, five under colonial rule (in 1922, 1946, 1951, 1954, and 1960) and four after colonial rule: the 1963 republican constitution, the 1979 constitution of the Second Republic, the 1989 constitution intended for the Third Republic; and a 1995 constitution that will finally be introduced in greatly amended form before power is transferred in 1999. Despite the expenditure of huge sums by both the Babangida and Abacha regimes on constitution-making, Nigeria experienced the anomaly of conducting national elections in 1998–1999 without a settled constitutional document.

In the United States, the U.S. Constitution is perceived as a living document and subject to interpretation. Even though the U.S. Constitution has been interpreted in various ways based on legal precedent and political expedience, the document itself has endured for over two hundred years with just twenty-seven amendments. In contrast, Nigerian constitutions have earned no such respect from military and civilian leaders, who have been unwilling to observe legal/constitutional constraints. Governance and policy-making in this context are conducted within fragile institutions that are often swamped by personal and partisan considerations. Military rule has bolstered these tendencies and personalized governance and policy-making. With this in mind, we discuss key elements of recent periods of military rule, their continued influence in the present, and the institutions projected for the Fourth Republic.

Federalism and State Structure

Nigeria's First Republic experimented with the parliamentary model, in which the executive is chosen directly from the legislative ranks in a manner inspired by the British system. The First Republic was relatively decentralized, with the locus of political power in the three federal units, the Northern, Eastern, and Western Regions. The Second Republic constitution, which went into effect in 1979, adopted a U.S.-style presidential model. The consensus among Nigeria's constitutional planners for the next Republic is that its structure should continue to be a variant of the U.S. model. In this view, democratic Nigeria should possess a presidential system with a strong executive who is constrained by a system of checks and balances on authority; a bicameral legislature; and an independent judicial branch charged with matters of law and constitutional interpretation. In addition, Nigeria should have a federal structure comprising states and local government units empowered to enact their own laws within their individual jurisdictions, but limited in scope by the constitution and federal laws. Together, these units should constitute a single national entity.

Nigeria's federal system thus operates with three levels of government. The first or highest is the national government, and, as in the U.S. federal system, state and local levels of government as well. Like the national government, each of the thirty-six state governments and 774 local governments in Nigeria has an executive branch and a legislative branch, although the legislatures are usually disbanded under military rule. The judicial system also resembles that of the United States, with a network of local and district courts as well as state-level courts.

Under a true federal system, the formal powers of the different levels of government would be clearly delineated, and the relationships among and between them defined. In Nigeria, by contrast, these institutions have been radically altered by military rule. The dominance of central government authority, particularly the executive, has been enhanced to suit the expedience of the junta of the moment. So while Nigerian federalism remains a subject of political and social discourse, in large part because of its ethnic overtones and federal character (see next section), the military is not a unit of governance in the traditional design of a federal structure. The control of oil wealth by this centralized command structure has further cemented economic and political control in the center, resulting in a skewed federalism in which states enjoy nominal powers but in reality are totally dependent on the central government. In other words, Nigeria under military rule has been a federation in name only. In reality, the nation has been governed as a unitary state, with the federal constituent parts acting primarily as administrative appendages of the center.

Federal Character

Numerous attempts have been made to arrive at some form of elite accommodation to moderate some of the more divisive dimensions of cultural pluralism. For example, recruitment of local elements into the army shortly after independence followed a quota system. Through such a system it was hoped the army would reflect the country's complex ethnic makeup. A similar practice, reflecting what Nigerians now refer to as **federal character**, was introduced into the public service and formally codified in Section 14(3) of the 1979 constitution:

> The composition of the Government of the Federation or any of its agencies and the conduct of its affairs shall be carried out in such manner as to reflect the federal character and the need to promote national unity, and also to command national loyalty thereby ensuring that there shall be no predominance of persons from a few states or from a few ethnic or other sectional groups in that government or any of its agencies.

Federal character has also come to be applied in university admissions, and as a requirement for private companies that do business with the government. Many businesses and organizations therefore feature their own hiring programs to promote ethnic balance.

Because federal character is also perceived as a tool of ethnic management, disputes about its application have tended to focus on ethnic representation rather than on representation of state interests. Although this principle was originally regarded as a positive Nigerian contribution to governance in a plural society, its application has tended to intensify rather than reduce intergroup rivalries and conflicts. In recent years there have been calls for the use of merit over federal character in awarding public-sector jobs.

Most of the resistance to federal character has come from southern Nigerians, whose historically higher levels of education and income have left many of them bitter that they have been passed up for job promotion or admission to the best universities in favor of northerners. For many southerners, federal character has become synonymous with "northernization," a presumed strategy of the north to control both the government and the economy. Northern professionals, meanwhile, express frustration that they are often assumed to be incompetent by their southern counterparts.

The Executive

Evolution of Executive Function

In the Second Republic, the earlier parliamentary system was replaced by a presidential system based on the U.S. model. The president was chosen directly by the electorate rather than indirectly by the legislature. The rationale for the change was based on the experience of the First Republic; the instability and ultimate failure of that government, which was less a result of the parliamentary model per se than of underlying societal cleavages, left a bitter legacy. In addition, there was a widespread belief that a popularly elected president, a truly national figure, could serve as a symbol of unity. Finally, the framers of the Second Republic's constitution believed that placing the election of the president in the hands of the electorate rather than parliament would mitigate the effects of a lack of party discipline in the selection of the executive.

Current Challenges: Nigeria's "Federal Character"

What is Nigeria's "federal character"? Federal character, in principle, is an affirmative action program to ensure representation of all ethnic and regional groups, particularly in the civil service. Although federal character is regarded as a euphemism for ethnic balancing, in practice it has provoked ethnic instability, rivalry, and conflict. Federal character goes beyond federalism in the traditional Western and territorial sense, although it definitely contains a territorial element. Federalism as a principle of government has a positive connotation (especially in regard to mitigating ethnic conflict); however, federal character elicits unevenness and inequality in Nigerian politics.

The pursuit of ethnic balancing has had numerous ill effects, several of which are identified by Nigerian scholar Peter Ekeh. First, federal character has created benefit-seeking and autonomy-seeking groups in areas where they did not previously exist. Second, federal character and federalism have overloaded the political system in terms of personnel and other costs. Federal character has also "invaded the integrity of the public bureaucracy" by ignoring merit. Finally, the thirty-six states that currently exist in Nigeria are vying for control of the center in order to extract the greatest benefits, using federal character's ethnic quotas as a lever. None of these conditions is likely to change in the near future, whether a military or a civilian government is in power. Federal character, and everything that goes with it, appears

to be a permanent part of Nigeria's political and social landscape.

Despite the methods of its institution and reform, ironically, the federal system has enjoyed wide support within Nigeria historically. With the national question unanswered, however, the federal structure endures increasing strain. At the conclusion of the civil war in 1970, many assumed that the question of national unity had been finally settled. Thus attempts to include clauses on the right to secede into the constitutions of 1979 and 1989 were roundly rejected by the drafting committees. Yet the Abubakar transition period featured a number of public debates about secession, particularly among the Yoruba. Other widely held beliefs are now questioned by some elements in society. For example, will Nigeria continue to be a secular state as outlined in the 1979 constitution and persist as a federation to accommodate the country's ethnic, cultural, and religious heterogeneity? Some northerners have advocated turning Nigeria into an Islamic state, prompting fear among many Christians.

To resolve these issues, some Nigerians have called for a national conference to review the basis of national unity and even to consider the restructuring of Nigeria into a loose confederation of autonomous states, perhaps along the lines of the First Republic. Such calls have been ignored by the military, which refused to permit any debate on the viability of a united Nigeria in the 1994–1995 constitutional conference, thus maintaining the geographic status quo. General Abubakar also ignored renewed calls for a national conference when he initiated his transition program in 1998. Key members of some of the nascent political parties have indicated that they will include such a conference in their platforms.

Source: See Ekeh, "The Structure and Meaning of Federal Character in the Nigerian Political System" in *Federal Character and Federalism in Nigeria*, ed. Peter P. Ekeh and Eghosa E. Osaghae (Ibadan: Heinemann, 1989).

In rejecting British parliamentarism for U.S.-style presidentialism, and a two-term limit, the framers of the 1979 constitution of the Second Republic argued that the new arrangement would lead to a more focused and effective executive. According to them, the U.S. model would also ensure (through the exercise of checks and balances and separation of powers) that no single arm of government would gain so much power as to put the liberties of citizens at risk. It was

argued also that presidentialism would promote political integration, since it authorized the head of the executive branch to appoint individuals from outside the legislature to the cabinet.

The Second Republic's experiment with presidentialism lasted for only four years before it was ended by the 1983 coup. Although political scientists continue to debate the relative merits of parliamentarism versus presidentialism,[12] that coup did not indict the presidential model as such. The return of military rule in 1983 further concentrated power in the hands of the chief executive, the head of state Major-General Muhammadu Buhari, until his removal in a 1985 palace coup. His successor, General Babangida, although obviously unelected, assumed the title of president, the first Nigerian military ruler to do so. After ousting Shonekan in November 1993, Sani Abacha also assumed the title of president.

The Executive under Military Rule and Future Civilian Governments

The styles and leadership approaches among Nigeria's seven military heads of state have varied widely. The military regime of General Gowon (1966–1975) was initially consensual, but as he clung to power for five years after the Biafran war, his authority declined and he increasingly relied on a small group of advisers. Although all have talked of "transitions to democracy," only General Obasanjo as a military ruler (1976–1979) and General Abubakar (1998–1999) have fulfilled the pledge of yielding power to an elected government. Buhari's coup in 1983 was initially welcomed by popular support in the wake of the abuses during the Second Republic. Many Nigerians today look back on the Buhari regime as a brief period during which the government exercised some discipline. He was, however, disliked for his authoritarian methods, the suspension of political liberties and outlawing of political activities, and for the extensive use of security services against political opponents.

After a few years of relatively consensual governance, the Babangida regime (1985–1993) drifted into the repressive policies of the Buhari era. Abacha outdid them all, however, and his harsh authoritarian rule included the 1994 suspension of habeas corpus and the hounding of outspoken Nigerians into exile. General Abubakar began like many of his predecessors, moving quickly to release political prisoners, institute a rapid democratization program, and curb the abuses of the security services. Fortunately for Nigeria, his decision to transfer power within less than a year guaranteed that his regime would not follow the usual pattern of decay, authoritarianism, and corruption.

Under both civilian and military administrations, appointments to most senior positions have been made by the president, or head of state, without seeking legislative approval. Even with the tumultuous events in Nigeria since Babangida stepped aside in August 1993, patron-client relationships remain fundamental to Nigeria's politics. Not surprisingly, therefore, ethnic, religious, and regional constituencies pay close attention to the pattern of appointments to the executive branch. Under the 1989 constitution, the proposed Third Republic would have included an executive similar to the U.S. model with several checks and balances. The U.S. presidential model is the one being followed in the Fourth Republic, although some of the innovations in Abacha's 1995 constitution (which he never formally issued), such as a rotational presidency among sections of the country, have been dropped. Whether the provisions of the eventual constitution of the Fourth Republic will be respected through implementation, however, remains to be seen. Nigeria's political history and recent experience suggest that the country will again experience the unchallenged rule of an executive president and his handpicked cabinet, ineffectually checked by a weak legislature and judiciary, both vulnerable to executive and clientelist pressures.

The Military as Executive Branch

As a result of its long years in power, the military has emerged as a central component of executive authority in Nigeria. As a consequence, the armed forces have been structurally weakened. Unlike their professional counterparts in other countries, Nigeria's military lacks camaraderie, discipline, a clear command structure, and unity of purpose. Since 1966 a distinction has developed between the military-in-government (officers appointed to political posts) and the military-in-barracks, who perform traditional military duties. Senior officers in the latter group have increasingly called for a withdrawal of the armed forces from politics and the restoration of military professionalism.

Coups conducted against military governments have often resulted from intramilitary tension. Several such attempts have failed, followed invariably by the execution or dismissal from the service of individuals implicated or suspected of disloyalty. Keenly aware of this, Babangida protected himself by constantly shuffling military personnel. Command and other major postings were dictated largely by questions of loyalty to his regime, resulting in the rapid advance of northern officers like himself. Increasingly under Babangida and then Abacha, the gulf between junior officers and the inner circle of northern military elites widened. The former were beset by a lack of prestige and inadequate pay, whereas many of the latter, including Abacha himself, profited greatly from their control of state resources.

One major consequence of these developments has been the loss by the Nigerian military of its non-political status. It is no longer considered by many Nigerians as a temporary, politically neutral alternative to civilian rule. As an institution, the military has been transformed from an instrument that guarantees national defense and security into another predatory apparatus similar to, but more powerful than, political parties. Three decades after the first military coup of January 1966, most Nigerians now believe that the country's political and economic development has been profoundly hampered by military domination and misrule. Since the late 1980s civil society groups have insisted that the military's withdrawal from public life is imperative if progress is to be made in virtually all areas of public life.

The Bureaucracy

The bureaucracy is related to and affects all aspects of Nigerian government. Although we referred to the Nigerian bureaucracy in the previous two sections, it is necessary to explain further how the Nigerian bureaucracy came to be bloated, inefficient, and corrupt. The colonial system relied greatly on an expanding bureaucracy to govern Nigeria. As government and society were increasingly "Africanized," the bureaucracy became a way to reward individuals in the patrimonial, prebendalist system. Bureaucratic growth was no longer determined by function and need; increasingly, individuals were appointed on the basis of patronage, ethnic group, and regional origin rather than merit. Administrative departments also became politicized as the government insulated and protected itself by installing civil servants who were loyal to and beholden to it.

Military governments in particular looked for allies in the bureaucracy, whose skills they needed for the complex tasks of governing. As successive

military governments since 1967 increased the number of states, while also launching grandiose public projects, the capabilities of the bureaucracy declined, while its size steadily increased. It is conservatively estimated that federal and state government personnel increased from a modest 72,000 at independence to well over 1 million by the mid-1980s.

Para-statals

The largest component of the national bureaucracy in Nigeria is the state-owned enterprises, or **para-statals**, which increased from 75 entities to 500 over the same period. Para-statals in Nigeria are corporate enterprises owned by the state and established to provide specific commercial and social welfare services. They are situated between institutions that engage in traditional government operations, such as customs or the postal service, and those in the private sector that operate primarily for profit. In organizational terms, such para-statals are similar to private enterprises in having their own boards of directors. In principle they are autonomous of the government that established them. In reality, however, such autonomy is limited, since their boards are appointed by, and ultimately answerable to, the government through the supervising government ministry.

In general, para-statals are established for the following reasons. First, they serve as public utilities that provide services which government departments cannot handle effectively but which the government is reluctant to pass on to private businesses. They include ports, waterworks, telecommunications, defense industries, hydroelectric power, and petroleum exploration and extraction. A second rationale for the establishment of para-statals is the need to accelerate economic development by controlling the "commanding heights" of the economy, including steel production, petroleum and natural gas, and certain areas of agriculture. Third, para-statals are intended to provide basic utilities and services (water, electricity, public transportation, agricultural support) to citizens at a low cost. These costs are held below the level of charges for the same services needed by private firms to generate profit.

Finally, there is a nationalist dimension that relates to issues of sovereignty over sectors perceived sensitive for national security. In this regard, para-statals

Institutional Intricacies: *Corporatism*

Corporatism has varying definitions and interpretations, but may be defined broadly as a system of interest-group aggregation whereby interest groups are hierarchically ordered in terms of their relationship with the state and licensed or controlled by the state. European or societal corporatism allows the national government greater access to information about various groups in society. Societal corporatism usually connotes a coherent and efficient state bureaucracy and describes a set of centralized interest organizations that bargain with the state. Many Africanist scholars, however, have argued that the concept of corporatism does not apply in Africa because the state is fragmented. State, local, and national agencies operate at

cross-purposes in pursuit of different goals, and lack centralization and coherence. A few, notably Julius Ihonvbere and Tim Shaw, have argued, however, that a state corporatist model can be applied to Nigeria.

The theoretical debate notwithstanding, the Nigerian state has endeavored to institute corporatist-like controls over various societal interest groups, including labor and business, in what might be labeled state corporatism, a variety of corporatism consistent with the authoritarian aspects of military rule. A blatant example of Nigeria's state corporatism was the 1994 attempt to control organized labor by firing the union heads and replacing them with Abacha's cronies. Unlike most environments of societal corporatism in which labor leaders with the support of their consitutents agree to cooperate with government, much of the rank and file of Nigerian labor refused to cooperate with the Abacha regime. His decimation of the union leadership was, however, effective in reducing the threat posed by trade unions to his rule.

Source: Julius Ihonvbere and Tim Shaw, "Corporatism in Nigeria" in *Corporatism in Africa: Comparative Analysis and Practice*, ed. Julius Nyang'oro and Tim Shaw (Boulder, Colo.: Westview Press, 1989).

are intended to provide services in economic areas that the government wishes to keep from the control of foreign capital and expertise. The para-statal structure is seen as a way to reduce dependence on foreign multinational firms in such industries as air transportation, seaport management, steel and petroleum production, power generation, and mass communication.

In Nigeria para-statals such as commodity boards and the Nigerian National Petroleum Corporation (NNPC) have served as major instruments of the interventionist state. They have been used to co-opt and hierarchically order business and societal interests for the purpose of controlling both society and economy —a form of governance usually called **state corporatism**. Because they are not motivated by profit, are protected by the state, and are frequently managed by administrators whose jobs are based on their personal connections rather than on managerial ability, the track record of Nigerian para-statals is littered with inefficiency, cronyism, and corruption. Most para-statal enterprises in Africa, just as in Nigeria, are a tremendous drain on the economy. It is not surprising, there-

fore, that one of the major requirements of the economic structural adjustment programs (see Section 2) is the privatization of most of these enterprises.

Although laudable in principle, in practice frequently mismanaged privatization programs have led to a continuation of problems. Without concerted and genuine efforts at privatization, Nigerian para-statals will likely continue to fall far short of the original expectations that they would contribute to economic development and efficient provision of services. Moreover, unless they are greatly reduced in number, they will contribute to the politics of patronage and resource allocation conducted along class and ethnic lines.

Other State Institutions

Other institutions of governance and policy-making, including the federal judiciary and subnational governments (incorporating state and local courts), operate within the context of a strong central government dominated by an all-powerful chief executive.

The Judiciary

At one time, the Nigerian judiciary enjoyed relative autonomy from the executive arm of government. Aggrieved individuals and organizations could take the government to court and expect a judgment based on the merits of their case. This situation changed as each successive military government demonstrated a profound disdain for judicial practices, and eventually undermined not only the autonomy but also the very integrity of the judiciary as a third branch of government.

The principal instrument used by the Babangida and Abacha regimes to achieve this outcome was a spate of repressive decrees that contained clauses disallowing judicial review. Such clauses were regularly inserted in government decrees barring any consideration of their legality by the courts as well as any actions taken by government officials under them. Other methods included intimidation by the security services, the creation of parallel special military tribunals that could dispense with various legal procedures and due process, and disrespect for courts of record. Through the executive's power of appointment of judicial officers to the high bench as well as the executive's control of funds required for the running of the judiciary, the government can manipulate and dominate the courts at all levels. Even in more routine civil and criminal actions, the courts are subject to political interference. In addition, what was once regarded as a highly competent judiciary has been undermined severely by declining standards of legal training as well as bribery. Deprived of adequate resources and the protections afforded the judiciary in Western societies, the judiciary has become an instrument of military regimes rather than an independent branch of government.

Any remaining doubts about this development were dispelled on July 22, 1993, when, in what analysts labeled "judicial terrorism," the Supreme Court endorsed a government position that literally placed all actions of the executive beyond the pale of judicial review. In a landmark judgment on a suit that sought judicial review of Babangida's decision to annul the June 12 election, the court ruled that it lacked jurisdiction, thereby bowing to the argument that any decree of a military government cannot be legally challenged. The judiciary in Nigeria has effectively ceased to be the last bastion for the protection of the rights of Nigerian citizens. The prolonged detention and death of Moshood Abiola after he declared himself president in June 1994, combined with the multiple changes in presiding judges hearing challenges to his detention, further eroded public confidence in the judiciary. The detention and hanging of Ken Saro-Wiwa and eight other Ogoni activists in 1995 underscored the politicization and compromised state of the judicial system. The military did not even bother to make a legal argument before a court of law. Instead, the military arranged its own court, consisting primarily of military officers, for the nine accused civilians. Not surprisingly, this sham court returned a guilty verdict; within forty-eight hours of the verdict, the nine had been hung, an action that was itself a violation of the automatic review procedure for death penalty decisions under Nigerian law.

State and Local Judiciaries

The judiciaries at the state level are subordinate to the Federal Court of Appeal and the Supreme Court. Some of the states in the northern part of the country with high Muslim populations maintain a parallel court system based on the Islamic *shari'a* (divine law). Similarly, some states in the Middle Belt and southern part of the country have subsidiary courts based on customary law. Each of these, in turn, maintains an appellate division. Otherwise, all courts of record in the country are based on the English common law tradition, and all courts are ultimately bound by decisions handed down by the Supreme Court. As noted earlier, however, the decisions of all courts may be effectively overruled by the military government.

Because it has been a source of continuing debate in Nigerian politics, the subject of *shari'a* deserves mention. For several years, some northern groups have participated in a movement to apply *shari'a* to all of Nigeria, and some even advocated that it be made the supreme law of the land. In 1977 northern groups led a boycott of the Constituent Assembly when it began drafting the Second Republic constitution, demanding stronger emphasis on *shari'a* in that national document. Although the military government of Obasanjo blocked the expansion of *shari'a*, provisions were made that allowed the appointment of several judges qualified in Islamic personal law to the federal Court of Appeal and the Supreme Court. Demands for a broader application of Islamic law were made during the drafting of the 1989 constitution, but these were again thwarted. At present, *shari'a* courts have jurisdiction only in civil proceedings and in questions of Islamic personal law.

The application of *shari'a* has sparked heated debate. On the one hand, Muslims view *shari'a* as a way of life. On the other, southerners and Christians consider the very presence of *shari'a* on a national level threatening to their own interests and beliefs, and another example of northern domination. The attempt under Babangida to alter Nigeria's status from observer to full membership in the Organization of Islamic Conference in 1986 also prompted fears that the secular nature of the state was endangered.

It is hoped that some of the professionalism and dignity engendered by independence will revert to the judiciary in the next Republic. New budgetary arrangements will be needed to protect the institutional interests of the judiciary vis-à-vis the executive. Moreover, the executive will need to be encouraged to respect judicial autonomy as a vital component of democratic governance. Unfortunately, the experience of the judiciary during periods of civilian party politics, although not as devastating as during military rule, does not bode well for the restoration of an autonomous judiciary and respect for the rule of law in the near future.

State and Local Government

Because the creation of new states and local governments opens new channels to the oil wealth accumulated at the federal level, localities are constantly clamoring for more. Sensing opportunities to buy support for their regimes, Babangida and Abacha nearly doubled the number of states and tripled that of local governments (see Table 5 on page 583). Although they touted these moves as answering the national question by increasing opportunities for local self-determination, probably only Lagos and Kano states could survive without federal subsidies.

Debate over the 1995 constitution, therefore, raised the idea of cutting the number of states, but no one wanted to be the first to give up theirs. In response, constitutional planners raised the notion of six zones in Nigeria to correlate roughly with the major ethnic regions in the country—Hausa-Fulani, Igbo, Yoruba, and three minority-dominated areas. The only concrete purpose of the zones that the Abacha administration publicly discussed was to delineate the regions among which the presidency was to rotate. This notion of a rotational presidency was presented as yet another attempt to answer the national question, but was set aside by the Abubakar government in 1999.

Virtually the entire process of constituting and reconstituting this federal arrangement, including the addition of a third level of government, consisting of 774 local governments by 1996, has occurred under either colonial or military rule. The initial motivation to create additional subnational units in the federation was to bring government closer to the people, foster development, and accommodate the demands of minority ethnic groups for their own units. In addition, creating more states addressed the key structural flaw of the First Republic's weak federalist arrangement of three (and in 1963, four) regions: the Northern Region was larger territorially and in population terms than the others combined. Breaking the north into states was intended to blunt its influence on the federal government, although it has subsequently retained a greater number of states than the south.

As mentioned, however, adding more states to the federation was also clearly an intrinsic part of a strategy of state corporatism, designed to keep the many subnational units financially dependent on and beholden to the central government. Such practices were employed by the Babangida and Abacha military regimes to divide and control the Nigerian population rather than to enhance popular participation. In sum, the Nigerian experience has promoted a distributive approach to federalism. The lofty claims for federalism as a way of promoting unity through diversity are lost amid the intense competition among "local communities and elites for access to national patronage in the form of oil revenues which are collected, and then appropriated or redistributed, by the federal administration"[13] through the states (see Table 6 on page 584).

State governments are generally weak and dependent on federally controlled revenues. Most of them

Table 5

Political Divisions, 1963–1996					
1963	*1967*	*1976*	*1987*	*1991*	*1996*
Northern Region	North Central	Kaduna	Kaduna Katsina	Kaduna Katsina	(Northwest zone) Kaduna Katsina
	Kano	Kano	Kano	Kano	Kano
	North-Western	Sokoto	Sokoto	Jigawa Sokoto	Jigawa Sokoto Zamfara
				Kebbi	Kebbi
	Benue-Plateau	Niger Benue-Plateau	Niger Benue-Plateau	Niger Benue Plateau	(North-central zone) Niger Benue Plateau Nassarawa
	West-Central	Abuja Kwara	Abuja Kwara	FCT (Abuja)[a] Kwara Kogi[b]	FCT (Abuja) Kwara Kogi
	North-Eastern	Bauchi	Bauchi	Bauchi	(Northeast zone) Bauchi Gombe
		Borno	Borno	Borno Yobe	Borno Yobe
		Gongola	Gongola	Adamawa Taraba	Adamawa Taraba
Eastern Region	East-Central	Anambra	Anambra	Anambra Enugu	(Southeast zone) Anambra Enugu Ebonyi
		Imo	Imo	Imo Abia	Imo Abia
	South-Eastern	Cross River	Cross River Akwa Ibom	Cross River Akwa Ibom	(South-south zone) Cross River Akwa Ibom
	Rivers	Rivers	Rivers	Rivers	Rivers Bayelsa
Mid-West Region	Mid-Western	Bendel	Bendel	Edo Delta	Edo Delta
Western Region	Western	Ogun Ondo	Ogun Ondo	Ogun Ondo	(Southwest zone) Ogun Ondo Ekiti
		Oyo	Oyo	Oyo Osun	Oyo Osun
Lagos[c]	Lagos	Lagos	Lagos	Lagos	Lagos

[a]Abuja replaced Lagos as the federal capital in December 1991, although its boundaries were first delineated in the 1970s.
[b]Kogi state was created by combining parts of Benue and Kwara states.
[c]Lagos was excised from the Western Region in 1954 and became the federal capital. In 1967 it also became capital of the new Lagos state, which included Badagry, Ikeja, and Epe districts from the Western Region.

Source: From *Politics and Economic Development in Nigeria* by Tom Forrest. Copyright © 1993, 1995 by Westview Press Inc. Reprinted by permission of Westview Press, a member of Perseus Books, L. L. C.

Table 6

Percentage Contribution of Different Sources of Government Revenue to Allocated Revenue, 1980–1996

	Oil Revenue Petroleum Profits Tax	Mining Rents and Royalties	Non-Oil Revenue Customs and Excise Duties	Other	Total
1980	58.1	25.7	12.3	3.9	100.0
1981	55.5	19.6	20.4	4.5	100.0
1982	44.5	27.3	21.5	6.7	100.0
1983	35.7	33.4	18.9	12.0	100.0
1984	44.8	32.4	15.2	7.6	100.0
1985	47.8	30.0	14.7	7.5	100.0
1986	40.5	25.3	14.6	19.6	100.0
1987	50.6	25.4	14.3	9.7	100.0
1988	46.7	31.5	15.9	5.9	100.0
	Oil Revenue (Combined)		Non-Oil Revenue	Other	Total
1992	86.2		8.4	5.4	100.0
1993	84.0		8.0	8.0	100.0
1994	79.3		9.1	11.6	100.0
1995	53.2		8.1	38.7[a]	100.0
1996	51.1		10.6	38.3[a]	100.0

[a]Beginning in 1995, the Nigerian government began including surplus foreign exchange as federally collected revenue in its accounting.

Sources: Federal Ministry of Finance and Economic Development, Lagos. From Adedotun Phillips, "Managing Fiscal Federalism: Revenue Allocation Issues," *Publius: The Journal of Federalism* 21, no. 4 (Fall 1991), 109. Nigerian Federal Office of Statistics, *Annual Abstract of Statistics: 1997 Edition.*

would be insolvent and unable to sustain themselves without substantial support from the central government, because of the states' weak resource and tax base. In the same way that states depend on federal handouts, local governments have remained dependent on both state and federal governments. This practice has continued despite reforms of the local government system initiated by the Babangida regime in 1988, supposedly to strengthen that level of government. The state and local governments have the constitutional and legal powers to raise funds through taxes. However, Nigerians, especially those in self-employment, trade, and other informal sector activities, share a pronounced unwillingness to pay taxes and fees to a government with such a poor record of delivering basic services. Moreover, experience seems to support the belief that most funds paid to government, at all levels, will be misused or simply stolen. The result is a vicious cycle. Government is sapped of resources and legitimacy, and cannot adequately serve

the people. Communities, in turn, are compelled to resort to self-help measures to protect these operations and thus withdraw further from the reach of the state. Because very few individuals and organizations pay taxes, even the most basic government functions cannot be performed (see Table 7 on page 585).

Although intergovernmental relations tend to be less confrontational under military rule because of its unitary command structure, conflict between subnational and national governments is inevitable. During the civilian Second Republic (1979–1983), conflicts developed between the federal and state governments, mostly over access to economic resources. About 90 percent of state incomes were received directly from the federal government, which includes a lump sum based on oil revenues, plus a percentage of oil income based on population. One of the challenges confronting the Fourth Republic is to develop a more effective federal system that would devolve more resources to state and local governments. These governmental units

Table 7

Share of Total Government Expenditure								
	1961	*1965*	*1970*	*1975*	*1980*	*1987*	*1992*	*1996*
Federal government	49%	53%	73%	72%	66%	75%	72%	74%
State government	51%	47%	27%	28%	34%	25%	28%[a]	26%[a]
Total expenditure (Naira millions)	336	445	1,149	10,916	21,349	29,365	128,476	327,707

[a]Note that 67% of state spending in 1992 and 49% in 1996 came from federal government oil earnings, part of which are allocated annually to all the states roughly in proportion to their population size.

Sources: Central Bank of Nigeria, *Annual Report and Statement of Accounts;* Federal Office of Statistics, *Abstract of Annual Statistics* (Lagos: Federal Government Printer, 1961, 1965, 1970, 1975, 1980, 1987, and 1997). From Izeubuwa Osayimwese and Sunday Iyare, "The Economics of Nigerian Federalism: Selected Issues in Economic Management," *Publius: The Journal of Federalism* 21, no. 4 (Fall 1991), 91. 1990s percentage calculations by Darren Kew.

must, however, generate more resources of their own to increase the efficiency of both their administrations and private economic sectors.

The Policy-Making Process

Nigeria's prolonged experience with military rule has resulted in a policy process based on top-down directives rather than on consultation, political debate, and legislation. Formal powers are concentrated in the military ruler. Much of the policy input process (to the extent it exists) comes to the president and his "cabinet" through informal channels and networks where clientelist practices flourish.

Because of their influence in recruitment and promotions, as well as through their own charisma or political connections, senior officers often develop a network of supporters of the same or lower rank, creating what is referred to as a "loyalty pyramid."[14] Once in power, the men at the top of these pyramids in Nigeria have access to tremendous oil wealth, which is passed on through the lower echelons of the pyramid to reward support. Often these pyramids feature ethnic or religious affiliations (see the discussions of corruption in Section 2 and prebendalism in Section 4), such as the "Kaduna Mafia" of officers from the Middle Belt, but pyramids like the "Babangida Boys" or "Abacha Boys" included a patchwork of officers from beyond the Middle Belt or northern sections of their leaders. In addition, the well-developed pyramids have allies or personal connections in the bureaucracy, business, or elsewhere in the private sector.

When the military seizes power, divisions within its ranks can become as politicized as those among the political parties in a civilian legislature. Thus a hierarchical institution structured to perform a single function—national security—over time will see its institutional solidarity and identity in constant tension with the politics of loyalty pyramids. As the regime struggles to address Nigeria's mammoth problems, whatever legitimacy the regime first gained in its claim to end corruption or to save the integrity of the state tends to be replaced by a legitimacy based on the tool that lifted it to power in the first place: the gun.

The personal ambitions of loyalty pyramid leaders eclipse the unified corporate mission of the military to "save" the nation. In time, personal ambition is the defining characteristic of the regime, with its only check being another coup. Most civilian leaders, of course, also have strong personal ambition, but if the democratic system is strong, their choices are constrained by the desire to be reelected. In most military regimes, the executive is constrained only by the balance of power among the loyalty pyramids within the armed forces, and the weakness of the overall economic and political systems that existed before the coup. Rather than addressing national problems, military regimes end up spending most of their time trying to solidify their shifting sources of power among the loyalty pyramids, which in Nigeria no leader or coalition of pyramids has been able to sustain indefinitely. Thus, in the end military regimes are no more stable, no less corrupt, no more effective economic managers than the civilians.

In many African countries, a coup signifies the ascension of one particular loyalty pyramid into power, often at the expense of others. Nigeria's first coup in 1966 appeared to signal the rise of a group of Igbo officers under General Ironsi, although he tried to maintain a more nationalist image. General Gowon, on the other hand, helped to establish a collegial (or consensus) model of military governance in which important decisions were made by an ethnically balanced body consisting of the leaders of the major loyalty pyramids. Because of the Biafran civil war, the young Gowon, a Christian from the Middle Belt and without much of a loyalty pyramid of his own, was picked by his senior officers to be a compromise head of state.Using this collegial model, Gowon successfully oversaw the reintegration of Biafra into Nigeria. The Muhammed and Obasanjo regimes also employed this model, as did Buhari and, at first, Babangida.

General Babangida, however, signified the turning point within the military when national concerns became increasingly subsumed by personal ambitions. He was a master at playing the different loyalty pyramids against each other, lavishing the nation's oil wealth on friends and buying the support of opponents he could not crush. Although Babangida's Armed Forces Ruling Council (AFRC) was initially tailored in the collegial fashion to reflect the ethnic and religious balance in the nation, he gradually replaced AFRC members with officers of northern descent who, more important, were his "boys." By the early 1990s the AFRC was quickly becoming a one-man operation with only one agenda: personal aggrandizement and enrichment. Babangida managed to survive two coups (of which the public was aware) but could not withstand the public outcry over his annulment of the June 1993 election, combined with pressure spearheaded by the Abacha faction within the military for him to step aside. Once in power, General Abacha made little pretense of accommodating other factions, ruthlessly centralizing nearly all government decision-making and spreading little of the largesse for which Babangida was famous.

Abacha's personal bonanza with the nation's revenues dispelled the notion that the military was a cohesive, nationalist institution capable of governing Nigeria more efficiently than the civilians. Young people fought for entrance to the military academies as the preferred career path to wealth and power, and private groups sprouted up—with the active support and participation of Abacha supporters in the military—to "demand" that the General stay on as a civilian president. Fearful of the growing tide of resentment within the military, Abacha rarely left the presidential fortress at Aso Rock in Abuja, almost never gave public speeches, and allowed only a cadre of closest supporters to meet with him regularly to make government policy decisions. Officers that showed a shred of independence or professionalism found their names on the next retirement list, were transferred to Liberia and Sierra Leone to fight in ECOMOG, or were even indicted for participating in coup plots that were likely fabricated. A parallel structure of junior officers fiercely loyal to Abacha acted as his gatekeepers, circumventing and humiliating the military's normal chain of command.

General Abubakar took the reins in June 1998 of a military that was a cohesive institution in name alone. The exact course of events has yet to be made public, but a number of senior officers with some remaining professionalism and concern for the integrity of the armed forces, and perhaps for the nation, appear to have rallied behind Abubakar, then chief of defense staff, to be head of state. Although Abubakar was once considered a "Babangida boy" and could not have ascended the height of the military command by being an absolute professional, he seemed intent on restoring the integrity of the military by returning it to the barracks. Within a month he had removed most of the "Abacha boys" from positions of power, instigated internal investigations into the money they had stolen, and reenergized the democratization process. He himself, however, did not appear to have the extensive loyalty pyramids of his predecessors and employed the collegial model to balance those of his current allies. Nonetheless, Abubakar's precarious position was quickly strengthened by the public and international support he won by releasing political prisoners and instituting a rapid transition program, making the likelihood of a countercoup attempt remote.

Yet regardless of whether the professional and pro-democratic inclinations of General Abubakar and his allies were genuine, others in the military clearly yearned for their turn at the top. Younger officers had spent at least fifteen years getting law degrees and Ph.D. degrees, and seeking traditional titles and chieftaincies. They had tasted power as military governors, built their own loyalty pyramids, and seen the lavish living of their predecessors, while still retaining the perspective that civilians are ineffective leaders. These men had made career investments that counted on military rule, and may not give up those ambitions lightly. Furthermore, the civilian government in 1999 inherited huge economic problems and social divisions that were certain to stretch its fragile institutions to the limits. Any chaos that results may offer ample excuses for a military entrepreneur to make his move. The civilian politicians appear well aware of this danger, but whether they will be able to resist by forging a new role with the military, as well as a sustainable coalition of support with civil society groups and public constituencies, remains to be seen.

Section ❹ Representation and Participation

Representation and participation are two vital components in modern democracies; however, Nigeria clearly is not yet a democracy. As noted, Nigerian legislative bodies have been ineffectual in practice; fraud, elite manipulation, and military interference have marred the party system and elections. Nevertheless, other modes of participation exist in Nigerian society outside the official structures. An important focus of this section is the unofficial (nongovernmental) methods of representation and participation through the institutions of civil society. Whereas the institutions of political society include such entities as parties, constitutions, and legislatures, those of **civil society** include professional associations, trade unions, religious groups, and various interest groups.

The Nigerian experience described in this section emphasizes the complex nature of the relationship between representation and participation. It shows that formal representation does not necessarily enhance participation. In fact, there are situations in which the most important modes of political participation are found outside of, and in opposition to, the institutional modes such as elections and legislatures.

The Legislature

Not surprisingly, Nigeria's legislature has been a victim of the country's political instability. Legislative structures and processes have not operated free of abuse, neglect, or peremptory suspension by the executive arm for any significant length of time since independence. As a consequence, the legislature has not become a vital component of a democratic system and there is little understanding of the functions and responsibilities of the legislature.

Until the first coup in 1966, Nigeria operated its legislature along the lines of the British model with an elected lower house and a smaller upper house composed of individuals selected by the executive. Then for the next thirteen years under military rule, legislative functions were performed by a supreme military council, which initiated and passed decrees at will. During the second period of civilian rule, 1979–1983, the legislature was similar to the United States system. As in the United States, Nigeria employed a bicameral structure, with both houses (Senate and House of Representatives) consisting of elected members. The Fourth Republic that began on May 29, 1999, maintained a U.S.-inspired legislative system and a separately elected president and vice president.

Beginning with the 1983 coup led by Muhammadu Buhari, Nigeria has witnessed a succession of military councils under different names (the Supreme Military Council; the Armed Forces Ruling Council; the National Defense and Security Council; and most recently, the Provisional Ruling Council, or PRC, under Abacha) that performed the function of approving decrees issued by the military administrations. The roles and powers of these institutions varied. Usually, however, they rubber-stamped decisions made by the head of state as the system became progressively autocratic.

As part of the Babangida regime's transition program, the civilian members of the National Assembly elected in July 1992 actually held meetings until mid-1993. Once seated, however, they were barred by military decree from deliberating on issues other than those dealing with uncontroversial topics. Part of the interim national government arrangement, which only lasted from August to November 1993, was that full powers of legislation would be granted to the Senate and House of Representatives. When Abacha took over, however, he dismissed both houses as well as all other elected officials at the state and local levels.

Only one woman sat among the 91 senators and two among the 593 representatives in the Third Republic, and only eight women were elected in 1999 to sit in the Fourth Republic's National Assembly. This reflects the limited political participation of Nigerian women in formal institutions, as discussed in Section 2. Election to the Senate is on the basis of equal state representation, with three senators from each of the thirty-six states, plus one senator from the federal capital territory, Abuja. The practice of equal representation in the Senate is identical to that of the United States, except that Nigerian states elect three senators instead of two. Another difference is the election of a senator from Abuja Capital Territory, whereas Washington, D.C., has no such representation. Election to the Nigerian House of representatives is also based on state representation but weighted to reflect the relative size of each state's population, again after the U.S. example.

An innovation made in the halting transition to the Third Republic is that local government structures were to be granted greater autonomy from state control. The lessons from Nigeria's past, however, will weigh on future developments: on the whole, the federal executive has dominated the other branches of government. Subordination of the legislature to the executive is partly a consequence of the frequency of military coups. It is standard practice among coup leaders to replace all elected legislatures with ruling councils, handpicked by the military executive. Indeed, General Abacha's first act as head of state in November 1993 was to abolish all political institutions, including the duly elected national and state legislatures. He allowed the local governments elected in 1997 to take office but not the state and national assemblies elected in 1997 and 1998.

To summarize, Nigerian legislatures under military government were either powerless or nonexistent. However, even under elected civil administrations, Nigerian legislatures have been subjected to great pressure by the executive and never assumed their full constitutional role. Because the executive and majority interests in the assembly have belonged to the same party, this influence has been easily exercised through the actions of party machines and by outright bribery. The history of independent Nigeria reveals a subverted national legislature that has never effectively represented the electorate. Underlying all this is a political economy skewed in favor of an executive branch, and the dependence of legislators on the executive for their allowances and the resources to meet the relentless demands from their constituents for jobs, contracts, and other favors.

The Party System and Elections

The unfortunate legacy of the party and electoral system since independence in 1960 was that political parties were associated with certain regions and ethnic groups. This extreme factionalization was further encouraged by the tendency of most Nigerians to perceive politics as a zero-sum (or winner-take-all) struggle for access to scarce state resources. Unlike Mexico and, to some extent, India, Nigeria did not develop an authoritarian de facto single-party system after independence that might have transcended some of these social cleavages. Instead, the multiparty system reinforced and deepened existing social divisions.

Nigeria's use of a "first-past-the-post" plurality electoral system produced legislative majorities for parties with strong ethnic and regional identities. All of the parties of the First and Second Republics were more attentive to the welfare of the regions from which they drew most support than to the development of Nigeria as a whole. Control of the center, or at least access to it, ensures access to substantial financial resources. In a polity as potentially volatile as Nigeria, however, these tendencies intensified political fragmentation and persistent resentment among the losers.

Nigerian parties during the First Republic were dominated by the three largest ethnic groups. During subsequent democratic experiments, many of the more recent parties could trace their roots to their predecessors in the First Republic. Although the name of a given party may have changed, its leadership and the areas from which it drew its strongest support remained fairly consistent. For example, the victorious NPN of the Second Republic, under the leadership of Shehu Shagari, was the political heir of the northern-dominated NPC of the First Republic. Similarly, the runner-up UPN of the Second Republic can be connected to the western-based Action Group of the First Republic. The Second Republic's NPP drew on the legacy of the NCNC of the First Republic, the strongest party of the former Eastern Region. The four-year experiment with a two-party system from 1989 to 1993 and the election of Abiola in 1993 demonstrated the potential within Nigeria to move beyond ethnicity. Abiola won a number of key states in the north, including the hometown of his opponent. Once the election was annulled, however, the more familiar north-south divisions reemerged, fostered by both the regime and Abiola's most determined advocates.

The Two-Party Mandate

In its wavering steps toward the civilian Third Republic, General Babangida's administration in October 1989 announced a landmark decision to establish, by decree, two political parties. The state provided initial start-up funds and wrote the constitutions and manifestos of these parties. According to the government, its decision to form the parties followed the failure of various political associations to satisfy the requirements set by the government for registration as political parties. Based on this controversial decision, the National Republican Convention (NRC) and the Social Democratic Party (SDP) emerged, designed by the government to be "a little to the right and a little to the left," respectively, on the political-ideological spectrum.

The NRC and SDP were the only two parties allowed to operate legally until Abacha seized power in November 1993. Significantly, the NRC and SDP were modeled after their Western counterparts, the Republican and Democratic parties in the United States and the Conservative and Labour Parties in Britain, with two vital differences. First, the U.S. and

British party structures emerged after years of voluntary interaction. They were not decreed into existence by the state, as in Nigeria. Second, although two parties dominate the political arena in the United States and Britain, they are not the sole parties, and significantly there are no legal restrictions on the formation of additional parties. In Nigeria the two-party limitation was explicit, and no association other than the two recognized parties could contribute to party funds or election expenses of candidates.

Interestingly, the elections that took place between 1990 and 1992 at local, state, and federal levels indicated that, despite their inauspicious beginnings, the two parties cut across the cleavages of ethnicity, regionalism, and religion in their membership and electoral performance. The election results also suggested that some of the old interethnic factionalism was reappearing, although a substantial measure of interethnic cooperation contributed to the victory of Moshood Abiola, a southern Muslim, in the June 12 presidential election. As shown in Table 8 on pages 590–591, northern-based parties dominated the first and second experiments with civilian rule. Given this historical trend, it is significant that a southerner was able to win the presidency in 1993—the first time in Nigeria's history that a southerner defeated a northerner in elections to lead the nation. Southerners, therefore, perceived the decision by the northern-dominated Babangida regime to annul the June 12 elections as a deliberate attempt by the military and northern interests to maintain their decades-long domination of the highest levels of government.

The annulment, and the regional and ethnic tension that followed it, resuscitated the belief that Nigerian party and electoral processes could not overcome ethnic and cultural cleavages. The SDP was linked in terms of its membership and leadership to a southern-dominated Second Republic alliance of the Unity Party of Nigeria, UPN (mainly Yoruba), and the Nigerian Peoples Party, NPP (mainly Igbo). However, it also attracted splinter elements of the Second Republic's Peoples Redemption Party, PRP (organized and located around Kano city in northern Nigeria), and the Great Nigerian People's Party, GNPP (organized around the Kanuri northeast). Similarly, the NRC was seen as having its roots in northern forces that were the core of the National

Table 8

Federal Election Results in Nigeria, 1959–1999

1959 Federal Parliamentary Elections[a]

	No. of Seats	NPC	NCNC/NEPU Alliance	AG	Others
Total	310	134	89	73	14
Percent	100	43.2	28.7	23.6	4.5

Distribution of Parliamentary Seats after 12/64 and 3/65 Elections[b]

	No. of Seats	NPC	NNDP	NCNC	AG	NPF	Independent
Total	312	162	36	84	21	4	5
Percent	100	51.9	11.6	26.9	6.7	1.3	1.6

1979 General Elections, House of Representatives[c]

	No. of Seats	GNPP	UPN	NPN	PRP	NPP
Total	449	43	111	168	49	78
Percent	100	9.6	24.7	37.4	10.9	17.4

1979 Senate Elections[d]

	GNPP	UPN	NPN	PRP	NPP
Seats won (out of 95)	8	28	36	7	16
Percent	8.4	29.5	37.9	7.3	16.9

1979 Presidential Election[e]

		Ibrahim (GNPP)	Awolowo (UPN)	Shagari (NPN)	Kano (PRP)	Azikiwe (NPP)
Actual vote	16,846,633	1.68 million	4.92 million	5.69 million	1.74 million	2.81 million
Percent	100	10.0	29.2	33.8	10.3	16.7
No. states won	25%	3	6	12	2	3

Requirements for victory: plurality of popular vote, plus at least 25% of the vote in two-thirds (66.66%) of the nineteen states. Note that Shagari reached this level in just twelve of nineteen states (63.16%); however, a favorable ruling by the Federal Elections Commission (FEDECO) ensured his victory.

1983 House of Representatives Elections[f]

	No. of Seats	NAP	GNPP	UPN	NPN	PRP	NPP
Total	450[g]	0	0	33	264	41	48
Percent	100	0	0	7.3	58.7	9.1	10.7

1983 Senate Elections[h]

	NAP	GNPP	UPN	NPN	PRP	NPP
Seats won (out of 96)[i]	0	1	16	61	5	13
Percent	0	1.0	16.7	63.6	5.2	13.5

1983 Presidential Election[j]

		Tunji Braithwaite (NAP)	Waziri Ibrahim (GNPP)	Obafemi Awolowo (UPN)	Shehu Shagari (NPN)	Hassan Yusuf (PRP)	Nnamdi Azikiwe (NPP)
Actual Vote	25,454,967	.289 million	.641 million	7.91 million	12.05 million	1.04 million	3.53 million
Percent	100	1.1	2.5	31.1	47.3	4.1	13.9
No. states won (25%)	–	0	0	7	16	1	4

Requirements for victory: plurality of popular vote, plus at least 25% of the votes in two-thirds of the nineteen states.

Table 8 (continued)

Federal Election Results in Nigeria, 1959–1999

1991 State Government Elections [k]

	Total Gubernatorial Seats		Total State House Majorities [l]
SDP	14		17
NRC	16		11

1992 National Assembly and Senate Elections

	Total National Assembly Seats		Total Senate Seats
SDP	276		38
NRC	317		53

1993 Presidential Election (annulled by military)

	Percentage of Popular Vote		States Won (out of 30)
SDP (Abiola)	58		19
NRC (Tofa)	42		11

1998 Local Government Elections [m]

	Total Council Chairs (out of 774)		Total States with Majority (out of 36, plus FCT)
PDP	426		28 (including FCT)
APP	172		2 (one tied with PDP)
AD	95		6
Others	6		0

1999 State Gubernatorial and House of Assembly Elections

	Total Governor Seats (out of 36)		House of Assembly Majorities (out of 36)
PDP	21		23
APP	9		8
AD	6		5

1999 National Assembly Elections [n]

	Senate (out of 109)	House (out of 360)
PDP	59	206
APP	24	74
AD	20	68

1999 Presidential Election

	Percentage of Votes Cast
PDP (Obasanjo)	62.78
APP/AD (Falae)	37.22

[a] Adapted from Richard Sklar, *Nigerian Political Parties: Power in an Emergent African Nation* (New York: NOK Publishers, 1983), 36.

[b] Adapted from Larry Diamond, *Class, Ethnicity and Democracy in Nigeria: The Failure of the First Republic* (Syracuse: Syracuse University Press, 1988), 227.

[c] Figures from Richard A. Joseph, *Democracy and Prebendal Politics in Nigeria* (London: Cambridge University Press, 1987), 126.

[d] Figures from Joseph, 125.

[e] Adapted from Joseph, 127.

[f] Adapted from Toyin Falola and Julius Ihonvbere, *The Rise and Fall of the Second Republic* (London: Zed Books, 1985), 221.

[g] One seat added for FCT.

[h] Adapted from Falola and Ihonvbere, 220.

[i] One seat added for FCT.

[j] Adapted from Falola and Ihonvbere, 220.

[k] All 1991–1993 election results are from Larry Diamond, Anthony Kirk-Greene, and Oyeleye Oyediran, eds., *Transitions Without End: Nigerian Politics and Civil Society under Babangida* (Boulder, Colo.: Lynne Rienner, 1997).

[l] Two of the State Houses of Assembly were evenly split between SDP and NRC.

[m] Preliminary results, *The Guardian* (Lagos), Dcember 9, 1998.

[n] Preliminary results, *The Guardian* (Lagos), February 24, 1999. Six Senate and twelve House seats required by-election runoffs or court rulings.

Table 9

List of Acronyms Used in Table 8	
AD	Alliance for Democracy
AG	Action Group
APP	All People's Party
GNPP	Great Nigerian People's Party
NAP	Nigerian Advance Party
NCNC	National Convention of Nigerian Citizens (formerly, National Council of Nigeria and the Cameroons)
NEPU	Northern Elements Progressive Union
NNDP	Nigerian National Democratic Party
NPC	Northern People's Congress
NPF	Northern Progressive Front
NPN	National Party of Nigeria
NPP	Nigerian People's Party
NRC	National Republican Convention
PDP	People's Democratic Party
PRP	People's Redemption Party
SDP	Social Democratic Party
UPN	Unity Party of Nigeria

Party of Nigeria (NPN), which dominated the central government in the Second Republic under the leadership of Shehu Shagari. Thus, even before the 1993 election debacle, and despite statistics indicating a fairly diverse (especially for Nigeria) support base for each party, the SDP was informally regarded as the "Southern" Democratic Party and the NRC as the "Northern" Republican Convention.

Abacha's Ambition and Abubakar's Promise

Nigerians in general greeted General Abacha's 1993 coup and subsequent banning of the SDP and NRC with expressions of anger, while the response of party members, with a few exceptions, was muted. Southern-based human rights and pro-democracy groups, in alliance with student unions and other organizations, launched street demonstrations, while trade union strikes brought the economy to a halt by mid-1994. With the unions crushed and Abiola in jail by the end of 1994, Abacha started his own transition program. His plan began with a constitutional conference in 1994–1995, a third of whose members were

government appointees while the others were elected in electoral contests largely ignored by the public. To the nation's surprise, the conference passed a motion that the military should relinquish power by January 1996—a resolution orchestrated by retired General Shehu Yar'Adua, who had been General Obasanjo's deputy head of state as well as an SDP presidential contender. The military used bribery and pressure to have the resolution reversed. In March 1995, Yar'Adua found himself accused of plotting a coup with Obasanjo and a score of other Abacha opponents. Unlike Obasanjo, Yar'Adua did not survive his incarceration, as he died in prison in December 1997 under suspicious circumstances.

Without publicizing the constitution produced by the conference, General Abacha announced a new transition timetable in October 1995, which featured a series of elections from the local to the federal levels over the following three years in a manner reminiscent of the Babangida program. The military promptly fell behind this schedule, taking nearly a year before even allowing new parties to form. Once the ban on political associations was lifted, some of the Second Republic party structures resurfaced and applied for accreditation with the election commission. To general surprise, not only was a party favored by northern oligarchs not registered but most of the other parties led by powerful figures were also denied. In late 1996 the Abacha government registered only five parties, most of whose members had no public constituency and little political experience. By the time local government elections were held in January 1997, again behind schedule, the few people who did vote had little idea for whom they were voting; and some of the candidates confessed publicly that they had never even seen their party's manifesto.

During 1997 the five parties, which Chief Bola Ige, Second Republic governor of Oyo state, branded "five fingers of a leprous hand," began to clamor for General Abacha to run for president. Public participation in delayed state assembly elections in December 1997 was abysmal, as each of the parties proclaimed, one after another, that Abacha was their candidate. Despite strong resistance from some of its leaders, the fifth party finally succumbed to pressure and nominated Abacha in April 1998, making the presidential elections scheduled for August 1998 a mere referendum, which received the endorsement of the Chief Justice of the Supreme Court as being legally permissible. The transition process had become a travesty. Throughout the Abacha transition, military influence or active involvement in the parties was common. Key generals in the ruling regime would orchestrate party policies and provide supplementary funding for the already government-funded groups. The government actively disqualified party candidates just days before the casting of ballots, and peremptorily reversed some election results.

In 1996–1997, condemnation of the Abacha government came primarily from Lagos-based human rights and pro-democracy groups, exiles abroad, international nongovernmental organizations, and foreign governments. By April 1998, once Abacha's plan to be proclaimed president became a certainty, domestic opposition increased. A group of former governors and political leaders from the north (many former NPN and PRP members) publicly petitioned Abacha not to run for president. They were later joined by colleagues from the south, forming what they called the Group of 34 (G-34). Human rights and pro-democracy organizations began again to form alliances to organize protests, and critical press coverage recovered some of its former boldness. General Babangida in late May also voiced his opposition to Abacha's continuing as president. Nevertheless, public disenchantment and apathy were so pervasive after years of economic struggle and broken political promises that the only real obstacle to Abacha's plan for "self-succession" was whether the military would allow it.

Rumors of Abacha's ill health had circulated for a year, but his sudden death on June 8, 1998, was still a great surprise. The following day General Abubakar, Chief of Defense Staff, was sworn in as head of state. Shortly thereafter he promised a speedy transition to democracy and began releasing political prisoners. There were immediate calls for Abiola's release and his appointment to head an interim government of national unity. Abiola's death by heart attack on July 7, 1998, removed the last obstacle to the holding of entirely new elections, the preferred option of the Abubakar administration. New parties quickly formed, and even Yoruba political leaders agreed by August to participate, although they insisted that the next president should be a Yoruba to compensate their

people for having been robbed of their first elected presidency.

Once again, political associations centering on well-known personalities emerged around the country, and intense bargaining and mergers among the smaller groups took place. The G-34, the prominent group of civilian leaders who had condemned Abacha's continuation plans, tried to transform itself into a political party. They created the People's Democratic Party (PDP) in late August, minus most of the key Yoruba members of G-34, who joined a primarily Yoruba-based Alliance for Democracy (AD). At least twenty more parties applied for certification to the electoral commission, INEC, many of which were truly grassroots movements, including a transformed human rights organization and a trade union party. The Abubakar administration evidently played no role in party formation, nor did it provide government funds for their functioning, unlike its two predecessors, the Babangida and Abacha regimes.

For the first round of party registration, INEC required that parties have offices in twenty-four of the thirty-six states and pay a 1 million naira registration fee. Nine parties met these qualifications in October 1998, the most prominent of which were PDP, AD, and the All People's Party (APP); the latter included a mixture of groups from the Middle Belt, the southeast, and the far north. The next INEC hurdle required that parties earn at least 5 percent of the votes in two-thirds of the states in the December 1998 local government elections in order to proceed to the state and federal levels. This turned out to be an ingenious way of reducing the number of parties for the most important elections, and also to oblige them to try to broaden their appeal. As a consequence, only three parties competed in the elections for the federal legislature and the presidency in February 1999, with the AD and APP forming an alliance against the PDP for the purpose of the presidential vote.

In comparison to the failed experiments of Babangida and Abacha, the transition process under Abubakar moved ahead peacefully, if problematically. One important exception was the continuing unrest in the southern Niger Delta region. A number of minority groups there, who in some local government areas had engaged in a small-scale civil war since 1997, complained of being excluded from the process. In

September 1998 they seized several production sites from multinational oil corporations and demanded more local government access, development projects, and a greater share of the oil wealth. Bayelsa state elections were disrupted and had to be rescheduled, as were some local government contests in the region. Voter turnout in the Niger Delta region for the presidential and National Assembly elections was abysmal, while the political parties fraudulently inflated the returns.

Most of the registered parties rely on elite-centered structures established during previous civilian governments and transition programs. The PDP includes core members of the northern establishment NPN and the northern progressive PRP of the Second Republic. From the Second Republic, the AD drew key individuals from the Yoruba-dominated UPN, and the APP from the GNPP (a Kanuri–Middle Belt dominated party). The latter also featured southern politicians who had prominent roles in the five Abacha parties. Demonstrating the cross-ethnic alliances that have been forged and reworked despite the political disruptions of a quarter-century, only the AD reflected a specific ethnic configuration. General Obasanjo and other Yoruba leaders joined PDP. In a fiercely contested nomination battle, Obasanjo was chosen as the PDP's presidential nominee, defeating Second Republic Vice President Alex Ekwueme, who is Igbo. Obasanjo then went on to defeat the AD/APP alliance candidate, Chief Olu Falae, in the presidential contest in February 1999.

APP is truly a multiethnic collection, drawing northern politicians of royal lineage, northeastern and Middle Belt minorities, Igbo business moguls, and southern minority leaders. AD appears to be as Yoruba-centric as its Second Republic UPN and First Republic AG predecessors. Yet, like these earlier parties, it has attracted dynamic politicians from other areas, such as Alex Nwankwo, an Igbo. It is important to note the political pragmatism of the Abubakar administration (and the INEC) in registering the AD, despite its ethnoregional base, and allowing it to compete for the presidency in alliance with the APP. It made sense to accommodate rather than alienate the Yoruba people on account of the deep sense of grievance toward the federal government provoked by the 1993 annulment of Abiola's victory and the

subsequent five years of bitter conflict. The rapidity of the Abubakar-supervised electoral process benefited civil and military politicians with access to substantial financial resources. The civil society groups that led much of the struggle against the Abacha dictatorship found themselves at a disadvantage in trying to influence, and participate in, this process. The Obasanjo government will have to find ways to avoid alienating these groups—including trade unions, student associations, pro-democracy/human rights NGOs, and women's organizations—as a disaffected constituency outside the political structures of the Fourth Republic.

Military rule has shown a tendency to exacerbate ethnoregional and clientelist factionalization and has retarded the development of a party and electoral system in Nigeria. As Larry Diamond has argued, progress toward the evolution of multiethnic parties was being made during both the First and the Second Republics. In each case, this progress was terminated by military intervention. The nineteen-state structure and various electoral provisions of the Second Republic requiring broad ethnic representation in parties contributed to these advances, despite the chaotic conflicts among individuals and factions in the various parties.[15] These issues and challenges emerged once again in the 1998–1999 transition. A key question that arises is whether the party and electoral system will have the breathing space to overcome its many deficiencies or whether it will be subjected to so much top-down manipulation that it loses credibility and efficacy once again.

The requirement by the Abubakar government's electoral commission that registered parties win 5 percent of the local government election votes in two-thirds of the states in order to advance to the state level was an example of judicious political engineering. Nigeria still has to get this process right, namely, party formation through bargaining and negotiation nudged along by enabling rules and legislation. At the start of the Fourth Republic, the leadership of the parties essentially comprises arrangements of convenience among powerful individuals who retain their own resource and client bases and lack a common ideology or clear policy agenda. That is, however, how party systems began in many countries that now possess stable two- or three-party systems with periodic alternation in power. An important question, therefore, is whether Nigeria will get beyond the initial disorderly stage of party formation during the Fourth Republic or see it decay once again into confusion.

Political Culture, Citizenship, and Identity

Traditionally, institutions that represent and mobilize society in the political sphere include legislatures, political parties, and trade unions. In the process, they help to shape, organize, and express political culture and identities, thus nurturing qualities of citizenship. For all but ten years since independence in 1960, however, these institutions in Nigeria have been proscribed and disbanded (in the case of legislatures and political parties) or muzzled (in the case of labor unions). Their roles have been largely assumed by other groups and institutions, including ethnic and religious organizations, the mass media, and professional and trade groups.

The basic units of socialization are mainly family, community, and peer groups; thus it is not surprising that ethnic, religious, and educational institutions have assumed a large role in the organization and expression of political attitudes and culture. Although these institutions can be a positive force, they often possess elements that complicate the political process. In many of these circles, the state (federal government) is regarded as an amoral entity. The state's unwillingness or inability to deliver appropriate services to the populace, its rampant corruption, and the frequency of military coups have fostered a political culture of apathy and alienation among many Nigerians, and militant opposition among particular communities and groups.

Modernity Versus Traditionalism

The terrain of political culture, citizenship, and identity is a contested arena within Nigeria. The interaction of modern (colonial, Western) elements with traditional (precolonial, African) practices has created the duality of a modern sociopolitical system that rests uneasily on traditional foundations. In other words, traditional elements have been modernized and modern elements traditionalized, so that individual Nigerians straddle two worlds that are each undergo-ing constant evolution. On one hand, the strong elements in communal societies that promoted accountability have been weakened by the intrusion of Western culture oriented toward individuality. On the other hand, the modern state has been unable to free itself from rival ethnic claims organized around narrow, exclusivist constituencies.

As a result, exclusivist identities have come to dominate Nigerian political culture and define the nature of citizenship. Individuals tend to identify with their immediate ethnic, regional, and religious (or subethnic, subregional, and subreligious) groups rather than with state institutions, especially during moments of crisis. Nigerians usually seek to extract as many benefits as possible from the state but hesitate when it comes to performing basic civic duties such as paying taxes or taking care of public property. In short, entirely missing from the relationship between state and citizen in Nigeria is a fundamental reciprocity—a working social contract—based on the belief that there is a common interest that binds them.

Religion

Religion has been a persistent basis of conflict in Nigerian history. Islam first began to filter into northeast Nigeria in the eleventh and twelfth centuries, spread to Hausaland by the fifteenth century, and greatly expanded in the early nineteenth century. In the north, Islam first coexisted with, then gradually supplanted, indigenous religions. Christianity arrived later but expanded rapidly through missionary activity in the south dating from the early nineteenth century. The amalgamation of northern and southern Nigeria in 1914 brought together the two regions and their belief systems.

These religious cultures have consistently clashed over political issues, such as during the *shari'a* debate. For most Muslims it represents a way of life and supreme (personal) law that transcends secular and state law; for many Christians it threatens the secular nature of the Nigerian state and their position within it. The pull of religious versus national identity becomes even stronger in times of economic hardship. The Babangida period corresponded with a rise in both Islamic fundamentalist movements and

Current Challenges: **Prebendalism**

Prebendalism, the peculiarly Nigerian version of corruption, is an extreme form of clientelism that refers to the practice of mobilizing cultural and other sectional identities by political aspirants and officeholders for the purpose of corruptly appropriating state resources. Prebendalism is an institutionalized pattern of political behavior that justifies the pursuit of and the use of public office for the personal benefit of the officeholder and his clients. The official public purpose of the office becomes a secondary concern. As with clientelism, the officeholder's "clients" are a specific set of elites to which he is linked, typically by ethnic or religious ties, and this linkage is key to understanding the concept. There are thus two sides involved in prebendalism, the officeholder and the client; and expectation of benefits by the clients (or supporters) perpetuates the prebendalist system. Prebendalism explicitly involves the abuse of the public realm, and therefore its inevitable consequence is the bankrupting of the state's coffers. In the context of prebendalism, a civilian or military officeholder, for example, might award state contracts to clients solely on the basis of their financial support, without regard to merit or due consideration of more qualified proposals. As practiced in the Babangida era, when official corruption occurred on an unprecedented scale, prebendalism deepened sectional cleavages and eroded the resources of the state. It also discouraged genuinely productive activity in civil society and expanded the class of individuals who live off state patronage.

As long as prebendalism remains the norm of Nigerian politics, a stable democracy will be elusive. These practices are now deeply embedded in Nigerian society and therefore are difficult to uproot. The corruption resulting from prebendalist practices is blamed in popular discourse for the enormous flight of internally generated capital into numbered accounts in overseas banking institutions. The lion's share of the US$12.2-billion Gulf War windfall is believed to have been pocketed by Babangida and senior members of his regime and the Central Bank, an example of the magnitude of the systematic pilfering of public resources. General Abacha continued this pattern and is accused of diverting US$4 billion from the Nigerian Central Bank. There are so many officeholders in Nigeria who indulge in these practices, albeit at less gargantuan levels, that Transparency International regularly listed Nigeria during the 1990s among the most corrupt countries.

evangelical Protestantism. Where significant numbers of southern Christians are living in predominantly Muslim states (for example, Kaduna state), many clashes have erupted, with great loss of life and the extensive destruction of churches, mosques, and small businesses.

The Press

The plural nature of Nigerian society, rather than the emergence of a shared political culture, can be seen in virtually all aspects of public life. The Nigerian press, for instance, has long been one of the liveliest and most irreverent in Africa. The Abacha regime moved to stifle its independence, banning several publications and threatening suspension of others. Significantly, most of the Nigerian press has been based in a Lagos-Ibadan axis in the western part of Nigeria and has frequently been labeled "southern." In 1994, Abacha closed several of the most influential and respected southern Nigerian newspapers and magazines, including the *Guardian*, *Concord* (owned by Abiola), and *Punch*, leaving less critical and more biased publishers intact. In this regard, he was following the nefarious example of his predecessor Babangida, especially during the final and increasingly conflictual years of his rule. A northern paper, the *New Nigerian* published in Kaduna, succumbed at times to overt sectionalism. The fact that the media are sometimes regarded as captives of ethnic and regional constituencies has weakened their capacity to resist attacks on their rights and privileges. More recent developments in Nigeria have been the emergence of independent television and radio stations and the steadily increasing use of the Internet.

Interests, Social Movements, and Protest

Issues relating to political attitudes, political culture, and identities are still dominated and defined largely by elite and male urban-based interests. These interests include ethnic as well as professional and associational groups. The few non-elite groups, such as urban-based market women's associations, often serve as channels for disseminating the decisions and agendas of male-dominated groups. In essence, non-elite and rural elements continue to be marginalized and manipulated by elites and urban groups. Lacking competence in the language of public discourse, namely English, and access to financial networks, non-elites have difficulty confronting, on their own, the decision-making centers of the state and society.

Elite and non-elite Nigerians alike come together in civic organizations and interest groups such as labor unions, and student and business associations. Because the political machinery has usually been in the hands of the military, Nigerian citizens have sought alternative means of representation and protest in an effort to have an impact on political life. Historically, labor has played a significant role in Nigerian politics, as have student groups and various radical and populist organizations. Business groups, on the other hand, have frequently supported and colluded with corrupt civilian and military regimes. In the last year of the Abacha regime, however, the business class through mechanisms like *Vision 2010* called for concrete policies to end such arbitrary rule.

Labor

Continuous military pressure since 1983 has forced a decline in the once independent and powerful role of organized labor in Nigerian politics. The Babangida regime implemented strategies of state corporatism designed to control and co-opt various social forces such as labor. Organized labor, which played an important role in challenging governments during both the colonial and postcolonial eras in several African countries, now has difficulty sustaining such actions in Nigeria. Whenever the leadership of the Nigerian Labour Congress (NLC), to which all unions compulsorily belong, took a vigorous stand against the government (as happened in the strike action against the Abacha regime in summer 1994), the government sacked the leaders and appointed conservative replacements. The Nigerian labor movement has been vulnerable to reprisals by the state and private employers. First, the state has always been the biggest single employer of labor in Nigeria as well as the recognized regulator of industrial relations between employers and employees. Second, ethnic, regional, and religious divisions have often hampered labor solidarity while being deliberately manipulated by the state.

The first attempt to establish a corporatist structure for organized labor was made in 1978 under the military government of Olusegun Obasanjo, which, as mentioned earlier, used a conflict within the labor movement to impose a single central labor organization, the NLC. This policy of centralization and co-optation was carried further under Babangida, who ensured that only candidates endorsed by the government were elected to lead the more powerful unions. The result has been a waning of trade union militancy and a steady decline in the role of labor as a political, ideological, and social force.

If allowed to function without such manipulation and control by the government, however, the labor movement can regain its vitality. That potential was demonstrated during the summer of 1994, when pro-democracy strikes by the National Petroleum Employees Union (NUPENG) and other sympathetic labor groups significantly reduced oil production and nearly brought the country to a halt before the Abacha regime arrested and disbanded its leadership. One of General Abubakar's first reforms was to remove the government-appointed union administrators and allow the unions to elect their own leaders. Labor still claims an estimated 2 million members across Nigeria and remains one of the most potent forces in civil society. It therefore has a great stake in the consolidation of constitutional rule during the Fourth Republic and the protections that would allow it to organize and act freely on behalf of its members and, more broadly, the masses of disadvantaged people in Nigeria.

The Business Community

Associational and professional life has remained vibrant. Nigeria has a long history of entrepreneurialism and business development. Stifling this spirit, however, is its history of capitalism based on the appropriation of state resources. Its business class is often characterized as "pirate capitalists" because of such tendencies and the high level of corrupt practices. Many wealthy individuals have served in the military or civilian governments, or indirectly protect their access to state resources through sponsoring elected officials. Nevertheless, as the economic and political conditions in Nigeria deteriorated, the state offered fewer avenues for businesspeople and could no longer provide even the necessary infrastructure for business development.

Private interests have proved surprisingly resilient as organized groups have emerged to represent the interests of the business class and to promote economic development generally. Increasingly, such efforts occur without direct state sponsorship as groups of enterprising capitalists create interlinked business associations. These associations have proliferated throughout Nigeria and, in many areas, represent diverse groups from butchers, to manufacturers, to car-hire firms. In a number of cases, they have demonstrated social responsibility by building roads, schools, market stalls, and similar infrastructure, all of which reduces demands on government revenue. As discussed in Section 2, business associations in the 1990s emerged as a leading force in promoting economic reform in Nigeria, as well as in raising related issues.

Many local or regional groups are also members of national organizations. National business associations, such as the Nigerian Association of Chambers of Commerce, Industry, Mines, and Agriculture (NACCIMA), the largest in the country, have taken an increasingly political stance by pressing the military leadership to resolve the June 12 crisis and by forging networks with other groups through *Vision 2010*. In their bid to reduce uncertainty, halt economic decline, and protect their economic interests, large business associations increasingly perform what are clearly political roles. It will be interesting to observe if they maintain or step back from such prominent activities during the Fourth Republic.

Other Social Groups

Student activism continues to be an important feature of Nigerian political life. University and other higher-level student groups play an important political role. Along with their teachers, they suffered government harassment, banning, and attempts to engineer divisions in their unions and associations, including countless closings of the universities, during the Babangida and Abacha regimes. By 1996 the military, using the usual tactics of pressure and bribery, succeeded in dividing the students into pro- and anti-government factions in an effort to reduce their effectiveness in the democracy struggle. Professional associations of doctors and lawyers have also become champions of human rights, reflecting a tendency characteristic of societies confronting repressive governments. They often support campaigns conducted by social rights organizations, which have proliferated since the founding of the Civil Liberties Organization (CLO) in 1987.

The activities of these organizations have increased significantly since the introduction of the economic structural adjustment program (SAP). Marginal groups, including women and the young, the urban poor, and people in rural areas, have perceived an imbalance in the distribution of the benefits and burdens generated by the SAP program. Not surprisingly, the flagrant display of wealth by senior members of the military has alienated these groups and encouraged a "culture of rage"[16] among youths, artisans, the urban poor, and the unemployed.

This rage over economic hardship and military oppression led to a sharp increase in the number of human rights groups and other nongovernmental organizations (NGOs) in the 1990s. Greater funding for NGOs from governments and private foundations in Europe and the United States assisted the growth of this sector, most notably in the south but gradually in the north as well. They generally focus on such issues as civil protection, gender law, health care, media access, and public housing. Most are urban-based, although efforts to develop rural networks are under way.

The personality conflicts, ethnic divisions, and intense competition for funding hampered the challenge posed by these civil society organizations to military dictatorship. Pro-democracy efforts by NGOs peaked in the 1993–1994 struggle over the nullification of the June 12 election, when they managed to stage successful stay-home strikes in Lagos and several other southern cities. The Campaign for Democracy in 1993, and then the National Democratic Coalition (NADECO) in 1994, built an antimilitary front among the NGOs that also included students, academics, some labor unions, and other groups. As Abacha moved forward with his "self-succession" campaign in 1997–1998, once again this

sector was able to mount numerous street demonstrations and other protests to counter the regime's orchestration. Nigeria's prospects for building a sustainable democracy during the Fourth Republic will depend, in part, on the willingness of many of these advocacy groups to increase their collaboration and maintain a high level of vigilance and activism.

Section ⑤   Nigerian Politics in Transition

After winning Nigeria's freest and fairest presidential election on June 12, 1993, Moshood Abiola returned to Nigeria to try to negotiate a peaceful transfer of power. He was imprisoned in 1994 and died in 1998, just days before his expected release. On the positive side, the popular success in pressuring military strongman Babangida to step aside in August 1993 underscored the resilience and vitality of Nigeria's democratic forces. Moreover, the failure of Babangida's tactics—which reflect the essence of neopatrimonial rule, or **patrimonialism**, in which "the chief executive maintains authority through personal patronage, rather than through ideology or law"[17]—reveals that patrimonialism does not inevitably succeed in countries like Nigeria. However, the long history of patrimonial rule and prebendal politics in Nigeria does not bode well for economic or democratic political reform. As Goran Hyden has argued, "While patrimonialism may provide stability in the short-run, it tends to block the road to constitutional development and reform. As a result, changes in the system are difficult without resorting to unconstitutional means."[18]

The popular vote on June 12, 1993, provided a radical departure from the sectionalism of the past and offered a refreshing opportunity to develop a more national political agenda. The June 12 vote was as much a protest against the military as a ruling group and against Babangida as a discredited leader as it was an endorsement of Moshood Abiola for president. June 12 was a historical breakthrough, the day the ordinary people of Nigeria rose against the ethnic, religious, and regional prejudices, and the divisive politics with which colonialism and the political class had oppressed them for half a century. In doing this, they took a great step toward making Nigeria a truly

viable and democratic polity. However, this historical opportunity was allowed to slip away on account of the cynical campaign by those who created the political impasse to ethnicize and regionalize it. This campaign by the Abacha regime placed ethnicity, religion, and regionalism firmly back on the agenda. Following the sudden deaths in mid-1998 of both Abacha and the elected president he had imprisoned, Abiola, Nigeria was rushed through a hasty transition in which ethnic and regional issues predominated in the choice of candidates and in the conduct of elections. Nigeria's Fourth Republic must find ways of developing a truly national political process in which mobilization and conflicts along ethnic, regional, and religious lines gradually diminish.

Political Challenges and Changing Agendas

The Nigerian transition has been halting in part because it was planned and directed from above. This approach contrasts sharply with the popular-based movements that unseated autocracies in central and eastern Europe beginning in 1989. Promises of democratic transition have been made periodically during Nigeria's political history as a ploy by the military to stabilize and legitimize their governments. General Abubakar was determined to complete the second such transition in 1999, although ensuring that the military's interests are well-protected under civilian rule. His rapid transition program, however, has produced a tenuous democratic government that faces daunting tasks of restoring key institutions, securing social stability, and reforming the economy.

Nigeria faces enormous political challenges. One must question the peculiar nature of a transition imposed and manipulated, or at best, refereed, from above by military rulers. The continuing strength and influence of collective identities defined on the basis of religion or ethnicity are often more binding than national (that is, all-Nigerian) ones. These identities have previously been used to mobilize support at the local level, and they foster divisive politics at the federal level. The parasitic nature of the Nigerian economy is a further source of instability. Rent-seeking and other unproductive, often corrupt, business activities are accepted norms of wealth accumulation.

Nonetheless, Nigerians are sowing seeds of change in all of these areas. Attitudes toward the military in government have shifted dramatically. The decline in the appeal of military rule can be attributed to the abysmal performances of the Babangida and Abacha regimes in economic policies and governance. Many now recognize that the military, despite its important contributions to national security, is incapable of promoting economic and social progress in Nigeria. In fact, military rule has resulted in the greatest erosion of national cohesion since the civil war in the late 1960s. General Abubakar's handling of the 1998–1999 transition improved the credibility of the military, but as details of Abacha's theft mounted, so also did awareness of the ravages of military rule.

The nature and outcome of the battle against patrimonialism will help to determine the direction of political and economic change in Nigeria. For now, it is enough to note that the political crisis since 1993 provided the opportunity for an embattled people to challenge patrimonial rule by attacking its very lifeline: earnings from oil exports that go directly to the state's coffers.

Foreign pressure played an important role in maintaining the quest for democracy and sustainable development. In recent years major external forces have been more forthright and decisive in supporting civil society and democratization in Nigeria. The United States, Britain, and some member states of the European Union were very visible in exerting pressure on Babangida to leave and in applying modest sanctions in support of democracy. This has been made possible, in part, by a changing international environment, especially the willingness of the major industrial countries and the international financial institutions

to support democracy in the Third World in Africa. Nigeria's increasingly weak economy and enormous debt, now estimated at US$32 billion, has made it susceptible to this kind of pressure. It is important to note, however, that although diplomatic pressures were applied to the Abacha regime, economic sanctions were never seriously threatened by the international community, allowing Abacha considerable breathing room.

Western commitment to development and democracy in Africa is not guaranteed. Much of the initiative for Africa's growth, therefore, still needs to emerge from within. In Nigeria, such initiatives will depend on substantial changes in the way Nigerians do business. As Larry Diamond has warned, "If there is to be any basis for self-sustaining growth and peaceful, democratic politics, there must be a transition from pirate capitalism to a more sophisticated and effective nurture capitalism. Nigeria must develop, for the first time, a basis of production and accumulation outside of oil and outside the state."[19] In other words, there must be a gradual replacement of the current political, economic, and social elite that derives its power and resources from state patronage by an elite that derives its economic power from diversified sources and through private initiatives outside the state system. Indeed, as Hyden has indicated, it is becoming increasingly clear that constitutional governance will be difficult to enthrone in much of Africa "without a concomitant rise of a bourgeoisie ready to defend those principles."[20]

In addition, the project of building a coherent nation-state out of competing nationalities remains largely unfinished and under constant siege by resurgent ethnonationalism and religious fundamentalism. The challenge here is to achieve a proper balance between ethnic-based symbols and institutions and those of a transethnic nature. Ethnic consciousness cannot be eliminated from society, but ethnicity should not become the main basis for political competition. Even though the opposition activities by human rights and pro-democracy activists in 1993 and 1994 were remarkable, they never coalesced into a truly national movement. These urban-based efforts did achieve a measure of success in their efforts to link up with mass associations, including some trade unions, market women, artisans, and other guild associations.

And it was the actions of these latter elements that paralyzed the economy after the arrest and detention of Moshood Abiola in June 1994.

Events since the annulment of the June 12, 1993, election demonstrate that civil society is no longer willing to be a passive vehicle for elite intrigue in Nigerian politics. The Babangida regime was unprepared for the widespread condemnation of this action and by the frequent demonstrations and riots. Pressure for a complete transition to democratic rule did not cease when Babangida tapped Ernest Shonekan to lead an interim "civilian" administration before stepping down in August 1993. For the first time in independent Nigeria's history, the elite could not control street-level politics—"people power" had been unleashed and could not be fully suppressed. The Nigerian elite was in disarray and the people filled the void by supporting militant civic and trade union leaders.

Nevertheless, the reach of most civic groups in Nigeria paled in comparison with the obtrusive state security apparatus put in place by Babangida and used effectively by Abacha. Babangida's security forces ensured that Nigerian politics resembled that of several Latin American countries in the 1960s and 1970s with recourse to state terrorism, disappearances, and the penetration of educational, associational, and opposition groups. In the later months of 1994, Nigeria's security services were responsible for an unprecedented wave of political terror as militant trade unionists and pro-democracy activists were harassed and detained, and their properties set on fire.

Although there was renewed optimism after Babangida was forced from office, the Abacha coup reignited grave doubts about whether Nigeria could escape the military's firm hold on power. One question persists: Can an army that has enjoyed the spoils of uncontested power for most of the period of independent nationhood voluntarily relinquish power? The transition supervised by General Abdulsalami Abubakar in 1998 and 1999 gave some grounds for hope, but the role of the military in Nigeria's politics remains an urgent and contested issue.

A review of Nigerian politics up to the fall of the Second Republic lamented that "since a democratic route to nationhood, in the context of Nigeria's social pluralism, is a parlous one, and an authoritarian route has not been seriously attempted, Nigerian society is left to oscillate between the broadening of democratic participation and the freezing of such practices with the reimposition of military rule."[21] That statement was made before Nigerians experienced heightened authoritarianism under Babangida and Abacha.

When the Second Republic collapsed in December 1983, the assumption among Nigerians was that it was unlikely that Nigeria would produce a dictator in the fashion of Togo's Eyadema, Uganda's Idi Amin, the Central African Republic's Bokassa, or Zaire's Mobutu Sese Seko. Although they came very close to that reality under Babangida, Nigerians were forced to confront it under Abacha. Here is a pertinent remark made in 1993 by a Nigerian businessman:

> The silence of an elite too anxious to protect what little gains they have made, caused us to so severely jeopardize the future of our children. . . . We have to pay tribute to the activists, for it could have been worse without them. We must dedicate ourselves to preventing this from happening again. Unless we say never again, we will wake up one day and a psychopath in uniform will usurp authority, use and abuse power to plunder the nation and dare us speak.[22]

As it turned out, Abacha was such a ruler who usurped authority, used and abused power, plundered the nation mercilessly, and punished those who dared speak. Will Nigeria be able, having witnessed the perils of unaccountable government, to prevent such a tragedy from happening again?

As indicated in Section 1, Nigerian politics has been characterized by turmoil and periodic crises since the British relinquished colonial power in 1960. Forty years later, the country still lacks a stable and orderly political system. Its retrogression is evidenced by the stagnation and decline of major productive sectors, infrastructure and institutions, the heightened sociopolitical tension, an increasingly irresponsible elite, and an expanding mass culture of despondency and rage. Although Nigeria completed a series of elections in February 1999, and a handover of power to an elected government on May 29, 1999, it would be premature to classify it as a democratic polity. The person elected president on February 27, 1999, Olusegun Obasanjo, is a former military ruler whose party received extensive financial support from other retired military officers, including the same individual who annulled the 1993 elections, Ibrahim Babangida. Although international observers accepted the results as fair, all the elections of the 1998–1999 transition were marred by irregularities. It is more appropriate to regard Nigeria as having just begun a possible evolution away from a nondemocratic system. Whether this transition will be completed depends on the realization of substantial progress in overcoming deep structural problems.

Two possible scenarios are apparent. Now that General Abubakar has successfully handed over power to an elected civilian government in May 1999, the restored democratic system must manage its internal contradictions sufficiently to govern. Moreover, although it benefited from a military-supervised transition, the Obasanjo government must engineer a thorough transformation of the armed forces into a constitutional and professional entity.

As in the past, issues of governance are certain to be filtered through an intense struggle among the parties for control of the government. Within a short time, the party that comes to power, while addressing the main interests of its members and supporters, will have to utilize the new democratic institutions without abusing them. Opposition parties, meanwhile, will have to accept the procedural limits of democratic institutions while promoting alternative policies in the federal legislature and state-level governments. The military will have to be depoliticized and restored to its constitutional and professional role in a democratic system.

One of the critical issues the new democracy will face is what Nigerians call the national question. There have been insistent calls for a genuine national conference to restructure the federation, rewrite the constitution, and renegotiate control of the oil wealth. Persistent discontent among the Yoruba, along with the low-intensity civil war in the Niger Delta, will likely force the new government to permit debate on the structure of the Nigerian federation, perhaps within narrow parameters. Unlike Nigeria's previous democratic experiments, the new democracy will include the activities of a highly mobilized civil society. Business interests, which have become more vocal and active through the Economic Summits and *Vision 2010*, will continue their efforts to move government economic policy in a free-market direction. Labor unions will regain their independence and most

advance alternatives to the business agenda that would include demands for a more active role of the state in addressing the steep decline in the value of wages and in social welfare. Some religious institutions, especially Islamic, will raise challenges, once again, to the avowed secular nature of the Nigerian state. The many advocacy groups in civil society are likely to be much more vigilant and outspoken than during the last period of civilian rule. A vigorous articulation of health, education, human rights, and women's interests can be anticipated, and a concerted attempt to counter the usual emphasis on narrow elite and ethnic concerns.

This optimistic scenario is full of ifs, and is clouded by the continued threat of military intervention. A weak democracy could fall prey to the narrow, parochial interests of individuals in powerful positions who are willing, once again, to foment ethnic and religious divisions. Rather than serving the nation's interest in broad-based economic development, the new leaders may spend most of their time trying to consolidate power within their parties and the government while seeking to siphon government funds for their own uses. The military is no longer a coherent organization, which might permit the new democracy an extended grace period. Generals Abacha and Babangida left the armed forces rife with division and rivalry, and they may be incapable of, resuming power in the near future.

Unlike Nigeria's previous democratic experiments, the new democracy will enjoy the independent participation of a more highly mobilized civil society. Business, well organized and active through the Economic Summits and *Vision 2010*, is certain to continue its efforts to move government economic policy in a free-market direction. Labor unions will regain their independence and most likely resist the business agenda. Religious institutions will seek to debate the secular nature of the Nigerian state, while the media are likely to renew their reputation as the most freewheeling in Africa. NGOs will continue to lobby for their targeted issues (health, local development, human rights, women's rights) and will serve as watchdogs over the government and the military. The strong articulation by civil society of these interests can force the new government to respond in ways that strengthen democratic institutions and move politics away from narrow elite or ethnic concerns.

Nigerian Politics in Comparative Perspective

Theoretical insights from the historical experiences of one country or region are seldom fully applicable to another; and political scientists are wary about stretching concepts so far as to suggest that one polity can be modeled after another. Given this caveat, the study of Nigeria has important implications for the study of African politics and, more broadly, of comparative politics. The Nigerian case embodies a number of key themes and issues that can be generalized to increase social science knowledge, and these themes deserve careful consideration. We can learn much about how democratic regimes are established and achieve stability by understanding the pitfalls Nigeria has encountered. By analyzing the historical dynamics of Nigeria's ethnic conflict, for example, we can identify institutional mechanisms that may be effective in reducing ethnic conflict in other states. We can also learn much about how viable and sustainable economies are developed by contrasting their evolution with Nigeria's. Each of these issues, in turn, offers comparative lessons for the major themes explored in this book: a world of states, governing the economy, the democratic idea, and the politics of collective identities.

A World of States

Nigeria exists in two worlds of states—one in the global political economy and the other within Africa. We have addressed at length Nigeria's position in the world. Economically, Nigeria was thrust into the world economy in a position of weakness, first as a British colony and later as an independent nation. Despite its resources and the potential of oil to provide the investment capital needed to build a modern economy, Nigeria has grown weaker. It has lost much of its international clout and, in place of the respect it once enjoyed in diplomatic circles, Nigeria now gets criticism for persistent human rights abuses. Although calls for stringent sanctions have been loud, these have elicited mainly symbolic actions, such as the denial of visas to government officials.

In a continent that comprises more than 10 percent of the world's population, there remain vast resources (for indigenous consumption and export), large poten-

tial markets, and many opportunities to achieve greater prominence in the world of states. This chapter began by quoting the statement, "As Nigeria goes, so goes the rest of sub-Saharan Africa." Instead of leading the continent, Nigeria has been left behind in such respects as national cohesion, state capabilities, economic growth, and democratization.

The future of democracy, political stability, and economic renewal in other parts of Africa, and certainly in West Africa, will be greatly influenced, for good or ill, by unfolding events in Nigeria. Beyond the obvious demonstration effect, the economy of the West African subregion can be revitalized by resumed growth of the Nigerian economy. International political, scholarly, and business attention has shifted steadily to the south of the continent, focusing chiefly on South Africa and its stable neighboring states of Botswana and Namibia. That shift portends a greater danger of marginalization, as Africa becomes divided into a zone of prosperity that attracts investment and a zone of decay.

Governing the Economy

Nigeria provides important insights into the political economy of underdevelopment. At independence in 1960, Nigeria was stronger economically than its Southeast Asian counterparts. Independent Nigeria appeared poised for growth, with a wealth of natural resources, a large population, and the presence of highly entrepreneurial groups in all regions of the country. Today, Nigeria is among the poorest countries in the world in terms of per capita income, while many of its Asian counterparts have joined the ranks of the newly industrializing nations. One critical lesson Nigeria teaches is that a rich endowment of resources is not enough to ensure economic development. In fact, it may encourage rent-seeking behavior that undermines more productive activities.

Other variables are critically important, notably political stability (if not necessarily democracy) and a strong developmentalist ethic. Such a developmentalist ethic, and an institutional structure to enforce it, can set limits to corrupt behavior and constrain the pursuit of short-term personal gain at the expense of national economic growth. Institutions vital for the pursuit of these objectives include a professional civil service, an independent judiciary, and a free press. Nigeria has had each of these, yet they were gradually undermined and corrupted. The public "ethic" that has come to dominate the Nigerian political economy has been prebendalism. Where corruption is unchecked, as in Nigeria, the Philippines under Ferdinand Marcos, or in Latin American countries such as Mexico and Venezuela, economic development suffers accordingly.

Nigeria also demonstrates that sustainable economic development requires sound economic policy. Without export diversification, commodity-exporting countries are buffeted by the price fluctuations of one or two main products. This situation, of course, can be traced back to overreliance on primary commodity-export-oriented policies bequeathed by the British colonial regime. Yet other former colonies, such as Malaysia and Indonesia, have managed to diversify their initial export base. Nigeria, in contrast, has substituted one form of commodity dependence for another; and it has allowed its petroleum industry to overwhelm completely all other sectors of the economy. Nigeria even became a net importer of products (for example, palm oil and palm nuts) for which it was once a leading world producer. In comparative perspective, we can see that natural resource endowments can be tremendously beneficial. The United States, for example, has parlayed its endowments of agricultural, mineral, and energy resources into one of the world's most diversified modern economies. Meanwhile Japan, which is by comparison poorly endowed with natural resources, has one of the strongest economies in the world, achieved in large part through its unique developmental strategies. Each of these examples illustrates the primacy of sound economic policies.

The Democratic Idea

As mentioned earlier, many African countries have experienced transitions from authoritarian rule. With the end of superpower competition in Africa, and the withdrawal of support from the former Soviet Union and the United States for Africa's despots, many African societies experienced a resurgence of popular pressures for greater participation in political life and for more open forms of governance. Decades of authoritarian, single-party, and military rule in Africa

have left a dismal record: arbitrary imprisonment and silenced political opposition; harassment of civic, professional, and religious institutions; stifled public discourse and free speech; and bankrupted treasuries and mismanaged economies. At the same time, a handful of elites have acquired large fortunes through wanton corruption. The examples, sadly, are plentiful. Consider Nigeria's "missing" US$12.2 billion windfall in oil revenues after the Gulf War in 1991; or the fact that Zairian president Mobutu Sese Seko's "personal" wealth was estimated to be several billion dollars, perhaps as much as half the external debt of the entire country. Or that Kenya's president Daniel Arap Moi is considered among the richest men in Africa, a group to which Ibrahim Babangida and the late Sani Abacha of Nigeria belong. The devious ways in which these fortunes were acquired and dispensed make it difficult to give concrete figures. They do, however, suggest that the exercise of postindependence authoritarian rule in Africa has contributed to economic stagnation and decline. The difficulty that such countries as Kenya, Cameroon, Togo, and Zimbabwe have experienced in moving to democratic systems is a reflection, among other factors, of the ruling elites' unwillingness to cede control of the political instruments that made possible their self-enrichment.

Nigeria exemplifies the harsh reality of authoritarian and unaccountable governance. Corruption, fraud, and mismanagement, and the restriction of political liberties, were tolerated in the past by populations numbed into complacency by political repression and the daily struggles for economic survival. Nigerians have endured six military regimes, countless attempted coups, and a bloody civil war that claimed over 1 million lives. They have also seen a once prospering economy reduced to rubble. Today, democracy has become a greater imperative because only such a system provides the mechanisms to limit abuses of power and render governments accountable.

Collective Identities

Nigeria presents an important case in which to study the dangers of ethnically based competition in a society with deep cultural divisions. How can multiethnic countries manage their diversity? What institutional mechanisms can be employed to avert tragedies such as the 1967–1970 civil war, or the continuing conflicts that have brought great suffering to the former Yugoslavia and Rwanda? This chapter has suggested institutional reforms such as proportional representation, decentralization, and a strengthened federal system that can contribute to reducing tensions and minimizing conflict.

Insights from the Nigerian experience may explain why some federations persist and help to identify the factors that can undermine them. Nigeria's complex social situation, and its varied attempts to create a nation out of its highly diverse population, enhance our understanding of the politics of cultural pluralism,[23] and the difficulty of accommodating sectional interests under conditions of political and economic insecurity. As described in this chapter, federal character in Nigeria has been distorted into a form of ethnic and regional favoritism and a tool for dispensing patronage. Yet, the country has benefited in some ways from the attention devoted to creating state and local governments, and from giving people in different regions a sense of being stakeholders in the entity called Nigeria.

The challenges that Nigeria will face in the next century concern not only its people's frustrated hopes for a better life, stable government, and a democratic political order but also the potential contributions that this country and its people could still make to the entire continent, and to the world at large, if only an exit can be found from the cycle of endless woe.

Key Terms

authoritarian
legitimacy
accountability
unfinished state
autocracy
jihad
acephalous societies
emirs
warrant chiefs
interventionist
indirect rule
clientelism
rents
structural adjustment
program

international financial
institutions
balance of payments
privatization
self-determination
Economic Community of
West African States
federal character
para-statals
state corporatism
shari'a
civil society
prebendalism
patrimonialism

Suggested Readings

Achike, Okay. *Public Administration: A Nigerian and Comparative Perspective.* London: Longman, 1978.

Adamolekun, L. *Politics and Administration in Nigeria.* London: Hutchinson, 1986.

Agbaje, Adigun. *The Nigerian Press: Hegemony and the Social Construction of Legitimacy, 1960–1983.* Lewiston, N.Y.: Edwin Mellen Press, 1992.

———. "Twilight of Democracy in Nigeria." *Africa Demos* 3 (no. 3): 5. Atlanta: Carter Center of Emory University, 1994.

Bienen, Henry. *Political Conflict and Economic Change in Nigeria.* London: Frank Cass, 1988.

Crook, Richard, and A.M. Jerve, eds. *Government and Participation: Institutional Development, Decentralization and Democracy in the Third World.* Bergen, Norway: Chr. Michelsen Institute, 1991.

Decalo, Samuel. *Coups and Army Rule in Africa.* 2d ed. New Haven: Yale University Press, 1990.

Diamond, Larry. *Class, Ethnicity and Democracy in Nigeria: The Failure of the First Republic.* London: Macmillan, 1988.

———. "Nigeria's Search for a New Political Order." *Journal of Democracy* 2, no. 2 (Spring 1991): 54.

Ekeh, Peter P., and Eghosa E. Osaghae, eds. *Federal Character and Federalism in Nigeria.* Ibadan: Heinemann, 1989.

Forrest, Tom. *Politics and Economic Development in Nigeria.* Boulder, Colo.: Westview Press, 1993.

Healey, J., and M. Robinson. *Democracy, Governance and Economic Policy: Sub-Saharan Africa in Comparative Perspective.* London: Overseas Development Institute, 1992.

Hodgkin, Thomas. *Nigerian Perspectives.* London: Oxford University Press, 1975.

Horowitz, Donald L. *Ethnic Groups in Conflict.* Berkeley: University of California Press, 1985.

Jackson, Robert H., and Carl G. Rosberg. *Personal Rule in Africa.* Berkeley: University of California Press, 1982.

Joseph, Richard A. *Democracy and Prebendal Politics in Nigeria: The Rise and Fall of the Second Republic.* Cambridge: Cambridge University Press, 1987.

Kew, Darren. "Political Islam in Nigeria's Transition Crisis," *Muslim Politics Report* (Council on Foreign Relations: New York), May-June 1996.

Lewis, Peter M. "Endgame in Nigeria? The Politics of a Failed Democratic Transition." *African Affairs* 93 (1994): 323–340.

Lewis, Peter M., Barnett R. Rubin, and Pearl T. Robinson. *Stabilizing Nigeria: Pressures, Incentives, and Support for Civil Society.* New York: Century Foundation, for the Council on Foreign Relations, 1998.

Nyang'oro, Julius, and Tim Shaw, eds. *Corporatism in Africa: Comparative Analysis and Practice.* Boulder, Colo.: Westview Press, 1989.

Ogwu, U. Joy, and Adebayo Olukoshi, eds. "Special Issue: The Economic Diplomacy of the Nigerian State." *Nigerian Journal of International Affairs* 17, no. 2 (1991).

Onoge, Omafume, ed. *Nigeria: The Way Forward*. Ibadan: Spectrum Books, 1993.

Oyediran, Oyeleye, ed. *Nigerian Government and Politics Under Military Rule*. London: Macmillan, 1979.

Oyovbaire, Sam E. *Federalism in Nigeria: A Study in the Development of the Nigerian State*. London: Macmillan, 1985.

Sklar, Richard L. *Nigerian Political Parties: Power in an Emergent African Nation*. New York: NOK Publishers, 1983.

Turok, Ben, ed. *Alternative Development Strategies for Africa*. Vol. 3: *Debt and Democracy*. London: Institute for African Alternatives, 1991.

Watts, Michael, ed. *State, Oil, and Agriculture in Nigeria*. Berkeley: University of California Press, 1987.

Wunsch, James S., and Dele Olowu, eds. *The Failure of the Centralized State: Institutions and Self-Governance in Africa*. Boulder, Colo.: Westview Press, 1990.

Young, Crawford. *The Rising Tide of Cultural Pluralism: The Nation-State at Bay?* Madison: University of Wisconsin Press, 1993.

Endnotes

[1] Peter Ekeh, "Colonialism and the Two Publics in Africa: A Theoretical Statement," *Comparative Studies in Society and History* 17, no. 1 (January 1975).

[2] Obafemi Awolowo, *Path to Nigerian Freedom* (London: Faber and Faber, 1947), 47–48.

[3] Billy J. Dudley, *An Introduction to Nigerian Government and Politics* (Bloomington: Indiana University Press, 1982), 71.

[4] The following discussion is based on Michael J. Watts, ed., *State, Oil, and Agriculture in Nigeria* (Berkeley: University of California Press, 1987), 61–84.

[5] Watts, 71.

[6] Watts, 66.

[7] Watts, 69.

[8] Dele Olowu, "Centralization, Self-Governance, and Development in Nigeria," in *The Failure of the Centralized State: Institutions and Self-Governance in Africa*, ed. James S. Wunsch and Dele Olowu (Boulder, Colo.: Westview Press, 1990), 211.

[9] Billy J. Dudley, *Instability and Political Order: Politics and Crisis in Nigeria* (Ibadan: Ibadan University Press, 1973), 35.

[10] J. Isawa Elaigwu, "The Nigerian Federation and Future Prospects," in *Nigeria: The Way Forward*, ed. Omafume Onoge (Ibadan: Spectrum Books, 1993), 32–33.

[11] Douglas Rimmer, "External Trade and Payments," in *Nigeria Since 1970: A Political and Economic Outline*, ed. Anthony Kirk-Greene and Douglas Rimmer (London: Hodder and Stoughton, 1981), 136.

[12] See Juan Linz, "The Perils of Presidentialism," *Journal of Democracy* 1, no. 1 (1990): 51–69; and responses in "Debate—Presidents vs. Paliaments," *Journal of Democracy* 1, no. 4 (1990); 73–91.

[13] William D. Graf, *The Nigerian State: Political Economy, State Class and Political System in the Post-Colonial Era* (London: James Currey, 1988), 205.

[14] Samuel Decalo, *Coups and Army Rule in Africa*, 2d ed. (New Haven: Yale University Press, 1990), 18.

[15] Larry Diamond, "Introduction: Roots of Failure, Seeds of Hope," in *Democracy in Developing Countries*, Vol. 2: *Africa*, ed. Diamond et al. (Boulder, Colo.: Lynne Rienner, 1988), 10.

[16] Adigun Agbaje, "Adjusting State and Market in Nigeria: The Paradoxes of Orthodoxy," *Afrika Spectrum* 27, no. 2 (1992): 132.

[17] Michael Bratton and Nicolas van de Walle, "Neopatrimonial Regimes and Political Transitions in Africa," *World Politics*, vol. 46 (July 1994): 453–489.

[18] Goran Hyden, "Reciprocity and Governance in Africa," in *The Failure of the Centralized State: State Institutions and Self-Governance in Africa*, ed. James S. Wunsch and Dele Olowu (Boulder, Colo.: Westview Press, 1990), 265.

[19] Larry Diamond, "Nigeria: Pluralism, Statism and the Struggle for Democracy," in *Democracy in Developing Countries*, Vol. 2: *Africa*, ed. Diamond, Lipset, and Linz (Boulder, Colo.: Lynne Rienner, 1988), 85.

[20] Goran Hyden, "Reciprocity and Governance in Africa," in *The Failure of the Centralized State: State Institutions and Self-Governance in Africa*, ed. James S. Wunsch and Dele Olowu (Boulder, Colo.: Westview Press, 1990), 263.

[21] Richard A. Joseph, *Democracy and Prebendal Politics in Nigeria* (Cambridge: Cambridge University Press, 1987).

[22] *The Guardian*, July 16, 1993, 17.

[23] Crawford Young. *The Politics of Cultural Pluralism* (Madison: University of Wisconsin Press, 1976), and Crawford Young, ed., *The Rising Tide of Cultural Pluralism: The Nation-State at Bay?* (Madison: University of Wisconsin Press, 1993).

CHAPTER 13

Iran

Ervand Abrahamian

Islamic Republic of Iran

Land and Population

Capital	Tehran	
Total Area (square miles)	634,562 (slightly larger than Alaska)	
Population	68.9 million	
Annual Population Growth Rate (1998)	2.04%	
Urban Population	59%	
Ethnic Composition	Persian	51%
	Azerbaijani	24%
	Gilaki and Mazandarani	8%
	Kurd	7%
	Arab	3%
	Other	7%
Major Languages	Farsi (Persian)	58%
	Turkic and Turkic dialects	26%
	Kurdish	9%
	Other	7%
Religious Affiliation	Shi'a Muslim	89%
	Sunni Muslim	10%
	Zoroastrian, Jewish, Christian, and Baha'i	1%

Economy

Domestic Currency	Rial	
Total GNP (US$)	$113.5 billion	
GNP per capita (US$)	$1780	
GNP per capita at purchasing power parity (US$)	$5530	
GNP average annual growth rate (1996–1997)		3.2%
GNP per capita average annual growth rate	1996–1997	1.2%
	1980–1995	−0.2%
	1965–1980	2.9%
Income Gap: GDP per capita (US$)	Data not available for Iran	
Structure of Production (% of GDP)	Agriculture	21%
	Industry	37%
	Services	42%
Labor Force Distribution (% of total)	Agriculture	32%
	Industry	25%
	Services	43%
Exports as % of GDP	21%	
Imports as % of GDP	16%	

Society

Life Expectancy	Female	69.1
	Male	67.9
Doctors per 100,000 people		62.5
Infant Mortality per 1000 live births		33
Adult Literacy	Female	59.3%
	Male	77.7%
Access to Information and Communications (per 1000 people)	Radios	228
	Televisions	134
	Telephone Lines	76
	Personal Computers	
	Data not available for Iran	
Women in Government and Economy		
Seats in parliament held by women		4.9%
Women at ministerial level		3%
Women as % of total labor force		24.0%
Female business administrators and managers		4.0%
Female professional and technical workers		33.0%
1998 Human Development Index ranking (out of 174 countries, 1 = highest)		78

Political Organization

Political System   Theocracy (rule of the clergy) headed by a cleric with the title of Supreme Leader. The clergy rule by divine right.

Regime History   Islamic Republic since the 1979 Islamic Revolution.

Administrative Structure   Centralized administration with 28 provinces. The Interior Minister appoints the provincial governor-generals.

Executive   President and his cabinet. The president is elected by the general electorate every four years. The president chooses his cabinet ministers, but they need to obtain the approval of the *Majles* (parliament).

Legislature   Unicameral. The *Majles,* formed of 270 seats, is elected every four years. It has multiple member districts with the top runners in the elections taking the seats. Bills passed by the *Majles* do not become law unless they have the approval of the clerically dominated Council of Guardians.

Judiciary   A Chief Judge and a Supreme Court independent of the executive and legislature but appointed by the Supreme Leader.

Party System   The ruling clergy restrict all party and organizational activities.

Note: Some of the categories and data used for Iran are different than for other countries in *ICP* because the World Development Report (World Bank) does not gather full statistics for Iran.

Politics in Action

In 1997 the Iranian people surprised the world—not to mention their own establishment—by electing as president a relatively unknown liberal cleric named Muhammad Khatami. Khatami was not a senior cleric with the exalted title of Grand Ayatollah ("Sigh of God") or a simple **ayatollah**, but a middle-ranking hojjat al-Islam ("Proof of Islam"). In the election, he had vigorously campaigned on the theme of creating a viable civil society and improving the "sick economy." He had stressed the importance of an open society that would protect individual liberties, freedom of expression, women's rights, political pluralism, and most essential, the rule of law. He had even authored books applauding such liberal thinkers as Locke, Voltaire, and Rousseau. It was as if he were transferring into practical politics principles found in political science textbooks. His electoral campaign had also stressed the need to have a dialogue with the West, especially with the United States. This was a far cry from the early days of the Iranian Revolution, when Grand Ayatollah Ruhollah Khomeini, the leader of that revolution, had denounced the United States as the "Great Satan" and had encouraged a group of university students to take over the U.S. embassy compound. This takeover, which lasted 444 days, involved fifty-two officials and became famous as the "hostage crisis." It prompted a break in U.S.-Iranian diplomatic relations. It also helped terminate Jimmy Carter's presidency.

Khatami's electoral success in 1997 was especially surprising because much of the religious establishment had openly endorsed his conservative rival. Most commentators, both inside and outside the country, had predicted the easy win of the conservative candidate. The conservatives controlled an impressive array of newspapers, radio stations, television programs, state institutions, quasi-state foundations, clerical organizations, and tens of thousands of prayer pulpits. They warned that any opening up of the system could endanger the whole regime and that Khatami could become another Gorbachev, the Soviet leader who had inadvertently presided over the demise

of the Soviet Union by initiating political reform. Even the Supreme Leader of the Islamic Republic, Ayatollah Ali Khamenei, had implicitly endorsed the conservative candidate. In the upset election, Khatami won a landslide victory, obtaining 70 percent of the vote in a campaign that drew nearly 80 percent of the electorate. In U.S. presidential elections, by contrast, less than 50 percent of eligible voters vote. Much of Khatami's vote came from women, university students, and youth throughout the country, and from the armed forces. He followed up his victory by liberalizing the press, promising the establishment of political parties, and initiating a "dialogue" with the United States on the Cable News Network (CNN). He even bolstered the case for liberalization by citing *Democracy in America*, the famous book by the nineteenth-century French traveler Alexis de Tocqueville. Khatami further followed up his electoral victory by assuring the West that Iran had no intention of implementing the *fatwa* (religious decree) that Ayatollah Khomeini had placed on Salman Rushdie, the Muslim-born British writer. Khomeini had condemned Rushdie to death on the grounds that his book *Satanic Verses* blasphemed Islam and thus proved that its author was an apostate from Islam—a capital offense according to a very narrow interpretation of the Islamic law.

The 1997 presidential elections vividly illustrated the main dilemmas confronting the Islamic Republic established by Ayatollah Khomeini in the aftermath of the 1979 revolution. The republic is a mixture of **theocracy** and democracy, a political system based on clerical authority as well as on popular sovereignty, on the divine right of the clergy as well as on the rights of the people, on concepts derived from early Islam as well as from Montesquieu's separation of powers. The country has regular elections for the presidency and the *Majles* (Parliament), but a clerically dominated **Guardian Council** determines who can and cannot run in these elections. The president is the formal head of the executive branch of government, but he can be overruled, even dismissed, by the chief cleric known as the **Supreme Leader**. The president appoints the

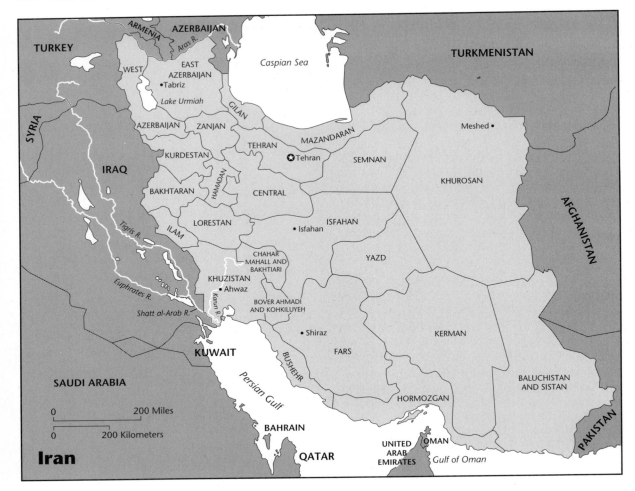

Iran

Minister of Justice, but the whole judiciary is under the supervision of the Chief Judge, who is appointed directly by the Supreme Leader. The *Majles* is the legislative branch of government, but its bills do not become law unless the Guardian Council deems them compatible with Islam and the Islamic constitution. In short, the political system is built both on vox dei (the voice of God) and on vox populi (the voice of the people).

Geographic Setting

Iran—three times the size of France, slightly larger than Alaska, and much larger than its immediate neighbors—is notable for two geographical features.

The first is that much of its territory is inhospitable to agriculture. A vast arid zone known as the Great Salt Desert covers much of the central plateau from Tehran to Afghanistan and Pakistan. A mountain range known as the Zagros takes up the western third of the country. Another range, the Elborz, stretches across the north. Rain-fed agriculture is confined mostly to the northwest and the Caspian provinces. In the rest of the country, population settlements are located mostly on oases, on the few rare rivers, and on constructed irrigation networks. Only pastoral nomads can survive in the semiarid zones and in the high mountain valleys. Thus 67 percent of the total populaton of 69 million is concentrated in 27 percent of the land—mostly in the Caspian provinces, in the northwest, and in such cities as Tehran, Qom, Isfahan, Shiraz, and Ahwaz. In the past, the inhospitable environment was a major obstacle to economic development. In recent decades, this obstacle has been circumvented by oil revenues. Iran is the second largest oil producer in the Middle East, and the fourth largest in the world. Its oil wells help fuel the West, especially by France, Italy, Germany, and Japan. These oil revenues account for the fact that Iran is now urbanized and partly industrialized, and can be described as a developing rather than a stagnant society. Nearly 60 percent of the population lives in urban centers; 68 percent of the labor force is employed in industry and services; 60–75 percent of adults are literate; life expectancy has reached 68 years; and the majority enjoy a standard of living well above that of populations in Asia and Africa.

Iran's second notable geographical feature is that it lies on the crossroads between Central Asia and Asia Minor, between the Indian subcontinent and the Middle East, between the Arabian Peninsula and the Caucasus Mountains. This has made the region vulnerable to invaders—Indo-Europeans in the distant past (they gave the country the name of Iran, Land of the Aryans); Islamic Arab tribes in the seventh century; and a series of Turkic incursions in the Middle Ages. The present populaton reflects these historic invasions. Some 51 percent of the country speaks Persian (**Farsi**) as a first language—Persian is an Indo-European language; 27 percent speak various dialects of Turkic, mainly Azeri and Turkoman; 8 percent speak Gilaki or Mazandarani, distant Persian dialects; 7 percent speak Kurdish, another Indo-European language; and 1–3 percent speak Arabic. Although Iranians have traditionally called their country Iran and their main language Farsi, Europeans since the Middle Ages have referred to the country as Persia, associating it with the dominant language and the central province of Fars. In 1935, Iran formally asked the international community to cease calling the country Persia.

Critical Junctures

Although modern Iran traces its roots to the ancient Iranian empire of the sixth century B.C. and its Islamic religion to the Arab invasions of the seventh century, its current national identity, geographical boundaries,

Critical Junctions in Modern Iran's Political Development

1921	Colonel Reza Khan's military coup
1925	Establishment of the Pahlavi dynasty
1941–1945	Allied occupation of Iran
1951	Nationalization of the oil industry
1953	Coup against Mosaddeq
1963	White Revolution
1975	Establishment of the Resurgence Party
February 1979	Islamic Revolution
1979–1981	U.S. hostage crisis
December 1979	Referendum on the constitution
January 1980	Bani-Sadr elected president
March 1980	Elections for the First Islamic *Majles*
1980–1988	War with Iraq
June 1981	President Bani-Sadr ousted
October 1981	Khamenei elected president
1984	Elections for the Second Islamic *Majles*
1988	Elections for the Third Islamic *Majles*
1989	Khomeini dies; Khamenei appointed Supreme Leader; Rafsanjani elected president
1992	Elections for the Fourth Islamic *Majles*
1996	Elections for the Fifth Islamic *Majles*
1997	Khatami elected president on reform platform

particular interpretation of Islam—**Shi'ism**—and political system were formed by four more recent critical junctures: the Safavid (1501–1722), Qajar (1794–1925), and Pahlavi (1925–1979) dynasties, and the Islamic Revolution of 1979, which led to establishment of the current Islamic Republic.

The Safavids (1501–1722)

Modern Iran, with its Shi'i Islamic identity and its present-day boundaries, can be traced to the sixteenth century, when the Safavid family conquered the territory with the help of fellow Turkic-speaking tribes and established their dynasty. They revived the ancient Iranian titles of Shah-in-Shah (King of Kings) and Shadow of God on Earth, and proceeded to forcibly

Background: *Islam and Shi'ism*

Islam, with some 1 billion adherents, is the second largest religion in the world. Islam means literally "submission to God," and a Muslim is someone who has submitted to God—the same God that Jews and Christians worship. Islam has one central tenet: "There is only one God, and Muhammad is His Prophet." Muslims, in order to consider themselves faithful, need to perform the following four duties to the best of their ability: give to charity; pray every day facing Mecca, where Abraham is believed to have built the first place of worship; make a pilgrimage at least once in a lifetime to Mecca which is located in modern Saudi Arabia; and fast during the daytime hours in the month of Ramadan to commemorate God's revelation of the Qur'an (Koran, or Holy Book) to the Prophet Muhammad. These four, together with the central tenet, are known as the Five Pillars of Islam.

From its earliest days, Islam has been divided into two major branches—the Sunnis and the Shi'is. The Sunnis, meaning literally "followers of tradition," are by far in the majority worldwide. The Shi'is, literally "partisans of Ali," constitute less than 10 percent of Muslims worldwide and are concentrated in Iran, southern Iraq, Azerbaijan, and southern Lebanon.

Although both branches accept the Five Pillars, they differ mostly over who should have suceeded the Prophet Muhammad (d. 632). The Sunnis recognized the early dynasties that ruled the Islamic empire with the exalted title of Caliph ("Prophet's Deputy"). The Shi'is, however, argued that as soon as the Prophet died, his authority should have been passed on to Imam Ali, the Prophet's close companion, disciple, and son-in-law. They further argue that Imam Ali passed his authority to his direct male heirs, the third of whom, Imam Husayn, had been martyred fighting the Sunnis in 680, and the twelfth of whom had supposedly gone into hiding in 941. They refer to the latter as the Mahdi, the Hidden Imam, and believe him to be the Messiah who will herald the end of the world. Furthermore, they argue that in his absence the authority to interpret the *shari'a* (religious law) should be in the hands of the senior clerical scholars—the ayatollahs. Thus, from the beginning, the Shi'is harbored ambivalent attitudes toward the state, especially if the rulers were Sunnis or lacked genealogical links to the Twelve Imams. For Sunnis, the *shari'a* is based mostly on the Qur'an and the teachings of the Prophet. For Shi'is, it is also based on the teachings of the Twelve Imams.

---

convert their subjects to Shi'ism. Although small Shi'i communities had existed in this area since the beginning of Islam, the vast majority had adhered to the majority Sunni branch. The Safavid motivation for this drastic conversion was to give their state and population a distinct identity separate from the surrounding Sunni powers—the Ottomans in the west, the Uzbeks in the north, and the Afghans in the east.

By the mid-seventeenth century the Safavids had succeeded in converting nearly 90 percent of their subjects to Shi'ism. Sunnism survived among the peripheral tribal groups—Kurds in the northwest, Turkomans in the northeast, Baluchis in the southeast, and Arabs in the southwest. It should be noted that the Safavids, despite their conquests, failed to capture from the Ottomans the two most holy Shi'i places located in modern Iraq: Karbala, the site of Imam Husayn's martyrdom, and Najaf, the main theological center.

In addition to the Sunni minority, Safavid Iran contained small communities of Jews, Zoroastrians, and Christians (Armenians and Assyrians). These small minorities lived mostly in Isfahan, Shiraz, Kerman, Yazd, and Azerbaijan. Jews had lived in Iran since ancient times, predating the great diaspora prompted by the Roman destruction of Jerusalem. Zoroastrians were descendants of those who retained their old religion after the Arab invasions. The Christians had lived in the northwest long before the advent of Islam. To strengthen their foothold in central Iran, the Safavids transported there some 100,000 Armenians, encouraging them to become craftsmen and merchants, especially in the lucrative silk trade. The Safavids, like most Muslim rulers but unlike medieval Christian kings, tolerated religious minorities as long as they paid special taxes and accepted royal authority. According to Islam, Christians, Jews, and Zoroastrians were to be tolerated as legitimate **People of the Book**. They were respected both because they were mentioned in the Holy **Qur'an** and because they had their own sacred texts—the Bible, the Torah, and the Avesta.

The Safavids established their capital in Isfahan, a Persian-speaking city, and recruited Persian scribes into their court administration. Such families had helped administer the ancient Iranian empires. They proceeded to govern not only through these Persian scribes and Shi'i clerics but also through local magnates—tribal chiefs, large landowners, religious notables, city merchants, guild elders, and urban ward leaders.

The Safavid army was formed mostly of tribal cavalry led by local chieftains. Financial constraints prevented the Safavids from creating a large bureaucracy or an extended standing army. Their revenues came mostly from land taxes levied on the peasantry. In theory, the Safavids claimed absolute power—Europeans labeled them Oriental despots. In reality, their power was limited, since they lacked a central state and had no choice but to seek the cooperation of many semi-independent local leaders. The central government was linked to the general population not so much through coercive institutions as through provincial and hereditary notables. It survived for the most part because the society below was sharply fragmented by lack of communications, geographical barriers (especially mountains), and regional, tribal, communal, and ethnic differences. Moreover, some of the senior clerics resided in Najaf, safely out of royal reach. The monarch did not control society. Rather, he hovered over it, systematically orchestrating its many existing rivalries.

The Qajars (1794–1925)

The Safavid dynasty collapsed in 1722 when Afghan tribesmen invaded the capital. The invasion was followed by a half century of civil war until the Qajars, another Turkic tribe, reconquered much of Iran. The Qajars moved the capital to Tehran and re-created the Safavid system of central manipulation and court administration, including the Persian scribes. They also declared Shi'ism to be the state religion even though they, unlike the Safavids, did not boast of genealogical links to the Twelve Imams. This was to have far-reaching repercussions. Since these new shahs did not pretend to wear the Imam's mantle, the Shi'i clerical leaders could claim to be the main interpreters of Islam. In addition, many of them safeguarded their independence from the state by continuing to reside in Iraq and collecting religious contributions directly from the faithful in Iran. These contributions came mainly from wealthy merchants.

Qajar rule coincided with the peak of European imperialism. The Russians seized parts of Central Asia and the Caucasus from Iran, and extracted a series of major economic concessions, including a monopoly to fish for sturgeon in the Caspian Sea and exemption from import duties, internal tariffs, and the jurisdiction of local courts. The British Imperial Bank won the monopoly to issue paper money. The Indo-European Telegraph Company got a contract to extend communication lines through the country. A British citizen named D'Arcy bought the exclusive right to drill for oil in the southwest. The later Qajars also borrowed heavily from European banks to meet lavish court expenses. By the end of the century, these loans had become so heavy that the Qajars were obliged to guarantee repayments by placing the country's entire customs service under European supervision. Iranians felt that their whole country had been auctioned off, that their merchants faced unfair competition, and that the shah had given away far too many concessions, or capitulations, as they called them.

These resentments culminated in the constitutional revolution of 1905–1909. The revolution began with shopkeepers and moneylenders demonstrating against the Europeans' being placed in charge of the customs collections. They suspected that the shah would renege on local debts in favor of repaying his foreign loans. They also protested that the government was not doing enough to protect native merchants and local industries. The protests intensified when the government tried to lower sugar prices by publicly whipping two major merchants after sugar prices rose out of control as a result of the disruptions of the 1905 Russian revolution.

The protests peaked in 1906, when some 14,000 took sanctuary inside the gardens of the British legation in Tehran and demanded a written constitution. After weeks of haggling, the shah conceded because the British legation advised compromise and because the unpaid Cossack Brigade, the regime's sole standing army, threatened to join the protesters. Led by Russians and named after the tsar's praetorian guards, the Cossack Brigade was the only force in Iran resembling a disciplined army. A British diplomat commented, "The shah with his unarmed, unpaid, ragged, starving soldiers, what can he do in face of the menace of a general strike and riots?"[1]

The 1906 constitution, modeled after the Belgian one, introduced essential features of modern government into Iran: elections, separation of powers, laws made by a legislative assembly, and the concepts of popular sovereignty and the nation (*mellat*). It also generated a heated debate, with some arguing that democracy was inherently incompatible with Islam and others countering that true Islam could not be practiced unless the government was based on popular support. Some even argued in favor of secularism—complete separation of religion from politics, church from state, clergy from government authority, the affairs of the next world from those of this world.

While retaining the monarchy, the new constitution centered political power in a national assembly called the *Majles*. It hailed this assembly as "the representative of the whole people" and guaranteed two seats to the recognized religious minorities—the Jews, the Zoroastrians, and the Christians. Significantly, no seats were given to the Baha'is, a nineteenth-century offshoot of Shi'ism. The clerical leaders deemed the Baha'is to be apostates from Islam and Baha'i to be a "sinister heresy linked to the imperial powers."

The constitution endowed the *Majles* with extensive authority over all laws, budgets, treaties, loans, concessions, and the composition of the cabinet. The ministers were accountable to the *Majles*, not to the shah. "Sovereignty," declared the constitution, "is a trust confided (as a divine gift) by the people to the person of the shah." The constitution also included a bill of rights guaranteeing citizens equality before the law, protection of life and property, safeguards from arbitrary arrest, and freedom of expression and association.

Although the constitution was modeled on a liberal secular system of government, it made some concessions to Shi'ism. Shi'ism was declared Iran's official religion. Only Shi'is could hold cabinet posts. Clerical courts retained the right to implement the *shari'a* (religious law), especially in family matters. A Guardian Council formed of senior clerics was given veto authority over parliamentary bills deemed un-Islamic. In short, popular sovereignty was to be restricted by a clerical veto power. In actual fact, this Guardian Council was not convened until the 1979 Islamic Revolution. Divisions within the clerical establishment as well as opposition from parliament prevented the convening of this Guardian Council.

The initial euphoria that greeted the constitutional revolution gave way to deep disillusionment in the subsequent decade. Pressures from the imperial powers continued, and a devastating famine after World War I took some 1 million lives, almost 10 percent of the total population. Internal conflicts polarized the *Majles* into warring liberal and conservative factions. The former, mostly members of the intelligentsia, championed social reforms, especially the replacement of the *shari'a* with a modern law code. The latter, led by landlords, tribal chiefs, and senior clerics, vehemently opposed such reforms, particularly land reform, women's rights, and the granting of full equality to religious minorities.

Meanwhile, the central government, lacking any real army, bureaucracy, or tax-collecting machinery, was unable to administer the provinces, especially the regions inhabited by the Kurds, Turkomans, and Baluchis. Some tribes, equipped with modern breech-loading European rifles, had more firepower than the central government. Moreover, during World War I, Russia and Britain formally carved up Iran into three zones. Russia occupied the north; Britain the south. Iran was left with a small "neutral zone" in the middle.

By 1921, Iran was in complete disarray. The shah was gathering his crown jewels to flee south. The British, in their own words, were hoping to "salvage" some "healthy limbs" in their southern zone. Left-wing rebels, helped by the young communist regime in Russia, had taken over the Caspian province of Gilan and were threatening nearby Azerbaijan, Mazandaran, and Khurason. According to a British diplomat, the propertied classes, fearful of bolshevism, were anxiously seeking a savior on horseback.[2]

The Pahlavis (1925–1979)

The savior appeared in February 1921 in the person of Colonel Reza Khan, the recently appointed commander of the 3000-man Cossack Brigade. Carrying out a typical military coup, he replaced the cabinet and, while paying lip service to the monarch, consolidated power in his own hands, especially the post of commander in chief of the armed forces. Four years later, he emerged from behind the throne, deposed the Qajars, crowned himself Shah-in-Shah in the style of his hero Napoleon, and established his own Pahlavi dynasty, adopting a name associated with the glories of ancient Iran. This was the first nontribal dynasty to rule the whole of Iran. To forestall opposition from Britain and the Soviet Union, he assured both countries that Iran would remain strictly nonaligned. A compliant *Majles* endorsed this transfer of power from the Qajars to the Pahlavis.

Reza Shah ruled with an iron fist until 1941, when the British and the Soviets invaded Iran to forestall Nazi Germany from establishing a foothold there. Reza Shah promptly abdicated in favor of his son, Muhammad Reza Shah, and went into exile, where he soon died. In the first twelve years of his reign, the young shah retained control over the armed forces but had to live with a free press, an independent judiciary, competitive elections, assertive cabinet ministers, and boisterous parliaments. He also had to confront two vigorous political movements: the communist Tudeh (Masses) Party; and the National Front, led by the charismatic Dr. Muhammad Mosaddeq (1882–1967).

The Tudeh drew its support mostly from working-class trade unions. The National Front drew its support mainly from the salaried middle classes and campaigned to nationalize the British-owned oil company that had a monopoly over the drilling, refining, and sale of all petroleum in Iran. Mosaddeq also wanted to sever the Shah's links with the armed forces. He argued that according to the constitution the monarch should reign, not rule, and that the armed forces should be supervised by cabinet ministers responsible to parliament. In 1951, Mosaddeq was elected prime minister and promptly nationalized the oil industry. The period of relative freedom, however, ended abruptly in 1953, when royalist officers overthrew Mosaddeq and installed the shah with absolute power. Since this 1953 coup was financed by the U.S. Central Intelligence Agency (CIA) and the British, it intensified anti-British sentiment and created a deep distrust of the United States. It also made the Shah appear to be a puppet of the foreign powers. Muhammad Reza Shah began to rule much in the style of his autocratic father until overthrown by the 1979 Islamic Revolution.

During their fifty-four-year rule, the Pahlavis built a highly centralized state, the first in Iran's history. This state rested on three pillars: the armed forces; the bureaucracy; and the extensive patronage system. The armed forces grew from fewer than 40,000 men in 1925 to 124,000 in 1941, and to over 410,000 in 1979. In 1925 the armed forces had been formed of a motley crew of cossacks, city policeman, and gendarmes (rural policemen). By the mid-1930s they had the power to disarm the tribes and impose the will of the state on the provinces. By 1979 they constituted the fifth largest army in the world, the largest navy in the Persian Gulf, the largest air force in western Asia, and one of the best-equipped tank brigades in the Third World. They were supplemented with a pervasive secret police known as SAVAK—the Persian acronym for the Organization to Protect and Gather Information for the State.

The bureaucracy expanded from a haphazard collection of hereditary scribes—some without fixed offices—to twenty-one ministries employing over 300,000 civil servants in 1979. The Interior Ministry (the main bureaucracy) appointed the provincial governors, town mayors, district superintendents, and village headmen. Since it also appointed electoral supervisors, it could rig *Majles* elections and thus provide the Shah with rubber-stamp parliaments. The constitutional laws of 1906–1909 survived, at least in theory. The Education Ministry grew twentyfold and by 1979 administered 26,000 primary schools with some 4 million children, and 1850 secondary schools with 740,000 pupils. Meanwhile, the Ministry of Higher Education administered 750 vocational schools with 227,000 students; and thirteen universities with 154,000 college students.

The Justice Ministry supplanted the *Shari'a* with a European-style civil code and the clerical courts with a modern judicial system. This went from district courts through provincial courts all the way up to a Supreme Court. To practice in these courts, lawyers and judges had to pass government-administered exams based on European jurisprudence. The system was further secularized in the 1960s, when the Shah decreed a controversial Family Protection Law. This contradicted the *shar'ia* on a number of points. It raised the marriage age to twenty for men and eighteen for women. It allowed women to override spousal objections and work outside the home if they got court permission. It restricted polygamy by stipulating that husbands could marry more than one wife only if they first obtained permission from previous wives and the courts. For some, the state had extended its arm to reach into the most intimate area of existence—family life.

Other ministries experienced similar expansion. For example, the Transport Ministry built an impressive array of bridges, ports, highways, and railroads known as the Trans-Iranian Railway. The Ministry of Industries financed the construction of numerous factories specializing in consumer goods. The Agricultural Ministry attained prominence in 1962, when the Shah made land reform the centerpiece of his much-heralded White Revolution. The government bought land from large absentee owners and sold it to small farmers through low-interest long-term mortgages. It also undertook the task of transforming small farmers into modern commercial entrepreneurs by providing them with fertilizers, cooperatives, distribution centers, irrigation canals, dams, and tractor-repair shops. The White Revolution included the extension of the vote to women, the Family Protection Law, and a Literacy Corps to eradicate illiteracy in the countryside. Thus, by 1979, the state had set up a modern system of communications, initiated a minor industrial revolution, and extended its reach into even the most outlying villages.

The state also controlled a number of major institutions: the National and the Central banks; the planning organization in charge of five-year plans; the Industrial and Mining Development Bank, which channeled money to private entrepreneurs; the National Radio-Television network, which monopolized the airwaves—by the 1960s most villages had access to transistor radios; and most important, the National Iranian Oil Company, which grew from a leasing firm in the 1950s to become a large exploring, drilling, refining, and exporting corporation.

The Pahlavi state was further bolstered by court patronage. Reza Shah, the son of a small landowner, used coercion, confiscations, and diversion of irriga-

tion water to make himself one of the largest landowners in the Middle East. In the words of a British diplomat, Reza Shah had an "unholy interest in property," especially other people's property.[3] This wealth transformed the Shah's court into a large military-landed complex providing patronage for the thousands employed in its numerous palaces, hotels, casinos, charities, companies, and beach resorts. This patronage system further grew under Muhammad Reza Shah, especially after he established his tax-exempt Pahlavi Foundation. By the 1970s the Pahlavi Foundation controlled 207 large companies active in tourism, insurance, banking, agribusiness, mining, construction, and manufacturing. The network was handy for rewarding friends and penalizing adversaries.

Although the Pahlavi state looked impressive, it lacked solid foundations. The drive for secularization, centralization, industrialization, and social development won some favor from the urban propertied classes. But arbitrary rule, especially the 1953 coup, the disregard for constitutional liberties, and the stifling of independent newspapers, political parties, and professional associations, produced widespread resentment, particularly among the clergy, the intelligentsia, and the urban masses. In short, this state was strong in the sense that it controlled new instruments of coercion and administration. But it was weak in terms of its failure to link the new state institutions to the country's social structure. The Pahlavi state, like the Safavids and the Qajars, hovered over, rather than embedded itself into, the society. What is more, much of the civil society that had existed in traditional Iran had now been swamped by the modern state.

As if the Pahlavi state did not control enough of society, in 1975 the Shah announced the formation of the Resurgence Party. He declared Iran to be a one-party state and threatened those refusing to join the party with exile and imprisonment. In heralding the new order, the Shah replaced the traditional Islamic calendar with a new royalist one, jumping from the Muslim year 1355 to the royalist year 2535; 2500 years were allocated to the monarchy in general and 35 years for the Shah's own reign. The King of Kings and the Shadow of God also accrued two new titles: Guide to the New Great Civilization and Light of the Aryans (*Aryamehr*).

Leaders: *Ayatollah Ruhollah Khomeini*

Ruhollah Khomeini was born in 1902 into a landed clerical family well known in central Iran. During the 1920s he studied in the famous Fayzieh Seminary in Qom with the leading theologians of the day, most of whom were scrupulously apolitical. He taught at the seminary from the 1930s through the 1950s, avoiding politics even during the mass campaign to nationalize the British-owned oil company. His entry into politics did not come until 1962, when he, along with most other clerical leaders, denounced Muhammad Reza Shah's White Revolution. Forced into exile, Khomeini taught at the Shi'i center of Najaf in Iraq from 1964 until 1978. During these years, he developed his own version of Shi'i populism by incorporating socioeconomic grievances into his sermons and denouncing not just the Shah but the whole ruling class. Returning home triumphant in the midst of the Iranian Revolution, he was declared the Supreme Leader, the Founder of the Islamic Republic, the Guide for the Oppressed Masses, and Imam of the Muslim community. In the past, Iranian Shi'is, unlike the Arab Sunnis, had reserved the special term *Imam* only for Imam Ali and his Twelve direct heirs, whom they deemed to be semidivine and thereby infallible. For many Iranians in 1979, Khomeini was charismatic in the true sense of the word—a man with a special gift from God. Khomeini ruled as Imam and Supreme Leader of the Islamic Republic until his death in 1989.

The Resurgence Party was designed to create yet another organizational link with the population, especially with the **bazaars** (traditional marketplaces), which unlike the rest of society, had managed to retain their guilds and thus escape direct government control. The Resurgence Party promptly established bazaar guilds as well as newspapers, women's organizations, professional associations, and labor unions. It also prepared to create a Religious Corps, modeled on the Literacy Corps, to go into the countryside to teach the peasants "true Islam." The state was venturing into areas in which previous rulers had feared to tread.

The Resurgence Party promised to establish an "organic relationship between rulers and ruled"; "synthesize the best of capitalism and socialism"; and chart the way toward the New Great Civilization. It also praised the Shah for curbing the power of the "medieval clergy," eradicating vestiges of class warfare, and having the authority of a "spiritual guide" as well as a world-renowned statesman. For his part, the Shah told an English-language newspaper that the party's philosophy was "based on the dialectical principles of the White Revolution" and that nowhere in the world was there such a close relationship between a ruler and his people. "No other nation has given its commander such a carte-blanche [blank check]."[4] The terminology, as well as the boast, revealed much about the Shah at the height of his power.

The Islamic Revolution (1979)

On the eve of the revolution, an Iranian paper published in Paris printed a long denunciation of the Pahlavis entitled "Fifty Indictments of Treason During Fifty Years of Treason."[5] It charged the Pahlavis with establishing a military dictatorship with the help of the CIA; trampling over the constitution; creating SAVAK; rigging parliamentary elections; organizing a fascistic one-party state; taking over the religious establishment; and undermining national identity by disseminating Western culture. It also accused the regime of inducing millions of landless peasants to migrate into urban shantytowns; widening the gap between rich and poor; funneling money away from the small bourgeoisie into the pockets of the wealthy comprador bourgeoisie (the entrepreneurs linked to foreign companies and multinational corporations); wasting resources on bloated military budgets; and granting new capitulations to the West—the most controversial being the extension of diplomatic immunity to U.S. military advisers.

These grievances were given greater articulation when Ayatollah Ruhollah Khomeini began to formulate a new version of Shi'ism from his exile in Iraq. Khomeini's version of Shi'ism has often been labeled Islamic **fundamentalism**, but would be better described as Shi'i populism or political Islam. The term *fundamentalism*, derived from American Protestantism, implies religious dogmatism, intellectual inflexibility and purity, political traditionalism, social conservatism, rejection of the modern world, and the literal interpretation of scriptural texts. Khomeini, however, was less concerned about literal interpretations of the Qur'an than about fanning grievances against the elite and resentment against the United States. By 1979 he was more of a political revolutionary than a social conservative.

Khomeini began to denounce monarchies in general and the Pahlavis in particular as part and parcel of the corrupt elite exploiting the oppressed masses. The oppressors, he said, comprised large landowners, high-ranking military officers, corrupt courtiers, wealthy foreign-connected capitalists, and millionaire palace dwellers. The oppressed, on the other hand, were the masses, especially the landless peasants, the wage earners, the shantytown poor, and the self-employed in the bazaars. His proclamations often echoed the promise of the Bible and the Qur'an that "the poor (meek) shall inherit the earth."

In calling for the overthrow of the Pahlavi monarchy, Khomeini injected a radically new meaning into the old Shi'i term *velayat-e faqih* (**jurist's guardianship**). He argued that jurist's guardianship gave the senior clergy all-encompassing authority over the whole community, not just over widows, minors, and the retarded, as had been the interpretation previously. He insisted that only the senior clerics had the competence to understand the *shari'a;* that the divine authority given to the Prophet and the Imams had been passed on to their spiritual heirs, the clergy; and that throughout history the clergy had championed the rights of the people against bad government and foreign powers. He further insisted that the clergy were the people's true representatives, since they lived among them, listened to their problems, and shared their everyday joys and pains. He also claimed that the Shah intended to confiscate religious endowments, replace Islamic values with "cultural imperialism," and force women to go unveiled and thus "naked" into the streets. In fact, the last Shah had merely encouraged women to unveil; he had never outlawed the veil nor banned the full covering known as the chador. These pronouncements added fuel to an already explosive situation.

Iran now needed a few sparks to ignite the revolution. These came in the form of minor economic difficulties and pressure from international human rights organizations to curb SAVAK. In 1977–1978 the Shah tried to deal with a 20 percent rise in consumer prices and a 10 percent decline in oil revenues by cutting construction projects and declaring war against "profiteers," "hoarders," and "price gougers." Not surprisingly, shopkeepers felt that the Shah was diverting attention from court corruption and planning to replace them with government-run department stores, and that he was intending to destroy the bazaar, which some felt was the "the real pillar of Iranian society."

The pressure to curb SAVAK came from Amnesty International, the United Nations, and the Western press as well as from the recently elected Carter administration in the United States. In 1977, after meeting with the International Commission of Jurists, the Shah permitted Red Cross officials to visit prisons and allowed defense attorneys to attend political trials. In the words of Khomeini's first prime minister, Mehdi Bazargan, this international pressure allowed the opposition to breathe again after decades of suffocation.[6]

This slight loosening of the reins, coming in the midst of the economic recession, sealed the fate of the Shah. Political parties, labor organizations, and professional associations—especially lawyers, writers, and university professors—regrouped after years of being banned. Bazaar guilds regained their independence from the government party. College, high school, and seminary students, especially in the religious center of Qom, took to the streets to protest the quarter century of repression. On September 8, 1978, known as Bloody Friday, troops in Tehran fired into a crowded square, killing hundreds of unarmed demonstrators. By late 1978 a general strike brought the whole economy to a halt, paralyzing not only the oil industry, the factories, the banks, and the transport system but also the civil service, the media, the bazaars, and the whole educational establishment. The oil workers vowed that they would not export any petroleum until they had exported the "Shah and his forty thieves."[7]

Meanwhile, in the urban centers, local committees attached to the **mosques** (Muslim places of worship) and financed by the bazaars were distributing food to the needy, organizing militias known as the ***pasdaran*** (revolutionary guards), and setting up ad hoc courts to retain some semblance of law and order, since the whole judicial structure and the police had melted away. Equally significant, the antiregime rallies were now attracting as many as 2 million protesters. The largest of them was held in Tehran in December 1978 on the day commemorating the martyrdom of Imam Husayn at Karbala in 680. Protesters demanded the abolition of the monarchy, the return of Khomeini, and the establishment of a republic that would preserve national independence from imperialism and give workers and peasants social justice in the form of decent wages, land, and a proper standard of living.[8] Some soon forgot these economic demands, claiming that the Islamic Revolution was made by fundamentalists.

Although these rallies were led by pro-Khomeini clerics, they had valuable support from a broad spectrum of organizations: the National Front; the Tudeh; the Fedayin, a Marxist guerrilla group; the Mojahedin, a Muslim guerrilla group formed of religious but lay radicals; university and high school students; lawyers, writers, and women's organizations; and many well-financed bazaar merchants and guilds. A secret Revolutionary Committee set up by the pro-Khomeini clerics in Tehran tried to coordinate the strikes and protests that erupted, mostly spontaneously, in the provincial cities. The Revolutionary Committee was in daily phone contact with Khomeini in exile and disseminated his speeches through clandestine tape cassettes. This was a revolution made in the streets and moved along by audiotapes.

After a series of such mass rallies in late 1978, the *Washington Post* concluded that the "disciplined and well-organized marches lent considerable weight to the opposition's claim of being an alternative government."[9] Similarly, the *Christian Science Monitor* stated that the "giant wave of humanity sweeping through the capital declared louder than any bullet or bomb could the clear message, 'The Shah must go.'"[10] Confronted by this opposition and aware that increasing numbers of soldiers were deserting to the opposition, the Shah decided to leave Iran. A year later, when in exile he was dying of cancer, there was much speculation, especially in the United States, whether he could have mastered the upheavals if he had been healthier, possessed a stronger personality, and received full support from the United States. But even a healthy man with an iron will and full foreign backing would not have been able to deal with 2 million demonstrators, a massive general strike, and defections from his own army rank-and-file.

On February 11—three weeks after the Shah's departure and ten days after Khomeini's return—armed groups, especially of the Fedayin and the Mojahedin supported by air force cadets, broke into the main army barracks in Tehran, distributed arms, and then assaulted the main police stations, the jails, and eventually the national radio-television station. That same evening, the radio station made the historic announcement: "This is the voice of Iran, the voice of true Iran, the voice of the Islamic Revolution." A few hours of street fighting had completed the destruction of the fifty-four-year-old dynasty that claimed a 2500-year-old heritage.

The Islamic Republic (1979 to the Present)

Seven weeks after the February revolution a nationwide referendum replaced the monarchy with an Islamic Republic. Of the 21 million eligible voters, 20 million—97 percent—endorsed the change. Liberal and lay supporters of Khomeini, including Mehdi Bazargan, his first prime minister, had hoped to offer the electorate a third choice—that of a Democratic Islamic Republic. But Khomeini overruled them on the grounds that the term *democratic* was redundant because Islam itself was democratic. The structure of this new republic was implicitly left to Khomeini, who was now hailed not only as a Grand Ayatollah but also as the Leader of the Revolution, the Founder of the Islamic Republic, the Guide for the Oppressed Masses, the Commander of the Armed Forces, and most potent, the **Imam** ("Infallible Leader") of the Muslim community.

The constitution itself was drawn up in late 1979 by a constituent body named the Assembly of Religious Experts (*Majles-e Khebregan*). Although this seventy-three-man assembly was elected by the general public, almost all secular organizations as well as clerics opposed to Khomeini boycotted the elections on the grounds that the state media were controlled, independent papers had been banned, and voters were being intimidated by club-wielding vigilantes known as the **Hezbollahis** ("Partisans of God").

The Shah's statue
on the ground,
February 1979.
Source: © Abbas/
Magnum Photos.

The vast majority of those elected, including forty hojjat al-Islams and fifteen ayatollahs, were pro-Khomeini clerics. They proceeded to draft a highly theocratic constitution vesting much authority in the hands of Khomeini in particular and the clergy in general—all this over the strong objections of Prime Minister Bazargan, who wanted a French-style presidential republic that would be Islamic in name but democratic in structure.

Khomeini submitted this clerical constitution to a national referendum in December 1979, at the height of the American hostage crisis. In fact, some suspected that the whole crisis had been engineered to undercut the Bazargan government which favored keeping cordial ties with the United States. As soon as Bazargan threatened to submit his own secular constitution to the public, the state television network—controlled by the clerics—showed him shaking hands with U.S. policymakers. Meanwhile Khomeini declared that the U.S embassy—the "den of spies"— was plotting a repeat performance of the 1953 coup. A month after the embassy break-in and Bazargan's resignation, Khomeini submitted the theocratic constitution to the public, insisting that all had

the duty to endorse it—99 percent of those voting endorsed it. The turnout, however, was not so impressive. Of the 21 million eligible voters, only 16 million participated despite the concerted efforts of all the authorities, including the mass media, the local mosques, and the revolutionary guards. The clerics had won their constitution but at the cost of eroding the republic's broad consensus.

In the first decade after the revolution, the clerics were able to further consolidate power for the following reasons. Few could afford to challenge Khomeini's overwhelming charisma. The Iraqi invasion in 1980—prompted by Sadaam Hussein's ambition to obtain vital border regions—rallied most of the population behind the regime; after all, the homeland had been violated by a foreign invader. The price of petroleum on the world market shot up, providing ample oil revenues. Thus, despite war and revolution, the new regime was able to continue the social programs launched by the previous one. In fact, in the 1980s modern amenities, especially electricity, indoor plumbing, televisions, telephones, refrigerators, motorcycles, and medical clinics, made their first significant appearance in the countryside.

The second decade after the revolution, however, brought the clerics serious challenges. Khomeini's death in June 1989 removed his decisive presence. His successor as Supreme Leader, Khamenei, lacked not only his popularity and political experience but also his scholastic credentials. Khamenei had been considered a mere **hojjat al-Islam** until the government-controlled press elevated him to the rank of ayatollah just before his appointment as Supreme Leader. Few senior ayatollahs deemed him their equal. The UN-brokered Iraqi cease-fire in 1988 ended the immediacy of the foreign danger. The drastic fall in world oil prices after 1984 strained state finances and placed a sharp brake on social and economic development. What is more, some clerics within the system began to call for liberalization, revitalization, and opening up of Iran to the West.

Themes and Implications

Historical Junctures and Political Themes

These historical junctures have shaped contemporary Iran, the way it grapples with the democratic idea, Iran's role in the world of states, its attempts to govern the economy and meet rising expectations as well as its aspiration to overcome internal division with a sense of a collective Shi'i Iranian identity.

By far the most important challenge facing the republic is that of reconciling Islam with democracy. Iran has been Muslim since the seventh century and Shi'i Muslim since the sixteenth century. It has also aspired to attain democracy, mass participation, and popular sovereignty since the 1905 constitutional revolution. The dual sentiments for Islam and for democracy culminated in the 1979 Islamic Revolution and appeared to be reconcilable as long as the vast majority supported Khomeini and accepted his notion of the jurist's guardianship. Rights of Man did not seem to contradict the Divine Right of the Clergy. As Khomeini liked to repeat, there was no contradiction between Islam and democracy because the vast majority supported the clerics, had faith in them, respected them as the true interpreters of the *shari'a*, and wanted them to oversee the activities of all state officials. Islam and democracy, however, now appear less reconcilable because the public has lost its enthusiasm

for the clergy, especially since the death of Khomeini. Thus some of his followers have continued to give priority to his concept of theocracy while others have begun to emphasize the need for democracy. In other words, Khomeinism has divided into two divergent branches—political liberalism and clerical conservatism.

The issue of democracy is compounded by the very nature of the *shari'a*. Democracy is based on the two principles that all are equal, especially before the law, and that all individuals have inalienable natural rights, including the right to choose their own religion. The *shari'a*, as conventionally interpreted, rejects both. Formulated in the seventh century, the *shari'a* is based on the principle of inequality, especially between men and women, between Muslims and non-Muslims, between legitimate minorities, known as the People of the Book, and illegitimate ones, known as unbelievers and idol-worshipers. In addition, the *shari'a*, like all religious law, considers rights to be derived from God rather than nature and deems the individual to be subordinate to the religious community. This is of special concern for Muslims who lose their faith or join another religion, since the *shari'a* can condemn them to death as apostates. This is no mere technicality; over 250 Baha'is and over 400 leftist political prisoners have been executed on the grounds of being religious apostates. The latter were hanged after admitting that they did not believe in God, the Resurrection, and the divinity of the Qur'an. But there are plenty of moderate clerics who want to reform the *shari'a* to make it compatible with the modern concepts of individual freedom and human rights. They also favor treating nonbelievers in the traditional fashion: "don't ask, don't tell."

The Islamic Republic is determined to remain the dominant power in the Persian Gulf, even though it attained this position under the Shah mainly thanks to U.S. assistance. In his last years, the Shah had been known as the American policeman in the Persian Gulf. By denouncing the United States as an "arrogant imperialist," by canceling military agreements with the West, and by condoning the taking of U.S. diplomats as hostages, Khomeini carried out a diplomatic revolution in the Middle East. This prompted Saddam Hussein to launch the Iraq-Iranian War. When ministers suggested referring to the Persian Gulf as the

Muslim Gulf to improve relations with Arab countries, all of whom call it the Arab Gulf, Khomeini responded that it should remain what it had always been—the Persian Gulf. Khomeini was as much an Iranian nationalist as a revolutionary Muslim.

Before dying, Khomeini initiated policies that have made it difficult for his successors to improve relations with the West, especially the United States. He called for revolutions throughout the Muslim world, denouncing Arab rulers in the region, particularly in Saudi Arabia, as the "corrupt puppets of American imperialism." He strengthened the navy, buying nuclear submarines from Russia. He launched a research program to build medium-range missiles and nuclear weapons. He denounced the proposals for Arab-Israeli negotiations over Palestine. He sent money as well as arms to Muslim dissidents abroad, particularly Shi'i groups in Lebanon, Iraq, and Afghanistan. He permitted the intelligence services to assassinate some one hundred exiled opposition leaders living in Western Europe. And most important, he issued a *fatwa* against the British writer Salman Rushdie. These policies helped isolate Iran not only from the United States but also from the European Community, human rights organizations and the United Nations. Khomeini's heirs have had to grapple with this heritage, especially since these acts have direct bearing on economic development and the prospects for obtaining foreign investment.

The Islamic Republic began with the conviction that it could rapidly develop the economy if it relied less on oil exports and more on agriculture and manufacturing. It blamed the Shah for the one-export economy, the migration of peasants into the towns, the increasing gap in incomes, the continued high illiteracy rate, the lack of medical and educational facilities, and, in general, the low standard of living. It also blamed the former regime for failing to make Iran self-sufficient and instead making it vulnerable to the vagaries of the world economy by building assembly plants rather than factories that would produce industrial goods.

The new regime soon discovered that although it was relatively easy to narrow the gap between town and country, the underlying problems of developing the economy were formidable. The state remains heavily dependent on oil and thus on the fluctuations of the international petroleum market. Peasants continue to migrate because of geographical pressures, notably the lack of agricultural land and water for irrigation. Industry remains limited because of the lack of capital. Real per capita income has fallen due to forces outside the control of the state. The real price of oil has plummeted; by 1999 it was less than it had been before the dramatic quadrupling of prices in 1974. Meanwhile, the population has grown to almost 69 million. In other words, the population has doubled since the revolution while oil income has stagnated. Not surprisingly, the republic continues to struggle with such financial problems as inflation, high unemployment, and capital shortages. Some decision-makers advocate conventional state-interventionist strategies: price controls, five-year plans, and further redistribution of wealth through high taxation and social investment. Others advocate equally conventional laissez-faire strategies: open markets, removal of state controls, more business incentives, and the wooing of foreign capital. Some clerics now openly admit that religion does not have answers to such problems as inflation, unemployment, and the volatility of oil prices. This is a sharp contrast to the early days of the revolution, when Khomeini had confidently declared that Islam had all the solutions and that economics was a subject worthy of donkeys.

Finally, the Islamic Republic began with a broad collective identity, since 99 percent of Iran's population is Muslim. But this major asset was squandered somewhat in the two decades after the revolution. The stress on Shi'ism naturally alienated the Sunnis, who constitute some 9 percent of the population. The triumph in neighboring Afghanistan of the ultraconservative Sunni organization the Taliban further complicated the situation. The Taliban has been supporting Sunni dissidents in Iran; Iran, in turn, has been arming Shi'i dissidents inside Afghanistan. Moreover, the regime's insistence on building the constitution around Khomeini's notion of theocratic government has antagonized many of the top clerics, who rejected this theory of government, as well as lay secular Muslims, who lead most of the political parties. Similarly, the inadvertent association of Shi'ism with the central Persian-speaking regions carries with it the potential danger of eventually alienating the important Turkic minority in Azerbaijan. Thus the Iranian regime, like most developing states, has to solve the problem of how to allocate scarce economic resources without exacerbating ethnic, regional, and sectarian differences.

Implications for Comparative Politics

The Iranian Revolution, the emergence of Islam in Middle Eastern politics, and the collapse of the Soviet Union convinced many Americans that a new specter was haunting the West—Islamic fundamentalism. By the mid-1990s some experts on international relations were predicting that a new "clash of civilizations" would replace the Cold War; that the fault lines in world politics would no longer be over economics and ideology but over religion and culture; and that the main clash would be between the West and the Islamic world, headed by the Islamic Republic of Iran. Islam was deemed a major threat not only because of its size but also because it was "inherently bellicose," and "militant," and bore a historic grudge against the West.

These dire predictions turned out to be gross exaggerations. It is true that the Islamic Republic began denouncing the United States, arming militants in other parts of the Middle East, and calling for a struggle, sometimes termed a *jihad* (crusade), against the West. But these rhetorical denunciations became muted as time passed—the election of Khatami indicates this. The call for Muslim unity fell on deaf ears, especially in Sunni countries. The external assistance was limited to Shi'is in Afghanistan, Iraq, and southern Lebanon. Islam proved to be not a monolith; the Muslim international turned out to be, at most, a Shi'i international. What is more, Iranians themselves, including the clerics, divide sharply into ultraconservatives, conservatives, liberals, and radicals. They even use the Western terms left, right, and center to describe themselves. Iran shows that the notion of Muslim politics has as little meaning as that of Christian politics. In the same way that one does not study the Bible to understand modern Europe, one does not need the Qur'an to analyze Middle Eastern politics.

It is true that Iran is a major power in the Middle East. It has the region's second largest army, a large land mass, human resources, a respectable GNP, and oil production. It has the largest navy in the Persian Gulf. In the days of the Shah, this navy safeguarded the flow of oil to the West. It now poses a threat to the same flow of oil. It also has plans, predating the Islamic Revolution, to build nuclear weapons. But it is also true that Iran is in many ways a much weakened power. It has the GNP of New Jersey, hardly a replacement of the Soviet threat to the United States. Its armed forces are a mere shadow of their former selves. The eight-year conflict with Iraq has made them war-weary. The officer ranks have been decimated by constant purges. Their hardware has been depleted by war, use, and obsolescence, and the regime has difficulty financing arms purchases. In the last years of the Shah, military purchases accounted for 17 percent of the gross domestic product. They now take less than 2 percent. Moreover, a U.S. fleet cruises the Persian Gulf, counterbalancing the Iranian navy, and plans to build nuclear weapons are bogged down in financial, technical, and logistical problems. Iran is unlikely to obtain nuclear weapons—not to mention nuclear capabilities—in the forseeable future.

It is true that Iran has viewed itself as the vanguard of the Islamic world. But that world turned out to be as illusory for its champions as for its detractors. It is formed not of one unitary bloc but of many rival states, each with its own national self-interest as defined by its own local elites. In theory, these rulers stress the importance of unity and solidarity. In reality, they pursue traditional power politics. They give priority to the protection of their own states, even if this involves allying with non-Muslim states against rival Muslims ones. For example, at the height of the American hostage crisis, Iran obtained military equipment from Israel and the United States to pursue the war against Iraq. Similarly, in recent years, Iran has sided with India against Pakistan; Armenia against Azerbaijan; Russia against Chechnya. It has also actively opposed the Afghan Taliban, mainly because the latter is backed by Pakistan and Saudi Arabia, Iran's regional rivals. Those who see the future as a clash of civilizations and a replay of the medieval Christian-Muslim wars forget that the crusaders themselves, both Muslim and Christian, were often divided, with some siding against their own co-religionists. One Muslim world exists no more now than it did in the days of the medieval crusaders.

Section ❷ Political Economy and Development

State and Economy

In 1993 billboards appeared in Tehran announcing the return of Coca-Cola after a fourteen-year absence. In its initial enthusiasm for economic self-sufficiency, the Islamic Republic had ousted Coca-Cola and many other multinational corporations. Although some leaders continued to warn against Western consumerism and cultural imperialism, the regime as a whole was now eager to market this and other hallmarks of international capitalism. Iran, despite its anti-Western stance, was being reintegrated into the world economy.

The Economy in the Nineteenth Century

The integration of Iran into the world system began in a modest way in the latter half of the nineteenth century. Before then, commercial contact with the outside world had been limited to a few luxury goods and the famous medieval silk route to China. A number of factors account for this nineteenth-century integration: the economic concessions granted to the European powers; the opening up of the Suez Canal and the building of the Trans-Caspian and the Batum-Baku railways; the laying of telegraph lines across Iran to link India with Britain; the outflow of capital from Europe after 1870; and, most important, the Industrial Revolution in Europe and the subsequent export of manufactured goods to the rest of the world.

In the course of the nineteenth century, Iran's foreign trade increased tenfold. Over 83 percent of this trade was with Russia and Britain; 10 percent with Germany, France, Italy, and Belgium; and less than 7

Coca-Cola being sold in Iran. *Source:* Rad Eslami/Gamma Liaison.

percent with countries in the Middle East. Exports were confined to carpets and agricultural products, including silk, raw cotton, opium, dried fruits, rice, and tobacco. Imports were mostly tea, sugar, kerosene, and such industrial products as textiles, glassware, guns, and other metal goods. Also in this period, modest foreign investment flowed into banking, fishing, carpet weaving, transport, and telegraph communications.

Contact with the West had far-reaching repercussions. It produced what later became known as economic dependency: the overreliance of the underdeveloped world on the developed; the vulnerability of poor countries to sudden fluctuations in rich economies; and the export of raw materials, whose prices often stagnated or declined, in return for the import of finished products, whose value invariably increased. Some claim that this dependency lies at the root of present-day economic underdevelopment in much of Africa, Latin America, and Asia (including the Middle East).

The nineteenth-century influx of mass-manufactured goods devastated some traditional handicrafts, especially cotton textiles. According to a tax collector in Isfahan, the import of cheap, colorful cotton goods damaged not only the local weavers, dyers, and carders but also the thousands of housewives who in the past had supplemented their family incomes with cottage industries and home spindles.[11] They naturally blamed foreign imports for their plight. Carpet manufacturers, however, benefited, since they found a ready market in Europe and North America.

Moreover, the introduction of cash crops, especially cotton, tobacco, and opium, reduced the acreage available for wheat and other cereals. Many landowners ceased growing food and turned to commercial export crops. This paved the way for a series of disastrous famines in 1860, 1869–1872, 1880, and 1918–1920. Opium cultivation was particularly encouraged by British merchants eager to meet the ever-rising demands of the Chinese market brought about by the notorious Opium Wars.

Furthermore, the competition from foreign merchants, together with the introduction of the telegraph and the postal systems, brought the many local merchants, shopkeepers, and workshop owners together into a national middle class aware for the first time of their common statewide interests against both the central government and the foreign powers. In short, the bazaars were transformed into a propertied middle class conscious of its national grievances. This awareness played an important role in the constitutional revolution.

The Oil Economy

The real integration of Iran into the world system came in the twentieth century. Its main engine was oil. British prospectors struck oil in Khuzistan in 1908, and the British government in 1912 decided to fuel its navy with petroleum rather than coal. It also decided to buy most of its fuel from the Anglo-Iranian Oil Company, in which it was a major shareholder. Iran's oil revenues increased modestly in the next four decades, reaching US$16 million in 1951. After the nationalization of the oil industry in 1951 and the agreement with a consortium of U.S. and British companies in 1955, oil revenues rose steadily, from $34 million in 1955 to $5 billion in 1973, and after the quadrupling of oil prices in 1974, to over $20 billion in 1975 and $23 billion in 1976. Between 1953 and 1978, the cumulative oil income came to over $100 billion.

Oil became known as Iran's black gold. It financed over 90 percent of imports and 80 percent of the annual budget, and far surpassed total tax revenues. In contrast, domestic taxation provides the Japanese government with over 75 percent of its revenues. Oil also enabled Iran not to worry about feeding its population, a problem confronting many poor countries. Instead it could undertake ambitious development programs that other states implemented only if they could squeeze scarce resources from their populations. In fact, oil revenues created what is known as a **rentier state**, a state obtaining a lucrative income by exporting raw materials or leasing out oil wells. Iran as well as Iraq, Algeria, and the Gulf states received enough money from their wells to be able to disregard their internal tax bases. The state became relatively independent of society. The society, in turn, had few inputs into the state. Little taxation meant little representation. It also meant that the state was totally reliant on one commodity whose price was determined by the world market.

Muhammad Reza Shah tried to diminish the dependency on oil by encouraging other exports and attracting foreign investment into nonoil ventures. Neither policy succeeded. Despite some increase in carpet and pistachio exports, oil continued to dominate. On the eve of the 1979 revolution, it still provided 97 percent of the country's foreign exchange. The new nonoil industries faced difficulties finding export markets. Furthermore, Iran failed to draw external capital despite the much-publicized 1955 Law for the Attraction and Protection of Foreign Investments. Even after the oil boom, foreign firms, mostly U.S., European, and Japanese, invested no more than US$1 billion. Much of this was not in industry but in banking, trade, and insurance. In Iran, as in the rest of the Middle East, Western companies grew weary of investing large fixed assets, because of government corruption, high labor costs, the limitations of the internal market, and the fear of potential instability and outright confiscations. Apparently, the companies did not share their governments' confidence that Iran was an island of stability.

Oil revenues financed Muhammad Reza Shah's development projects. It is true—as the opposition liked to publicize—that some revenue was squandered on palaces, royal extravagances, bureaucratic waste, outright corruption, ambitious nuclear projects, and ultrasophisticated weapons too expensive even for many NATO countries. But it is also true that significant sums were channeled into socioeconomic development. Gross national product (GNP) grew at the average rate of 9.6 percent every year from 1960 to 1977, making Iran one of the fastest developing countries in the Third World at that time. The land reform project—the linchpin of the White Revolution—created over 644,000 moderately prosperous farms (see Table 1). The number of modern factories tripled from fewer than 320 to over 980 (see Table 2). Enrollment in primary schools grew from less than 750,000 to over 4 million; in secondary schools from 121,000 to nearly 740,000; in vocational schools from 2500 to nearly 230,000; and in universities from under 14,000 to more than 154,000. The Trans-Iranian Railway was completed, linking Tehran with Tabriz, Meshed, Isfahan, and the Gulf. Roads were built connecting most villages with the provincial cities.

The expansion in health services was equally impressive. Between 1963 and 1977 the number of hospital beds increased from 24,126 to 48,000;

Table 1

Land Ownership in 1977

Size (hectares)	No. of Owners
200+	1300
51–200	44,000
11–50	600,000
3–10	1,200,000
Landless	700,000

Note: 1 hectare is equal to approximately 2.47 acres.

Source: E. Abrahamian, "Structural Causes of the Iranian Revolution," *Middle East Research and Information Project*, no. 87 (May 1980), 23.

Table 2

Number of Factories

Size	1953	1977
Small (10–40 workers)	Fewer than 1000	More than 7000
Medium (50–500 workers)	300	830
Large (over 500 workers)	19	159

Source: E. Abrahamian, "Structural Causes of the Iranian Revolution," *Middle East Research and Information Project*, no. 87 (May 1980), 22.

Table 3

Industrial Production

Product	1953	1977
Coal (tons)	200,000	900,000
Iron ore (tons)	5000	930,000
Steel (tons)	—	275,000
Cement (tons)	53,000	4,300,000
Sugar (tons)	70,000	527,000
Tractors (no.)	—	7700
Motor vehicles (no.)	—	109,000

Source: E. Abrahamian, "Structural Causes of the Iranian Revolution," *Middle East Research and Information Project*, no. 87 (May 1980), 22.

medical clinics from 700 to 2800; nurses from 1969 to 4105; and doctors from 4500 to 12,750. These improvements, together with the elimination of epidemics and famines—mainly due to food imports— lowered infant mortality and led to a population explosion. In the two decades prior to the 1979 revolution, the overall population doubled from 18 million to nearly 36 million. This explosion gave the country a predominantly youthful age structure. By the mid-1970s half the populaton was under sixteen years of age. This was to have repercussions in the street politics of 1977–1979.

Society and Economy

Socioeconomic development, however, did not necessarily make the Shah popular. On the contrary, the way this development was implemented tended to increase his unpopularity. The Industrial and Mining Development Bank channeled over US$50 billion of low-interest loans to court-connected entrepreneurs, industrialists, and agribusinessmen. The Shah, like most conservative economists, believed that if enough benefits were extended to the rich, some of them would gradually trickle down into the lower levels of society. But in Iran, as elsewhere, the benefits got stuck at the top. By the mid-1970s, Iran had one of the worst income distributions in the world.[12] Similarly, land reform, despite high expectations, created a small stratum of prosperous farmers but left the vast majority of peasants landless or nearly landless; over 1.2 million received less than 10 hectares (approximately 24.7 acres), not enough to survive as independent farmers (see Table 1). Not surprisingly, many flocked to the urban shantytowns in search of work.

The factories drew much criticism on the grounds that they were assembly plants and poor substitutes for real industrial development (see Table 3 on page 626). The medical programs still left Iran with one of the worst doctor-patient ratios and child mortality rates in the Middle East. The educational expansion created one place for every five university applicants; failed to provide primary schools for 60 percent of children; and had no impact on 68 percent of illiterates. In fact, the total number of illiterates rose because of the population explosion. The priority given to the capital by the regime increased the dis-

parities between Tehran and the provinces. By the mid-1970s, Tehran contained half the country's doctors and manufacturing plants. According to one comparative study, the per capita regional product in the richest provinces was ten times more than in the poorest ones. Iran—after Brazil—had the highest regional disparity in the developing world.[13] According to another study, the ratio of urban to rural incomes was 5 to 1— again, making it one of the worst in the world.[14]

These inequalities created a **dual society**. On one side was the modern sector, headed by the elites with close ties to the oil state. On the other side was the traditional sector comprising the clergy, the bazaar middle class, and the rural masses. Each sector, in turn, was sharply stratified into unequal classes. Thus, Iranian society was divided vertically into the modern and the traditional, and horizontally into a number of urban as well as rural classes (see Figure 1 on page 628).

The upper class—the Pahlavi family, the court-connected entrepreneurs, the military officers, and the senior civil servants—constituted less than 0.01 percent of the population. In the modern sector, the middle class—namely, professionals, civil servants, salaried personnel, and college students—formed about 10 percent of the population. The bottom of the modern sector—the urban working class, which included factory workers, construction laborers, peddlers, and unemployed—constituted over 32 percent. In the traditional sector, the middle class—bazaar merchants, small retailers, shopkeepers, workshop owners, and well-to-do family farmers—made up 13 percent. The rural masses—landless and near-landless peasants, nomads, and village construction workers— made up about 45 percent of the population.

Government statistics show the rising inequality between classes and between regions. In 1972 the richest 20 percent of urban households accounted for 47.1 percent of total urban family expenditures; by 1977 it accounted for 55.5 percent. In 1972 the poorest 40 percent accounted for 16.7 percent of urban family expenditures; by 1977 it accounted for 11.7 percent (see Table 4).

These inequalities fueled resentments against the ruling elite, which, however, were expressed more in cultural and religious terms than in economic and class terms. Articulating these resentments was a

The society was divided sharply not only into horizontal classes, but also into vertical sectors—the modern and the transitional, the urban and the rural. This is known as a dual society.

Figure 1

Iran's Class Structure in the Mid-1970s

Upper Class

Pahlavi Family; Court-Connected Entrepreneurs; Senior Civil Servants and Military Officers	0.1%

Middle Class

Traditional (Propertied)	13%	Modern (Salaried)	10%
Clerics Bazaaris Small Factory Owners Commercial Farmers		Professionals Civil Servants Office Employees College Students	

Lower Classes

Rural	45%	Urban	32%
Landed Peasants Near Landless Peasants Landless Peasants Unemployed		Industrial Workers Wage-Earners in Small Factories Domestic Servants Construction Workers Peddlers Unemployed	

gadfly writer named Jalal Al-e-Ahmad (1923–1969). A former communist who had rediscovered his Shi'i roots in the 1960s, Al-e-Ahmad shook his contempo-

Table 4

Measures of Inequality of Urban Household Consumption Expenditures

	Percentage Share in Total Expenditures		
Year	Poorest 40%	Middle 40%	Richest 20%
1972	16.7	36.2	47.1
1977	11.7	32.8	55.5

Source: V. Nowshirvani and P. Clawson, "The State and Social Equity in Postrevolutionary Iran," in *The Politics of Social Transformation in Afghanistan, Iran, and Pakistan*, ed. M. Weiner and A. Banuazizi (Syracuse, N.Y.: Syracuse University Press, 1994), 248.

raries by publishing a polemical pamphlet entitled *Gharbzadegi* (*The Plague from the West*). He argued that the ruling class was destroying Iran by blindly imitating the West, neglecting the peasantry, showing contempt for popular religion, worshipping mechanization, regimentation, and industrialization, and flooding the country with foreign ideas, tastes, luxury items, and mass-consumption goods. He stressed that Third World countries such as Iran could survive this "plague" of Western imperialism only by returning to their cultural roots and developing a self-reliant society, especially a fully independent economy. Al-e-Ahmad inspired the long search for cultural authenticity and economic self-sufficiency.

These themes were developed further by another young intellectual, Ali Shariati (1933–1977). Studying in Paris during the turbulent 1960s, Shariati was influenced by Marxist sociology, Catholic liberation theology, the Algerian revolution, and most important, Frantz Fanon's theory of Third World revolutions as laid out in his famous book, *Wretched of the Earth.* Shariati returned home with what can be called a fresh and revolutionary interpretation of Shi'ism, echoes of which would later appear in Khomeini's writings.

Shariati argued that history was a continuous struggle between oppressors and oppressed. Each class had its own interests, its own interpretations of religion, and its own sense of right and wrong, justice and injustice, morality and immorality. To help the oppressed, Shariati believed, God periodically sent down prophets, such as Abraham, Moses, Jesus, and Muhammad. In fact, Muhammad had come to launch a dynamic community in "permanent revolution" toward the ultimate utopia—a perfectly classless society in this world.

Although Muhammad's goal had been betrayed by his illegitimate successors, the Caliphs, his radical message had been preserved for posterity by the Shi'i Imams, especially by Imam Husayn who had died to show future generations that human beings had the moral duty to fight oppression in all places at all times. Shariati equated Imam Husayn with Che Guevara, the famous Latin American guerrilla killed in Bolivia in 1967. According to Shariati, the contemporary oppressors were the imperialists, the feudalists, the corrupt capitalists, and their hangers-on, especially the "tie-wearers" and "the palace dwellers," the carriers of the "Western plague." He also criticized the conservative clerics who had tried to transform revolutionary religion into an apolitical public opiate. Shariati died on the eve of the 1979 revolution, but his prolific works were so widely read and so influential that many felt that he rather than Khomeini was the true theorist of the Islamic Revolution.

Iran and the International Political Economy

Iran under the Shahs

The oil boom in the 1970s gave the Shah the opportunity to play a significant role in international politics. As the second most important member of the Organization of Petroleum Exporting Countries (**OPEC**), Iran could cast decisive votes for raising or moderating oil prices. At times, the Shah curried Western favor by moderating prices. At other times, he pushed for higher prices to finance his ambitious projects and military purchases. These purchases rapidly escalated once President Richard Nixon began to encourage U.S. allies, such as the Shah, to take greater responsibility in policing their regions. Moreover, Nixon's secretary of state, Henry Kissinger, openly argued that the United States should finance its ever-increasing oil imports—most of them from the Persian Gulf—by exporting more military hardware. The Shah was now able to buy from the United States almost any ultrasophisticated weapon he desired. Arms dealers began to jest that the Shah read their technical manuals in the same way that some other men read *Playboy*. The Shah's arms buying from the United States jumped from US$135 million in 1970 to a peak of $5.7 billion in 1977. Between 1955 and 1978, Iran spent more than $20.7 billion on U.S. arms alone.

This military might gave the Shah a reach well beyond his immediate boundaries. He invaded and occupied three small but strategically located Arab islands in the Straits of Hormuz, thus controlling the oil lifeline through the Persian Gulf. He talked of establishing a presence well beyond the Gulf on the grounds that Iran's national interests reached into the Indian Ocean. "Iran's military expenditures," according to a 1979 U.S. congressional report, "surpassed those of the most powerful Indian Ocean states, including Australia, Indonesia, Pakistan, South Africa, and India."[15]

In the mid-1970s the Shah dispatched troops to Oman to help the local sultan fight rebels. He offered Afghanistan US$2 billion to break its ties with the Soviet Union, a move that probably prompted the Soviets to intervene militarily in that country. The Shah, after supporting Kurdish rebels in Iraq, forced Baghdad to concede to Iran vital territory on the Shatt al-Arab estuary. This had been a bone of contention between the two countries ever since Iraq had come into existence after World War I. A U.S. congressional report summed up Iran's overall strategic position: "Iran in the 1970s was widely regarded as a significant regional, if not global, power. The United

States relied on it, implicitly if not explicitly, to ensure the security and stability of the Persian Gulf sector and the flow of oil from the region to the industrialized Western world of Japan, Europe, and the United States, as well as to lesser powers elsewhere."[16]

These vast military expenditures, as well as the oil exports, tied Iran closely to the industrial countries of the West, and to Japan. Iran was now importing millions of dollars' worth of rice, industrial tools, construction equipment, pharmaceuticals, tractors, pumps, and spare parts. The bulk of the rice and wheat, and a substantial portion of the tractors, medicines, and construction equipment, came from the United States. Trade with neighboring and other Third World countries was insignificant. In the words of the Department of Commerce in Washington, "Iran's rapid economic growth [provided America with] excellent business opportunities."[17]

The oil revenues thus had major consequences for Iran's political economy, all of which paved the way for the Islamic Revolution. They allowed the Shah to pursue ambitious programs that inadvertently widened class and regional divisions within the dual society. They drastically raised public expectations without necessarily meeting them. They made the rentier state independent of society. They also made the state highly dependent on oil prices and imported products. Iran was no longer a simple rentier state, but an oil-addicted one, vulnerable to the vagaries of the world petroleum market. Economic slowdowns in the industrial countries could lead to a decline in their oil demands, which, in turn, could diminish Iran's ability to buy such essential goods as food, medicine, and industrial spare parts. One of the major promises made by the Islamic Revolution was to end this economic dependency on oil and the West.

The Islamic Republic

The Islamic Republic began with high hopes of rapidly developing the economy, and at the same time becoming fully independent of oil and the West. The results have been mixed, illustrating the constraints the political economy places on society. The Pahlavi monarch and the Islamic Republic may have differed in many respects, but they governed the same economy and therefore faced similar financial problems.

The main problem plaguing the Islamic Republic has been instability in the world oil market. This instability has occurred despite the efforts of OPEC to preserve prices by limiting production and setting quotas for its members. The price of a barrel of oil—which had quadrupled from US$5 to $20 in 1974— peaked to $40 in 1980, but plummeted thereafter, reaching $18 in 1985, hovering around $12–$14 in the late 1980s and 1990s, and descending to a new low of $10 in 1999. This meant that Iran's oil revenues—which continued to provide the state with 80 percent of its hard currency and 75 percent of its total revenues—fell from $20 billion in 1978 to $13 billion in the late 1980s. In 1998 they hit a new low of $10.5 billion. Iran is still a rentier state and remains vulnerable to the vagaries of the international petroleum market. Oil, which had brought considerable riches before the revolution, produced relative deprivation in the 1980s and 1990s.

The decline in the world price of oil was due to a number of factors outside Iran's control: the slackening of the demand in the industrialized countries (especially with the recession in the late 1990s); the glutting of the international market by the entry of non-OPEC producers, such as Britain and Mexico; and the tendency of some OPEC members to preserve their revenues by cheating on their production quotas. Iran's oil revenues were also affected by the Iraqi war and the failure of the national oil company to raise production. In some years, Iran was not able to meet even its OPEC quotas. To raise production, Iran needs an influx of capital and new deep-drilling technology, both of which can be found only in the West.

This oil crisis has been compounded by the population explosion, the Iraqi war, and the flight of some 3 million Iranians. The annual population growth rate which had hit 2.5 percent in the late 1970s, jumped to nearly 4 percent by the late 1980s, mainly because the new regime initially encouraged large families. This was the highest rate in the world, causing a major strain on government resources, especially on social services and food imports. The Iraqi war not only hurt the oil industry but also wrought as much as US$600 billion in property damage—whole border cities were flattened. It also caused half a million Iranian casualties. The revolution itself frightened many professionals and highly skilled technicians as well as wealthy entrepreneurs and industrialists into fleeing to the West. Of course, they took their portable assets.

The overall result was a twenty-year economic crisis. Gross national product fell 50 percent. Per capita income declined 45 percent. Inflation hovered around 20–30 percent every year. The value of real incomes, including salaries and pensions, went down as much as 60 percent. Unemployment hit 20 percent—over two-thirds of entrants into the labor force could not find jobs. The absolute number of illiterates increased. Peasants continued to flock to the urban shantytowns. Tehran grew from 4.5 million to 12 million people. The total number of families living below the poverty level increased. By the late 1990s over 9 million urban dwellers lived below the official poverty line.[18] Shortages in foreign exchange curtailed vital imports, even of essential manufactured goods. The value of the currency plummeted: the rial, which had been worth 1.3 cents in 1979, was no more than 0.016 cents on the black market in 1998. What is more, the regime that came to power advocating self-sufficiency is now heavily indebted to foreign banks. Its external debt has jumped from zero to over US$30 billion, forcing it to constantly renegotiate foreign loans.

Despite this on-going economic crisis, the regime scored some notable successes, especially after the Iraqi war ended. The Reconstruction Ministry, established mainly for the rural population, built 30,000 miles of paved roads, 40,000 schools, and 7,000 libraries. It also brought electricity and running water to more than half of the country's 50,000 villages. The five-year plan organization continued to build more dams and irrigation canals. The Agricultural Ministry gave farmers more favorable prices, especially for wheat. Thus by the late 1990s most independent farmers had such consumer goods as radios, televisions, refrigerators, and pickup trucks. The extension of social services also narrowed the gap between town and country, and between the urban poor and the middle classes. The literacy rate rose from 50 percent to nearly 66 percent. The infant mortality rate fell from 104 per 1000 in the mid-1970s to 25 per 1000 in the late 1990s. Life expectancy climbed from 55 to 68 years, one of the best in the Middle East. On the whole, the poor are better off now than their parents were.

The Islamic Republic regime has also made major strides toward population control. At first, it closed down birth control clinics, claiming that Islam approved of large families and that Iran needed workers. But it reversed direction once the ministries responsible for social services felt the full impact of this growth. The regime also realized that only food imports could meet the rising demands. In 1989 the regime declared that Islam favored healthy rather than large families and that one literate citizen was better than ten illiterate ones. It reopened birth control clinics, cut subsidies to large families, and announced that the ideal family should consist of no more than two children. It even took away social benefits to those having more. By 1994 the regime boasted that it had reduced annual rate of population growth to 1.8 percent—the true figure was probably closer to 2.8 percent. Whatever the figure, it is an impressive accomplishment. It is also a sign that the regime is highly pragmatic when it comes to economic issues.

Section ❸ Governance and Policy-Making

Iran is unique in the contemporary world. Its system of government is not presidential, parliamentary, military, monarchical, or a one-party dictatorship. Instead, it is a theocracy with some concessions to democracy. It is a theocracy for the simple reason that the clergy— in other words, the theocrats or the theologians— control most of the important positions. The system nevertheless contains an element of democracy, since some high officials, including the president, are elected directly by the public. Although this combination is unprecedented, similar ones are likely to emerge in other parts of the Middle East if more Islamic countries have similar mass revolutions. So far the others that label themselves Islamic republics are products of either guerrilla wars, like Afghanistan, or of military coups, like Pakistan and Sudan.

Leaders: *Ayatollah Ali Khamenei*

Ali Khamenei succeeded Khomeini as Supreme Leader in 1989. He was born in 1939 in Meshed into a minor clerical family originally from Azerbaijan. He studied theology with Khomeini in Qom and was briefly imprisoned in 1962. Active in the opposition movement in 1978, he was given a series of influential positions immediately after the revolution even though he held only the middle-level clerical rank of hojjat al-Islam. He became Friday prayer leader of Tehran, head of the revolutionary guards, and in the last years of Khomeini's life, president of the republic. After Khomeini's death, he was elevated to the rank of Supreme Leader even though he was neither a Grand Ayatollah nor a recognized senior expert on Islamic law. He had not even published a theological treatise. The government-controlled media, however, began to refer to him as an ayatollah. Some ardent followers even referred to him as a Grand Ayatollah qualified to guide the world's whole Shi'i community. After his elevation he built a constituency among the regime's more die-hard elements—traditionalist judges, conservative war veterans, and antiliberal ideologues. Before 1989 he often smoked a pipe in public—a mark of an intellectual—but put away the habit when he became Supreme Leader.

Organization of the State

The Iranian state rests on the Islamic Constitution designed by the Assembly of Religious Experts immediately after the 1979 revolution. It was amended in April–June 1989 during the very last months of Khomeini's life by a Council for the Revision of the Constitution handpicked by Khomeini himself. These amendments, in turn, were ratified by a nationwide referendum in July 1989, immediately after Khomeini's death. The final document, totaling 175 clauses and some forty amendments, is a highly complex mixture of theocracy and democracy.

The preamble of the 1979 constitution affirmed faith in God, Divine Justice, the Qur'an, the Resurrection, the Prophet Muhammad, the Twelve Imams, the eventual return of the Hidden Imam (the Mahdi), and of course Khomeini's doctrine of jurist's guardianship. All laws, institutions, and state organizations were to be based on these "divine principles."

The Supreme Leader

The constitution named Khomeini to be the Supreme Leader for life on the grounds that the public overwhelmingly respected him as the "most just, pious, informed, brave, and enterprising" of the most senior clerics. It further described him as the Leader of the Revolution, the Founder of the Islamic Republic, and most important, the Imam of the whole community. It stipulated that if no single Supreme Leader emerged after his death, then all his authority would be passed on to a leadership council of two or three senior clerics. After Khomeini's death, however, his followers so distrusted the other senior clerics that they did not set up such a council. Instead, they elected one of their own, Ali Khamenei, a middle-ranking cleric, to be the new Supreme Leader. All of Khomeini's titles, with the exception of Imam, were bestowed on Khamenei. The Islamic Republic has often been described as the regime of the ayatollahs (high-ranking clerics). It would be more aptly described as the regime of the hojjat al-Islams (middle-ranking clerics), since few senior clerics want to be associated with it. None of the grand ayatollahs and few of the ordinary ayatollahs ever subscribed to Khomeini's novel notion of jurist's guardianship. On the contrary, most disliked his radical populism and political activism.

The constitution gives wide-ranging authority to the Supreme Leader. Described as the link between the branches of government, he mediates between the legislature, the executive, and the judiciary. He "determines the interests of Islam," "supervises the implementation of general policy," and "sets political guidelines for the Islamic Republic." He can eliminate presidential candidates as well as dismiss the duly elected president. He can also grant amnesty. As commander in chief, he can mobilize the armed forces, declare war and peace, and convene the Supreme Military Council. He appoints and dismisses the commanders of the army, navy, air force, and revolutionary guards.

The Supreme Leader can nominate and remove the Chief Judge, the chief prosecutor, and the revolutionary tribunals. He can also remove lower court judges. Even more important, he nominates six clerics to the powerful twelve-man Guardian Council. This council can veto parliamentary bills. It has also obtained (through separate legislation) the right to review all candidates for elected office, including the presidency and the *Majles*. The other six on the Guardian Council are jurists nominated by the Chief Judge and approved by the *Majles*.

The Supreme Leader is also authorized to fill a number of important nongovernment posts: the preachers (**Imam Jum'ehs**) of the main mosques, the director of the National Radio-Television network, and the heads of the main religious foundations, especially the **Foundation of the Oppressed**, much larger than the old Pahlavi Foundation. The Foundation of the Oppressed administers most of the assets of the former Pahlavi Foundation as well as some of the real estate confiscated from the old elite. The Supreme Leader has obtained more constitutional powers than the Shah had ever dreamed of.

The later constitutional amendments expanded and transformed the Assembly of Religious Experts into a permanent eighty-six-man house. Packed by clerics, the assembly not only elected Khamenei as Khomeini's successor but also reserved the right to dismiss him if it found him "mentally incapable of fulfilling his arduous duties." In effect, the Assembly of Religious Experts has become an upper chamber to the Islamic *Majles*. It is elected every four years, and its members are required to have a seminary degree equivalent to an M.A. degree. Figure 2 on the following page illustrates the hierarchy established by the constitution.

The general public elects the *Majles*, the president, and the Assembly of Religious Experts. But the Supreme Leader and the cleric-dominated Guardian Council decide who can compete in these elections.

Since the whole constitution is based on Khomeini's theory of jurist's guardianship, it gives wide-ranging judicial powers to the Supreme Leader in particular and to the clerical strata in general. Laws are supposed to conform to the *shari'a*, and the clergy, particularly the senior jurists, are regarded as

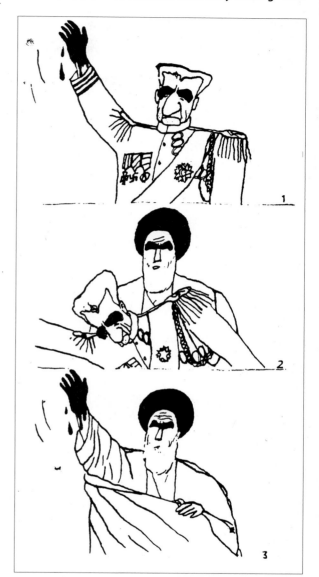

The Shah turning into Khomeini, from an émigré newspaper. *Source:* Courtesy *Nashriyeh.*

the ultimate interpreters of the *shari'a*. In fact, the constitution makes the judicial system the central pillar of the state, overshadowing the executive and the legislature. Bills passed by the Islamic *Majles* are reviewed by the Guardian Council to ensure that they conform to the *shari'a*. All twelve members of this Guardian Council are either clerics or lay jurists

The general public elects the *Majles*, the president, and the Assembly of Religious Experts. But the Supreme Leader and the cleric-dominated Guardian Council decide who can compete in these elections.

Figure 2

The Islamic Constitution

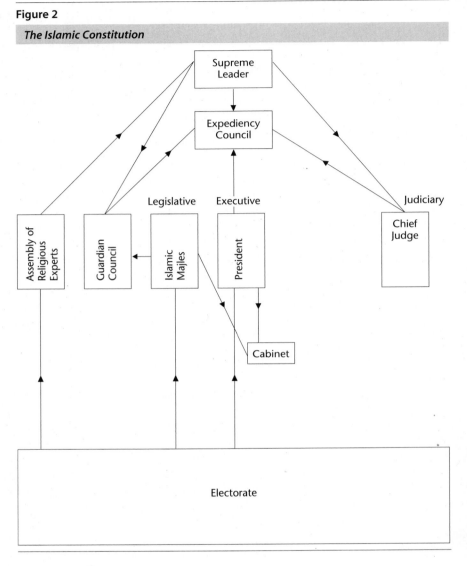

knowledgeable in the *shari'a*. The justice minister is chosen by the president but needs the approval of both the *Majles* and the Chief Judge. The judicial system itself has been Islamized all the way down to the district courts, with seminary-trained jurists replacing university-educated judges. The Pahlavis purged the clergy from the judicial system; the Islamic Republic purged the university-educated from the same judiciary.

The Executive

The President and the Cabinet

The constitution—particularly after the amendments—concentrates a considerable amount of power in the presidency. The president is described as the chief executive and the highest state official after the Supreme Leader. He is chosen every four years through a national election. He must be a pious Shi'i and faithful to the principles of the Islamic Republic. He cannot be elected to more than two terms. He draws up the annual budget and supervises economic matters by chairing the planning and budget organization. He can propose legislation to the *Majles*. He conducts the country's internal and external policies. He signs all international treaties, laws, and agreements. He chairs the National Security Council, which is responsible for all defense matters. He selects the cabinet, whose ministers have increased to twenty-two. The new members head the ministries of Reconstruction, Intelligence, Heavy Industries, and Culture and Islamic Guidance. The president can also select an indefinite number of vice presidents.

The president, moreover, appoints most of the senior officials, including the provincial governors-general, regional governors, town mayors, and ambassadors. Furthermore, as head of the executive, he names the directors of the many large public organizations—the National Iranian Oil Company, the National Electricity Board, and the main banks, airlines, mines, insurance companies, and shipping firms, most of which were nationalized immediately after the revolution.

Although during the revolution Khomeini often promised that trained officials would run the executive, in fact clerics have dominated the presidency. Of the four presidents since the revolution, three have been clerics: Khamenei, Rafsanjani, and Khatami. The exception, Abol-Hasan Bani-Sadr, was ousted in 1981 precisely because he described the regime as "a dictatorship of the mullahtariat" modeled on the communist "dictatorship of the proletariat."

The Bureaucracy

The president, as the chief of the executive branch, heads a huge bureaucracy. In fact, this bureaucracy continued to proliferate after the revolution even though Khomeini had often taken the Shah to task for having a bloated government. It expanded, for the most part, to provide jobs for the many college and high school graduates. On the eve of the revolution, the ministries had 300,000 civil servants and 1 million employees. By the early 1990s they had over 600,000 civil servants and 1.5 million employees. The Iranian

revolution, like many others, ended up creating a bigger bureaucracy.

Of the new ministries, Culture and Islamic Guidance censors the media and enforces "proper conduct" in public life; Intelligence has replaced SAVAK as the main security organization; Heavy Industries manages the recently nationalized factories; and Reconstruction has the dual task of expanding social services and taking "true Islam" into the countryside. Its mission is to build bridges, roads, schools, libraries, and mosques in the villages so that the peasantry will learn the basic principles of Islam. "The peasants," declared one cleric, "are so ignorant of true Islam that they even sleep next to their unclean sheep."[19]

The clergy dominate the bureaucracy as they do the presidency. They have monopolized the most sensitive ministries, Intelligence, Interior, Justice, and Culture and Islamic Guidance, and have given posts in other ministries to their relatives and protégés. These ministers appear to be highly trained technocrats, sometimes with higher degrees from the West, but in fact are powerless individuals chosen by, trusted by, and related to, the ruling clergy.

Semipublic Institutions

The Islamic Republic has set up a number of semipublic institutions. They include the Foundation for the Oppressed, the Alavi Foundation (named after Imam Ali); the Martyrs Foundation; the Pilgrimage Foundation; the Housing Foundation; the Foundation for the Publication of Imam Khomeini's Works; and the Fifteenth of Khordad Foundation, which commemorates Khomeini's 1963 denunciation of the White Revolution. Although these organizations are supposedly autonomous, their directors are clerics appointed personally by the Supreme Leader. According to some estimates, their annual income may be as much as half of the government's budget.[20] All are exempt from paying state taxes and can buy foreign currencies, especially U.S. dollars, at highly favorable exchange rates subsidized by the oil revenues. A large part of their assets is property confiscated from the old elite.

The largest of these institutions, the Foundation for the Oppressed, administers 140 factories, 120 mines, 470 agribusinesses, 100 construction companies, and over 2700 urban real estate properties. Many of these businesses previously belonged to entrepreneurs, senior bureaucrats, and high-ranking officers who either fled the country after the revolution or were judged by the clerical courts to be "active counterrevolutionaries." The foundation also owns the country's two leading newspapers, *Ettela'at* and *Kayhan*. *The Guardian* (London) estimated that in 1993 the foundation employed some 65,000 and had an annual budget of US$10 billion.[21] According to an Iranian economist, this was as much as 10 percent of the government budget.[22] Its present director is the former head of the *pasdaran*. During the revolution, he served as Khomeini's chauffeur.

The Alavi Foundation, based in Meshed, is the next largest. As the direct heir to the Pahlavi Foundation, it administers the vast assets that belonged to the Shah. The Martyrs Foundation, in charge of helping war veterans, controls property of the old elite that was confiscated in 1979 but not handed over to the Foundation for the Oppressed. It also receives an annual subsidy from the government. These three foundations together own some 20 percent of the country's private assets, employ over 150,000, and administer vast economic empires including 7800 hectares of farmland, 270 orchards, 230 commercial companies, and 90 cinemas. They can be described as states within a state, but with the important caveat that the same clerical elite that controls the state also controls these foundations.

Other State Institutions

The Military

The clergy have taken special measures to control the military. The Supreme Leader has the constitutional authority to appoint the joint chiefs of staff and the leading commanders. Khomeini and Khamenei filled the post of Defense Minister with their own confidants, who reported directly to them, bypassing the president and the cabinet. Moreover, the regime placed chaplains in military units to watch over the officers as well as to minister to the spiritual needs of the troops. They resemble the network of ideological officers, known as commissars, established in communist-bloc countries to forestall military coups.

Furthermore, the regime has built a new army, the *pasdaran* (revolutionary guards). Created as a voluntary militia in 1979, the revolutionary guards expanded rapidly during the Iraq war to parallel the existing armed forces. They obtained their own officers, uniforms, budgets, munitions factories, recruitment centers, and draftees. According to the constitution, the regular army defends the borders, while the revolutionary guards protect the republic. The Defense Minister, who is in charge of both, comes from the revolutionary guards. Most senior field officers are volunteers raised from the ranks because of their ideological commitment. The revolutionary guards are supplemented with a militia of underage and overage volunteers known as the Basej-e Mostazafin ("Mobilization of the Oppressed"). It is estimated that the regular army contains some 200,000 men; the *pasdaran* another 200,000; and the **basej** some 3 million.

The Judiciary

The Islamic Republic regime Islamized the judiciary by enacting a penal law based on an extremely narrow reading of the *shari'a*, so narrow that it prompted many modern-educated lawyers to resign in disgust, charging that it contradicted the UN Charter on Human Rights. It permitted injured families to demand blood money on the biblical and Qur'anic principle of "an eye for an eye, a tooth for a tooth, a life for a life." It mandated the death penalty for a long list of "moral transgressions," including adultery, homosexuality, apostasy, drug trafficking, and habitual drinking. It sanctioned stoning, live burials, and finger amputations. It divided the population into male and female, Muslims and non-Muslims, and treated them unequally. For example, in court, the evidence of one male Muslim is equal to that of two female Muslims. The regime also passed a "law on banking without usury" to implement the *shari'a* ban on all forms of interest-taking and interest-giving.

Although the law was Islamized, the modern centralized judicial system was not dismantled. For years, Khomeini argued that in a truly Islamic society the local *shari'a* judges would pronounce final verdicts without the intervention of the central authorities. Their verdicts would be swift and decisive. This, he insisted, was the true spirit of the *shari'a*. After the revolution, however, he discovered that the central state needed to retain ultimate control over the justice system, especially over life and death. Thus, the new regime retained the appeals system, the hierarchy of state courts, and the power to appoint and dismiss all judges. State interests took priority over the spirit of the *shari'a*.

Practical experience also led the regime to gradually broaden the narrow interpretation of the *shari'a*. To permit the giving and taking of interest, without which modern economies would not function, the regime allowed banks to offer attractive rates as long as they avoided the taboo term *usury*. To meet public sensitivities as well as international objections, the courts rarely implemented the harsh corporal punishments stipulated by the *shari'a*. They adopted the modern method of punishment, imprisonment, rather than the traditional one of corporal public punishments. By the early 1990s those found guilty of breaking the law were treated much as they would be in the West, fined or imprisoned rather than flogged in the public square.

Although the Islamic Republic is a theocracy, some regime supporters argue that it is compatible with democracy. According to the constitution, the government represents the general electorate. The Supreme Leader is chosen by the Assembly of Religious Experts, who, in turn, are elected by the general population. This is viewed as a two-stage popular election. The legislature also has a considerable constitutional role (see Section 4). According to Hojjat al-Islam Rafsanjani, one of the architects of the constitution, the *Majles* is the centerpiece of the Islamic constitution. It has many prerogatives, including that of enacting or changing ordinary laws (with the approval of the Guardian Council), investigating and supervising all affairs of state, and approving or ousting the cabinet ministers."[23] Some add that the public, by voting with their feet in the mass demonstrations of 1978–1979, implicitly favored a type of democracy that would be confined within the boundaries of Islam. Another architect of the constitution has argued that the Iranian people, by carrying out an Islamic Revolution, had determined for future generations that democracy in Iran should be placed within the rubric of jurist's guardianship.[24] Yet another declared that if he had to choose between the people and jurist's guardianship, he would not hesitate to choose the latter, since it came directly from God.[25] On the eve of the initial referendum for the constitution, Khomeini himself insisted that democracy and jurist's guardianship in no way contradicted each other: "This constitution, which the people will ratify, is in no way a contradiction with democracy. Since the people love the clergy, have faith in the clergy, want to be guided by the clergy, it is right that the supreme religious authority oversee the work of the prime minister or of the president, to make sure that they don't make mistakes or go against the law: that is the Qur'an."[26]

Subnational Government

Although Iran is a highly centralized state, it is divided into provinces, districts, subdistricts, townships, and villages. Provinces are headed by governors-general, districts by governors, subdistricts by lieutenant governors, towns by mayors, and villages by headmen.

The Islamic constitution promised elected councils on each level of administration. The constitution declares that the management of local affairs in every village, town, subdistrict, district, and province would be under the supervision of councils whose members would be elected by the people of the locality. It also declares that governors-general, governors, mayors, and other local officials appointed by the government have an obligation to abide by the decisions of the local councils. These clauses were incorporated because of mass demonstrations organized in late 1979 by the left—notably the Mojahedin and the Fedayin—demanding the formation of elected councils.

Despite the promises, no steps were taken to hold elections for such councils until 1999. Thus local government was left in the hands of government officials. Although these officials did not have to contend with elected councils, they did have to oblige local notables, especially officers of the revolutionary guards, court judges, and Imam Jum'ehs with their mosque pulpits. Each gave them considerable headaches. In 1999 the newly elected president took concrete measures to hold elections for these local councils.

The Policy-Making Process

The policy-making system is highly complex in part because of the complex constitution and in part

The clerical regime and its two stilts—the sword and the oil wells. *Source:* Courtesy *Mojahed* (in exile).

indignations under the Shah, and most important, shared the same vested interest in preserving the Islamic Republic. Moreover, most had studied at the same seminaries and came from the same lower-middle-class backgrounds. Some were even related to each other through marriage and blood ties.

But once the constitution was in place, the same clerics drifted into two loose but identifiable blocs: the Society (*Majmu'eh*) of the Militant Clergy, and the Association (*Jam'eh*) of the Militant Clergy. The former can be described as populists, radicals, or statists; the latter as conservatives or supporters of laissez-faire. The statists hoped to consolidate lower-class support by redistributing wealth, eradicating unemployment, raising wages, nationalizing enterprises, confiscating large estates, implementing ambitious social programs, rationing and subsidizing essential goods, and placing price ceilings on many consumer commodities. In short, they espoused the creation of a comprehensive welfare state. The conservatives hoped to retain middle-class support, especially in the bazaars, by removing price controls, lowering business taxes, cutting red tape, encouraging private entrepreneurs, opening up the market, and balancing the budget, even at the cost of sacrificing subsidies and social programs.

The conservative free-marketers were labeled middle-roaders and traditionalists. The statists were labeled progressives, fast-walkers, seekers of new ideas, clergy favoring the oppressed, and followers of the Imam's line. The free-marketers often denounced their rivals as extremists, leftists, and pro-Soviet Muslims. The statists countered by denouncing the free-marketers as medievalists, rightists, capitalist jurists, mafia bazaaris, and pro-American Muslims. Both could bolster their arguments with apt quotes from Khomeini and the Qur'an.

This polarization created a major constitutional gridlock, since the Islamic *Majles* was dominated by the radical clerics while the Guardian Council was controlled by the conservative clerics. Khomeini had appointed conservatives to the Guardian Council to preserve his links with the bazaars and to build bridges to the grand ayatollahs, who distrusted his whole revolutionary movement. Between 1981 and 1987 over one hundred bills passed by the *Majles* were vetoed by the Guardian Council on the grounds that they vio-

because factional conflicts within the ruling clergy have added more amendments over the years, making the original constitution even more cumbersome. Decisions originate in diverse places. They are modified by pressures coming from diverse directions. And they can be blocked by a number of diverse state institutions. In short, the decision-making process is highly fluid and diffuse, often reflecting the regime's factional divisions.

The clerics who destroyed the old order remained united while building the new one. They were convinced that they alone had the divine mandate to govern. They formed a distinct social stratum as well as a cohesive political group. They followed the same leader, admired the same texts, cited the same potent symbols, remembered the same real and imaginary lated the *shari'a*, especially the sanctity of private property. The vetoed legislation included a labor law, land reform, nationalization of foreign trade, progressive income tax, control over urban real estate transactions, and confiscation of the property of émigrés whom the courts had not yet found guilty of counter-revolutionary activities. Introduced by individual deputies or cabinet ministers, these bills had received quick passage because the radical statists controlled the crucial *Majles* committees and held a comfortable majority on the *Majles* floor. Some ultraconservatives had countered by encouraging the faithful not to pay taxes and instead to contribute to the grand ayatollahs of their choice. After all, one could find no mention of income tax anywhere in the *shari'a*.

Both sides cited the Islamic constitution to support their positions. The free-marketers referred to the long list of clauses protecting private property, promising balanced budgets, and placing agriculture, small industry, and retail trade in the private sector. The statists referred to an even longer list promising education, medicine, jobs, low-income housing, unemployment benefits, disability pay, interest-free loans, and the predominance of the public sector in the economy.

To break the constitutional gridlock, Khomeini boldly introduced into Shi'ism the Sunni concept of *maslahat*—"public interest" and "reasons of state." In the past, Shi'i clerics had denounced this as a Sunni notion designed to bolster the illegitimate Caliphs. Khomeini now claimed that a truly Islamic state could safeguard the public interest by suspending important religious rulings, even over prayer, fasting, and the pilgrimage to Mecca. He declared public interest to be a primary ruling; the others mere secondary rulings. In other words, the state could overrule the highest-ranking clerics and their interpretations of the sacred law. It could destroy a mosque in the name of public interest. It could confiscate private property in the name of public interest. It could cancel religious contracts in the name of public interest. It could nationalize and raise income taxes in the name of public interest. Khomeini also argued that the Islamic state had absolute authority, since the Prophet Muhammad had exercised absolute (*motalaq*) power, this power had passed to the Imams, and the Islamic Republic now represented the Hidden Imam. Never before had a Shi'i religious leader claimed such powers for the state, especially at the expense of fellow clerics.

As a follow-up, Khomeini set up a special Expediency Council for Determining the Public Interest of the Islamic Order. It is known simply as the Expediency Council. Khomeini himself remained above the fray so as not to be too closely identified with his radical or his conservative followers. He gave this Expediency Council the task of resolving the conflicts between the Islamic *Majles* and the Guardian Council. He packed the council with thirteen clerics, including the president, the Chief Judge, the speaker of the *Majles*, and six jurists from the Guardian Council. The Expediency Council soon passed many of the more moderate bills favored by the statists. These included a new income tax, banking legislation, and a much-disputed labor law providing workers in large factories with a minimum wage and some semblance of job security.

After Khomeini's death, the constitutional amendments institutionalized this Expediency Council. The new Supreme Leader was authorized not only to name all its members but also to determine its size, tenure, and jurisdiction. Khamenei expanded it to twenty-six members, packed it with eight of his own clerical supporters (none of them prominent ayatollahs), and allowed it to hold meetings in secret. He also extended its jurisdiction, allowing it to initiate entirely new laws and not restrict itself to resolving the existing differences between the *Majles* and the Guardian Council. In effect, the Expediency Council is now a secretive supraconstitutional body accountable only to the Supreme Leader. In this sense, it has become a powerful body rivaling the Islamic *Majles*. Laws can now originate in the Expediency Council as well as in the *Majles*.

Section ❹ Representation and Participation

The Legislature

The Islamic Republic's constitution is undoubtedly a theocratic document. Nevertheless, in recognizing the importance of democracy and popular participation, it leaves some space for civil society and organizations outside government control. The constitution stipulates direct elections for the presidency, for the Assembly of Religious Experts, and most important, for the Islamic *Majles*, which is defined by the constitution as the legislative branch. In describing this branch of government, the constitution uses the term *qanun* (statutes) rather than *shari'a* (divine law) so as to gloss over the fundamental question of whether law is derived from God or the people. The rationale is that the divine law (*shari'a*) comes from God, but statutes (*qanuns*) are made by the people's elected representatives.

The Islamic *Majles*, described by the constitution as "representing the nation," contains 270 deputies elected every four years through secret and direct balloting. All adults over the age of fifteen, including women, can vote. The *Majles* has considerable authority. It can pass *qanun* as long as the Guardian Council deems it compatible with the *shari'a* and the Islamic constitution. It can interpret legislation as long as these interpretations do not contradict the judicial authorities. It chooses six of the twelve-representatives on the Guardian Council, but it is limited to a list drawn up by the Chief Judge.

It can investigate at will cabinet ministers, affairs of state, and public complaints against the executive and the judiciary. It can remove cabinet members—with the exception of the president—through a parliamentary vote of no confidence. It can withhold approval for government budgets, foreign loans, international treaties, and cabinet appointments. It can hold closed debates, provide its members with immunity from arrest, and regulate its own internal workings, especially the committee system.

Although the 1989 constitutional amendments weakened the *Majles* vis-à-vis the presidency and the Expediency Council, the *Majles* nevertheless remains highly important. In recent years, the *Majles* has revamped the annual budget, criticized government policies, modified development plans, and forced the president to replace his cabinet ministers as well as the director of the National Radio-Television network. In 1992, 217 deputies circulated an open letter that explicitly emphasized the prerogatives of the *Majles* and thereby implicitly downplayed those of the Supreme Leader. The latter's supporters promptly issued a counterblast reminding the *Majles* that the Islamic Republic was based on Khomeini's concept of jurist's guardianship.

The powers as well as the limitations of the *Majles* can be seen in how bills are passed into legislation. They can be drawn up by the Expediency Council or introduced in the *Majles* by a deputy, a cabinet minister, or a parliamentary committee. Bills passed by the *Majles* need the approval of the Guardian Council. In addition, all bills, whether originating in the Expediency Council or the Islamic *Majles*, need the Supreme Leader's final approval.

Political Parties

Political parties cannot function in Iran without a license from the Interior Ministry, even though the constitution guarantees the freedom to organize, and the *Majles* in 1980 approved a bill recognizing the right of political parties to function. This bill was shelved by the Guardian Council. By 1999 only one party had obtained a license—the Servants of Reconstruction, formed by associates of former president Rafsanjani. Two others, the Islamic Labor Party and the Islamic Iran Participation Front, both formed in 1999 by associates of President Khatami, had applied for licenses. The following parties function in exile, especially in Europe.

- **The Liberation Movement.** Established in 1961 by Mehdi Bazargan, who became Khomeini's first premier in 1979, the Liberation Movement is a moderate Islamic party similar in some ways to the Western European Christian Democrats. Since 1981 the regime has tightly controlled its activities because it opposed continuation of the war with

Iraq, criticized the arbitrary confiscation of private property, and denounced the clergy for interfering in politics. The Liberation Movement, despite its religiosity, advocates secularism and the strict separation of mosque and state.

- **The Mojahedin.** Formed in 1971 as a guerrilla organization to fight the old regime, the Mojahedin tried to synthesize Marxism and Islam. It interpreted Shi'i Islam to be a radical religion favoring equality, social justice, martyrdom, and redistribution of wealth. Immediately after the revolution, the Mojahedin attracted a large following among college and high school students, especially when it began to denounce the clergy for establishing a new dictatorship. The regime retaliated with mass executions and forced the Mojahedin to move their base of operations into Iraq. Not unexpectedly, the Mojahedin became associated with the national enemy and thereby lost much of its appeal within Iran.
- **The Fedayin.** Formed in 1971, the Fedayin modeled itself after the Marxist guerrilla movements of the 1960s in Latin America, especially those inspired by Che Guevara and the Cuban revolution. Losing more fighters than any other organization in the guerrilla war against the Shah, the Fedayin came out of the revolution with much revolutionary mystique and popular urban support. But it soon lost much of its strength because of massive government repression and a series of internal splits.
- **The Tudeh.** Established in 1941, the Tudeh is the mainstream communist party of Iran, fully supporting the policies of the former Soviet Union. Although the Tudeh supported the Islamic Republic as a "popular anti-imperialist state," it was banned, and most of its organizers were executed during the period 1983–1989. It survives mostly in Europe.

Elections

The constitution promises that all elections, including those for the Islamic *Majles*, will be free. In practice, however, *Majles* elections have become increasingly more regulated, manipulated, and controlled. The Guardian Council routinely eliminates candidates on the grounds that they are not sufficiently committed to the principles of the Islamic Republic. For example, in 1996 the Guardian Council excluded over 44 percent of some 5000 parliamentary candidates by questioning their loyalty to the concept of jurist's guardianship. The National Radio-Television network, the main source of information for the vast majority of people, favors some candidates, ignores others, and denounces yet others. The Interior Ministry bans dissident organizations, especially their newspapers and meetings, with the claim that they are anti-Islamic and antirevolutionary. Ballot boxes are placed in mosques, and the revolutionary guards supervise voting. Neighborhood clerics are on hand to help illiterates complete their ballots. Club-wielding gangs, the Hezbollahis, assault critics of the regime. By-elections are timed to coincide with high religious holidays. The Supreme Leader inevitably denounces those tempted to abstain as "secret agents of the devil." The electoral law, based on a winner-take-all majority system rather than on proportional representation, which guarantees some seats to any party that wins a certain percentage of the vote, was designed to minimize the voice of the opposition, particularly in the early days of the republic, when there was an opposition.

The Islamic Republic has had five *Majles* elections so far: 1980, 1984, 1988, 1992, and 1996. These elections have gone from being relatively free to being completely controlled. If the 1997 presidential campaign is an indication, the next *Majles* elections, due in 2000, may turn out to be more free.

The First Majles

In the election for the First *Majles* in 1980, there were over 4400 candidates, over forty parties, over two hundred dailies and weeklies, and thousands of workplace organizations in the bazaars, campuses, high schools, factories, and offices. The parties represented the whole range of the political spectrum from the far right, through the center, to the extreme left. The revolution had shattered the state, liberating scores of social and political groups. It was as if, after years of silence, every professional and occupational association, every political party and ideological viewpoint, and every interest and pressure group rushed into the open to air its views, print its newspapers and broadsheets, and field its parliamentary candidates.

On the right was the Islamic Republican Party (IRP). It was founded immediately after the revolution by Khomeini's closest disciples. The IRP had the support of two highly conservative religious groups that had survived the old regime: the Fedayan-e Islam and the Hojjatieh Society. It also had the support of the Islamic Association of Bazaar Guilds, the Islamic Association of Teachers, the Islamic Association of University Students, the Association of Seminary Teachers of Qom, and most important, the Association of the Militant Clergy in Tehran. The Islamic Republican Party championed Khomeini's notion that the clergy had the divine mandate to rule.

At the center was the Liberation Movement, headed by Mehdi Bazargan. Bazargan had been appointed prime minister in February 1979 by Khomeini himself but had resigned in disgust ten months later when the revolutionary guards had permitted students to take over the U.S. embassy. The Liberation Movement favored free markets, limited government, nonalignment without bellicose attacks on the United States, and a pluralistic political system in which all parties—religious and nonreligious, right and left—would be able to function and compete in fair and open elections. The Liberation Movement also favored a regime built on its own liberal interpretation of Islam, one in which the clergy would guide and advise rather than rule. Bazargan was a former member of Mosaddeq's National Front, the organization instrumental in nationalizing the oil industry in 1951. But Bazargan, unlike Mosaddeq, liked to sprinkle his speeches and bolster his ideas, concepts, and arguments with quotations from the Qur'an, the Prophet, and the Twelve Imams.

Closely allied with the Liberation Movement was the National Front, a mere shadow of its former self, and its offshoots, the National Party and the Democratic National Front. These parties, like the Liberation Movement, favored liberal democracy and were led by Western-educated, middle-aged professionals and technocrats. But unlike the Liberation Movement, they avoided making political use of Islam. Like their deceased mentor Mosaddeq, they preferred to separate politics from religion and to treat the latter as primarily a private matter. The Liberation Movement can be defined as a liberal Muslim party, and the National Front and its offshoots as liberal secular parties.

The left was fragmented even more into religious and nonreligious groups. The religious included such Muslim yet anticlerical ones as the People's Mojahedin, the Movement of Militant Muslims, and the Movement for the Liberation of the Iranian People. The nonreligious included a number of Marxist and ethnic parties: the Tudeh, the Majority and Minority Fedayin, the Kurdish Democratic Party, and at least a dozen small Marxist-Leninist parties. To complicate matters further, Bani-Sadr, who had been elected president in January 1980, was distancing himself from the Islamic Republican Party by fielding a number of his own candidates.

Many of these political parties had their own student, labor, professional, and women's organizations. For example, in the early years of the revolution, there were over a dozen women's organizations in Tehran alone. Among them were the Society of Militant Women, the Islamic Association of Women, the Union of National Women, the Union of Women Lawyers, the Union of Democratic Women, the Women for Justice, and the Society of Islamic Revolutionary Women. Each was affiliated with one of the larger political parties.

Not surprisingly, the elections for this First *Majles* were extremely lively, even though the IRP manipulated the state machinery, especially the Interior Ministry and the National Radio-Television network. On the eve of the voting, the Minister of the Interior forthrightly declared that all were free to run but that only "true Muslims" would have their credentials accepted in the forthcoming parliament.[27] Some 80 percent of the electorate participated in the first round.

The main contestants were, on the one hand, the IRP and its clerical and bazaar affiliates and, on the other hand, President Bani-Sadr, the Mojahedin, and their secular-leftist allies. The competition was so intense in some constituencies, particularly Kurdistan, Kermanshah, West Azerbaijan, and the Caspian provinces, that the Interior Ministry stepped in, impounded the ballot boxes, harassed candidates, and postponed the second round indefinitely. The second round was not held until late 1981. By then, the regime had cracked down on the opposition, forcing Bani-Sadr into exile, banning many leftist parties, and executing hundreds of Mojahedin organizers.

Of the 216 deputies elected in 1980, 120 were

supporters of the IRP, 33 of Bani-Sadr, and 20 of the Liberation Movement, while 33 described themselves as independent. The independents included two Kurdish Democrats and five National Front leaders. The latter had their parliamentary credentials promptly rejected on the grounds that documents found in the recently occupied U.S. Embassy "proved" them to be U.S. spies. The IRP had won only 35 percent of the popular vote but had collected over 60 percent of the filled seats. The Mojahedin, on the other hand, had won 25 percent of the popular vote but had not obtained a single seat. The electoral law based on majority rather than proportional representation had paid off for Khomeini.

Once the IRP carried out the second round and replaced the purged members, including Bani-Sadr's supporters, it gained a solid majority. This included 105 clerics—more than 38 percent of the *Majles*—making it by far the highest clerical representation in Iran's parliamentary history. Most were medium-ranking clerics serving as court judges and town preachers (Imam Jum'ehs). The others were white-collar employees and high school teachers, some of whom were seminary graduates. Over 90 percent came from the propertied middle class. Their fathers had been clerics, bazaar merchants, guild elders, or small farmers.

The Second Majles

The elections for the Second *Majles* in 1984 were carried out under very different circumstances. The "spring of the Iranian Revolution" was over. The opposition—including the Liberation Movement—was now banned. The IRP monopolized the political scene, manipulating the state and controlling a vast array of organizations, including large foundations, local mosques, revolutionary guards, and thousands of town preachers. Not surprisingly, it won a landslide victory, leaving a few seats to independent-minded clerics with their own local followings. Also not surprisingly, voter participation fell sharply to less than 60 percent, even though the voting age was reduced from sixteen to fifteen and even though Khomeini declared that abstaining was tantamount to betraying Islam.

Over 54 percent of the 270 deputies were clerics, almost all middle-ranking. Most of the nonclerics had Ph.D.'s, M.A.'s, B.A.'s, associate degrees, or high school diplomas. Only eleven had not completed high school. Twenty-seven of the lay members had at one time or another attended a seminary. As before, most were in their late thirties or early forties.

In 1987, Khomeini dissolved the IRP in preparation for the Third *Majles*. No reason was given, but the decision was probably prompted by the conflict between the statists and the free-marketers. The party's central committee was divided sharply into radicals demanding land reform, progressive taxation, and more nationalization, on the one hand, and conservatives favoring the bazaar, the industrial employers, and the reduction of state expenditures, on the other. One radical deputy claimed that "the party had been infiltrated by opportunistic time-servers pretending to be devout followers of the Imam's Line."[28] In the *Majles*, the radicals could muster 120 votes; the conservatives some 90; the remainder moved back and forth between these poles.

Moreover, the IRP's monopoly of power had aroused concern. Some drew parallels with the Resurgence Party and remembered how the clergy had unanimously denounced the Shah's totalitarian drive to take over the whole society. Furthermore, provincial clerics with their own power bases lobbied Khomeini against the IRP. They feared the party not only for its economic radicalism but also for its drive to centralize power. Finally, as far as Khomeini himself was concerned, the IRP had accomplished its main purpose: eliminating the Mojahedin, the National Front, the Tudeh, and the Liberation Movement.

In dissolving the IRP, Khomeini declared the clergy to be free to establish two competing organizations as long as both remained diligent against imperialism, advocated neither communism nor capitalism, and agreed to preserve Islam, the Islamic Revolution, the Islamic Republic, and jurist's guardianship. "Political differences," he commented, "are natural. Throughout history our religious authorities have differed among themselves. . . . Besides Iranians should be free to express themselves."[29] He could have added, "within reason and within the context of Islam as defined by myself."

In preparation for the Third *Majles* elections in 1988, the radicals left the Association of the Militant Clergy to form their own Society of the Militant

Clergy. From then on, there were two rival clerical organizations: on one side, the statists with their association and five major newspapers, including the two largest national papers, *Kayhan* and *Ettela'at*; on the other side, the conservative free-marketers with their society and a newspaper called *Resalat* (*Message*). Both had adherents in the seminaries and among the local Imam Jum'ehs. This was political pluralism, but a pluralism limited to the Khomeinist clerics and their protégés, who subscribed fully to their interpretation of Shi'ism. This theocracy resembles an oligarchy, the rule of numerous notables, more than a totalitarian state headed by a one-party dictatorship.

The Third, Fourth, and Fifth Majleses

The radicals won the lackluster elections for the Third *Majles*. In the new parliament, there were eighty-six clerics—a 23 percent decline from the previous assembly. This, however, did not signify the demise of clerical power. Some prominent clerics had gone on to higher positions, especially to the Assembly of Religious Experts. Many of the new lay deputies were young protégés of the clerics recruited into their fold from the students who had taken over the U.S. Embassy. The conservative clerics who did not run in these elections went on to occupy other influential positions as heads of religious foundations, preachers in the city mosques, and editors of mass newspapers.

Although the radical clerics began the Third *Majles* with a clear majority, their influence soon ebbed because of Khomeini's death in 1989 and because Khamenei and Rafsanjani, the new Supreme Leader and president, respectively, began to adopt free-market policies as soon as the war with Iraq ended. During the war, these two had been vocal advocates of price controls, rationing, high taxes, nationalization, and large government budgets. Now, with the ceasefire, they argued that the only way to revive the war-torn economy was to encourage private enterprise, open up the market, and cut government expenditures.

Rafsanjani launched the new course in giving his eulogy for Khomeini.[30] He played down Khomeini's role as a charismatic revolutionary who had led the downtrodden. Indeed, the word *oppressed* was hardly mentioned. Instead, he praised Khomeini as a world-famous statesman who had restored Iran's national sovereignty. He also praised him as a highly reputable scholar-theologian who had intellectually "awakened the moribund seminaries" from their "medieval graves." This ran counter to the prevailing notion that Shi'i Islam was by definition a revolutionary creed against all forms of despotism and exploitation.

In the following months, Rafsanjani—and to a lesser extent Khamenei—stressed that the revolution had been "guilty of excesses." They asked their followers to put away "childish slogans." They talked increasingly of realism, stability, efficiency, managerial skills, work discipline, expertise, individual self-reliance, modern technology, entrepreneurship, and business incentives. They warned that the worst mistake a state could make was to spend more than it earned. Rafsanjani declared, "Some people claim that God will provide. They forget that God provides only for those willing to work." Khamenei sermonized on how Imam Ali, the founder of Shi'i Islam, had taken great pride in his plantations. Khomeini had often depicted Imam Ali as a humble water carrier; Khamenei now depicted him as an entrepreneurial plantation owner.

To ensure that the change of economic course would go smoothly, Khamenei handed over the two main newspapers, *Kayhan* and *Ettela'at*, to the conservative free-marketers and authorized the Guardian Council to monitor the 1992 *Majles* elections. The Guardian Council announced that all candidates had to prove their "practical commitment to the Supreme Leader and the Islamic Republic." The Guardian Council further restricted the campaign to one week, permitting candidates to speak in mosques and run newspaper advertisements but not to debate each other in open forums. The head of the Guardian Council announced that he would use pesticides to cleanse parliament of anyone with "difficult attitudes." Seventy-five radical candidates withdrew. Forty were disqualified by the Guardian Council. Only a handful of radicals were allowed to be elected. Voter participation dropped to a new low. In Tehran less than 55 percent of the eligible voters bothered to cast ballots despite Khamenei's pronouncement that it was the "religious obligation of everyone to participate."

Ayatollah Khalkhali, a vocal radical, was barred from running on the grounds that he did not have appropriate theological training. Yet the same Khalkhali had been considered qualified enough from 1978 to 1987 to sit as a high court judge dispatching hundreds of political prisoners to their deaths. Khalkhali retorted that his candidacy had been rejected by rightists who had sat out the revolution but were now weaseling their way into the Guardian Council. He warned that "true servants of the revolution," like himself, had been subjected to a political purge as a prelude to a future physical purge. Another disqualified candidate, who had earlier dismissed any talk of human rights as a "foreign conspiracy," now complained that the Guardian Council had grossly violated the UN Charter on Human Rights. It had failed to inform him of the charges brought against him; it had given him insufficient time to respond; and it had denied him the right to defend himself in a proper court of law.

The Guardian Council responded that its decisions had been kept out of the mass media in order to protect state secrets and the public reputations of the unqualified. The purged were expected to be grateful for this sensitivity. It also argued that it had followed precedent, reminding the radicals that they themselves had used similar procedures to keep out "undesirables" from the previous three parliaments—undesirables such as the Mojahedin, the Fedayin, the Tudeh, the National Front, the Liberation Movement, and the "pseudo-clerics," who did not believe in jurist's guardianship.

The purge was relatively easy to carry out. For one thing, the extensive powers entrusted to the Supreme Leader by the Islamic constitution left the radicals vulnerable. As Hojjat al-Islam Mohtashami, a leading radical, complained, the institution of jurist's guardianship was now being used to clobber revolutionary heads. When radicals complained that they were being slandered as traitors for merely questioning free-market economics, their opponents countered that disobedience to the Supreme Leader was tantamount to disobedience to God. They argued that only proponents of "American Islam" would dare question the decisions of the Supreme Leader. They also reminded them that the new oath of office required parliamentary deputies to obey the Supreme Leader as "the Vice Regent of the Hidden Twelfth Imam." Khamenei may not have inherited Khomeini's title of Imam, but he had obtained the new exalted position of the Hidden Imam's Spokesman.

What is more, the conservatives effectively used populist rhetoric against the radicals. They described them as the "newly moneyed class" and the "Mercedes-Benz clerics." They accused them of misusing official positions to line their own pockets, open slush funds and secret foreign accounts, give lucrative contracts to their friends, sell contraband, and deceive the masses with unrealistic promises. "They," exclaimed one conservative, "act like a giant octopus, giving with one tentacle but taking away with the others." They also placed the responsibility for the country's economic malaise squarely on the shoulders of the radicals. They argued that a decade of statist policies had further increased poverty, illiteracy, inflation, unemployment, and slum housing. Before the revolution, these problems were blamed on the Pahlavis. Now they were blamed on the "extremist pseudo-clerical radicals."

The purge was so decisive that the radicals suspended the activities of their Society of the Militant Clergy soon after the elections for the Fourth *Majles*. Some went to head foundations and libraries. Some took up seminary positions. Others began to write for newspapers, occasionally arguing that the public should choose its Supreme Leader and that the Guardian Council should stay out of the whole electoral process. Yet others remained politically active, mildly criticizing the regime and quietly awaiting a better day.

This expectation was not far-fetched, for the majority in the Fourth *Majles* divided into two blocs once it had implemented a series of probusiness reforms. These reforms included relaxation of price controls, liberalization of imports, trimming of the ration list, disbanding of courts that penalized hoarders and price gougers, return of some confiscated real estate, withdrawal of all bills associated with land reform, income redistribution, and nationalization of foreign trade, and setting up a stock exchange in Tehran and free-trade zones in the Persian Gulf.

One bloc, named after the newspaper *Resalat*, supported highly conservative cultural policies as well as laissez-faire economics. It favored strict control over the media, the silencing of liberal intellectuals, and the rigid implementation of the dress code for women. It was also reluctant to challenge the financial privileges of the large foundations or open up the economy to international and émigré capital—foreign competition was seen as a threat to the bazaar economy. These conservatives could muster some 170 votes in the *Majles*. The other bloc, while also advocating laissez-faire, favored more active wooing of foreign capital and greater cultural liberalization. It was also eager to balance the budget by downsizing the large clerical foundations and by cutting state expenditures, especially for food and fuel subsidies. This bloc could muster some 40 votes. The remaining 60 members were independent deputies from the provinces. They sometimes voted with the majority, sometimes with the minority.

The first bloc, which can be described as the cultural conservatives, enjoyed the support of Khamenei, the Supreme Leader. The second bloc, the cultural liberals, had the backing of president Rafsanjani. To get a working majority, Rafsanjani had no choice but to water down his own preferences. He had to remove his own brother from the directorship of the National Radio-Television network. He could take no more than modest measures to privatize some five hundred large enterprises, trim the foreign-exchange privileges of the huge clerical foundations, and cut the social subsidies that absorbed much of the oil revenue. Moreover, he was unable to increase business taxes— all the taxes raised by the bazaar guilds together still constitute less than 9 percent of the government's annual tax income. Rafsanjani had to shelve his daring bill designed to attract foreign investment. This bill would have raised the share that foreign interests could own in Iranian enterprises from 49 percent to 100 percent. It would have been a total policy reversal, since the revolutionaries had relished accusing the Shah of selling the country to foreign capitalists. Rafsanjani now argued that he could not jump-start the ailing economy without the injection of massive foreign capital. The bill, however, met stiff resistance from conservatives fearful that foreign capital would swamp the bazaars.

Not surprisingly, Rafsanjani's supporters entered the Fifth *Majles* elections with their own party, Servants of Reconstruction. It was endorsed by ten cabinet ministers, four vice presidents, the governor of the Central Bank, and even more important, the mayor of Tehran. The latter was highly popular because he had made the city into a livable place by building highways, libraries, and parks, often from gardens confiscated from the former elite. Supported by the radical clerics, the Servants of Reconstruction won over 80 seats. Some 140 seats went to the conservatives, many endorsed by the Association of the Militant Clergy. The Fifth *Majles* turned out to be a repeat performance of the lackluster Fourth *Majles*.

Political Culture, Citizenship, and Identity

In theory, the Islamic Republic should be a highly viable state. After all, Shi'ism is the religion of both the state and the vast majority of the population. It can be described as the central component of popular culture. The Islamic constitution guarantees basic rights to religious minorities as well as to individual citizens. All citizens, regardless of race, color, language, or religion, are promised the rights of expression, worship, and organization. They are guaranteed freedom from arbitrary arrest, torture, and police surveillance. In short, the Islamic constitution incorporates the concept of individual rights as developed in the West; according to the constitution, civil society is not a foreign notion in twentieth-century Iran.

The constitution gives specific guarantees to the recognized religious minorities. Although Christians (Armenians and Assyrians), Jews, and Zoroastrians form 1 percent of the total population, they are allocated five *Majles* seats. They are permitted their own places of worship, their own community organizations, including schools, and their own marriage, divorce, and inheritance laws. The constitution, however, is ominously silent about the Baha'is and the Sunnis. The former are deemed apostates; the latter, fellow Muslims theoretically equal in rights to the Shi'i Muslims.

The constitution also gives guarantees to non-Persian speakers. Although 83 percent of the population understands Persian, thanks to the educational system, over 50 percent continue to speak non-Persian languages at home, languages such as Azeri, Kurdish, Turkic, Gilaki, Mazandarani, Arabic, and Baluchi. The constitution promises them rights unprecedented in Iranian history. It declares that "local and native languages can be used in the press, media, and schools." It also declares that local populations have the right to elect provincial, town, and village councils. These councils can watch over the governors-general and the town mayors as well as their educational, cultural, and social programs. They cannot be dismissed by the central government.

These generous promises are honored more in theory than in fact. The local councils—the chief institutional safeguard for the provincial minorities—were not convened until mid-1999. Subsidies to non-Persian publications and radio stations are meager. Jews have been so harassed as "pro-Israeli Zionists" that more than half—40,000 out of 80,000—have left the country. Armenian Christians have had to accept Muslim principals in their schools, end coeducational classes, adopt the government curriculum, abide by Muslim dress codes, including the veil, and close their community clubs to Muslims. Christians, on the whole, are viewed as "contaminated" with Western culture. The Christian population has declined from over 300,000 to less than 200,000.

The Baha'is, however, have borne the brunt of religious persecution. Their leaders have been executed as "apostates" and "imperialist spies." Adherents have been fired from their jobs, had their property confiscated, and been imprisoned and tortured to pressure them to convert to Islam. Their schools have been closed, their community property expropriated, and their shrines and cemeteries bulldozed. It is estimated that since the revolution one-third of the 300,000 Baha'is have left Iran. The Baha'is, like the Jews and Armenians, have migrated mostly to Canada and the United States, especially New York and California.

The much larger Sunni population, which forms as much as 9 percent of the total, has its own reasons for being alienated from the regime. The state religion is Shi'ism. High officials have to be Shi'i. Citizens have to subscribe to Khomeini's concept of government—a notion derived from Shi'ism. Few institutions cater to Sunni needs. There is not a single Sunni mosque in the whole of Tehran. And the regime tends to overlook the existence of Sunnis among the Kurds, Turkomans, Arabs, and Baluchis. It is no accident that in the period 1979–1981 the newborn regime faced its most serious challenges in precisely these areas—among the Sunni Kurds, Turkomans, Arabs, and Baluchis. It succeeded in crushing their revolts by rushing in tens of thousands of revolutionary guards from the Persian Shi'i heartland of Isfahan, Shiraz, and Qom.

Thus one can generalize that the Islamic Republic has its strongest cultural roots in the Persian Shi'i heartland. Its weakest roots are among the non-Shi'is—the Sunnis, Baha'is, Jews, Christians, and Zoroastrians. Its base among the Azeris, who are Shi'i but not Persian speakers, remains to be tested. In the past, the Azeris, who form 24 percent of the population and dwarf the other minorities, have not posed an ethnic problem. They are part and parcel of the Shi'i community. They have prominent figures, such as Khamenei, in the Shi'i hierarchy. Many Azeri merchants, professionals, and workers live throughout the regions of Iran. In short, Azeris can be considered well integrated into Iran. But the 1991 creation of the Republic of Azerbaijan out of the Soviet Union has raised new concerns, since some Azeris on both sides of the border have begun to talk of establishing a larger unified Azerbaijan. It is no accident that in the recent war between Azerbaijan and Armenia, Iran favored the latter. So far, the concept of a unified Azerbaijan has little appeal among Iranian Azeris.

Interests, Social Movements, and Protest

The regime has also violated most of the constitution's clauses promising to respect individual rights and civil liberties. It has closed down newspapers, professional associations, labor unions, and political parties. It has banned demonstrations and public meetings. It has incarcerated tens of thousands without due process. It has systematically tortured prisoners to extract false confessions and public recantations. And it has executed some 25,000 political prisoners, most of them without due process of law. The United Nations, Amnesty International, and Human Rights Watch have all strongly criticized Iran for violating the UN Charter on Human Rights as well as the Islamic constitution itself. Most of the victims have been Kurds, military officers from the old regime, and leftists, especially members of the Mojahedin and Fedayin. The Islamic Revolution, like some others, has devoured its own children.

Although the violation of individual liberties has affected the whole population, it arouses special resentment among the modern middle class, the traditionally minded Shi'is, women, and minorities. The modern middle class, which forms as much as 10 percent of the total population, has been secular and even anticlerical ever since the 1905 revolution. Little love is lost between it and the Islamic Republic. Not surprisingly, most of those executed have been teachers, engineers, professionals, and college students. Members of the intelligentsia who join the regime are regarded by their colleagues as betrayers of their class.

The traditionally minded Shi'is had difficulty accepting Khomeini's populist version of Islam, including his concept of jurist's guardianship. At the time of the revolution, none of the grand ayatollahs subscribed to this theory of government. After the revolution, few of them were willing to be associated with the Islamic Republic. And after Khomeini's death, even fewer were willing to give his successor a helping hand. The grand ayatollahs—some residing in Iraq, others in Iran—could still influence large numbers of pious Muslims, especially from the older generation. Just because the state is Shi'i does not automatically mean it enjoys the allegiance of all Shi'is. The new theocracy is haunted by the old Shi'i distrust of the state.

Finally, some women harbor grievances against the Islamic Republic, especially against the conservative clerics who control the *Majles* and the judiciary. Although the Western press has dwelled on the veil, Iranian women consider the veil one of their lesser problems. Given a choice, many would most likely continue to wear the veil, since they consider it practical and customary. More important to women are their work-related grievances. They have been purged from some offices and occupations. They are the last hired and the first fired. They are discriminated against in pay scales. They are encouraged to stay home, raise children, and do housework. To add insult to injury, the law treats them as wards of their male relatives, requiring them to have legal guidance from their fathers, husbands, or brothers. Even adult women are not allowed to travel without written permission from their male relatives.

Women have countered by publishing newspapers, forming organizations, and waging parliamentary campaigns. They have managed to raise the marriage age to fifteen, implicitly contradicting the *shari'a*. After the Islamic Revolution, the marriage age for women had been abolished. They have persuaded President Rafsanjani to establish a parliamentary Women's Commission. They have tried to restrict polygamy by encouraging the signing of marriage contracts in which the husband gives up the right to have multiple wives. These contracts can also give wives the right to divorce their husbands. Women have persuaded universities to reopen fields closed to them immediately after the revolution, such as geol-ogy, architecture, agriculture, veterinary medicine, and law. They have lobbied to get women back into the judiciary, but so far they have succeeded only in family courts. They have also persuaded the expediency Council that divorced women should be entitled to half the family property accumulated during the marriage. Immediately after the revolution, women's share in the labor force fell from 13 to 8 percent. By the mid-1990s it had rebounded to 13 percent. Even more impressive, women now constitute over 40 percent of university students, 45 percent of medical doctors, and 25 percent of the government labor force. Some observers have started to talk of the emergence of Islamic feminism and even of fundamentalist feminism.

These social pressures—together with the fact that the constitution recognized individual rights, that mass participation made the revolution, and that the concept of democracy made inroads into Iran from the beginning of the twentieth century—have forced the ruling clergy to make important concessions. By the late 1990s the government had recognized the existence of some one hundred organizations. These licensed organizations include clubs belonging to the recognized minorities, bazaar guilds and chambers of commerce, the Islamic Association of Students, the Islamic Women's Association, and the Workers' House, a center in Tehran for factory employees who support the regime. Most of these organizations are controlled by clerics; all accept the legitimacy of the regime. Other state-approved organizations include the Teachers of the Qom Seminaries, the Society of the Militant Clergy, and the Association of the Militant Clergy. At most, less than 1 percent of the population belongs to these organizations. The increasing distrust of the public is reflected in the official stamps issued to commemorate the revolution. In the early 1980s the commemorative stamps were full of energy and depicted demonstrators realistically. By the late 1980s the commemorative stamp designs were highly abstract and stylized. The crowds have become stylized as well as regimented and controlled.

Society has managed to preserve some semblance of independence from the state because the country's 200,000 clerics are sharply divided. They are divided not only into the conservative Association of the Militant Clergy and the radical Society of the Militant Clergy but also into many informal groups, some supporting ultraconservative ayatollahs, some supporting radical ones, and many keeping their distance from all politics. They prefer to do what clerics have done throughout the ages—preach, teach, study, tend the sick, and bury the dead. This division has given society a breathing space. Conservatives have tried to woo financial and electoral support from bazaar guilds, chambers of commerce, and farmers' associations. Radicals have tried to win over the Islamic Association of Students, the Islamic Association of Teachers, the Islamic Women's Association, and the Workers' House.

The extent, as well as the limitations, of these interest group politics can be seen in the passage of the labor law, which took a full eleven years. Immediately after the revolution, the labor minister, who was a free-market conservative, drafted a bill proposing that almost all labor issues be resolved by employers and employees themselves. His attitude was that the state should not be involved in private contracts and that good Muslim employers did not need government regulations to tell them how to treat their employees. Besides, a society that had the Qur'an, the *shari'a*, and jurist's guardianship did not require a Western-style labor law. He even proposed to do away with child labor restrictions, the minimum wage, mandatory holidays, and the weekly day of rest. This bill caused such outrage that it had to be withdrawn. Most of the outrage came from the radical clerics in parliament and their friends outside, especially the Workers' House and the Islamic Workers' Association. The head of the Workers' House warned that such a backward bill would drive factory employees into the arms of the Marxist parties.

The radical clerics came up with their own fairly comprehensive labor law, which guaranteed pensions, disability pay, health insurance, annual holidays, maximum work hours, a minimum wage, job security, and government arbitration. The bill, however, made no mention of independent labor unions. The Workers' House helped pass the bill through the *Majles* in 1986 by holding a series of mass rallies, especially on May Day, the international workers' day. The bill was promptly vetoed by the Guardian Council on the grounds that it was un-Islamic and violated the sanctity of private property. It was precisely this veto that prompted Khomeini to create the Expediency Council in 1987. The labor minister who had drafted this bill later admitted that the Expediency Council eventually endorsed the legislation in 1989 because of the direct intervention of Hojjat al-Islam Ahmad Khomeini, the Imam's son.[31] The regime that claims to represent the oppressed masses had taken a full decade to enact a fairly mild labor law. But the fact that it had been enacted against the opposition of the employers and the bazaars was a clear indication that interest group politics had taken root in the Islamic Republic.

Section ⑤ Iranian Politics in Transition

Political Challenges and Changing Agendas

On the eve of the 1997 presidential elections, *The Economist* (London) published a special survey on Iran predicting the certain victory of Hojjat al-Islam Ali-Akbar Nateq-Nuri, the Speaker of the *Majles*.[32] The journal was confident of this prediction because Nateq-Nuri was overwhelmingly favored by the religious establishment. The detailed survey provided much information on the regime's leading personalities but did not mention Khatami, who proved to be the victor. The survey, as well as the whole election, illustrates the pitfalls of making predictions about a regime that is based on two inherently contradictory principles—theocracy and democracy.

Before the elections, the Guardian Council did what it had habitually done. It weeded out the candidates, leaving only two serious ones: Nateq-Nuri and

Leaders: *Sayyid Muhammad Khatami*

Muhammad Khatami was elected president of the Islamic Republic in 1997. He was born in 1944 into a prominent clerical family in central Iran. His father, an ayatollah, was a close friend of Khomeini. His mother came from a prosperous landed family. He studied theology in Qom and philosophy at Isfahan University. At the outbreak of the revolution, he was in charge of a Shi'i mosque in Germany. After the revolution, he first headed a state publishing house, then sat in the *Majles*, and then served as Minister of Culture and Islamic Guidance. Arousing the wrath of the conservatives, he resigned from the last post in 1992 and took up the teaching of philosophy at Tehran University. He uses the title sayyid and wears a black turban to indicate that he is a male descendant of the Prophet. Although a cleric by appearance and training, he seems to many more like a university professor interested in political philosophy.

Khatami. In weeding out the candidates, the Guardian Council made sure it eliminated all secular and lay liberal voices. The Council was confident that in a two-man race Nateq-Nuri would win. He was well known, having served in a number of parliaments. He had been close to Khomeini, who had at one time named him Minister of Interior. He had presided over a number of revolutionary tribunals. Moreover, he was backed by an impressive array of clerical organizations, interest groups, and newspapers: the Association of the Militant Clergy; the Foundation of the Oppressed; the National Radio-Television network; the newspapers *Resalat*, *Kayhan*, and *Ettela'at*; the Chamber of Commerce; the Chamber of Bazaar Guilds; the Association of Farmers; and of course, his own conservative bloc in the *Majles*. Furthermore, he was endorsed by most of the Imam Jum'ehs and members of the Guardian Council. Many also felt that he had been implicitly endorsed by the Supreme Leader himself.

In contrast, Khatami had the support only of the Servants of Reconstruction; their newspaper *Hamshahri* (*Fellow Townsman*); the revived Society of the Militant Clergy and its paper *Salam* (*Greetings*); the Islamic Association of Students; the Islamic Women's Association and its paper *Zanan* (*Women*); and the Workers' House and its paper *Kar va Kargar* (*Work and Worker*). The popular mayor of Tehran served as the chairman of his electoral campaign. Khatami also received the support of a number of small but independent intellectual journals.

Khatami pitched his campaign at youth, women, middle-class professionals, and the urban working class. He appeared at bus stops, supermarkets, and schools. He drove around in his own small car. He was photographed using the Internet and playing table tennis, his favorite sport after soccer. He gave interviews to *Zanan*, whereas his opponent considered such behavior too demeaning. When asked by *Zanan* if his wife drove a car, he confessed that he wished she did since he would like to do less driving himself. His speeches stressed the importance of the rule of law, civil society, political pluralism, toleration, greater openness, and fewer social restrictions. In an appeal to the radical clerics, the urban poor, and the organized working class, he stressed economic justice, job creation, and welfare programs.

His intellectual supporters were more explicit in their criticisms of the conservatives. For example, Abdol-Karim Soroush, a popular lecturer who at Khomeini's behest had helped purge the universities, now stressed the importance of human rights, popular will, and intellectual freedom. He argued that religion and politics should be kept separate for the benefit of both. Politics debased religion into a false ideology. And religion in the hands of a political elite inevitably became a tool of oppression. He also argued that conservatives had used the issue of "cultural imperialism" to silence new voices, that innovative ideas had come not from the seminaries but from such intellectuals as Shariati and Bazargan, and that Iran should become a full-fledged democracy in which Islam would be recognized as the religion of the majority. In other words, Iran should become secular in structure but Islamic in name, just as Bazargan had advocated years earlier. Not surprisingly, Hezbollahis often disrupted his public lectures.

Khatami's electoral themes struck the right note. Whereas 16.4 million voters had participated in the 1989 presidential election and 16.7 million in the election of 1993, over 29 million voted in 1997. Almost 70 percent supported Khatami. This was a resounding yes for him, and, at the same time, a resounding no to the whole establishment. According to journalists, the main concerns for the youth that flocked to the polls were jobs, education, university places, household goods, and freedom in everyday life—freedom from the vigilante Hezbollahis and the *basej*. They also wanted the freedom to go to parties, dance, date, listen to music, watch videos, and own satellite-television dishes. According to the same journalists, most of the revolutionary guards also voted for Khatami. The generation raised after the revolution has had enough of social control and religious guidance. In other words, youth find the clerical revolution to be middle-aged.

Khatami followed up his victory with a number of liberal measures. He placed his own supporters and those of Rafsanjani in charge of the important ministries of Interior, Culture and Islamic Guidance, Labor, and Foreign Affairs. He licensed the Servants of Reconstruction, stressed the importance of political parties, and promised to enact the long-awaited law legalizing political parties. He scheduled elections for local councils—elections that should have been held two decades ago. He encouraged his *Majles* supporters to draft a bill stripping the Guardian Council of the power to vet electoral candidates. He eased the censorship on books, newspapers, films, and television. He criticized fellow believers for the tendency to place their hopes on the Hidden Imam. He declared that the "sick economy" needed social as well as financial reforms. He removed the prison system from the control of die-hard conservatives. He warned Hezbollahis not to disrupt meetings. He freed from house imprisonment a number of grand ayatollahs. He moved the *basej* from the wealthier suburbs of northern Tehran. He permitted the launching of a number of liberal newspapers—one, *Jam'eh* (*Society*) grew overnight to a circulation of over 100,000, outselling the established papers. In addition, he used the cable television station CNN to appeal directly to the West, especially to the U.S. public. He expressed admiration for the United States, especially for its tradition of religious toleration. He also expressed "pity" over the hostage-taking "tragedy." He was clearly trying to break the ice in order to persuade the United States to lift its embargo and allow U.S. oil companies to return to Iran.

This new course did not have smooth sailing. Despite the landslide victory, the president's constitutional powers were sharply limited from all sides—by the Supreme Leader, the judiciary, and the *Majles*. Khamenei undermined the rapprochement with the West by continually denouncing the United States as well as the Israeli-Palestinian peace process. He also removed the jurisdiction of the national police from the Interior Ministry. One of the clerical foundations upped the bounty it had offered to anyone killing Salman Rushdie. The judiciary banned licensed newspapers and arrested associates of Khatami and Rafsanjani. For example, the popular mayor of Tehran was hauled to court on trumped-up corruption charges. The *Majles* forced Khatami to place conservatives in charge of the ministries of Justice, Intelligence, and Defense. It also forced the resignation of Khatami's Interior Minister and drafted a new electoral law raising the voting age from fifteen to sixteen. Meanwhile, Hezbollahis assaulted a number of Khatami supporters, including ministers and venerable Imam Jum'ehs. One of the injured was the Supreme Leader's brother, who was Khatami's close friend. To top it all, a group of assassins, probably organized by the Intelligence Ministry, killed four prominent lay intellectuals. By early 1999 it was clear that Khatami could not pursue his liberal agenda unless he won the *Majles* elections scheduled for 2000. To do that he would need to strip the Guardian Council of the power to vet parliamentary candidates, but for that he would need a parliamentary majority. In other words, Khatami reached a constitutional dead end. So far the theocratic features of the constitution have proved to be stronger than the democratic ones.

Iranian Politics in Comparative Perspective

Iran is both like and unlike the rest of the Third World. Unlike most Third World countries, it is an old state with institutions that go back to the ancient world. Unlike most others, it is not a newly independent country since it was never formally taken over by the imperial powers. It remained officially independent,

Leaders: *Hojjat al-Islam Ali-Akbar Hashemi Rafsanjani*

Ali-Akbar Rafsanjani was born in 1934 into a fairly prosperous business and farming family in the heartland of the Shi'i and Persian-speaking provinces. He studied in Qom with Khomeini, found himself in prison four times during the 1960s, set up a number of commercial companies, including one that exported pistachios, and wrote a book praising a nineteenth-century prime minister who had made an aborted attempt to industrialize the country. Nevertheless, Rafsanjani remained active enough in clerical circles to be considered a hojjat al-Islam. After the revolution, he became a close confidant of Khomeini and attained a number of cabinet posts, culminating with the presidency in 1989. After serving two four-year terms, the maximum allowed by the constitution, he was given the chairmanship of the powerful Expediency Council. In some ways, his institutional power rivals that of President Khatami, but not, of course, that of Supreme Leader Khamenei.

even at the height of European imperialism. Unlike some others, it has a religion that links the elite with the masses, the cities with the villages, the state with the citizenry. Shi'ism, as well as Iranian identity, serves as social cement, giving the population a collective identity. Unlike most Third World countries, it possesses rich oil resources and thus has the potential for rapid economic development. And unlike most others, it has produced two popular upheavals in the twentieth century: the constitutional and the Islamic revolutions. In both, the citizenry actively intervened in politics, overthrowing the old regime and shaping the new. The Islamic Republic and the 1905 constitution were authentic home products, not foreign imports.

Yet Iran shares some problems with other Third World countries. It has failed to establish a full-fledged democracy. Its economy remains underdeveloped, highly reliant on one commodity, and unable to meet rising expectations. Its collective identity is strained by internal fault lines, especially those of class, ethnicity, and interclerical conflicts. And its ambition to enter the world of states as an important player has been thwarted by international as well as internal and regional realities. In fact, this ambition has helped to undermine democracy and economic development in Iran.

Democracy has been constricted by theocracy. Some argue that Islam made this inevitable. But Islam, like Christianity and the other major religions, can be interpreted in ways that either support or oppose democracy. Islam, as interpreted by some Muslims, stresses the importance of justice, equality, and consultation. It has a tradition of tolerating other religions. Its *shari'a* explicitly protects life, property, and honor. In practice, it has often separated politics from religion, statutes from holy laws, spiritual affairs from worldly matters, and the state from the clerical establishment.

Moreover, the theocracy in Iran originates not in Islam but in jurist's guardianship, a new concept developed by Khomeini. On the whole, Sunni Islam considers clerics to be theological scholars, not a special stratum. This helps explain why the Iranian regime has found it difficult to export the revolution to the rest of the Muslim world. The failure of democracy in Iran should be attributed less to Islam than to the confluence of crises in 1979–1981 that allowed a small group of clerics to seize power. Whether they remain in power into the twenty-first century depends not so much on Islam but on how they handle the opposition, their own differences, and most important, the country's economic problems.

The Islamic Republic is sharply divided on how to manage an economy beset by rising demands, falling petroleum revenues, and the nightmarish prospect that in the next two generations the oil wells will run dry. Most clerics favor the conventional capitalist road to development, hoping to liberalize the market, privatize industry, attract foreign capital, and encourage the propertied classes to invest. Others envisage an equally conventional statist road to development, favoring central planning, government industries, price controls, high taxes, state subsidies, national self-reliance, and ambitious programs to eliminate poverty, illiteracy, slums, and unemployment. Khatami has charted a third road, combining elements of state intervention with free enterprise. This is strikingly similar to the social democracy favored in other parts of the world.

As the clock ticks, the population grows, oil revenues stagnate, and the per capita national income falls. The economic problems that undermined the monarchy could well undermine the Islamic Republic. Only time will tell whether social discontent will be expressed through apolitical channels, such as drug addiction, emigration, and quietist religion; through radical clerics remaining within the regime; through insurrectionary organizations, through ethnic-based movements, or through reformist movements such as Khatami's electoral campaign.

Iran's collective identity has come under great strain in recent years. The emphasis on Shi'ism has antagonized Sunnis as well as non-Muslims. The emphasis on clerical Shi'ism has further alienated all secularists, including lay liberals, radical leftists, and moderate nationalists. Furthermore, the emphasis on Khomeini's brand of Shi'ism has alienated Shi'is who reject the whole notion of jurist's guardianship. And the elevation of Khamenei as the Supreme Leader has antagonized many early proponents of jurist's guardianship. In short, the regime has used slicing tactics on itself, gradually reducing its social base to a bare minimum. It is, however, possible that reformist movements such as that of Khatami could help rebuild the collective national identity.

Finally, the Islamic Republic's attempt to enter the international arena as a militant force has been counterproductive. It has diverted scarce resources to the military, especially the revolutionary guards. It has frightened Saudi Arabia and the Gulf sheikhdoms into the arms of the United States. It has prompted the United States to isolate Iran, discouraging investment and preventing international organizations from extending economic assistance. It has also frightened the neighboring secular states such as Turkey, Tadzhikistan, and Azerbaijan. It has strained relations with some other Third World countries. Moreover, Iran has discovered that its brand of Islam is not exportable to the Sunni world. The West may perceive Iran as the vanguard of the Islamic radicalism that is spreading throughout the Middle East and North Africa. But the Sunni world sees Iran much more as a unique Shi'i phenomenon. Only the future will show whether the 1979 Islamic Revolution can be repeated elsewhere.

Key Terms

ayatollah	mosques
fatwa	*pasdaran*
theocracy	Imam
Majles	Hezbollahis
Guardian Council	hojjat al-Islam
Supreme Leader	*jihad*
Farsi	rentier state
Shi'ism	dual society
People of the Book	OPEC
Qur'an	Imam Jum'ehs
shari'a	Foundation of the
bazaars	Oppressed
fundamentalism	*basej*
jurist's guardianship	*maslahat*

Suggested Readings

Abrahamian, E. *Iran Between Two Revolutions*. Princeton, N.J.: Princeton University Press, 1982.

——. *Khomeinism*. Berkeley: University of California Press, 1993.

——. *Tortured Confessions: Prisons and Public Recantations in Modern Iran*. Berkeley: University of California Press, 1999.

Akhavi, S. *Religion and Politics in Contemporary Iran*. Albany: State University of New York Press, 1980.

Bakhash, S. *Reign of the Ayatollahs*. New York: Basic Books, 1984.

Baktiari, B. *Parliamentary Politics in Revolutionary Iran*. Gainesville: University Press of Florida, 1966.

Bill, J. *The Eagle and the Lion*. New Haven, Conn.: Yale University Press, 1988.

Chehabi, H. *Iranian Politics and Religious Modernism*. Ithaca, N.Y.: Cornell University Press, 1990.

Cottam, R. *Nationalism in Iran*. Pittsburgh: University of Pittsburgh Press, 1964.

Dabashi, H. *Theology of Discontent: The Ideological Foundation of the Islamic Revolution in Iran*. New York: New York University Press, 1993.

Esposito, J. *The Iranian Revolution: Its Global Impact*. Miami: University Press of Florida, 1990.

Fischer, M. *Iran: From Religious Dispute to Revolution*. Cambridge, Mass.: Harvard University Press, 1980.

Foran, J. *Fragile Resistance: Social Transformation in Iran from 1500 to the Revolution*. Boulder, Colo.: Westview Press, 1993.

———. *A Century of Revolution: Social Movements in Iran.* Minneapolis: University of Minnesota Press, 1994.

Green, J. *Revolution in Iran.* New York: Praeger, 1982.

Halliday, F. *Iran: Dictatorship and Development.* London: Penguin, 1979.

Heiss, M. *Empire and Nationhood: The United States, Great Britain, and Iranian Oil, 1950–1954.* New York: Columbia University Press, 1997.

Huntington, Samuel P., *The Clash of Civilizations and the Remaking of the World Order.* New York: Simon & Schuster, 1996.

Kazemi, F. "Civil Society and Iranian Politics." In *Civil Society in the Middle East,* ed. A. Norton. Vol. 2. Leiden: Brill, 1996.

Keddie, N. *Roots of Revolution.* New Haven, Conn.: Yale University Press, 1981.

———. *Iran and the Muslim World.* London: Macmillan, 1995.

Mackey, S. *The Iranians: Persia, Islam, and the Soul of a Nation.* New York: Penguin, 1996.

Milani, M. *The Making of Iran's Islamic Revolution.* Boulder, Colo.: Westview Press, 1994.

Mottahedeh, R. *The Mantle of the Prophet.* New York: Simon and Schuster, 1985.

Najmabadi, A. *The Story of the Daughters of Quchan.* Syracuse, N.Y.: Syracuse University Press, 1998.

Paidar, P. *Women and the Political Process in Twentieth-Century Iran.* Cambridge: Cambridge University Press, 1995.

Rahema, A., and S. Behnab. *Iran after the Revolution.* London: Tauris, 1995.

Ramazani, R. *Revolutionary Iran.* Baltimore: Johns Hopkins University Press, 1986.

Schirazi, A. *The Constitution of Iran.* London: Tauris, 1997.

Weiner, M., and A. Banuazizi, eds. *The Politics of Social Transformation in Afghanistan, Iran, and Pakistan.* Syracuse, N.Y.: Syracuse University Press, 1994.

Endnotes

[1] Quoted in E. Browne, *The Persian Revolution* (New York: Barnes and Noble, 1966), 137.

[2] British Financial Adviser to the Foreign Office in Tehran, *Documents on British Foreign Policy, 1919–39* (London: Government Printing Office, 1963), First Series, XIII, 720, 735.

[3] British Minister to the Foreign Office, *Report on the Seizure of Lands,* Foreign Office 371/Persia 1932/File 34-16007.

[4] *Kayhan International,* November 10, 1976.

[5] Editorial, "Fifty Indictments of Treason During Fifty Years of Treason," *Khabarnameh,* no. 46 (April 1976).

[6] M. Bazargan, "Letter to the Editor," *Ettela'at,* February 7, 1980.

[7] *Iran Times,* January 12, 1979.

[8] "Text of the Mass Rally of Ashura," *Khabarnameh,* December 15, 1978.

[9] *Washington Post,* December 12, 1978.

[10] *Christian Science Monitor,* December 12, 1978.

[11] Mirza Hosayn Khan Tahvildar-e Isfahan, *Jukhrafiha-ye Isfahan* (*The Geography of Isfahan*) (Tehran: Tehran University Press, 1963), 100–101.

[12] International Labor Organization, "Employment and Income Policies for Iran" (Unpublished report, Geneva, 1972), Appendix C, 6.

[13] A. Sharbatoghilie, *Urbanization and Regional Disparity in Post-Revolutionary Iran* (Boulder, Colo.: Westview Press, 1991), 4.

[14] *Wall Street Journal,* November 4, 1977.

[15] U.S. Congress, *Economic Consequences of the Revolution in Iran* (Washington, D.C.: U.S. Government Printing Office, 1979), 184.

[16] U.S. Congress, *Economic Consequences of the Revolution in Iran,* 5.

[17] U.S. Department of Commerce, *Iran: A Survey of U.S. Business Opportunities* (Washington, D.C.: U.S. Government Printing Office, 1977), 1–2.

[18] Cited in H. Amirahmadi, *Revolution and Economic Transition* (Albany: State University of New York Press, 1960), p. 201.

[19] Cited in *Iran Times,* July 9, 1993.

[20] J. Amuzegar, *Iran's Economy Under the Islamic Republic* (London: Taurus Press, 1994), 100.

[21] Cited in *Iran Times,* July 9, 1993.

[22] Amuzegar, *Iran's Economy,* 101.

[23] A. Rafsanjani, "The Islamic Consultative Assembly," *Kayhan,* May 23, 1987.

[24] S. Saffari, "The Legitimation of the Clergy's Right to Rule in the Iranian Constitution of 1979," in *British Journal of Middle Eastern Studies* 20, no. 1 (1993): 64–81.

[25] Ayatollah Montazeri, *Ettela'at,* October 8, 1979.

[26] O. Fallaci, "Interview with Khomeini," *New York Times Magazine,* October 7, 1979.

[27] *Kayhan,* March 6, 1980.

[28] *Kayhan,* April 21, 1987.

[29] *Kayhan-e Hava'i,* November 16, 1988.

[30] A. Rafsanjani, Friday sermon, *Kayhan,* November 4, 1989.

[31] Interview with the former Labor Minister, *Salam,* January 9–25, 1993.

[32] "Survey of Iran," *The Economist,* January 18, 1997.

Glossary*

5 percent rule   provision of the German electoral law requiring all parties to win at least 5 percent of the vote to obtain seats for representation.

abertura (*apertura* in Spanish)   in Brazil, refers to the period of authoritarian liberalization begun in 1974 when the military allowed civilian politicians to contest for political office in the context of a more open political society. (See **glasnost.**)

accommodation   an informal agreement or settlement between the government and important interest groups that is responsive to the interest groups' concerns for policy or program benefits.

accountability   a government's responsibility to its population, usually by periodic popular elections and (in **parliamentary systems**) by parliament having the power to dismiss the government by passing a motion of no-confidence. In a political system characterized by accountability, the major actions taken by government must be known and understood by the citizenry. (See **democracy.**)

acephalous societies   literally "headless" societies. A number of traditional Nigerian societies, such as the Igbo in the precolonial period, lacked executive rulership as we have come to conceive of it. Instead, the villages and clans were governed by committee or consensus.

administrative court   court that hears cases from private citizens and organizations involving allegations of bureaucratic violations of rules and laws. In Germany, the third branch of the court system, consisting of the Labor Court, the Social Security Court, and the Finance Court. In France, the highest administrative court is the Council of State.

administrative guidance   in Japan, informal guidance, usually not based on a statute or formal regulation, that is given by a government agency, such as a ministry and its subdivisions, to a private organization, such as a firm, or a lower-level government. The lack of transparency of the practice makes it subject to criticisms as a disguised form of collusion between a government agency and a firm.

---

*Note: Boldface terms *within* a definition can be found as separate entries in the Glossary.

amakudari   a Japanese practice, known as "descent from heaven," in which government officials retiring from their administrative positions take jobs in public corporations or private firms under their own ministry's jurisdiction.

Amerindian   original peoples of North and South America; indigenous people.

ancien régime   the monarchical **regime** that ruled France until the Revolution of 1789, when it was toppled by a popular uprising. The term is used to describe long-established regimes in other countries ruled by undemocratic elites.

anticlericalism   opposition to the power of churches or clergy in politics. In some countries, for example, France and Mexico, this opposition has focused on the role of the Catholic church in politics.

appropriations   government spending that must be approved by Congress each year. All such spending must begin with a bill proposed in the House of Representatives.

Articles of Confederation   the first governing document of the United States, agreed to in 1777 and ratified in 1781. The Articles centralized almost all power in the states and made the national government dependent on voluntary contributions by the states and the agreement of all states for important national activities.

Asia Pacific Economic Cooperation   a regional organization of Asian and Pacific rim nations established in 1989 to promote cooperation among member states, especially in foreign investment and the standardization and compilation of statistical data. Currently composed of eighteen members (including the United States and Canada) APEC advocates "open regionalism."

Asian Development Bank (ADB)   a regional bank established in 1966 to promote economic development in and cooperation among nations in Asia. The bank mediates public and private investments in and loans for selected developmental projects. The current members include 56 nations and areas in Asia and 16 others, including the United States.

Association of Southeast Asian Nations (ASEAN)   an organization formed in 1967 to promote regional economic and political cooperation. In 1995, ASEAN consisted of six member states: Brunei, Indonesia, Malaysia, the Philippines,

A1

Singapore, and Thailand. Laos, Myanmer, and Vietnam were expected to join the organization shortly.

asymmetrical federalism   a system of governance in which political authority is shared between a central government and regional or state governments, but where some subnational units in the federal system have greater or lesser powers than others.

authoritarian   (See **authoritarianism.**)

authoritarianism   a system of rule in which power does not depend on popular legitimacy but rather on the coercive force of the political authorities. Hence there are few personal and group freedoms. It is also characterized by near absolute power in the executive branch, and little if any legislative and judicial controls. (See **autocracy, fascism, patrimonialism.**)

autocracy   a government in which one or a few rulers has absolute power, thus, a **dictatorship.** Similar to **authoritarianism.**

autonomous region   in the People's Republic of China, a territorial unit equivalent to a province that contains a large concentration of ethnic minorities. These regions have some autonomy in the cultural sphere but in most policy matters are strictly subordinate to the central government.

autonomous republic   a territorial unit in the Soviet Union which was a constituent unit of the **union republic** within which it was located; autonomous republics were populated by a large national (**ethnic**) group, after which the autonomous republic was generally named. They enjoyed little actual autonomy in the Soviet period. Once Russia adopted its new constitution in 1993, those autonomous republics within Russian territory became constituent units (now called republics) of the Russian Federation.

Ayatollah   literally, God's symbol. High-ranking clerics in Iran. The most senior ones—often no more than half a dozen—are known as Grand Ayatollahs.

balance of payments   an indicator of international flow of funds, it shows the excess or deficit in total payments of all kinds between or among countries. Included in the calculation are exports and imports, grants, and international debt payments.

basej   Persian word for mobilization used to describe the volunteer army of young and old men formed in Iran to help the regular army and revolutionary guards in the war against Iraq.

Basic Law *(Grundgesetz)*   German document establishing the founding of the Federal Republic of Germany (West Germany) in 1949. Similar to a written constitution.

bazaar   an urban marketplace where shops, workshops, small businessmen, and even export-importers are located.

bicameral   a legislative body with two houses, such as the U.S. Senate and the U.S. House of Representatives. Just as the Constitution divides responsibilities between branches of the federal government and between the federal and state governments, it divides responsibilities between the House and the Senate.

Bill of Rights   the first ten amendments to the Constitution (ratified in 1791) which establish limits on the actions of government. Initially, the Bill of Rights only limited the federal government. The 14th amendment and subsequent judicial rulings extended the provisions of the Bill of Rights to the states.

Brahmin(s)   highest caste in the Hindu caste system, who traditionally dominated the Hindu society of India.

bureaucracy   an organization structured hierarchically, in which lower-level officials are charged with administering regulations codified in rules which specify impersonal, objective guidelines for making decisions. In the modern world, many large organizations, especially business firms and the executives of developed states, are organized along bureaucratic lines.

bureaucratic authoritarianism   a term developed by the Argentine sociologist, Guillermo O'Donnell, to interpret the common characteristics of military-led authoritarian regimes in Brazil, Argentina, Chile, and Uruguay in the 1960s and 1970s. According to O'Donnell, bureaucratic authoritarian regimes led by the armed forces and key civilian allies emerged in these countries in response to severe economic crises. Repression in these regimes varied from the relatively mild forms that constricted civil rights and other political freedoms in Brazil, to the much harsher policy of forced detention, mass exile, and widespread killing that characterized the military regimes of Argentina (1976–1983) and Chile (1973–1989).

bureaucratic rings   a term first developed by the Brazilian sociologist and president Fernando Henrique Cardoso that refers to the highly permeable and fragmented structure of the state bureaucracy which allows private interests to make alliances with mid-level bureaucratic officers. By shaping public policy to benefit these interests, bureaucrats gain the promise of future employment in the private sector. While in positions of responsibility, bureaucratic rings are ardent defenders of their own interests.

bushi   the warrior class in medieval Japan, known also as *samurai.* The class emerged around the tenth century A.D. and a dominant band established Japan's first warrior government in the twelfth century. The last warrior government was overthrown in the Meiji Restoration of the mid-nineteenth century.

cabinet the ministers who direct executive departments. In **parliamentary systems,** the cabinet and high-ranking subcabinet ministers (also known as the government) are considered collectively responsible to parliament.

cadre a person who occupies a position of authority in a **communist party-state;** cadres may or may not be communist party members.

capital flight transferring assets from those denominated in a national currency into those denominated in a foreign currency (e. g. Russian rubles into US dollars) outside the process of regular trade or commerce.

caste system India's Hindu society is divided into castes. According to the Hindu religion, membership in a given caste is determined at birth. Castes form a rough social and economic hierarchy. (See **Brahmins, untouchables.**)

central planning (See **command economy.**)

chancellor the German head of government. Functional equivalent of prime minister in other parliamentary systems.

charisma the ability of a leader to attract an intensely devoted following because of personal characteristics that supporters believe endows the charismatic leader with extraordinary and heroic qualities.

checks and balances a governmental system of divided authority in which co-equal branches can restrain the actions of other branches. For example, the president must sign legislation for it to become law, after both branches of Congress pass the bill in the same form. The Supreme Court can review the Constitutionality of this legislation.

citizen action groups formed in Germany in the 1970s, forerunner of the Greens Party.

civil servants state employees who make up the bureaucracy.

civil society refers to the space occupied by voluntary associations *outside* the state, for example, professional associations (lawyers, doctors, teachers), trade unions, student and women's groups and religious bodies, and other voluntary association groups. The term is similar to **society,** although civil society implies a degree of organization absent from the more inclusive term *society.*

clientelism (or **patron-client relations**) an informal aspect of policy-making in which a powerful patron (for example, a traditional local boss, government agency, or dominant party) offers resources such as land, contracts, protection, or jobs in return for the support and services (such as labor or votes) of lower status and less powerful clients; corruption, preferential treatment, and inequality are characteristic of clientelist politics. (See **partimonialism, prebendalism.**)

co-determination German legal mechanism which authorizes trade union members in firms with 2,000 or more employees to have nearly 50 percent of the seats on the firm's board of directors.

cohabitation the term used by the French to describe the situation in the Fifth Republic when a president and prime minister belong to opposing political coalitions.

Cold War the term designates the hostile relations that prevailed between the United States and the USSR from the late 1940s until the demise of the Soviet Union in 1991. Although an actual (hot) war never directly occurred between the two superpowers, they clashed indirectly by supporting rival forces in many wars occurring in the Third World.

collectivization a process undertaken in the Soviet Union under Stalin in the late 1920s and early 1930s, and in China under Mao in the 1950s, by which agricultural land was removed from private ownership and organized into large state and collective farms.

command economy a form of **socialism** in which government decisions ("commands") rather than market mechanisms (such as supply and demand) are the major influences in determining the nation's economic direction; also called **central planning.**

Commonwealth the association of independent states which evolved from the British Empire, including the United Kingdom and former British colonies or dependent territories.

communism a system of social organization based on the common ownership and coordination of production; according to Marxism (the theory of German philosopher Karl Marx, 1818–1883), communism is a culminating stage of history, following **capitalism** and **socialism.** In historical practice, leaders of China, the Soviet Union, and other states who have proclaimed themselves seeking to achieve communism have ruled through a single party, the communist party, which has controlled the state and society in an authoritarian manner, and have applied **Marxism-Leninism** to justify their rule.

communist (See **communism.**)

communist party-state   a type of **nation-state** in which the communist party attempts to exercise a complete monopoly on political power and controls all important state institutions. (See **communism.**)

communitarianism   a tradition of political thought that emphasizes the relationship between individuals and communities and the contribution to democracy that can be played by the shared set of social bonds that are fostered by community.

comparative politics   the study of the domestic politics, political institutions, and conflicts of countries. Often involves comparisons among countries and through time within single countries, emphasizing key patterns of similarity and difference.

comparativists   political scientists who study the similarities and differences in the domestic politics of various countries (see **comparative politics**).

Confucianism   a social philosophy based on the teachings of the Chinese sage, Confucius (c. 551–479 B.C.) that emphasizes social harmony, righteous behavior toward others, and deference to one's superiors. Confucianism remains a major source of cultural values in the countries of East Asia, including China and Japan.

conservative   the belief that existing political, social, and economic arrangements should be preserved. Historically, this has involved a defense of the inequalities (of class, race, gender, and so on) that are part of the existing order; often used to identify the economic and social policies favored by right-of-center parties.

Constitution   the governing document of the United States, drafted in 1787 and ratified in 1788. The Constitution has been amended 27 times since ratification.

constitutional monarchy   system of government in which the head of state ascends by heredity, but is limited in powers and constrained by the provisions of a constitution.

constitutionalism   a political system characterized the existence of clear, predictable, fair, and stable laws enforced by an impartial and powerful judiciary. Also called the rule of law.

constructive vote of no confidence   provision in the German political system of requiring any opposition party or group of parties to have an alternative majority government that would replace the current one. This provision was placed into the Basic Law in 1949 to avoid the Weimar practice of voting governments out of office and producing numerous political crises.

convergence criteria   targets adopted by member states of the European Union designed to encourage governments to limit budget deficits, public debt, and inflation in preparation for the launching of a common European currency (the **euro**).

convoy system   the practice among Japanese banks and securities firms of cooperating and helping each other, like members of a truck convoy, under the government's watchful eye. Companies in financial trouble too serious to be solved with the help of other members of the convoy are bailed out by the government.

cooptation   incorporating activists into the system while accommodating some of their concerns.

corporatism   a pattern of organizing interests and influencing public policy in which the state gives favored status to certain **interest groups;** typically involves tripartite (three-way) consultations among representatives of business, labor, and government over economic policy. Corporatism can occur in both **democratic** and **authoritarian** settings. However, it is usually criticized for the fact that it limits open debate and representative processes. (See **neo-corporatism, state corporatism.**)

corporatist philosophy   (See **corporatism.**)

country   a territorial unit controlled by a single state. Countries vary in the degree to which groups within them have a common culture and ethnic affiliation. (See **ethnicity, nation-state, state.**)

danwei   a Chinese term that means "unit" and is the basic level of social organization and a major means of political control in China's **communist party-state.** A person's *danwei* is most often his or her workplace, such as a factory or an office.

decentralization   policies that aim to transfer some decision-making power from higher to lower levels of government, typically, from the central government to subnational governments.

Declaration of Independence   the document asserting independence from Great Britain signed in Philadelphia on July 4, 1776.

democratic centralism   a system of political organization developed by V. I. Lenin and practiced, with modifications, by all **communist party-states.** Its principles include a hierarchical party structure in which (a) party leaders are elected on a delegate basis from lower to higher party bodies; (b) party leaders can be recalled by those who elected them; and (c) freedom of discussion is permitted until a decision is taken, but strict discipline and unity should prevail in implementing a decision once it is made. In practice, in all communist parties in China, the Soviet Union, and elsewhere, centralizing elements tended to predominate over the democratic ones.

democratic corporatism   a set of institutions or forums that bring representatives from employers, trade unions, and government together to negotiate issues affecting workplaces, industry structure, and national economic policy.

demokratizatsiia   the policy of democratization identified by former Soviet leader Mikhail Gorbachev in 1987 as an essential component of *perestroika.* The policy was part of a gradual shift away from a vanguard party approach toward an acceptance of **liberal** democratic norms. Initially, the policy embraced multicandidate elections for the soviets and a broadening of political competition within the Communist Party itself; after 1989 it involved acceptance of a multiparty system.

deregulation   the process of dismantling state regulations which govern social and economic life. Deregulation increases the power of private actors, especially business firms.

détente   a relaxation of tensions between formerly hostile nations that moves them toward more normal diplomatic relations. Often used to describe a thaw in the **Cold War** beginning in the 1960s.

developmental state   a **nation-state** in which the government carries out policies that effectively promote national economic growth.

developmentalism   an ideology and practice in Latin America during the 1950s in which the state played a leading role in seeking to foster economic development, through sponsoring vigorous **industrial policy.** [See **import substituting industrialization (ISI).**]

dictatorship   (See **autocracy, authoritarianism, totalitarianism.**)

dirigisme   a French term denoting that the state plays a leading role supervising the economy. *Dirigisme* differs from **socialism** or **communism** in that, under a system of *dirigisme,* firms remained privately owned. At the other extreme, *dirigisme* differs from the situation where the state has a relatively small role in economic governance.

dirigiste   (See *dirigisme.*)

distributive policies   policies that allocate resources into an area that policymakers perceive needs to be promoted. For example, leaders today believe that school children should have access to the internet. In order to accomplish this goal, telephone users are being taxed to provide money for schools to establish connections to the internet (which uses, in large part, telephone lines).

distributive policies   transfer resources from one group to another in the society.

divided government   different branches of government being controlled by different parties.

Domei   the Japanese Confederation of Labor founded 1964 through the merger of several federations of rightwing labor unions opposed to the leftist labor organization, *Sohyo.* Dominated by private sector unions and closely allied with the Democratic Socialist Party, *Domei* advocated harmonious management-labor relations and a **corporatist** relationship with the government. *Domei* was disbanded in 1987 when all its affiliated unions joined *Rengo* at its founding.

dual economy   an economy that is sharply divided into a modern and a traditional sector.

dual rule   a system of administration used in China (adapted from the Soviet Union) that places a government body under the authority of both a higher level government organization and a communist party organization.

dual-structure system   a structure of an industrial economy characterized by a sharp division between a modern corporate sector composed of large and powerful enterprises on the one hand and a traditional small-business sector, on the other. The latter tend to be dependent on and often controlled by the former. The pre–World War II Japanese economy was characterized by such a structure.

Economic Community of West African States (ECOWAS)   the organization established in 1975 among the sixteen governments in West Africa. The goals of ECOWAS are to strengthen and broaden the economies in the region through the removal of trade barriers among its members (such as import quotas and domestic content laws) and freedom of movement for their citizens and monetary cooperation.

economic liberalization   attempts to dismantle government controls on the economy.

Economic Miracle   denotes a period of rapid economic growth, such as occurred in France, Germany, and Japan during the 1950s and 1960s (and, for Japan, through the 1980s).

ejidatario   recipient of *ejido* land grant in Mexico.

ejido   land granted by Mexican government to organized group of peasants.

Emergency (1975–1977)   the period when Indian Prime Minister Indira Gandhi suspended many formal democratic rights and ruled in an **authoritarian** manner.

emir   traditional Islamic ruler. The emir presides over an "emirate," or kingdom, in Northern Nigeria.

euro   the European Union's single currency unit introduced January 1, 1999 by eleven of the fifteen member states.

executive   the agencies of government which implement or execute policy. The highest levels of the executive in most countries is a president or prime minister and cabinet. The top executive officeholders supervise the work of administrative departments and bureaux.

export-led growth   economic growth generated by the export of a country's commodities. Export-led growth can occur at an early stage of economic development, in which case it involves primary products, such as the country's mineral resources, timber, and agricultural products; or at a later stage, when industrial goods and services are exported.

Farsi   Persian word for the Persian language. Fars is a province in central Iran.

fatwa   Islamic term for religious decree.

favelas   in Brazil, huge shanty towns of homes made out of cardboard, wood from dumps, and blocks of mortar and brick. These shanty towns create rings of extreme poverty around cities like Rio de Janeiro and São Paulo. Similar shanty towns can be found in other Latin American cities, although terms to describe them may vary by country. In Peru, for example, these shanty towns are called *barriadas*.

federal character   Nigeria's version of "affirmative action," applied to the civil service and all government agencies to ensure representation of all ethnic and regional groups and to prevent the dominance of any one group. In practice, federal character has tended to promote the employment of northern Nigerians at the expense of southerners.

Federal Reserve Board   the U.S. central bank established by Congress in 1913 to regulate the banking industry and the money supply. Although the president appoints the chair and Board of Governors (with Senate approval), the Board operates largely independently. Many criticize its policies as reflecting the needs of banks and international capital over the needs of citizens, particularly workers.

federal system   (See **federalism.**)

federalism   a system of governance in which political authority is shared between a central government and regional or state governments. The powers of each level of government are usually specified in a federal constitution.

Fiscal Investment and Loan Program (FILP)   known also as Japan's "second budget," FILP draws its funds mainly from deposits collected by the national postal savings system, premiums paid into the public life insurance program, and contributions to public pension programs. The funds are allocated to public and semipublic enterprises, and amounted to nearly two-thirds of Japan's regular annual budget in 1993.

Foundation of the Oppressed   a clerically controlled foundation set up after the revolution in Iran. It owns much of the confiscated assets of the old elite. Its profits are supposed to go to charity and education.

framework regulation   German style of regulation in which the general patterns of public policy are outlined, but specific details of policy are left to policy-makers' discretion as long as they remain within the general framework.

franchise   the right to vote.

free market   the absence of government regulation of the economy. Relative to other advanced democracies, the United States has traditionally had a more free market economy. (See **laissez-faire.**)

free trade   international commerce that is relatively unregulated or constrained by tariffs (special payments imposed by governments on exports or imports).

fundamentalism   a term recently popularized to describe radical religious movements throughout the world. It is widely believed that these movements interpret the fundamental texts of their religion literally and intend to recreate their religion's early societies. Iranian leader Khomeini hardly fits this definition of fundamentalism.

fusion of powers   a constitutional principle that merges the authority of branches of government, in contrast to the principle of **separation of powers.** In Britain, for example, Parliament is the supreme legislative, executive, and judicial authority; the fusion of legislature and executive is also expressed in the function and personnel of the cabinet.

gender   social division based on the cultural and political significance ascribed to sexual difference.

gender gap   politically significant differences in social attitudes and voting behavior between men and women.

glasnost   Gorbachev's policy of "openness" or "publicity," which involved an easing of controls on the media, arts, and public discussion, leading to an outburst of public debate and criticism covering most aspects of Soviet history, culture, and policy.

globalization   the intensification of world-wide interconnectedness associated with the increased speed and magnitude of cross-border flows of trade, investment and finance, and processes of migration, cultural diffusion, and communication.

grandes écoles   prestigious and highly selective schools of higher education in France that train top civil servants, engineers, and business executives.

grands corps   elite networks of graduates of selective training schools in France.

grassroots democracy   term used to describe activist, local political action, and community control. Used frequently by the Greens Party in Germany and many **social movements** elsewhere.

Great Leap Forward   a movement launched by Mao Zedong in 1958 to industrialize China very rapidly and thereby propel it toward **communism.** The Leap ended in economic disaster in 1960, causing one of the worst famines in human history.

Great Proletarian Cultural Revolution   the political campaign launched in 1966 by Chairman Mao Zedong to stop what he saw as China's drift away from socialism and towards capitalism. The campaign led to massive purges in the Chinese Communist Party, the widespread persecution of China's intellectuals, and the destruction of invaluable cultural objects. The Cultural Revolution officially ended in 1979 after Mao's death and the arrest of some of his most radical followers.

green revolution   a strategy for increasing agricultural (especially food) production, involving improved seeds, irrigation, and abundant use of fertilizers.

guanxi   a Chinese term that means "connections" or "relationships," and describes personal ties between individuals based on such things as common birthplace or mutual acquaintances. *Guanxi* are an important factor in China's political and economic life.

Guardian Council   a committee of twelve jurists created by the Iranian constitution. It has the authority to veto any parlimentary bill it considers to be un-Islamic and against the constitution.

guerrilla warfare   a military strategy based on small bands of soldiers (the guerrillas) who use hit-and-run tactics to attack a numerically superior and better-armed enemy.

health insurance funds   a semipublic system in Germany that brings all major health interests together to allocate costs and benefits by way of consultation and group participation.

hegemonic power   a state that can control the pattern of alliances and terms of the international order, and often

shapes domestic political developments in countries throughout the world.

Hezbollahis   literally means the partisans of God. The term is used in Iran to describe religious vigilantes. In Lebanon, it is used to describe the Shi'i militia.

Hindus   India's main religion is Hinduism, and its adherents are called Hindus.

hojjat al-Islams   literally, the proof of Islam. Medium-ranking clerics in Iran.

household responsibility system   the system put into practice in China beginning in the late 1970s in which the major decisions about agricultural production are made by individual farm families based on profit motive rather than by a **people's commune** or the government.

Imam   leader. Iranians traditionally used this title only for the twelve early Infallible Leaders of Shi'ism. During the Islamic Revolution, this title was used for Khomeini to elevate him above the other Grand Ayatollahs.

Imam Jum'ehs   prayer-leaders in Iran's main urban mosques on Fridays. Appointed by the clerical hiearchy in Qom, these prayer-leaders enjoy considerable authority in the provinces of Iran.

import substituting industrialization (ISI)   strategy for industrialization based on domestic manufacture of previously imported goods to satisfy domestic market demands. (See **developmentalism.**)

Indian Administrative Service (IAS)   India's civil service, a highly professional and talented group of administrators who run the Indian government on a day-to-day basis.

indicative planning   a term used to describe the development of a national economic plan which *indicates* what the plan specifies as desirable priorities for economic development. Indicative planning can be distinguished from plans developed under **command economies.**

indigenous groups   population of Amerindian heritage in Mexico.

indirect rule   a term used to describe the British style of colonialism in Nigeria in which local traditional rulers and political structures were used to help support the colonial governing structure.

industrial policy   a generic term to refer to a variety of policies designed to shape leading sectors of the economy and enhance competeviness, especially for industries that are considered strategic to national interests. Countries differ substantially regarding the degree to which their states consciously pursue industrial policies.

informal sector (economy)   an underground economy.

insider privatization   a term used in relation to Russia to refer to the transformation of formerly state-owned enterprises into **joint-stock companies** or private enterprises in which majority control of the enterprise is in the hands of employees and/or managers of that enterprise.

interest groups   organizations that seek to represent the interests—usually economic—of their members in dealings with the government. Important examples are associations of occupational groups, such as farmers, or business firms in a particular sector (for example, steel producers or aircraft manufacturers).

International Financial Institutions (IFIs)   generally refers to the International Bank for Reconstruction and Development (The World Bank) and the International Monetary Fund (IMF), but can also include other international lending institutions. [See **structural adjustment program (SAP).**]

interventionist   an interventionist state acts vigorously to shape the performance of major sectors of the economy.

interventores   in Brazil, allies of Getúlio Vargas picked by the dictator during his first period of rulership to replace opposition governors in all the Brazilian states except Minas Gerais. The *interventores* represented a shift of power from subnational government to the central state. (See **politics of the governors.**)

iron rice bowl   a feature of China's socialist economy that provided guarantees of lifetime employment, income, and basic cradle-to-grave benefits to most urban and rural workers. Economic reforms beginning in the 1980s aimed at improving efficiency and work motivation sought to smash the iron rice bowl and link employment and income more directly to individual effort.

iron triangles   a term coined by students of American politics to refer to the relationships of mutual support formed by particular government agencies, members of Congressional committees or subcommittees, and interest groups in various policy areas. Synonymous with "cozy triangles," the term has been borrowed by some students of Japanese politics to refer to similar relationships found among Japanese ministry or agency officials, Diet (parliament) members, and special interest groups.

jihad   Islamic "holy war" against nonbelievers. One of the fundamental duties required of Muslims, although its interpretation varies widely.

joint-stock company   a business firm whose capital is divided into shares which can be held by individuals, groups of individuals, or governmental units. In Russia, formation of joint-stock companies has been the primary method for privatizing large state enterprises.

judicial review   the prerogative of a high court (such as the U.S. Supreme Court) to nullify actions by the executive and legislative branches of government that, in its judgment, violate the constitution.

Junkers   reactionary land-owning elite in nineteenth-century Prussia. Major supporters of Bismarck's attempts to unify Germany in 1871.

jurist's guardianship   Khomeini's concept that the Iranian clergy should rule on the grounds that they are the divinely appointed guardians of both the law and the people. He developed this concept in the 1970s.

keiretsu   a group of closely allied Japanese firms that have preferential trading relationships, and often interlocked directorates and stock-sharing arrangements. The relationships among *keiretsu* member firms have been regarded as collusive and harmful to free trade by some of Japan's principal trading partners.

Keynesian demand management   named after the British economist John Maynard Keynes, an approach to economic policy in which state economic policies are used to regulate the economy in an attempt to achieve stable economic growth. During recession, state budget deficits are used to expand demand in an effort to boost both consumption and investment (and create employment); during periods of high growth, when inflation threatens, cuts in government spending and a tightening of credit are used to reduce demand.

Keynesianism   (See **Keynesian demand management.**)

koenkai   usually translated as "support association," *koenkai* is a Japanese campaign organization for a particular candidate, consisting mainly of the candidate's relatives, friends, alumni, coworkers, and their acquaintances. Networks of *koenkai* organizations are far more important and effective than political parties in assisting politicians' election campaigns. Since it costs politicians a great deal to maintain these networks, *koenkai*-centered elections thus encourage corruption.

krai   one of the six territorial units in the Russian Federation which are defined by the constitution of 1993 to be among the 89 members of the federation, with a status equal to that of the republics and *oblast'*. Like the *oblasts'*, during the Soviet period, the *krai* were defined purely as territorial-administrative units within a particular **union republic** of the Soviet Union. A *krai* differed from an *oblast'* in that part of its border was on an external boundary of the USSR and/or it included a mixture of diverse ethnic territories. Generally a *krai* is a geographically large unit, but relatively sparsely populated.

Kulturkampf "cultural struggle" between Protestant and Catholic forces in late-nineteenth-century Germany.

laissez-faire the doctrine that government should not interfere with commerce. Relative to other advanced democracies, the United States has traditionally taken a more laissez-faire attitude toward economic regulation. Regulation has, however, increased in the 20th century. (See **free market.**)

land reform the process of reducing gross inequalities in the ownership of farm land by either confiscating or buying it from large owners and redistributing it to those who have little or no land.

law-based state a state where the rule of law prevails, so that actions of the government as well as of nongovernmental actors are subject to the requirements of the law. The creation of a law-based state in the Soviet Union was one of the explicit goals of Gorbachev's reform process, thus limiting the ability of state agencies or the Communist Party of the Soviet Union arbitrarily to circumvent laws or legal provisions.

legitimacy a belief by powerful groups and the broad citizenry that a state exercises "rightful" authority. In the contemporary world, a state is said to possess legitimacy when it enjoys consent of the governed, which usually involves democratic procedures and the attempt to achieve a satisfactory level of development and equitable distribution of resources. (See **democracy.**)

liberal (See **liberalism.**)

lifetime employment the practice common among Japanese government agencies and large business firms to keep newly hired high school and university graduates on payroll until they reach mandatory retirement age. As a rule, however, the practice applies only to male employees and, moreover, is on the decline in contemporary Japan, where both the general population and workforce are rapidly "graying" and the ratios of temporary, part-time, and female employees are rising.

Lok Sabha the lower house of parliament in India where all major legislation must pass before becoming law.

luan a Chinese term meaning "chaos." It conveys the fear of China's leaders and many of its people that without strong central leadership the country would collaspe into **anarchy.**

macroeconomic policy government policy intended to shape the overall economic system at the national level by concentrating on policy targets such as inflation, or growth.

mafia a term borrowed from Italy and widely used in Russia to describe networks of organized criminal activity that pervade both economic and governmental structures in that country and that involve activities such as the demanding of protection money, bribe-taking by government officials, contract killing, and extortion.

Maharajas India's traditional rulers—monarchs—who retained their positions under British tutelage during the colonial period but who were removed from power when the Indian **republic** was established.

Majles Arabic term for assembly used in Iran to refer to the parliament.

Manifest Destiny the public philosophy in the late 19th century that the United States was not only entitled, but destined to occupy all of the territory from the Atlantic to the Pacific.

maquiladora factories that produce goods for export, often located along the U.S.-Mexican border.

Marbury v. Madison the 1803 ruling by the Supreme Court that the federal courts inherently had the authority to review the constitutionality of acts passed by Congress and signed by the president. This ruling, initially used sparingly, placed the courts centrally in the constitutional system of **checks and balances.**

market reform a strategy of economic transformation embraced by the Yeltsin government in Russia and the Deng Xiaoping government in China that involves reducing the role of the state in managing the economy and increasing the role of market forces. In Russia, market reform is part of the transition to **post-communism** and includes the extensive transfer of the ownership of economic assets from the state to private hands. In China, market reform has been carried out under the leadership of the Chinese Communist Party and involves less extensive privatization.

maslahat Arabic term for advisable or prudent. It is now used in Iran to refer to reasons of state or what is best for the Islamic Republic.

mestizo a person of mixed white, indigenous (Amerindian), and sometimes African descent.

middle-level theory seeks to explain phenomena in a limited range of cases, in particular, a specific set of countries with particular characteristics, such as parliamentary regimes, or a particular type of political institution (such as political parties) or activity (such as protest).

military dictatorship a political system in which unelected military officers hold **executive** power and repress all forms of dissent and opposition. (See also **authoritarianism.**)

Minamata Disease organic mercury poisoning caused by eating contaminated river fish and clams, which produces paralysis of limbs and speech impairment. Occurred in Japan in the 1950s and 1960s as a result of industrial firms' discharge of toxic wastes. The disease is regarded as one of the most tragic examples of the widespread industrial pollution that characterized postwar Japanese society at the height of its dramatic economic growth.

mir a traditional form of communal peasant organization in Russia that survived until the collectivization campaign of the late 1920s and which involved a periodic redistribution of strips of land among families of the commune.

moderating power *(poder moderador)* a term used in Brazilian politics to refer to the situation following the 1824 constitution in which the monarchy was supposed to act as a moderating power, among the executive, legislative, and judicial branches of government, arbitrating party conflicts, and fulfilling governmental responsibilities when non-royal agents failed.

monetarism an approach to economic policy that assumes a natural rate of unemployment determined by the labor maket, and rejects the instrument of government spending to run up budgetary deficits for stimulating the economy.

money-based privatization a second phase in the privatization of state-owned enterprises in the Russian Federation. This phase commenced in 1994. In contrast to the first phase, which was voucher privatization (see **privatization voucher**), money-based privatization permitted firms to sell shares for cash or investment guarantees. Shares owned by the state could also be sold at auctions for cash, providing a potential source of state revenue. (See **privatization, spontaneous privatization.**)

mosque Muslim place of worship, equivalent to church, temple, or synagogue.

most different case analysis The logic of most different case analysis is that, by comparing cases that differ widely, one seeks to isolate a factor or factors (termed the independent variable or variables) that both cases share—despite their differences in other respects—that might explain an outcome (or dependent variable).

Muslim(s) followers of Islam.

nationalism an ideology that seeks to create a **nation-state** for a particular community; a group identity associated with membership is such a political community. Nationalists often proclaim that their **state** and **nation** are superior to others.

nationalization the take-over by the government of privately owned business firms.

nation-state distinct, politically defined territory with its own **state,** relatively coherent culture, economy, and ethnic and other social identities. (See **country.**)

Nazi acronym for Adolph Hitler's National Socialist German Worker's Party.

neoliberalism a term used to describe government policies aiming to promote free competition among business firms within the market, notably, **liberalization** and **monetarism.**

new social movements grassroots associations that may be differentiated from more established social movements and from interest groups by their greater tendency to raise basic questions about social values, social goals, and political styles; examples include environmentalism, women's rights, peace, and gay rights.

New State *(Estado Novo)* in Brazil, an authoritarian government led by Getúlio Vargas in 1937 that legitimized its rule through **state corporatism,** massive public sector investment through **para-statals,** and paternalistic social policies.

nomenklatura a system of personnel selection utilized in the Soviet Union and China under which the Communist Party maintains control over the appointment of important officials in all spheres of social, economic, and political life. The term is also used to describe individuals chosen through this system and thus refers more broadly to the privileged circles in the Soviet Union and China.

nonaligned bloc a group of countries that refused to ally with either the United States or the USSR during the **Cold War** years.

nongovernmental organization (NGO) a private group that seeks to influence public policy and deal with certain problems that it believes are not being adequately addressed by governments; examples include Amnesty International (human rights), Oxfam (famine relief), and Greenpeace (the environment).

non-tariff barriers (NTBs) policies designed to prevent foreign imports in order to protect domestic industries, such as quotas, health and safety standards, packaging and labeling rules, and unique or unusual business practices. A form of **protectionism** that does not use formal tariffs.

oblast' one of 49 territorial units in the Russian Federation which are defined by the constitution of 1993 to be among the 89 members of the federation, with a status equal to that of the republics and **krai**. An *oblast'* generally lacks a non-Russian national/ethnic basis. During the Soviet period, the *oblasts'* were defined purely as territorial-administrative units located within a particular **union republic** of the Soviet Union.

okrug one of 10 territorial units in the Russian Federation that are defined by the constitution of 1993 to be among the 89 members of the federation with a status equal to that of the republics, **oblasts,** and **krai.** An okrug generally was originally formed due to the presence of a non-Russian national/ethnic group residing in the territory. Alongside their status as equal units of the Russian Federation, most of the okrugs are physically located within and constituent parts of an oblast or krai. This situation has created ambiguity regarding the relationship between the okrug and the oblast or krai they are located in.

oligarchy narrowly based, undemocratic government, often by traditional elites. (See **autocracy, authoritarianism.**)

OPEC Organization of Oil Exporting Countries. Iran is one of its leading members.

overlapping responsibilities (policy) refers to the unique pattern of German federalism in which federal and state governments share administrative responsibility for implementation of public policies.

panchayats the lowest level of local government in India.

para-statals state-owned, or at least state-controlled, corporations, created to undertake a broad range of activities, from control and marketing of agricultural production to provision of banking services, operating airlines, and other transportation facilities and public utilities. (See **interventionist.**)

parliamentary democracy system of government in which the chief executive is answerable to the legislature and may be dismissed by it. Parliamentary democracy stands in contrast to a presidential system, in which the chief executive is elected in a national ballot and is independent of the legislative branch.

parliamentary sovereignty a constitutional principle of government (principally in Britain) by which the legislature reserves the power to make or overturn any law without recourse by the executive, the judiciary, or the monarchy; only parliament can nullify or overturn legislation approved by parliament; and parliament can force the cabinet or the government to resign by voting a motion of no-confidence.

party democracy a term used to describe the strong role that German political parties are allowed to play in the Federal Republic. Unlike the American Constitution where parties are not mentioned, the Basic Law explicitly enables political parties to play a crucial linking role between citizen and state.

pasdaran Persian term for guards used to refer to the army of revolutionary guards formed during Iran's Islamic Revolution.

patrimonialism (or **neopatrimonialism**) a system of governance in which a single ruler treats the state as personal property (patrimony). Appointments to public office are made on the basis of unswerving loyalty to the ruler. In turn, state officials exercise wide authority in other domains, such as the economy, often for their personal benefit and that of the ruler, to the detriment of the general population. (See **authoritarianism, autocracy, prebendalism.**)

patrimonial state (See **patrimonialism.**)

patron-client relations (or **network**) (See **clientelism.**)

People of the Book the Muslim term for recognized religious minorities such as Christians, Jews, and Zoroastrians.

people's communes large-scale rural communities that were in charge of nearly all aspects of political, social, and economic life in the Chinese countryside from the late 1950s until the early 1980s when they were disbanded and replaced by a system of household and village-based agricultural production.

perestroika the policy of "restructuring" embarked upon by Gorbachev when he became head of the Communist Party of the Soviet Union in 1985. Initially, the policy emphasized decentralization of economic decision-making, increased enterprise autonomy, expanded public discussion of policy issues, and a reduction in the international isolation of the Soviet economy. Over time, however, restructuring took on a more political tone, including a commitment to *glasnost* and *demokratizatsiia.*

personalist politicians demagogic political leaders who use their personal charisma to mobilize their constituency.

personalized proportional representation German voters cast two votes on each ballot: the first for an individual candidate; and the second for a list of national/regional candidates grouped by party affiliation. This system has the effect of personalizing list voting because voters have their own representative but also can choose among several parties.

petrodollars revenue earned from the sale from petroleum, often circulating internationally as US dollars.

police powers powers, traditionally held by the states, to regulate public safety and welfare. Police powers are the form of interaction with government that most citizens most often experience. These remain the primary responsibility of the states and localities.

political action committee (PAC) a narrow form of interest group that seeks to influence policy by making contributions to candidates and parties. PACs emerged because of an effort to limit corporate and union contributions to candidates for federal offices. Since these are prohibited, corporations, unions, and others channel their contributions through PACs, which may contribute to candidates (up to specified dollar limits).

political culture the attitudes, beliefs, and symbols that influence political behavior; often defined in terms of specific national political-cultural orientations.

political development the stages of change producing more modern and effective political institutions.

political economy the study of the interaction between the state and the economy, that is, how the state and political processes affect the organization of production and exchange (the economy), and how the organization of the economy affects political processes.

political institutions the formal rules, structured relationships, and organizations within the state, and, more broadly, within the political sphere. Some key examples are the executive, legislature, judiciary, military, and political parties.

politics of the governors in Brazil, refers to periods of history in which state governors acquire extraordinary powers over domains of policy that were previously claimed by the federal government. The term refers most commonly to the Old Republic and the current state of Brazilian federalism. (See **federalism.**)

populism gaining the support of popular sectors. When used in Latin American politics, this support is often achieved by manipulation and demagogic appeals.

prebendalism patterns of political behavior that rest on the justification that official state offices should be competed for, and then utilized for the personal benefit of office holders as well as of their support group or clients. Thus, prebendal politics is sustained by the existence of **patron-client networks.** (See **patrimonialism, clientelism.**)

predominant-party system a multi-party political system in which one party maintains a predominant position in parliament and the control of government for a long period of time.

prefects French administrators appointed by the minister of the interior to coordinate state agencies and programs within the 100 French departments or localities. Prefects had enormous power until decentralization reforms in the 1980s transferred some of their responsibilities to elected local governments.

presidentialization the increasing role of the presidency in French politics. The result is that the process of choosing a president has an important impact on political parties, elections, public opinion, and the careers of professional politicians.

privatization the sale of state-owned enterprises to private companies or investors. Those who support the policy claim that private ownership is superior to government ownership because for-profit entities promote greater efficiency. Privatization is a central component of **structural adjustment programs (SAPs)** to curtail the losses associated with these enterprises and generate state revenue when they are sold. For Russia, see **spontaneous privatization.**

privatization voucher a certificate worth 10,000 rubles issued by the government to each Russian citizen in 1992 to be used to purchase shares in state enterprises undergoing the process of privatization. Vouchers could also be sold for cash or disposed of through newly created investment funds.

proletariat the industrial working class which, according to Marxism-Leninism, is destined to seize power and replace capitalism with socialism.

proportional representation (PR) a system of political representation in which seats are allocated to parties within multimember constituencies, roughly in proportion to the votes each party receives. PR usually encourages the election to parliament of more political parties than single-member district winner-take-all systems.

protectionism government policies that aim to prevent imported goods from competing with a country's domestic industries. The most common example is tariffs, a tax on imported, but not domestic, products.

pyramid debt a situation when a government or organization takes on debt obligations at progressively higher rates of interest in order to pay off existing debt. In some cases, a structure of pyramid debt can result in a default on the entire debt obligation if interest owed becomes unmanageable.

quangos acronym for quasi-nongovernmental organizations, the term used in Britain for nonelected bodies that are outside traditional governmental departments or local authorities. They have considerable influence over public policy in areas such as education, health care, and housing.

Qur'an the Muslim Bible.

Rayja Sabha India's upper house of parliament; considerably less significant politically than the *Lok Sabha.*

redistributive policies   policies that take resources from one person or group in society and allocate them to a different, usually more disadvantaged, group in the society. The United States has traditionally opposed redistributive policies, at least to the disadvantaged, but many distributive policies transfer resources from one group to another in the society.

referendum   an election in which citizens are asked to approve (or reject) a policy proposal.

regulations   the rules that explain the implementation of laws. When Congress passes a law, it sets broad principles for implementation, but how the law is implemented is determined by regulations set by other government organizations and agencies. The regulation-making process allows interested parties to influence the eventual shape of the law in practice.

Rengo   the General Confederation of Japanese Labor founded in 1987 under the leadership of private-sector unions. The largest labor organization in Japanese history, *Rengo* consists today of 80 industrial unions with the combined membership of about 7.6 million.

rentier state   a country that obtains much of its revenue from the export of oil.

rents   above-market returns to a factor of production. Pursuit of economic rents (or "rent-seeking") is profit-seeking that takes the form of nonproductive economic activity.

republic   in contemporary usage, a political regime in which leaders are not chosen on the basis of their inherited background (as in a monarchy). A republic may but need not be **democratic.** For Russia, see **autonomous republic.**

reservations   jobs or admissions to colleges reserved by the government of India for specific social groups, particularly underprivileged groups.

revolution   the process by which an established political regime is replaced (usually by force and with broad popular participation) and a new regime established that introduces radical changes throughout society. Revolutions are different from **coups d'état** in that there is widespread popular participation in revolutions, whereas coups d'état are led by small groups of elites.

scheduled castes   the lowest caste groups in India, also known as the untouchables.

Self-Defense Forces (SDF)   inaugurated in Japan as a Police Reserve Force with 75,000 recruits in August 1950, following the outbreak of the Korean War. Known by the present name since 1954, the SDF today consists of approximately 250,000 troops equipped with sophisticated modern weapons and weapons systems. The constitutional status and operational mandates of these forces are controversial.

self-determination   the right of a sovereign state or an ethnic or other group that shares cultural and historical ties to live together in a given territory and in a manner they desire. It is often the basis of the claim by a state or group for political independence and cultural autonomy.

semipresidential system (regime)   a regime which combines elements of a **presidential system** and a **cabinet** or parliamentary government. In a semipresidential regime there is neither a complete separation of powers between executive and legislature, as in a presidential system, nor a **fusion of powers,** as in a **parliamentary system.** The elected president exercises extensive power but shares control of the executive and policy-making powers with a prime minister and government responsible to parliament.

separation of powers   an organization of **political institutions** within the **state** in which the executive, legislature, and judiciary have autonomous powers and no one branch dominates the others. This is the common pattern in **presidential systems,** as opposed to **parliamentary systems,** in which there is a **fusion of powers.**

sexenio   six-year administration of Mexican presidents.

shari'a   Islamic law derived mostly from the Qur'an and the examples set by the Prophet Mohammad, but more broadly, the totality of **Muslim** belief and practice; the legal foundation of Islamic theocracy.

Shi'ism   a branch of Islam. It literally means the followers or partisans of Ali. The other main branch of Islam is known as Sunnism, or the followers of tradition.

shock therapy   a variant of **market reform** which involves the state simultaneously imposing a wide range of radical economic changes, with the purpose of "shocking" the economy into a new mode of operation. Shock therapy can be contrasted with a more gradual approach to market reform.

Sikh(s)   an important religious minority group in India.

single member plurality system   electoral systems in which candidates run for a single seat from a specific geographic district. The winner is the person that receives the most votes whether or not that person won a majority. Single member plurality systems, unlike systems of proportional representation, increase the likelihood that two national coalitional parties will emerge.

social class   common membership in a group whose boundaries are based on a common economic location, notably, occupation and income. Members of the same social class often share similar political attitudes.

Social Market Economy term describing the German economy which combines an efficient competitive economy with generous welfare state benefits for large segments of the population.

social movements grassroots associations which demand reforms of existing social practices and government policies. Social movements are less formally organized than **interest groups.** (See **new social movements.**)

social security national systems of contributory and non-contributory benefits to provide assistance for the elderly, sick, disabled, unemployed, others similarly in need of assistance. The specific coverage of social security, a key component of the welfare state, varies by country.

socialism in a socialist regime, the state plays a leading role in organizing the economy and most business firms are publicly owned. A socialist regime, unlike a **communist party-state,** may allow the private sector to play an important role in the economy and be committed to political pluralism. In **Marxism-Leninism,** socialism refers to an early stage in development of **communism.** Socialist regimes can be organized in a **democratic** manner, in that those who control the state may be chosen according to democratic procedures (see **social democracy, democratic socialism**). They may also be governed in an undemocratic manner, when a single party, not chosen in free competitive elections, controls the state and society.

socialist democracy the term used by the Chinese Communist Party to describe the political system of the People's Republic of China. Also called the people's democratic dictatorship. The official view is that this type of system, under the leadership of the Communist Party, provides democracy for the overwhelming majority of people and suppresses (or exercises dictatorship over) only the enemies of the people. Socialist democracy is contrasted to bourgeois (or capitalist) democracy, which puts power in the hands of the rich and oppresses the poor.

Sohyo the General Council of Trade Unions of Japan founded in 1950 by 17 leftwing industrial unions drawn mainly from public sector. Throughout the 1950s and 1960s, *Sohyo* was closely allied with the Japan Socialist Party and played a prominent role in a series of campaigns on controversial issues, such as Japanese rearmament and the United States-Japan Mutual Security Treaty. *Sohyo's* influence began to decline in the mid-1970s and it was absorbed by *Rengo* in 1989.

spontaneous privatization a process, which occurred in the late 1980s and early 1990s in Russia, in which existing managers or ministry bureaucrats transformed promising state-owned enterprises into privatized entities in their own hands, without the existence of a clear legal framework for doing so. (See **privatization.**)

spring labor offensive an annual event in Japan since 1955, the spring labor offensive refers to a series of negotiations between labor unions in major industries and management that take place each spring. The wage increases and changes in working hours and working conditions negotiated in this manner set the standards for management-union negotiations in other industries in the given year.

state a unified political entity; the state comprises a country's key political institutions that are responsible for making, implementing, enforcing, and adjudicating important policies in that country. States have also been defined as those institutions within a country that claim the right to control force within the territory comprising the country and to make binding rules (laws) which citizens of that country must obey. (See **civil society, society.**)

state capitalism strategy in which government guides industrial and agricultural development and sets political conditions for its success.

state corporatism an **authoritarian regime** in which the **state** requires all members of a particular economic sector to join an officially designated **interest group.** Such interest groups thus attain public status and they participate in national policy-making. The result is that the state has great control over the groups, and groups have great control over their members. (See **corporatism, neocorporatism.**)

state formation the historical development of a **state,** often marked by major stages, key events, or turning points (critical junctures) which influence the contemporary character of the state.

state-led economic development the process of promoting economic development via the use of governmental machinery.

statism a situation in which the state intervenes extensively to direct economic and social activity within a country.

structural adjustment program (SAP) medium-term, generally 3–5 year, programs (which include both action plans and disbursement of funds) established by the World Bank intended to alter and reform the economic structures of highly indebted, **Third World** countries as a condition for receiving international loans. SAPs often involve the necessity for **privatization,** trade **liberalization,** and fiscal restraint. [See **International Financial Institutions (IFIs).**]

Supreme Commander for the Allied Powers (SCAP) the official title of General Douglas MacArthur during 1945–1951, when he led the Allied Occupation of Japan.

Supreme Leader the head of the Islamic Republic of Iran.

suspensive veto if the German *Bundesrat* votes against a bill, the *Bundestag* can override the *Bundesrat* by passing the measure again by a simple majority. If, however, a two-thirds majority of the *Bundesrat* votes against a bill, the *Bundestag* must pass it again by a two-thirds margin.

Taisho Democracy a reference to Japanese politics in the period roughly coinciding with Emperor Taisho's reign, 1919–1925. The period was characterized by the rise of a popular movement for democratizaton of government by the introduction of universal manhood suffrage and the reduction of the power and influence of authoritarian institutions of the state.

technocrats career-minded bureaucrats who administer public policy according to a technical rather than a political rationale. In Mexico and Brazil, these are known as the *técnicos* (for contrasting concepts, see **clientelism, patrimonial state, prebendalism**).

theocracy a state dominated by the clergy who rule on the grounds that they are the only interpreters of God's will and law.

totalitarianism a political system in which the state attempts to exercise total control over all aspects of public and private life, including the economy, culture, education, and social organizations, through an integrated system of ideological, economic, and political control. The term has been applied both to **communist party-states** and **fascist** regimes such as Nazi Germany.

township and village enterprises (TVEs) non-agricultural businesses and factories owned and run by local governments and private entrepreneurs in China's rural areas. TVEs operate largely according the market forces and outside of the state plan.

typology a method of classifying by using criteria which divide a group of cases into smaller numbers. For example, in this book, we use a typology of countries which distinguishes among established democracies, transitional democracies, and non-democracies.

unfinished state a **state** characterized by instabilities and uncertainties that may render it susceptible to collaspe as a coherent entity.

union republic one of fifteen territorial units which constituted the **federal system** of the Soviet Union and which subsequently became independent states with the break-up of the Soviet Union in December 1991.

unitary state by contrast to the **federal systems** of Germany, India, Canada, or the United States, where power is shared between the central government and state or regional governments, in a unitary state (such as Britain) no powers are reserved constitutionally for subnational units of government.

untouchables the lowest caste in India's **caste system**, whose members are among the poorest and most disadvantaged Indians.

vanguard party a political party that claims to operate in the "true" interests of the group or class it purports to represent, even if this understanding doesn't correspond to the expressed interests of the group itself. The communist parties of the Soviet Union and China are good examples of vanguard parties.

vertically divided administration also known as "sectionalism," the term refers to the extreme autonomy of each Japanese government agency or its subdivision, a situation that seriously interferes with "horizontal" coordination between two or more agencies or their subdivisions.

volatility the tendency for change in a political situation, especially as applied to electoral results and changes in the share of votes between parties from one election to the next.

warrant chiefs employed by British colonial regime in Nigeria: A system in which "chiefs" were selected by the British to oversee certain legal matters and assist the colonial enterprise in governance and law enforcement in local areas.

Watergate the collective name for the various scandals of President Nixon and his senior aides, which included a break-in at the Democratic National Committee housed in the Watergate Hotel in Washington, D. C.. Nixon and his aides used the institutions of the federal government to reduce the opportunity of his opponents to win elections. Congress learned from their experience with investigating Watergate that investigations could dampen popular support for the presidency.

welfare state not a form of state, but rather a set of public policies designed to provide for citizens' needs through direct or indirect provision of pensions, health care, unemployment insurance, and assistance to the poor.

Westminster model a form of **democracy** based on the supreme authority of parliament and the **accountability** of its elected representatives; named after the parliament building in London.

works councils legally mandated workplace organizations that provide collective representation for workers with their employers. Separate organization from the trade unions.

zaibatsu giant holding companies in pre–World War II Japan, each owned by and under the control of members of a particular family. The largest were divided into a number of independent firms under the democratization program during the postwar occupation but were later revived as *keiratsu,* although no longer under the control of any of the original founding families.

zamindars landlords who acquired private property rights during British rule of India and retained their property in the modern period.

zoku members of the Japanese Diet (parliament) with recognized experience and expertise in particular policy areas such as agriculture, construction, and transportation, and close personal connections with special interests in those areas.

Zollverein 1834 Customs Union among various pre-unification German states. Fostered economic cooperation which led to nineteenth-century German unification (1871).

About the Editors and Contributors

Ervand Abrahamian is Professor of History at Baruch College and the Graduate Center of the City University of New York. His recent publications include *Khomeinism: Essays on the Islamic Republic* (University of California Press, 1993), and *Tortured Confessions: Prisons and Public Recantations in Modern Iran* (University of California Press, 1999).

Christopher S. Allen is an Associate Professor at the University of Georgia, where he teaches courses in comparative politics and political economy. He has held research fellowships at the Harvard Business School, Johns Hopkins University, and from the German Marshall Fund. He is the editor of *The Transformation of the German Political Party System* (Berghahn, 1999), and is currently working on a study of democratic representation in parliamentary and presidential systems.

Joan DeBardeleben is Professor of Political Science and Director of the Institute of European and Russian Studies at Carleton University in Ottawa, Ontario. She has published widely on Russian politics and on environmental policy and politics in post-Communist countries. Her recent publications include *Russian Politics in Transition* (Houghton Mifflin, 1997), and, with Peter J. Stavrakis and Larry Black, *Beyond the Monolith: The Emergence of Regionalism in Russia* (Johns Hopkins University Press, 1997).

Louis DeSipio is an Assistant Professor of Political Science at the University of Illinois at Urbana-Champaign. He is the author of *Counting on the Latino Vote: Latinos as a New Electorate* (University Press of Virginia, 1996) and, with Rodolfo O. de la Garza, of *Making Americans/Remaking America: Immigration and Immigrant Policy* (Westview Press, 1998). He is also the author and editor of a six-volume series on Latino political values, attitudes, and behaviors published by Westview Press.

Shigeko N. Fukai is Professor of Political Science in the Faculty of Law at Okayama University (Japan). She has written on Japan's land problems and policy-making, Japan's role in the emerging regional economic order in East Asia, and Japan's electoral and party politics.

Haruhiro Fukui is Professor Emeritus at the University of California, Santa Barbara, and currently teaches political science and international relations at Nanzan University (Japan). His recent work includes contributions to *The Rise of East Asia: Critical Visions of the Pacific Century* (Routledge, 1997), and *Passages to Power: Legislative Recruitment in Advanced Democracies* (Cambridge University Press, 1997).

Merilee S. Grindle is Edward S. Mason Professor of International Development at the John F. Kennedy School of Government, Harvard University. She is a specialist on the comparative analysis of policy-making, implementation, and public management in developing countries and has written extensively on Mexico. Her most recent book is *Challenging the State: Crisis and Innovation in Latin America and Africa* (Cambridge University Press, 1996).

Richard A. Joseph is Asa G. Candler Professor of Political Science at Emory University. He has written extensively on Nigerian politics and governance in sub-Saharan Africa in general. He is the author of *Democracy and Prebendal Politics in Nigeria: The Rise and Fall of the Second Republic* (Cambridge University Press, 1987), and editor of *State, Conflict, and Democracy in Africa* (Lynne Rienner, 1999).

William A. Joseph is Professor of Political Science at Wellesley College and an Associate of the Fairbank Center for East Asian Research at Harvard University. His research focuses on contemporary Chinese politics and ideology. He is co-editor of *New Perspectives on the Cultural Revolution* (Harvard University Press, 1991), and contributing editor of *The Oxford Companion to Politics of the World* (Oxford University Press, 1993) and the Asia Society's China Briefing series.

Mark Kesselman is Professor of Political Science at Columbia University. A specialist on the French and European political economy, his recent publications include contributions to *The Mitterand Era: Policy Alternatives and Political Mobilization in France* (Macmillan, 1995), and *Mitterand's Legacy, Chirac's Challenge* (St. Martin's, 1996). He is the co-author of *A Century of Organized Labor in France* (St. Martin's, 1997).

Darren Kew is a Ph.D. candidate at the Fletcher School of Law and Diplomacy at Tufts University. In 1996–1997 he taught at the Universities of Lagos and Kano (Bayero) in Nigeria on a Fulbright grant. His dissertation focuses on the role of civil society in democratization and conflict resolution in Nigeria.

Atul Kohli is Professor of Politics and International Affairs at Princeton University. His principal research interest is the comparative political economy of developing countries, especially India. He is the author of *Democracy and Discontent: India's Growing Crisis of Governability* (Cambridge University Press, 1990). His current research involves a comparative analysis of industrialization in South Korea, Brazil, India, and Nigeria.

Joel Krieger is Norma Wilentz Hess Professor of Political Science at Wellesley College. His publications include *British Politics in the Global Age: Can Social Democracy Survive?* (Polity, 1999), and *Reagan, Thatcher, and the Politics of Decline* (Oxford University Press, 1986). He was also editor-in-chief of *The Oxford Companion to Politics of the World* (Oxford University Press, 1993).

Peter Lewis is Associate Professor at the School of International Service, American University. He has written extensively on Nigerian political economy, as well as on broader regional issues of participation, democratic transition, and economic adjustment in Africa. He is currently working on a study of the comparative political economies of Indonesia and Nigeria.

Alfred P. Montero is Assistant Professor of Political Science at Carleton College. His recent publications include contributions to *Democratic Brazil: Actors, Institutions, and Processes* (University of Pittsburgh Press, 1999), and articles in the *Journal of Interamerican Studies and World Affairs, Current History,* and *Hemisphere.* He is currently writing a book on subnational industrial policy in Brazil and Spain.

Scott Taylor is Gwendolen M. Carter Lecturer in African Politics at Smith College. His writings focus on African political economy and business-government relations. He is currently writing a book entitled *Business and the State in Southern Africa.*

Index*

*Numbers in boldface indicate the page where a key term is defined.